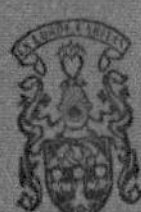

GEORGE
WATSON'S
—COLLEGE—

HISTORY
DEPARTMENT

Understanding Italian Renaissance Painting

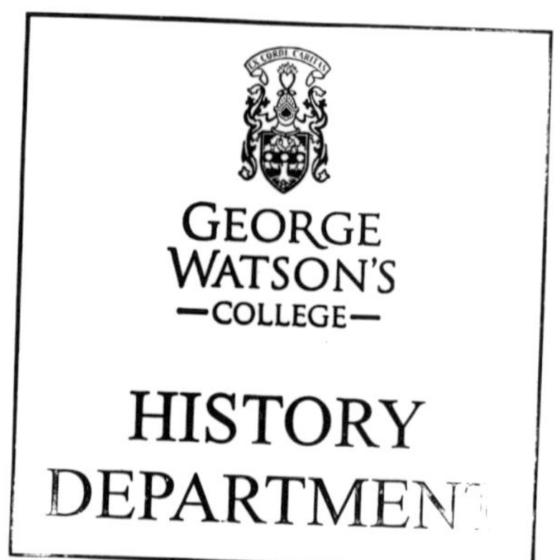

on the cover

Cosmè Tura
The Muse Erato (or Spring)
c. 1460, London, National Gallery

page 6

Leonardo da Vinci
Lady with an Ermine
1485–90, Cracow, Muzeum Czartoryskich

Translated from the Italian *Come Leggere l'Arte del Rinascimento*
by Donald Pistolesi

Colour separations by Die Keure, Bruges

Design by Studio Zuffi

Any copy of this book issued by the publisher as a paperback is sold
subject to the condition that it shall not by way of trade or otherwise
be lent, resold, hired out or otherwise circulated without the publisher's
prior consent in any form of binding or cover other than that in which
it is published and without a similar condition including these words
being imposed on a subsequent purchaser.

First published in the United Kingdom in 2010 by
Thames & Hudson Ltd,
181A High Holborn,
London WC1V 7QX

www.thamesandhudson.com

Copyright © 2010 Ludion and the author

All Rights Reserved. No part of this publication may be reproduced
or transmitted in any form or by any means, electronic or mechanical,
including photocopy, recording or any other information storage and
retrieval system, without prior permission in writing from the publisher.

British Library Cataloguing-in-Publication Data
A catalogue record for this book is available from the British Library

ISBN: 978-0-500-97703-3

Printed and bound in China

Stefano Zuffi

Understanding Italian Renaissance Painting

A Guide to the Artists, Ideas and Key Works

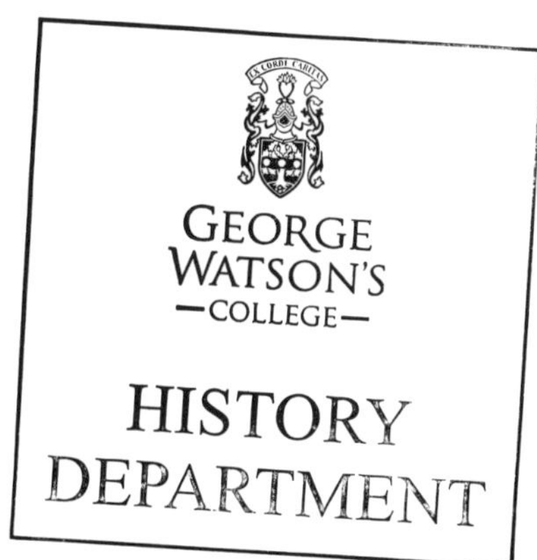

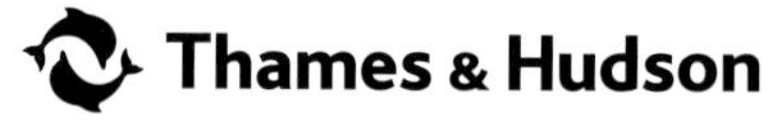

CONTENTS

Introduction 7

Index of Themes, Topics and Techniques 10

Chronology of Italian Renaissance Painting, 1400–1600 12

Index of Artists and their Works 396

Photographic Credits 399

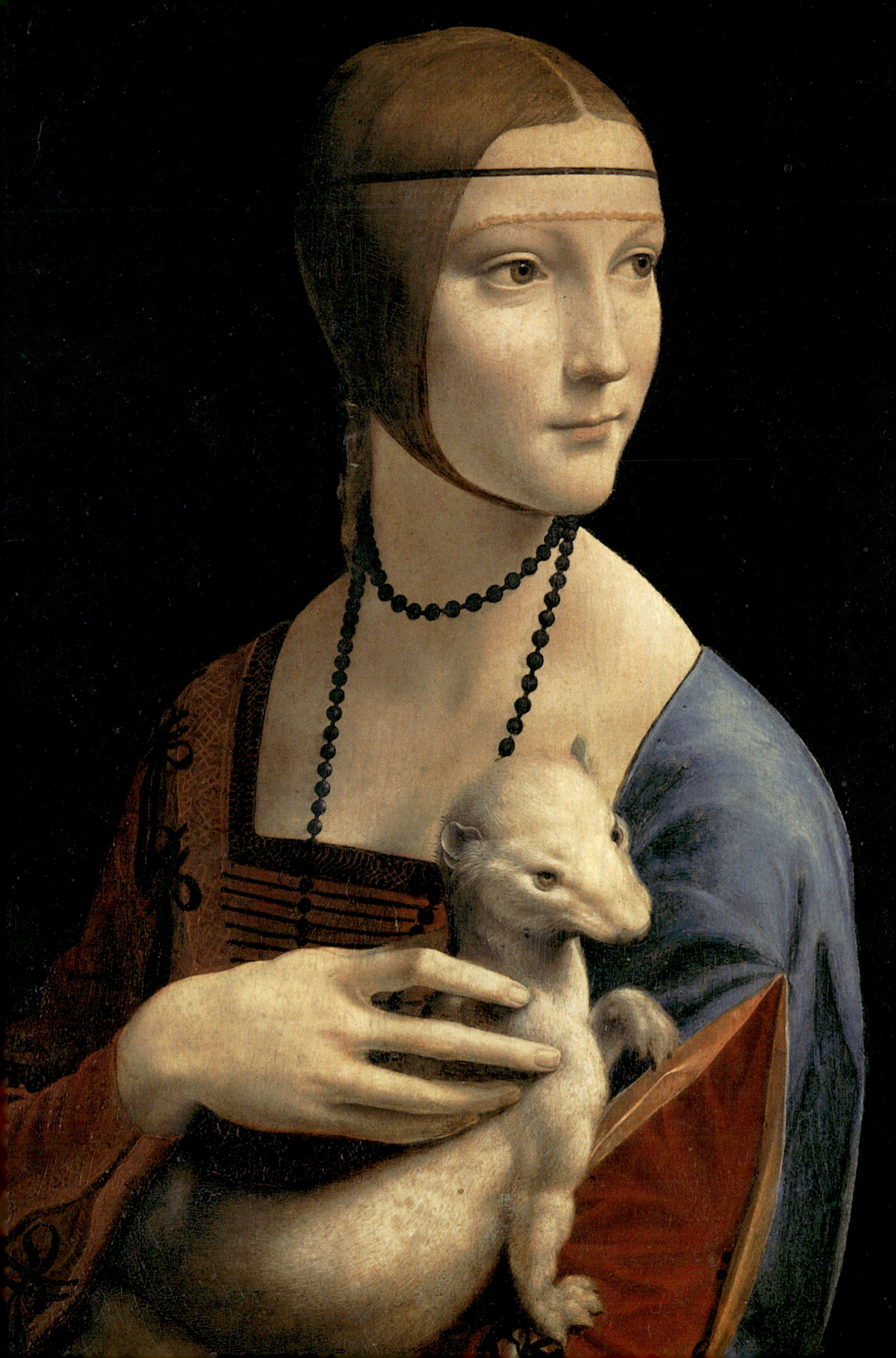

INTRODUCTION

Of all the categories and periods that have been devised to make sense of the sweep of art history, the 'Italian Renaissance' is perhaps the most coherent. Whereas artists in the Middle Ages were not consciously 'medieval', artists in Italy between 1400 and 1600 very deliberately worked to bring about renewal. This renewal was intellectual, stylistic, technical and philosophical. It involved the revival of the study of the human figure and its proportions; a new emphasis on drawing as the foundation of art; the use of perspective to enhance the impression of depth and realism; and an enthusiastic rediscovery of the rich heritage of the classical world. The names of its great masters are well known: Botticelli and Mantegna, Perugino and Leonardo, Raphael and Michelangelo, Correggio and Titian. Their masterpieces, which today hang in galleries across the world, reflect a true golden age of art, a period of staggering innovation.

At the heart of the Renaissance was the humanist culture that had first found expression in the works of Dante and Giotto in the early 14th century. From that moment onwards more and more emphasis would be placed on humankind, and less on the divine – a major departure from the medieval worldview that placed God at the heart of everything. Humanism also encouraged study of the literature and art of Ancient Greece and Rome, much of which had been lost (or frowned upon) in the Middle Ages. This trend, soon bolstered by intellectuals and philosophers keen to escape the strictures of medieval thought, produced a vein of artistic brilliance and innovation that lasted right through to Caravaggio.

The crucible of the Renaissance was Florence, and by the second half of the 15th century – the era of Lorenzo de' Medici, known as 'the Magnificent' – the Tuscan city had become the meeting place of poets, philosophers and artists. It was here that ancient Roman mythology was given new life in the works of Botticelli while Antique architecture was revived by Alberti and Brunelleschi, and Antique sculpture by Donatello. Meanwhile, a resplendent Venice reigned as Queen of the Seas and the minor courts of Urbino, Mantua and Ferrara fostered artistic talent and had intellectual influence out of all proportion to their size. The Milan of the Sforzas was in many respects the heart of the Western world, and the patronage of its wealthy elite gave Leonardo considerable opportunities. The Kingdom of Naples was the hub of Mediterranean trade and cultural exchange, from where Italian Renaissance ideas were exported further afield. As is clear from this list, 'Italy' was still not a single country, but rather a collection of occasionally warring states, each with its own dialect, currency and customs. This fragmentation was expressed in a number of different 'schools' of art, which placed emphasis on particular characteristics. Nonetheless, the whole of the Italian peninsula offered untold possibilities for artists.

Importantly, these courts also offered a chance to artists to participate in intellectual debate, which in time led to the elevation of their status. In this sense, the Renaissance sees the birth of the modern artist, an independent *thinker* as well as a craftsman. Renaissance painting frequently combines the intellectual rigour of geometry with poetics. As a result of this new stature, by the 16th century, artists were courted by popes, dukes and emperors, and offered extravagant privileges. An early chronicler of these artists, Giorgio Vasari, characterized this period as one of great geniuses; no doubt he was thinking of Leonardo, Raphael and Michelangelo. With Leonardo in particular, the Middle Ages finally came to an end, and all of Europe adopted the 'modern manner' as a model. Italy's artistic primacy was universally accepted and uncontested.

By the early 16th century, however, a serious political and economic crisis was developing across Europe. Challenged by France, Germany and the Ottomans in the east, the Italian peninsula grew increasingly peripheral in world affairs. The dream of reviving the political power and splendour of Rome, the principal pursuit of Pope Julius II (1503–13), was short-lived, and although it resulted in the magnificent Vatican works of Raphael and Michelangelo, the Protestant Reformation was just around the corner. Things continued to go downhill until the Sack of Rome in 1527. This bloody pillaging of the Eternal City by mutinous troops of Emperor Charles V marked a traumatic end to the humanist dream of a world of beauty and harmony.

Nonetheless, it did not mark the end of the Renaissance from an artistic point of view – quite the opposite. Sixteenth-century Italian artists and intellectuals, fully aware of the divisive political situation, sought to forge a common form of expression. While the power and influence of many once-proud states declined across the Italian peninsula (only the Most Serene Republic of Venice managed to preserve its full independence), painting flourished, building on the incredibly rich inheritance of Raphael and Leonardo. The output of two remarkably long-lived artists, Michelangelo and Titian, illustrates the radical changes in taste that occurred as the 16th century wore on. The innovation continued, and even a late Renaissance artist such as Caravaggio was able to find radical new ways of expressing old stories amid the climate of reinvigorated Catholicism fostered by the Counter-Reformation.

This book represents an entirely fresh approach to this exciting story.
Each double-page spread introduces a single painting, in various media,
arranged chronologically according to when it was created. We begin with
Gentile da Fabriano's *Valle Romita Polyptych* (1405–10) and end with
Caravaggio's *The Rest on the Flight into Egypt* (*c.* 1595). Every painting
is reproduced in full as well as through a number of details, with captions
that explain its content, technique or symbolism, while every artist is
introduced with a short biography.

Artists are referred to by the most familiar form of their name in English.
This may be a birth name, a nickname, an anglicized version of their
name, or a religious epithet. Other names in use during an artist's lifetime
are given in brackets at the start of his or her biography. The dimensions
of works of art are given in the form height × width (× depth).

The works in this book have been chosen not only for their intrinsic
importance and beauty but also as the visual embodiments of a series
of key themes, topics and techniques (as indicated by the title of each
spread) that together encapsulate and explain the timeless genius of Italian
Renaissance painting.

INDEX OF THEMES, TOPICS AND TECHNIQUES

A

Academy 324
Allegory 316
Allusion 242
Altarpiece 210
Ambiguity 306
Anatomy 170
Animals 30
Antiquarian 354
Apotheosis 366
Apprehension 284
Archaeology 120
Architecture 188
Astronomy 198
Atmosphere 178
Awe 288

B

Balance 156
Battle 68
Bizarrerie 380

C

Caricature 370
Cassone 36
Cenacolo 44
Ceiling 212
Central Axis 50
Central Plan 194
Ceremony 62
Chiaroscuro 302
Classicism 152
Collecting 286
Colorito 200
Colour 32
Composition 208
Contrapposto 248
Council of Trent 374

Counter-Reformation 356
Court 76
Crisis 312
Culture 114
Cupid 296

D

Delicacy 282
Detail 150
Diagonal 382
Dispersal of Artists 300
Divine Proportions 172
Dome 268
Donors 134
Double Portrait 220
Drama 270
Dynamism 246
Dynasty 158

E

The East 196
Ekphrasis 154
Eloquence 266
Equestrian Portrait 336
Eroticism 298
Expressionism 86

F

Family 326
Fashion 328
Female Nude 344
Flemish Artists 108
Foreshortening 116
Fresco 34
Friendship 254

G

Gallery 390
Genre Painting 386
Gentleman 230
Geometry 106
Gesture 216
Gold Ground 42
The Golden Section 38
Grace 124

H

Half-length Figure 264
Harmony 176
Hierarchy of the Arts 260
Historicized Portrait 304
Humanism 100

I

Iconographic Programme 186
Idea 138
Ideal City 118
Idyll 224
Illusion 232
Illustrious Men 52
Intellectuals 228
International Gothic 28
Internationalism 112

K

Kiss 294

L

Landscape 376
Leonardesque 146
Library 40
Line 90
Literature 262
Luxury 14

M

Maestà 56

Male Nude 278

Mankind 18

Mannerism 276

Medals 102

Melancholy 318

Michelangelesque 338

Mirror 244

Monochrome 250

Movement 74

Movements of the Soul 160

Myth 272

N

Narrative 140

Naturalism 372

Nature 206

Neo-Platonism 132

Nepotism 330

Night Scene 360

Non finito 332

Northern Europe 202

O

Obsession 292

Ovid's *Metamorphoses* 78

P

Palladianism 362

Papacy 256

Pastorale 350

Patron 104

Perfection 236

Perspective 22

Politics 66

Polyptych 12

Popularism 378

Portico 26

Portrait 148

Power 322

Preparatory Cartoon 226

Private Devotion 136

Procession 70

Profile 80

Provincial 364

Psychological
    Indeterminacy 164

R

Realism 358

Reclining Nude 222

Relationship among
    Figures 258

Replicas 130

Rhetoric 240

Rhythm 24

Rivalry 252

Romanists 340

S

Sacra Conversazione 274

Sacra Rappresentazione 234

Scream 388

Self-portrait 168

Semicircle 218

Sensuality 308

Sfumato 180

Shadow 110

Sinuosity 334

Smile 192

Sobriety 20

Spatial Depth 122

Square Panel 46

Stage Scenery 320

Still Life 368

Stories 60

Studiolo 184

Students of Squarcione 72

Style 142

Sunset 392

Symbolism 128

Symmetry 96

T

Telero 162

Theatre 352

The Three Ages of Man 238

Tondo 190

Torsion 280

Treatises 348

Triumph of Death 48

Triptych 144

Trompe l'oeil 82

U

Ugliness 204

Ut pictura poesis 346

V

Vanishing Point 58

Veduta 166

Venus 88

Vitruvius 174

Volume 16

W

Women Artists 342

Workshop 92

Polyptych

Gentile da Fabriano
Valle Romita Polyptych
1405–10

Tempera on panel,
157.2 × 79.6 and 117.5 × 40 (× 4)
and 48.9 × 378 (× 4) cm

Milan, Pinacoteca di Brera

Gentile da Fabriano

Fabriano, Ancona, 1370/80–Rome, 1427

Gentile da Fabriano, a native of the Marche region in central Italy, was the most sought-after and revered artist of the first quarter of the 15th century. His first important work was the *Valle Romita Polyptych*, today found in the Pinacoteca di Brera, Milan. In 1408, Gentile visited Venice, where he painted frescoes in the Ducal Palace. Although they are lost today, their influence on Venetian art of the first half of the 15th century was profound. After a stay in Lombardy, Gentile returned to the Marche region, and then in 1419 he went to Florence where he came in contact with the incipient humanist movement as well as Antique sculpture. His most famous work, the sumptuous *The Adoration of the Magi* (see pages 14–15), now in the Uffizi Gallery, Florence, dates from 1423. The *Quaratesi Polyptych* came soon after. Following brief stays in Siena and Orvieto, in early 1427 Gentile was summoned to Rome to begin the decoration of the basilica of St John Lateran. He died shortly after beginning work. Significantly, he bequeathed his brushes and the commission to Pisanello.

The polyptych or multi-panelled painting originated in the 14th century but remained the most widespread type of altarpiece throughout the 15th – at least until it was replaced by the single-scene altarpiece employing the rules of perspective. Italian polyptychs seldom include the painted and sculpted figures and movable wings and doors typical of those painted north of the Alps. The distribution of panels around a large central scene (often devoted to the Madonna), is perfectly symmetrical; figures of saints appear at the sides, while at the bottom narrative scenes often appear in a series of panels called a predella. More opulent examples include a higher second register of panels and an ornamental moulding at the top, often incorporating images of the Crucifixion or Christ Blessing. This polyptych by Gentile da Fabriano was produced for the convent of Valle Romita. The original frame has been lost, and opinions differ as to whether the polyptych should be displayed in an imitation Gothic frame or unframed, directly on the wall.

Precious and Fragile: Polyptych Fragments

Italian polyptychs are rich, complex structures that required skills in carpentry as well as in painting. The scenes were often painted on a gold ground and mounted in ornately carved gilt frames, sometimes designed by the same painter but more often the product of a specialized workshop. Many frames were destroyed, especially in the 18th and 19th centuries, in part due to changing tastes, but also because the panels could be sold separately, sometimes to recover the pure gold in which they were covered. The dispersal of the panels to different collections has made it difficult to reconstitute original groupings.

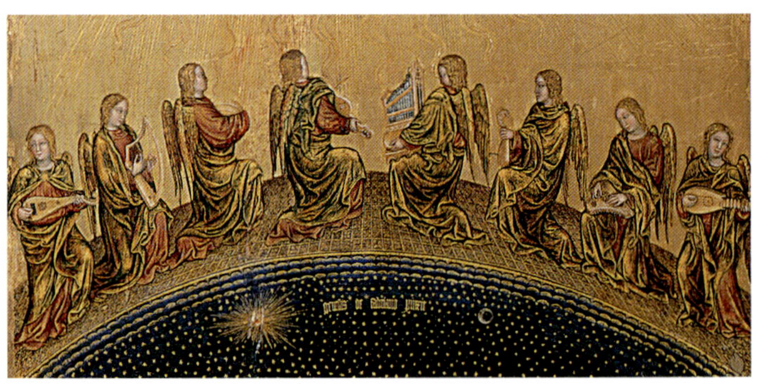

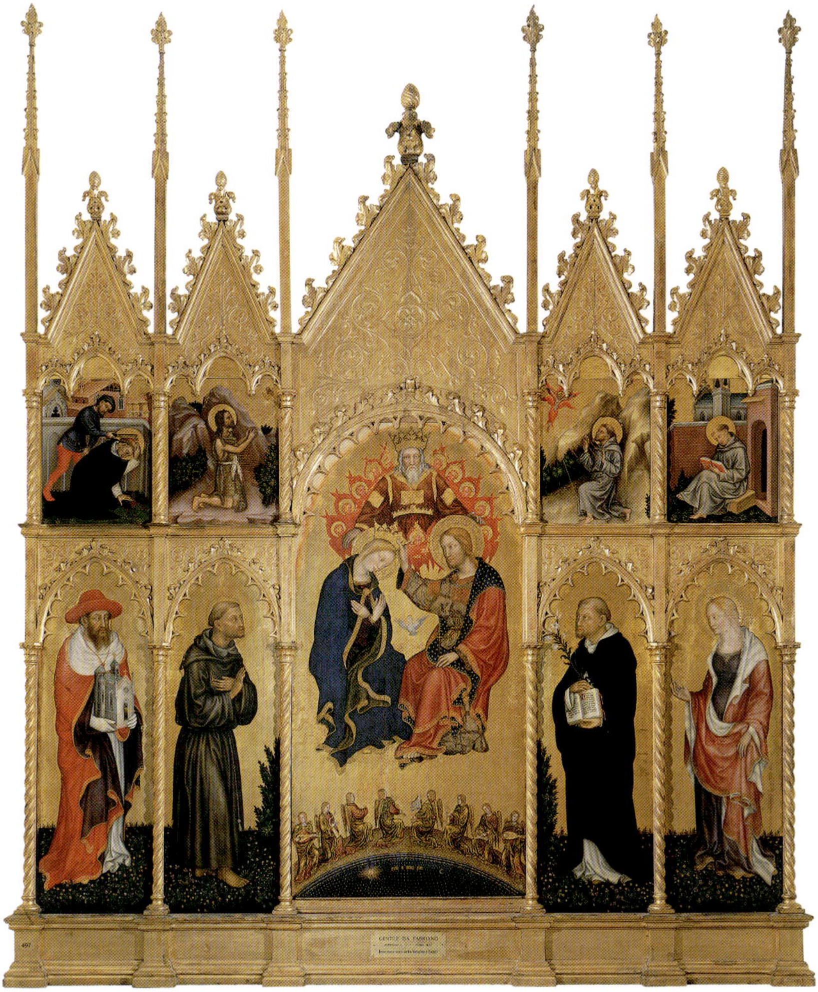

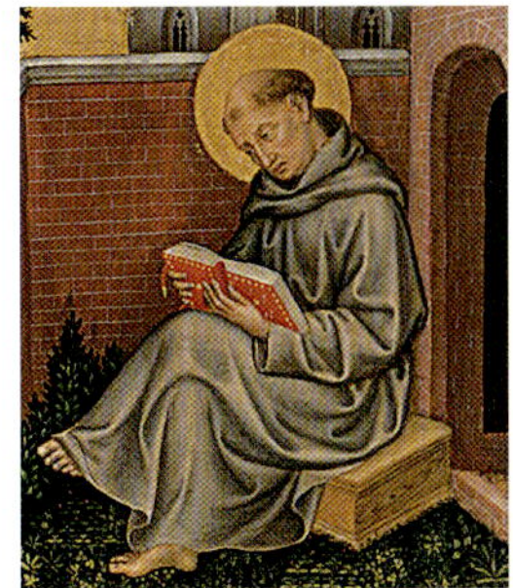

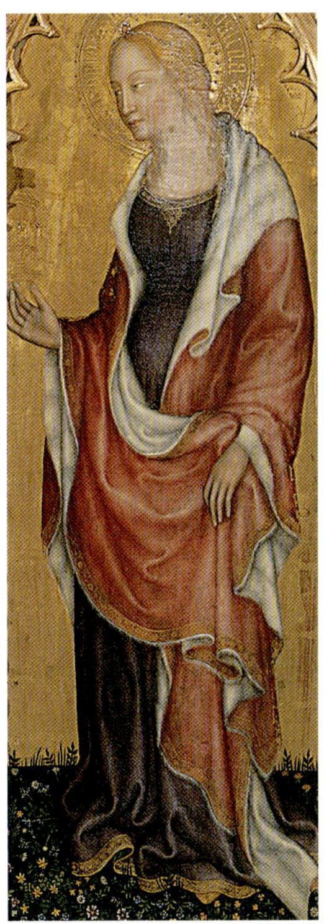

▲ The focus of this polyptych is the Coronation of the Virgin, in which Christ crowns his mother Queen of Heaven.

◄ The orchestra of angels is arrayed just above the vault of heaven. The mandolin, psalter and organ are all depicted in detail. Beneath the angels, stars shine in the deep-blue sky, and the painter's signature glows between the sun and the moon.

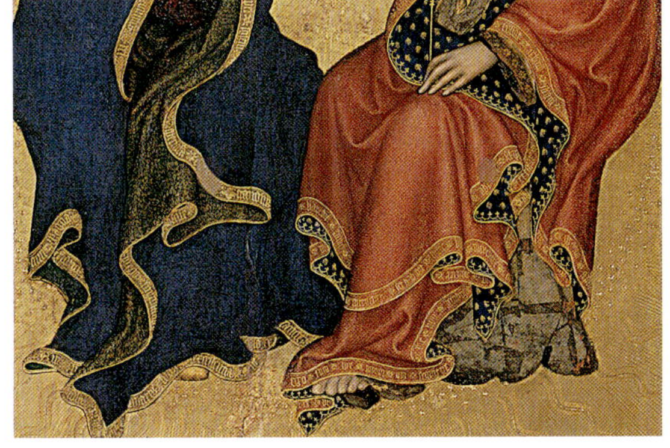

▲ The cloaks of Mary and Christ are coloured with costly materials: lapis lazuli and pure gold and silver leaf. The drapery falls in intricate folds, and a prayer is embroidered along the border of the Madonna's robes.

▲ St Jerome, St Francis, St Dominic and St Mary Magdalene face the central panel. Dressed in fur-lined clothing, the slender, blonde Magdalene is the picture of an elegant maiden.

13

Luxury

Gentile da Fabriano
The Adoration of the Magi
1423

Tempera on panel, 300 × 282 cm
Florence, Galleria degli Uffizi

For artist biography, see page 12.

In the first decades of the 15th century, Italian painting still largely adhered to the International Gothic style. Although Brunelleschi and Donatello had attempted to direct Florentine sculpture and architecture towards a new style based on the example of Antiquity, Florentine painters remained enthralled by the visual delight of precious colours and precisely depicted details. The journey of the Three Wise Men or Magi, with retinues of exotic servants, sumptuous costumes and splendid gifts for the Christ Child, offered the perfect excuse for a dazzling depiction of luxury. Gentile da Fabriano's radiant panel, painted for the Florentine church of Santa Trinita, marks a high point in the painter's career and reflects the wealth of the patron who commissioned it, Palla Strozzi, who at the time was probably the richest man in Florence.

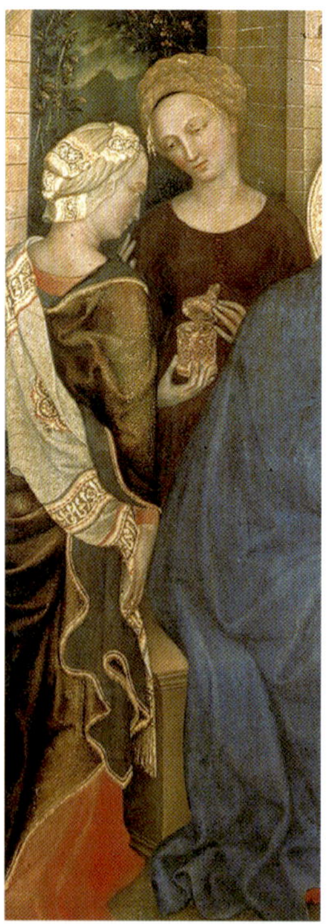

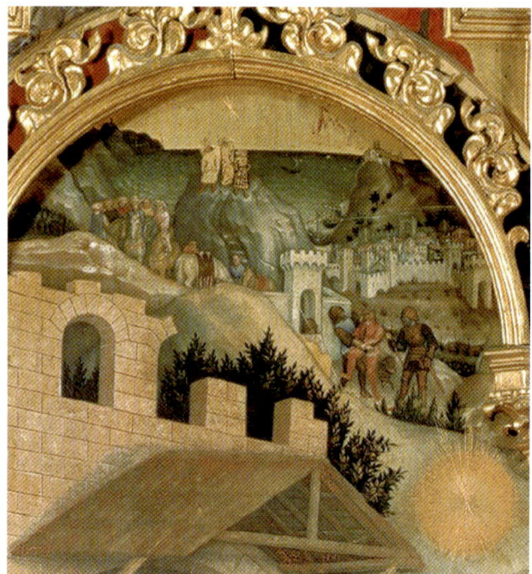

◄ The painting is conceived as a long narrative. Patient viewers can follow the various stages of the journey of the Magi, finding details in the distance as well. For example, on a rocky plateau under the upper left arch, the Three Wise Men try to interpret the position and direction of the comet, which gleams with a refined effect against the small patch of gold ground.

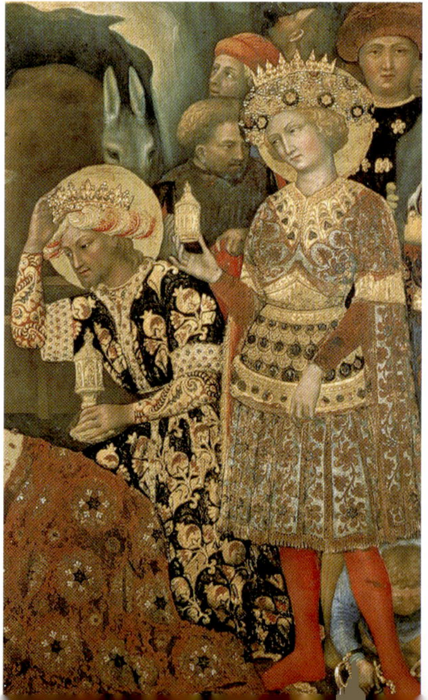

◄ ► The costumes are particularly elegant and luxurious – not only those of the Magi and their retinue, but also those of the midwives (who do not appear in the biblical account) whose flowing, gold-embroidered robes fall in elegant, winding folds. The cloaks and garments of the Magi, made of extraordinary fabric stitched in gold and adorned with silver-thread embroidery, are the height of luxury. Late Gothic artists often designed court costumes, and Gentile da Fabriano's Magi model the most sumptuous fashions of the early 15th century.

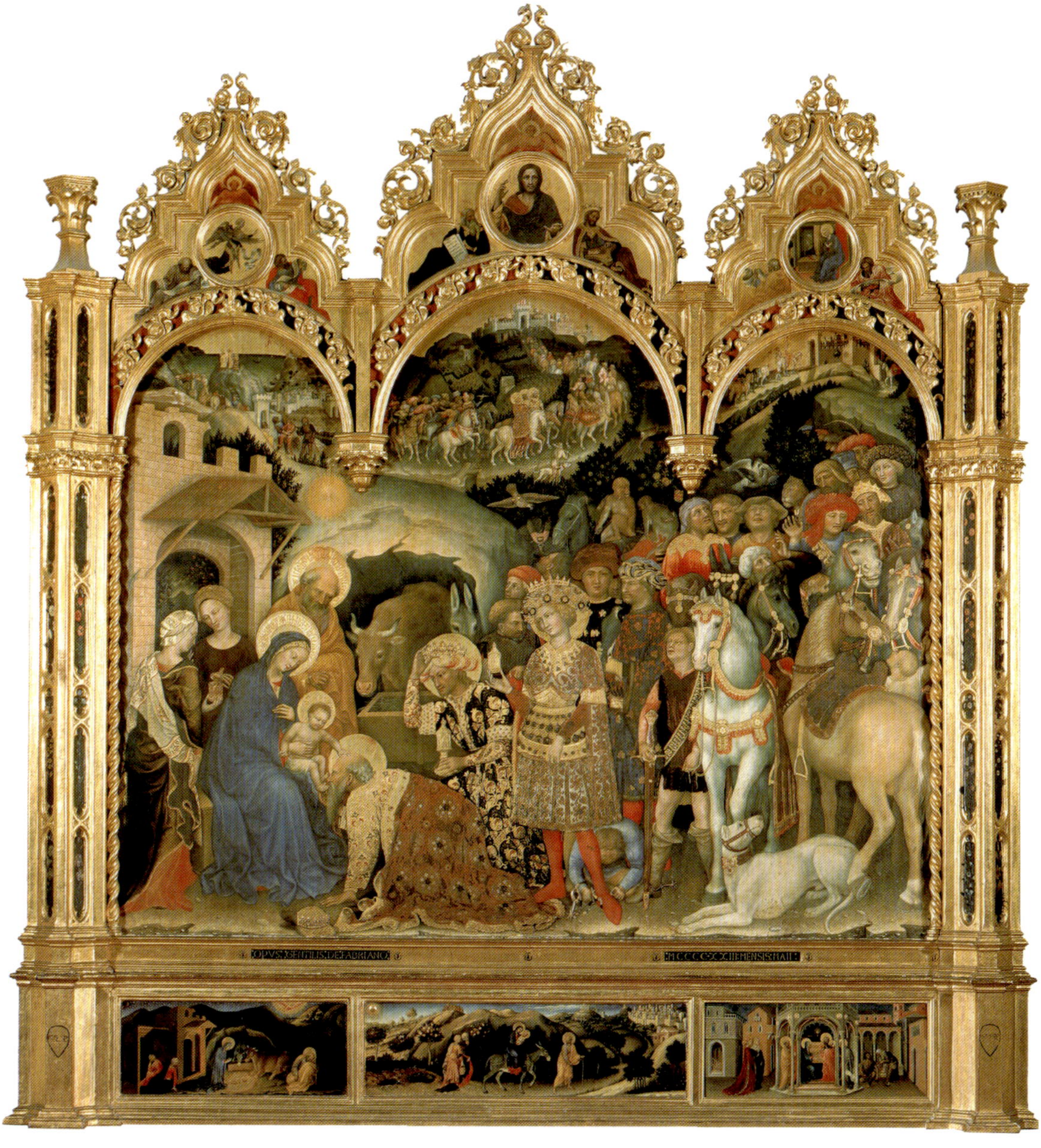

► This magnificent painting should not be seen only as a display of pomp, however, since it carries some weighty messages. In the middle of the procession, a leopard (an exotic animal that members of the Italian nobility often kept in their menageries) hisses and snarls at the horses, symbolizing a violent, savage world – while the birth of Jesus marks a new era of peace and love.

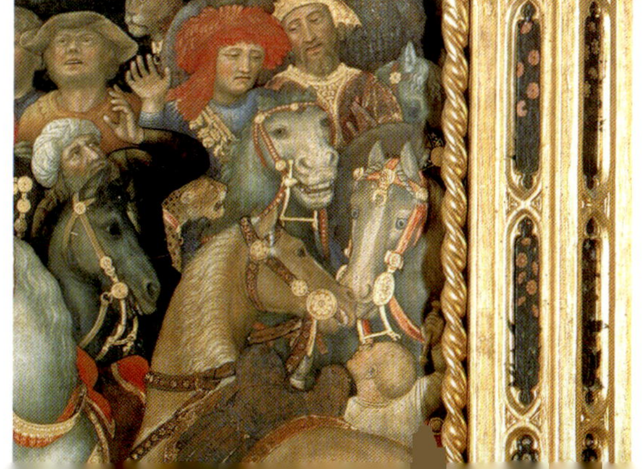

Volume

Masaccio
The Tribute Money
Detail from the *Stories of Peter*
1424–8

Fresco, 255 × 598 cm

Florence, Santa Maria del Carmine,
Brancacci Chapel

Masaccio

(Tommaso di Giovanni)

San Giovanni Valdarno, Florence, 1401–
Rome, 1428

Masaccio, a boy from the countryside
whose real name was Tommaso, was
the first to apply the new thinking of
Donatello and Brunelleschi to painting.
Though he died aged just 27, his influence
was enormous. His first major work was
the San Giovenale triptych in the small
town of Cascia di Reggello (1422); after
this Masaccio moved to Florence where
he came into contact with Masolino
da Panicale. Together, the two painters
executed the *Madonna and Child with
St Anne* (1424; now in the Uffizi) and,
immediately after, began the frescoes
in the Brancacci Chapel at Santa Maria
del Carmine. They divided tasks and
scenes. Masaccio gave the figures a solid
volume, and placed them in urban spaces
or wild landscapes. Masaccio continued
this approach in his subsequent works,
such as the large polyptych with a gold
ground for the Carmelite church in Pisa
(1425; the panels are dispersed among
various museums) and the fresco of *The
Trinity* in Santa Maria Novella in Florence
(1427). At the end of 1427, Masaccio
went to Rome and died soon after of
unknown causes.

Soon after Gentile da Fabriano painted the *Adoration of the Magi* (see pages 14–15), the Florentine Masaccio proposed a radically different approach to painting. In contrast to the spectacular richness of the International Gothic style, his style is severe and strictly focused on the arrangement of solid figures within a landscape setting. Of course, the difference of medium must be taken into account – Gentile painted on panel, Masaccio in fresco. Nonetheless, while Gentile da Fabriano's figures crowd together in a lively manner, almost giving the impression they are climbing on top of one another, Masaccio's Apostles are imposing, geometric figures. Through the use of perspective and shadow he defines the volumes with remarkable clarity, and every figure occupies its own space.

A Complicated History

The frescoes of the Brancacci Chapel were fraught with problems from the outset. Although the two collaborators (Masolino and the younger Masaccio) had already worked together, their styles were very different, and combining them proved difficult. Then work on the chapel broke off suddenly, and the frescoes remained unfinished for about 60 years, until 1485, when Filippino Lippi completed them. In the 18th century, fire ravaged the church of Santa Maria del Carmine. The Brancacci Chapel, miraculously, was spared, though it did suffer smoke damage. In 1989, cleaning revealed the brilliant original colours, which had been so dulled down by soot and repainting that generations of visitors and art historians had believed that Masaccio's palette was dark and earth-toned. Masaccio's contributions now appear as he originally painted them: with colours as pure and clear as Masolino's.

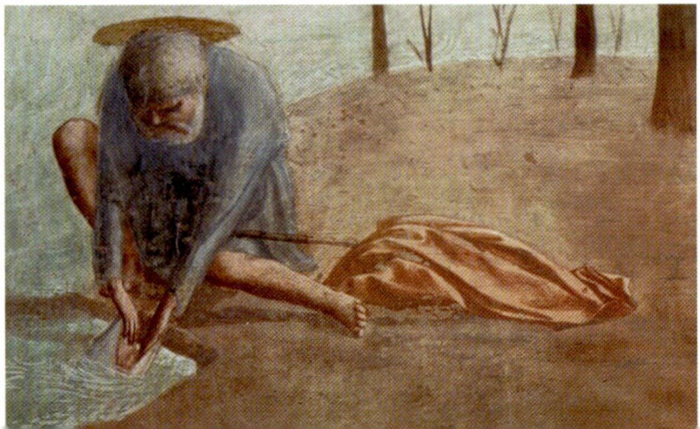

◄ Masaccio's use of solid, volumetrically defined forms is particularly effective in the static, solemn figures, but he also experimented with more relaxed and dynamic poses, like that of St Peter: his yellow cloak removed, he crouches bare-legged by the river to catch the fish whose stomach holds a silver coin.

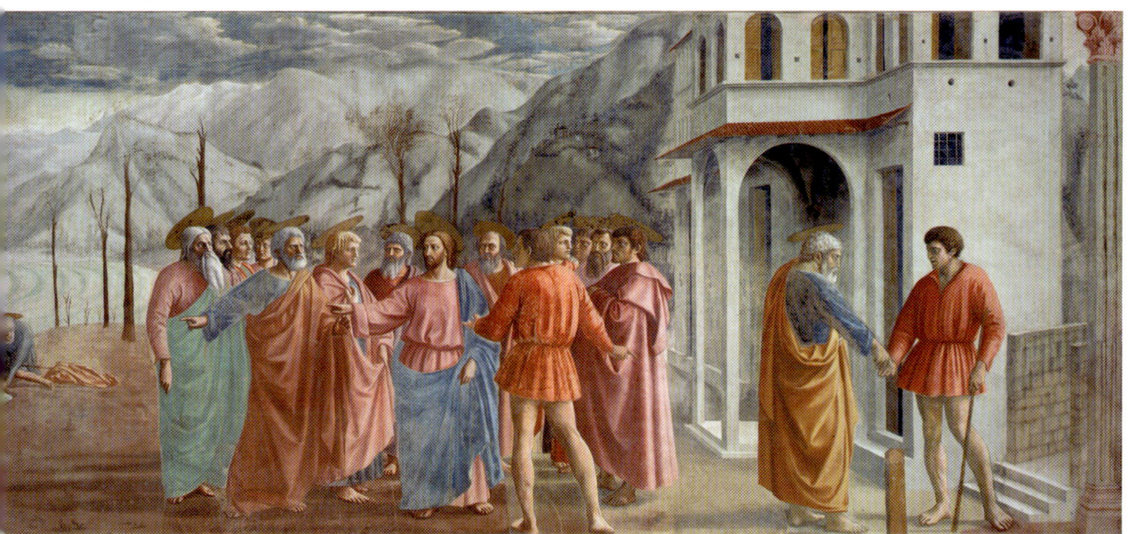

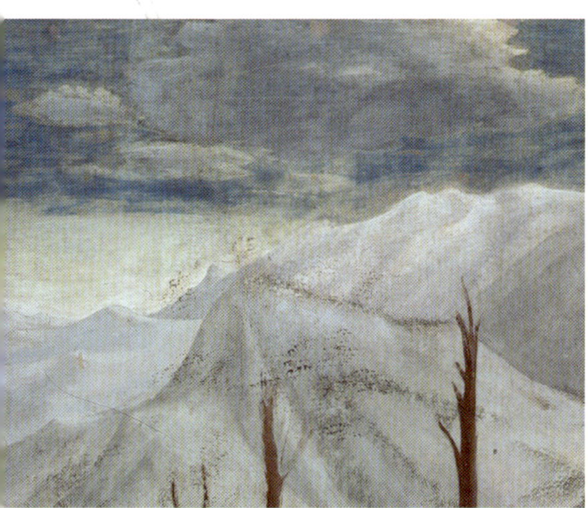

◄▲ Masaccio depicts three successive moments in a single, drastically simplified landscape: in the centre, Christ suggests that Peter should catch a fish; at the left, Peter does so; and at the right, he hands the coin – his tribute money – to the satisfied tax collector.

▼ The patron who commissioned this cycle of paintings, Felice Brancacci, was a tax collector, and so for him this scene had great personal significance.

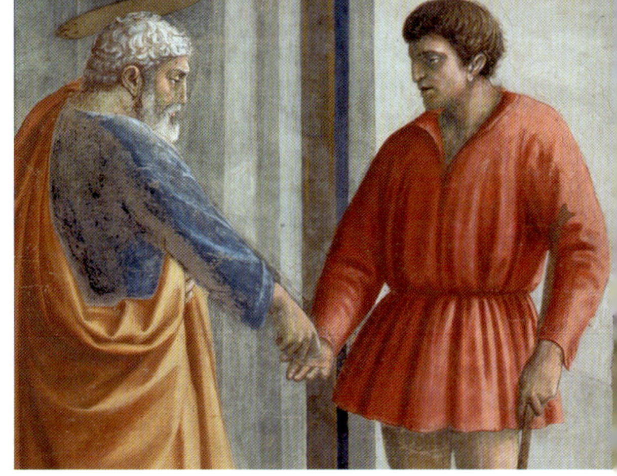

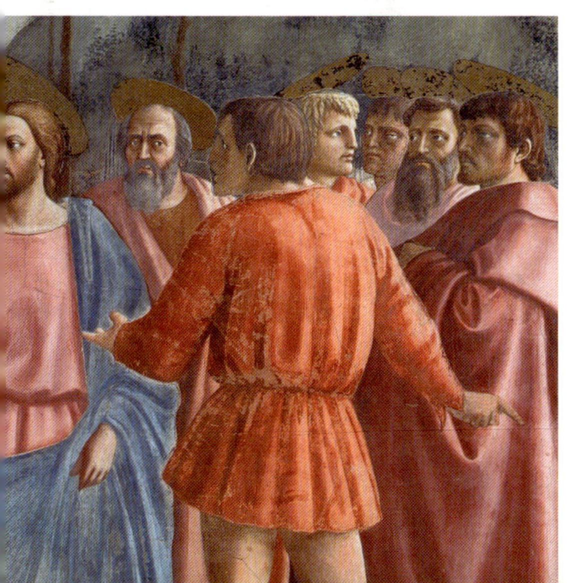

◄ The group of the Twelve Apostles (to which the tax collector, wearing a short red tunic, is added in the foreground) forms a circle around Christ, who turns to Peter with an assured gesture. The mass and arrangement of this group has caused it to be likened to the Colosseum in Rome.

Mankind

Masolino
The Temptation of Adam
1424–8

Fresco, 208 × 88 cm

Florence, Santa Maria del Carmine,
Brancacci Chapel

Masaccio
The Expulsion from Eden
1424–8

Fresco, 208 × 88 cm

Florence, Santa Maria del Carmine,
Brancacci Chapel

Masolino

(Tommaso di Cristofano Fini)

Panicale in Valdelsa, Siena, 1383–
Florence, 1440

Masolino had a peripatetic career as an artist, and perhaps the impossibility of identifying him with a particular school makes it harder to perceive his role in early humanism. He was a pupil of Ghiberti and the teacher of Masaccio, and active from Florence to Lombardy and from Umbria to Rome. The result of his early artistic collaboration with Masaccio is memorable: the Brancacci Chapel at the church of Santa Maria del Carmine. In 1425, Masolino came into contact with Cardinal Branda Castiglione whose patronage would continue until the end of his career. Masolino went to Hungary in the cardinal's entourage and in 1428 moved on to Rome to paint his private chapel in the basilica of San Clemente with frescoes of *The Story of St Catherine of Alexandria*. In 1435, again called upon by Branda Castiglione, Masolino went to Castiglione Olona, in Lombardy, where he decorated the chancel of the collegiate church, the baptistery (see pages 26–7) and some rooms in the cardinal's palace.

Masaccio

For artist biography, see page 16.

Early 15th-century Florentine art recast mankind as the conscious protagonist of history and maker of its own destiny. This type of thought had first become popular a century earlier, in the time of Giotto and Dante, but was checked by the devastating plague of 1348 and the subsequent return to a more God-focused and mystical view of the world. But now improved economic and social conditions, combined with a newly regained serenity, spurred intellectuals and artists to view man once again as the 'measure of all things'. The renewed interest in classical Antiquity became the basis for the movement called 'humanism', centred on the dignity, beauty, and physical and moral aspects of mankind. The two depictions of the first humans, Adam and Eve, by Masolino and Masaccio in the entrance of the Brancacci Chapel reflect this new emphasis.

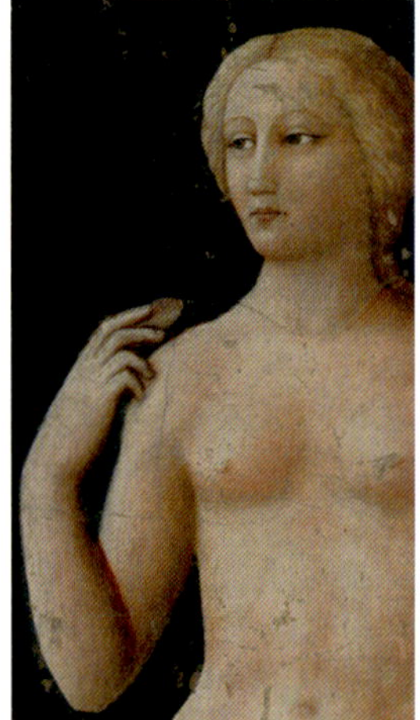

◄ The poses and expressions chosen by Masolino are serene and noble, inspired by classical statuary. Eve's body is luminous, as yet untouched by the shadow of sin.

▼ The features of the serpent's face clearly are those of a woman.

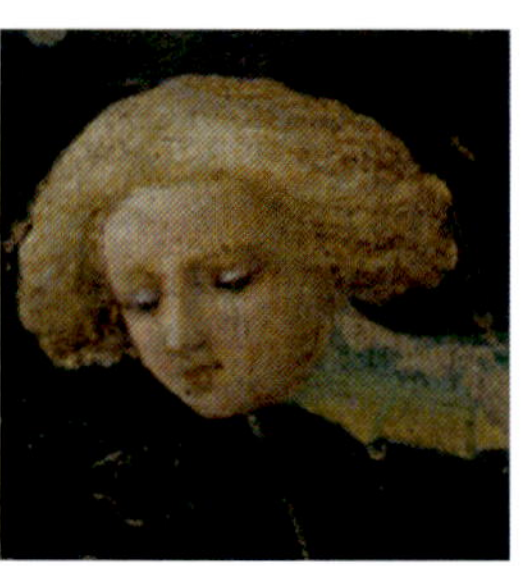

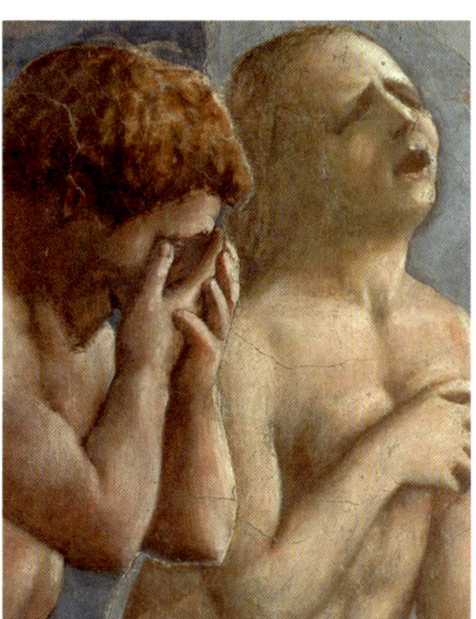

▲ Masaccio's Adam and Eve have lost the radiant grace of Masolino's figures. Instead, he captures the drama of the scene, investing the figures with an intense new physicality, restoring strength and independence to human nature. The heavy shadows give the figures a clearly defined volume.

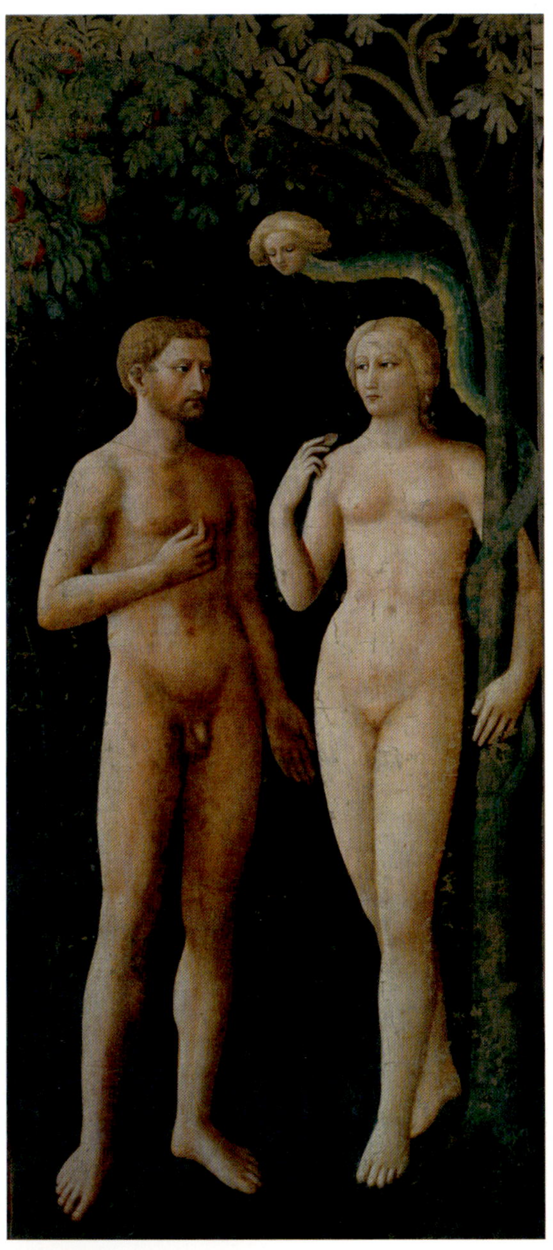

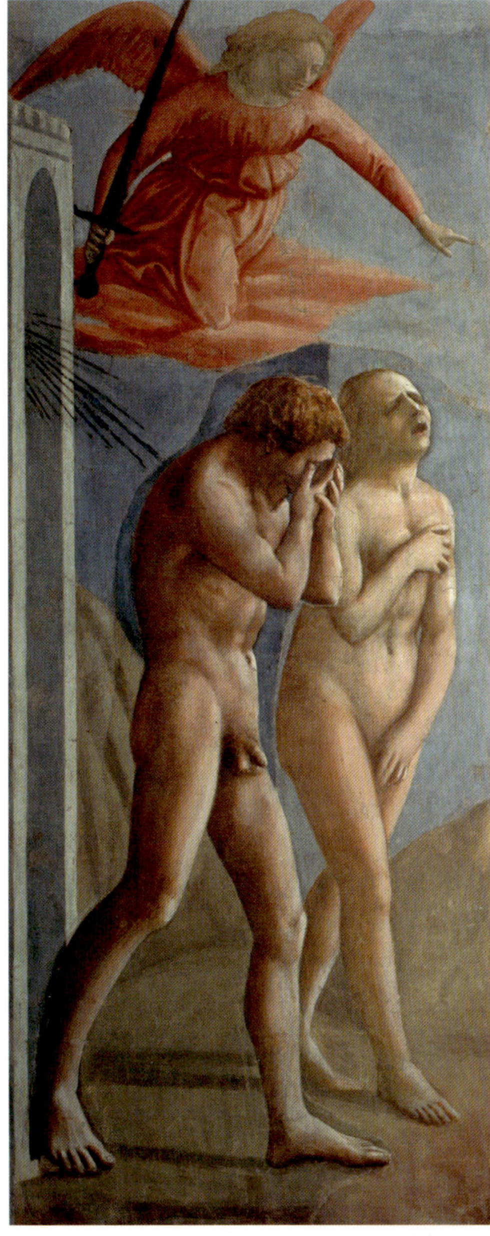

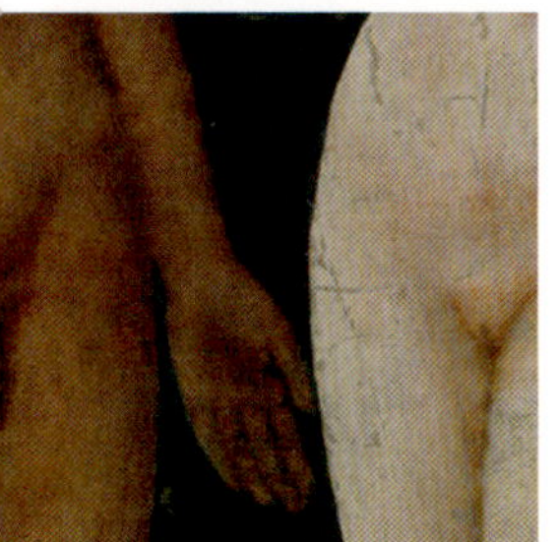

▲ ◄ Masolino's Eve is shown in the *contrapposto* pose in which the weight of the body falls on one foot, causing a tilting of the pelvis and shoulders. Masolino is not hesitant about showing their genitals.

▲ ► Expelled from Eden's gate by an angel sent by God, Adam and Eve face a bleak, inhospitable world. Masaccio uses shadow to convey a sense of weight.

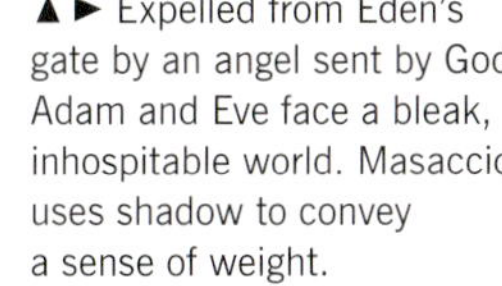

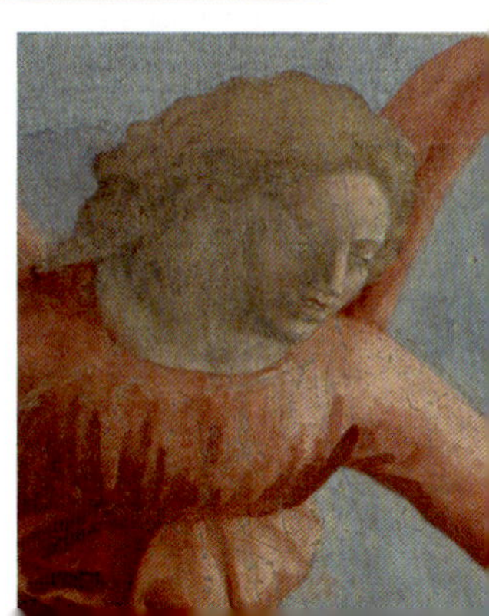

Sobriety

Masaccio
The Adoration of the Magi
Predella of the *Pisa Polyptych*
1426

Tempera on wood panel, 21 × 61 cm
Berlin, Gemäldegalerie

For artist biography, see page 16.

While the richly ornate late Gothic style remained in fashion in courts throughout the Italian peninsula, in Florence, a more measured form of expression and decoration prevailed in the art of Brunelleschi, Donatello and Masaccio. Their aim was to reflect the political order of the Florentine republic, which was controlled by a small group of powerful merchant and banking families, foremost among them the Medici. Scenes that even a few years before would have been the perfect vehicles for depictions of majestic luxury were now expected to express the sober, austere and deeply 'moral' attitudes of Florence's ruling class.

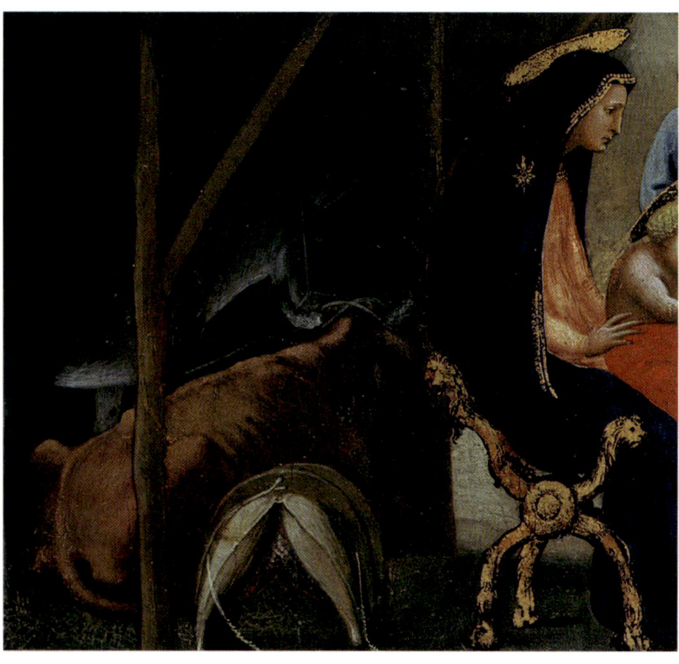

▲ Only three years after Gentile da Fabriano painted his *Adoration of the Magi* (see pages 14–15) in Florence, Masaccio conceived the same scene in an entirely different way, with fewer figures, restrained gestures, sober costumes, an almost total absence of gold and garish colours, and details drawn from real life. In this detail, Masaccio draws a parallel between the Madonna's folding stool and the donkey's pack saddle.

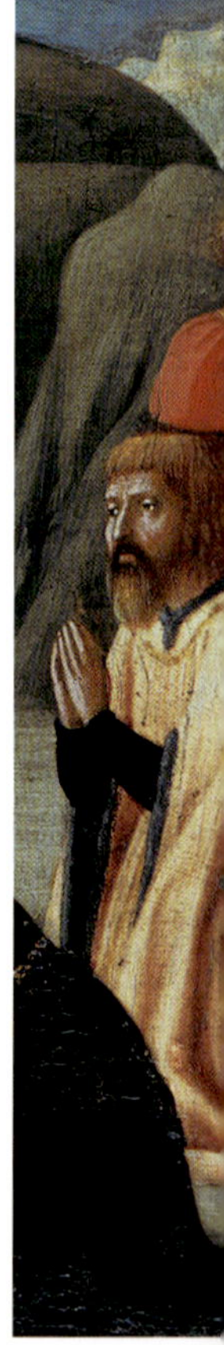

► The polyptych to which these panels belonged has long since been dismantled. The separate panels are now to be found in museums in Berlin, London, Los Angeles, Naples and Pisa.

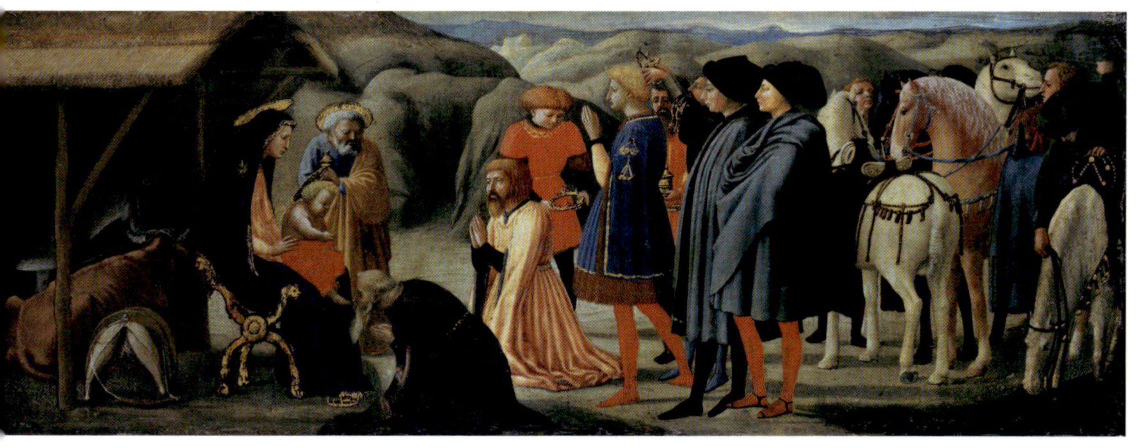

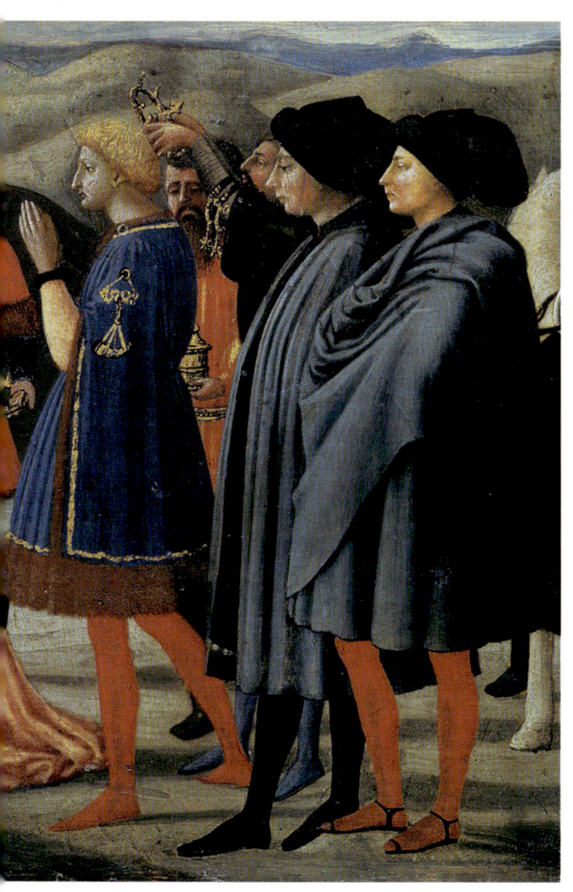

▲ This long, narrow painting is part of a polyptych; specifically, it is a predella, a horizontal panel running along the bottom of the altarpiece.

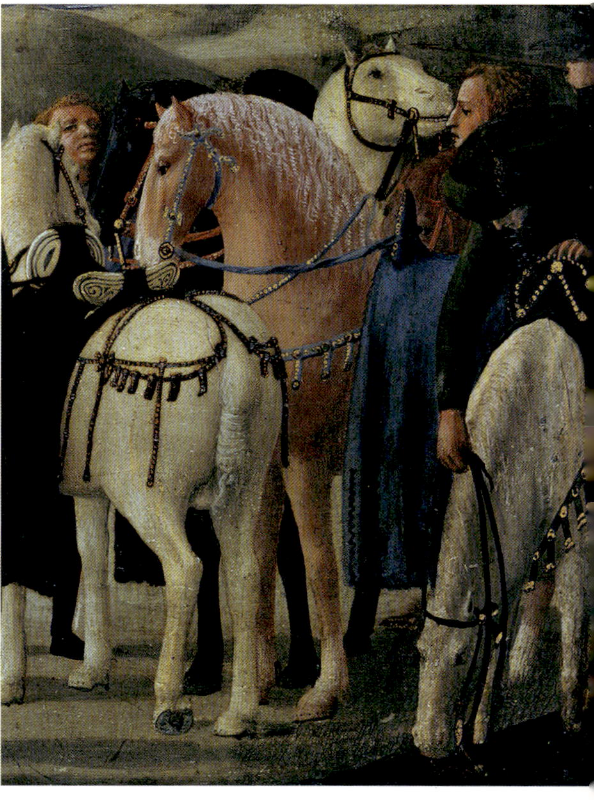

◄▲ In the visual arts as well as in performances of liturgical drama, the procession of the Magi often included exotic animals, lavishly uniformed pages and other sumptuously arrayed figures. But Masaccio limits the scene to the basics. The most prominent figures are two silent, stolid middle-class Tuscans wrapped in severe dark cloaks and wearing black headpieces. The horses' harnesses and trappings, too, are relatively simple: the painter was more interested in defining the animals in perspective.

Masaccio
The Trinity
1426

Fresco, 667 × 317 cm

Florence, Santa Maria Novella

For artist biography, see page 16.

Masaccio's final and most intense masterpiece is dominated by the influence of Brunelleschi. In fact, the architect may even have helped plan the architectural background. This fresco can be found in the Dominican church of Santa Maria Novella, in Florence. The perspectival setting imitates the opening of a deep niche with a barrel vault. Depicted as monumental, geometric volumes, the solemn figures are arranged to form a pyramid, with God at the top and the two kneeling donors at the bottom. They are in turn distributed along the lines of an imaginary pyramid.

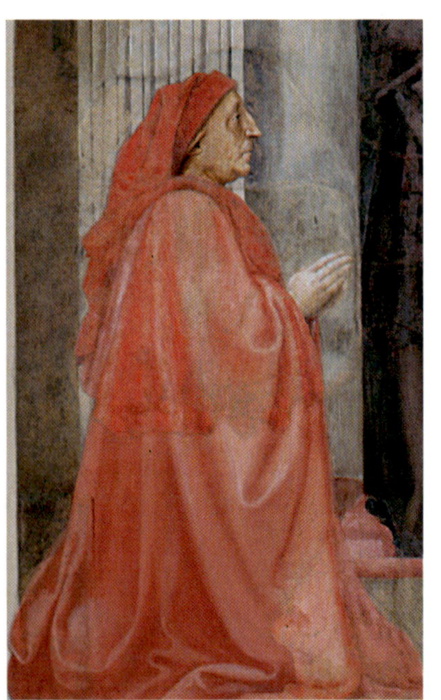

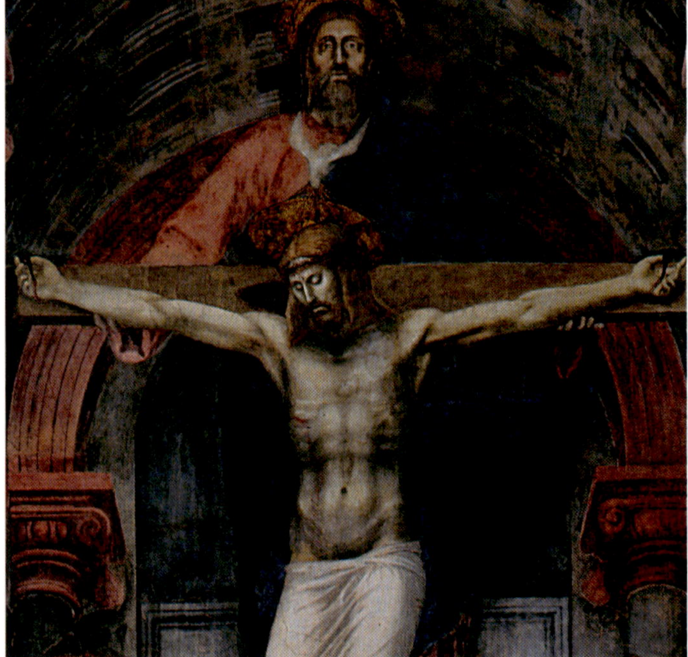

◄ The donors, already fairly advanced in years, kneel outside the *trompe-l'oeil* niche, at the base of tall Corinthian pilasters. They are probably Domenico de' Lenzi and his wife.

▲ At the centre, a solemn God supports Christ on the Cross. A white dove, symbol of the Holy Ghost, flutters between the heads of the Father and the Son.

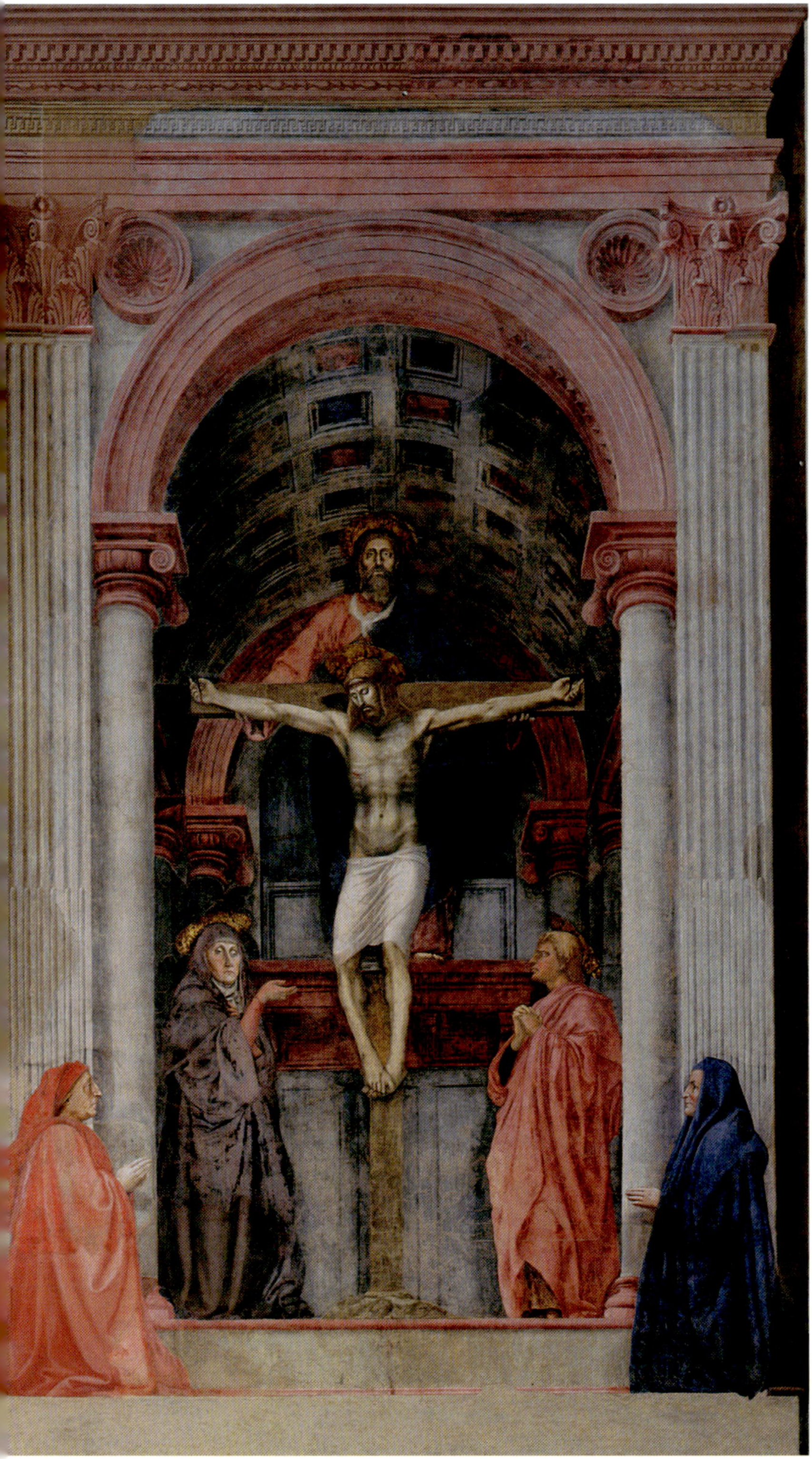

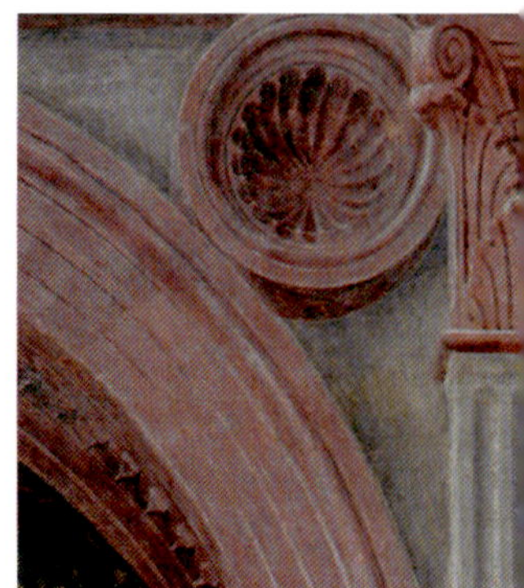

▲ The architectural details are meticulous, while the shadows increase the illusion of three-dimensionality.

▼ The two kneeling donors are reduced to pyramids themselves. Perspective is planned using simple geometric shapes arranged on a plane.

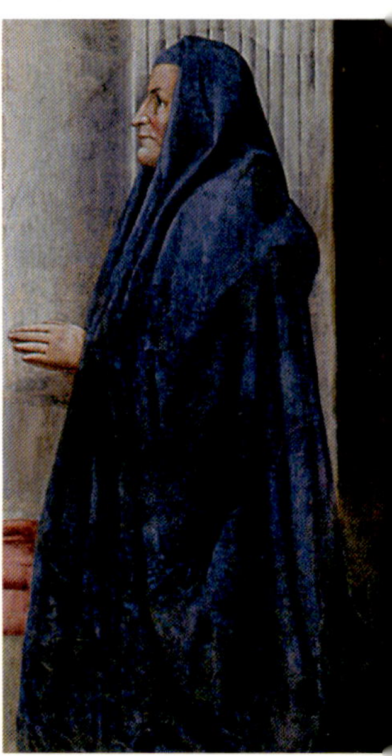

Rhythm

The Nine Heroes
c. 1430

Fresco

Manta, Cuneo, Sala Baronale of Castello

While Florentine art was moving towards the definition of 'solid' volumes arranged in a geometric space, the rest of Italy continued to uphold late Gothic taste. In frescoes decorating the residences and castles of the ruling class, a love of decoration prevailed over the dry, mathematical quest for convincing perspective and naturalism. Late Gothic painting, just like tapestries of the period, shows us, instead, a narrative that rhythmically unfolds along a wall, involving the viewer in a tale in which noble heroes and enchanting heroines stroll across fields of flowers, bearing armorial shields. The scene is exceedingly contrived, but it does make for an easily understood and beautifully decorative work.

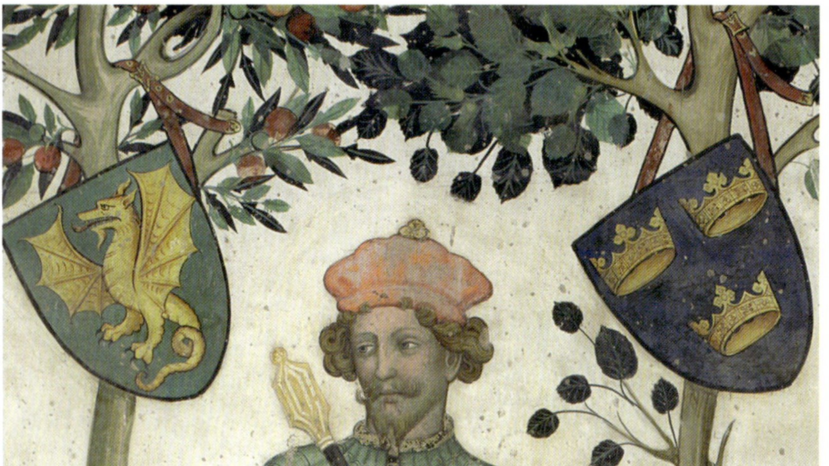

◀ The shields hanging from the trees bear heraldic arms and emblems. The code of heraldry, which may seem remote and complicated today, was a language shared by 15th-century courts. Symbols, shapes and colours had an immediately recognizable meaning and defined the rank, origin, nationality and characteristics of a family.

▶ The position of the feet establishes the pose and the relationships among the figures. The anonymous late Gothic painter was not interested in creating spatial depth but in showing a succession of people, rhythmically linked as though in a great ballet.

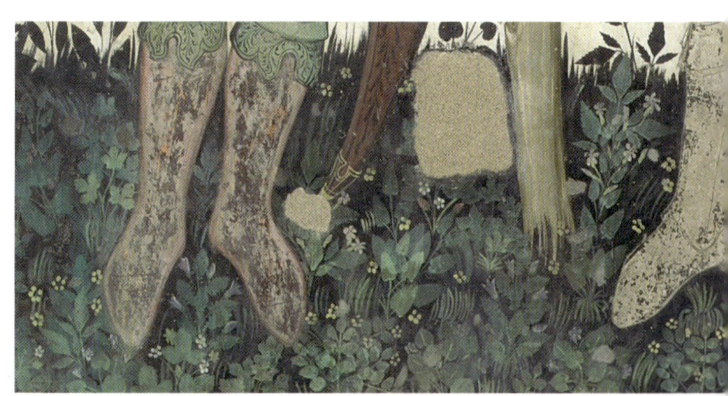

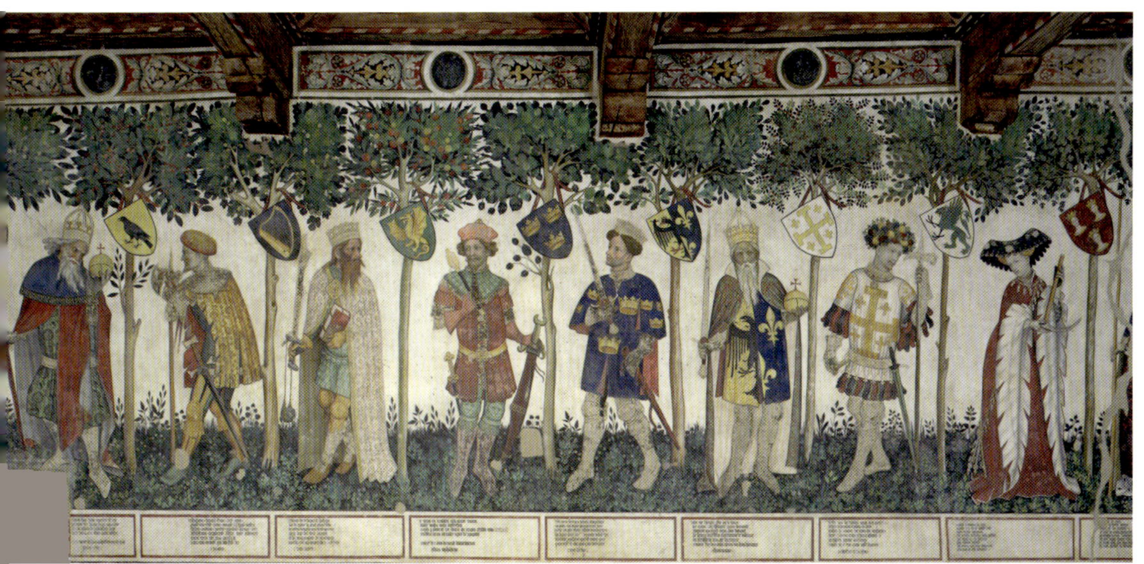

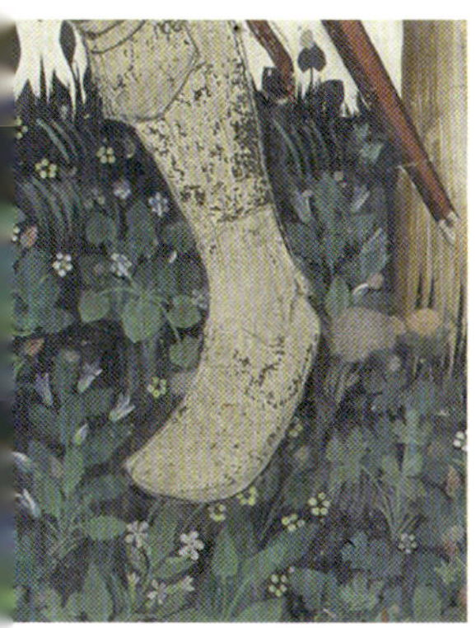

► The slender tree trunks between the figures give the wall a regular rhythm. The linear division is complemented by panels below, with poetic texts referring to each character, and reinforced by the prominent armorial shields. The painter was able to introduce variety into this simple schematic division through the figures' fanciful costumes, bizarre hairstyles and graceful movement.

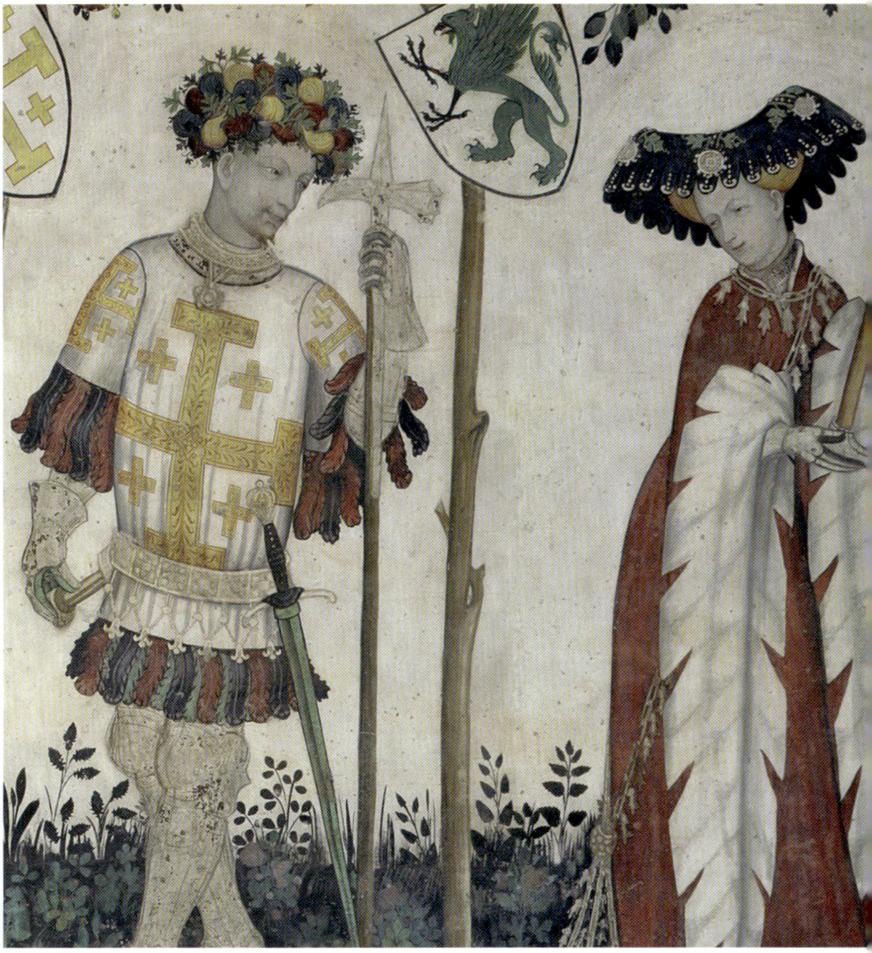

Portico

Masolino
The Banquet of Herod
Detail from *The Story of*
St John the Baptist
1435

Fresco, 380 × 473 cm

Castiglione Olona, Varese, baptistery

For artist biography, see page 18.

As artists travelled, and as they attempted to meet the exacting requests of their well-informed patrons, the rules of perspective gradually spread throughout Italy. One superb application of this new science can be found in a series of frescoes carried out by Masolino at the request of Cardinal Branda Castiglione in the town of Castiglione Olona, north of Milan. His pleasing narrative scenes, set amid long classical colonnades, were a far cry from the local Lombard tradition.

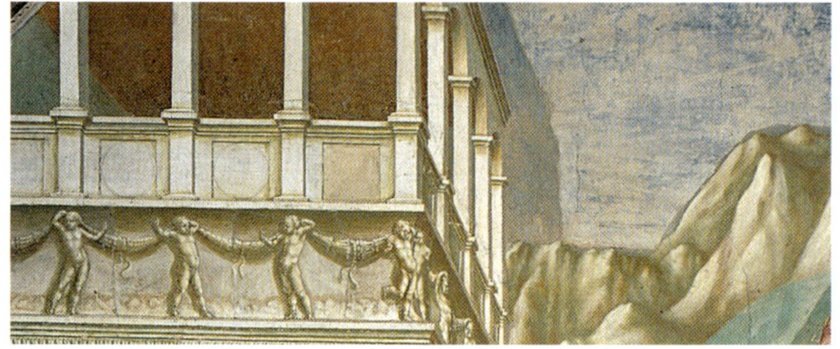

► The sides of Roman sarcophagi were often decorated with putti carrying garlands of leaves, a motif seized upon by Florentine artists in the early 15th century. Here, Masolino transfers the motif to the architecture, accentuating the contrast between the elegantly decorated galleries and the rugged mountains in the background.

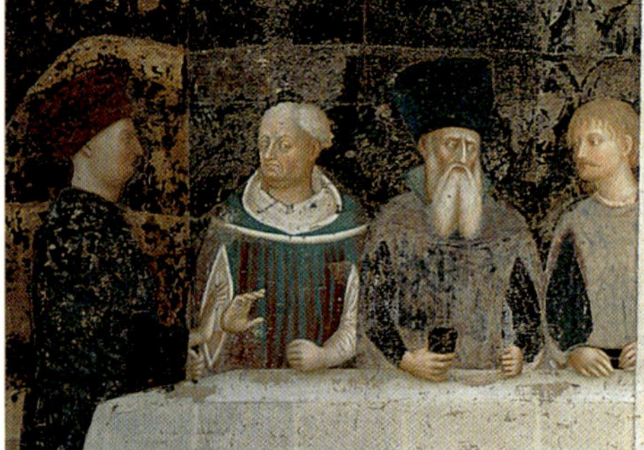

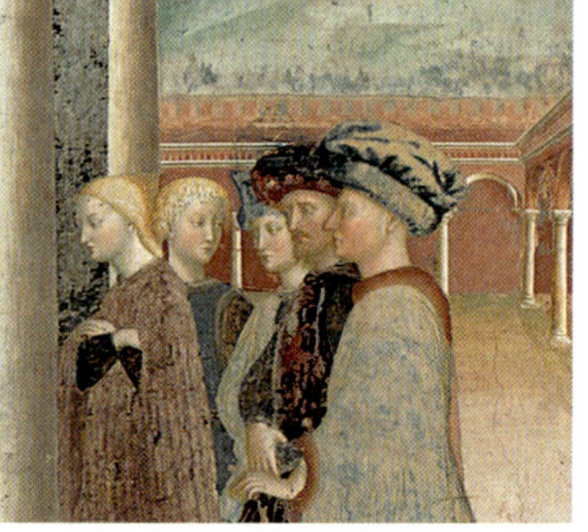

► Part of a cycle on the life of St John the Baptist, this fresco is on the back wall of the baptistery, in an empty, ill-lit square. Using receding colonnades with series of white columns, Masolino sought to create the illusion of a brighter, more spacious setting. The light colours of the faces, sky and buildings, and the airy distribution of the scene's figures, contribute to the effect.

▲ The portico serves to organize the space and guide the reading of an episode. This complex narrative unrolls in three scenes: King Herod's banquet at the left, the delivery of John the Baptist's head to Herodias on the right and the tomb with the saint's remains in the background. The architecture guides the viewer's eye through the visual narrative.

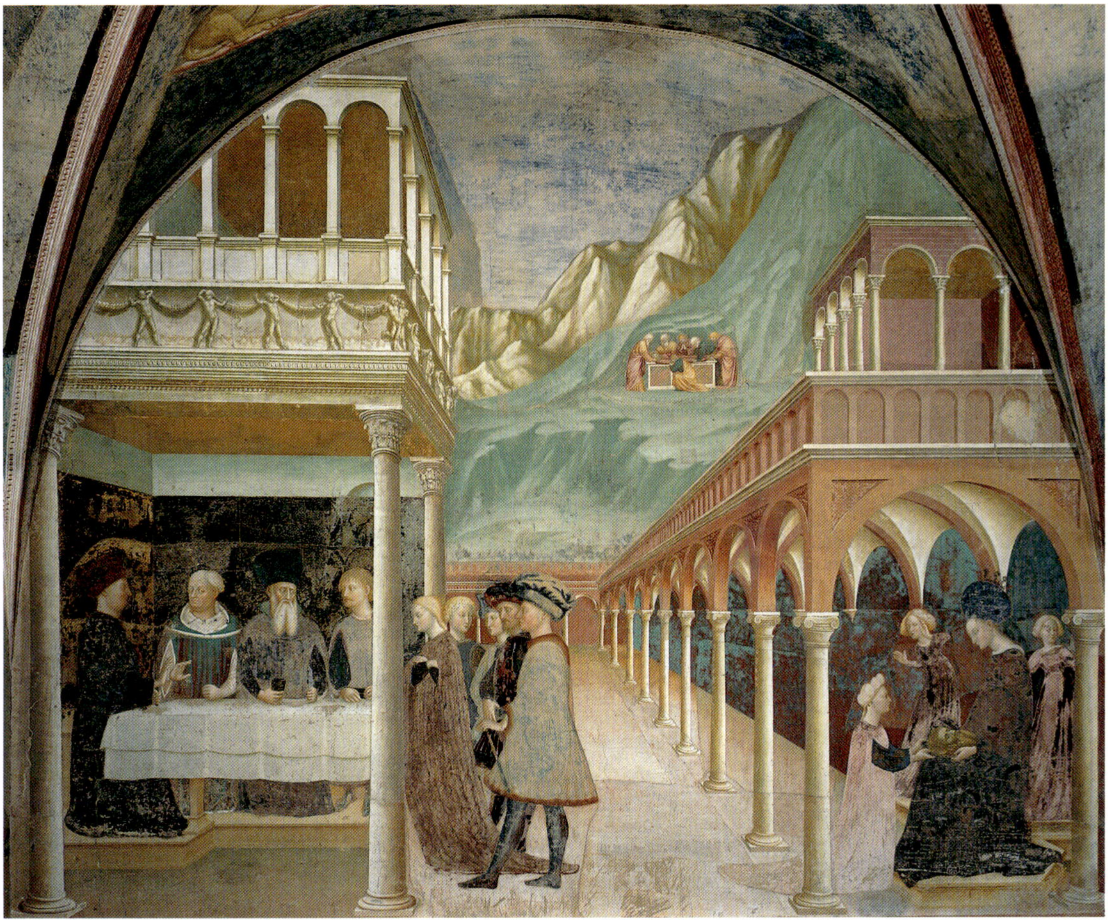

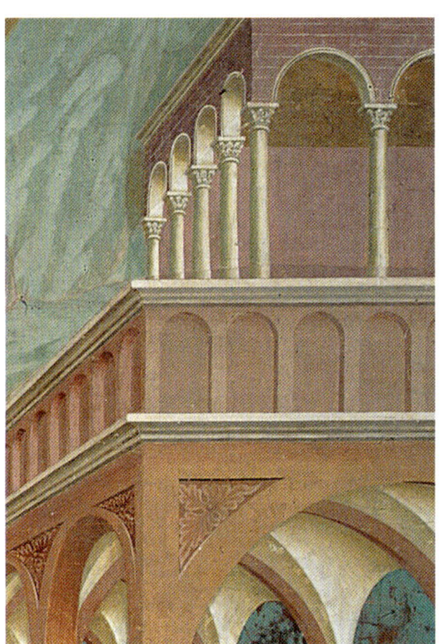

► Working for a cultivated, well-informed patron, but in a region still clinging to late Gothic taste, Masolino created a cycle of refined compromise: the architecture, clearly described in perspective, is inspired by Brunelleschi's latest style, but the richness of the costumes, the poses (often in profile), the women's hairstyles and the calculated elegance of the gestures recall the International Gothic approach. The fresco by Pisanello depicting St George and the Dragon at the church of Sant'Anastasia in Verona makes an interesting comparison (see pages 28–9).

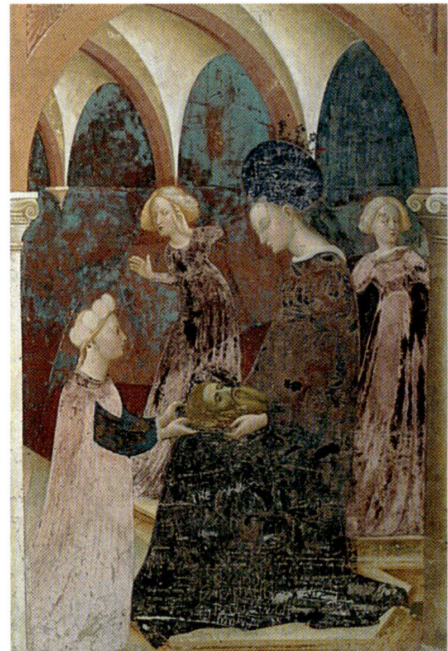

International Gothic

Pisanello
St George and the Dragon, right side
1436–8

Entire fresco, 223 × 620 cm
Verona, Sant'Anastasia

Pisanello

(Antonio Pisano)

Verona, c. 1395–Mantua, 1455

A captivating painter, Pisanello belongs to the sumptuous International Gothic period but also showed great openness to the advances of humanism and perspective. The son of a merchant from Pisa (hence his nickname), Pisanello was trained in the Veneto, first in Verona and then in Venice. Around 1420, he collaborated with Gentile da Fabriano, whom he followed to Florence in 1423. In 1427, he went to Rome to complete the frescoes at St John Lateran that had been interrupted by Gentile's death. In the meantime, he had launched a career as a panel painter in Verona. Pisanello successfully developed patrons in the wealthy courts of Ferrara, Rimini, Mantua and, later, Milan and Naples, alternately painting fresco cycles and producing commemorative medals. His outstanding drawings include studies from nature and designs for clothing. The most important of his extant works is the large scene of *St George and the Dragon* (1436–8) in the church of Sant'Anastasia in Verona. (The frescoes at the palace of the Duke of Mantua are poorly conserved.) After the mid-15th century, Pisanello's fame rapidly declined. He probably died in Mantua, where in the following year Andrea Mantegna took over his position as court painter.

The traditional conception of the 'old' Gothic and the 'new' humanism is simplistic, and can lead to the false conclusion that there was a single moment of change. In fact, there are many fascinating examples of transition and exchange between the styles. A student and successor of Gentile da Fabriano, Pisanello was the main artistic figure in various Italian cities and courts, including Verona, Mantua, Ferrara, Rimini, Milan and Naples. An exceptional draughtsman, skilled stylist and unsurpassed designer of medals – Pisanello showed a taste for ornament, curves and great detail – all characteristics of the late Gothic style. This was a deliberate choice, dictated not by a lack of knowledge of the rules of perspective (which he applied with precision at times) but by a conscious, expressive intent.

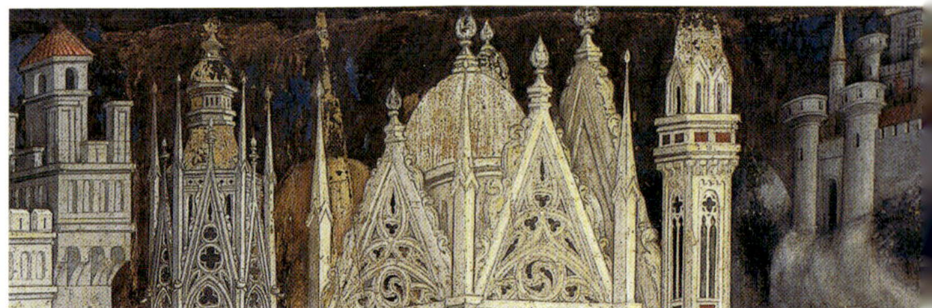

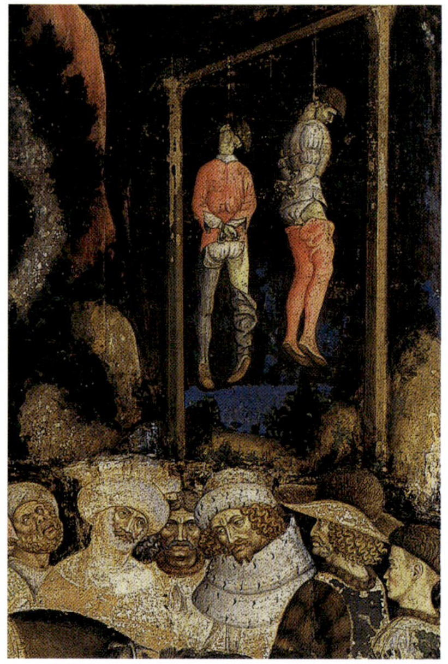

▲ Unlike Masolino, Pisanello creates a background of Gothic architecture full of steeples, openwork and ornament. He does not seek a model in porticoes in the style of Brunelleschi, but in the exuberant 14th-century Scaligere Arches – well-known in the Veneto as the tombs of Verona's prominent citizens.

◄ As in romances and poems of the period, Pisanello surrounded the main subject with 'minor' episodes and figures that heighten the viewer's curiosity. Here we see a macabre detail of two hanged men.

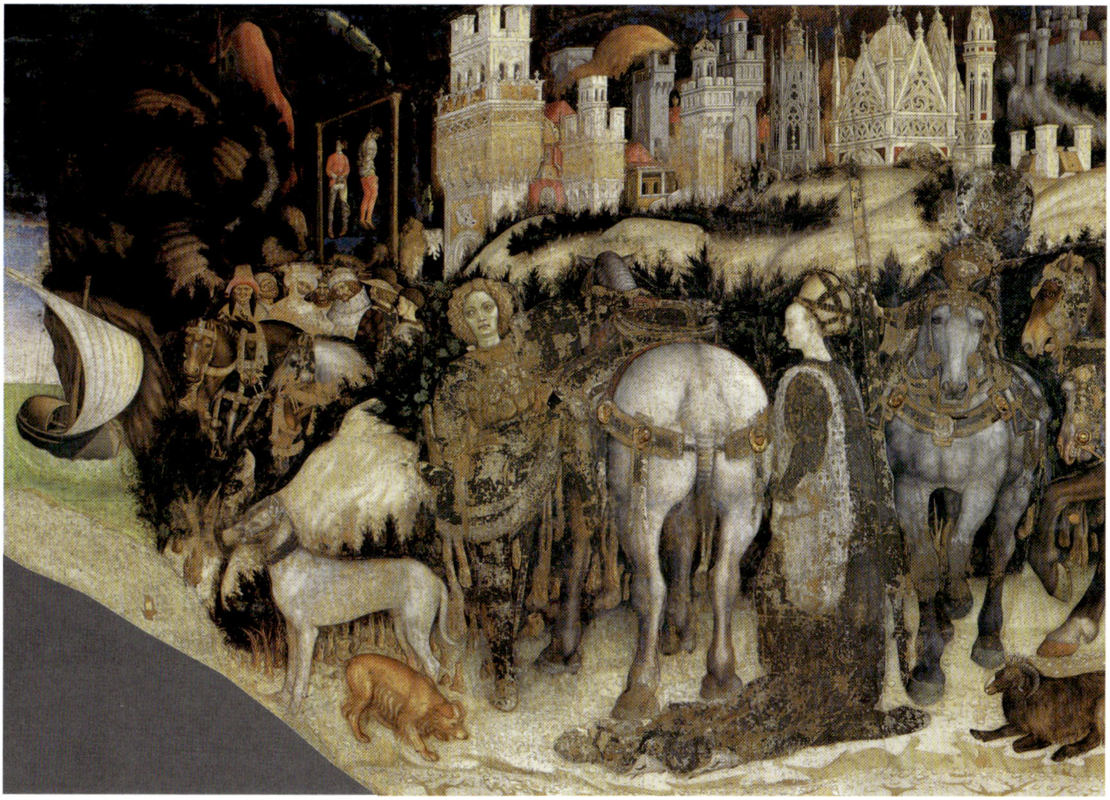

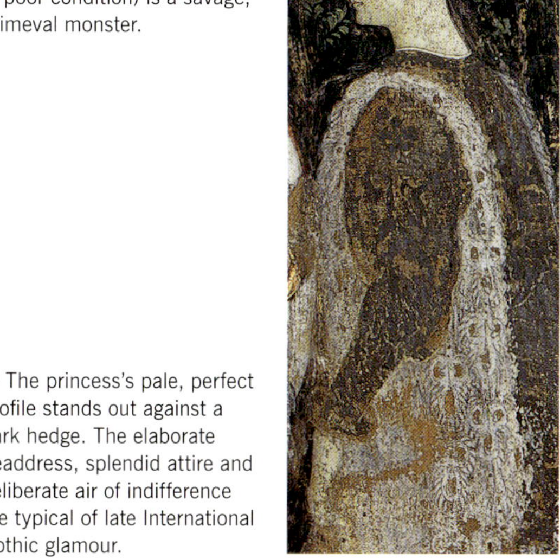

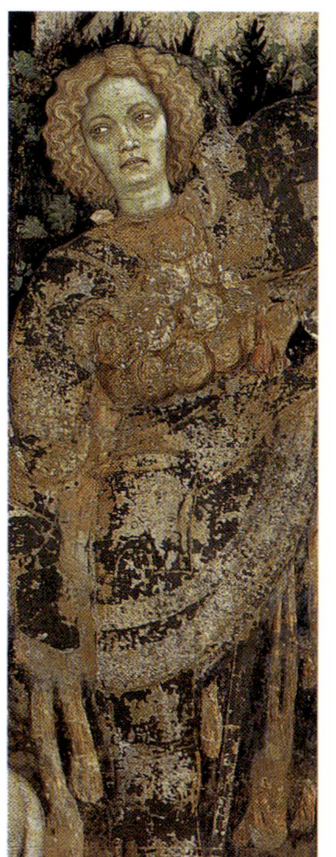

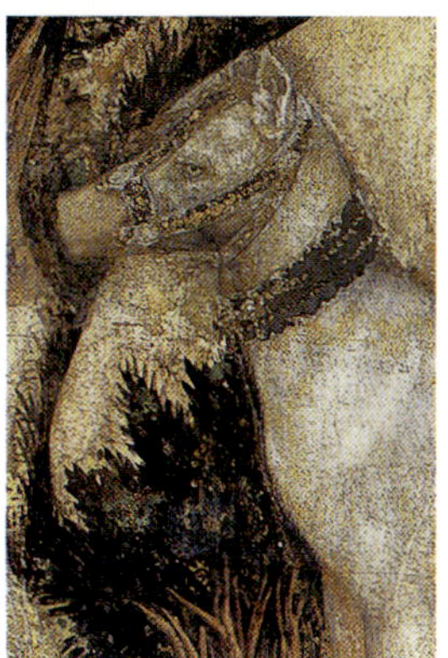

◄ The muzzled dog and the horses with opulent gold harnesses symbolize a benevolent, domesticated nature, hospitable to mankind. On the other hand, the dragon to the left of the arcade (today in poor condition) is a savage, primeval monster.

◄ St George was thought of as the perfect medieval hero: a 'spotless, fearless' knight who didn't hesitate to confront the dragon in order to save the princess. Pisanello fixes the moment when St George mounts his horse, determined to pursue his noble mission.

► The princess's pale, perfect profile stands out against a dark hedge. The elaborate headdress, splendid attire and deliberate air of indifference are typical of late International Gothic glamour.

Animals

Pisanello
The Vision of St Eustace
c. 1438

Tempera on wood panel, 55 × 65 cm
London, National Gallery

For artist biography, see page 28.

Fifteenth-century art often shows great interest in the world of nature. Plants and animals were depicted and discussed in treatises on botany, pharmacology, the hunt and veterinary medicine. Owning a zoological park, or at least a selection of horses and thoroughbred dogs, was a common ambition of the well-to-do gentleman. Real and fantastic creatures populate the heraldry of aristocratic families, invoking a rich symbolism that ranges from astrology to Christianity and the attributes by which saints were recognized. Late Gothic taste stimulated a new observation of nature, even if artists still had to rely on drawings or other images of more exotic animals. Pisanello was an extraordinary interpreter of the animal kingdom.

► The stag with a crucifix between its antlers that miraculously appears during a hunting party is common to the legends of St Eustace, a Roman army general, and St Hubert, a Flemish bishop. However, the image of the encounter between the patron saint of hunters and the miraculous stag developed independently of the historical figures Eustace and Hubert and the appearance of the main figure in this painting does not correspond to either saint.

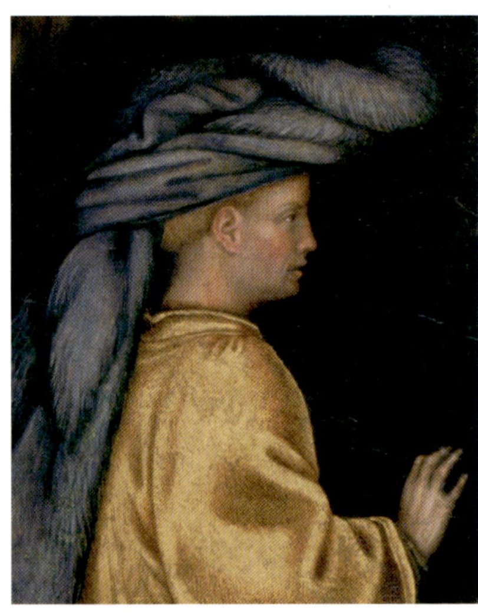

▼ At the lower edge of the painting is a banderole or scroll that was probably meant to contain the painter's signature, but it is blank. With a remarkable sense of humour, Pisanello has echoed the scroll's curves in the arched body of a greyhound as it pursues a hare. They are the most dynamic figures in the whole composition – almost all of the other animals are standing still.

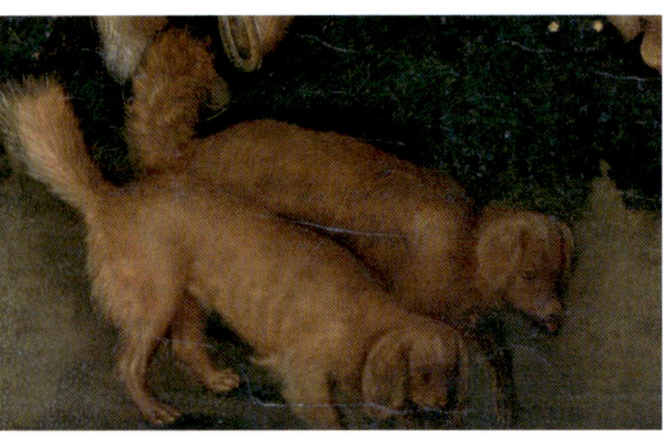

◄ Hunting was by far the preferred recreation in late Gothic courts, and the nobility spent fabulous sums to maintain packs of pedigree dogs. In this painting, Pisanello included no fewer than five different kinds of dog bred to point, flush and chase the various wild animals that appear in the scene.

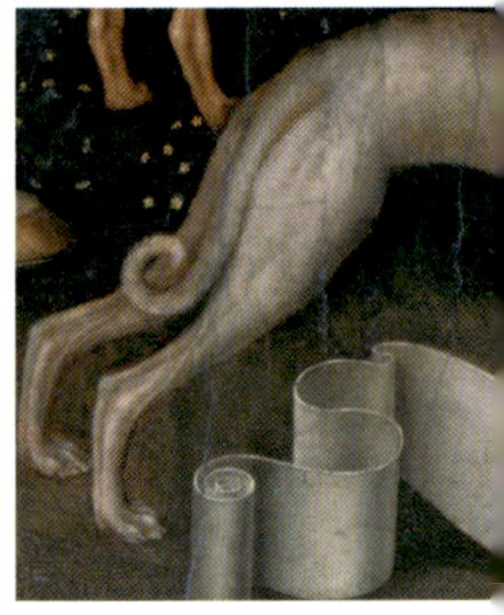

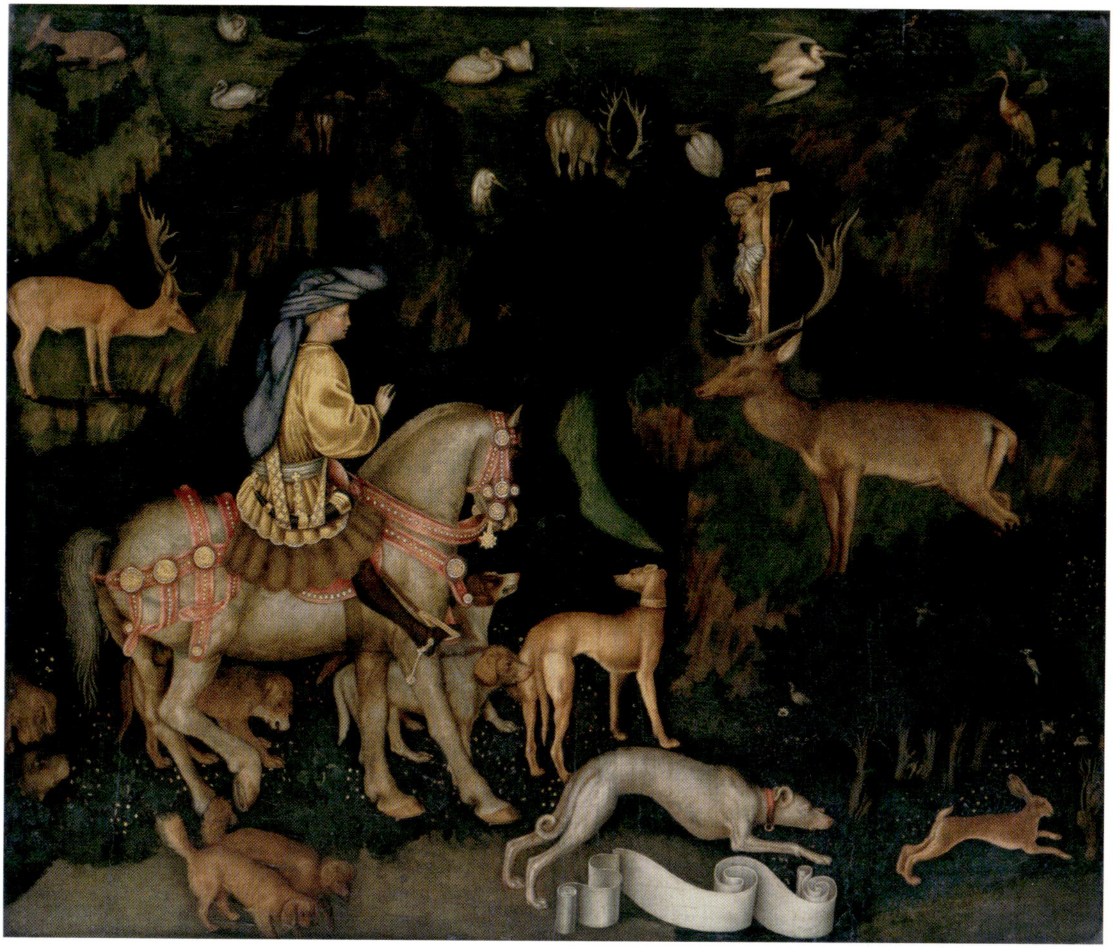

► In Pisanello's fairy-tale forest setting, bears, stags, hares and various species of bird live side-by-side amid flowers and dense shrubbery. Each of the animals is accurately reproduced from life. Before Leonardo, Pisanello was the greatest draughtsman of nature in Italian art.

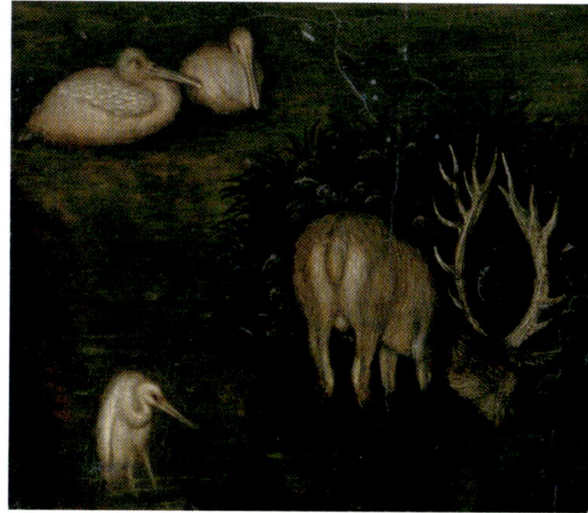

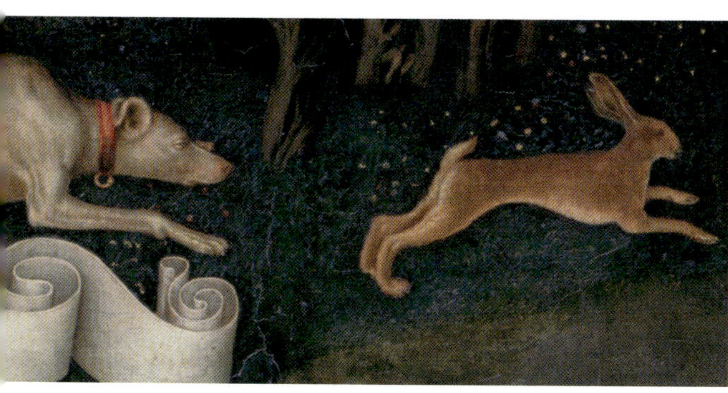

Colour

Fra Angelico
The Deposition (Santa Trinita Altarpiece)
c. 1436–40

Tempera on panel, 176 × 185 cm

Florence, Museo di San Marco

Fra Angelico

(Fra Giovanni da Fiesole,
real name, Guido di Pietro)

Vicchio di Mugello, Florence, *c.* 1395–
Rome, 1455

An important figure in the Dominican
Order, Fra Angelico was one of the most
sensitive interpreters of religious themes,
but also aware of the latest trends:
perfectly able to use perspective, he
transferred to large-format paintings the
splendid sense of colour he had learned
during his training as a miniaturist. Fra
Angelico's devotion to celestial mysticism
did not isolate him; in fact, he worked
with the most advanced artists of
the time, for example, on the *Linaioli
Tabernacle* (1433; Florence, Museo di
San Marco), on which he collaborated
with Lorenzo Ghiberti. Between 1439
and 1442, he executed the splendid
series of frescoes at the convent of
San Marco, with the help of the school
where Benozzo Gozzoli was a pupil. In
1446, at the request of Pope Nicholas
V, he painted frescoes in the chapel of
St Stephen and St Lawrence in Rome,
one of the first 'modern' projects in the
Vatican complex. The following year he
worked on the decoration of the chapel
of St Brizio in Orvieto cathedral, but left
it unfinished. Luca Signorelli completed
the frescoes some fifty years later (see
pages 170–1). Back in Florence, Fra
Angelo returned to work at the Dominican
convent of San Marco. In 1453, he was
again called to Rome, where he remained
until his death two years later. He was
officially beatified at the end of the
20th century by Pope John Paul II.

Because gold grounds had largely been abandoned but also
because of the darkening of the Brancacci Chapel frescoes, it
has often been thought that the perspective paintings of the
early humanist era were less luminous and colourful than those
of the late Gothic. This was not always so: Fra Angelico, who
began his career as a miniaturist, constructed his compositions
in a 'modern' manner but made them shine with bright, clean
colours. The pigments he used were obtained by grinding
precious materials like pure gold, lapis lazuli, malachite and
cochineal into a fine powder. For a painter motivated by a profound faith, these colours reflected the beauty of Creation. For
less devout patrons, such prestigious works of art were proof of
wealth, power and good taste.

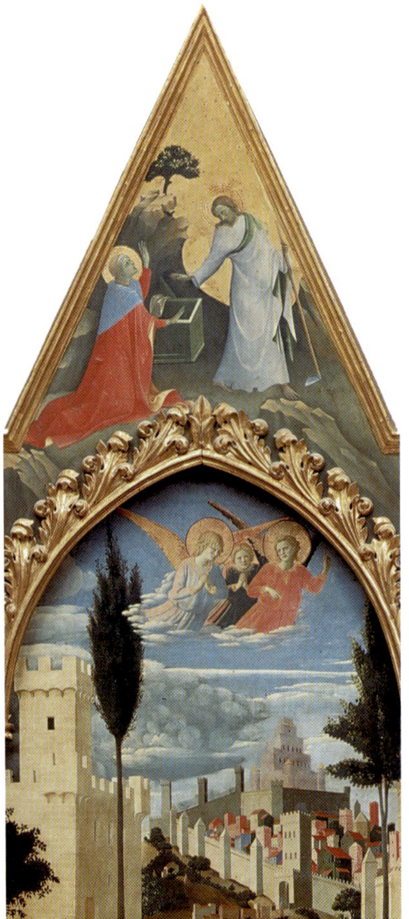

► Fra Angelico inherited a
panel from about 15 years
earlier, divided into three
fields, similar to that used
by Gentile de Fabriano for
The Adoration of the Magi
(see pages 14–15). The
essential difference lies in
the openness of the luminous
landscape in the distance,
between the walled city of
Jerusalem and a view of hills
on the right. Gold is reserved
for the haloes and a few
details; all the other colours
are from nature.

◄ Fra Angelico completed
this painting left unfinished by
his teacher, Lorenzo Monaco,
who died in 1424. The
pointed apexes attest to the
early phase of its execution,
still tied to the late Gothic.
The open landscape under
a blue sky and the geometric
volumes of the architecture
mark a significant transition
away from the flat gold ground
used by Lorenzo Monaco,
however.

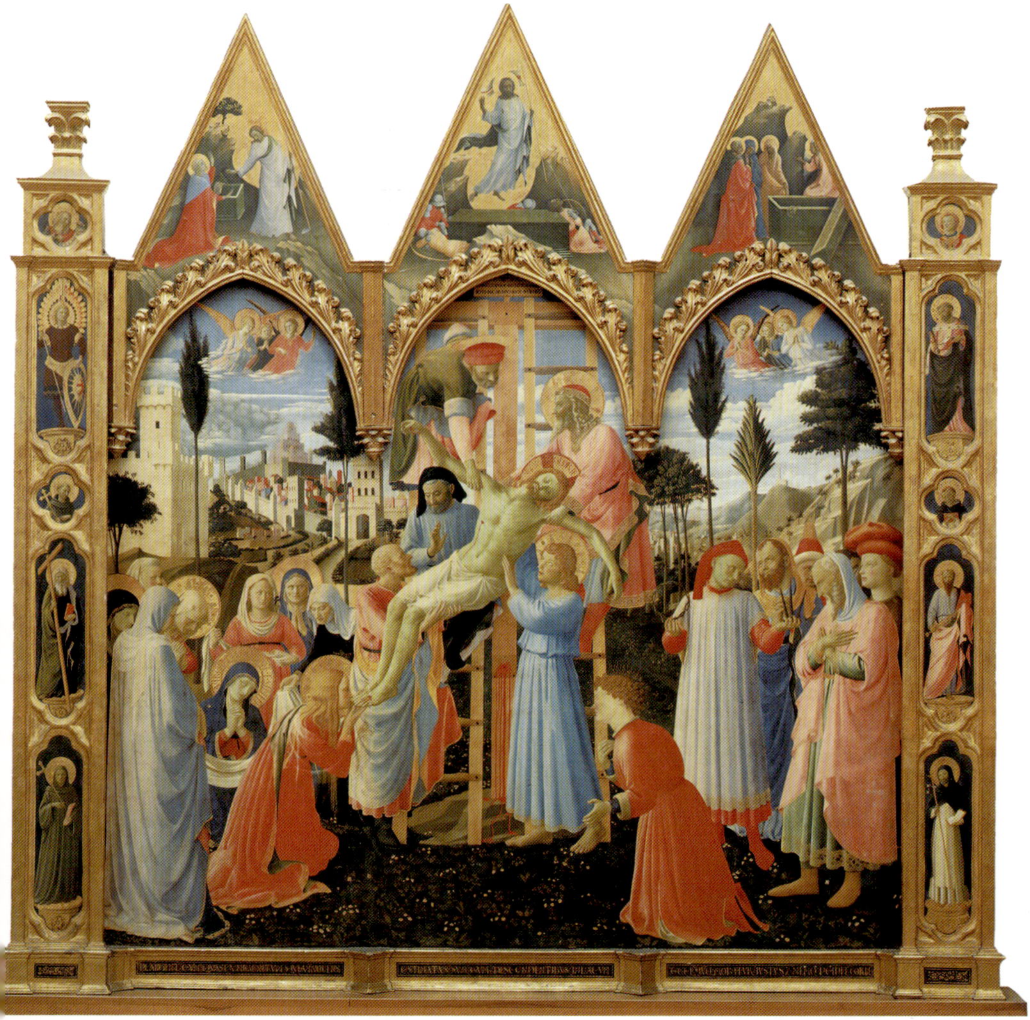

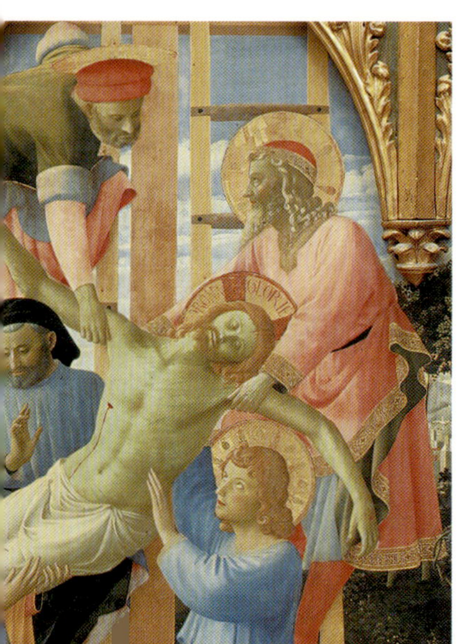

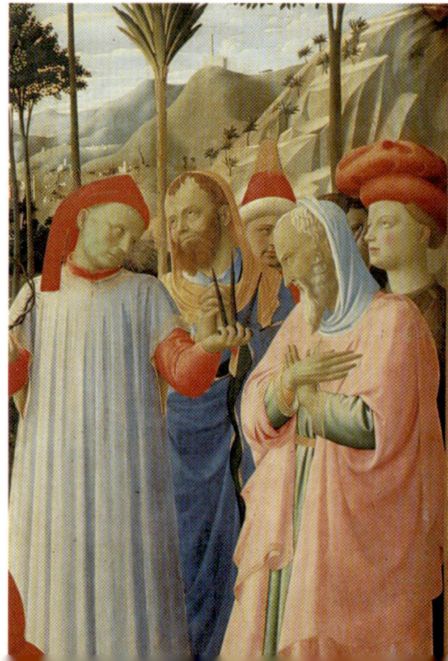

► *The Deposition* is one of the most significant works from Fra Angelico's mature period, since it represents a perfect 'modern' compromise between the abundant luxury of the late Gothic period and the geometrical volumes of Masaccio.

Fresco

Fra Angelico
The Mocking of Christ
1439

Fresco, 188 × 164 cm
Florence, Museo di San Marco

For artist biography, see page 32.

In no other country was the fresco such a widespread and important medium as it was in Italy. Durable, economical and quickly executed – colour is applied directly to an area of wet plaster, which must be completed in a single day – the large scale stimulates the painter's imagination. Despite the differences of technique, materials and dimensions between the two media, many 15th-century Italian painters were equally at ease with fresco and panel painting. Fra Angelico is a good example of this flexibility. At the convent of San Marco in Florence, he painted impressive frescoes on the walls of his Dominican brothers' cells, as well as panels rich with gold and sumptuous colours.

The Various Methods of Preparing Fresco: Sinopia, Incision and Cartoon
The painting of a fresco required a great deal of preparation. While the master prepared the sketches for the composition (sometimes shown to the patron for approval), scaffolds were built and the wall to be frescoed smoothed with a layer of wet plaster. The composition could then be laid out on the prepared wall, either by drawing the image directly onto the plaster with a special reddish-brown chalk (sinopia) or by transferring a full-size preparatory drawing (cartoon) executed in the studio, using guidelines incised in the plaster. At the start of each day, a thin layer of lime plaster was spread over the area to be painted during the next few hours. At this point, the master arrived on the scene for the actual execution. Fresco could only be accomplished during the warm months and when the humidity was low, not only to avoid the discomfort of working in the cold and damp, but above all to allow the plaster to dry evenly and so ensure consistent, well-preserved colours.

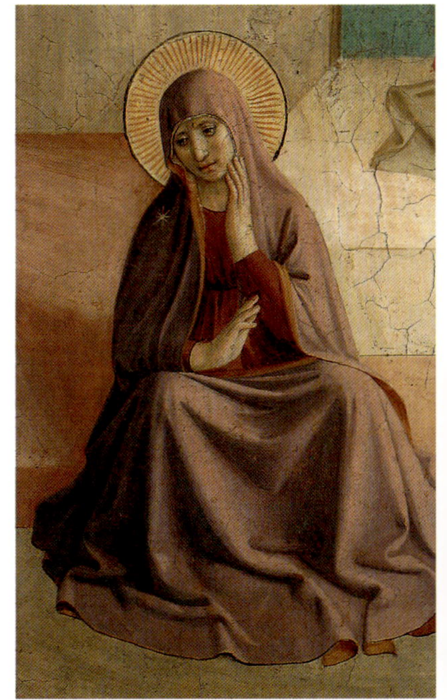

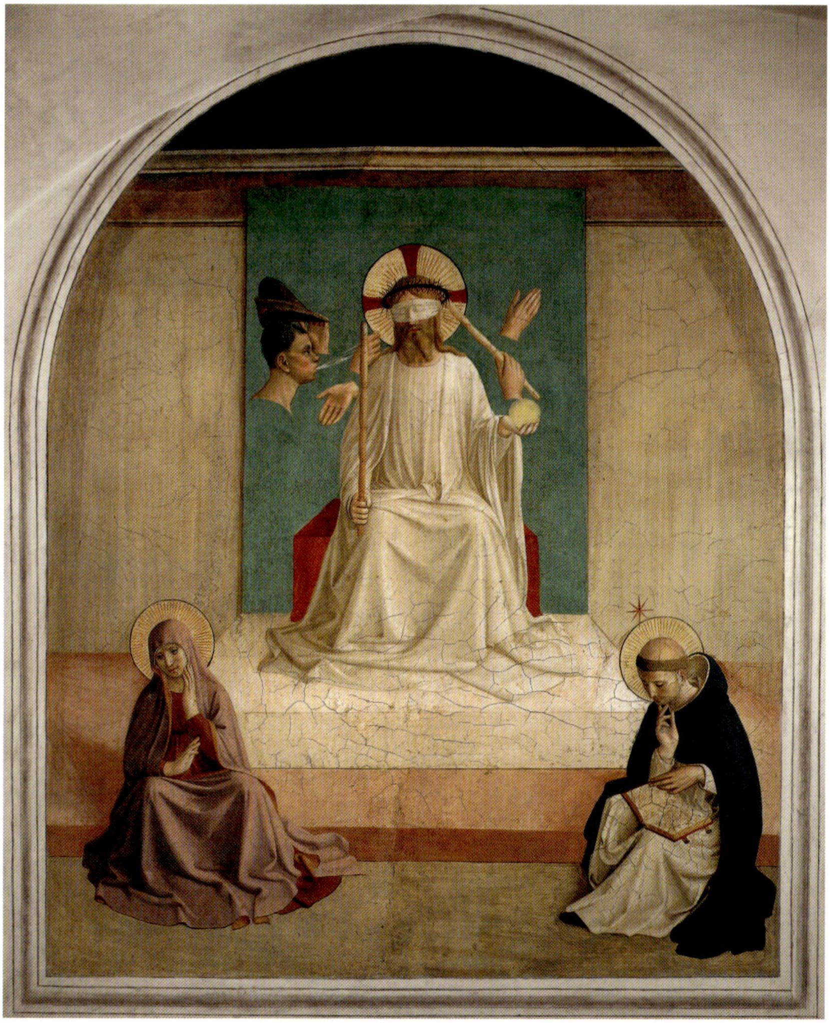

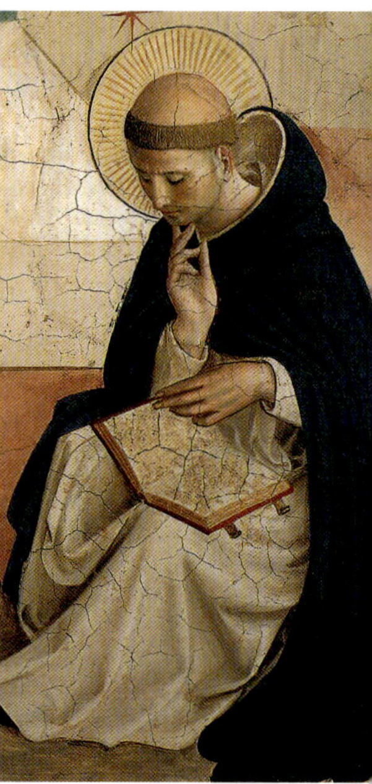

◄ The Dominican convent of San Marco in Florence occupies a group of buildings designed by Michelozzo, the same architect who created the nearby Palazzo Medici. The monks' cells are on the first floor and open onto a spacious corridor. The interiors are dimly lit, and for this reason Fra Angelico favoured light tones in the frescoes, often using white. These paintings provided a visual aid for the monks' prayer.

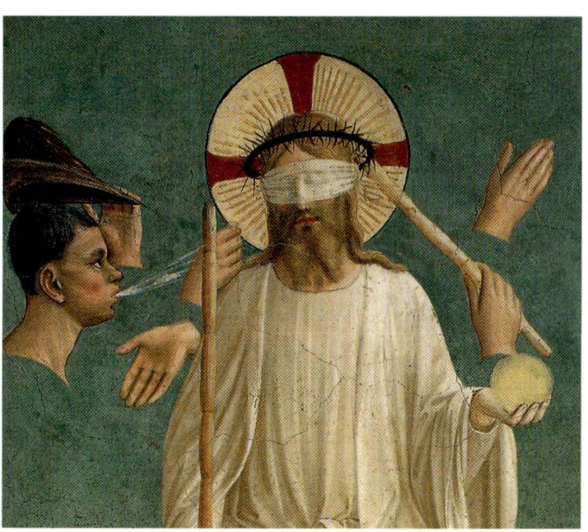

◄ The painter effectively and concisely depicted the cruel outrages, harsh blows and derision suffered by Christ. The thin blindfold that allows the viewer to intuit the eyes of Christ, closed in an expression of resignation and forgiveness, is an additional refinement.

Cassone

Giovanni di Ser Giovanni
Adimari Cassone
c. 1440

Tempera on panel, 63 × 280 cm
Florence, Galleria dell'Accademia

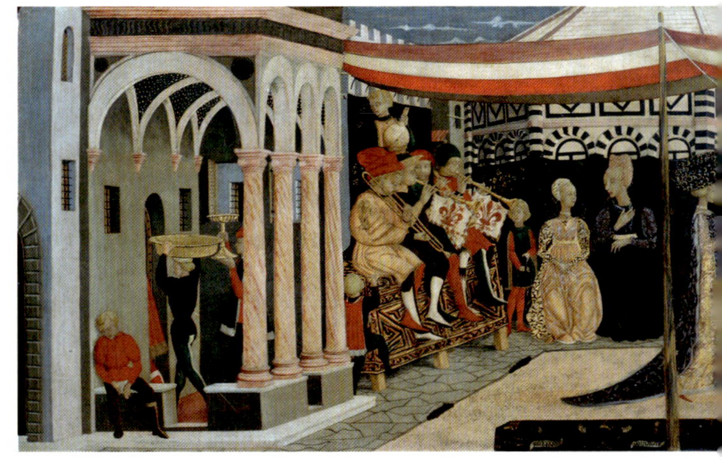

Giovanni di Ser Giovanni

('Lo Scheggia')

San Giovanni Valdarno, Arezzo, 1406–
Florence, 1486

Giovanni, who outlived his elder brother Masaccio by many years, returned to their grandfather's traditional activity of making *cassoni*: painted chests typical of Tuscany. Nicknamed 'Lo Scheggia', Giovanni also specialized in the pictorial decoration of wedding chests and *deschi de parto*, trays that were made to celebrate births in aristocratic families. The one painted by Giovanni for the birth of Lorenzo de' Medici is today in the Metropolitan Museum of Art in New York. This type of appealing, decorative object, rich in gilding and descriptive detail, clearly shows how Giovanni's style differs from the austere, concentrated style of his brother.

The workshop production of 15th-century Italian painters was far more varied and eclectic than is generally thought. Besides executing panels and frescoes, painters often designed garments, costumes, decorative scenery for feasts and receptions, and valuable objects and ornamental details of every kind. The decoration of furniture, including the chests (*cassoni*) in which brides kept their trousseaus, was a common activity. These were often the most prized items of furniture in the palazzos of the nobility and the wealthy. The fronts and sometimes also the tops of these elegant examples of cabinetry were painted with delightful allegorical or mythological scenes, often showing a taste for charming narrative detail but little concern for perspective. Giovanni di Ser Giovanni, nicknamed 'Lo Scheggia', was one of the most brilliant specialists in this type of luxury item.

► The setting is unmistakably Florence: in the background is the silhouette of the baptistery, clad in white and green marble, the symbol of the city. Furthermore, the banners on the trumpets bear a red lily in a white field, the city's heraldic symbol.

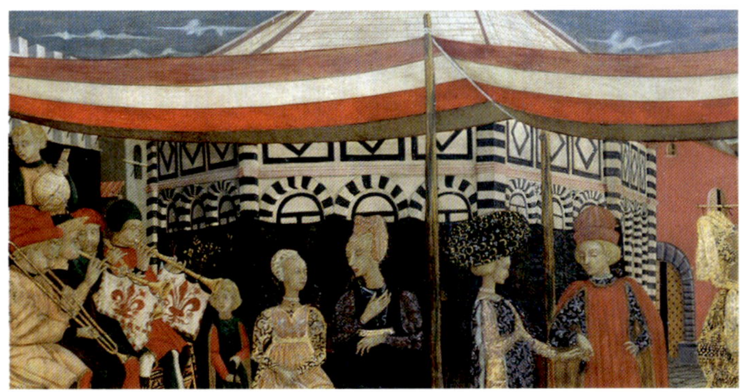

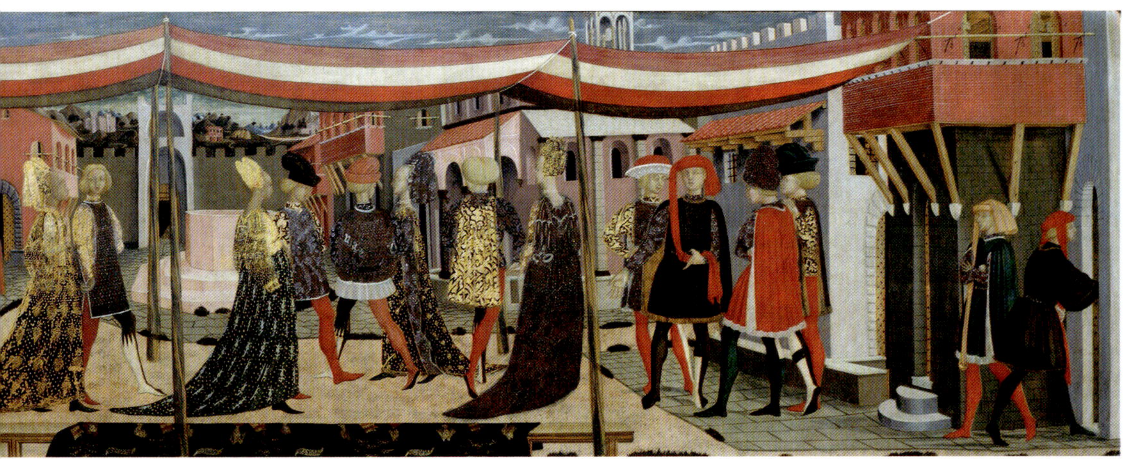

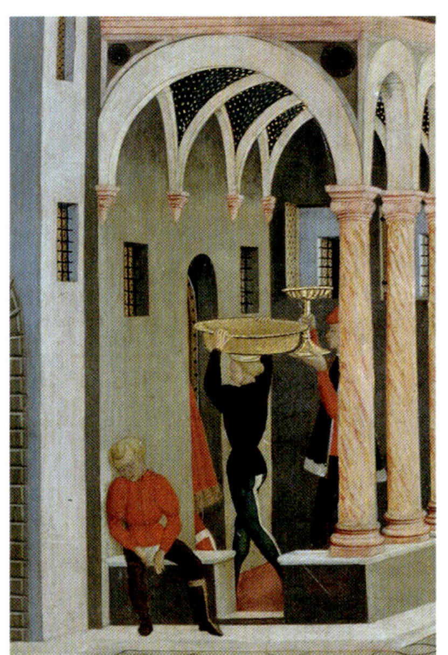

▲ This famous panel, which offers one of the liveliest images of Florentine high society in the mid-15th century, is traditionally considered to be the front of a *cassone* painted to mark the marriage of a member of the noble Adimari family.

◄► Many details, especially the porticoes, balconies and doors, make it clear that the painter was conversant with the rules of perspective.

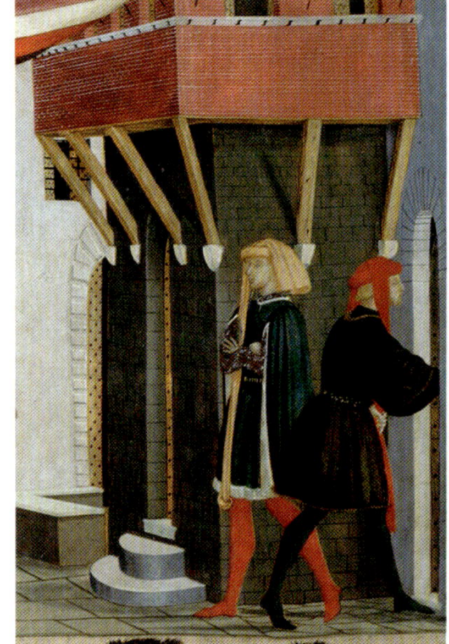

◄ The many animated figures, the colours and the cut of the dresses with long trains, the complicated hairstyles, the abundant gold and the festive rhythm of the dancing that takes place beneath a canopy, still belong to the rich late Gothic taste.

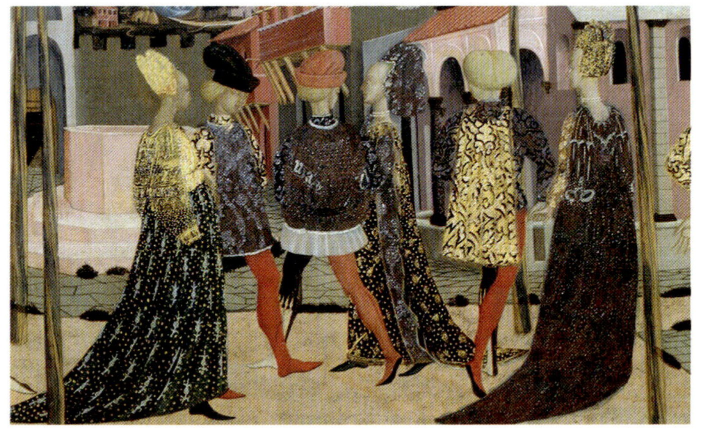

The Golden Section

Filippo Lippi
The Annunciation
c. 1442

Tempera on panel, 175 × 183 cm
Florence, San Lorenzo

Filippo Lippi

Florence, *c.* 1406–Spoleto, Perugia, 1469

A leading figure of the Florentine art scene in the central decades of the 15th century, as a young man Filippo Lippi took vows as a Carmelite brother. He painted frescoes in the Carmelite convent in Florence and passionately studied the works of Masolino and Masaccio. In 1434 he stayed in Padua, and later made a trip to Flanders. New experiences enriched his style, although he did not abandon his basic adherence to geometric perspective. In 1441, with the monumental *Coronation of the Virgin* (today in the Uffizi Gallery), Filippo showed Florence that he was a most effective painter of altarpieces and sacred scenes. He left the Carmelite Order because of his relationship with Lucrezia Buti (they had a son, Filippino Lippi). In 1452 Filippo went to Prato, where he executed the frescoes in the sacristy of the cathedral. In his last creative phase, once again in Florence, Filippo continued to paint highly esteemed sacred works, like the *Nativity* for the Chapel of the Magi in the Medici Palace (today in Berlin). He died in Spoleto, leaving the frescoes at the cathedral unfinished. His son, Filippino, completed them.

Spurred on by the rediscovery of philosophical and poetical texts in Greek and Latin, 15th-century Italy sought to revive the human, expressive and moral values of classical Antiquity. Higher education was not, however, directed towards humanistic subjects but rather towards mathematics – indispensable in a period when almost every city had a different system of weights, measures and currency. Among the geometrical devices applied by artists (though also recognized and valued by patrons) was the Golden Section, a system of ratios that was felt to be aesthetically pleasing. This rule was fundamental to the mathematical construction of perspective since a well-calibrated balance between each component of a painting determined the height of the horizon line as well as the scale.

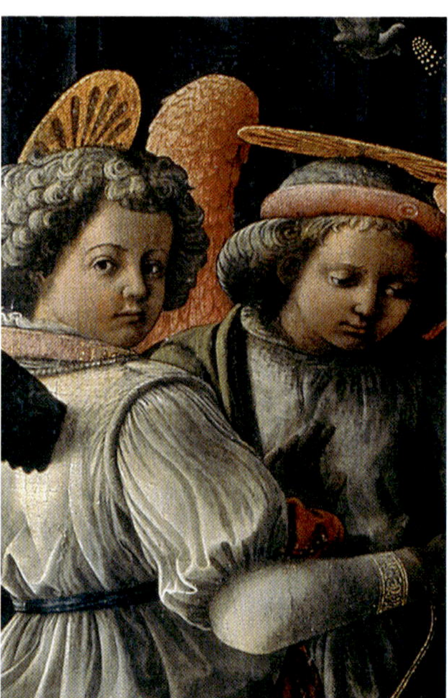

▼ The scene is divided in two by a smooth, flat pilaster that supports two symmetrical arches. Every element of the work (figures, architectural setting and background) is measured within a strict perspective structure. The concept of the Golden Section is based on a specific proportional relationship between a part and the whole.

▲ Commissioned by Niccolò Martelli, the altarpiece is in the Medici family's favourite church. Filippo Lippi thus made contact with the ruling family, showing himself to be one of the most knowledgeable and experimental artists in Florence, even when following complex geometric rules.

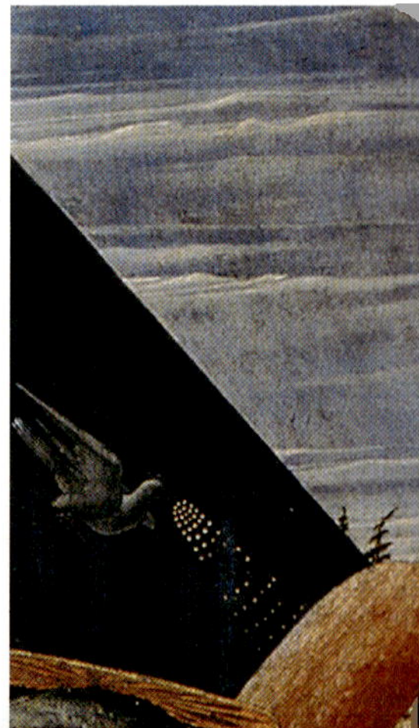

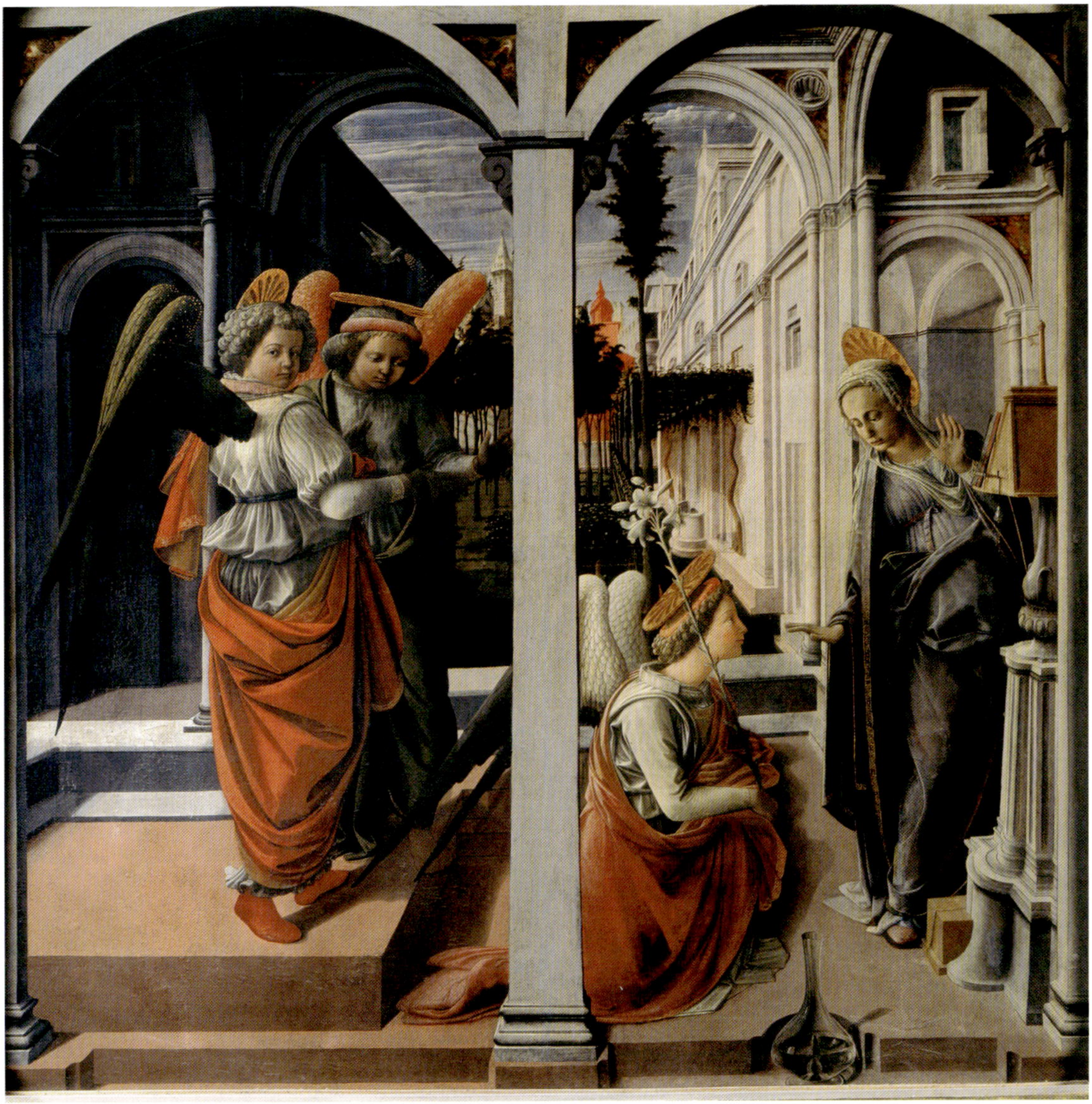

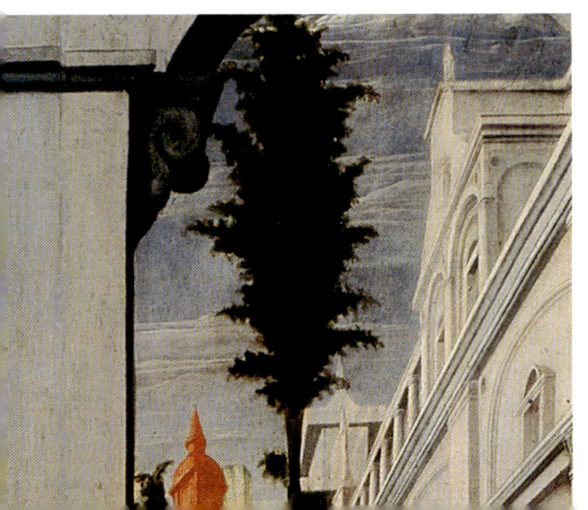

► The bottle of water in the foreground is a symbolic reference to the 'spotless' purity of Mary, but also a challenge to Flemish painting of the period, which was celebrated for its fascinating realistic details.

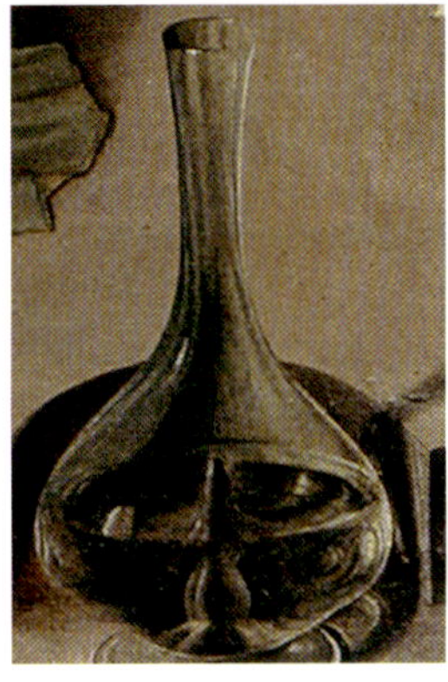

Library

Niccolò Antonio Colantonio
St Jerome in his Study
c. 1444

Oil on panel, 125 × 151 cm
Naples, Museo Nazionale di Capodimonte

Niccolò Antonio Colantonio

Active in Naples between 1440 and 1470.

Little is known about this painter, who was active in the mid-15th century in Naples and is believed to have been the teacher of Antonello da Messina. At that time, the great southern city was the main centre for collecting and studying international art, which was well represented by paintings and tapestries in the collections of the Angevins and Aragonese royal families. Colantonio offers an intelligent synthesis of Flemish, Provençal and Spanish influences. In his analytical concern for details, even the clothing and landscapes that he painted directly recall the models of Van Eyck and Van der Weyden, but show a fuller, surer sense of space and volume.

The spread of humanistic thought brought with it a desire to collect books and to organize them systematically in spacious, well-lit libraries under conditions conducive to study. The mid-15th-century invention in Germany of movable type reached Italy somewhat later but the impact was just as dramatic, allowing private individuals to put together libraries that would rival those of convents and dukes. Paintings offer some impressive images of *studioli* – rooms designed and decorated to house not only books, maps, documents and clerical records but also scientific instruments, small valuable objects and refined artworks that reflected the personal taste of their owner.

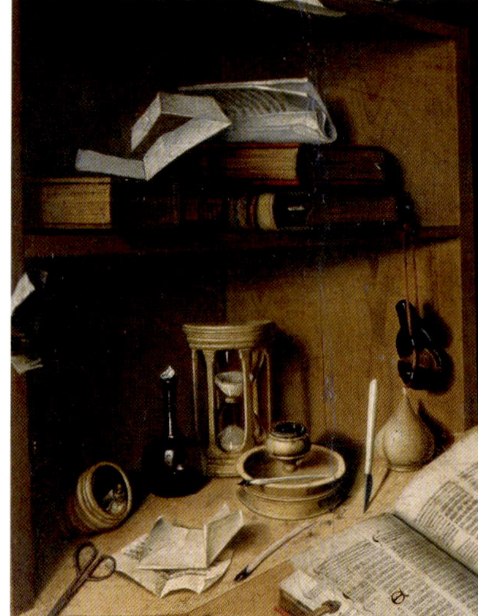

◄ In addition to books and papers (among which a certain disorder reigns), St Jerome's library includes writing implements and materials, such as tempered quills, an inkwell, various colours of ink and blank writing paper. There is also a clepsydra, or water clock, a reminder that time must not be wasted, urging the man of letters to concentrate on the passing minutes. The library depicted here is not a large one open for consultation by scholars, but a private space.

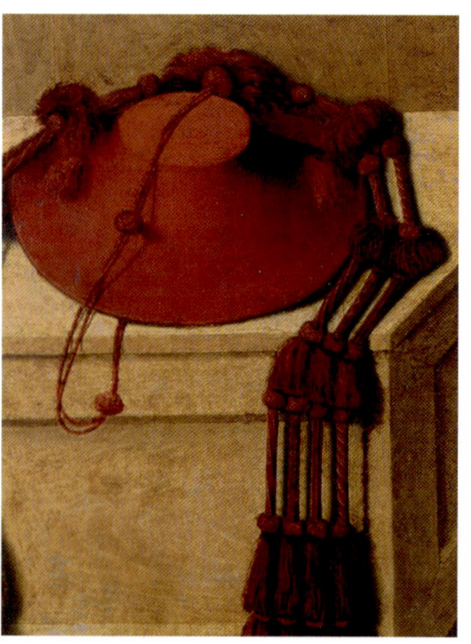

◄ A red cardinal's hat with tassels is prominently placed on a wooden chest in the foreground. St Jerome, who is represented in paintings in various ways, is shown here as a humanist, a man of letters.

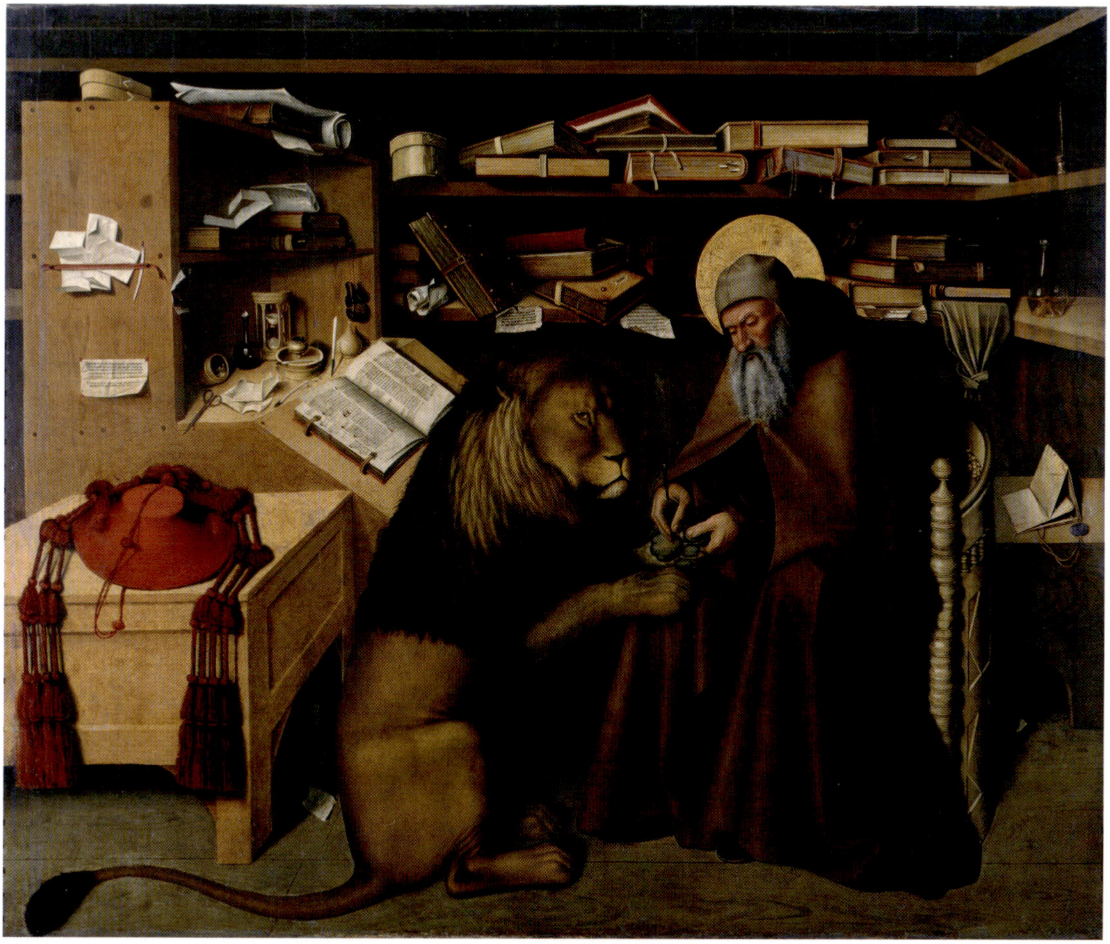

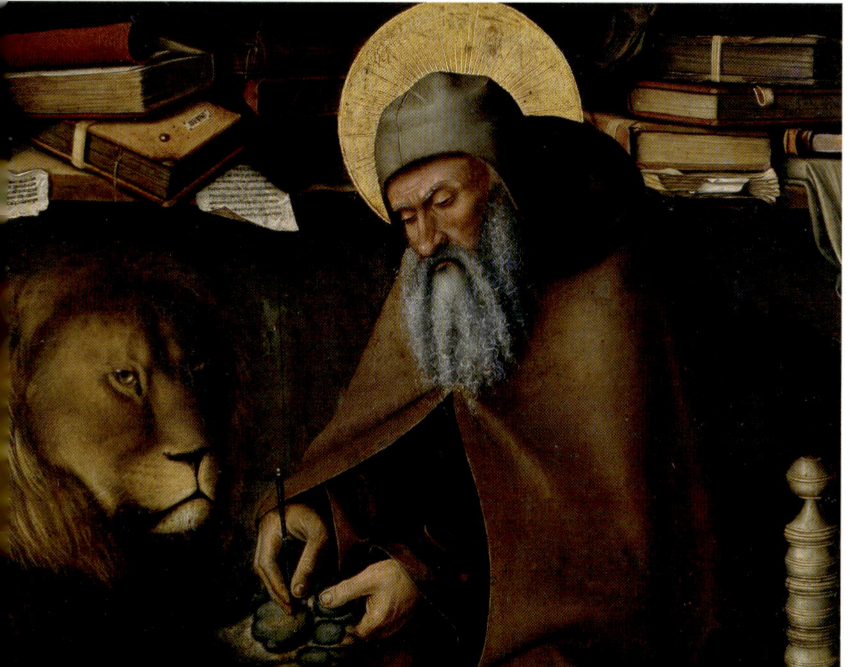

▲ This is the best-known
painting from a series that
once formed a polyptych in
the large Franciscan church
of San Lorenzo in Naples.
The subdued, brown tones,
which recall the colour of the
Franciscan habit, lend the
painting a calm, sober mood
in keeping with the chromatic
range of the parchment,
wooden shelves and old
leather bindings.

◄ According to legend, St
Jerome removed a thorn from
the paw of a lion that, out of
gratitude, became the saint's
meek, inseparable companion.

Gold Ground

Piero della Francesca
Madonna of Mercy
Central panel of the *Polyptych of the*
Madonna of Mercy
1445–62

Oil and tempera on panel, 134 × 91 cm
Sansepolcro, Arezzo, Museo Civico

Piero della Francesca

Sansepolcro, Arezzo, 1416/17–92

The best-known of the second generation
of humanist painters, Piero della
Francesca provided a new approach to
painting with a theoretical basis. He saw
a close link between art and geometry,
between poetical expression and carefully
applied mathematical rules. Piero began
his career in Florence and, in 1439, he
worked with Domenico Veneziano on a
fresco cycle that has been almost entirely
lost. After this early work in Florence, he
was active in 'the provinces'. During the
1440s Piero alternated periods of work
in Sansepolcro with stays in other cities,
among them Rome, Rimini and Ferrara,
where he came into contact with the
architect Leon Battista Alberti and Rogier
van der Weyden. In 1452, he began the
frescoes of the *Story of the True Cross*,
a landmark in Italian art, in the church of
San Francesco, Arezzo. During the 1460s,
Piero was active mainly in Urbino, at the
court of Duke Federico da Montefeltro.
During this period he produced a number
of masterpieces and came into close
contact with international artists and
developments in geometry, perspective
and algebra. He lost his sight in the
mid-1470s and returned to Sansepolcro,
where he devoted himself to completing
his treatises on mathematics and painting.
Piero della Francesca died the same day
that Columbus reached the New World,
12 October 1492.

During the 15th century, Italian painters gradually abandoned the traditional gold ground in favour of architecture and
landscape settings. The transition was slow, as the pure gold
leaf – embellished with patterning, like rich drapery – had been
used to give paintings a precious appearance since the Middle
Ages. Artists also used it to suggest supernatural light surrounding divine figures such as the Virgin Mary, Jesus and saints – an
effect heightened by flickering votive candles placed before the
painting. Even the most innovative 15th-century Italian painters (from Masaccio to Mantegna, Fra Angelico to Piero della
Francesca) continued to paint panels with gold elements. In
this case, however, the artist combined the traditional ground
with new concepts of space, geometry, light and volume.

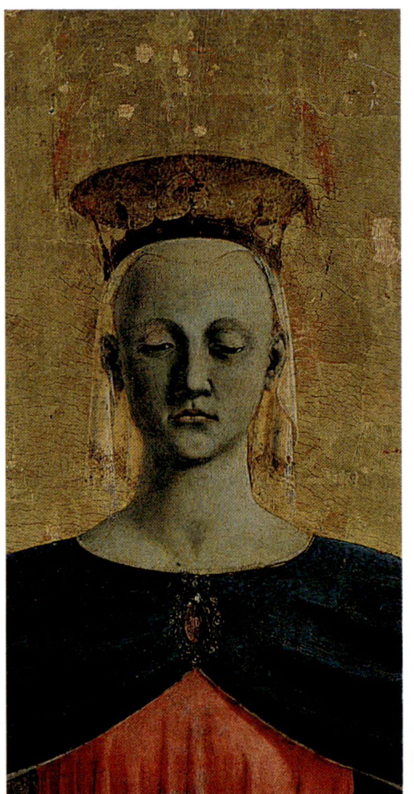

◄ The *Polyptych of the*
Madonna of Mercy is
interesting for its noticeable
stylistic contradictions, which
provide clues to understanding
the complicated relationship
between artists and their
patrons. In small towns such
as Sansepolcro, a gold ground
was still an inalienable feature
of sacred and devotional
painting. Furthermore,
tradition required the
Madonna to be larger than
the worshippers gathered
under the protection of her
cloak. Although Piero della
Francesca certainly followed
these traditions, he added
completely novel elements
such as the idealized, perfect
oval shape of Mary's face and
the representation of the halo
in perspective.

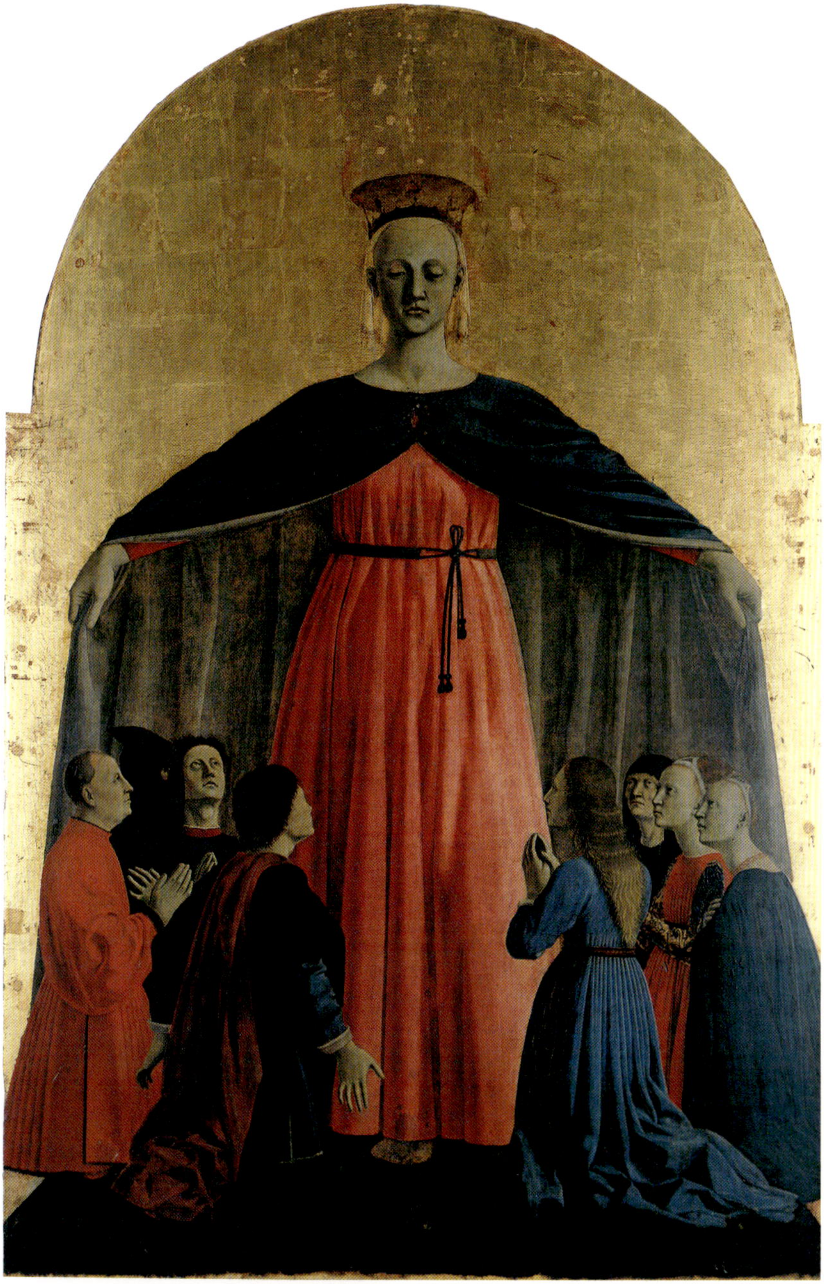

◄ The *Madonna of Mercy*
is the central component
of a large polyptych that
the Confraternita della
Misericordia of Sansepolco
commissioned from Piero
della Francesca in 1445,
and which he carried out
many years later with the
participation of assistants.
Though its frame has been
lost and in some places it is
in poor condition, it remains
in the painter's native city.
The extraordinary beauty
of the parts painted by
Piero della Francesca are
heightened by the contrast
with the precious gold ground.

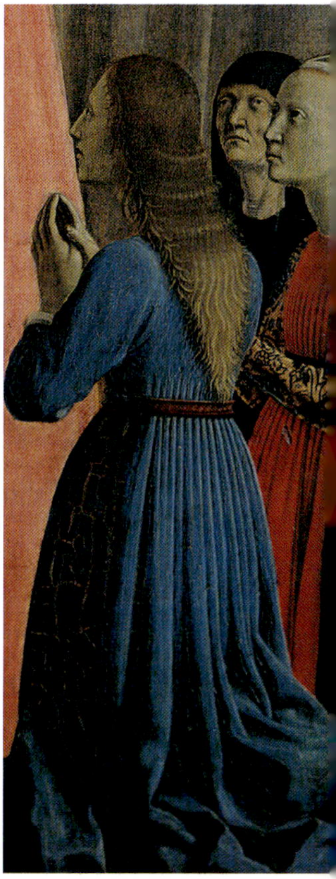

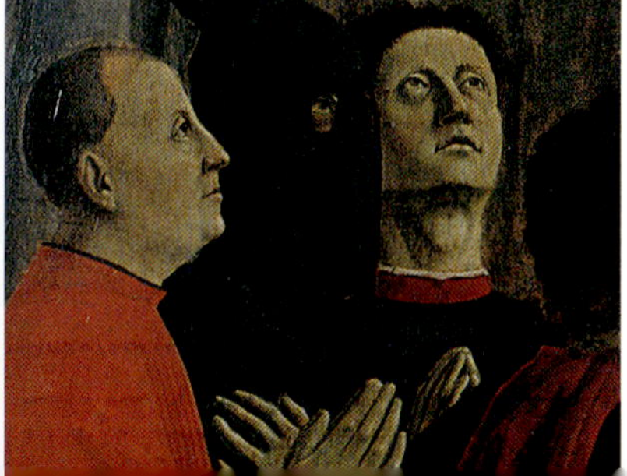

◄► The figure of the Madonna, motionless
and stark against the dense gold ground, is
obviously idealized. However, the worshippers
who kneel beneath her cloak are portrayed
with greater naturalism. Among them, wearing
red, is the patron who commissioned the
polyptych. A member of the Confraternita
della Misericordia, his face is hidden by a
black hood.

Cenacolo

Andrea del Castagno
The Last Supper
1445–50

Fresco, 453 × 975 cm

Florence, Cenacolo di Sant'Apollonia

Andrea del Castagno

Castagno nel Mugello, Florence, 1421–
Florence, 1457

A sober, intense exponent of Florentine humanist art, Andrea del Castagno is especially noted for the expressive force of his drawing and the realistic energy of his figures, modelled with heavy shadow. In 1439, he is recorded in Florence among the pupils of Domenico Veneziano. Not long after, in 1442, he went to Venice, probably on the advice of his master, and painted frescoes in the apse of the chapel of San Tarasio at San Zaccaria. This was a pioneering example of Tuscan humanist art in Venice, where painting still followed Gothic and even Byzantine models. Back in Florence, Andrea stood out among the most brilliant and active mid-century artists, but unfortunately his career was cut short by his premature death. In the cathedral of Santa Maria del Fiore, he provided cartoons for the glass in the oculi of the dome and painted monochrome frescoes on the *Monument to Niccolò da Tolentino* (1456). Two other important frescoes can be found in the church of the Santissima Annunziata. The most complex masterpiece is the decoration of the Cenacolo di Sant'Apollonia, with its vast, impressive *The Last Supper* (1445–50). The cycle of *Illustrious Men and Women*, today in the Uffizi Gallery, is also very well known.

The word *cenacolo* (refectory) refers to the long, rectangular dining hall in monastic communities. The smaller walls of these refectories were often frescoed with two Gospel scenes directly related to the function of the room and the symbolic relationship between the food consumed and Christ's sacrifice: the Last Supper and the Crucifixion. Every time they dined together, the monks were reminded of the Passover meal eaten by Jesus and his Apostles, which culminated in the mystical offering of the body and blood of Christ in atonement for the sins of the world ('Take and eat ye all of this'), immediately before Jesus' betrayal by Judas. The decoration of a refectory wall was a good commission for 15th-century painters, offering unique challenges and opportunities. The genre reached its climax with *The Last Supper* painted by Leonardo da Vinci in Milan.

► Andrea del Castagno painted two brick walls at the edges of the scene. The simplicity of the brick strongly contrasts with the richness of the variegated marble cladding of the hall's interior. The benches along the side walls terminate with statues of chimaeras, fabulous creatures that are part woman and part animal.

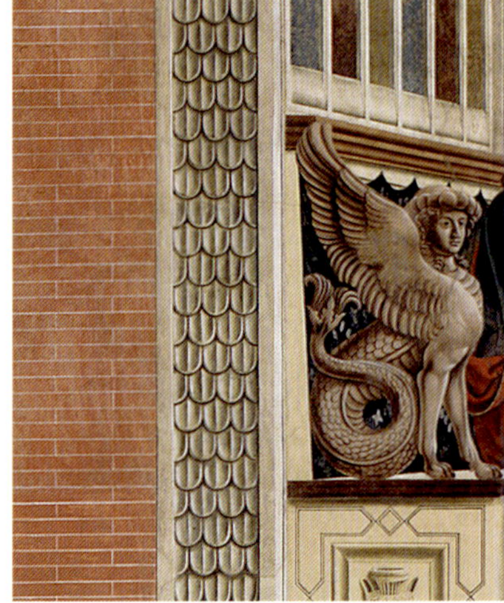

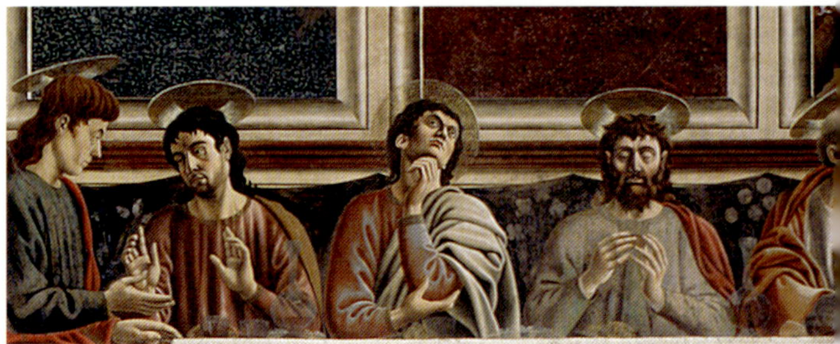

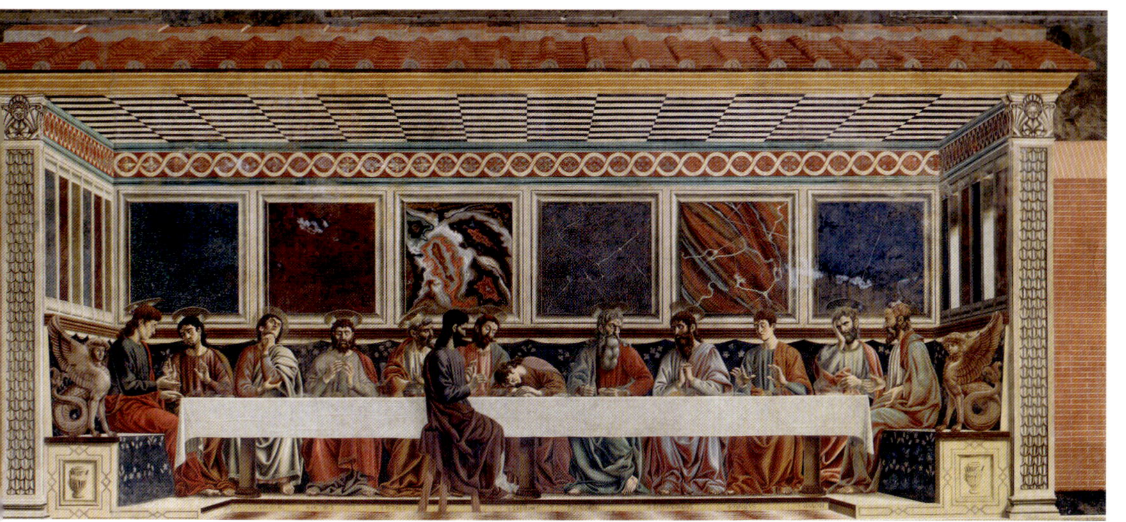

► The fresco in the refectory of the convent of Sant'Apollonia is a remarkable example of the use of geometric perspective. The ceiling, floor and walls are conceived as a sumptuously decorated and coloured three-dimensional 'box', while the long table covered with a smooth white tablecloth provides an element for gauging the depth of the space. The relationship between Andrea del Castagno and Piero della Francesca, who were both involved in research into perspective, was particularly strong.

▼ Andrea del Castagno chose to depict a moment of suspended meditation. Christ has just announced his imminent betrayal. The Apostles do not react energetically, but instead seem to wonder silently, withdrawn into themselves, motionless and solemn like statues. The focus of the composition is on the four central figures: Christ, who blesses and gently caresses John, who has slumped forward; Judas, dressed in dark clothing and shown in profile, seated alone on the near side of the table; and behind him, Peter.

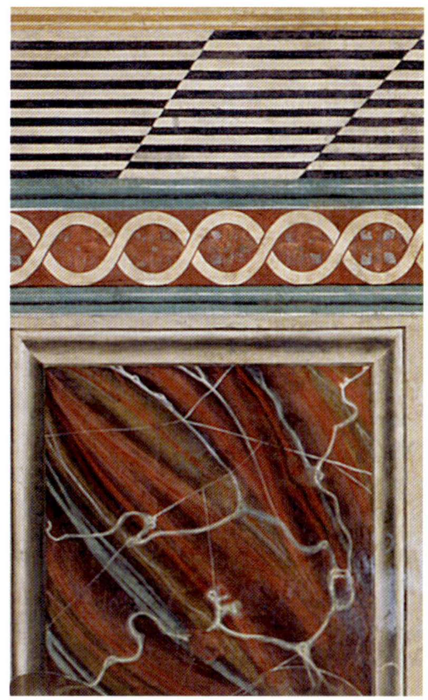

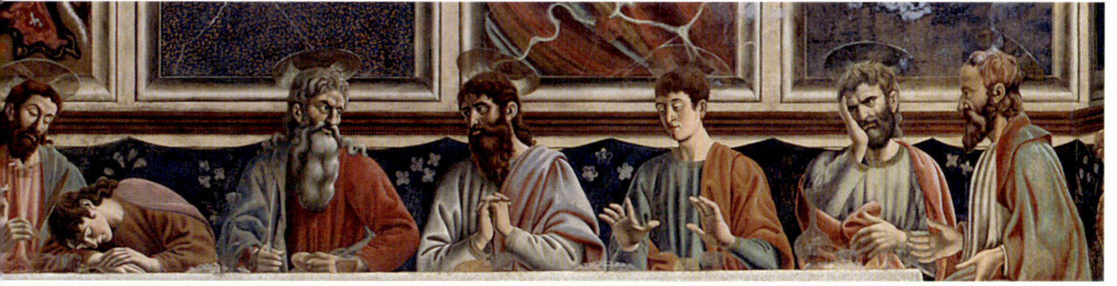

Square Panel

Domenico Veneziano
Santa Lucia de' Magnoli Altarpiece
1445–8

Tempera on panel, 209 × 216 cm
Florence, Galleria degli Uffizi

Domenico Veneziano

(Domenico di Bartolomeo)
Venice, *c.* 1410–Florence, 1461

A Venetian by birth and a great innovator, Domenico was one of the artists most committed to the philosophy behind humanist Florentine art. He proved to be a point of reference for an entire generation of artists. He succeeded in combining the various lessons of his training, which took place in the 1420s not in his native city of Venice but between Rome and Florence, under Gentile da Fabriano, Masolino, Pisanello and Masaccio. Among his early works the most outstanding is a *tondo*, *The Adoration of the Magi* (Berlin, Gemäldegalerie), painted for the church of Sant'Egidio in Florence in collaboration with Andrea del Castagno and Piero della Francesca. Just after completing the *tondo* he began the frescoes (almost all now lost) at the same church. Domenico's masterpiece, the *Santa Lucia de' Magnoli Altarpiece* (Florence, Uffizi Gallery), confirmed that the single-panel altar painting had definitively replaced the polyptych.

The transition from the polyptych to the single-panel altar painting was a significant moment in the history of religious painting. Although it had occasionally appeared in earlier centuries, in the second half of the 15th century the single altar painting became the standard. Its success was directly related to the spread of the rules of perspective – in fact, the change from a gold ground to architectural or natural settings occurred at almost exactly the same time. Unlike the polyptych, the unified altar painting gathered all the figures in a single, organically composed space. Considerations of space, volume and geometry were crucial, as was the realistic relationship between the figures and their setting. Yet again, the initial steps were taken in Florence, where influential and authoritative scholars such as Leon Battista Alberti explicitly recommended the single square picture.

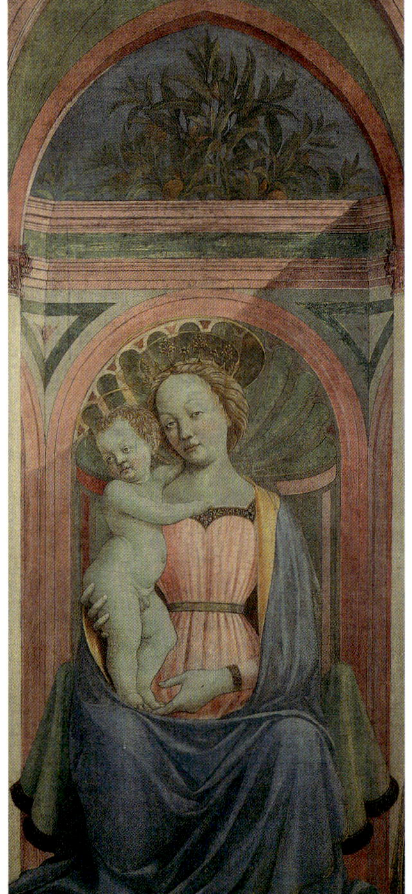

► Domenico Veneziano sought a compromise between the tradition of the triptych and the 'modern' single panel. The bright, symmetrical scene is framed by a portico with three arches that allude to the customary three-part division. Nonetheless, behind the portico he suggests a spacious courtyard, with niches and arches that enclose the entire composition within a unified space.

◄► At the centre of the composition, the Madonna and Child are framed by two very different arches: the slender, pointed portico is still Gothic, while the shell-shaped niche is in the new, classical style. The painter made the bold choice to unify the painting's varied, complex architecture by colouring the structural elements in green and light pink.

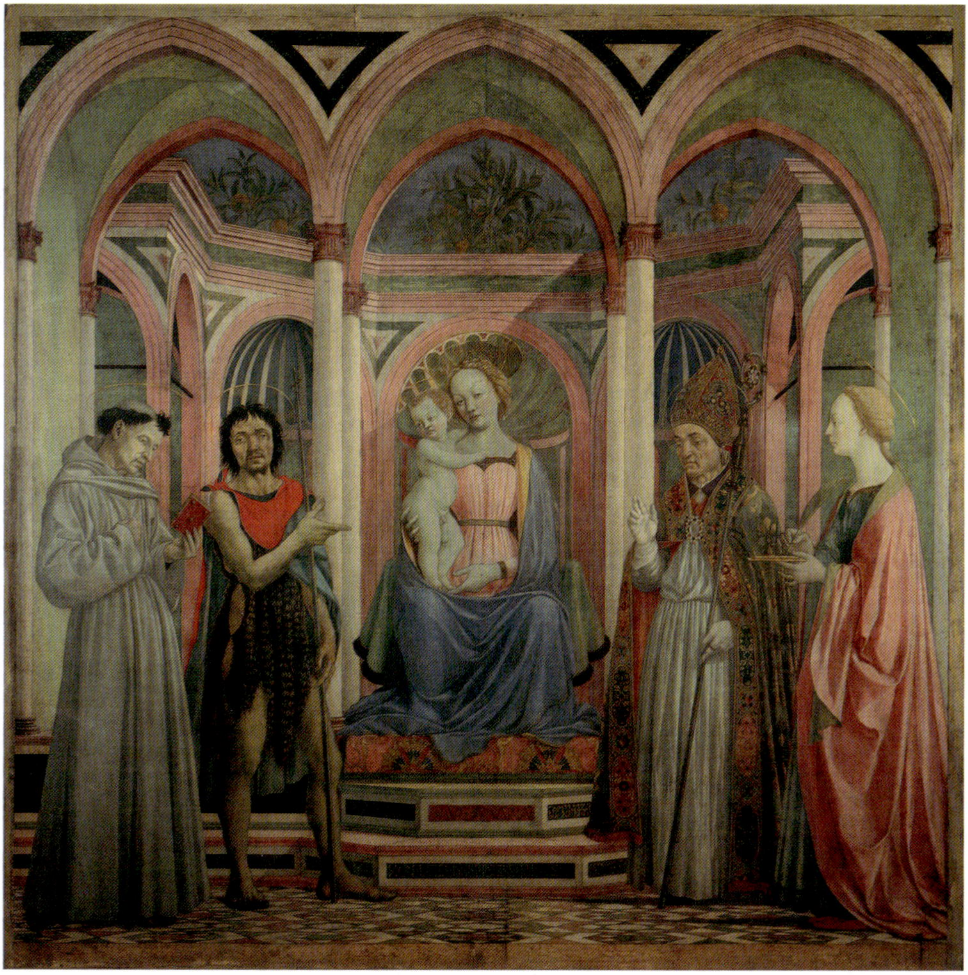

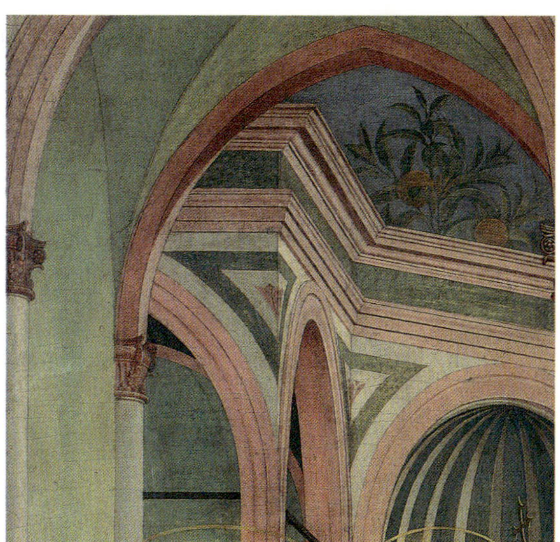

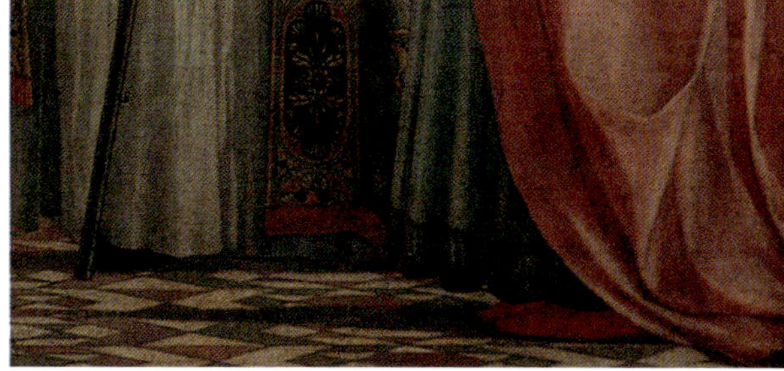

▲ The floor is decorated with complicated geometric figures. The white, green and pink marble is inlaid in a lozenge pattern, arranged by Domenico Veneziano in a way that emphasizes his flawless mastery of perspective. The figures' shadows (above are those of St Zanobi and St Lucy) suggest weight and volume and indicate that the light comes from the side.

Triumph of Death

Unknown artist
Triumph of Death
c. 1446

Fresco (detached), 600 × 642 cm

Palermo, Galleria Regionale
della Sicilia di Palazzo Abatellis

The medieval motif of Death that sweeps away all, obliterating social distinctions, remained popular throughout the Renaissance, often appearing under the guise of the 'Danse Macabre' or Dance of Death. In Italy as in all of Europe, war, disease, famine and capital punishment made death an everyday 'spectacle'. From popular dances to religious plays, from the meditations of philosophers to artworks commissioned by the aristocracy, the macabre image of the skeleton bearing a scythe recurs constantly. In pre-humanistic Italian culture, the poet Petrarch took up the theme and, in a more comforting vision, placed the triumph of death after that of love and chastity but before that of fame, time and eternity. This large fresco in Palermo, still suffused with the International Gothic taste, is one of the most complete and imposing scenes of its kind.

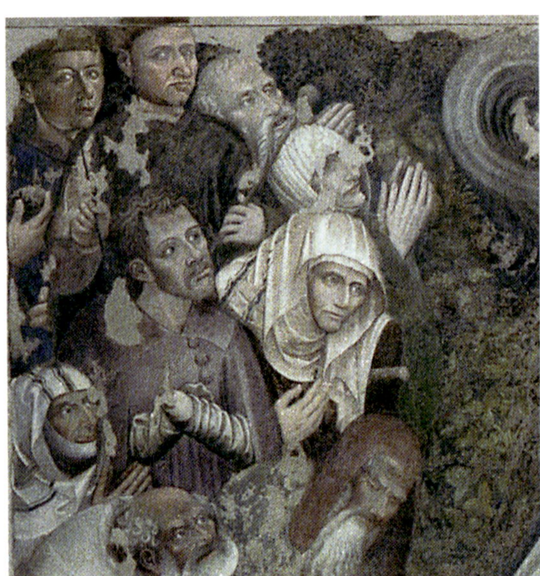

▲ At the middle left, some people seem to be invoking Death. One theory is that the two standing male figures who face the viewer could be the Burgundian painter Guillaume Spicre, the presumed author of the fresco, and his assistant, who holds a tray of colours and may be the young Antonello da Messina.

▼ Palazzo Sclafani, the fresco's original location, was the site of a hospital, a setting in which the theme takes on even greater significance. Death, the clear protagonist, hurls arrows as he gallops across the scene on an emaciated horse. The image of the starved horse so profoundly affected Picasso that he used it in *Guernica*.

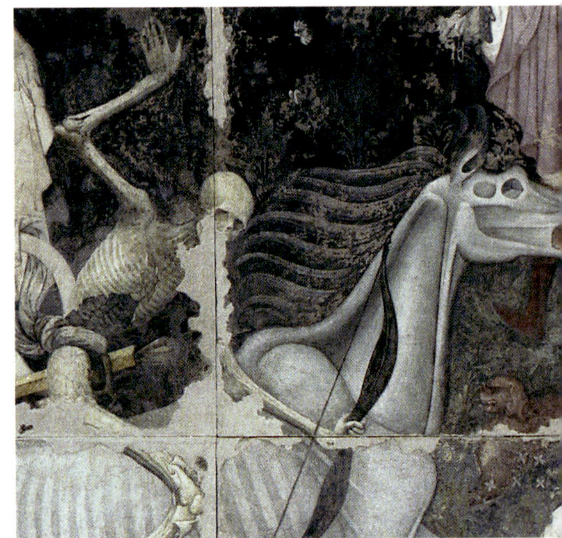

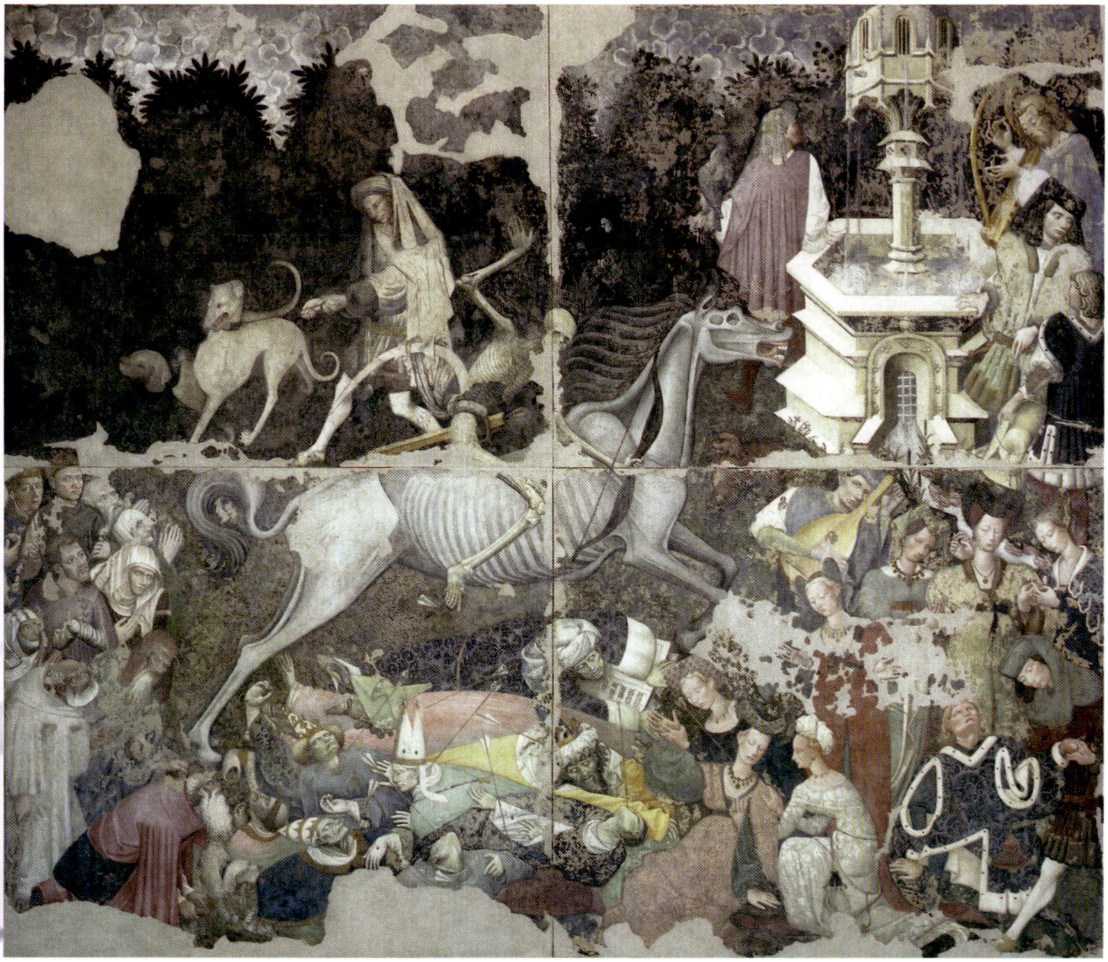

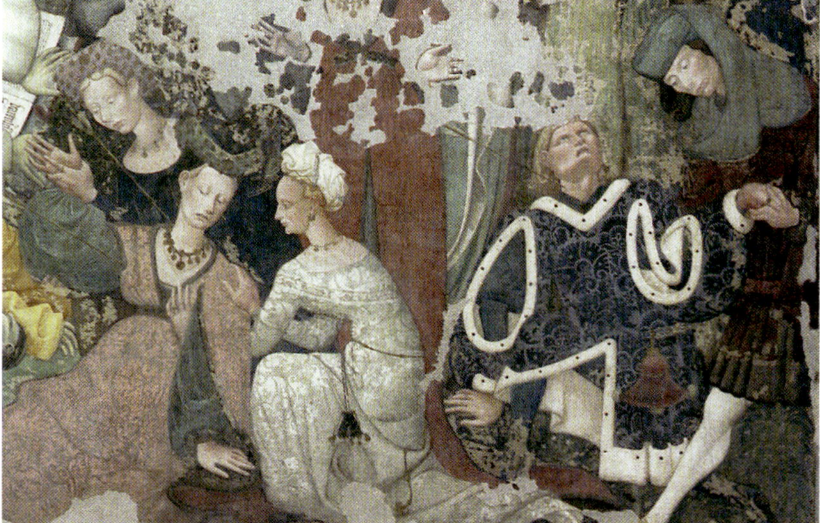

► In keeping with medieval tradition, Death strikes down everyone. In the centre of the scene, popes and sovereigns have fallen in a disorderly heap, while the whole right-hand portion of the fresco is occupied by a group of young men and beautiful ladies. As they enjoy the pleasures of youth, elegance and wealth, Death's arrows cruelly rain down on them.

Central Axis

Piero della Francesca
The Baptism of Christ
1448

Tempera on panel, 167 × 116 cm
London, National Gallery

For artist biography, see page 42.

The geometric organization of 15th-century Italian painting often called for strict symmetry, based on a horizon line and an imaginary vertical dividing the scene in half. The perspective depends upon a grid constructed on the basis of these two elements. (Flemish painting of this period was almost entirely based, instead, on the direct observation of the real world.) Some Italian painters sought to hide the perspective grid, but others made an explicit, almost didactic, feature of it. This is especially true of Piero della Francesca, who, even in a painting set outdoors and rife with splendid effects of natural light, uses light – divine light – to underscore the importance of the central axis.

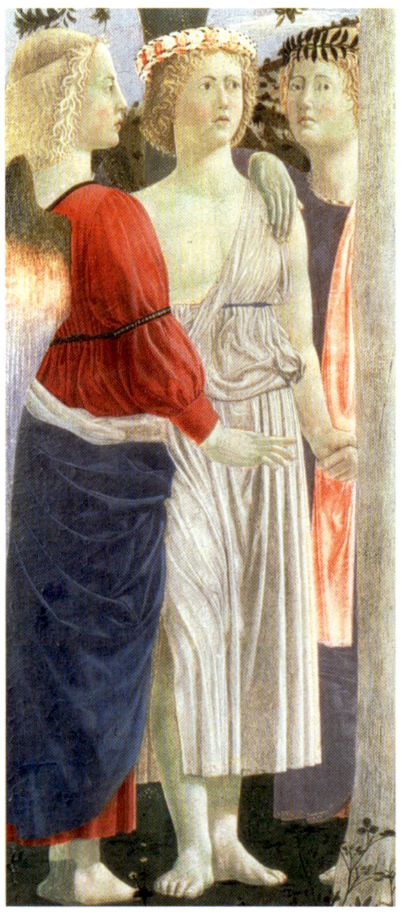

◀ At the left of the panel is a group of three angels. Although often present in paintings of the Baptism of Christ, here they scarcely seem to be involved. Their erect, dignified stance confirms the scene's axiality, with the middle angel, dressed in a white tunic in the Antique style, facing the trunk of a leafy tree.

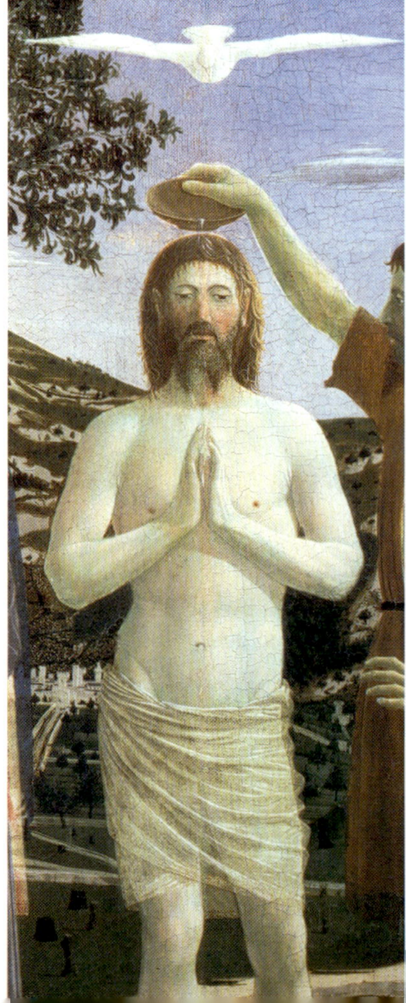

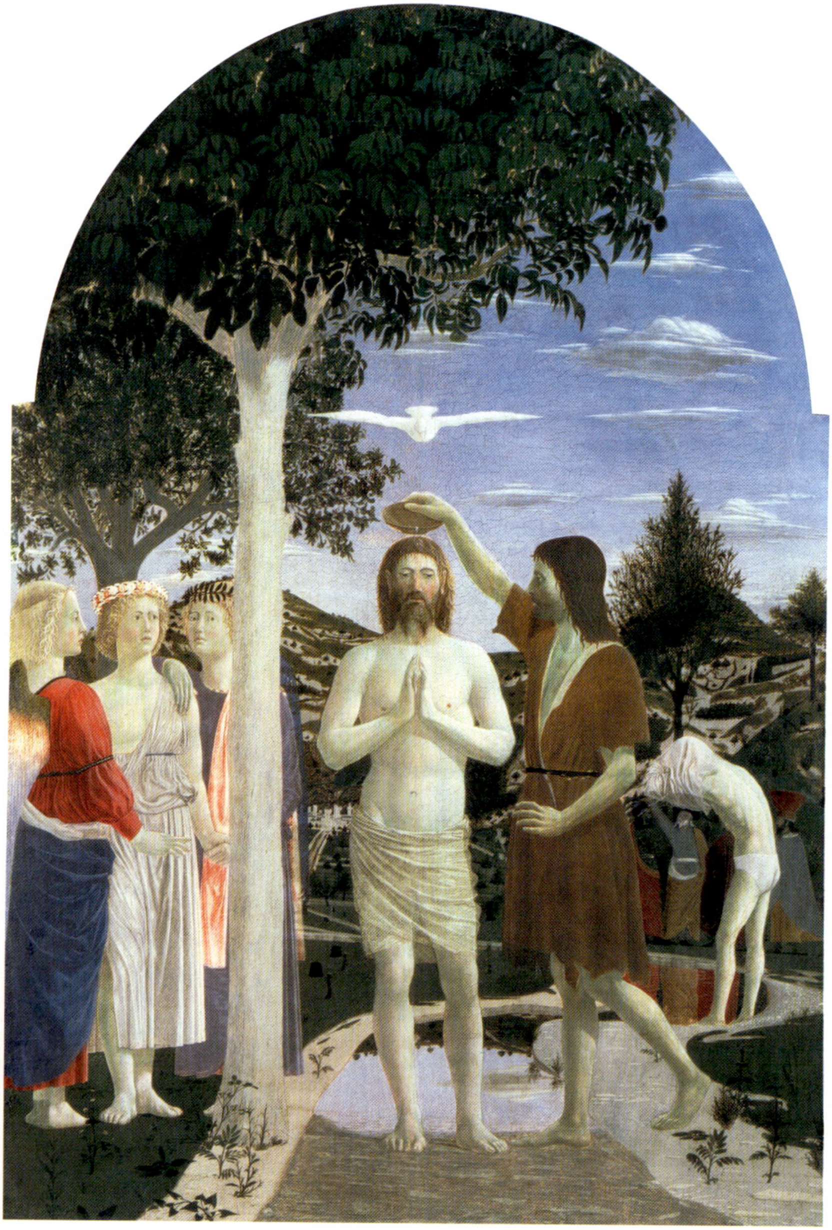

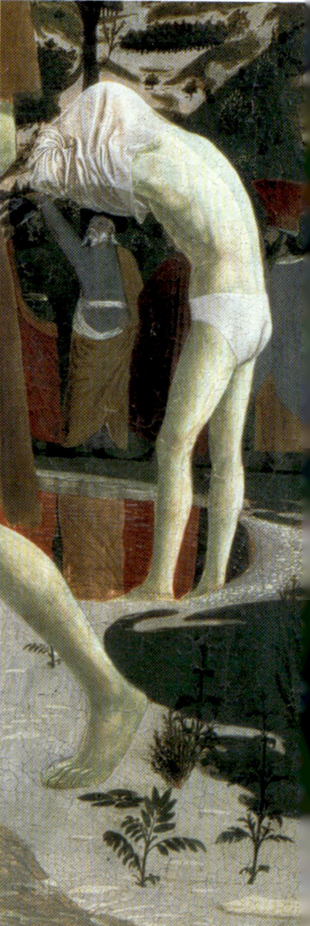

◄▲ The absolute axiality of Christ, motionless at the centre
of the composition, was further accentuated by the painting's
original location at the centre of a triptych with wings painted
by Matteo di Giovanni, who came from the same town as
Piero della Francesca. The tree trunk with smooth, light bark
reinforces the frontal pose of Christ, above whose head the
mystic dove of the Holy Spirit hovers, motionless and
with outspread wings.

Illustrious Men

Andrea del Castagno
Dante, Boccaccio and Pipo of Ozora
1449–51

Fresco transferred to panel,
250 × 154 (× 3) cm

Florence, Galleria degli Uffizi

For artist biography, see page 44.

'We are like dwarfs on the backs of giants.' This is the spirit that galvanized the humanists: to perceive the greatness of the leading figures of history and find in their example the inspiration to extend the horizon of civilization. The celebration of 'illustrious men' is a strong tradition in 15th-century humanistic culture, giving rise to collections of literary biographies and painting cycles populated with commanders, emperors, poets and thinkers as well as heroines, famous queens and women of the ancient world. Programmes of this type decorated the private apartments of the powerful. On the ceiling of the Camera degli Sposi, the heart of the Gonzaga residence in Mantua, Mantegna painted busts of the Roman emperors, while the Duke of Urbino's study originally had 28 portraits of famous figures painted by Justus of Ghent and Pedro Berruguete, half of which remain in situ and half of which were removed to the Louvre. The genre culminated in the early 16th century with Raphael's frescoes in the Stanza della Segnatura at the Vatican.

Poets and Soldiers: Curious Bedfellows

How is the fame of a historical personality measured? Even in the most advanced centres of humanistic culture, it was difficult to resist the fascination of a military commander, particularly if his exploits were still fresh in memory – a consideration that perhaps contradicts our image of 15th-century society as particularly sophisticated and classical. Italy, constantly threatened by large and small wars, celebrated brutal but victorious military leaders alongside its great poets. Lined up in a row along the left aisle of Florence Cathedral, for example, are two allegorical paintings of mercenary captains on horseback and a panel with Dante, who radiates light upon his city. In Andrea del Castagno's fresco cycle, images of literati alternate with those of famous captains. Filippo Buondelmonti (1369–1426), known as Pipo of Ozora in English and by his Tuscan surname Pippo Spano, was first an administrator and treasurer, then the brave and merciless commander of the army of King Sigismond of Hungary. He led Hungarian foot soldiers and cavalrymen in dramatic raids and sieges in the Veneto.

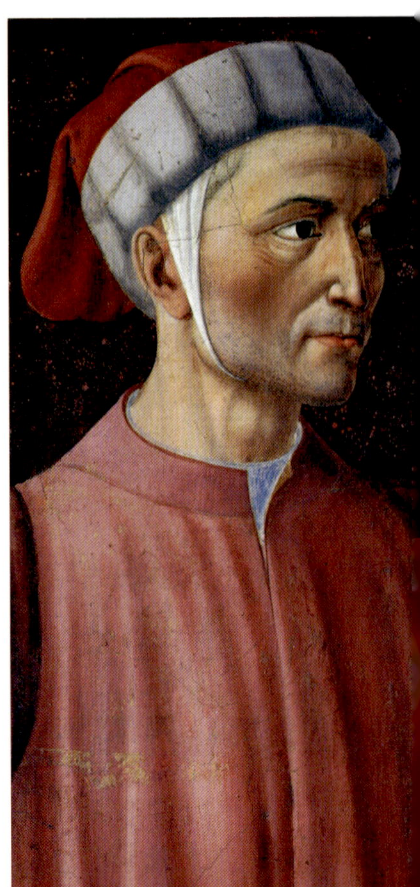

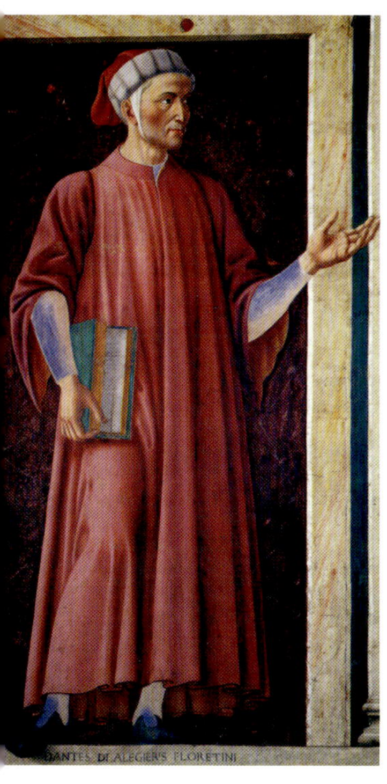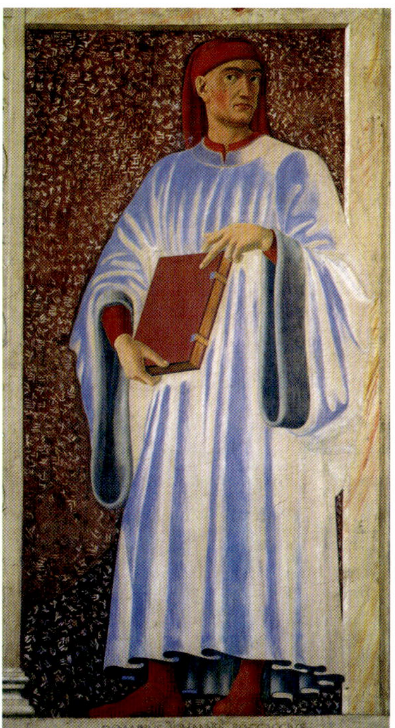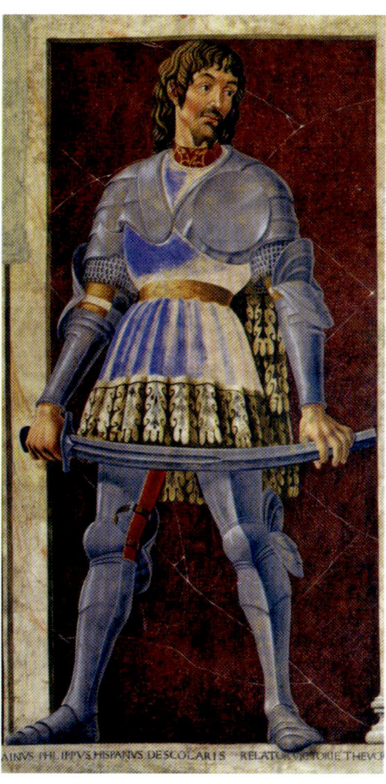

◄▲ The cycle by Andrea del Castagno includes nine figures, who are united by a sort of 'civil passion' against tyranny: three commanders (Pipo of Ozora, Farinata degli Uberti and Niccolò Acciaioli), three women (Queen Esther and Queen Tomyris, both adversaries of the Persians, and the Cumaean sibyl) and the three great Tuscan poets (Dante, Petrarch and Boccaccio).

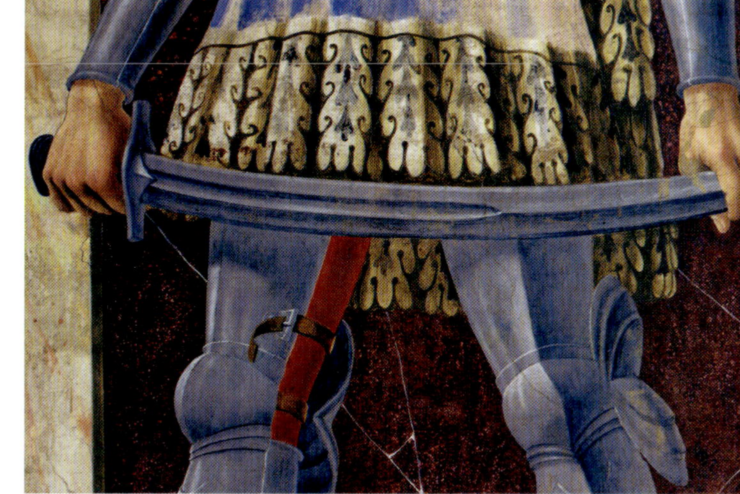

▼ The folds of Boccaccio's cloak fall in regular scrolls that seem to protrude from the painting. As often happens in the works of Andrea del Castagno, the characters have a sculptural grandeur and stand out strongly in the space.

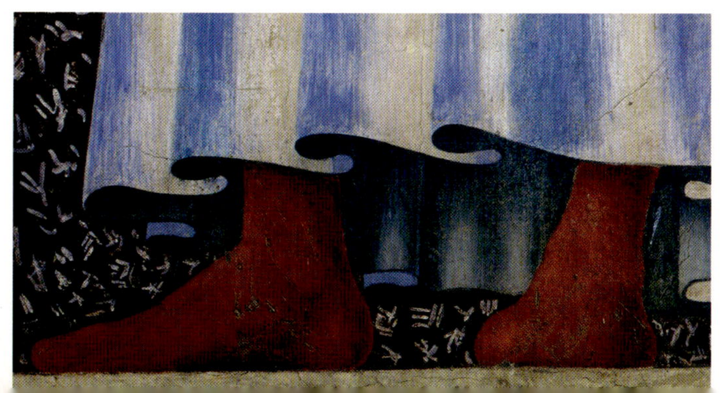

▲ The foreign scimitar and vaguely exotic decorative fringe allude to Pipo of Ozora's exploits in Eastern Europe. The famous figures are set against a background of precious variegated marble, of red and purple, colours that have always symbolized nobility and power.

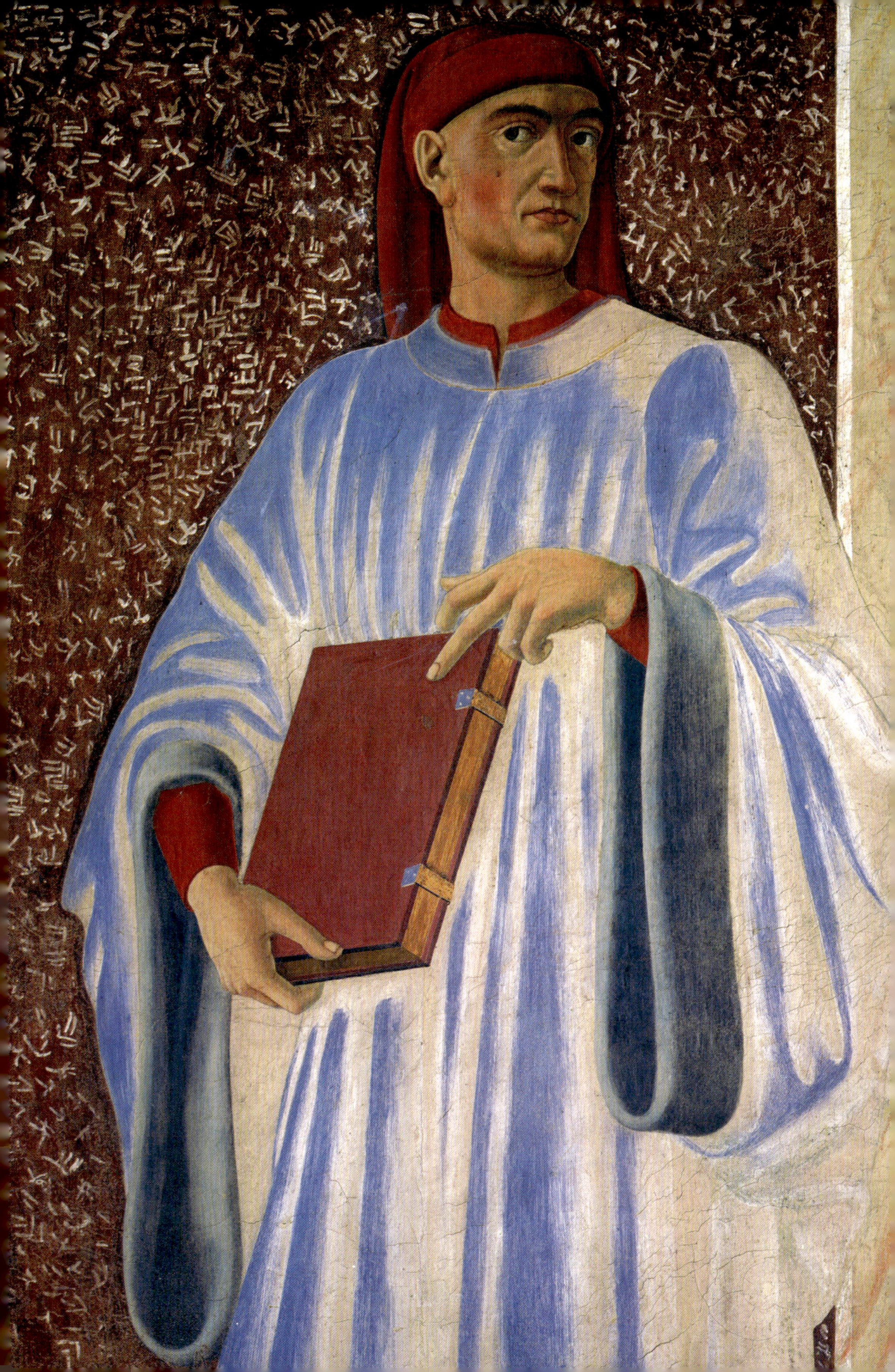

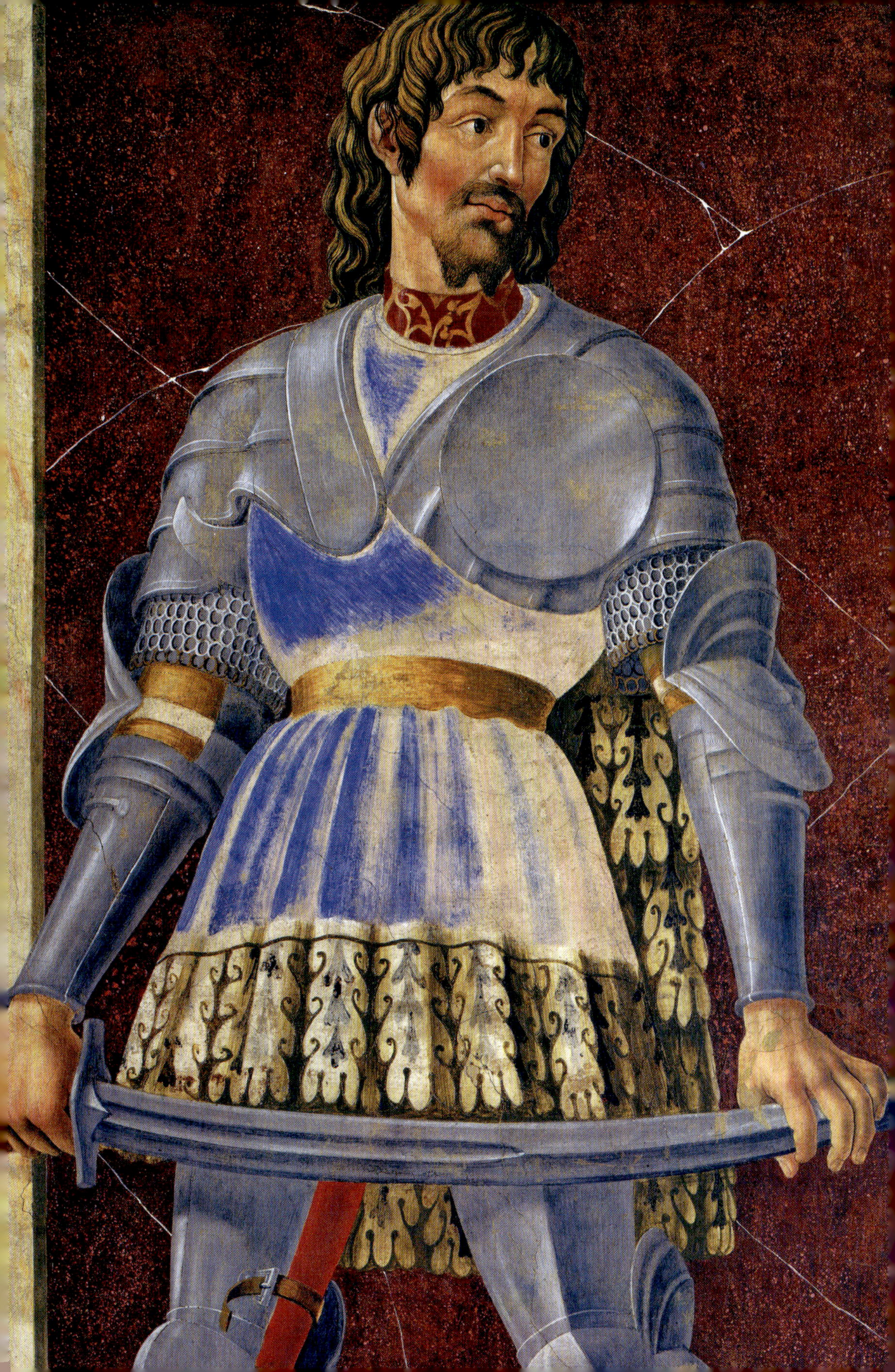

Maestà

For artist biography, see page 32.

The Virgin Mary is the central figure in most Italian Renaissance religious paintings. Devotional images of the Madonna encompass a range of expressions, from the tenderness of the Nativity to the agonized suffering she shows in the Pietà. For altar paintings and celebratory frescoes, the favourite model was the solemn, noble *Maestà* (majesty), handed down from the Middle Ages. In it, the Madonna appears as the Queen of Heaven, seated on a throne and holding the baby Jesus in her arms. Beside her are saints, the dignitaries of the heavenly court, while angels act as pages and musicians. The architectural setting normally reflects the scene's solemnity. In addition to the Madonna's throne, it often includes an Oriental rug and a room (or the interior of a church) with marble walls.

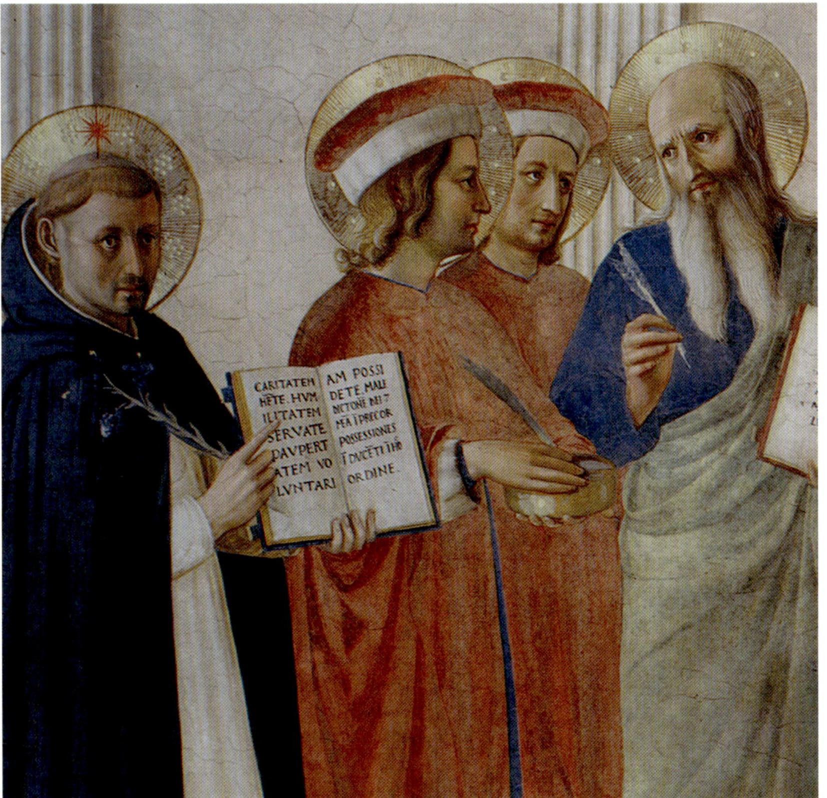

◄► This fresco can be found in a corridor, outside cell 25 in the convent of San Marco. Among the eight saints symmetrically flanking the Madonna and Child are the brothers Cosmas and Damian, dressed in red: the contemporary fashion. Both physicians, the two saints were also considered protectors of the Medici family, who effectively ruled Florence. The saint at the far left is Dominic, founder of the monastic order to which Fra Angelico belonged.

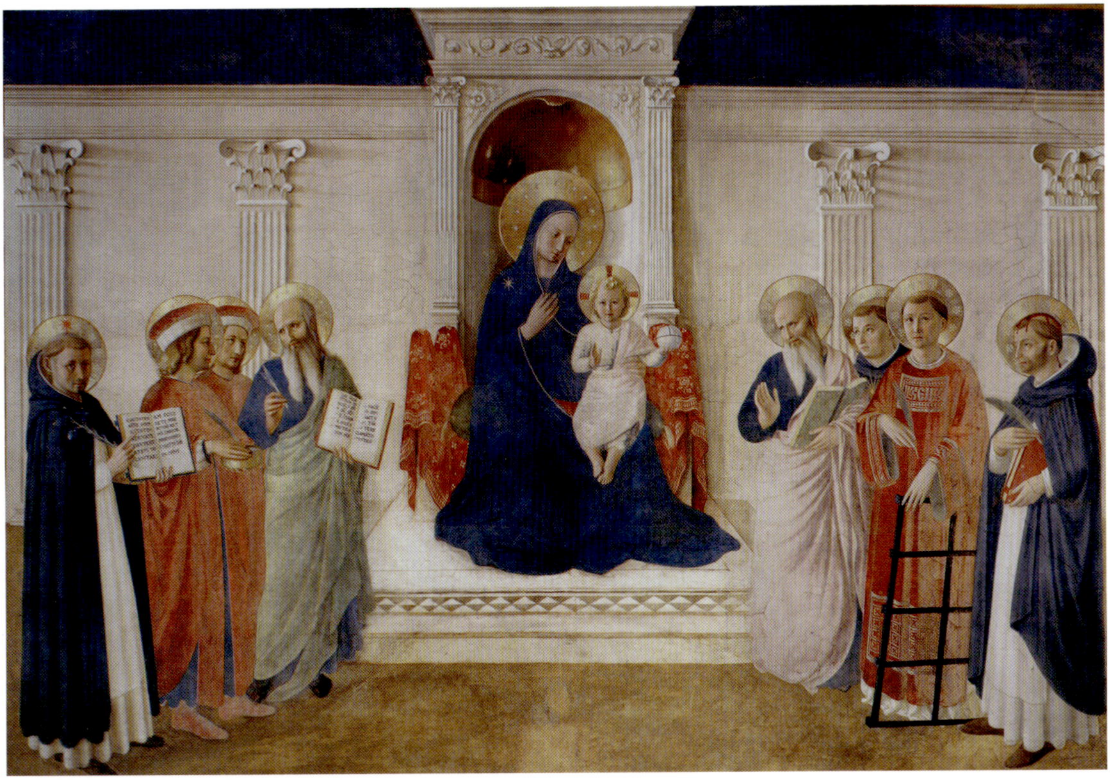

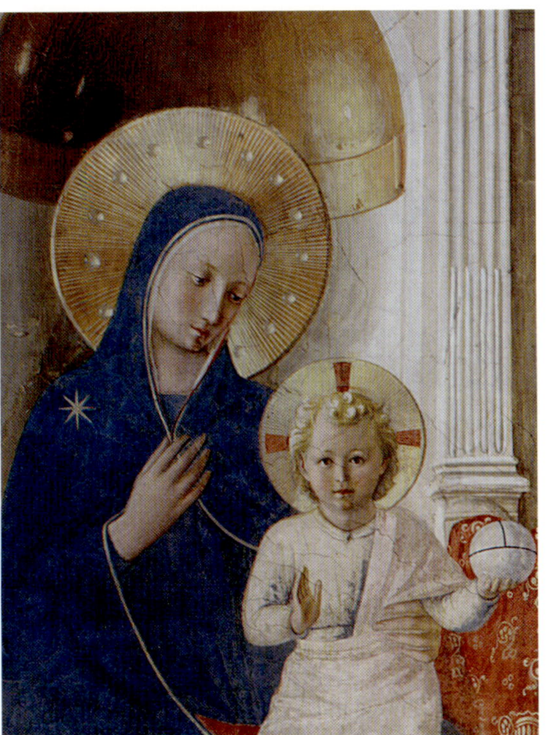

◄ The infant Jesus is presented frontally, raising his right hand in a gesture of blessing and holding in his left a globe, symbolizing his authority over the whole world. The haloes add to their regal appearance as well as the solemnity of the scene.

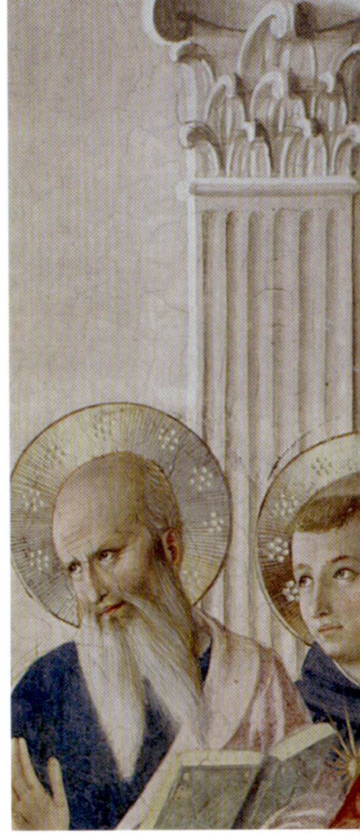

► This fresco gets its popular title from the long shadows cast by the Capitals.

Vanishing Point

Filippo Lippi
The Annunciation
1450

Tempera on panel, 203 × 186 cm
Munich, Alte Pinakothek

For artist biography, see page 38.

In 1450, the humanist architect Leon Battista Alberti completed his treatise *On Architecture*, the concluding volume in a cycle that included similar studies of painting and writing. A man of profound classical learning, trained in Tuscany but willing to take advantage of opportunities to work in other cities such as Rome, Rimini, Ferrara and Mantua, Alberti played a fundamental role in the study and success of humanistic art. His treatises were indispensable in clearly codifying the geometric rules on which one-point perspective was based. According to Alberti, a painting should be conceived of as a 'window' through which the viewer regards the scene. All the lines of the painting tend to converge towards a single point in the centre of the composition, called the 'vanishing point': it is the imaginary place where parallels meet, an effect easily verified by observing railway tracks or a long, tree-lined avenue. In the centre of some frescoes, there is even a small hole at the spot where a nail was hammered in to mark the vanishing point. Strings tied to the nail helped the painter to draw the figures and architecture in proper perspective. The vanishing point is usually set at the viewer's eye level.

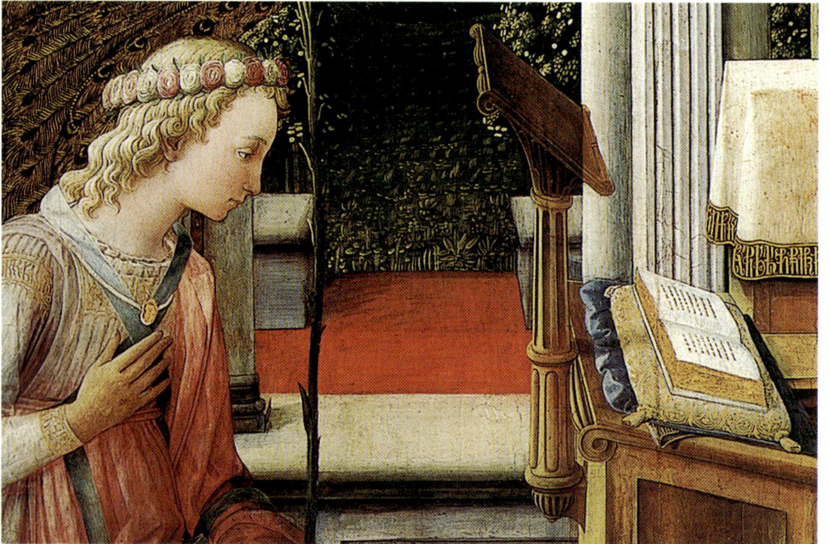

◄ The clean outline of the angel closely recalls the idealized Florentine profile portraits of women at the time. Filippo Lippi depicts the individual objects faithfully but is mindful of the requirements of perspective and the vanishing point. The lectern, and atop it the book resting on a cushion, are set on the diagonal and guide the eye towards the vanishing point at the exact centre of the composition.

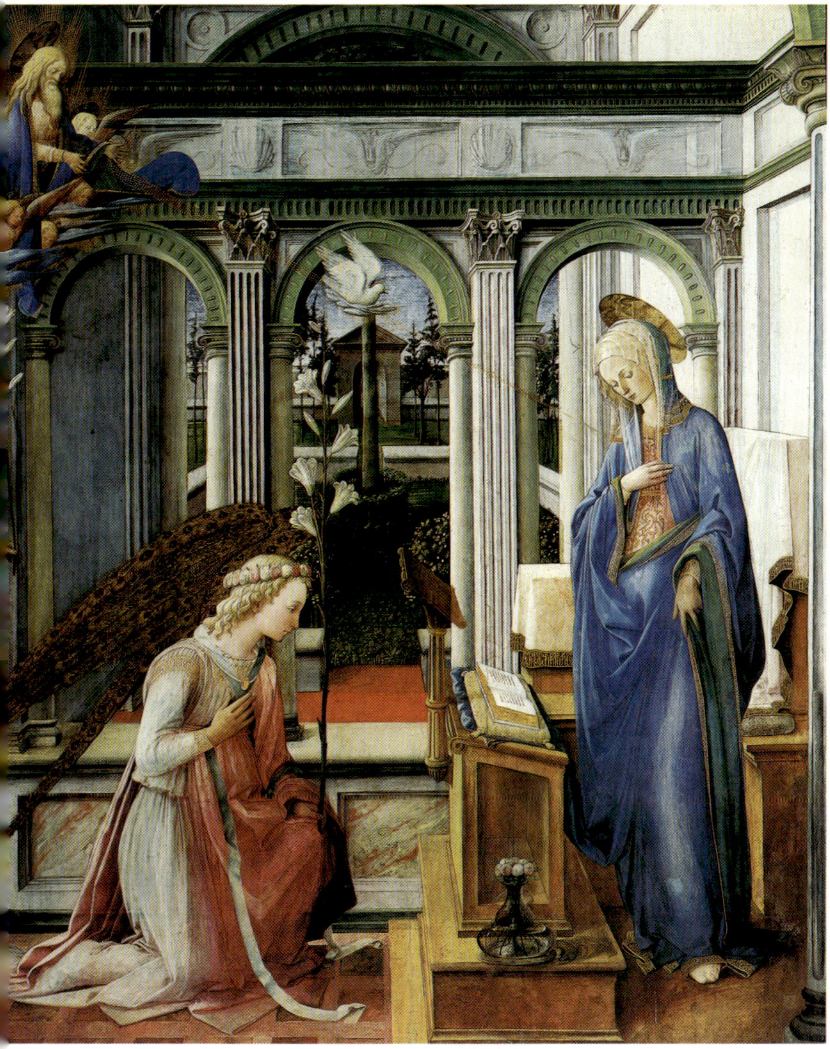

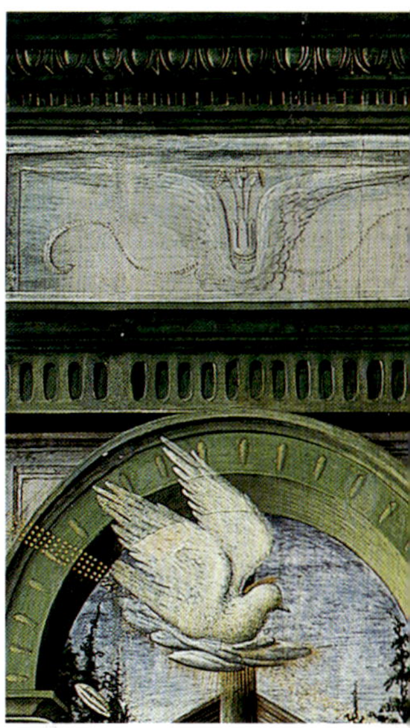

▲ The dove of the Holy Spirit glides along the ray of light that emanates from God the Father, cutting the scene on the diagonal. The dove marks the central arch of the portico and the painting's perspectival axis.

◄ The details are not simply part of the narrative, nor are they mere demonstrations of the painter's skill. They often have a precise symbolic meaning: the transparent vase with roses, for example, refers to Mary's virginal purity.

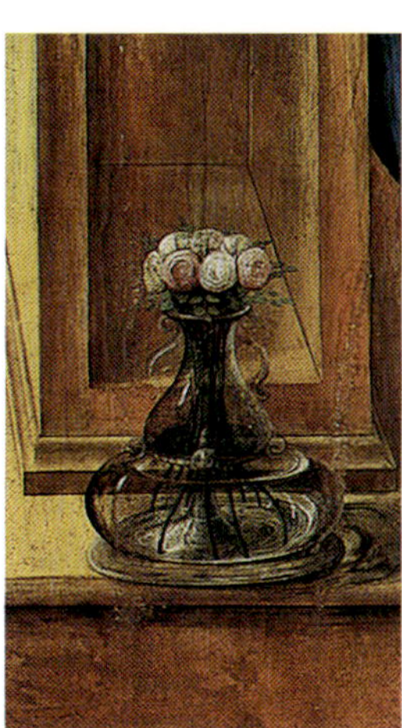

► The Annunciation was one of the most frequently depicted sacred scenes in 15th-century art, especially in Tuscany. Even in a relatively simple treatment of the theme, showing only two figures, painters could choose various psychological and narrative approaches. In this case, Mary meekly acquiesces to the divine announcement, 'Ecce ancilla Domini' – 'Behold the handmaiden of the Lord'.

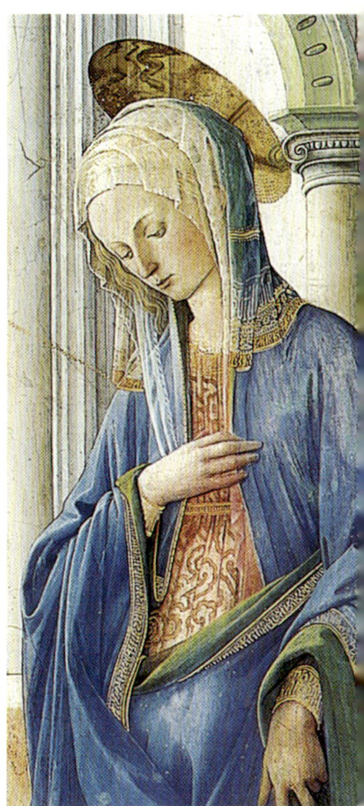

Stories

Piero della Francesca
The Combat of Heraclius and Khosrau
Detail from the *Story of the True Cross*
c. 1452

Fresco, 329 × 747 cm
Arezzo, San Francesco

For artist biography, see page 42.

Italian painting, and not only that of the Renaissance, typically favours paintings of 'history'. The term 'history painting' refers generally to any subject matter that implies a story: religious scenes, mythological episodes, literary tales and historical events. The frequent availability of large surfaces, such as walls to be frescoed, fostered the development of a type of painting showing figures in action, as opposed to the static portraits and altar paintings of the period. Yet even the action in dramatic battle scenes appears planned, calculated, measured. It was not until the turn of the 16th century – thanks above all to Leonardo da Vinci – that exaggerated or accentuated gesture, truly dynamic movement and intensely characterized expression would appear in art.

The *'Story of the True Cross'* and the *Golden Legend*
Piero della Francesca's frescoes in Arezzo tell the story of the tree from which Christ's Cross was made, and the complicated succession of events leading to Empress Helen's discovery of the relic of the True Cross centuries later. Biblical episodes, legends and historical facts are conflated in a rambling mystical account that was particularly appreciated by the Franciscan monastic community. The literary source for this depiction is found in the Golden Legend, *a volume compiled in the late 13th century by Jacopo of Voragine (today the town of Varazze, in Liguria). In this book, the learned Dominican recounts in great detail the lives of the saints and episodes connected to particular devotions, such as that of the True Cross. Drawing from the Bible, the apocryphal Gospels, hagiographic accounts of the lives and martyrdom of saints, popular tradition and other sources, Jacopo put a wealth of incidents, episodes, symbols, situations and characters at artists' disposal. For centuries, the* Golden Legend *was the main reference for sacred subject matter in art.*

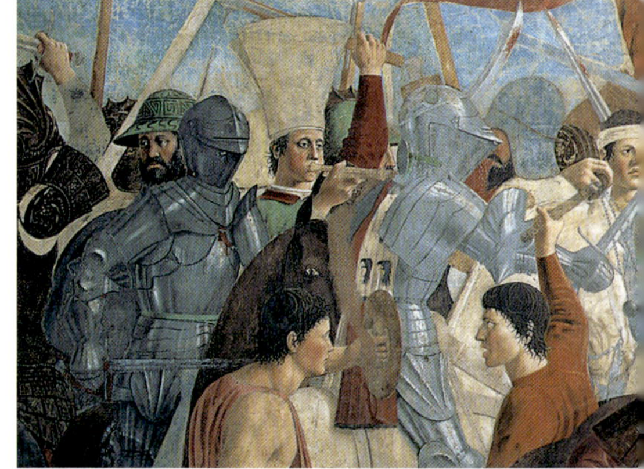

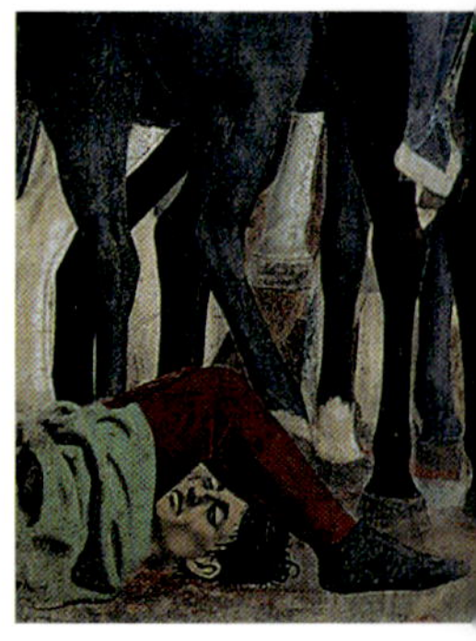

▶ At first sight, the battle does not seem particularly bloody. However, closer examination reveals macabre details such as dismembered corpses amid the horses' hoofs, a dying man dragging himself along the ground spattered with drops of blood and, at the far left, Khosrau's son impaled at the throat.

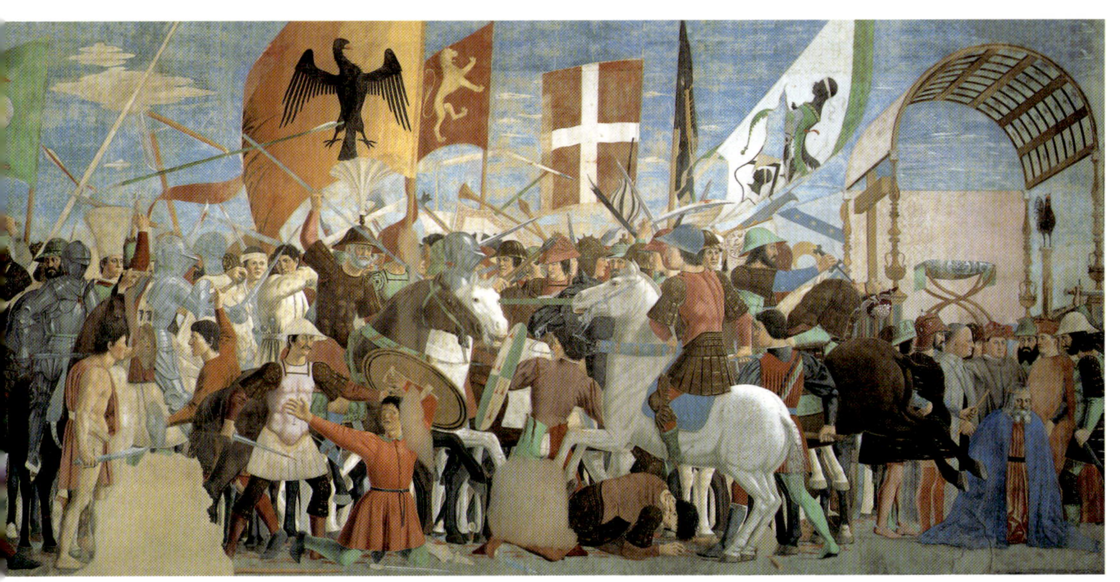

▼ In history painting, unlike propagandistic art (or films today), the 'hero' is indistinguishable from the 'villain'. On foot or on horseback, bare-chested or wearing armour, young or old, everyone is entangled in a deadly fray as the contending armies' banners wave above. Piero della Francesca describes the scene with an apparently impassive neutrality, coolly delineating expressions and poses.

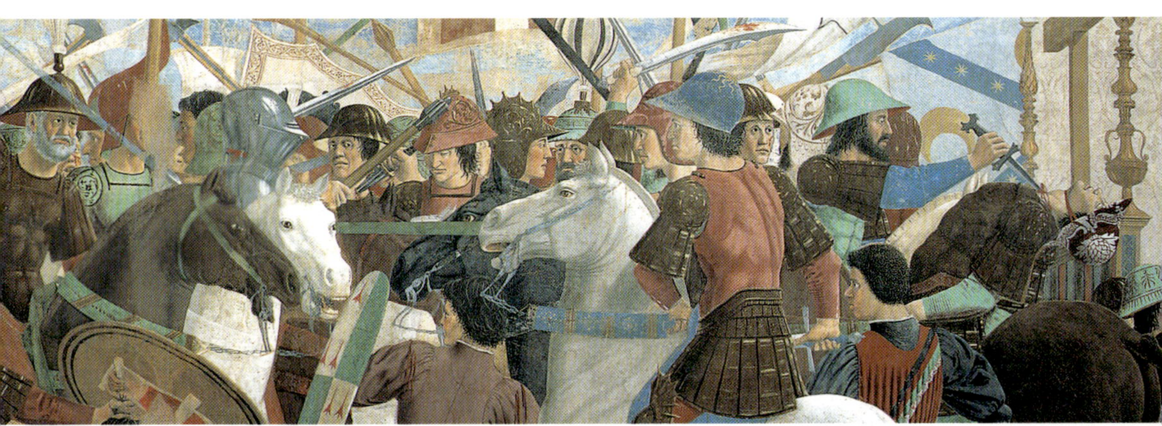

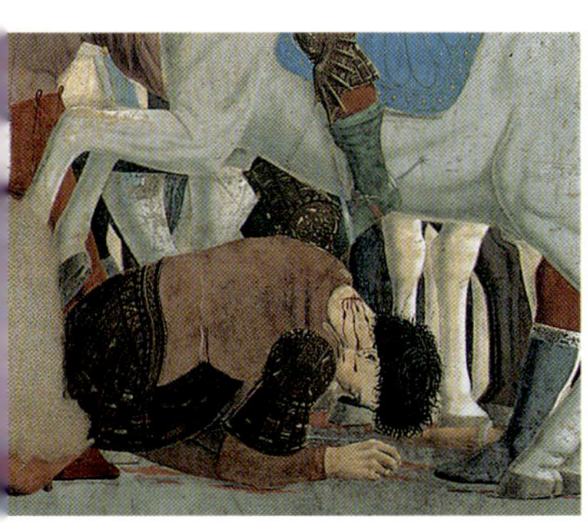

► The two battles that Piero della Francesca painted in Arezzo depict authentic historical facts, not legends. This scene recalls the defeat of the Persian King Khosrau II by the Byzantine Emperor Heraclius in the year 628. On the right of the painting the defeated king, on his knees, is surrounded by his conquerors.

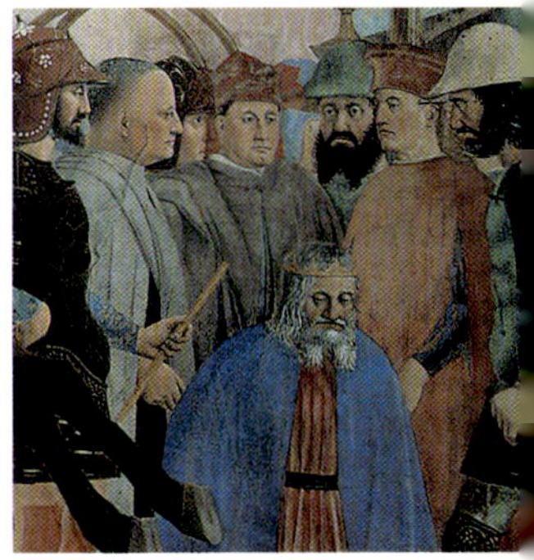

Ceremony

Piero della Francesca
Solomon and the Queen of Sheba
Detail from the *Story of the True Cross*
c. 1452

Fresco, 336 × 747 cm
Arezzo, San Francesco

For artist biography, see page 42.

As seen on the preceding pages devoted to the same fresco cycle, Piero della Francesca conceived the unfurling of dramatic events as a sort of solemn ritual. His figures' gestures are calm and meaningful, conveying an immediate, noble eloquence. This sense of official or even sacred ceremony is heightened by the simple but majestic buildings, the grandeur of the urban scenes and the stately landscape setting. Other great 15th-century Italian painters shared this way of conceiving a vast scene as a whole. This was because such a scene could combine the conscious application of perspective with the celebratory requirements of the ruling aristocracy. It replaced the gold and jewels of late Gothic painting with a composed 'nobility', an elegant sobriety immediately perceived as symbolizing total self-restraint and unquestioned power.

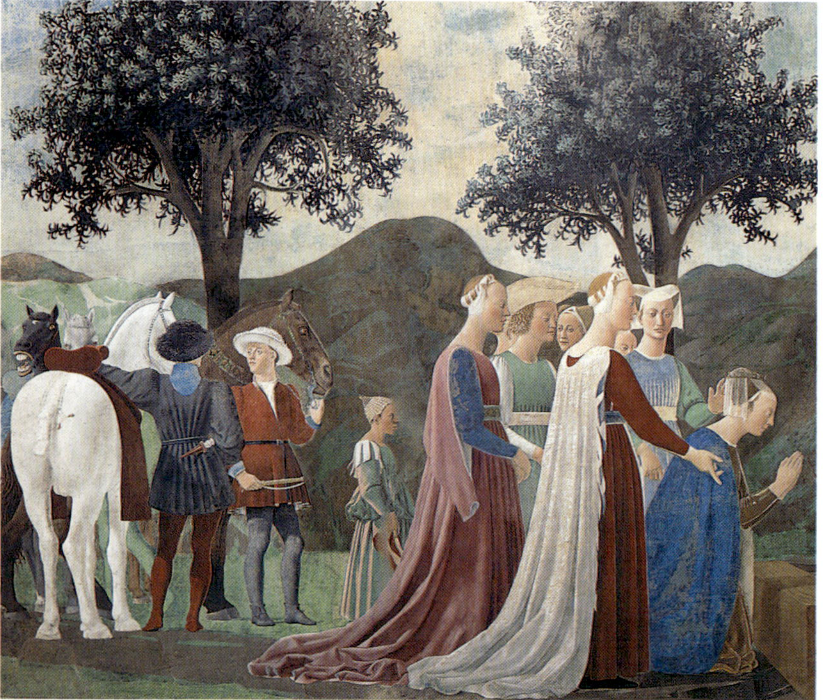

◀ The wood of the Tree of Life – that is, the tree from the Garden of Eden – was first used for a bridge and later for Christ's cross. The Queen of Sheba was on her way to Jerusalem to meet Solomon when she arrived at the bridge. Sensing the miraculous nature of the wood she dismounted and knelt in prayer. Piero della Francesca's depiction of the queen's retinue is delightful: ladies in sumptuous garments, weary-looking pages and well-groomed horses of different colours.

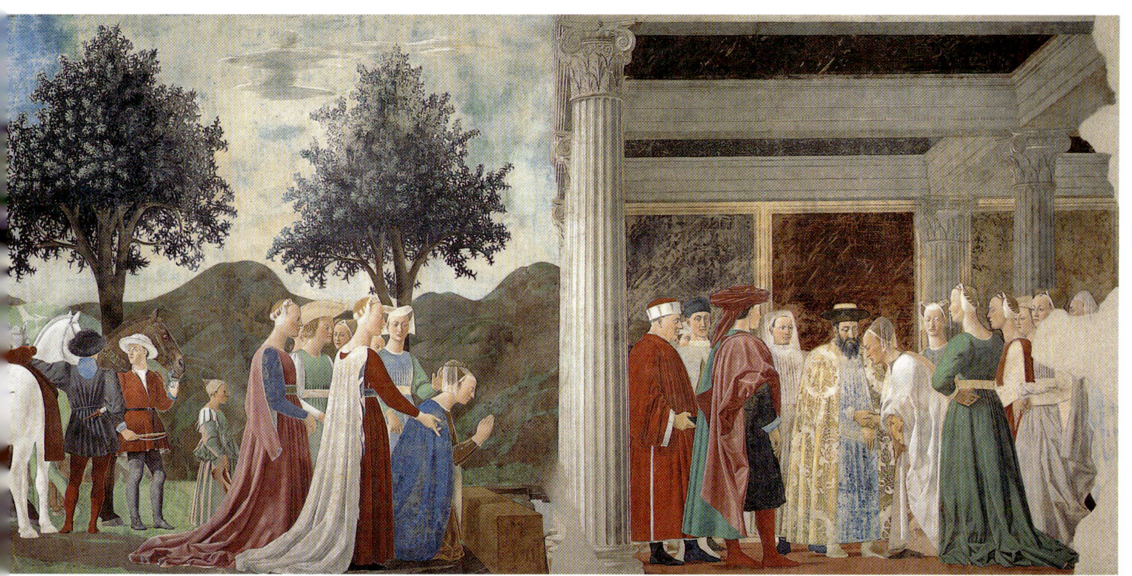

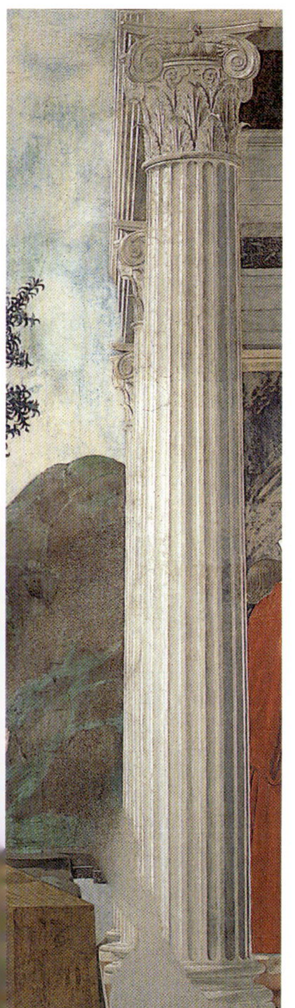

◄▲ The long scene is divided into two successive episodes. To make it easier to distinguish the two, Piero inserted a fluted column in the centre, clearly dividing the space. The left scene is set in an expansive, hilly landscape; the right within the elegant chambers of a regal residence. The meeting of the Queen of Sheba and the wise Solomon, in the right half of the fresco, takes place in an atmosphere of proper diplomatic protocol, with official delegations watching as the two sovereigns express affectionate mutual esteem. Their clothing is appropriate to their rank, but without late Gothic luxuriousness.

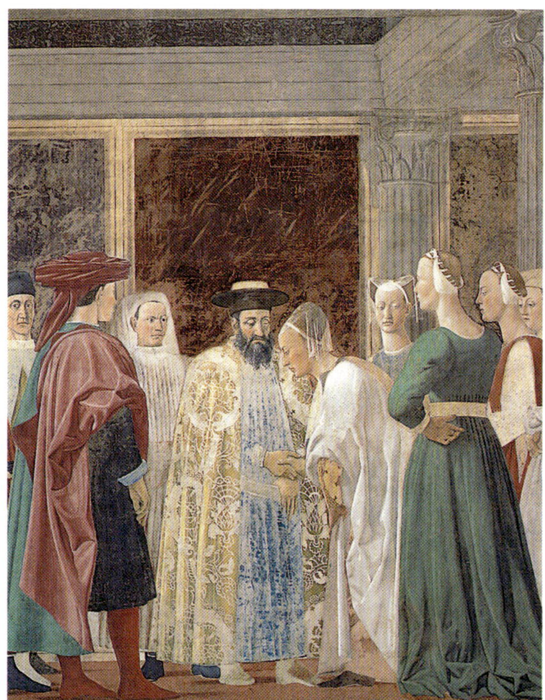

▲ The queen bows before Solomon, who courteously takes her hand and invites her to rise. Piero della Francesca includes the queen's ladies-in-waiting (see detail on the following pages).

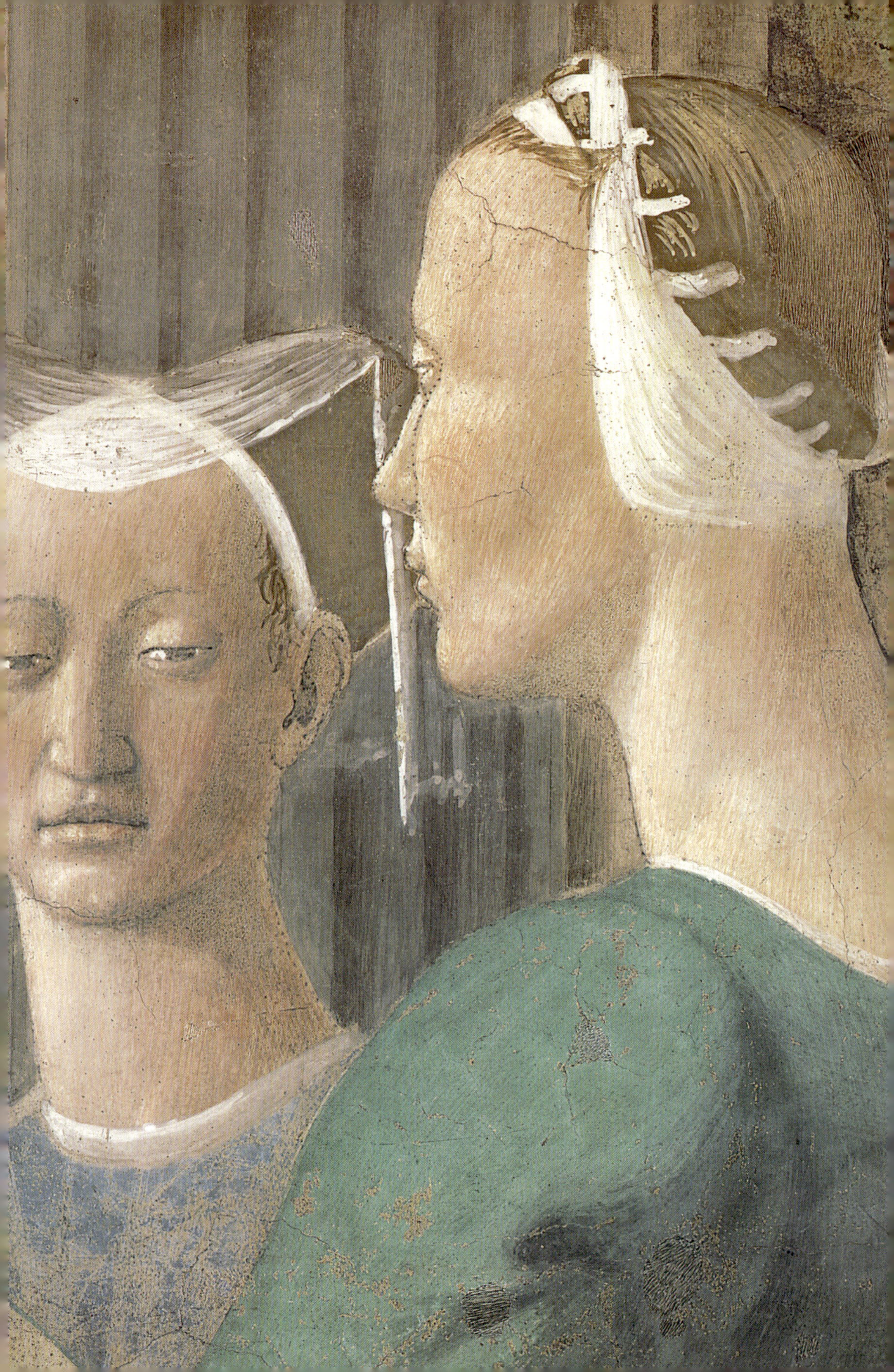

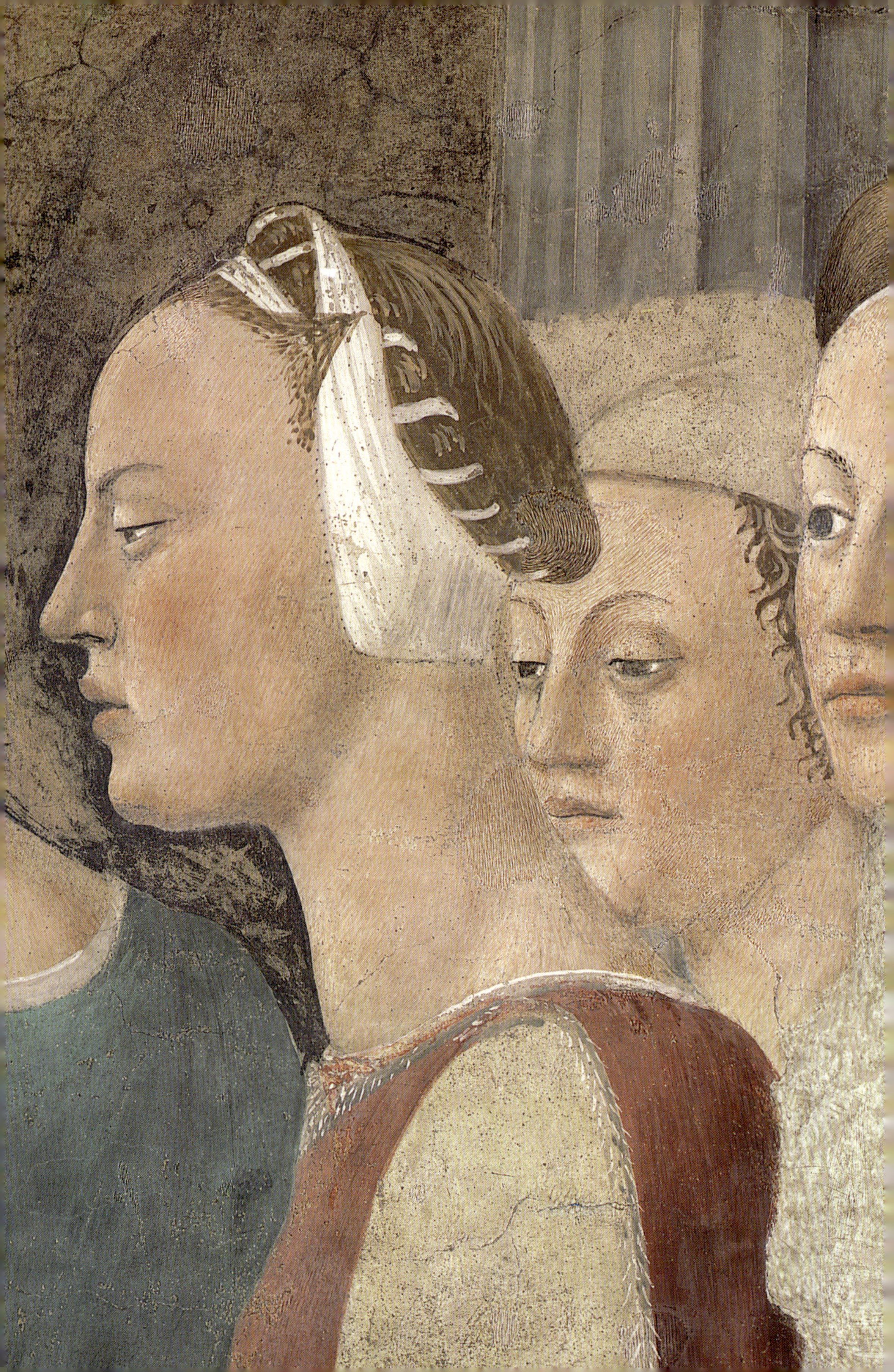

Piero della Francesca
The Flagellation
c. 1455

Oil and tempera on panel, 58.4 × 81.5 cm
Urbino, Galleria Nazionale delle Marche

For artist biography, see page 42.

The ability of images to popularize ideas and propagate political agendas has been exploited for thousands of years. During the 15th century, the Italian peninsula was divided into various independent states whose relationships constituted a complex web of alliances and rivalries, desires for conquest and proud claims to local power. All, of course, set against the background of what was happening north of the Alps. Many 15th-century paintings refer to facts, people and situations connected with the history and politics of the time, even if they are sometimes disguised beneath a pretext of traditional sacred subject matter. The exact meanings, allusions and symbolism contained in these paintings are not always entirely comprehensible today. An example is the mysterious and fascinating *Flagellation* by Piero della Francesca, which some have read as an allegory of a bloody conspiracy to conquer the small but strategic duchy of Urbino.

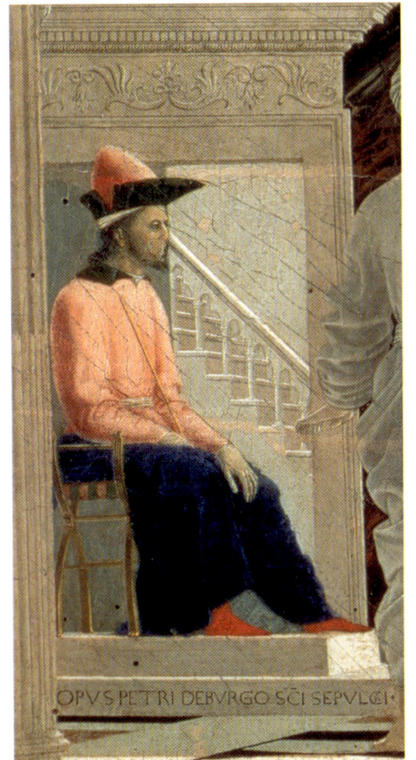

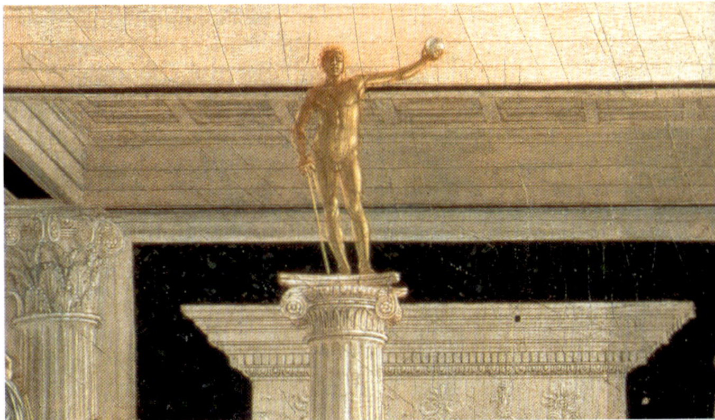

◄ One of the figures witnessing the Flagellation of Christ could be Pontius Pilate, but he is dressed exactly like the Byzantine Emperor John VII Palaeologus, known in Italy for having taken part in the Council of Ferrara and Florence (1438–9) and often portrayed in paintings and on medals.

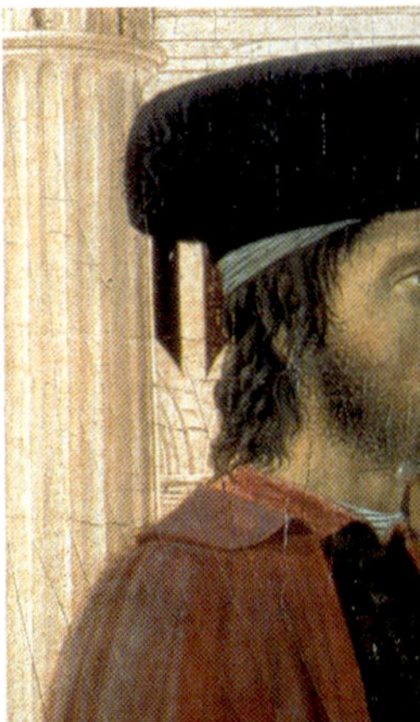

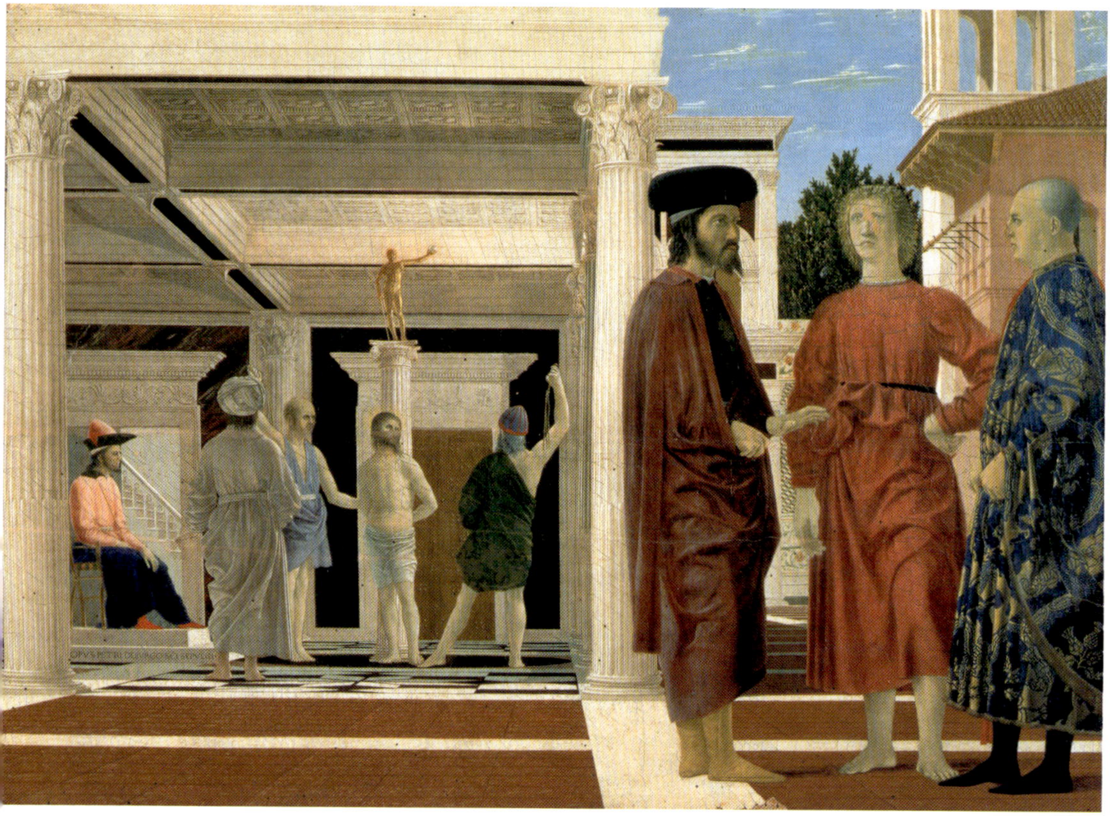

◄ The magnificent classical coffered ceiling clearly indicates the depth of the space and is also a vehicle for showing the effects of light – an indispensable element in successful perspective. The fluted Corinthian column in the centre neatly divides the two zones in which the figures stand: inside (middle ground) and outside (foreground).

▼ The identity of the three main figures remains a mystery despite much study by specialists. One particularly intriguing hypothesis is that Federico da Montefeltro commissioned this scene to commemorate the conspiracy of 1444 in which his stepbrother Oddantonio, the legitimate duke, was assassinated by treacherous courtiers.

► At the right, spring sunshine fills the cloudless sky. The diffuse light and the perfect arrangement of the urban setting demonstrate Piero della Francesca's mastery of both perspective and light effects.

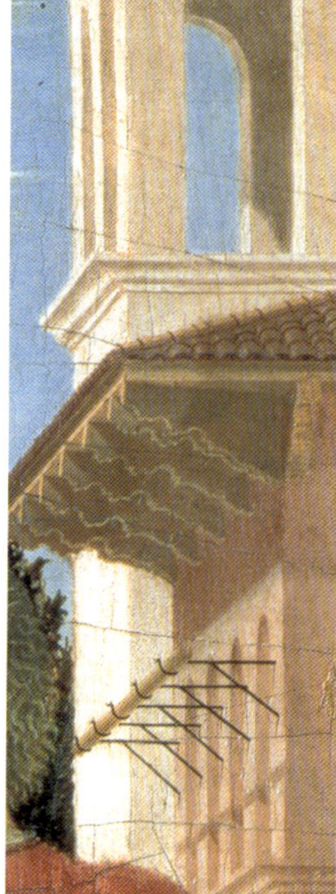

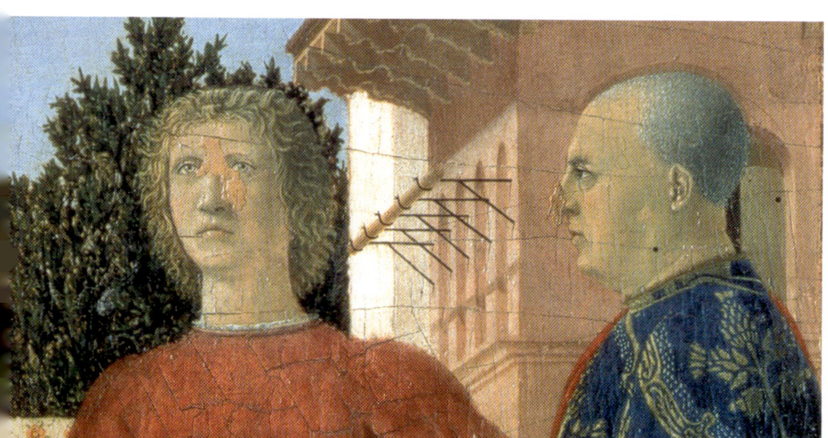

Battle

Paolo Uccello
The Battle of San Romano
c. 1456

Tempera on panel, 182 × 220 cm
London, National Gallery

Paolo Uccello

(Paolo di Dono)
Florence, 1397–1475

A bold exponent of complex perspective but also a captivating narrator of legendary exploits, Paolo Uccello started out in Florence during the 1420s and, through the frescoes in the so-called Green Cloister of Santa Maria Novella, soon gained prominence among the lively personalities in that artistic community. In 1425, Uccello began a long stay in northern Italy. In Venice, he took part in the decoration of the basilica of San Marco, executing cartoons for mosaics and inlaid marble floors, while in Bologna he painted a fresco in the church of San Martino. Back in Florence, from 1436 he worked in the cathedral of Santa Maria de Fiore, where he painted a fresco depicting John Hawkwood and *tondos* with the prophets surrounding the clock, and made cartoons for the stained glass in the dome. The three well-known panels of *The Battle of San Romano*, today divided among the Uffizi Gallery, the Louvre and the National Gallery, London, were painted to decorate a room in Palazzo Medici. Nonetheless, the painter's Florentine career gradually waned, and around 1465 he left his native city for Urbino and the court of Federico da Montefeltro, where he executed the *Profanation of the Host* as the predella of a large altarpiece by Justus of Ghent.

As already seen in Piero della Francesca's frescoes in Arezzo, when depicting battles, 15th-century Italian painting did not seek to portray agitated, dramatic action. This is confirmed in the celebrated series of three scenes painted by Uccello for the Medici's Florentine residence. The encounter between the Florentine and Sienese cavalry and footsoldiers is a bloody one, with dead bodies and hideous wounds. Yet viewers feel they are looking at a scene from a fairy tale or an aristocratic tournament rather than the illustration of a specific, dramatic historical event. Uccello concentrated on the individual figures, horses and even details of weapons and clothing, perfectly applying perspective, though he paid less attention to the composition as a whole, which is unbalanced and chaotic.

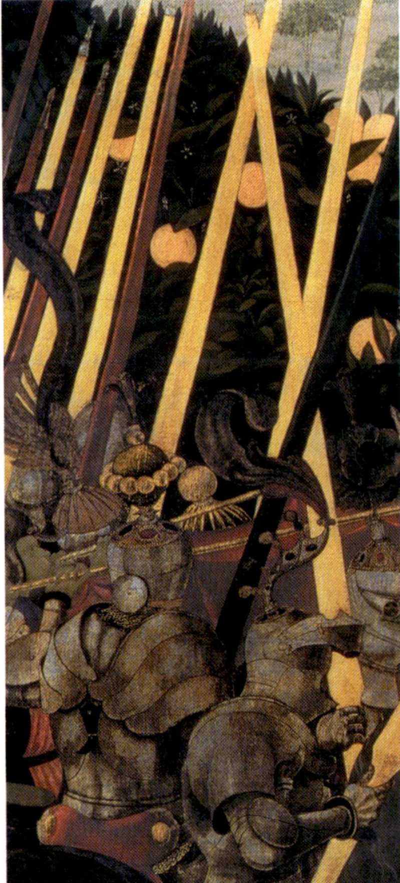

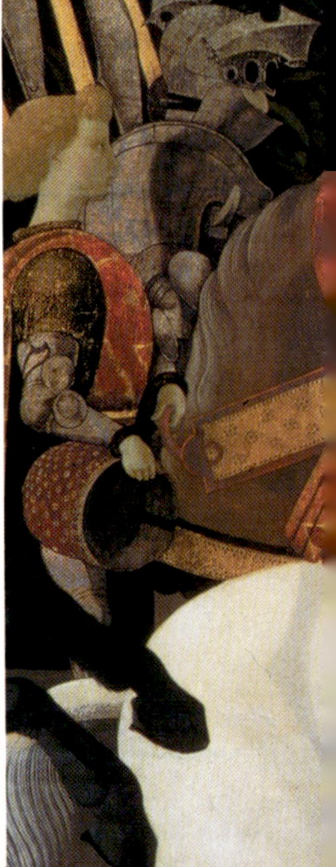

◄ Colourful lances rise above the clashing figures in all three of Paolo Uccello's panels depicting the battle, which was fought on 1 June 1432.

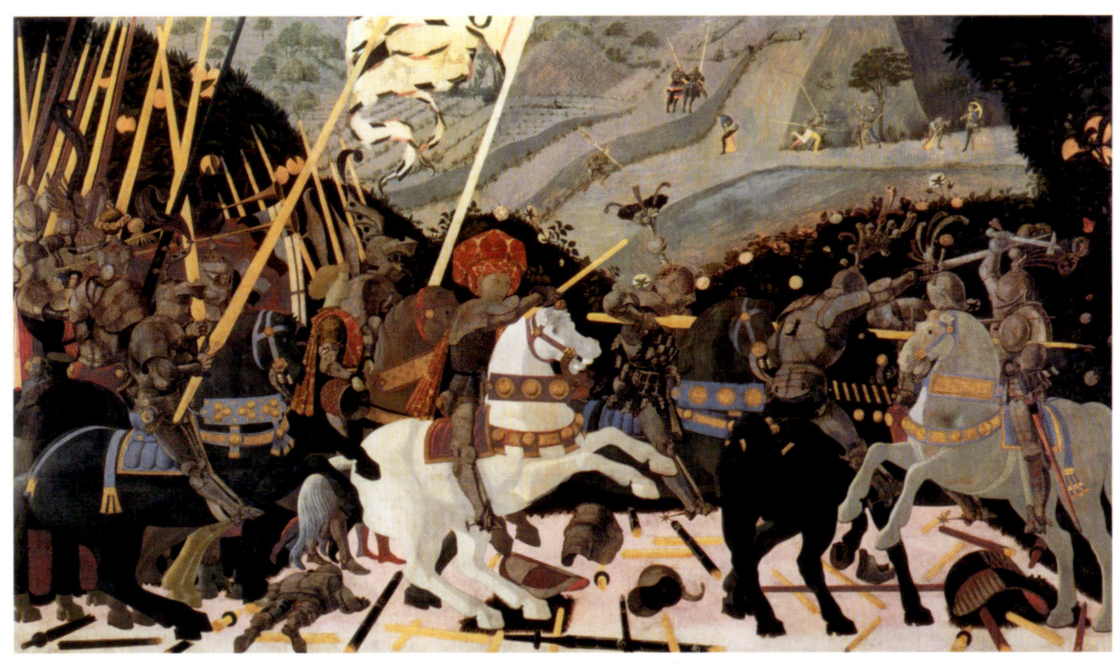

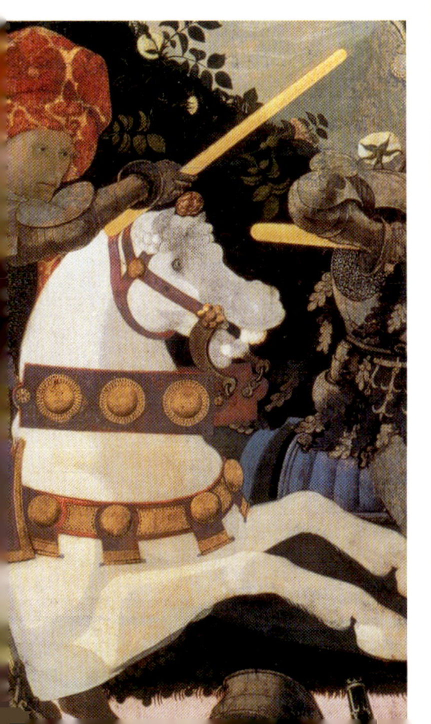

▼ The commander of the Florentine militia, Niccolò da Tolentino, is easily identifiable by his large, faceted headpiece, baton of command and white horse. The mercenary captain was further honoured in Florence by a fresco by Andrea del Castagno in the cathedral.

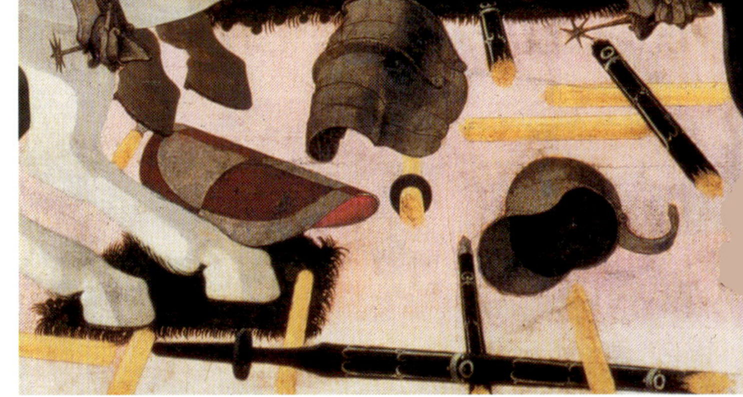

▲ Uccello's quest for correct geometric perspective can be seen in the broken lances on the ground, which define a sort of geometric grid. They create a controlled and planned structure for the painting.

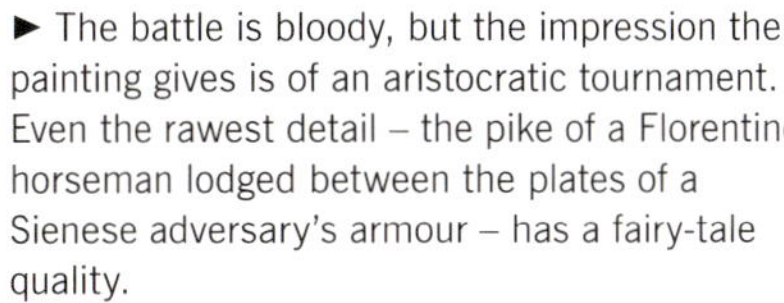

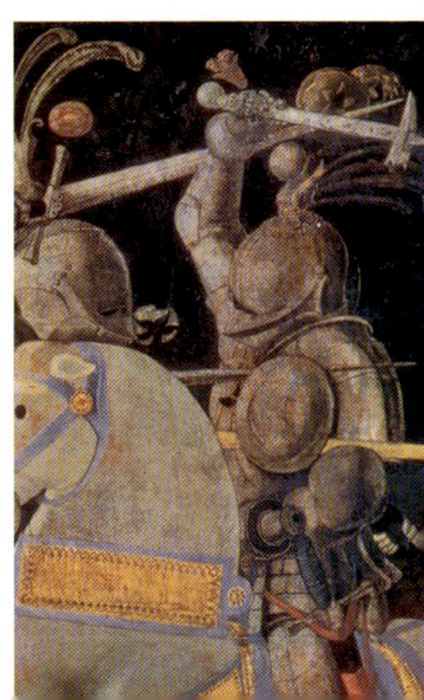

► The battle is bloody, but the impression the painting gives is of an aristocratic tournament. Even the rawest detail – the pike of a Florentine horseman lodged between the plates of a Sienese adversary's armour – has a fairy-tale quality.

Procession

Benozzo Gozzoli
The Procession of the Magi
1459

Fresco

Florence, Palazzo Medici Riccardi, Chapel of the Magi

Benozzo Gozzoli

(Benozzo di Lese)

Florence, c. 1421–Pistoia, 1497

A pupil of Fra Angelico in the convent of San Marco in Florence, Benozzo Gozzoli followed his teacher in his successive undertakings in Rome and Orvieto. Benozzo developed an independent career, and his simple, festive style was especially admired in the provinces, though he enjoyed success in Florence as well. In 1450, he was at Montefalco in Umbria, where he painted a fresco cycle in the church of San Fortunato and San Francesco. After a trip to Rome and various projects in Tuscany, Lazio and Umbria, in 1458 he received a commission to decorate the private chapel in the Palazzo Medici in Florence. There his opulent *Procession of the Magi* also serves as a joyful celebration of the family. Between 1464 and 1466, he resided in San Gimignano, where he executed frescoes in the collegiate church and the church of Sant'Agostino. The subsequent series of stories from the Old Testament in the Campo Santo of Pisa (1468–84) was, unfortunately, almost entirely lost during the Second World War. After a series of works in Florence and smaller Tuscan centres, he died in Pistoia in the plague of 1497.

In Italian cities of the Renaissance, marriages between aristocratic families, official visits of illustrious guests, religious processions, popular festivals and solemn feasts were most often celebrated with parades and processions. These were an opportunity to display lavish clothing, richly harnessed horses, groups of trumpeters and other musicians; they would also often include guards in full dress, exotic animals, servants in livery and temporary decorations such as wooden triumphal arches, false façades painted on canvas, ornamental statuary of papier mâché and so on. Painters wove these these dazzling urban spectacles in sumptuous paintings; in the case of Benozzo Gozzoli, they serve as the backdrop to the Story of the Magi.

The Italian Sojourn of the Byzantine Emperor John VIII Palaeologus

On 8 February 1438, a high-level embassy disembarked in Venice from Constantinople: Emperor John VIII Palaeologus was accompanied by the Orthodox patriarch Gennadius II and the extremely cultivated cardinal of Nicea, Johannes Bessarion. The Byzantine delegation was headed for Ferrara to take part in a Council called by Pope Eugene IV in an attempt to reconcile the Eastern and Western branches of the Christian Church and present a common front against the now unstoppable Ottoman advance. The initiative was too late to prevent the fall of Constantinople (renamed Istanbul) in 1453, but it had a noticeable effect on Italian culture. The imperial entourage, Byzantine ceremonial, unusual costumes and high rank of the guests made this an important contact between Italian humanism and the sophisticated traditions of the East. Before then, few Italian intellectuals understood Greek. In 1439, the Council was moved to Florence, where the presence of the Byzantine delegations unmistakably influenced its art history.

▶ The image of the Magi as they proceed together along the same street effectively symbolizes Medicien 'good government'. Cosimo I, founder of the Medici dynasty and considered the Pater Patriae of Florence, and his son Piero the Gouty may be recognized astride the two mounts in this detail from the east wall – the one with the greatest political overtones.

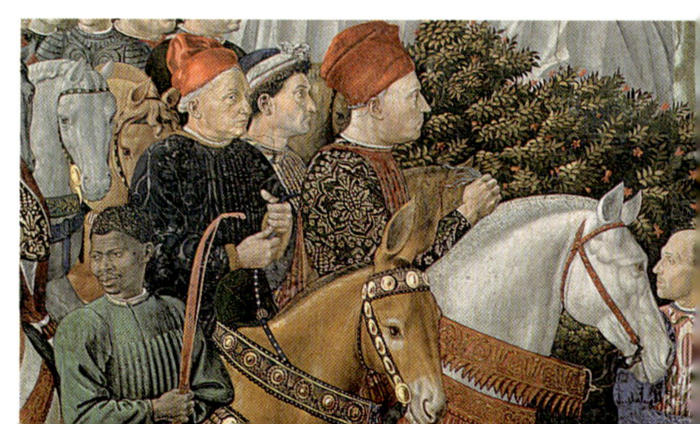

"""

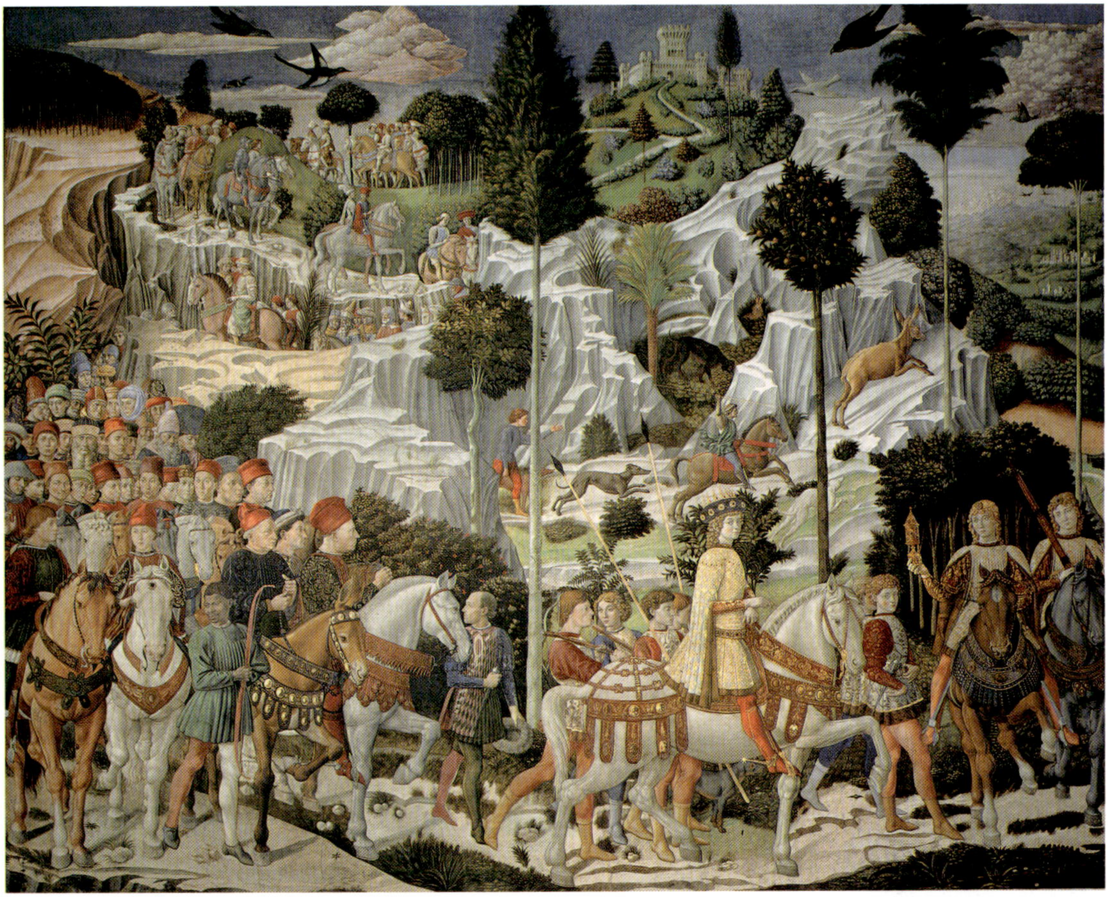

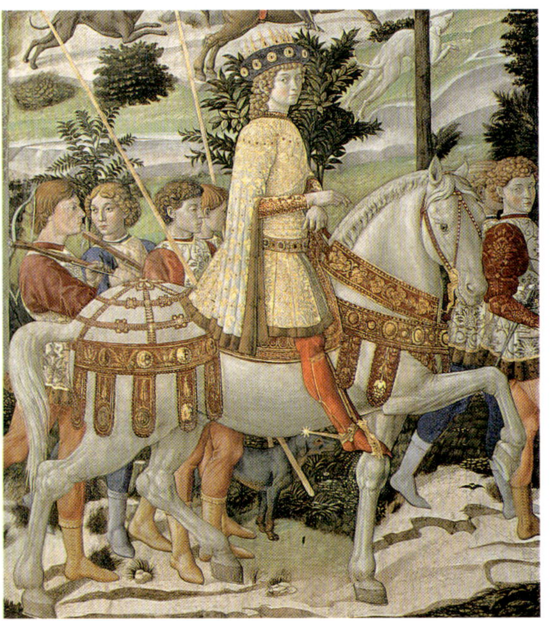

◄ Radiant colours heighten the opulent garments and precious details. Many of the main figures are portraits of members of the Medici family. The splendidly attired boy has been identified as the young Lorenzo the Magnificent.
In some parts of the scene, Benozzo has concentrated many figures in a small space, with an effect not unlike that of the late Gothic *Adoration of the Magi* painted a quarter of a century earlier in Florence by Gentile da Fabriano.

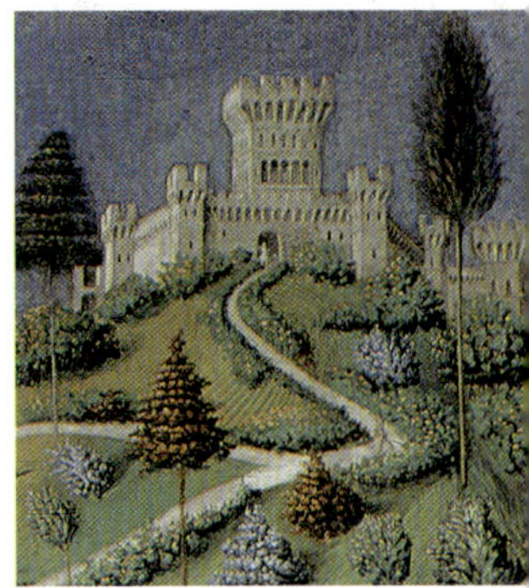

▲ In the upper part of the scene, the Magi's lavish entourage wends its way amid fantastic landscapes with castles, villages, cliffs and animals, all set against a blue sky with just a few clouds.

Cosmè Tura
The Muse Erato (or *Spring*)
c. 1460

Oil on panel, 116 × 71 cm
London, National Gallery

Cosmè Tura

Ferrara, *c*. 1430–95

The extremely original art of Cosmè
Tura, the main representative of the
Ferrarese school in the 15th century,
was born out of the remarkable cultural
atmosphere created by the Dukes of Este.
After founding a university, the rulers of
Ferrara invited masters of high standing
to their court including Jacopo Bellini,
Pisanello, Rogier van der Weyden, Piero
della Francesca and Alberti. Tura trained
in the humanistic culture of Padua (not
far from Ferrara), where he came into
contact with the young Mantegna. Back
in Ferrara, he became the court painter of
Ercole and Borso d'Este and never left the
city again. He supervised the decoration
of the Estes' residences, including the
frescoes of the Hall of the Months in
Palazzo Schifanoia. Among his most
important works are the organ door at
the cathedral (1469; Ferrara, Museo del
Duomo) and the magnificent *Roverella
Polyptych* (1470–4), which has since
been dismantled and dispersed among
various Italian and foreign museums.

The seat of a prestigious university, home to the tomb of Saint
Anthony, and heir to an extraordinary pictorial tradition that
included the Scrovegni Chapel frescoed by Giotto, Padua was
the foremost centre for the diffusion of humanistic culture in
northern Italy. An intellectually open-minded city, towards the
middle of the 15th century it welcomed great Tuscan masters
such as Filippo Lippi, Paolo Uccello and above all Donatello,
who remained for a decade and left several extraordinary
bronzes. The most active art workshop in Padua was the one
run by Francesco Squarcione. A tailor, embroiderer and indifferent painter, Squarcione directed and trained a group of
highly gifted young artists, all of whom left Padua in the space
of a few years to become the leading figures in the renewal of
painting in various cities: Andrea Mantegna in Mantua, Cosmè
Tura in Ferrara, Carlo Crivelli in the Marche, Vincenzo Foppa
in Milan, Marco Zoppo in Emilia and Michael Pacher in Alto
Adige. Each painter developed his own individual talent but
with certain common technical and formal elements.

Signs of Recognition: A Code among Old Workshop Mates
*Even today, members of associations and alumni of famous
colleges and universities will display signs of recognition (badges,
pins, neckties) showing that they belong to an in-group. The
brief phase of humanistic painting in Padua was concentrated
in the 1450s. Immediately after, all of Squarcione's most brilliant
students left the city, and several decades passed before important
paintings – a group of frescoes by the young Titian – were once
again being produced there. Nevertheless, even working in
different cities, the 'Squarcioneschi' adopted special signs of
recognition, not just a common style but specific details they
frequently inserted in their compositions, such as garlands of
greenery and fruit hung in the top part of larger works, extremely
realistic little animals depicted in the foreground and ornamental
strings of red balls and glass beads dangling behind the figures.*

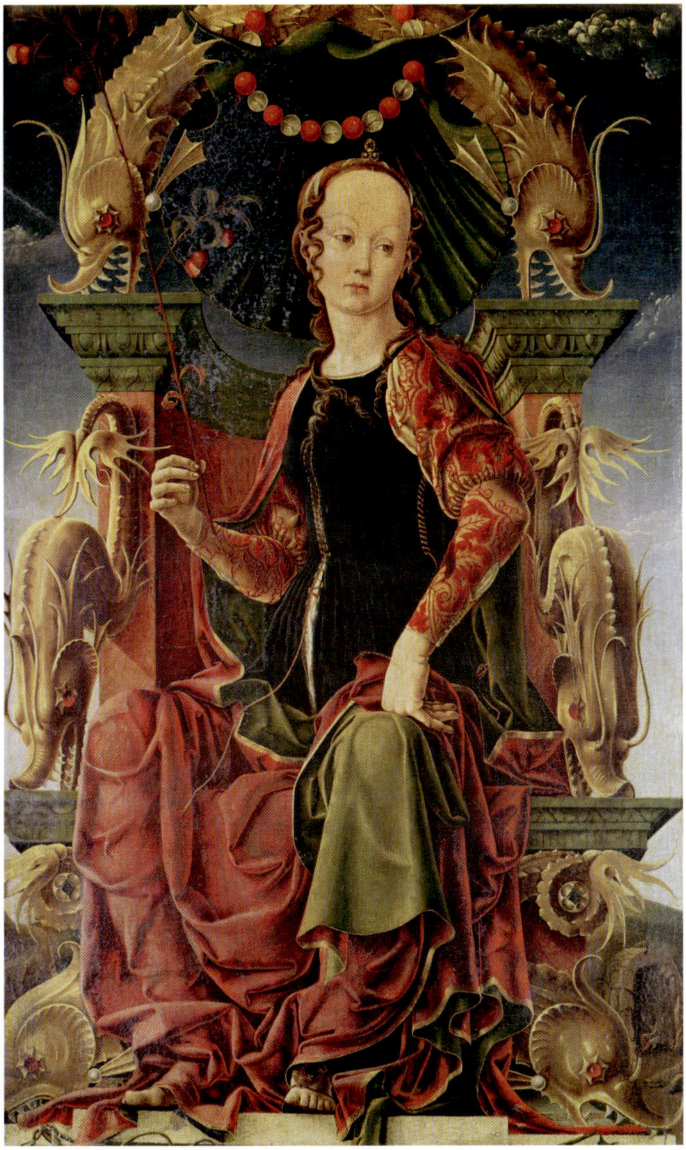

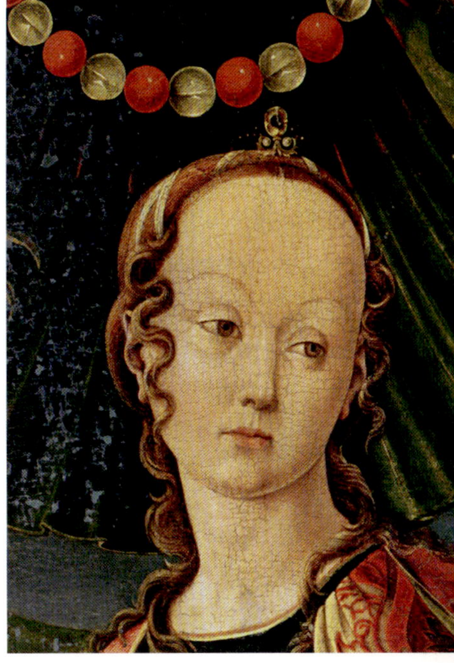

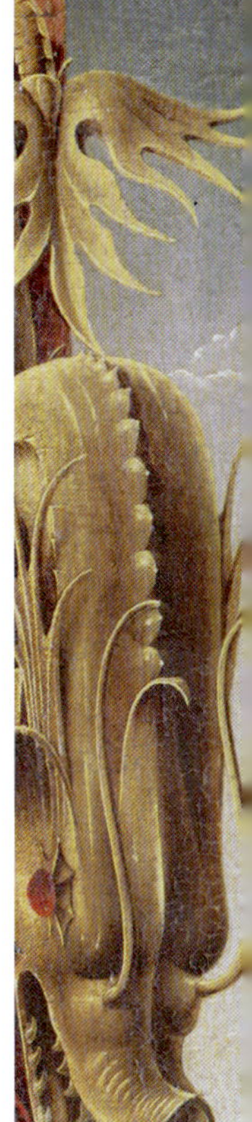

◄ ▲ Patient reconstruction by critics has made it possible to retrace the nine panels that decorated the 'Camerino delle Muse' in the Este residence of Belfiore, now dispersed among several museums (London, Budapest, Milan and Ferrara). The work of artists of various origins and talents, these paintings depict the classical Muses. Tura's contribution is certainly the most original and significant. Above the head of Erato (the muse of love poetry) hangs a string of beads, a decoration typical of Squarcione's pupils.

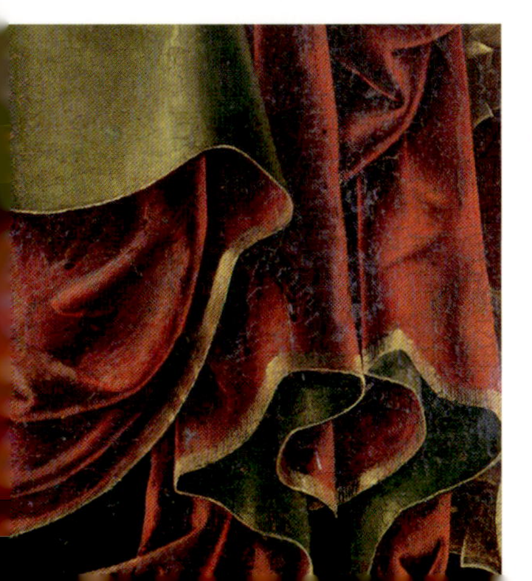

◄ Another distinctive characteristic of the group of painters trained in Padua in the mid-15th century is the depiction of turbulent, complicated drapery. Tura carried this feature to the extreme, curling and folding drapery into twisted, pointy wrinkles.

► The Muse's throne is decorated with odd, somewhat disturbing dolphins. Tura's invented creatures seem to be made of metal, with sharp edges and points and open mouths baring sharp teeth. The eyes, made of large rubies, sparkle threateningly.

Movement

Filippo Lippi
The Dance of Salome
**Detail from the *Story of St John
the Baptist***
1460

Fresco, approx. 770 cm

Prato, Cathedral

For artist biography, see page 38.

The action that unfolds in 15th-century Italian painting is most often fluid and rhythmic. In this respect they look to the Antique Roman sarcophagi frontals still found throughout Italy, and particularly in Rome and the central regions. Large frescoes depicting multiple episodes led artists to emphasize rhythmic relationships or highlight a specific moment, rather than simply proceed from left to right. In these cases, the sequence in which the scenes unfold is obvious from gestures and movements.

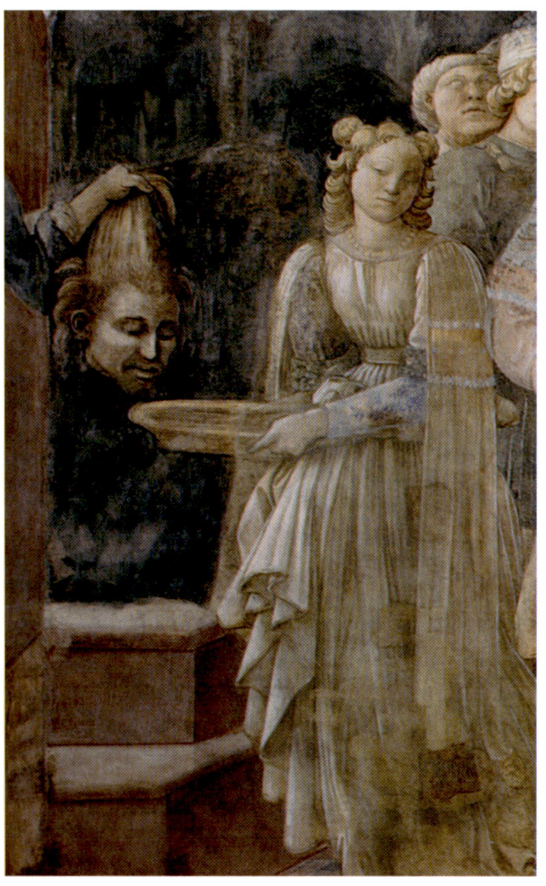

◄ Salome, the beautiful young daughter of Herodias, appears three times in this scene: in the centre, she seduces King Herod with her dance; at the left, she receives the severed head of John the Baptist on a platter; and at the right, she offers the macabre trophy to her mother. The approach is not too different to Masaccio's in *The Tribute Money*.

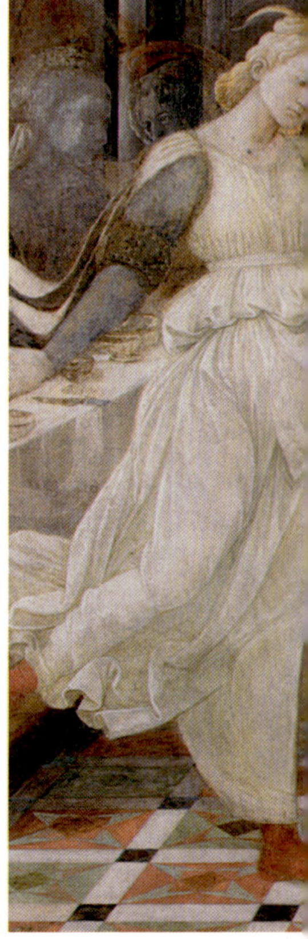

► The sensual Salome, in a flowing, light-coloured dress, establishes the sense of movement and sets the scene's character. In the centre, she dances gracefully, with intensity.

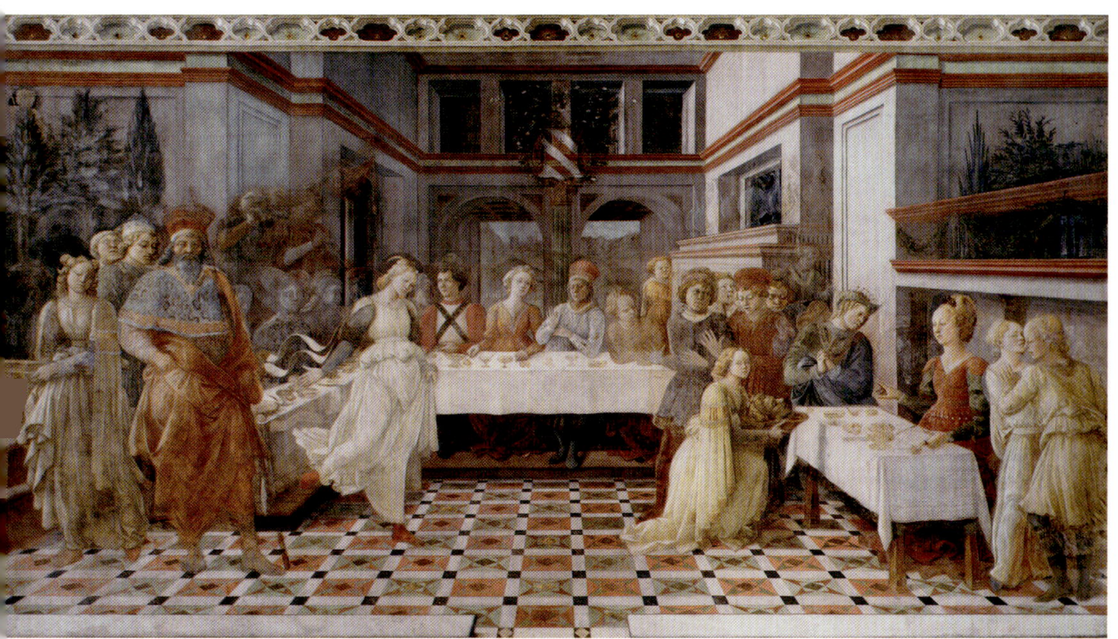

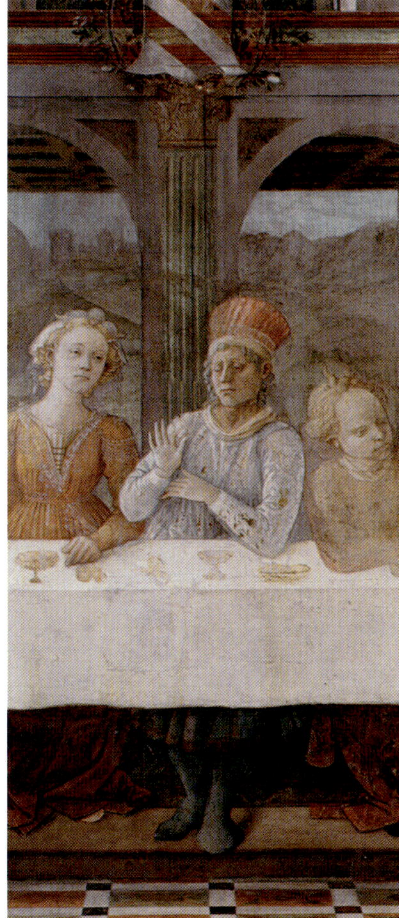

► After the middle of the 15th century, Tuscan painting began to make more effort to combine the rigid geometry of perspective with narrative rhythm. Perhaps painters felt the need to compete with Lorenzo Ghiberti's spectacular 'Gates of Paradise', bronze door for the Florence Baptistery, which he completed by 1452. In its ten large panels depicting biblical scenes, the sculptor achieved a perfect balance between buildings in perspective and figures in action. The desire to underscore both the flawless definition of the space and the fluidity with which the scene unfurls is also evident in Filippo Lippi's frescoes in Prato. King Herod, seated just in front of the room's central column, leans backward, introducing a note of animation into the architecture's absolute symmetry.

▼ Salome's dynamism contrasts sharply with the cold determination of Herodias, who seems indifferent to the sight of the severed head of John the Baptist, while her two handmaids are aghast.

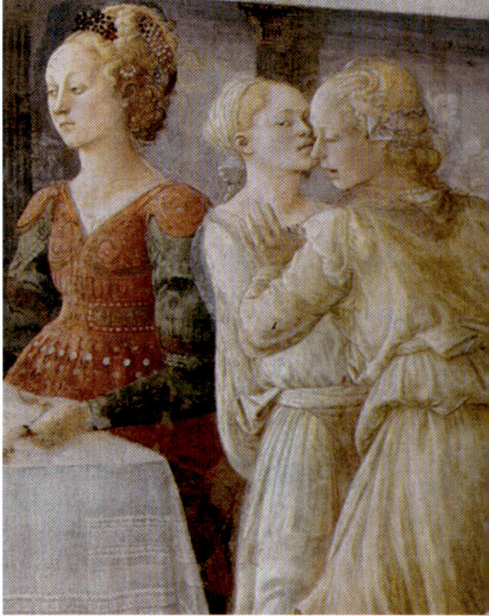

Court

Andrea Mantegna
The Court of the Gonzagas
1465–74

Tempera on wall, 805 cm wide

Mantua, Palazzo Ducale,
Camera degli Sposi

Andrea Mantegna

Isola di Carturo, Padua, 1431–Mantua,
1506

Mantegna was the first painter in northern
Italy to show a desire to abandon all
Gothic traditions and turn decisively
towards the innovations of perspective
and classical monumentality. A precocious
talent, Mantegna grew up in Padua during
the years when great Tuscan masters
such as Donatello and Uccello were in
the city. The frescoes of the Ovetari agli
Eremitani Chapel are his first success.
In 1451 he married Nicolosia, the sister
of Gentile and Giovanni Bellini, beginning
a relationship with the leading family
of Venetian artists. After completing
the painting for the high altar of the
basilica of San Zeno in Verona (1457–9),
Mantegna moved to Mantua to take up
the office of painter to the Gonzaga family.
The decoration of the Camera degli Sposi,
a true masterpiece in the court art of the
second half of the 15th century, is the
culminating work of Mantegna's career
and the one that best illustrates his style.
Mantegna never adopted the technique
of tonal colour and *sfumato*, preferring a
lucid visual precision supported by incisive
drawing and the memory of Antiquity.

Beginning in the mid-15th century, a shift in taste saw several
Italian courts offer important commissions to humanistically
oriented architects, painters and sculptors. In Mantua, the
Gonzagas initiated a stylistic revolution by patronizing Leon
Battista Alberti and especially Mantegna, who settled there permanently in 1460. Though the specific tasks of the court painter
did not change (for example, they were still involved in producing temporary decorations for festivals), state portraits, sacred
commissions and especially fresco cycles in official residences,
all show signs of perspectival experimentation and references
to classical Antiquity. In just a few decades, it became a matter
of pride for the more ambitious courts to show how up-to-date
they are in rejecting the decorative splendour of the Gothic.

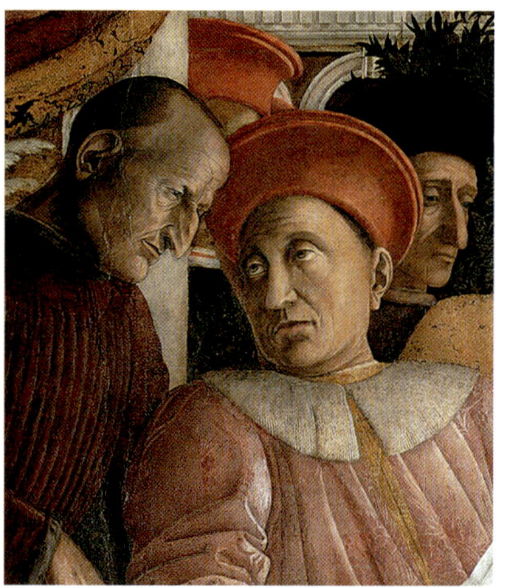

◄ The main character,
the centre of gravity around
which court life revolved,
was Marchese Ludovico II
Gonzaga. Mantegna has
placed him neither in the
middle of the composition
nor in a frontal pose. Still,
the interplay of postures
and gazes, and the general
structure of the image,
direct attention towards
the main figure.

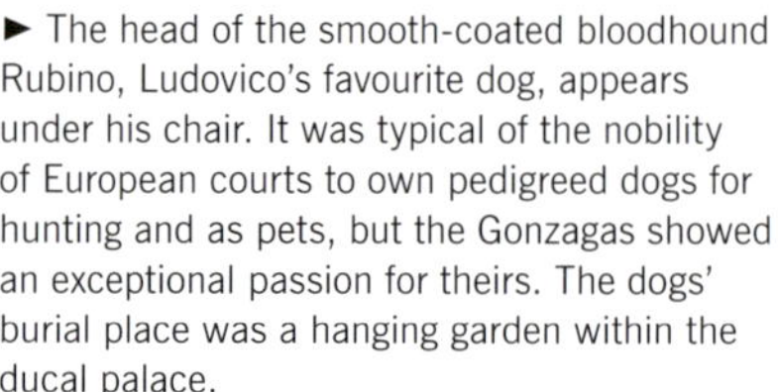

► The head of the smooth-coated bloodhound
Rubino, Ludovico's favourite dog, appears
under his chair. It was typical of the nobility
of European courts to own pedigreed dogs for
hunting and as pets, but the Gonzagas showed
an exceptional passion for theirs. The dogs'
burial place was a hanging garden within the
ducal palace.

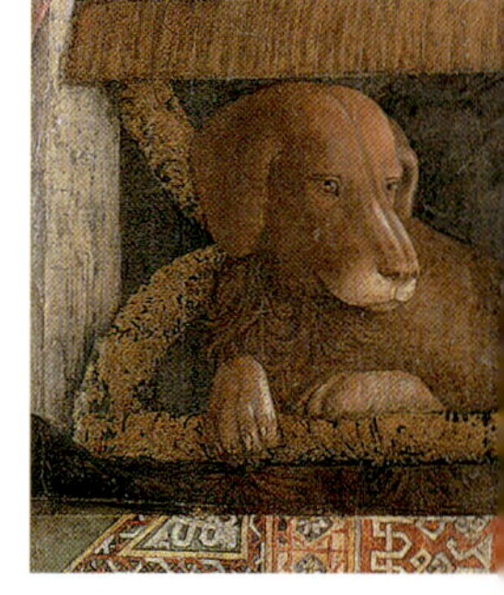

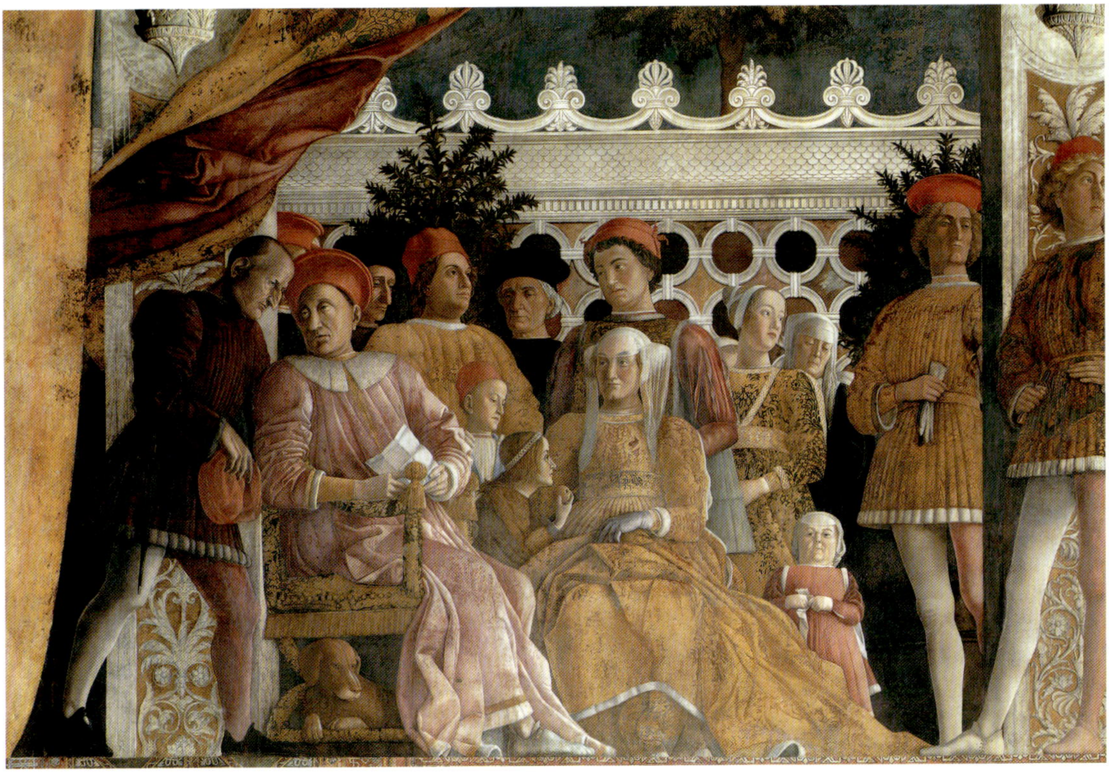

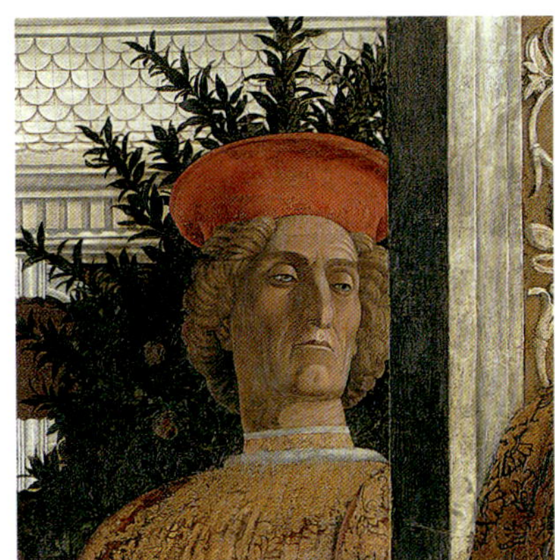

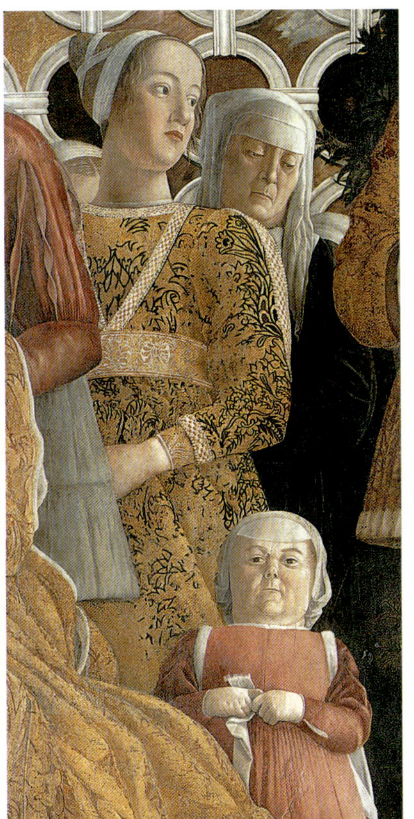

◀ The spectacle of luxury and variety took centre stage in 15th-century courts. Aristocratic families were always very large. Sons and daughters were valuable pawns in marriage alliances with other families or else could be launched on prestigious ecclesiastical careers. Numerous relatives, preceptors and servants of every type and rank revolved around the nucleus of the immediate family. Barbarina (the most graceful of Ludovico's daughters), her old nurse and, in the foreground, the dwarf are particularly noticeable in this group portrait. In Mantua, as in other courts, dwarfs played a special role: a somewhat bitter 'joke' of nature, they were considered refined buffoons, endowed with a vein of ironic melancholy.

▲ Even in this 'modern' image, Mantegna emphasizes the Mantuan court's luxury with clothing of sumptuous gold fabric, red hats and fashionable details like the pages' two-tone tights.

Ovid's *Metamorphoses*

Antonio del Pollaiuolo
Apollo and Daphne
c. 1465

Tempera on panel, 30 × 20 cm
London, National Gallery

Antonio del Pollaiuolo

(Antonio Benci)

Florence, *c.* 1431–Rome, 1498

Called 'Pollaiuolo' because his father was a chicken and egg vendor, this remarkably versatile artist worked as a painter, bronze sculptor and goldsmith as well as a pioneer of burin engraving in Italy. Whatever the medium, Pollaiuolo employed a clean, fine, expressive line to depict excited animation and dramatic action. He was one of the first artists in Florence to depict scenes from mythology, in both painting and bronzes. However, he also made altar paintings, such as the *Coronation of the Virgin* for the church of Sant'Agostino in San Gimignano. In Rome during the second part of his career, Pollaiuolo was above all occupied with monumental bronze sculptures, including two important sarcophagi for Pope Sixtus IV (1484–92) and Pope Innocent VIII (1492–8) at the basilica of St Peter.

If the main literary source for sacred painting was the *Golden Legend*, the basic reference for Greco-Roman mythological subjects was undoubtedly the *Metamorphoses* of the Roman poet Ovid (43 BC–AD 18). The epic poem gathers together more than two hundred stories, or fables, about the transformations of gods, nymphs and humans into animals, plants or natural phenomena. Humanist authors often turned to this huge pool of literary material to produce versions that were shortened, adapted or moralistic (that is, related to the Christian faith). The growing appreciation of Ovid's text among the wealthiest and most cultivated classes resulted in an ever-greater output of paintings, initially in small format, conceived as refined illustrations to the best-known myths. The popularity of the *Metamorphoses* continued throughout the Renaissance and Baroque eras.

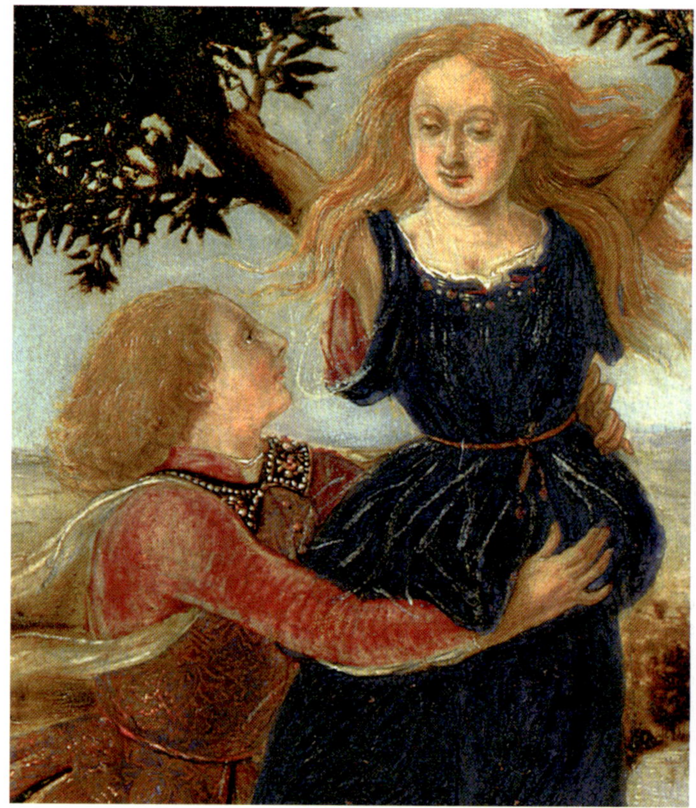

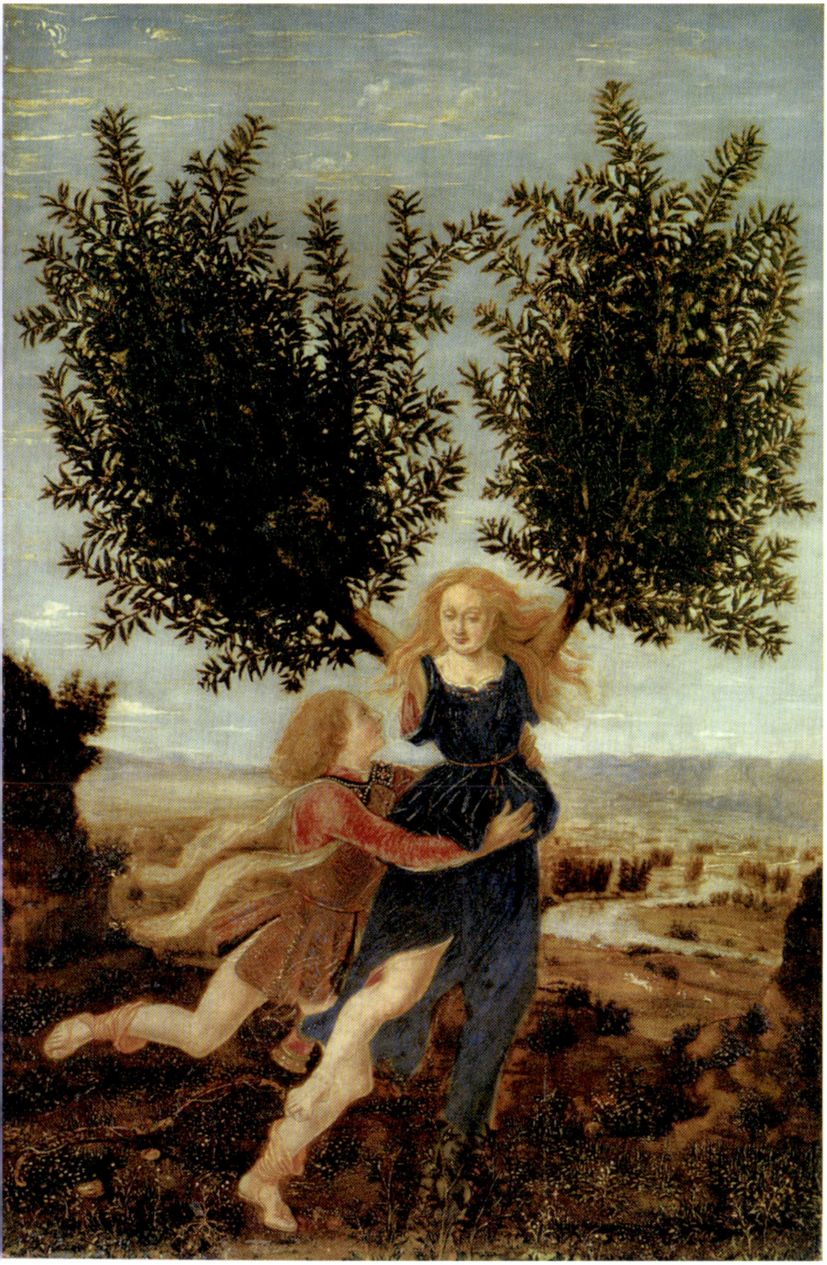

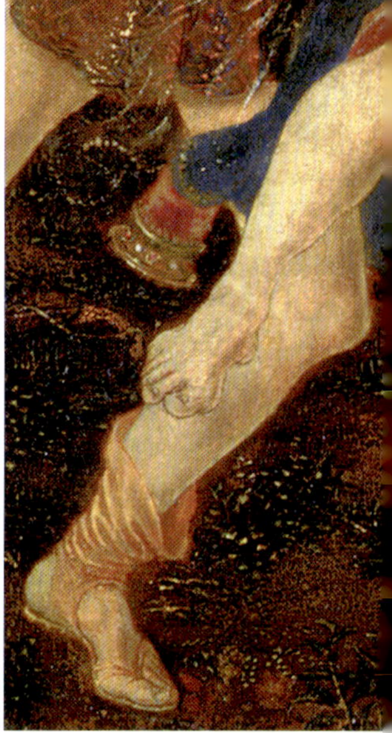

◀ Ovid's subject is often the contrast between adventure-seeking gods and bashful nymphs. In their attempts to conquer or to flee, they often assumed – or were given – new physical forms.

▲ One of the most famous 'metamorphoses' is that of the beautiful nymph Daphne, long pursued by Apollo. Once the god caught up with her, in order not to yield to him, she turned herself into a laurel tree. From then on, laurel leaves and branches of this tree were the sign of Apollo, god of music and poetry, and the laurel wreath became the symbol of poets.

Profile

Piero della Francesca
The Urbino Diptych (Portrait of
Federico da Montefeltro and
Battista Sforza)
1465–72

Tempera on panel, 47 × 33 cm
(each panel)

Florence, Galleria degli Uffizi

For artist biography, see page 42.

One of the most noticeable differences between Italy and the Netherlands, the two most artistically advanced regions in 15th-century Europe, has to do with portrait painting. While the Flemish painters Jan van Eyck and Robert Campin had already taken up the frontal and three-quarters pose, Italian artists still portrayed the nobility in profile, a court tradition derived from imperial Roman medals. Even artists in the vanguard painted their subjects in profile until after the middle of the 15th century. Lacking the direct relationship that a mutual gaze establishes with the viewer, a profile tends to look somewhat unnatural. Antonello da Messina (heavily influenced by Netherlandish art) introduced the three-quarters pose to Italy, where it spread alongside realistic portrait busts sculpted in marble and terracotta. It found full acceptance in the last two decades of the 15th century, thanks to Leonardo.

Federico da Montefeltro, Part Blind but Ever Watchful

Federico da Montefeltro (1422–82) ruled the small, hilly territory in the Marche region, not particularly rich but important because it controlled highways along the Adriatic. Made a duke in 1444 after the murder of his half-brother Oddantonio in a conspiracy, Federico proved to be an excellent military commander as well as a man sincerely open to humanistic culture: the ducal palace in Urbino became a model of the new architecture and a cosmopolitan centre for the most recent developments in art. His marriage to Battista Sforza widened the duchy's boundaries and initiated a complicated period of alliances and rivalries. In 1454, however, Federico orchestrated the Peace of Lodi, which inaugurated an era of peaceful accord among the Italian states. It may have been during a tournament organized to celebrate the agreement that Federico suffered a wound that altered his appearance: a lance pierced his helmet, putting out an eye. Disfigured, Federico decided to have the bridge of his nose amputated to broaden the field of vision of his remaining eye. For this reason he is always depicted in strict profile, showing his 'good' side.

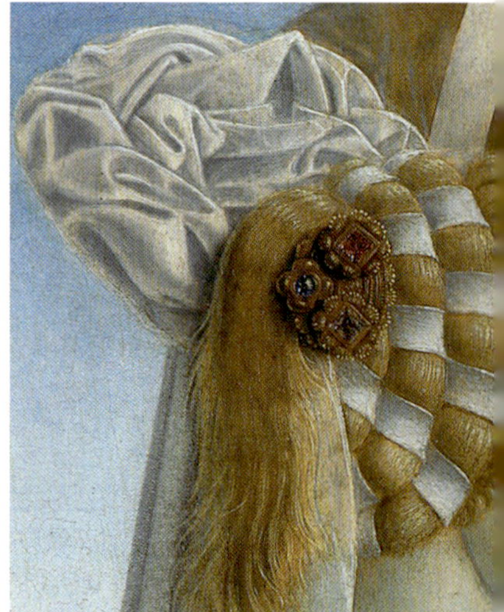

▲ Battista Sforza's elaborately styled, long, blonde hair assumes an idealized circular form. Intertwined with a white cloth in three concentric turns, it is fastened to the top of her head with a ribbon. A piece of gold jewellery set with large, coloured stones holds it in place.

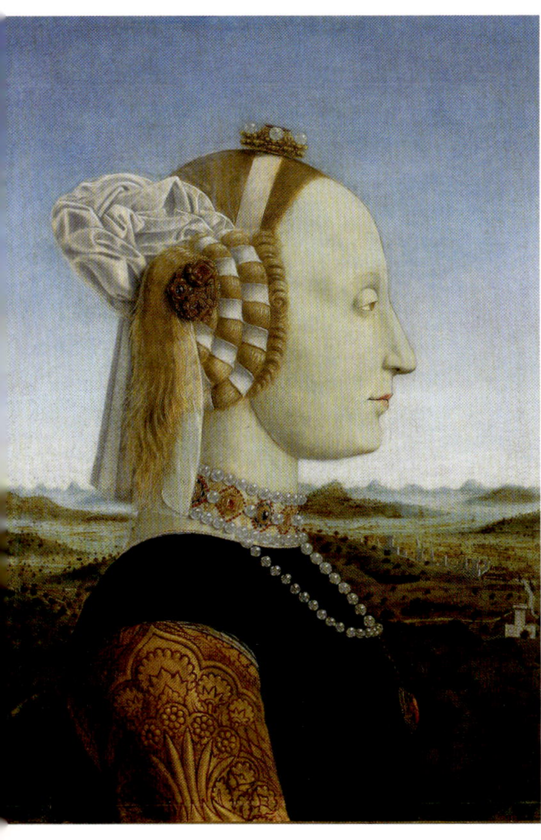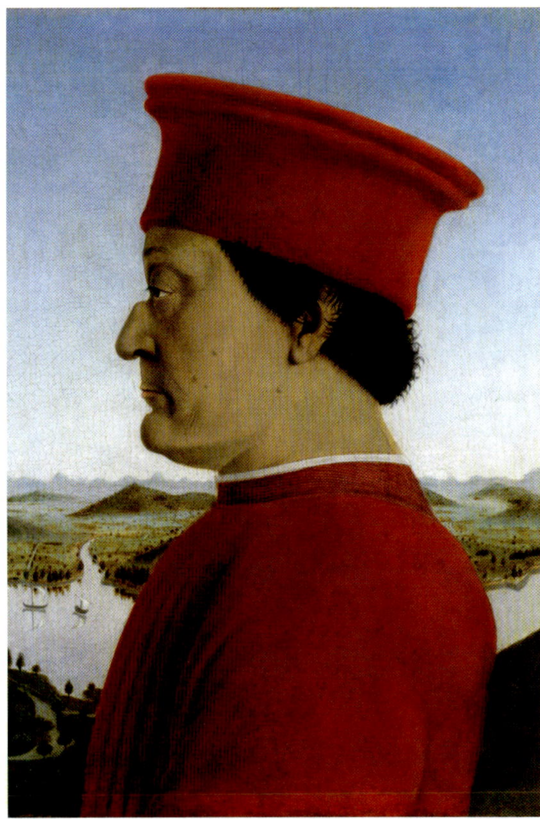

▲▼ Piero della Francesca emphasizes the serene grandeur of the duke and duchess of Urbino, counterbalancing the finely detailed style of their portraits with a distant, hazy landscape wrapped in a faint pearly mist. The castle with its turreted wall refers to the powerful fortifications in the Montefeltro region.

► Federico da Montefeltro's clearly defined profile is unmistakable as a work of the Italian Quattrocento. The chromatic and linear simplicity of the costume and hat are the result of an artificial treatment of the duke's head along lines essentially forming a cube, while the profile of the duchess has a circular tendency.

▼ The landscape in the portrait of Federico does not depict a specific place, but rather suggests the hills that surround Urbino and drop down to the Adriatic.

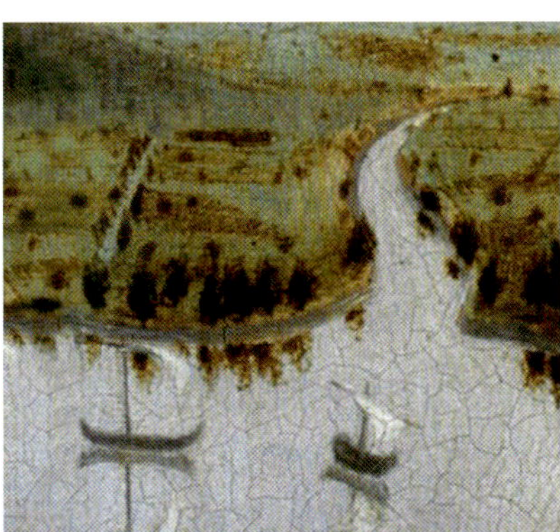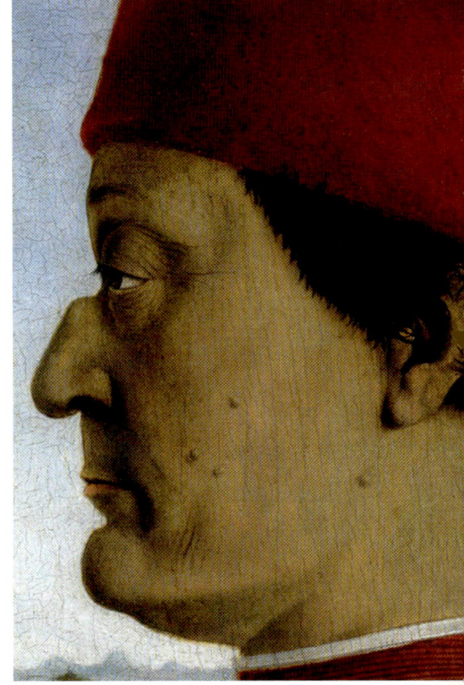

Trompe l'oeil

Andrea Mantegna
Oculus in the Ceiling of the Camera degli Sposi
1465–74

Fresco, 270 cm (diam.)

Mantua, Palazzo Ducale,
Camera degli Sposi

For artist biography, see page 76.

As more artists acquired an understanding of the mathematical basis of perspective and its use became widespread, works of increasingly spectacular illusionism became possible. Andrea Mantegna was particularly fascinated by applied geometry and used his knowledge to become one of the most brilliant, inventive painters of the 15th century. Taking advantage of the creative freedom granted to him by the Gonzagas, Mantegna introduced some surprising innovations to the refined taste of the northern Italian court, including monochromatic paintings, *trompe l'oeil* imitations of low relief, the use of canvas as a support, the revisiting of themes from Antiquity and engravings. His main interest, however, remained experimentation with perspective, as can be seen in the so-called Camera degli Sposi, the heart of the ducal residence. Mantegna not only painted a portico along the walls (with curtains variously open or closed), but also, in the centre of the ceiling, imitated an oculus, with figures leaning over the edge – an extraordinary virtuoso perspective effect.

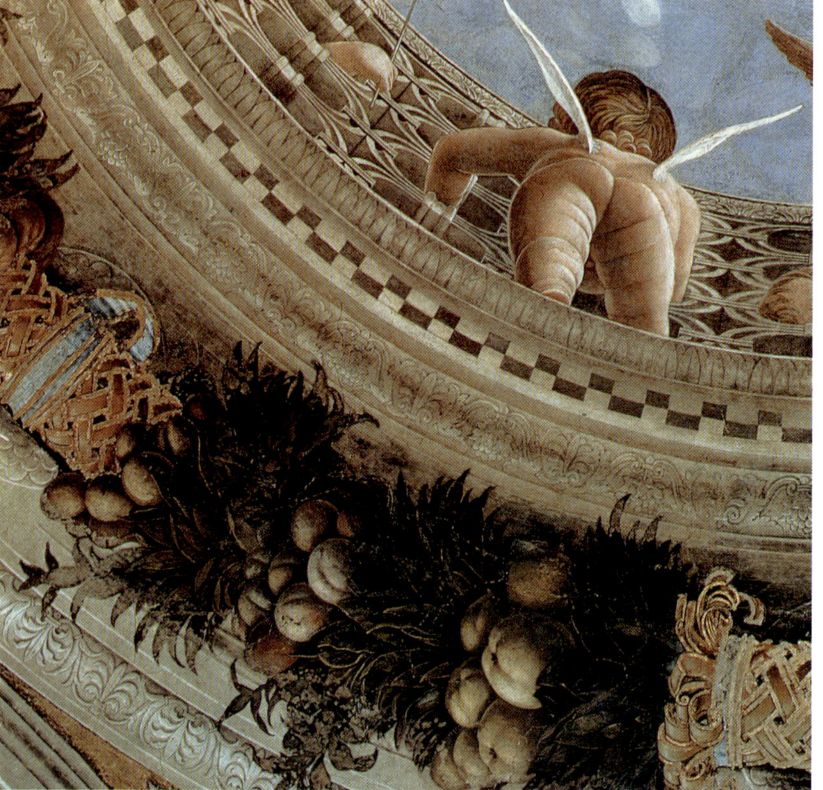

◄ The ceiling of the Camera degli Sposi is the first humanistic example of *trompe l'oeil*. Mantegna's fresco imitates a large, circular opening with a balcony. The winged putti climbing on the frame and leaning through the ringed openings of the balustrade are irreverant, apparently not caring that their buttocks are seen by viewers standing below. The ornamental band that runs beneath the oculus, made up of rich garlands of foliage and fruit tightly bound with gold ribbons, seems to hang into the room. Interwoven garlands are a common motif in the work of the painters trained in the Padua workshop of Squarcione (see page 72).

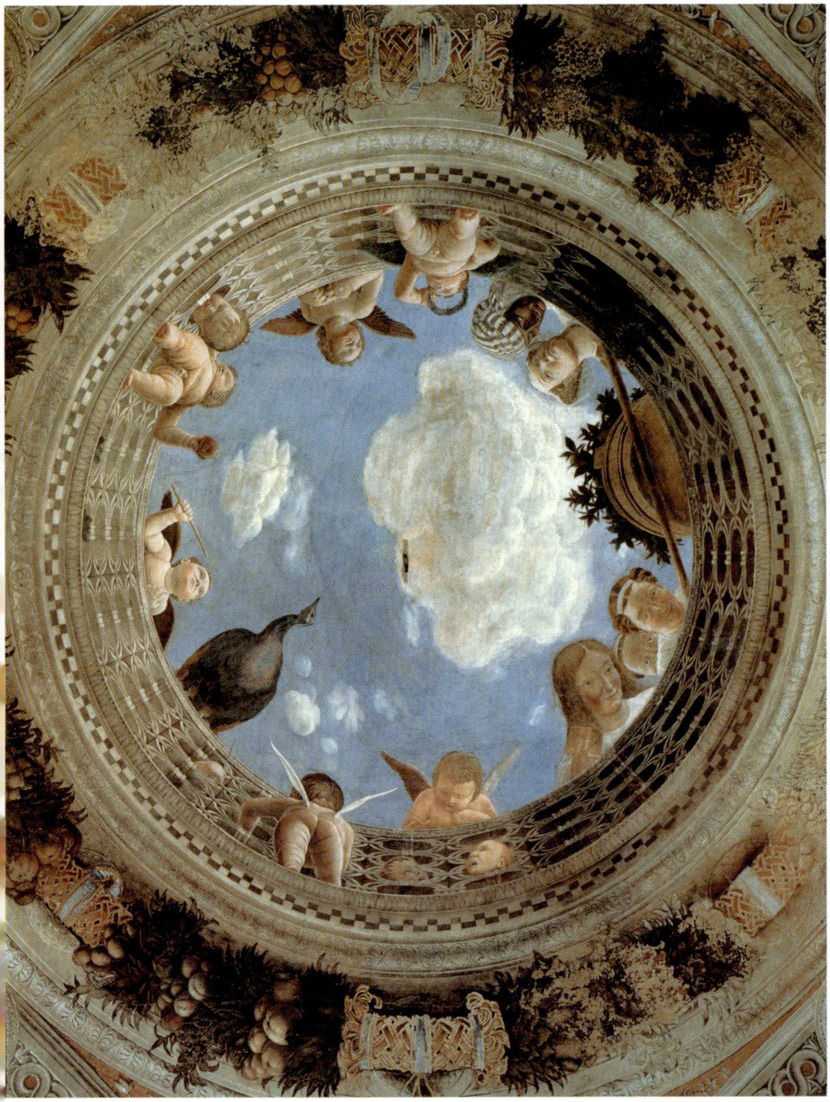

▼ The fresco's most impressive detail is the large tub used as a planter for a small citrus tree. Supported by a slender rod that does not appear very strong, the heavy object extends over the edge of the marble balustrade. In this way, Mantegna introduces a theme of precariousness that Giulio Romano, also working in Mantua, would develop 60 years later.

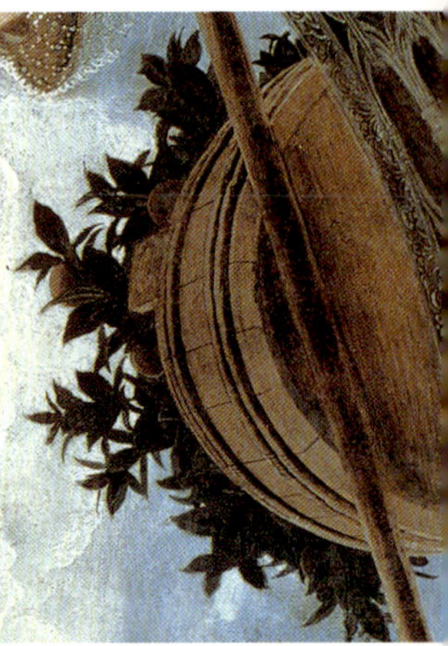

◄ The innovation and virtuosity displayed throughout the decoration wof the Camera degli Sposi extends to its circular form and the utter naturalness of the putti and peering ladies arranged around the balcony. The clouds that float across the sky add to the sense of movement throughout the entire composition.

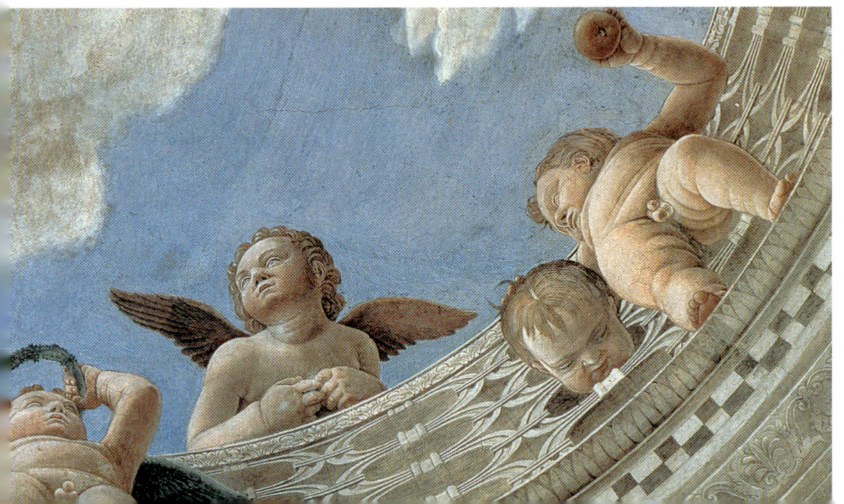

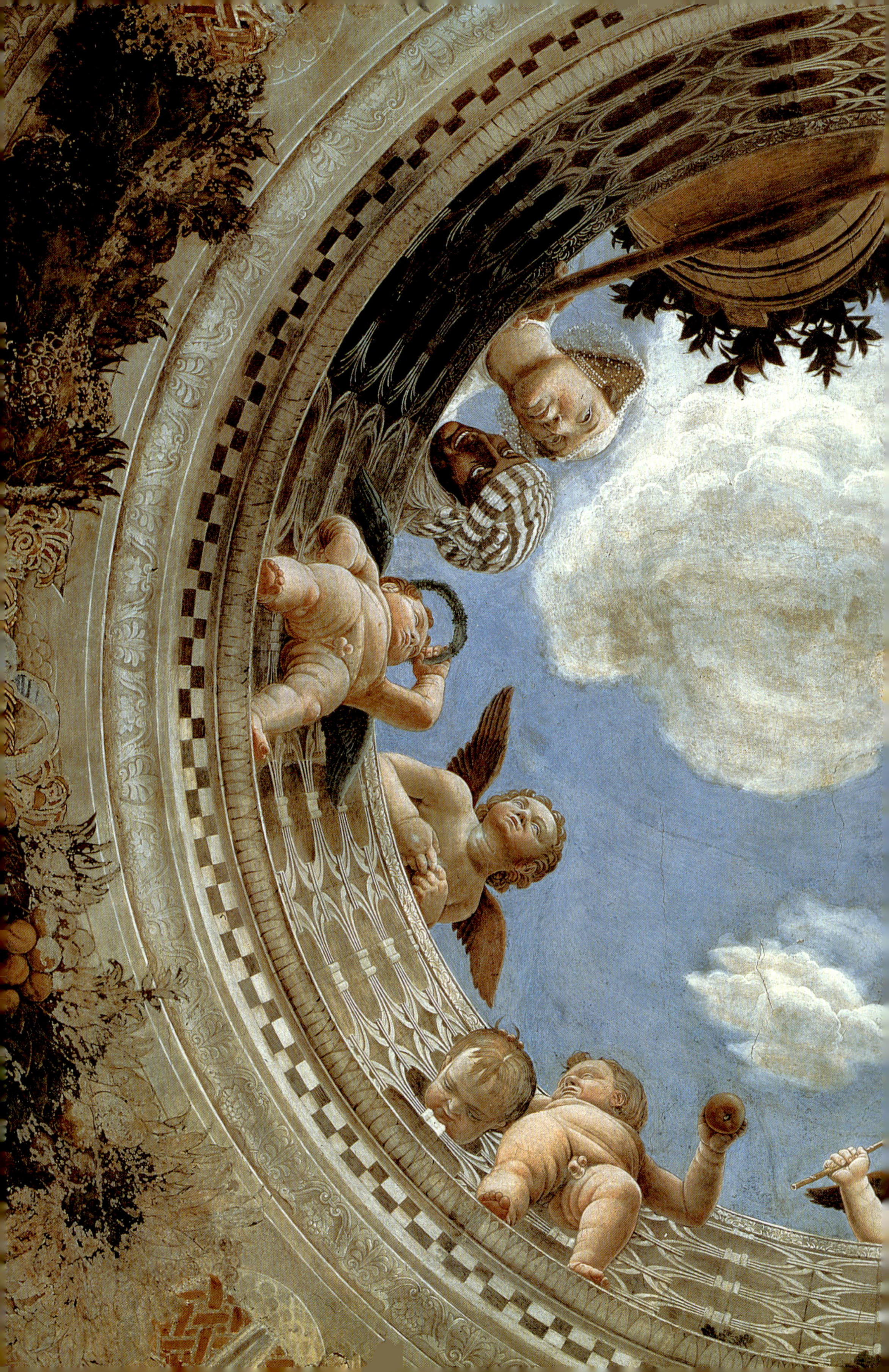

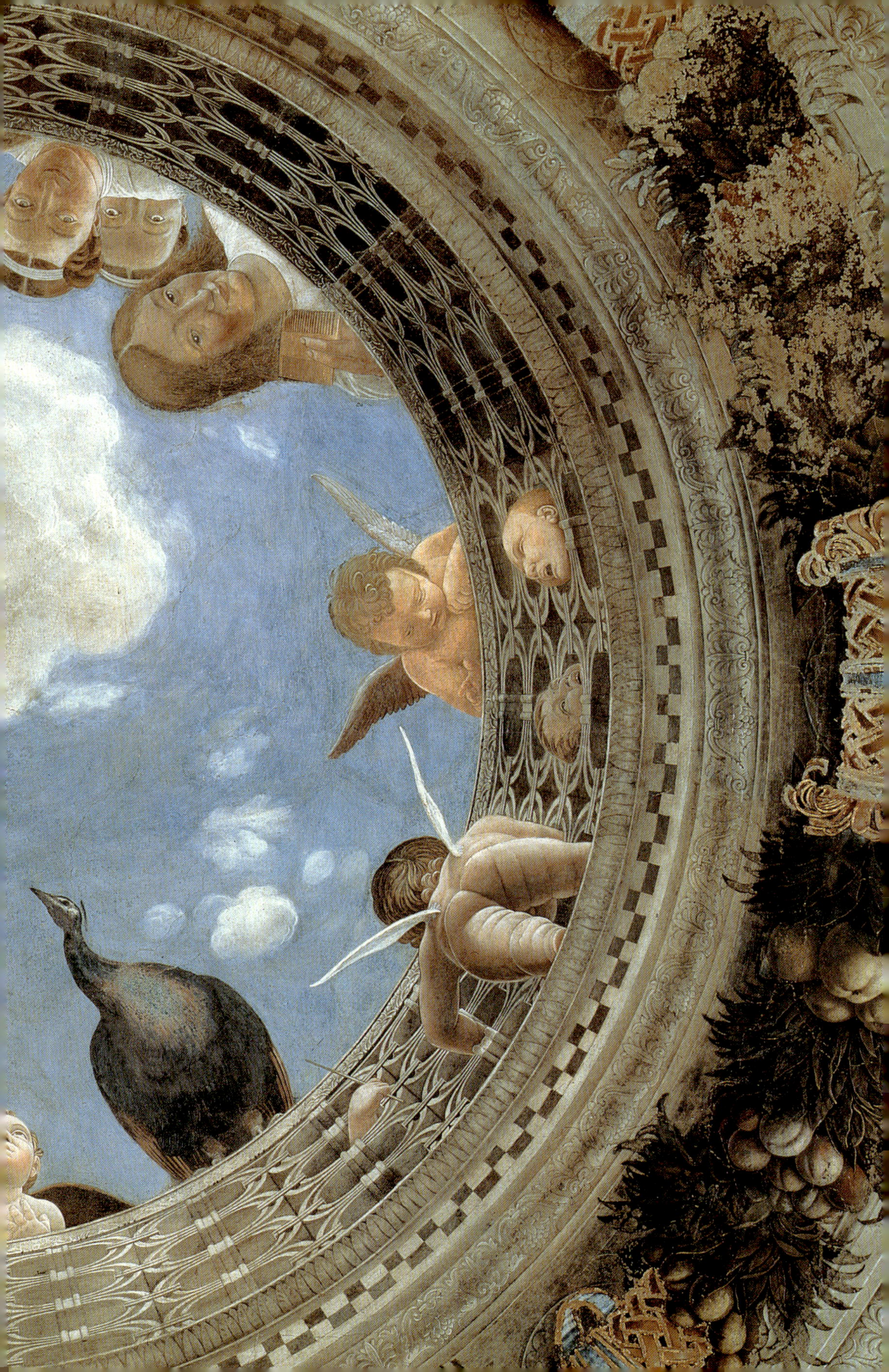

Expressionism

While Florentine art of the mid-15th century tended to be balanced and impassive, other schools of Italian painting showed a new expressiveness. Ferrara is a good example. One of the most fascinating courts of the Italian Renaissance, it was critical in the development of the visual art, urbanism and literature. In the absence of a solid local painting tradition, the dukes of the house of Este had prepared the ground by inviting various masters (Jacopo Bellini, Pisanello, Alberti, Piero della Francesca and Rogier van der Weyden, among others) to Ferrara and financing the studies of Cosmè Tura in Padua. With the maturity of Tura, the growth of Francesco del Cossa and the sudden emergence of Ercole de' Roberti a little later, the Ferrara school, with a surge of rough, grotesque and ingenious expressiveness, made its mark on 15th-century Italian painting.

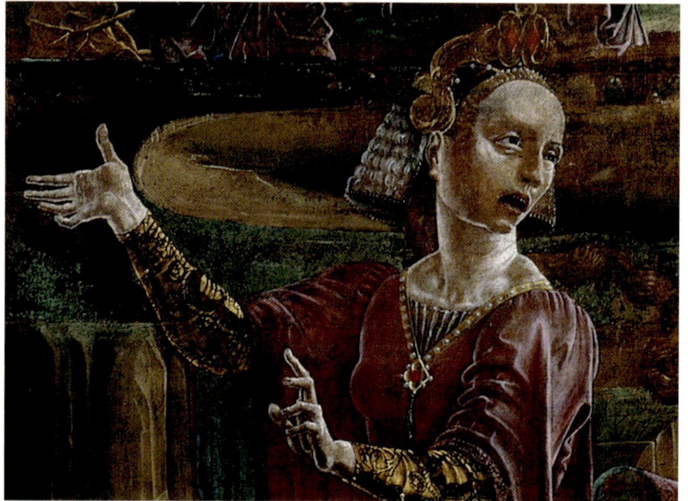

◄ St George heroically slaying the dragon to save the princess is one of the most frequently depicted scenes in 15th-century court art. But Tura transforms it into an episode charged with chaos and drama through his intense focus upon the gestures, facial expressions and general disarray. The princess seems terrified rather than relieved by the sudden appearance of the mounted saint.

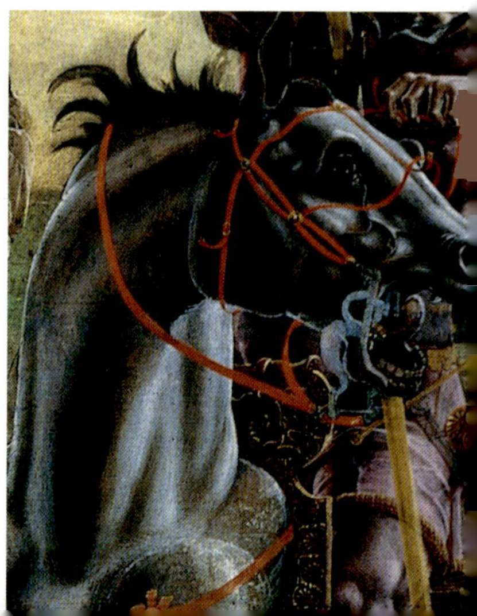

► The cry of the princess is echoed by the desperate whinny of the horse. Up on its hind legs, St George's rearing steed, with swollen veins, dilated nostrils and a wide-open mouth, seems confused and frightened by the dragon. The effect is marked by its bridle. The thin, red trappings look like rivulets of blood running down the animal's head.

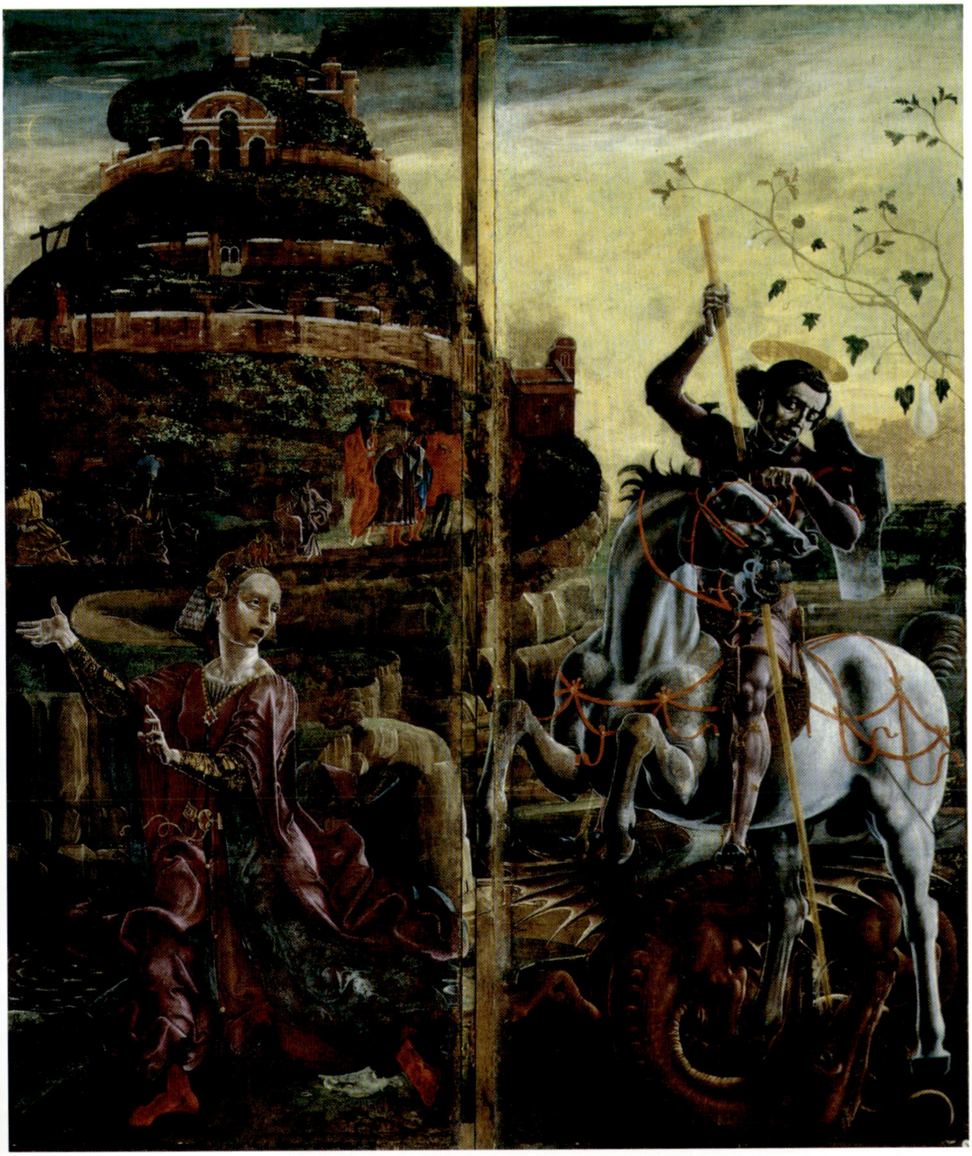

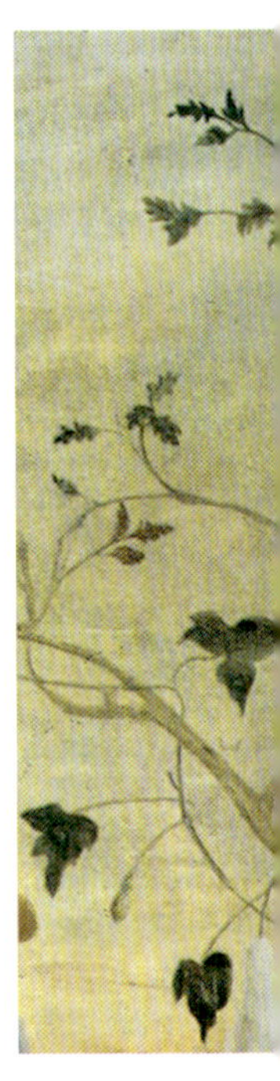

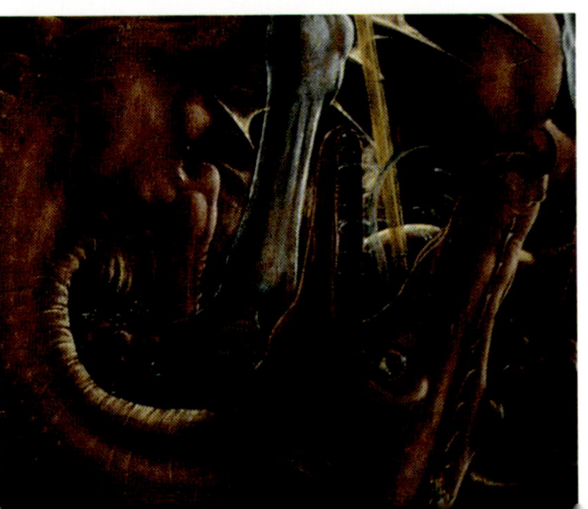

► The writing, wounded dragon shows Tura's expressive inventiveness. With a long, gnarled spine, and wings like sharp blades, the monster has the look of a machine. Through the artist's use of colour and light, he seems to be made of gleaming copper. The glassy eye and sparse, needlelike teeth heighten the impression that this is a diabolical contraption, not a living creature.

◄ The rays of the setting sun colour the sky with a yellowish tinge that evokes the earlier effect of a gold ground. A slender, twisting vine at the upper right intensifies the harsh, tense atmosphere.

Venus

Francesco del Cossa
The Triumph of Venus
Detail of the *Month of April*
c. 1470
Fresco, 191 × 320 cm
Ferrara, Palazzo Schifanoia

Francesco del Cossa

Ferrara, *c.* 1436–1477/8

Cossa was an influential figure in the Ferrara school of painting, and without doubt one of the most original and independent artists in the 15th-century Italian courts. An associate of Cosmè Tura, Cossa developed a narrative style that was less rough than that of his older colleague. The *Month of March* and the *Month of April* are the best preserved of the scenes that he painted in the *salone* of Palazzo Schifanoia in Ferrara. In them, Cossa successfully managed the complex combination of mythological scenes, astrological references and details from the contemporary life of the duke, court, city and countryside. Dissatisfied with his payment from the Este family, Francesco del Cossa left Ferrara for Bologna soon after 1470. There he executed important altar paintings for the basilica of San Petronio and the ambitious *Grifoni Polyptych* (now divided among various museums), on which he collaborated with Ercole de' Roberti. Cossa died at the age of about 40, in an outbreak of the plague.

The resurgence of Greek and Roman mythology in 15th-century art was gradual but unstoppable. During the Middle Ages, it had been considered 'dangerous' to depict the ancient gods, except in scenes closely connected with astronomy or counterbalanced by the inclusion of Christian figures. Humanism revived the values of classical culture and prompted the rediscovery of ancient art. Neo-Platonic philosophy, the most important intellectual movement of the second half of the 15th century, promoted a 'humanized', moral reading of mythology, in harmony, and not in opposition to, Christian precepts. Thus, after more than one thousand years, Olympian figures reappeared in *cassone* and miniature painting, large panel paintings and frescoes. The goddess of love, Venus, met with the greatest success.

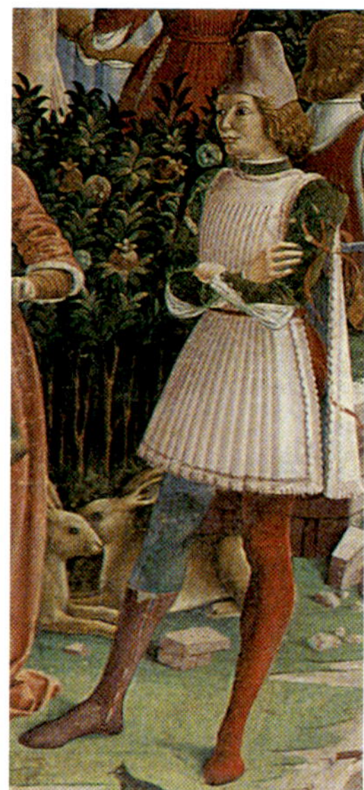

◀ A sense of humour permeates the Palazzo Schifanoia frescoes, even the most solemn classical scenes. Cossa depicts various aspects of the reign of love, including this detail of a companionless boy who stands with his arms folded, watching the others kiss and embrace. His elegant clothing, the attire of a true ladies' man, serves no purpose.

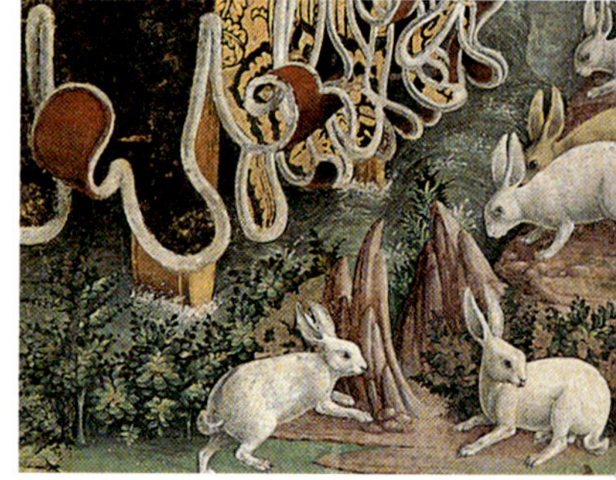

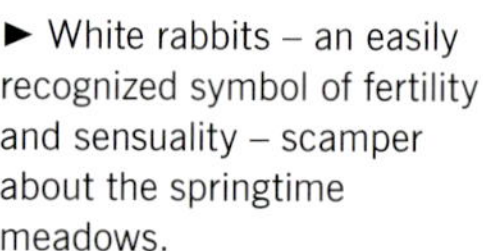

▶ White rabbits – an easily recognized symbol of fertility and sensuality – scamper about the springtime meadows.

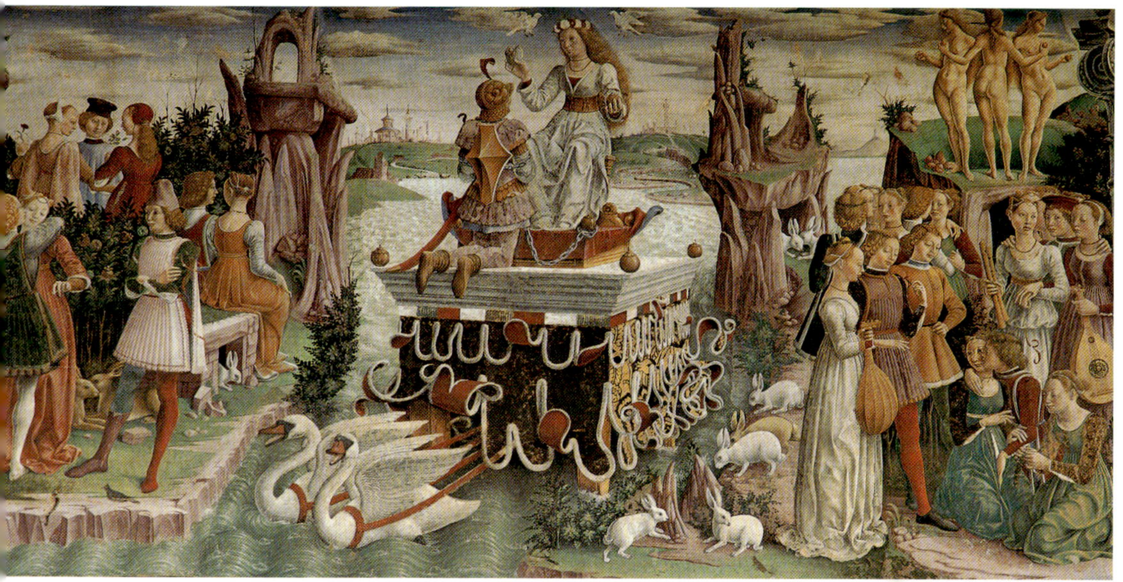

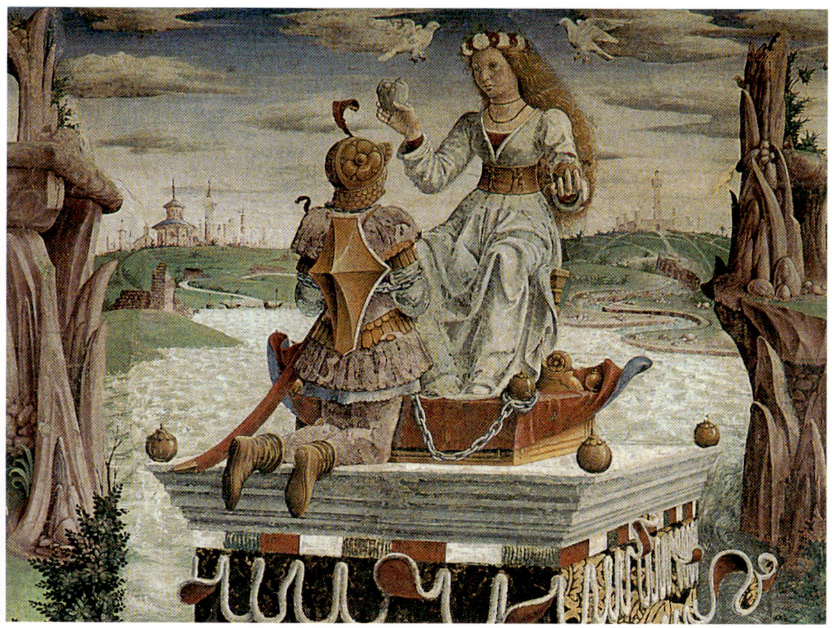

▲ Venus, the goddess of love, rides in a luxurious boat pulled by two white swans and flanked by white doves in flight. Mars, in chains, kneels at her feet. Despite his weapons and armour, the lord of war yields to the power of seduction.

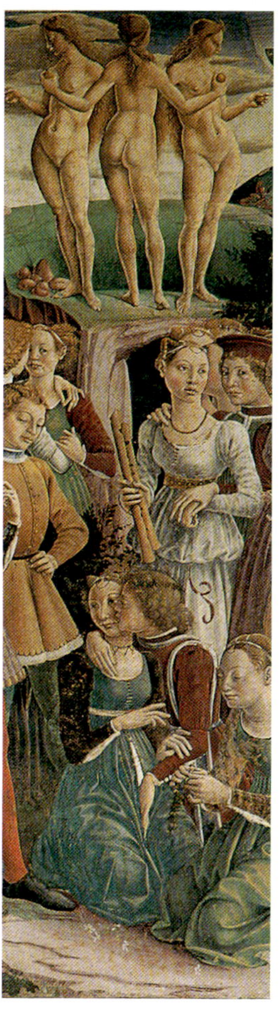

► The mythological tone of the allegory is heightened by the inclusion of the Three Graces, derived from ancient representations. Cossa puts the nude goddesses in the distance, however, making room for the numerous young men and women dressed in the attire of his period.

Line

Antonio del Pollaiuolo
Portrait of a Woman
c. 1470

Tempera on panel, 46 × 34 cm
Milan, Museo Poldi Pezzoli

For artist biography, see page 78.

Throughout the Renaissance, Tuscan painting sought to achieve perfection through the mastery of line. The authors of the great treatises, for example Giorgio Vasari who wrote *Lives of the Painters* (and who also founded the Accademia del Disegno – Drawing Academy – in Florence), affirmed the importance of drawing. The profile portrait, although beginning to yield to more realistic frontal poses, remained a favoured vehicle for demonstrating one's draughtsmanship. The natural grace of the Florentine aristocracy's most beautiful young women, as well as exquisite attention to fashion, make-up and hairstyles, offered artists an ideal pretext for displaying the supreme elegance of a stroke drawn against a neutral background.

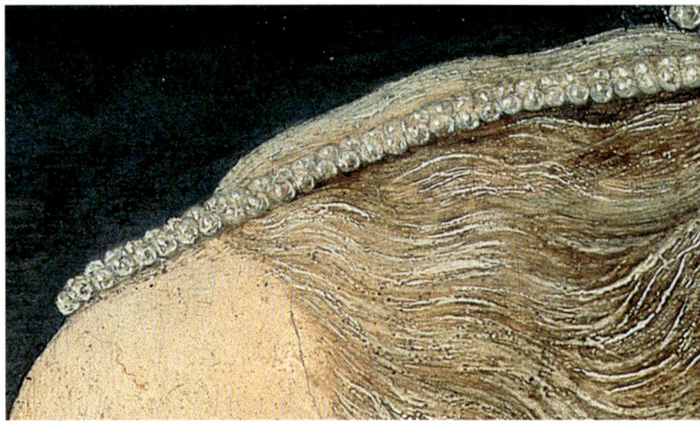

▲ In the *Divine Comedy*, Dante had extolled the juxtaposition of opalescent pearls and a young woman's smooth, pure, white forehead. Fashionable young 15th-century women shaved the hair directly above the forehead to make it appear higher and rounder.

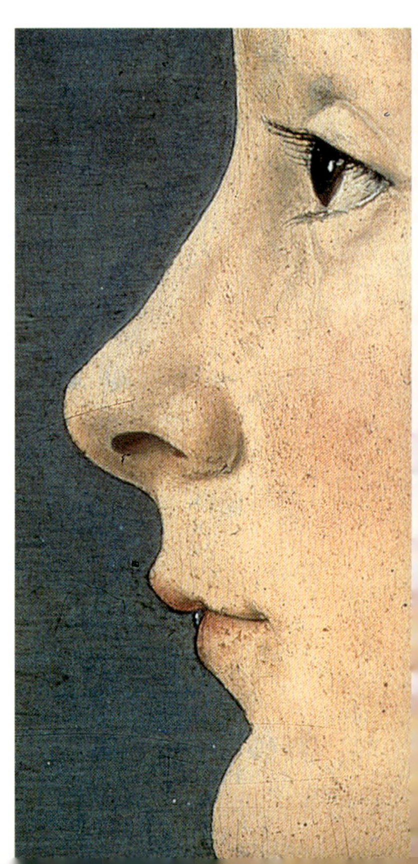

► The line drawn around the profile is easily discernible. Against the background of a distant sky with small clouds, without any points of reference to establish scale, the young lady's face and bust assume an almost abstract character.

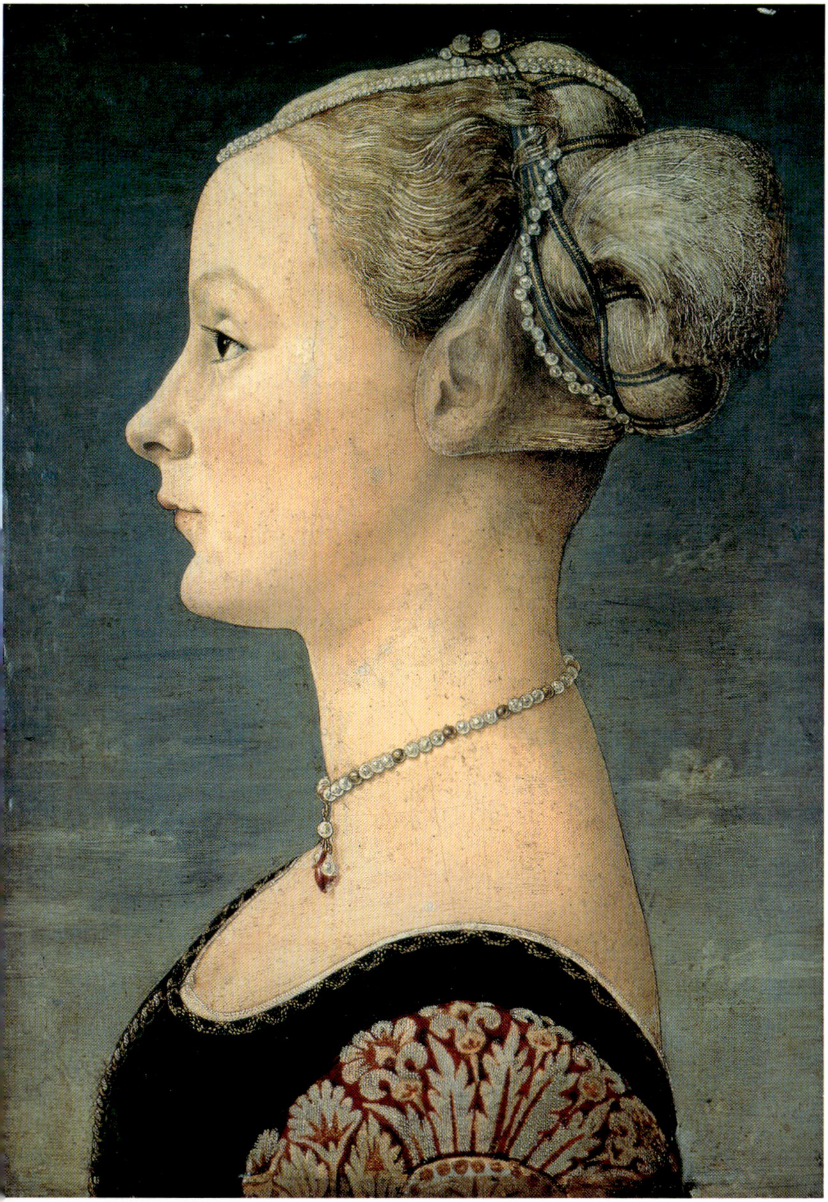

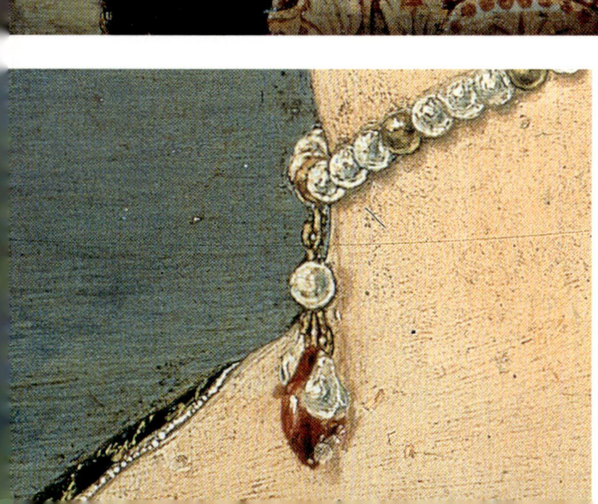

◀ The enthusiasm for flowing line prompted Pollaiuolo not only to idealize the woman's features but also to tamper with anatomical accuracy: the neck, highlighted by a necklace of pearls and gold beads, is unnaturally long.

▼ The refined hairstyle provided Pollaiuolo with a further opportunity to show off his skill. A narrow blue and gold ribbon, fastened at the top of the head by a piece of jewelry, is entwined with a strand of pearls that gathers up the thick, blonde locks, exposing the nape. A hairnet covers the ear.

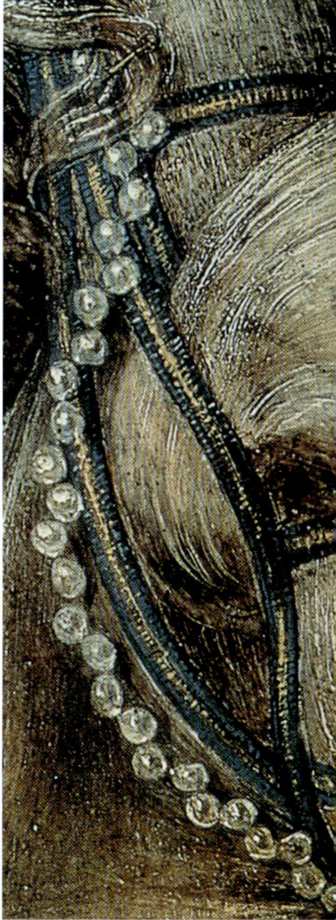

**Andrea del Verrocchio and
Leonardo da Vinci**
The Baptism of Christ
1470–80

Oil and tempera on panel, 177 × 150 cm
Florence, Galleria degli Uffizi

Andrea del Verrocchio

(Andrea di Francesco di Cione)
Florence, 1435–Venice, 1488

Verrocchio is the perfect example of a
multifaceted late 15th-century artist.
In his workshop, a crucible of Florentine
art at this time, pupils such as Leonardo
and Perugino tried their hands at various
techniques, materials and styles. Owing
to the considerable number of paintings
that came out of his workshop, efforts to
attribute works by distinguishing which
students were involved, and to what
degree, are often inconclusive. Today,
Verrocchio is particularly admired for
his work as a goldsmith and sculptor.
Some examples are the porphyry and
bronze Medici tomb in the Old Sacristy
at San Lorenzo, the silver relief *Altar of
St John* (Florence, Museo dell'Opera del
Duomo), the *Incredulity of St Thomas*
for Orsanmichele (1483) and the famous
*Equestrian Monument to Bartolemeo
Colleoni* in the Campo San Zanipolo,
Venice (1488).

Leonardo da Vinci

For artist biography, see page 130.

Documents, portraits, biographies and contemporary testi-
monies allow us to reconstruct events in the lives of many
Italian Renaissance artists. Some became popular personalities, the subjects of anecdotes, some of which have survived.
Nevertheless, we must not allow too Romantic a vision of these
artists. In the Renaissance, an artwork was not considered the
unique and unrepeatable expression of a single creative individual but the result of a well-organized workshop. The most
successful artists worked in teams, with rigorously subdivided
roles and tasks. The collaboration of pupils and assistants with
varying levels of autonomy is more easily recognized in larger
works, such as fresco cycles and altarpieces. Usually, however,
the master would strive to make the assistants' hands as consistent and indistinguishable from one another as possible. *The
Baptism of Christ*, a product of Verrocchio's extremely active
Florentine workshop, is a notable exception in this regard, since
we can discern different hands.

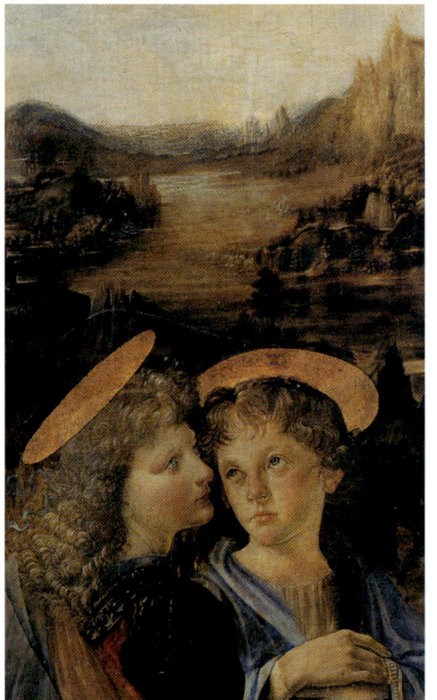

◄ Not all art historians
agree as to how much of the
Baptism Verrocchio himself
painted, and what proportion
is from the hand of his
emerging student Leonardo.
Lingering doubts about the
authorship of the figure of
Christ seem to confirm that
the creation of an altarpiece
in a 15th-century workshop
was a group undertaking.
Still, the hand of Leonardo is
undeniable in the left part of
the painting, particularly in
the landscape of water and
mountains (with its typical
sfumato atmosphere), and
in the angel shown in profile,
with long, blonde hair painted
with exceptional finesse
(unlike the dull-gold haloes).

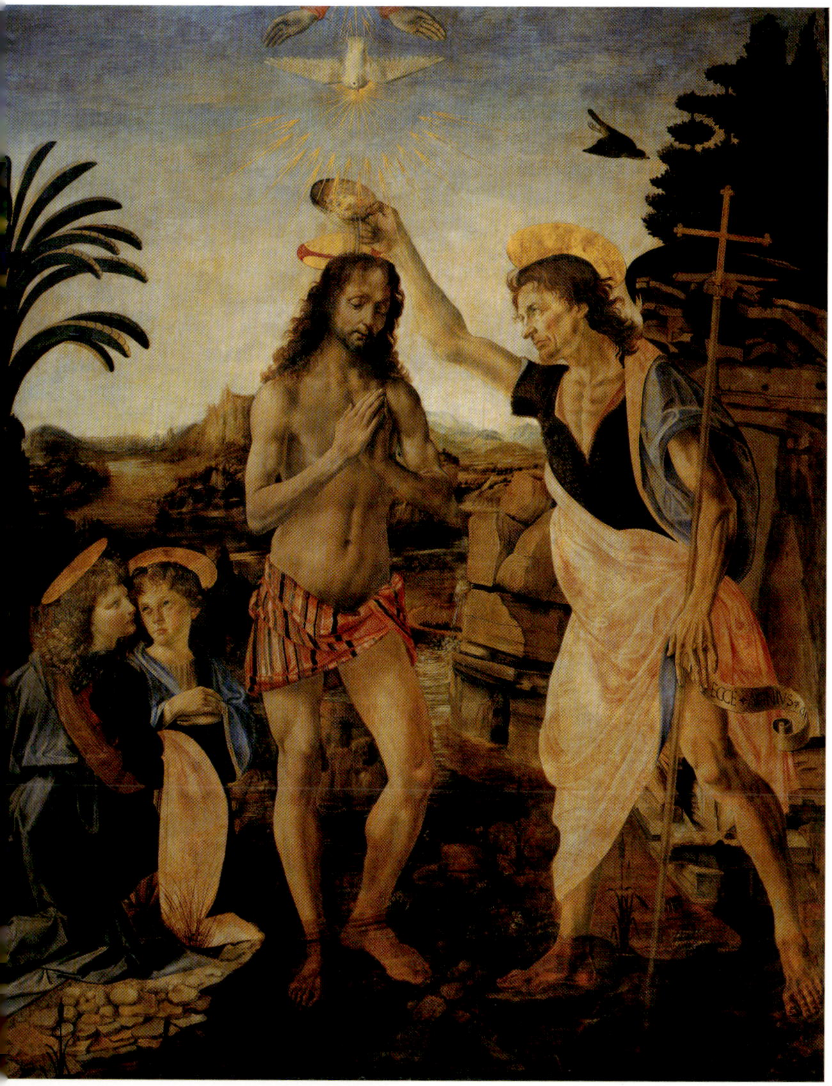

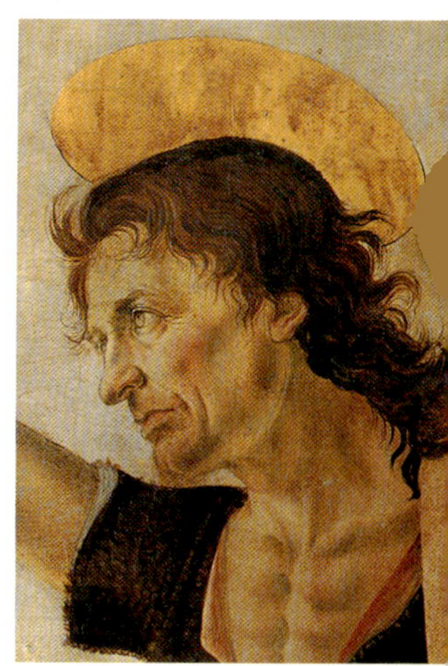

▲ Verrocchio's workshop was the most famous and efficient of any in Florence in the second half of the 15th century. The master delineated the general outlines of the composition and also executed the main figures (the figure of John the Baptist unmistakably shows Verrocchio's solid, almost sculptural treatment), leaving the completion of the painting to assistants.

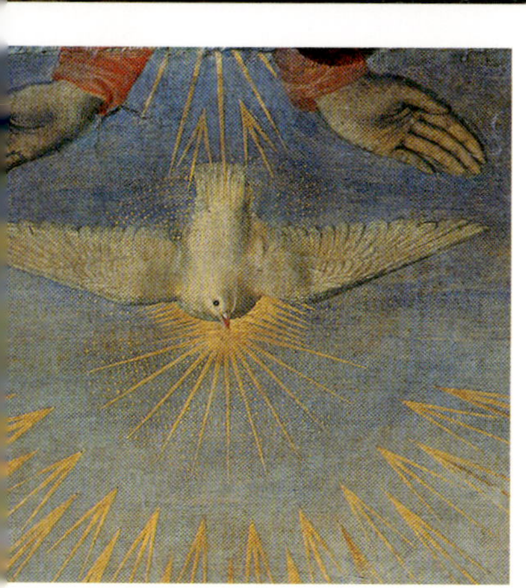

◄ The hands of God the Father and the dove, symbolizing the Holy Ghost, appear at the top of the panel. Their dry and somewhat stiff style betray the participation of an unidentified pupil who, to judge from the mediocre execution, does not seem to have been destined for a brilliant career.

► The fine painting of the brook in which Christ's feet and ankles are immersed is quite different. The transparency of the water, the pebbles on the riverbank, and the ripples and eddies on the surface are unmistakable signs of the scientific and pictorial research of the young Leonardo.

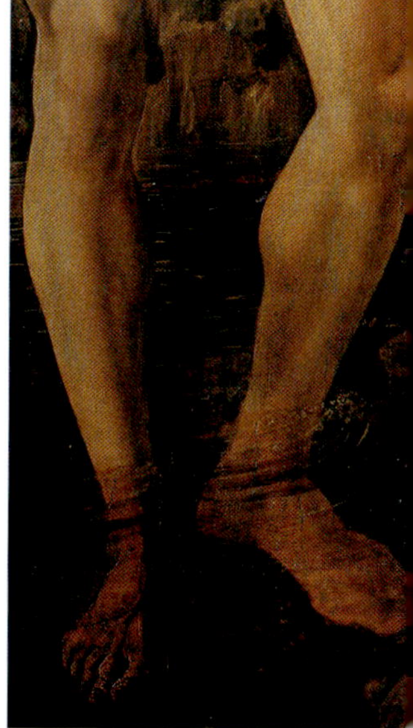

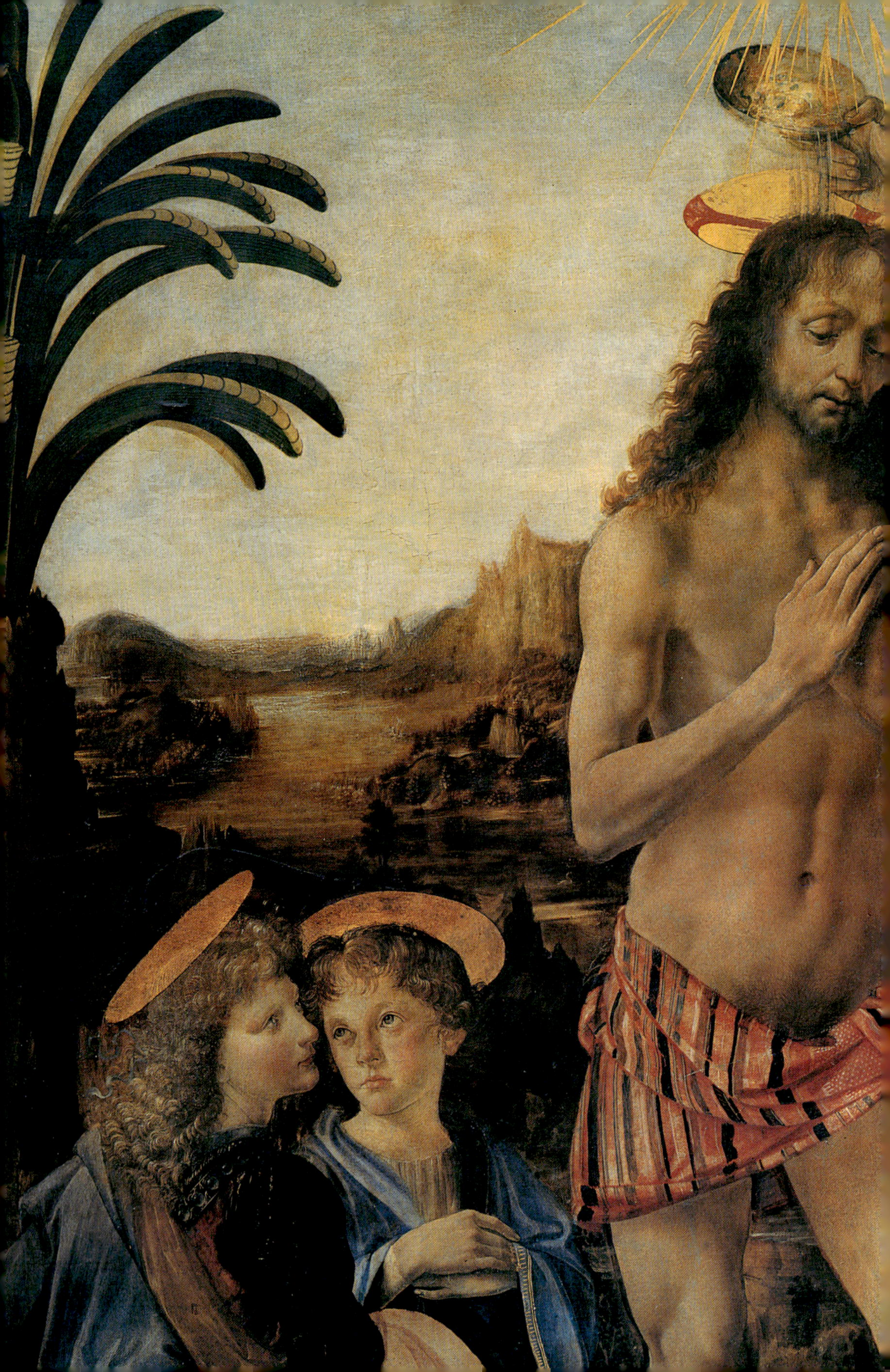

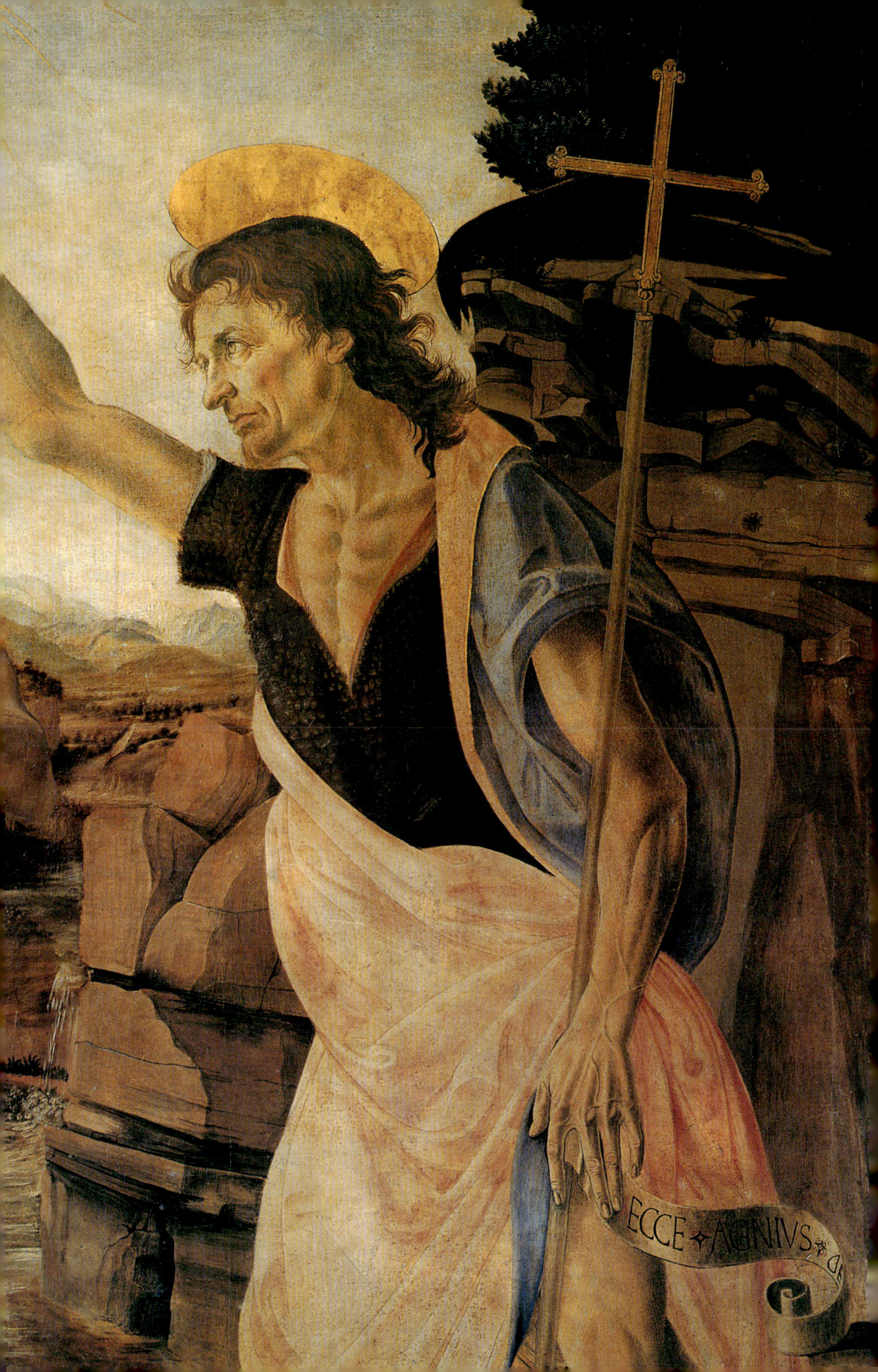
ECCE · AGNVS · D

Symmetry

Piero della Francesca
Montefeltro Altarpiece
1472–4

Oil on panel, 248 × 170 cm
Milan, Pinacoteca di Brera

For artist biography, see page 42.

Throughout his entire career as a painter and author of treatises, Piero della Francesca devoted himself to the demonstration and definition of the rules of perspective. His treatise *On perspective in painting* was the fundamental theoretical text for painting in the second half of the 15th century. Piero preferred essentially static compositions, avoiding overly dramatic movements and exaggerated gestures that might upset the balance of a carefully ordered scene. One of his inalienable concepts was absolute symmetry in the construction of the image. In this regard, the *Holy Conversation with Federico da Montefeltro,* one of the last works the painter completed before losing his sight, is essentially a manifesto. Up to the second decade of the 16th century, perfect symmetry would remain the most telling characteristic of Italian altarpieces and religious scenes.

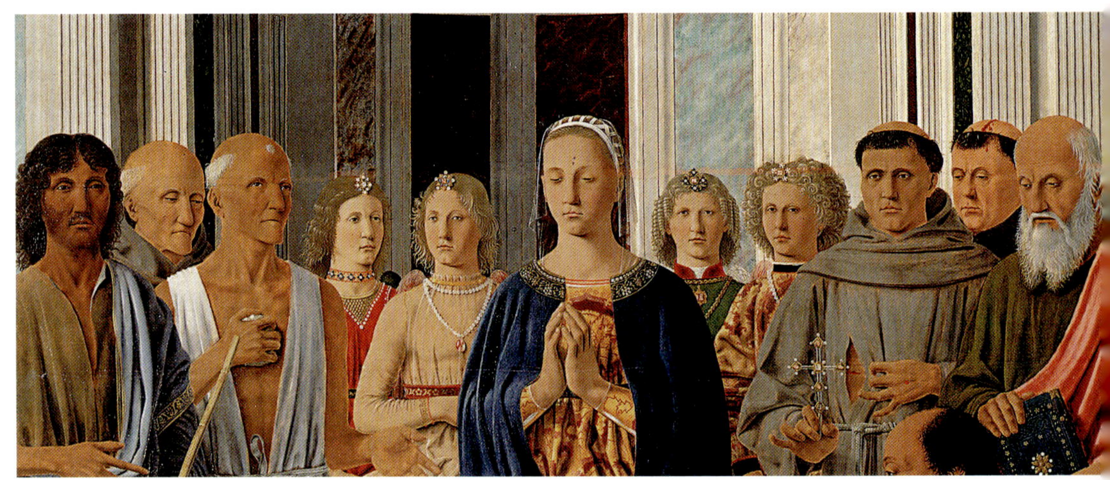

▲ The Virgin's eye level almost exactly aligns with that of the saints to either side of her, while the four angels behind Mary are arranged symmetrically. The purity of the architecture and the total absence of movement in the figures make this image a model of clear, almost abstract, intellectual conception.

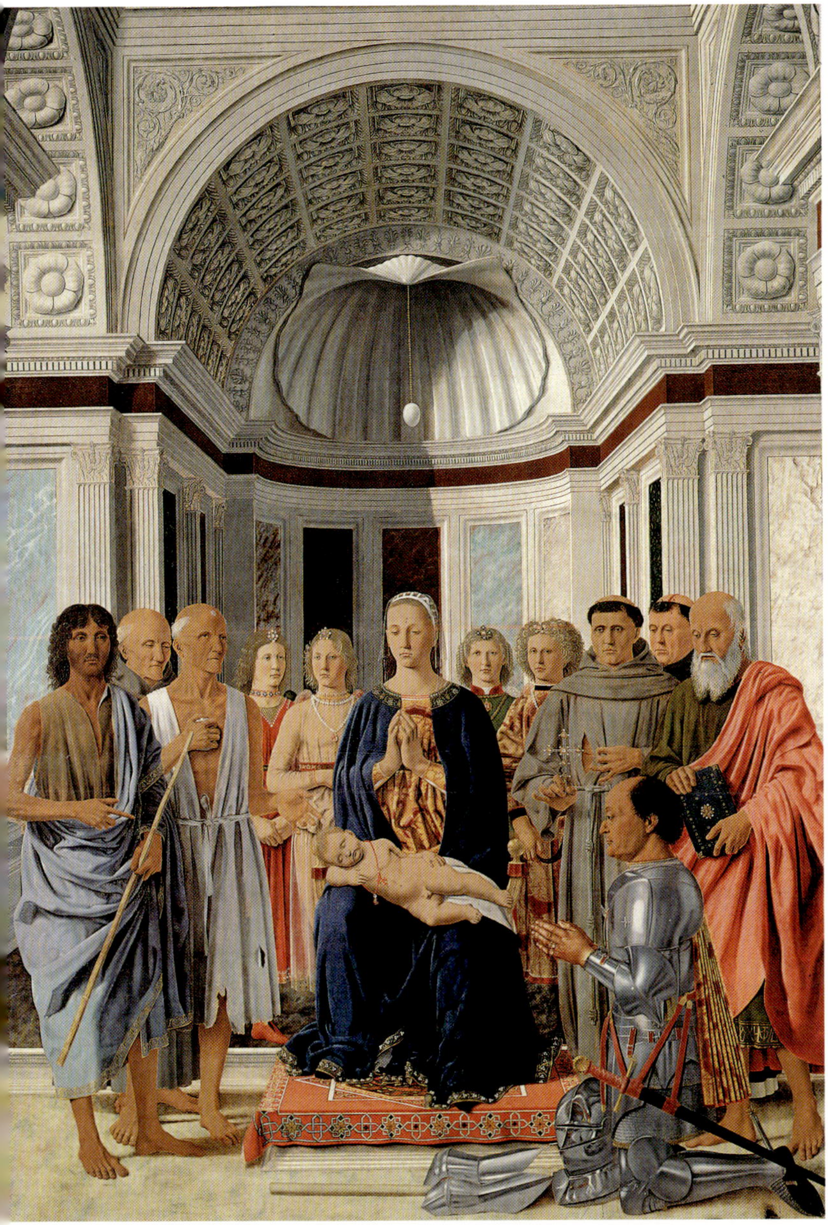

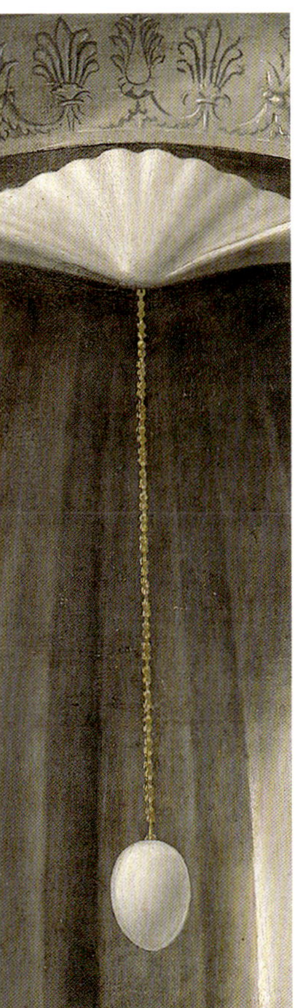

▼ The most famous detail is the ostrich egg hanging on a chain in the apse. A symbol of the birth of Christ and also a reference to the Montefeltro family coat of arms, its smooth, geometrical form is repeated in the volume of the Madonna's head.

◄ The only asymmetrical element (and for this reason easily spotted) is the portrait of Duke Federico da Montefeltro, kneeling in profile. His helmet and gloves gleam in the foreground.

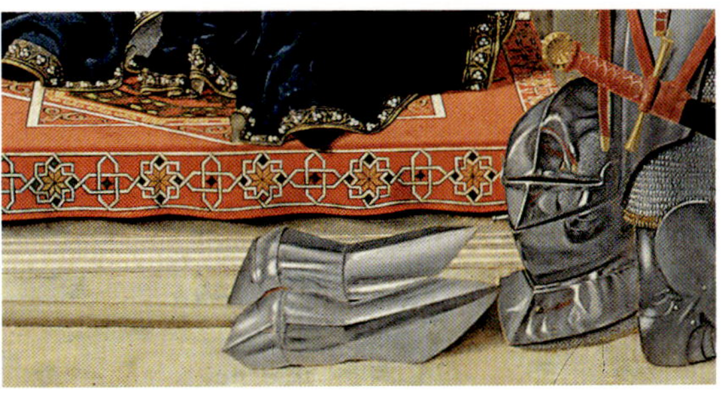

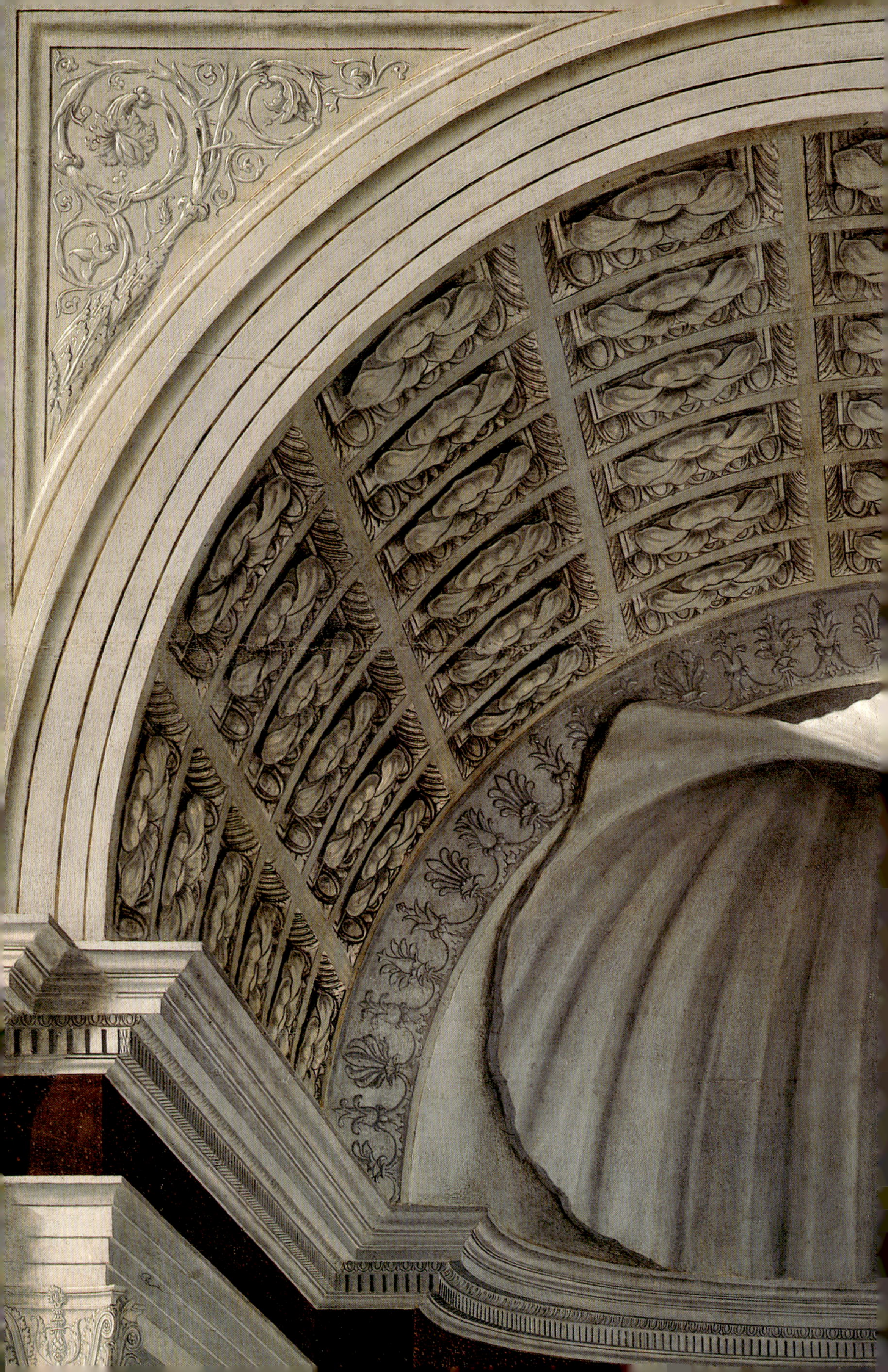

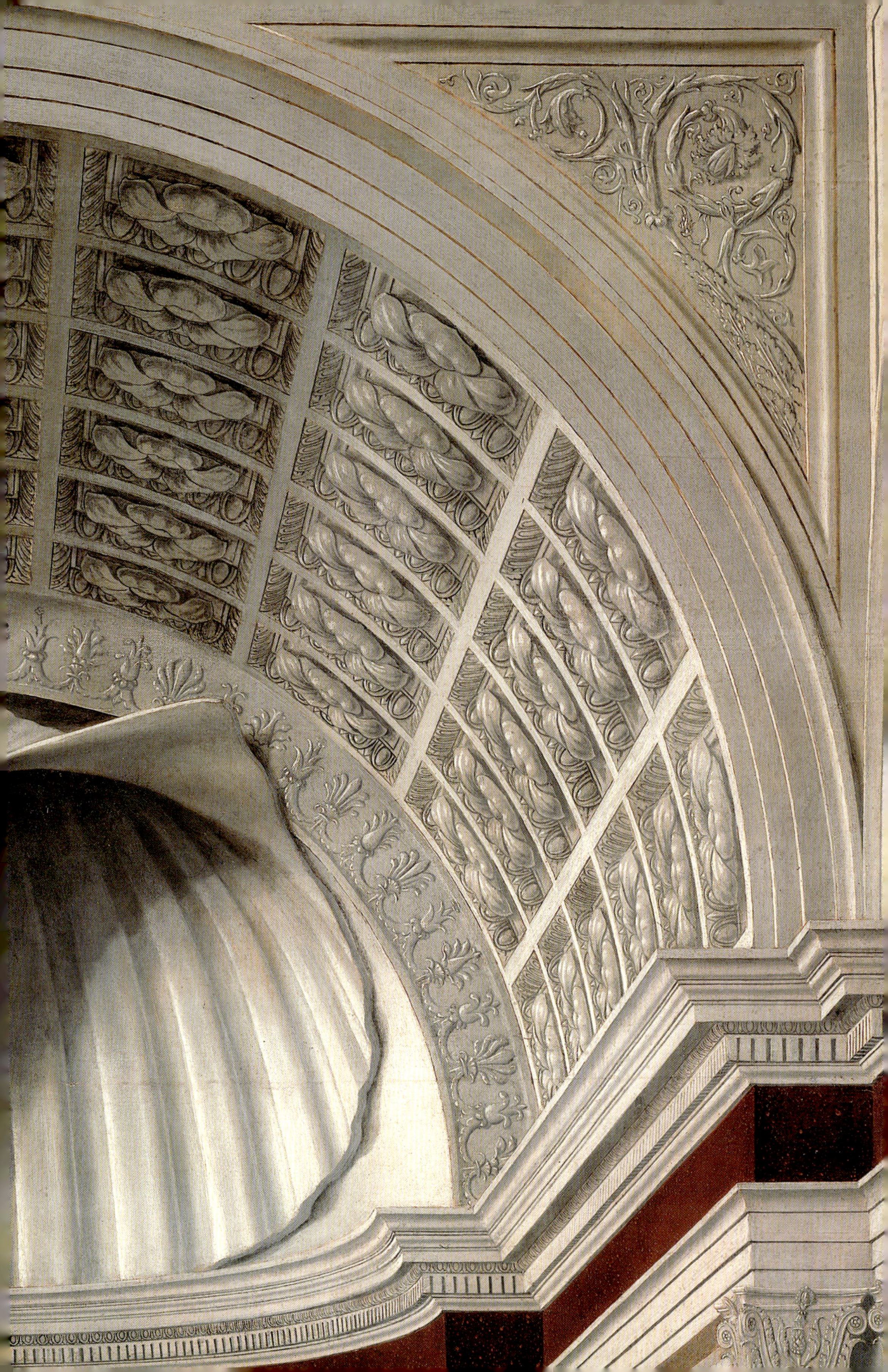

Humanism

Antonello da Messina
St Jerome in His Study
1474

Oil on panel, 46 × 36.5cm
London, National Gallery

Antonello da Messina

(Antonello di Antonio)
Messina, *c.* 1435–79

Despite the loss of some works by Antonello da Messina and uncertainty about dating others, this artist signals a turning point in 15th-century Italian painting. Antonello trained in Naples where he studied Flemish and Provençal painting in the large royal collections. He concentrated (though not exclusively) on two themes: the Crucifixion and half-length portraits of men in three-quarters view, with the sitter turning towards the viewer. Antonello remained at the juncture of Italian perspective and northern realism, alternating periods in Sicily with a gradual northward move up the peninsula. He studied the works of Piero della Francesca in Tuscany and the Marche region learning to impart solid monumentality to his figure groups and to organize scenes according to the rules of geometry. His career reached its high point with a stay in Venice (1474–8), where he painted his most impressive works – for example the *San Cassiano Altarpiece*, whose surviving sections are in Vienna, and the *St Sebastian* today in Dresden – which showed the local school, especially Giovanni Bellini, the way to exploit colour. In the last years of his life, Antonello returned to Sicily where he created, among other works, the beautiful *Annunciation of Siracusa*.

A dubious etymology connects the word 'Gothic' to the root *Got* – God. The dizzying height of the medieval cathedrals, the heavenward thrust of the pilasters and spires that disappear into the distance, the extremely expressive images all suggest other-worldly, celestial aims. In contrast, the culture of humanism sought out and celebrated the human dimension. Returning to the motto of the Greek philosopher Protagoras ('Man is the measure of all things'), the humanists restored dignity to human existence. Through intelligence, study and a capacity for discernment, humankind could bring order to nature and understand the meaning of things. Thus, humanity could construct a world to 'the measure of man' – beautiful and harmonious. This marvellous painting by Antonello da Messina is a sort of 'manifesto' of humanistic culture: St Jerome, who translated the Bible and is considered the prototype of the scholar, is depicted in a study appropriate for the work of a man of letters.

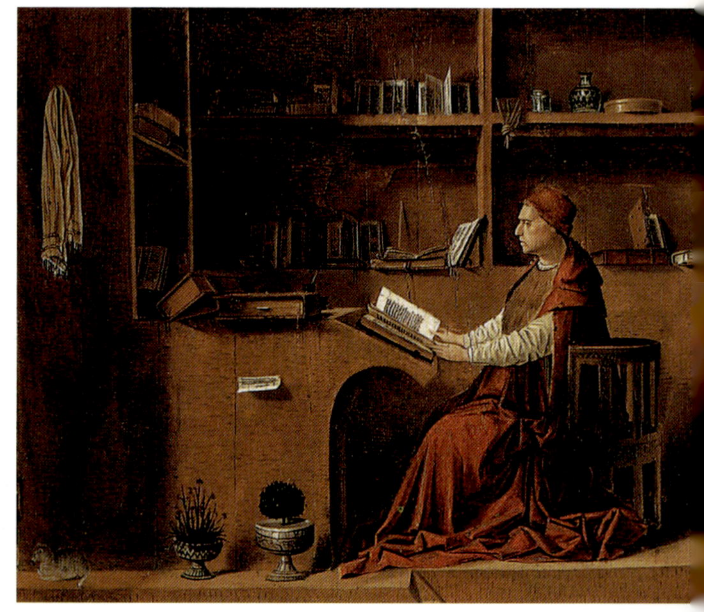

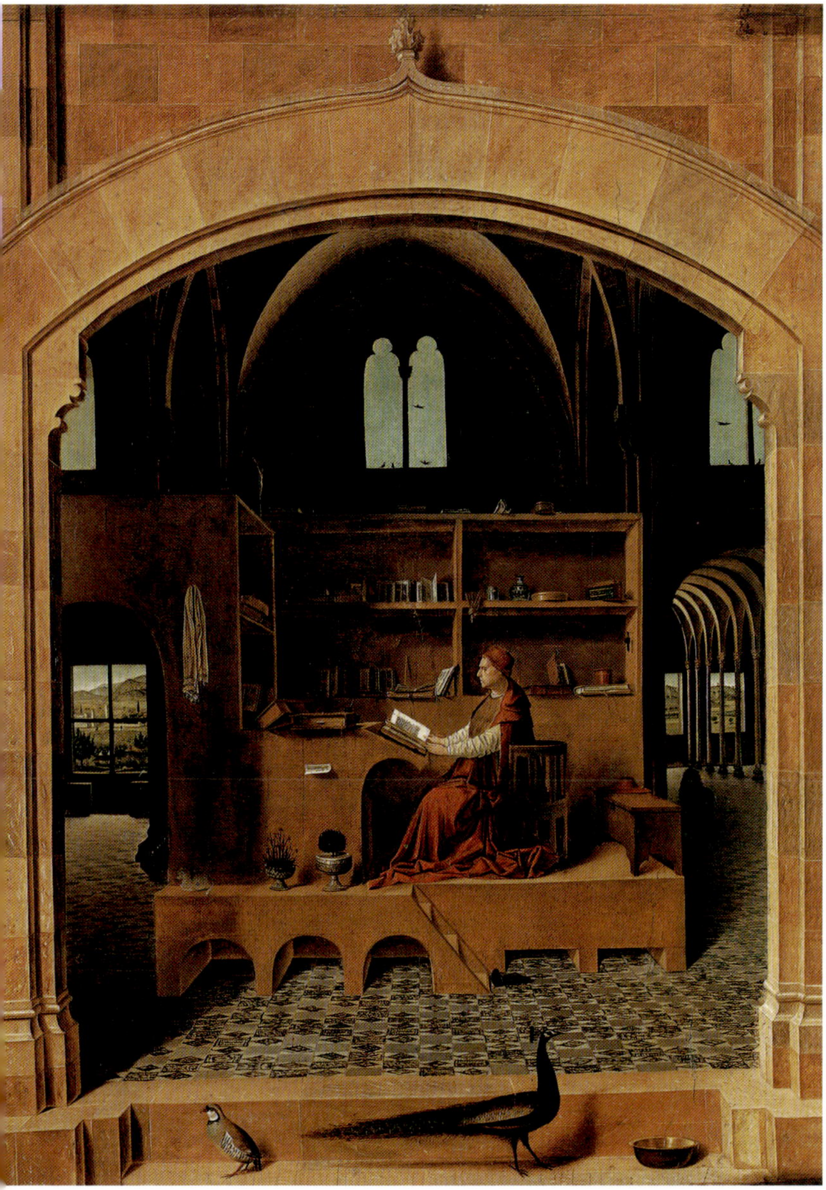

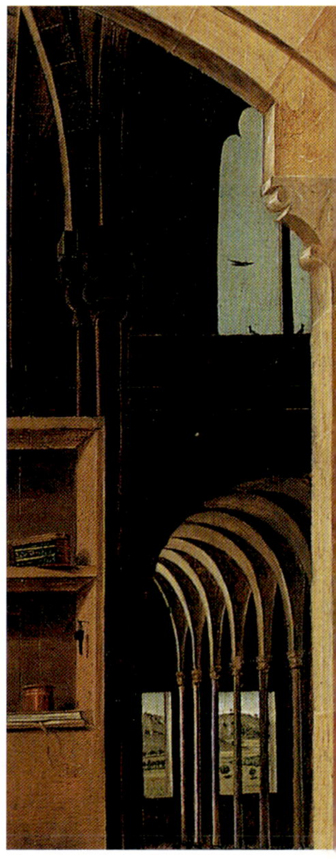

▲ Spring daylight streams into this architectural space through several windows placed at two different heights, creating a complicated but subtle effect. Because of its meticulous execution, the painting was long thought to be by a Flemish master.

◄ Within his isolated, well-lit and comfortable room the humanist saint can read and write amid the perfume of aromatic plants and the songs of swallows, and take pleasure in turning over the crackling parchment pages of old books.

► Antonello reverses Alberti's concept: his painting is a window that opens onto the inside; as two birds strut across the windowsill.

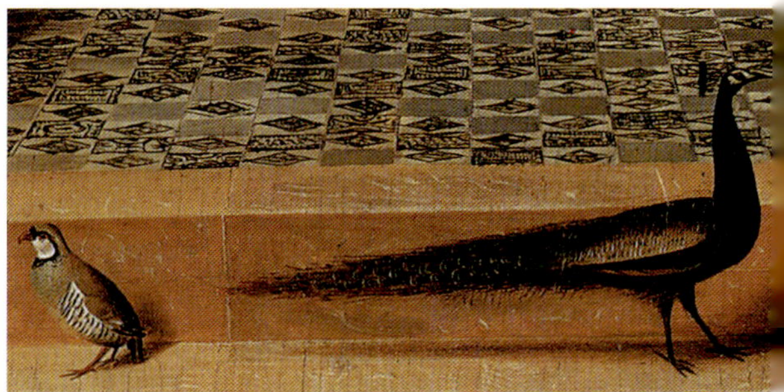

Medals

Sandro Botticelli
*Portrait of a Man with a Medal
of Cosimo the Elder*
1474

Tempera on panel, 57.5 × 44 cm
Florence, Galleria degli Uffizi

Sandro Botticelli

(Alessandro di Mariano Filipepi)
Florence, 1445–1510

Botticelli's famous allegories, illustrating the 'golden age' of Lorenzo the Magnificent and the Neo-Platonic culture of Florence, represent a refined, erudite and serene highpoint of the Italian Renaissance. The artist trained in Filippo Lippi's workshop during the 1460s, and in 1466 he became a collaborator of Andrea del Verrocchio. Like the young Perugino and, before him, Leonardo, Botticelli repeatedly treated the theme of the Madonna and Child. In 1472 he enrolled in a guild in Floence along with his friend Filippino Lippi. A series of portraits of the Medicis indicates Botticelli's increasing contact with the ruling family. In 1477, he painted an allegory of Spring, launching a cycle probably meant for a cousin of Lorenzo the Magnificent. In 1482, Botticelli was in Rome to take on the role of principal designer for the decoration of the Sistine Chapel. After his return to Florence, Lorenzo the Magnificent's favourite painter executed frescoes, altarpieces and sacred and profane paintings, all characterized by an extremely elegant use of line. In 1492, with the death of Lorenzo and the upheaval fomented by the Dominican friar Savonarola, Botticelli's works begin to show an intense spiritual agitation, almost a foreshadowing of the impending Mannerism.

Numismatics, the collection and study of coins and medals, was a favourite intellectual activity during the Renaissance. To possess a complete series of Roman coins with portraits of the emperors indicated one's refinement and love of Antiquity. For this reason, and also to display personal power and commemorate particular honours or events, Italian Renaissance nobles often commissioned medals, typically in bronze. The front always depicted the patron, in strict profile. The reverse, however, could feature allegorical motifs, heraldry or a memorable event. Medals conveyed political values and made suitable gifts for diplomats and visiting dignatries. While they were produced by specialized craftsmen, painters sometimes provided drawings and designs. The medals cast by Pisanello remain unsurpassed for their creative freedom of invention and technical perfection.

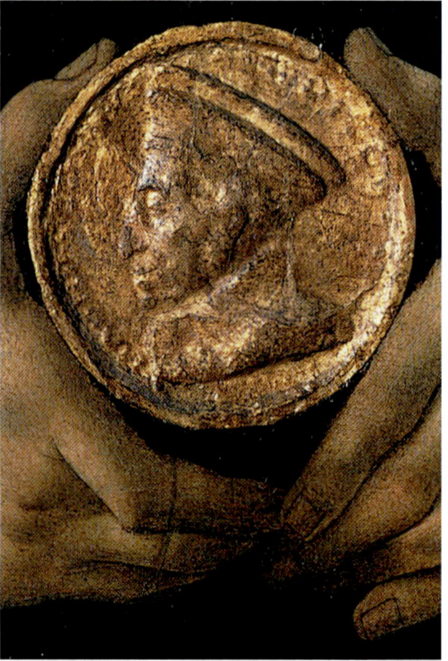

◄ The large medal is a realistic relief, executed in gold paste and inserted into the painting. The young man who holds the medal is shown frontally, while the portrait of Cosimo the Elder is in profile.

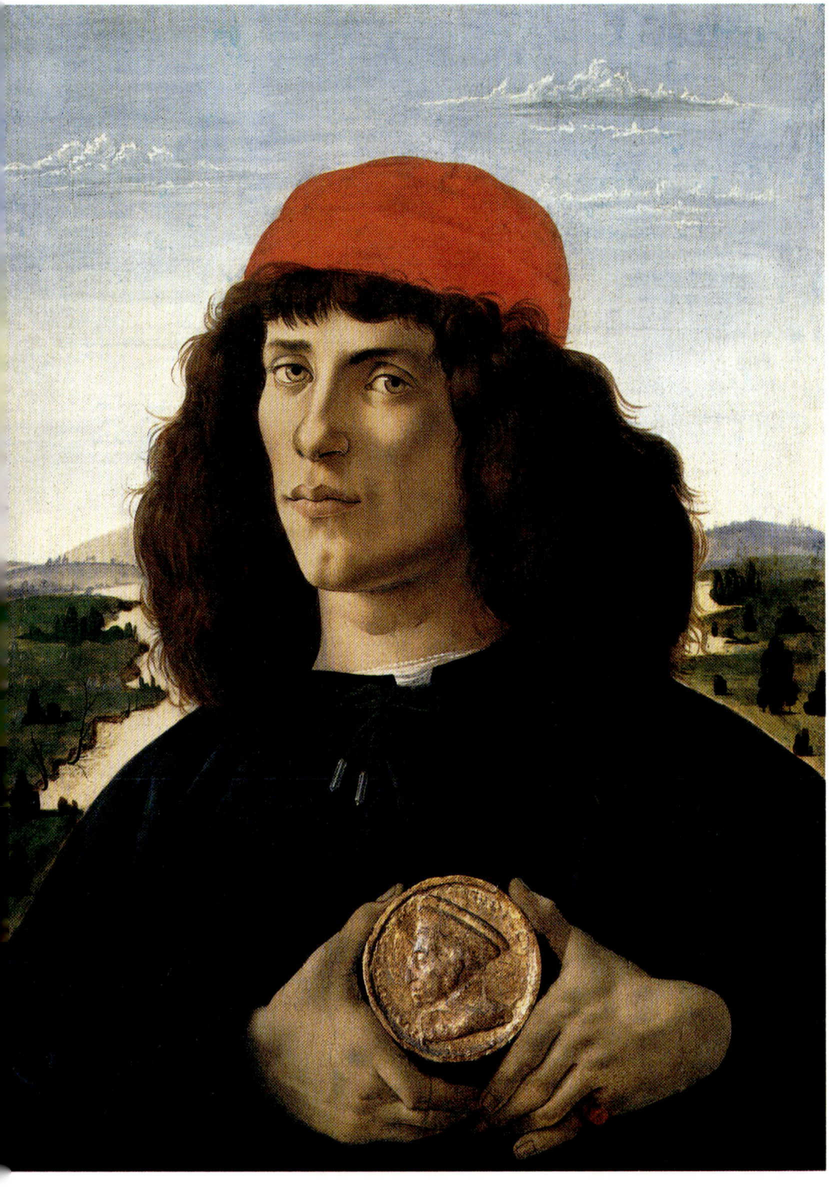

◄ In an unusual twist, we do not know the identity of the young man portrayed by Botticelli, while we can easily recognize the person represented on the medal as Cosimo de' Medici, considered the true founder of Florence's ruling family.

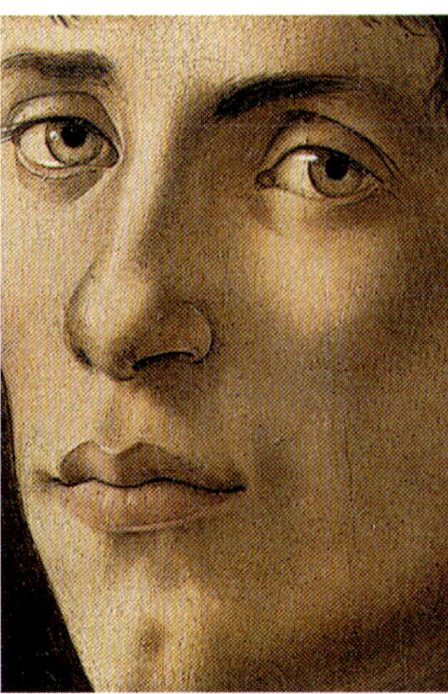

▲ The young man's cleanly incised features, which seem to express a vague sadness, are characteristic of Florentine male portraits from the second half of the 15th century.

► Botticelli was not concerned with depicting a detailed landscape. His contemporaries, starting with his rival Leonardo, called these anonymous backgrounds 'dismal'.

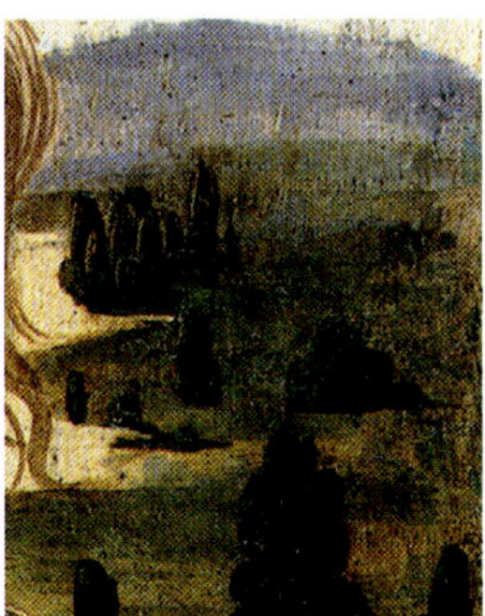

Patron

Sandro Botticelli
The Adoration of the Magi
1475

Tempera on panel, 111 × 134 cm
Florence, Galleria degli Uffizi

For artist biography, see page 102.

While it is fascinating to pore over the lives of the great painters, it is also important to consider those who commissioned the works, determining the subject, dimensions, medium and even colours and style. In the centuries prior to the birth of the commercial art market and private collecting, patrons – that is, those who paid for paintings or sculptures, generally for churches or public places – played a decisive role in the career of an artist. Especially during the 15th and the early 16th centuries, it was not unusual for patrons to be portrayed in the work, generally off to the side in an attitude of contemplation and prayer. Sometimes the wife or children were also represented and every now and again the patrons actually participated in the action of the scene, broadening their involvement to the historical context – as is the case in this *Adoration of the Magi*, which Botticelli painted as a celebration of the Medici family.

► Not all of the many figures portrayed by Botticelli have been identified. Among those that have been, however, are the poet Angelo Poliziano (in a red hat, inviting a dignified young man to kneel) and, beside him, in an attitude of devotion, the young humanist Giovanni Pico della Mirandola. Starting from the pretext of a sacred subject, the painting becomes a collective celebration of a politically and culturally powerful group.

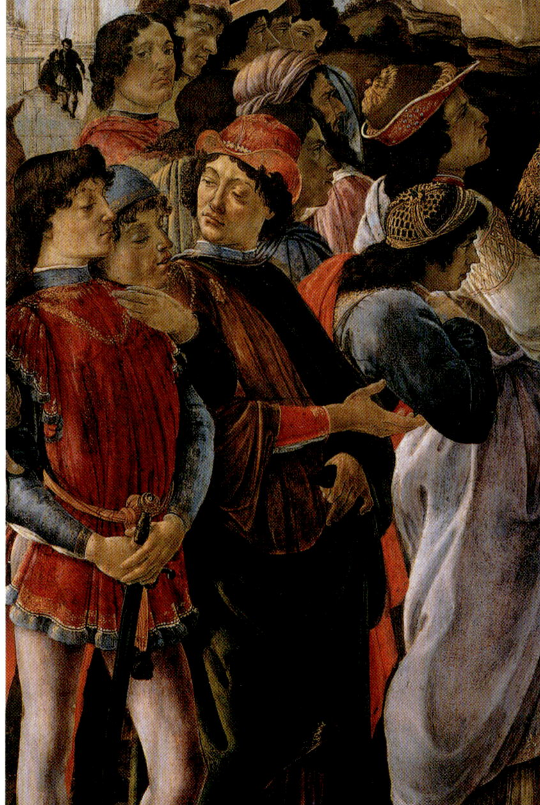

► The Medici commissioned several versions of the Adoration of the Magi, a subject frequently chosen by Florentine patrons because it offered opportunities to include family portraits. The procession frescoed about fifteen years earlier by Benozzo Gozzoli in the chapel of Palazzo Medici in Florence (see pages 70–1) is a famous example of this 'family' subject.

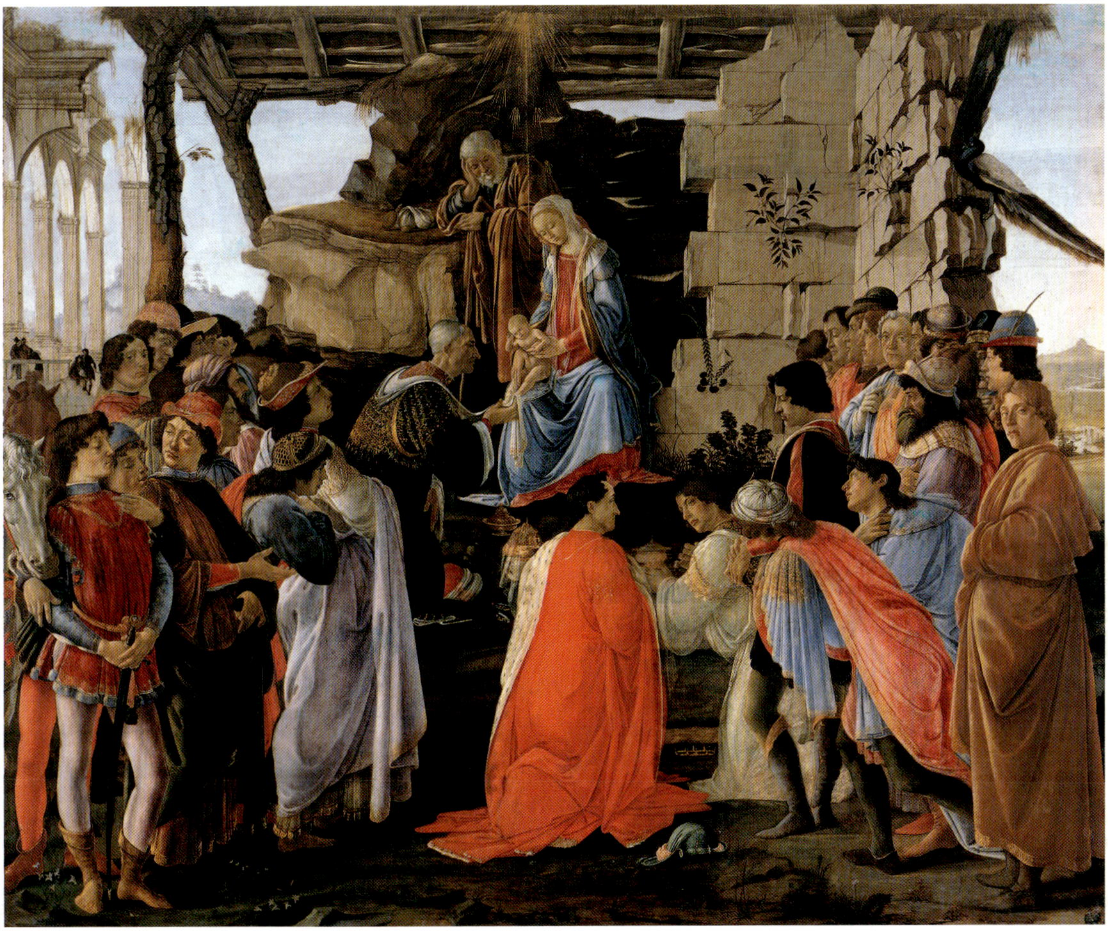

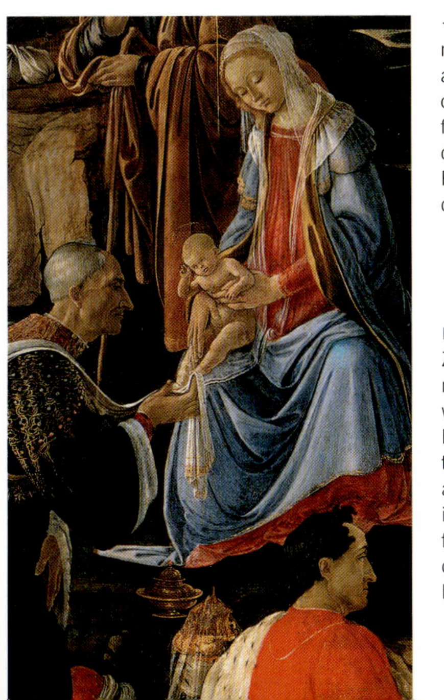

◀ All the most illustrious members of the household are portrayed, beginning with old Cosimo, presented as the first Wise Man, and in the centre of the scene, his son Piero the Gouty, in a red cloak, seen from behind.

▶ The patron was Gaspare Zanobi del Lama, the older man in the middle ground who turns towards the viewer. In front of him are Lorenzo the Magnificent, wearing blue, and the dark-haired Giuliano, in profile. The figure on the far right wrapped in a yellow cloak may well be Botticelli himself.

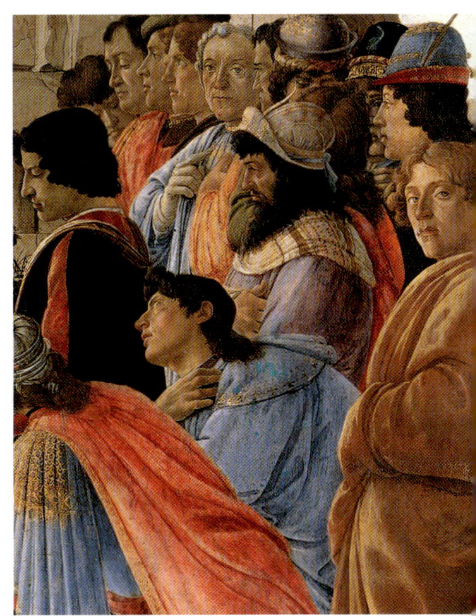

Geometry

Antonello da Messina
The Virgin Annunciate
c. 1476

Oil on panel, 45 × 34.5 cm

Palermo, Galleria Regionale
della Sicilia di Palazzo Abatellis

For artist biography, see page 100.

The application of the strict rules of geometry in 15th-century Italian paintings did not preclude innovation or feelings of intensity. In some cases, the perspectival 'grid' itself is used for expressive purposes. Antonello da Messina travelled widely and saw a broad range of painting styles from abroad as well as from Italy. His clearly defined, simple forms (here, for example, the perfect oval of the face and the pyramid formed by the cloak) are accompanied by a rare psychological sensitivity. The somewhat uncommon theme of the painting is the moment immediately following the Annunciation (a more frequently depicted subject). Alone, Mary meditates on the angel's news.

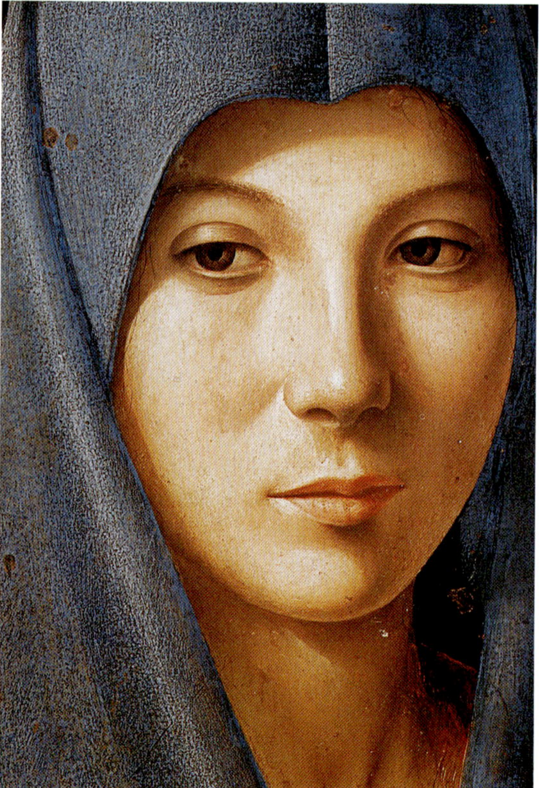

◄ Mary's fresh, smooth face emphasizes her purity. The heavy blue veil, creased at the centre of her forehead, aligns with the vertical axis of her nose.

► On more than one occasion Antonello da Messina used the figures' hands to introduce movement and action into highly geometric images. Mary holds her veil closed with her left hand, while the right reaches forward, foreshortened, in a gesture that may be interpreted variously as acceptance, expectation, suspense or perplexity.

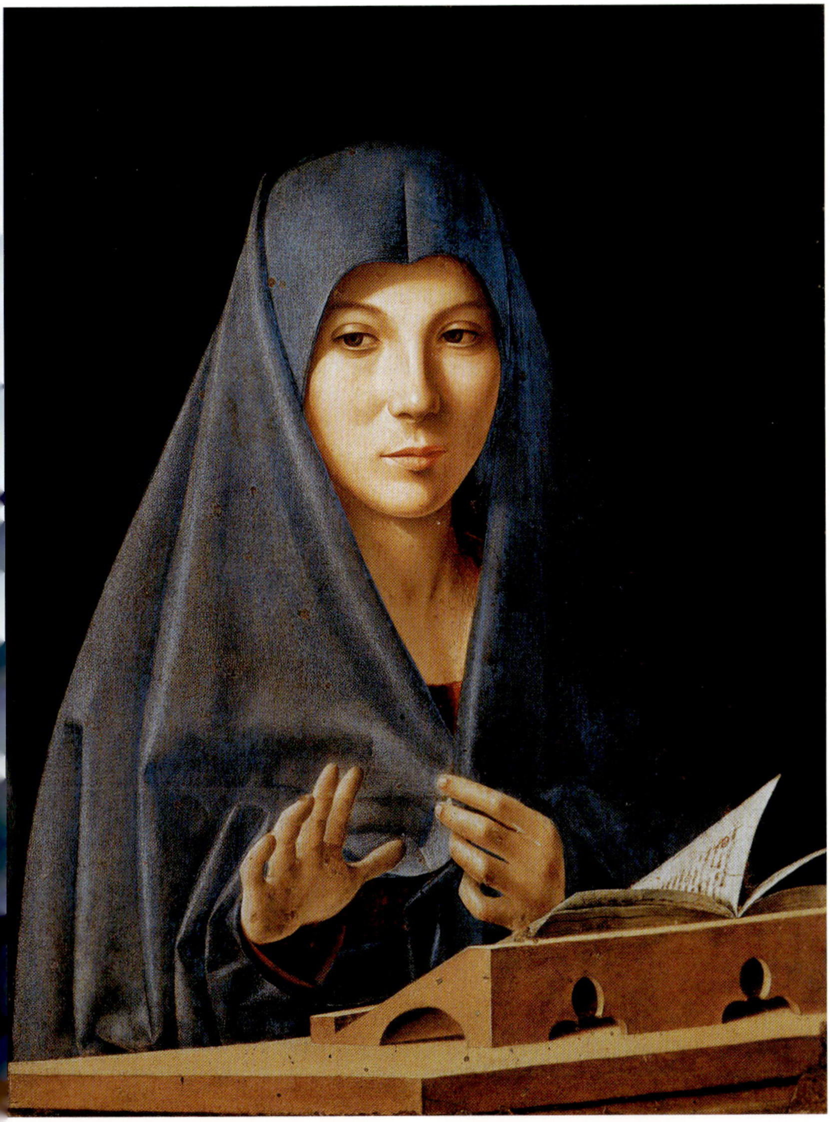

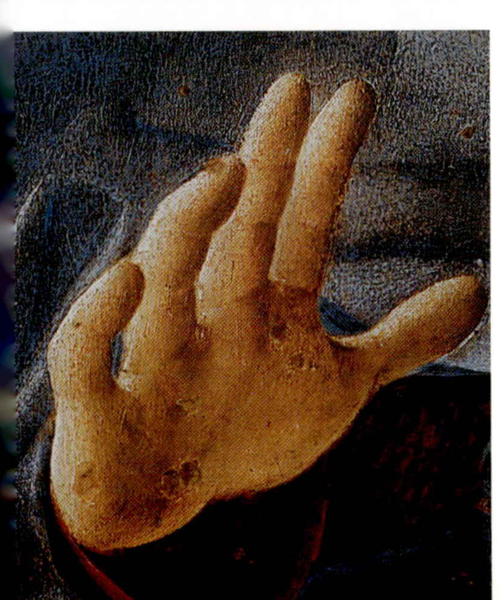

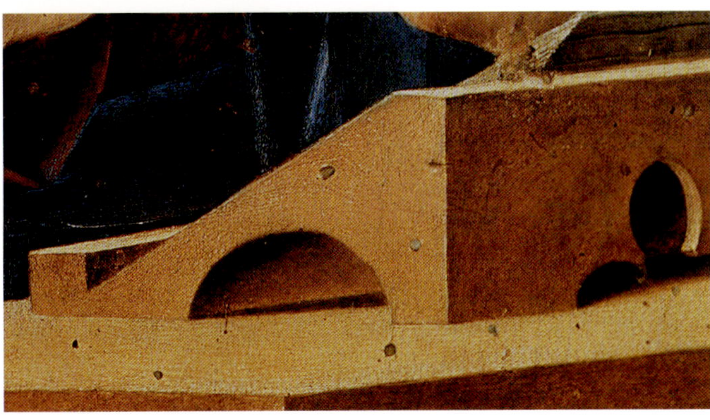

▼ The simple wooden lectern contributes to the strict geometry of the painting. The lectern, resting on a surface of the same light-coloured wood, is placed so that the light, surfaces, angles and curved openwork are all clearly defined.

Flemish Artists

Hugo van der Goes
Portinari Triptych
c. 1475

Oil on panel, 253 × 586 cm

Florence, Galleria degli Uffizi

Hugo van der Goes

Ghent, *c.* 1440–Rood Klooster, Brussels, 1482

One of the most interesting and troubled Flemish masters of the second half of the 15th century, Van der Goes enrolled in the painters' guild in Ghent in 1467, but around 1475 his profound faith led him to enter the Augustinian monastery of Rood Klooster as a lay brother. He lived there until his death. However, his secluded life did not prevent him from working. His fame attracted many notable figures to the monastery, and the painter enjoyed special privileges that allowed him to converse with his illustrious guests. The *Portinari Triptych*, executed *c.* 1475 and sent to Florence in 1483, marks the high point of his career as a painter. The arrival of this Flemish masterpiece in the main centre of Italian humanism prompted great interest among Florentine artists. The growing emotional difficulties of the artist are recorded in the monastery's archives. As the result of his severe depression, Van der Goes's style became increasingly nervous and deeply felt, as shown by the dramatic *Death of the Virgin* in Bruges.

The cultural relationship between central Italy and the cities of the Netherlands reflects the lively commercial and financial network that linked Bruges and Ghent with Florence, Milan, Genoa and other Italian cities. Thus it was inevitable that artists of the two main European schools should meet and influence each other. The Italian painters were above all interested in the Flemish school's achievement of luminosity through the use of colours diluted with flax oil, as well as by their portrait poses and taste for descriptive detail. Many factors fostered this cross-over: Rogier van der Weyden's trip to Ferrara, Florence and Rome; the collection of the King of Naples; the international patronage of Federico da Montefeltro; the direct relationship between the duchies of Milan and Burgundy; the trade activity of the Genoese; and the presence in Flanders of Florentine banks and merchants (the Arnolfinis, Tanis, Portinaris), who were generous patrons and connoisseurs of art. The arrival in Florence of an absolute masterpiece like Hugo van der Goes's triptych was the climax in a cultural relationship in which, at least to begin with, Flanders still prevailed. But in the following century, the situation was reversed in favour of the Italians.

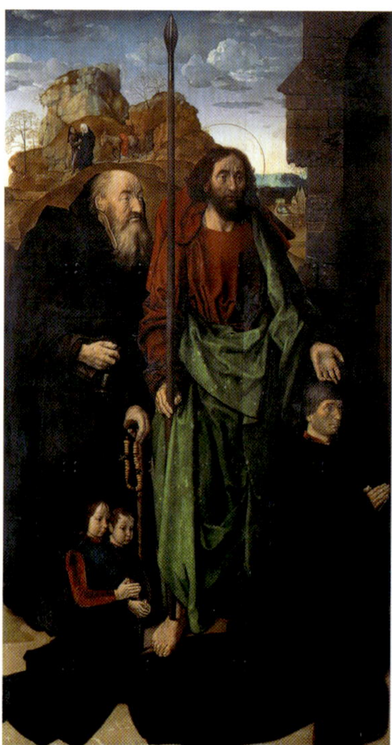
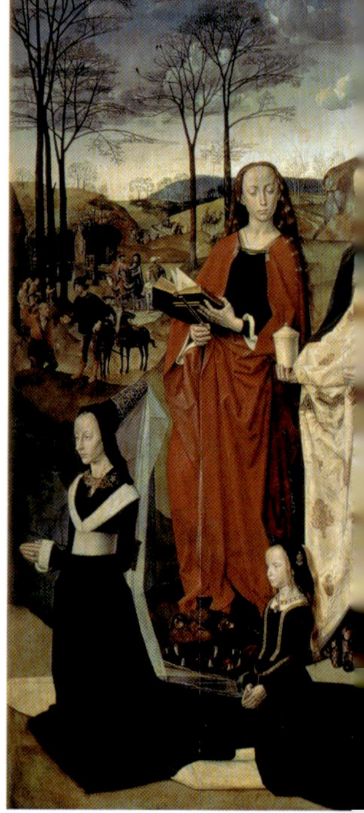

► The triptych's lateral wings, hinged in the Flemish tradition, depict the patrons and their patron saints. Tommaso Portinari and his wife, Maria Baroncelli, are shown along with their children in an attitude of prayer. A Florentine art lover who also had his portrait painted by Hans Memling, Portinari was director of the Medici bank in Bruges.

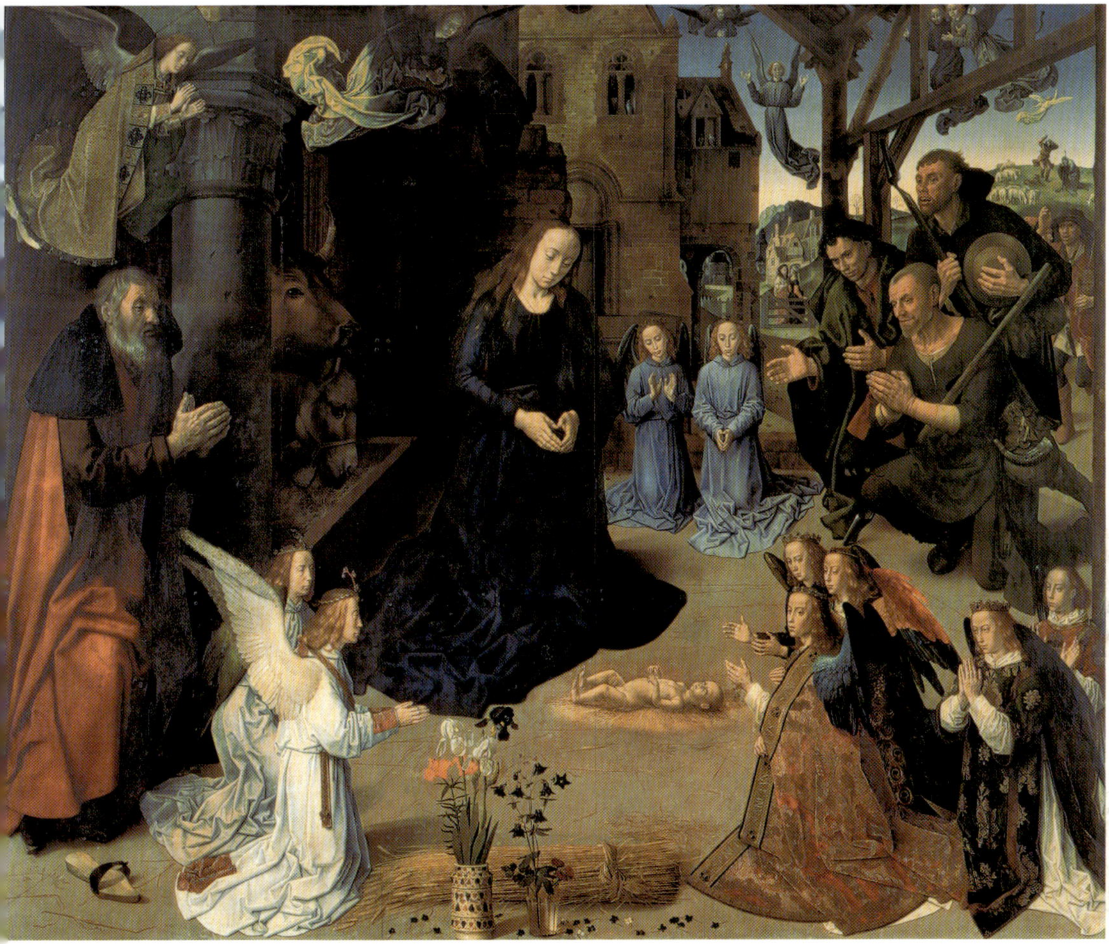

> The painting's meticulously refined execution, a remarkable example of Flemish realism and the possibilities of oil painting, caused an immediate reaction in Tuscan art circles. The painters in the orbit of Lorenzo the Magnificent sought to emulate the highly effective, particularized style of the Flemish artists in rendering facial expressions, surfaces and materials.

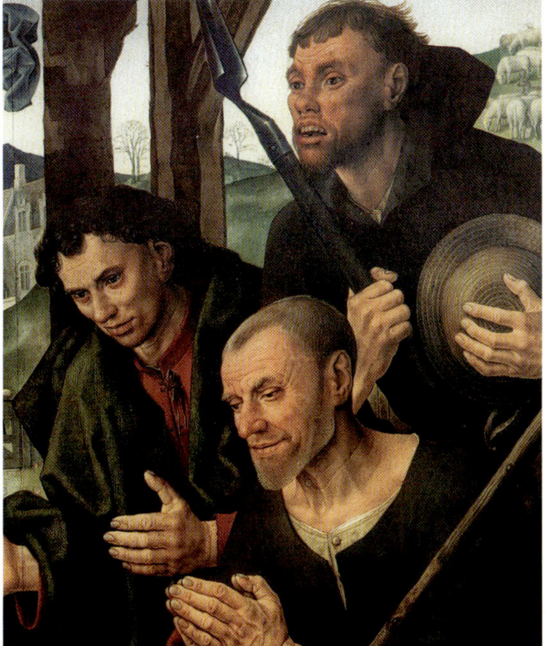

▲ The iconography of the triptych's central scene is relatively rare in Italy: it is not, properly speaking, a Nativity, but an Adoration of the Child. All of the figures (Joseph, Mary, the angels and shepherds), with their hands joined in prayer, surround the Infant Jesus, who has been laid on the ground. It is not a narrative episode but a mystical, symbolic scene. The unusual foreground details of two vases of flowers and bundled spikes of grain allude to Christ's future sacrifice.

Shadow

Antonello da Messina
St Sebastian
1476

Oil on panel transferred to canvas,
171 × 85.5 cm
Dresden, Gemäldegalerie

For artist biography, see page 100.

In the new Italian painting, shadows play an indispensable role, lending figures and forms their three-dimensionality and concreteness, indicating the source and direction of light, and defining architectural masses. Before Giotto, medieval painters completely ignored shadows. The figures in a sacred scene stood like cut-outs, beyond time and space. Attributing a solid volume to the human figure meant recognizing that it occupied space, a physical place, in the world and in history. Therefore, humanistic painting accentuated the effect of shadows not simply to demonstrate a theorem or create a pictorial illusion, but to convey the dignity of humankind.

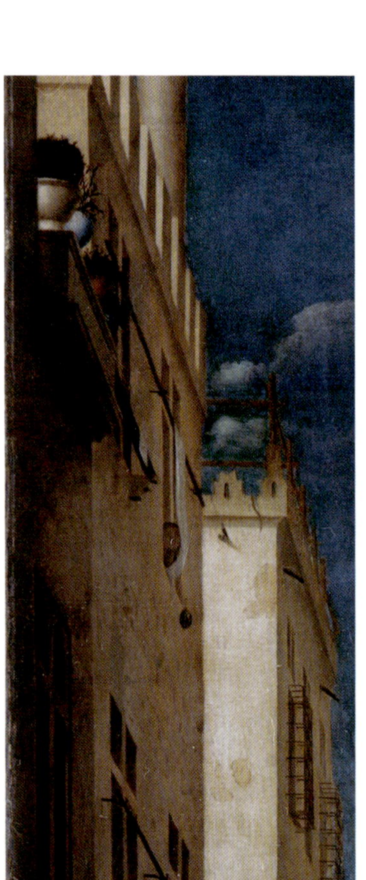

◄ The light flows down from the left. The façades in the compact block of buildings at the side are in shadow. Originally, this *St Sebastian* panel was combined with another representing St Roche, which has been lost. In all probability, it depicted a symmetrical architectural scene.

▼ Overcome by the afternoon heat, a soldier stretches out for a nap, lying on a step at the back of the square. The foreshortened figure contrasts with the fluid line of the woman's silhouette. Dressed in blue, she holds a baby in her arms.

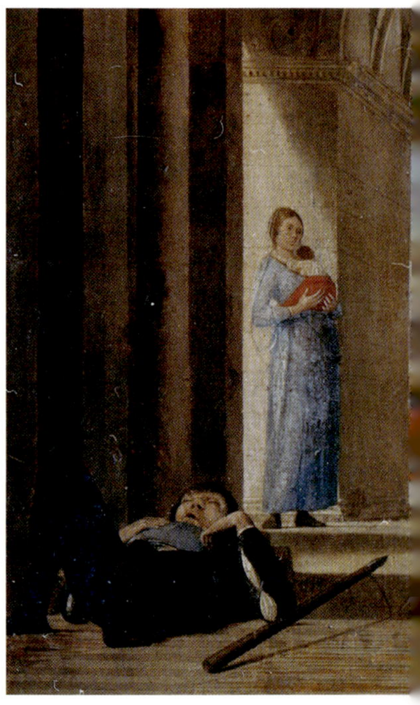

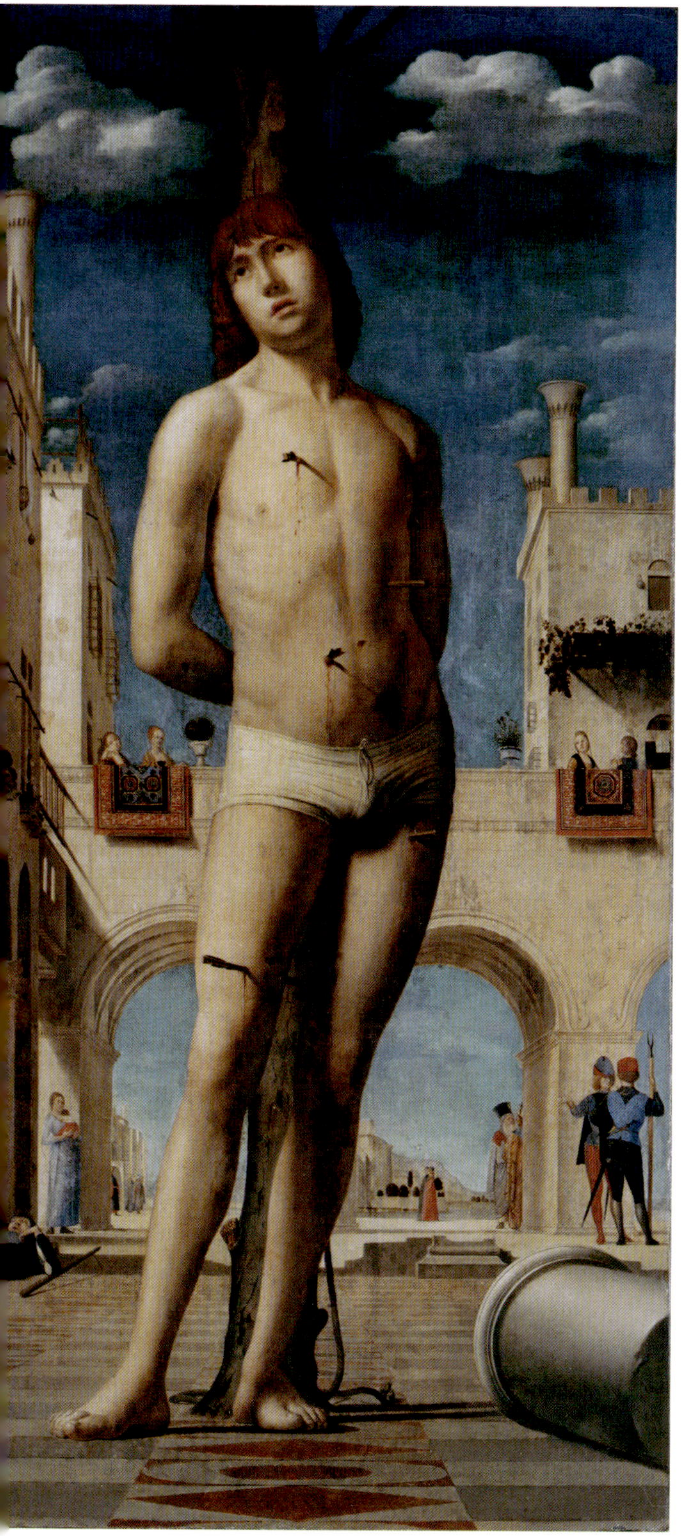

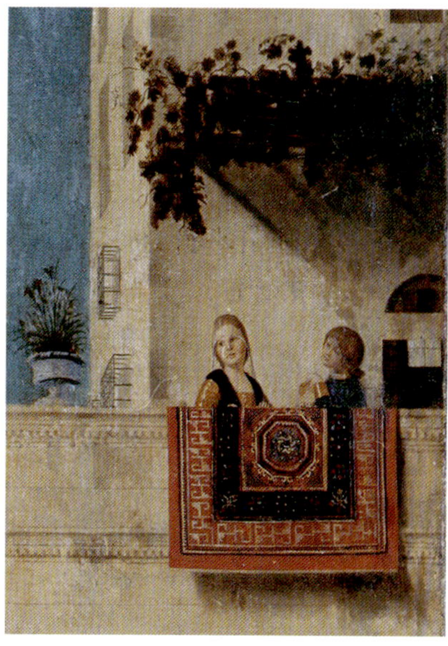

▲ Executed during the Sicilian painter's Venice sojourn of 1474–8, the painting demonstrates knowledge of Flemish art, especially in the care taken with each detail.

◄ ▼ Only five short arrows from a crossbow pierce St Sebastian's splendid youthful body. Drops of blood flow from each wound. The shafts that protrude from his chest and abdomen are placed like the gnomon of a sundial, as if their shadows were measuring the hours of the day on the face of a clock.

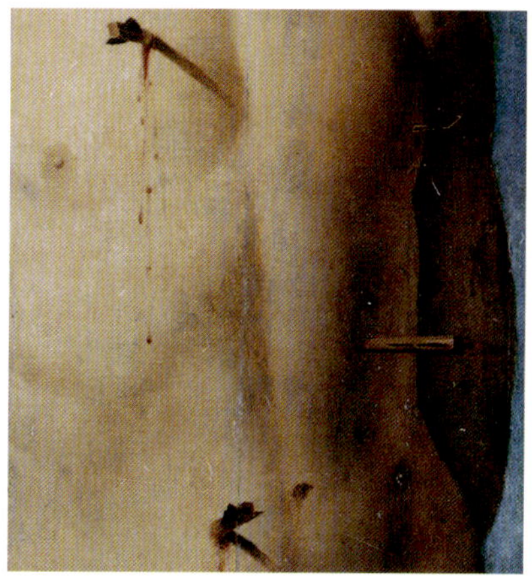

Internationalism

Pedro Berruguete
Portrait of Federico da Montefeltro
1476

Oil on panel, 134 × 77 cm
Urbino, Galleria Nazionale delle Marche

Pedro Berruguete

Paredes de Nava, Palencia, c. 1450–
Avila, c. 1504

A clear example of the tendency towards international dialogue in art during the second half of the 15th century, the Spaniard Berruguete took Flemish painting as his model and spent the most important part of his career in Italy. Trained under Fernando Gallego, like most masters on the Iberian peninsula at the time, he drew inspiration from northern models, in particular the tradition of Van Eyck. In 1474, he moved to Italy where, in the cosmopolitan atmosphere of the highly refined court of Urbino, Berruguete collaborated with Justus of Ghent on a series of images of illustrious persons for the *studiolo* of Federico da Montefeltro. He also painted an important full-length portrait of the duke seated at a reading stand with his son Guidobaldo beside him. When the artist returned to Spain in 1483, he again took up painting altarpieces for various churches in Castile, adapting himself to a taste that still expected a gold ground and exaggerated decoration.

Fifteenth-century Italy is often described as a mosaic of independent states in continual conflict over control of bordering territories. Art was a means of acquiring prestige and asserting a city or region's identity, and the many schools of painting throughout Italy, each with its own distinct character, reflect this political situation. While the larger cities could rely mainly on local artists, the smaller centres increased their ranks by inviting masters from other cities or even other nations. Perhaps the best example of this growing internationalism was the small but splendid city of Urbino, which attracted artists from Tuscany, Spain, Flanders, Dalmatian, Umbria, Venice and Lombardy.

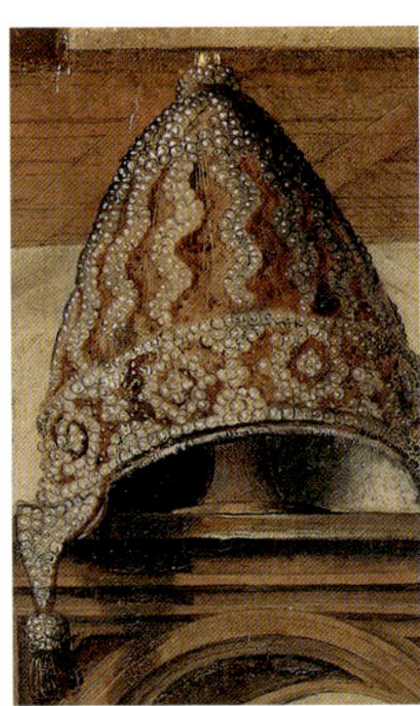

◄ In this official portrait by the Spanish painter Berruguete, one of the most visible symbols of Federico da Montefeltro's efforts at international diplomacy is the pearl-studded tiara, a personal gift from the Sultan of Constantinople.

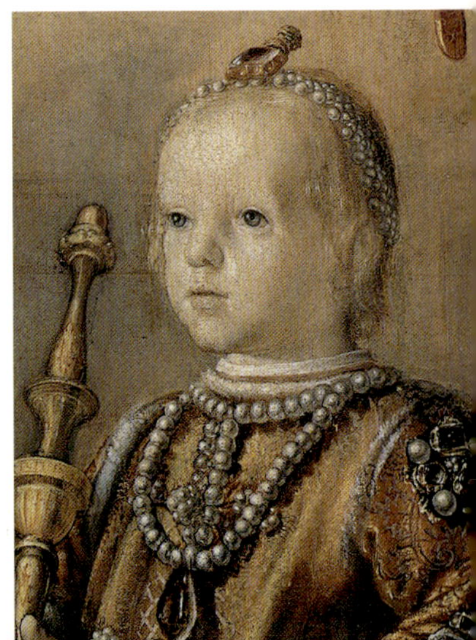

► Federico's son Guidobaldo, heir to the duchy, stands beside him. Berruguete contrasts the child's innocent face with weighty insignia of power such as the lavish pearl ornaments and the baton of command, which the child holds like a plaything.

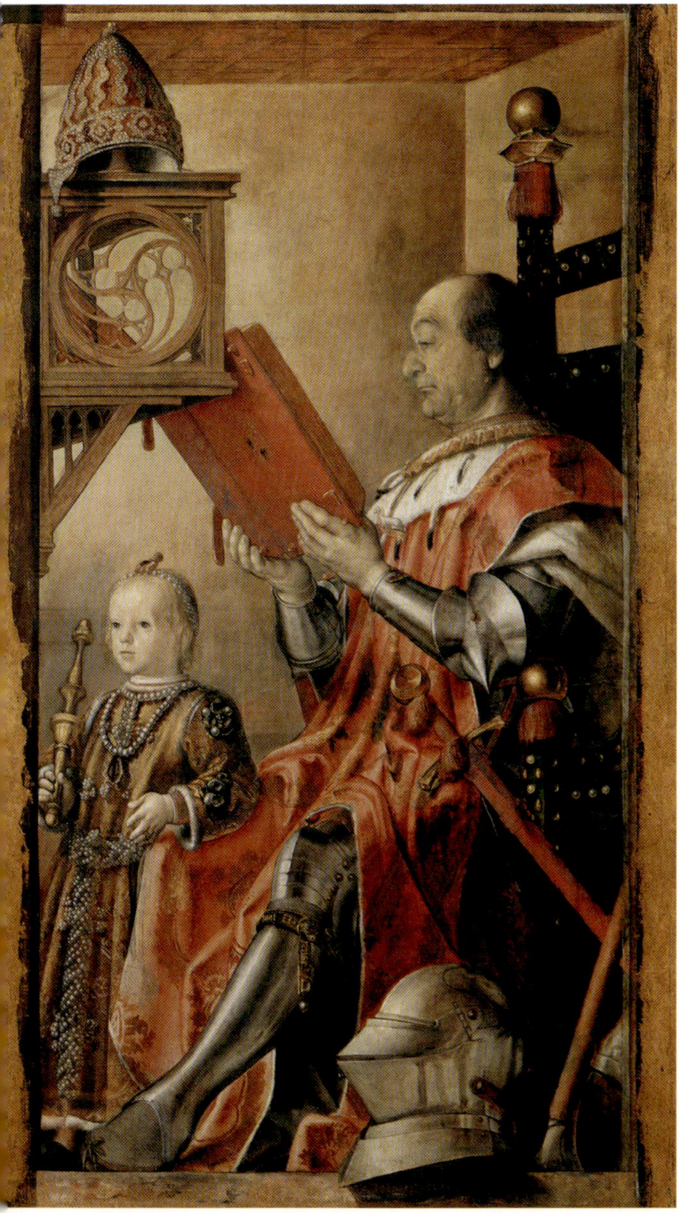

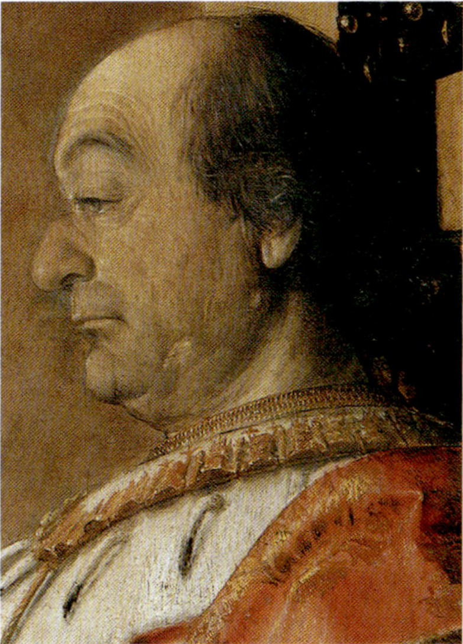

◀▼ Wrapped in an ermine-bordered cloak topped by the collar of the Golden Fleece – the Holy Roman Empire's highest insignia of honour – Federico is portrayed as an intellectual sovereign, intently reading, a member of the most select international aristocracy. On the other hand, the Duke of Urbino also presents himself as a man of action: he wears armour under his cloak, a sword hangs at his side and at the lower right, his helmet and baton of command are ready, leaning against the armchair.

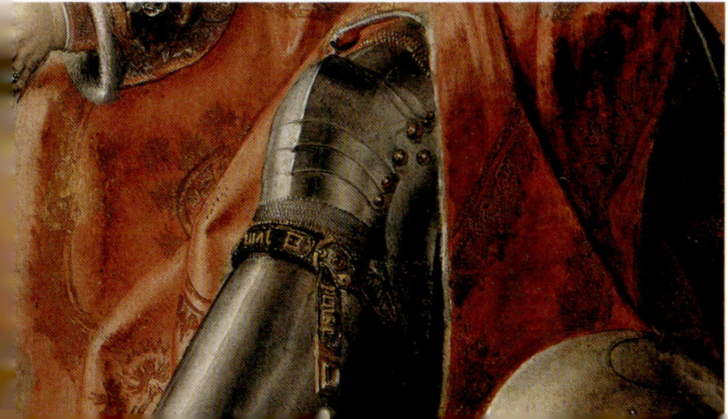

◀ The duchy of Urbino occupied a small, hilly territory between Romagna and the Marche region, near the Adriatic Sea. To offset the marginality of his domain, Federico invited intellectuals and artists from various areas to his palace, and he himself cultivated the air of a nobleman with a great openness to the larger world beyond. On his left leg, he displays the Order of the Garter which he received from the King of England.

Culture

Melozzo da Forlì
Pope Sixtus IV Appoints Bartolomeo Platina Prefect of the Vatican Library
1477

Fresco, detached and transferred to canvas, 370 × 315 cm
Vatican City, Rome, Musei Vaticani

Melozzo da Forlì

(Melozzo di Giuliano degli Ambrogi)
Forlì, 1438–94

The loss of many documented works poses an obstacle to our knowledge of one of the earliest and most sensitive interpreters of Piero della Francesca's innovations. After spending his early years in his native city of Forlì, in 1469 Melozzo first went to Rome, after which he stayed for an extended period at the cultivated, cosmopolitan court in Urbino. In 1475, he returned to Rome and, as *pictor papalis* to Sixtus IV, decorated the Vatican Library. Of these frescoes, the commemoration scene survives (today in the Vatican Museums). For Giuliano della Rovere, the future Pope Julius II, he frescoed the apse of the basilica of the Santi Apostoli with *Christ the Redeemer in a Concert of Angels*. Several remaining fragments of the composition, which were removed when the church was restyled in the Baroque era, are at the Quirinale and the Vatican Museums. Around 1484, assisted by an efficient workshop, Melozzo frescoed the chapel of the Tessoro in the sanctuary of Loreto, his last important surviving work. Forlì's subsequent work in Rome and Ancona has all been lost.

This imposing scene formerly greeted visitors at the entrance to the Vatican Library, designed as a model humanistic library and headed by one of the most celebrated men of letters of the period. In the Middle Ages, libraries were most often connected to monasteries and religious institutions, but by the 15th century a growing number of book collections belonged to aristocratic courts, individual intellectuals and bibliophiles. The printing press, introduced to Italy in the late 15th century by German immigrants, gradually reduced the cost of books, and although monastic centres continued to produce hand-illuminated codices for the elite, the reading and book-buying public grew wider. Soon translations of Latin and Greek classics became available (indispensable for someone like Leonardo da Vinci, who had only a rudimentary knowledge of Latin) as well as inexpensive pocket editions.

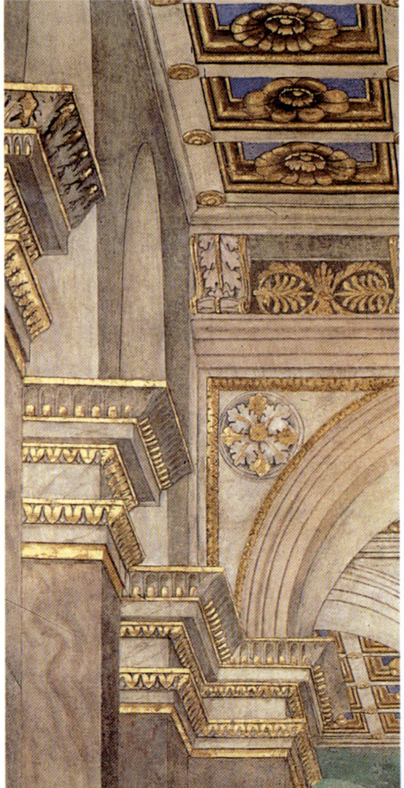

◄ The setting, with a coffered blue and gold ceiling, is an idealized architecture in perspective, based on the example of Alberti. Its clarity, classicism and nobility are an obvious reflection of the 'enlightenment' that the library could provide.

► Kneeling in profile, the humanist Bartolomeo Sacchi, known as Il Platina, is vested by the pope with the responsibility of directing the new Vatican Library. Attending the ceremony are the laymen Giovanni della Rovere, Girolamo Riario and, beside them, Cardinal Raffaele Riario and Cardinal Giuliano della Rovere – all members of the pope's family

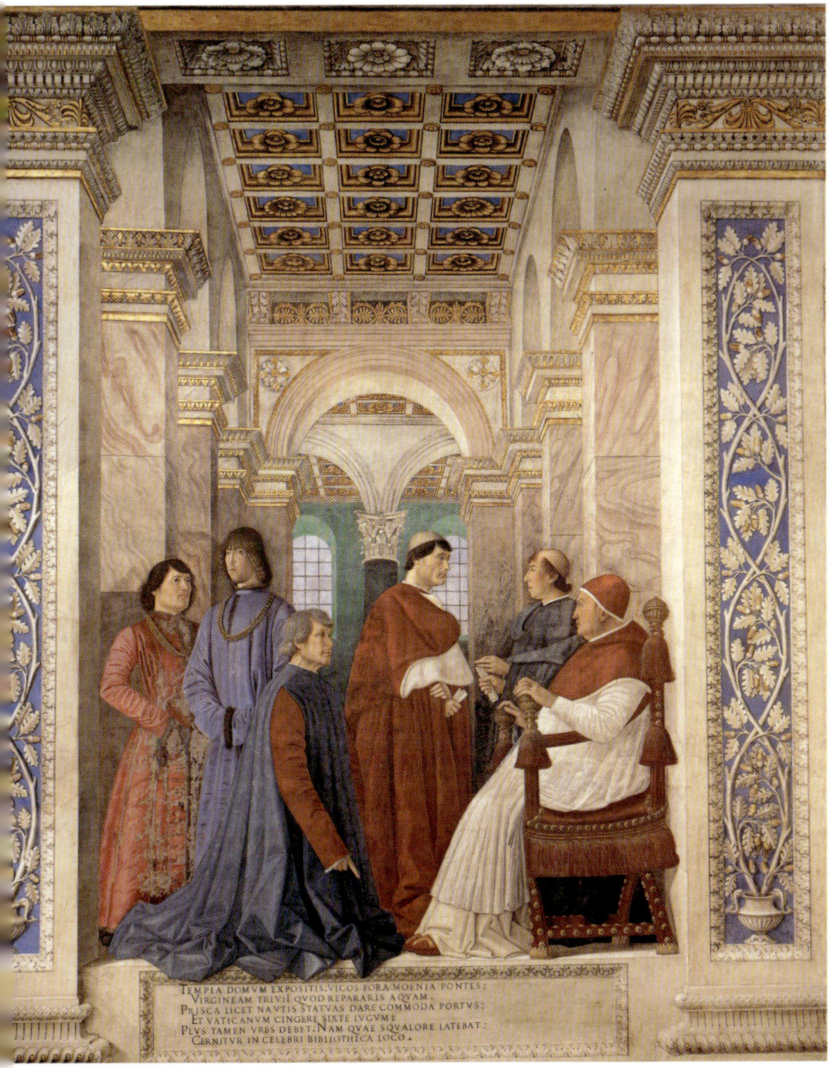

◄ Only one panel from Melozzo's frescoes for the library has survived, but fortunately it is the one that celebrates the founding. The Vatican Library was rebuilt in new quarters in the late 16th century, curiously, at the bidding of a pope who had assumed the name of his 15th-century predecessor – Sixtus V.

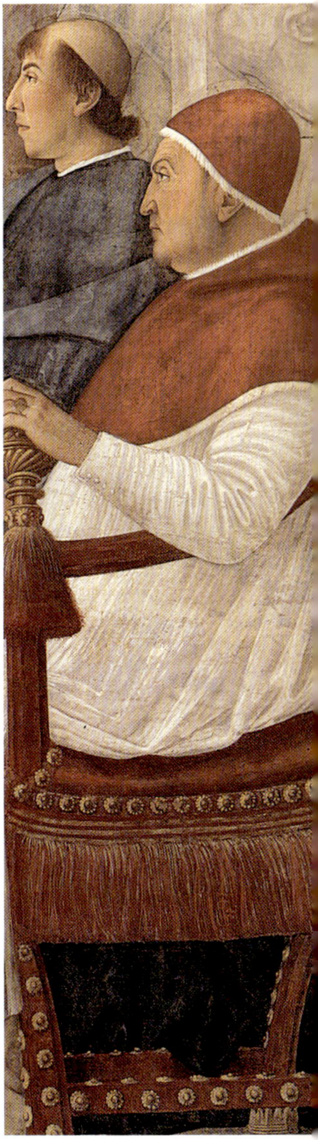

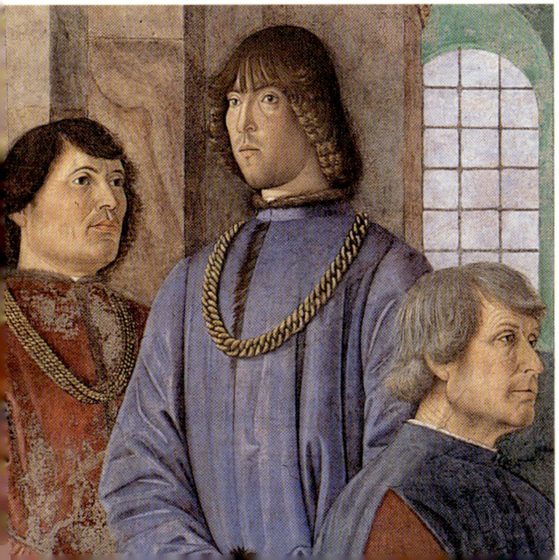

► The initiatives of Sixtus IV (pope from 1471 to 1484) were critical in making Rome the definitive centre of Renaissance art and culture. One of the first measures he provided for was a spacious library to be headed by celebrated humanists. The painted decoration was done by Melozzo da Forlì.

Foreshortening

Andrea Mantegna
The Dead Christ
c. 1480

Tempera on canvas, 66 × 81 cm
Milan, Pinacoteca di Brera

For artist biography, see page 76.

As discussed earlier, the Venetian Andrea Mantegna was among the boldest innovators in the use of perspective, especially during his long period of activity in Mantua for the Gonzagas. He was at his most daring just as Florentine painters were beginning to rely on well-established formulas. One of Mantegna's most famous and to a certain extent mysterious works is *The Dead Christ.* The lifeless figure of the crucified Christ, ready for the tomb, is presented from an unusual viewpoint, aggressively distorted. It is quite likely that the canvas was meant to be seen not from straight on, but from below.

► The gloomy, half-lit setting intensifies Christ's pallor. Mantegna's chromatic range is limited to a few tones based on grey and pink.

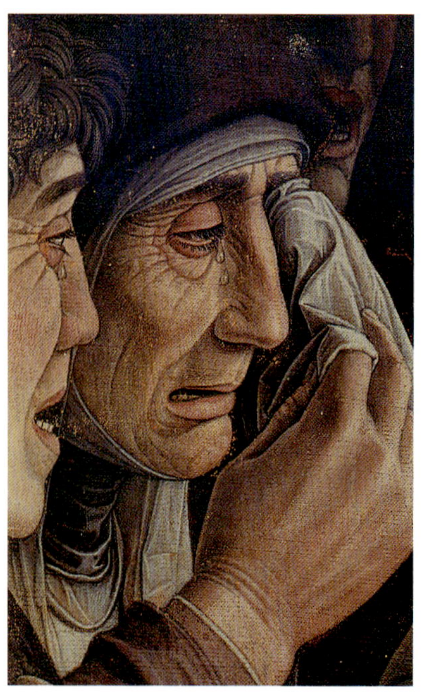

◄ At the left, with features so contracted and distorted in grief that they resemble tragic Greek masks, are Mary, St John and a third figure, perhaps Mary Magdalene, whose face can be only partially seen.

► In the foreground, Mantegna presents a detail not previously seen in painting – the soles of Christ's feet. The wounds from the nails are clean and dry.

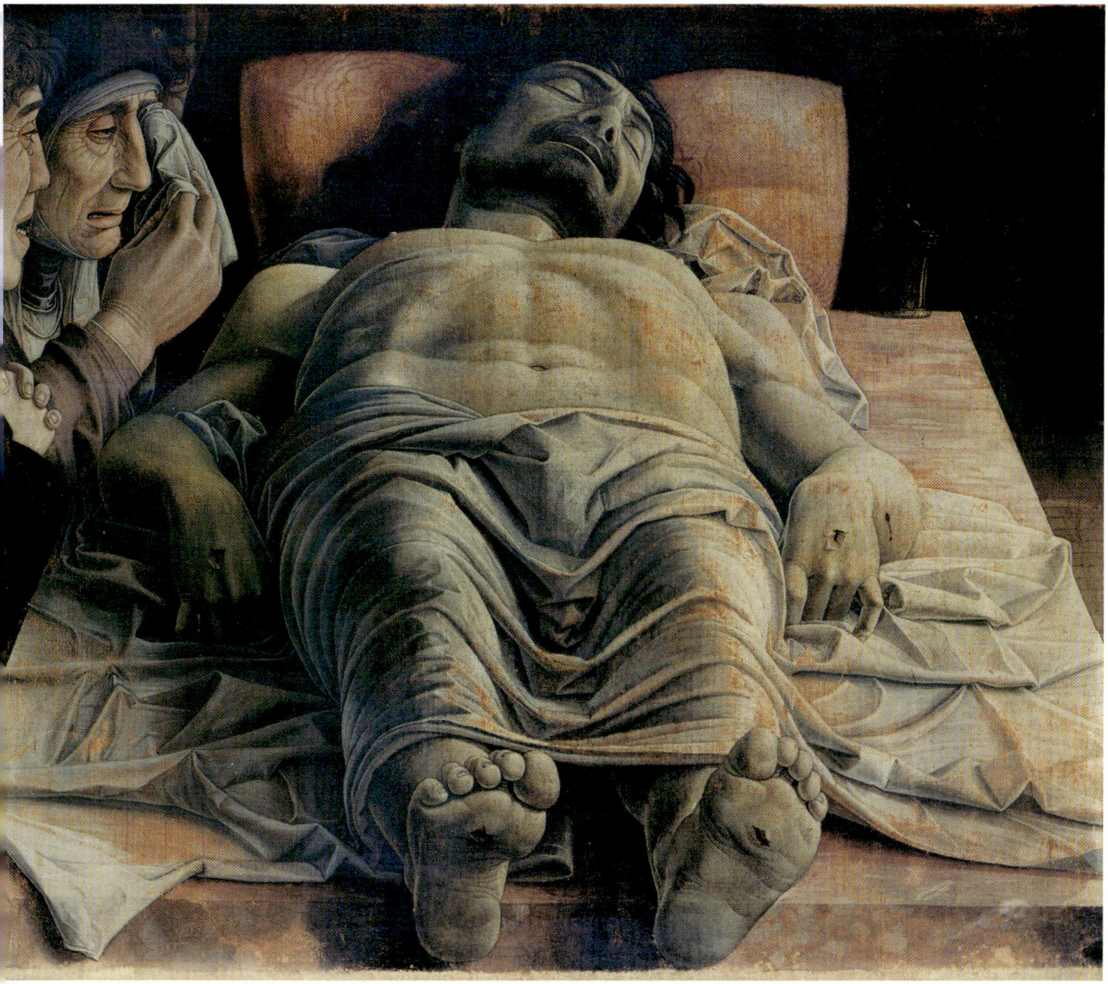

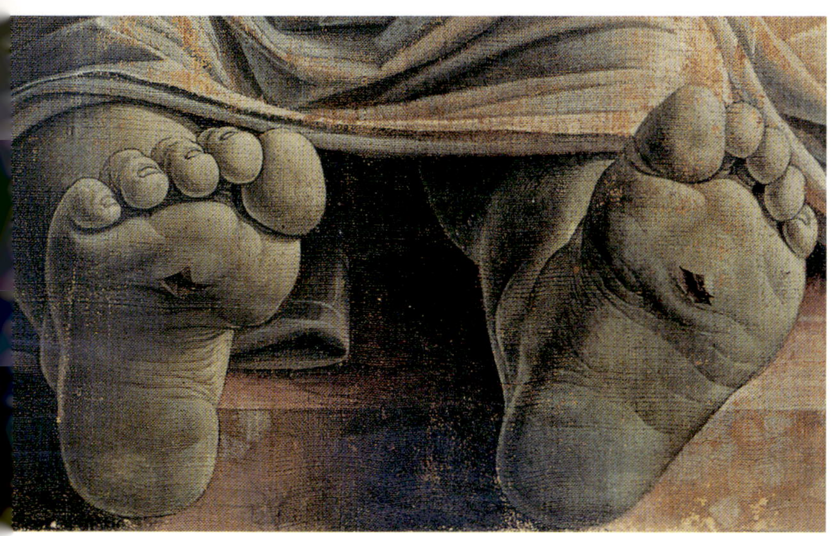

▲ Scholarly opinion is
divided as to the date and
original purpose of this
painting, which is probably
the 'Foreshortened Christ'
listed in the inventory drawn
up by the painter's son at
his father's death. According
to one intriguing hypothesis,
Mantegna painted this
dramatic, experimental canvas
for the lower part of his own
funerary monument in the
Mantuan church of
Sant'Andrea.

Ideal City

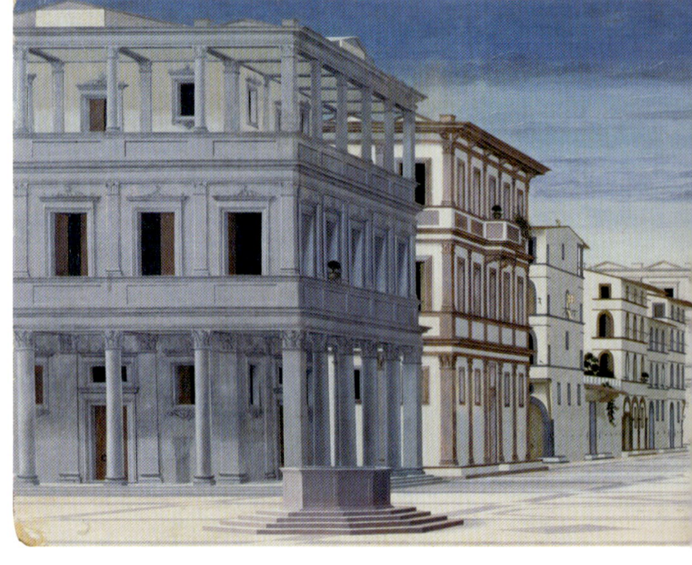

One of the dreams of humanist intellectuals was the creation of an 'ideal city', an urban framework patterned according to man's physical and moral requirements that eloquently expressed a clear, peaceful and harmonious vision of the world and society. Very few projects of this nature were actually carried out during the 15th century. The most important are the small town of Pienza, near Siena, designed by Bernardo Rossellino for Pope Pius II, and the exemplary urban development of Ferrara designed by Biagio Rossetti for Duke Ercole I d'Este. Some fascinating painted utopias, the fruit of the sophisticated court of Urbino have also survived. Among the many unrealized plans for new cities, the most interesting are the projects designed by Filarete and Leonardo da Vinci for the dukes of Milan.

▼ The regularity of the layout of dense, urban spaces does not preclude variety in the height and features of individual buildings. By today's standards, the 'ideal city' of the 15th century provided for very few green spaces, though potted plants on the balconies add a hint of nature.

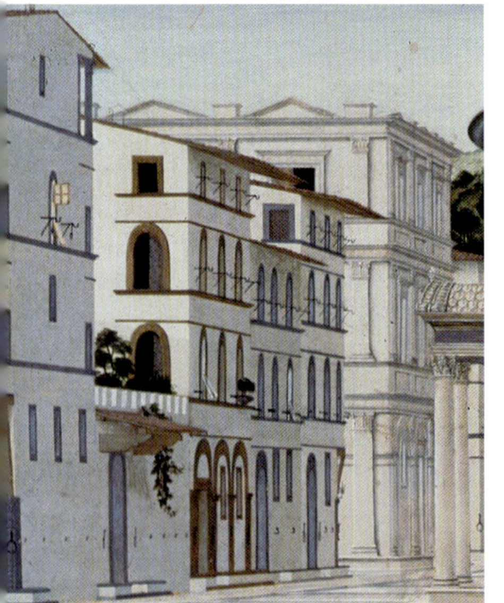

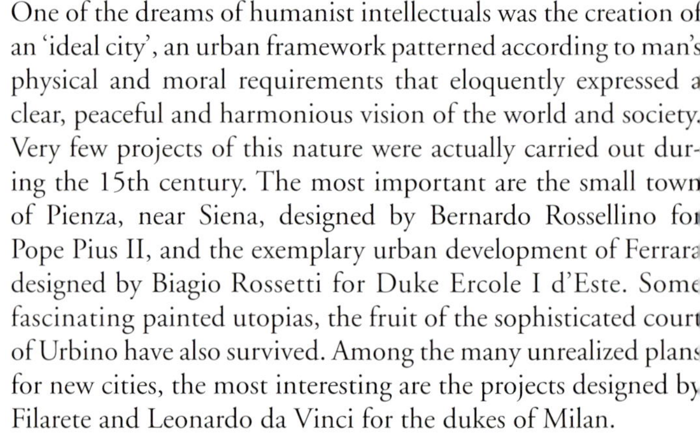

► The large circular building in the centre of the composition is probably not a house of worship but a civic structure (the façade of a church appears at the back of the square, to the right). Surrounded by a Corinthian colonnade, it has marble cladding perfectly attuned to the austere aesthetic of the square. Close adherence to the concepts of Alberti suggests that the great architect may have directly inspired, if not actually executed, this painting.

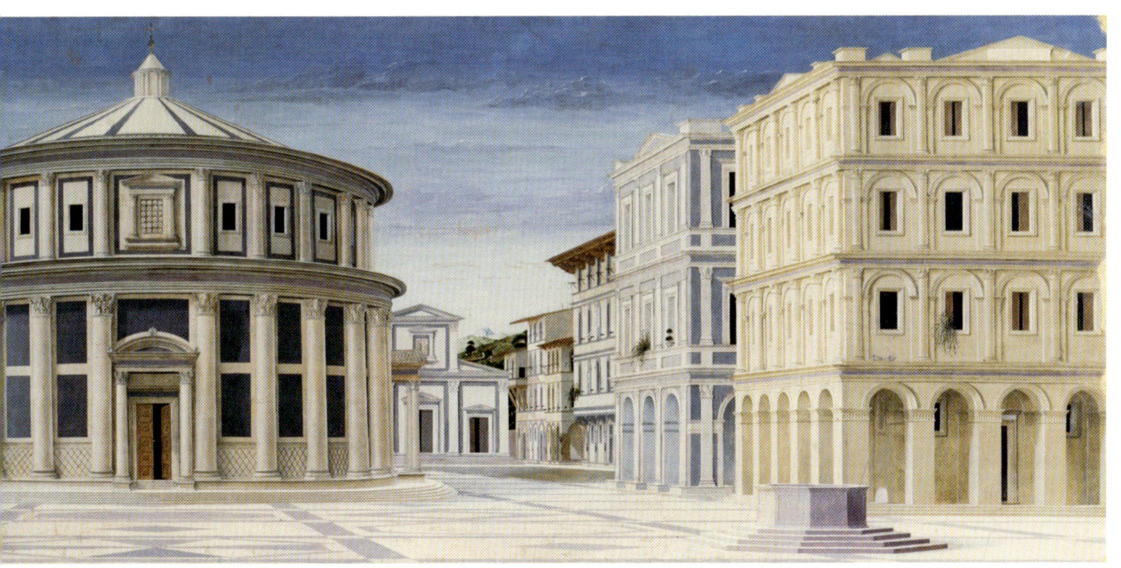

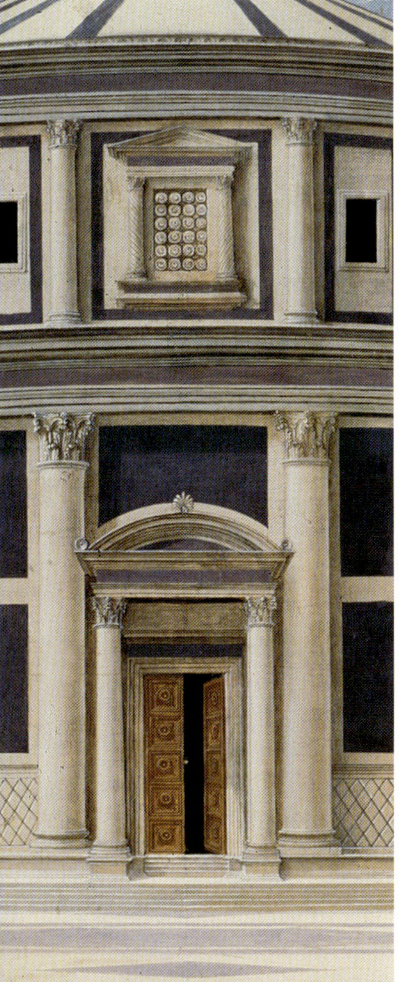

▲ The panel in Urbino is part of a cycle that includes two other similar urban views, today in Berlin and Baltimore. It is believed that the three panels, painted on poplar wood, were originally designed to be inserted into the backs of furniture or in the wainscoting of a room in the ducal palace of Urbino. None of the three panels contains figures.

▼ Two octagonal fixtures (the plinths of monuments or, more likely, wells) are set symmetrically in the square, paved in a linear, geometric pattern. The faceted surface of the octagons clearly indicates the direction of the light.

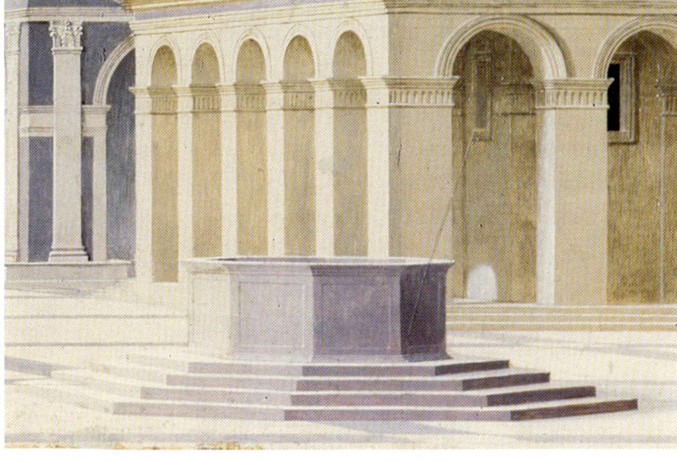

Archaeology

Andrea Mantegna
St Sebastian
1480

Tempera on canvas, 275 × 142 cm

Paris, Musée du Louvre

For artist biography, see page 76.

A characteristic passion of the humanists was the study of classical Antiquity. Of course, imposing Roman ruins could be seen in many parts of Italy, but apart from a handful of admiring experts, no organized field of archaeological study, conservation or protection existed. This would change in the early decades of the 16th century, but until then excavations and the collection of ancient fragments were anything but systematic. Even so, to demonstrate a direct awareness of classical sculpture was a form of intellectual distinction. Andrea Mantegna was typical in this regard. He had long desired to make a study trip to Rome, he signed his name in ancient Greek characters, and several of his works contain reproductions of headstones, sculptural fragments and elements of classical architecture.

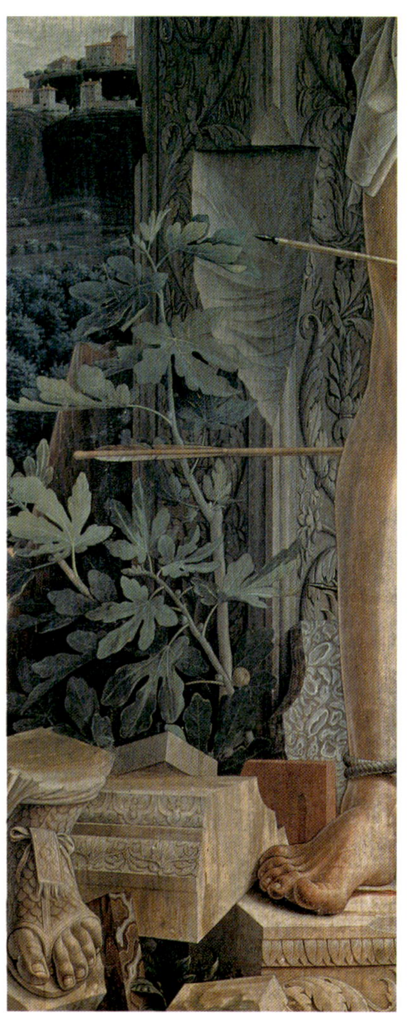

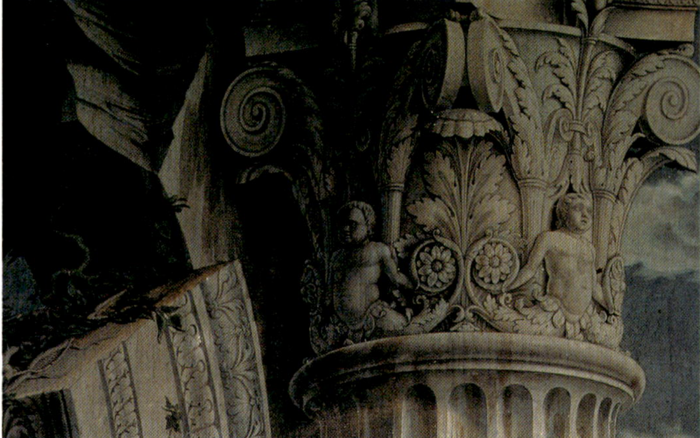

◄ Against a background of classical ruins, Mantegna juxtaposes the saint's right foot with a fragment of a marble sculpture, as if to draw attention to the ancient sculptors' perfect reproduction of nature.

▲ The fascinating jumble of architectural remains and stone vestiges surrounding St Sebastian expresses both beauty and precariousness. An enthusiastic student and collector of ancient sculpture, Mantegna bemoaned the lack of a systematic, rational approach to the study and preservation of archaeological sites.

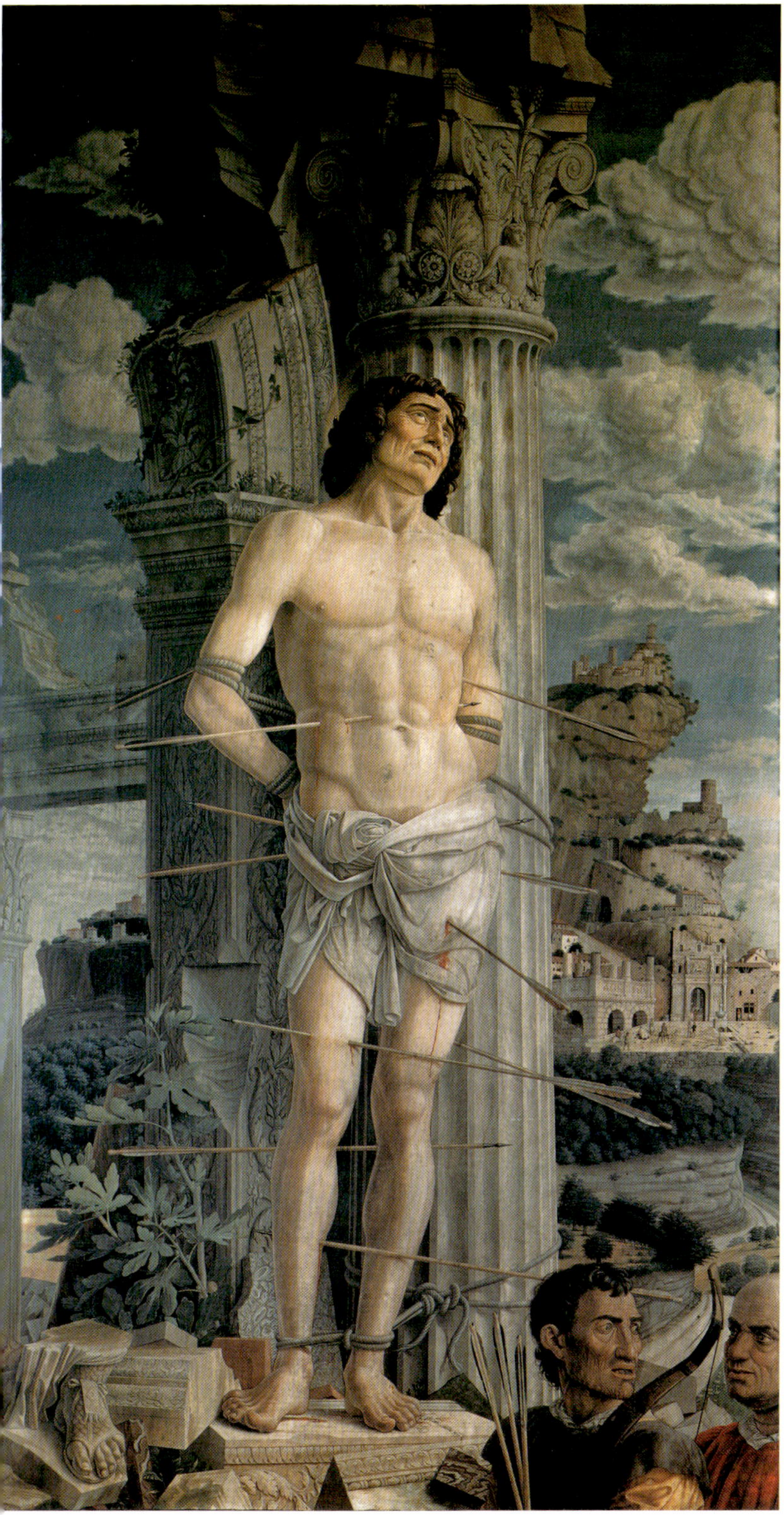

▼ It is difficult to say whether
the buildings of the city in the
background are grandiose
ancient ruins or incomplete
contemporary constructions.
Mantegna probably intended
to suggest a possible continuity
between past and present.

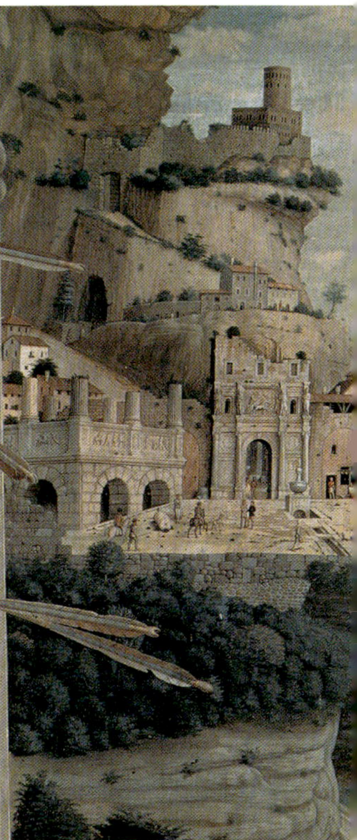

Spatial Depth

Pietro Perugino
The Delivery of the Keys
Detail from the *Story of Christ*
1481–2

Fresco, 335 × 540 cm

Vatican City, Musei Vaticani,
Sistine Chapel

For artist biography, see page 152.

Just when painters in the Veneto region were beginning to open the backgrounds of their paintings to landscape and atmosphere, central Italian masters were creating vast architectural spaces based on central linear perspective. This fresco shows Christ instituting the office of the papacy by giving the keys to St Peter – the most symbolically charged theme in the Sistine Chapel, where the election of the pope is held. Pietro Perugino, born in Umbria but closely linked to the Florentine milieu, sets the perfectly symmetrical scene in an immense paved square, with a domed church in the centre flanked by two triumphal arches that are accurately based on classical ruins.

The Walls of the Sistine Chapel, a Collective Affirmation of the Florentine School

In 1481, Pope Sixtus IV called the best painters working in Florence to Rome to fresco the Sistine Chapel, which had just been built at the centre of the architectural complex at the Vatican. The decoration of this chapel, the setting for the most solemn papal ceremonies, was to include a series of scenes on the life of Moses and the life of Christ (to juxtapose episodes from the Old and New Testaments), and, above these, portraits of the popes. To make the cycle balanced and harmonious, the painters were to adhere to common rules of proportion and colour – but the various masters' styles nonetheless remain easily recognizable. Perugino and Botticelli were the main figures in a group that also included Ghirlandaio, Cosimo Rosselli and Luca Signorelli (and conspicuously excluded the 30-year-old Leonardo). Each artist had his own group of assistants and collaborators so they could all work simultaneously and drastically reduce execution time. The Sistine Chapel wall frescoes are historically significant: they signal the collective triumph of the Florentine school in the age of Lorenzo the Magnificent, inaugurate the stupendous period of the High Renaissance at the papal court, and mark the distinctions between Leonardo and his Tuscan colleagues.

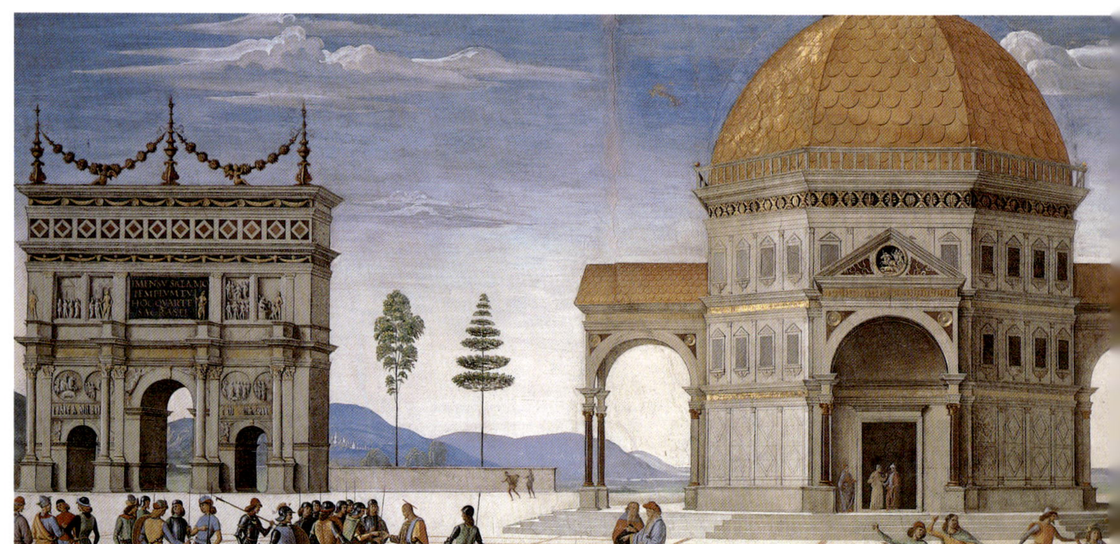

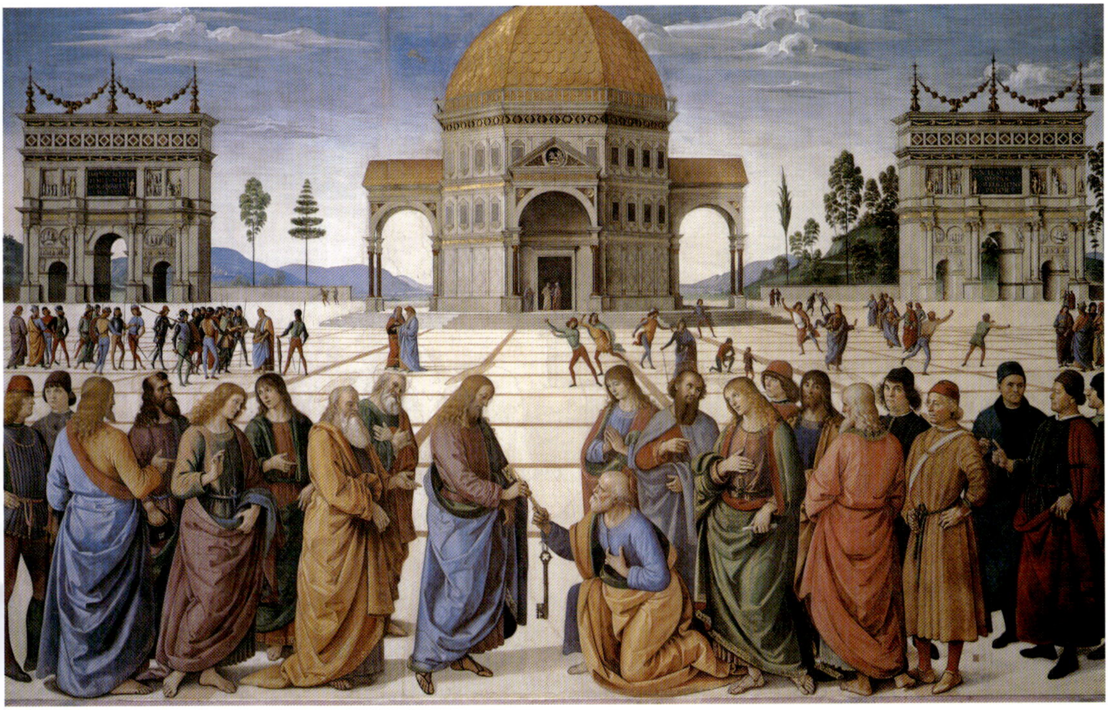

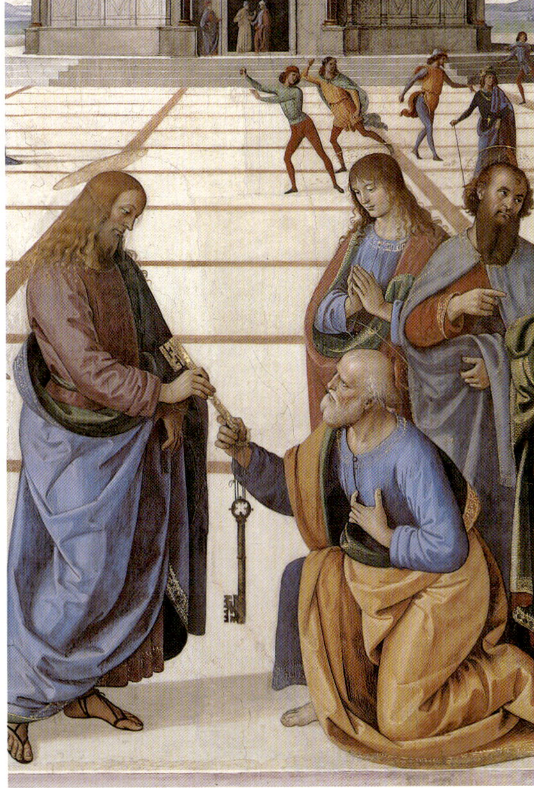

▼ The Temple of Jerusalem, depicted as an example of the late 15th-century exploration of centrally planned architecture, dominates the vast urban esplanade, framed between two classical triumphal arches. The buildings symbolize the continuity of Christianity with its Jewish and Greco-Roman roots.

► This scene was conceived as a synthesis of the message of the entire cycle, which aimed to celebrate the historical function of the Church and the supremacy of the pope using the stories of Christ and Moses. Throughout the chapel, the frescoes are rife with complex references and allusions to current times and even include contemporary figures.

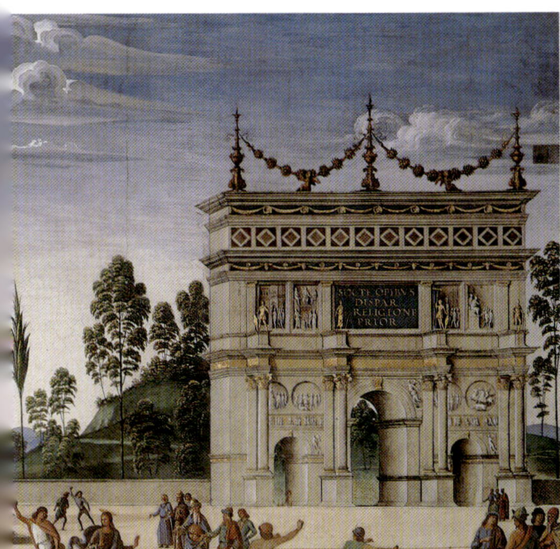

Grace

Sandro Botticelli
Spring (Primavera)
c. 1482

Tempera on panel, 203 × 314 cm
Florence, Galleria degli Uffizi

For artist biography, see page 102.

The term 'grace' as used (frequently) by Renaissance writers refers to two things: an overall physical quality (not just beauty but also harmonious gestures, natural movements, even spontaneous accord between dress and hairstyle) and social attribute (good manners and pleasant, well-informed conversation that is never forced or affected). A well-known personification of these qualities from classical mythology and Hellenistic sculpture is the group of Graces, three smiling maidens who join hands. Botticelli, interpreter of the aesthetic and moral ideals of the Medici's Florence, included a memorable version of the Three Graces in the largest and most complicated of his classical allegories: the same 'grace' that was required of young women was also a highly desirable quality in painting.

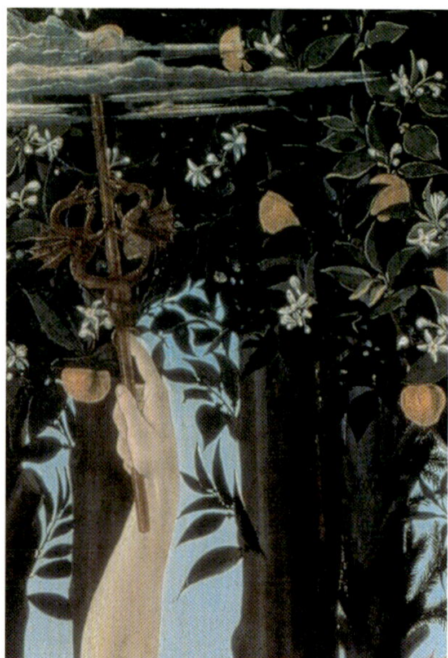

▲ At the far left, the god Mercury clears the sky of clouds with his symbol, the caduceus, a rod with two intertwined serpents. The complicated allegory, which has never been completely unravelled, was apparently addressed to a young and promising scion of the Medici family for didactic purposes.

▼ Although Botticelli borrowed the motif of the Three Graces from Hellenistic culture, he freely reworked it, capturing the three young women in elegant, dance-like movement. Each detail, from hairstyles to veils, from laced fingers to gazes, speaks of grace, elegance and harmony.

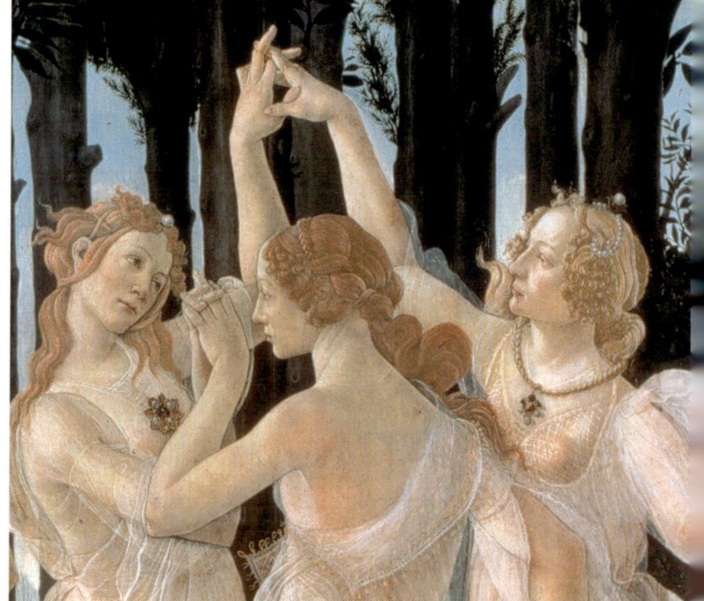

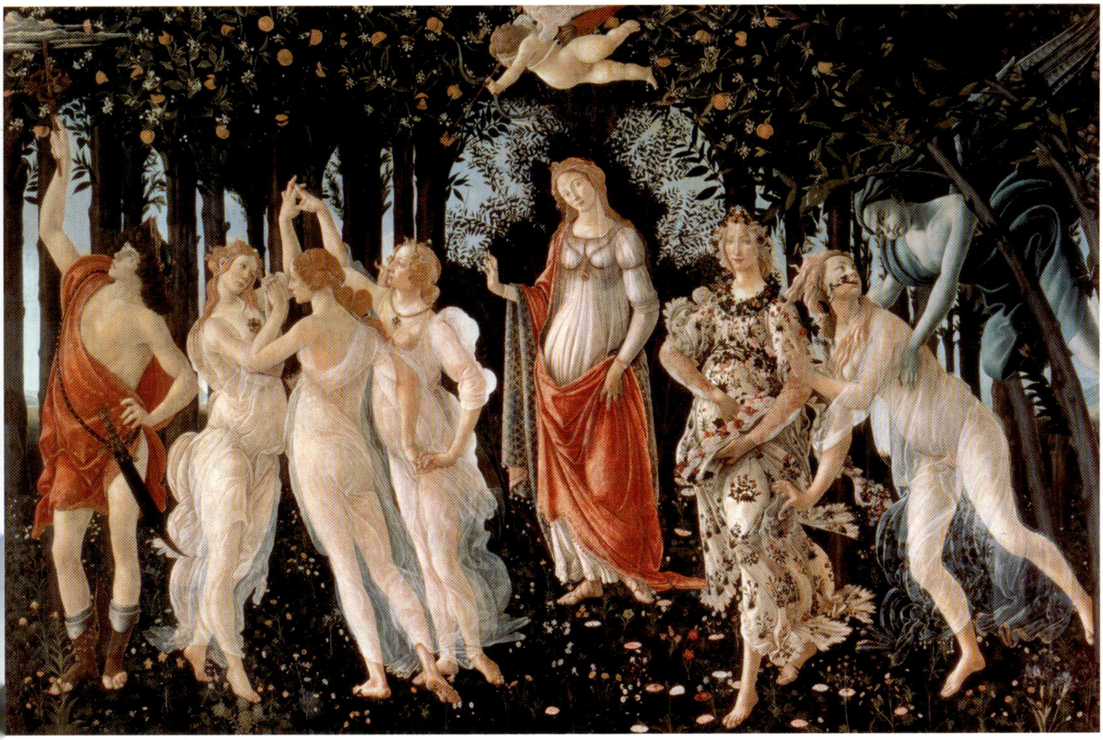

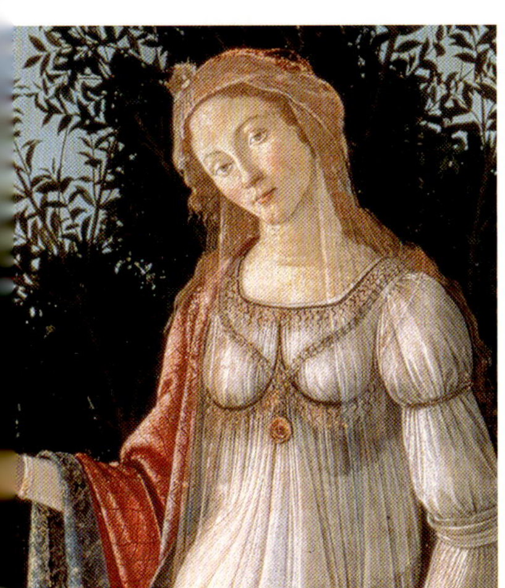

▲ The luminous figure of Venus is the lynchpin of the composition. With a welcoming gesture, the goddess stands out against a dense, dark green bush, which reaches towards the bright sky. According to the most widely shared opinion, Venus symbolizes virtue, around which harmony reigns.

▼ The impetuous Zephyr pursues his betrothed, Chloris. As the spring breeze touches her, she is transformed into Flora and strews the world with flowers. Around 150 different botanical species may be counted in the painting, each observed with the thorough precision of a herbal.

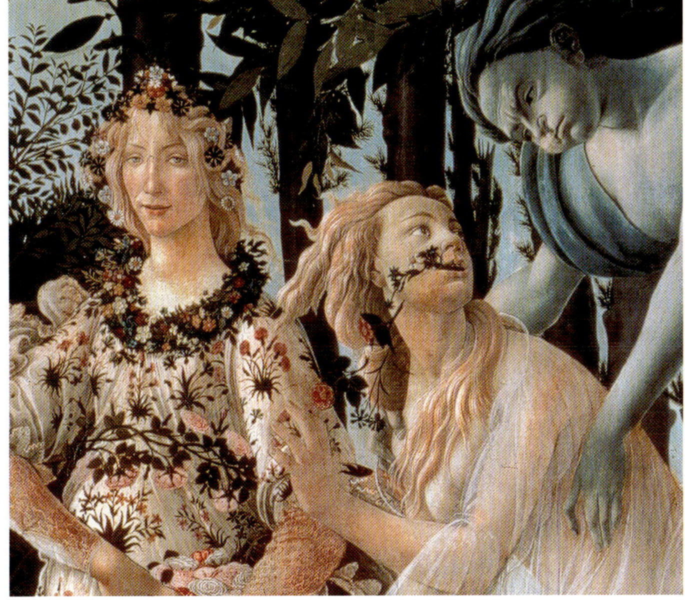

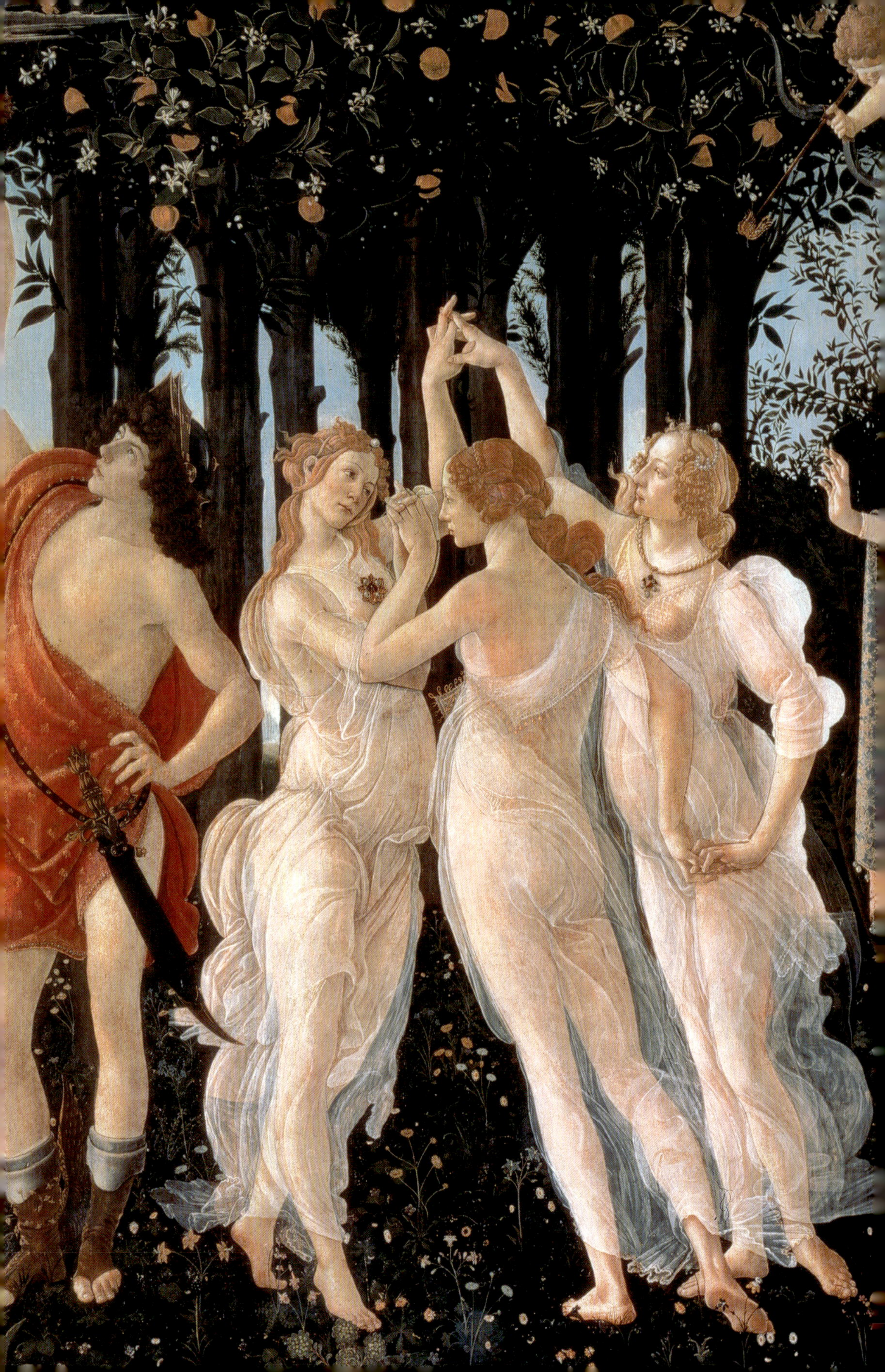

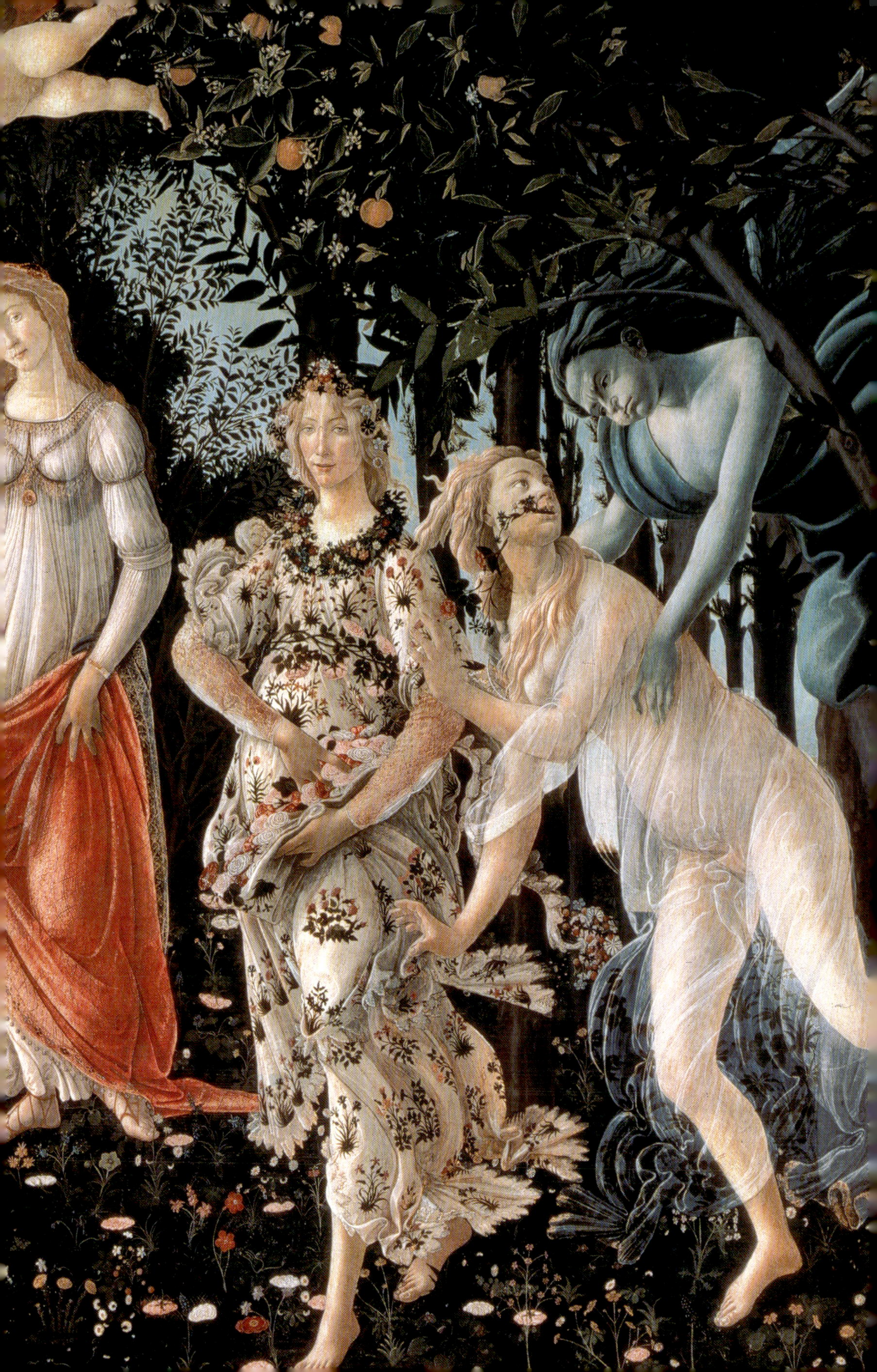

Symbolism

Sandro Botticelli
Pallas and the Centaur
c. 1482

Tempera on canvas, 207 × 148 cm
Florence, Galleria degli Uffizi

For artist biography, see page 102.

Some well-known Italian Renaissance works challenge even the most learned experts in the complexity of their symbolism and iconology. The fruit of an elitist, refined and even exclusive culture, these paintings harbour hidden meanings that contrast with the apparent significance of the figures and the symbols, and the immediate splendour of the image. Hidden in the works of the leading figures of the High Renaissance, from Botticelli to Giorgione, Mantegna to Raphael, Leonardo to Perugino, are symbols and references that we struggle to grasp today. Without specific documents – for example, a literary text or a contract from a patron – we must seek answers in other written sources from the period but seldom find a unanimously accepted interpretation. The subject of this painting is not drawn from ancient mythology and has no direct relationship to other works where Botticelli evidently celebrates the supremacy of intelligence over brute force. Here he presents a richer, more subtle web of intellectual, dynastic and political references connected with the history and culture of Florence in the time of the Medici.

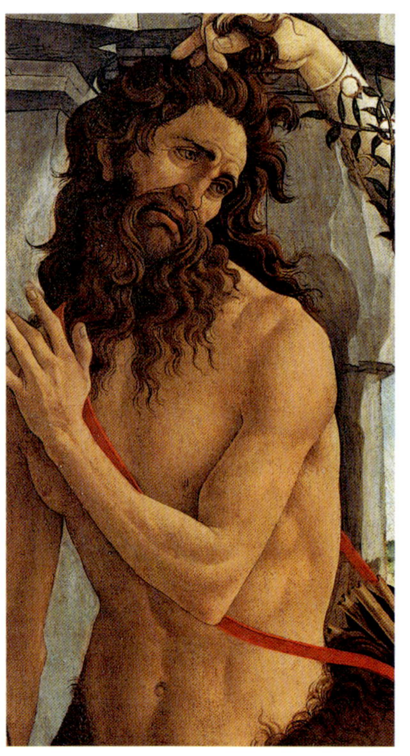

◄ With a gentle but firm hand, Pallas Athena holds a centaur by the hair; the mythical being, half man and half horse, is tamed by the goddess of wisdom. During the Renaissance, the small but refined Republic of Florence enjoyed seeing itself in figures that had managed to overcome powerful, threatening enemies through courage and intelligence – like David, who defeated Goliath, and Judith, who seduced and beheaded Holofernes.

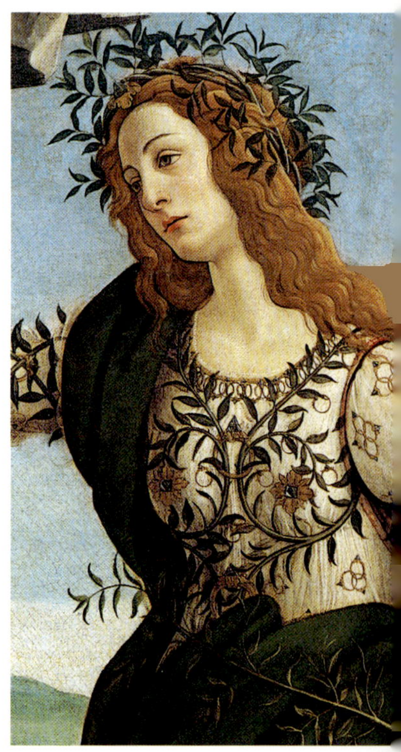

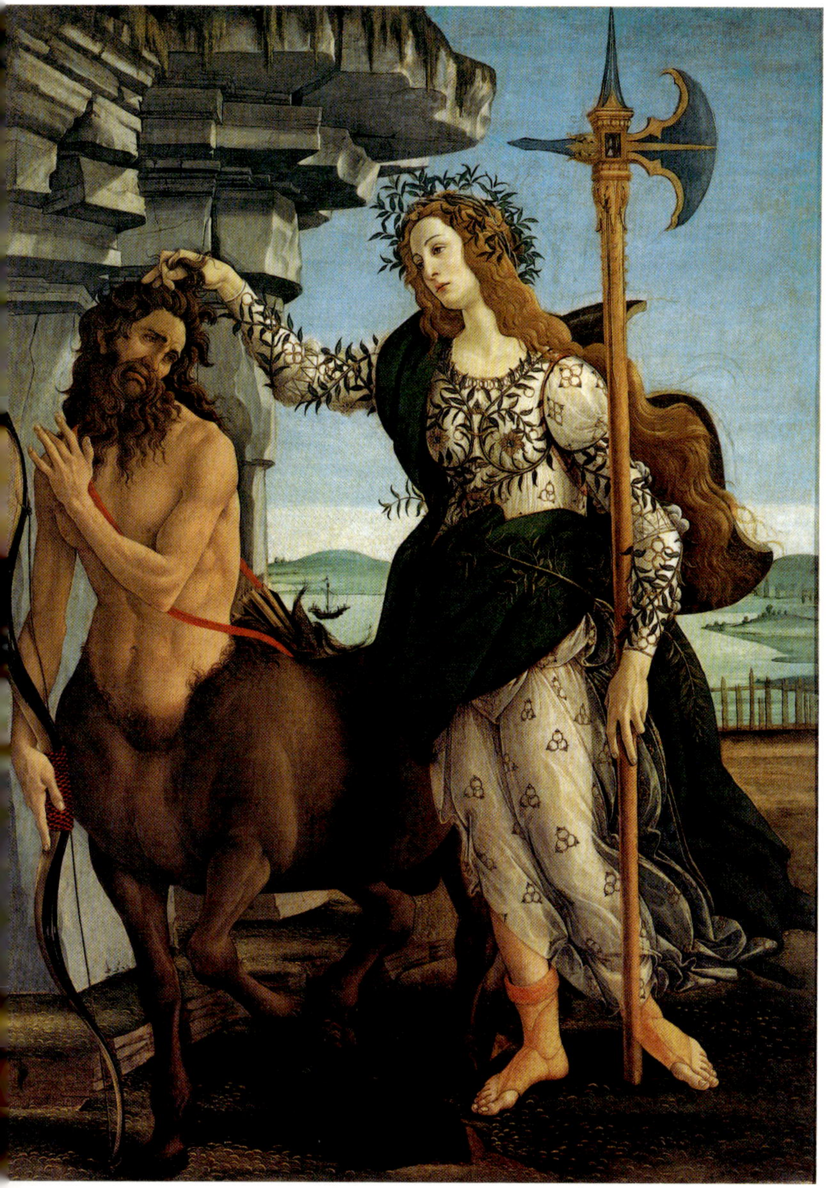

◄ Pallas Athena is the goddess of learning and
culture. On her head and breast, she wears
laurel branches, a reference to poetry but also
a tribute to Lorenzo the Magnificent. The exact
interpretation of the individual subjects is
still open to debate. However, the painting's
symbolic meaning is obvious: the harmony
of man and the world brought about by the
victory of reason, intelligence and beauty over
animal savagery and arms. This sums up the
entire programme of Italian humanism, even
if it was often thwarted by the rivalry of the
minor states that carved up the territory.

► The motif of three
intertwined rings is a nod
to the heraldry of the Medici.
Executed for the Medici's
villa at Castello under the
supervision of the philosopher
Marsilio Ficino, the cycle
was intended for the young
Lorenzo de Pierfrancesco
de' Medici, a cousin of
Lorenzo the Magnificent.

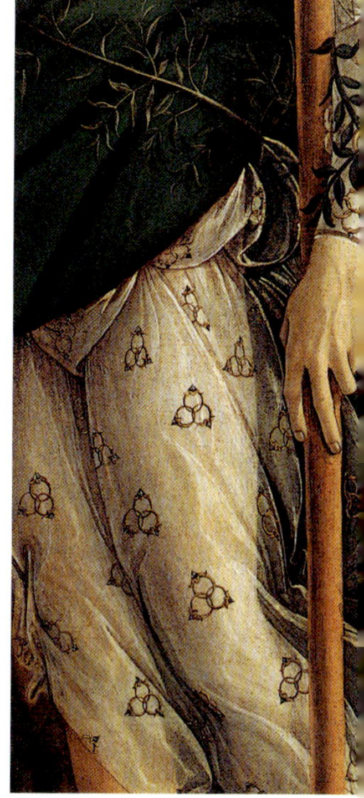

Replicas

► **Leonardo da Vinci**
The Virgin of the Rocks
1483–4

Oil on panel transferred to canvas,
199 × 122 cm

Paris, Musée du Louvre

► ► **Leonardo and the De Predis brothers**
The Virgin of the Rocks
1503

Oil on panel, 189.5 × 120 cm

London, National Gallery

Leonardo da Vinci

Vinci, Florence, 1452–Cloux, Amboise,
1519

The 'universal genius' *par excellence*,
active in many scientific and artistic
fields, Leonardo followed an intellectual
path in painting that created a new
picture of the world, man and nature,
based on the serene certainties of
15th-century humanism. Trained in
Florence, in the workshop of Andrea
del Verrocchio, Leonardo learned
various artistic techniques, all founded
upon drawing. From the outset, he
demonstrated a predisposition for
portraits and the careful observation of
nature. In 1482, he went to the court
of Duke Ludovico il Moro in Milan, where
he spent much of his career. His interest
in the natural sciences and technology
spilled over into painting, and he filled
notebooks with annotations and sketches
(the 'Codices'). *The Virgin of the Rocks*
(begun in 1483) and *The Last Supper*
at the church of Santa Maria delle Grazie
(1494–8) date from his first period
in Milan. Leonardo fled the city when
French troops invaded, passing through
Mantua and Venice on his return to
Florence. Back in his native city, he met
Michelangelo and the young Raphael,
painted the *Mona Lisa* and continued the
technological, geographical and scientific
investigations he had begun in Milan.
In 1506, he returned to Lombardy and
completed the *Virgin with St Anne*, today
at the Louvre. In 1513, he accepted the
invitation of Francis I to settle in France,
taking with him some paintings as well
as his thousands of pages of notes
and drawings.

Some artistic genres, for example medals and prints, are based upon the production of multiple 'originals'. Similarly, 15th-century artisans used moulds to produce series of terracotta reliefs. They would then 'personalize' the reliefs with colours gilding and various additions. Creating multiple 'originals' o paintings obviously required a different process. In time a distinction emerged between a 'copy' (more or less faithful to the original) and a 'replica' (often with some variations, executed directly by the same artist or under his supervision in the workshop). This latter type of production became frequent in the 16th century when Titian, in particular, perfected it. An early example can be found in the two paintings of *The Virgin of th Rocks*. This altarpiece was commissioned by the church o San Francesco Grande, but for some reason the first version was never delivered. After much legal wrangling the second version was finally completed with the De Predis brothers and delivered to the church by 1507.

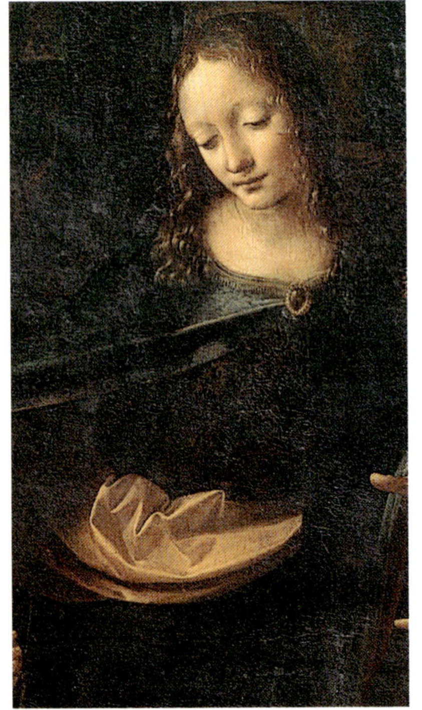

◄ The gazes and gestures between the figures of the group, linking them together, already show Leonardo's interest in the 'movements of the soul'. The first version is a fascinating example of Leonardo's delicate, blended touch. The painting (or more precisely the second version, which remained in Milan whi Leonardo apparently kept the first one with him) influenced the course of art in Lombard For decades, artists imitated the figures and proposed new ones, using a broad variety of forms and techniques. Thi represented a transition from 'replica' to 'copy'.

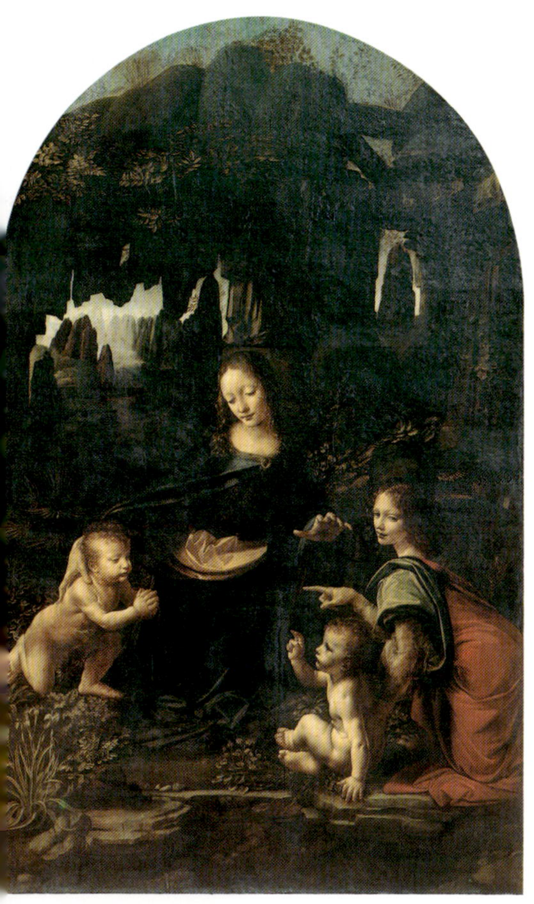

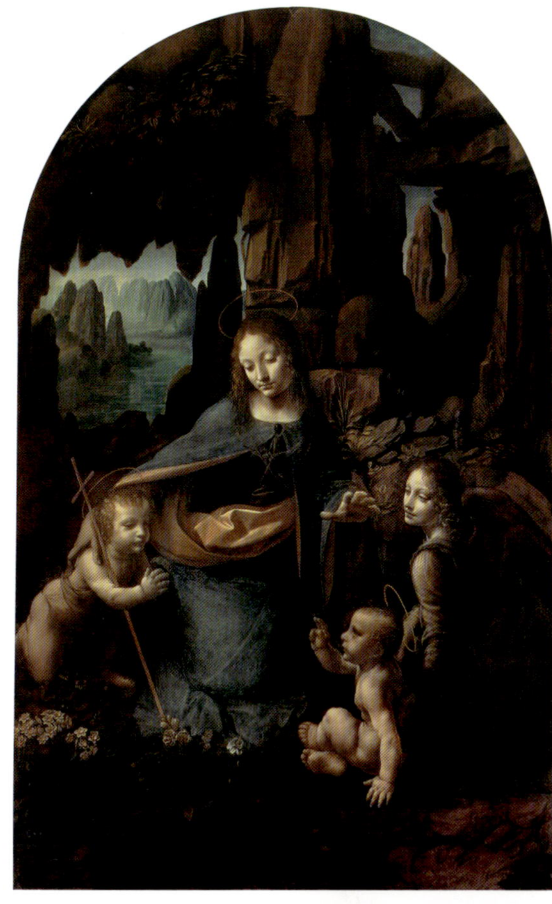

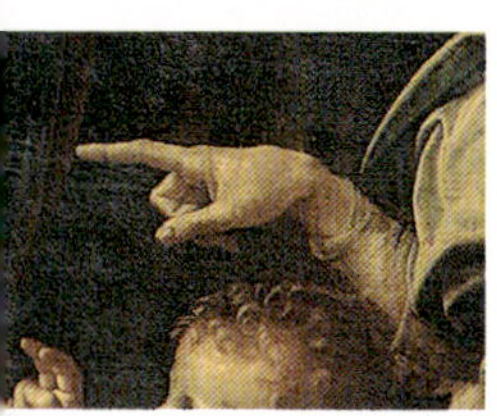

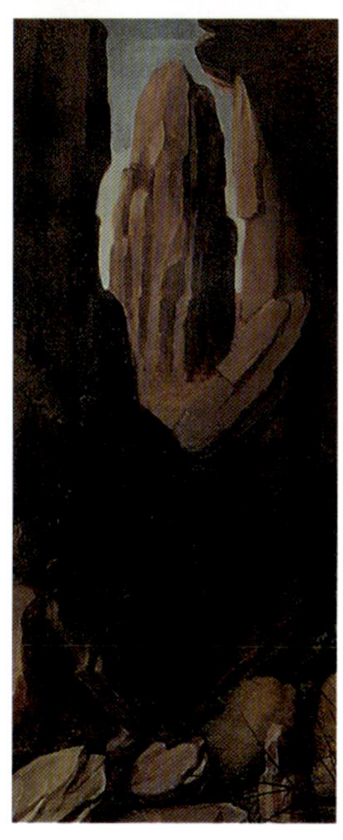

▲ *The Virgin of the Rocks* represents the meeting of St John the Baptist with the Infant Jesus, in the presence of Mary and an angel. The scene takes place among rocks in a damp cave, perhaps an allusion to the purity of Mother Earth's womb. Light filters through openings in the background, which reveal a typical Lombard landscape of lakes and mountains.

◄ The angel's index finger, which points towards Mary's lap, has disappeared completely in the second version.

▼ ► In the second version of the painting, the natural world (flowers, plants, stones) is defined with a cool, almost metallic clarity. The same incisiveness may be observed in the definition of the contours and features of the figures.

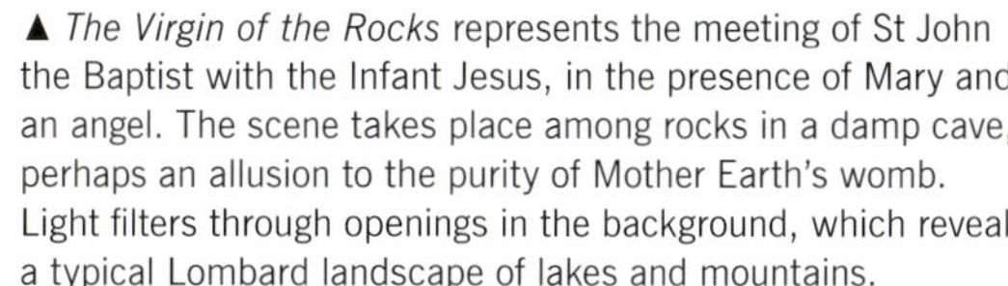

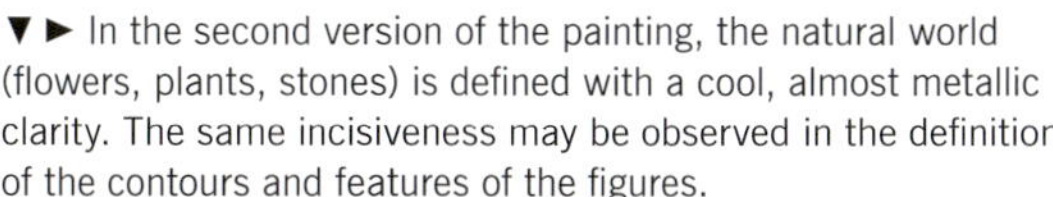

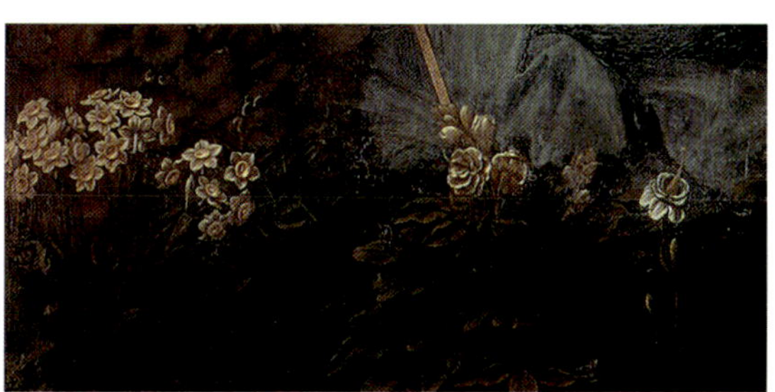

Neo-Platonism

Sandro Botticelli
The Birth of Venus
c. 1485

Tempera on canvas, 184.5 × 285.5 cm

Florence, Galleria degli Uffizi

For artist biography, see page 102.

The allegorical scenes produced by Botticelli for the Medici and their circle were the first Renaissance paintings in which scenes from classical mythology were represented on the large scale previously reserved for religious subjects. A female nude, such as Venus, was an extraordinary novelty previously only found in scenes of Adam and Eve. Not surprisingly, in the time of the severe moral reform preached by Fra Girolamo Savonarola after the death of Lorenzo the Magnificent, paintings of this type would be condemned as intolerably profane and lascivious. The openness to classical themes in late 15th-century art was related to Neo-Platonic philosophy, disseminated through contact with Byzantine intellectuals. A driving centre was the 'academy' founded in 1459 by Marsilio Ficino at the behest of Cosimo de' Medici in the villa at Careggi, at the gates of Florence. Renaissance Neo-Platonism proposed a humanistic Christian interpretation of the Platonic doctrines, in particular regarding human consciousness and the unity of spirit and intellect.

▼ In his writings, Ficino saw the mythological episode of Venus's birth out of the sea as a cosmogonic ideal, the poetic transposition of the divine origin of the world and the beauty of creation. Venus emerged, fully grown and perfect, from the sea. On a shell propelled by gentle breezes, she heads from Cythera to Cyprus, the two 'islands of love', as roses are scattered in the air.

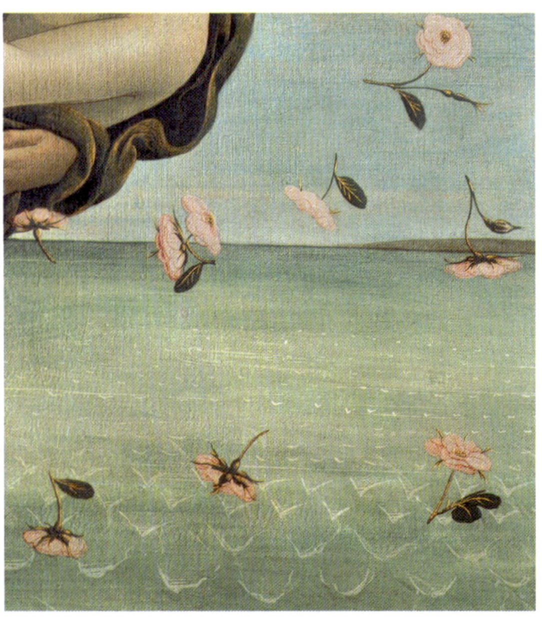

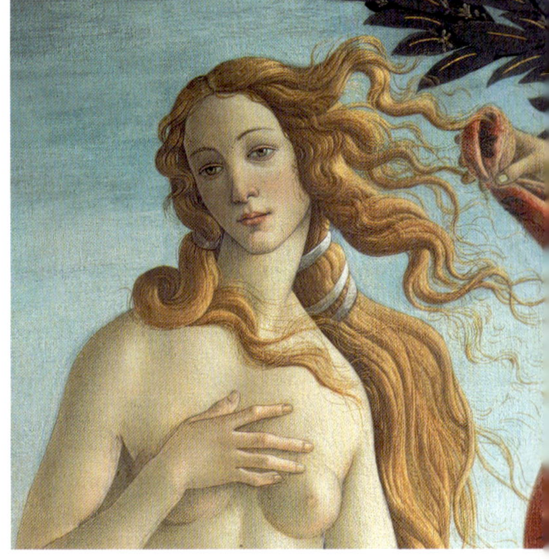

▲ According to Ficino, we should recognize the goddess Venus as the personification of *humanitas*, a combination of 'temperance and honesty, fascination and splendour'. Like *Spring* (see pages 124–5), this painting was probably executed for Lorenzo di Pierfrancesco de' Medici.

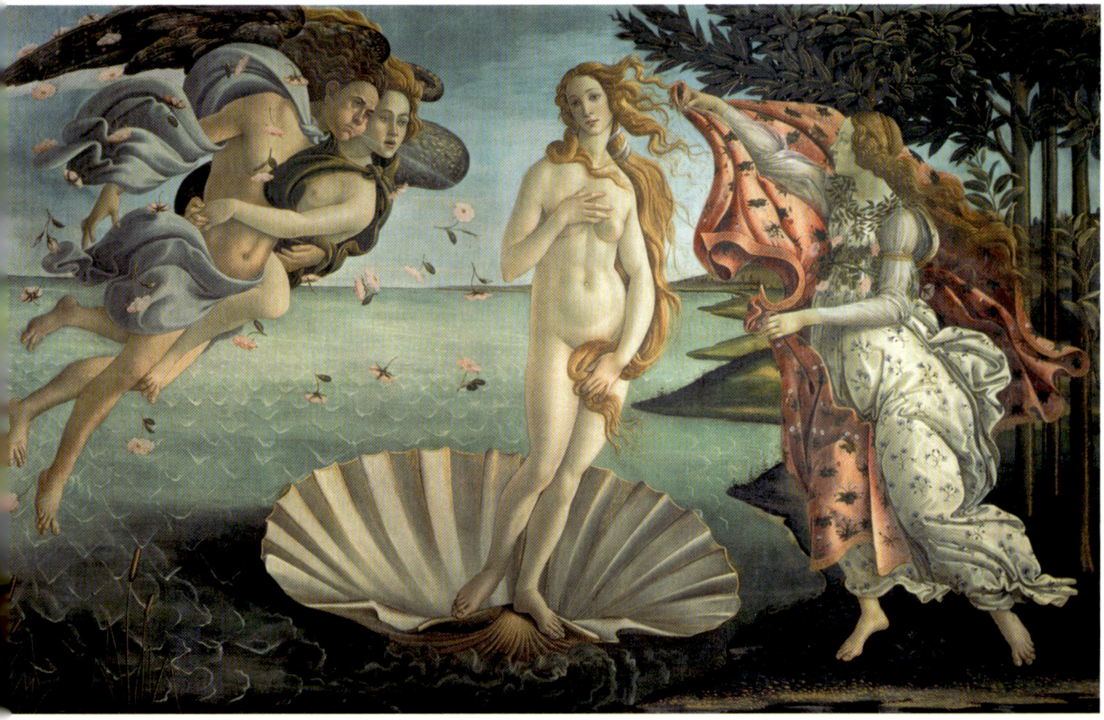

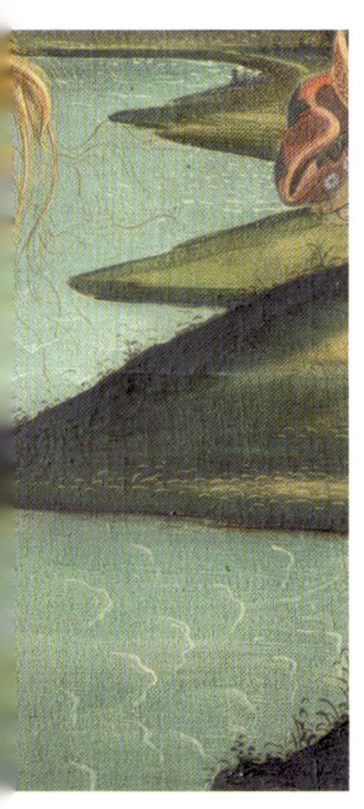

▲ The most influential
intellectual in 15th-century
Tuscany, Marsilio Ficino
(1433–99) was well versed
in Greco-Roman philosophy
and poetry. He proposed that
classical myths should be read
in a symbolic way in order
to recognize the moral and
spiritual continuity between
Plato and Christianity. Tutor to
the Medici family and a guiding
light of humanism, Ficino was
so convinced of the perfect
harmony between classical
culture and Christianity that
at the age of 40 he took vows
and was ordained a priest.

◄ The coastal seascape
of inlets and gulfs follows
a linear course, to which
perspective has been only
loosely applied.

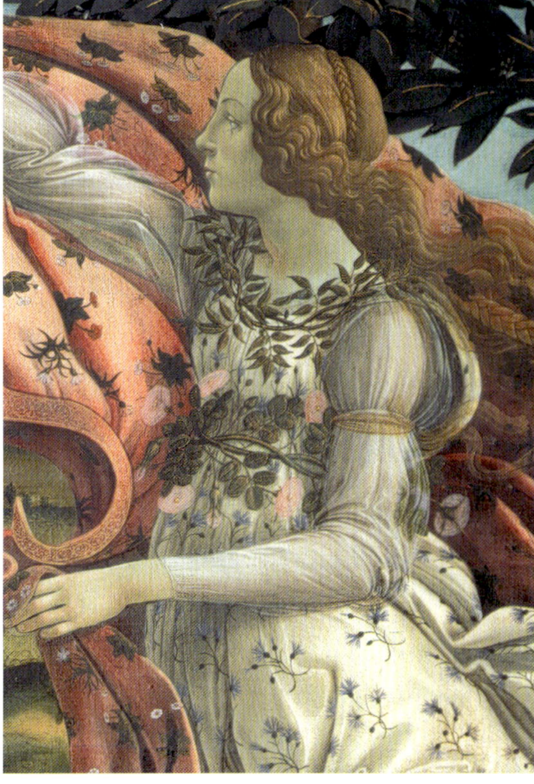

► A nymph prepares to cover
the goddess's nudity with a
cloak. The laurel wreaths and
fleurs-de-lis on her dress once
again refer to the Medici and
Florence.

Filippino Lippi
The Vision of St Bernard
1482–6

Oil on panel, 210 × 195 cm
Florence, Badia Fiorentina

Filippino Lippi

Prato, *c.* 1457–Florence, 1504

Critics and the public alike are currently rediscovering the importance of Filippino Lippi in Florentine art of the second half of the 15th century. He is by no means a second-rate figure, but a master of great originality and expressive intensity. From an early age he worked with his father, Filippo Lippi, after whose death he finished the frescoes in the Spoleto Cathedral. Filippino then worked with Botticelli with whom he shared much stylistically. Though maintaining contact with Botticelli during the 1480s, Filippino achieved a clearly defined, independent role in Florence. During this period, he completed the frescoes that Masaccio and Masolino had begun at the Brancacci Chapel (*c.* 1485) and in 1488 was called to Rome to paint frescoes in the Carafa Chapel at Santa Maria sopra Minerva. After returning to Florence, Filippino recognized the crisis in humanism caused by the death of Lorenzo the Magnificent (1492) and the preaching of Savonarola, and expressed his uneasiness in paintings that brimmed with tension and symbols.

In sacred paintings of the Renaissance, the donor is often portrayed half-length, in the lower foreground, almost always with hands clasped and absorbed in kneeling contemplation. This attitude of humility and prayer is meant to remind the viewer of the individual's devotion, offsetting the pride implicit in the impulse to have one's portrait inserted into a work displayed in church. In such representations the donor does not emphasize a costly privilege but is presented as a simple worshipper. This pose had lasting success, in particular after the Counter-Reformation, when depictions of figures in prayer (lay donors, clerics, saints, sometimes even the Madonna) were offered as models for the devout.

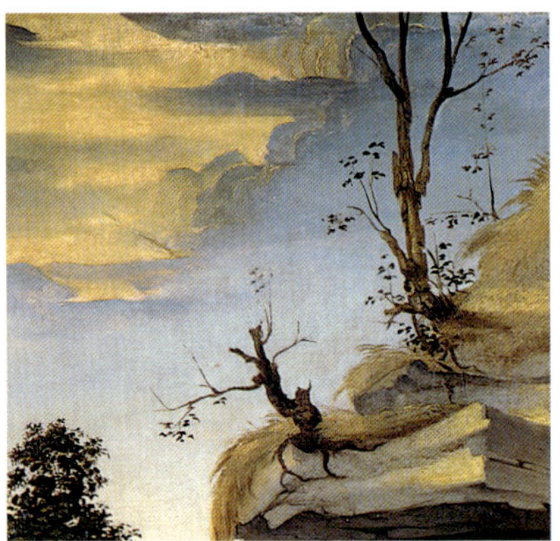

◀ This panel by Filippino and the analogous subject painted by Perugino (see pages 156–7) make a striking comparison. The donor evidently asked Filippino Lippi for a dramatic, tense and anxious interpretation. The result is entirely different from Perugino's balanced vision.

▶ Competing with the Flemish painters in minute detail and vivid colour, Filippino began to introduce a melancholy uneasiness that seems to eat away at the figures. It became a characteristic of the last phase of his production. Painted for a church in the outskirts of Florence, this altarpiece was so famous that during the 1529 siege of the city it was removed for safe keeping to the church of Badia. It remains there today.

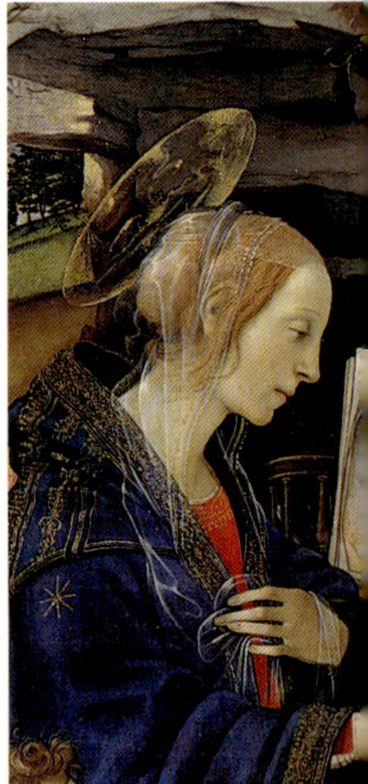

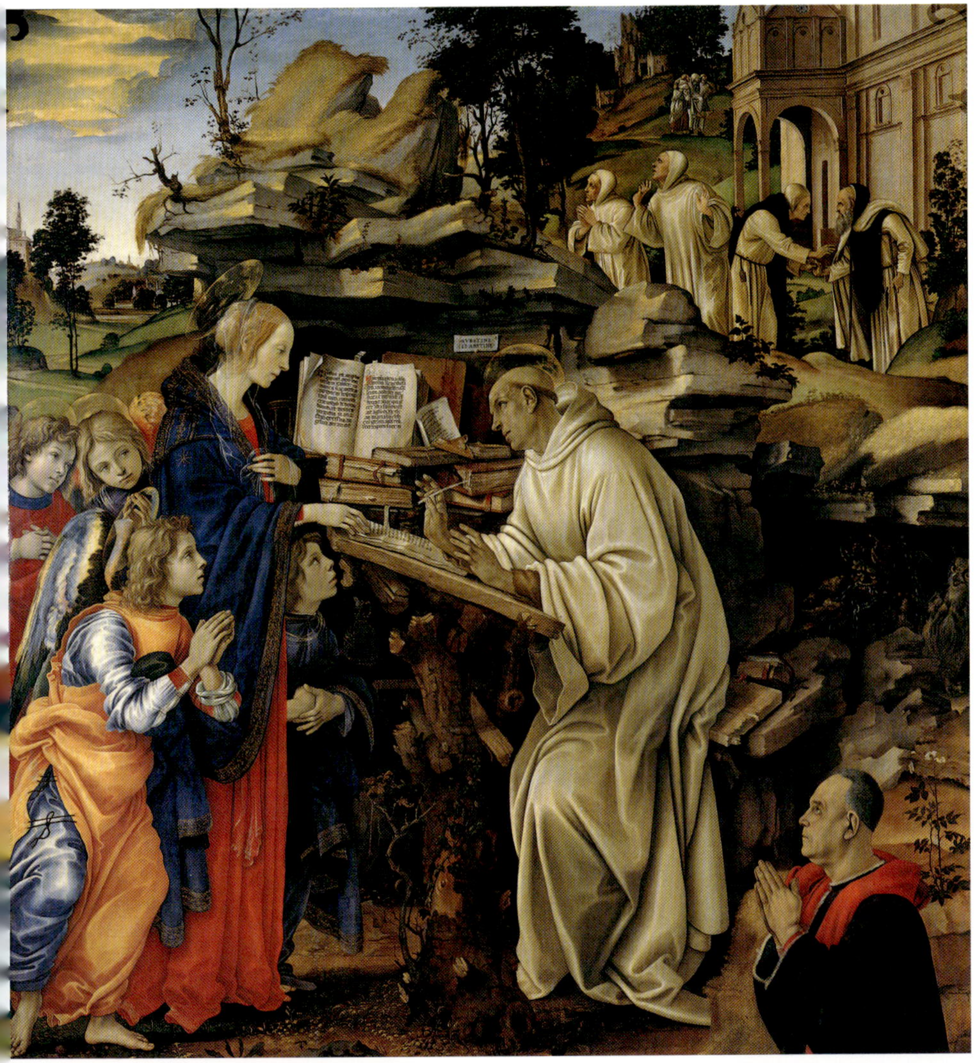

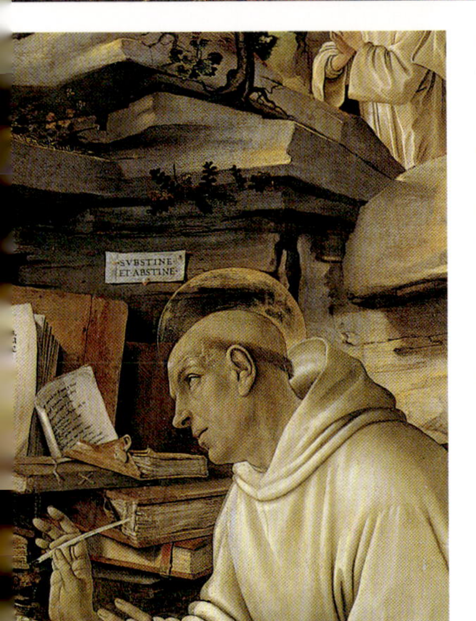

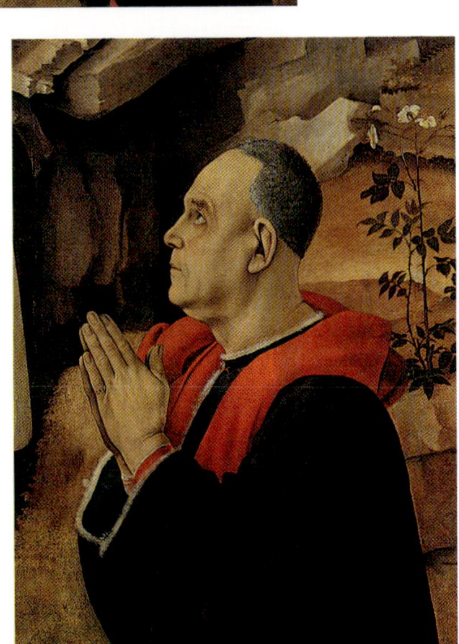

▶ Pietro dal Pugliese, who commissioned the work, assumes an attitude of worshipful devotion; from his pose we infer that he is kneeling. The portrait was much admired by Vasari, who wrote, 'All he lacks is speech.' Interestingly, Gaspare Zanobi del Lama, the patron who commissioned *The Adoration of the Magi* from Botticelli (see pages 104–5), was boldly inserted in the narrative but not represented in prayer.

Private Devotion

Bergognone
Madonna of the Milk
c. 1485

Oil on panel, 61 × 44 cm

Bergamo, Accademia Carrara

Ambrogio Bergognone

(Ambrogio da Fossano)

Fossano (Cuneo), 1453–Milan?, 1523

Ambrogio Bergognone was a founder, along with Vincenzo Foppa, of the late 15th-century Lombard school of painting. His style suggests a knowledge of Flemish art and his surname suggests that he may have trained at the court of Burgundy. After painting a number of small pleasant panels in his youth, from 1488 to 1494 Bergognone worked on a major commission that included altar paintings as well as frescoes for the Carthusian monastery in Pavia. In 1496 he created frescoes at the church of San Satiro in Milan, designed by Bramante (the frescoes are now at the Pinacoteca di Brera). Bergognone's full stylistic maturity, characterized by a compositional monumentality and knowledge of perspective, derives from his collaboration with Bramante. Later Bergognone worked in Milan (where he executed many frescoes at San Simpliciano and Santa Maria della Passione), Lodi, Bergamo and once again at the Carthusian monastery in Pavia.

The history of Italian painting is rich in fresco cycles and large-scale public works. In addition to these, however, artists produced many smaller paintings for a more limited, private audience. These works, unfettered by grandiose concepts, establish a more intimate relationship with the viewer. Many were created for private devotion, to assist the faithful in their efforts to commune with God. Therefore, such paintings presented realistic contexts, situations and descriptive details. The humble yet poetic image of everyday life demonstrated in this charming Madonna is typical of Lombard painting. In this regard, the Renaissance masters of Milan, Brescia and Bergamo are the forerunners of Caravaggio.

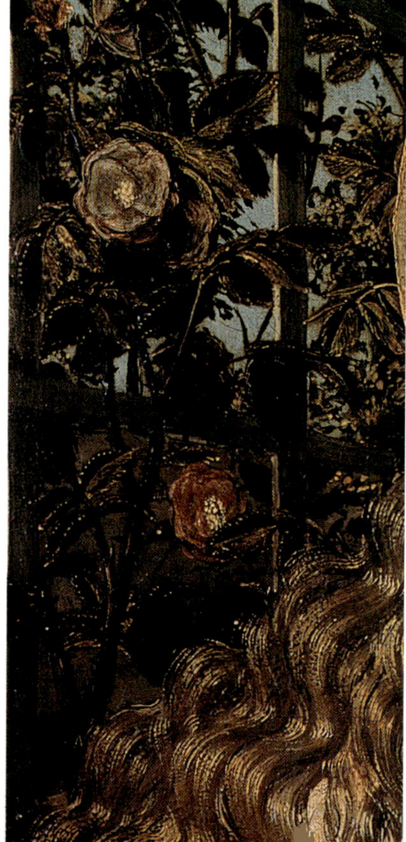

▶ The details of the painting are not purely decorative but have specific devotional references. The rose is an attribute of Mary (called the Mystic Rose in prayers), while the long, unfastened hair indicates the young maiden's virginity.

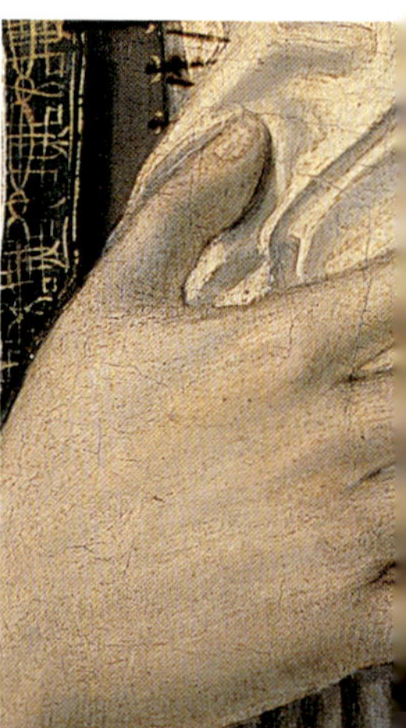

▶ The theme of Mary nursing the Infant Jesus gives a human, domestic dimension to her motherhood. It presents an obvious contrast with solemn altarpiece scenes in which the Madonna sits enthroned and surrounded by angels and saints in a lofty architectural setting.

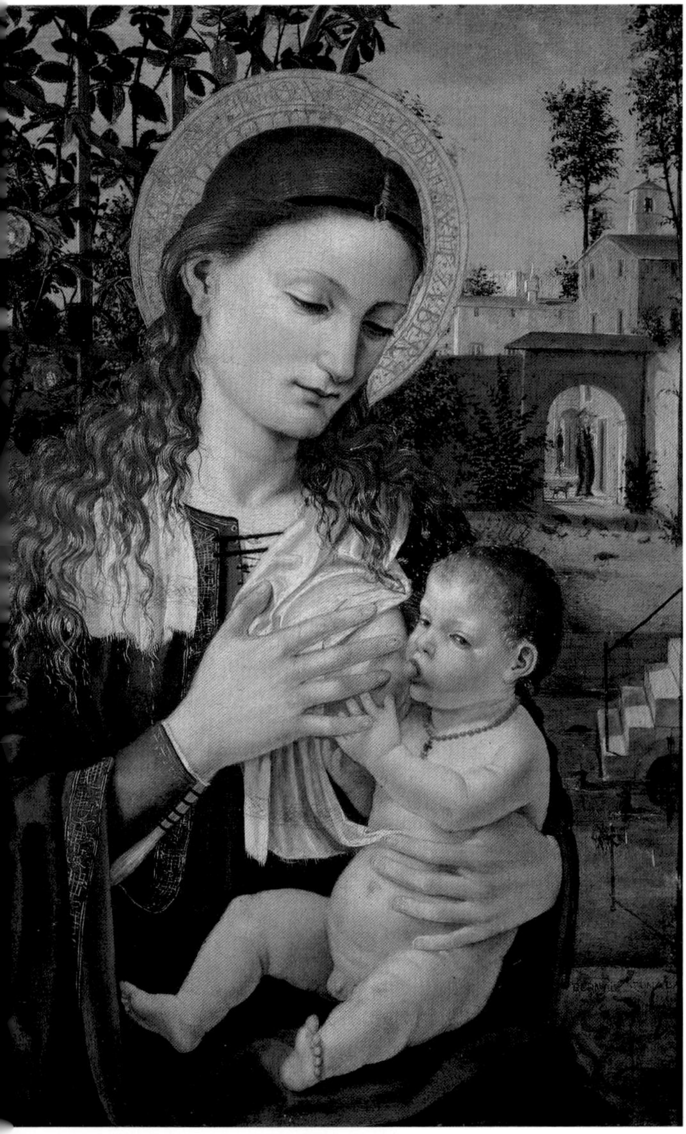

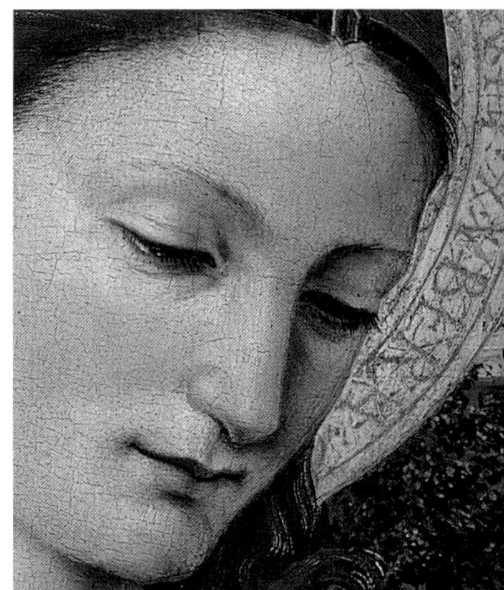

▲ Mary's gaze and gesture are remarkably realistic: smiling attentively, she presses her breast to assist the Infant Jesus. The nipple and cloth are further realistic details.

▼ With an attention to detail that reveals his awareness of Flemish art, Bergognone evokes the atmosphere of rural Lombardy by carefully describing a yard where hens and chicks forage.

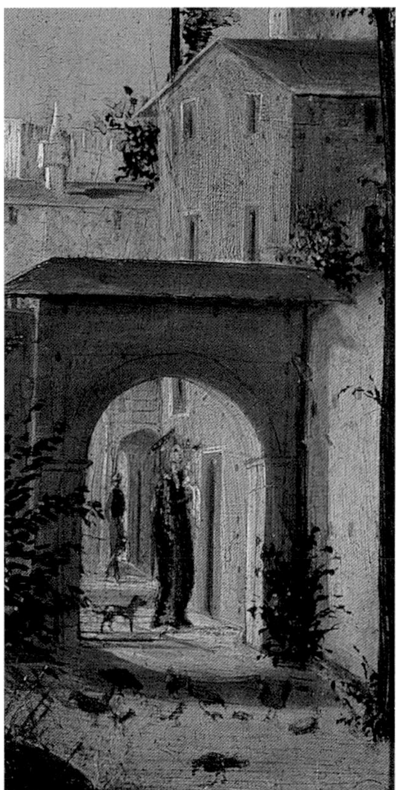

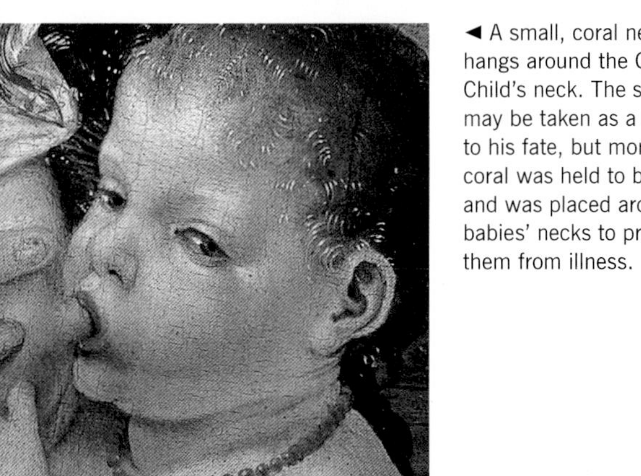

◄ A small, coral necklace hangs around the Christ Child's neck. The small cross may be taken as a reference to his fate, but more generally, coral was held to be charmed and was placed around babies' necks to protect them from illness.

Idea

Leonardo da Vinci
Lady with an Ermine
1485–90

Oil on panel, 54.8 × 40.3 cm

Cracow, Muzeum Czartoryskich

For artist biography, see page 130.

According to Giorgio Vasari, Leonardo initiated a new era in art, one in which figures acquired 'movement and breath'. But it was not only a question of expressing physical vitality. Leonardo probed the spirit of his subjects, revealing their passions. It was the birth of the depiction of the internal 'idea'. After Leonardo, Renaissance artists could no longer limit themselves to reproducing what they saw with their eyes but had to apply their intellect and skill to the further interpretation of the world, nature, consciousness and inner human sensations. The painting known as *Lady with an Ermine* is a portrait of the beautiful, intellectual mistress of Ludovico il Moro, Duke of Milan. It is an exceptionally penetrating psychological study, accomplished through the complex interplay of torsions and movements of the upper body, neck, head and eyes, which turn towards an invisible source of light.

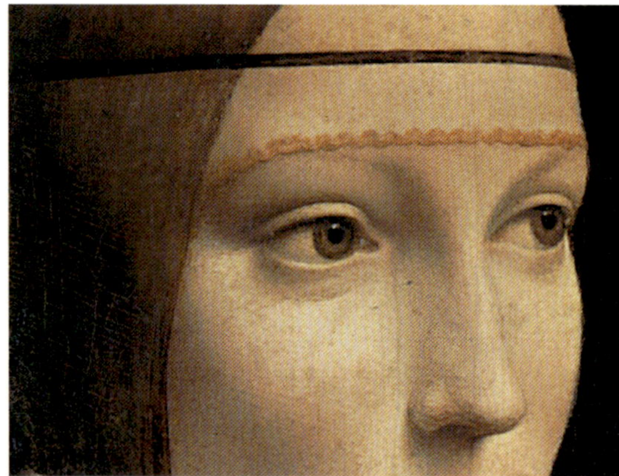

◄ 'She seems to be listening, not speaking': thus the court poet Bernardo Bellincioni praised Leonardo's portrait, alluding to the young woman's lifelike gaze and introspection, silently expressed through painting. She slowly turns her intelligent eyes in a brilliant, intense gaze that ignites the faint smile on her lips and implies the strength of her intellect. In an almost exclusively masculine culture, this is one of the earliest and most explicit pictorial tributes to feminine intelligence.

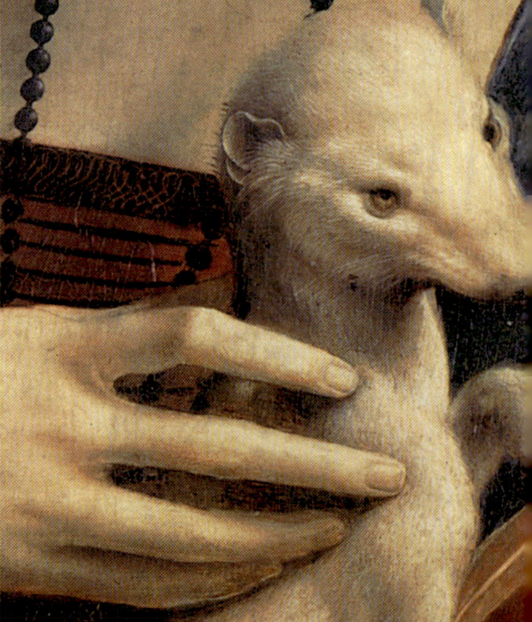

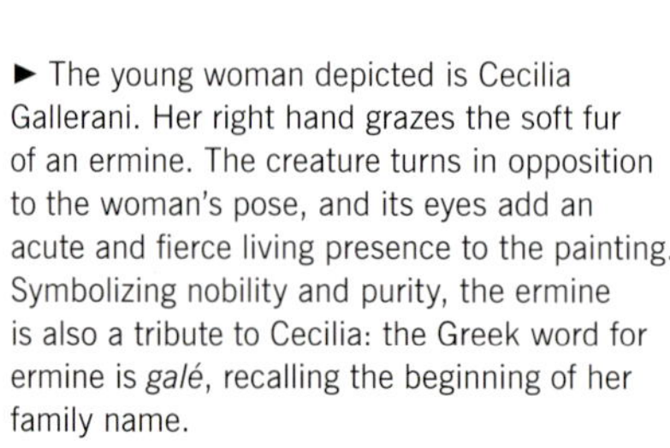

► The young woman depicted is Cecilia Gallerani. Her right hand grazes the soft fur of an ermine. The creature turns in opposition to the woman's pose, and its eyes add an acute and fierce living presence to the painting. Symbolizing nobility and purity, the ermine is also a tribute to Cecilia: the Greek word for ermine is *galé*, recalling the beginning of her family name.

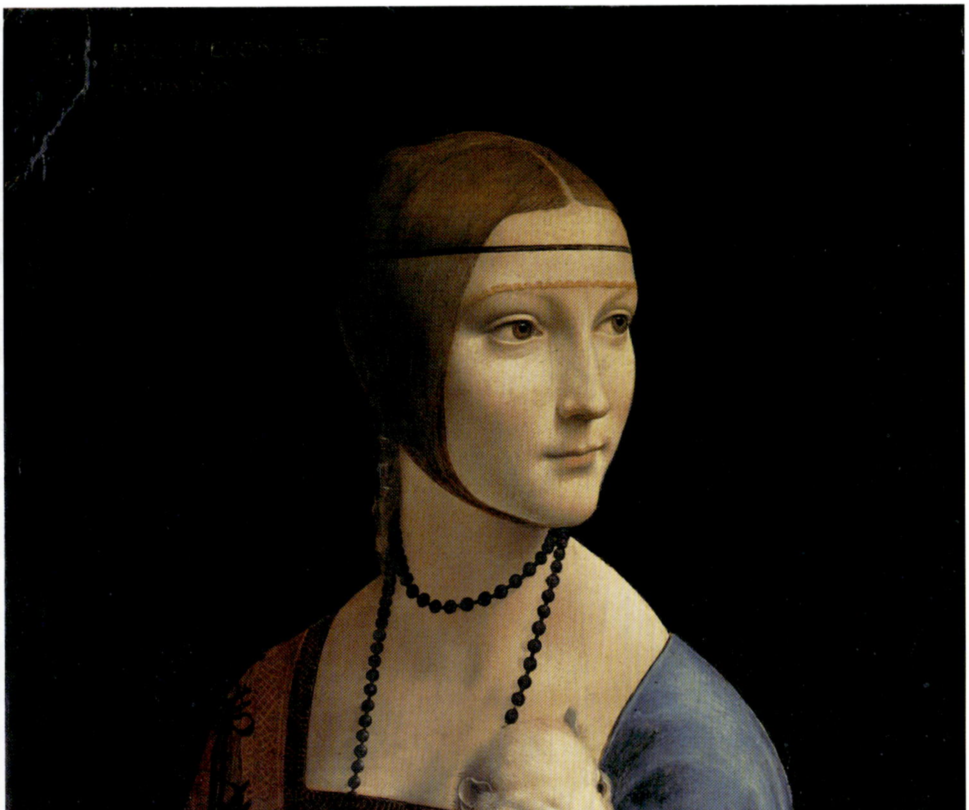

► The subject's overall dynamism is implicit in her turn towards an invisible source of light, suggesting a perfect harmony between the 'movement of the soul' and that of the body.

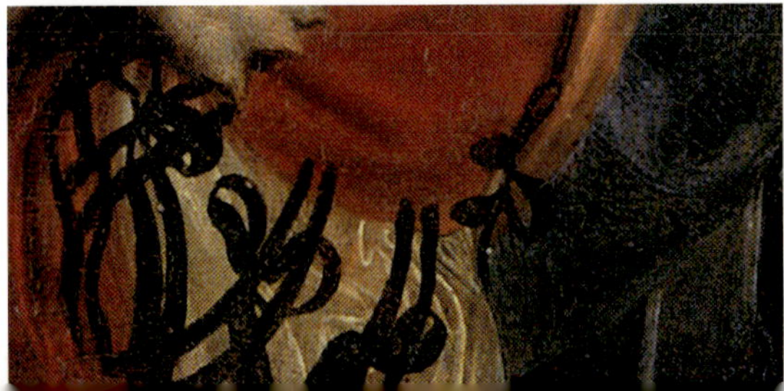

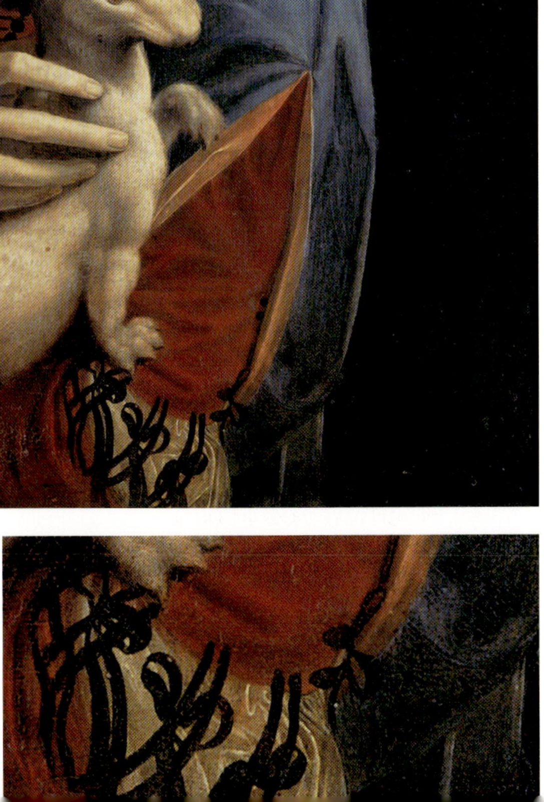

Narrative

Domenico Ghirlandaio
The Birth of the Virgin
Detail from the *Story of the Virgin*
1486–90
Fresco
Florence, Santa Maria Novella

Domenico Ghirlandaio

(Domenico di Tommaso Bigordi)
Florence, 1449–94

A felicitous creator of images, Ghirlandaio was in his element when executing large-scale fresco cycles. He grew up with Perugino and Botticelli in the workshop of Andrea del Verrocchio, and obtained the backing of the Vespucci family (the most powerful in Florence after the Medici) for whom he executed various works in the church and convent of Ognissanti. In 1475, he painted the delicate *Story of St Fina* in the collegiate church of San Gimignano. His important position in the Florentine school is clear: he was called to Rome in 1481 to paint two frescoes in the Sistine Chapel. When he returned to Florence, he executed works of increasing significance, such as the decoration of the Sala dei Gigli in the Palazzo Vecchio (1483), the frescoes and altarpiece of the Sassetti Chapel at Santa Trinita (1485), the start of the frescoes in the spacious Tornabuoni Chapel, and the main chapel in Santa Maria Novella. This last work was completed in 1490 with the participation of the workshop in which Michelangelo trained.

Even at the height of the Italian Renaissance, the majority of the population was illiterate. Moreover, the language of the Church was Latin, which was little understood by the people. Therefore, painting – especially in public places such as churches – continued to play an important role in the dissemination and explanation of the faith to ordinary people. Fresco cycles offered an economical and effective means of visual communication. The Dominican brothers, whose order made preaching one of its basic aims, were perfectly aware of this, as is demonstrated by the series of paintings in the Florentine convent of Santa Maria Novella. Between the mid-14th century and the early 16th, the church, cloisters and annexed chapels of the Dominican complex acquired frescoes by Nardo de Cione, Andrea di Bonaiuto, Masaccio, Paolo Uccello, Domenico Ghirlandaio, Filippino Lippi and Jacopo Pontormo.

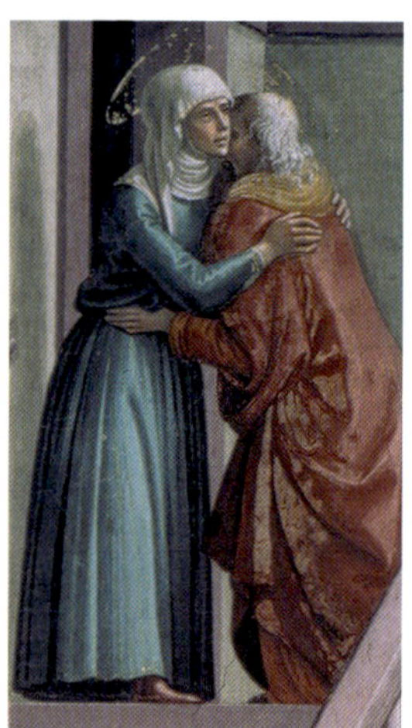

◄ At the upper left, Ghirlandaio skilfully inserts a bit of 'back story' drawn from the apocryphal gospels to complement the narrative; Mary's parents, Joachim and Anne, anxiously and affectionately embrace upon Joachim's return from voluntary exile in the desert. This chaste embrace marks the moment of Mary's conception – the Immaculate Conception.

► Ghirlandaio sets the scene of Mary's birth in a realistic, noble environment of his period. Some women have come to visit the new mother and her daughter. The first in line, shown in profile, is Ludovica, daughter of the cycle's patron, Giovanni Tornabuoni.

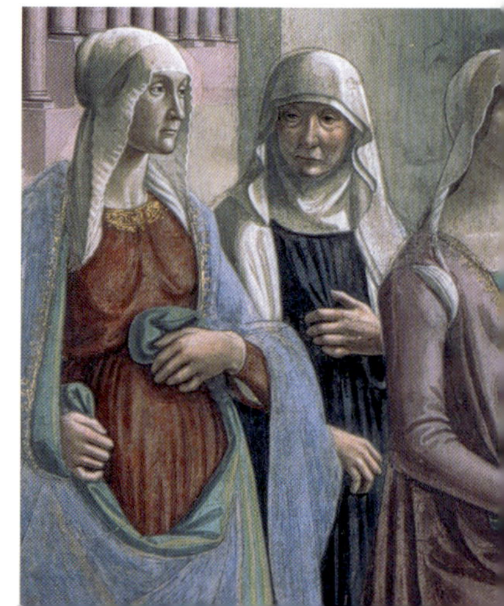

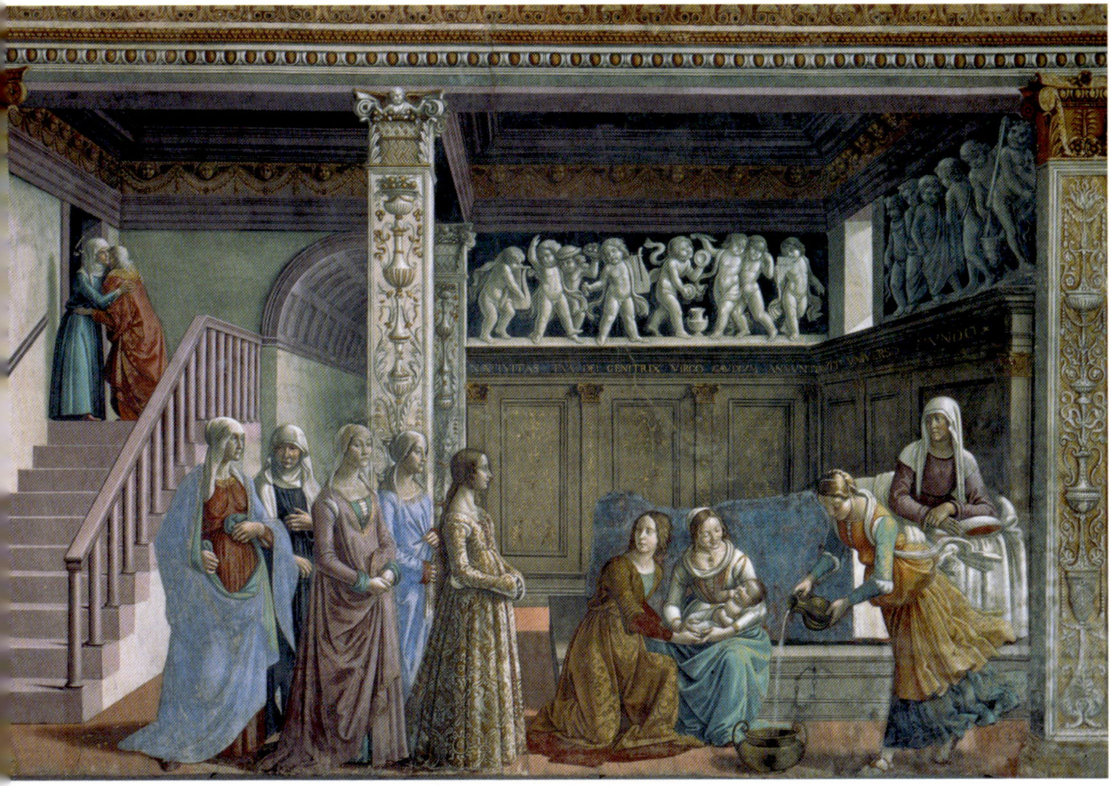

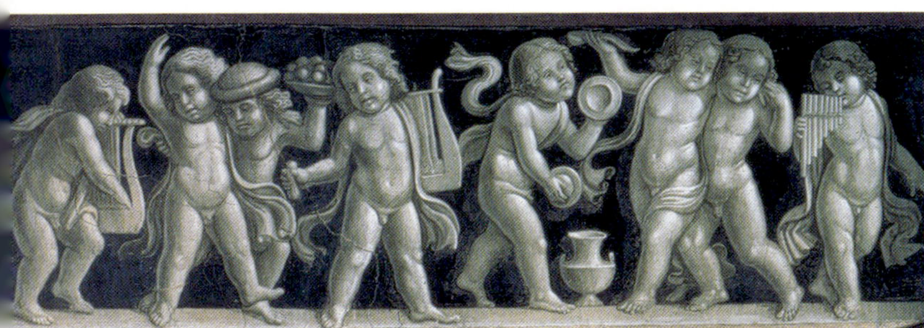

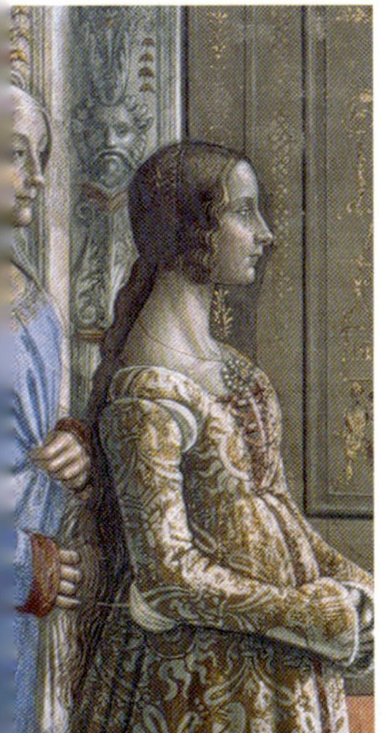

◄ St Anne's bedroom is sumptuously decorated with inlaid wood panels and relief friezes, recalling the terracotta relics of the Della Robbia brothers. The dancing putti add a further note of animation to the fresco.

► Among the Florentine painters of the second half of the 15th century, Ghirlandaio and Benozzo Gozzoli were the most inclined to paint extensive narrative cycles, taking delight in storytelling and decoration. The young women who look after the newborn combine grace and naturalism, while the baby spontaneously puts a finger into her mouth.

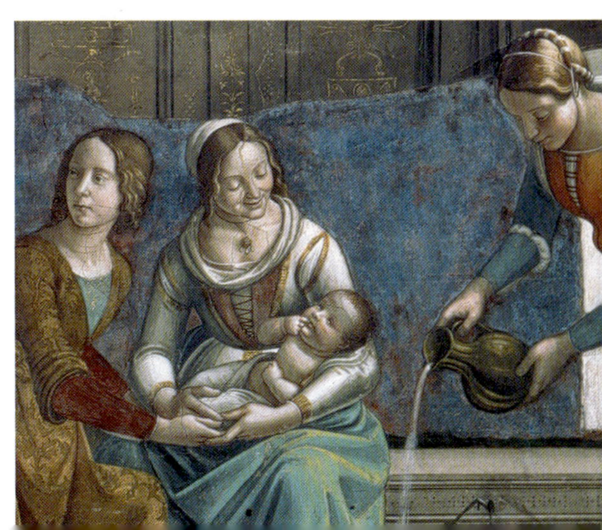

Domenico Ghirlandaio
Portrait of Giovanna Tornabuoni
1488

Tempera on panel, 76 × 50 cm
Madrid, Museo Thyssen-Bornemisza

For artist biography, see page 140.

The 'style' of a portrait was in large part dictated by the social conventions of the city in which it was produced, as well as the status of the subject. In Milan, Leonardo was moving decisively towards the expression of 'movements of the soul' (see *Lady with an Ermine*, pages 138–9) while in Florence, artists remained bound to the traditional profile view. As this masterpiece shows, Ghirlandaio was perfectly aware of the limitations of this pose, but contrary to Leonardo's style at the same time in a different city, he transformed the figure into a sophisticated, almost abstract image, a model of absolute elegance.

▼ Giovanna degli Albizzi, whose statuesque classical beauty was portrayed in paintings and medals, was one of the most celebrated young ladies in Florence. Her brief marriage to Lorenzo Tornabuoni ended with her death in childbirth at the age of twenty, in the same year that Ghirlandaio painted this portrait. Her tragic death was felt to mark the end of a happy era.

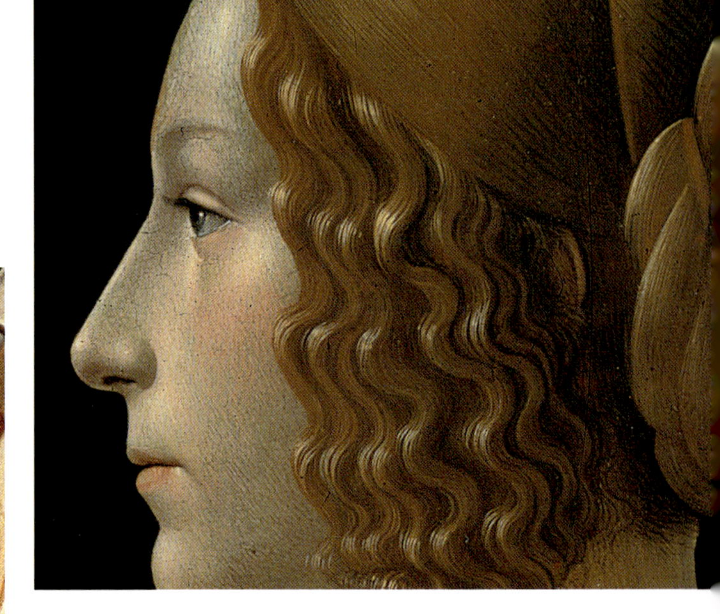

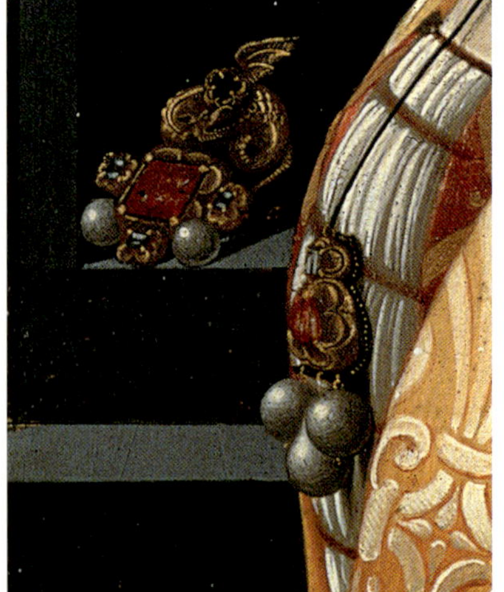

◄ Ghirlandaio gave depth to the austere architectural background by placing a rich piece of jewelry in a recess. It is difficult to determine whether the painting was done before or after the woman's tragic death – or perhaps during the pregnancy that cost her her life.

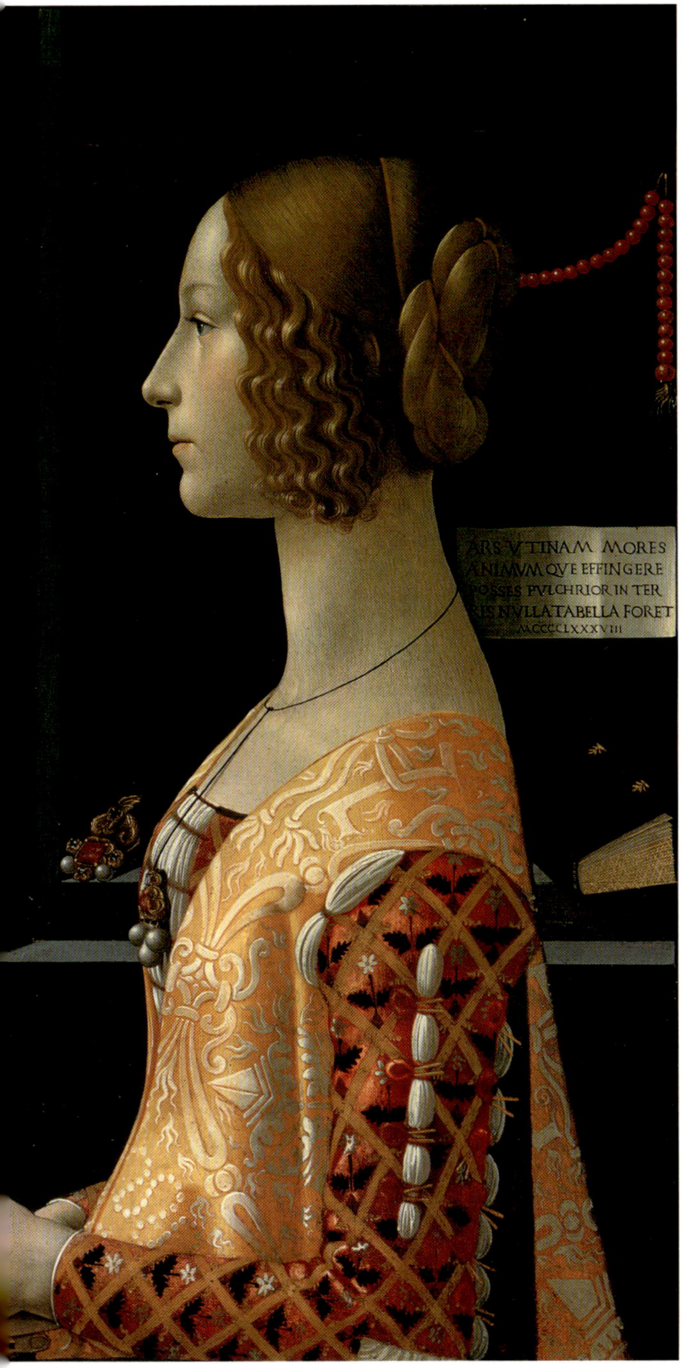

◄ ▼ Every detail of the costume, hairstyle, make-up and background expresses the quest for a particular refined style. Line, colour, light and composition all speak of a carefully established balance expressed in flowing naturalness. The portrait was painted two years after Giovanna degli Albizzi married Lorenzo Tornabuoni (a cousin of Lorenzo the Magnificent), uniting two of the richest families in Florence. The inscription in splendid Latin capitals praises the young woman's moral virtues, which could be represented in a painting, but never replaced.

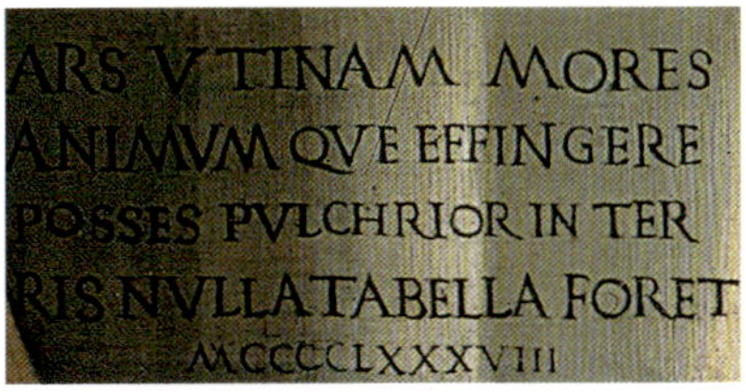

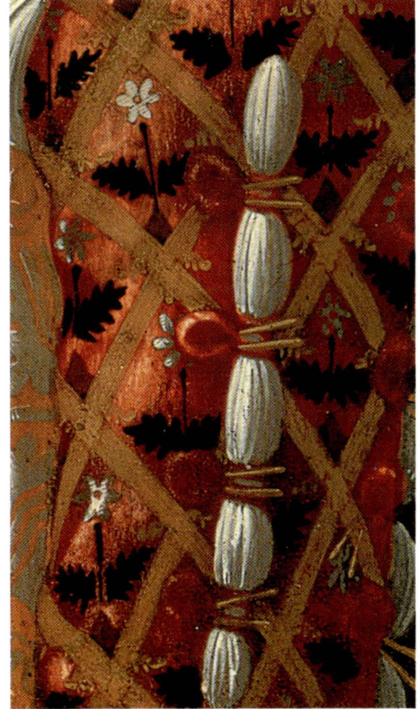

► The same sumptuous dress, in the latest fashion with puffed gathers in the sleeves tied back with cords, also appears in the portrait of Giovanna in the Tornabuoni Chapel frescoes.

Triptych

Giovanni Bellini
Virgin and Child with Saints
(Frari Triptych)
1488

Oil on panel, 184 × 79 cm and
115 × 46 cm (each of two side panels)
Venice, Santa Maria Gloriosa dei Frari

Giovanni Bellini

Venice, c. 1430–1516

Giovanni Bellini trained along with his
brother Gentile in the workshop of their
father, Jacopo. His sister's marriage to
Andrea Mantegna in 1451 further linked
him to the Venetian artistic community.
For a time, Giovanni Bellini and Mantegna
painted works on the same subject.
In comparison with his brother-in-law,
however, Bellini showed greater attention
to colour and light than to drawing, and
soon took up a quest for delicate, natural
atmosphere. The altarpiece depicting
the coronation of the Virgin, which he
painted for Pesaro (1471–4), confirms his
contact with Piero della Francesca, active
in nearby Urbino. Bellini's assimilation of
new trends continued with his study of
the innovations of Antonello da Messina,
who had arrived in Venice in 1474.
Appointed official painter to the Most
Serene Republic of Venice in 1483, Bellini
held the position for 33 years, until his
death. During this time, he painted some
of the most important altarpieces to be
found in Venetian churches.

As the 15th century progressed the traditional subdivided alta
painting became increasingly outmoded in the main art centre
in Italy: the age of the triptych and polyptych, with their gol
grounds, was coming to an end. However, the occasional trip
tych was still commissioned, and not only in provincial areas
The absence of a unified perspective among the various panel
was felt to be the greatest drawback, and so the most successfu
triptychs were those in which the artist made a convincing
transition from the central to the side panels. Mantegna hac
resolved the problem first in the 1450s, but the most effective
solution was the one employed by his brother-in-law Giovann
Bellini, which relied on a sensitive use of impalpable, pale light

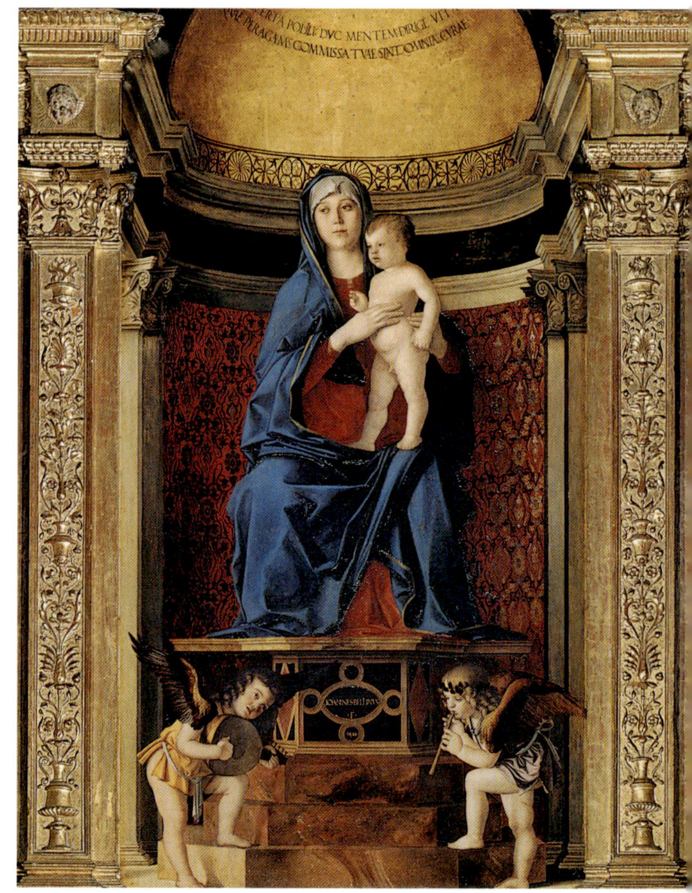

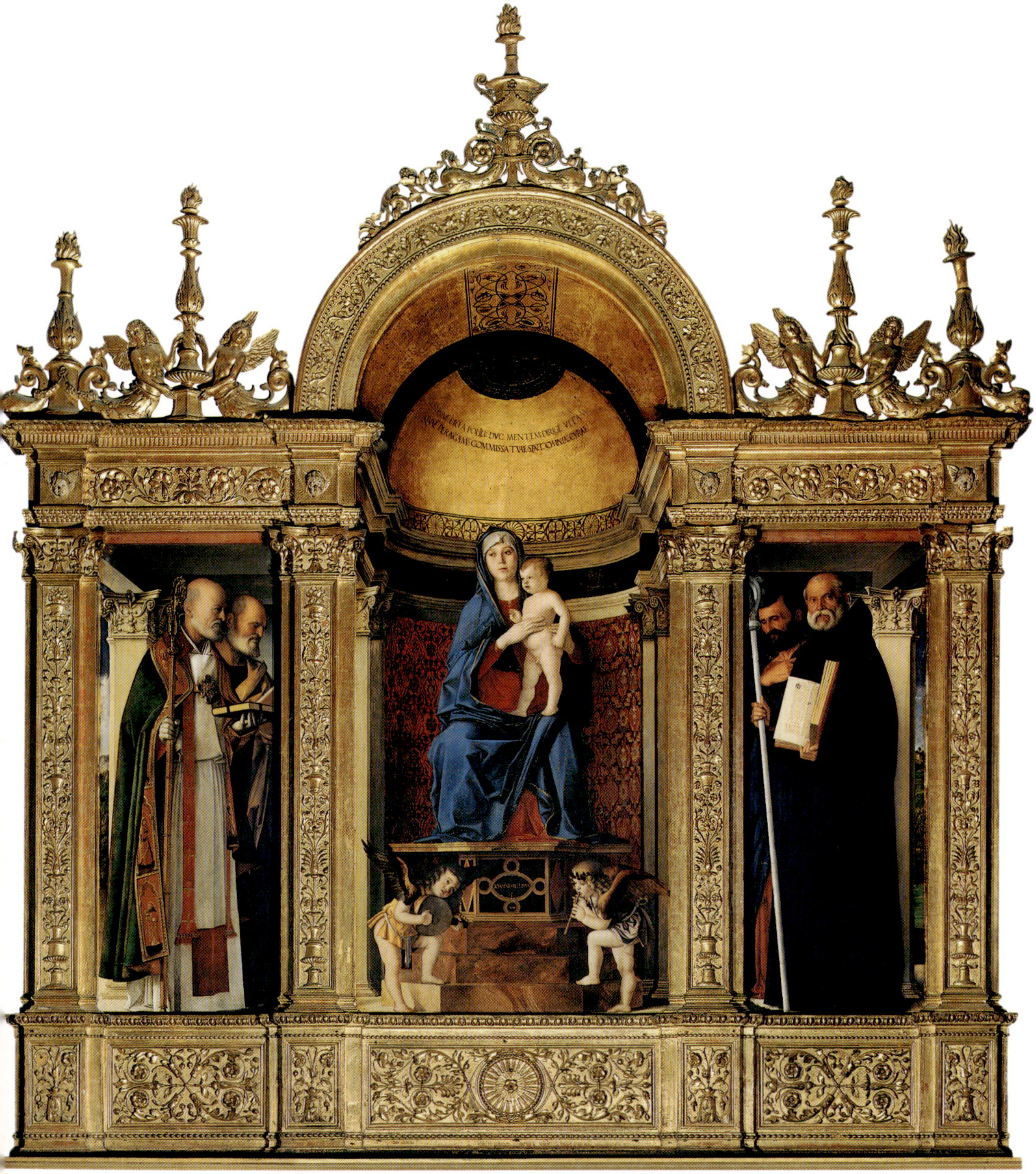

▲ Giovanni Bellini found
poetic way of combining
ıe geometric rigour of Piero
ella Francesca with diffused,
atural light. The symmetrical
rangement of the figures
ıd architecture is given
armth by the attenuated
ghting of the semidome,
hich simulates a gold-ground
osaic.

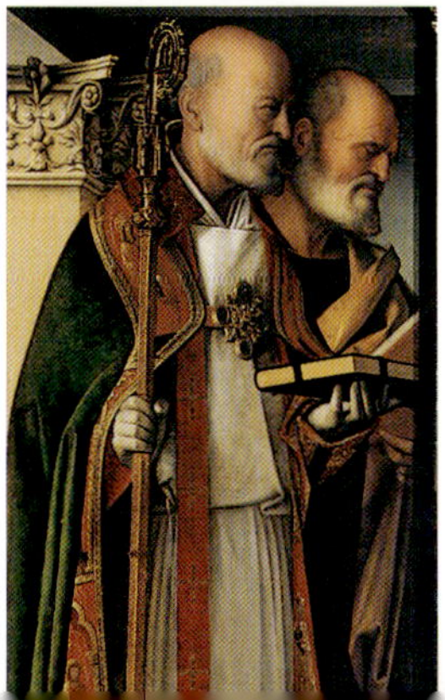

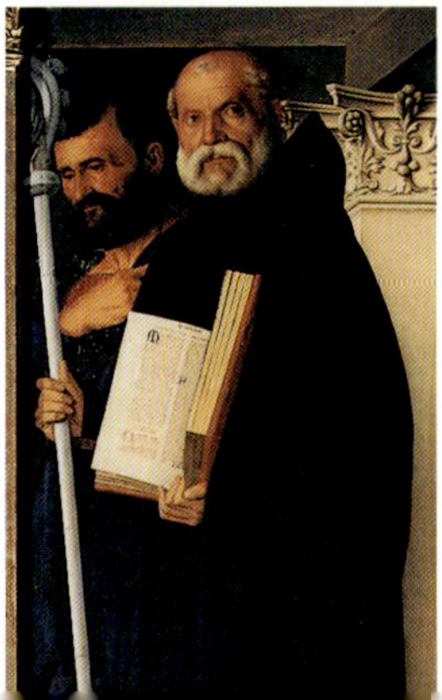

◄▲ Perfectly preserved in its original location (the sacristy of the basilica of the Frari), the triptych has also retained its original frame, which Giovanni Bellini himself designed. The architectural components of the wooden structure blend with those painted in the triptych's background.

Leonardesque

Giovanni Antonio Boltraffio
Madonna of the Rose
c. 1490

Oil on panel, 45.5 × 35.6 cm
Milan, Museo Poldi Pezzoli

Giovanni Antonio Boltraffio

Milan, 1466/7–1516

Boltraffio was one of Leonardo's favourite students, frequently mentioned in his notes beginning in 1490. He was from an old Milanese family, and was buried with full honours in the church of San Paolo in Compito under a tombstone that is now at the Castello Sforzesco, Milan (from this we learn that he died in 1516). His earliest work, on which he collaborated with Marco d'Oggiono, is an altarpiece depicting the resurrection of Christ commissioned for the Milan church of Santa Liberata in 1491 (today in Berlin). Besides Leonardo's influence, Boltraffio drew on other inspiring painters: Bramantino, Bergognone, Perugino and Francesco Francia. In 1500, Boltraffio executed a series of works for the Casio family in Bologna that demonstrate his mastery of a formal language all of his own. In 1502, and again in Milan, he painted *St Barbara* for the church of Santa Maria presso San Satiro (also in Berlin), and in 1508 he received a commission from Bassano da Ponte for an altar painting for the cathedral in Lodi (today in Budapest). Boltraffio's ability as a painter may also be appreciated in his many altars for private devotion (for example, the *Madonna and Child* at the Museo Poldi Pezzoli), and in the astonishing power of his many portraits, in which formal finesse is successfully interwoven with introspection. A wealth of archival documents regarding Boltraffio deal almost entirely with his private life, leaving unanswered many questions on the authorship and chronology of certain works.

Comparison of this painting with Bergognone's *Madonna of the Milk* (see pages 136–7) – which is of a similar period, technique, geographical origin, function and size – immediately reveals some telling differences. Bergognone's *Madonna* – its poetic Flemish influence laced with realism – belongs to the tradition of Lombardy; Boltraffio's was an overt tribute to Leonardo, who, after moving to the court of Duke Ludovico il Moro, became the absolute point of reference in Milanese art. It has been suggested that Leonardo himself advised and assisted his student Boltraffio with this panel. The raking light against a dark background, the reciprocal movement of the two figures, the child's soft, fleshy limbs and the perfect oval of the smiling Madonna all reflect Da Vinci's code, a visual repertoire that, from this time on, two generations of painters in Lombardy would repeat with unfaltering loyalty.

The Difficulty of Collaborating with Leonardo

Leonardo stated, 'I tell painters that no one should ever imitate the manner of another.' Given the horde of more or less slavish adherents and the many copies of his work in Milan, this statement has a paradoxical ring. Raised in the stimulating environment of Verrocchio's Florentine workshop, Leonardo was the first great Renaissance master to renounce the traditional sharing of work in workshop production, considering it a waste of time. In a famous aphorism, he reminded us that 'if you are alone, you are entirely your own'. Rather than encourage the training of young artists by involving them in the execution phase, Leonardo preferred to collect notes and suggestions that he planned to use in a lengthy treatise on painting (which he never finished). The exceptional power of concentration Leonardo devoted to each minuscule aspect of the world around him was an impassioned exercise, but so constricting that it created an intellectual isolation. Leonardo alternated whole days of uninterrupted work with long, inexplicable periods of apparently idle time. It was impossible for a pupil to follow so unpredictable a work rhythm.

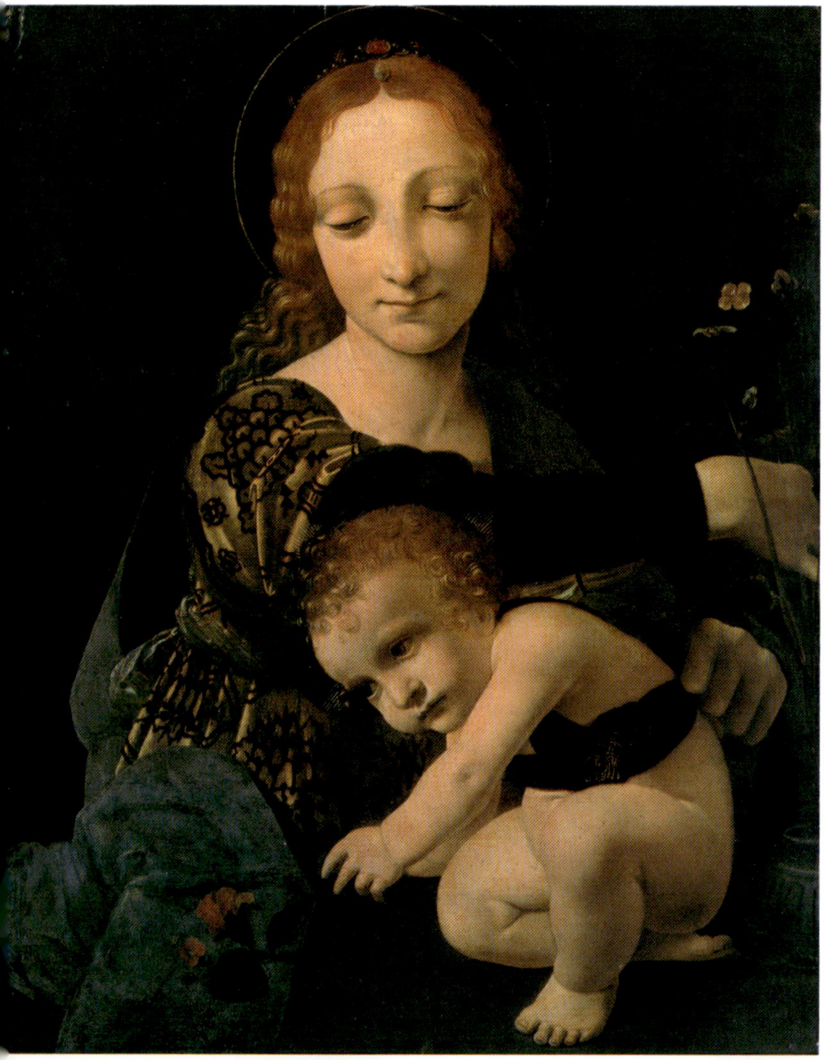

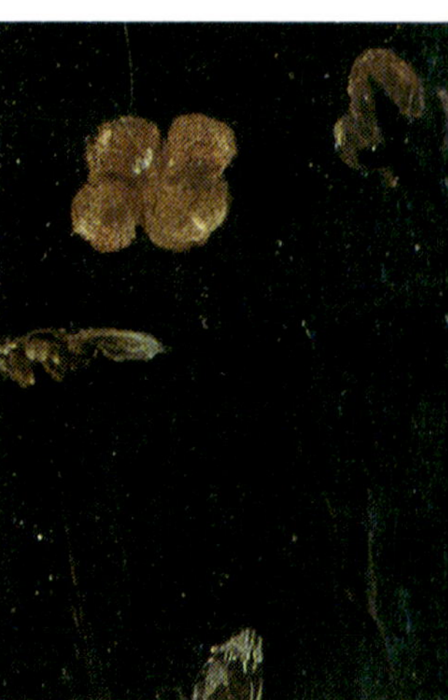

▼ Interest in botany is another characteristic of Leonardo's work in Milan, where he made many beautiful drawings of flowers, leaves and shrubs.

▼ The chubby, curly headed blond Christ Child is a model that Leonardo's imitators used over and over. Artists had treated children's anatomy somewhat carelessly before Leonardo.

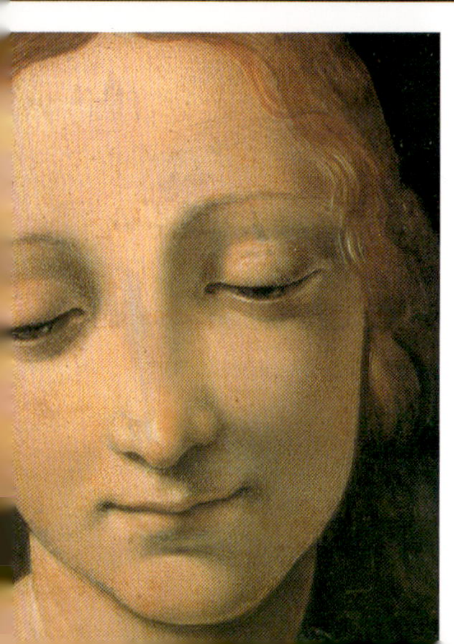

◄ Mary's features are unmistakable: the oval face, the perfect complexion, the hair parted in the centre revealing the forehead, the thin eyebrows and half-closed, downturned eyes.

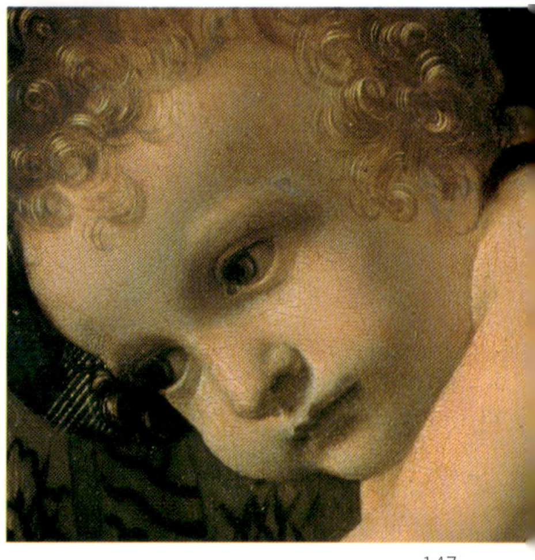

Portrait

Domenico Ghirlandaio
Portrait of a Grandfather and His Grandson
c. 1490

Tempera on panel, 62 × 46 cm
Paris, Musée du Louvre

For artist biography, see page 140.

In the late 15th century, Italian portraiture began to embrace new expressive opportunities. The profile pose, almost obligatory until just a few years before, was now optional, and realism sometimes resulted in some pitiless effects: the big pimply nose of this affectionate Florentine grandfather is a typical example. Painting was propelled in this direction by 'competition' from astonishingly lifelike portrait busts sculpted in marble, painted terracotta, wood and even wax. This painting by Ghirlandaio presents other ideas becoming key to Italian Renaissance portraiture: the close relationship between two people; the connection between generations, emphasized by the use of the same red in the clothing of both the child and the old man; the inevitable passage of time; and the interior setting, with a window opening onto a landscape.

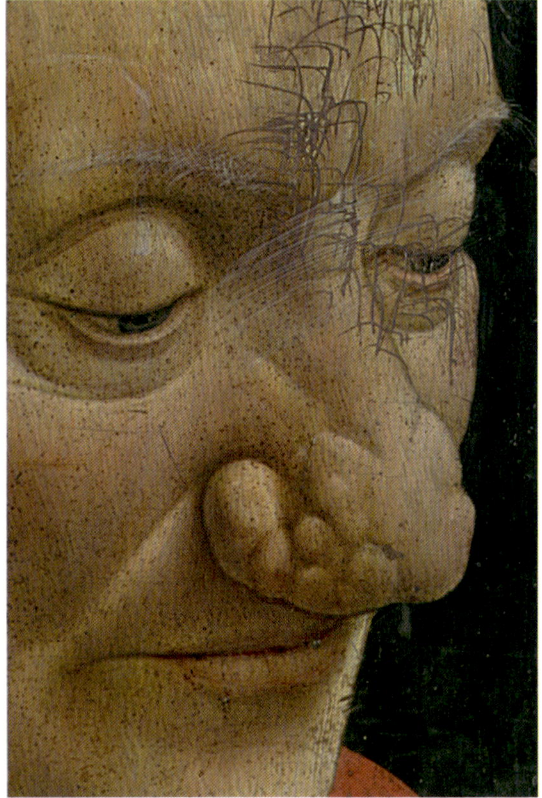

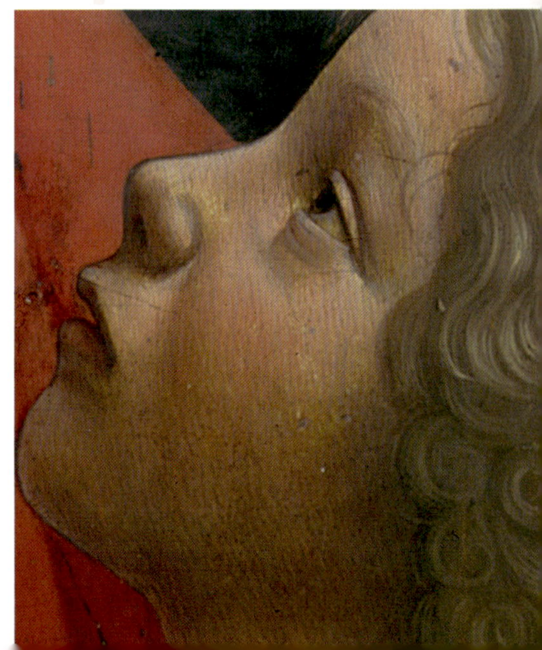

◀▼ The exchange of glances between a grand-father and grandson was a novelty in Renaissance portraits: there was no precedent for depicting such closeness between two people of different ages. This detail alone is enough to belie Ghirlandaio's reputation as a pleasing but perhaps simplistic painter.

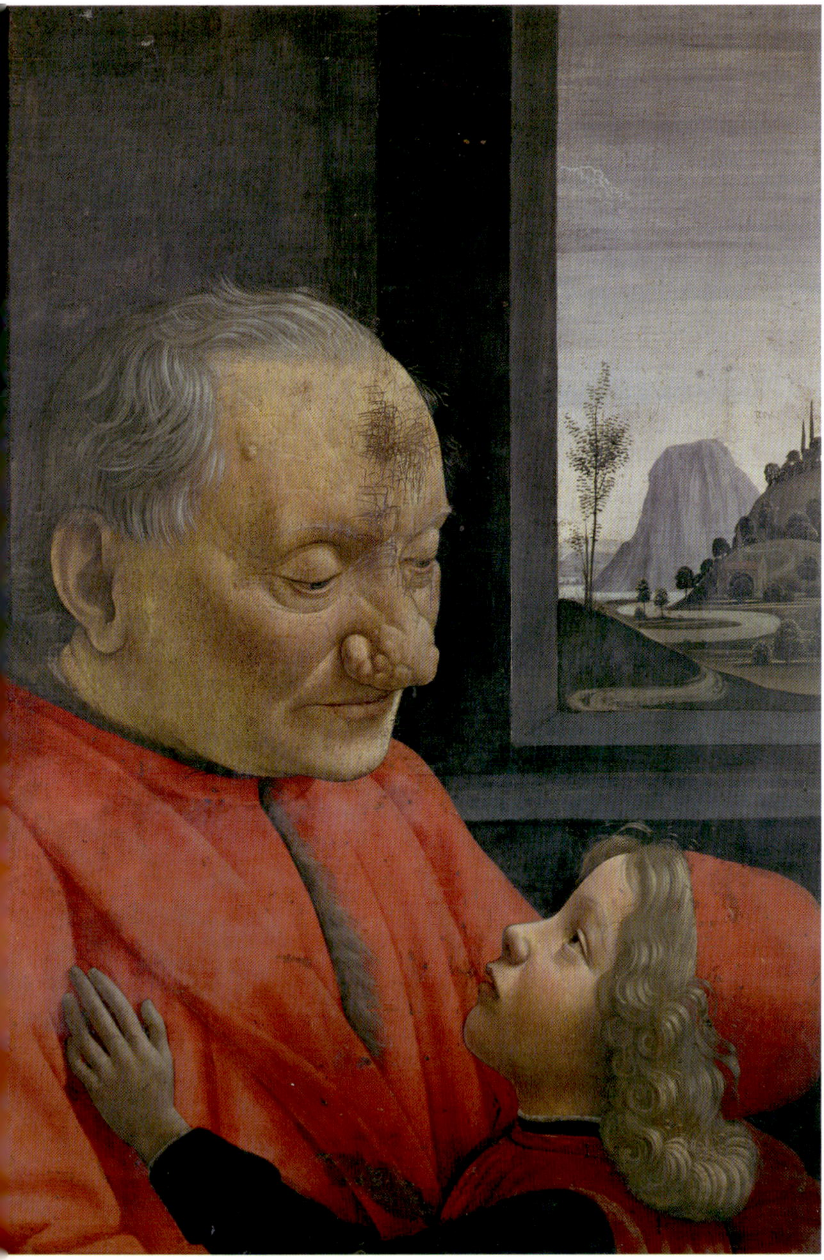

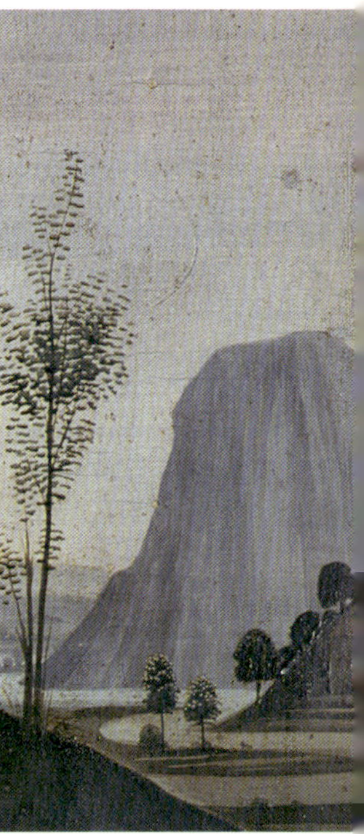

▲ Ghirlandaio was one of the most successful painters in Florence during the time of Lorenzo the Magnificent. Part of his fame rests upon his attention to detail in landscapes and still lifes, in both panel paintings and his highly esteemed fresco cycles.

▲ We have no information as to the identity of the two sitters, but a preparatory drawing today in Stockholm (and which had also passed through the collection of Giorgio Vasari) shows the grandfather's eyes closed and his features more rigid and contracted. It has been suggested that Ghirlandaio executed the portrait after the old man's death, making it a touching and tender memorial to his affection for his little grandson.

Carlo Crivelli
Madonna of the Candle
1490

Tempera on panel, 218 × 75 cm
Milan, Pinacoteca di Brera

Carlo Crivelli

Venice, 1430/5–Marche, 1494/5

Crivelli's career echoes the lively dialogue between 'centre' and 'periphery' in 15th-century Italy. Born in Venice, he trained first in the workshop of Vivarini and then in the humanistic setting of mid-century Padua. Crivelli's youthful misadventures forced him to leave Venice, however, and live first in Istria (1459) and then in the Marche region from 1468 until his death. Crivelli found a more congenial atmosphere in the provinces, and became one of Italy's most unique artists of the second half of the 15th century. Backed by a well-equipped workshop, Crivelli left radiant polyptychs and altarpieces in large, small and even very small centres throughout the region. He combined the modern rules of perspective and classical monumentality with a lavishly exuberant ornamental approach that wrapped everything in a fairy-tale atmosphere. Up until his death at the end of the 15th century he persistently used the antiquated gold ground.

Compared to the Northern schools, Italian painting is generally less rich in meticulous descriptive detail. The transition from International Gothic to Renaissance also signified a greater concentration on the main image through the selection of what was truly important and meaningful (and thus less emphasis on incidental detail). Significant exceptions abound, owing above all to masters active in relatively peripheral locations. This was the case with Carlo Crivelli. Born in the Veneto and trained in Padua under Francesco Squarcione just after the middle of the century. From 1468 he established himself in the Marche, a hilly region facing the Adriatic, where he remained until his death. Although Crivelli was perfectly aware of the rules of perspective, he willingly adapted to the expectations and tastes of his 'provincial' audience. Using the traditional technique of gold ground, he painted sumptuous polyptychs and included a wealth of narrative particulars.

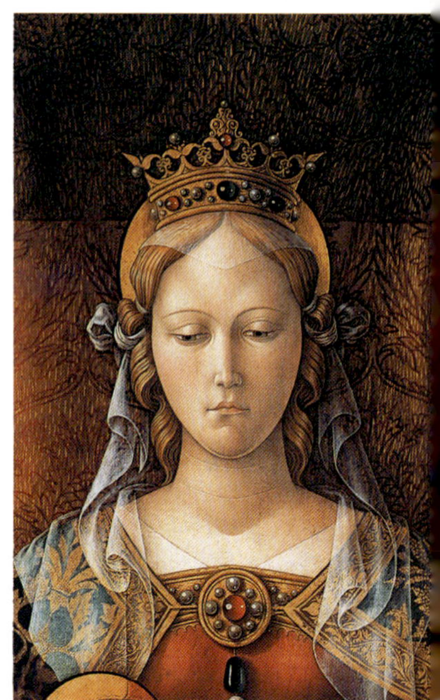

▼ The purity and pensive expression of the Virgin seem at odds with the painting's festive, lavish richness, brimming with gold and sumptuous detail.

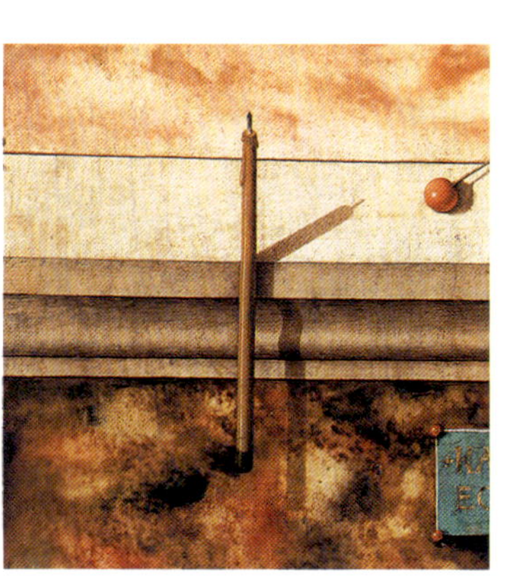

◄ The painting's title refers to a detail that might easily escape the viewer's attention: the thin, extinguished candle in the lower left.

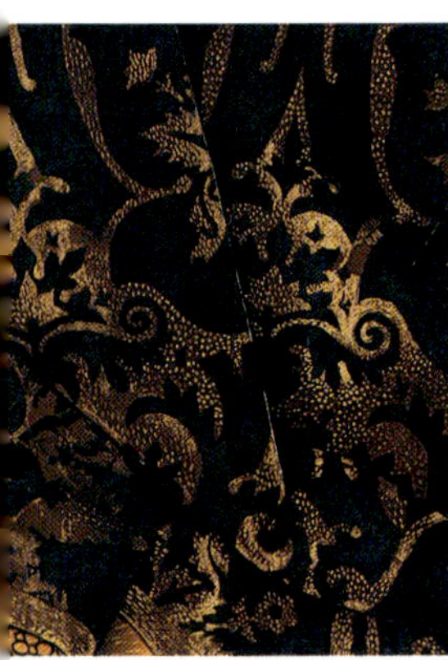

◄▼ Crivelli's paintings are filled with flowers, garlands of leaves and fruit and rare objects. The painter's exceptional skill in reproducing the tactile appearance of fabric is evident in his splendid rendering of the rich, heavy brocades with gold branch designs. The vase of lilies and roses symbolically recalls Mary's virtue.

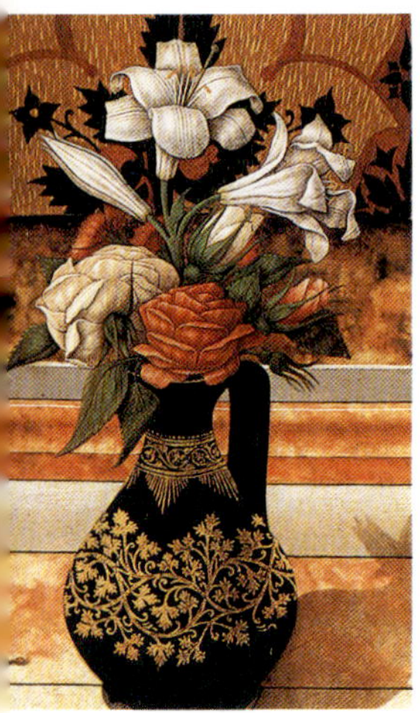

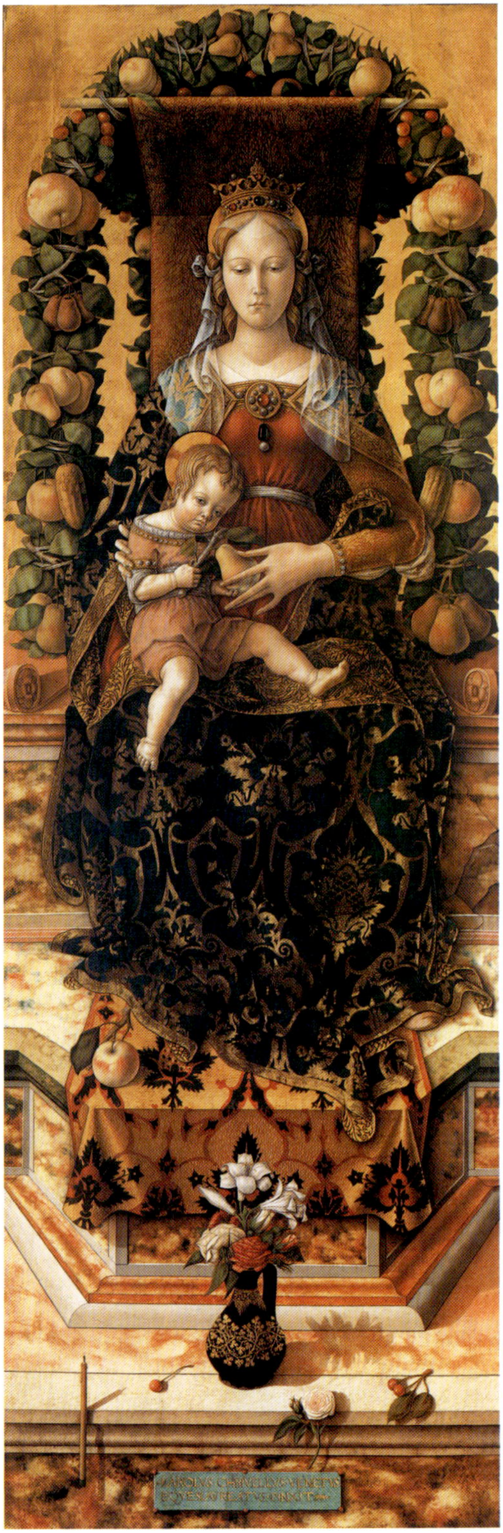

◄ ▲ The painting is signed *karolvs crivellus venetvs eqves lavreatvs pinxit* ('the Venetian Carlo Crivelli, a laurelled knight, painted it'). Specifying the painter's noble title emphasizes his social standing.

Classicism

Pietro Perugino
Apollo and Marsyas (or *Apollo and Daphnis*)
1490–5

Oil on panel, 39 × 29 cm
Paris, Musée du Louvre

Pietro Perugino

(Pietro Vannucci)

Città della Pieve, Perugia, c. 1450–
Fontignano, Perugia, 1524

Gentle, bright and never exaggerated,
Perugino's painting was extraordinarily
widely distributed. At the end of the
15th century, after the period of
expressive variety in local schools, his
style became the 'common language' of
Italian art. He grew up in Florence as a
pupil of Verrocchio alongside Botticelli
and later Leonardo, and in 1481 Pope
Sixtus IV called upon Perugino for the
decoration of the Sistine Chapel, where
he painted the emblematic *Delivery of
the Keys*. When he returned to Florence,
he painted altarpieces, frescoes and
portraits. Perugino's success spread
quickly, thanks to a formula consisting of
rhythmically elegant gestures, expressions
and compositions. Simple, fluid and
graceful, the images Perugino and his
workshop produced were in demand all
over Italy. Towards the end of the 15th
century, the young Raphael arrived in
Perugino's workshop. The culmination
of this period was the decoration of the
collegiate church of the Cambio in Perugia
between 1496 and 1501. After 1500,
however, Perugino's painting quickly fell
out of fashion, and he devoted himself
to producing repetitive work exclusively
in the provinces.

Lorenzo the Magnificent's favourite motto was *Le temps revien*
– Time returns. Literature of the period does not use the term
'Renaissance' (or even rebirth), but its sense can be clearly un
derstood in light of the poetic, artistic and philosophical climate
of the late 15th century. This refined little painting by Perugino
summarizes it effectively. Erroneously attributed in the past to
Mantegna and Raphael, it is an exquisite exercise in allegori
cal motifs, references to classical sculpture and the celebration
of the liberal arts of music, poetry and painting. The panel
was certainly meant for a highly cultivated and sophisticated
patron, perhaps Lorenzo the Magnificent himself. It allegori
cally celebrates the peace and harmony of Medici Florence,
which was seen by many as the heir to classical civilization.

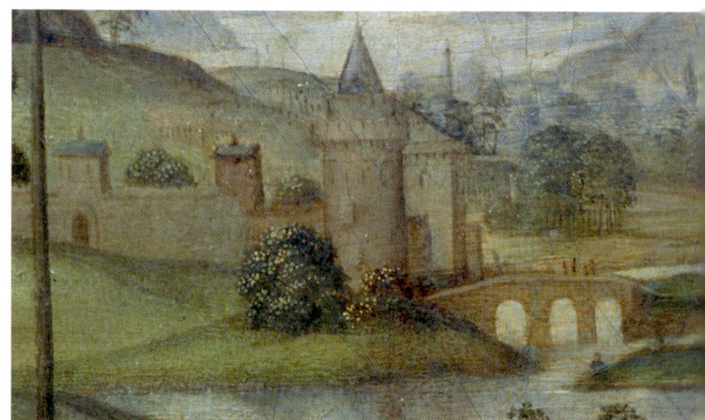

▲ The landscape with a
castle beside a bridge looks
very similar to that in *The
Lamentation* (see pages
164–5), confirming the
essential interchangeability
of some parts of Perugino's
paintings, regardless of
subject.

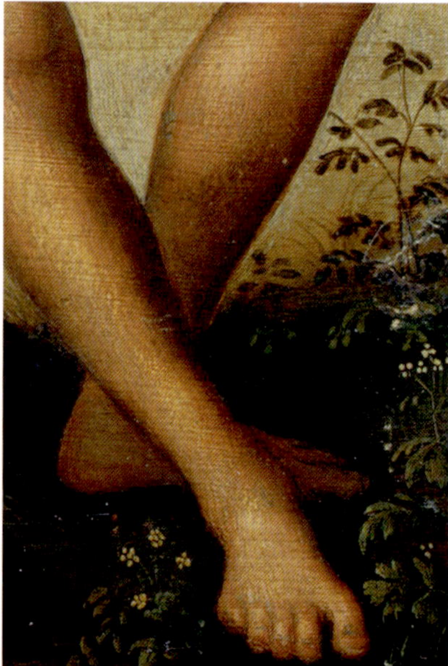

◄ The smooth, slender legs
of the shepherd who plays the
flute are based on a model by
Lysippus. The nudity of the
two figures is a homage to
classical art.

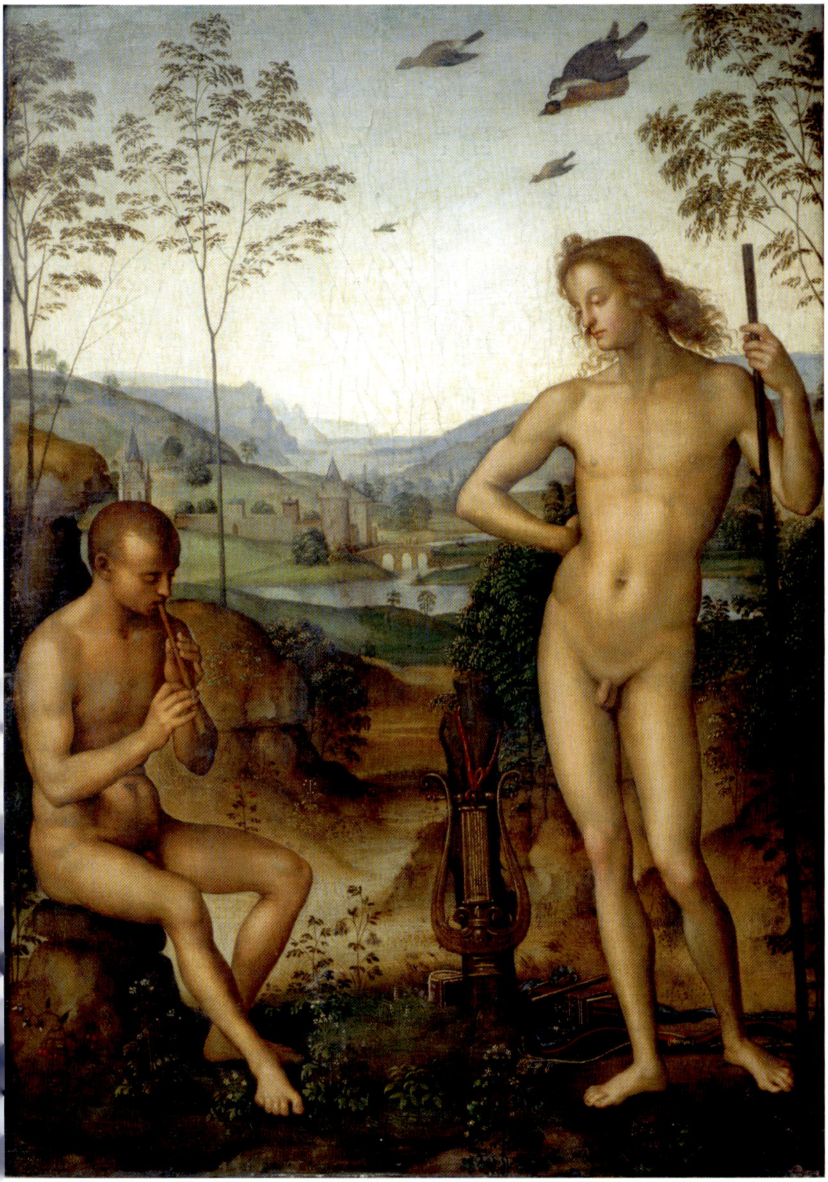

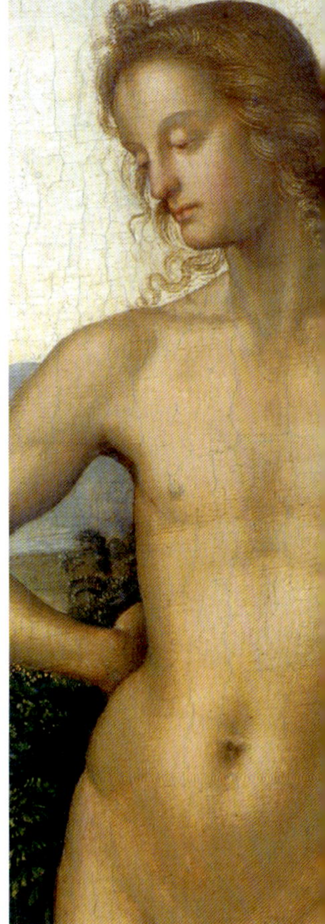

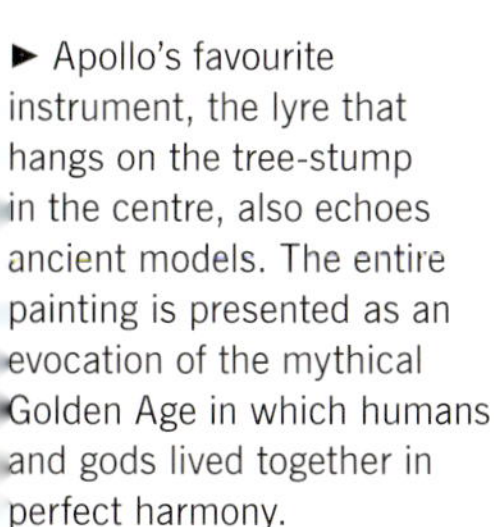

► Apollo's favourite instrument, the lyre that hangs on the tree-stump in the centre, also echoes ancient models. The entire painting is presented as an evocation of the mythical Golden Age in which humans and gods lived together in perfect harmony.

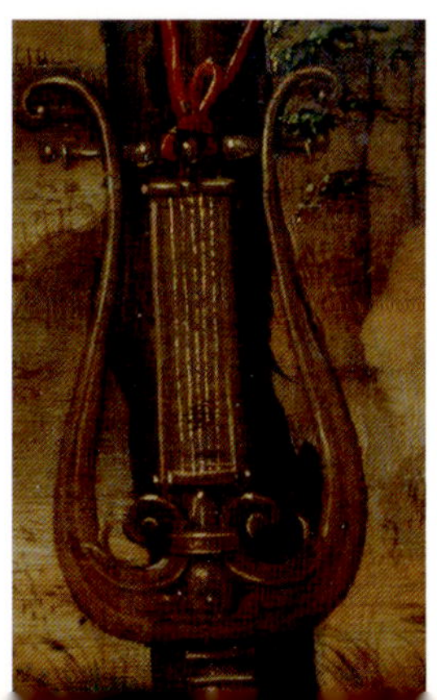

► Apollo's calm, balanced pose, leaning on a staff, derives directly from classical models. The elegant hint of *contrapposto* refers to Praxiteles, while the proportions of the slender body, elongated in comparison to his relatively small head, recall the canon of the Antique sculptor Lysippus.

Sandro Botticelli
The Calumny of Apelles
1494–5

Tempera on panel, 62 × 91 cm
Florence, Galleria degli Uffizi

For artist biography, see page 102.

Humanistic culture invited the comparison of different art forms with regard to their techniques, expressiveness and modes of enjoying them, even proposing a hierarchy. The visual arts, because they involved manual skill and technical knowledge of the 'trade', were often considered less 'noble' than poetry and musical composition. In their quest for full acknowledgment among the arts, painters turned their attention to a refined intellectual exercise known as *ekphrasis*. This Greek word refers to the literary description of a visual work of art – a practice common in Antiquity. Renaissance artists seized upon these ancient descriptions of ancient artworks and attempted to recreate them – in the process demonstrating the antiquity of their art, raising its status. The best-known case is Botticelli's reconstruction of an allegorical painting by the 4th-century BC Apelles, as described by the Greek author Lucian of Samosata.

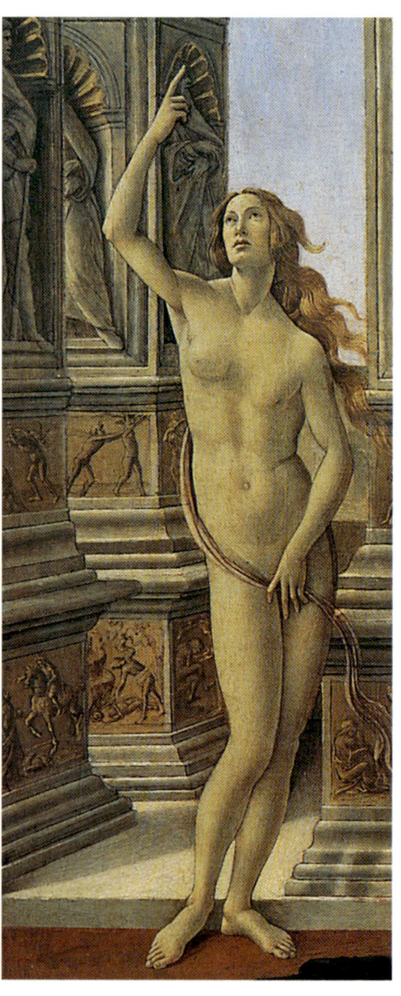

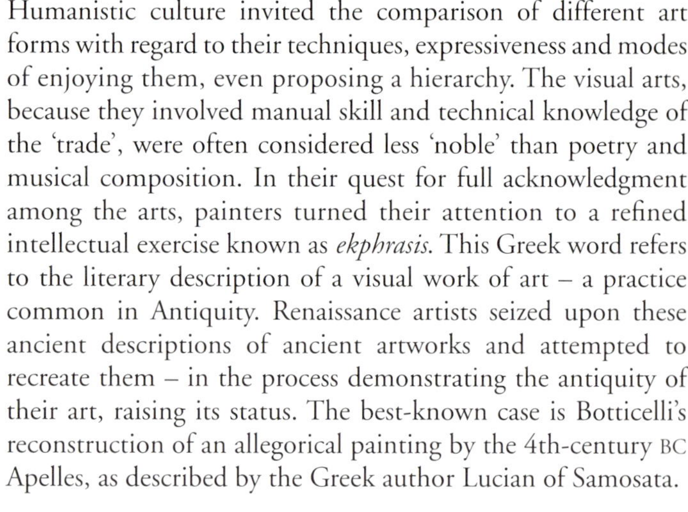

◀ On the left side of the painting, the stern, dark-robed figure of Remorse turns to look at the naked Truth – a figure that recalls the model in *The Birth of Venus* (see pages 132–3) – while she raises her eyes and one arm towards the sky.

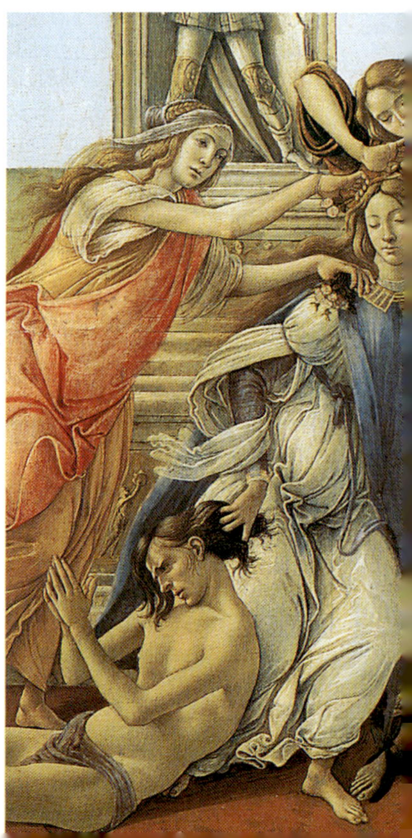

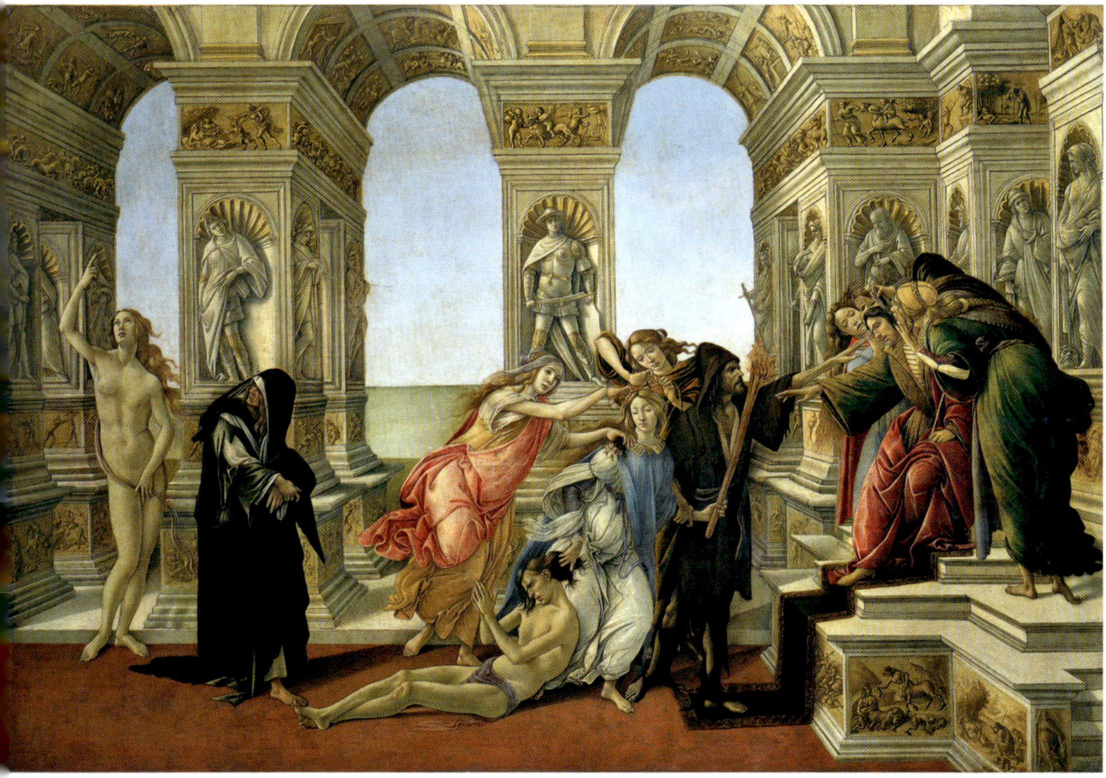

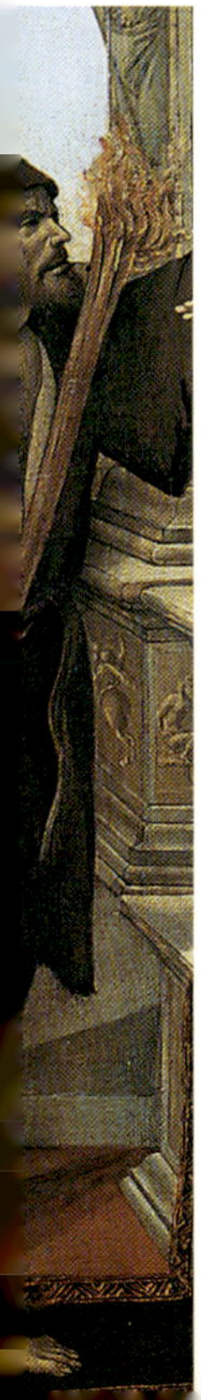

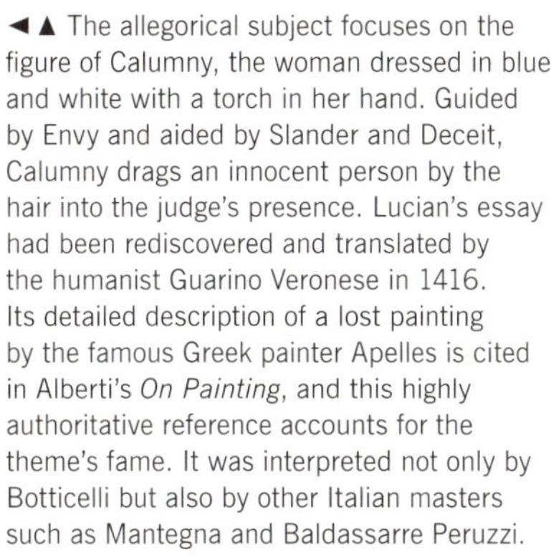

◄ ▲ The allegorical subject focuses on the figure of Calumny, the woman dressed in blue and white with a torch in her hand. Guided by Envy and aided by Slander and Deceit, Calumny drags an innocent person by the hair into the judge's presence. Lucian's essay had been rediscovered and translated by the humanist Guarino Veronese in 1416. Its detailed description of a lost painting by the famous Greek painter Apelles is cited in Alberti's *On Painting*, and this highly authoritative reference accounts for the theme's fame. It was interpreted not only by Botticelli but also by other Italian masters such as Mantegna and Baldassarre Peruzzi.

► Lending an ear to Ignorance and Suspicion, the judge condemns the innocent. Botticelli adds a new element to the literary description: the judge who relies on malicious counsellors is shown with a crown and a donkey's ears. These attributes identify him as King Midas, a canonical example of poor judgment. Thus Renaissance painting vies with classical literature.

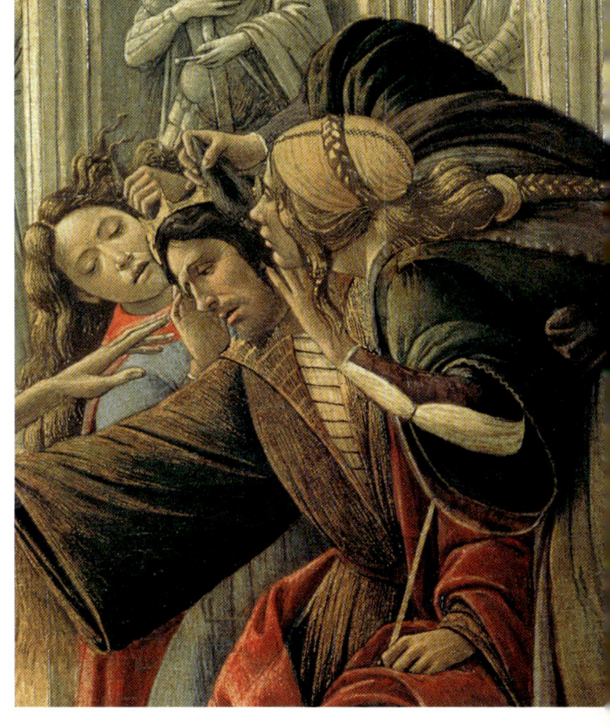

Balance

Pietro Perugino
The Virgin Appearing to St Bernard
1493–4

Oil on panel, 173 × 170 cm

Munich, Alte Pinakothek

For artist biography, see page 152.

In the two decades either side of the year 1500, Perugino was the most highly acclaimed painter in Italy. His works were admired and imitated throughout the entire peninsula, from Rome to Venice, from the duchy of Milan to the kingdom of Naples, from Umbria to Mantua. Perugino's success was so great that he had two workshops operating simultaneously, one in Florence (where he resided and worked for the most part) and another in Perugia. An expressive delicacy, which carefully avoids distortion and excess in the colours, expressions and poses, is an unmistakable feature of Perugino's painting. The figures are arranged in a pleasing, regular way amid calm architectural and natural settings.

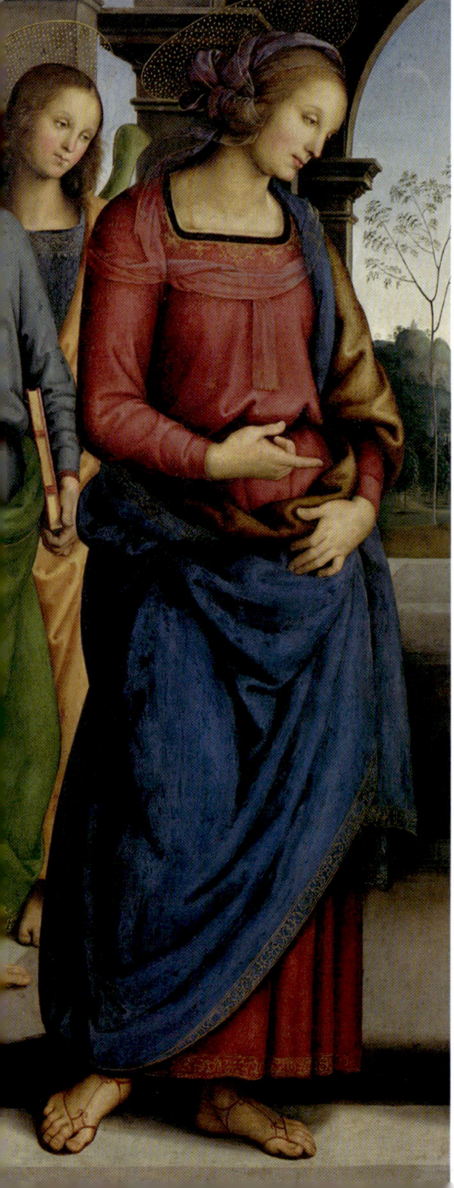

◄ The nature of mystical apparition stimulates the scene's sense of contemplation. Ten years earlier Filippino Lippi (see pages 134–5) had treated the same scene very differently. The figure of the Madonna was used by Raphael as the model for the *Marriage of the Virgin* (see pages 194–5).

▼ This painting shows a constant balancing of effects. The austere, grey columns are set against the distant view of the serene landscape, and the saint's cowl against the brighter colours of the angels' and Virgin's cloaks. Even the movement of the heads is calculated to create an alternation of subtle convergent and divergent movement.

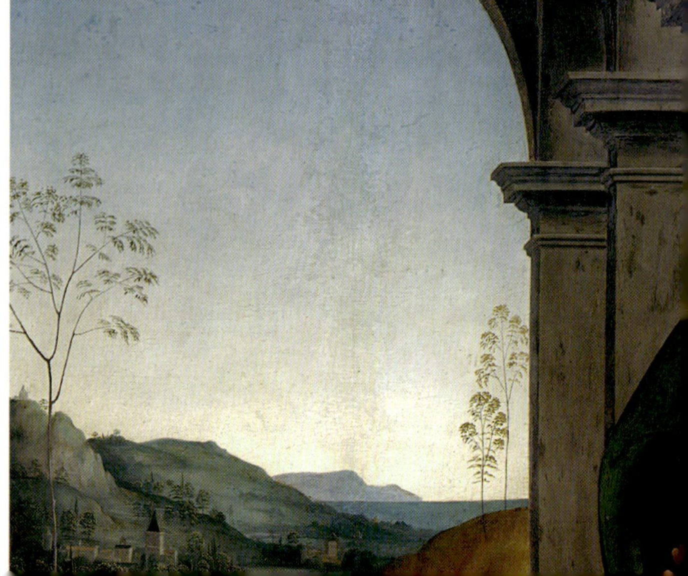

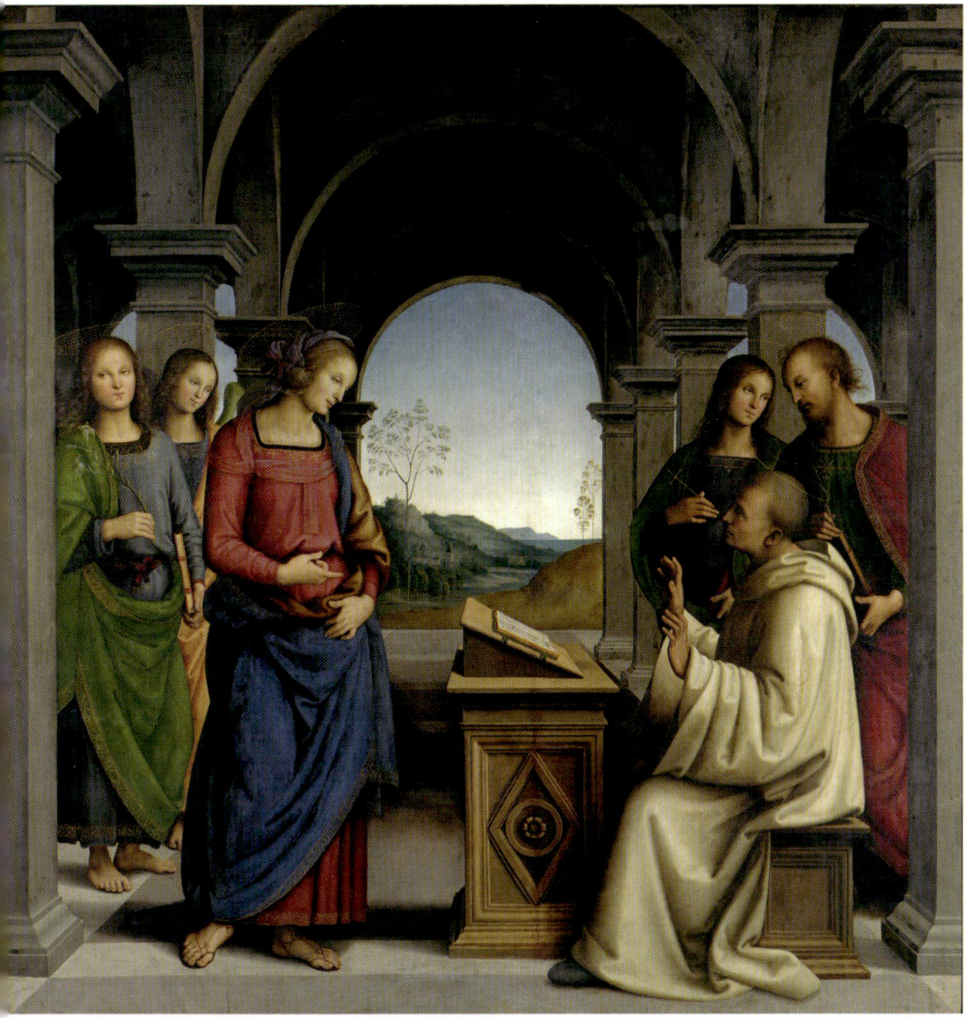

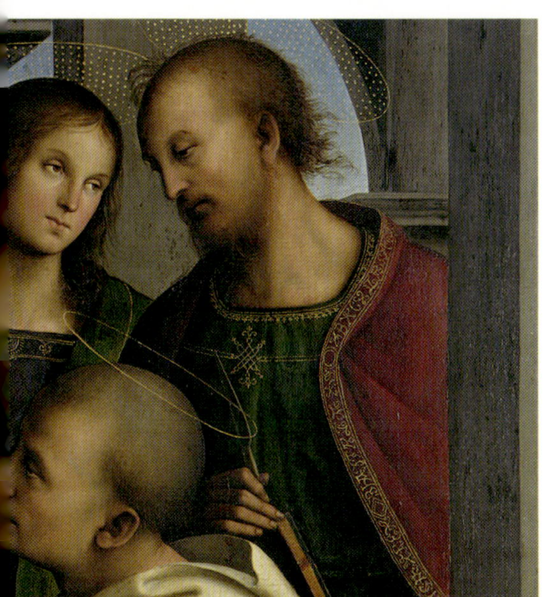

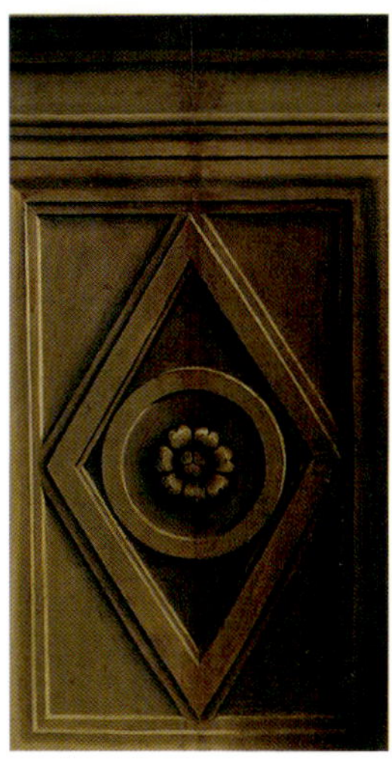

► St Bernard's lectern, with its simple, symmetrical decoration, enhances the sense of balance. This detail differs completely from the interpretation by Filippino Lippi, where the saint's books sit on a crude rustic wooden support.

Dynasty

Master of the Pala Sforzesca
Sforzesca Altarpiece
1494

Tempera and oil on panel, 230 × 165 cm
Milan, Pinacoteca di Brera

Master of the Pala Sforzesca

Active in Milan between 1480 and 1520

Despite scholarly research, no firm
identity has yet been determined for the
Lombard painter of this grandiloquent
altarpiece depicting the ducal family of
Milan (1494; today in the Pinacoteca
di Brera). A discrete, reconstructed group
of drawings, panel paintings and frescoes
by the anonymous painter belongs wholly
to the Lombardian school. It is highly
probable that he was among Bergognone's
collaborators in the decoration of the
Carthusian monastery of Pavia. His
traditional training is complemented by
references to the Ferrara school and,
above all, by his inevitable awareness of
the Milanese works of Leonardo da Vinci.

When painting needed to express a particular message
or reinforce political authority stylistic refinements took
second place to the needs of communication. For dynastic propaganda, the ambitious Duke of Milan, Ludovico
il Moro, turned not to his court painter Leonardo da Vinci
but to an anonymous Lombard master, less talented certainly
but who painted in a much simpler and more direct manner. The ducal family is posed kneeling before the Virgin in
a sumptuous setting full of luxurious details, amid gold,
gems and brocades. The scene is constructed along the customary central axis formed by the Virgin's throne, and quite
skilfully designed as a noble 'investiture' of the Duke of Milan
by the Queen of the Celestial Court.

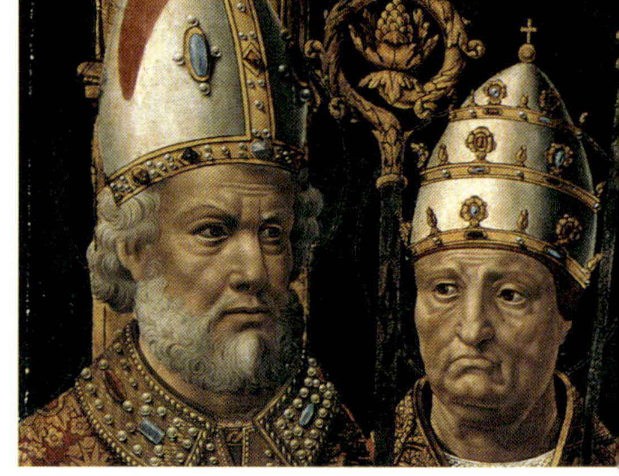

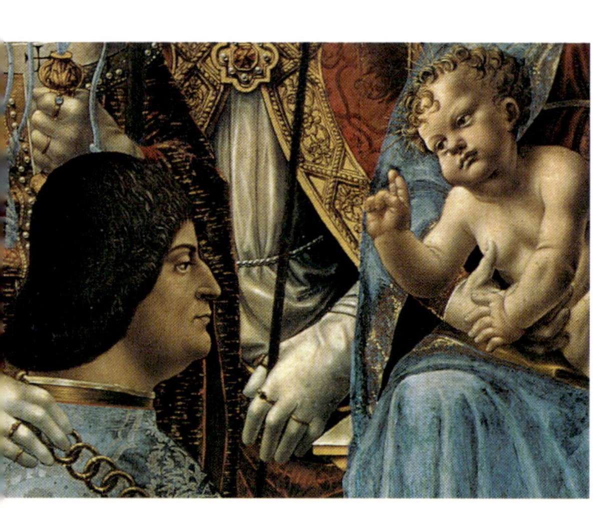

◄ Raising his right hand
in blessing, the Infant
Jesus turns towards the
Duke of Milan. In this way,
the painter alludes to the
divine protection enjoyed
by the Sforza family.

▲ The painting represents
the Madonna enthroned
among the four Doctors of
the Church. One of these, St
Ambrose (the bearded bishop
at the far left), is the patron of
the city of Milan. The saint's
right hand rests on Ludovico
il Moro's back, in an eloquent
gesture of protection.

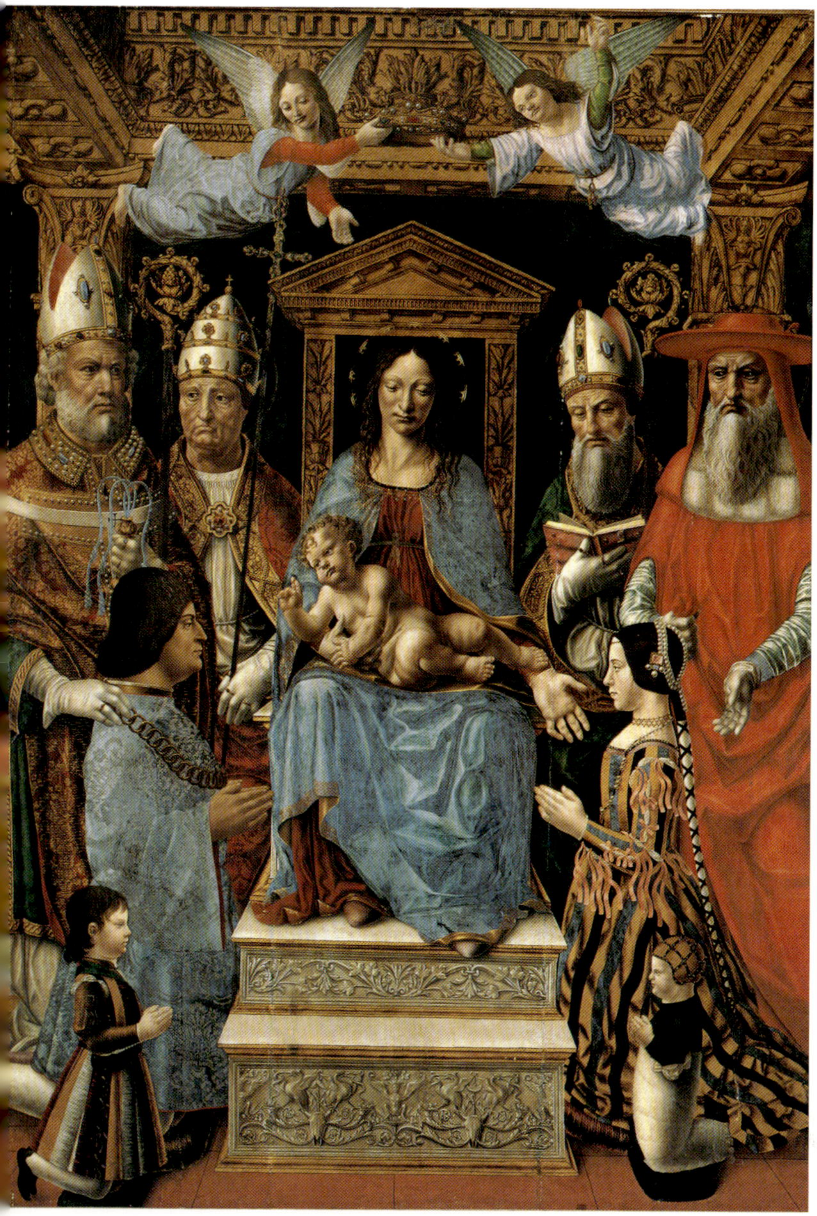

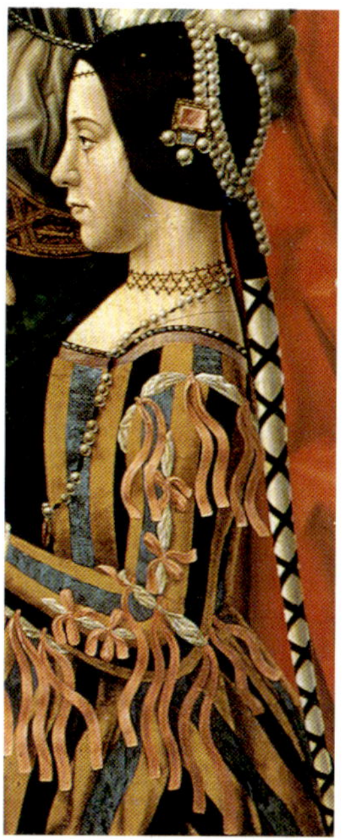

▲ Beatrice d'Este, the duke's wife, wears a dress that is itself a work of art. The young duchess – who, two years after this painting was made, died of a haemorrhage suffered at a ball – was famous for her original elegance. Her marriage to Il Moro took place in the context of matrimonial alliances of the time: Beatrice's brother Alfonso d'Este was the Duke of Ferrara, while her sister was the Marchesa of Mantua.

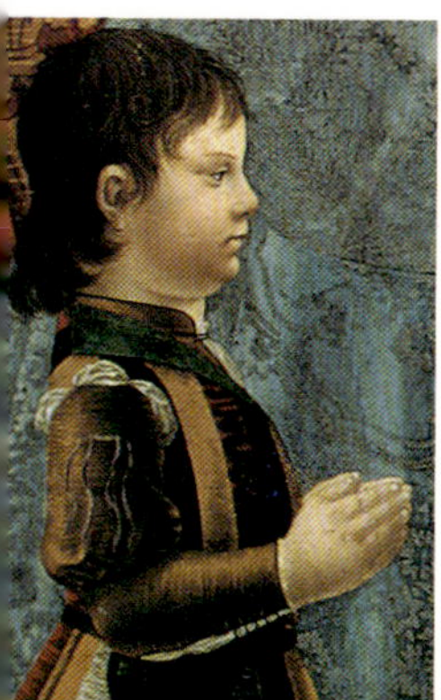

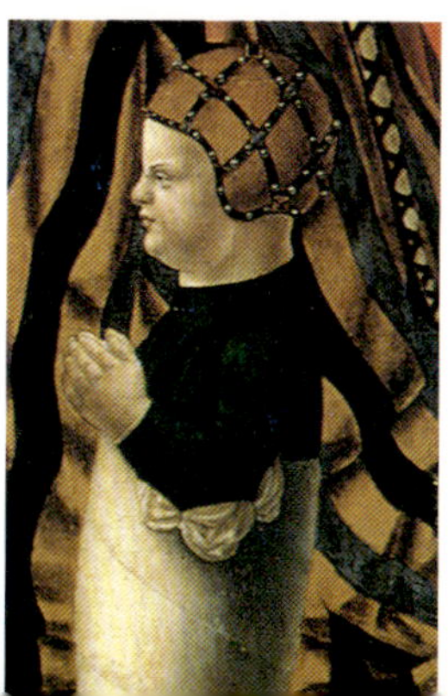

◄ Kneeling stiffly beside their parents, the little Francesco and Massimiliano (a very young child still wrapped in swaddling clothes) were a guarantee of dynastic continuity. The Sforza government was short-lived, however: in 1499, only five years after this altarpiece was painted, King Louis XII of France invaded the duchy of Milan. The following year, Ludovico il Moro was taken prisoner and exiled to France.

Movements of the Soul

Leonardo da Vinci
The Last Supper
1494–7

Oil on wall, 460 × 880 cm

Milan, Refectory of Santa Maria delle Grazie

For artist biography, see page 130.

Reacting decisively to the painting of Perugino and his followers (see pages 164–5), Leonardo imprinted his figures with a powerfully expressive eloquence, seeking to convey passions, emotions and thoughts through gestures and facial expressions. Despite the extensive deterioration caused by Leonardo's disastrous choice of medium, the recently restored *Last Supper* still shows the characteristic that made it a turning-point in art history: the physical and psychological action that stirs the figures. Each of the twelve Apostles reacts to Christ's words in a different way, expressing – as Leonardo wrote – his own 'movements of the soul'. This theme became almost an obsession with the painter, who defined painting as poetry without words. To intensify his depiction of the Apostles' emotions, the master carefully observed the sign language of the deaf while working on *The Last Supper*, and drew further inspiration from the facial expressions and hand gestures used by orators to reinforce their message.

'One of you shall betray me.'

Especially during his youth in Florence, Leonardo had the chance to see many depictions of The Last Supper *– a common subject in the history of painting – frescoed on the back walls of monastery refectories. This Gospel story, a key moment in Christianity, unfurls in a sequence of interconnected events. Christ, who has gathered his twelve Apostles in a large room for the Passover feast, performs the ritual actions that establish the sacrament of the Eucharist, that is, the offering of his body and blood in the form of consecrated bread and wine. He foretells of his imminent arrest and implicitly points to Judas as his betrayer. The moment chosen by Leonardo is not the most mystical, but it is by far the most dramatic. Christ speaks the words 'One of you shall betray me', and a storm of feeling breaks out among the Apostles: dismay, incredulity, anguish, perplexity, sadness, fear, resignation.*

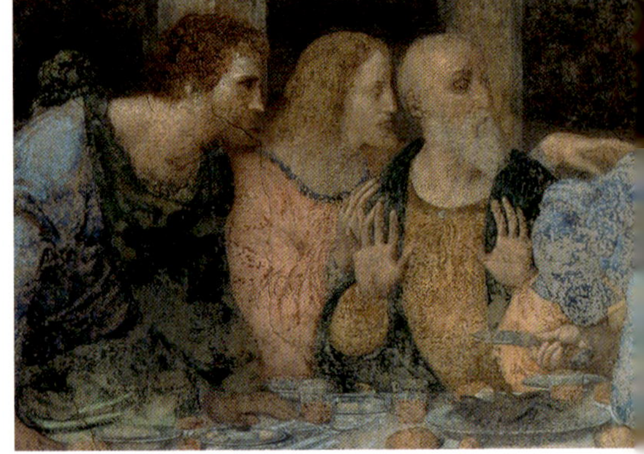

▲ Comparison with the fresco of this theme painted about half a century earlier by Andrea del Castagno (see pages 44–5) shows a substantial transition, from figures that are meditative and static to a dynamic composition where all the participants are involved simultaneously. Among other refinements, Leonardo places all twelve Apostles on the same side of the table. In all previous compositions, Judas was on the opposite side, separated from the others.

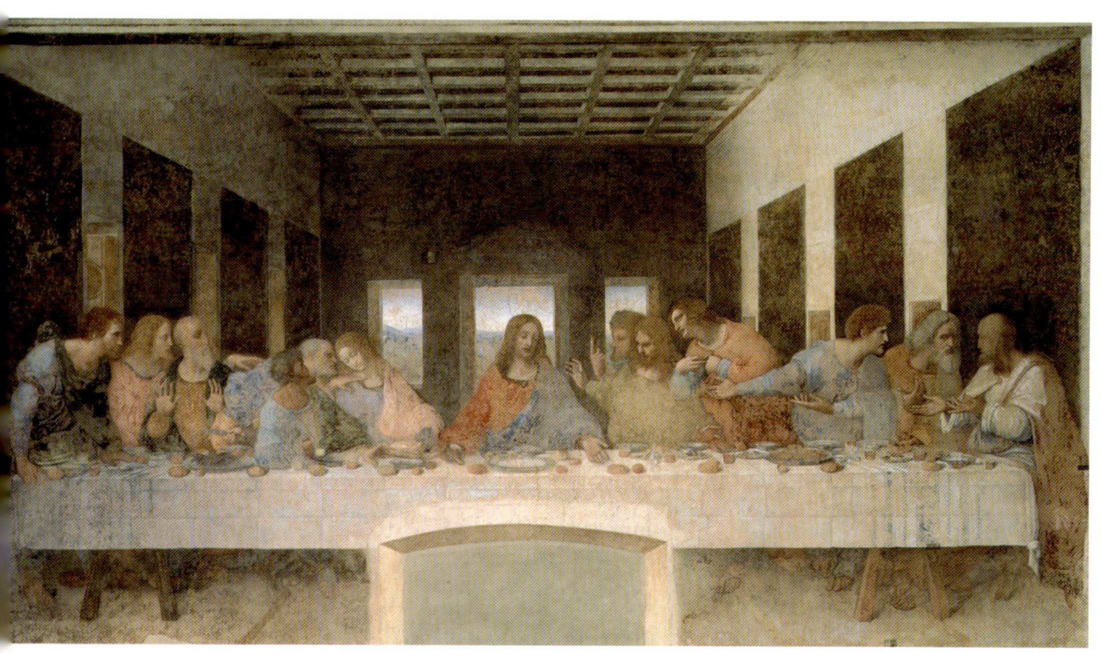

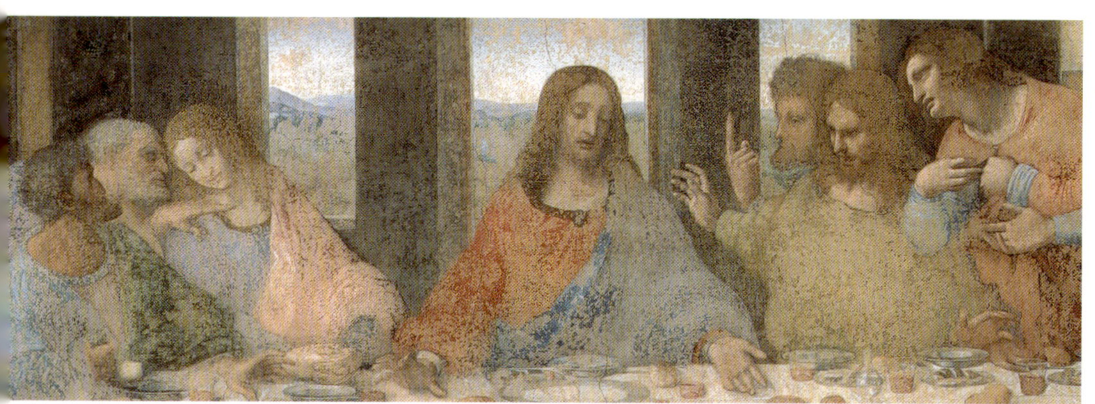

The Last Supper provides an impressive demonstration of Leonardo's ability to convey emotions through faces, hands and body motions. The brightly lit window in the centre of the composition frames Christ, around whom the Apostles seem to surge in waves, moving towards and away from him.

► The intensity of the Apostles' reactions fades the farther they are from the centre. The Apostles closest to Christ display urgent, animated gesture, while the figures at the far ends of the table, grouped, like the other Apostles, in threes, converse with relative calm.

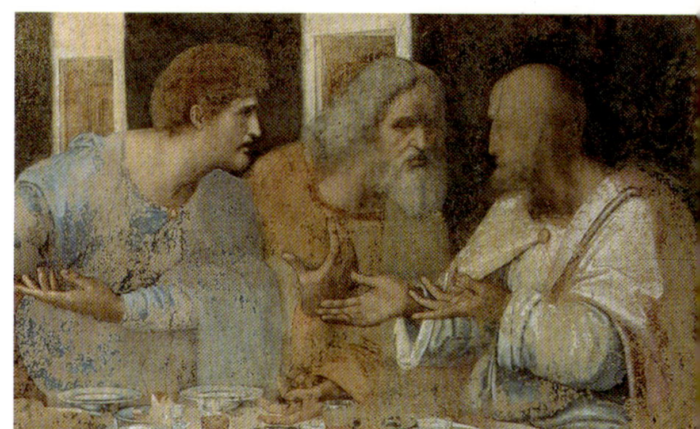

Telero

Vittore Carpaccio
The Meeting and Departure of the Betrothed Couple
1495

Tempera on canvas, 280 × 611 cm
Venice, Gallerie dell'Accademia

For artist biography, see page 184.

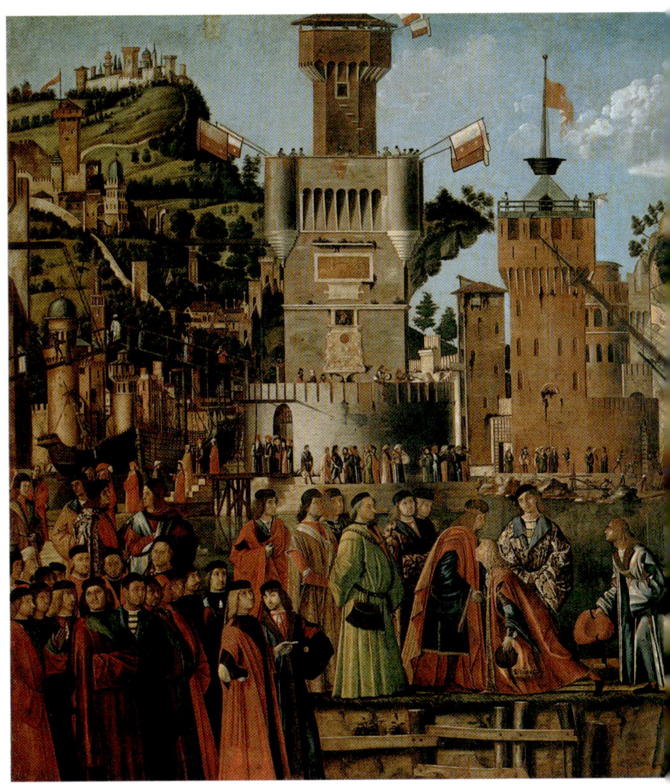

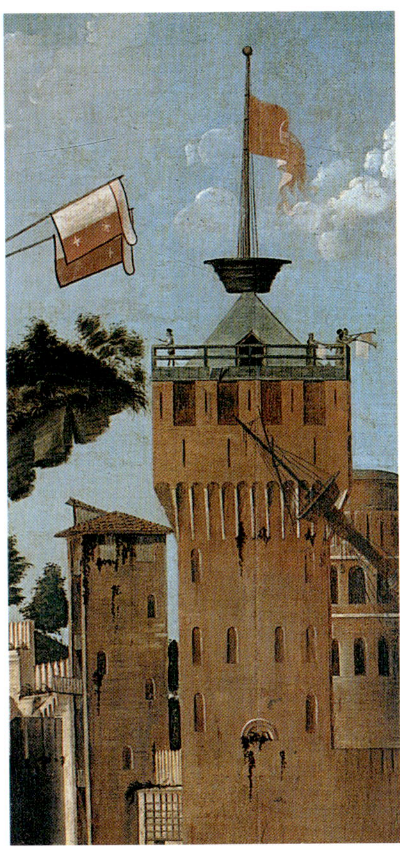

▲ The largest of the Sant'Orsola *teleri* is clearly divided in the centre by a banner fluttering above a standard. The skilful mixture of real and imaginary elements, such as the more than probable presence of many contemporary Venetian notables, gives the painting a mysterious ambiguity.

The climate of Venice has always been extremely problemat for the conservation of frescoes, which can be destroyed k damp, salty air in just a few years – as happened with the cyc that Giorgione and Titian executed on the exterior walls of th Fondaco dei Tedeschi. Reluctant to forgo opportunities to pai large, narrative scenes with episodes from the lives of the sain spreading across broad surfaces, the Venetians adopted the sy tem of *teleri*. The word *telero* refers to the special frames bu to accommodate large canvases and keep them at the corre tension. Organized in full cycles, these paintings completely f ceremonial settings, in particular the public areas of the Scuol confraternities to which tens of thousands of Venice's citize belonged. The founding of the oldest of these corporate cha table institutions dates back to the 13th century, but the Scuo were especially strong during the Renaissance, and proved to l active and demanding art patrons as well. Five 'Grandi' Scuo (San Marco, San Rocco, Carità, San Giovanni Evangelista ar Misericordia), as well as a host of smaller institutions, flourishe throughout the city.

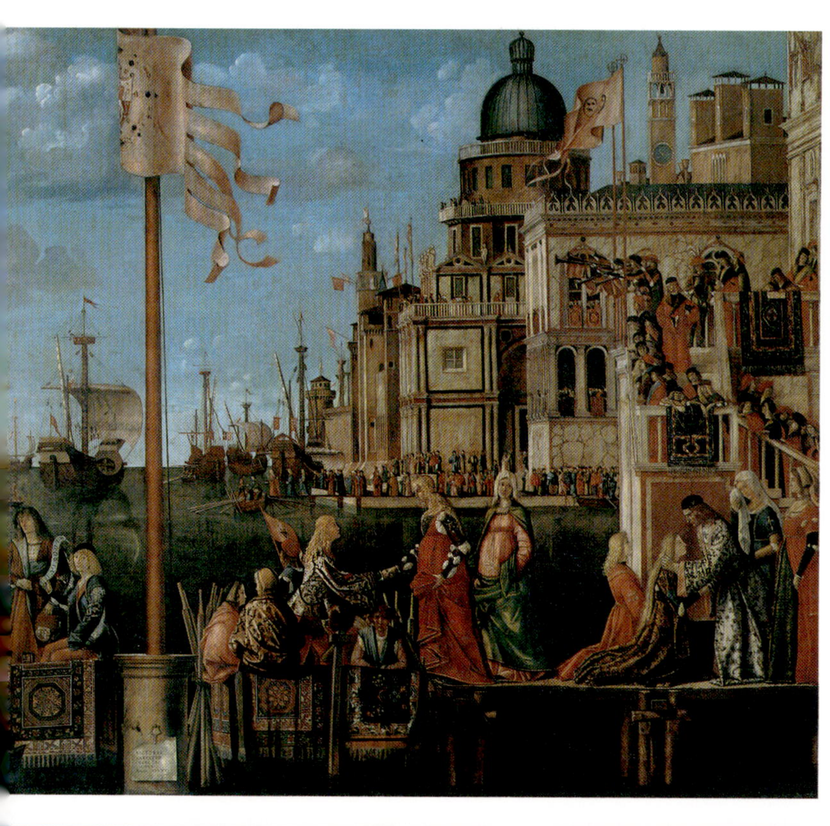

▼ Today, the paintings produced for the Scuola di Sant'Orsola are all displayed in a gallery of their own at the Gallerie dell'Accademia. Balancing reality and fantasy, Carpaccio rendered the tragic, romantic story of the beautiful princess Ursula and the young prince who seeks her hand in marriage.

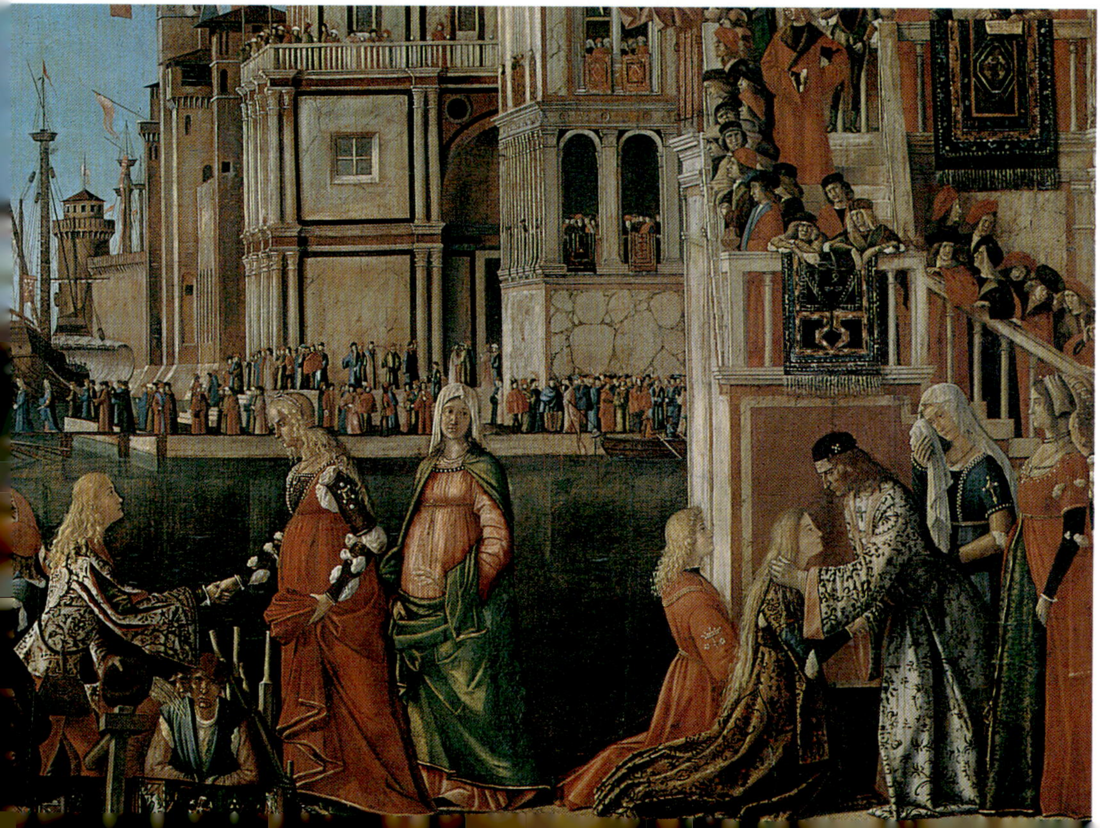

Psychological Indeterminacy

Pietro Perugino
The Lamentation
1495

Oil on panel, 214 × 195 cm

Florence, Galleria Palatina

For artist biography, see page 152.

In his quest for harmony and balance, Perugino avoided forceful, emotional characterization: even the most dramatic scenes unfold in gently lit natural or architectural settings, while feelings are conveyed through restrained gestures and controlled expressions. Perugino sought a tone halfway between quiet melancholy and gentle contemplation, without insisting on the psychology of the individual or the portrayal of affection. In this regard, *The Lamentation* is an exemplary work, highly admired and widely imitated for many years.

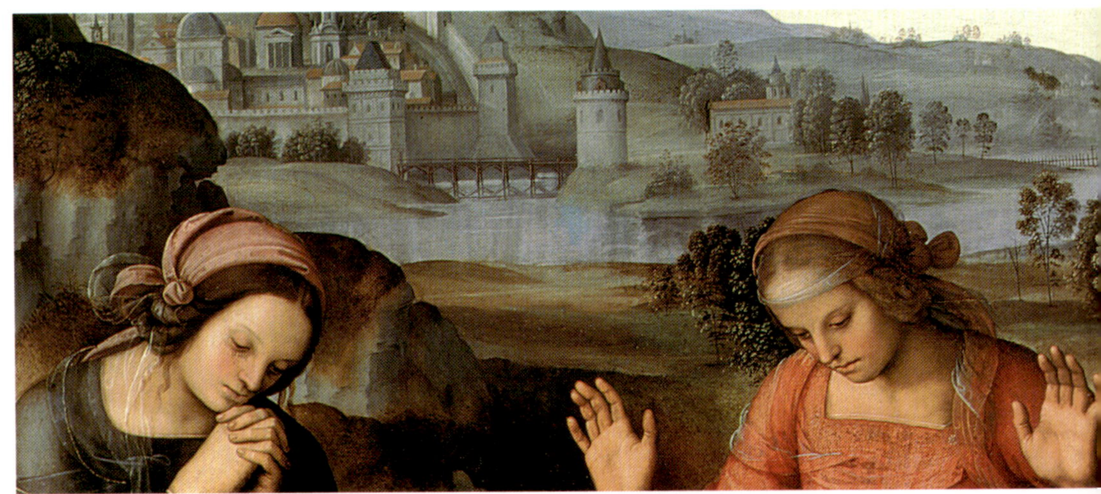

▲ The young women stand before a pleasant, peaceful landscape background, with clusters of trees, reflections in the water, rolling hills and meadows, and a distant walled city. The natural setting lends the entire painting with a mood of tranquillity.

► Even at the peak of the drama – Mary's lamentation over the body of her dead son – Perugino adheres to controlled facial expressions, and does not concern himself at all with emotions. Interpretations of the same theme by other painters and sculptors, especially those in northern Italy, accentuated the moments of poignancy.

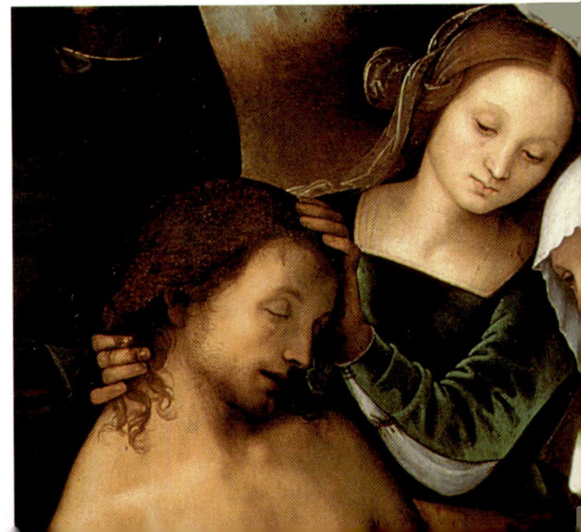

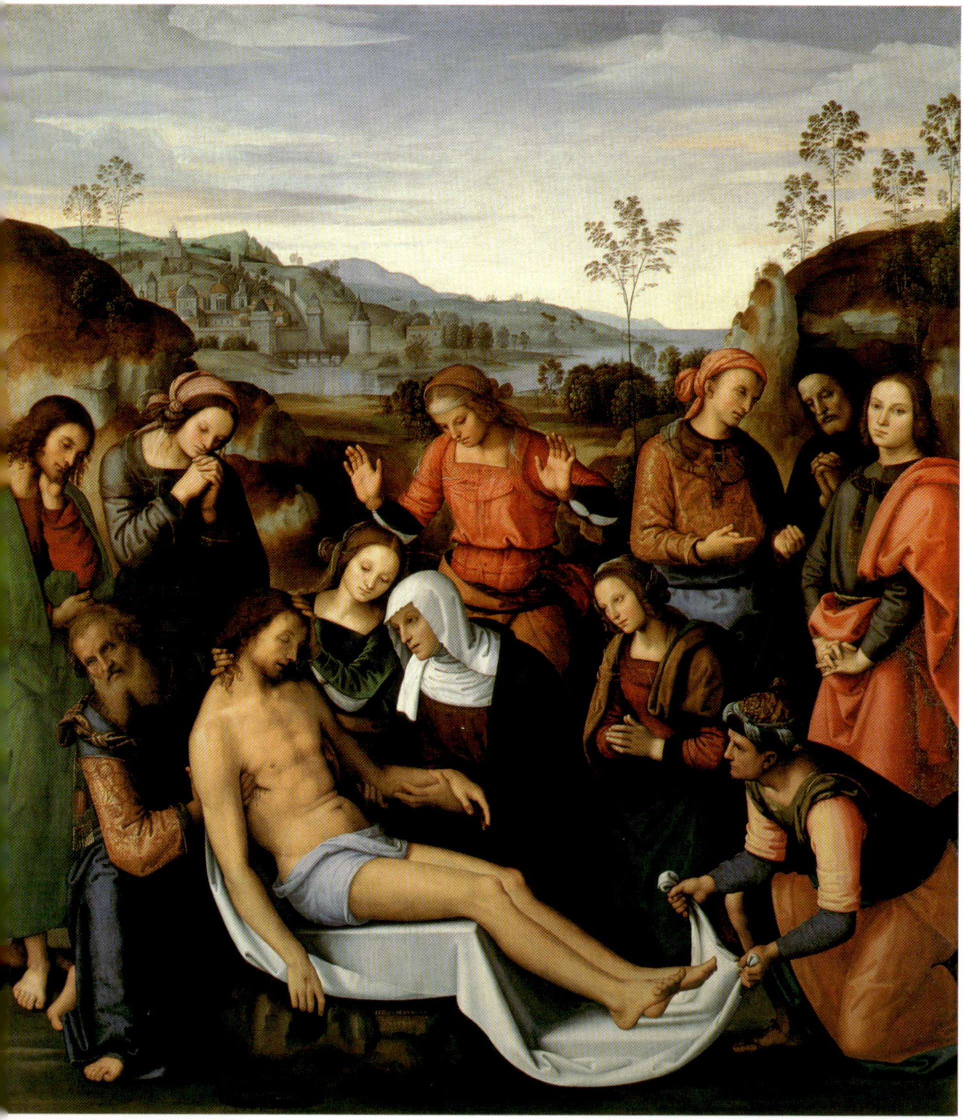

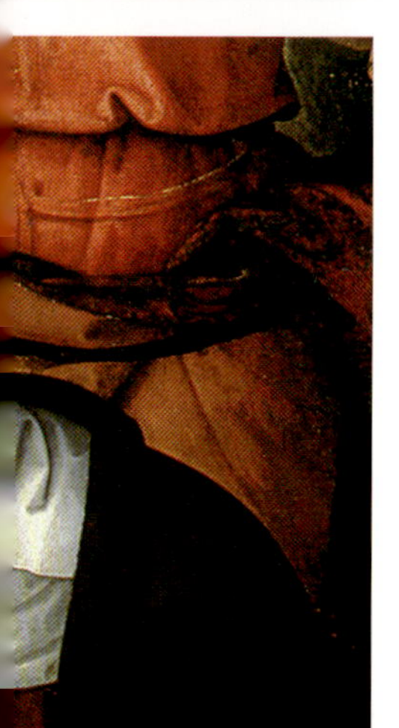

▶ Although immediately admired and copied because of its perfectly balanced composition and the refined execution, *The Lamentation* undeniably includes some essentially 'interchangeable' figures. The controlled poses and neutral facial expressions allowed Perugino to insert them into other compositions without difficulty.

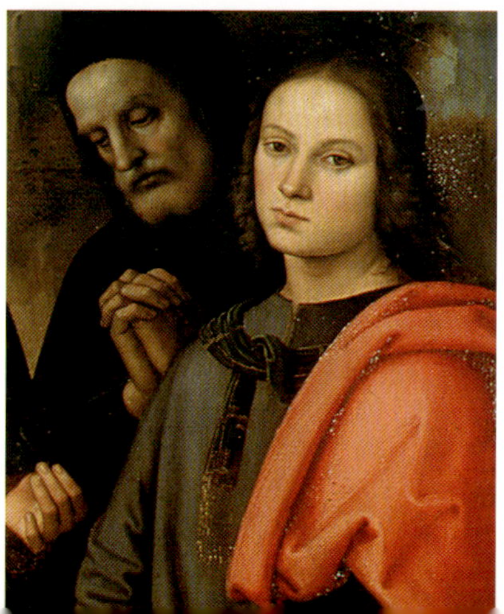

Veduta

Gentile Bellini
Procession in Piazza San Marco
1496

Tempera and oil on canvas, 367 × 745 cm
Venice, Gallerie dell'Accademia

Gentile Bellini

Venice, c. 1430–1507

The son of a painter, brother of Giovanni Bellini and the brother-in-law of Mantegna, Gentile began to work independently in the 1460s, obtaining official commissions from the Republic from 1466 on. Gentile Bellini was a 'portraitist' of persons and cities. We owe to him the first true views of Venice, observed and celebrated in the hour of its greatest splendour. Gentile was an outstanding draughtsman, driven by an intense curiosity in the world around him, and in 1479 he was invited to Constantinople on an artistic and diplomatic mission (see the *Portrait of the Sultan Mehmet II*, London, National Gallery). In 1496, he began the execution of his most important work, a cycle of narrative scenes for the Scuola di San Giovanni Evangelista, today at the Gallerie dell'Accademia, which form a rich document of the urban and social realities of Venice. He died before completing the large canvas of *St Mark Preaching in Alexandria* (Milan, Pinacoteca di Brera) for the Scuola di San Marco. His brother Giovanni finished it.

The landscape of the Veneto and, even more so, the incomparable urban setting of Venice, were obvious sources of inspiration for local painters. Vivid, immediate depictions of the Serenissima on the threshold of the 16th century can be found in the *teleri* that once decorated the Scuola di San Giovanni Evangelista. Venice is the setting for the episodes that concern the relic of the True Cross (which is one of the treasures conserved at the Scuola) and the people and places are recognizable. Scenes such as the *Miracle in Campo San Lio* by Giovanni Mansueti, the huge *Procession in Piazza San Marco* by Gentile Bellini and the *Miraculous Healing of the Possessed Man* by Vittore Carpaccio, with the view of the Grand Canal spanned by the old Rialto Bridge, offer invaluable documentation of the city as it was. They may be considered a precedent for the subsequent development of the *veduta* (view), a particular strain of landscape painting for which, several centuries later, Venice provided some of the favourite subjects.

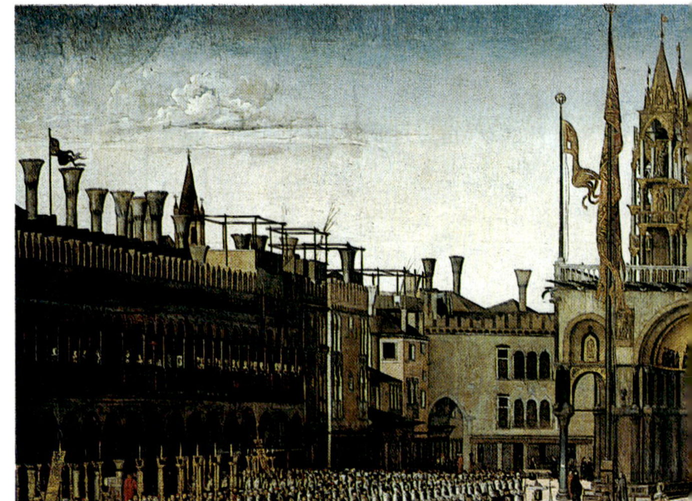

▲ This large scene may be considered one of the first realistic urban views in history. The huge façade of the basilica of San Marco is represented with meticulous exactitude, as are the other buildings in this spectacular setting, including the Gothic ducal palace. The one important exception is the bell tower, which has been depicted to the right of its actual location in order to leave more room for the advancing procession.

► The main subject of the scene is the solemn procession that moves through Piazza San Marco. The reliquary with the fragment of the True Cross is carried beneath a canopy, and the members of the confraternity wear long white robes.

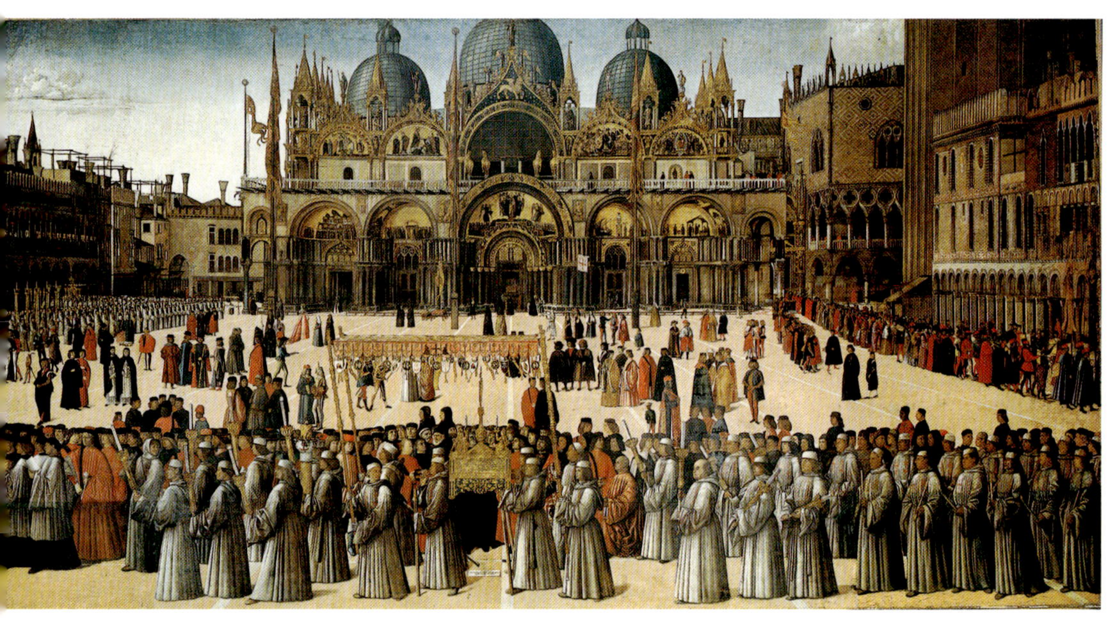

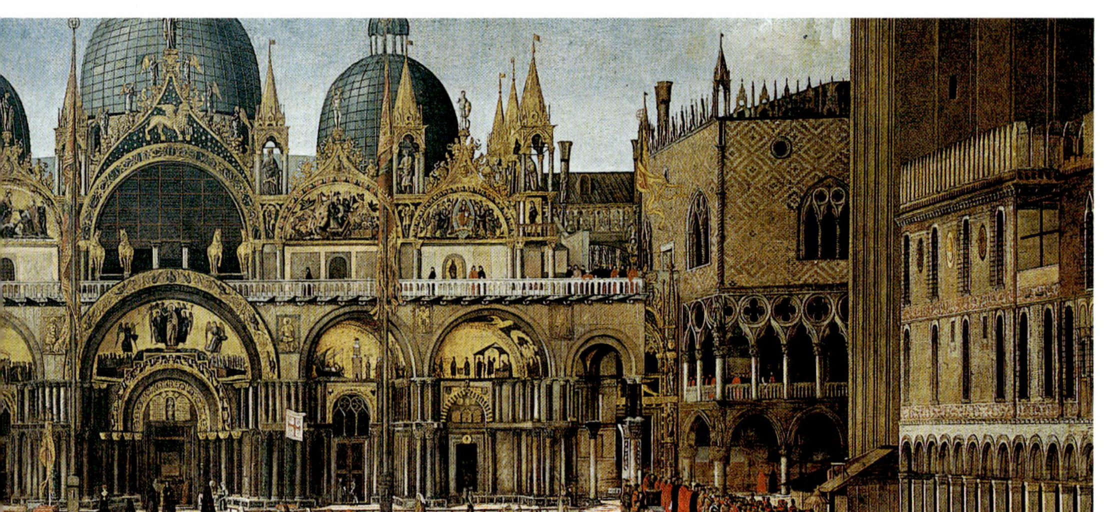

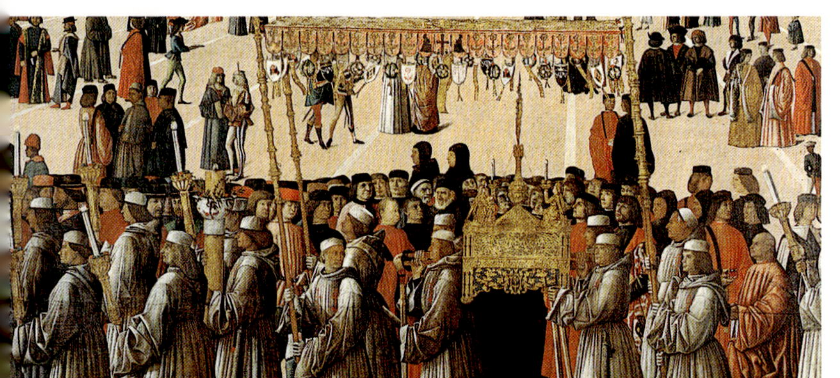

▲ This first *telero* from the cycle of the relic of the True Cross, conserved at the Scuola di San Giovanni Evangelista, faithfully represents the magnificent setting of Piazza San Marco, providing an eloquent image of Venice at the height of its power.

Self-portrait

Pietro Perugino
Self-portrait
1498–1500

Fresco, 40 × 30.5 cm
Perugia, Collegio del Cambio

Pinturicchio
Self-portrait
Detail from *The Annunciation*
1496–1501

Fresco
Spello, Perugia, Santa Maria Maggiore,
Baglioni Chapel

Pietro Perugino

For artist biography, see page 152.

Pinturicchio

(Bernardino di Betto)
Perugia, *c.* 1454–Siena, 1513

A representative of the delicate and highly regarded Umbrian school, Pinturicchio excelled in sumptuous fresco decorations. Trained in Perugia, he was Perugino's main assistant in the execution of the refined *Story of St Bernardino of Siena* (1473; Perugia, Galleria Nazionale dell'Umbria) and then at the Sistine Chapel (1481–2). Around the age of 30, Pinturicchio left Perugino's workshop and struck out on his own, alternating between Perugia and Rome, where he created his most important works, including the frescoes in Santa Maria d'Aracoeli, Santa Maria del Popolo and, especially, Pope Alexander VI's apartments in the Vatican (1492–5). Decorated in fresco, with gilding and applied stucco, the Vatican rooms reveal the strong influence of Roman murals, such as those in the Domus Aurea, and others that had recently been rediscovered. When Pinturicchio returned to Umbria, it was to paint both altarpieces and frescoes: the most outstanding are those at the Baglioni Chapel in Spello (1501). His crowning masterpiece is the Piccolomini Library, an annexe to the cathedral in Siena (1505), one of the most captivating early 16th-century settings. For this decorative undertaking, Pinturicchio made use of drawings by the young Raphael.

The artist achieved a far higher status in Renaissance Italy than anywhere else in Europe at this time. One indication of this is the frequency of signatures, sometimes followed by a brief annotation or simply the letter 'F', standing for the Latin *faciebat* (He made it). While Italian artists wanted to be identified as creators, putting their names on their work for others to see, in other nations the vast majority of painters remained essentially anonymous until the 16th century. Fifteenth-century Italian painters also sometimes inserted their own likeness into larger compositions, while the increasingly widespread custom of painting one's own portrait, a living presence, represented a further advance for Italian artists.

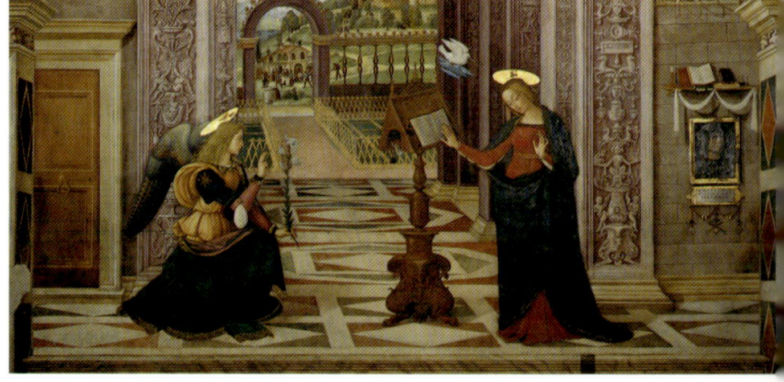

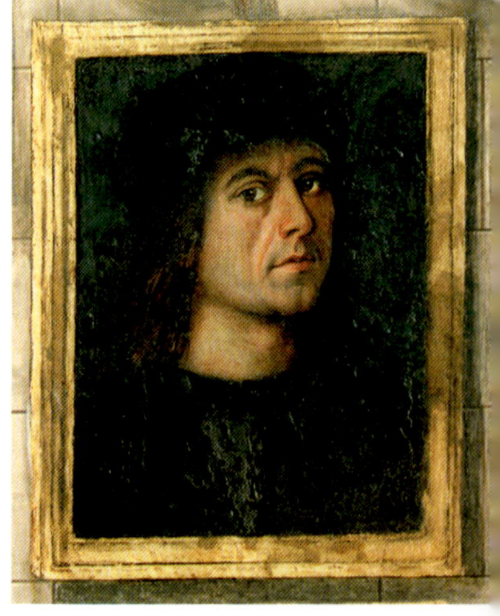

▲ ► Pinturicchio chose a spot for his self-portrait similar to the one that Pietro Perugino found: in a small painting-within-a-painting, in one of his most important fresco cycles, in the Baglioni Chapel in Spello.

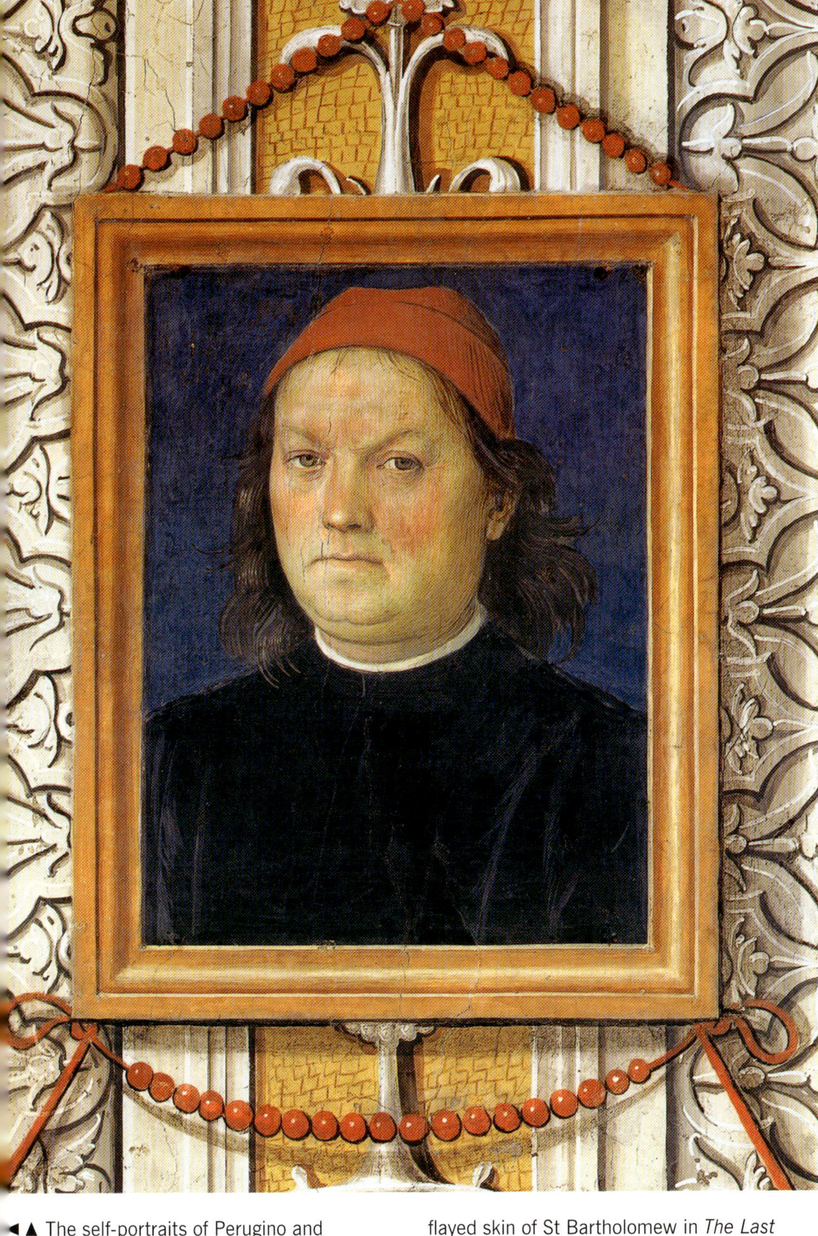

◀ ▲ The self-portraits of Perugino and Pinturicchio usher in the 16th century, which was a century of self-portraits. At the peak of the High Renaissance, Raphael painted himself among the scholars and philosophers in *The School of Athens*; Michelangelo, exhausted by the dramatic disillusionment of history and his life, painted himself as an old man on the flayed skin of St Bartholomew in *The Last Judgment* in the Sistine Chapel. The Mannerist Parmigianino's *Self-portrait in a Convex Mirror* is an exercise in virtuosity, while Titian's series of self-portraits shows the painter growing old but always aware of himself and his greatness, ready to face eternity clasping the paintbrush in his fist.

Anatomy

Luca Signorelli
The Resurrection of the Flesh
Detail from the *Story of the*
Apocalypse
1499

Fresco

Orvieto Cathedral, San Brizio Chapel

Luca Signorelli

Cortona, Arezzo, *c.* 1445–1523

Active in various central Italian localities in the late 15th century, Luca Signorelli was stylistically autonomous. Arezzo, Florence and Urbino were the stopping points in a youthful career, during which he was a pupil of Piero della Francesca and Antonio del Pollaiuolo, masters from whom he absorbed the rules of perspective and the expressive intensity possible through modelling. Luca Signorelli was called to Rome by Perugino to work on the frescoes in the Sistine Chapel where, through contact with the Umbrian artist, his style became less rough. He moved to Florence and took his place in the cultural milieu around Lorenzo the Magnificent. After Lorenzo's death, the painter left Florence to work in smaller centres, creating two memorable fresco cycles: the *Story of St Benedict* in the cloister of the abbey of Monteoliveto Maggiore (1496–8) and the *Apocalypse* in the San Brizio Chapel at the cathedral of Orvieto (1499–1504).

The Renaissance witnessed a new, more direct and scientific approach to nature. An example closely related to art is the study of anatomy. Medicine had long been faced with the strictures imposed by classical authors such as Aristotle. Because it was considered indecorous for a physician to touch a patient, 'quacks' performed operations, and scientific illustrations were so generic as to be completely useless. Leonardo da Vinci was the first artist to plan an illustrated treatise on human anatomy, for which he made extraordinary drawings based on his own dissections of cadavers. As demonstrated by the frescoes of Luca Signorelli, the new awareness of anatomy affected the study of the nude in painting. Artists turned to reality rather than to models of classical statuary and traditional diagrams.

Treatises and Illustrations Straddling Medicine and Art

After the pioneering treatise published in Bologna by Jacopo Berengario da Carpi (1521), medical and scientific illustration finally found a cornerstone in the volume by Andreas Vesalius (the Latinized name of the Belgian physician André Vésale), De humani corporis fabrica, *published in Basel in 1543 and illustrated with marvellous plates engraved by the German Johann Stephan Calcar, probably with the direct participation of Titian. The publication of this revolutionary volume corresponds to the heated debate initiated by Michelangelo's fresco of* The Last Judgment *in the Sistine Chapel, over the relationship between body and soul, flesh and spirit, physical and moral nudity.*

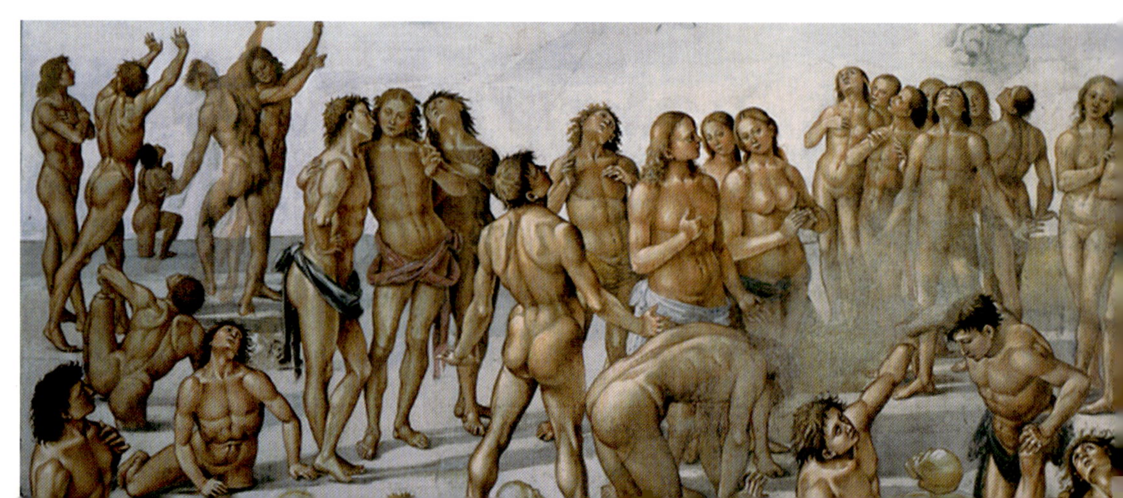

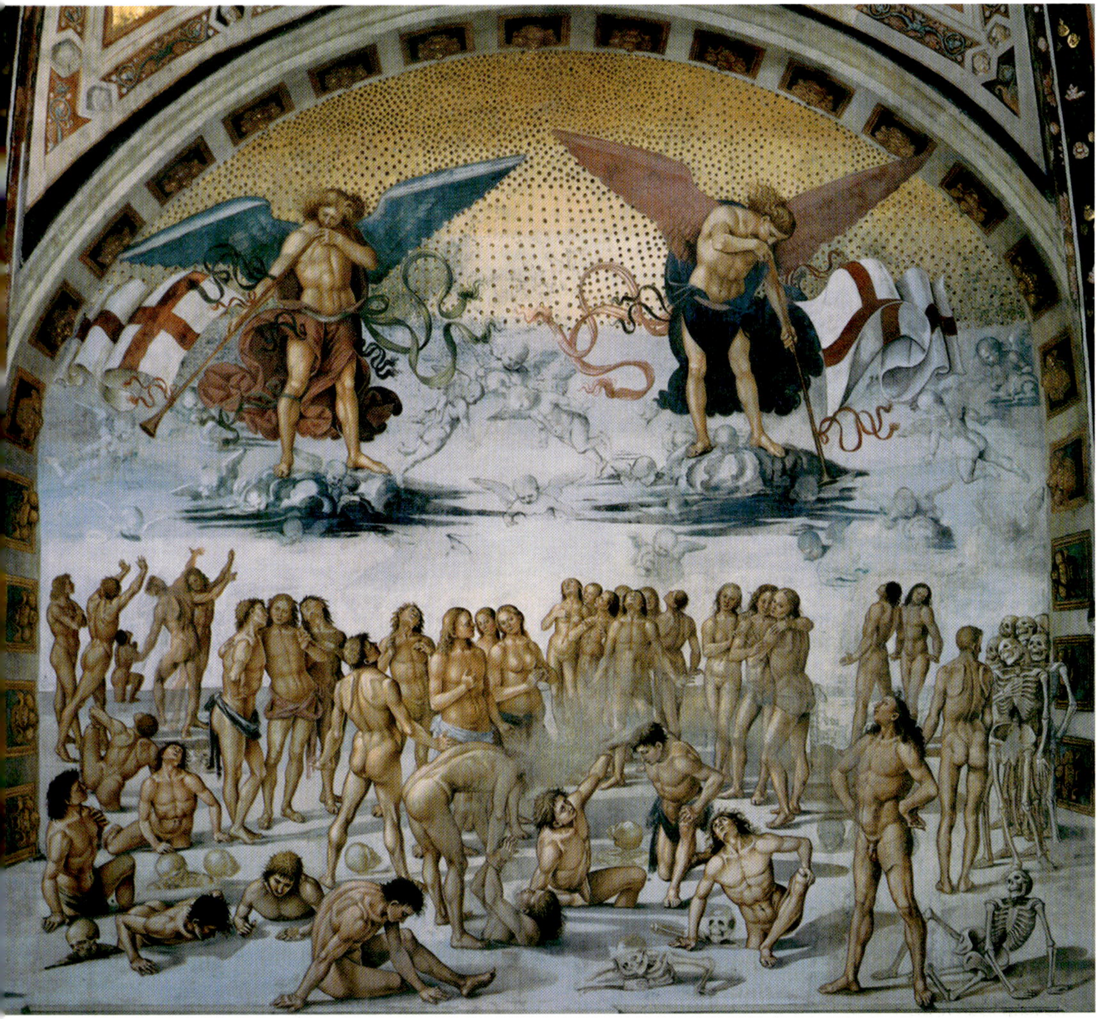

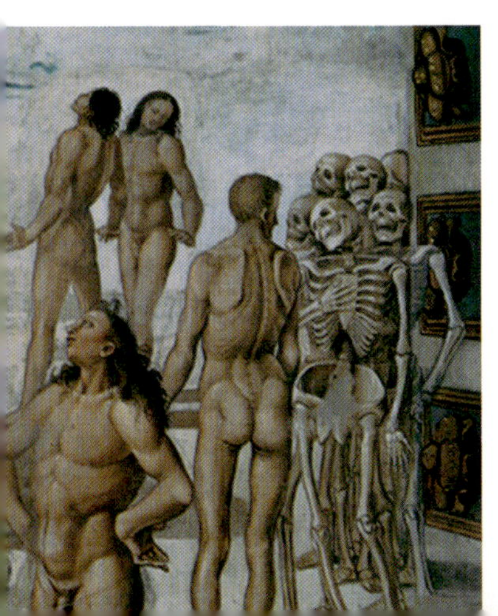

▲ ► In the mid-15th century Fra Angelico began the fresco cycle in the chapel of San Brizio, but painted only part of the ceiling. The large lunettes along the walls are a powerful visual invention of Luca Signorelli, who represented the *Story of the Apocalypse* leading up to the Last Judgment and the division of the damned and the blessed between Hell and Paradise. In this scene, at the sound of the trumpets played by two muscular angels, the dead rise from their tombs and the skeletons put on flesh, regaining their human appearance.

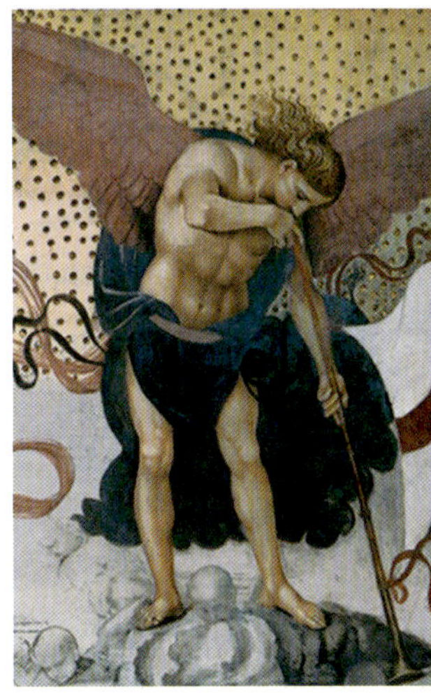

◄ This series of poses and attitudes provided an inventive repertoire of male and female nudes, and moved beyond the classical models derived from ancient reliefs and sarcophagi.

Divine Proportions

Jacopo de' Barbari
Portrait of Luca Pacioli
c. 1495

Oil on canvas, 99 × 120 cm

Naples, Museo Nazionale di Capodimonte

Jacopo de' Barbari

Venice, *c.* 1445–*c.* 1515

The information we have regarding the birth and death of the painter Jacopo de' Barbari is sketchy. In the early years of his career, he concentrated his activity in his native city, where he was in the circle of Alvise Vivarini. It was in Venice that de' Barbari met Dürer in 1495 and soon became his friend and profound admirer. Then came the controversial and well-known *Portrait of Luca Pacioli*, dated *c.* 1495, today in the Museo Nazionale di Capodimonte in Naples. In 1500, the artist moved to Germany where he worked until 1502 under the name of Jacob Walch in Nuremberg, in the service of Emperor Maximilian. Documentary evidence indicates that de' Barbari worked for the Elector of Saxony in Wittenberg from 1502 to 1504. Later, around 1510, he settled in Flanders, where he was a court painter to Marguerite of Austria. Among his most noteworthy works are about 20 engravings, including the famous *Perspective View of Venice* from 1500.

The Franciscan friar and mathematician Luca Pacioli was born around 1445 in Borgo Sansepolcro, also the birthplace of Piero della Francesca. Based on that great painter's studies, notes and conversations with him, Pacioli wrote *De divina proportione*, a treatise on solid geometry that was a great success, and not only in Italy. Leonardo da Vinci illustrated a lavish manuscript copy in 1497, during Pacioli's stay at the court of Ludovico il Moro in Milan, but the definitive edition dates from 1509. He was a professor of geometry at the University of Bologna in the early 16th century, and was considered the greatest theoretician on perspective and the proportions of the human body of the time. Even the German painter Albrecht Dürer, on his second trip to Italy, sought out Pacioli.

► Artists of the late 15th century repeatedly interpreted the complex, faceted geometrical solids and voids described in Luca Pacioli's treatise. In addition to Leonardo's illustrations for the codex of 1497 (today in the Biblioteca Ambrosiana in Milan), Fra Giovanni da Verona made intarsia panels.

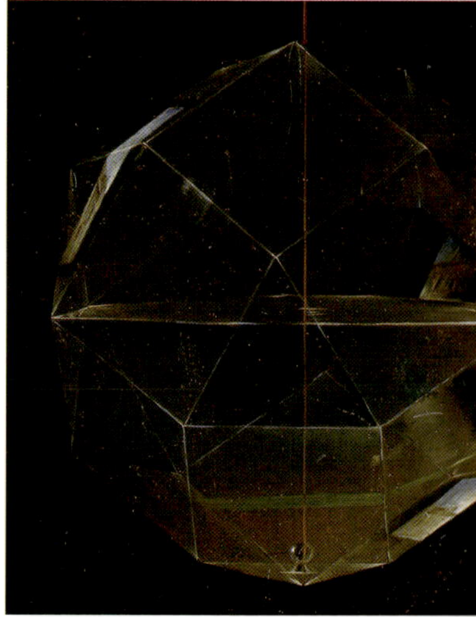

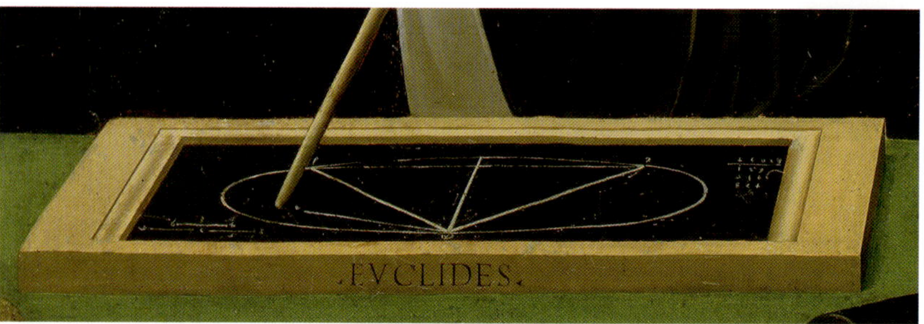

◄ The mathematician friar is demonstrating a Euclidean theorem (an equilateral triangle inscribed in a circle) with a slate blackboard and a pointer. Euclid's name is written on the edge of the blackboard.

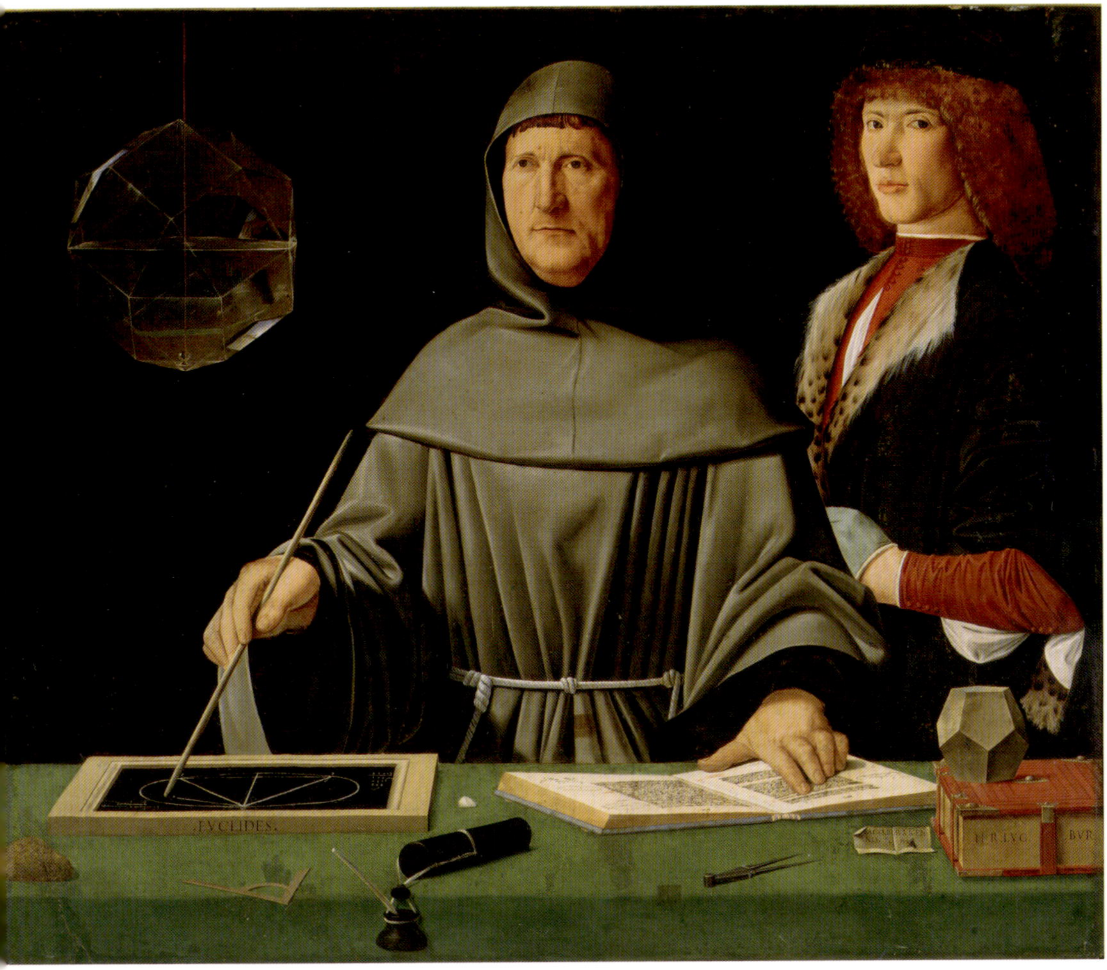

▼ *De divina proportione* was the most authoritative and influential treatise on mathematics in the late 15th century. Luca Pacioli also wrote *Summa de arithmetica* (published in 1494, a sort of encyclopaedia of mathematics consisting of a collection of math and logic games) plus a brief treatise on chess.

▲ The attribution of this painting to the Venetian painter Jacopo de' Barbari is still quite controversial. The aristocratic young pupil is perhaps Guidobaldo da Montefeltro, Federico's son, who had been portrayed beside his father as an infant in a painting by Pedro Berruguete (see pages 112–13).

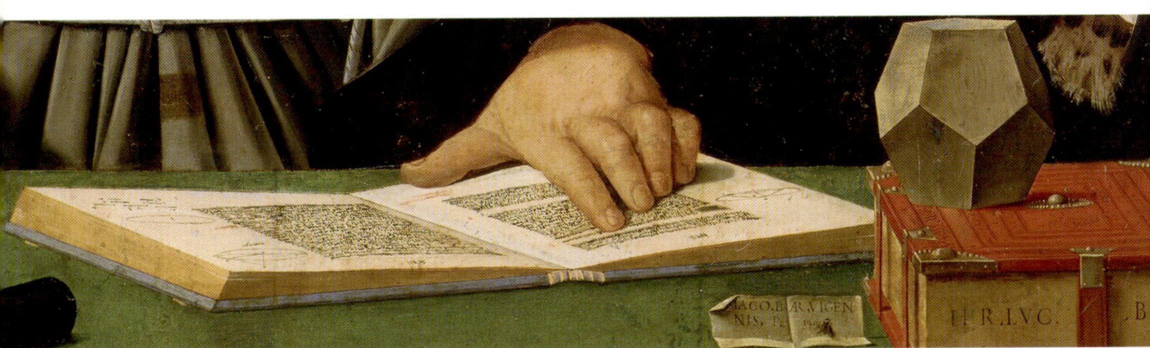

Vitruvius

Leonardo da Vinci
The Vitruvian Man
1500

Pencil and ink on paper, 34 × 24 cm
Venice, Gallerie dell'Accademia

For artist biography, see page 130.

The quest for an objective definition of beauty obsessed many Italian humanist artists. The method established by Vitruvius, a Roman architect and scholar who lived in the 1st century BC, inspired a doctrine based on the calculation of proportion and symmetry, whether in architecture or anatomy. In his treatise *On Architecture*, transcribed, published, translated and illustrated many times throughout the Renaissance, Vitruvius proposes an analogy between architectural construction and the human body: a man, his legs spread and his arms stretched wide, is inscribed within a square and a circle whose centre coincides with his navel. Other proportional systems were used, however. Cennino Cennini chose the face, divisible into three parts. Lorenzo Ghiberti, in his *Commentari*, proposed an elongated canon, based on a ratio of 1:9.5 between head and body. Alberti suggested placing the figure within a complicated geometric grid of six 'feet' divided into ten 'finger breadths', in turn divided into ten 'minutes'. In seeking the 'divine proportion', Luca Pacioli suggested dividing the human body according to the volumes of geometric solids. Leonardo has decided to illustrate Vitruvius' system.

Beyond Vitrivius: An Elusive Canon

Despite the effectiveness of his 'Vitruvian man', Leonardo remained very sceptical about the possibility of reducing the secret of beauty and harmony to a schematic relationship between the height of the head and the overall measurements of the body. In various drawings, he proposed measuring faces according to a regular grid but was mindful of the great variety of physical types, expressions and physiognomies found in nature. Thus, at the dawn of the 16th century a new canon emerged – one that respected the authority of the classics as well as recent scientific evidence for the infinite variations found in the natural world. Albrecht Dürer is the clearest and most fascinating case of an intellectual artist caught between the two opposing tendencies. Over many years he collected information directly from the authors of treatises and the Italian mathematicians, seeking to define objectively an ideal anthropometry based on a reliable and repeatable proportional 'grid'. Immediately after the artist's death in 1528, the results of his years of enquiry were published, in Latin and German, in a volume on the proportions of the human body. It was translated and reissued in various languages many times during the 16th century. Nonetheless, the illustrations are awkward: the correct application of norms results in cold robots, soulless dummies. In a note written in the last years of his career, Dürer himself had to admit, 'What beauty is, however, I do not know'.

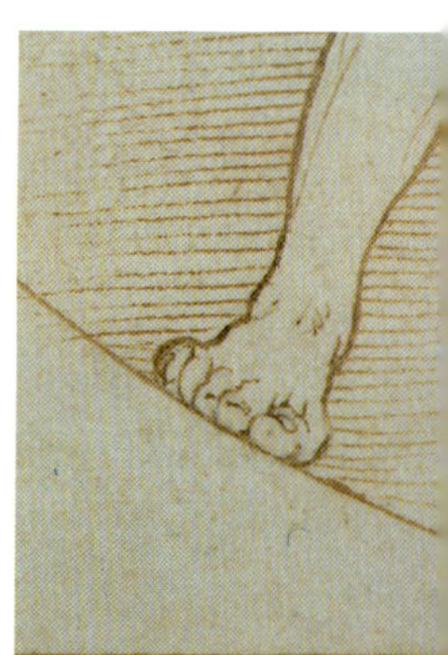

▼ The solution adopted by Leonardo is simple and ingenious. The man's legs are shown together (in which case the feet rest on the lower edge of the square) and slightly spread as well (in which case they reach the circumference of the circle).

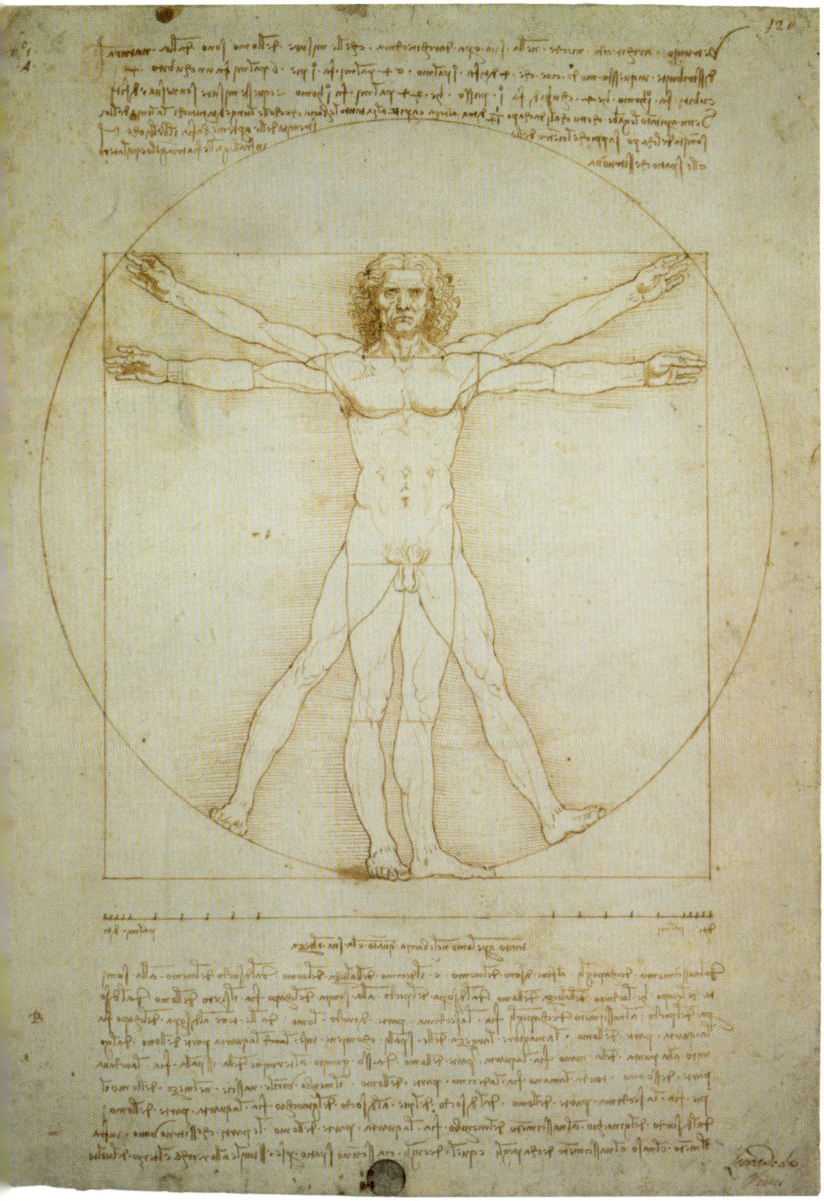

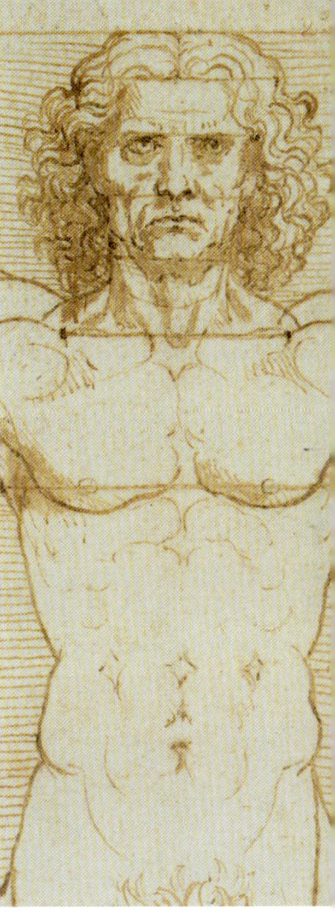

▲ The effectiveness of Leonardo's drawing results not only from the ingenious solution to the problem of the insertion of an 'idealized' male nude within both a circle and a square, but also in the figure's firm, decisive, assured expression, which seems to defy history and geometry.

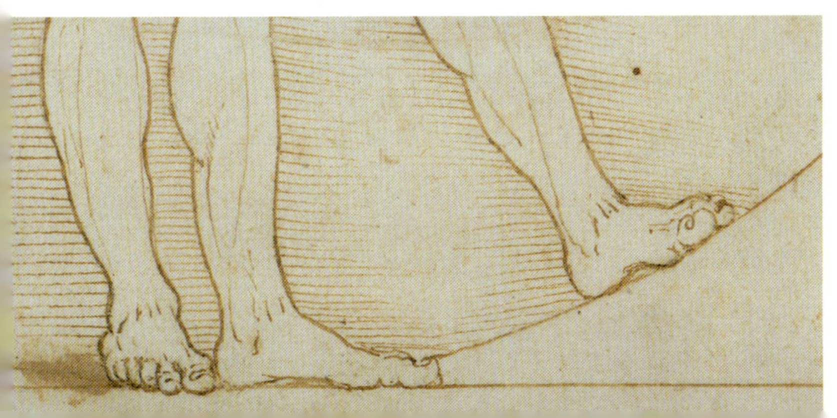

Harmony

Piero di Cosimo
The Death of Procris
c. 1501

Oil on panel, 65 × 183 cm
London, National Gallery

Piero di Cosimo

Florence, 1461/2–1521

A fascinating and whimsical artist, a true
eccentric of the Florentine school during
the transition from the 15th to the 16th
century, Piero di Cosimo created unusual
paintings on mythological subjects,
among them the story of 'Primitive Man'.
Even in more traditional sacred works,
however, he always included unexpected
details. His patronym derives from his
apprenticeship with Cosimo Rosselli,
who involved him in the decoration of
the Sistine Chapel at a young age. Piero
di Cosimo's subsequent career took place
mainly in Florence, where he worked for
the important Del Pugliese family. The
cultural references of his style are many
and varied: the clearly defined detail
comes from the example of the Flemish
painters; the naturalism of pose and
feature recalls Leonardo; and the nervous
instability of the figures and composition
can be related to Filippino Lippi. In the
early 16th century, Piero di Cosimo's
style grew even more eccentric, as he
increasingly distanced himself from the
heart of artistic debate.

The sense of suspension and waiting in Italian painting
from around 1501 can be related to the strained political
situation: the premature death of Lorenzo the Magnificent
(1492); the foreign conquest of the states of Milan (1494) and
Naples (1499); the controversial papacy of Pope Alexander
VI Borgia; and the first naval defeats of Venice, at the hands
of the Turks. Art began to function not as a reflection of the
world but as a way of escaping reality by imagining a setting
of beauty and harmony. Gradually, the humanistic projection
of an architecturally 'ideal city' was replaced by the image of
a poetical, utopian nature.

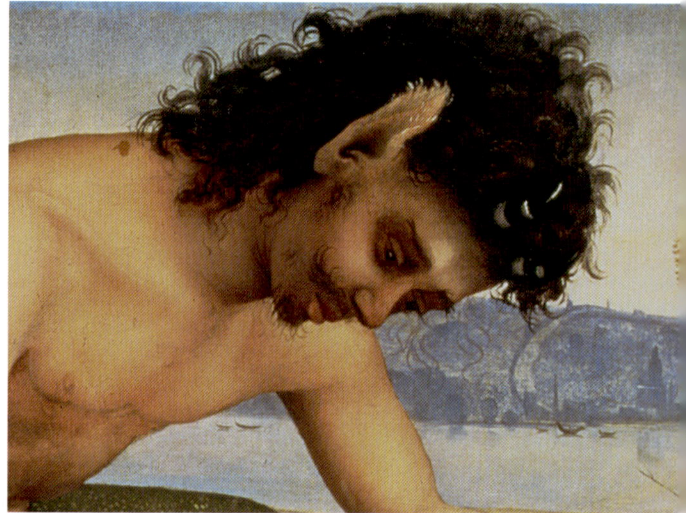

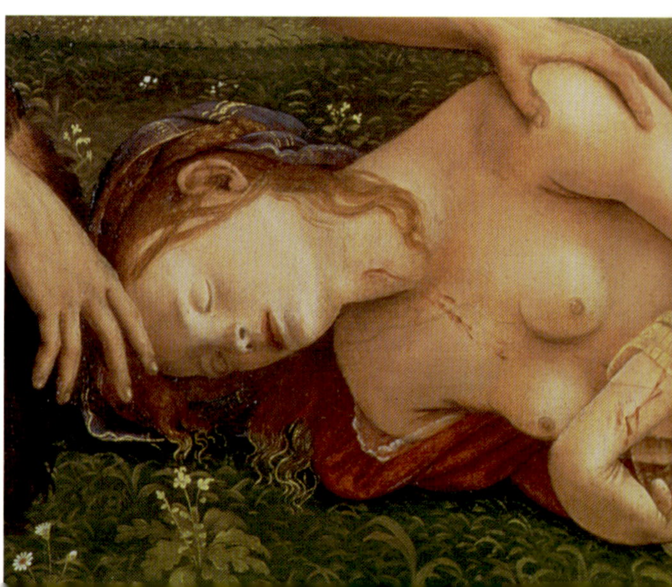

► Only a small wound on
the throat and a few drops of
blood tell us that the young
woman is not sleeping but
dead. The sense of serenity
tinged with sadness is
exemplified in the relationship
between the soft curves of
the semi-nude body and the
cool meadow dotted with
flowers. Even the satyr's gaze
and pose seem tender, his
semi-bestial nature mitigated
by the painting's quiet
tranquillity.

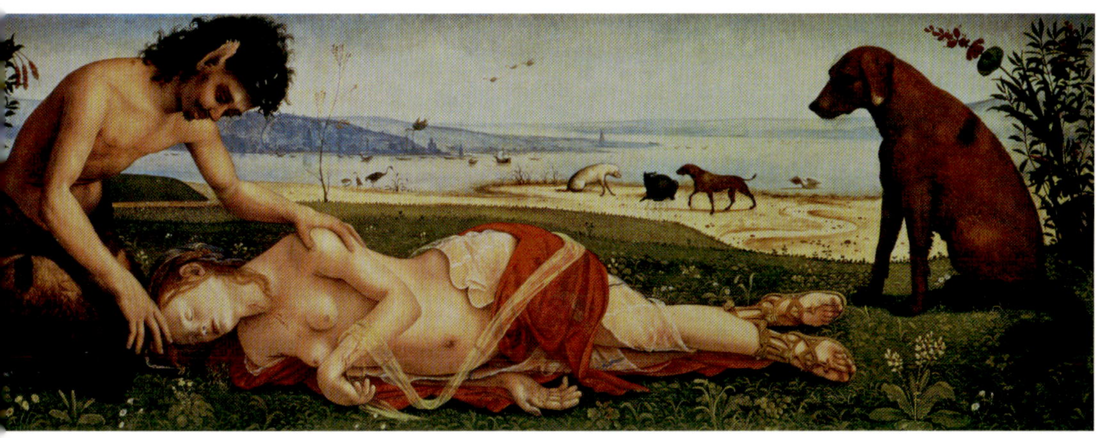

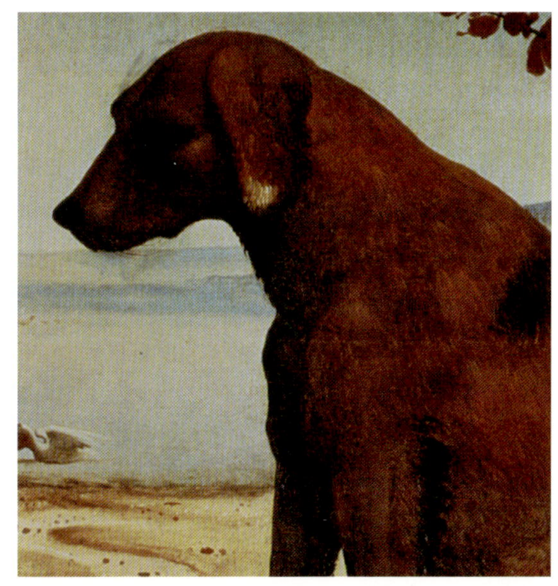

This painting likely represents the final scene in a tragic mythological tale of love and death. When Eos, goddess of the dawn, is spurned by Cephalus, a handsome hunter with whom she is infatuated, she arouses his jealousy towards his wife Procris. Courting Procris in disguise to test her faithfulness, Cephalus succeeds in seducing her. Out of shame, the nymph takes refuge in the woods with Diana, who gives her a magic arrow and a dog. Reconciled, she returns to Cephalus but jealous in turn, Procris spies on her husband during a hunting party. Mistaken for the prey, she is killed by the very arrow she gave to Cephalus. The absence of Cephalus from the painting led some critics to favour a more generic title, *Satyr Mourning Nymph.*

The dog's grief for its mortally wounded mistress underscores the close ties between humankind and animal. The painting is a full-blown solemn declaration of the universal harmony that would result from peace throughout the natural world.

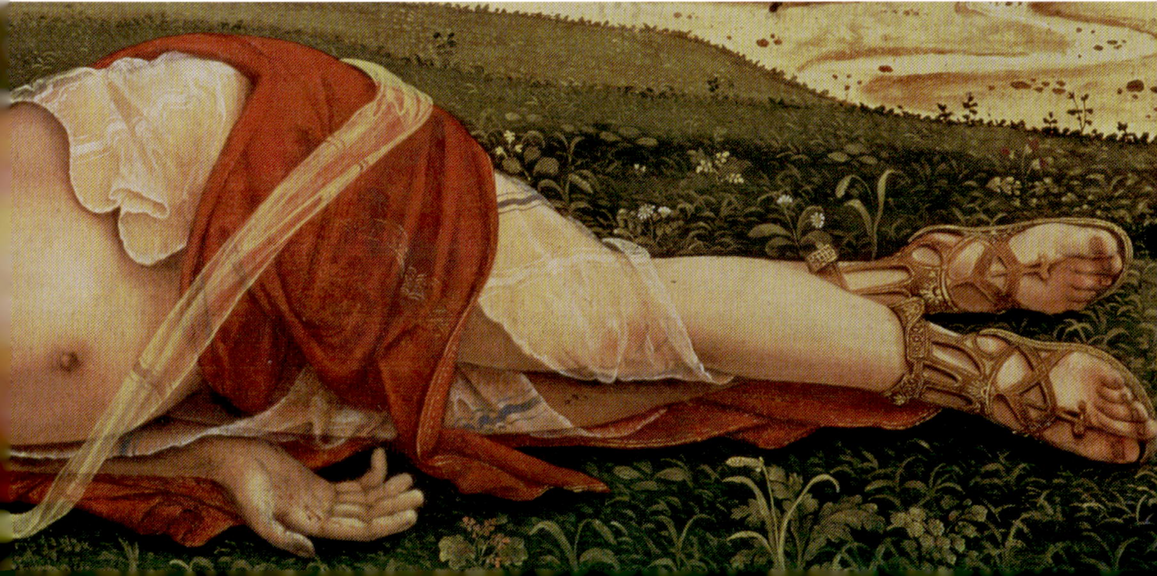

Atmosphere

Giovanni Bellini
Crucifixion with Cemetery
1501–3

Tempera on panel, 81 × 49 cm

Prato, Galleria di Palazzo degli Alberti,
Cariprato Collection

For artist biography, see page 144.

One of the most important achievements of late 15th-centur
painting is the representation of natural light on the land
scape. The spread of oil painting and admiration for th
transparency achieved by the Flemish school prompted th
most sensitive Italian masters to seek the effects of paintin
in the open air. Especially in the Veneto, less bound to th
tradition of architectural perspective than Tuscany, the stud
and evocation of atmospheric effects developed. The activit
of Giovanni Bellini was critical in this respect. Over the cours
of a long career, he gradually abandoned drawing and instea
used effects of light, shades of colour and various degrees c
gentle shadow to define figures in space. These captivating
delicate stylistic innovations initiated a radical shift in the a
of the Veneto and prompted a concentration on the natur
landscape, in particular the region's calm, hilly backdrop, do
ted with castles, towns and groves of trees.

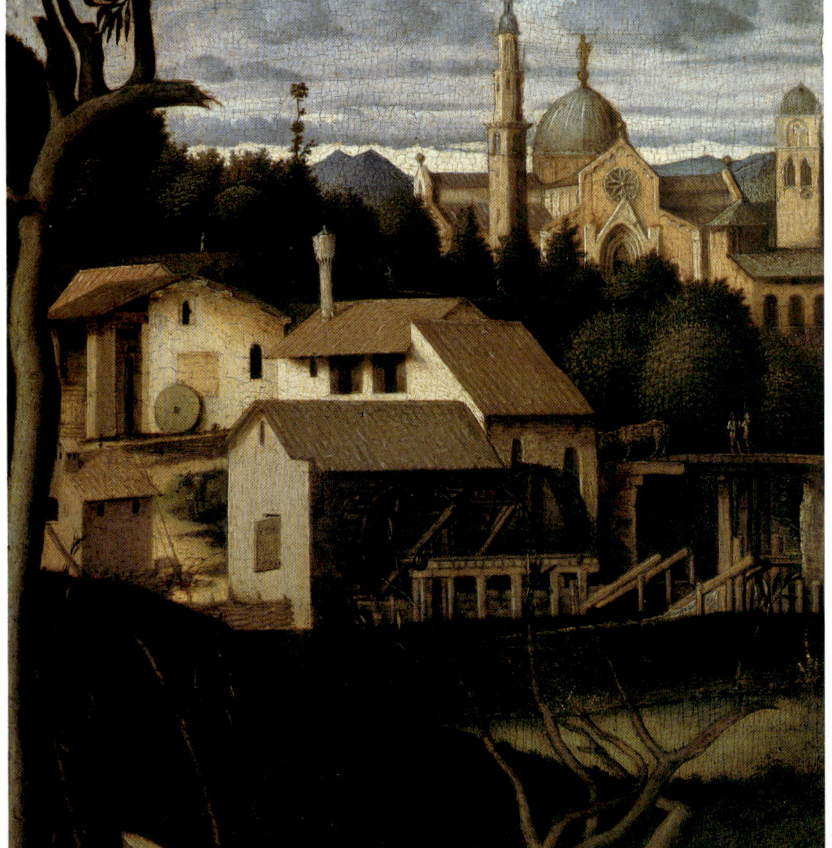

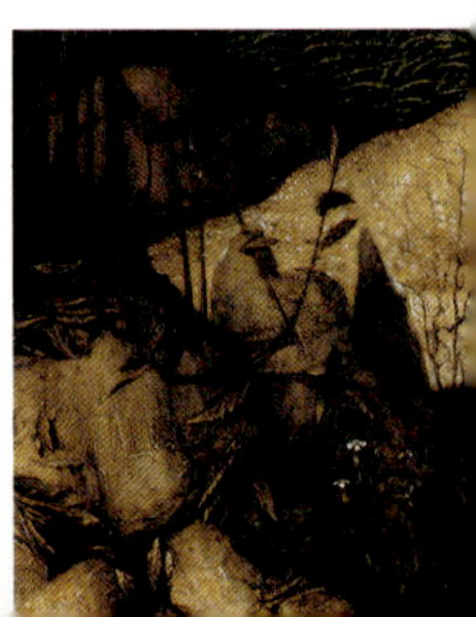

◄ The background of this panel by Giovanni Bellini freely but successfully combines real and imaginary buildings, churches and rust mills. Some monuments are easily recognizable: this deta shows the tall, narrow Torre dei Signori in Vicenza and behind it, the façade and be tower of the cathedral of San Ciriaco in Ancona. Thus, this is not a *veduta* like those painted by Giovanni's brothe Gentile (see pages 166–7) b in a way anticipates the gen of the *capriccio* (a landscape combining real and imaginar features).

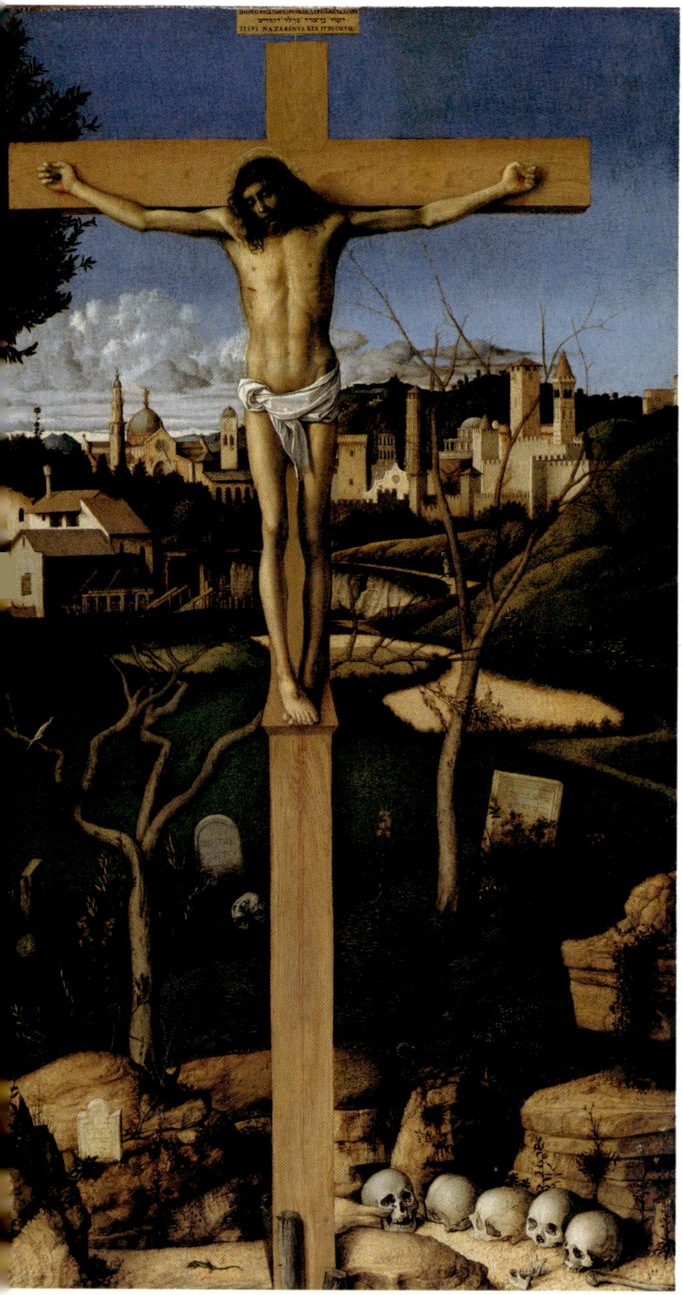

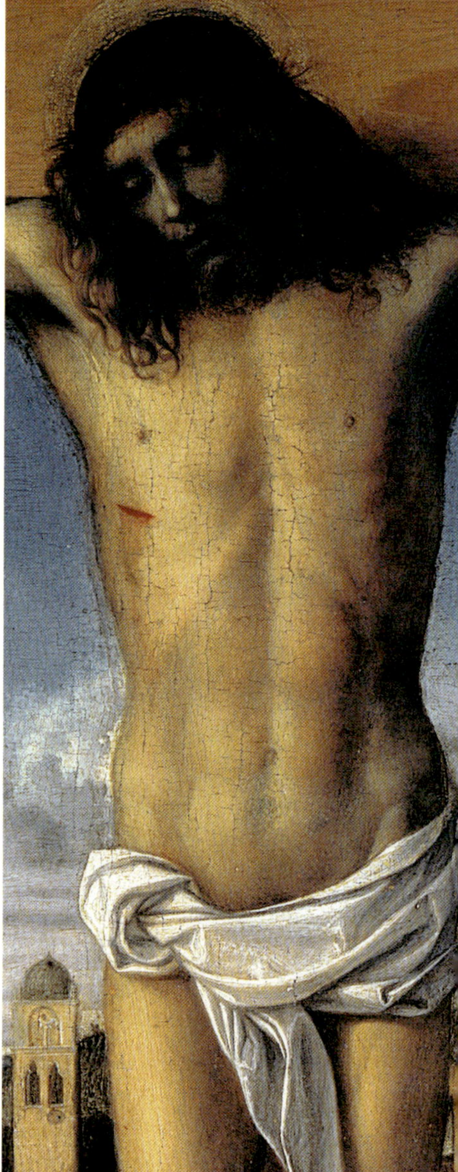

▼ The tall Cross raises Christ above the horizon line. Giovanni Bellini lets the natural atmosphere act on Christ's face and torso. A warm light, moving from left to right, seems to skim the smooth body and carve deep shadows on the pain-stricken face. The effect recalls Antonello da Messina's *St Sebastian* in Dresden (see pages 110–11).

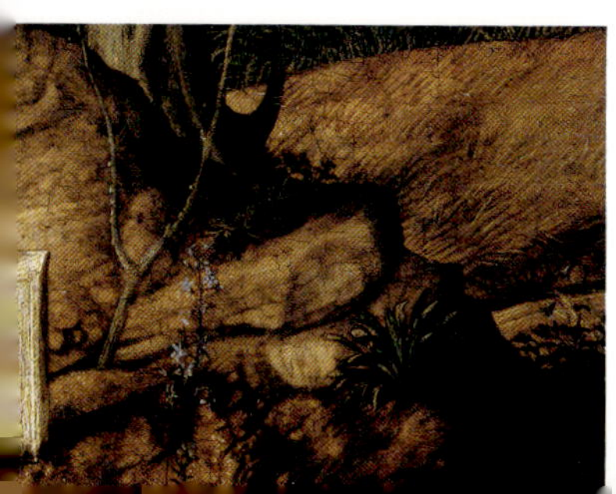

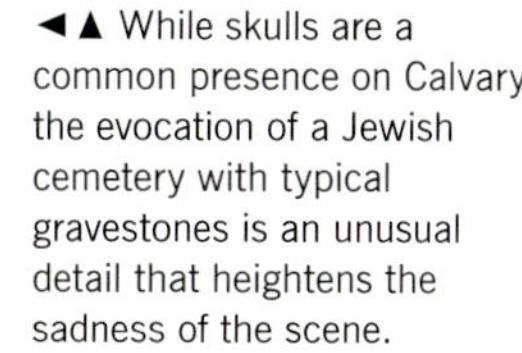

◄▲ While skulls are a common presence on Calvary, the evocation of a Jewish cemetery with typical gravestones is an unusual detail that heightens the sadness of the scene.

Sfumato

Leonardo da Vinci
The Virgin and St Anne
1501–10

Oil on panel, 168 × 130 cm

Paris, Musée du Louvre

For artist biography, see page 130.

Fifteenth-century painters tended to prefer clear lines, crisp shadows and enamel-like colours, but in the early 16th century the opposite tendency came to the fore, starting in northern Italy. Muted tones were now preferred and a naturalistic atmosphere circulated freely throughout the painting. Paradoxically, it was Leonardo, one of the greatest draughtsmen of all time, who first experimented with the values of brushstroke and colour in this way. The result of his experimentation was the concept of *sfumato* (from the Italian *fumo*, 'smoke'), often applied to the landscape background, where haze, clouds and humidity make outlines vague.

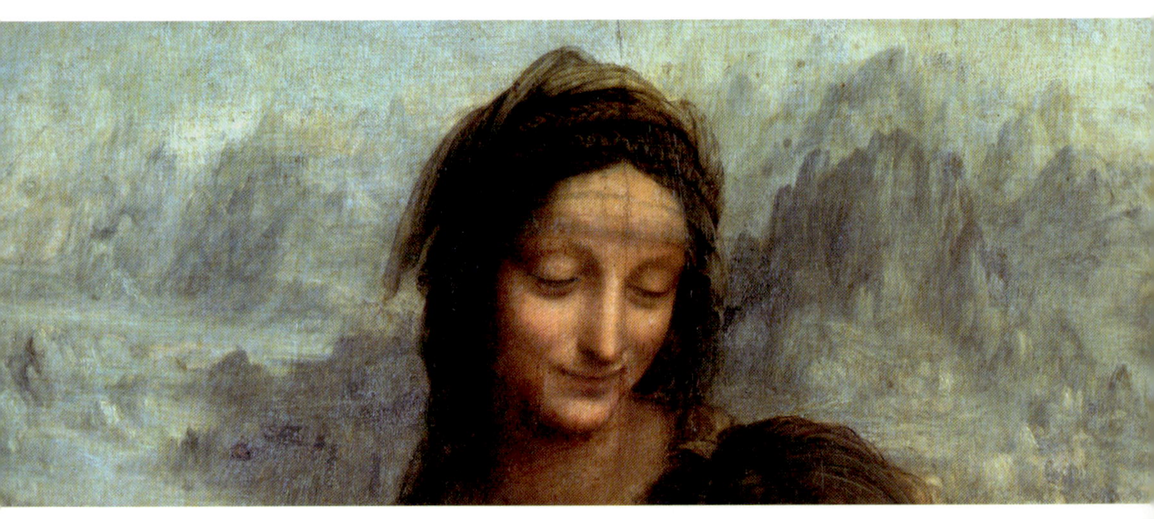

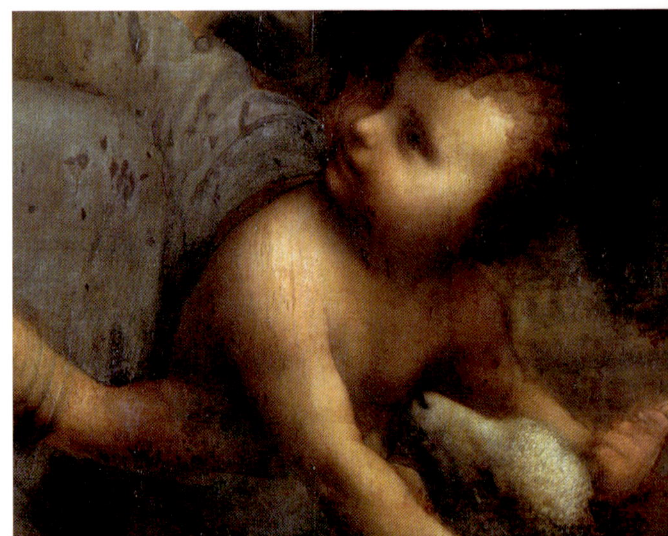

▲ The extraordinary sweetness of St Anne's smile is projected against a mountain background blurred by haze. A group of Lombard painters known as Leonardeschi gathered up Leonardo's ideas and independently developed them. The group included mainly masters in the Veneto, but also other northern Italian painters, such as Correggio.

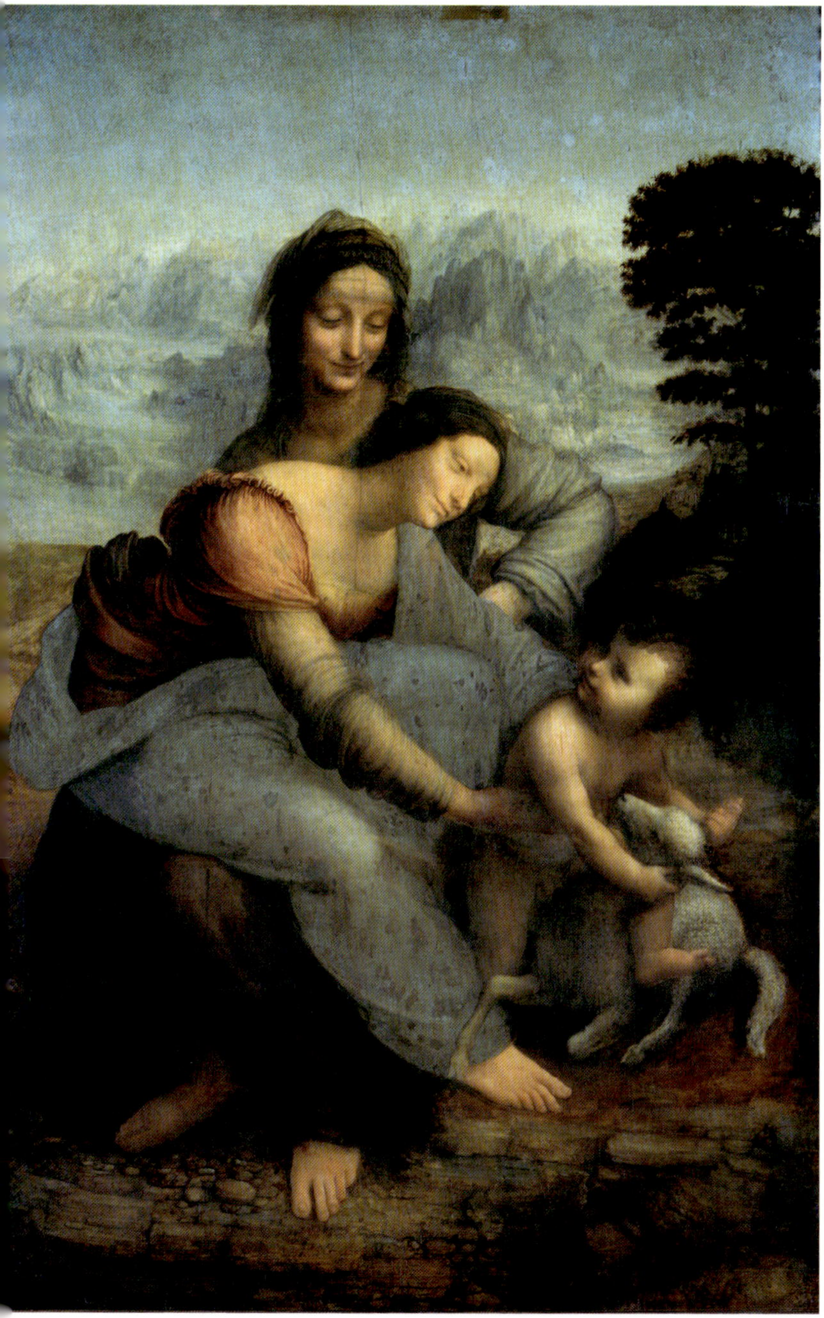

▲ The mysterious sweetness of the three divine figures' smiles is projected onto a dense natural background of trees, rocks and water – the result of the scientific and pictorial investigations Leonardo made during his second stay in Milan.

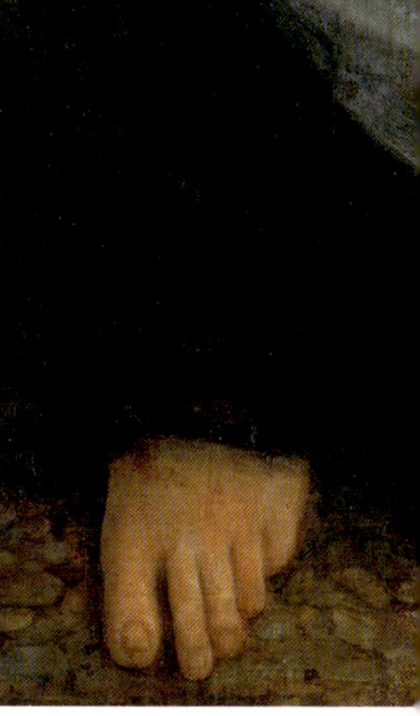

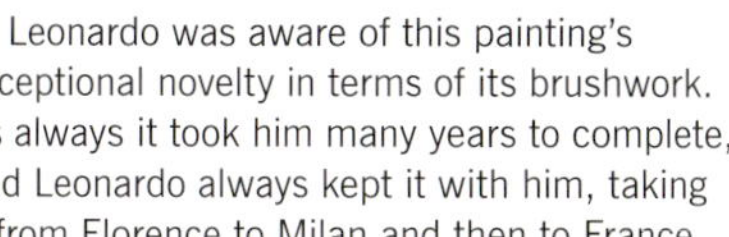
Leonardo was aware of this painting's exceptional novelty in terms of its brushwork. As always it took him many years to complete, and Leonardo always kept it with him, taking it from Florence to Milan and then to France.

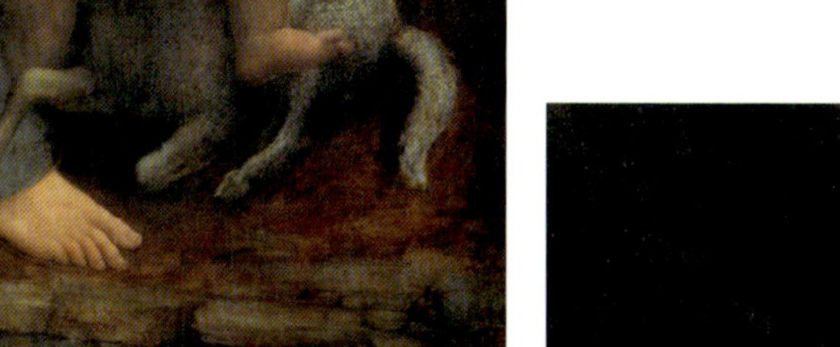
► The same *sfumato* technique may also be seen in details like the pebbles on the ground and the definition of the toes. Compare this with similar details in previous works by Leonardo (see pages 92–3) and Mantegna (see pages 116–17) in Milan.

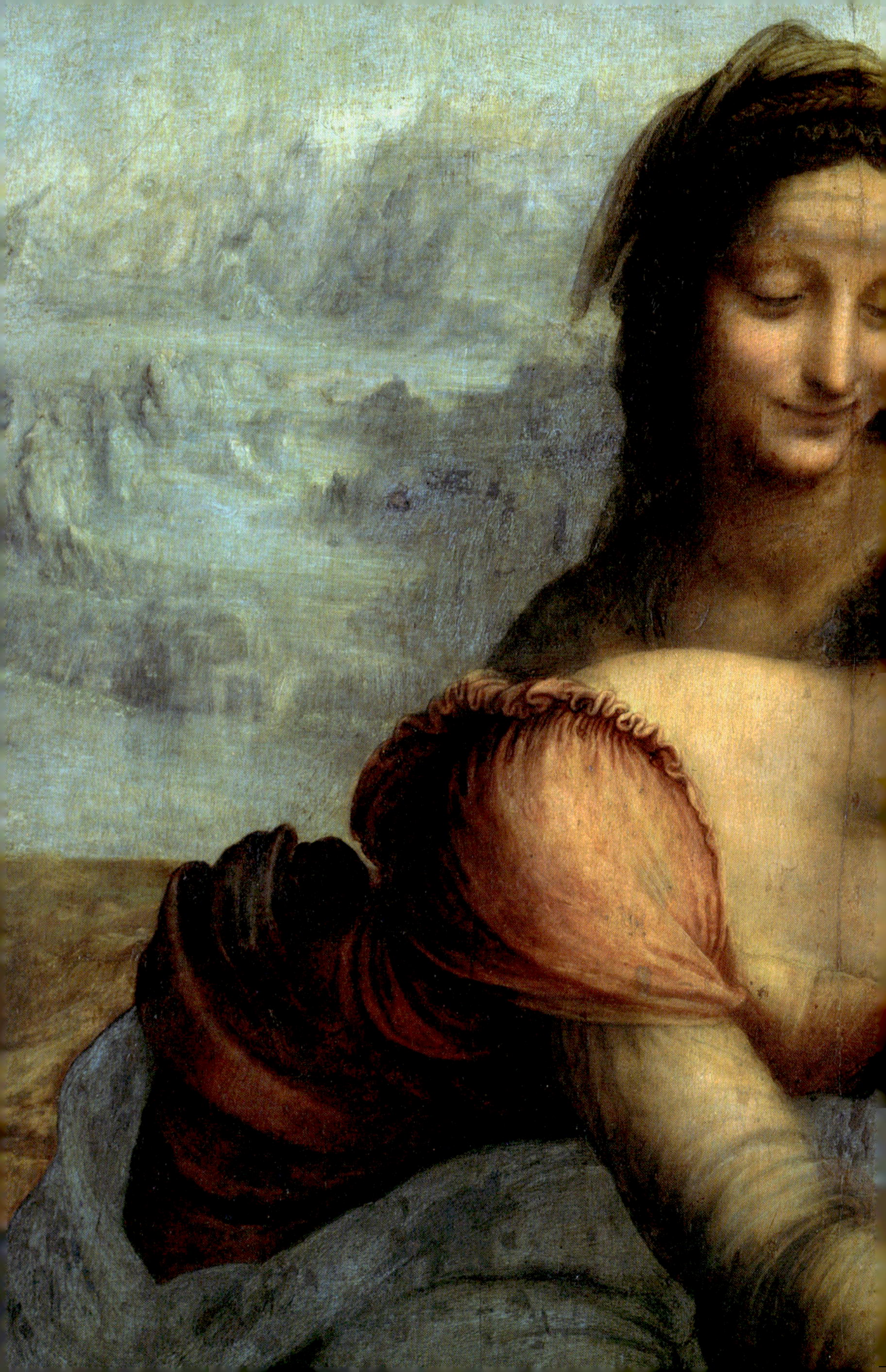

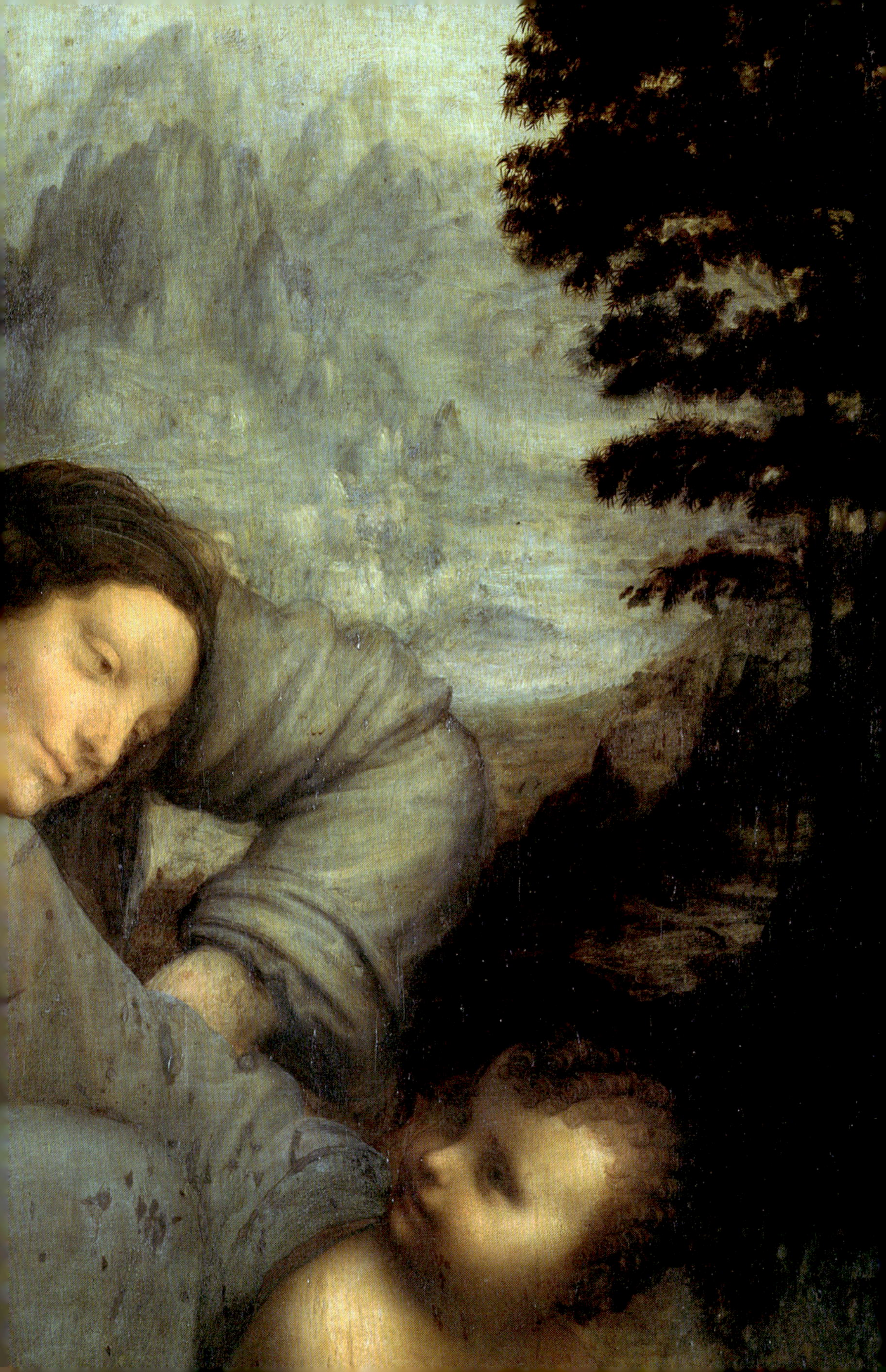

Studiolo

Vittore Carpaccio
St Augustine in his Study
c. 1502

Tempera on canvas, 141 × 210 cm
Venice, Scuola di San Giorgio

Vittore Carpaccio

Venice or Capodistria, 1460/5–1525/6

Carpaccio's name is above all associated with his immense *teleri*, the splendid narrative cycles the artist painted for the Venetian Scuole. Rich in descriptive detail inspired by contemporary reality, these paintings provide vivid and unique evidence of the city's splendour. Carpaccio's first major work, produced in 1490, was his cycle on the *Story of St Ursula* (today at the Gallerie dell'Accademia, Venice). This accomplished a balance between the narrative rhythm of the action and the ability to linger over myriad details of architecture, costume and physiognomy. His next cycle, for the Scuola di San Giorgio degli Schiavoni (1502–7), has remained at its original site, whereas the one painted a little later for the Albanesi (*Story of the Virgin*) and the one begun in 1514 for the Wool Guild (*Story of St Stephen*) were dismantled. Altarpieces for Venice and the provinces alternated with portraits and panels for private devotion, executed in a sustained style in which clean, precise drawing still prevailed over the tonal use of colour seen in Giorgione. Because of his 15th-century style, Carpaccio was increasingly relegated to the fringe of the Venetian school. His career ended in Istria.

Over the centuries, Italy's artistic heritage has suffered considerable destruction and fragmentation. But perhaps the most serious damage is the loss of the *studioli*, the private studies of nobles, prelates and intellectuals. The demise of the small duchies led to the dispersal on the antique market of paintings, sculptures, friezes, intarsias, scientific instruments, objects and furnishings of all types. Paintings such as this one are invaluable in reconstituting the appearance of the *studioli*, formed according to the personal tastes and enthusiasms of their owners. These may be considered the basic nucleus of private collecting and the origin of encyclopaedic museum collections, which in the late 16th century took the characteristic form of *Wunderkammern* (cabinets of curiosities).

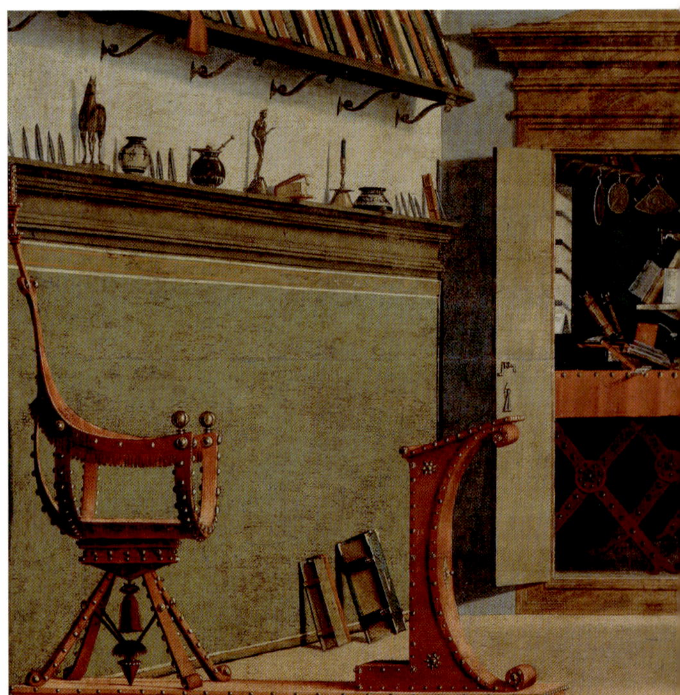

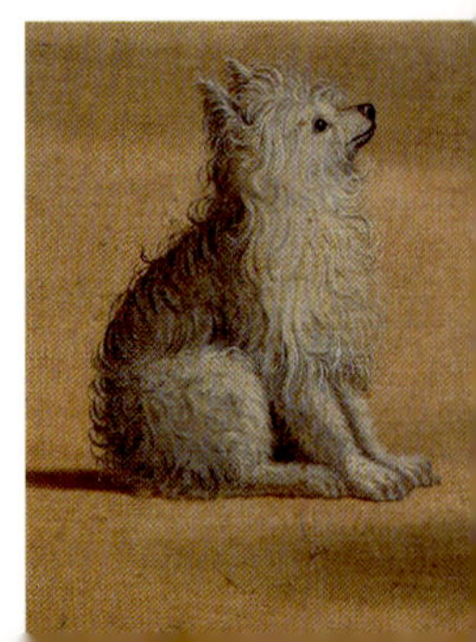

▲ This painting, which remained in its original location in the Venetian Confraternità dei Damalti, dedicated to St George, St Tryphon and St Jerome, offers a clear image of a humanist's studio, with books and curios (including small bronzes and ceramic vessels) neatly arranged on a shelf.

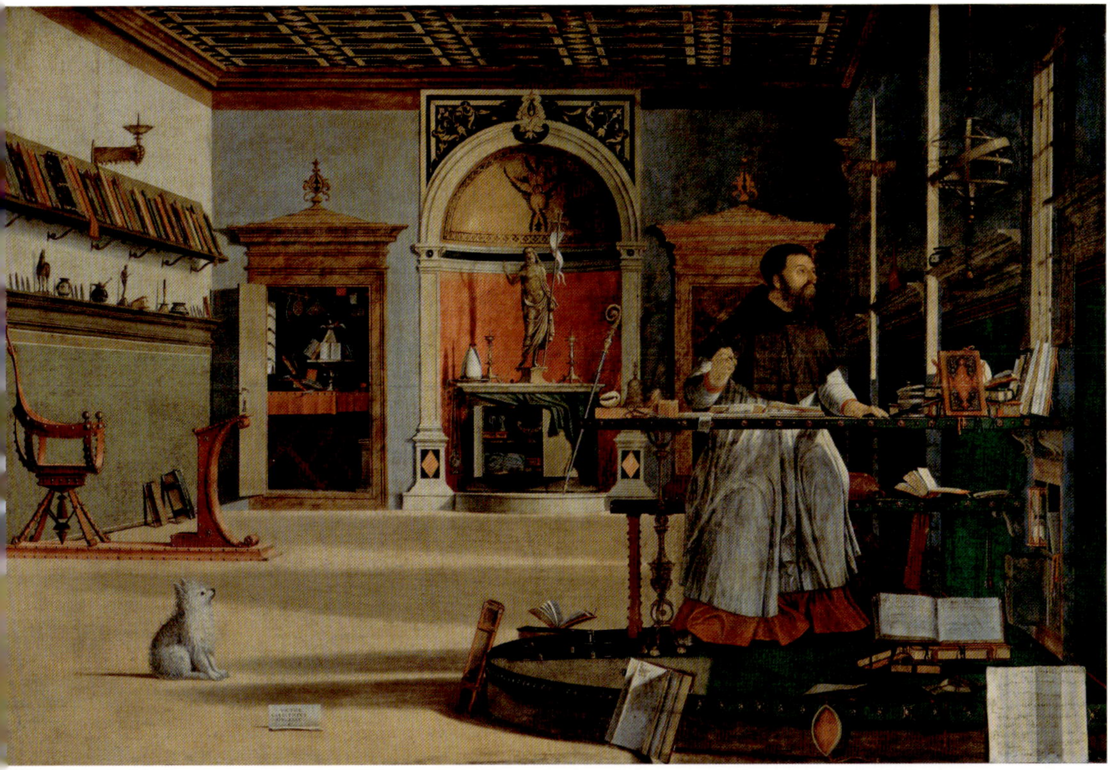

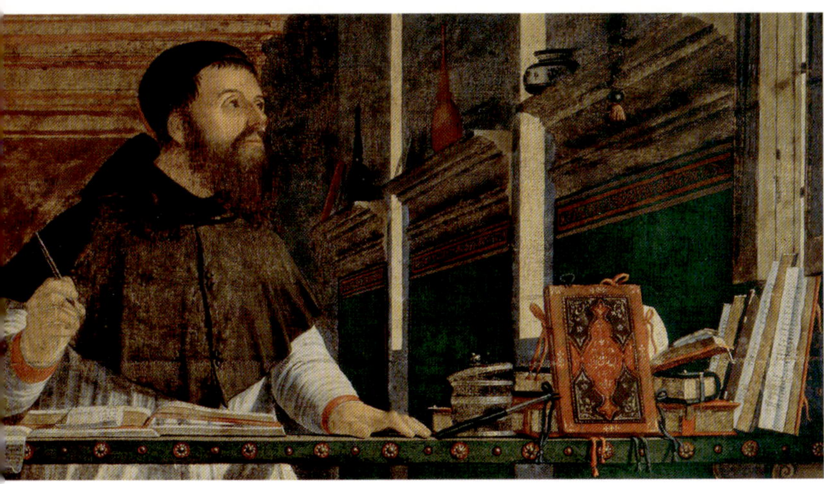

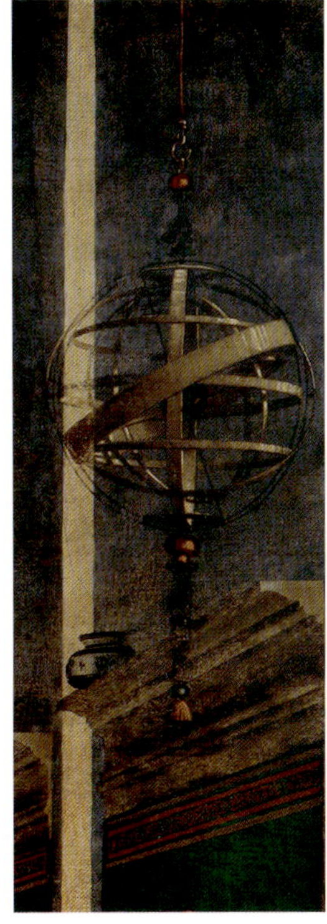

◄ This lively, endearing little dog is surely one of the most famous domestic animals in art history. The spitz was not introduced as a pet in Europe until the late 15th century.

▲ Identifying the subject of the painting raised some difficulty. Carpaccio has depicted the apparition of St Jerome in the form of light entering the window to 'illuminate' Augustine's understanding of the Holy Scriptures.

► An important aspect of intellectuals' private collections, sophisticated scientific instruments such as this armillary sphere were admired for both their functional value and their technical precision.

Andrea Mantegna
Minerva Expelling the Vices from the Garden of Virtue
c. 1502

Tempera on canvas, 160 × 192 cm
Paris, Musée du Louvre

For artist biography, see page 76.

While in many cases the subject and treatment of a painting could be agreed between the patron and artist, for certain important or complicated works or cycles another expert would be involved. A specific programme of images, figures and visual solutions would be agreed upon for the painter to follow. When the subject matter was sacred, theologians or representatives of the religious orders were involved. For mythological and profane paintings, intellectuals, literati, heraldry experts or even astrologers and alchemists intervened to suggest rare and esoteric references that we are not always able to understand today.

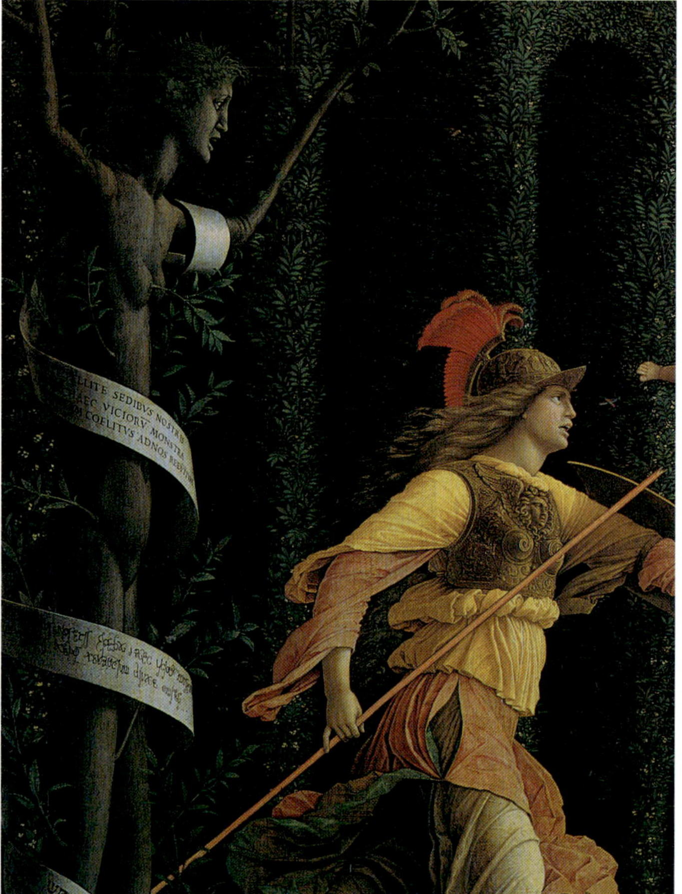

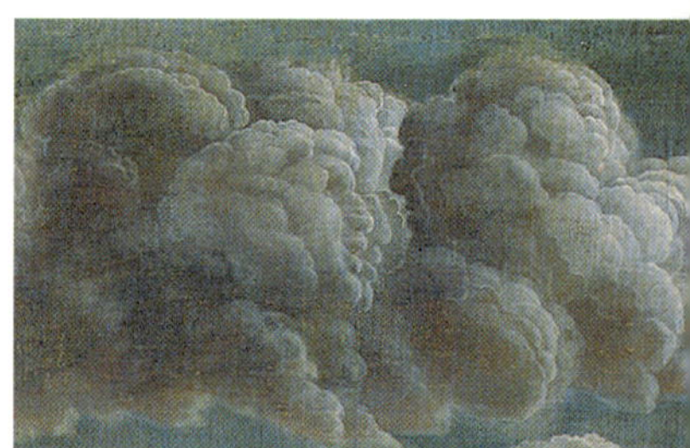

▲ Talking trees, clouds with human faces, anthropomorphic monkeys, allusions to the classical world and Christian virtues, beauty and monstrosity: the formulation of this painting was certainly guided by a precise programme devised by a humanist.

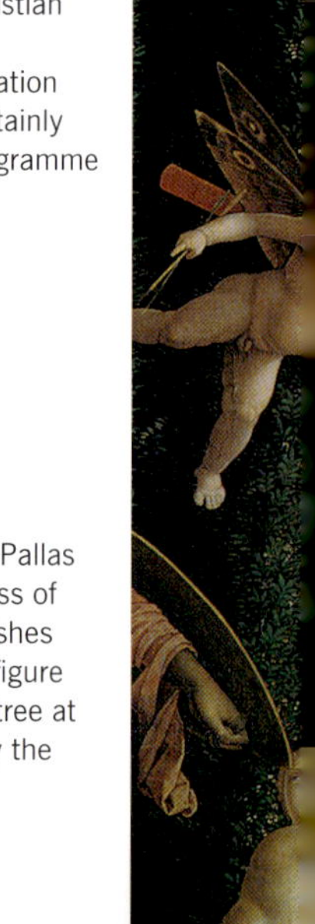

◄► The protagonist is Pallas Athena, classical goddess of wisdom, who re-establishes the reign of Virtue (the figure imprisoned in the olive tree at the left) by driving away the monstrous Vices.

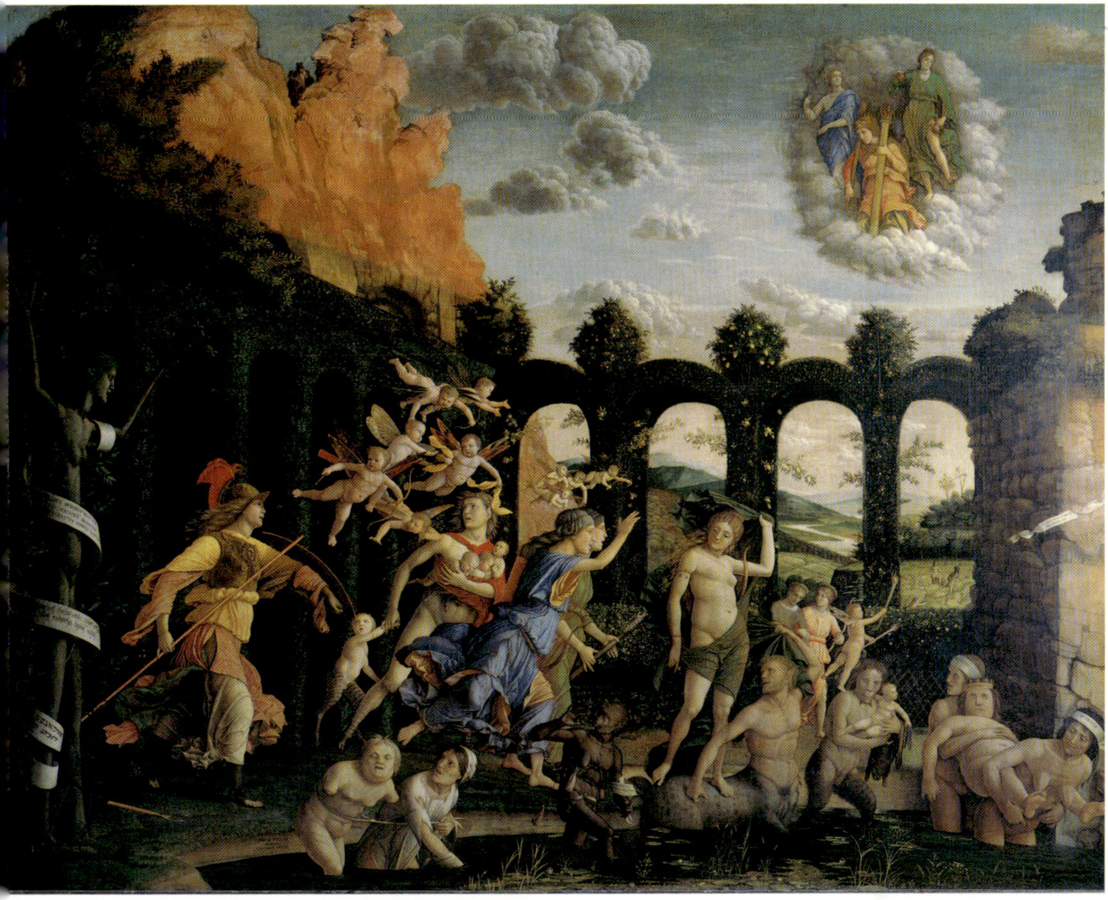

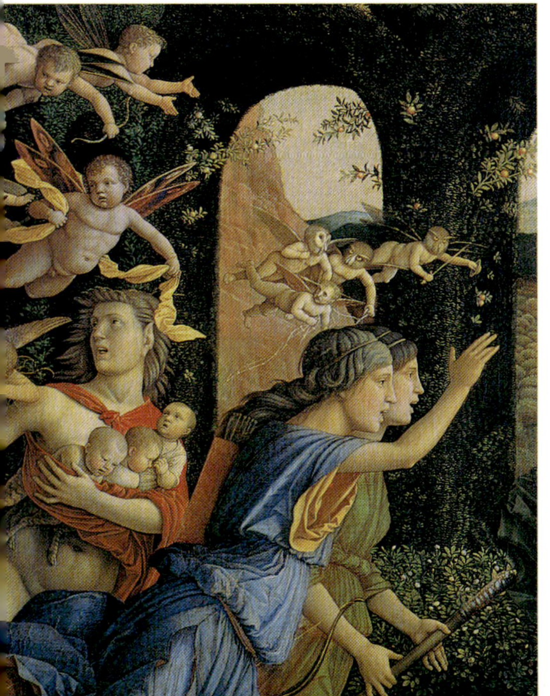

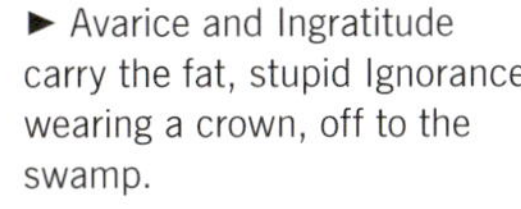

▲ This painting is the second work executed by Mantegna for the private study of Isabella d'Este in the Gonzagas' ducal palace in Mantua. The overall subject of the cycle (continued by Perugino and Correggio after Mantegna's death) is the praise of virtues of the marchesa, a refined patron of the arts. It is likely that the cultivated court poet and astrologer Paride Ceresara dictated the iconography.

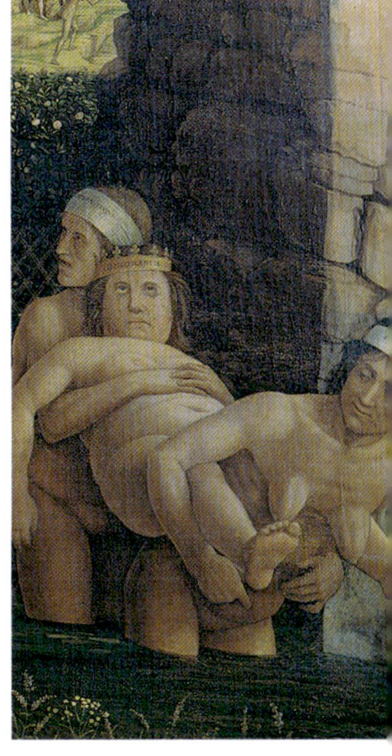

► Avarice and Ingratitude carry the fat, stupid Ignorance, wearing a crown, off to the swamp.

Architecture

Pinturicchio
Details from the *Story of Pius*
II Piccolomini
1503–8

Fresco
Siena Cathedral, Libreria Piccolomini

For artist biography, see page 168.

Throughout the Italian Renaissance, architects and painters were closely connected; indeed, many masters practised both disciplines. Only in the 16th century did the architect's activity take on a distinct, autonomous form, with its own set of treatises and a specific course of training. Before the introduction of technical drawings of plans, elevations and sections, building sites were still based on wooden scale models, of which only a few examples remain. Many Renaissance paintings depict architectural components that not only serve as a background or perspective frame, but also represent actual proposals that could be transformed into real buildings.

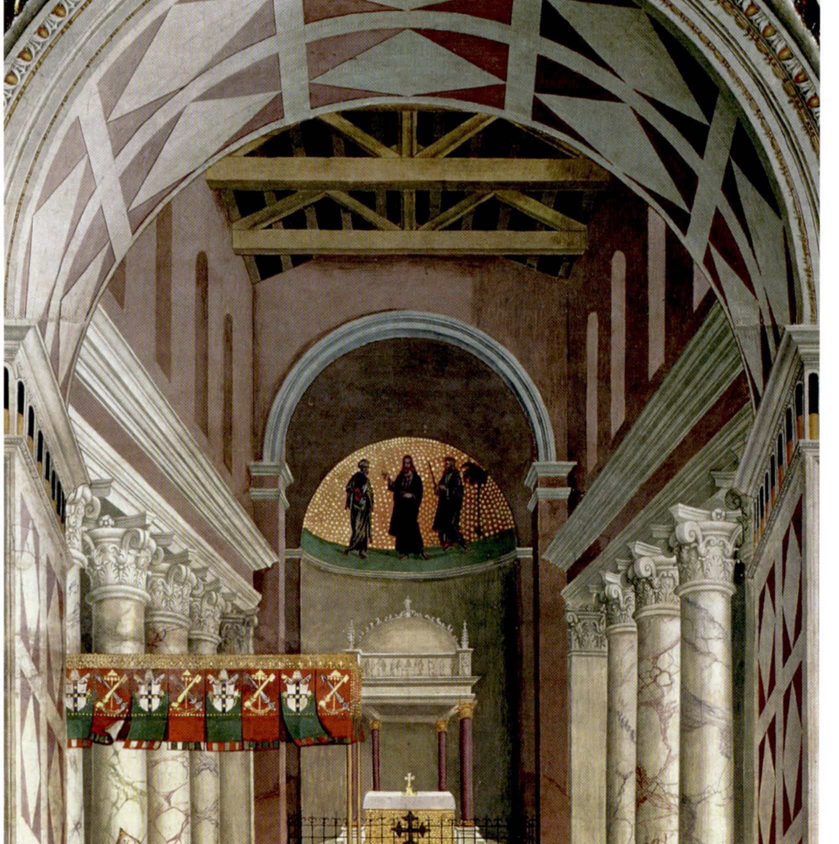

◄ Pinturicchio's frescoes decorate one of the most captivating settings of the early 16th century, the Library along the left side of Siena Cathedral. The Sienese Pope Pius III had this constructed to honour his predecessor and relative Pius II, the celebrated humanist who had built Pienza 50 years earlier. The subject is thus not legend but fairly recent history. Pinturicchio alternated and balanced reality with imaginary scenes. The detail to the left is of great historical importance, as it shows the interior of St Peter's basilica in Rome before Pope Julius II had it demolished to make way for a new building designed by Bramante. The young Raphael probably assisted Pinturicchio on this work.

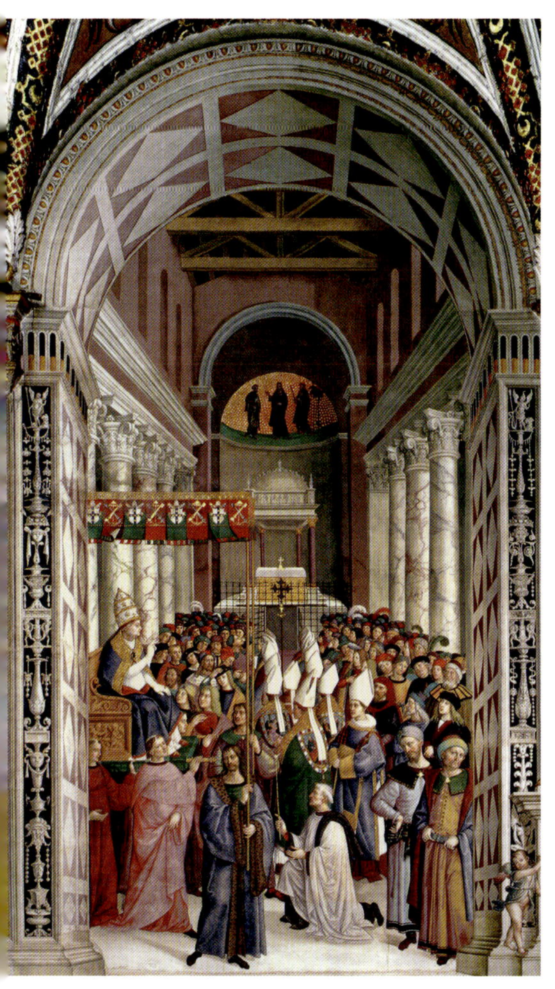

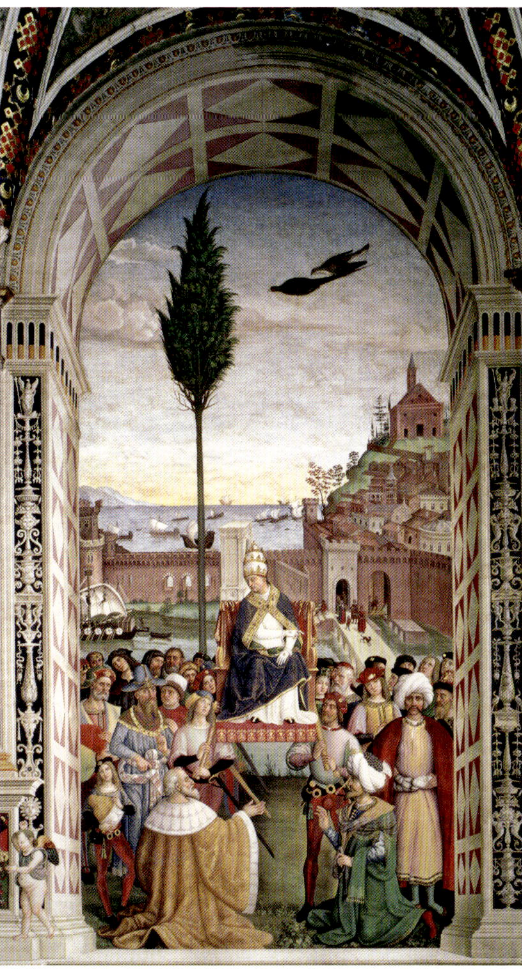

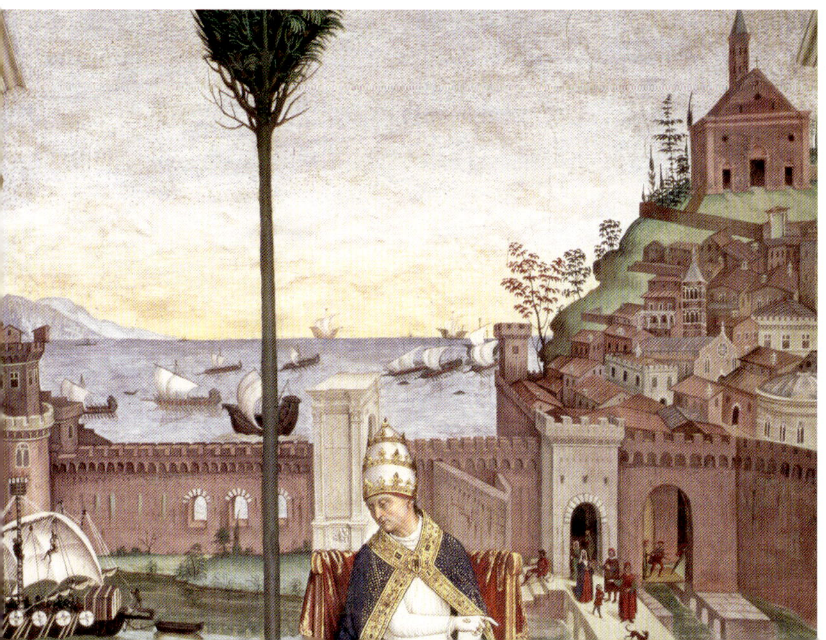

◄ The alternation of open architectural interior scenes with outdoor episodes allowed artists to depict various buildings and cities, identified by well-known landmarks. Pinturicchio shows a view of the city and port of Ancona. The Arch of Trajan is recognizable alongside the pope's head, but the painter restricted himself to recalling the presence of the cathedral isolated on the hill, forgoing the precise description of the Romanesque building in which Giovanni Bellini had indulged (see pages 178–9).

Tondo

Michelangelo Buonarroti
Doni Tondo
1503–4

Tempera on panel, 120 cm (diam.)
Florence, Galleria degli Uffizi

Michelangelo Buonarroti

Caprese, Arezzo, 1475–Rome, 1564

Foremost a sculptor but also a superb architect, painter and poet, Michelangelo is the epitome of 16th-century European art. Trained as a painter in the workshop of Ghirlandaio in Lorenzo the Magnificent's Florence, Michelangelo soon turned towards sculpture and created a group of masterpieces including the *Pietà* at St Peter's in Rome, the *David* now at the Accademia in Florence and the *Madonna of Bruges*. Painting occupied Michelangelo for most of the following period: in Florence he vied with Leonardo in the decoration (now lost) of Palazzo Vecchio and executed the *Doni Tondo*. Then, in Rome between 1508 and 1512, he began the exhausting and unforgettable fresco decoration of the Sistine Chapel's ceiling. After this, Michelangelo abandoned painting for more than twenty years, devoting himself to sculpture and architecture (the statues and projects for the mausoleum of Pope Julius II, the New Sacristy at the church of San Lorenzo in Florence, then the dome of St Peter's and the Piazza del Campidoglio in Rome). He took up his brushes again in the 1530s for the long gestation of the *Last Judgment* at the Sistine Chapel, a masterpiece that sums up the Renaissance and continues in two frescoes in the Pauline Chapel. In his old age, Michelangelo sculpted his last two marble *Pietàs*, one now at the Museo dell'Opera of the cathedral in Florence and the other at the Castello Sforzesco in Milan.

In his late twenties, Michelangelo treated the subject of this *tondo*, the Holy Family of Mary, Joseph and Jesus, in both sculpture and painting. The painting, executed for Agnolo Doni (who also commissioned Raphael), is the only surviving signed panel painting by Michelangelo. The bright, cold, enamel-like colours, the clearly drawn line around the figures and the tightly enclosed monumental composition are the antithesis of the *sfumato* proposed by Leonardo in Florence at the same time. Even in painting, Michelangelo affirmed his 'sculptural' conception of art: to obtain the image 'by removal', making the figures emerge from the background of the marble, and not 'by addition', with successive layers of colour or additions, as Leonardo did.

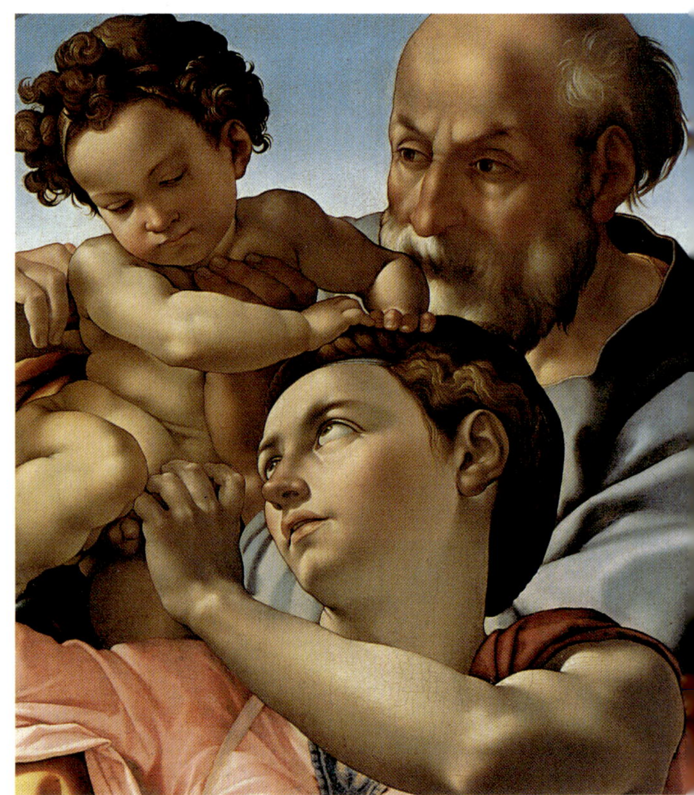

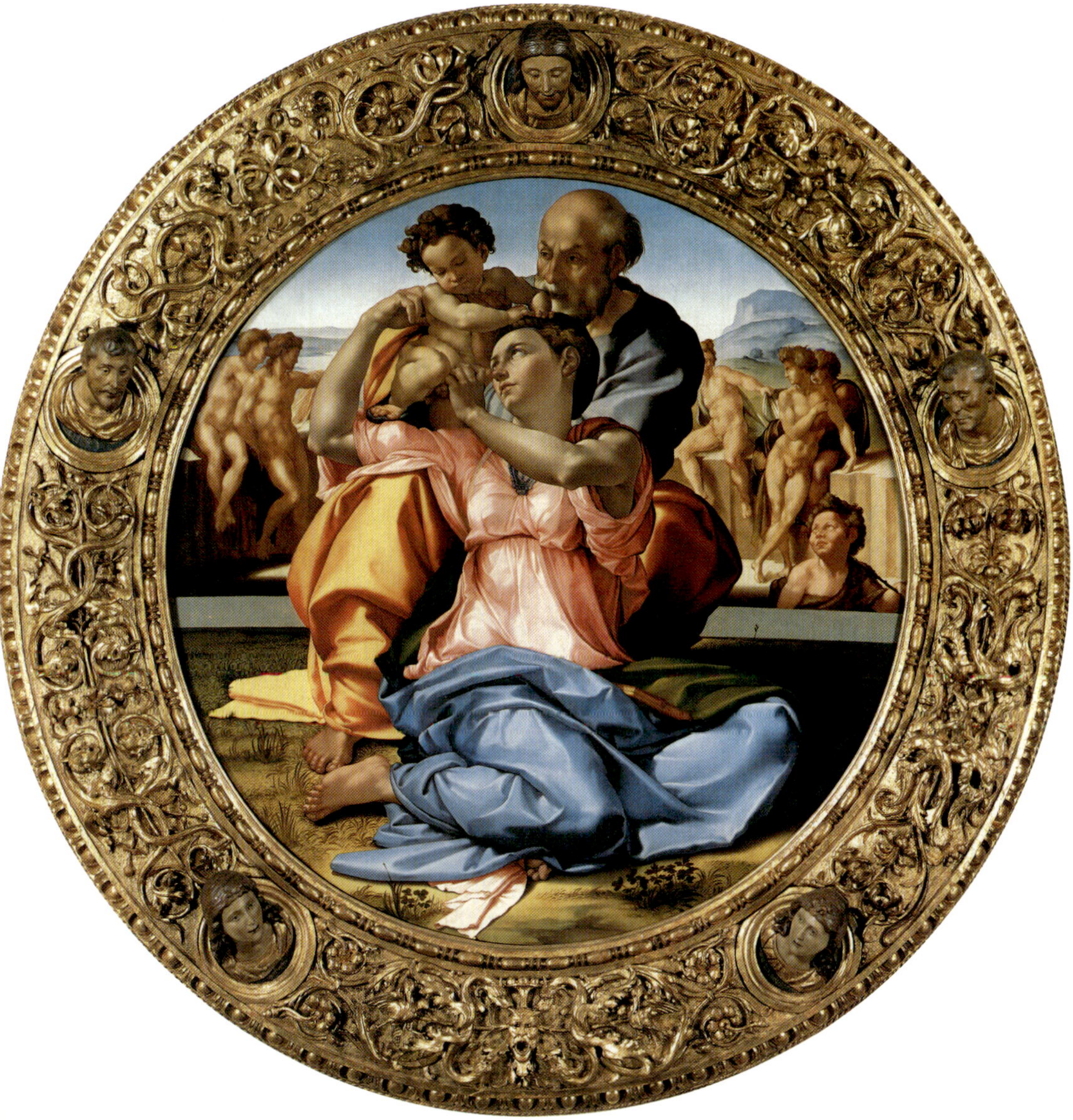

◄ Mary, Joseph and Jesus
re tightly bound in a knot of
estures and feelings powerful
nough to overcome even the
istorted poses and torsions.
he clear colours and the
utlines, decisively drawn
 sure, dark strokes, are an
xplicit polemical response
 Leonardo's *sfumato* (see
ages 180–1).

▲ ► The *tondo* is a traditional Florentine
format, frequently used by Botticelli. In this
case, the stupendous original gilt-wood frame
designed by Michelangelo himself has also
been preserved. Probably commissioned to
celebrate the bond between Agnolo Doni and
his wife, Maddalena Strozzi, the *tondo* shows
the Holy Family in a landscape, with a low wall
separating the three main figures from John
(mediator between human and divine) and a
row of youthful nudes.

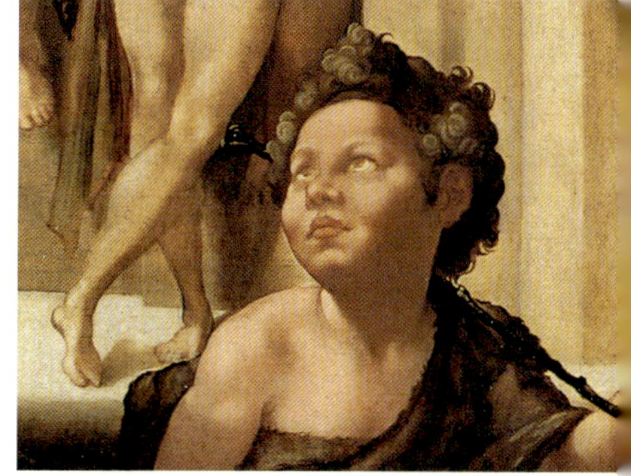

Smile

Leonardo da Vinci
Mona Lisa (La Gioconda)
1503–6

Oil on panel, 77 × 53 cm

Paris, Musée du Louvre

For artist biography, see page 130.

The polemical nature of Michelangelo's *Doni Tondo* in regard to Leonardo's painting is obvious from a comparison with this most famous portrait. The sitter is identified as Monna (Lady) Lisa, the wife of Francesco del Giocondo, and Leonardo began the piece in 1503 – though, as occurred with many of his most important paintings, Leonardo spread its execution over years. Furthermore, he never delivered it to the commissioner – which is unusual for a portrait – but always considered it an unfinished work, a painting eternally incomplete, and subjected it to an almost infinite series of retouches, reworkings, glazes and interventions. The portrait presents a seductive yet disturbing image, wrapped in the humid tremor of a misty landscape.

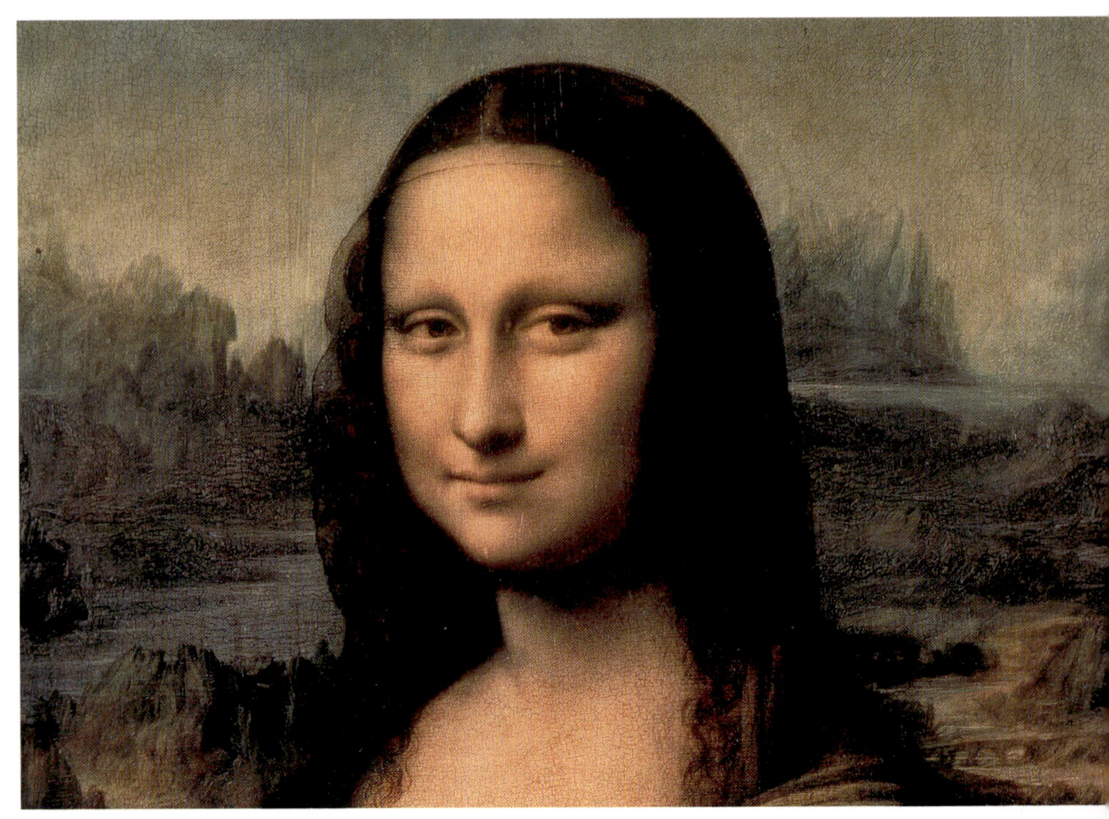

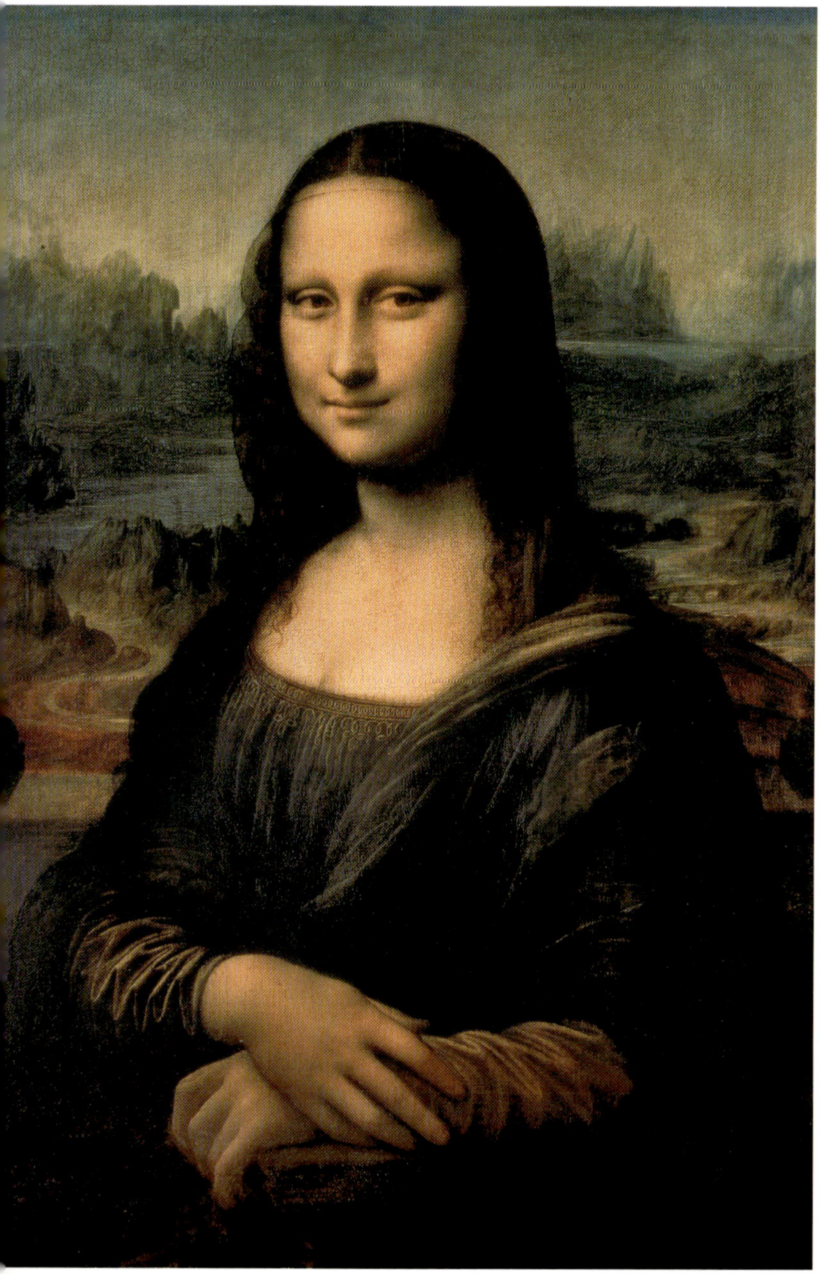

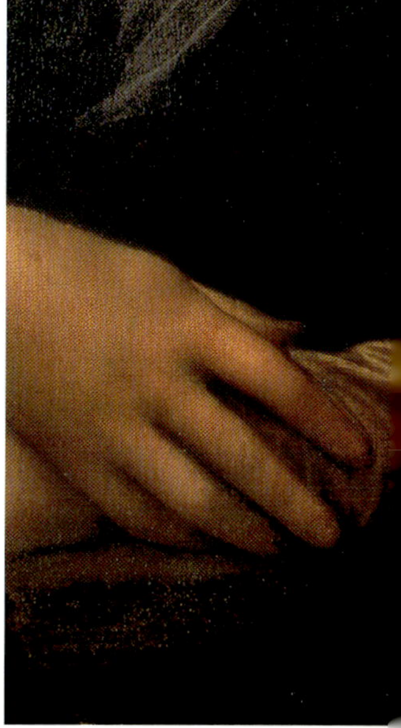

The ineffable Mona Lisa, with her faint suggestion of a smile, embodies a satisfied and serene 'movement of the soul' that we can share only by intuiting the reason behind it (the unsubstantiated suggestion has often been made that she is pregnant). Begun in Florence, continued during Leonardo's second Milanese period, then taken by the artist to France, the portrait is a synthesis of the studies, tensions and emotions of the last decades of the painter's life: his search for expression, his relationship with the landscape and atmospheric mists, and his manner of drawing that softens into chiaroscuro.

Central Plan

Raphael
The Marriage of the Virgin
1504

Oil on panel, 170 × 118 cm
Milan, Pinacoteca di Brera

Raphael

(Raffaello Sanzio)
Urbino, 1483–Rome, 1520

Considered the classic Renaissance painter, Raphael personifies the brief, fascinating stage of the so-called *cresta sottile*, the crest of the Renaissance wave, when a balance was achieved between the application of the rules of perspective, nature and an intense sweetness of expression. Raised in the artistic culture of Urbino where he imbibed the heritage of Piero della Francesca, Raphael completed his training by working with Perugino for a year or two. Endowed with an exceptional ability to absorb and process the ideas of other artists, he lived in Florence in dialogue with Michelangelo and Leonardo between 1504 and 1508. Among the many splendid works created in this period, his series of variations on the theme of the Virgin and Child is outstanding. In 1508, Pope Julius II called him to Rome to paint frescoes in his private apartment at the Vatican. From the Stanza della Segnatura (1508–11) to the Stanza di Eliodoro (1511–13) we can see a gradual expressive transition from harmoniously composed scenes ('the triumph of the beautiful, the good and the true') to more excitedly dramatic episodes. In Rome, Raphael created an impressive series of altarpieces, portraits and frescoes in which his large and efficient workshop took part. During the papacy of Leo X, Raphael was busy mainly with decorative projects (the Vatican loggias, Villa Farnesina) that anticipated the themes and solutions of incipient Mannerism.

The Renaissance saw a great revival of interest in centrally planned buildings – a theme that Rafael explored in painting and later through the construction of a church and a chapel in Rome. The most famous example can be found in *The Marriage of the Virgin*, now in Milan. The building that dominates the composition is raised on a stepped podium with sixteen sides, and is surrounded by a refined, columned portico. The elegance and cohesion of the structural elements demonstrate the 21-year-old Raphael's profound understanding of the 'new' architecture.

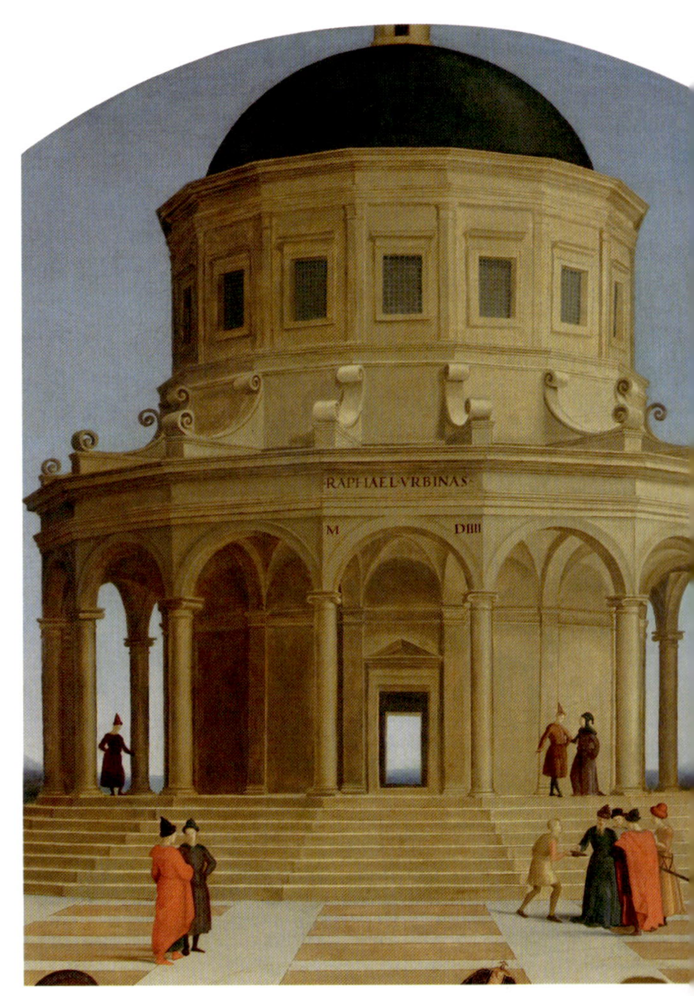

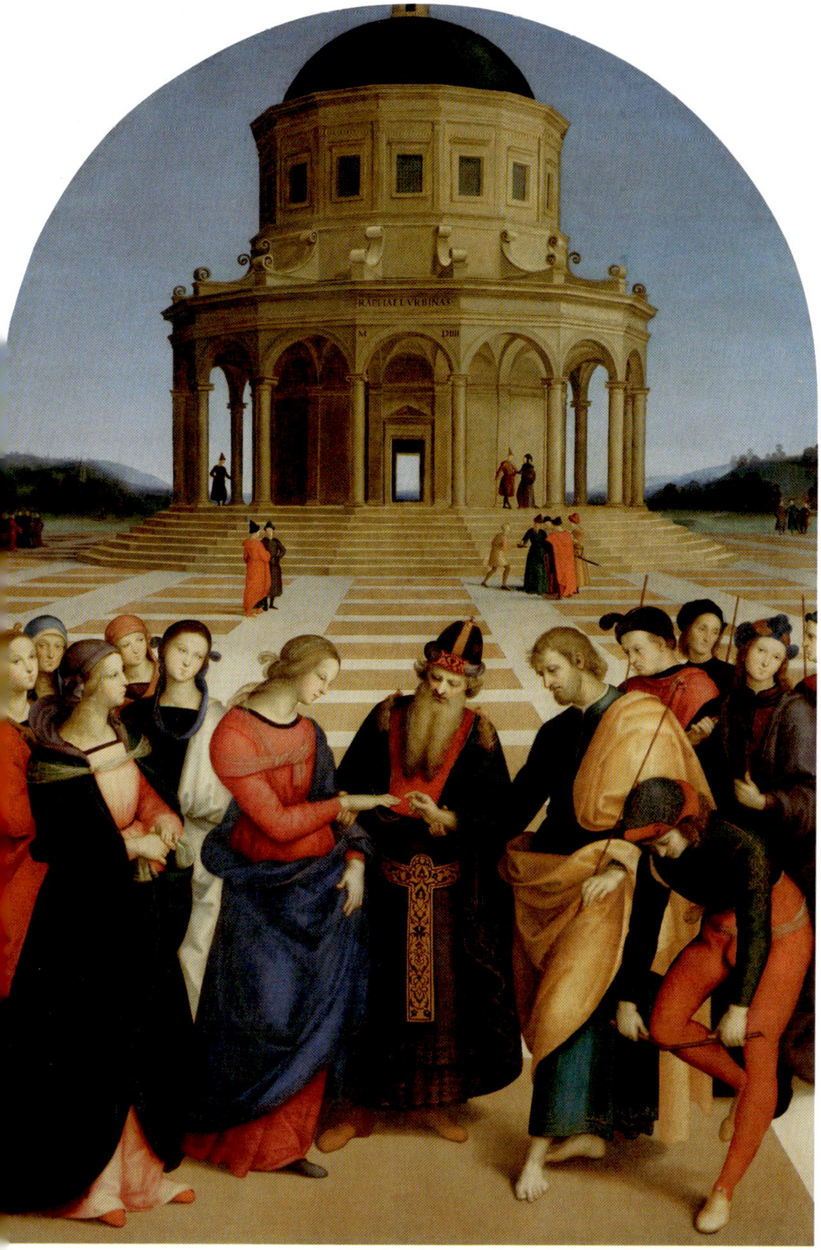

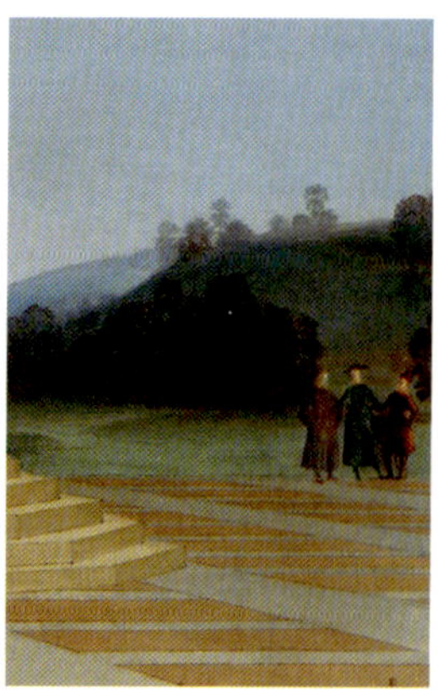

▲ For other painters, the temple would have served as a grand backdrop to a narrative scene (Raphael's teacher Perugino comes to mind; see pages 122–3). For Raphael, however, it became the image's main feature, the fulcrum of the space. The marble pavement around the church blends into the green of the meadows and the countryside. The reference to the architecture of Bramante and the perspective culture of the urban setting is combined with the search for a natural composition.

◀▼ The scene represents the moment when Joseph places a wedding ring on Mary's finger. For the figure of the Madonna, Raphael reused one of Perugino's models (see pages 156–7).

◀ The geometric figure of the semicircle is repeated in the central axis, in the shape of the panel, the dome, the central arcade, and so on. Light passes through the double door in the centre.

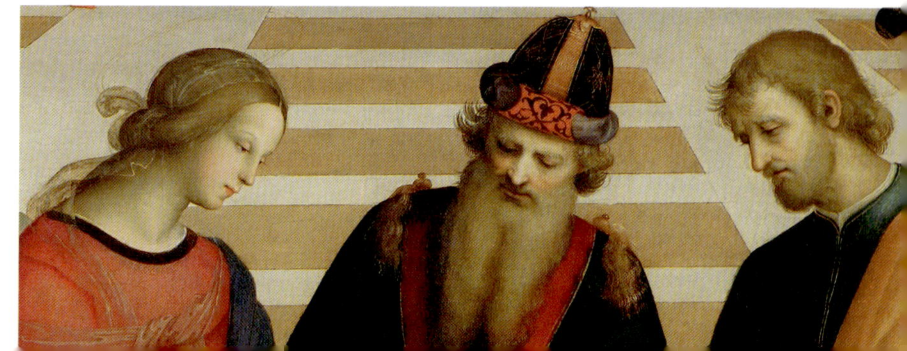

The East

Gentile and Giovanni Bellini
St Mark Preaching in Alexandria
1504–6

Oil on canvas, 347 × 770 cm

Milan, Pinacoteca di Brera

For artist biographies, see pages 166 and 144.

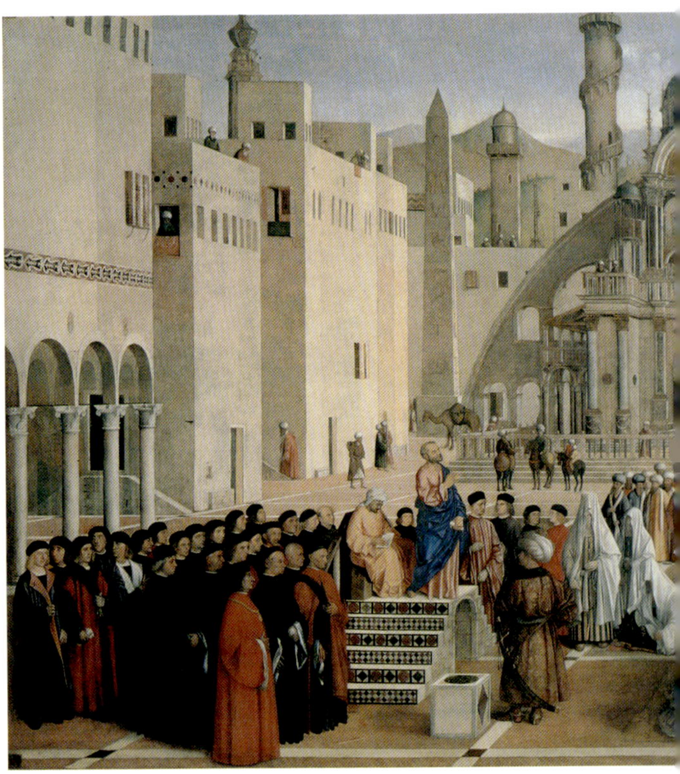

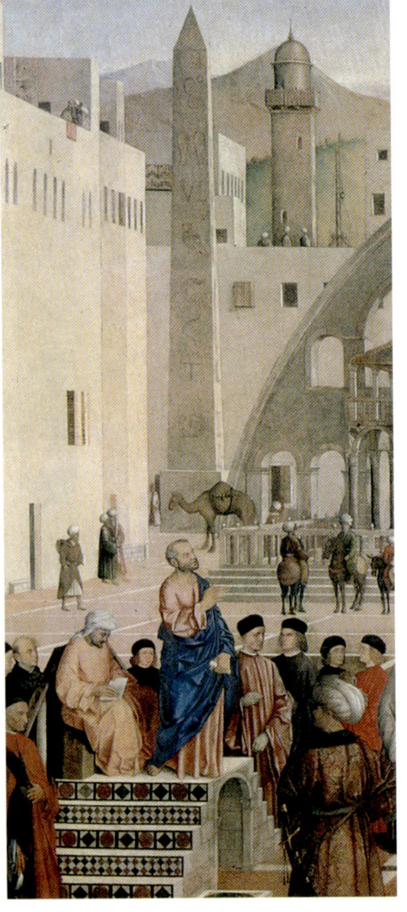

▲ The scene appears to be set in Alexandria, Egypt, as Gentile and Giovanni imagined it. St Mark, protector of the city of Venice, stands upon a bridge-shaped 'pulpit', and just above his head are a dromedary and an obelisk – unmistakable references to the East and ancient Egypt.

By the beginning of the 16th century the Ottoman Empire wa beginning seriously to threaten Venice, with naval battles con tinuously erupting. This prompted renewed attention to th East, and the resulting economic ties, diplomatic relation and artistic exchanges made certain aspects of Islamic architec ture and culture better known in Italy. Gentile Bellini had bee posted to the court of Sultan Mehmet II in Constantinople, fc example. While along the coast of Europe the Saracens wer considered a scourge unworthy of diplomatic efforts, th Most Serene Republic clearly thought quite differently abou the rich and varied culture from the East.

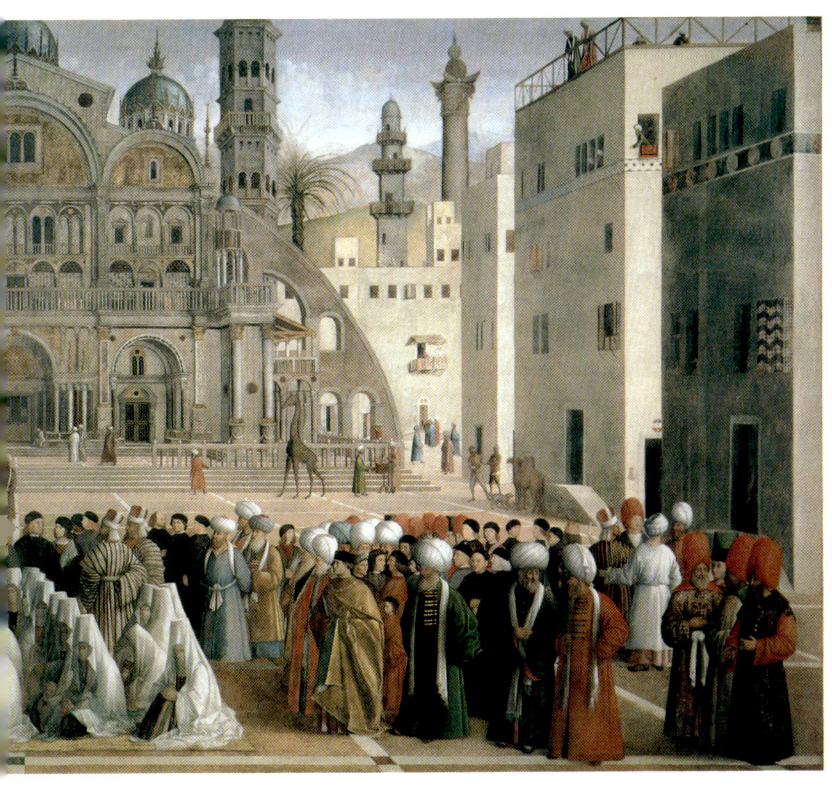

▼ The large canvas (measuring more than 26 square metres) is organized like a stage on which a host of characters appears: in the centre, the kneeling Arab women, all veiled in white, stand out. Some unusual figures are present amid the mostly Eastern costumes: Portuguese merchants and, in the group of turbaned men behind the seated women, even a portrait of Dante Alighieri. (The poet is buried in Ravenna, a city that had recently been conquered by the Venetians.)

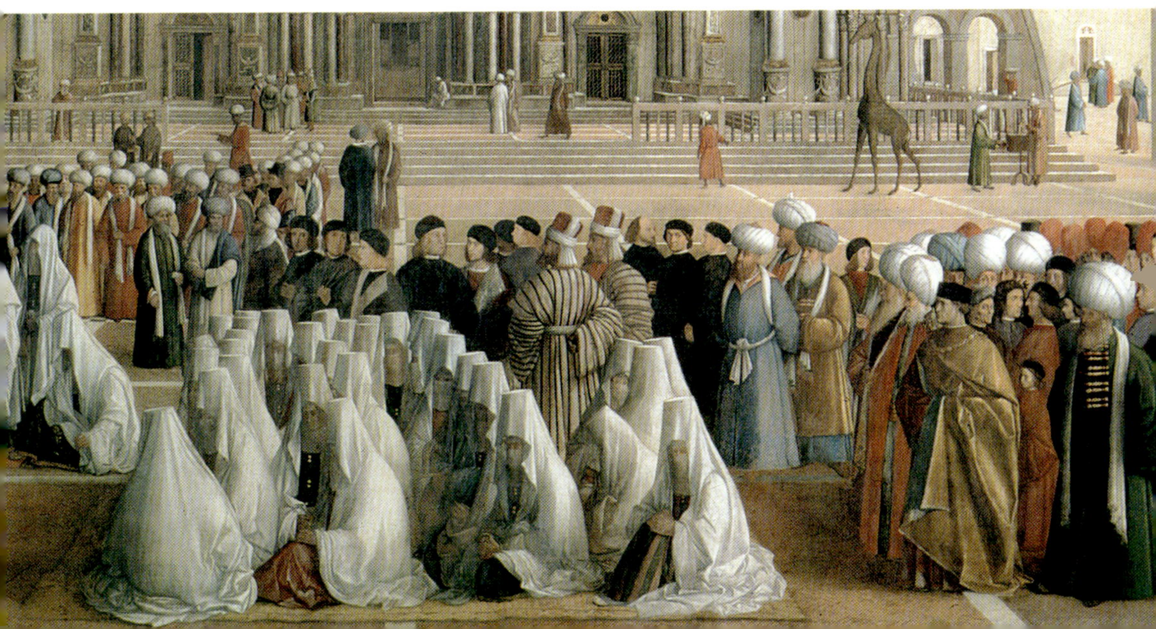

Astronomy

Giorgione
The Three Philosophers
c. 1504

Oil on canvas, 124 × 145 cm
Vienna, Kunsthistorisches Museum

Giorgione

(Giorgio da Castelfranco)

Castelfranco Veneto (Treviso), *c.* 1478–
Venice, 1510

Though we know little about Giorgione's
life, his importance in the development of
Venetian painting – especially in the shift
towards atmosphere and light – cannot
be overstated. Following the example of
Giovanni Bellini and Leonardo's *sfumato*,
around 1505 Giorgione rejected the
traditional approach to sacred scenes
and placed his *Castelfranco Altarpiece*
(see pages 200–1) out-of-doors. It was a
milestone in the development of *colorito*.
A new feeling for nature and landscape
inspired his masterpieces such as *The
Tempest* (see pages 206–7) and *The
Three Philosophers*. In 1508, Giorgione
reached the peak of his brief career with
the frescoes at the Fondaco dei Tedeschi
(German warehouse), now almost entirely
lost, near the Rialto Bridge. He worked
on them with the young Titian, the
most brilliant exponent of his circle
of collaborators and imitators (which
also included Sebastiano del Piombo).
Giorgione died of the plague in 1510,
when he was in his early thirties.

Those who were able to read the stars and celestial phenomena
were accorded great status and power, and astronomers played
a fundamental role at courts large and small throughout Italy.
This was a time, of course, when many still believed in predic-
tions and divinatory practices. An exceptional alignment of the
planets such as the one that occurred in 1504, the appearance
of comets and other unusual celestial events were viewed with
concern. The image of an astronomer clutching sheets of paper
and instruments recurs frequently in early 16th-century painting, especially in Italy and Germany.

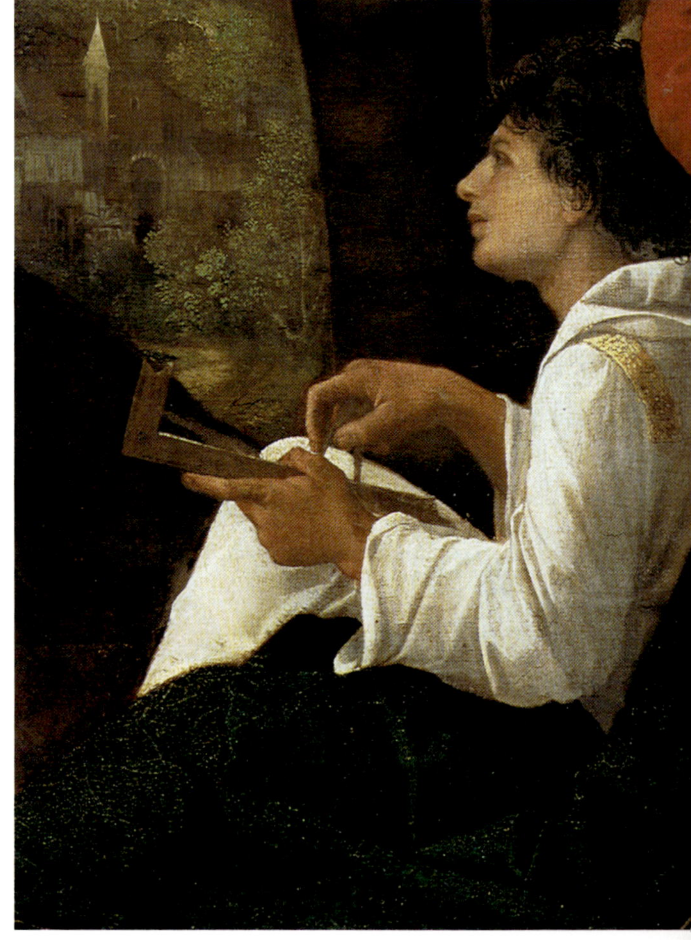

► The figures' sense of anticipation
led scholars to identify the three
astronomers as the Magi, witnessing
the first appearance of the star. The
youngest gazes intently at the landscape,
as if searching for some revelation, while
the other two are talking. In various other
interpretations, the painting is an allegory
of the human race, of philosophy and of
the Three Ages of Man, a common theme
in Venetian art.

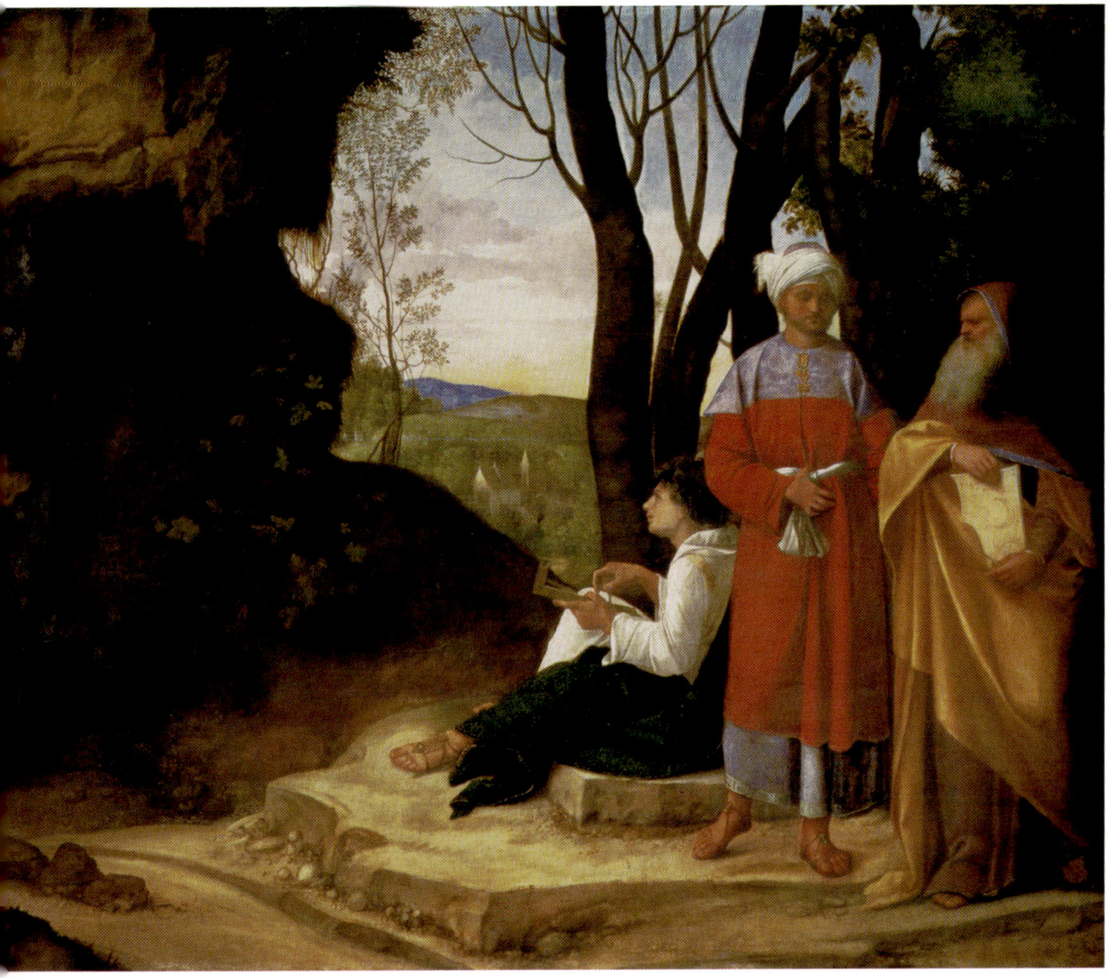

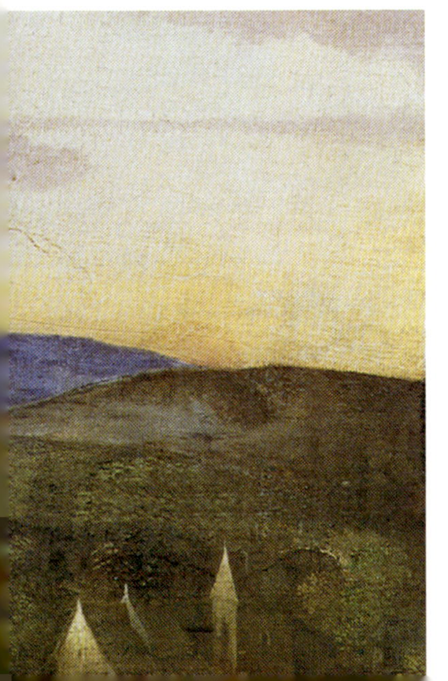

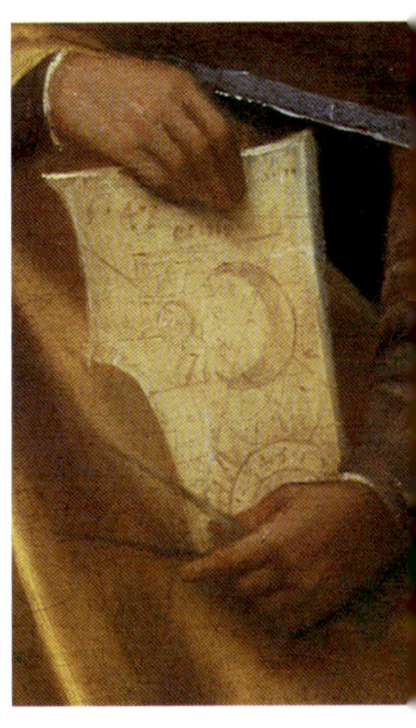

◄ ▲ This work ranks among the most captivating but also most mysterious paintings of the Renaissance. Prioritizing colour over line, the painter sensitively captures the transparency of the atmosphere, the secrets of the heavens and the enchantment of nature.

► The figures are certainly astronomers, or at least versed in interpreting the movements of the heavenly bodies, as confirmed by the charts and instruments held by two of the men.

Colorito

Giorgione
Castelfranco Altarpiece
1505

Oil on panel, 200 × 152 cm

Castelfranco Veneto, Treviso Cathedral,
Costanzo Chapel

For artist biography, see page 198.

As already discussed, Venetian painting chose a practical and poetical alternative to the Florentine school's focus on the study of drawing (*disegno*). This painting achieves its formal, spatial and emotional unity through transitions of light and merging planes of colour. Giorgione's only altar painting, the *Castelfranco Altarpiece* is not set in an architectural interior. The muted tones, the colours and the open, natural atmosphere are qualities that sum up the concept of *colorito*, a stylistic trend in the Veneto in which the image emerges from the background through a gradation of tones, which are smoothed by the lighting.

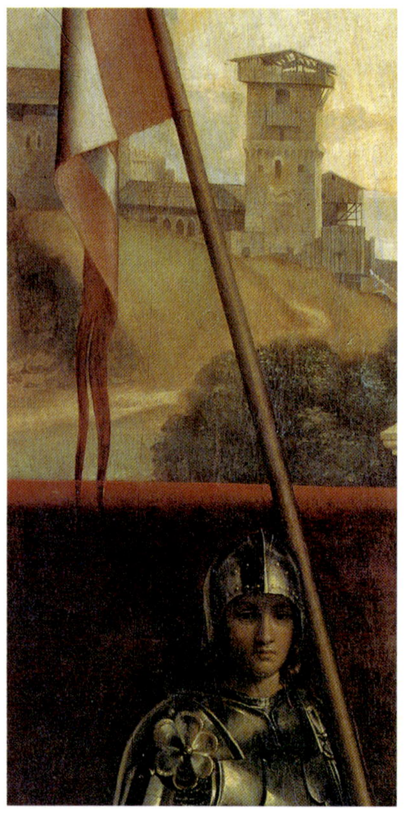

▶ The beautiful young Madonna is seated on a high throne. The painting's mood is sweetly melancholic, as is often the case in the paintings of Giorgione and Giovanni Bellini.

◀ A tall, velvet-covered balustrade separates the open countryside from the floor on which the saints and the Virgin's throne are placed. Because natural light prevails over drawing, the eye does not perceive a line or contour dividing the gold from the red, or the green from the blue of the sky. The light slowly glides along the stones of the tower in the background, seems to be absorbed by the velvet of the balustrade and then lightly touches St Liberale's burnished armour, which darkly gleams, its colour between silver and black.

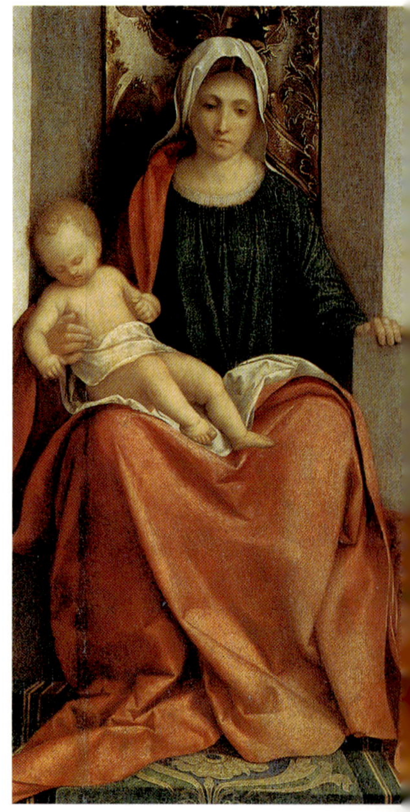

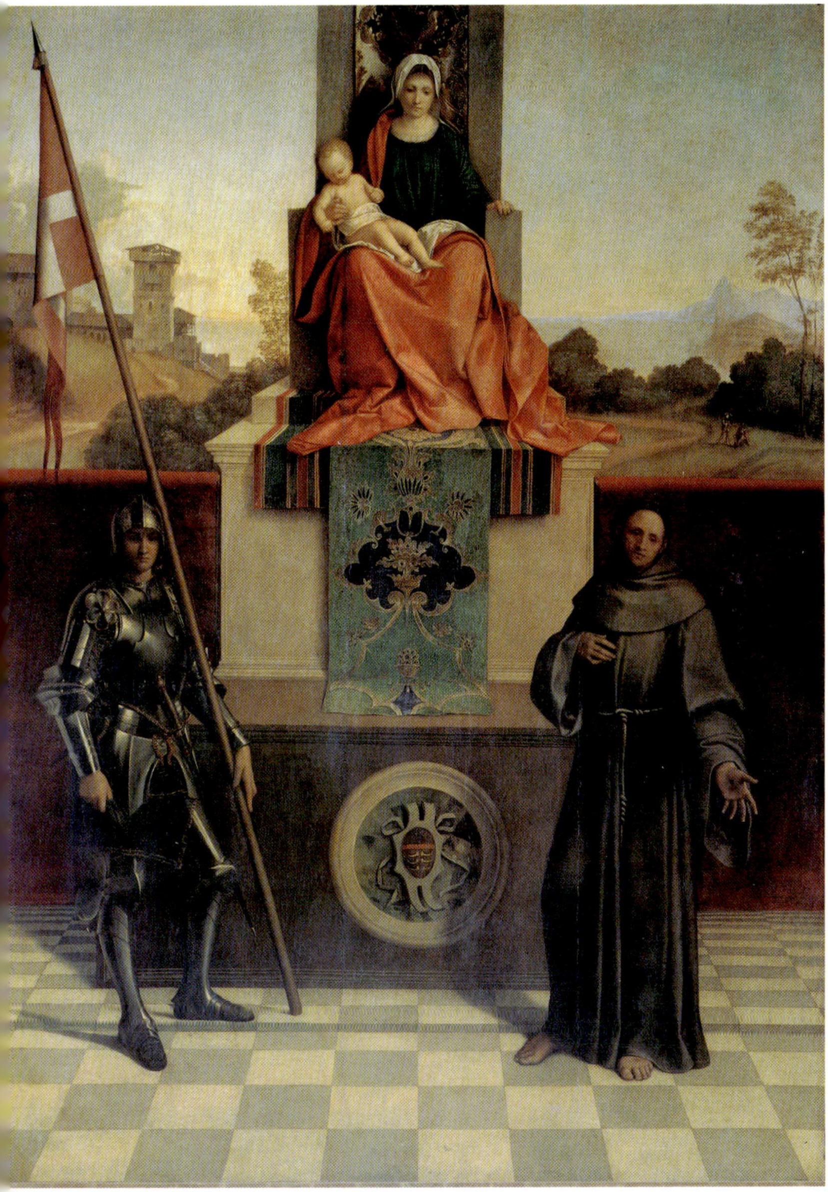

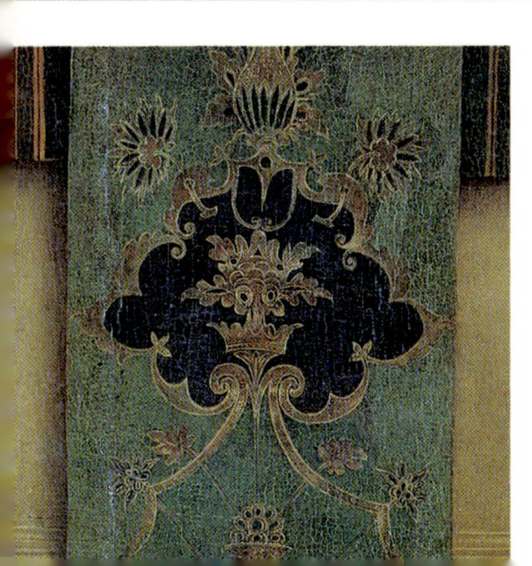

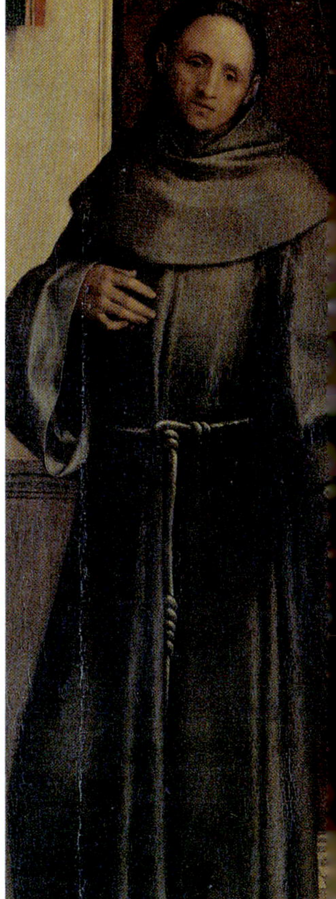

◄▼ Giorgione's only altarpiece is still in its original location, the funeral chapel of the Costanzo family in the cathedral of Castelfranco Veneto. His production, which included portraits, allegories and sacred subjects, mainly appealed to private collectors. While the altarpiece's setting in natural light is wholly innovative, the composition is a customary pyramidal one, with some variations: St Francis, on the right, stands slightly farther forward than St Liberale, the patron of Castelfranco.

◄ *Colorito* seeks an effect of chromatic blending and relegates outline drawing to a secondary role. Yet it does not preclude the execution of highly refined details, such as the damask panel adorning Mary's throne.

Northern Europe

Albrecht Dürer
The Feast of the Rosary
1506

Oil on panel, 162 × 194.5 cm
Prague, Národní Galerie

Albrecht Dürer

Nuremberg, 1471–1528

The greatest German artist of the Renaissance was a 'universal' master, interested in many different themes, formats and techniques, and involved in compiling treatises and technical writings. At the conclusion of his early training – under his father, a goldsmith, and then in the workshop of Michael Wolgemut – Dürer set out on a long study trip that broadened his vision to include a European perspective. He was absent from Nuremberg for four years, from April 1490 to May 1494. A journey to Venice rounded out his training, and he began an impressive career as a painter and engraver in the service of Maximilian of Augsburg. From 1505 to 1507, Dürer was back in Italy, staying at length in Venice just as the local school experienced a stylistic transition from the tradition of Bellini to the new generation of Giorgione and Titian. Subsequent compositions, always characterized by extreme concern for drawing, have a full monumental and perspectival scope. In 1521, he travelled to Antwerp and the Low Countries, where he came into contact with Gabriel Metsys and Lucas van Leyden.

► The iconographic theme of the work is the institution of the Feast of the Rosary. Aided by angels and a Dominican friar, Mary and the Child distribute crowns of roses to figures kneeling in prayer, beginning with the pope (an anachronistic portrait of Alexander VI, who had died three years earlier) and Emperor Maximilian I of Hapsburg.

The relationship between the Italian and Central European masters is an important subject in Renaissance art. The letters and paintings that Albrecht Dürer produced on his two voyages to Italy are direct proof of a strong mutual influence, but also of the differences and mistrust between Italy and the northern world. The most important result of Dürer's activity in Venice was the *Madonna of the Rose Garlands*, or *The Feast of the Rosary*, painted in 1506 for the church of San Bartolomeo, near the Rialto Bridge. This church was attended by Venice's German community, and some of its successful merchants and financiers are portrayed in the painting. The work has an immediate resonance and represents the best example of the exchange between Venetian and Northern European art.

► The portrait gallery included in the painting was an extraordinary lesson for early 16th-century Venetian painters.

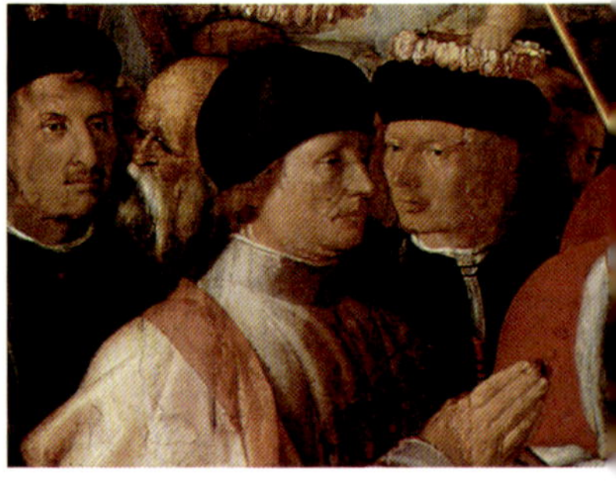

▼ The angel playing the lute at the foot of the Virgin's throne is an obvious homage to Venetian tradition. Angel musicians often appear in the altarpieces of Giovanni Bellini, Carpaccio and Lorenzo Lotto.

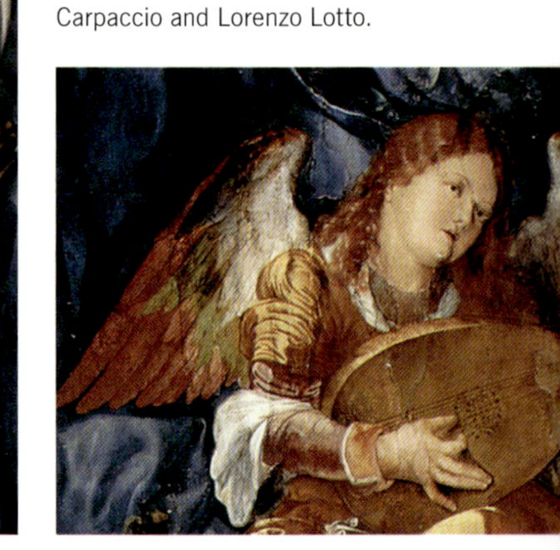

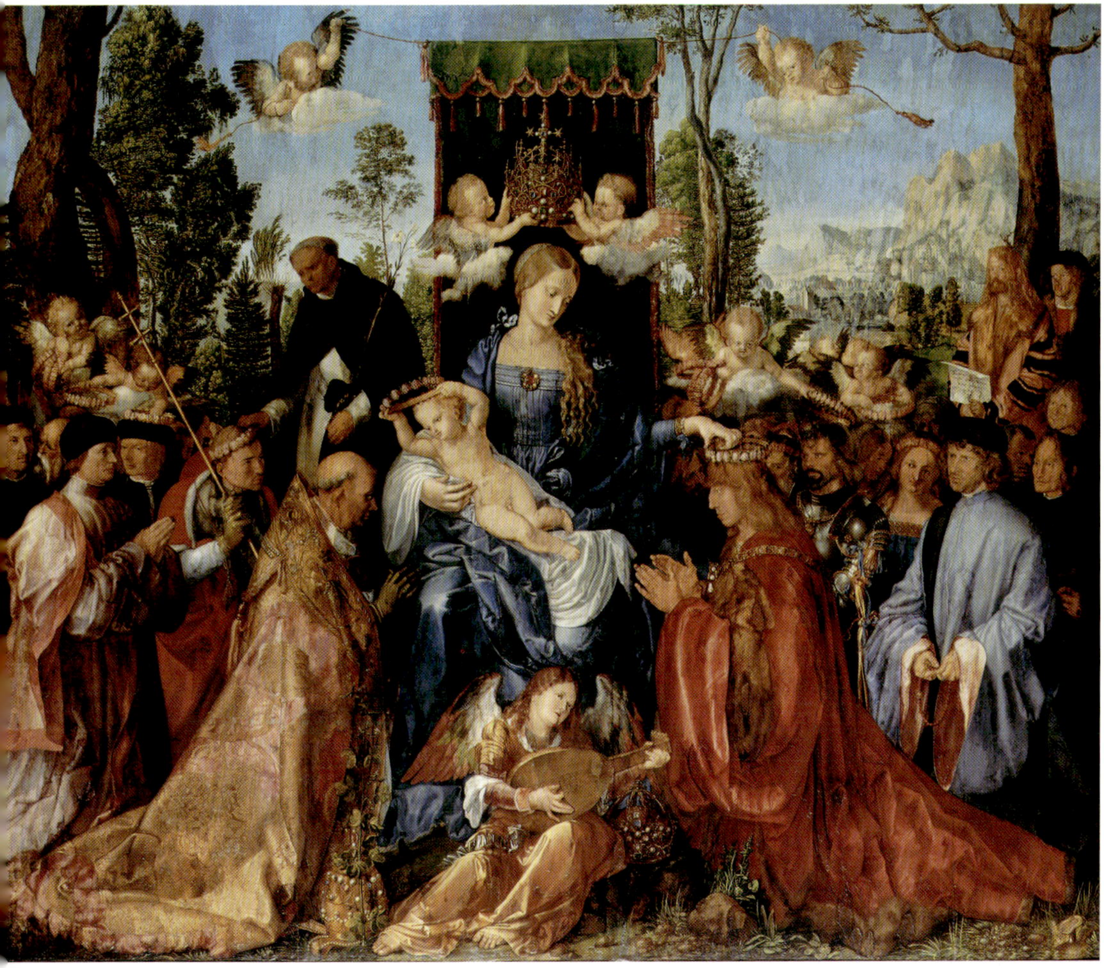

▼ Most of the people portrayed in this altar painting are Dürer's German contemporaries. Jacob Fugger, in a place of honour directly behind Emperor Maximilian, was an Augsburg banker and the president of the German community in Venice. Behind him is the architect Willem van Tetrode (known as Guglielmo Tedesco in Italy), who had just rebuilt the Fondaco dei Tedeschi after a devastating fire.

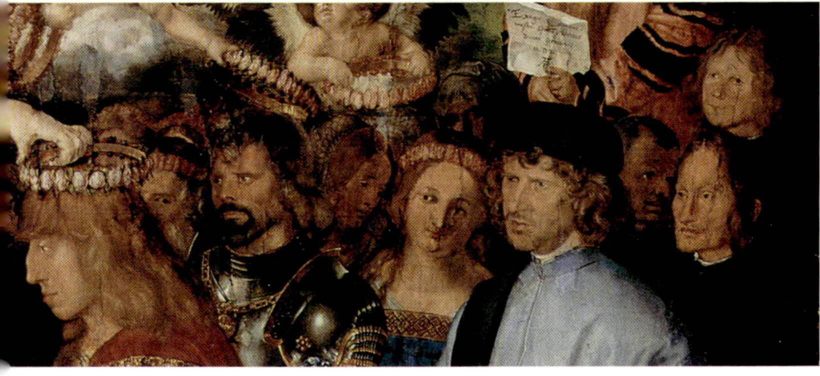

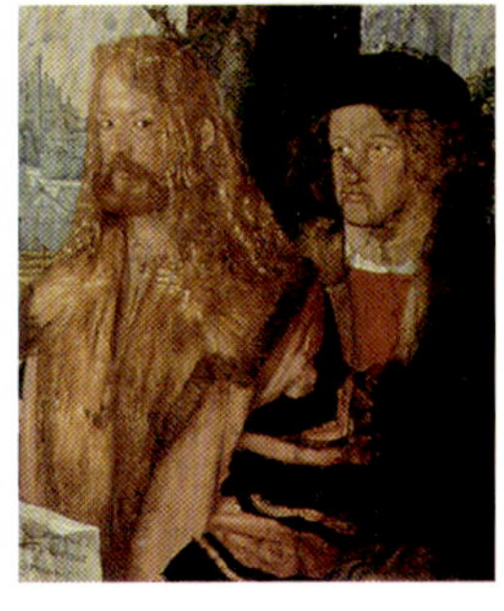

▲ Dürer's self-portrait appears, less conspicuously, in the background. A cartouche inscribed in Latin bears his signature and date, and indicates that the artist spent five months executing the altarpiece.

Ugliness

Giorgione
The Old Woman
1506

Oil on canvas, 68 × 59 cm
Venice, Gallerie dell'Accademia

For artist biography, see page 198.

The attention paid to 'ugliness' is one of the most obvious signs of the cultural transition from the 15th to the 16th century. The 'grotesque' heads drawn by Leonardo and contact with the great northern artists who came to Italy around 1500 (Dürer, Bosch, Metsys) provided the most direct visual precedents. But psychological motives came into play as well. In a rapidly changing international order, Italy's small states were faced with severe political, economic and military problems. The optimism of the humanists was running up against a harsh reality, prompting a sense that the era was coming to an end.

► The eyes, turned towards the viewer, are surrounded by deep furrows, the grey hair is thin and dry, the neck wrinkled and the mouth half-closed, as though she were wheezing. The old woman that Giorgione painted is an individual, charged with intensity and humanity, an independent and touching poetic invention utterly dissimilar to the allegories, burlesque caricatures and comic derivations found in Leonardo's 'grotesque' drawings. Looking at this portrait, one can detect the vestiges of a now irretrievably faded beauty.

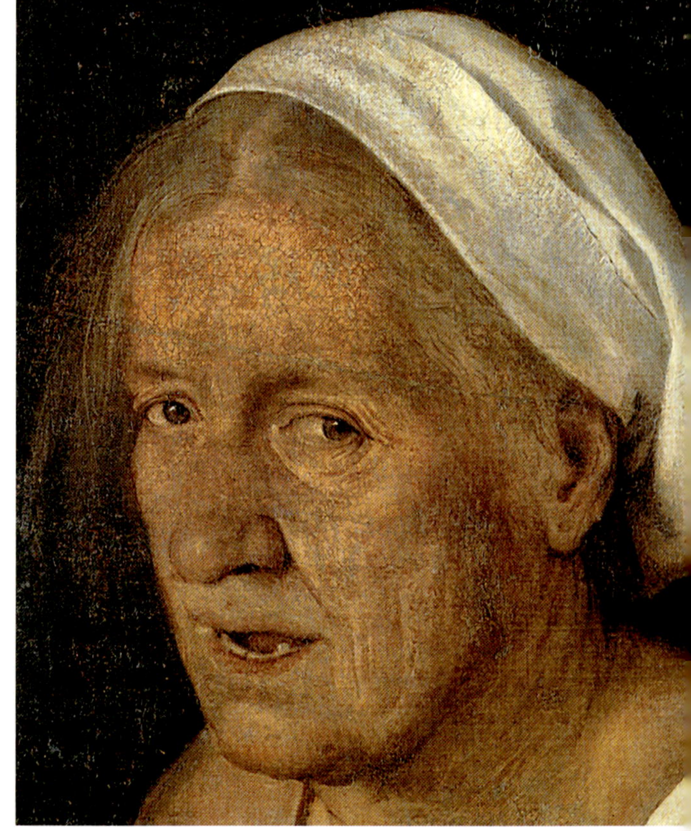

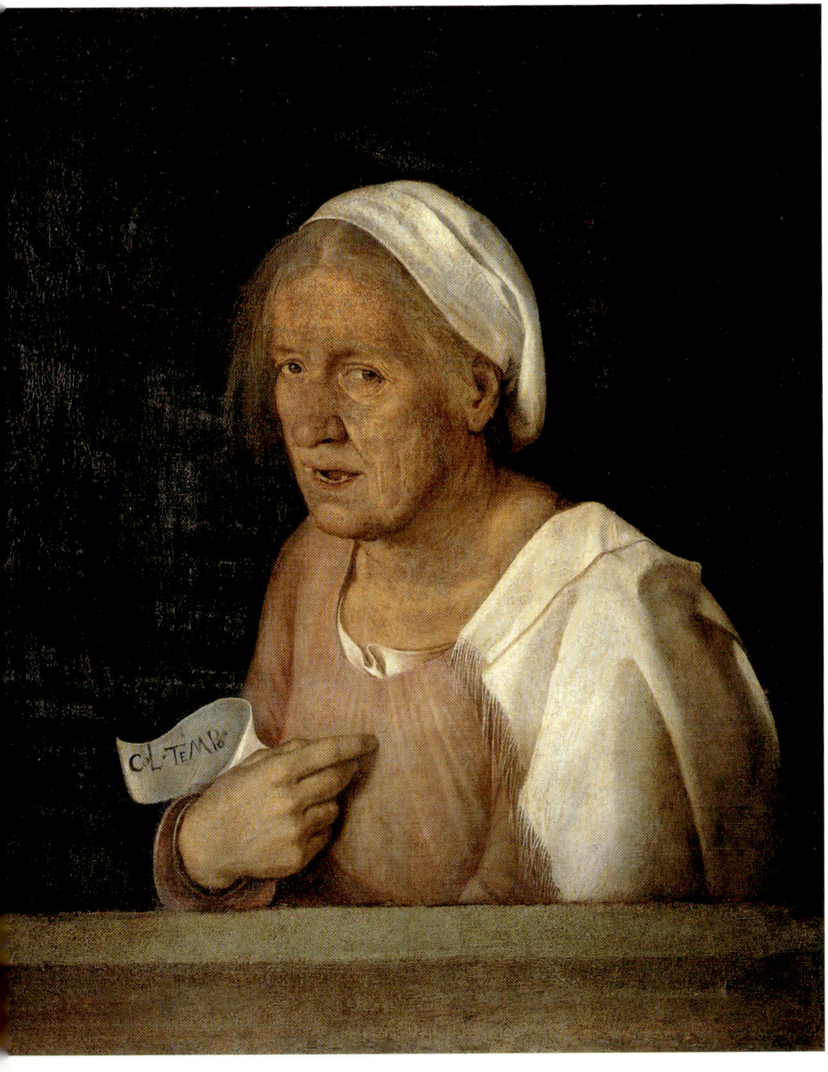

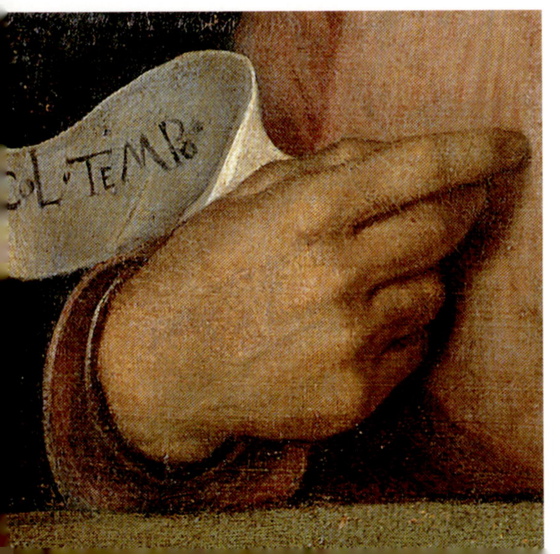

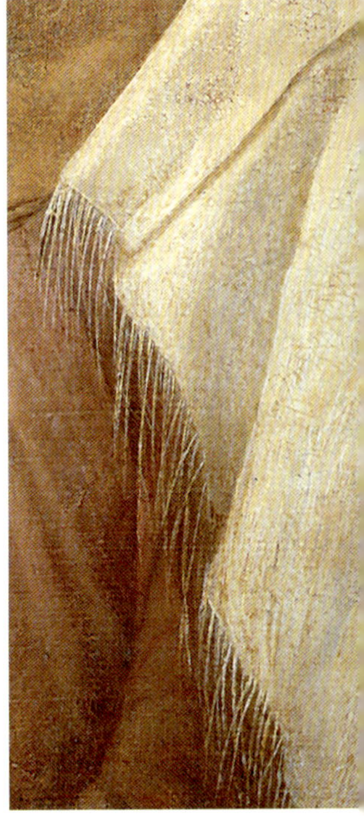

▲▼ Giorgione's placement of the figure in a pose most often used for aristocrats is hardly an accident. The woman emerges from a neutral background, in half-length and turned three-quarters behind a marble ledge. The painting may be compared with Titian's portrait of a man from a few years later (see pages 230–1), especially in the relationship of the man's extraordinary, richly quilted sleeve and the humble, fringed shawl thrown over the old woman's hunched back.

◄ The written warning, 'with time', is unambiguous. The old woman's face eloquently shows the devastating effects of time, which erodes beauty. Only fifteen years before, Lorenzo the Magnificent had used the French motto *le temps revient* (time returns) in a diametrically opposite sense, referring to humanism's faith in the return of a 'golden age'.

Nature

Giorgione
The Tempest
1506–8

Oil on canvas, 82 × 73 cm
Venice, Gallerie dell'Accademia

For artist biography, see page 198.

When painters in the Veneto began to manipulate colour – applying brushstrokes in superimposed layers for a soft blended effect – they achieved a new sense of light and atmosphere in the natural landscape. The deepening relationship between painting and nature is the key to reading the work of Giorgione, a profound innovator despite his early death. He further reduced the importance of outline drawing in favour of chromatic transitions of tone, with particularly effective results in works with contemplative, poetical and allegorical subjects.

From the Sea to the Land: Land Investments and Perspectives of the Venetian Nobility

At the beginning of the 16th century, two new factors impeded the traditional role of Venice as a centre for trade in the Eastern Mediterranean: the growing Ottoman strength and the opening of the Atlantic trade routes. Venetian patricians were thus prepared to abandon their sea routes and develop better land resources. An impressive farmland reclamation plan, promoted and directed by the influential Alvise Cornaro, provided new land for cultivation. Poets and authors praised the virtues of rustic life in various ways, and artists soon became open supporters of the idea. Painting offered the Venetians an idyllic image of rural 'leisures'. Thus began the so-called Civilization of the Villas, which would find its most brilliant interpreter mid-century in Palladio. At the same time, more and more painters were coming from the mainland to settle in Venice.

◄ The most credible iconographic hypotheses identify the two figures as Adam and Eve expelled from Eden. The lightning that pierces the clouds would represent the angel's flaming sword. However one interprets this painting, the undisputed main attraction is its portrayal of atmospheric effects, which had never before been given such importance in art.

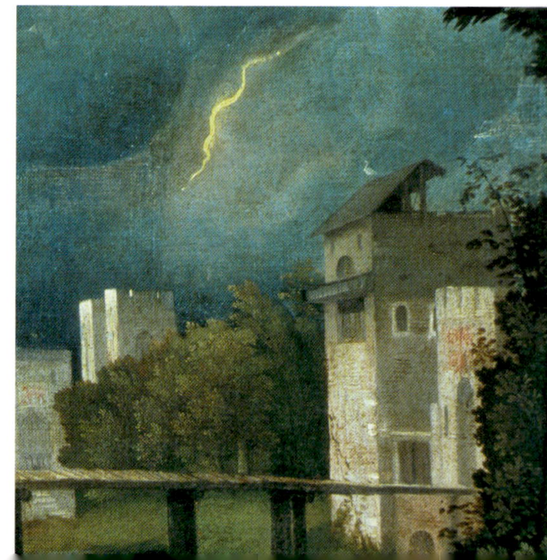

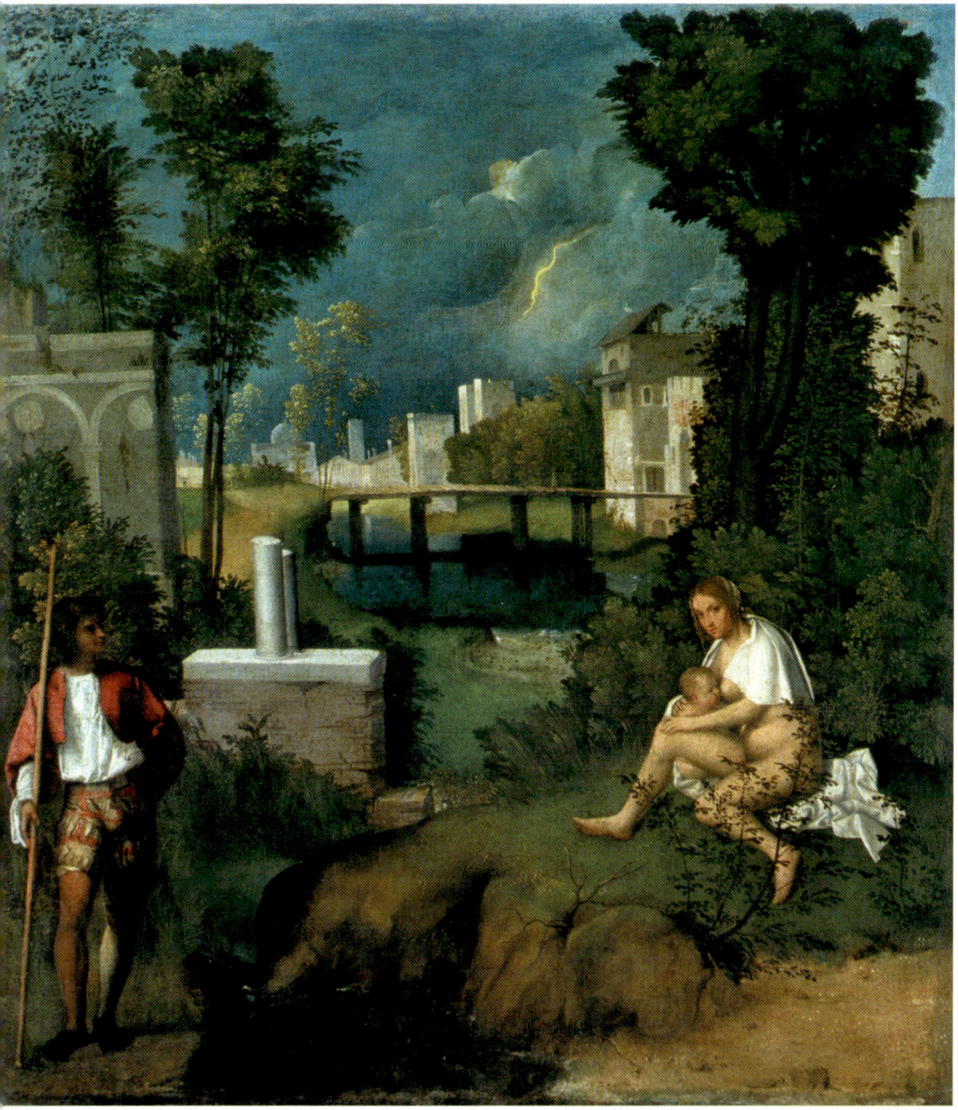

◄ ▲ In contemporary
documents this painting
is cited as a 'landscape on
canvas with a storm, a gypsy
woman and a soldier'. Even
then the narrative subject
seemed less important than
the image of nature and
the storm.

► Seeking a richer, softer
blending of colours that
merge into a natural whole,
Giorgione renounced minutely
defined details in the figures,
lush plant elements and
background houses and
architecture.

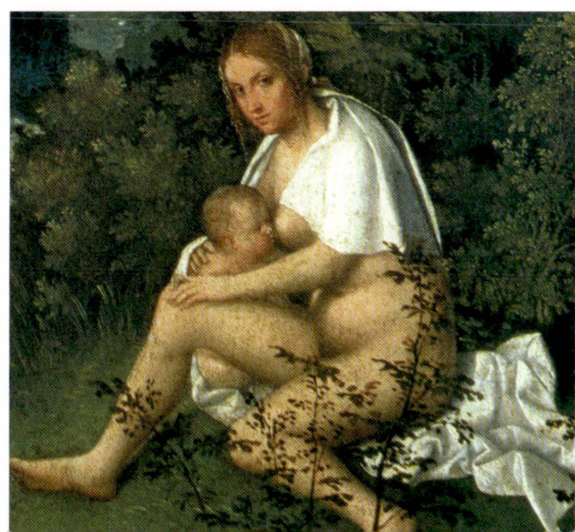

Composition

Raphael
*The Bearing of Christ's Body
to the Tomb*
1507

Oil on panel, 184 × 176 cm
Rome, Galleria Borghese

For artist biography, see page 194.

The construction of an image through a combination of single figures and groups of figures is a basic concept in Italian Renaissance painting. One of the most brilliant innovators in compositional structure, Raphael's increasingly complex, bold compositions appear spontaneous and natural. Surviving sketches and drawings make it possible to follow the process by which he put together certain key works. With the passing of time, and above all with the rise of Mannerism, the quest for daring poses and quotations from classical sculpture would make 'composition' a standard test for evaluating a painter's skill and inspiration.

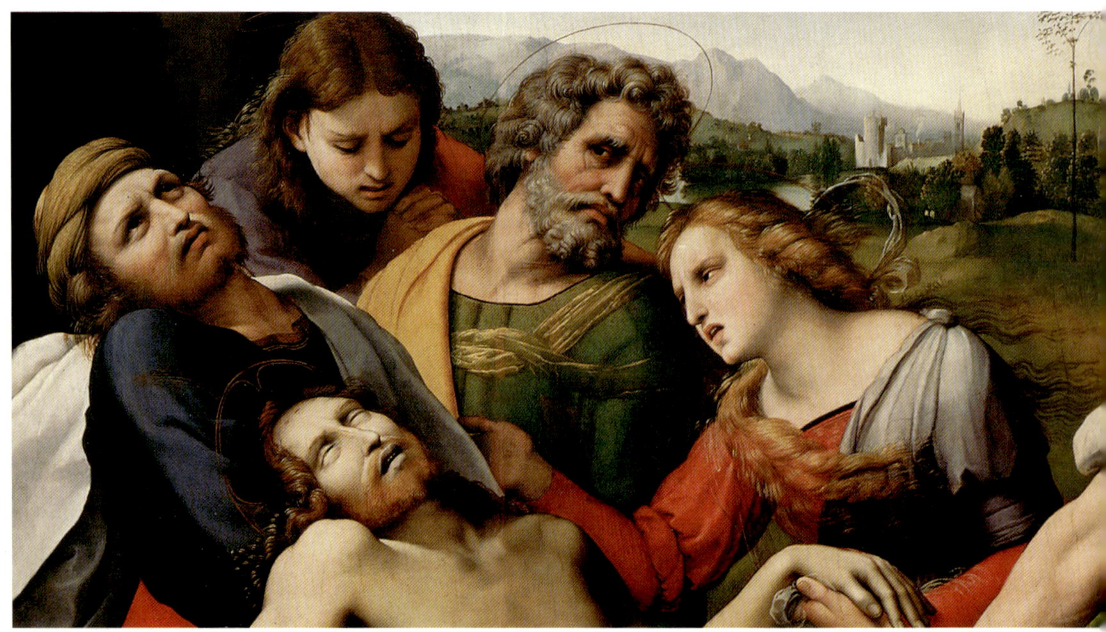

▲ This painting contains references to a dramatic contemporary event, the brutal murder of a young member of the Baglione family during a blood feud. The mother of the victim commissioned it to commemorate both an innocent's folly and a mother's torment. The composition's complex articulation, tense expressions, eloquent gestures, classical quotations and echoes of Michelangelo (particularly in the lifeless body of Christ and the woman sitting at the right who, with a twist of the upper body, turns to support the Madonna) make this work a declaration of maturity and power.

▶ Sometimes called a Deposition, the painting represents the exhausting transport of Christ's body to the tomb. The figures bearing the body are in full view.

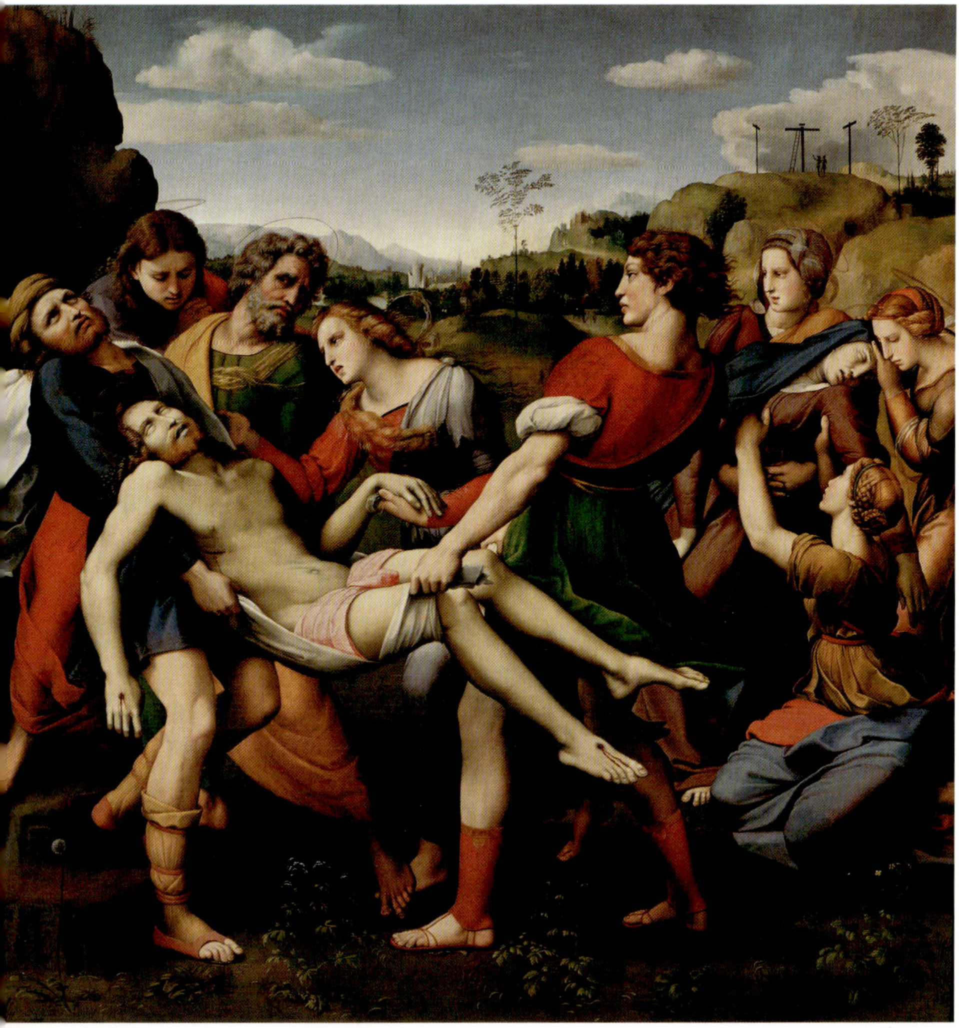

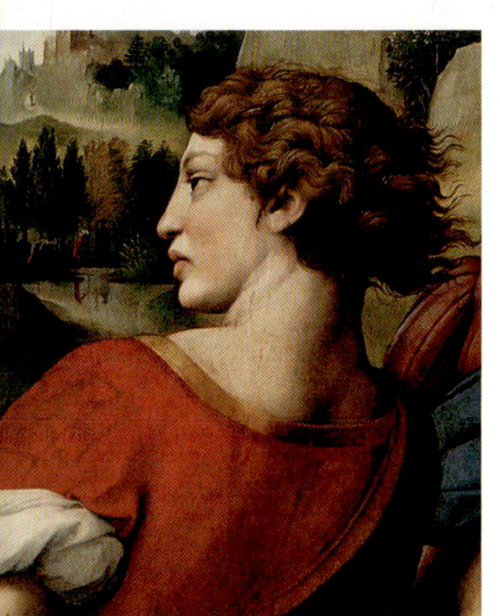

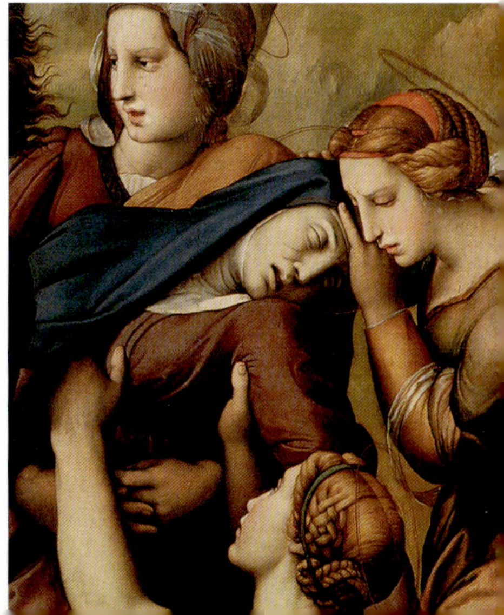

▶ Mary's swooning forms a self-contained episode. Raphael conceived this section independently, and its compositional link with the main group is not entirely effective. However, the work's success heralded a turning-point for Raphael, who soon left Florence to establish himself in Rome.

Altarpiece

Fra Bartolomeo della Porta
Apparition of God the Father to St Mary Magdalene and St Catherine
1508

Panel, transferred to canvas,
361 × 236 cm

Lucca, Pinacoteca Nazionale

Fra Bartolomeo della Porta

(Bartolomeo di Paolo del Fattorino)

Savignano, Prato, 1472– Florence, 1517

A key part of the Florentine school of
the late 15th century, Fra Bartolomeo
trained with Cosimo Rosselli and then
in 1500 opened a workshop with
Mariotto Albertinelli. A follower of
Savonarola, Fra Bartolomeo experienced
a profound mystical crisis, even more
intense than that experienced by
Botticelli. As a result, he abandoned
painting and took Dominican vows.
In 1504, at the monastery of San Marco
where Fra Angelico had worked before
him, Fra Bartolomeo returned to art.
The monk's habit did not prevent him
from travelling to learn about recent
developments in art or to execute
commissions in various regions. The
altarpieces he painted in the first decade
of the 16th century, such as the *Vision
of St Bernard* (Florence, Uffizi), seem
to rival even Raphael and Leonardo in
compositional scope and the delicate
rendering of atmosphere. After a trip
to Venice in 1508, his colours took on
a warmer, more compact tonality. His
subsequent development, in parallel
with the establishment of Andrea del
Sarto in Florence, saw an increase in
mystic monumentality and a heightened
sensitivity in the rendering of nature
and the landscape.

The early 16th century's most obvious innovation in the realm of
altar painting is the abandonment of the architectural setting that
enclosed the figures. The use of open backgrounds with natural
light – initiated by Leonardo and soon to become a characteristic
of painting in the Veneto – gradually spread to Tuscany and
other regions. During the first two decades of the 16th century, painters maintained the arrangement of figures in the now
traditional geometric schemes, but their quest for a new, more
dramatic expressiveness in the gestures and animated poses
was evident.

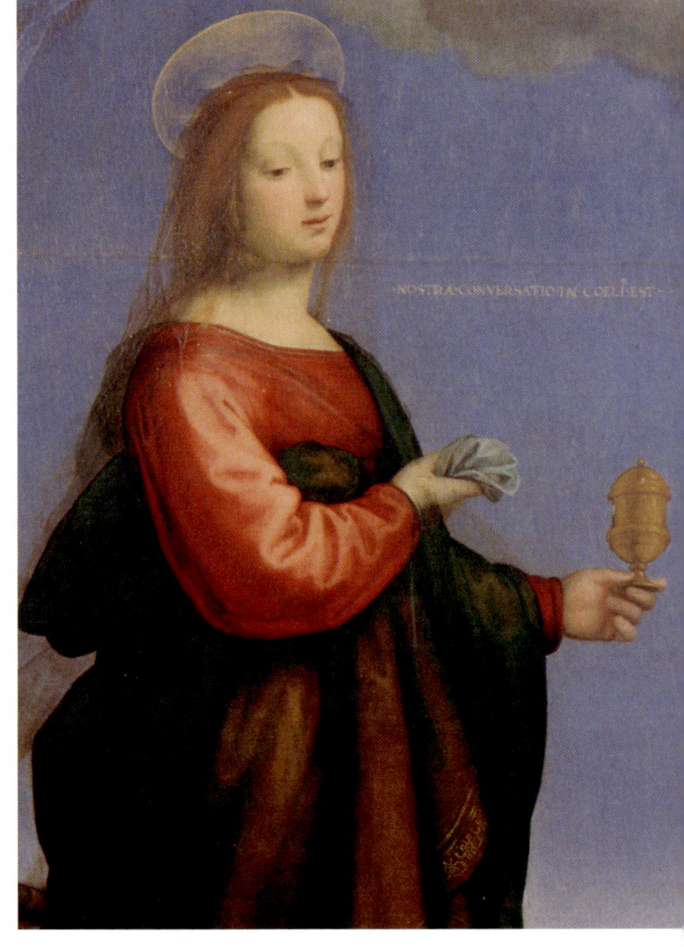

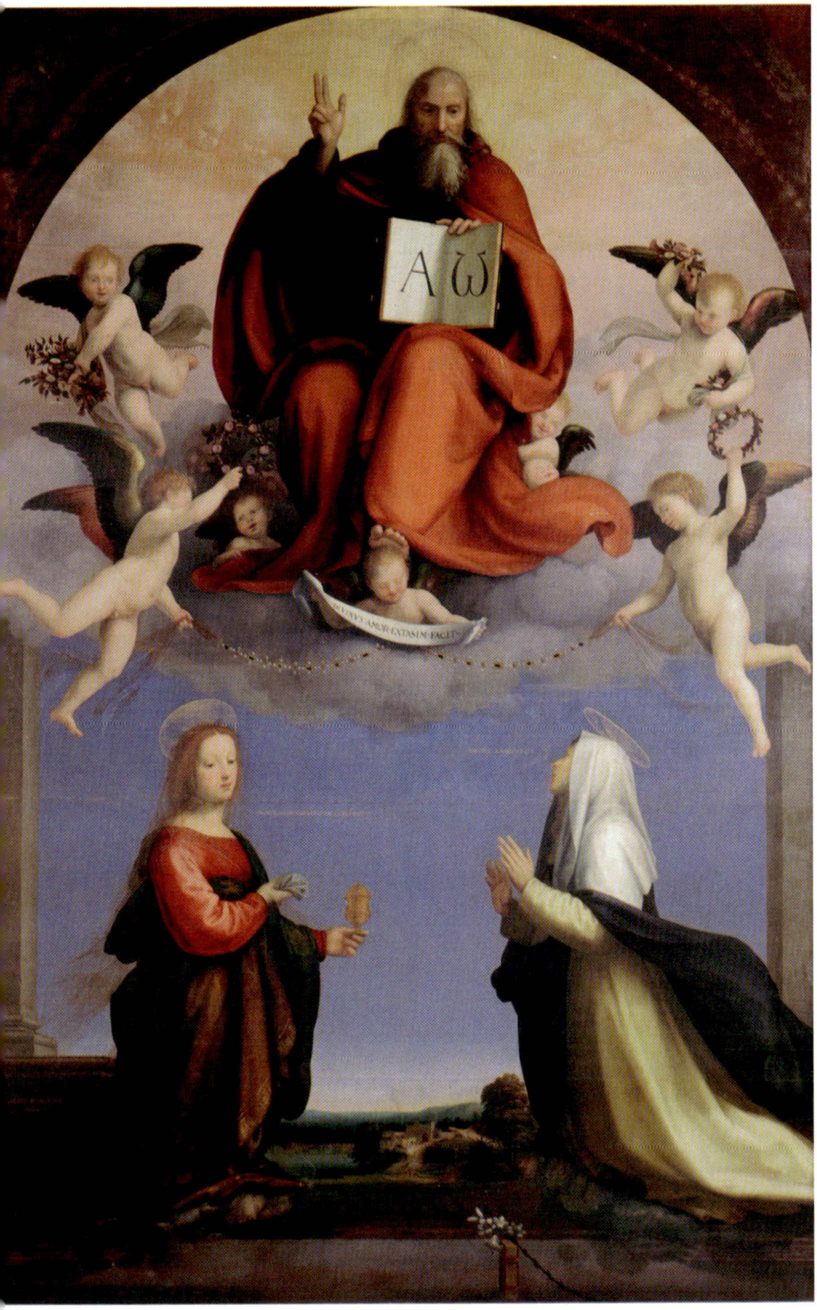

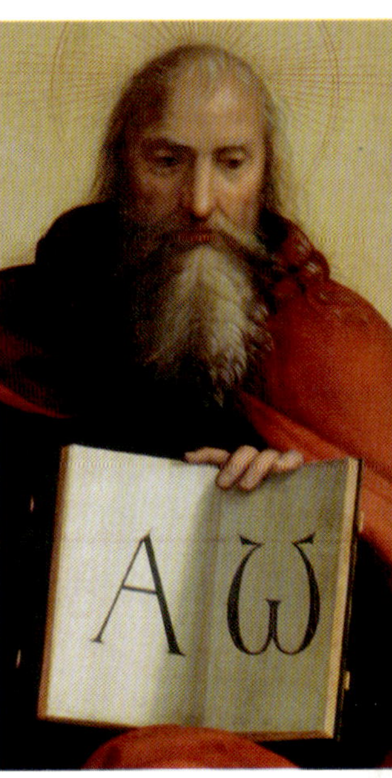

▲ The painting evokes
a solemn atmosphere,
confirmed by the frontal
figure of God the Father,
who is holding a book that
states that he is the 'Alpha
and the Omega, the beginning
and the end of all things.'

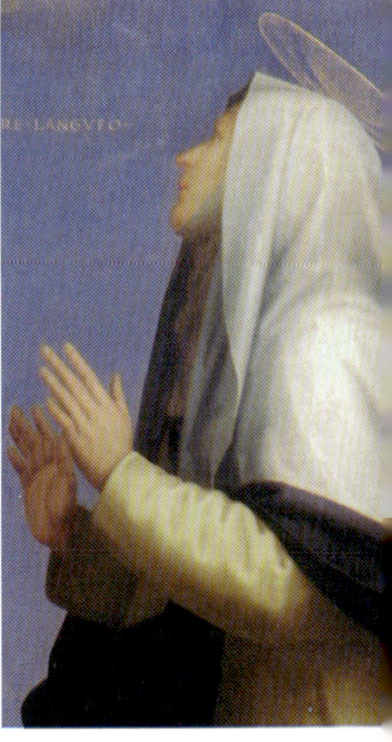

◄ The large altarpieces from the first years
of the 16th century are Fra Bartolomeo's
most innovative, showing a balance between
intense, impassioned mysticism and a delicate
harmony of light and colour. In this sense,
they are comparable to the contemporary
achievements of Raphael.

► Having entered the Dominican Order,
Fra Bartolomeo reflected the austere teachings
of Girolamo Savonarola in his painting. Though
set in a spacious gallery that opens onto a
natural landscape, this altar painting has
a perfectly clear compositional organization.

Ceiling

Michelangelo
Ceiling of the Sistine Chapel
1508–12

Fresco

Vatican City, Vatican Museums,
Sistine Chapel

For artist biography, see page 190.

The ceiling of the Sistine Chapel is one of the most magnif[i]cent and original masterpieces in art history. In it Michelangel[o] created an absolutely unified structure of unsurpassed expressiv[e] force. It follows neither the path of illusionism or *trompe l'oe[il]* blazed by Mantegna, Melozzo and Bramante, nor that of th[e] wall decoration in the old style adopted by Pinturicchio an[d] Raphael. Imitating an architectural framework that transform[s] the simple covering over the chapel into a complex, organi[c] whole, Michelangelo organized the vast space into a celebratio[n] of divine creation and the beauty of the human body. To hel[p] the overall organization, on the broad barrel vault Michelangel[o] painted five heavy beams that 'support' the ceiling and whic[h] incorporate the thrones of the prophets and sibyls.

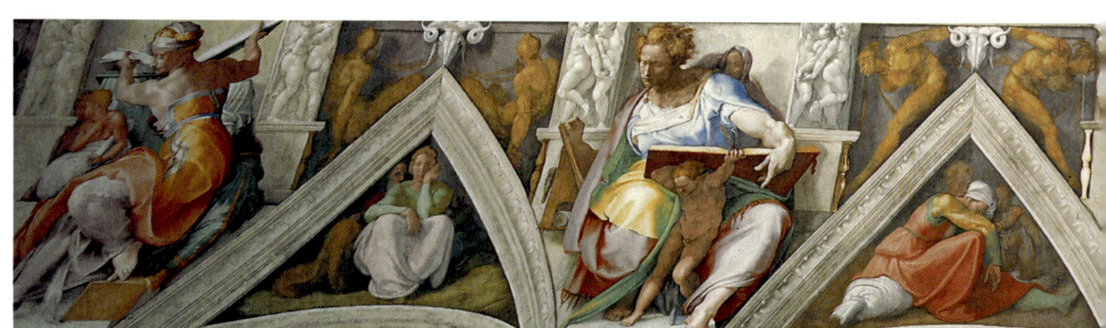

▲ The lunettes above the windows show the generations of Christ's ancestors, while the four large corner spandrels depict Old Testament scenes. The large figures of the prophets and sibyls, seated on high-backed marble chairs, are arranged on the curve of the ceiling.

► Nine scenes from Genesis, in alternating large and small rectangular fields, run down the centre of the ceiling, while nimble, athletic nudes flank the smaller fields. *The Creation of Eve* occupies the ceiling's centre.

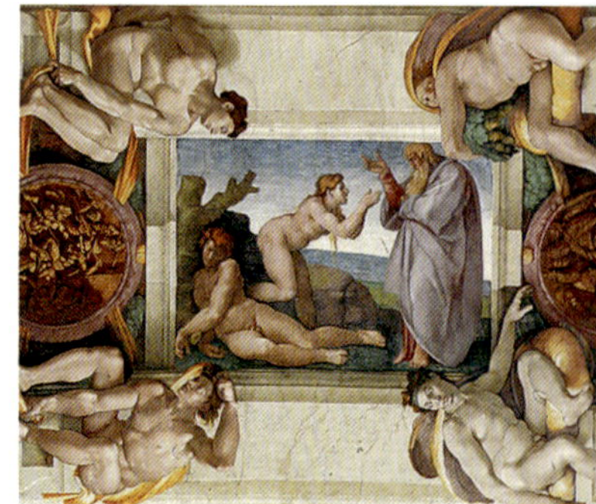

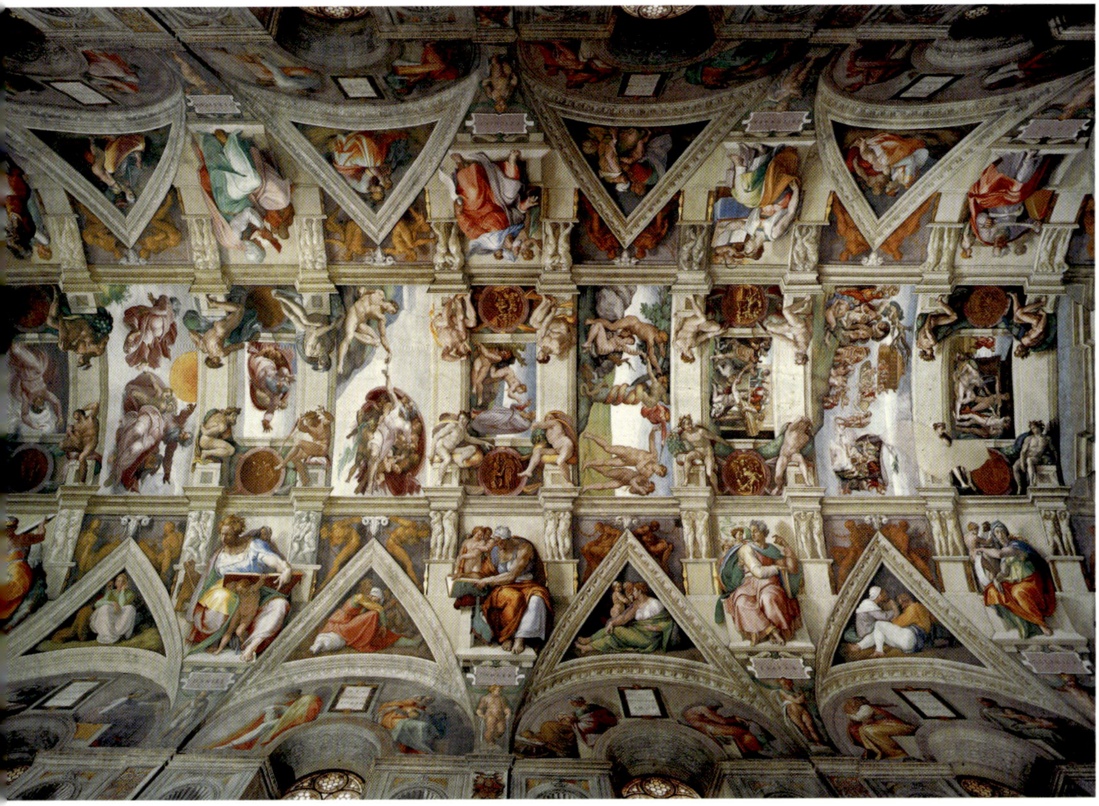

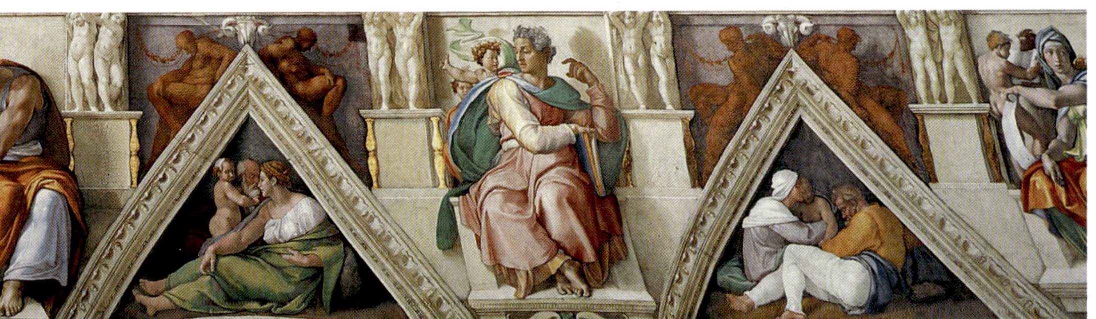

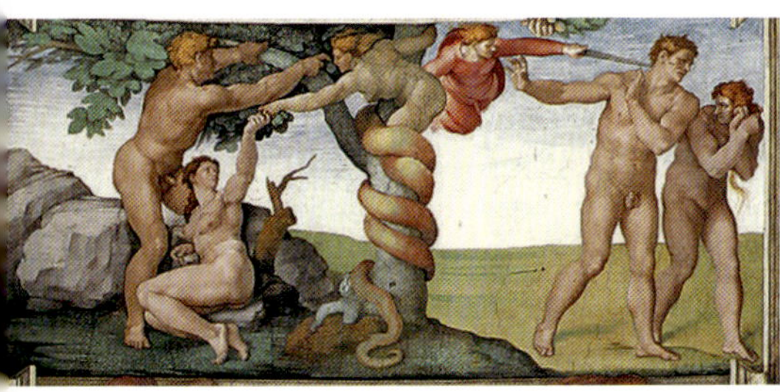

◄ Some of the larger scenes include two distinct, successive episodes, as if to invite viewers to shift their gaze from one part of the ceiling to the next. This is true of *The Fall of Man*, which is immediately followed by *The Expulsion from Eden*.

▲ Before Michelangelo's contribution, a simple, starry sky decorated the Sistine ceiling. Pope Julius II, who asked Michelangelo to paint the twelve Apostles, did not expect the complexity and innovation of the resulting cycle.

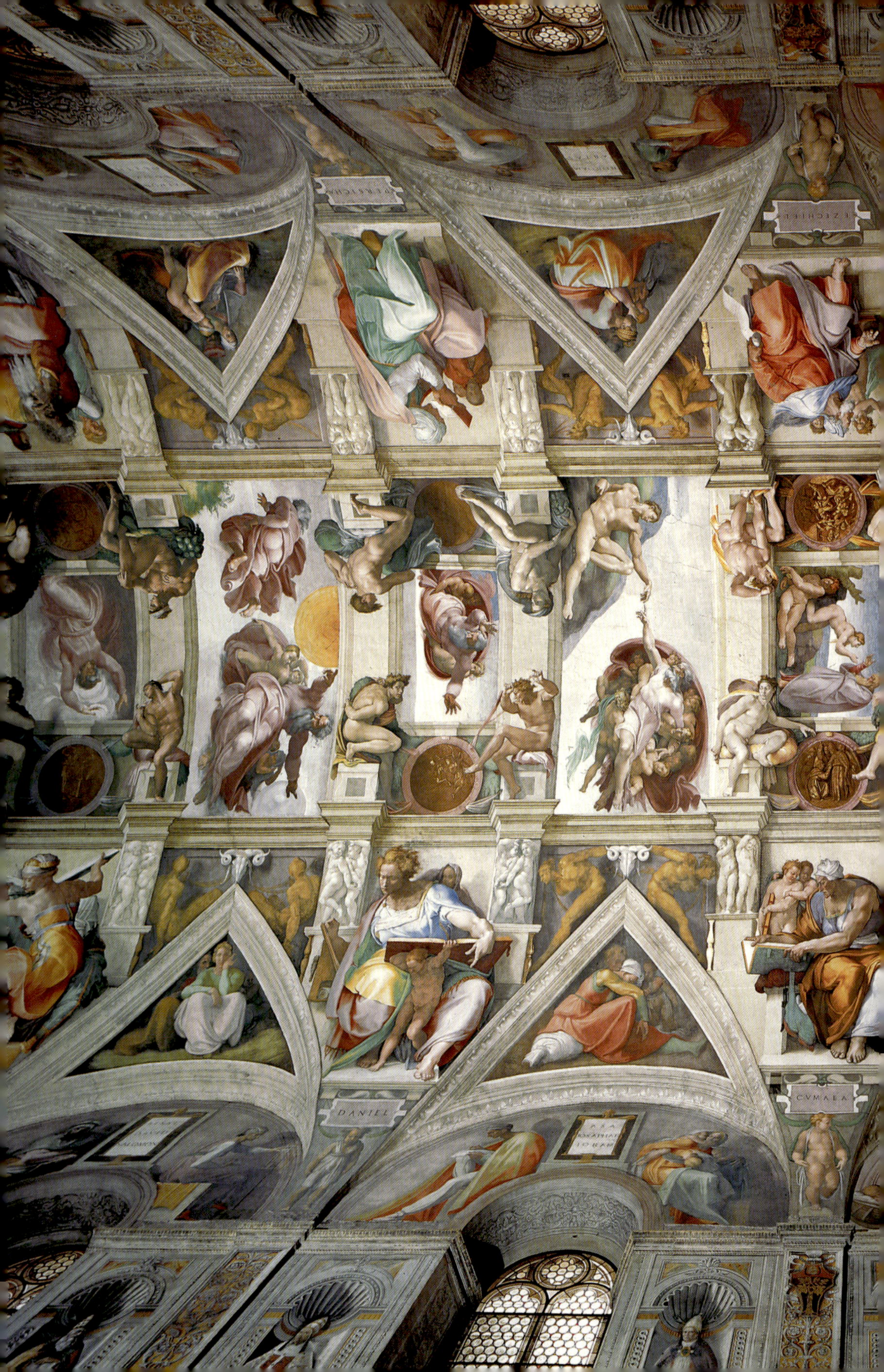

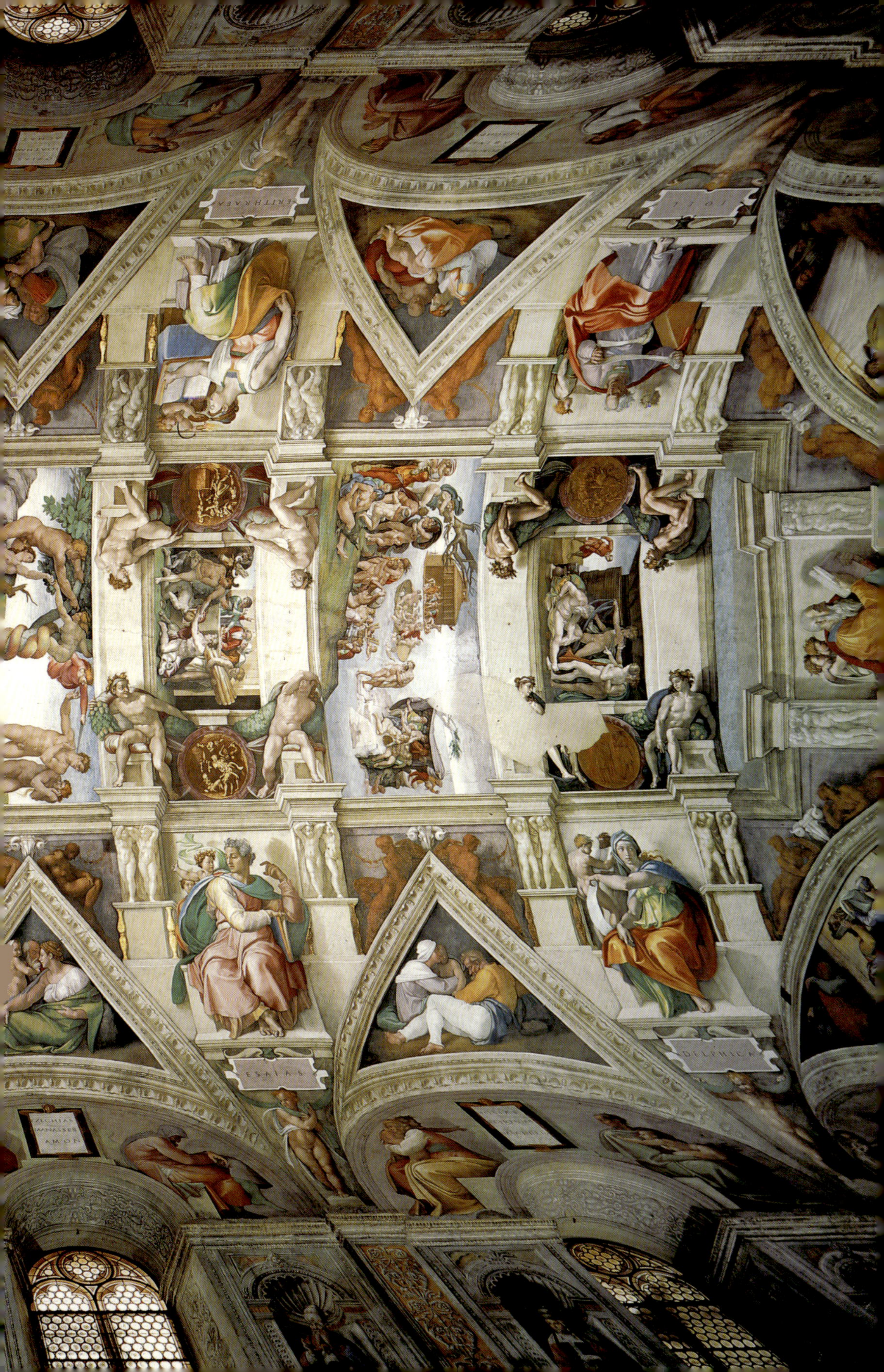

Gesture

The parallel activity of Raphael and Michelangelo at the Vatican around 1510 radically changed the history of painting, charging every figure with a new and profound meaning. Almost instantly, Botticelli's and Perugino's delicate figures seemed lifeless and hollow. The intensity, commanding monumentality and original compositional solutions were the basis of the new Renaissance manner. In the Sistine Chapel, Michelangelo introduced the concept of *terribilità* (awe) to painting. The irresistible power and will of God the Father dominates the ceiling – the gestures, the expressions and even the dimensions of the figures. The Creator hovers over the ceiling spaces. Every gesture is an order, each moment an explosion of force that reaches its peak in *The Creation of Adam*.

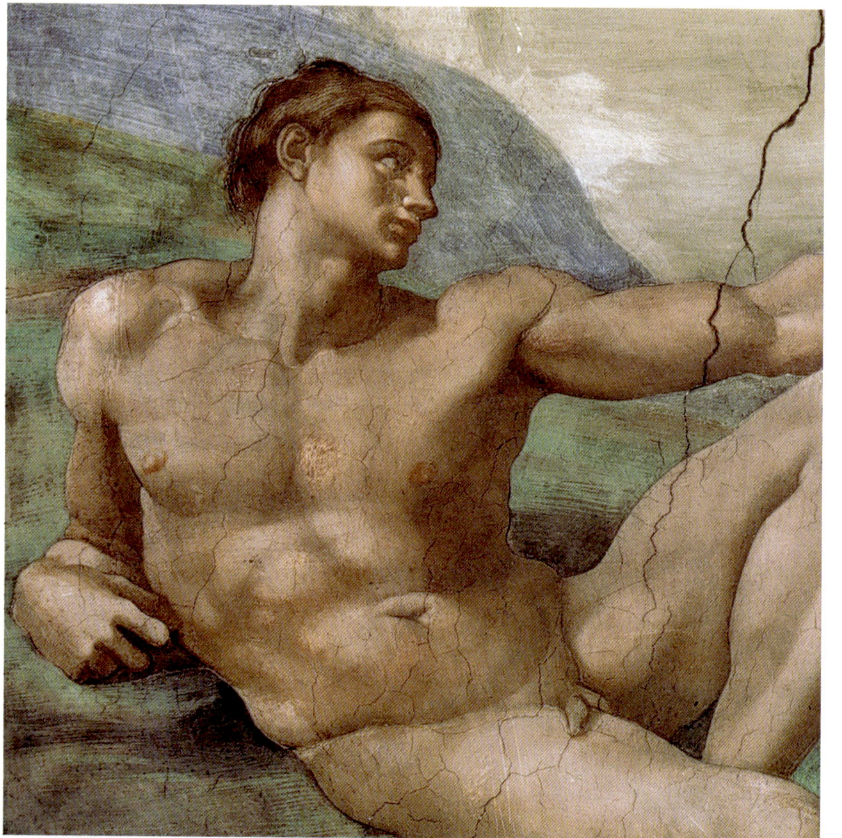

◄ The moving *Creation of Adam*, almost in the centre of the ceiling, is the pivotal point of the entire cycle conceived by Michelangelo. Brought to life by God the Father flying in the void, Adam slowly raises his strong, agile body from the bare earth. Still hesitant, his eyes are fixed on God's firm gaze. A silent exchange of looks, wills and power takes place.

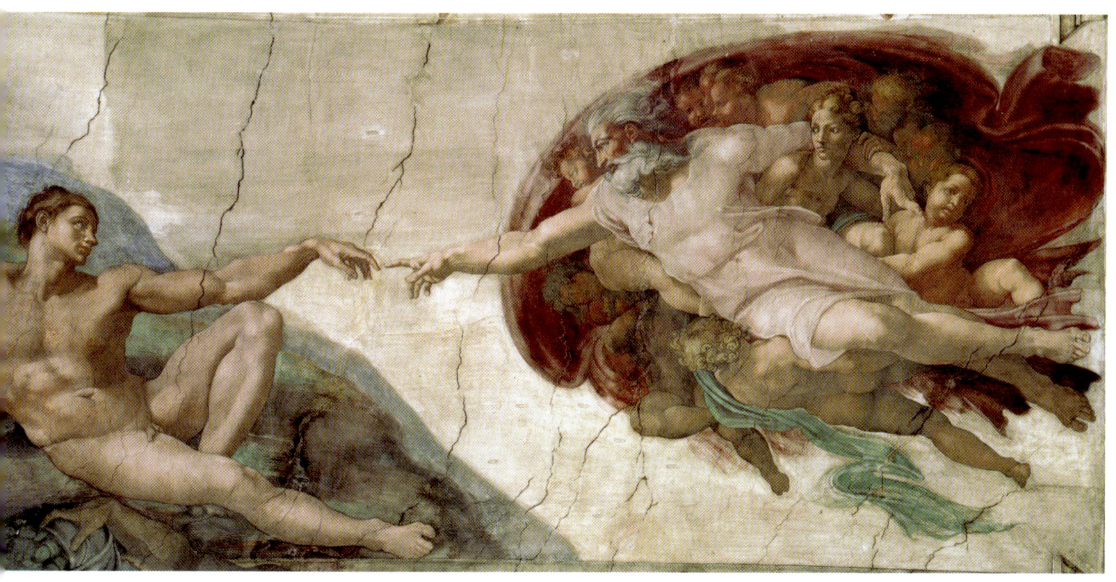

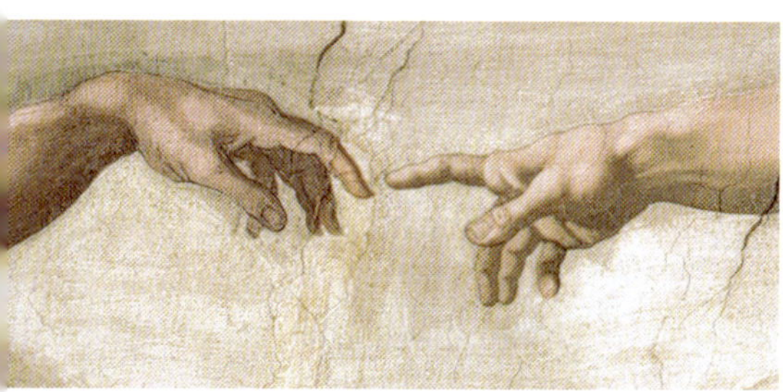

▲ A small yet immeasurable space separates the index finger of God from that of the first man. The subsequent scenes in Michelangelo's fresco seem to be the consequence of this fateful act.

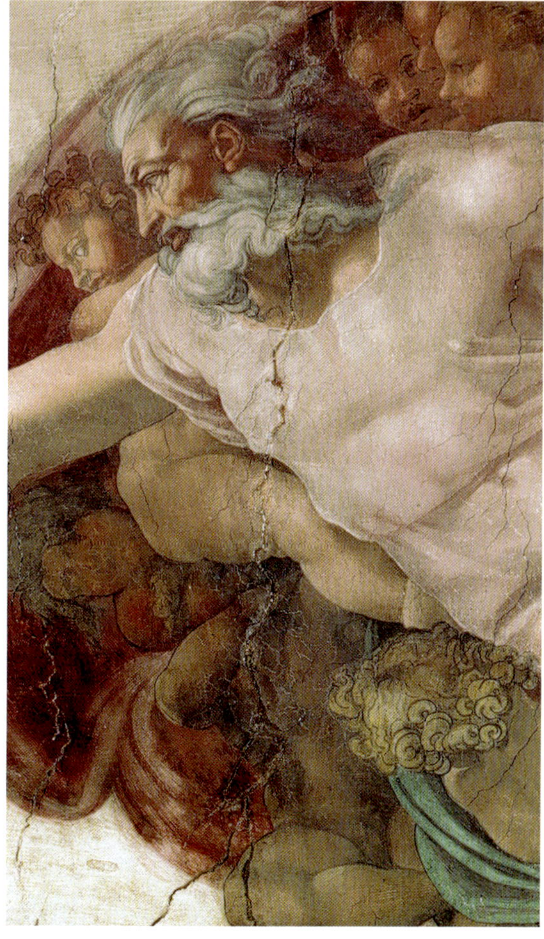

► God the Father, who appears old but robust and resolute, is an impressive figurative invention by Michelangelo. A small company of angels labours to sustain the Creator in flight, as an enormous, full, red cloak swells in the clear, bright sky.

Semicircle

Raphael
Disputation of the Holy Sacrament
1509

Fresco, approx. 770 cm (lower edge)

Vatican City, Musei Vaticani, Stanza della Segnatura

For artist biography, see page 194.

In 15th-century painting, series of figures are usually presented in a linear fashion, arranged in regular rows. Or, if the artist wanted to emphasize a hierarchy, they might use a triangular distribution. Raphael sought to overcome the somewhat monotonous simplicity of these compositions by using more dynamic groupings and taking advantage of the spatial depth. The walls of the Stanza della Segnatura show some of his innovative solutions. Without losing a sense of centrality and symmetry, Raphael arranged the figures on a flight of steps in *The School of Athens* (see pages 228–9), on the slopes of a hill in *Parnassus* and in a double semicircle in the *Disputation of the Holy Sacrament*.

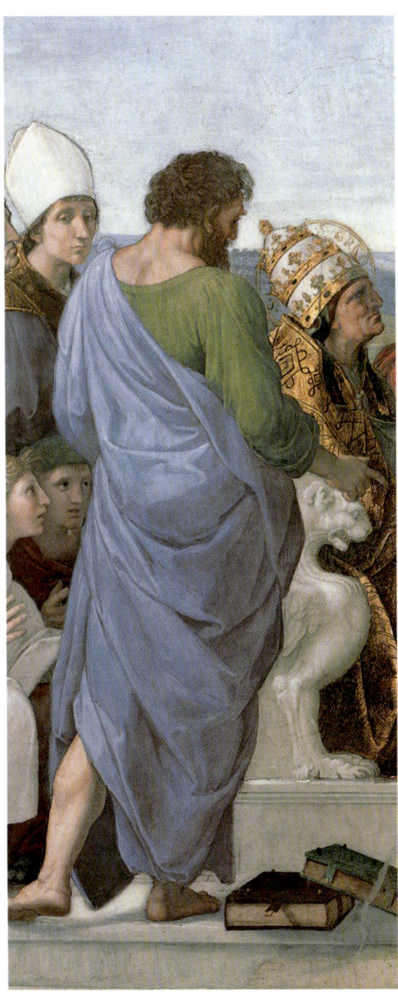

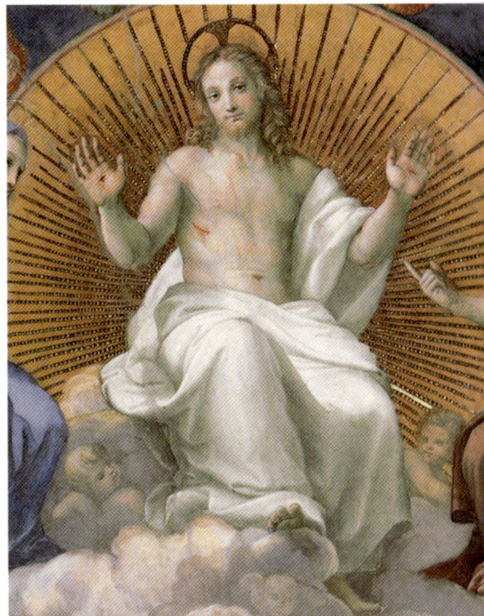

▶ Raphael painted the first large wall scene in the papal apartments at the Vatican on a semicircular lunette, on the same side of the room where theology books were kept. The artist illustrates various religious themes simply but effectively: the relationship between Father, Son and Holy Ghost; the connection between the Heavenly Church and the Church in the world; the central role of the Eucharist. The means Raphael chose to convey these concepts is a coherent composition based clearly and legibly on the superimposition of two semicircles and a vertical axis, explicitly anchored on the altar on which the consecrated host is exposed.

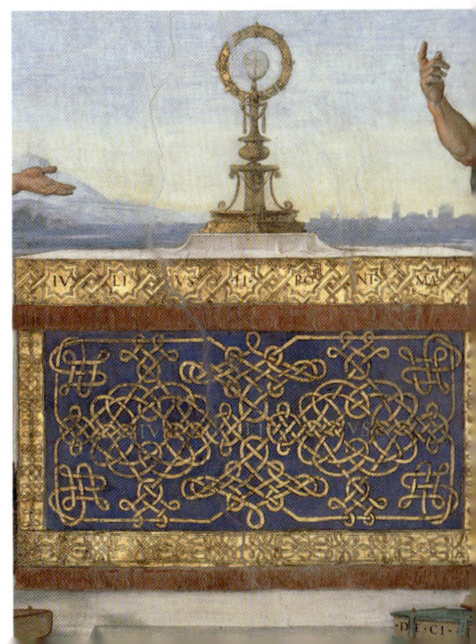

◀ The figures' gazes are vital to linking the two planes of the composition and to giving the viewers the feeling that they too are involved in the scene.

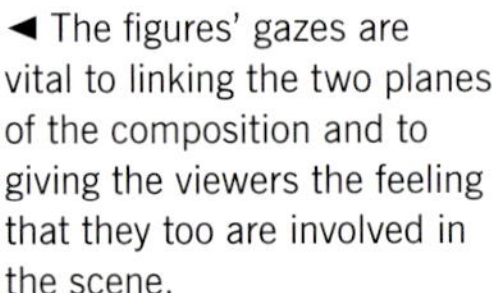

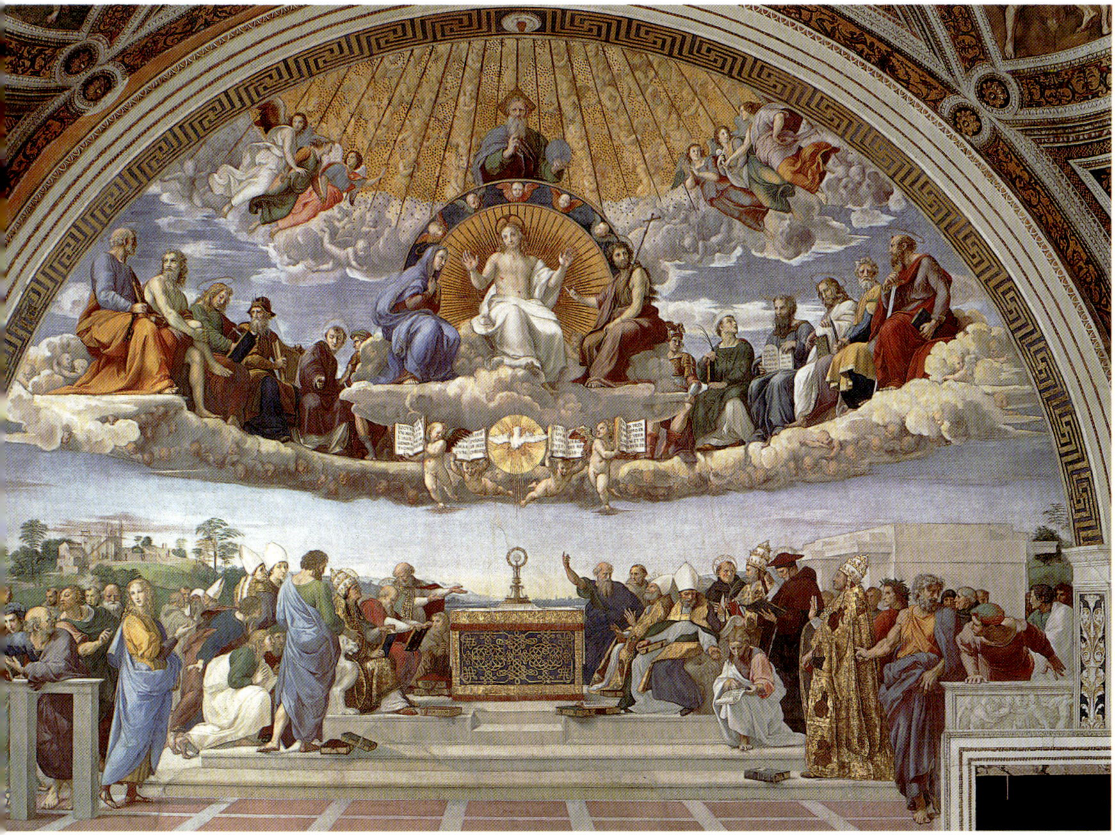

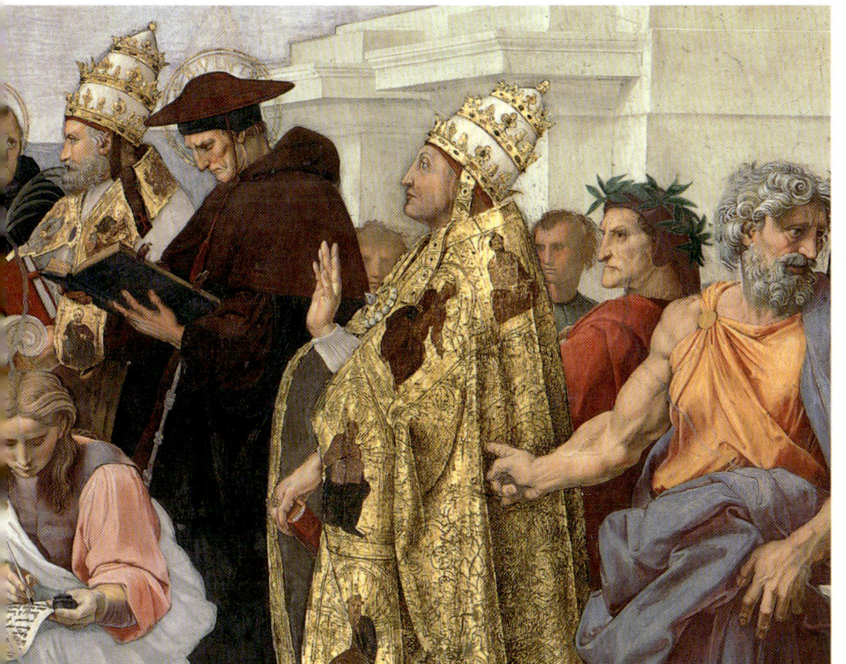

◄ Belief in Transubstantiation – that is, the transformation of the bread into the actual body of Christ – is one of the basic tenets of Catholicism. In dealing with so delicate a matter, Raphael undoubtedly had the assistance of a theologian, but he also had to avoid making a conversation among people who lived in different eras seem anachronistic. Many of the figures are recognizable through dress, attributes and well-known facial features; for example, the profile of Dante Alighieri, with a laurel wreath on his head.

Double Portrait

Giorgione
Double Portrait
1510

Oil on canvas, 80 × 67.5 cm

Rome, Museo di Palazzo Venezia

For artist biography, see page 198.

Multiple portraits are rare in 15th-century painting. Even in the case of married couples, separate portraits were painted, then placed alongside one another. However, in the early 16th century artists began to receive co missions for works combining two or more figures – a successful solution soon adopted in various regions of Italy. The double portrait implies an expressive and psychological relationship between the sitters, while the presence of additional figures requires more complex, thoroughly worked-out compositions.

▶ In double portraits, the combination of feelings and emotions can give rise to intriguing situations. The two young men portrayed here are unknown, but the painting has been related to the thoughts, feelings and poetry of the group of refined intellectuals with whom Giorgione was in contact.

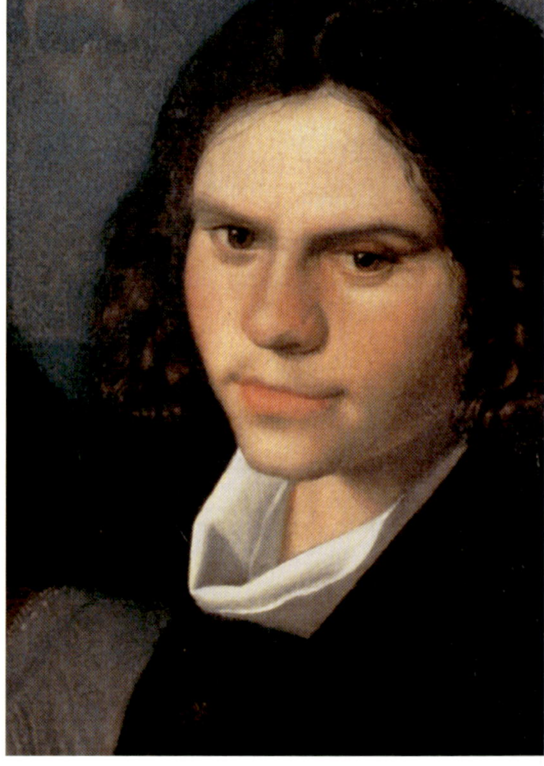

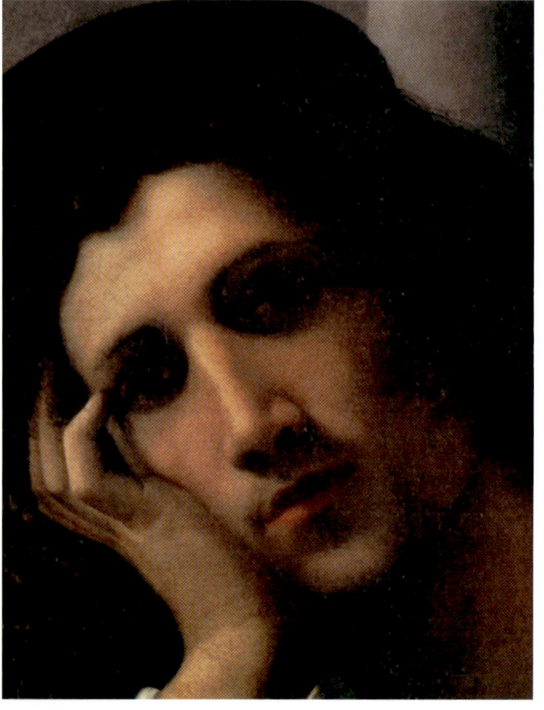

◀ The young man in the foreground presents an easily recognizable emotional type that is characteristic of the early 16th century: the face resting on the palm of the hand, the distant gaze and the tilt of the head are outward signs of 'melancholy'.

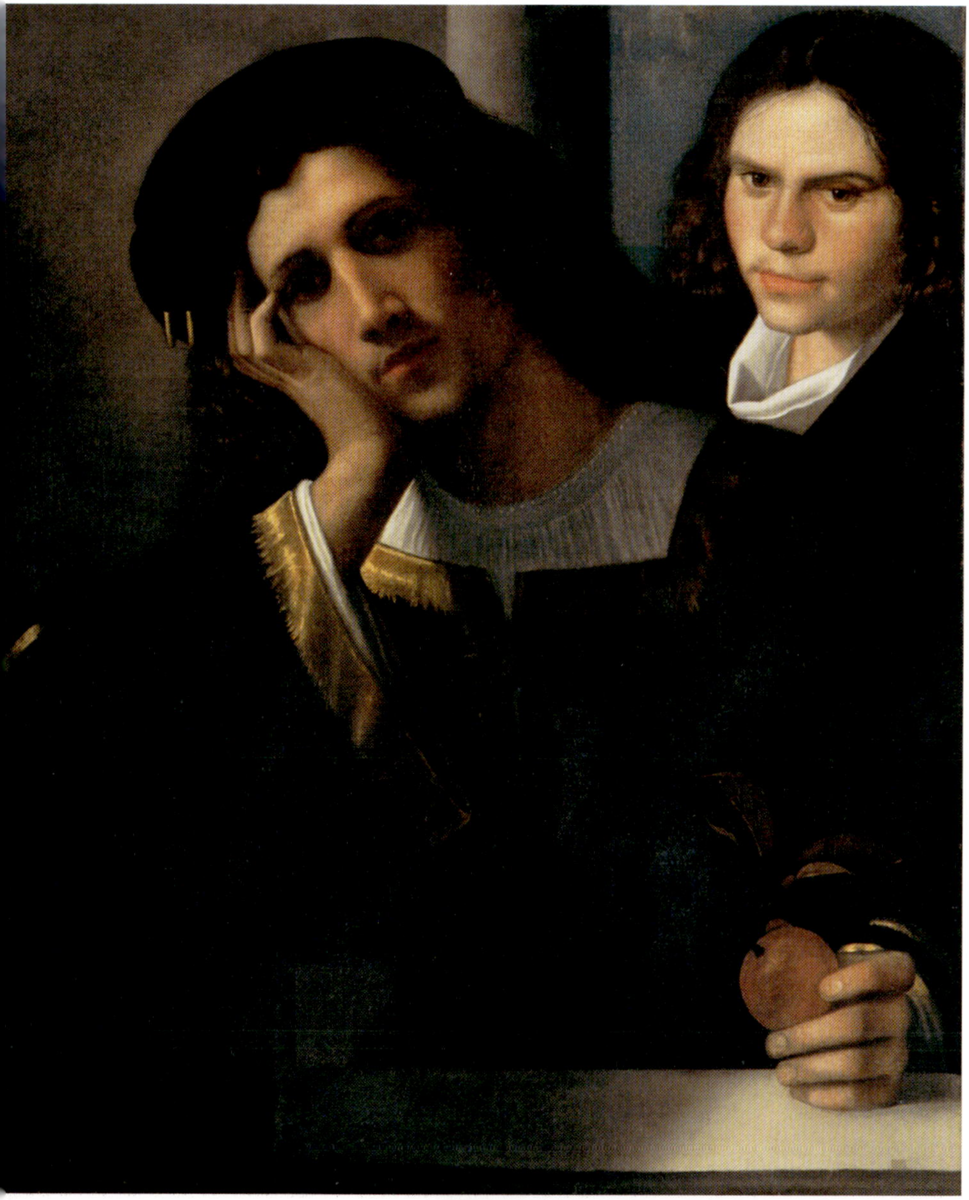

► The fruit held out by the melancholy young
man has been identified as a 'Seville' orange,
a bitter variety of the fruit. It suggests that
pleasure does not exist, particularly in love,
without a tinge of bitterness – a message that
is reinforced by the young man's pensive
expression.

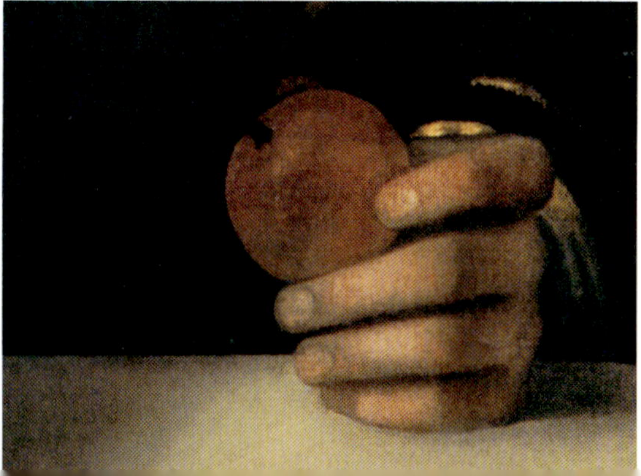

Reclining Nude

Giorgione and Titian
Dresden Venus
1510

Oil on canvas, 108 × 175 cm
Dresden, Gemäldegalerie

Demand for paintings with mythological or even frankly erotic subject matter increased as the advent of private collecting broadened the art market. Particularly in demand was the reclining female nude, a subject that spread rapidly throughout Europe, remaining remarkably popular until the 20th century. The Venetians' use of colour lends a special softness to the rendering of flesh tones, harmoniously balanced with natural light.

Giorgione

For artist biography, see page 198.

Titian

For artist biography, see page 224.

Giorgione or Titian?

Whether certain works should be attributed to Giorgione or Titian remains an unsolved puzzle. The two artists' collaboration was so close, especially in the period 1508–10, that attribution can be very difficult. While strong doubts persist for some canvases, the early Titian shows an energy, dynamism and richness of colour that Giorgione seems to reject in favour of more muted harmonies and feelings. Nevertheless, Giorgione's tragic early death in the plague of 1510 meant that some of his works were left unfinished. This is probably true of the Dresden Venus, *painted by Giorgione but completed by Titian with the addition of the white drapery. Giorgione's death was a further spur to the ambitious young Titian's rise to supremacy in the realm of Venetian painting.*

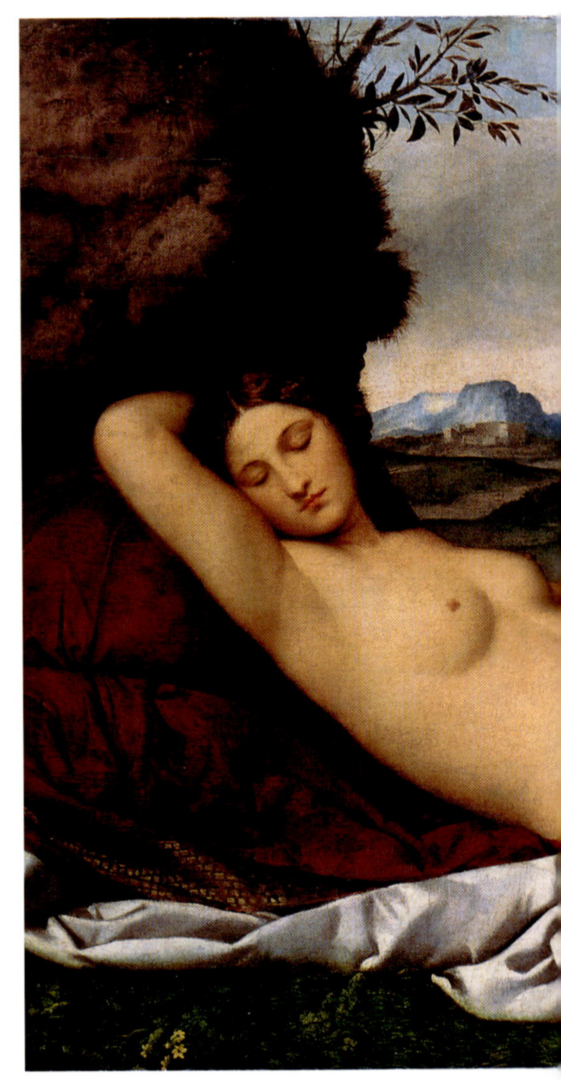

► The *Dresden Venus* is one of the first and most important examples of a genre that was destined to be highly successful in 16th-century Venetian painting. The young woman's body seems to follow the soft contours of the hills that stretch out in the quiet glimmer of the landscape. Far from suggesting Venus's sensuality, the image seems to signify the contemplative attitude Giorgione often demonstrates before beauty and nature.

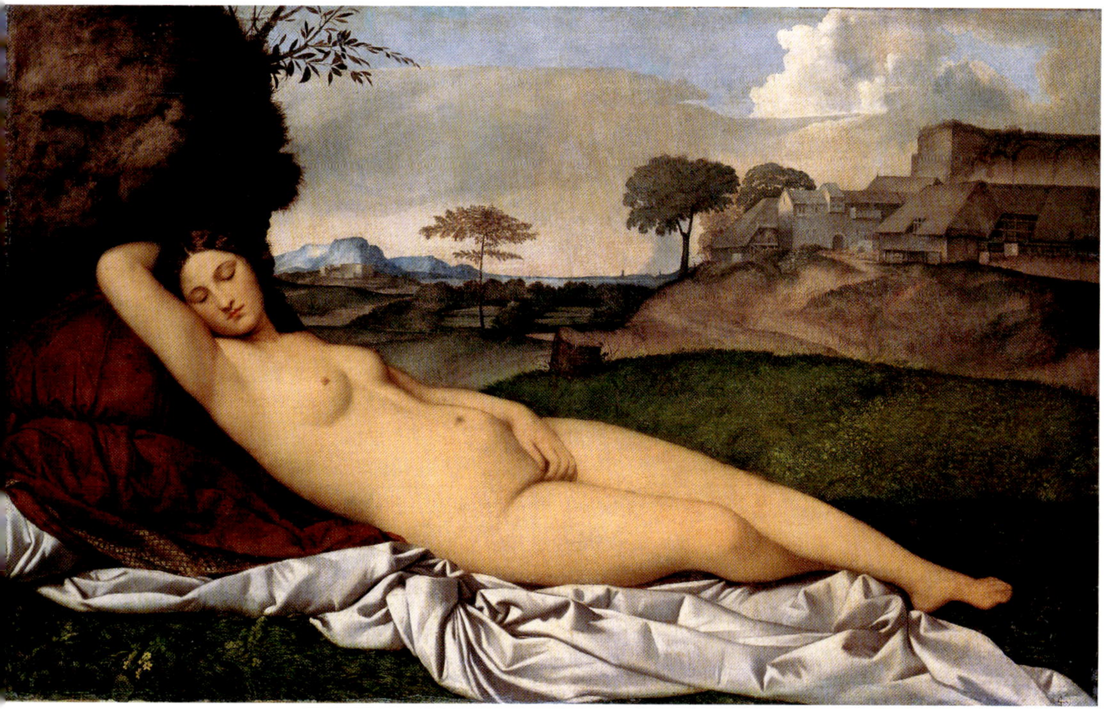

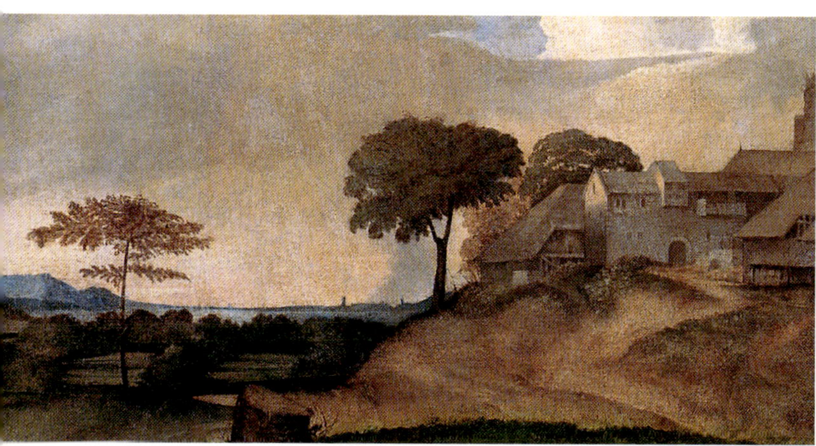

▲ The painting is cited in a 16th-century inventory as 'Venus with a small Cupid'. Although no obvious trace of the cupid is evident, X-ray photography reveals it was near the woman's feet, but was painted over.

◀ ▶ The sense of solemn natural harmony evoked by Giorgione in the relationship between the sleeping nude and the luminous countryside is made more active and dynamic by the contribution of Titian, who infused the painting with new chromatic energy by adding drapery – white and a strident red.

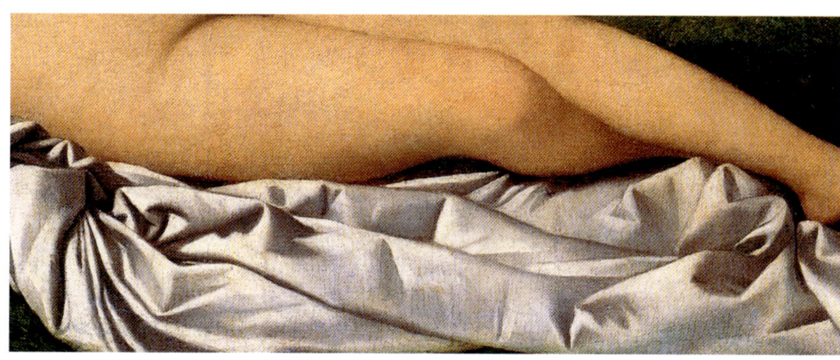

Idyll

Titian
Pastoral Concert
1510

Oil on canvas, 110 × 138 cm

Paris, Musée du Louvre

Titian

(Tiziano Vecellio)

Pieve di Cadore, Belluno, 1488/90–
Venice, 1576

Perhaps it would be an exaggeration
to call Titian the greatest painter of all
time, but certainly no one has had wider
or more lasting influence. A student
of Giorgione, the tremendous richness
of his colours and energy brought him
pre-eminence in the Venetian school
and oriented the style of 16th-century
Venetian painting towards warm, mellow
colour. In 1516, he became the official
painter of Venice, a position he retained
until his death 60 years later. Titian's
work for the Italian courts began in 1518
with a cycle of *Bacchanals* for Alfonso
d'Este, Duke of Ferrara. Soon after,
he worked for the Gonzagas, and then
the Della Roveres and Farneses. Titian
became the most sought-after court
portrait painter, and in 1530 his career
acquired an international scope: Emperor
Charles V became his most prestigious
patron, initiating a relationship with
the Spanish court that was upheld by
Philip II. Around 1540, Titian felt the
need to confront Mannerism directly.
A trip to Rome (1545–6) climaxed
with a not uncontroversial meeting
with Michelangelo. After two sojourns
in Augsburg, Germany, in the entourage
of Charles V, from 1551 on Titian
remained in the Veneto. His final Venetian
altarpieces alternate with canvases
for private devotion and mythological
paintings, interpreted as a mirror of
the human condition.

Fifteenth-century culture and art had sought to design an 'ideal
city', an urban and architectural space in man's measure; the
16th century rediscovered the fascination, mystery and repose
of nature. In celebrating the life of the countryside, poets and
authors took up the genre of the country idyll, which conjures up
a loving harmony that envelops landscape and figures. Explicit
reference to music evoked simple melodies full of feeling. Born
in the exclusive intellectual circles of which Giorgione was a
part, the 'pastoral' developed throughout the 16th century. With
Titian, it lost its initial tone of refined melancholy to express
a broad, powerful accord between humankind and nature, in
paintings rich with energy and dense colours.

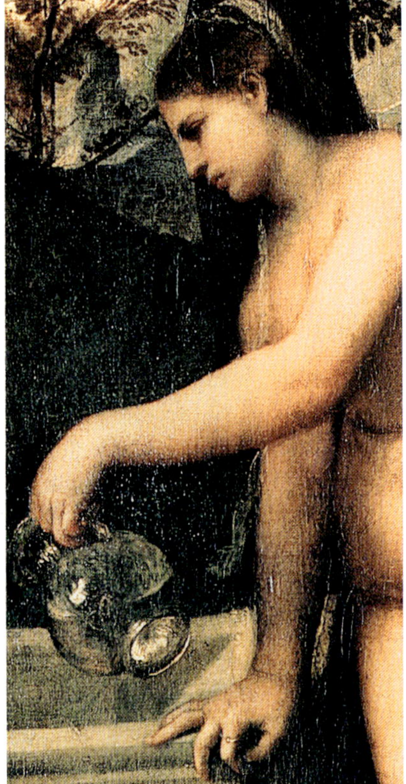

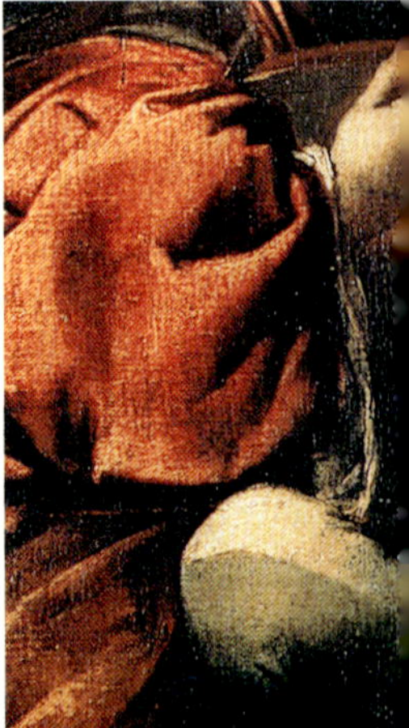

◄ This famous painting,
admired by the Impressionists,
has raised a problem of
attribution for the past two
centuries. Specialists have long
been divided as to whether it
should be ascribed to Giorgione
or Titian. Currently, most
scholars tend towards Titian.

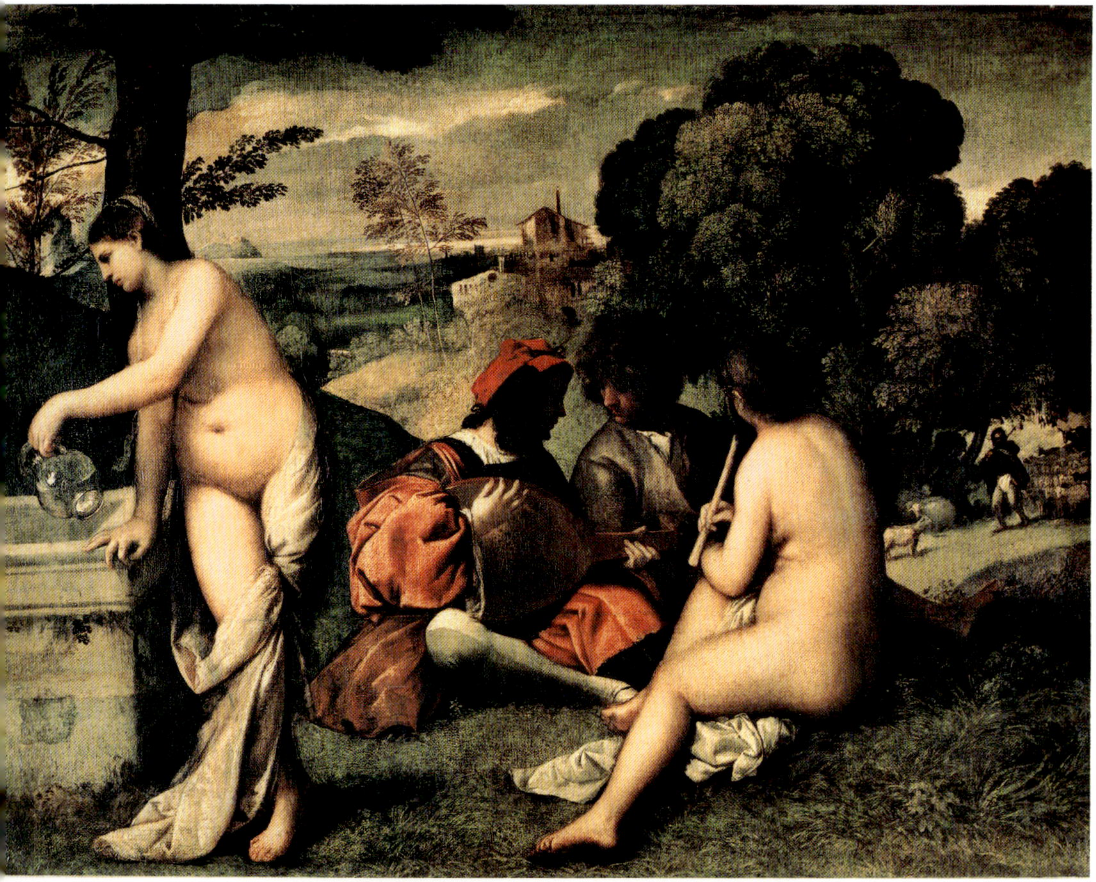

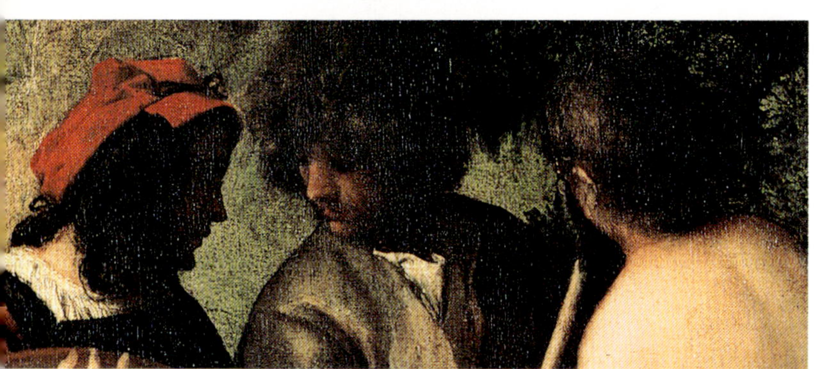

Sixteenth-century culture
ok up the theme of the
norous idyll as a combination
poetry, music and painting.
le madrigal, a love song
ccompanied by the lute,
ew out of this dialogue
nong the arts.

▲ The subject of this painting was born out
of the literary culture of a refined circle of
connoisseurs. Some art historians have
suggested that it should be read as an allegory
of the harmony of the Four Elements that
make up the world: air, water, fire and earth.

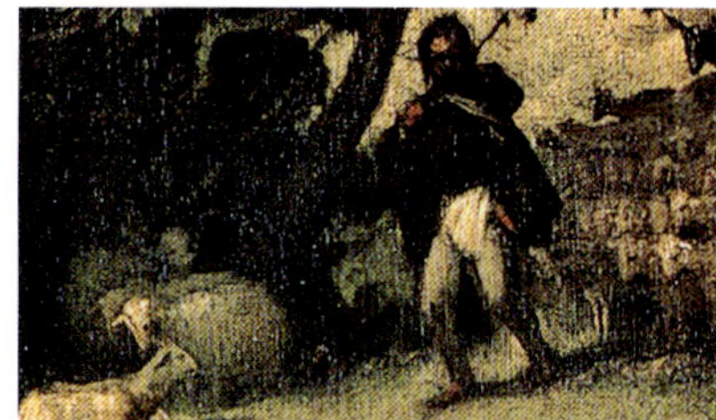

Raphael
Cartoon for the School of Athens
1510

Black chalk and white lead on paper,
285 × 804 cm

Milan, Pinacoteca Ambrosiana

For artist biography, see page 194.

Cartoons are drawings executed on sturdy paper in the sam
dimensions as the finished work. Their use became frequen
in the preparatory phase of fresco cycles, replacing the sinop
(a reddish drawing done directly on the wall) that had been th
traditional method in the medieval and late Gothic period
The transition to the cartoon coincided with the affirmatio
of drawing as the foundation of artistic creation. The cartoo
was a basic task of the master who held the commission. H
assistants attended to various stages of the operation, such a
accurately perforating the outline of the figures, applying th
cartoon to the wall to be frescoed, pouncing with fine carbo
powder and leaving incisions around the contours. Assistan
subsequently took part in laying out the colour and execu
ing the background or even complete sections. Therefore, a
certain times during the height of the Renaissance, the artist
cartoon became even more valuable and 'authentic' than th
final fresco.

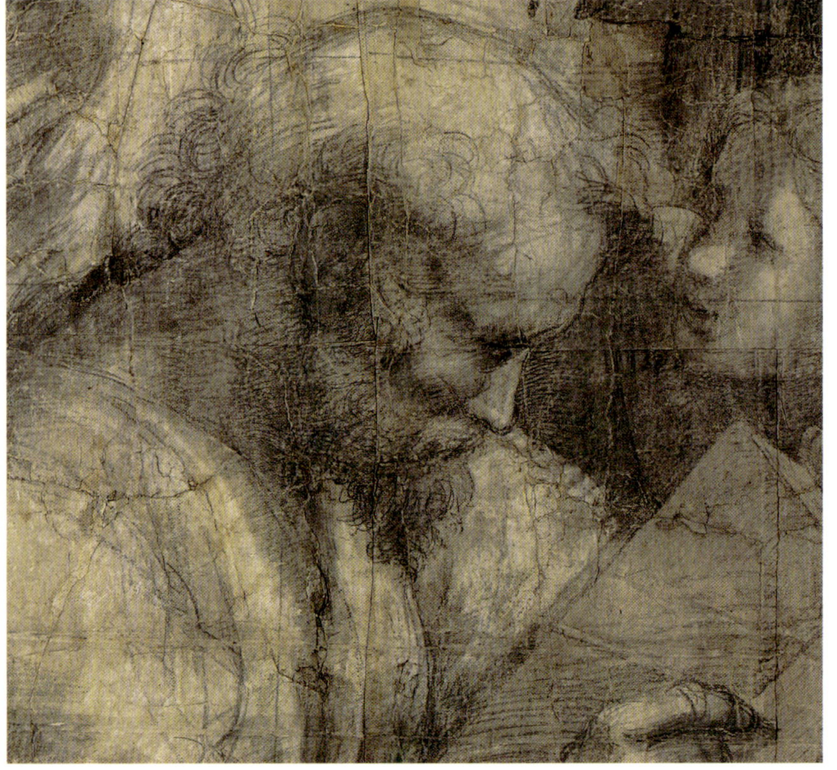

◄ The large cartoon in Milan
about eight metres wide, is
composed of various sheets
placed side by side. The join
are easily visible. The state c
conservation of the delicate
drawing, which is exhibited
in a microclimate under
proper lighting conditions,
is generally quite good.

► Comparison of the cartoo
and the finished fresco (see
pages 228–9) reveals the
extraordinary finesse of
Raphael's draughtsmanship
and the artist's concentratio
on the group of figures that
animate the scene: they are
defined with great care, whil
the architectural setting is
barely sketched.

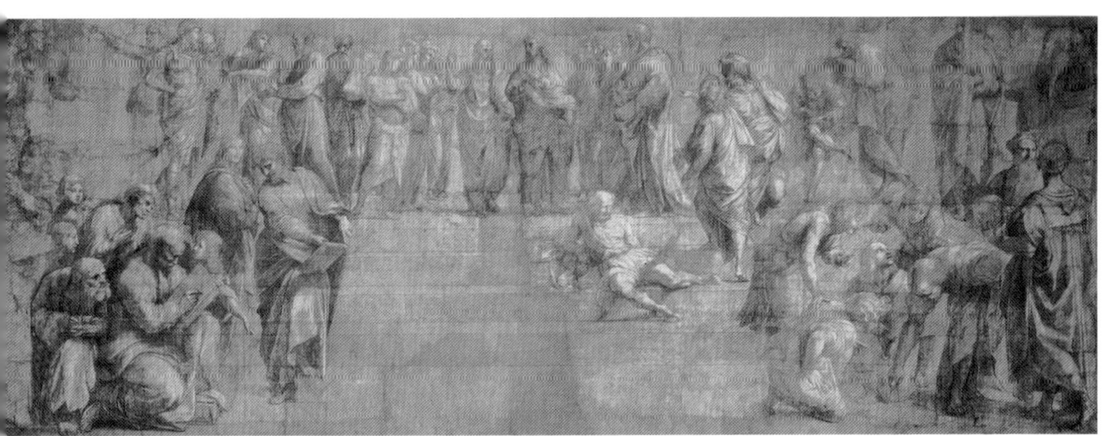

The conservation of the preparatory cartoon for *The School of Athens* (see pages 228–9), the second lunette Raphael painted in the Stanza della Segnatura at the Vatican, is an utter rarity. With a few exceptions, drawings of this type have all been lost. Some cartoons would become well known in their own right, as happened with two produced by Michelangelo and Leonardo for battle scenes in the main hall of Palazzo Vecchio.

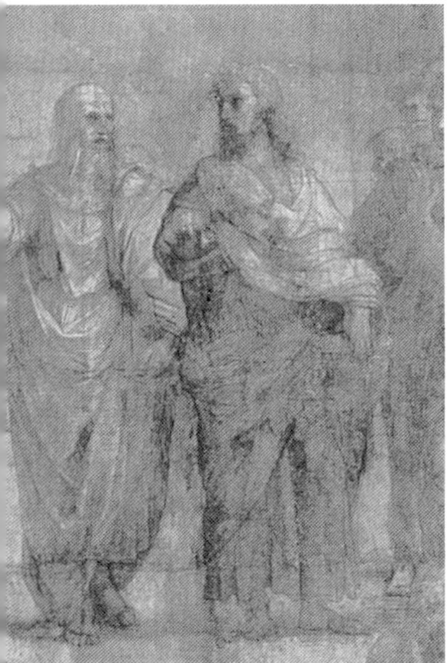

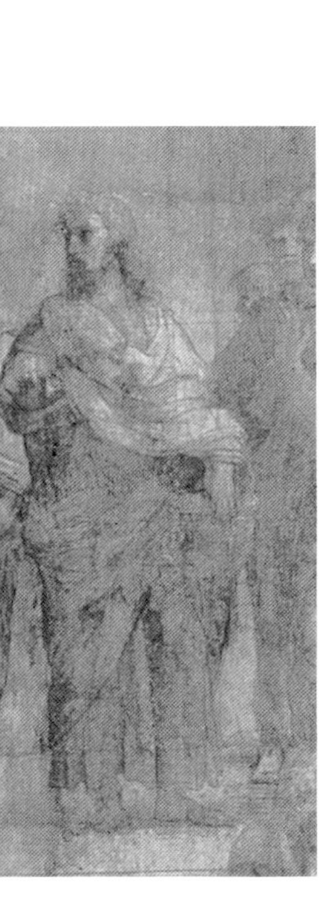

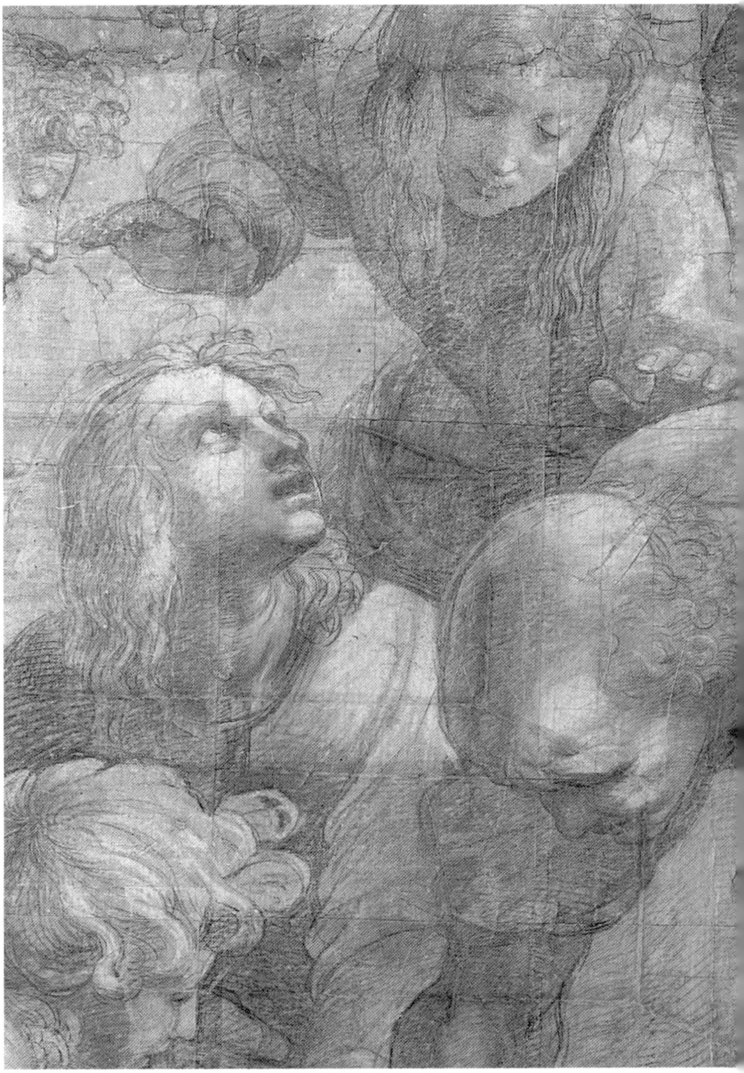

Intellectuals

Raphael
The School of Athens
1510–11

Fresco, approx. 770 cm (lower edge)
Vatican City, Rome, Musei Vaticani,
Stanza della Segnatura

For artist biography, see page 194.

In the early 16th century the area of the papal apartments that later became known as the Stanza della Segnatura housed the pope's private library, and was therefore a highly intellectual environment. The frescoes on the ceiling allude to the fourfold division of learning into theology, philosophy, poetry and law. The large lunettes, below which the bookshelves were arranged, present memorable events and outstanding figures of these respective disciplines. Imaginary encounters occur on the walls in celebration of intellect and culture through the millennia: theologians and saints congregate around the divine altar and philosophers gather in the 'temple of wisdom' as poets of all times stroll in the garden of Mount Parnassus.

Philosophy of the Past, Faces of the Present

In The School of Athens *ancient philosophers are dotted around the generous space of the proscenium in a theatrical arrangement. Raphael has ordered the composition rhythmically with the vaults of a huge building, a sort of temple of wisdom that recalls the architecture of Bramante's new basilica of St Peter. In the centre, Plato and Aristotle gesture towards the essence of their respective philosophical systems. Raphael succeeds in bringing the ancient world to life through the inclusion of many figures from his own time: Plato, with his index finger pointing to the sky, has the features of Leonardo; Michelangelo is the frowning, solitary Heraclitus; and Bramante becomes Euclid, compass in hand.*

▼ In the centre of the scene, Plato points towards the 'world of ideas', while Aristotle, with his open hand palm down, fixes his attention on concrete physical reality. Praising the Greek philosophers in the core of the Vatican signals a turning point in the humanist dialogue between classical culture and Christianity.

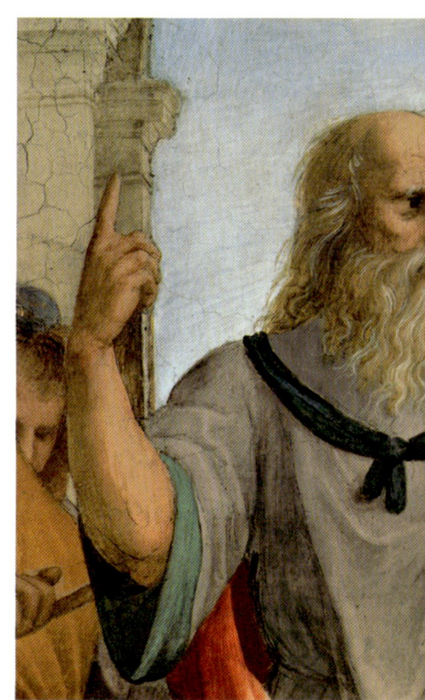

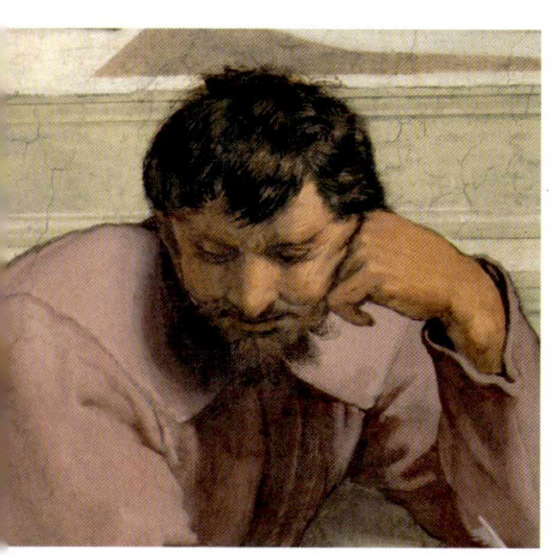

◄ While Raphael painted the Stanza della Segnatura, Michelangelo was not far away, busily working on the ceiling of the Sistine Chapel. Raphael decided to include a tribute to his great and solitary colleague, portraying him in the guise of Heraclitus who, as may be seen by comparing the preparatory cartoon (see pages 226–7), was not originally planned.

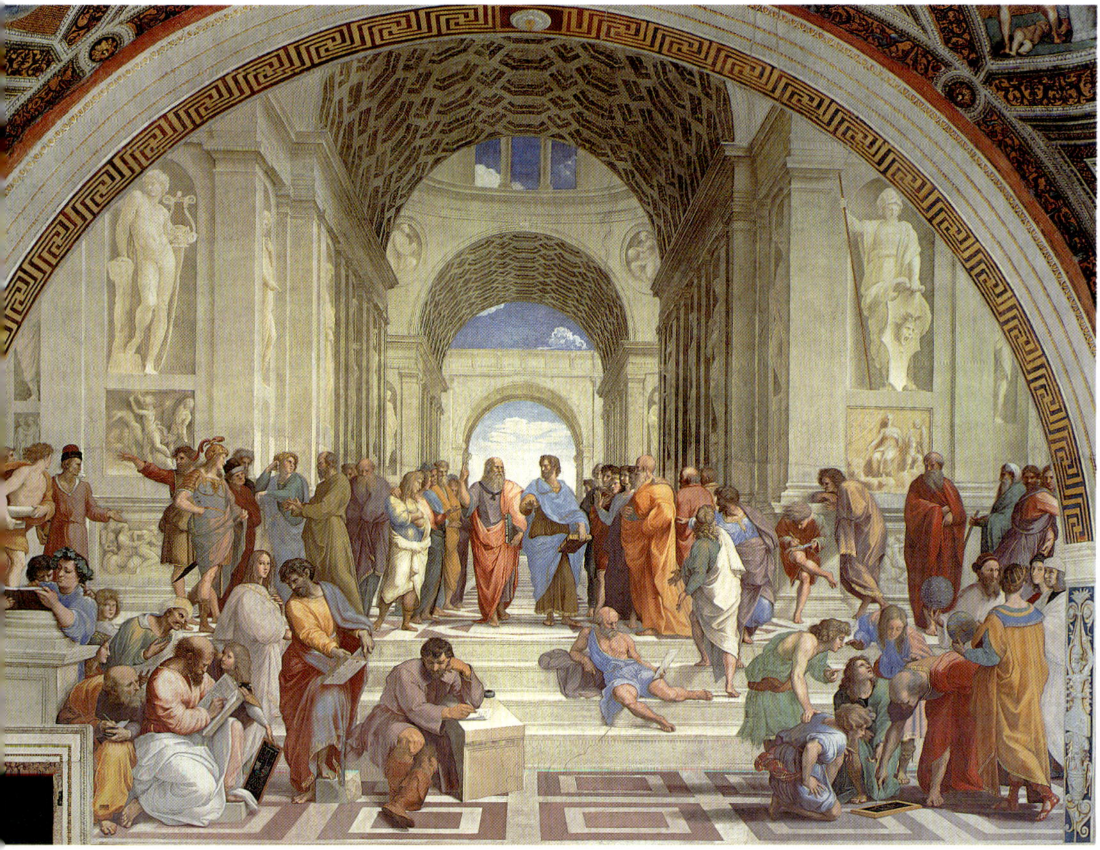

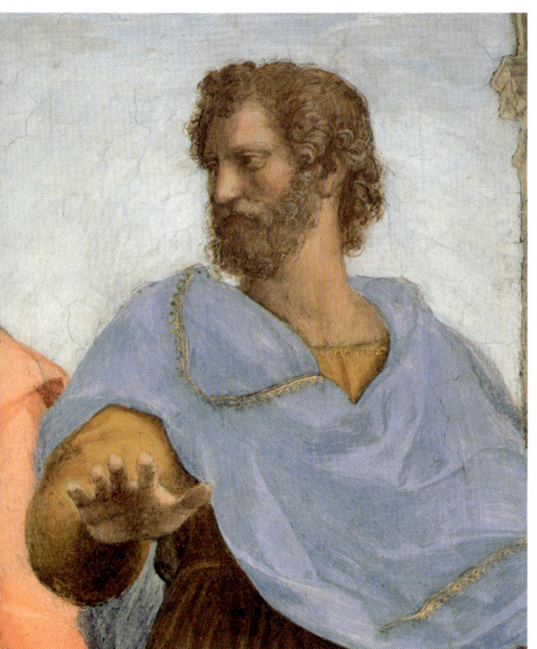

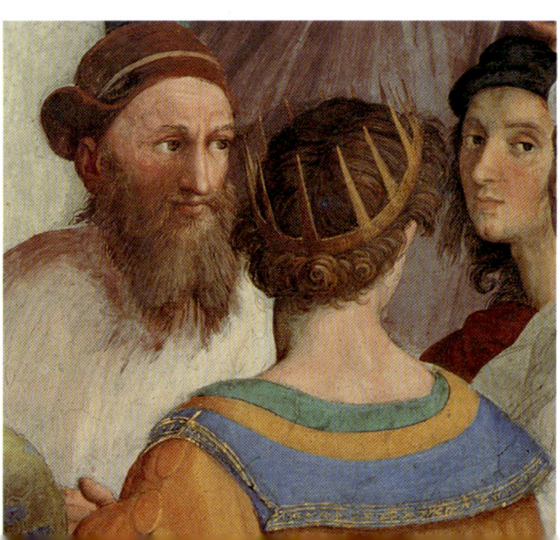

▼ The brightness of the colours, the luminosity of the setting, the elegance of the composition and the relaxed expressions and natural gestures of the figures transmit a sense of confidence and harmony. In keeping with the idea that the painter was first of all an intellectual, Raphael has inserted his own self-portrait among the philosophers and thinkers. At the time of this fresco, the painter from Urbino was 27 years old.

Gentleman

Titian
Portrait of a Gentleman (Ariosto)
1512

Oil on canvas, 84 × 69 cm
London, National Gallery

For artist biography, see page 224.

In one of history's not infrequent contradictions, while th small *signorie* declined in the face of the great internationa states, the Italian style prevailed throughout Europe as th absolute model of elegance and good taste in all fields. Artist now formed part of the intellectual elite. Bramante, Raphae and above all Michelangelo ventured into the realm of poetry others are remembered as fine singers and virtuoso lute play ers. From craftsman, the artist was transformed into a 'courtie and experienced a significant rise in social level. Assimilatin this new lifestyle of the courts, artists became participants o a par with the most powerful, refined and aristocratic patrons Treatises on 'good manners' were a characteristic phenomenon and Baldassare Castiglione's *Book of the Courtier* is a landmar in the genre.

A 16th-century Bestseller

A friend of Raphael, Baldassare Castiglione composed his Book of the Courtier *over a period of many years in a series of gradually expanded and reworked editions. The scene is set in Urbino, but it is easy to discern references to the Gonzaga court in Mantua. In the literary form of a polite but lively dialogue among various people, a gentleman from Mantua suggests 'modes, manners, words, gestures and adornments'. It is a veritable handbook, in which the concept of 'grace' and courtesy triumphs and is promptly applied to art. Castiglione sums it all up in one 'absolutely universal rule' that encapsulates the secret of the class of refined men: 'Insofar as one may, flee affectation as if it were a sheer and treacherous precipice; and, perhaps to propose a new idea, employ in all things a certain casual unconcern that will disguise artfulness and demonstrate what is done and said to be done effortlessly, as if giving the matter no thought.' The notion of 'casual unconcern' became a guiding principle in painting and sculpture at the height of the 16th century.*

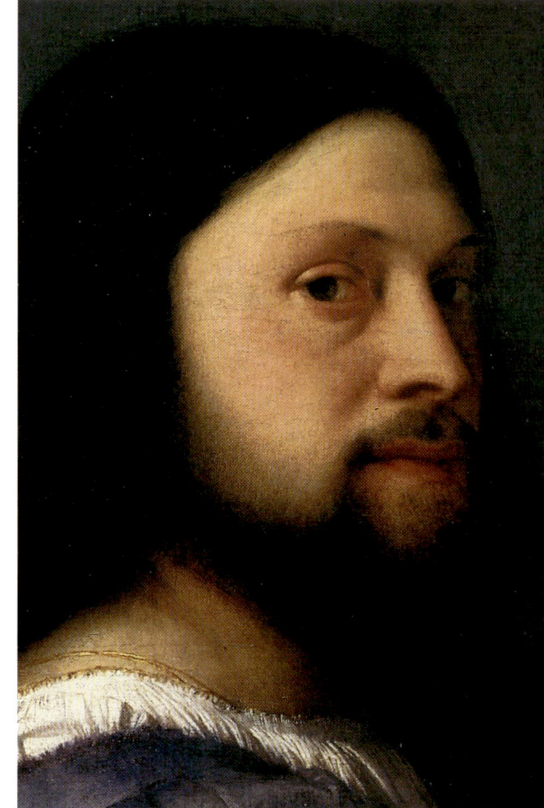

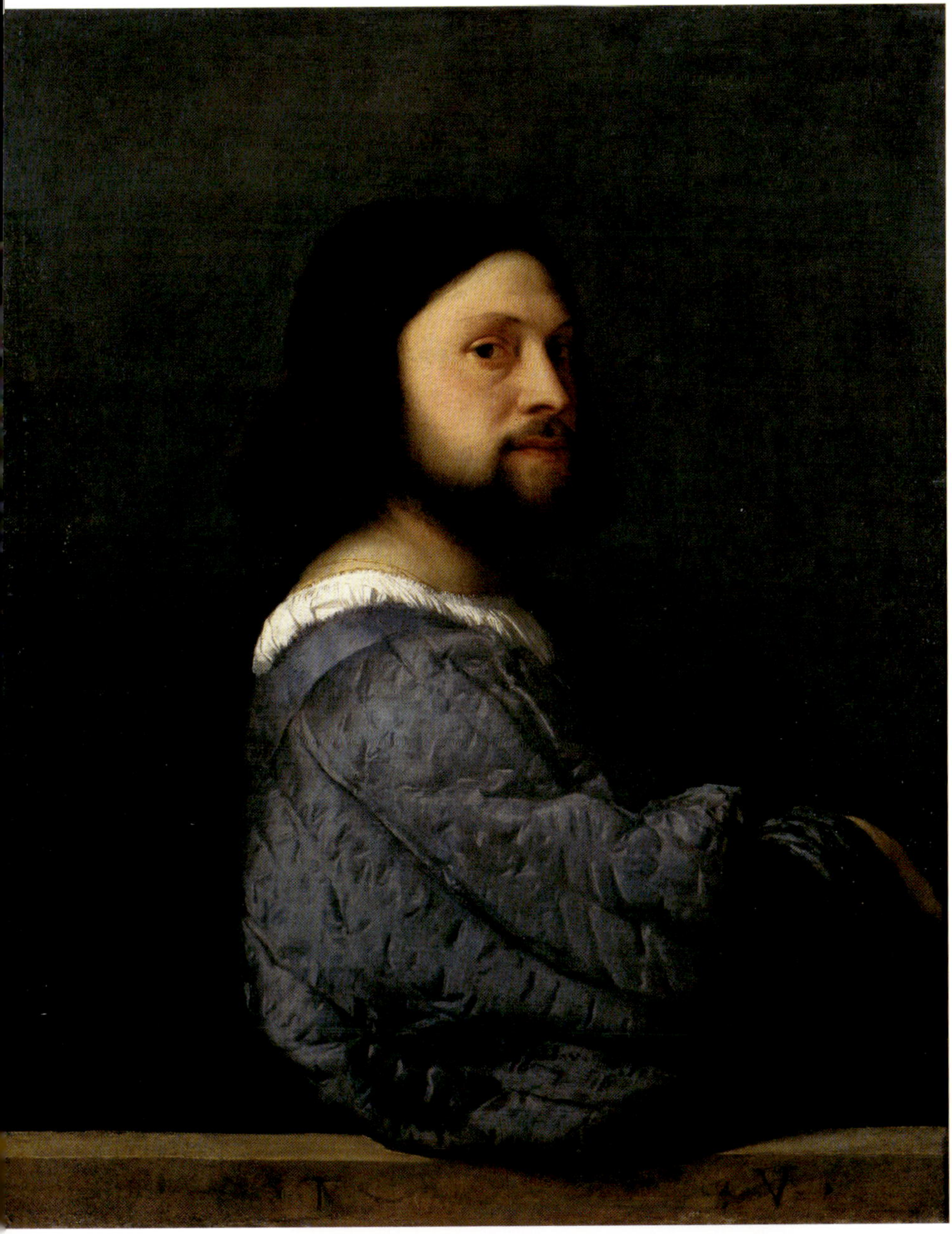

◄ ▲ This gentleman's identity
is unknown. For a time, he
was erroneously thought to
be the poet Ludovico Ariosto,
then a member of the
Barbarigo family and even
a self-portrait of Titian.

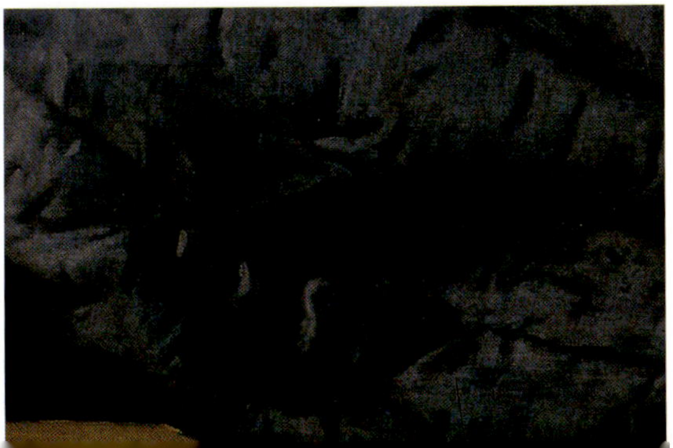

◄ The most noticeable
feature is no doubt the
splendidly full, quilted sleeve
in the foreground. The
position of the leaning arm
conveys apparent unconcern
but also awareness of the
fashionable attire.

Raphael
Sistine Madonna
1512–13

Oil on canvas, 269.5 × 201 cm
Dresden, Gemäldegalerie

For artist biography, see page 194.

The development of the concept of illusion occurred simultaneously with the transition from humanistic architectural perspective to atmospheric and tonal painting. A sense of depth wa no longer created through the depiction of three-dimensiona interiors but through the evocation of natural open spaces. Thi artifice was reinforced by the presence of close-up foregroun details (such as window ledges, balustrades, draperies), while moving towards the background, outlines blur and soften int cloudy skies and distant hazy landscapes. The arrangement o the figures also showed more movement and variety than th geometric schemes of 15th-century tradition.

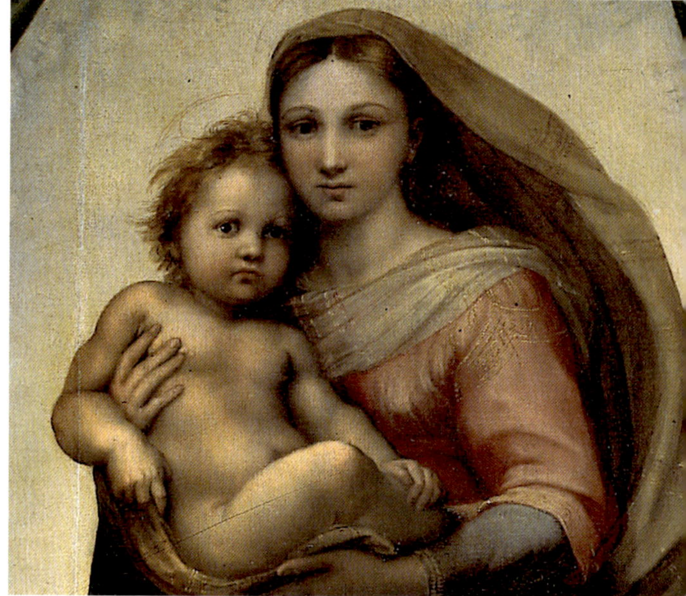

◄ The green drape, drawn like a theatre curtain, increases the illusionistic effect. Originally placed along the curve of the apse in the church of San Sisto in Piacenza, the painting was the same size and shape as the real windows beside it. Observing the picture close up, one notices that the clouds are partly formed of cherubs' faces.

▲ Aware of the beholder's point of view, Raphael simulated a window through which we see the Madonna and Child advancing towards us. The forward stride and gaze downward from above must have heightened the effect, which is only partially visible at the museum in Dresden, where the painting now hangs.

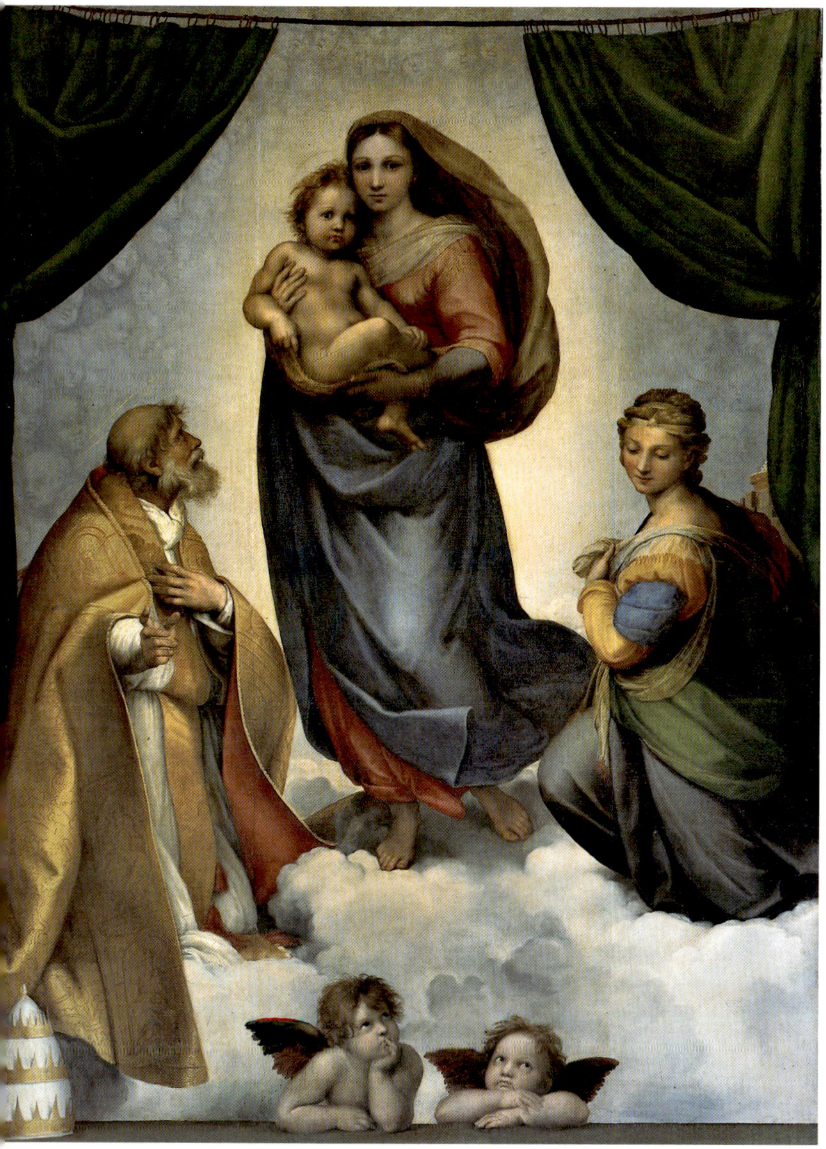

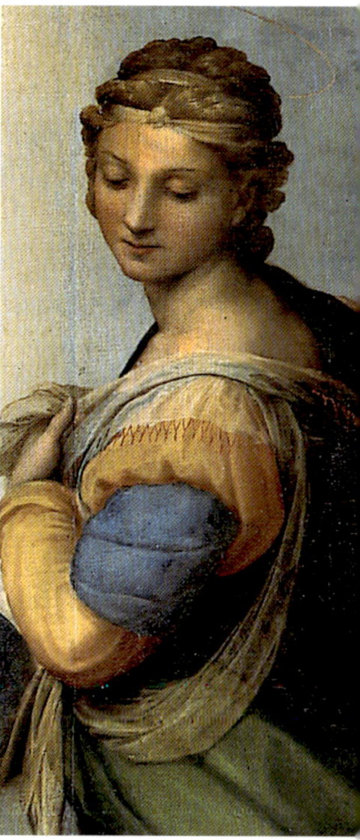

▼ Suspended in mid-air, the sweet St Barbara perfectly closes off the composition, her gesture matching that of St Sixtus on the opposite side. Once again, the gaze looking down from above connects the heavenly vision and ground level, where the viewer is located.

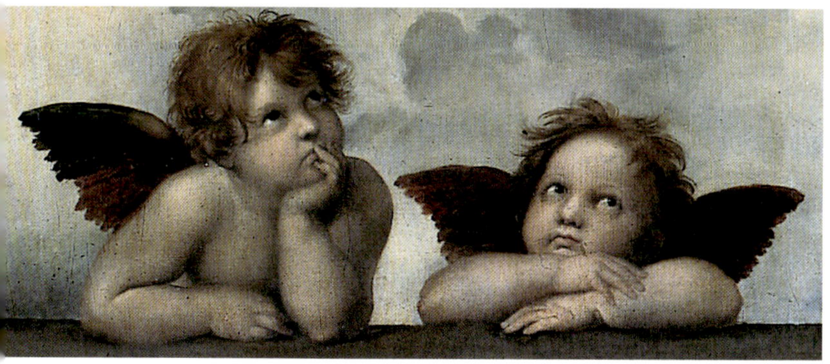

◄ Reproduced millions of times but almost always out of context, these two pensive little cherubs lean on the ledge of the imaginary window. St Sixtus's papal tiara is set on the same level at the far left.

Sacra Rappresentazione

Gaudenzio Ferrari
Crucifixion
Detail from the *Story of the Life and Passion of Christ*
1513

Fresco, 533 × 266 cm
Varallo, Vercelli, Santa Maria delle Grazie

Gaudenzio Ferrari

Valduggia (Vercelli), 1475/80–Milan, 1546

Considered by his contemporaries to be one of the supreme artists of the 16th century, Gaudenzio Ferrari has since been overlooked, perhaps because his masterpieces are in peripheral locations. Particularly in Varallo Sesia (the main town in a Piedmontese valley sheltered behind Mount Rosa), Gaudenzio executed paintings and sculptures for the main chapels at the Sacro Monte, in which he innovatively combined landscape, architecture, painting and sculpture. Gaudenzio reached artistic maturity with the frescoes on the large dividing wall of Santa Maria delle Grazie in Varallo (1513). Although related to the Lombard tradition, his style makes plentiful references to more modern art, demonstrating direct knowledge of the developments of the Renaissance in central Italy. The desire to involve viewers collectively through painting also inspired subsequent works like the frescoes and altarpiece at San Cristoforo in Vercelli (1529–34), the dome of the sanctuary of Saronno (1534–6) and the late paintings executed in Milan, in which Gaudenzio proposed moving beyond the noble but by now ever more distant model of Leonardo.

Participation in the *Sacra Rappresentazione* (Sacred Performance) of liturgical drama, a typical form of popular devotion, remained widespread throughout the Renaissance. The realism and pathos of the Passion of Christ staged in the streets and squares of large and small cities had an effect on visual art as well. Especially in northern Italy, the aim of some fresco cycles to involve worshippers fully is clear from the figures' eloquent gestures, direct expression of emotion and immediate realism.

The 'Sacri Monti'

A Sacro Monte (Sacred Mountain) is a series of chapels along the slopes of a hill. Inside the chapels, scenes from the life of Christ and the saints are represented realistically in sculptural groups and wall frescoes. Born in the Renaissance, Sacri Monti developed considerably during the Counter-Reformation and the 17th century. They are typical of Lombardy, but examples existed almost everywhere. Worshippers followed a kind of pilgrimage circuit that brought them 'into the presence' of the characters and settings of the sacred story. The first and most important Sacro Monte is the one at Varallo, not far from Mount Rosa. Its initial purpose was to recreate various localities of the Holy Land, to reconstitute the topography of Jerusalem, the Holy Sepulchre and other places in the life of Christ. Gaudenzio Ferrari, long active as a painter and sculptor at Varallo, played a critical role in the project. His expressive solutions, especially in the ingenious linking of sculpture and fresco, served as models for all subsequent examples.

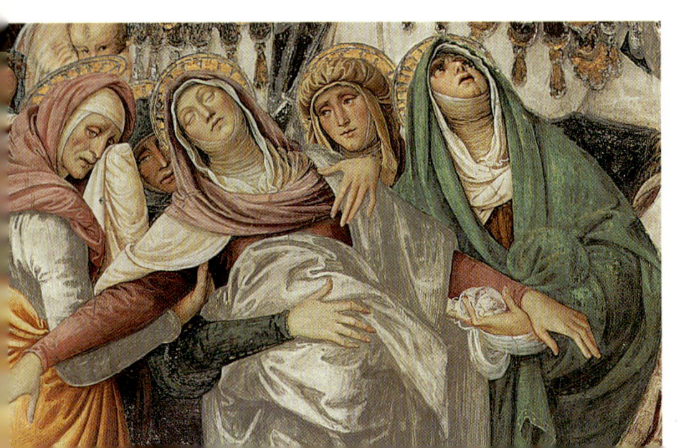

◄ As with Raphael (see pages 208–9), the swooning of Mary at the death of her Son is an independent subtheme that invites a strong emotional response. The women supporting Mary seem to form a single sculptural block. Gaudenzio Ferrari himself, sculpting the scene of the Crucifixion for the Calvary Chapel on the Sacro Monte ten years later, would depict Mary and the Holy Women around her as a compact and unified group in polychrome terracotta.

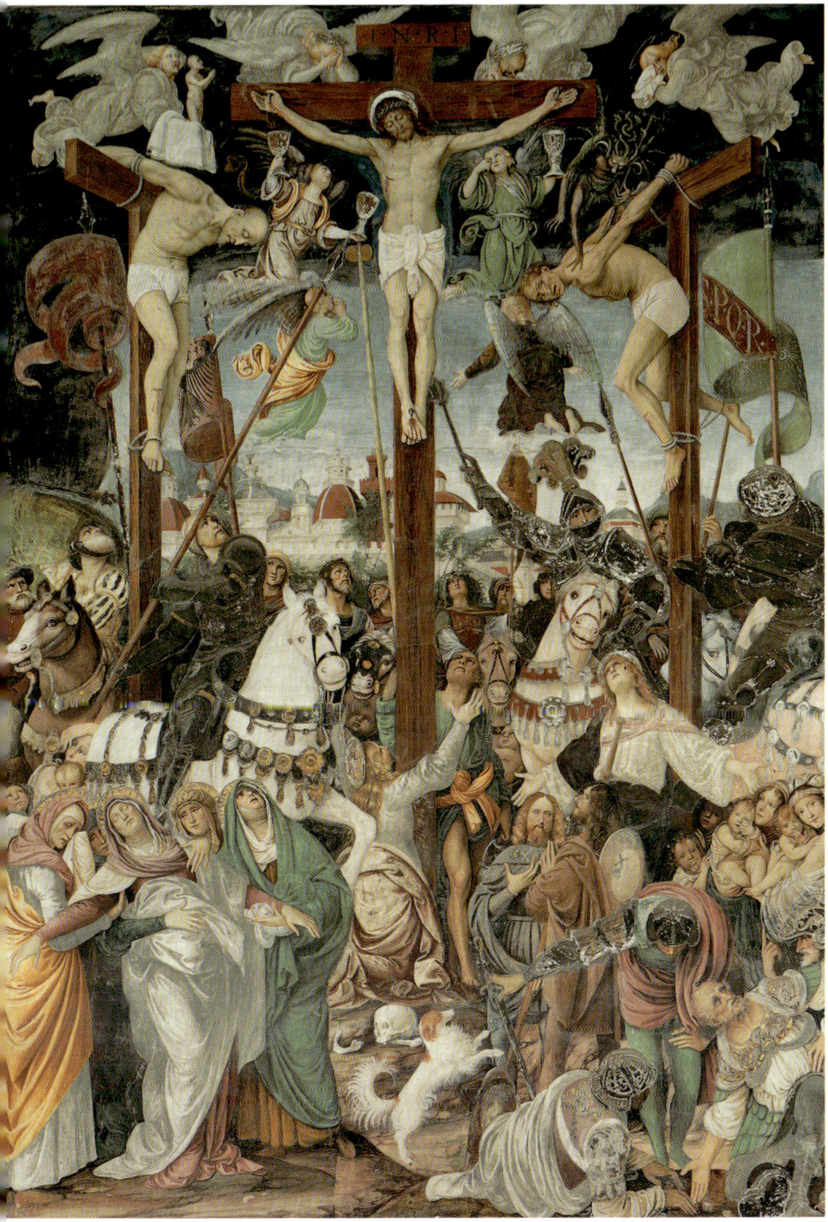

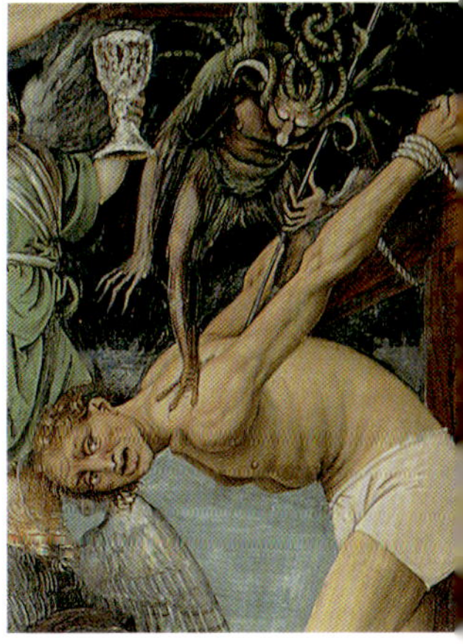

▲▼ At first glance, the crowded composition seems confused. But many details (like the devil standing on the bad thief and St John's sweeping gesture) aid in the unambiguous understanding of the role, identity and function of every single participant.

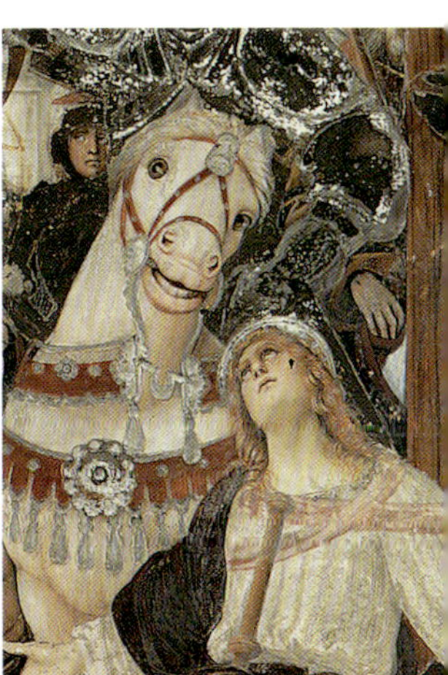

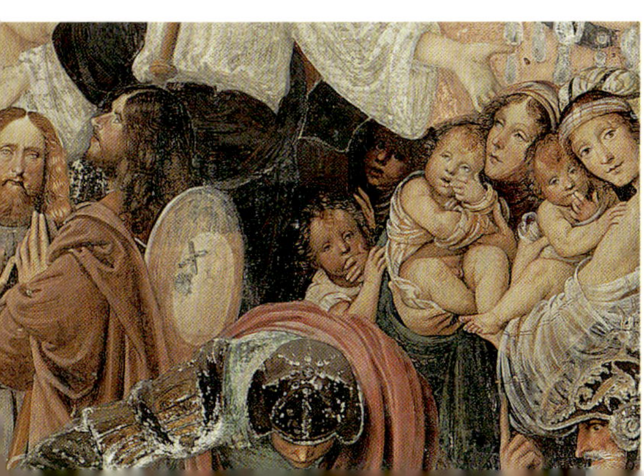

◄ The church of Santa Maria delle Grazie is on the edge of the residential area of Varallo, at the start of the path to the Sacro Monte. The rapidly developing devotional art complex enjoyed the strong participation of the people of Varallo, and Gaudenzio became its main artistic exponent.

Perfection

Raphael
Madonna of the Chair
1513

Oil on panel, 71 cm (diam.)
Florence, Galleria Palatina

For artist biography, see page 194.

Does it make sense to use the word 'perfection' in art history? As a measure of appraisal or as a critical category, is it actually useful? Probably not. For hundreds of years, artists and authors sought a system for measuring beauty with numbers and objective criteria, but all such attempts were doomed to failure. Raphael left no declaration of intent or treatise on art: his naturalness catches us off-guard, and it is no wonder that few have been able to imitate him. With a flowing line, he releases gestures, gazes, landscapes, light and colour in compositions of apparent simplicity. One after another, Raphael's Madonnas compose a gallery of enchantments – tender little gestures, the hint of a smile – but also prove his capacity to produce ever more varied and complicated poses, groupings, landscapes, lighting and situations.

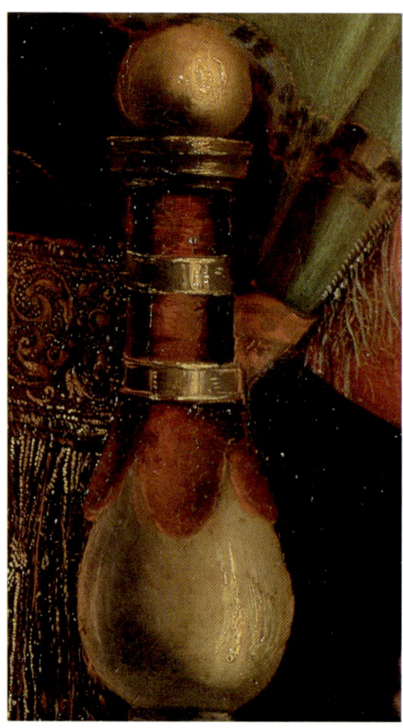

▲ The chair of the title is actually a small, elegant and refined seat. The turned and gilt knob and arm add circular elements to the painting.

► Mary's gaze is remarkably spontaneous. On her head she wears a form of turban.

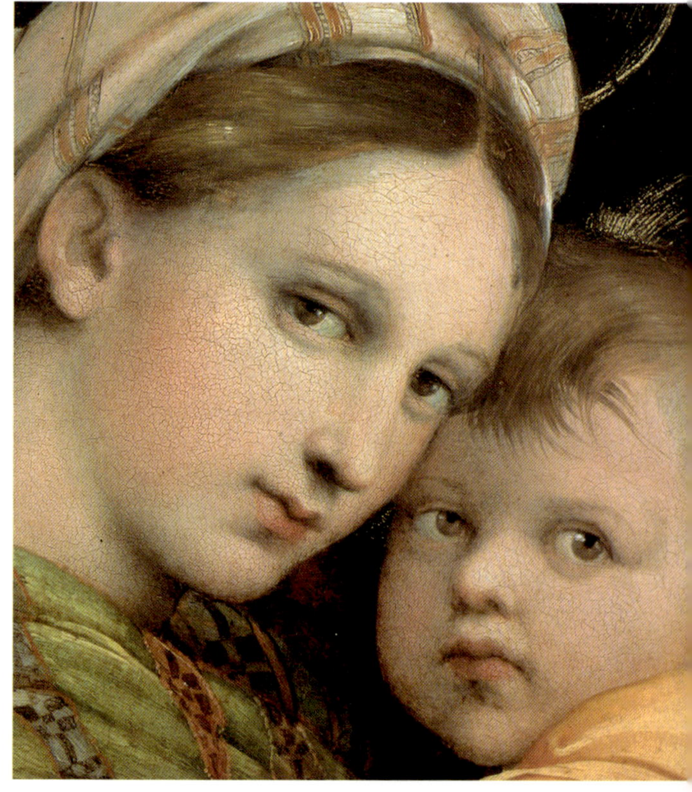

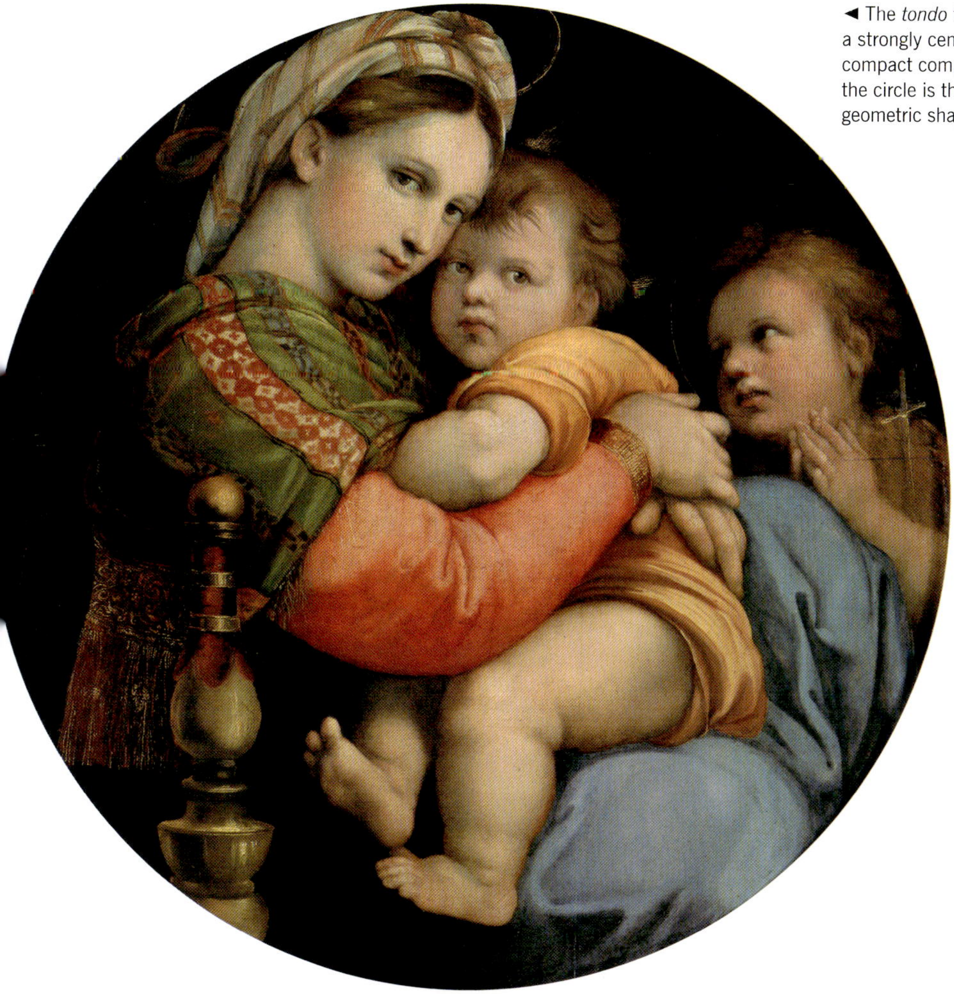

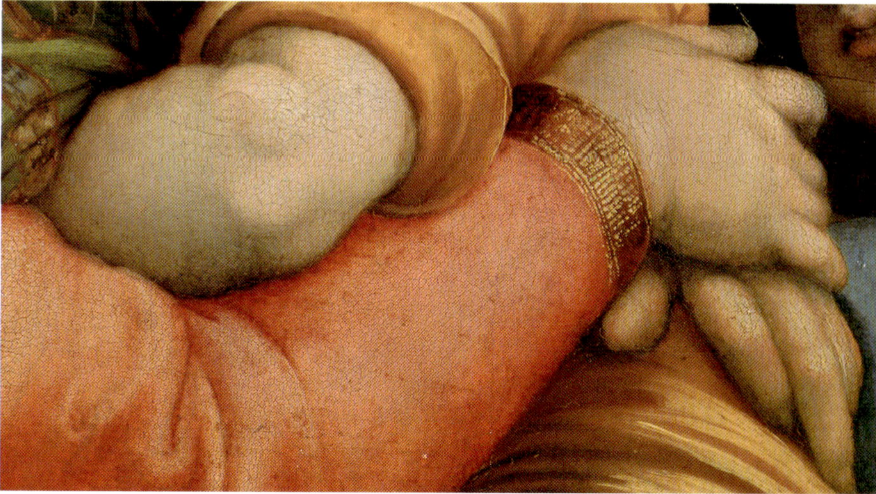

The composition pivots
on the Baby Jesus' elbow, at
almost the exact geometrical
centre of the *tondo*. The elbow
projects forward, towards the
viewer, and is heightened by
a ray of light.

The Three Ages of Man

Titian
The Three Ages of Man
1513

Oil on canvas, 90 × 151 cm
Edinburgh, National Gallery of Scotland

For artist biography, see page 224.

In the early 16th century, painting in the Veneto was sup‑
ported by the development of aristocratic collections, which
created a significant art market. To begin with, the genres mos
in demand were portraits and medium-format religious subject
set in natural backgrounds (precursors of pure landscape paint‑
ings). Secular subjects were soon introduced as well: moralis‑
tic compositions, concerts, female half-figures and favourite
mythological and literary themes. One very popular allegorica
subject was the Three Ages of Man, which allowed artists to
indulge their whims and populate compositions with figure
alluding to the stages of life: childhood, youth and old age.

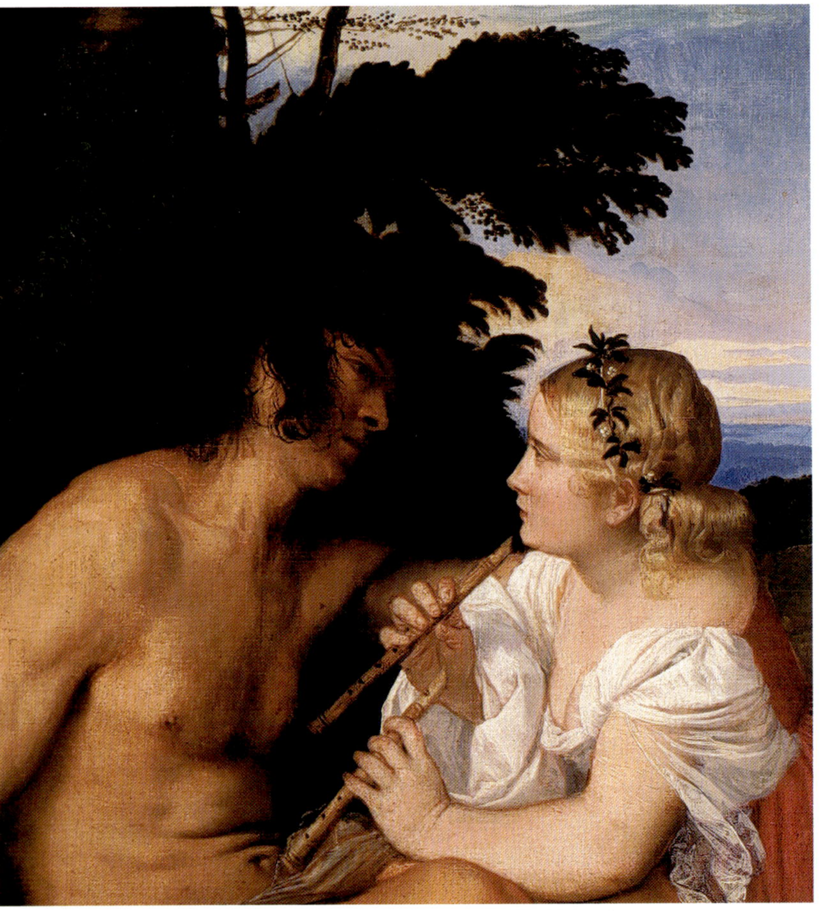

◄ Titian adds a deeply felt, buoyant sensuality to the theme of the inexorable passage of time. In his early twenties, the painter was experiencing the first successes of his long, brillian career, and was less given to literary and melancholy meditation than his friend Giorgione. The young Titian relegates the more admonitor aspects of the theme to the background and – much as in a poem by Lorenzo the Magnificent – invites us to enjoy the youth, love and beauty expressed in a paintir filled with luminous vitality. The intense gaze exchanged by the two young people, and the sexual allusion implicit in the flute the girl is holding, clearly indicate this.

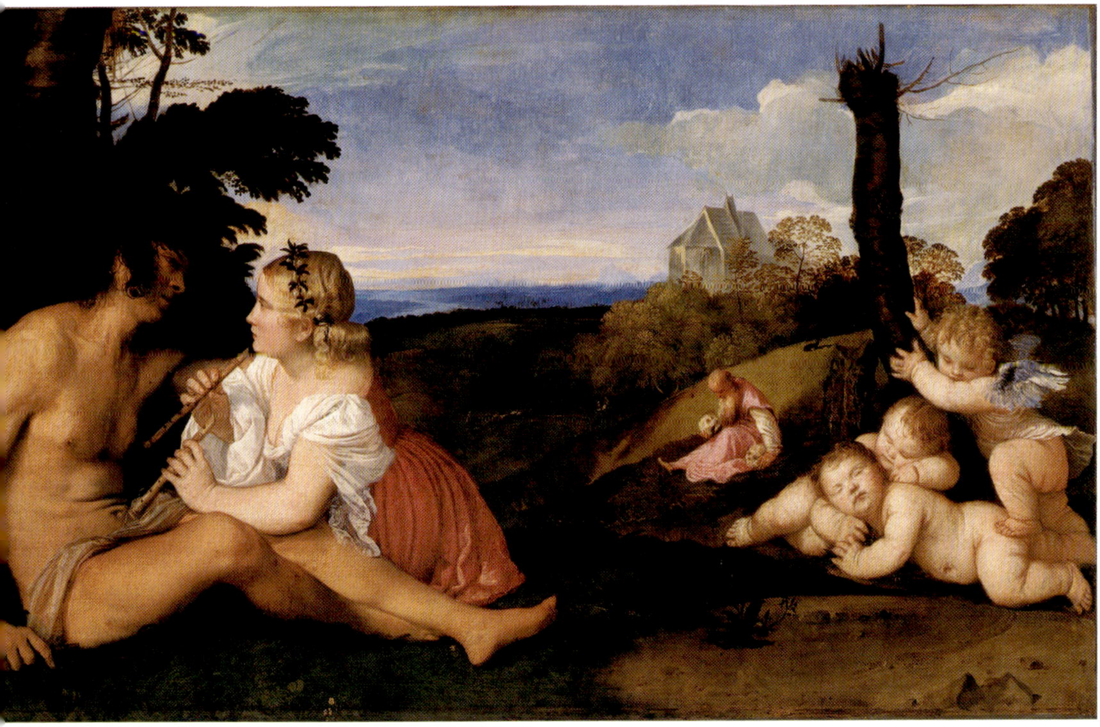

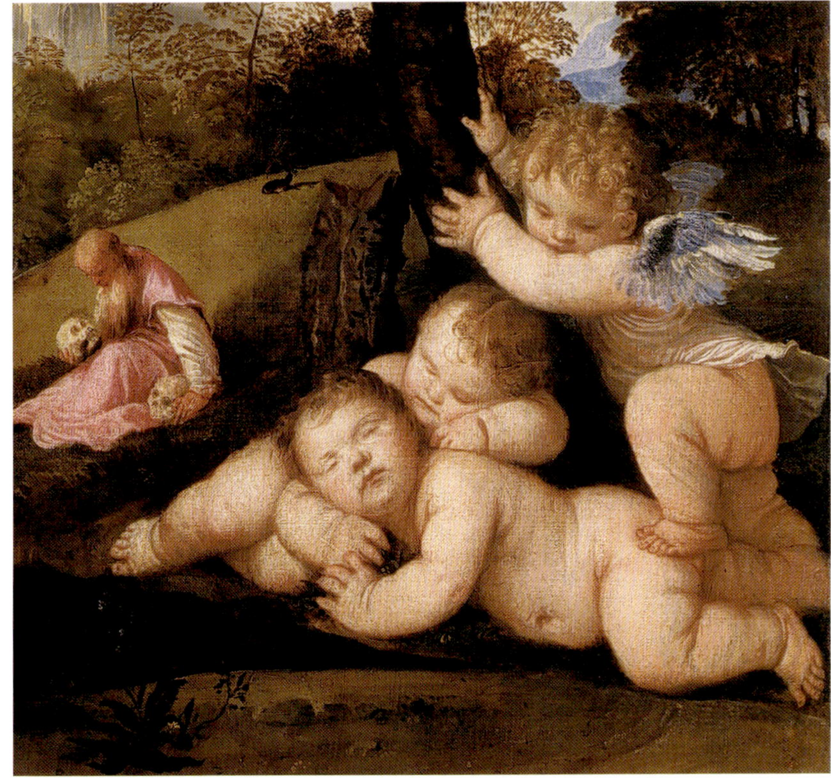

◄ While Cupid watches over two sleeping infants in the middle ground, a solitary bald and bearded old man meditates upon two skulls in the background. The theme of the painting is surely related to the poetical and literary interests of the intellectual circle around the influential poet and linguist Pietro Bembo. The painting known as *The Three Philosophers* (see pages 198–9) has also been taken to be an allegory of the Three Ages of Man.

Rhetoric

Raphael
The Fire in the Borgo
1514

Fresco, 670 cm (lower edge)
Vatican City, Rome, Musei Vaticani,
Stanza dell'Incendio di Borgo

For artist biography, see page 194.

After the death of Julius II in 1513, the Florentine Giovann
de' Medici, son of Lorenzo the Magnificent, was elected pop
and took the name Leo X. Once again Raphael became th
first to interpret the spirit of the new era. Systematic excava
tion had unearthed more and more examples of classical art
providing a wide variety of approaches, poses and decoration
Raphael demonstrated his deep ability to interpret the ancien
prototypes through controlled, elegant and stylistically flawles
painting in which the gestures and expressions of each indi
vidual figure convey an eloquent rhetoric. A fine example o
this is the decoration of the third Vatican Stanza, where Leo
X wished to recall historical episodes connected with his pre
decessors named Leo. The figures' expression of feelings and
the architecture are markedly theatrical.

**The Letter from Raphael and Baldassare Castiglione
to the New Pope**

*In 1514 Raphael and his friend Baldassare
Castiglione petitioned the new pope to safeguard
ancient monuments. At the time, Roman ruins
were still being treated as mere stone quarries.
The huge number of monuments Bramante had
demolished earned him the nickname 'mastro
Ruinante' (destroying master). Marble statues,
especially fragments, were smashed to produce
whitewash. Raphael and Castiglione understood
the importance of conserving vestiges of past
civilizations, and urged artists and intellectuals
to accept 'comparison with the Ancients'. To this
end, they asked the pope to establish standards and
provide legal instruments protecting works of art
and buildings. The letter of Raphael and Castiglione
thus proposed a first modern outline of laws for the
preservation of cultural heritage.*

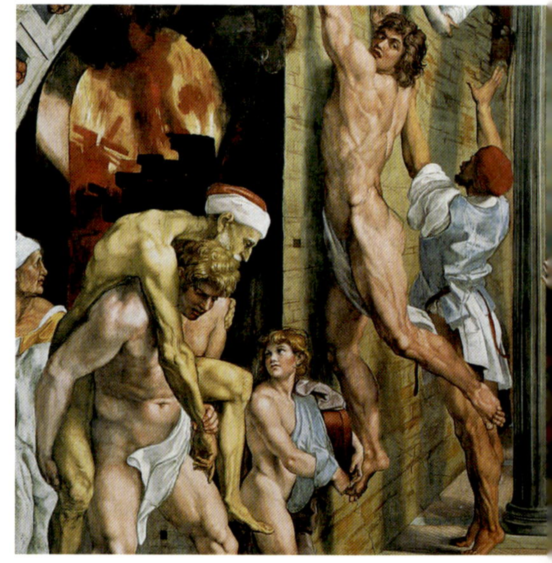

▲ In 1514, Raphael began the decoration of the
third Stanza for Leo X. It is known as the Stanza
dell'Incendio di Borgo (of the Fire in the Borgo),
after the subject of the main fresco, the only one
that Raphael carried out personally. This detail
shows a literary reference to the burning of
Troy – Aeneas fleeing with his father Anchises
on his back and his little son Ascanio at his side.

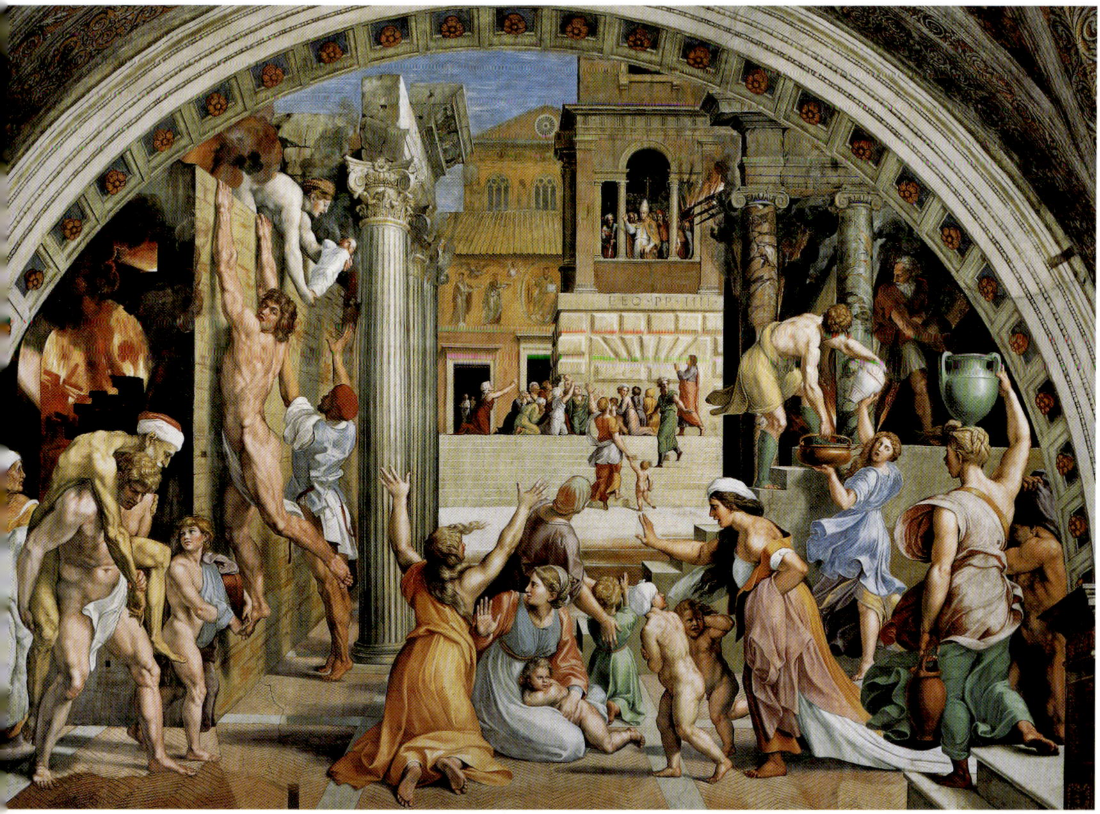

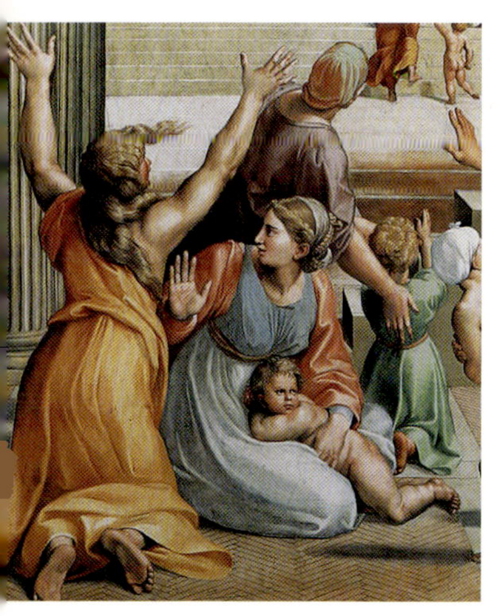

▼ The illustration of a fire in medieval Rome provided the occasion for an exhibition of rhetorical gestures, costumes and figures drawn from Antiquity and with a strongly theatrical flavour. Raphael's fresco was a source of inspiration for almost a century afterwards and offered a blueprint for Mannerist painters.

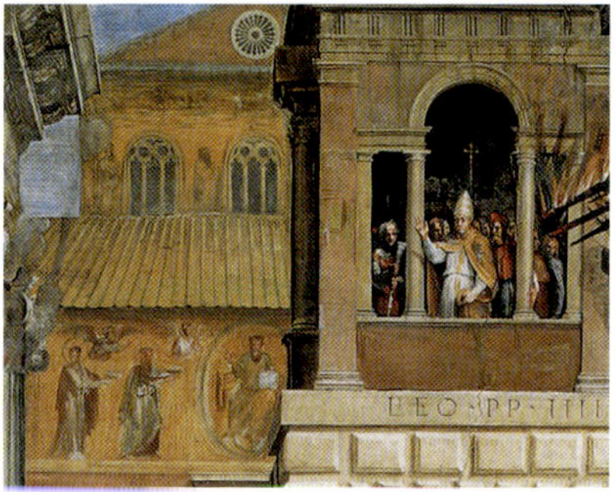

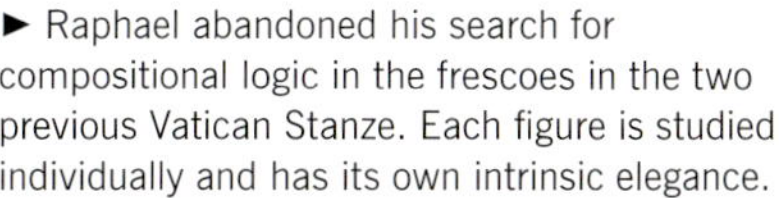

▲ All the episodes in the Stanza celebrate events that have a pope named Leo as their main character. Here, Leo IV leans from the loggia and miraculously extinguishes the fire ablaze in the Borgo quarter, behind the basilica of St Peter.

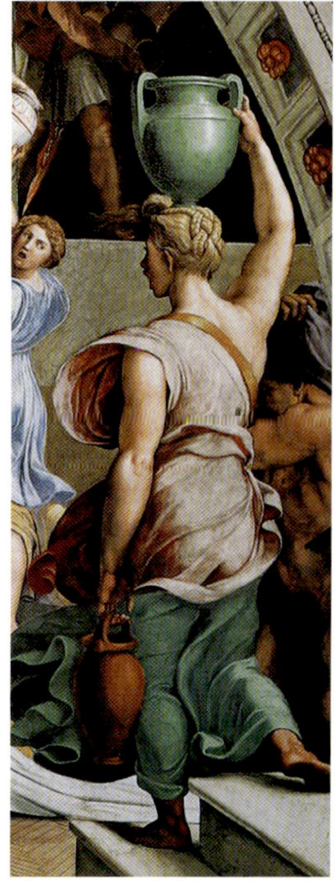

► Raphael abandoned his search for compositional logic in the frescoes in the two previous Vatican Stanze. Each figure is studied individually and has its own intrinsic elegance.

Allusion

Titian
Sacred Love and Profane Love
1514

Oil on canvas, 118 × 279 cm

Rome, Galleria Borghese

For artist biography, see page 224.

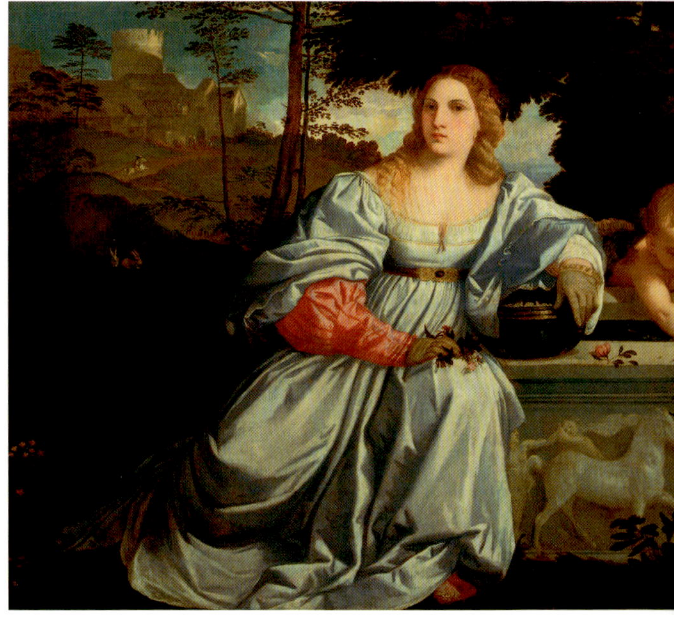

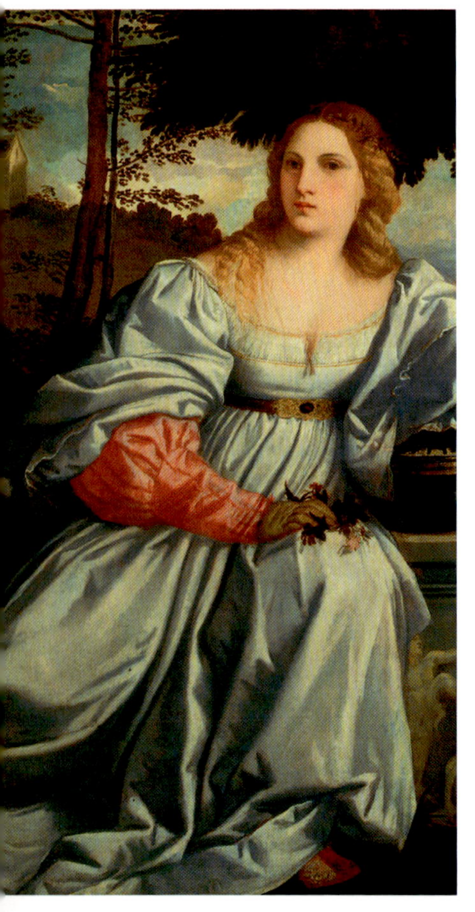

Renaissance painters always took their audience into account, and often created paintings for private individuals that are rife with personal references and allusions. We are not always able to understand all their symbolism, and the traditional titles are often misleading. A branch of art history called iconology deals with deciphering complicated messages and languages. Nonetheless, it would be an exaggeration to think that painters always used a mysterious 'secret code'. Identifying the correct reference (the recipient, occasion or possible literary source) can aid in understanding a work's meaning, which sometimes turns out to be simpler and clearer than had initially been thought.

◄ Various details of the two women's costumes, accessories and attitudes refer to different types of love and passion: sensuality and fidelity find a perfect union in matrimony. The clothed woman alludes to love in marriage; the nude woman elevates that same love to an eternal celestial plane, symbolized by the lamp.

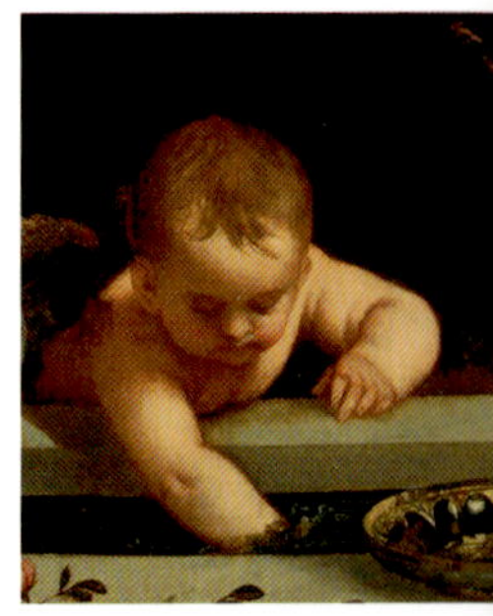

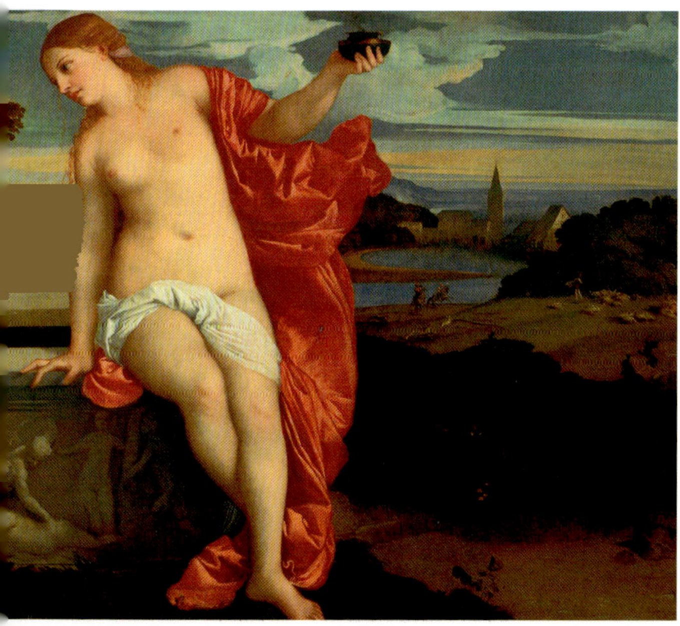

◄ The coat of arms on the fountain-sarcophagus in the centre of the painting is that of the influential Venetian aristocrat Niccolò Aurelio, who intended this painting to celebrate his marriage to Laura Bagarotto of Padua. This magnificent canvas thus belongs to a genre of 'occasional' paintings and invites an iconographic interpretation entirely related to the theme of marriage. The allegory's central subject is the celebration of love, interpreted with radiant breadth by the young Titian, who invites the eye to wander over a world of beauty and pleasure.

▼ In its evident harmony, the painting offers a continuous play of contrasts: death, represented on the sarcophagus, is counterbalanced by life, symbolized as a fountain; the clothed woman's reserve is counterbalanced by the nude's vivacity; the human figures contrast with the wilderness of the landscape background.

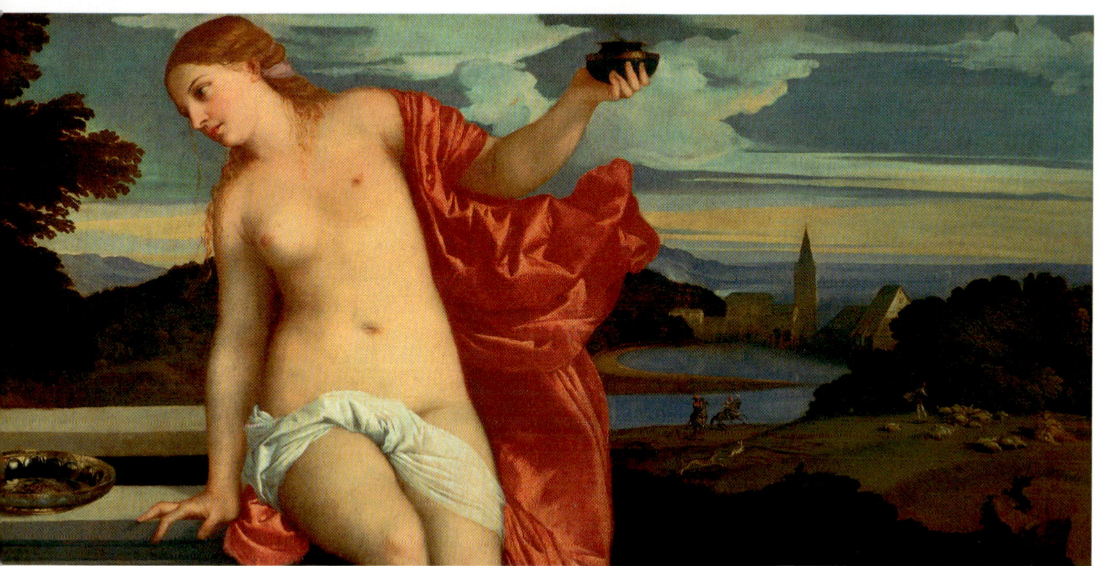

◄ The 'coinciding of chastity and sensuality' in matrimony is further alluded to through the Cupid stirring the fountain's waters.

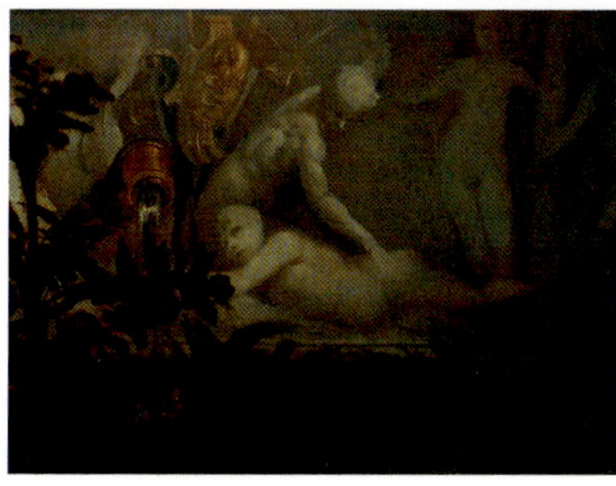

◄ The violent scene on the sarcophagus probably alludes to a tragedy suffered by the Bagarotto family. Laura Bagarotto's father, a well-known jurist, was put to death for his presumed betrayal of the Venetian state, only to be pardoned after his execution.

Mirror

Giovanni Bellini
Young Woman Combing her Hair
1515

Oil on canvas, 62 × 79 cm
Vienna, Kunsthistorisches Museum

For artist biography, see page 144.

During the first quarter of the 16th century, the mirror became an ambiguous presence in painting. As an attribute of Pride and Lust (two Deadly Sins), it had negative moral connotations, being a kind of professional tool of a sinful woman. However, in the context of an allegory of Prudence or Knowledge it might also be an instrument of virtue and knowledge. The results are often fascinating. In Venetian painting, the mirror affords the possibility to contemplate feminine beauty deeply, and from multiple points of view.

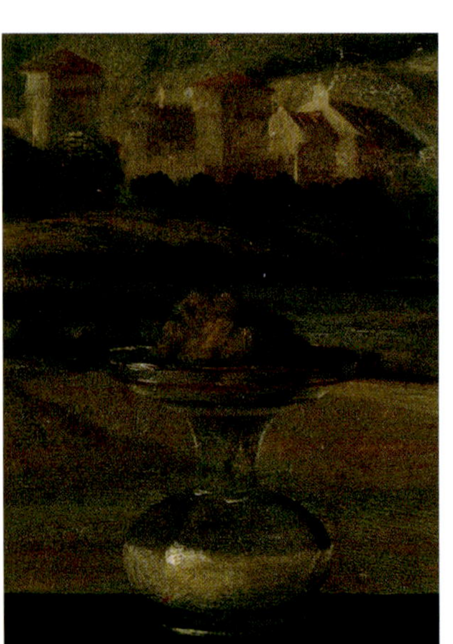

◄ A placid country landscape appears through the large window at the left. Bellini makes masterly use of colour to convey an impression of climate, atmosphere and nature.

▲ The girl's expression is quiet and concentrated: her nudity is luminous and modest. This would seem to exclude an interpretation of the mirror as a negative moral symbol here.

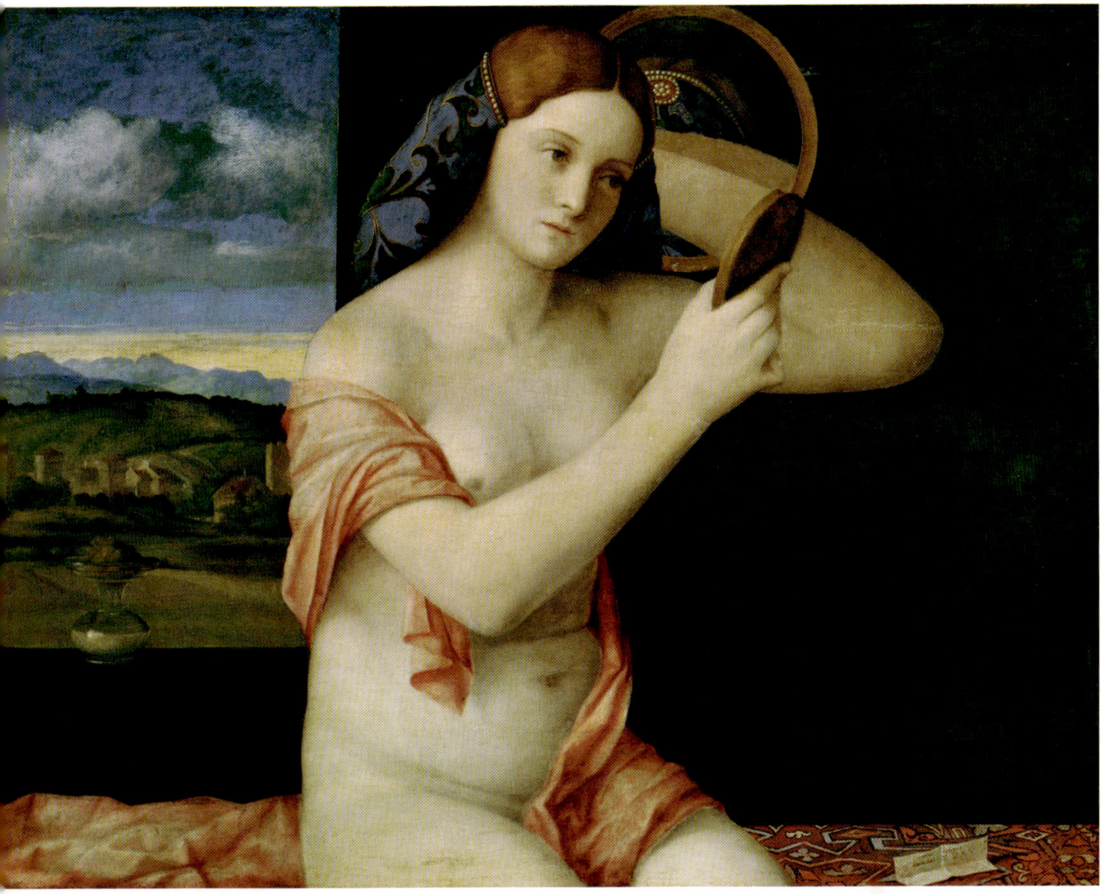

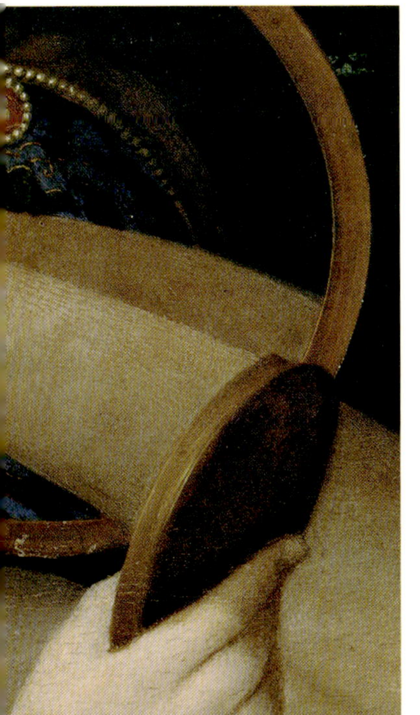

◄ ▲ The painting includes two mirrors. The larger one hangs on the wall; the other, smaller one is in the hand of the young woman who examines her hair. The double viewpoint this gives to the delicate, poetic canvas can be related to the discussion on the 'hierarchy' of the arts (see pages 260–1).

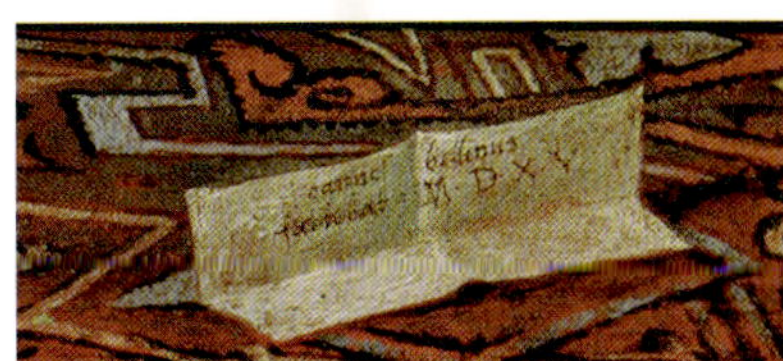

▲ A scrap of paper bears the painter's signature and the date. Bellini created this work when he was in his eighties, just before he died. It demonstrates the inexhaustible inventiveness of a painter who, at the close of his career, completed his first and only large female nude, barely grazed by the light, with a chaste and sweet purity.

Dynamism

Titian
The Assumption
1516–18

Oil on panel, 690 × 360 cm

Venice, Santa Maria Gloriosa dei Frari

For artist biography, see page 224.

The Assumption, the immense altarpiece painted for the high altar of the large Gothic church of the Franciscans in Venice confirmed Titian's supremacy in Venetian art. In the transition from Giorgione's calm, intimate vision to an astonishing new expression of extraordinary energy, this work marked a turning point. Titian made religious paintings that were no longer static images for contemplation by the devout, but scenes of impassioned, dramatic action. A dazzling vortex of light greets the Virgin, who ascends in a twisting pose. The excited gestures of the Apostles in the foreground indicate their amazement at this supernatural event.

A Painting That Sparked Controversy

The Assumption *presented a dilemma for the members of the Venetian artistic community who were not ready to accept the innovative import of Titian's altarpieces. Father Germano Casale, who commissioned the work, wondered whether the Apostles (for which Titian chose rude fishermen from the Laguna as models) showed sufficient 'decorum'. As Ludovico Dolce, Titian's first biographer (1557), wrote, 'The awkward painters and foolish herd who had never before seen anything but the cold, dead things of the Bellinis and the Vivarinis, without relief or movement, spoke much ill of this panel. Once their envy had subsided, people began to be amazed at the new manner found in Venice by Titian.' The Venetians' amazement was warranted:* The Assumption *stands out sharply from previous painting in the Veneto, forming the starting point for a 'new manner', which Dolce attempted to summarize: 'This panel contains the grandeur and awesomeness of Michelangelo, the peacefulness and graceful beauty of Raphael, and the true colours of nature.'*

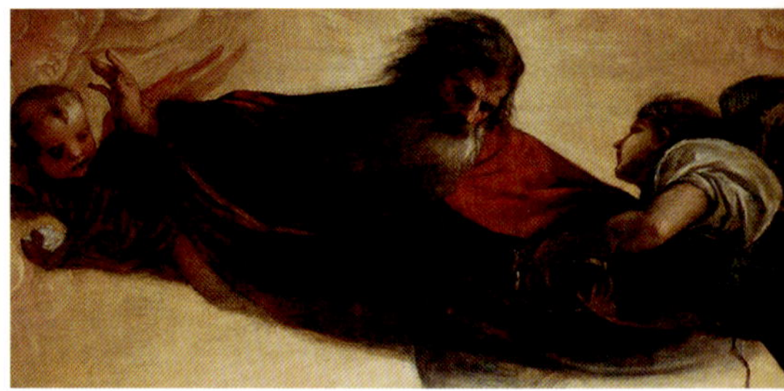

▲ Even the figure of God the Father, hovering diagonally at the top of the panel, emphasizes the composition's energy, which is also conveyed by the hot palette and strong contrasts of light.

▼ Titian's decision to use muscular fishermen from Chioggia as models for the Apostles caused a sensation. In response to traditionalist critics' concern, Titian pointed out that many of the Apostles were, in fact, fishermen.

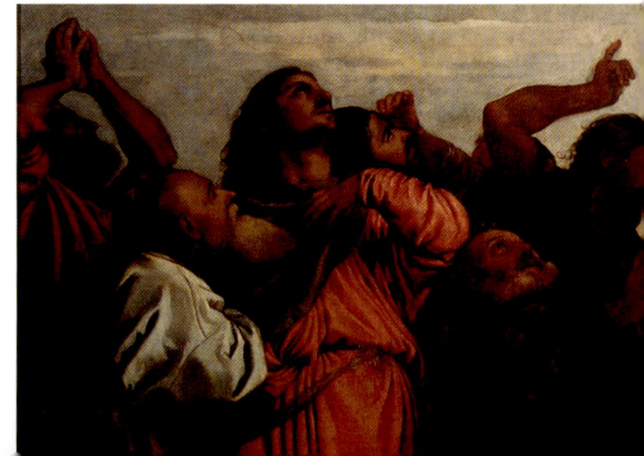

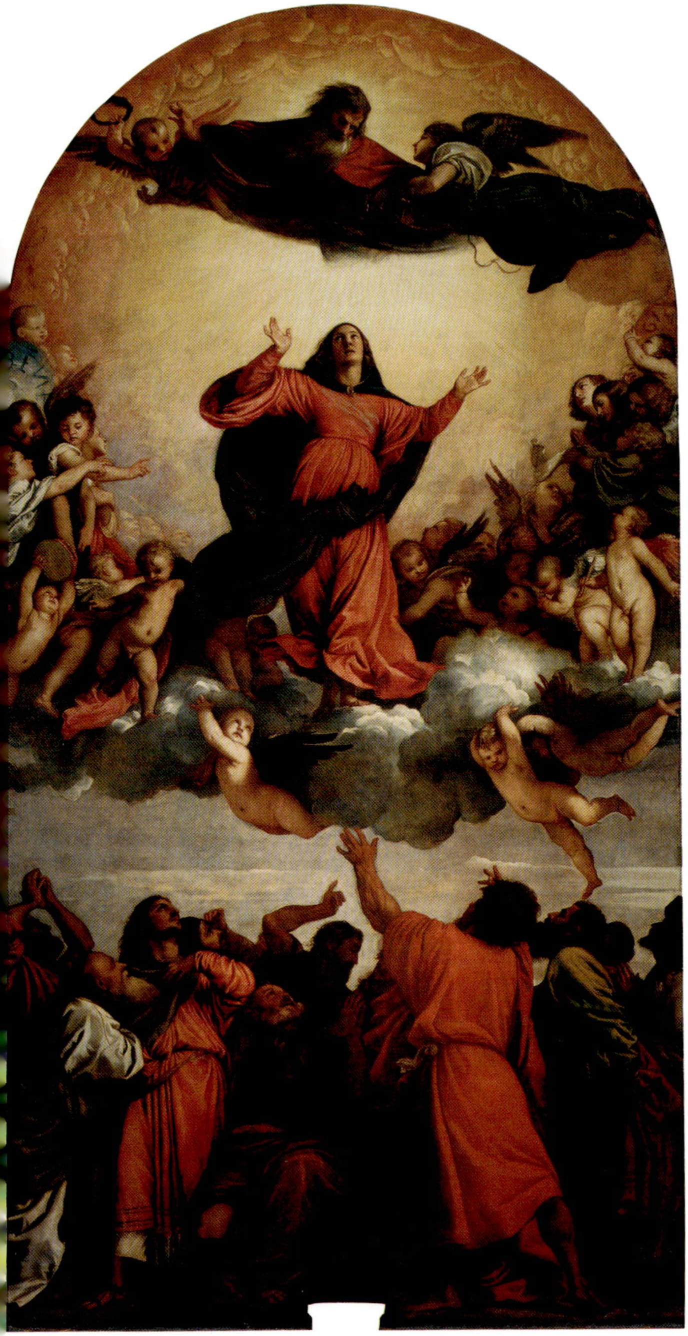

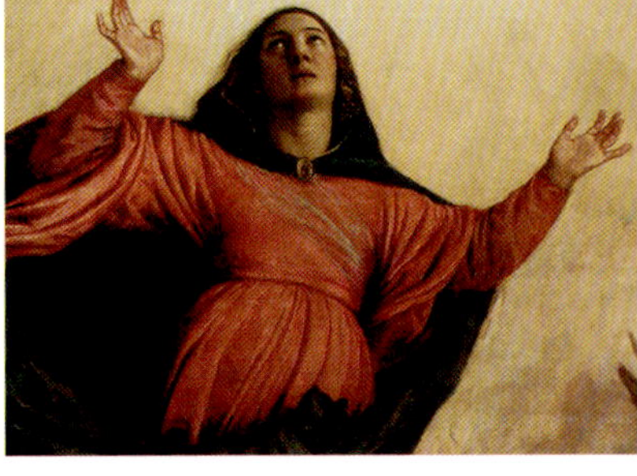

▲ The figure of Mary is revolutionary.
Traditional images of the Assumption had
generally depicted the Virgin motionless,
in prayer. Titian on the other hand infuses a
strong upward movement with a spiral rotation.

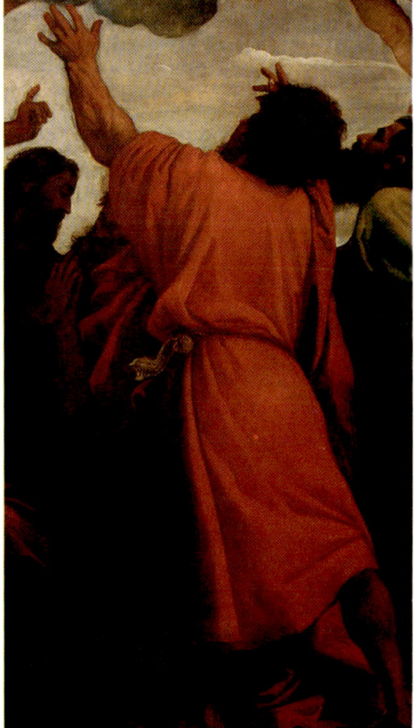

► The monumental, red-robed Apostle
who stretches out as if to embrace Mary
is the starting point for a spiral movement,
a whirling vortex that rises upward through
the centre of the painting and is mostly red,
a luminous colour.

Contrapposto

Andrea del Sarto
Madonna of the Harpies
1517

Oil on panel, 208 × 178 cm
Florence, Galleria degli Uffizi

Andrea del Sarto

(Andrea d'Agnolo)

Florence, 1486–1530

A link between the age of Lorenzo the Magnificent and early Mannerism, Andrea del Sarto promoted a well-mannered, wide-ranging modernization of Florentine painting, of which he is one of the key masters (at the time, Raphael, Michelangelo and Leonardo were working elsewhere). The son of a tailor (*sarto* in Italian, hence his surname), pupil of Piero di Cosimo and a skilful copyist in his youth, Andrea opened his own workshop in Florence in 1508. His first major commission was for frescoes in the Chiostrino dei Voti at the basilica of the Santissima Annunziata. After a trip to Rome to absorb the latest developments, Andrea began, in the cloister of the Scalzo, his original monochrome decoration. It was to become a fundamental work for the development of Florentine *disegno* (drawing) in the early 16th century. The *Madonna of the Harpies* (1517, Florence, Uffizi) preceded a brief sojourn in France, in the wake of Leonardo and in anticipation of Rosso Fiorentino. During the 1520s, thanks also to contact with the monks of Vallombrosa, the devotional intensity of his style increased. His masterpiece from this period is the decoration of the refectory of San Salvi.

The rediscovery and study of important sculptures from Antiquity prompted a quest for new, elegant, well-balanced poses. According to classical canons sanctioned by Lysippus and Praxiteles, the preferred posture is the *contrapposto*. In this the figure's centre of gravity is located at the navel, with the weight obviously falling onto one foot. If a figure's right arm is forward, the left leg is advanced, while the left arm and right leg are behind. Besides observing and measuring Greek and Roman statues during the 16th century, artists paid greater attention to human anatomy. Andrea del Sarto provides a number of masterly examples of the correct application of the classical schemas, but in a fluid, natural way that avoids being overly academic.

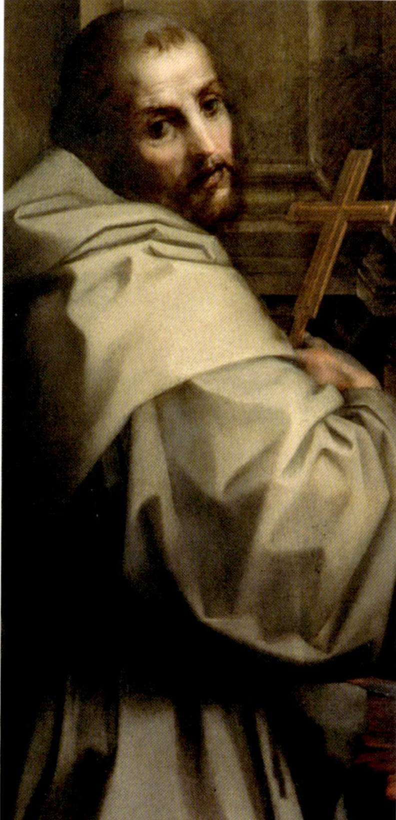

◄ The figures assume eloquent poses, but without the slightest anatomical strain, while the modelling is created by soft *sfumato* transitions that recall Leonardo. St Francis turns elegantly, his weight falling onto his left leg.

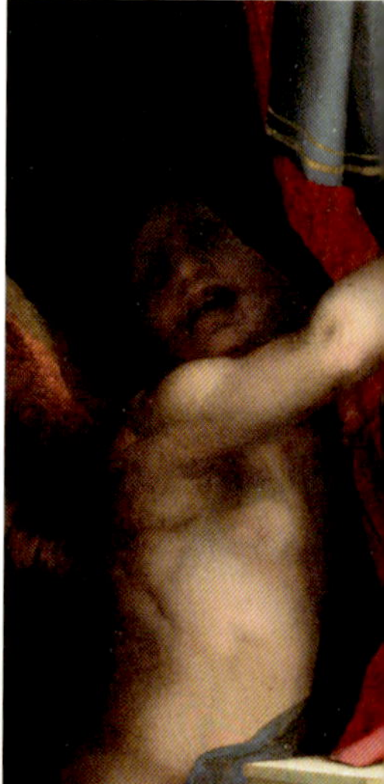

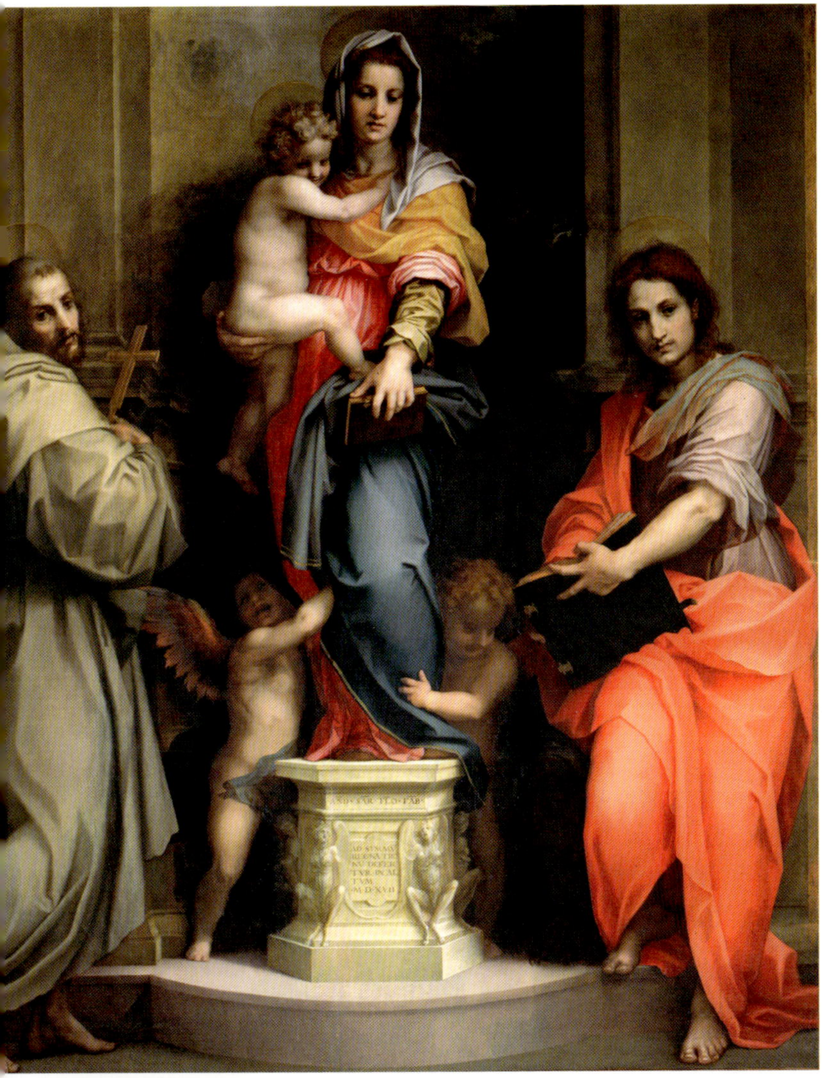

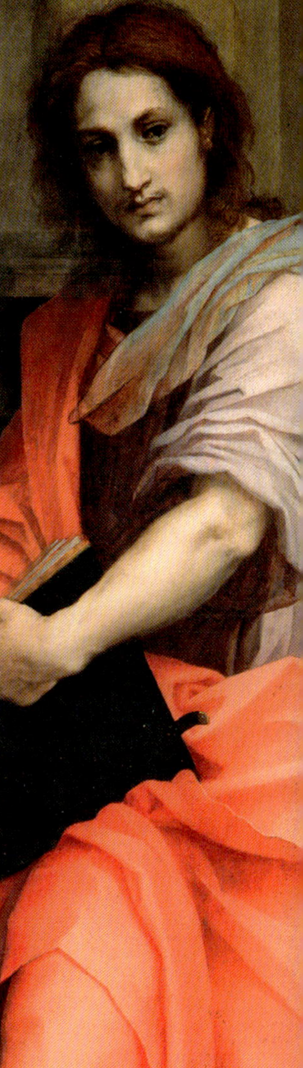

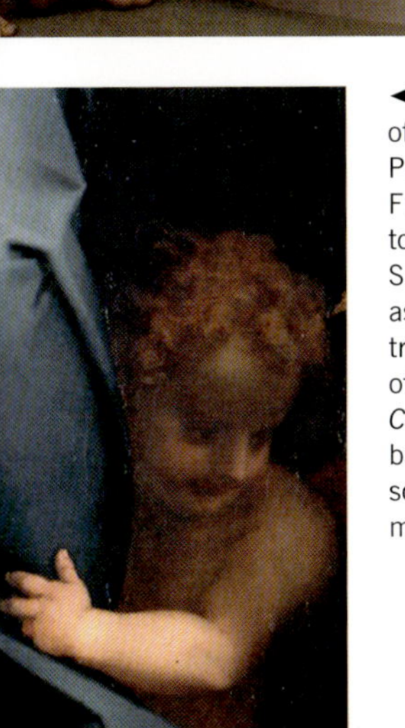

◀ Young Florentine painters
of the period, like Jacopo
Pontormo and Rosso
Fiorentino, immediately
took this panel, Andrea del
Sarto's most famous work,
as their model. The traditional
triangular arrangement
of the 15th-century *Sacra
Conversazione* against a sober
background is mediated with
softer modelling and greater
movement in the poses.

▶ St John the Evangelist's
energetic pose and obvious
musculature are related to
the prophets in Michelangelo's
frescoes at the Sistine
Chapel (see pages 212–15)
but adopt the classical
contrapposto pose.

Monochrome

Andrea del Sarto
Baptism of the People
1517

Fresco

Florence, Cloister of the Scalzo

For artist biography, see page 248.

During the 1510s, a period of political uneasiness, a difficult inter-generational exchange occurred in Florentine painting. In 1512, Louis XII, king of France, had restored the Medici to power, but discontent spread. Andrea del Sarto straddled a middle ground between the now declining humanistic certainties and the tensions of the new 'Mannerism'. With his predisposition for drawing, he proposed a graceful renewal of Florentine tradition, avoiding the polemical boldness of the early Mannerists (several of whom were his pupils). His monochrome frescoes are a memorable lesson in style: the soft light, faded half-tones, flowing composition and noble figures with delicately shaded outlines show the fully up-to-date approach of the painter, indisputably a leading figure in the artistic debate.

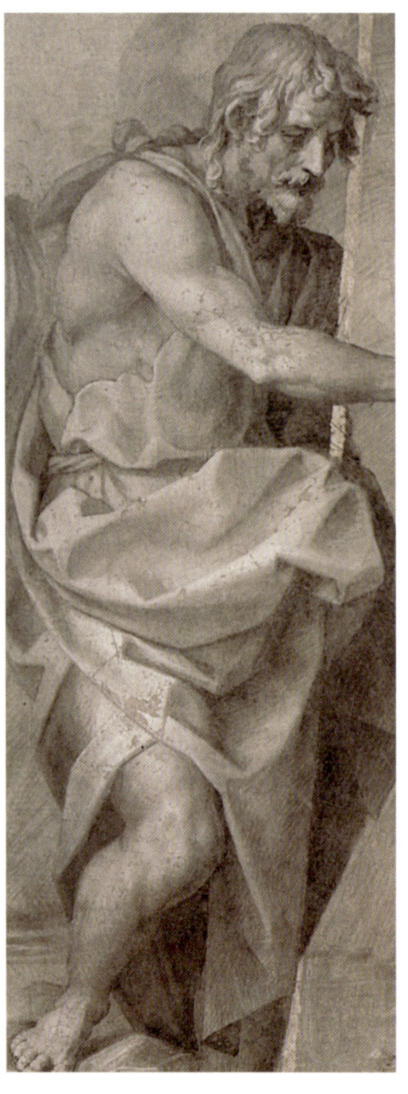

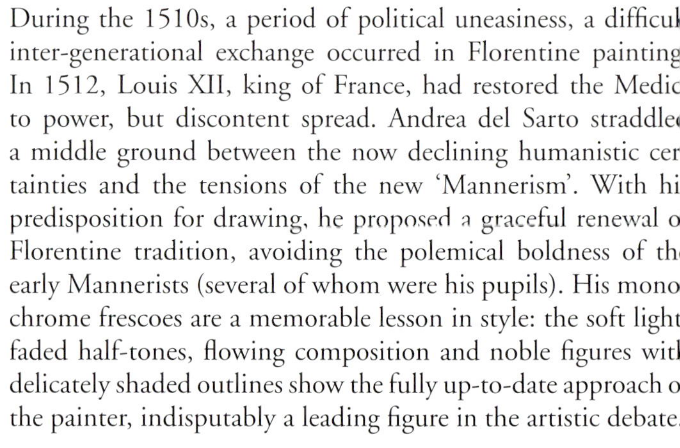

◄ The decision to decorate a cloister with monochrome frescoes was unusual but not unheard of. Uccello's frescoes in the so-called Green Cloister of Santa Maria Novella in Florence were an important precedent.

► Drawing had maintained its fundamental role throughout the history of Florentine painting. Andrea del Sarto's pictorial cycle, with its severe, refined tones of grey, can be seen as a rebuttal of the Venetian masters' exuberant eruption of colour. In fact, at exactly the same time as he was painting the monochromes in the cloister of the Scalzo, Titian was painting the highly coloured altarpiece of *The Assumption* in Venice (see pages 246–7).

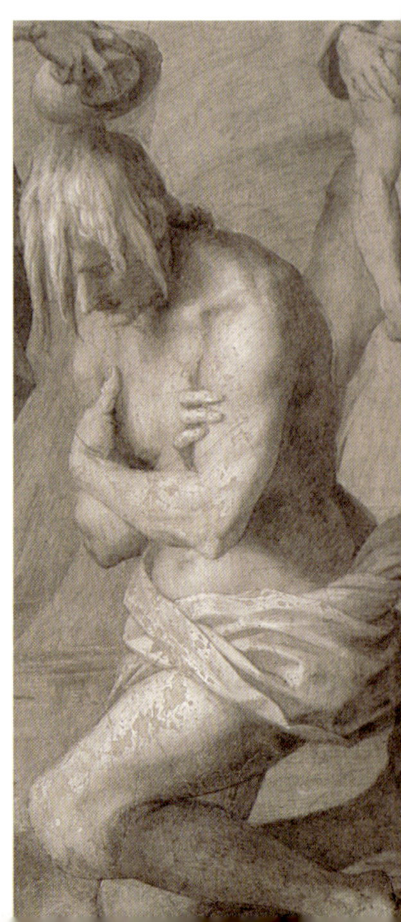

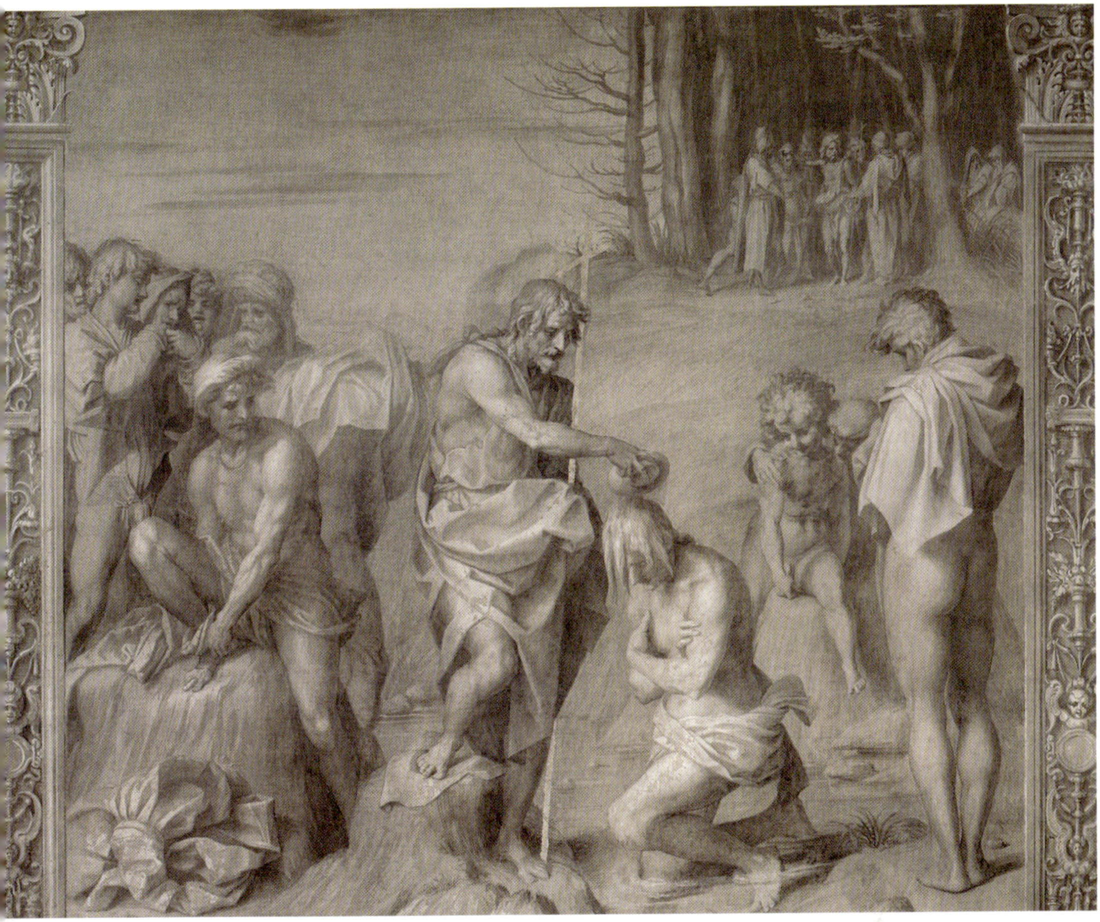

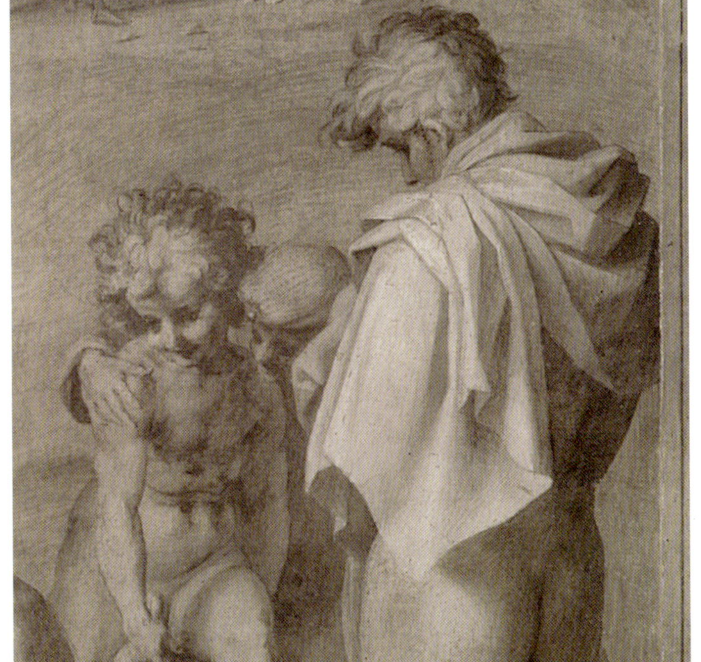

Andrea del Sarto was
considered an exemplary
master for most of the 16th
century. Preserved, imitated
and reused, his drawings
entered the collections of
connoisseurs and fine arts
academies. The single
figures, even more than
the compositions, are an
education in themselves.
For example, Jacopo
Pontormo, one of Andrea
del Sarto's most brilliant
pupils, soon borrowed the
seated nude boy with his
legs spread apart.

Rivalry

► **Sebastiano del Piombo**
The Raising of Lazarus
1517–19

Oil on canvas, 381 × 289 cm

London, National Gallery

►► **Raphael**
The Transfiguration
1518–20

Oil on panel, 405 × 278 cm

Vatican City, Rome, Pinacoteca Vaticana

From the very beginning of the 15th century, Florentine patron often pitted great artists against one another, taking advantag of their rivalry to spur them on to ever greater achievement This rivalry among painters became a defining characteristic i some fundamental stages of the Renaissance. Cardinal Giuli de' Medici, the future Pope Clement VII, knew the fruit of competition well and did not hesitate to commission twi altarpieces for his diocese of Narbonne, in France. He entruste their execution to Raphael and Michelangelo, fully aware tha each one would strive mightily to surpass his rival.

Sebastiano del Piombo

(Sebastiano Luciani, also called
Sebastiano Veneziano)

Venice, *c.* 1485–Rome, 1547

A leading figure in Venetian and Roman art, a colleague and rival of all the major artists of the first half of the 16th century, Sebastiano is perhaps less well known than he deserves to be. He grew up in the workshop of Giorgione, whose heir he aspired to be after the master's untimely death in 1510. However, competition from Titian led Sebastiano to accept an invitation to move to Rome, where he worked alongside Raphael at the Villa Farnesina. Without ever losing his typically Venetian sense of colour, Sebastiano became a faithful exponent of Michelangelo's ideas in painting. He used the latter's drawings and cartoons for *The Raising of Lazarus* (1519, London, National Gallery), a large altarpiece he painted in competition with Raphael's *Transfiguration*. Chosen as Clement VII's portraitist, Sebastiano was one of only a few artists who did not abandon Rome during the Sack of 1527 but remained at the pope's side. In recognition, he received the *officio di Piombo* (keeper of the papal seals) in 1531, an ecclesiastical benefit that made him wealthy. After that, his painting activity was limited to a small number of bravura portraits.

Raphael

For artist biography, see page 194.

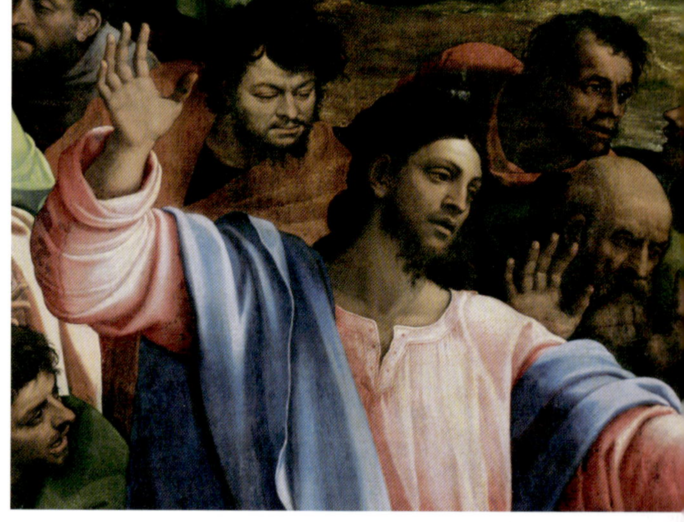

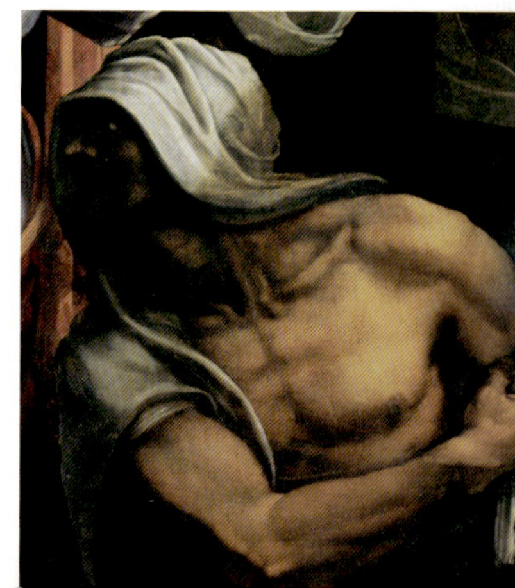

▲ ► *The Raising of Lazarus* is a highly rhetorical work, with monumental figures set against a cloudy landscape background. The duo of Sebastiano and Michelangelo could not conceal a certain cumbersomeness in the slightly overcrowded composition.

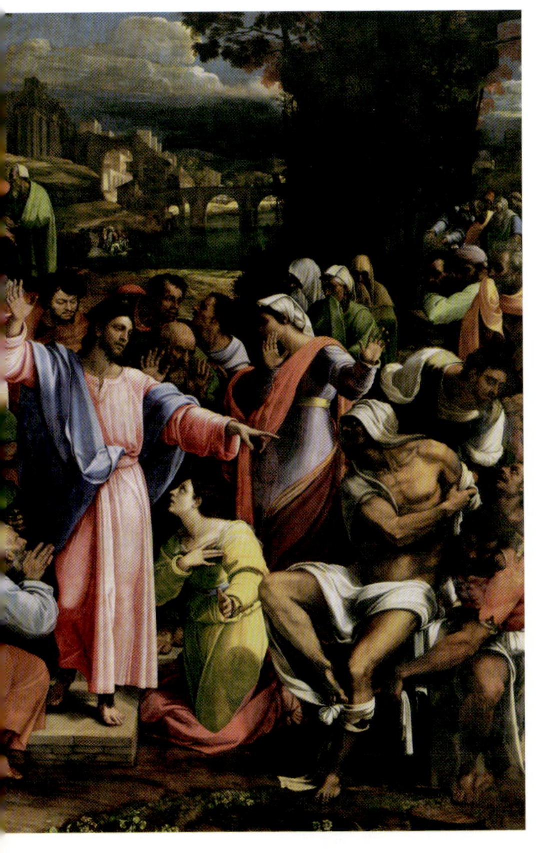

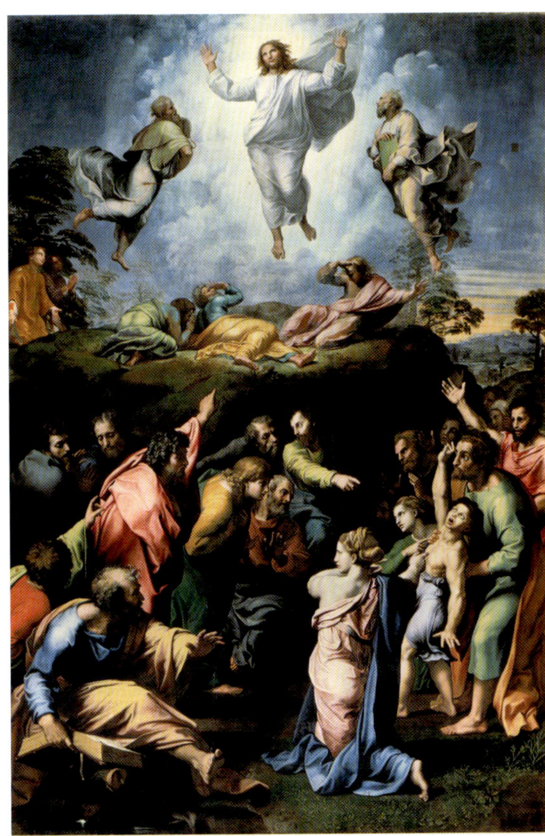

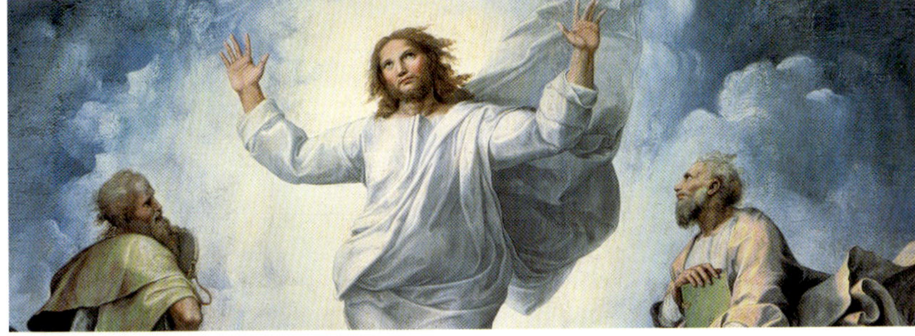

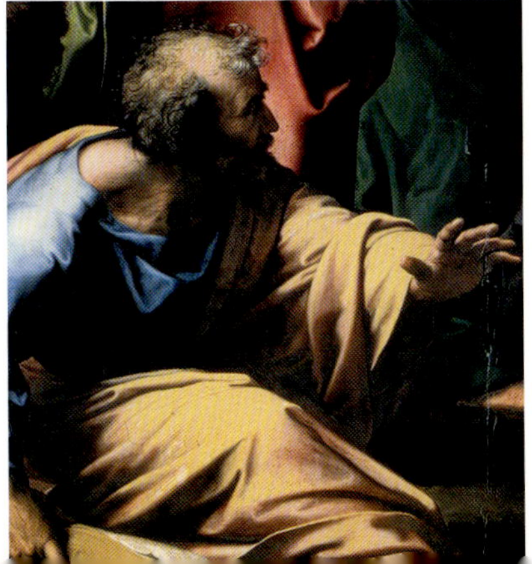

◄ ▲ Relying on a theatrical repertoire of gestures, expressions and feelings, Raphael succeeded in connecting two contrasting yet simultaneous scenes, the mystical Transfiguration above and, below, the hubbub surrounding the possessed boy – a scene whose high emotional key forges a link between Leonardo and Caravaggio.

Friendship

Raphael
Self-portrait with a Friend
1518

Oil on canvas, 99 × 83 cm

Paris, Musée du Louvre

For artist biography, see page 194.

Renaissance literature throughout Europe frequently concerned itself with the subject of friendship. The pleasure of sharing enthusiasms, ideas, feelings and solidarity is expressed especially often in 16th-century correspondence. Perhaps this is related to the growing religious and moral tension that pervaded the entire continent, creating a mood of doubt and reflection, or to the greater frequency and length of voyages over the new sea routes. Either way the same tendency can be found in portraits of various artists' friends and companions, which are characterized by relaxed poses, naturalistic expressions and gestures of mutual sympathy.

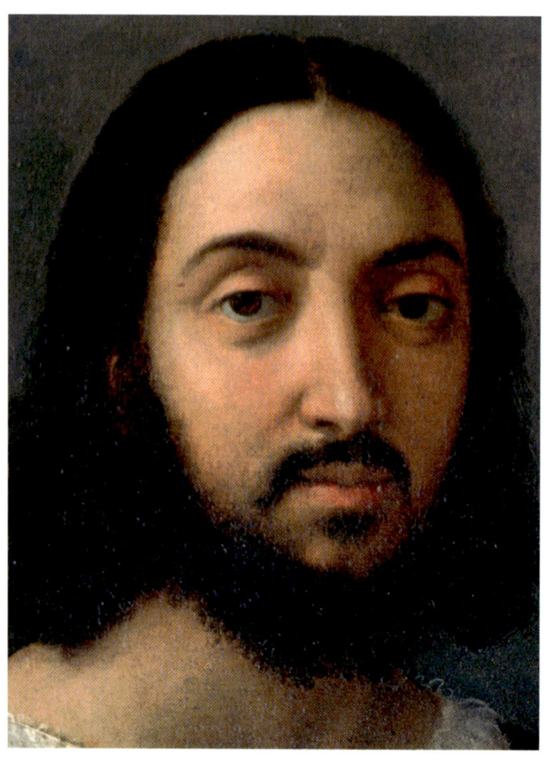

▲ This self-portrait of the bearded, 35-year-old Raphael shows a fuller, more mature face than the usual image of the master as youthful, clean-shaven and slender, for example in the detail of *The School of Athens* (see pages 228–9).

▼ The identity of the friend portrayed by Raphael is unknown. Among the many names suggested are Pietro Aretino and a number of artists (including Jacopo Pontormo, Baldassarre Peruzzi, the students Giulio Romano and Perino del Vaga), but so far none is convincing.

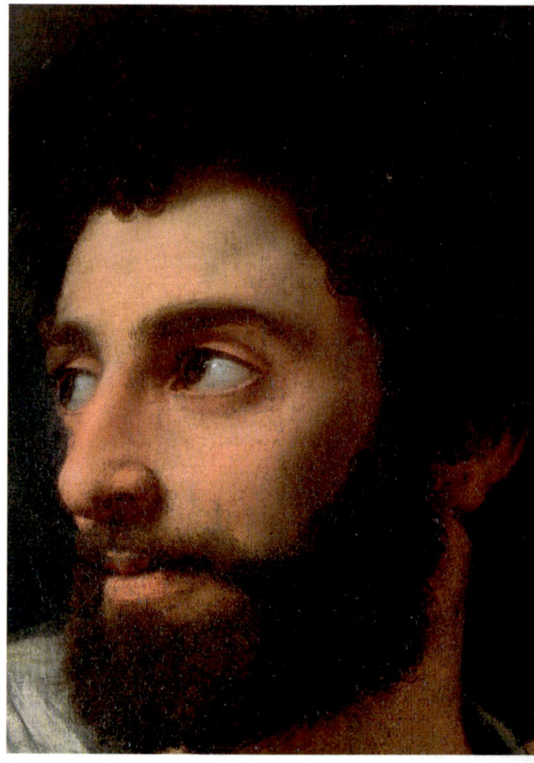

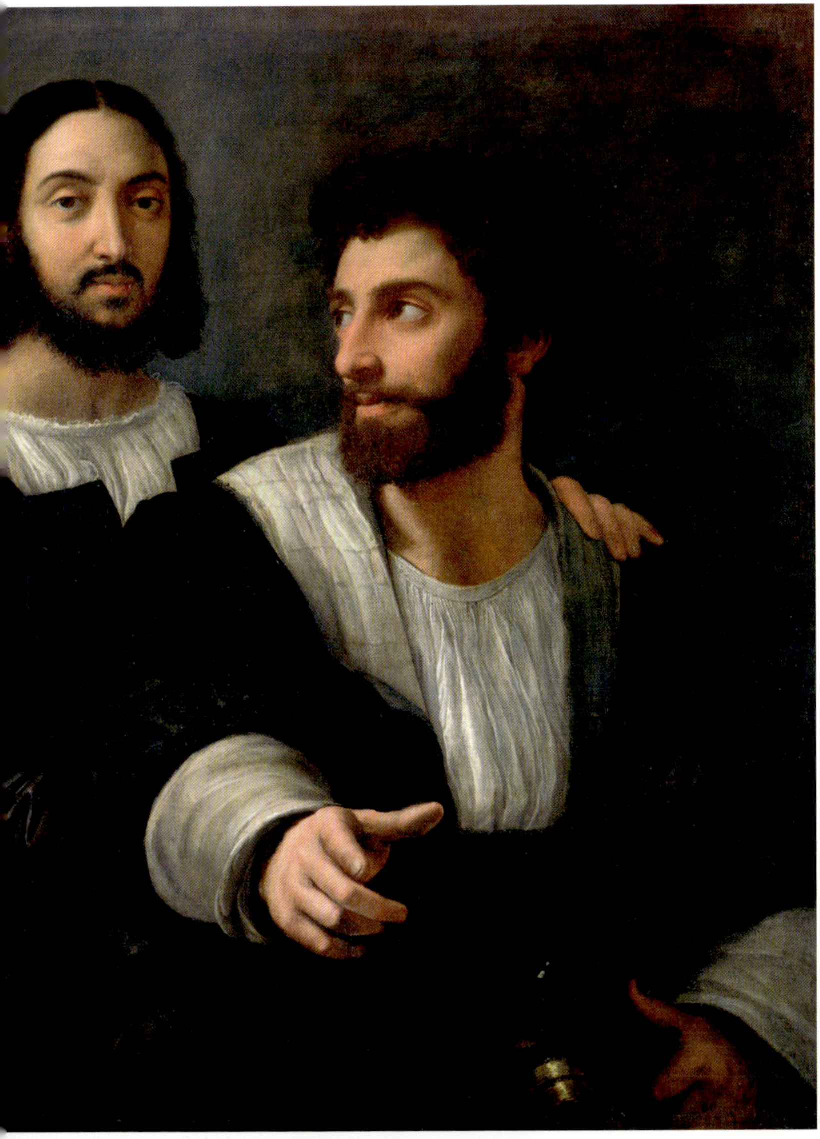

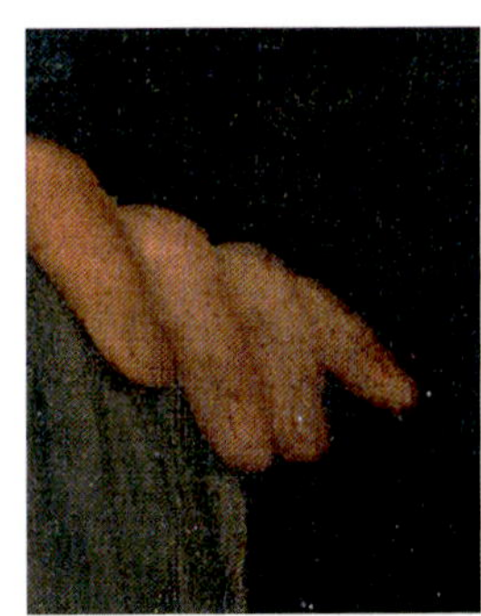

▲ The placement of a hand on the shoulder expresses confidence and spontaneity. The painting fits neatly into the dynamic of the 'double portrait' taken up by Giorgione (see pages 220–1) and others.

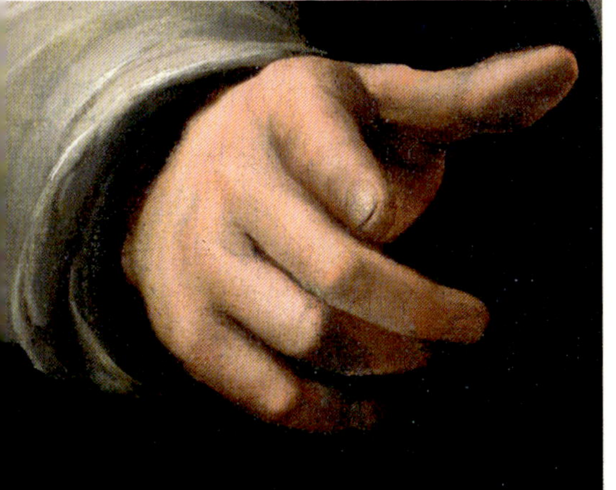

◄ The figure in the foreground is traditionally called Raphael's 'fencing master', although the only elements in support of this are the sword hilt and the gesture that could suggest a lunge.

Raphael
Portrait of Leo X with Two Cardinals
1518

Oil on panel, 154 × 119 cm

Florence, Galleria degli Uffizi

For artist biography, see page 194.

From the middle of the 15th century, the pope's role as an art patron continued to increase, in both the importance of the projects undertaken and the prestige of the masters involved. It reached a pinnacle in the first two decades of the 16th century when, thanks to Julius II and Leo X, the papal seat of the Vatican became Renaissance Europe's most extraordinary site of architectural and artistic activity. In addition, a splendid court of cardinals and high-ranking prelates revolved around the papal see, and they in turn were demanding and generous patrons and collectors. The Protestant Reformation and the Sack of Rome in 1527 brought this magnificent era to an abrupt end.

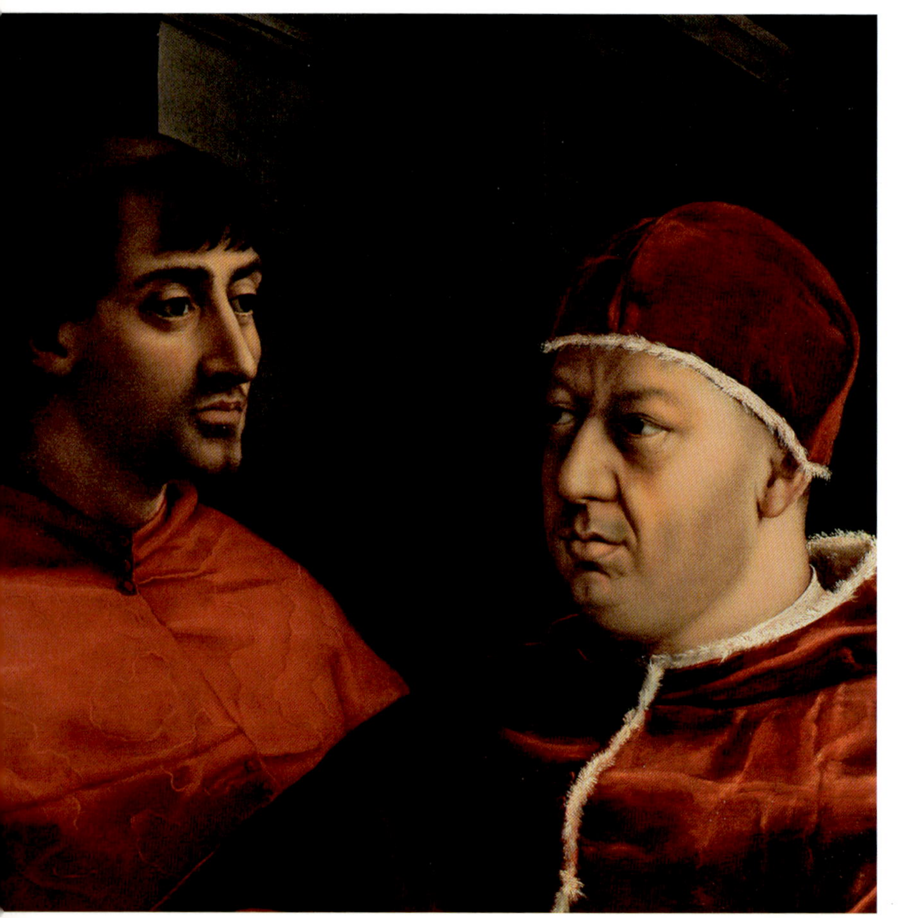

◄ With his usual capacity for political and psychological insight (enhanced by ten years' work inside the Vatican palaces), Raphael managed to convey a sense of dynastic succession. Beside the reigning pope is one of his relatives and successors: Cardinal Giulio de' Medici, who became Pope Clement VII after the brief interlude of the Dutch pope Adrian VI, from Utrecht.

► Raphael portrays Leo X, the son of Lorenzo the Magnificent and an art lover, patron and collector, with his hands on a fabulous illuminated Bible (the so-called Hamilton Bible, now in Berlin). In his left hand he holds a magnifying glass, with which he seems to have been examining the decorated page.

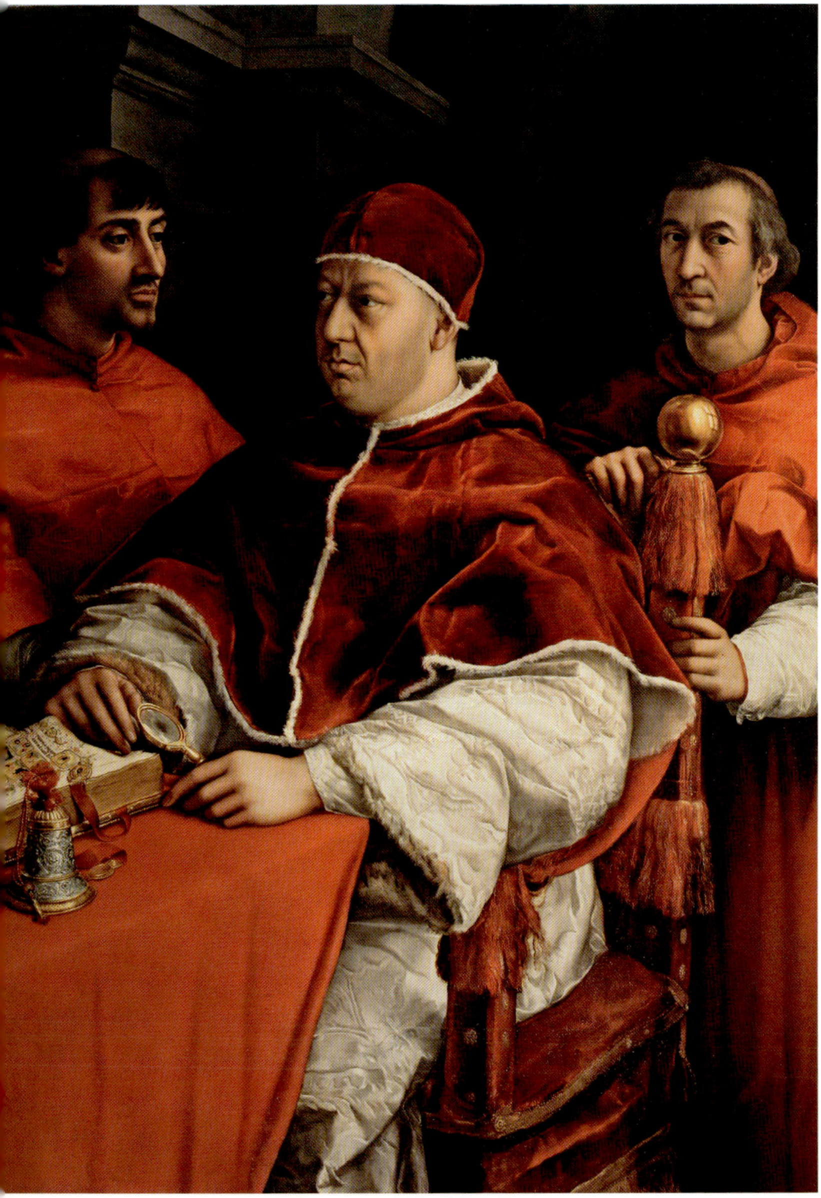

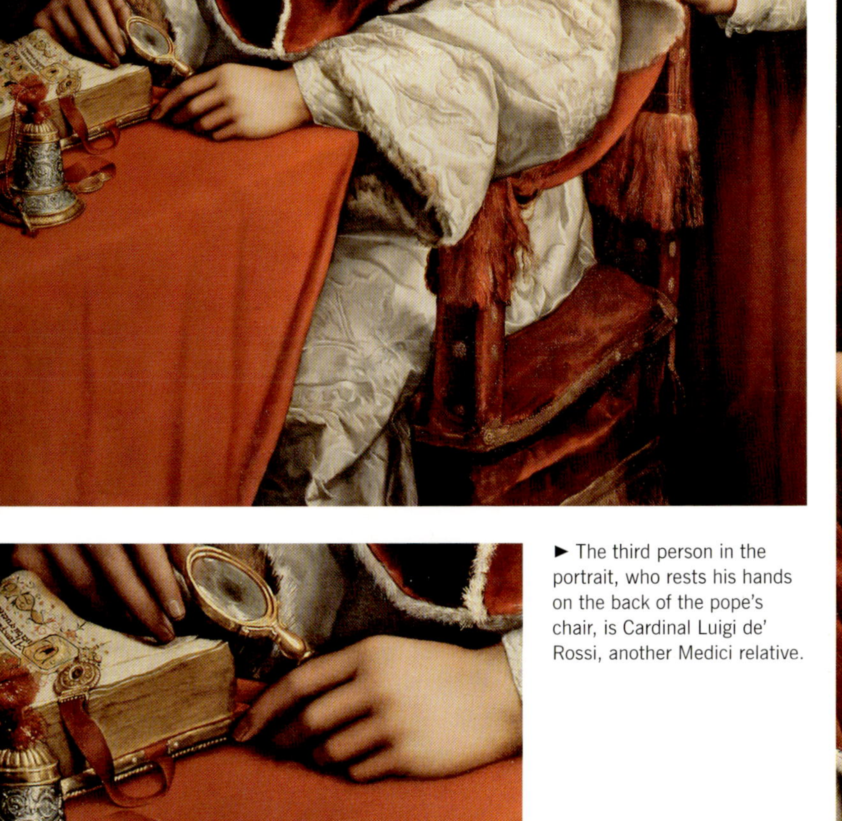

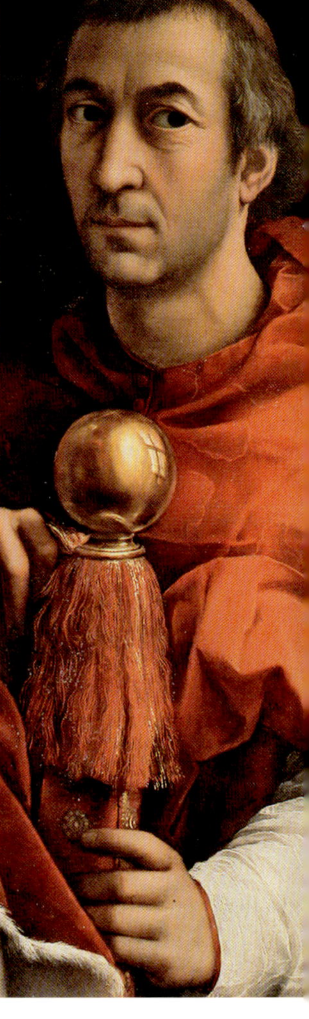

▶ The third person in the portrait, who rests his hands on the back of the pope's chair, is Cardinal Luigi de' Rossi, another Medici relative.

Titian
Pesaro Altarpiece
1519–25

Oil on canvas, 478 × 266 cm

Venice, Santa Maria Gloriosa dei Frari

For artist biography, see page 224.

With the altarpiece that Titian painted for the Pesaro family, h
introduced a substantial novelty into the genre. Abandonin
the late-15th-century geometrical arrangement of the *Sacr*
Conversazione, he shifted the Madonna's seat from the centr
towards the right. The group of figures (the family of Bisho
Jacopo Pesaro, with the household's patron saints and figure
alluding to military victories) is oriented towards the Virgin
The intensely luminous colours heighten the sense of inno
vation, the close dialogue among the figures and the unusua
articulation of the architectural elements, with two powerfu
columns that disappear beyond the top of the frame.

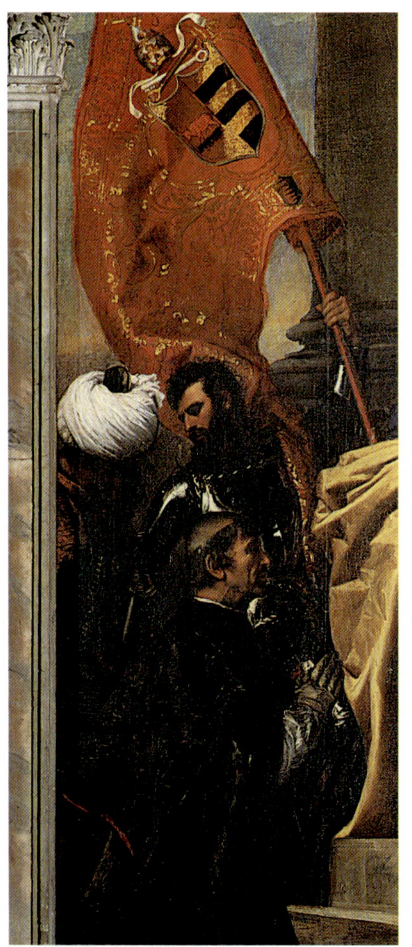

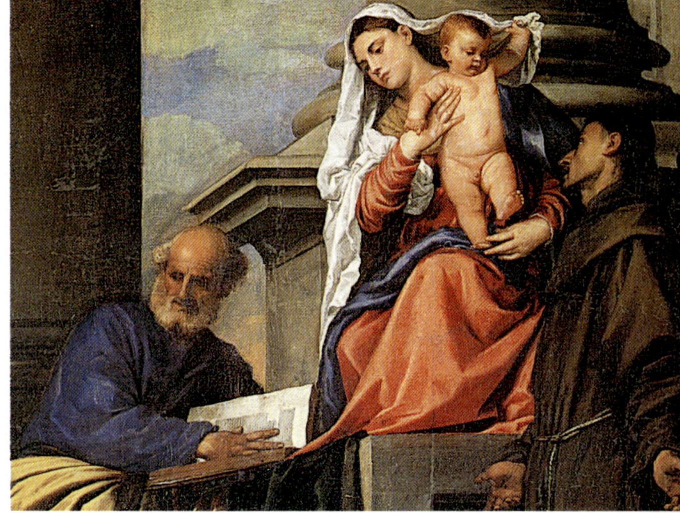

◄ The Pesaro family – with its household patron saints and figures alluding to the military victories of Jacopo, bishop of Paphos in Cyprus and a great admirer of Titian – turn towards the Madonna in a motion that revolutionized the canonical triangular arrangement of the *Sacra Conversazione*.

▲ The main group is composed of St Peter, who looks towards Jacopo Pesaro, the Virgin Mary, turning to the right, and the Infant Jesus, smiling at St Francis who opens his arms as if to protect the members of the Pesaro family. Titian has thus organized and articulated the interplay of gazes and gestures with a coherent narrative logic.

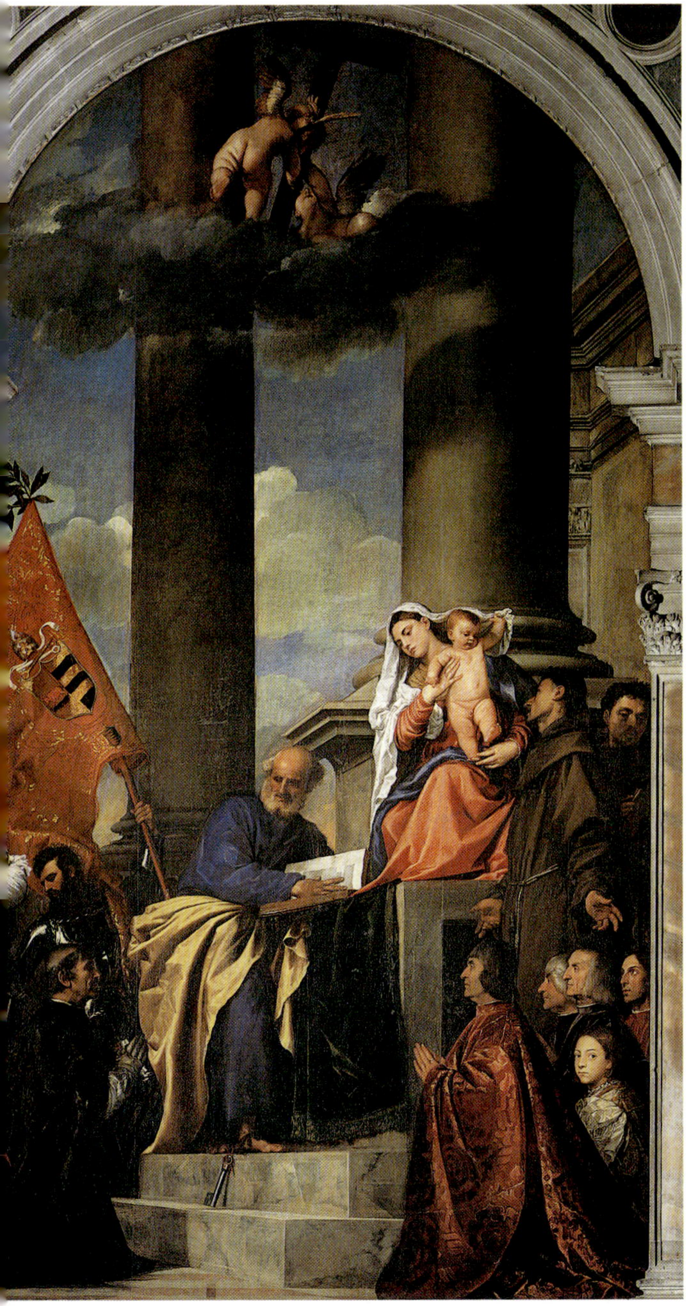

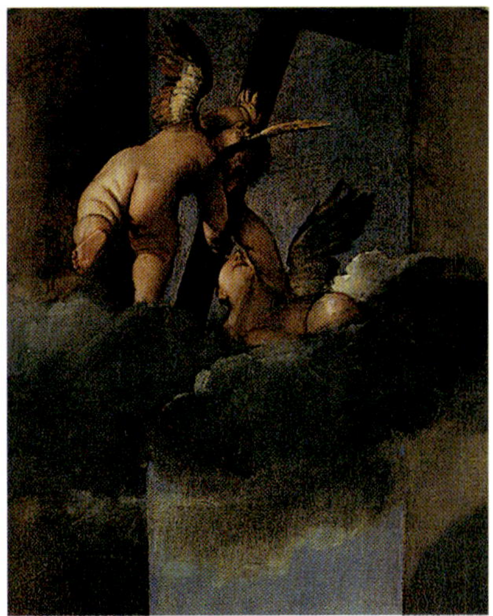

▲ The solemn architecture essentially consists of two immense columns that disappear above clouds where two little angels carry the Cross.

▼ The curious, lively gaze of the boy dressed in silver stands out amid the austere portraits of his relatives.

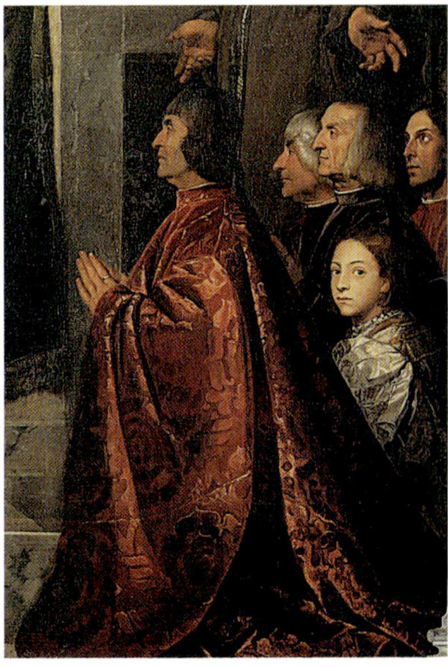

▲ Commissioned by Bishop Jacopo Pesaro, the altarpiece remains in its original site on the altar of the Concezione in the basilica of the Frari. It was the altar's placement along the left aisle of the Franciscan church that prompted Titian to shift the Madonna's seat from the centre towards the right, altering the usual symmetrical arrangement of the figures.

Hierarchy of the Arts

Giovanni Girolamo Savoldo
Portrait of a Man in Armour
(Self-portrait?)
c. 1520

Oil on canvas, 91 × 123 cm
Paris, Musée du Louvre

Giovanni Girolamo Savoldo

Brescia, 1480/5–*c.* 1548

Though Savoldo spent almost his entire career in Venice (where he began working in 1520), it is more accurate to consider him a representative of the Brescian school along with Romanino and Moretto – and not only because he had patrons in his native city. The role he played in the quest for direct realism and delicate psychological interpretation, typical of Renaissance artists in the Plain of Padano, is especially important. His most characteristic paintings depict devotional subjects for private collections, sometimes repeated in several versions. Savoldo's work from the 1520s gleams with silvery light effects and bright colours. In the few portraits and touching sacred works from the 1530s, this tendency to luminosity lessens, and he creates a more delicate expression of intimate poetical melancholy. Because of his elegant use of chiaroscuro and feeling for human truth, Savoldo is considered a predecessor of Caravaggio.

Sixteenth-century Italy was witness to some lively debate on the figurative arts, in which well-known authorities, intellectuals and artists expressed often harsh differences of opinion. At the beginning of the century, Leonardo and Michelangelo disagreed as to whether painting was superior to sculpture. Sculptors felt they deserved precedence, because their figures could be observed from different angles. In response, painters began painting images that incorporated mirrors, shiny metal and other reflective surfaces to provide multiple viewpoints. Such works, motivated by clearly polemical intent, exhibit an engrossing virtuosity.

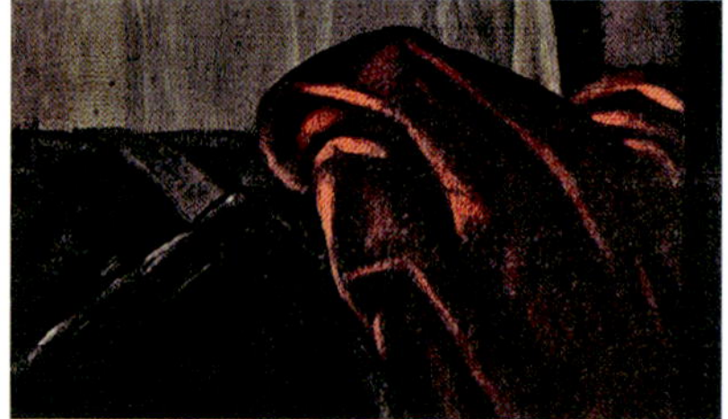

◀ The effects of light, in generally muted tones, are impressive. Savoldo was one of the first Renaissance artists to paint candlelit night scenes.

▶ The subject of this portrait (for a while thought to be an idealized portrait of the French military commander Gaston de Foix) has not been identified. It could be an imaginary figure or perhaps a self-portrait, made for a specific purpose. When considered in the context of the debate over the relative 'excellence' of painting and sculpture, this work becomes an argument in favour of painting. Following the precedent of a work by Giorgione (now lost, but described in contemporary sources), Savoldo used various means to show the human figure simultaneously from various points of view, with matchless virtuosity.

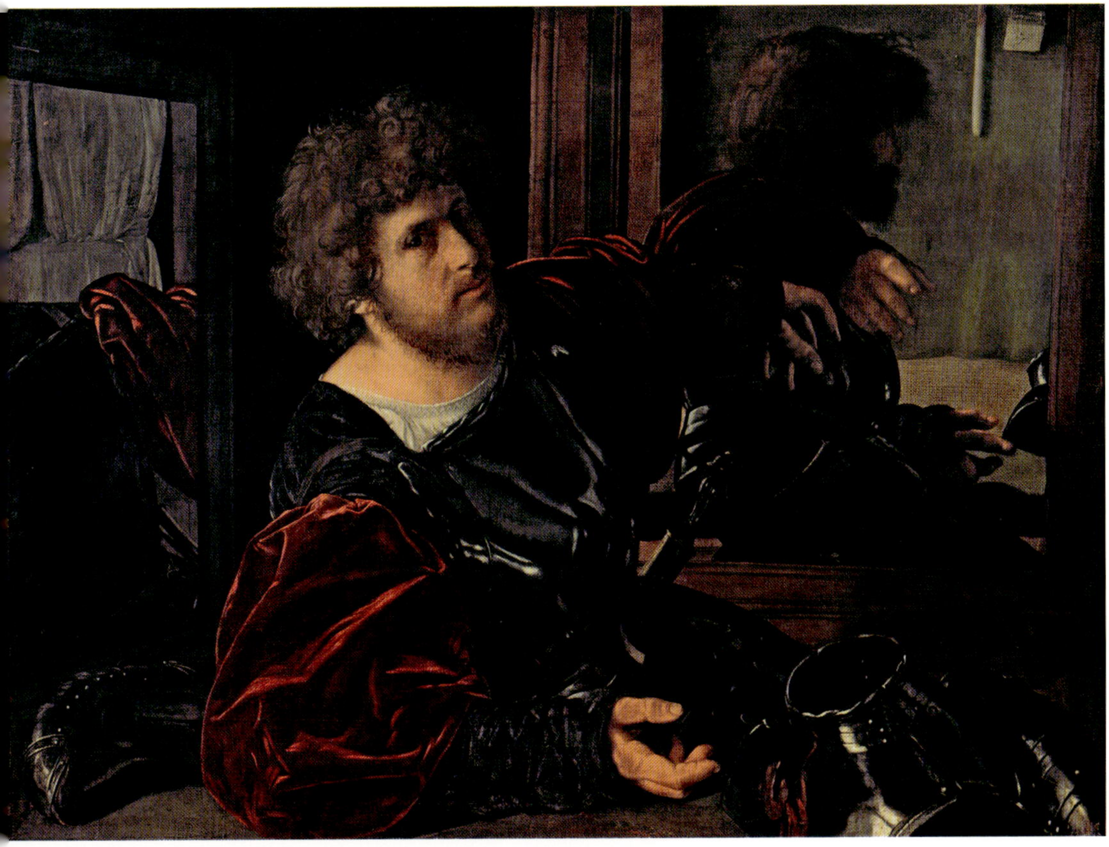

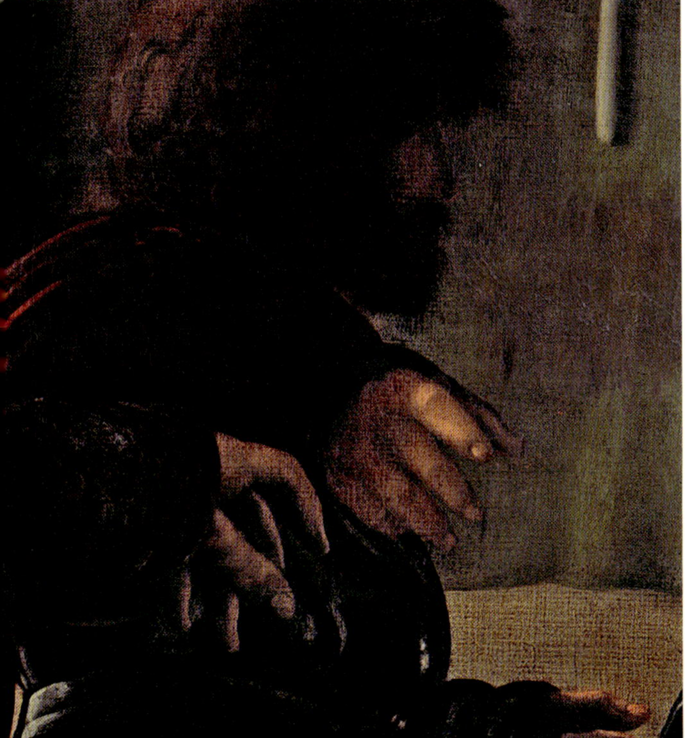

▲▼ Two mirrors, gleaming metal and other reflective surfaces multiply the image of the man in his armour. After moving to the Veneto, Savoldo became involved in the art scene and cultural debates of the Most Serene Republic, but remained ever mindful of Lombard naturalism while mastering the northern Italian painters' techniques of conveying light and atmosphere.

Literature

Dosso Dossi
Melissa
1520

Oil on canvas, 176 × 174 cm

Rome, Galleria Borghese

Dosso Dossi

(Giovanni di Niccolò Luteri)

Unknown locality between Mantua and
Ferrara (possibly Dosso Mantovano),
c. 1490–Ferrara, 1542

Perhaps the wittiest painter of the Italian
Renaissance, Dosso was the primary
master of the early 16th-century school
of Ferrara, which was influenced by the
taste of Duke Alfonso d'Este. Dosso
became the Este family's official painter
in 1514 and coordinated the duke's
decorative projects, which involved
Giovanni Bellini and Titian, among others.
Although working in a provincial city,
Dosso remained constantly up-to-date
through frequent trips to Venice, Rome
and Florence. He also received important
commissions in cities like Pesaro
and Trento. Dosso Dossi's production
alternated altarpieces with decorative
canvas and fresco cycles on literary and
mythological themes. He enlivened his
essentially Venetian style with a vivid
and independent narrative vein, developed
through a close relationship with Ludovico
Ariosto, a leading early 16th-century
Italian poet who was connected with
the court of Ferrara.

Despite the rapidly changing international order, some aristocratic Italian courts remained refined laboratories of art and poetry, even in the 16th century. Splendid art collections and an active literary life became a distinctive trait of the minor states that strove to maintain their autonomy and identity. The relationship between poets and painters was naturally close in the courts. Ferrara is a typical case: there, thanks above all to Duke Alfonso d'Este, the presence of the great writer Ludovico Ariosto (author of *Orlando Furioso*) spurred on and influenced the visual arts as well.

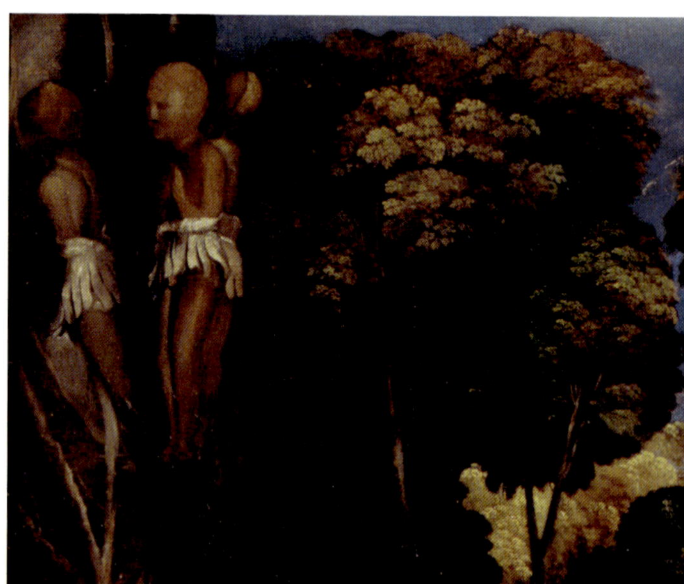

▲ In a fascinating example of visual
interpretation of a literary text, Dosso Dossi,
court painter to Duke Alfonso d'Este, illustrated
a passage from the epic poem that Ariosto had
composed in Ferrara. The good fairy Melissa
brings *Orlando Furioso* to a happy ending,
freeing the paladins from the spell of the evil
sorceress Alcina, who had transformed them
into harmless little dolls (visible at top left).

► For centuries art historians
misinterpreted the subject
of this fine painting as Circe
preparing to cast a spell.
However, this is not the
formidable enchantress from
the *Odyssey* but the 'good'
enchantress Melissa, who
cured Orlando of the furious
madness that gives Ariosto's
poem its title.

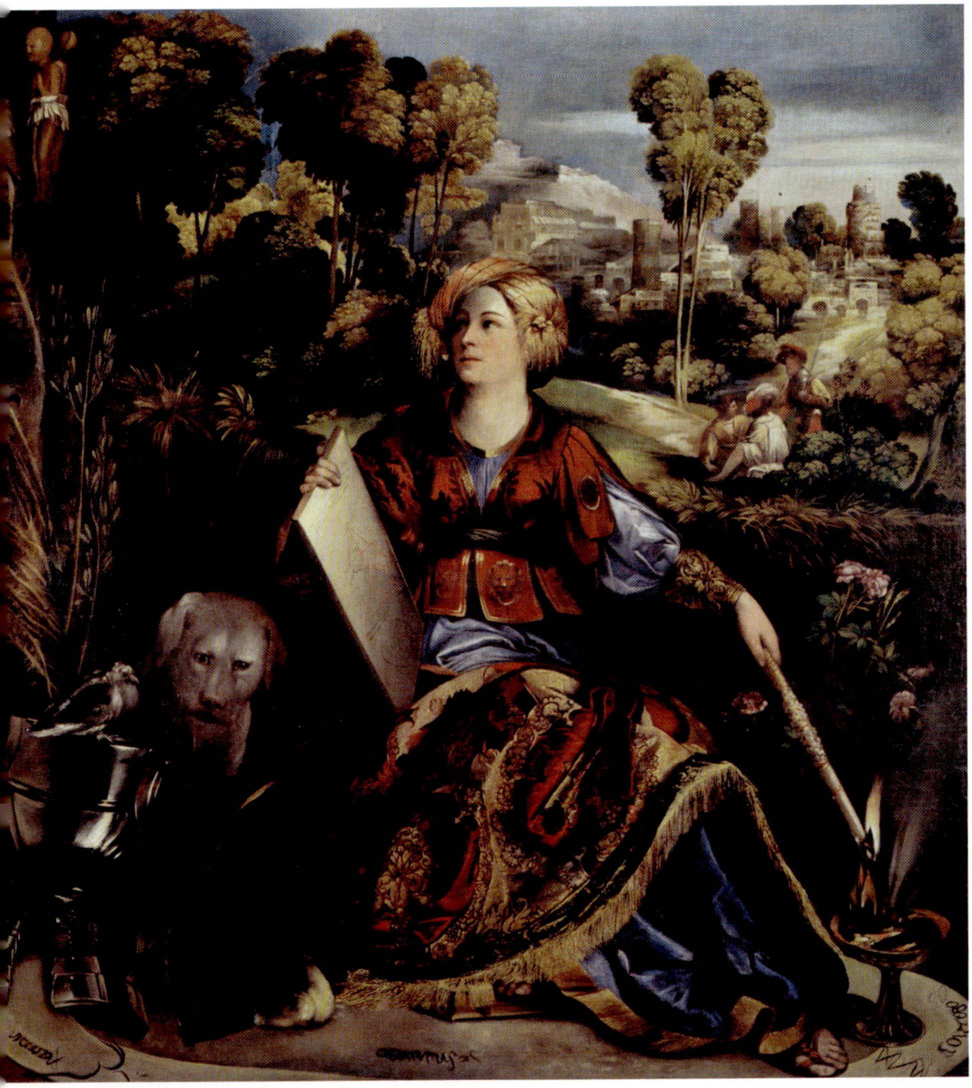

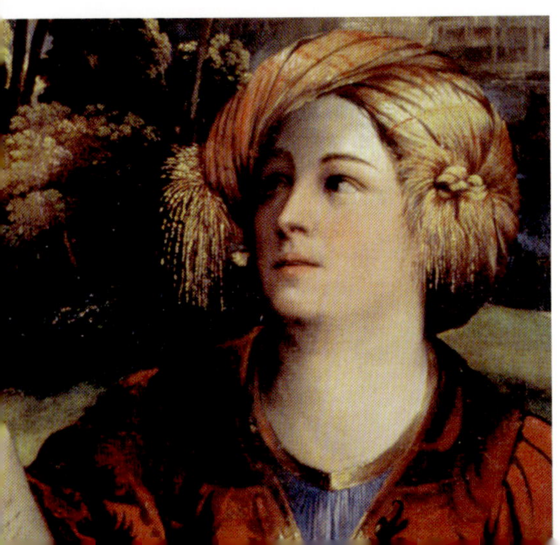

► The enchantress is immersed in a calm, luxuriant, sunlit natural setting, which somehow softens the power of the magic circle and other charms. In the background, a pleasant pastoral view unfolds: figures relax out-of-doors, as if at a picnic.

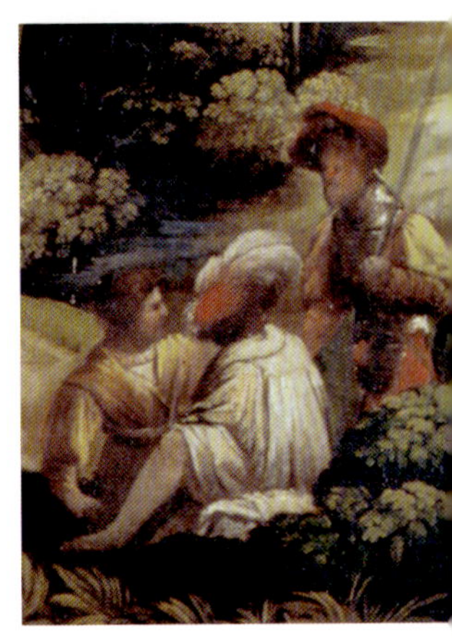

Half-length Figure

Palma Vecchio
The Three Sisters
1520

Oil on panel, 88 × 123 cm
Dresden, Gemäldegalerie

Palma Vecchio

(Jacopo Negretti)

Serina, Bergamo, *c.* 1480–Venice, 1528

Like many other inland artists active in Venice, Palma represents the 'moderate' painters of the Serenissima in the early 16th century. His nickname 'Vecchio' (elder) distinguishes him from his nephew of the same name, Jacopo Palma Giovane (younger), an outstanding Venetian painter of the late Renaissance. Palma Vecchio's paintings almost always present a serene, diffuse light, composition that fits well with the landscape, light colours and an atmosphere of calm beauty. A native of Bergamo, Palma Vecchio moved to Venice in 1510. His successful career developed along two distinct lines: he produced quiet, devout altar paintings for the churches of Venice and the Veneto, and secular canvases of voluptuous blondes for the private collectors.

► As confirmed by 16th-century handbooks on beauty, Venetian women lightened their hair by spending hours in the sun and using various products. If one carefully studies the women painted by Palma Vecchio, one gets the impression they are not entirely natural blondes.

The half-length figure, much appreciated by private collectors, became an essential feature of early 16th-century artistic production in Italy. Led by Titian, painters in the Veneto created an impressive number of delightful variations. Palma Vecchio painted charming sacred and secular ladies who reflected the Venetian ideal of calm, generous beauty – shapely blondes with thick, soft, free-flowing hair. This type of image usually showed young women in the foreground in half-length. Two particular variants – the reclining nude and the group of young bathers – were clearly meant for the art market.

The Social and Cultural Role of the Courtesan

Sumptuously adorned, raised on high platform shoes, dazzlingly beautiful but not shameless or vulgar, courtesans (cortigiane) are characteristic figures of the Venetian Renaissance. Their main purpose was to entertain men, but they did not restrict themselves to providing their clients with physical pleasure. Like the Japanese geisha, the Venetian courtesan received a thorough education in the humanities. Many were virtuoso performers on musical instruments, while others are still remembered in literary anthologies as refined poets. All were able to converse at an elevated level. Endowed with a strong sense of self, Venetian courtesans seem to prefigure 20th-century women's liberation from their secondary role in society and art. In the second half of the 16th century, however, with the stringent restrictions imposed by the Counter-Reformation, courtesans withdrew from public view, limited once again to the most physical and commonplace aspects of their profession.

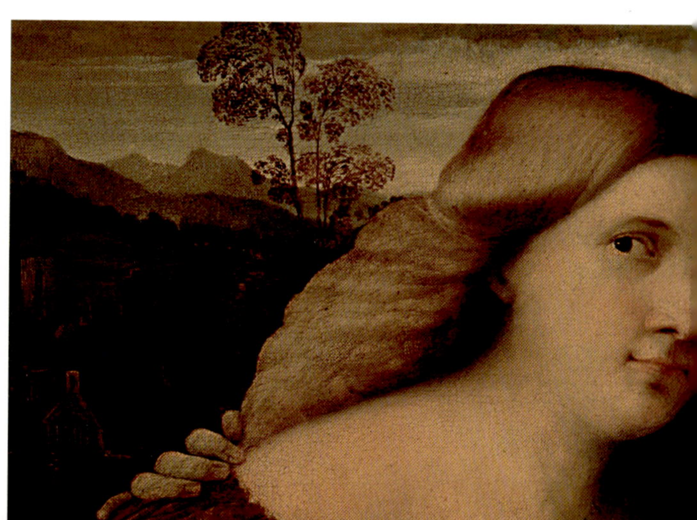

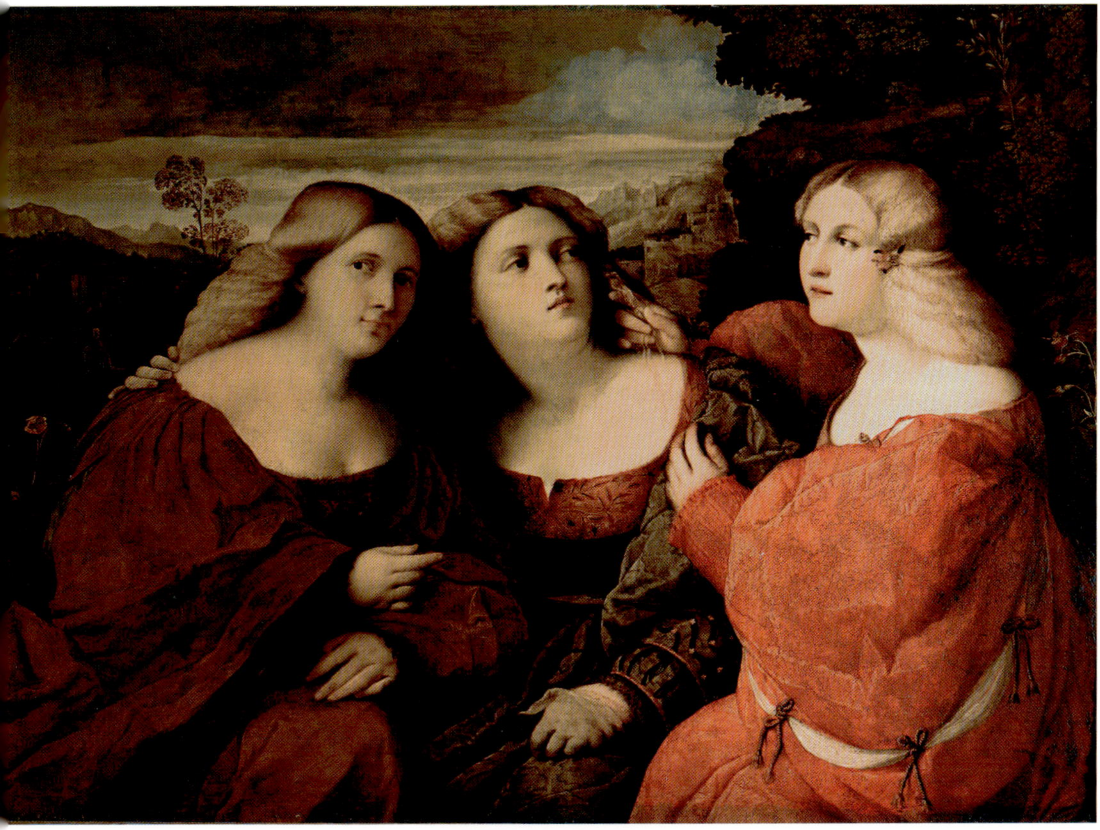

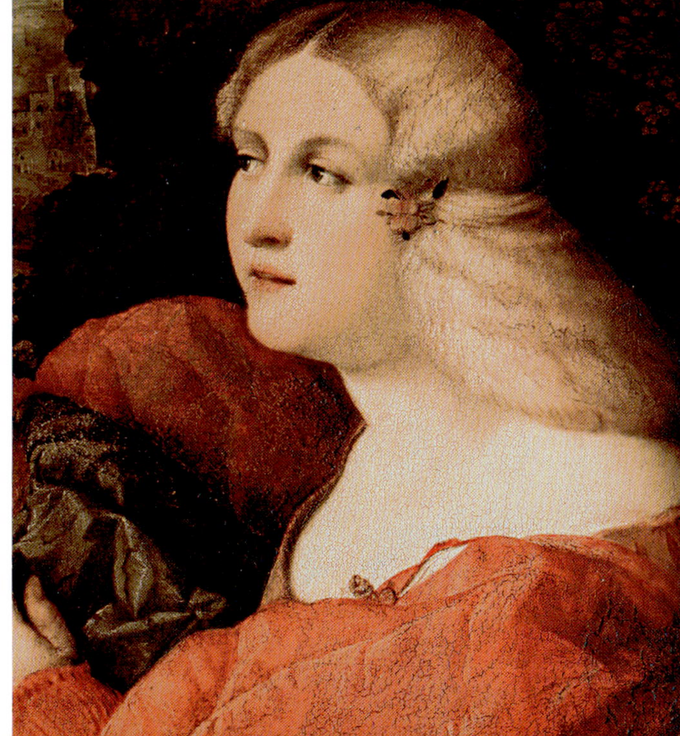

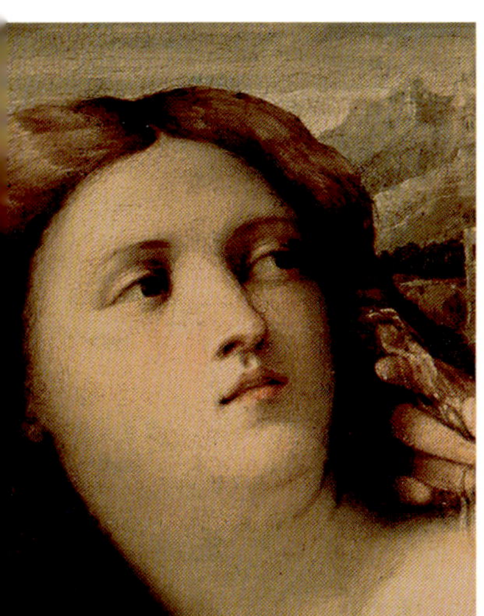

The full puff sleeves worn by the woman at the right echo the figure's roundness. Palma Vecchio always uses soft shapes and curved lines to suggest a generous buxomness and gentle, expansive beauty. It has been reported that the painter's favourite model was a girl named Violante, who may have been his daughter.

Eloquence

Pordenone
Crucifixion
1520–2

Fresco, 900 × 1200 cm

Cremona, Cathedral

Pordenone

(Giovanni Antonio de' Sacchis)

Pordenone, *c.* 1483–Ferrara, 1539

A likeable and resourceful 'provincial' artist, active throughout a wide area of northeastern Italy, Pordenone created not only spectacular fresco cycles but also notable altar paintings. He began working in his native region of Friuli around 1510. A trip to Rome rounded out his artistic culture, providing first-hand knowledge of Michelangelo and Raphael as well as the opportunity to admire the prints of Dürer. Beginning with the frescoes in the cathedral of Treviso, Pordenone embarked upon a series of commissions. Between 1520 and 1522 he was in Cremona, where he painted frescoes in the cathedral on the large counter façade and scenes of the Passion along the aisle. After that came works in Friuli (Spilimbergo, Pordenone), a first short stay in Venice and, in about 1530, other important painting cycles in Piacenza and Cortemaggiore, between Emilia and Lombardy. Contact with the work of Gaudenzio Ferrari, Correggio and Parmigianino gave his painting a new expressive content. Pordenone returned to Venice as an eminent artist, and, before his sudden, mysterious death on a trip to Ferrara, Titian looked upon him as a dangerous rival.

Covered with frescoes in the first half of the 16th century, the interior of the Romanesque cathedral of Cremona exhibits the work of various masters. The cycle on the Passion of Christ has a monumental rhythm and daring use of perspective, a result of Venetian style intersecting with the realism and popular pathos of the Lombard tradition. The cathedral's interior façade is entirely covered by the impressive *Crucifixion* painted by the energetic Friulian painter Pordenone. The scene's violence and drama unfurl with an all-encompassing theatricality. The swirling composition, with its strong tendency towards effects popular with Lombard audiences, differs greatly from the traditional arrangement of a Calvary.

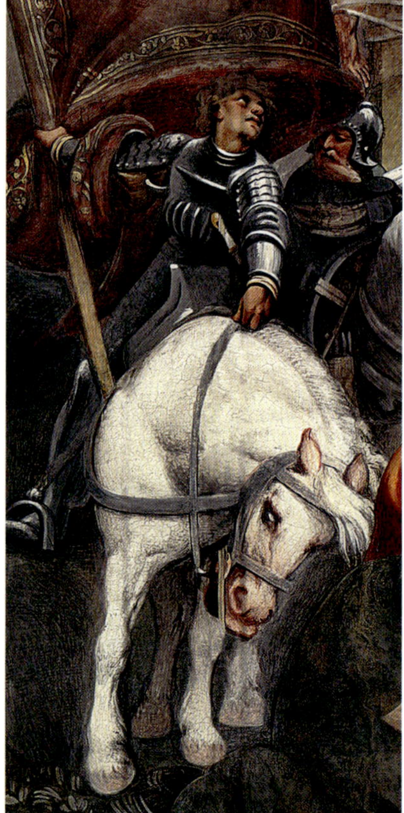

◄ The space of Pordenone's paintings often swells with figures and expansive drapery.

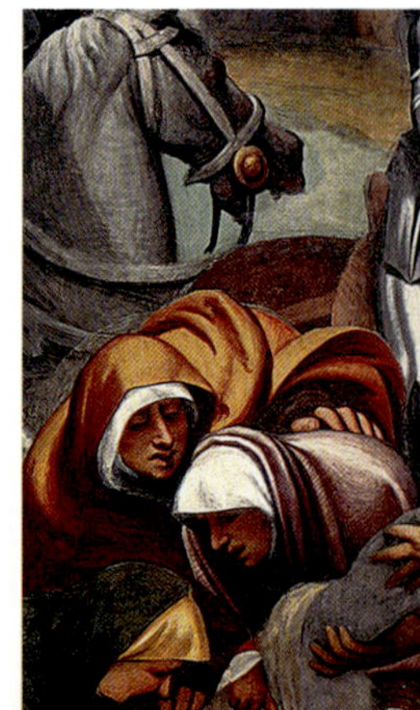

▼ The whole composition turns on the huge mercenary in the centre, wearing armour and holding a disturbing double-edged broadsword. As in the *Crucifixion* by Gaudenzio Ferrari (see pages 234–5), the group of women with the swooning Virgin Mary is essentially self-contained.

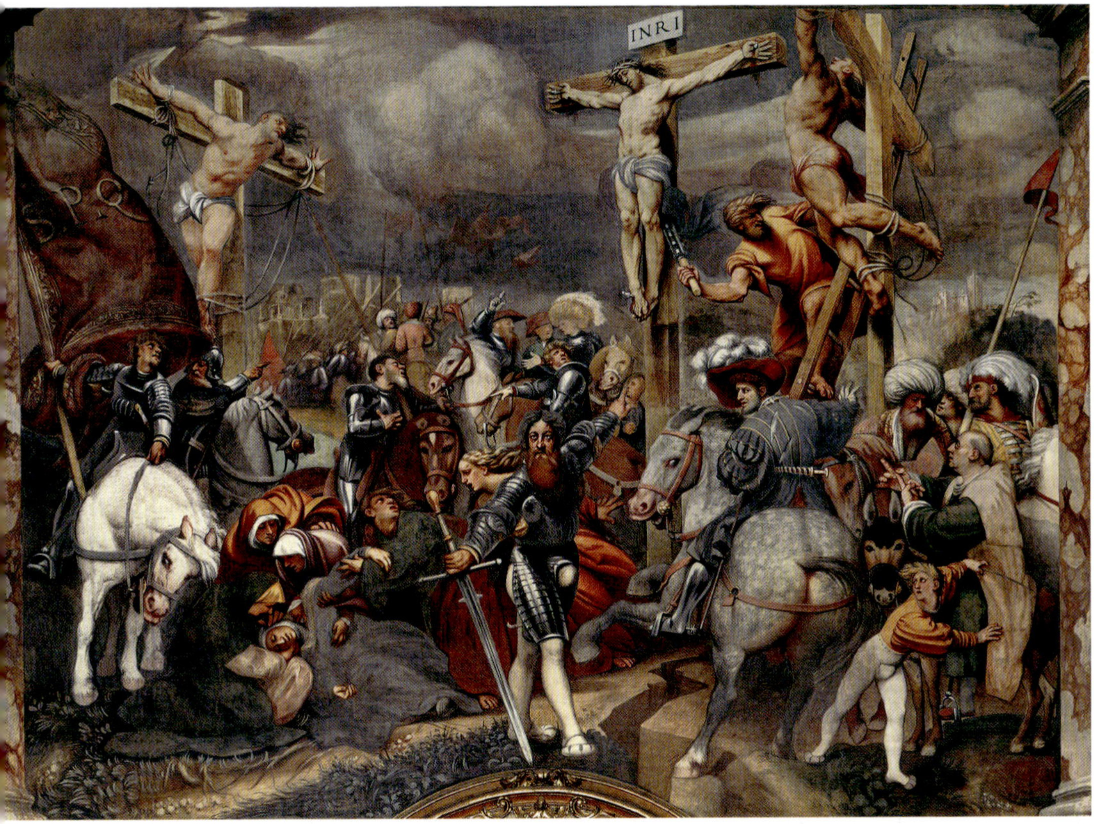

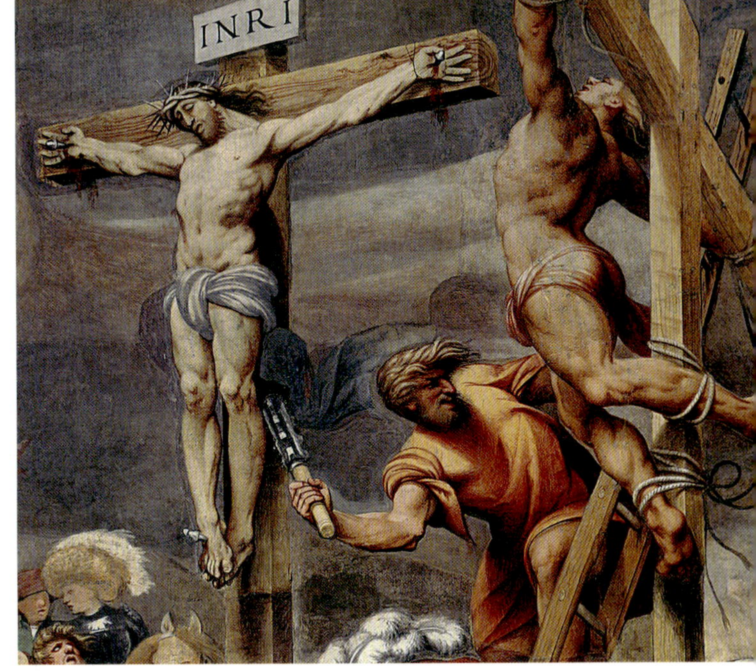

Pordenone employs various tactics to heighten the emotion: a gloomy, stormy atmosphere conjures darting effects of light; the three crosses are disposed asymmetrically and askew; the disorderly crowd stirs in agitation; the abruptly foreshortened horses have an almost demonic appearance; and the tormentors behave with appalling violence.

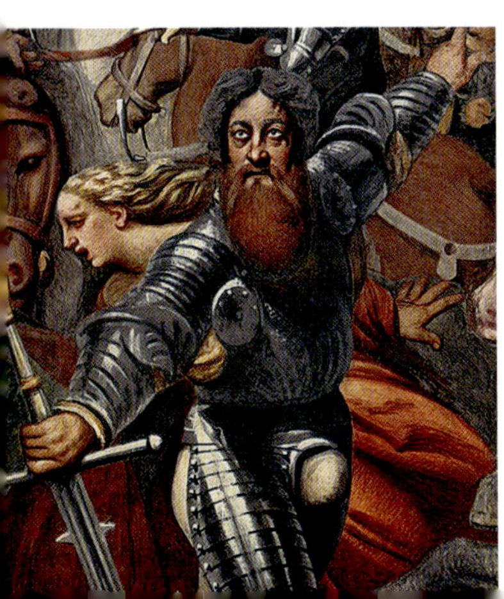

Dome

Correggio
The Vision of St John the Evangelist
1520–1

Fresco, 966 × 888 cm (oval)

Parma, San Giovanni Evangelista

Correggio

(Antonio Allegri)

Correggio (Reggio Emilia), *c.* 1489–1534

Concentrated in the city of Parma, Correggio's bright, joyful painting is not merely a pleasing, good-natured interlude at the height of the Renaissance: it provided a major source for Baroque art and a knowledgeable, skilled demonstration of an alternative to the great schools of Venice and central Italy. Correggio's training was particularly rich. Having grown up with the heritage of Mantegna in Mantua, he independently studied Leonardo, Raphael and the early 16th-century Venetian masters. A first, surprising result is the Camera della Badessa at the convent of San Paolo in Parma (1519). This marked the beginning of a magnificent and distinctive production that immediately continued with the frescoes in the Parmesan church of San Giovanni Evangelista, starting with the dome (1520–1). Then came freely and innovatively conceived altarpieces, with experiments in night scenes, interconnected gestures, smiling facial expressions and convincing colours. Correggio's career in Parma culminated with the *Assumption of the Virgin* in the dome of the cathedral. During the last years of his life, he went back to work for the Gonzaga family, painting two canvases for the *studiolo* of Isabella and four scenes on the Loves of Zeus.

In the spectacular frescoes that Correggio painted in Parma, h moved away from 15th-century models to lay the groundwor for the development of grand Baroque decoration, especially i the huge dome of San Giovanni Evangelista. There, he used *trompe l'oeil* effect: the scene appears to open onto a sky again which the figures are silhouetted. His stylistic reference was th ceiling of the Camera degli Sposi in Mantua, with Mantegna famous 'oculus' (see pages 82 3), but the result is complete different. From the glorification of humanistic perspective, h proceeds to an enveloping, luminous illusionism that antic pates Baroque art.

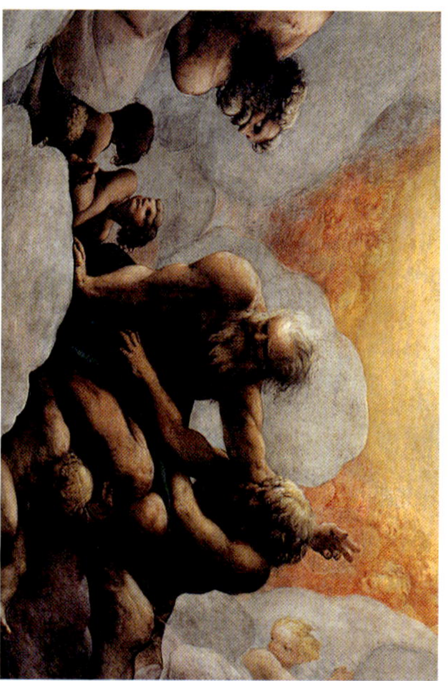

◄ This fresco is the crowning glory of the huge decorative project for the church of San Giovanni Evangelista, annexed to a large Benedictine monastery. In the relatively low and shallow dome, Correggio has represented the vision of St John, who saw Christ surrounded by the Apostles and angels in the sky.

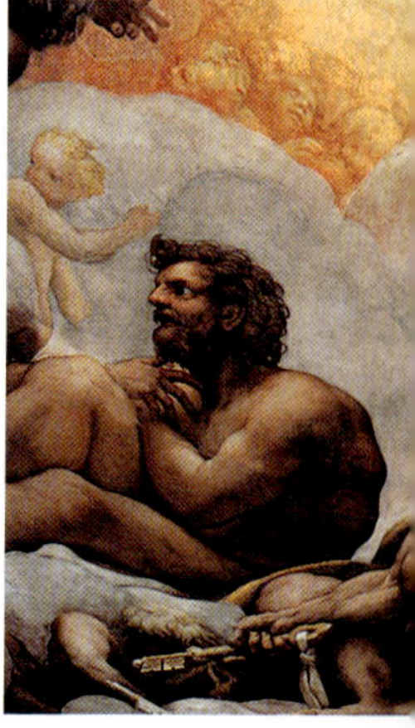

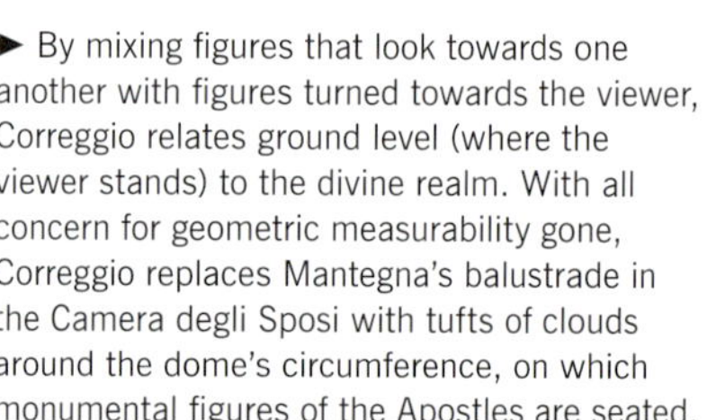

► By mixing figures that look towards one another with figures turned towards the viewer, Correggio relates ground level (where the viewer stands) to the divine realm. With all concern for geometric measurability gone, Correggio replaces Mantegna's balustrade in the Camera degli Sposi with tufts of clouds around the dome's circumference, on which monumental figures of the Apostles are seated.

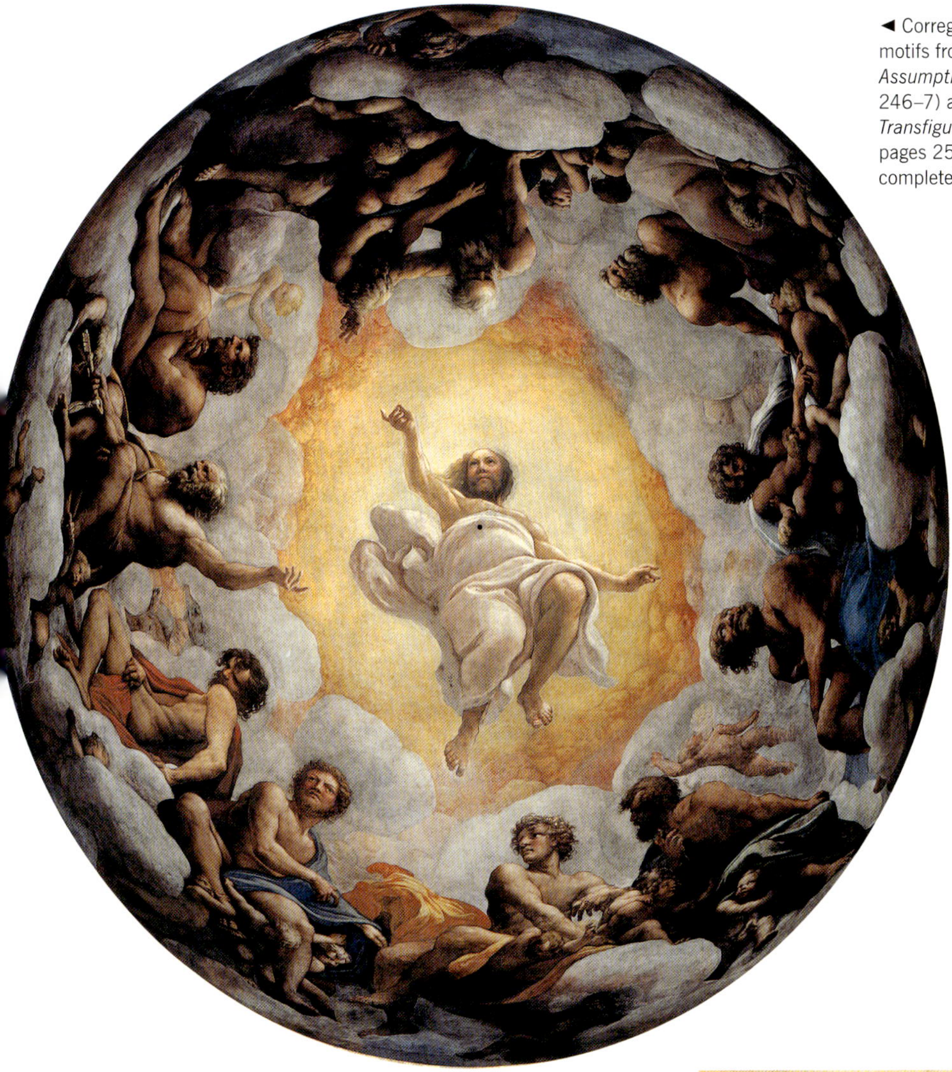

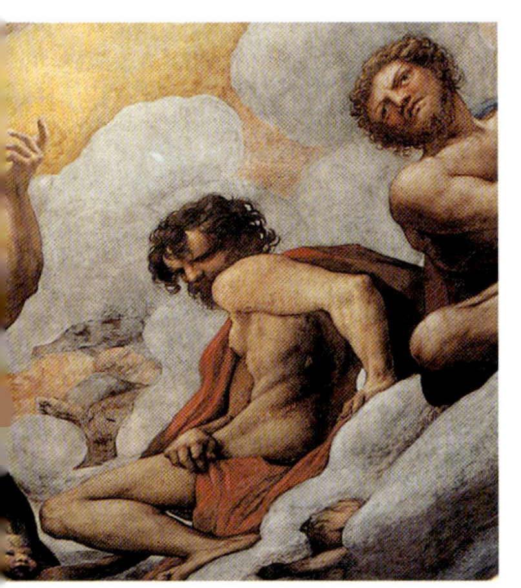

► In an innovative intuition,
Correggio lets the figure of
Christ, wrapped in white,
float in the circle of brilliant
light. The highly effective
foreshortening of the figure
gives the impression that
Christ is truly in motion
at the centre of the dome.

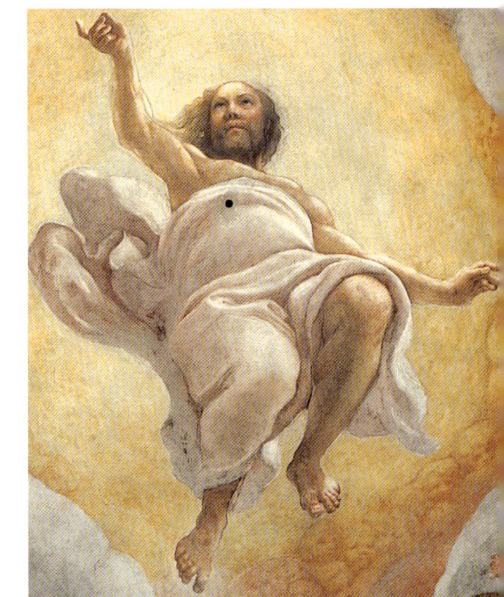

Drama

Rosso Fiorentino
The Deposition
1521

Oil on panel, 375 × 196 cm

Volterra, Pisa, Pinacoteca Civica

Rosso Fiorentino

(Giovanni Battista di Jacopo)

Florence, 1495–Fontainebleau, Paris, 1540

Rosso Fiorentino was an important disseminator of Mannerism to the European courts. A companion of Jacopo Pontormo in the workshop of Andrea del Sarto, Rosso made his start by painting frescoes in the Chiostrino dei Voti at Santissima Annunziata, a true laboratory of Florentine painting in the second decade of the 16th century. His figures often have bizarre, deformed faces that perplexed his patrons. *The Deposition* in Volterra (1521) shows a disconcerting aggressiveness, but above all an absolutely innovative freedom. His style soon evolved: within a few years Rosso left behind the influence of Florence (Jacopo Pontormo and Andrea del Sarto) and submitted to the Roman influence of Michelangelo and then Parmigianino. Profoundly affected by the Sack of Rome (1527), in 1530 Rosso left Italy for France. There he painted the magnificent gallery of the royal palace of Fontainebleau (1532–7) for Francis I.

Pope Leo X, a cultured, peace-loving individual, could n⟨ avert the Lutheran schism, which began in the same year th⟨ Raphael died (1520). This schism brought with it a profoun⟨ rethinking of the approach to art, resulting in Mannerisn⟨ The most radical proposals came from Tuscany. After studyir⟨ the works of Michelangelo and Raphael, Jacopo Pontormo an⟨ Rosso Fiorentino began to paint violently distorted versions ⟨ traditional poses. Their figures seem to be locked in contorte⟨ positions, their faces expressing ambiguous drama. Rosso's larg⟨ altarpiece in Volterra exemplifies early Tuscan Mannerisn⟨ with its misshapen figures and the metallic texture of its disco⟨ certingly harsh colours.

▼ Devoid of any landscape or atmospheric depth, the scene is set against a leaden sky, dense and heavy as an impenetrable cloak of varnished metal. The Florentine painter's icy, austere rendering is completely different from Gaudenzio Ferrari's and Pordenone's depictions of crowds of common people in their *Crucifixions*, painted in northern Italy in the same years (see pages 234–5 and 266–7).

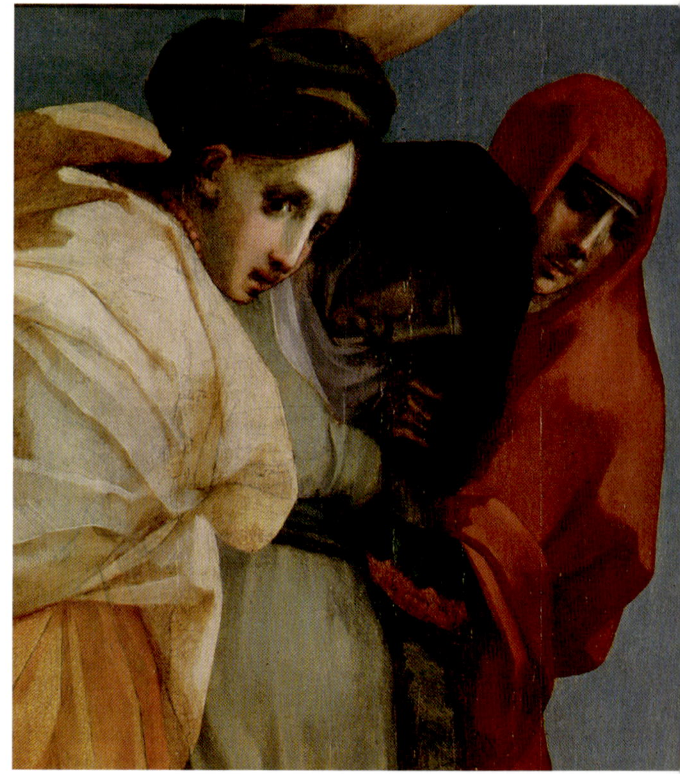

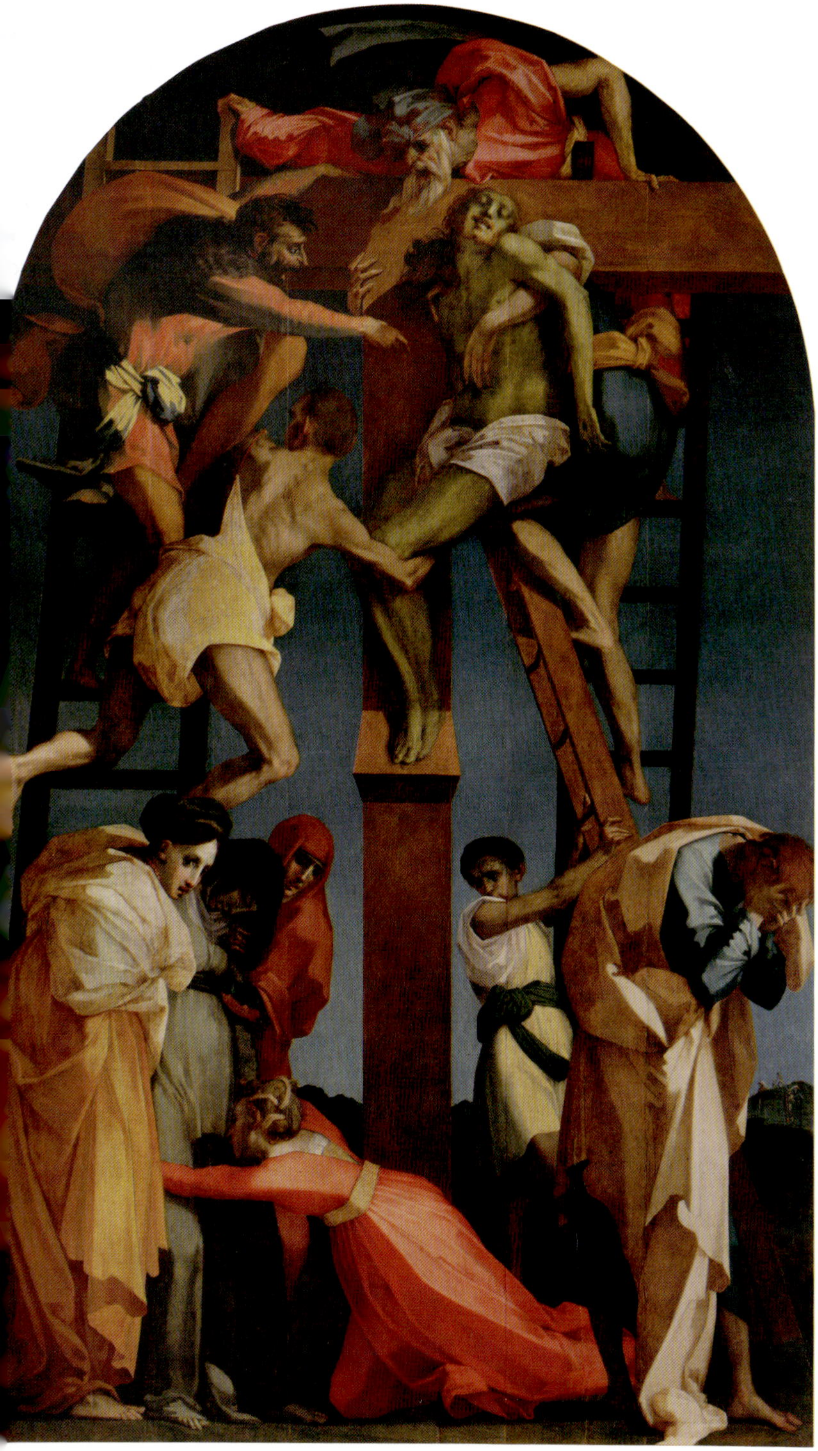

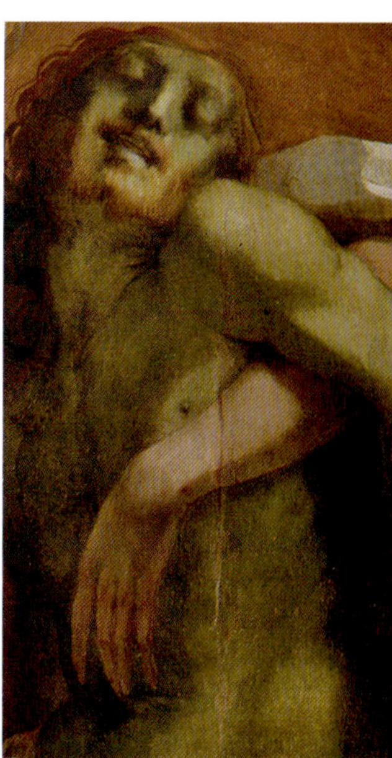

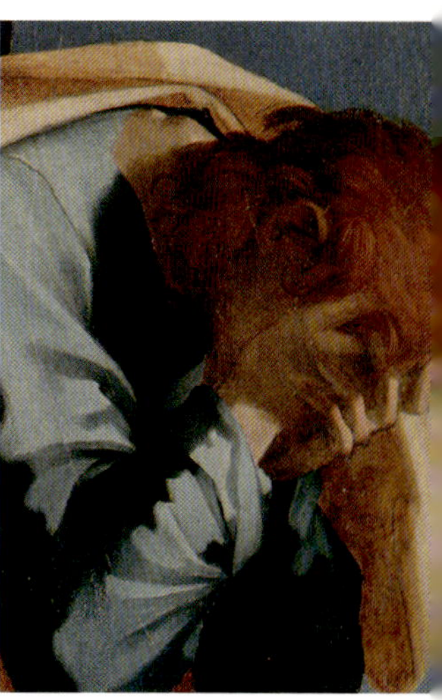

▲▼ A forced, incongruous
structure of ladders and
smooth planks encloses
stone-rigid figures in dramatic,
theatrical poses. The lifeless
body of Christ is livid and
dislocated, and St John
withdraws in despairing grief.

Myth

Titian
The Arrival of Bacchus on the Island of Andros
1521

Oil on canvas, 175 × 193 cm

Madrid, Museo Nacional del Prado

For artist biography, see page 224.

As Renaissance masters and their patrons more freely inte[r]-preted the literature of classical mythology, subjects draw[n] from secular sources became more common. In this Titia[n] played a particularly important role. The classical myths becam[e] a springboard for his free, lively painting style, rich in colou[r] and permeated with a delightful spirit of sensuality. The cyc[le] of *Bacchanals*, intended to decorate Duke Alfonso d'Est[e] Alabaster Chamber in Ferrara, comprised three paintings pl[us] substantial adjustments to a previous work by Giovanni Bellin[i]. Sadly, the dispersal of the Este collection after the duchy wa[s] relocated to Modena in 1598 has made it impossible to reconst[i]-tute the entire group.

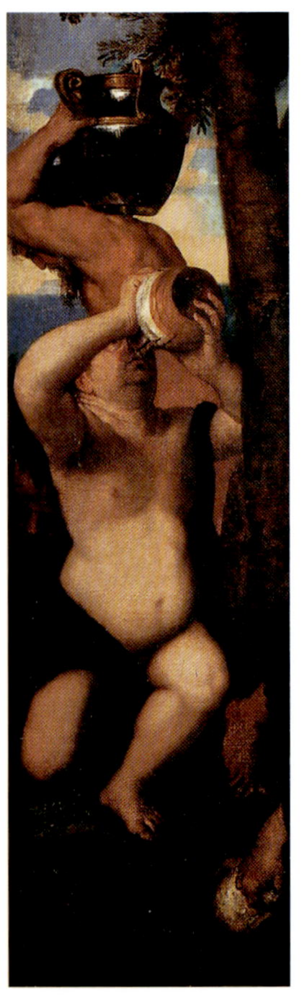

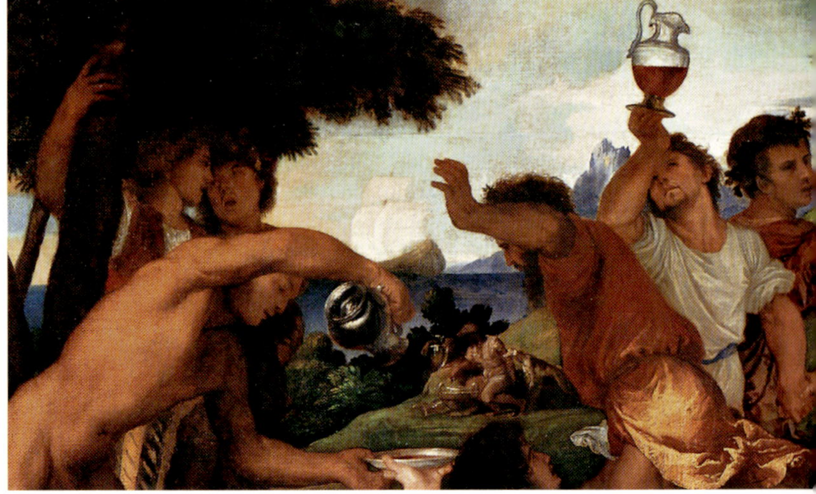

◀ ▲ Together with Giovanni Bellini's *Feast of the Gods*, retouched by Titian, the three *Bacchanals* were the highlights of Alfonso's study, which the duke evidently designed in open competition with the similar *studiolo* of his sister Isabella d'Este in Mantua (see pages 186–7). Like Isabella, Alfonso prescribed a highly literary iconographic programme, but while his sister had preferred paintings inspired by the arts and love, the Duke of Ferrara chose a high-spirited main character: the god of wine and mirth. This vibrant, wine-scented painting is ablaze with light and energy.

► Evidently with the permission of the exuberant patron of the *Bacchanals*, Titian allowed himself broad licence with conventions. A well-known example is the baby urinating in the foreground, just beside a sensual reclining nude.

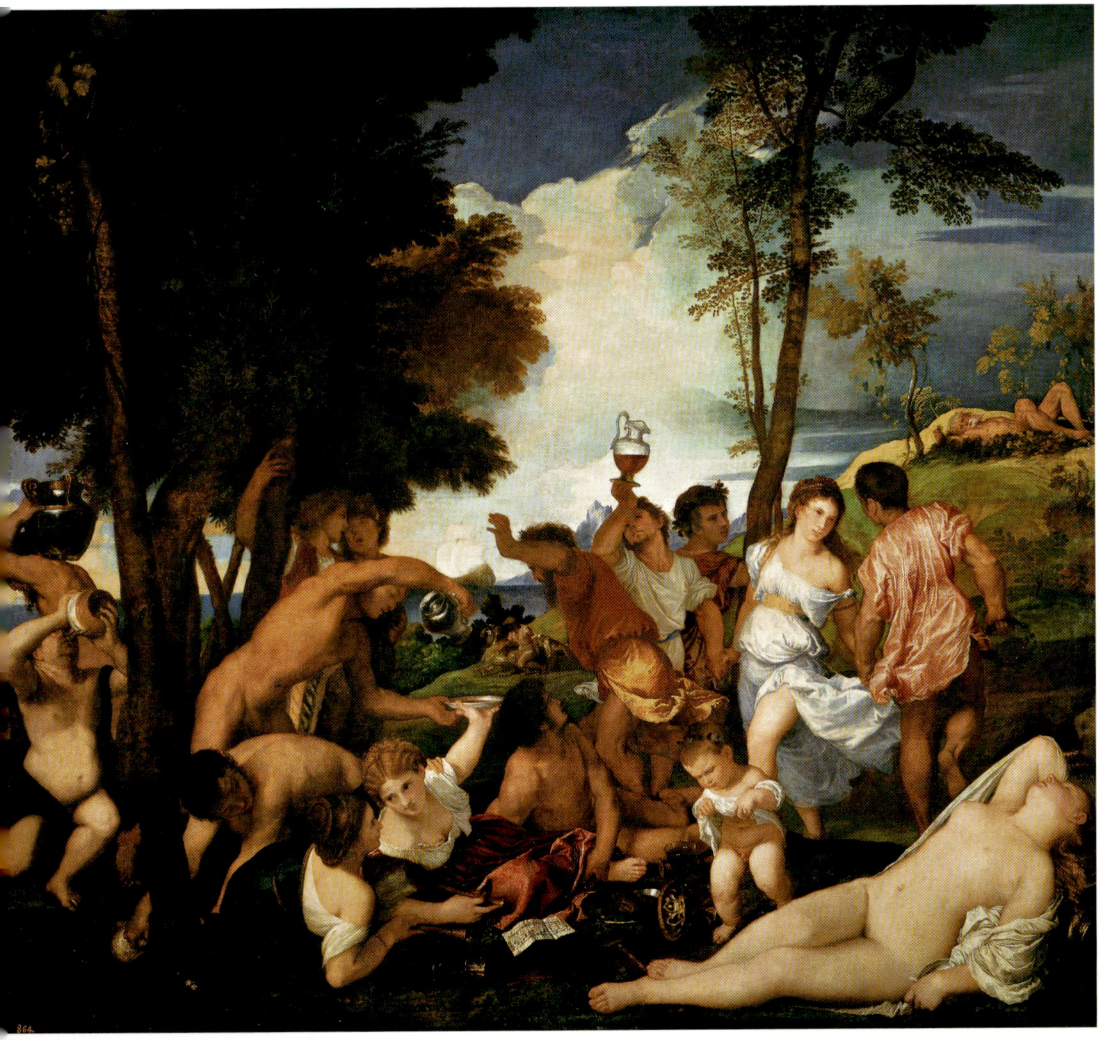

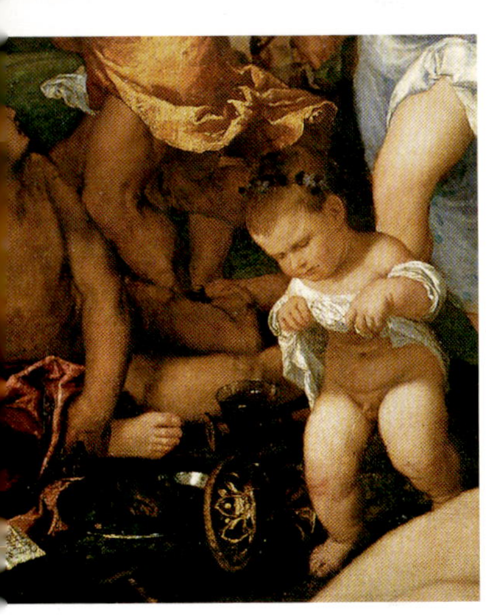

▶ An old man is lying in the grass by himself. This is not a melancholy reference to the 'Three Ages of Man' (see pages 238–9) but a ritual of regeneration through magic herbs, symbolizing the joy and youth brought by dance, love and wine.

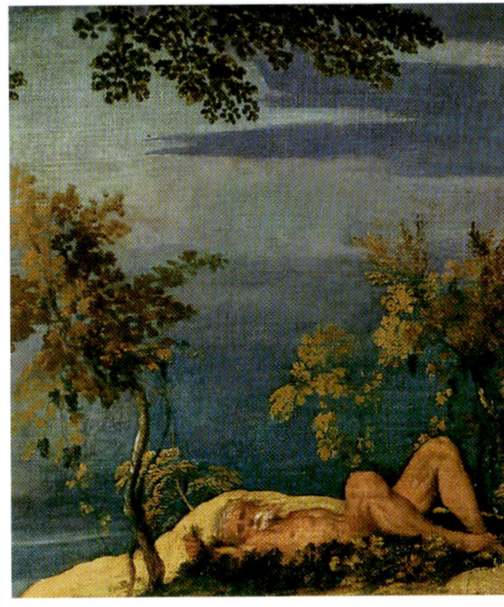

Sacra Conversazione

Lorenzo Lotto
Madonna and Child with Saints
(Sacra Conversazione)
1521

Oil on canvas, 300 × 275 cm
Bergamo, San Bernardino in Pignolo

Lorenzo Lotto

Venice, *c.* 1480–Loreto, 1556/7

A student of Giovanni Bellini, Lorenzo Lotto did not follow the success of *colorito*; rather, working in Treviso and the provinces, he painted in a style that shows his strong interest in northern painting and his remarkable capacity for psychologically penetrating portraiture. After a first stay in the Marche, he went to Rome where he worked alongside Raphael on the Vatican Stanze, but afterwards he became deeply disturbed. He returned to the Marche where he sought a style that could compete with the masters of the Veneto and central Italy. He settled in the peaceful city of Bergamo and there, between 1513 and 1525, he experienced his best years. He painted altarpieces, portraits and fresco cycles, executed brilliant cartoons for the inlaid wood choir stalls at Santa Maria Maggiore and came into contact with the freest and most original northern Italian interpreters of the Renaissance: Gaudenzio Ferrari, Correggio and Pordenone. Back in Venice in 1525, Lotto again painted magnificent portraits but found little time for them between religious commissions. Marginalized by the circle of painters then working in Venice, and advanced in years, he again returned to the Marche where he found peace and solitude at the Sanctuary of Loreto.

The enthroned Madonna flanked by various saints – th most usual form of altarpiece – is traditionally called a *Sac Conversazione* (Holy Conversation). However, this gener title seldom corresponds to the scene depicted, since the fig ures rarely actually 'converse' with each other. But in a contex where the form and function of altar paintings were bein reconsidered, Lorenzo Lotto introduced the theme of dialogu among the figures who express their emotional and affectiv relationship with eloquent gestures.

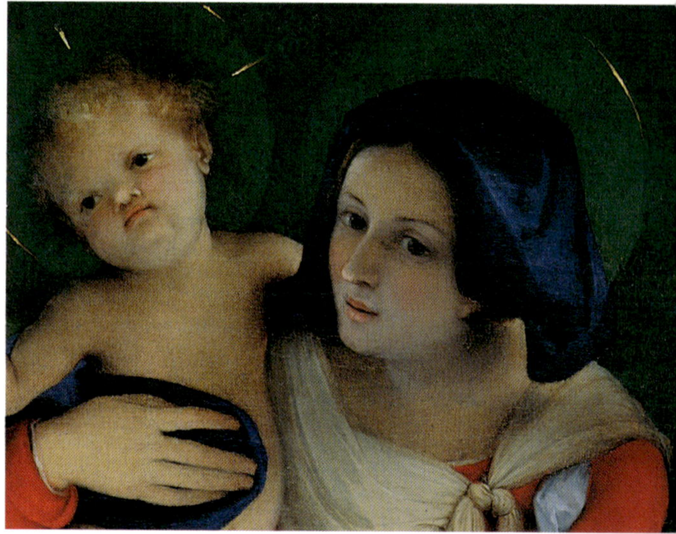

▲ The Madonna's gesture and the child's expression are not from the conventional repertoire. Because Lorenzo Lotto was working in the provinces, he could introduce innovations in this painting that might not have been accepted in Venice or another major city: for example, the green canopy puts the faces of the two main characters in shadow.

► Huddled uncomfortably at the foot of the Virgin's throne, an angel scribe suddenly leaves off recording the conversation and abruptly turns towards the viewer. It is a wry, direct gaze that insistently claims our attention and draws us into the scene.

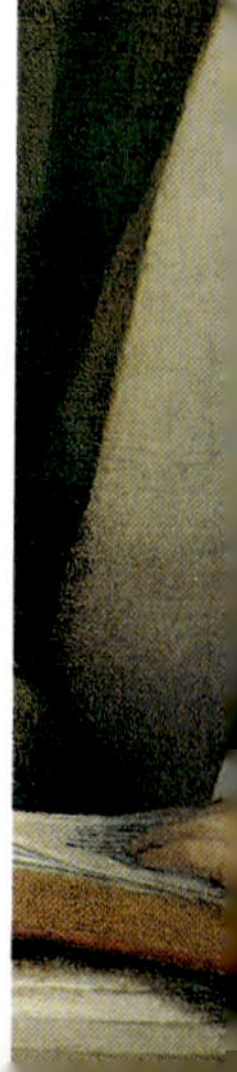

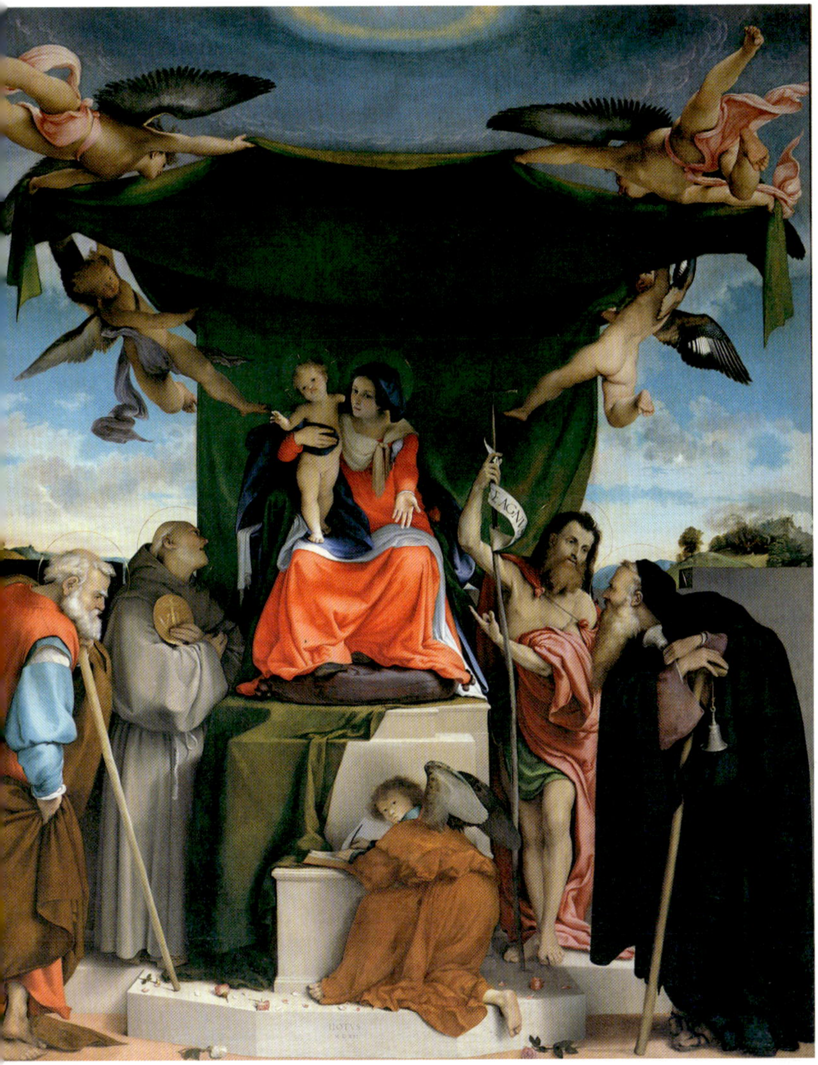

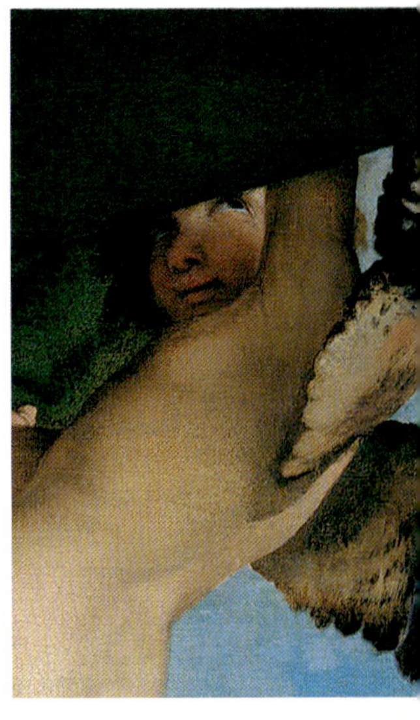

▲ While 15th-century altarpieces were enclosed within solid, symmetrical architectural spaces, this setting seems precarious, temporary, fleeting. To shelter Mary and the Child, four angels labour to stretch a large green canopy over them, but the drapery seems about to escape from their grip.

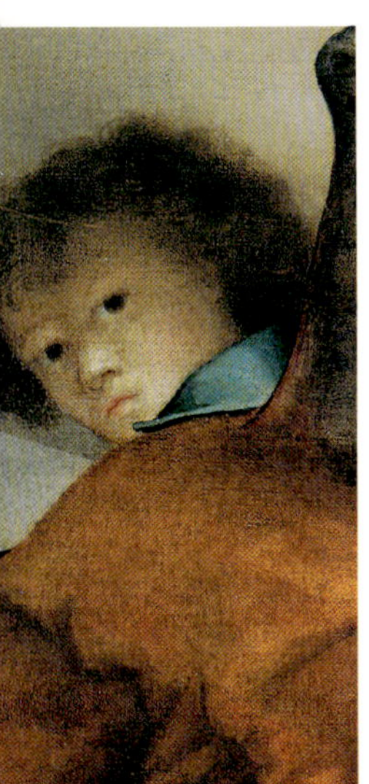

► The dialogue is particularly animated between John the Baptist and the old Anthony Abbot, two ascetic saints of resolute and prickly character. Both spent periods of penance in the desert, resisting physical and spiritual temptation.

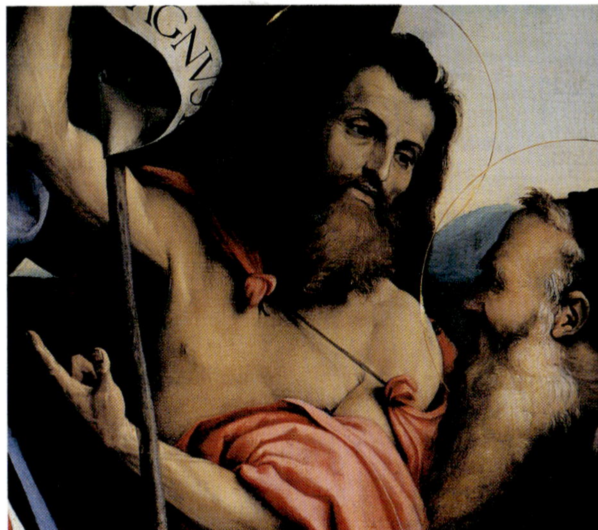

Mannerism

Jacopo Pontormo
*The Bearing of Christ's Body
to the Tomb*
1525–8

Oil on panel, 313 × 192 cm
Florence, Santa Felicita

Jacopo Pontormo

(Jacopo Carucci)

Pontorme, Florence, 1494–Florence,
1557

A master of the 'irregular', Jacopo
Pontormo led the way as Florentine
painting moved from the High
Renaissance to Mannerism. He is an
engaging figure not only because of the
drama of his paintings but also for the
contradictions and tensions that caused
this brilliant and courageous man to
lapse into fits of anxiety. He left written
accounts of his torment in a slender
diary, and the 'Life' compiled by Vasari
mentions it as well. A brilliant student
of Andrea del Sarto, Pontormo arrived
on the Florentine scene with the frescoes
at the Santissima Annunziata, which
express a strong inclination for novelty.
Drawn to Michelangelo and the prints of
Dürer, in the 1520s Pontormo was the
most sought-after and admired painter
in Florence. He received prestigious
commissions, such as the *Story of
Joseph* for the Borgherinis (today in the
National Gallery, London), the decoration
of the Medicean villa at Poggio a Caiano
and the frescoes in the cloister of the
Charterhouse (or Certosa) of Galluzzo
(1523–5). However, after the dramatic
siege of Florence (1529), Pontormo
became increasingly withdrawn, and
in the last years of his life he embarked
upon some ill-fated undertakings that
intensified his melancholy.

Jacopo Pontormo led the change in direction of Florentine
painting during the High Renaissance and, along with Rosso
Fiorentino, he was the first exponent of Mannerism, the style
that developed in the middle decades of the 16th century.
The frescoes in the cloister of the Charterhouse of Galluzzo and
the decoration of the Capponi Chapel decisively influenced the
campaign for new expressive effects. The altarpiece *The Bearing
of Christ's Body to the Tomb* for the altar of the Capponi Chapel
can be considered the 'manifesto' of Mannerism. As often happens in art history, Mannerism was initially an innovative style
that broke with tradition, but within a generation it had become the typical, even conventional, expression of Renaissance
courts internationally.

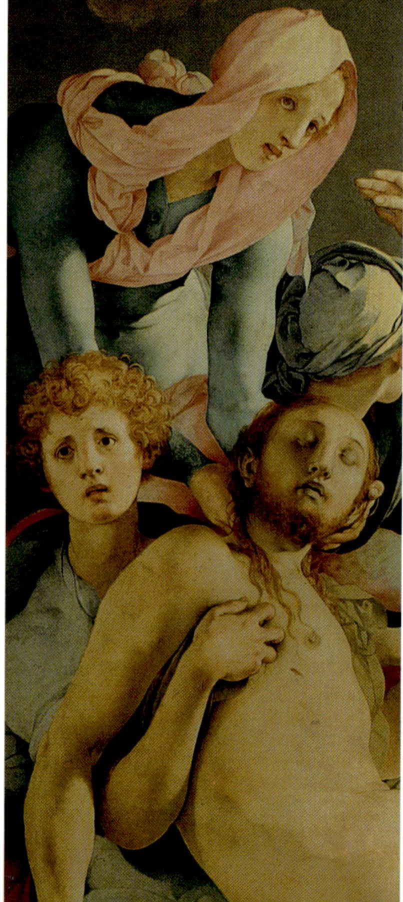

◄ The symmetrical structure
that regulated humanistic
painting collapses into an
intentionally ambiguous
composition. The figures,
with their highly charged
gestures and features, seem
to wander aimlessly in an
uncertain space of livid,
unreal colours.

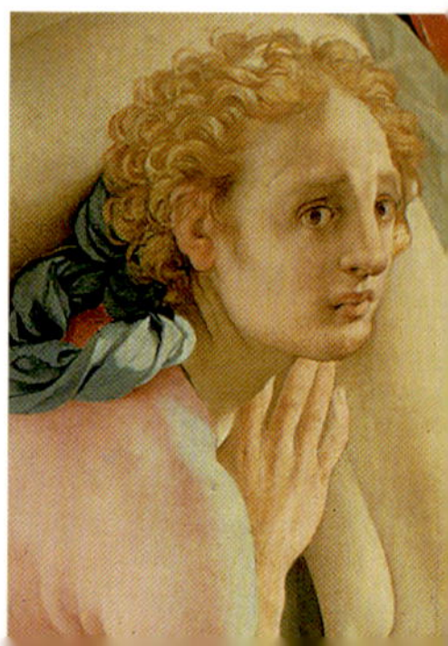

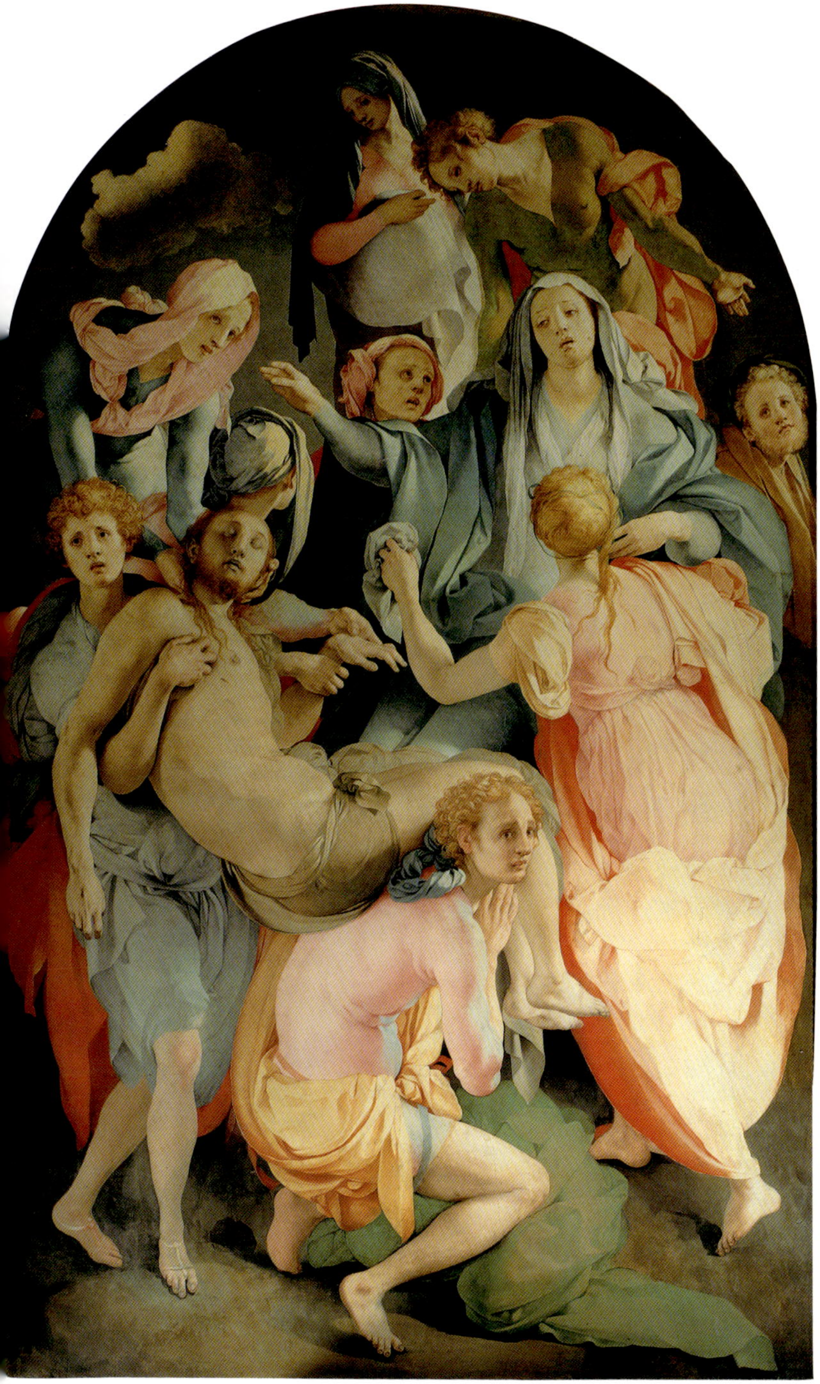

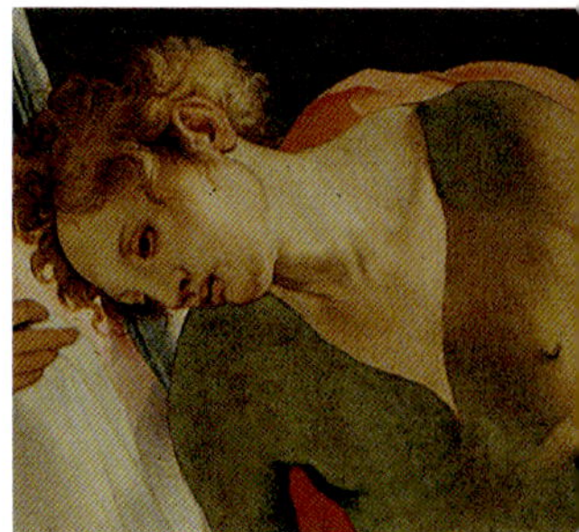

▲ Some figures, following
the panel's contours, are
distributed unnaturally around
the composition like an
ornamental frieze. Nothing
at all hints at a landscape,
backdrop or architecture.
The little cloud at the left
is unnaturally placed.

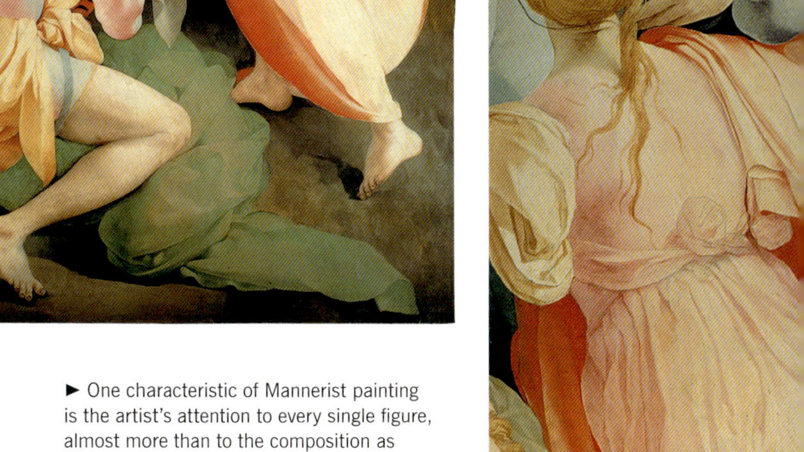

◄ The figure crouching in the foreground
turns towards the viewer with a beseeching
look of dismay. The whole painting gives an
impression of uncertainty and unease.

► One characteristic of Mannerist painting
is the artist's attention to every single figure,
almost more than to the composition as
a whole.

Male Nude

Rosso Fiorentino
The Dead Christ with Angels
1525

Oil on canvas, 133.5 × 104 cm
Boston, Museum of Fine Arts

For artist biography, see page 270.

Taking its cue from the example of Michelangelo, artistic doctrine in the 16th century considered the most elevated theme in painting to be the human figure – or more precisely the male nude, so long as it was in isolation or within a moralistic narrative. During Clement VII's papacy, before the catastrophic Sack of Rome, artists such as Parmigianino and Rosso Fiorentino were in the city, and sensual motifs and refined languor dominated painting. The narrative subject was almost inconsequential: the flawless rendering of anatomy, athletic musculature and expression of feeling were all that mattered.

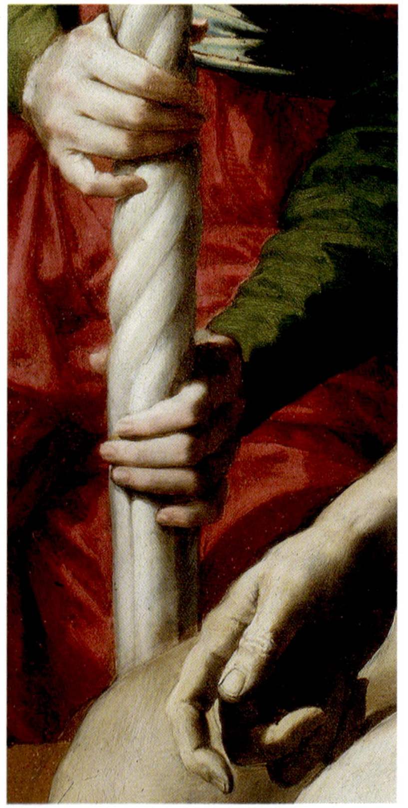

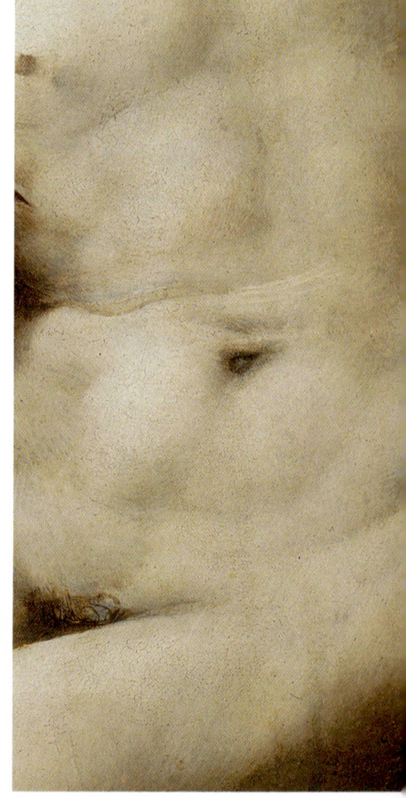

◄ The angels carry large, spiral candles, typical of those burned at funerals. The Mannerists considered spiral movement (called 'serpentine motion' by Vasari), to be the height of elegance. The series of curves and countercurves of Christ's limp body spectacularly confirm this.

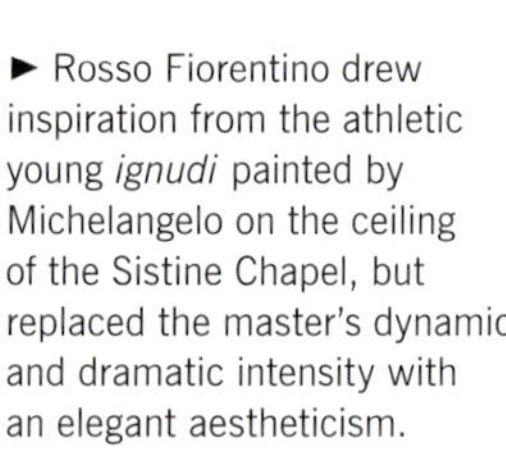

► Rosso Fiorentino drew inspiration from the athletic young *ignudi* painted by Michelangelo on the ceiling of the Sistine Chapel, but replaced the master's dynamic and dramatic intensity with an elegant aestheticism.

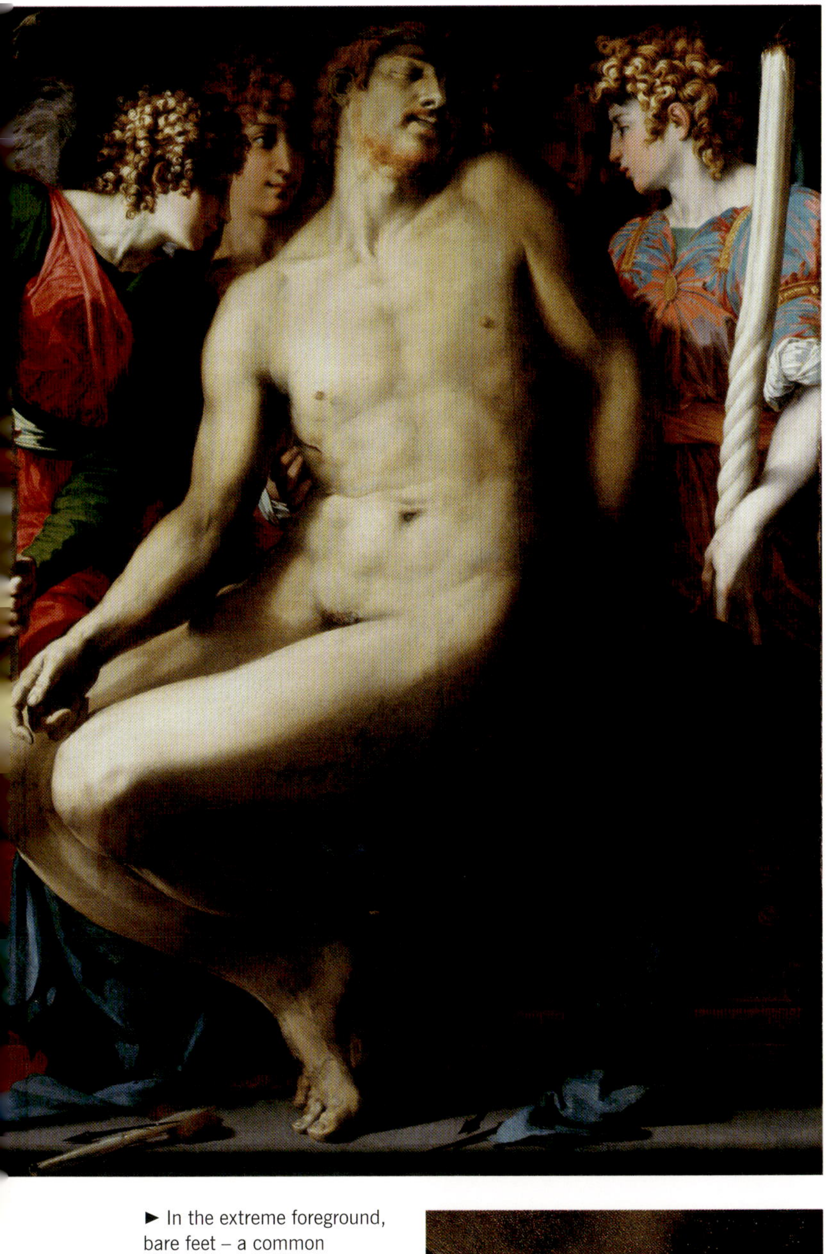

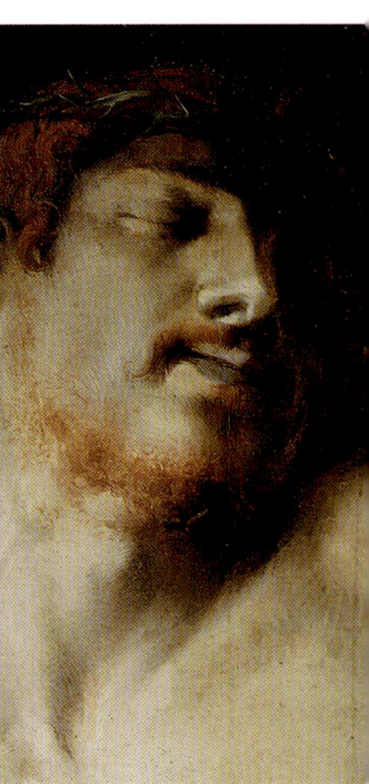

▲ Perfectly balanced between Christian pathos and classical exaltation of the male nude, this work remained a quintessential example of Mannerist painting throughout the 16th century.

► In the extreme foreground, bare feet – a common Mannerist detail – rest on the ground in a way that suggests and continues the spiral movement of the body. This is also found in the work of Parmigianino (see pages 296–7 and 306–7).

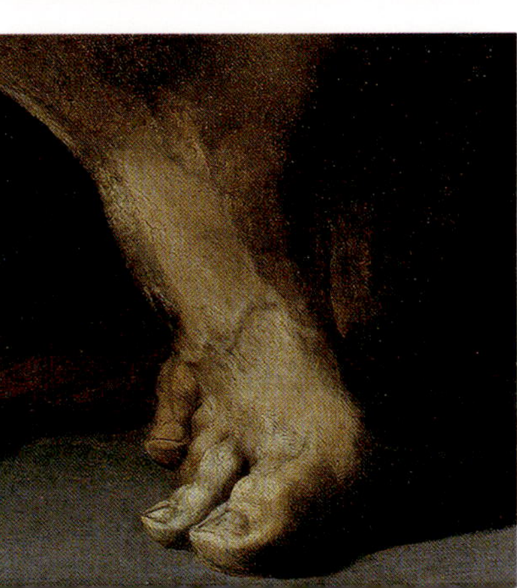

Torsion

Parmigianino
The Vision of St Jerome
1526–7

Oil on panel, 343 × 149 cm
London, National Gallery

Parmigianino

(Francesco Mazzola)

Parma, 1503–Casalmaggiore, Piacenza,
1540

In a succession of masterpieces from
the 1520s and 1530s, Parmigianino's
refined intellectual manner openly
competed with the gentle, joyful style of
his master, Correggio, and made Parma
a fascinating laboratory of Renaissance
art. By the age of 20 Parmigianino
had painted a major work with traits
that foreshadowed Mannerism: *The
Bath of Diana* at the Rocca Sanvitale
in Fontanellato, not far from Parma.
In 1524, he went to Rome and became
a leading spirit in the effervescent artistic
climate of Clement VII's court. Following
the Sack of Rome (1527), Parmigianino
returned north to Emilia where he spent
several years in Bologna before returning
in 1531 again to Parma. Unnaturally
elongated figures and twisting poses are
typical of his art from these years. In the
frescoes that he executed in the church
of the Madonna della Steccata, however,
his final scenes show a refined, stylized
classical inspiration.

One of the strangest painters of the early 16th century i
Italy, Parmigianino was a precocious student of Correggic
His psychological 'crises', his early death at the age of 37 an
his documented interest in alchemy made him a legendar
mysterious figure. More than anything, though, Parmigianino
reputation was built on his early experiments with comple
poses, torsion and vigorous twisting, and complicated, almo
unnatural gestures – all common in international Manneris
painting. Intellectual curiosity and virtuosity (evident in hi
flawless, nervous drawing style) were far more important to th
painter than nature and spontaneity. Although Parmigianin
grew up in the same cultural environment as Correggio, he ar
rived at completely different formal solutions during exactl
the same years.

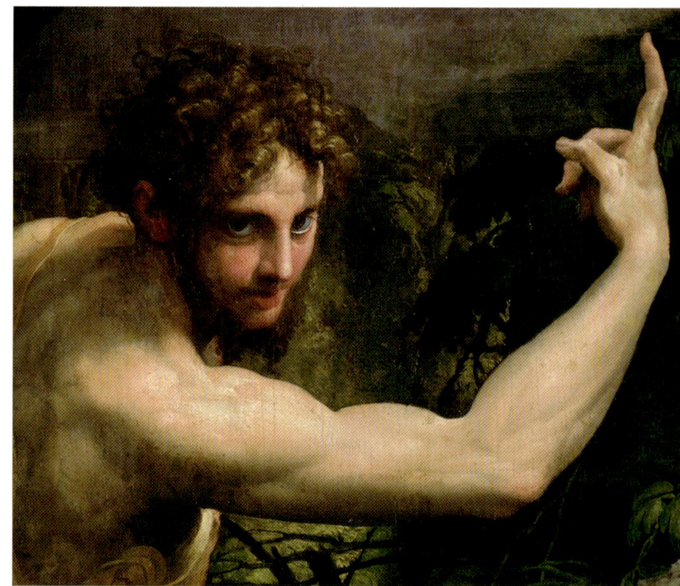

▲ John the Baptist's gesture is eloquent proof of the young
Parmigianino's virtuosity. Leaning dynamically towards the
viewer, the Baptist twists around to point towards the Madonna
and Child behind him. The index finger turned heavenwards,
a gesture also typically used by Leonardo, becomes nervous
and dramatic.

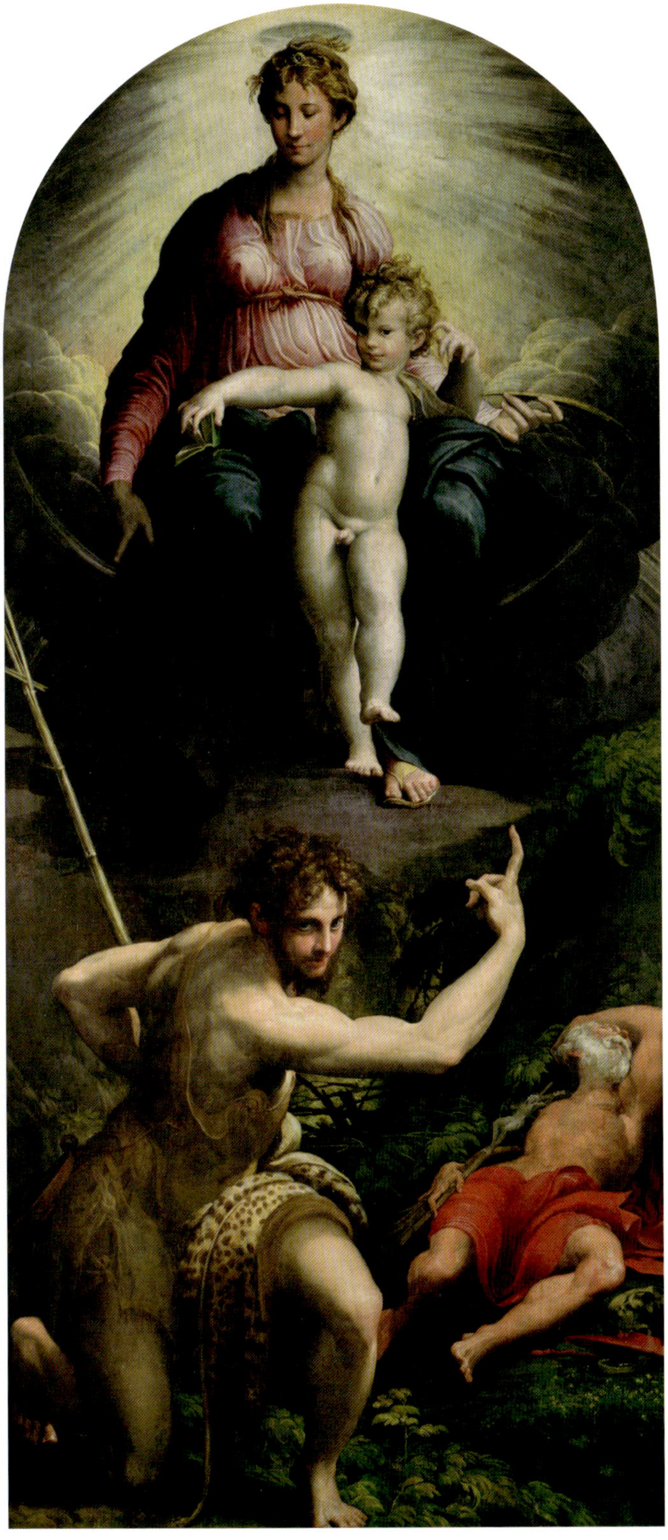

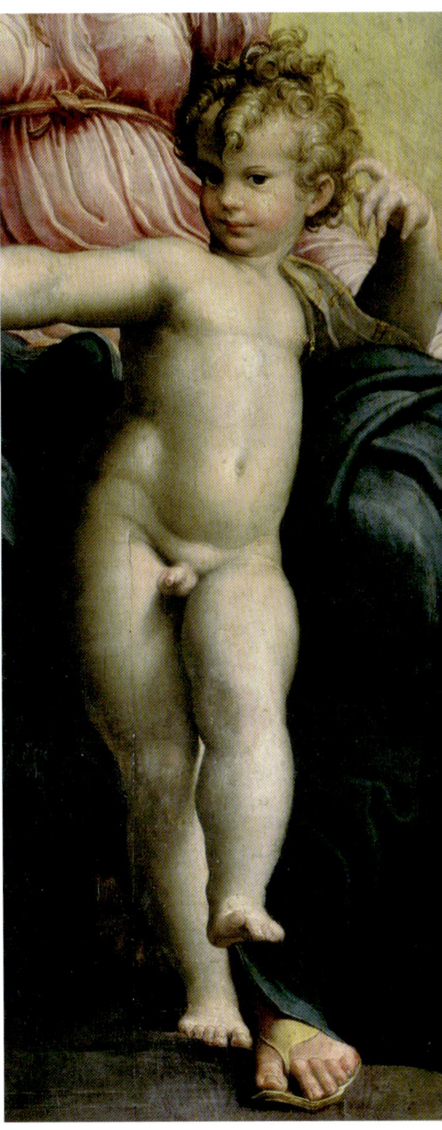

◄ ▲ St John's magnetic gaze contrasts with St Jerome's deep slumber. The infant Christ, held between Mary's knees and poised to take a step forwards, assumes a classical *contrapposto* posture (see pages 248–9).

Delicacy

Correggio
The Madonna with St Jerome
1527

Oil on panel, 235 × 141 cm

Parma, Galleria Nazionale

For artist biography, see page 268.

Correggio was certainly one of the most gracious Renaissance artists. In works such as this, created in his native city of Parma, his intentions are clear: to renew the compositional structure and emotional tone of the Renaissance altarpiece, but without resorting to the new standards of Mannerism. Starting from Leonardo – whose influence is recognizable in the Madonna's features and above all in the light that blurs the contours – Correggio conveys feelings of sweetness, serene abandon and smiling confidence. The splendid choice of palette, with delicate golden tones, anticipates Baroque painting.

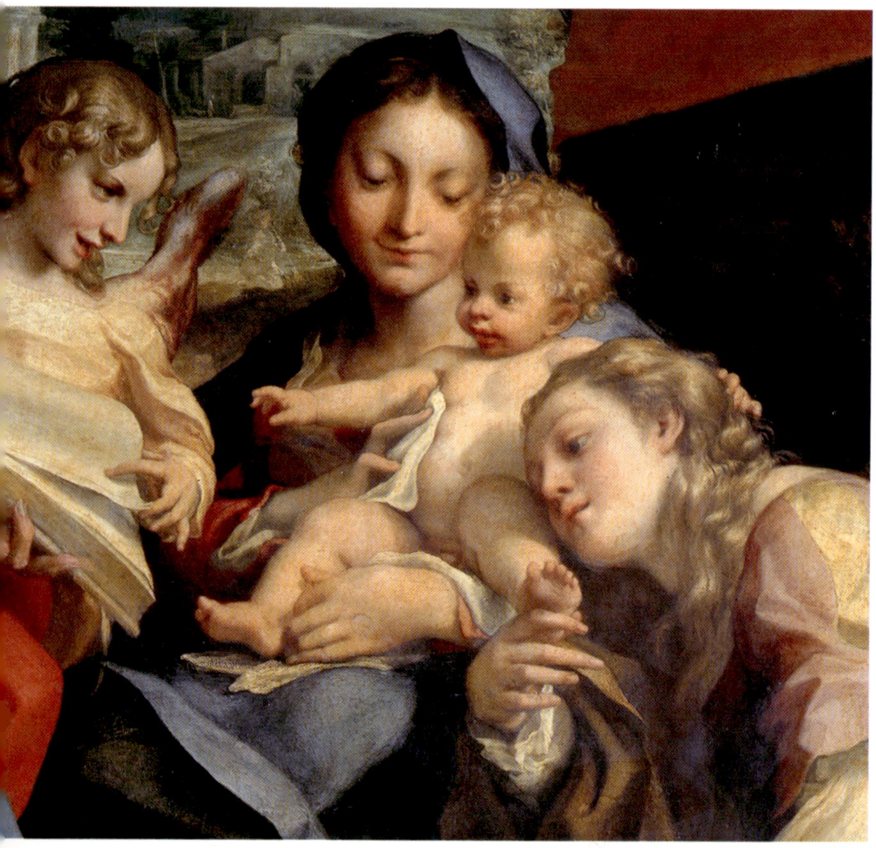

◄ Nicknamed *Il Giorno* (the Day) because of its diffuse midday light – as opposed to *La Notte* (the Night), a contemporary *Adoration of the Shepherds* – this is perhaps the best known of Correggio's altarpieces.

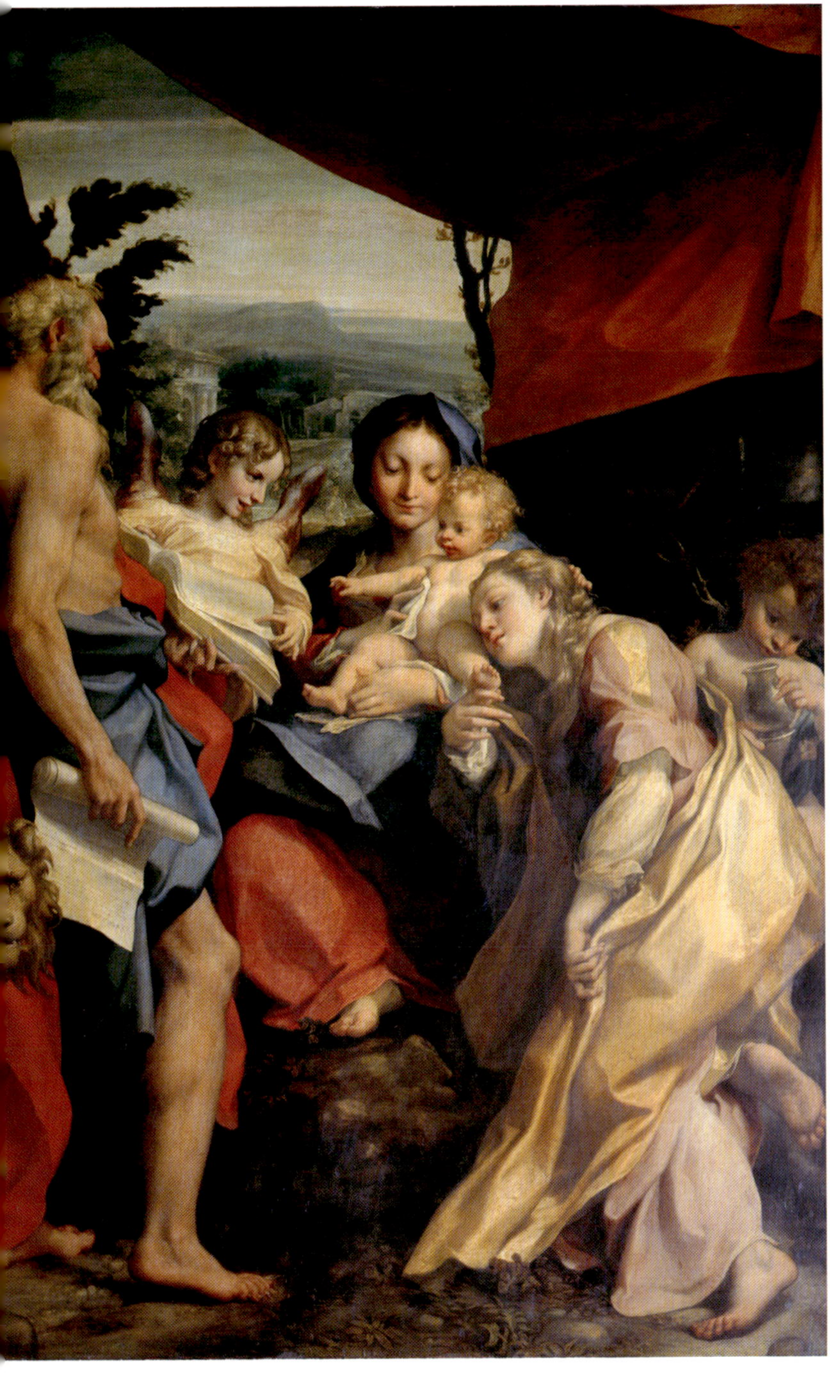

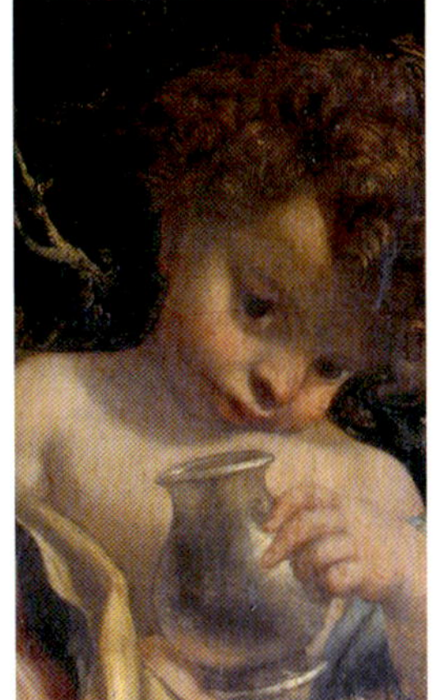

▲ It is illuminating to compare Correggio's appealing angels with the ambiguous cherubs in Parmigianino's paintings. Correggio's soft, delicate brushstroke is especially effective at bringing to life figures of great tenderness.

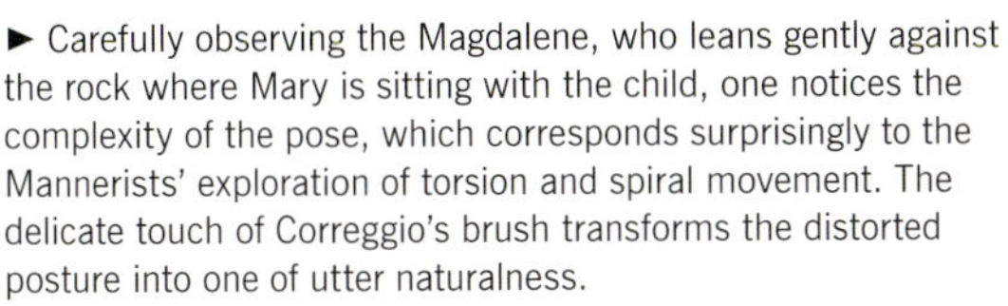

► Carefully observing the Magdalene, who leans gently against the rock where Mary is sitting with the child, one notices the complexity of the pose, which corresponds surprisingly to the Mannerists' exploration of torsion and spiral movement. The delicate touch of Correggio's brush transforms the distorted posture into one of utter naturalness.

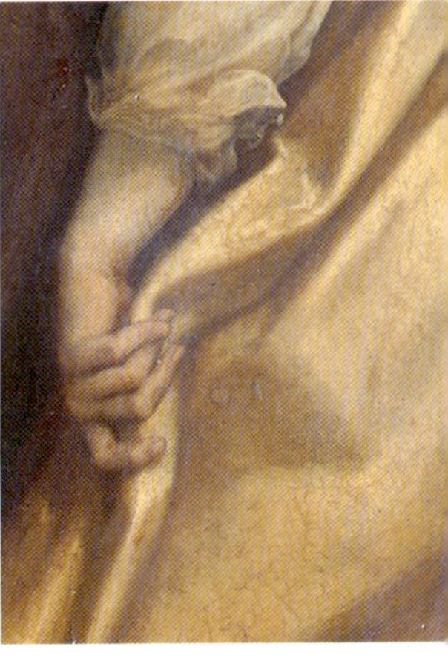

Apprehension

Lorenzo Lotto
The Annunciation
c. 1527

Oil on canvas, 166 × 114 cm

Recanati, Macerata, Museo Civico

For artist biography, see page 274.

Some artists gave theatrical expression to the uncertain mood produced by the tense political situation in Italy and Europe. Florence responded by giving birth to Mannerism while, in northern Italy, the Venetian Lorenzo Lotto rejected the poetical, contemplative, even ecstatic tone of many precedents and instead created an image of emotional tension: the famous leap of his anxiously fleeing cat sums up his art. He turned to one of the most frequently and diversely depicted themes in religious art, *The Annunciation*, to find inspiration for one of his freest and best-known expressions of creative originality and forthright inventiveness.

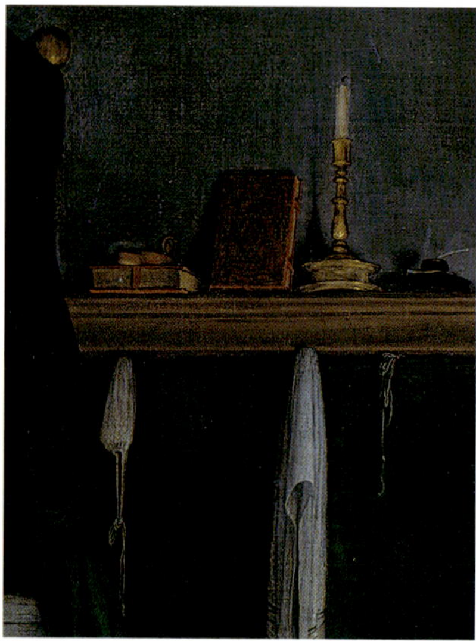

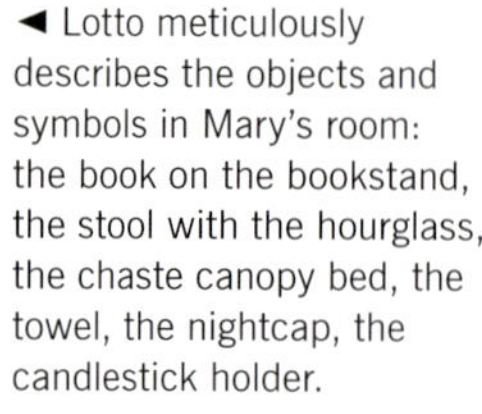

◄ Lotto meticulously describes the objects and symbols in Mary's room: the book on the bookstand, the stool with the hourglass, the chaste canopy bed, the towel, the nightcap, the candlestick holder.

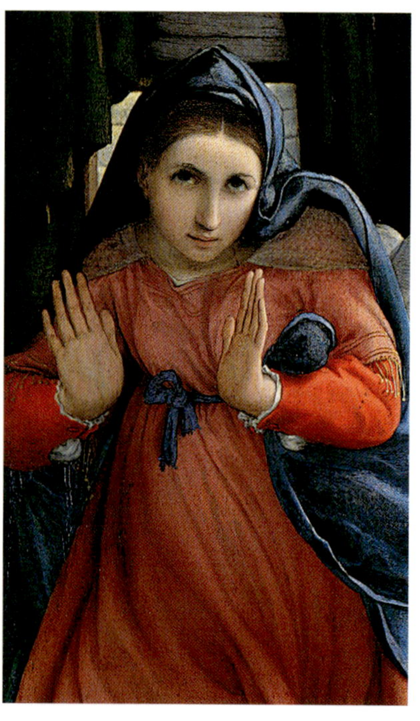

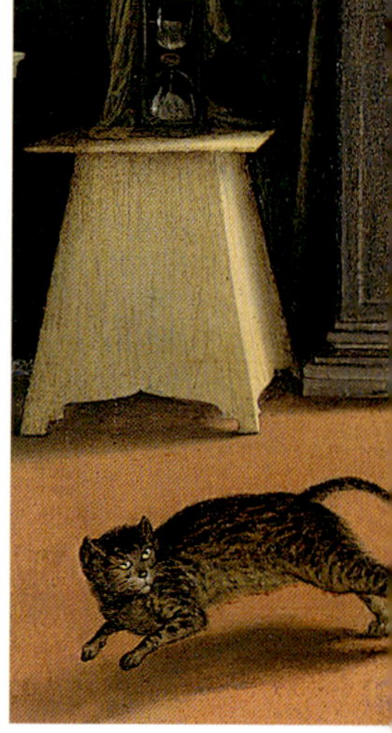

◄ Attention is focused on the Virgin Mary. Troubled and frightened by the sudden upheaval in her life, with her back to the angel, she turns towards us as if seeking our aid. She inspires tenderness with her big, dark, roaming eyes and fragile little hands.

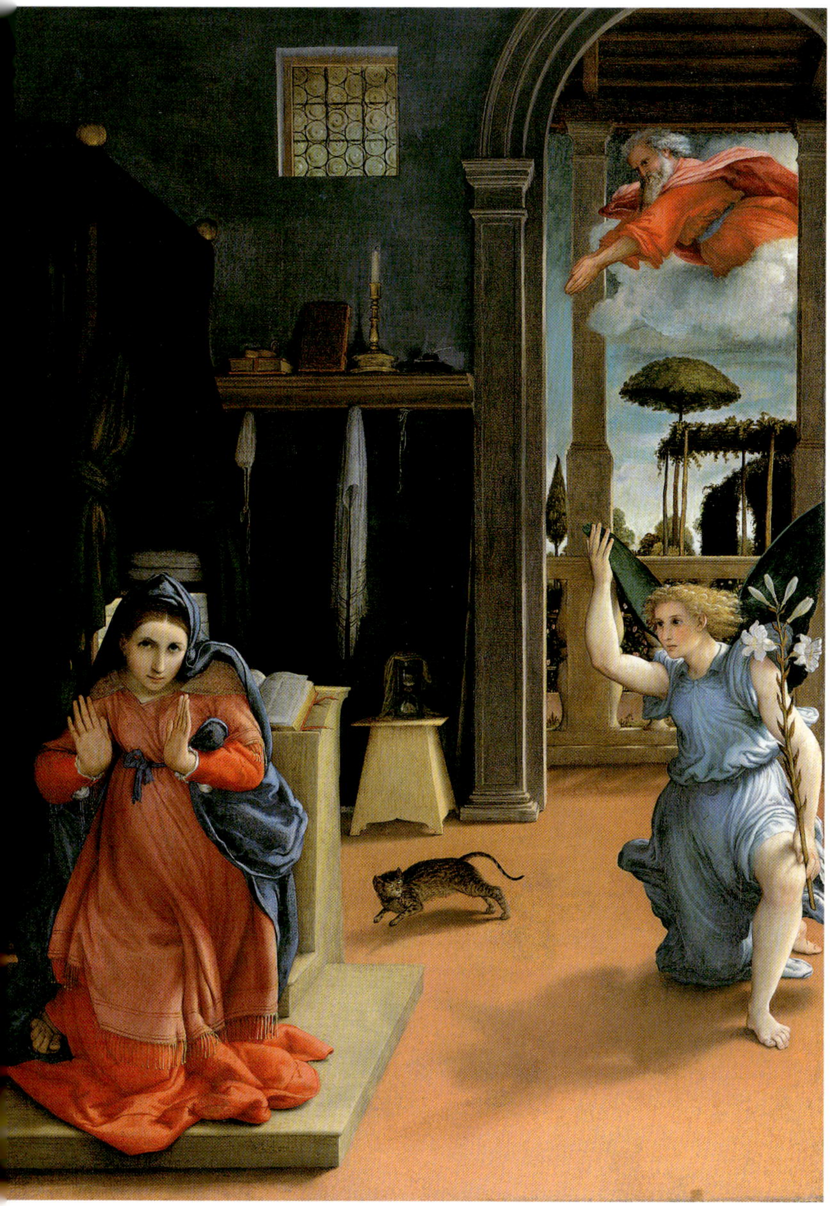

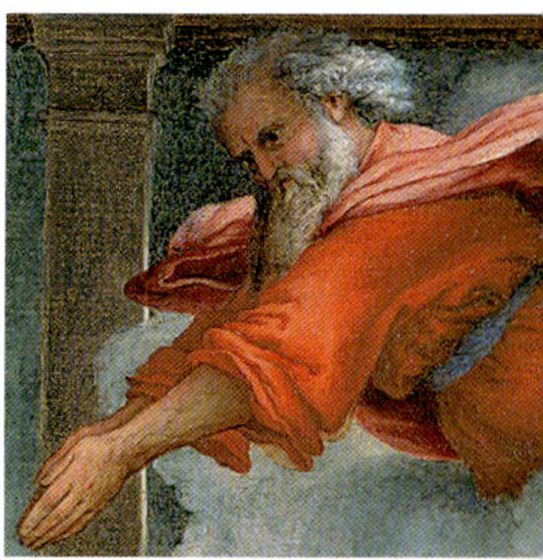

▲ In the background,
God the Father seems to be
diving in to shatter the silent
orderliness of Mary's room.
The gestures of God and the
archangel Gabriel are strong,
decisive, commanding –
the opposite of the Virgin's
trembling look of alarm.

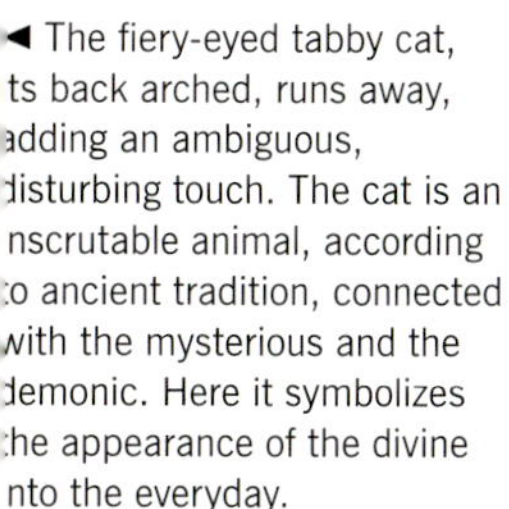

◄ The fiery-eyed tabby cat,
its back arched, runs away,
adding an ambiguous,
disturbing touch. The cat is an
inscrutable animal, according
to ancient tradition, connected
with the mysterious and the
demonic. Here it symbolizes
the appearance of the divine
into the everyday.

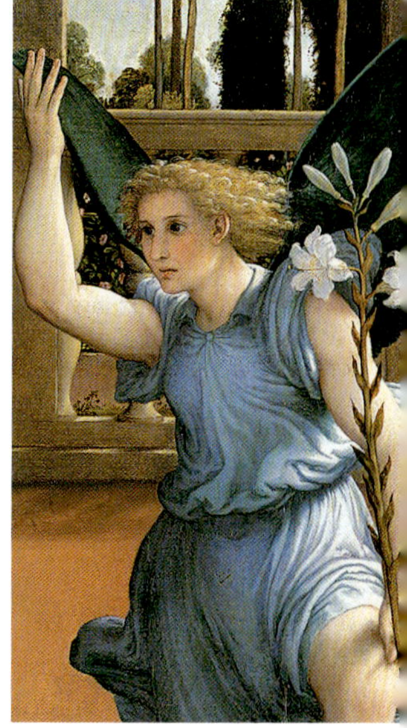

► A shudder of fear runs
through the scene. The
archangel's massive physical
presence, emphasized by the
shadow cast on the floor,
contrasts with the fragile,
frightened Mary.

Collecting

Lorenzo Lotto
Portrait of Andrea Odoni
1527

Oil on canvas, 114 × 101 cm

Hampton Court, London, Royal Collection

For artist biography, see page 274.

The growth of private collecting had its roots in antiquarianism – that is, the interest in excavations, Antiquity and the market for works of art and old objects – and was promoted by refined art dealers with an international clientele. The Italian cities of Venice and Rome, and later Antwerp and London to the north, contributed to the growth of private collections. As antiquarian tastes spread, the number of private collections swelled. Humanism's enthusiasm for the recovery of classical works encouraged a new intellectual attitude. This wonderful painting illustrates it well.

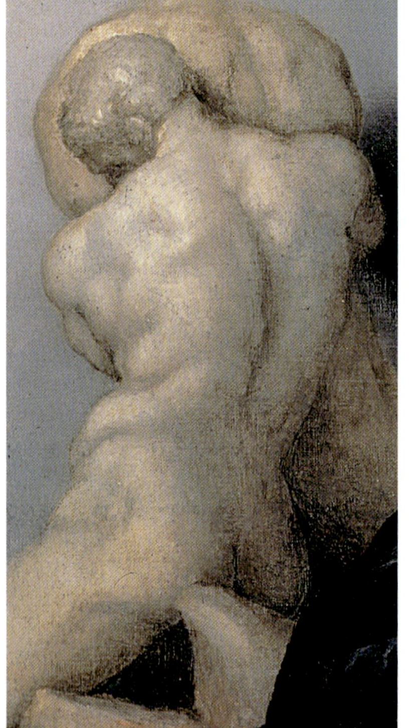

▶ Andrea Odoni was one of the most important collectors of art and antiquities in early 16th-century Venice and one of the few patrons of Lorenzo Lotto in that city.

◀ Despite the fact that the city of Venice was not of Roman origin, and so had no local archaeological finds at hand, its commercial strength and the amassing of fabulous private collections made it an important centre of the classical antiquities market.

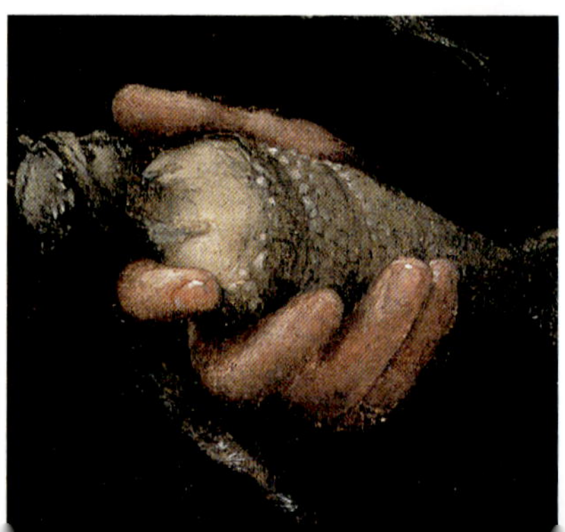

◀ Lotto shared Andrea Odoni's taste for ancient objects. The refined statuette in the foreground appears in other works by the painter, such as the intarsia panels in the choir of Santa Maria Maggiore in Bergamo.

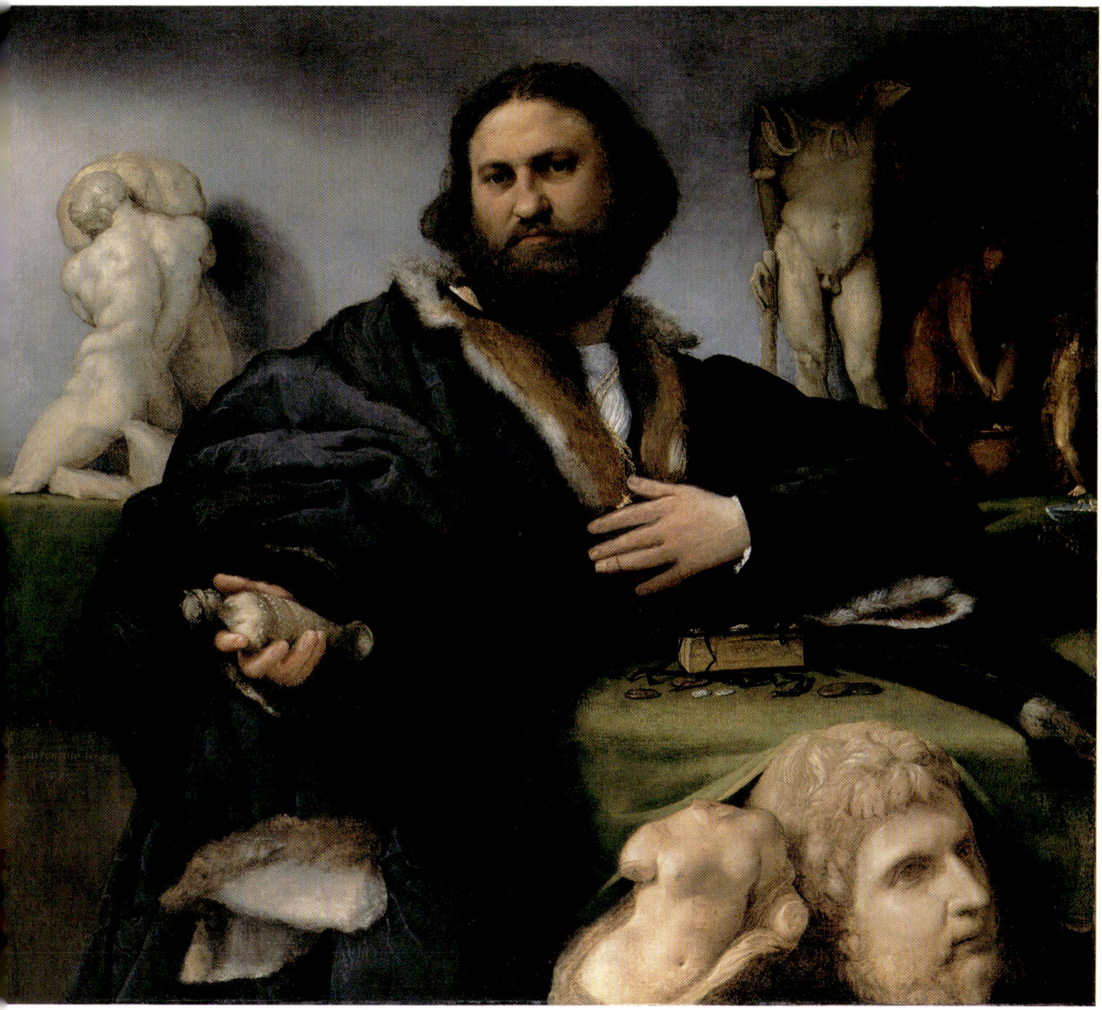

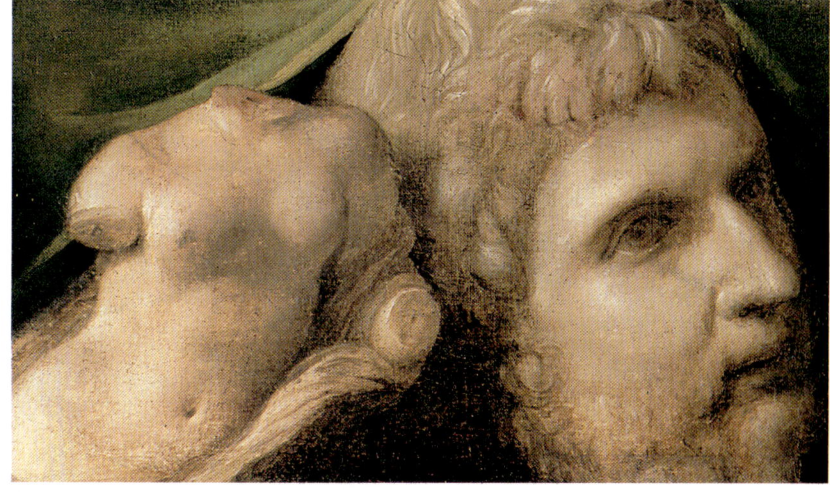

The gentleman makes a slow, broad gesture in a portrait with an unusual format. He is surrounded by his collection, which recalls an illustrious but now fragmentary past. The painting prompts regret for a lost civilization. The muted light, the sculptures' missing pieces, the pinkish yellow patina and the intentional blurring of the marble impart a note of melancholy to the portrait.

Awe

Giulio Romano
The Fall of the Titans
1527–8

Fresco

Mantua, Palazzo Te, Sala dei Giganti

Giulio Romano

(Giulio Pippi)

Rome, 1492/9–Mantua, 1546

When Raphael died in 1520, Giulio Romano, recognized as the most brilliant of the master's direct collaborators, took over the workshop, completing the major undertakings left unfinished at the Vatican. Following a period of activity as a painter and engraver, he moved to Mantua in 1524. There he dominated the final chapter in Renaissance Italian court art, setting aside the brush to devote himself to architecture and the organization of immense decorative projects that innovatively combined stucco and fresco. For the Gonzagas, he designed ambitious construction projects (the expansion of the ducal palace, the cathedral of Mantua and the abbey of San Benedetto Po) as well as ornamental works, including tapestry cartoons and metalwork – all of which enhanced the reputation and legacy of the court of Isabella and Federico Gonzaga. The most complex and significant undertaking remains the design and decoration of the Palazzo Te, in which every room presents new and increasingly elaborate ornamental solutions.

Vasari wrote that the painter-architect Giulio Romano, heir to Raphael's workshop and manner, had moved to Mantua in 1524 and that his activity there was 'varied, rich and full'. For more than 20 years, Giulio Romano designed and decorated the most important aristocratic and religious buildings in and around Mantua. Palazzo Te (1527–34), the 'villa of delight' on the edge of the historic city, is a fundamental model of international Mannerism. In the main rooms and enchanting 'secret' apartment of the garden, Giulio Romano boldly employed perspective and light, combined stucco and fresco and intertwined literary subjects and frankly erotic scenes. The single most famous and impressive example represents Zeus felling the Titans and striking them with lightning: the disproportionate figures echo the poses and *terribile*, or awe-inspiring, physicality of Michelangelo. This room is certainly one of the most famous and surprising in the Palazzo Te. Its door has almost no frame: visitors should be unaware of any seam between real space and painted architecture, reality and illusion.

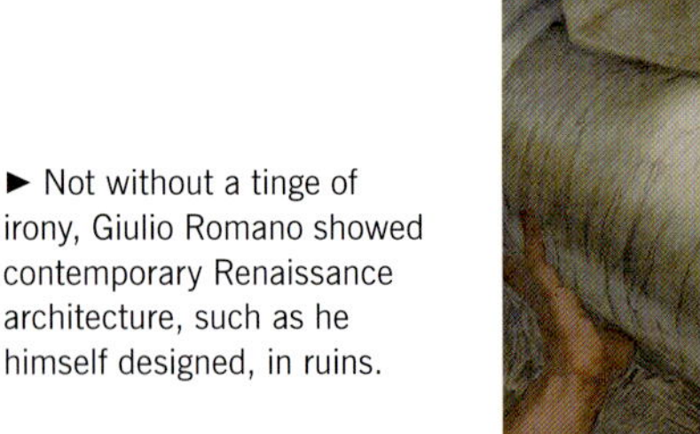

► Not without a tinge of irony, Giulio Romano showed contemporary Renaissance architecture, such as he himself designed, in ruins.

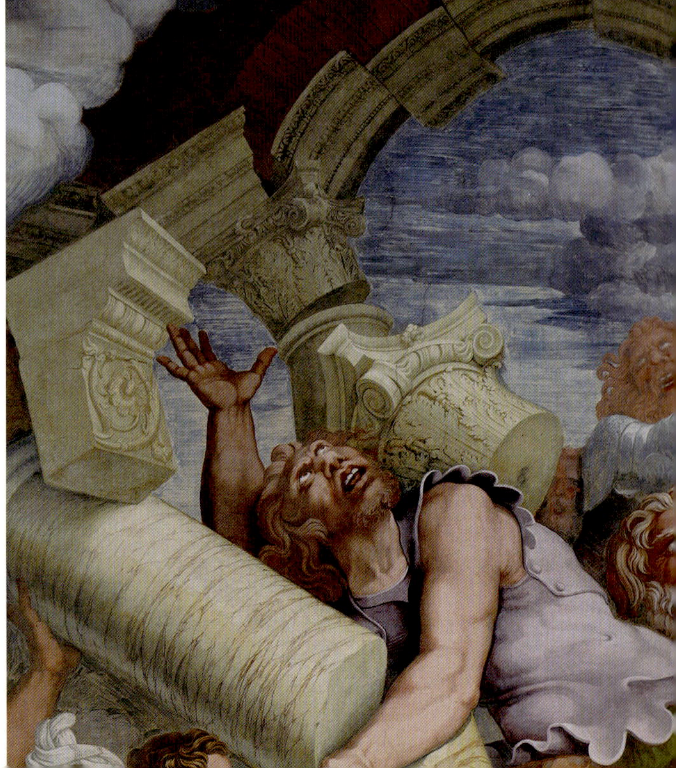

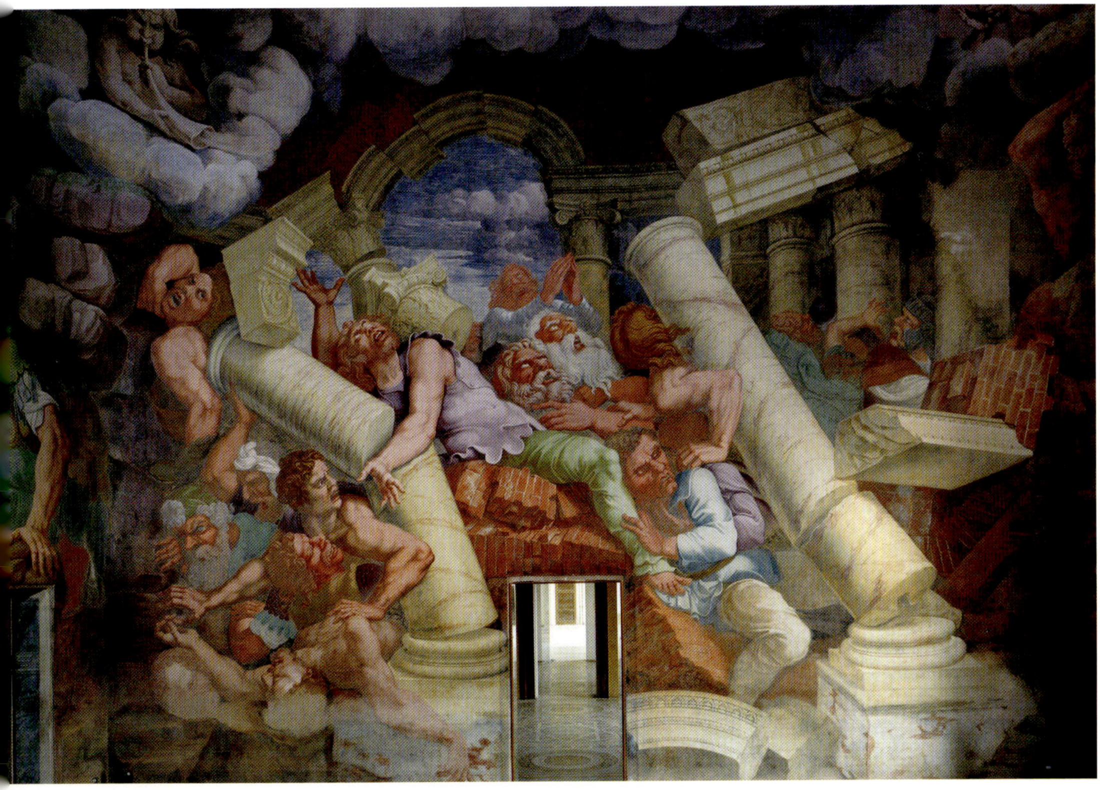

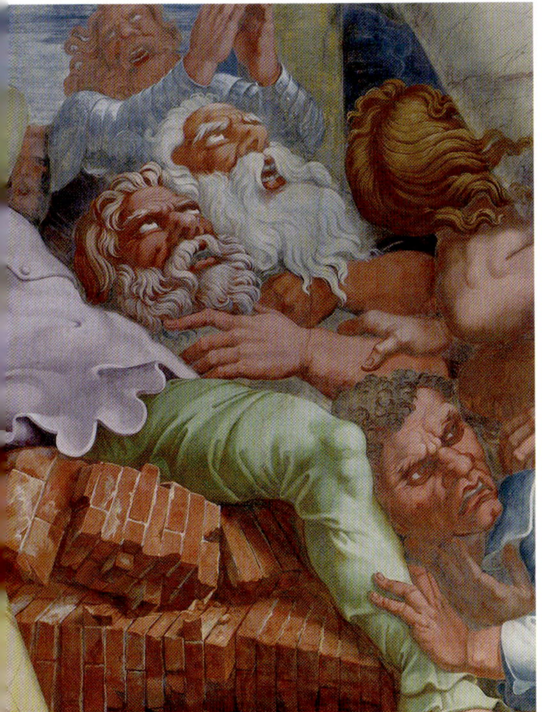

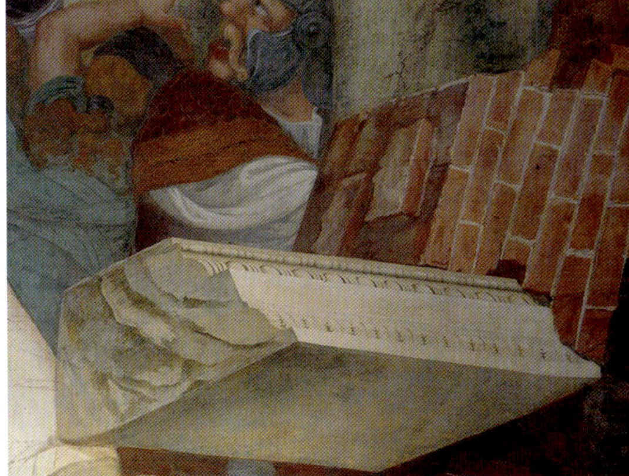

◄▲ The Titans look up, terrified. As seen on the following pages, Zeus, on the ceiling, hurls lightning bolts and slays his enemies. Beyond the dynastic celebration of his patron Federico Gonzaga (who liked to identify himself with Zeus), Giulio Romano involved the viewer in a catastrophic situation taking place at the same moment: the Sack of Rome. In this Mantuan room, the artist recreates the collapse of a world, the end of an era.

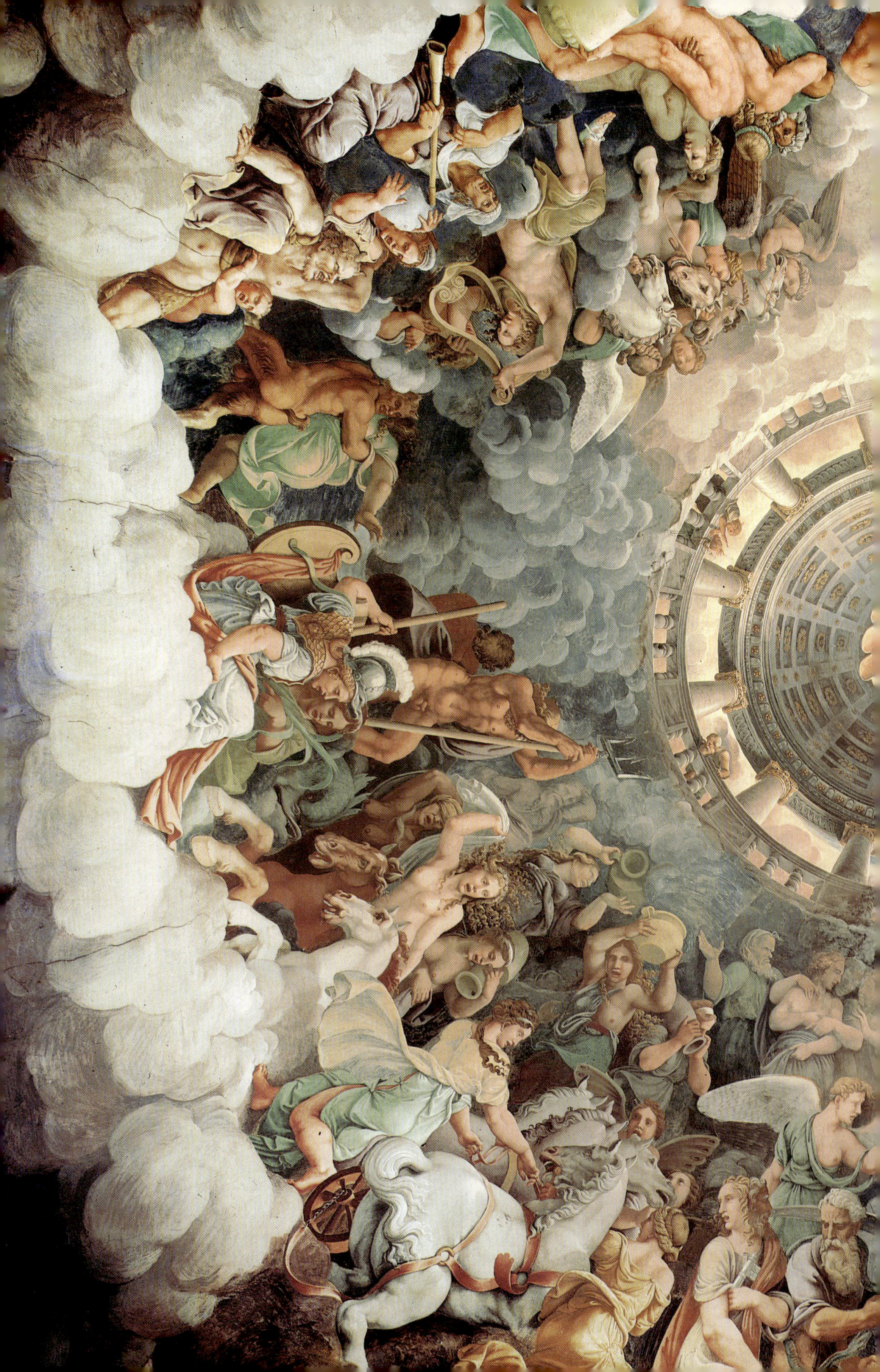

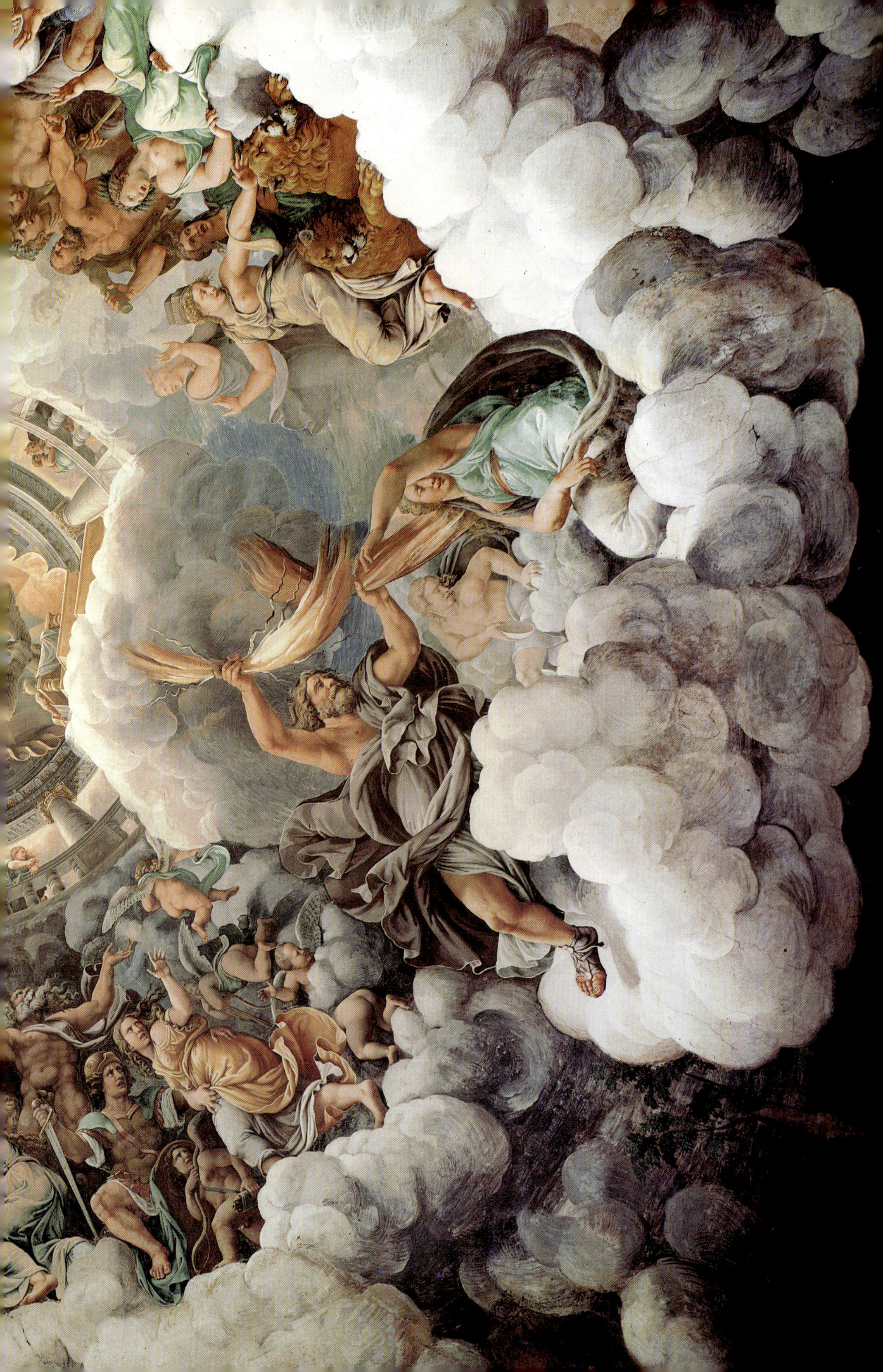

Obsession

Jacopo Pontormo
The Visitation
1528

Oil on panel, 202 × 156 cm
Carmignano, Prato, San Michele

For artist biography, see page 276.

Jacopo Pontormo studied gestures and expressions to the poir of obsession, and his observations led to some radical innov: tions. The tense, still gazes, the cold, clashing colours and th monumentality of the looming figures give his compositior an unnatural air. This disquieting *Visitation*, which remains i the small parish church of Carmignano, includes an unusu; embrace between the two cousins, seen both frontally and i profile, the colours of their clothing symmetrically inverted.

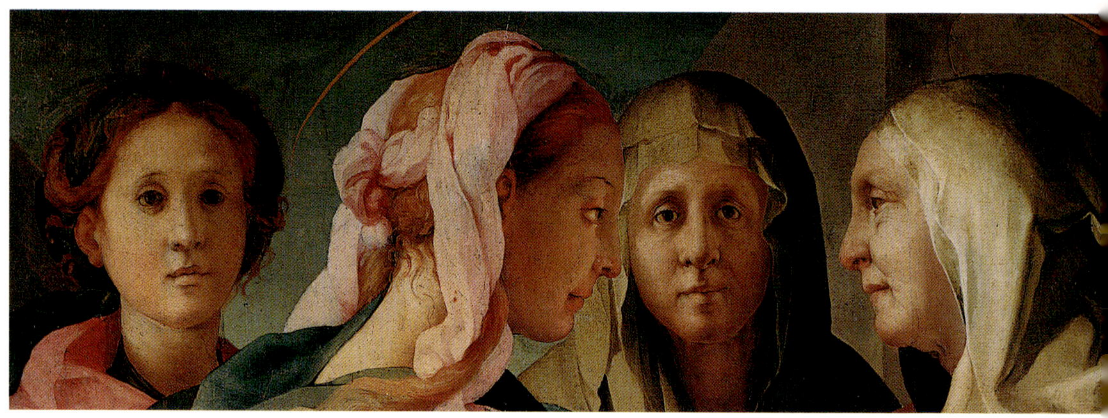

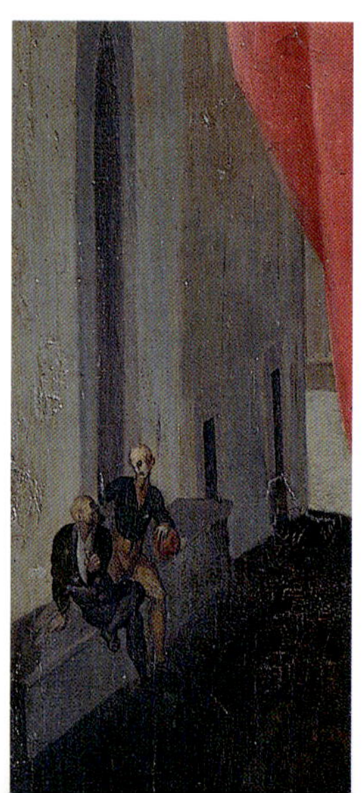

◄ The scene unfolds between two steep, narrow architectural wings: the square-blocked mass of the buildings encloses the scene, which is grey and suffocating, with almost no way out. It makes a stark comparison with the urban scenes in 15th-century paintings, which often open onto glimpses of the 'ideal city' (see pages 118–19).

▲ The two main figures of *The Visitation*, Mary and her aged cousin Elizabeth, are portrayed motionless, in profile. Lips closed, they gaze into each other's eyes. Pontormo's unique interpretation contrasts sharply with tradition. Two rapt figures in the background, who seem to be mysterious 'doubles' of Mary and Elizabeth, have been the subjects of various interpretations.

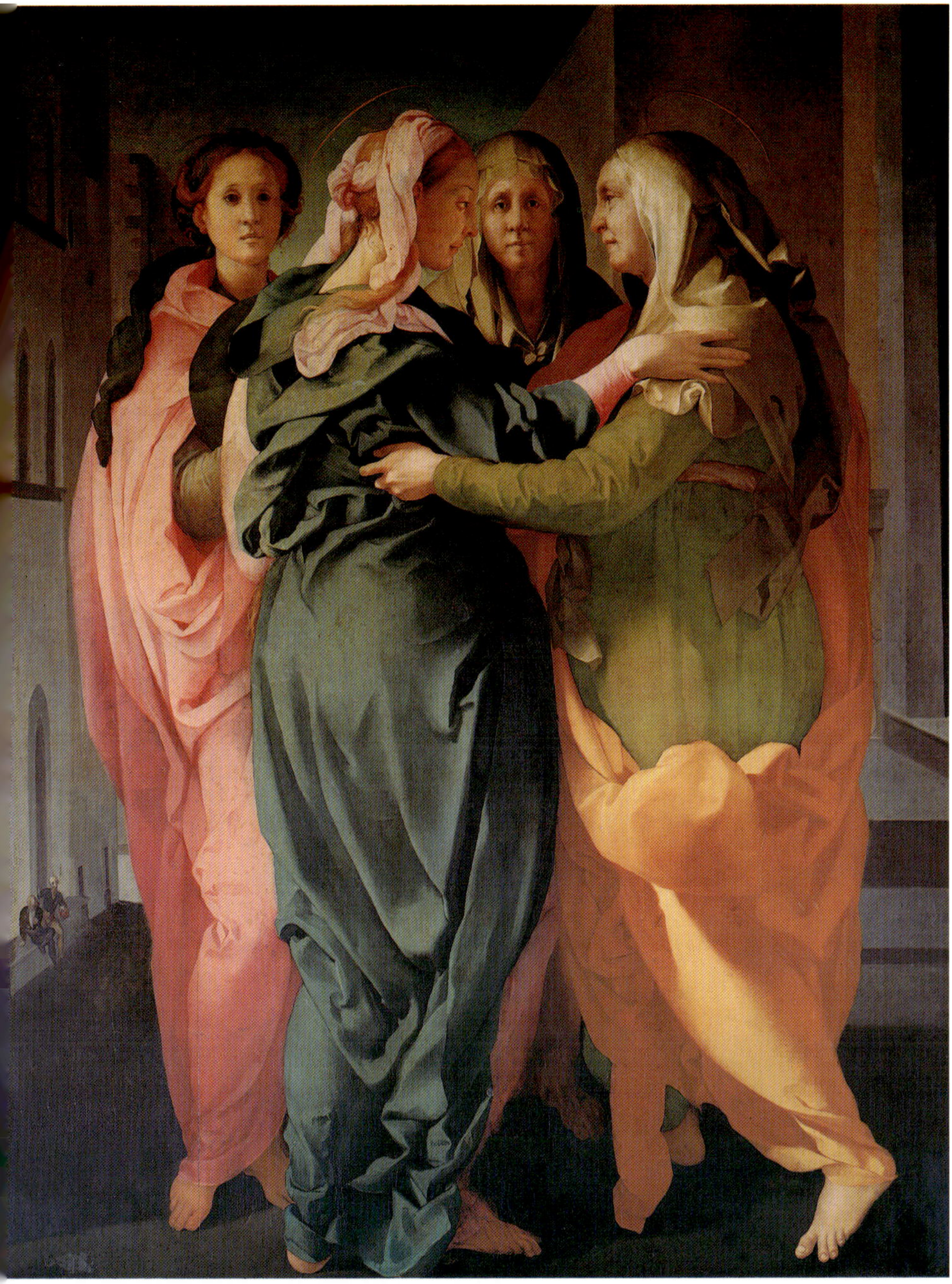

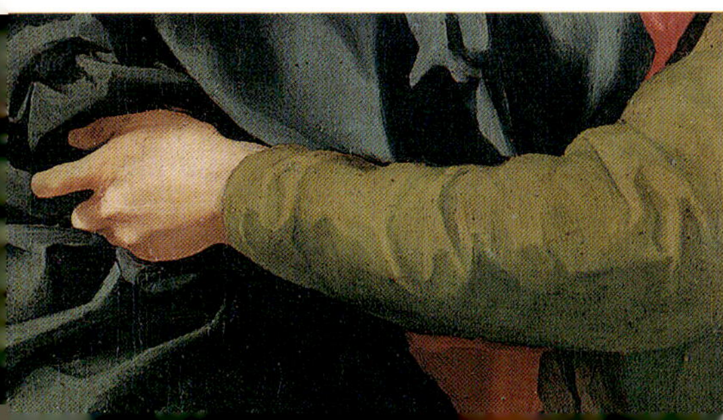

◄ The embrace of the two women, both pregnant, is charged with a dramatic intensity. In the Gospel passage, John the Baptist leaps in his mother Elizabeth's womb, knowing the Lord to be in the room.

Kiss

Correggio
Jupiter and Io
1530

Oil on canvas, 163.5 × 70.5 cm

Vienna, Kunsthistorisches Museum

For artist biography, see page 268.

Rediscovered in 16th-century literature, where it was exalted as a vehicle of the emotions, the kiss had up to that point been connected in painting with Judas's betrayal of Christ. Correggio, more than any other painter, restored the kiss's amorous significance. This painting is one of the four 'Loves of Jupiter', which also include *The Rape of Ganymede*, also in Vienna, the *Danae* at the Galleria Borghese in Rome (see pages 298–9), and *Leda and the Swan*, at the Gemäldegalerie in Berlin. With this cycle, painted for Federico Gonzaga but soon transferred to the collection of Emperor Charles V, sensual mythological painting in the Renaissance reached its pinnacle in passages of amorous abandon.

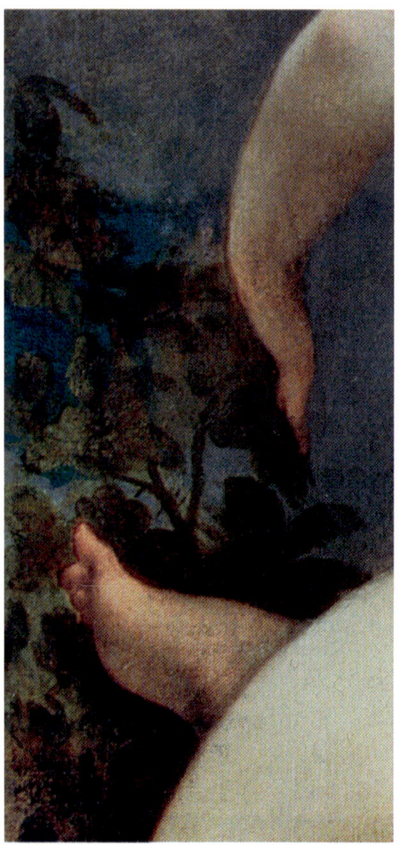

Correggio
Jupiter and Io
1530

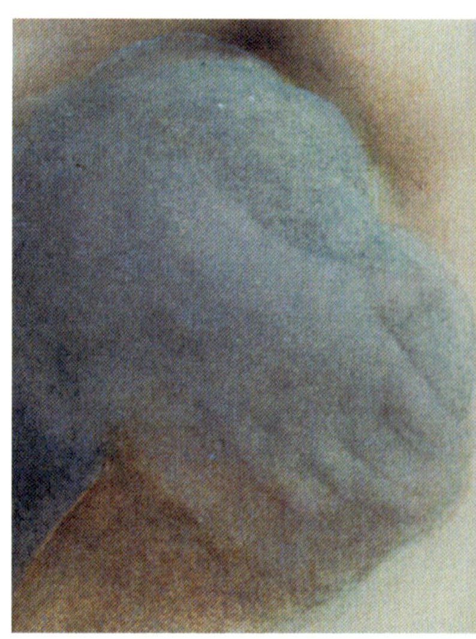

◄ To approach the nymph Io, whom he has surprised near a stream, Jupiter sends down a dense fog to cover the area and, assuming the form of a soft cloud, couples with the young woman. With surprising naturalness, Correggio describes Io's sensual pleasure as she abandons herself to the embrace and the kiss of the 'cloud' in which Jupiter hides.

▲ The soft, silken cloud truly appears to envelop the young woman's smooth body, clasping her gently, irresistibly. Upon contact with the cloud, a shiver of passion traverses her fleshy, luminous body and she swoons with love.

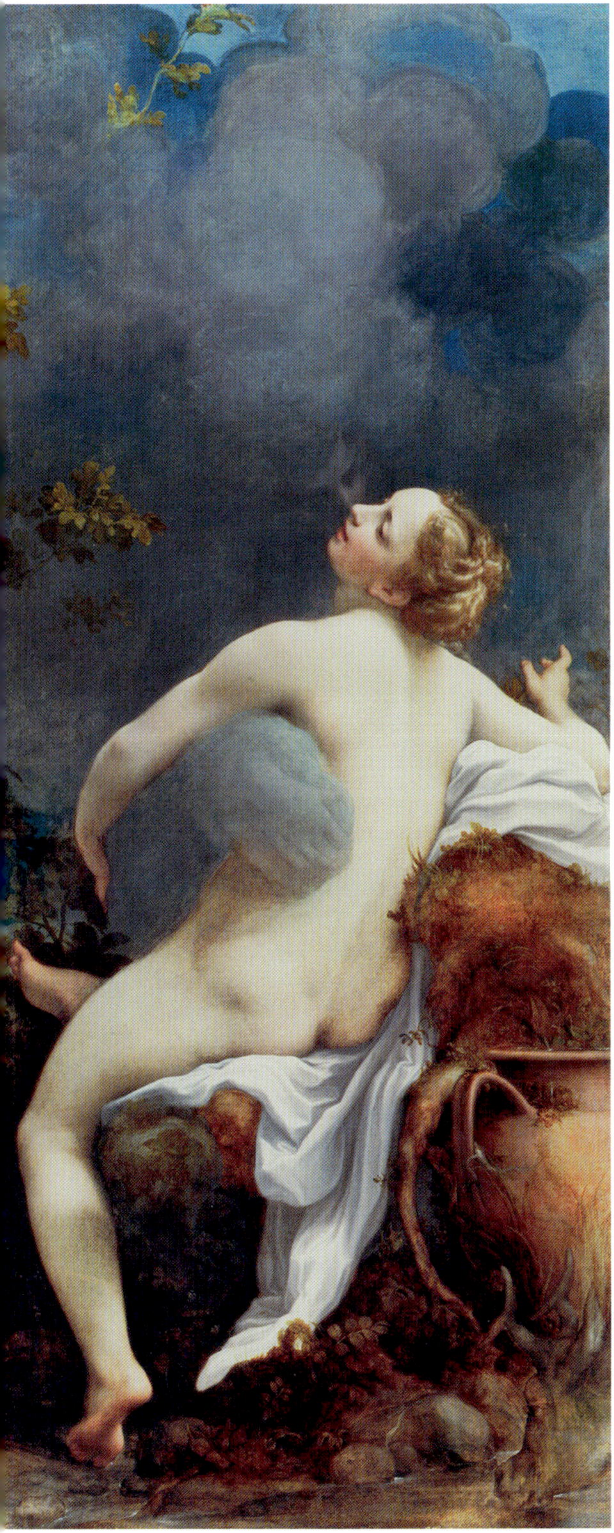

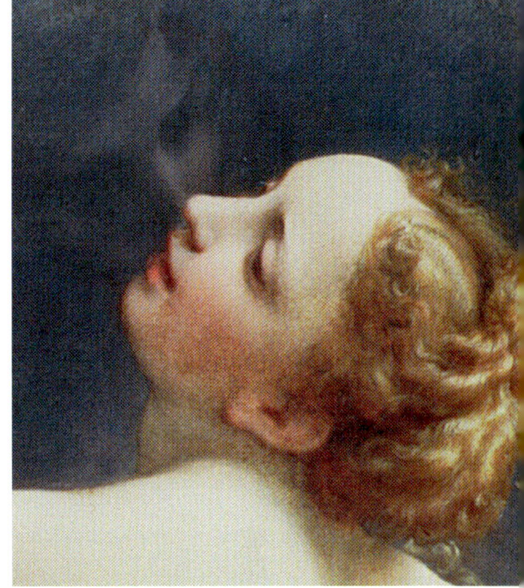

▲ Zeus's young man's features emerge from within the cloud. Correggio's graceful elegance and witty but sincere manner keep this scene from crossing the threshold of coarse eroticism.

▼ The handle of the urn and the root protruding from the ground appear to be explicit sexual references.

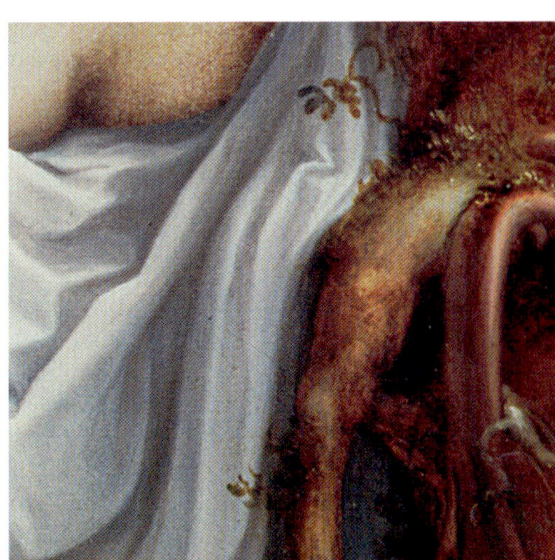

Cupid

Parmigianino
Cupid Carving His Bow
1530

Oil on panel, 135 × 65.3 cm

Vienna, Kunsthistorisches Museum

For artist biography, see page 280.

Cupid appears repeatedly in 16th-century art, variously po[r]trayed in refined intellectual allegories and explicitly erotic scene[s]. One of the most interesting and at the same time unsettli[ng] examples is by Parmigianino. Always in search of a 'new natur[e]', Parmigianino developed a subtle moral and allusive approac[h], replacing Correggio's softly defined light with a sharp, graph[ic] delineation of tapered, polished, almost unrecognizable form[s].

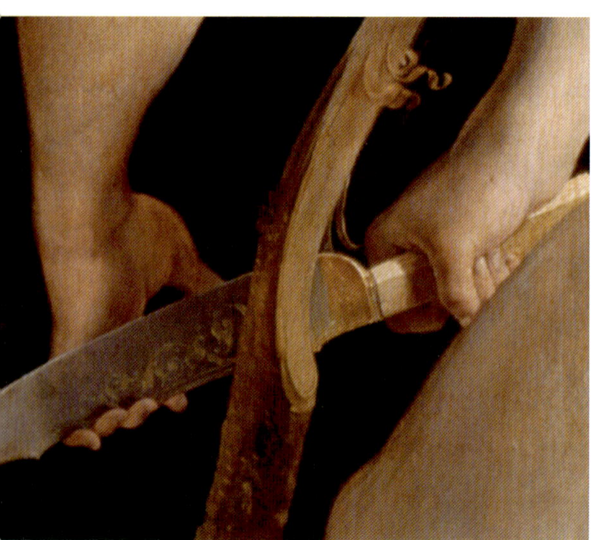

▲ This subject is unusual and almost unique in painting, although it did appear in poetry and madrigals: Cupid is whittling and smoothing his bow with a blade to make it more responsive and accurate. The adolescent god's slender but muscular physique shows a perfect knowledge of the works of Michelangelo and Raphael.

▶ Joy and Suffering: the two little cherubs below highlight the opposite emotions caused by love.

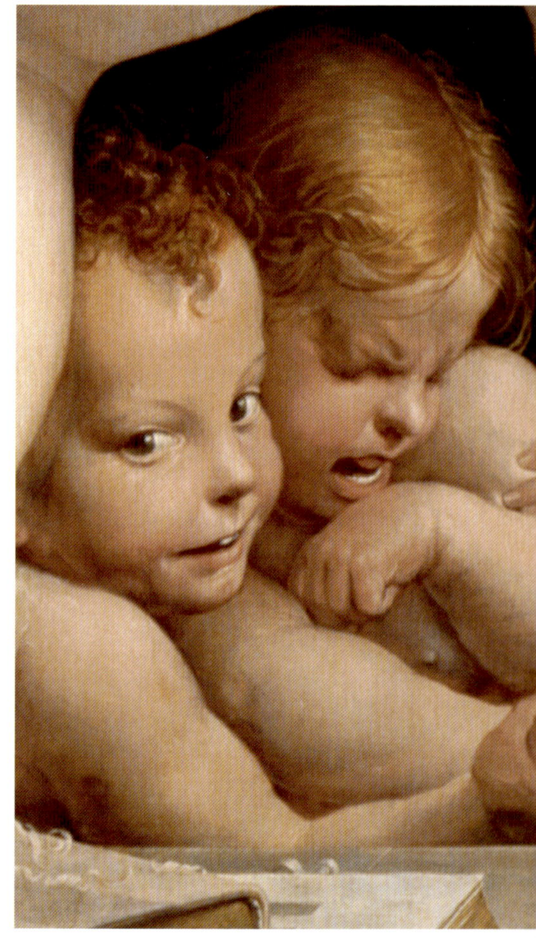

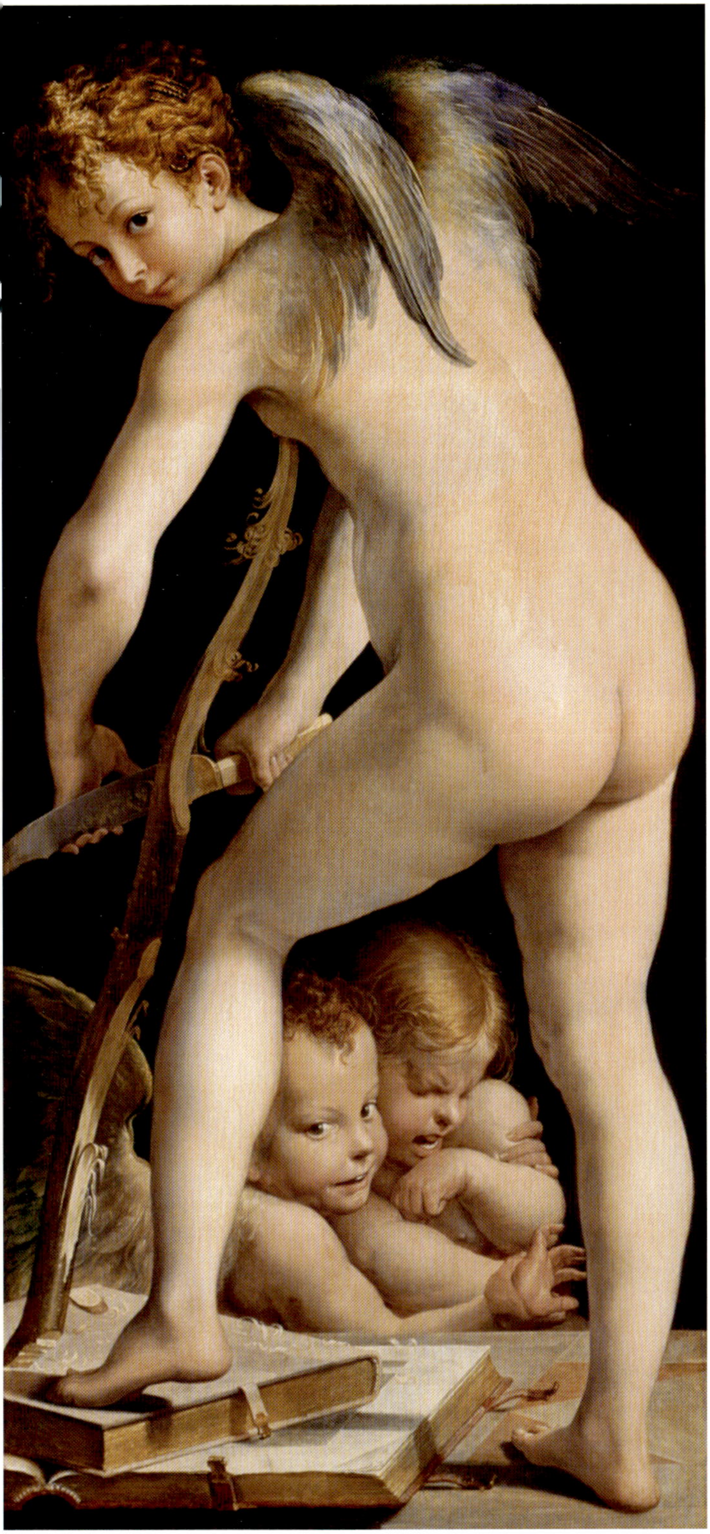

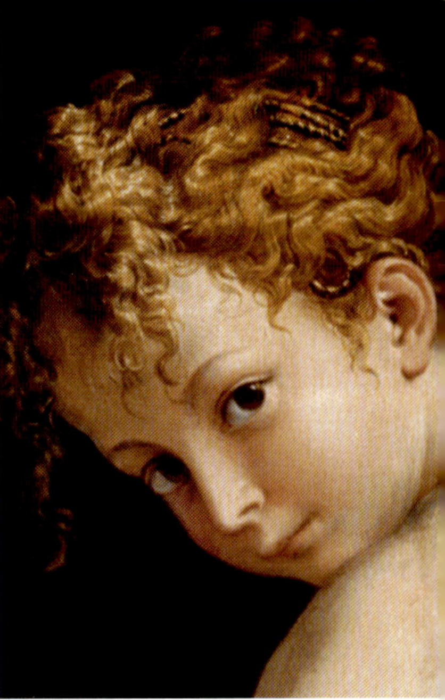

▲ Cupid's gaze is penetrating and pointed, like the arrows he shoots from his infallible bow. Parmigianino captures fleeting expressions and gives his figures a gaze that seems to connect, as if drawn by magnet, with the viewer's eyes (see pages 280–1).

▼ The large books being used as a footrest symbolize love's supremacy over all human knowledge, alluding to the classical theme of the Triumph of Venus, summarized in the Latin phrase *Amor omnia vincit*: Love conquers all.

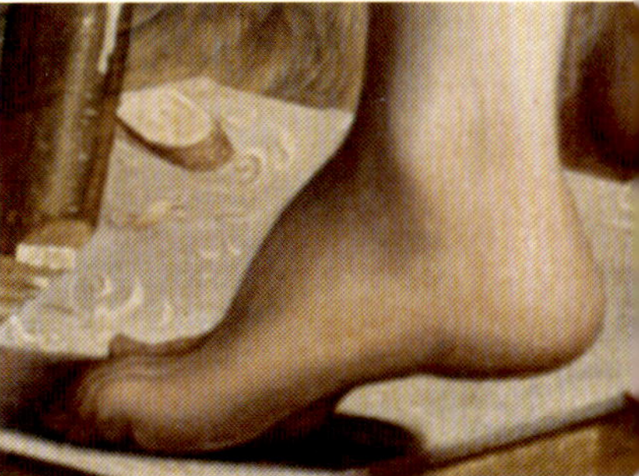

Eroticism

Correggio
Danae
c. 1531

Tempera on panel, 161 × 193 cm
Rome, Galleria Borghese

For artist biography, see page 268.

Sixteenth-century painters did not shy away from sensual subject-matter, especially when it had a mythological pretext. Danae, seduced by Zeus who comes to her bed in the form of a shower of gold, provided the subject of one of Correggio's masterpieces and one of the most explicitly erotic paintings in history. The young woman welcomes the golden rain with an unambiguous gesture, seconded by the presence of Cupid who draws back the sheet. Each curve of Danae's soft body, half-reclining on her bed, is an irresistible invitation. The painter's typical soft-textured flesh tones are executed in a mellow chiaroscuro. The canvas is one of four 'Loves of Jupiter' (see pages 294–5), a cycle produced by Correggio for Federico Gonzaga, who gave it to Emperor Charles V.

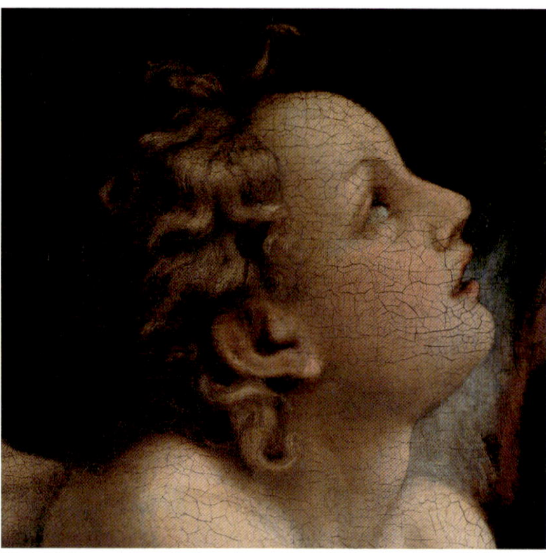

◄ Cupid's adolescent figure, seated on Danae's bed, adds a further note of eroticism. The full, round features derive from Raphael, while the delicate use of *sfumato* betrays attentive study of Leonardo. The light that softly models the nude figure is an eloquent essay on sensuality typical of Correggio.

▼ Rounded thighs, drapery being drawn aside, enticing cushions, swelling breasts, half-closed red lips, caressing shadows, cascading veils, quivering fingers, penetrating gazes: this is certainly one of the most erotic of Renaissance paintings. With an utter lack of prudery, it illustrates Jupiter's metamorphosis and conquest of the beautiful Danae, who has been locked in a tower.

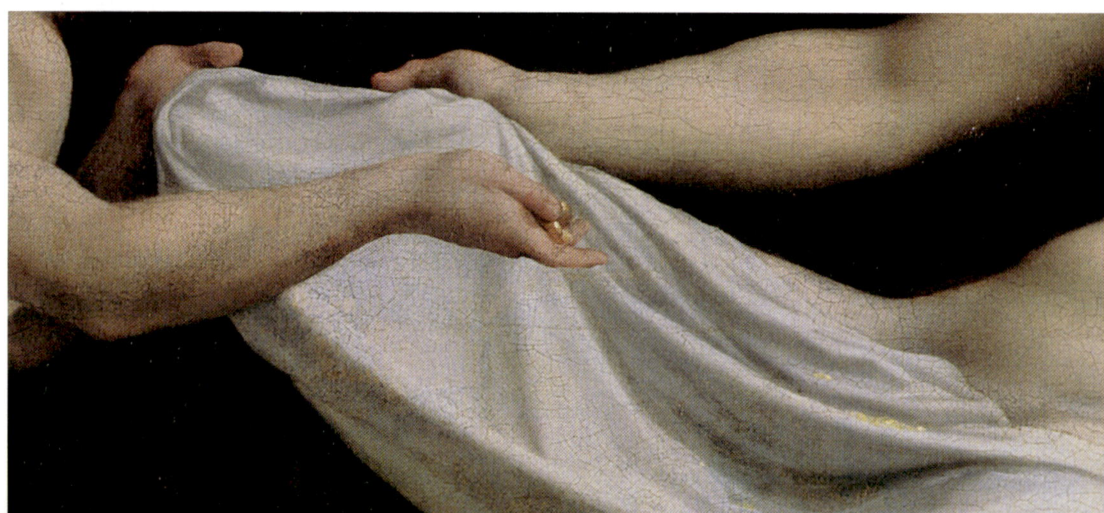

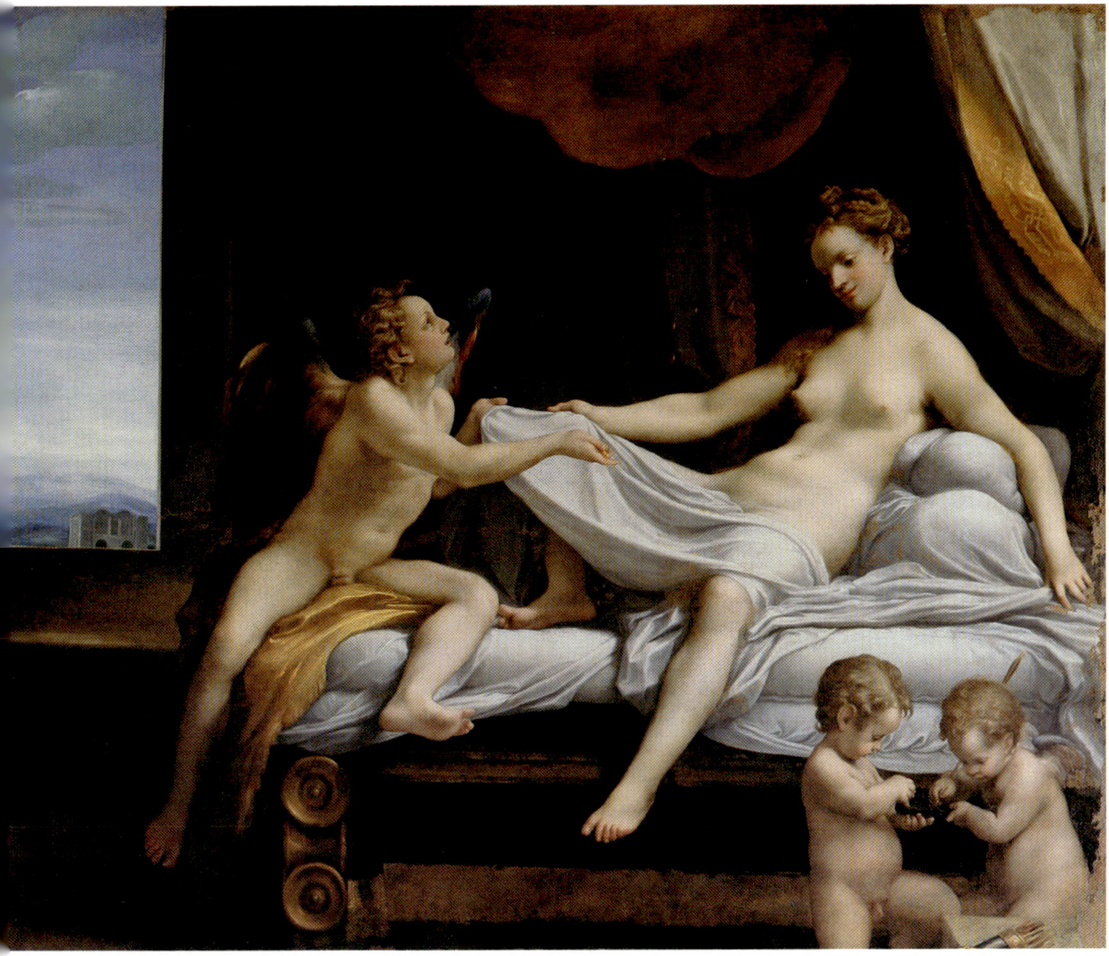

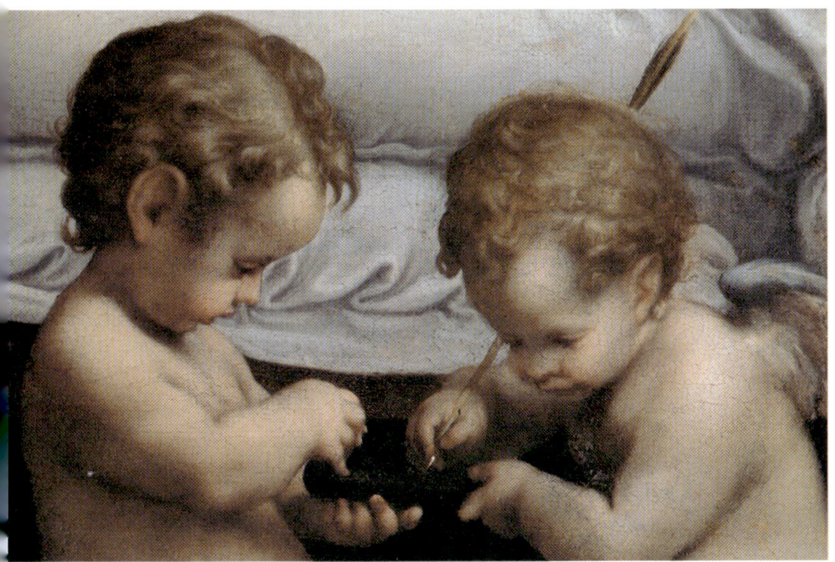

◄ The two little cherubs
playing with an arrow are
appealing and fresh. Their
fame rivals that of the cherubs
who appear in Raphael's
Sistine Madonna (see pages
232–3). Here Correggio
transforms the scholarly and
literary theme of the diverse
forms Love can assume into
immediately delightful charm.

Dispersal of Artists

Perino del Vaga

(Pietro Buonaccorsi)

Florence, 1501–Rome, 1547

Perino del Vaga has been called the 'missing link' in Genoese painting, coming between the last vestiges of the late Gothic and the advent of the Genoese school. After initial training in Florence, he entered Raphael's workshop and participated in the major decorative projects in Rome. He passed through Florence in 1527 and then moved to Genoa. Commissioned by Andrea Doria, Perino painted grand secular frescoes (comparable to those of Giulio Romano) and altarpieces, establishing himself as a leading figure in international Mannerism. Back in Rome in 1538, he was in contact with Michelangelo. With his elegant intellectual style, he asserted his status as one of the most important painters of the circle of the Farneses, for whom he created various interiors in the Vatican and the Castel Sant'Angelo.

The ebbing of Renaissance optimism initiated a period of crises and troubled reflections on humankind's destiny that resulted in a new concept of painting. The pillaging of Rome, which lasted several months over the spring and summer of 1527, profoundly affected art production. Only one great artist (Sebastiano del Piombo) remained by Pope Clement VII's side; all of the other leading artists fled. Raphael's former pupils were scattered to various Italian and foreign cities, where they decisively contributed to the spread of Mannerism. Giulio Romano now settled in Mantua, Sansovino took refuge in Venice, Rosso Fiorentino went to France, Parmigianino returned to Emilia. Perino del Vaga accepted the invitation to come to Genoa and became the leading artist in the age dominated by Andrea Doria.

The Sack of Rome, a Symbolic Turning-point

The Sack of Rome perpetrated in 1527 by Charles V's mercenaries was one of the most disastrous events in 16th-century Italian history. The pope was forced to abandon the Vatican palaces and take refuge in the Castel Sant'Angelo. The construction site of St Peter's was devastated and the basilica's ancient treasury looted. Thousands died, churches and palazzos were ruined, and many art treasures destroyed. In a Christendom shaken by the Reformation, it was interpreted as a terrible sign of the times. Some saw it as a dramatic but salutary penitential purification, while others hailed it as the undoing of a sinful city and age.

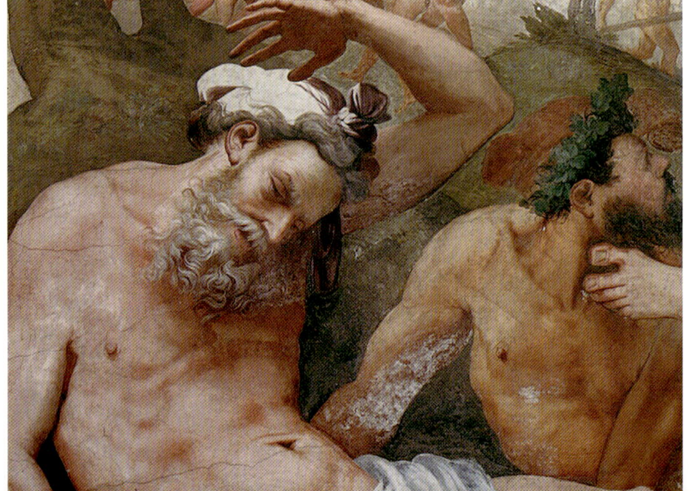

◄ Andrea Doria's artistic initiatives to revitalize Genoa focused on the Palazzo 'of the Prince', a splendid suburban residence where Perino del Vaga painted a series of frescoes celebrating the classical taste, similar in approach to what Giulio Romano had done in the Mantuan Palazzo Te. Pordenone and Domenico Beccafumi were also involved in the decoration, but their contributions have been lost.

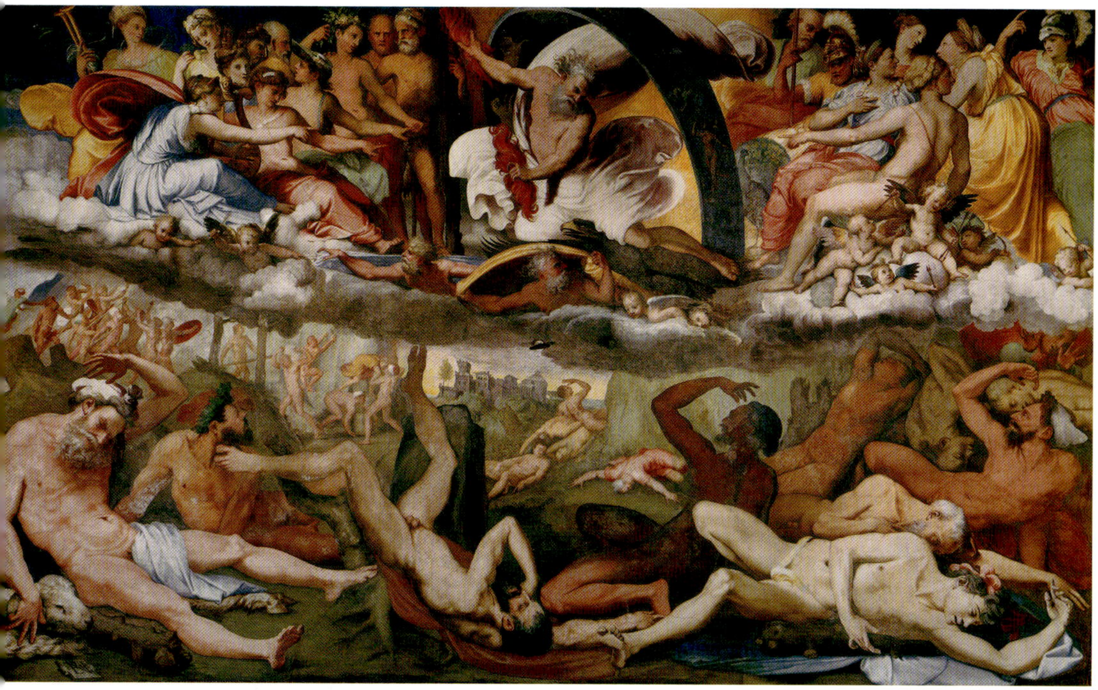

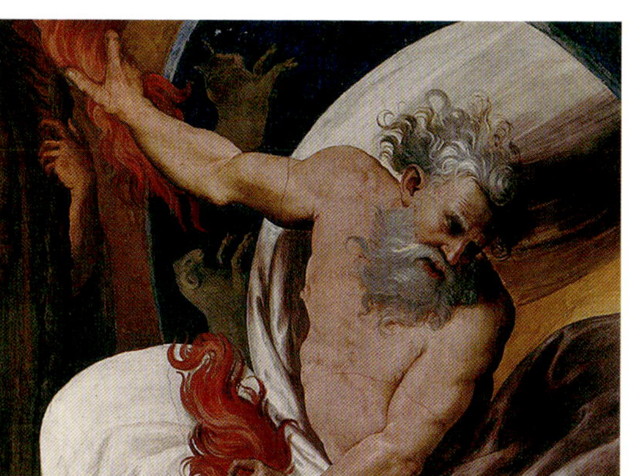

◄ Admiral Andrea Doria assumed political power in 1528, reformed the Republic of Genoa's administrative system and redefined diplomatic and financial agreements with Charles V's Spain. To give the city a modern architectural and visual look, he called upon Perino del Vaga, one of the most important artists from Raphael's workshop who fled the Sack of Rome.

▼ Along with well-documented stylistic references to Mannerism, Perino also brought to Genoa the sense of apprehension and gloom characteristic of artists personally affected by the ruinous events of the 1520s.

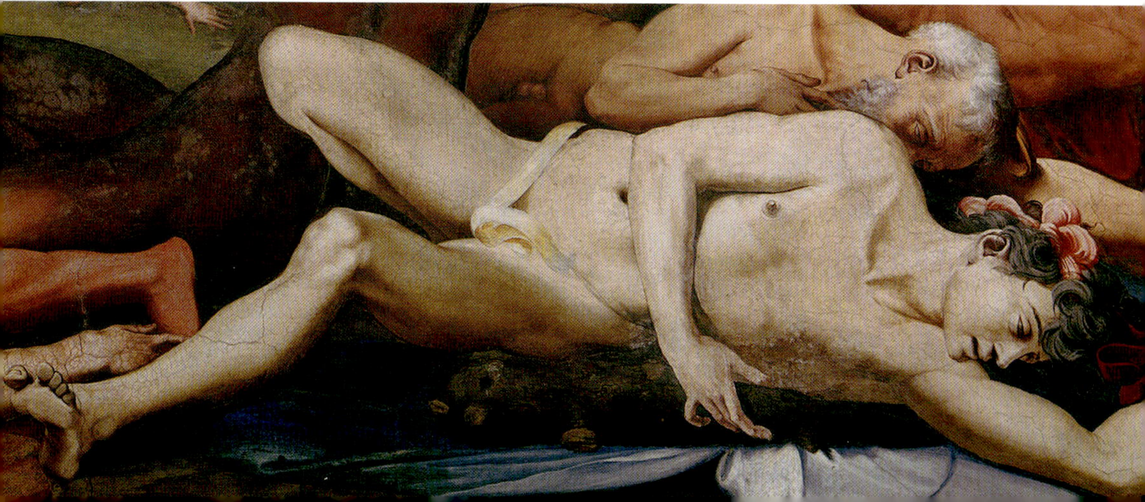

Chiaroscuro

Giovanni Girolamo Savoldo
St Matthew and the Angel
1534

Oil on canvas, 93 × 125 cm
New York, The Metropolitan
Museum of Art

For artist biography, see page 260.

In 1532, the last duke of Milan, Francesco II Sforza, com
missioned four paintings 'at night with fire' from the refine
Brescian painter Giovanni Girolamo Savoldo. At the time, suc
scenes were a fascinating novelty among collectors. Only one o
these paintings has so far been identified, *St Matthew and th
Angel*: it shows a magical night scene barely illuminated by th
light of a candle, focused entirely on the sweet angel and th
ecstatic yet solidly robust Evangelist. Now in its full maturit
the Italian Renaissance showed increasing interest in the noc
turnal and, consequently, in the search for sources of light an
gleaming fire.

◄ A window at the left opens
onto a landscape lit by a
silvery, full moon. Moonlight
grew so popular that it became
a truly 'classic' feature of
European Baroque art.

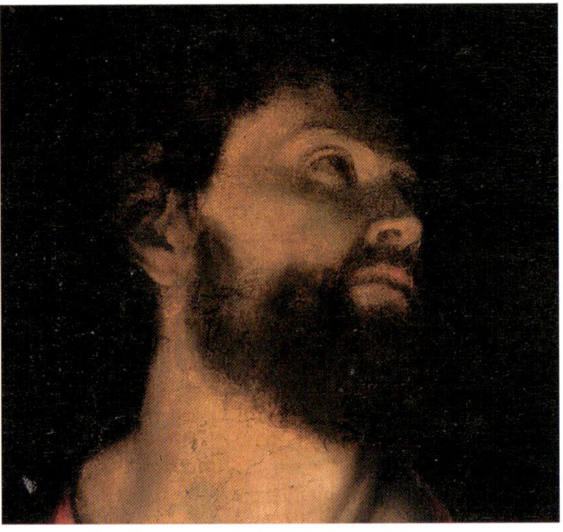

◄ Savoldo's refined work is
often reminiscent of Giorgion
in its use of softly contrasting
light and dark chiaroscuro.
The raking light that delicate
caresses the features of
St Matthew demonstrates
the Brescian painter's
extraordinary sensitivity to th
atmospheric effects of light.

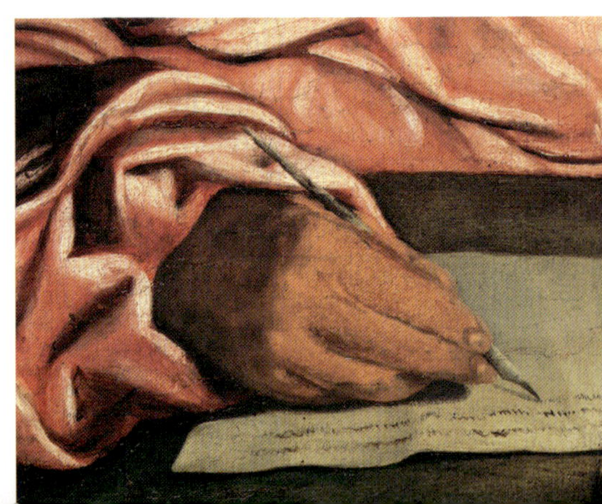

▼ By the light of an oil lamp
the Evangelist takes dictatior
from the angel. The flame, fi
and glowing coals became a
essential component in High
and late Renaissance paintin

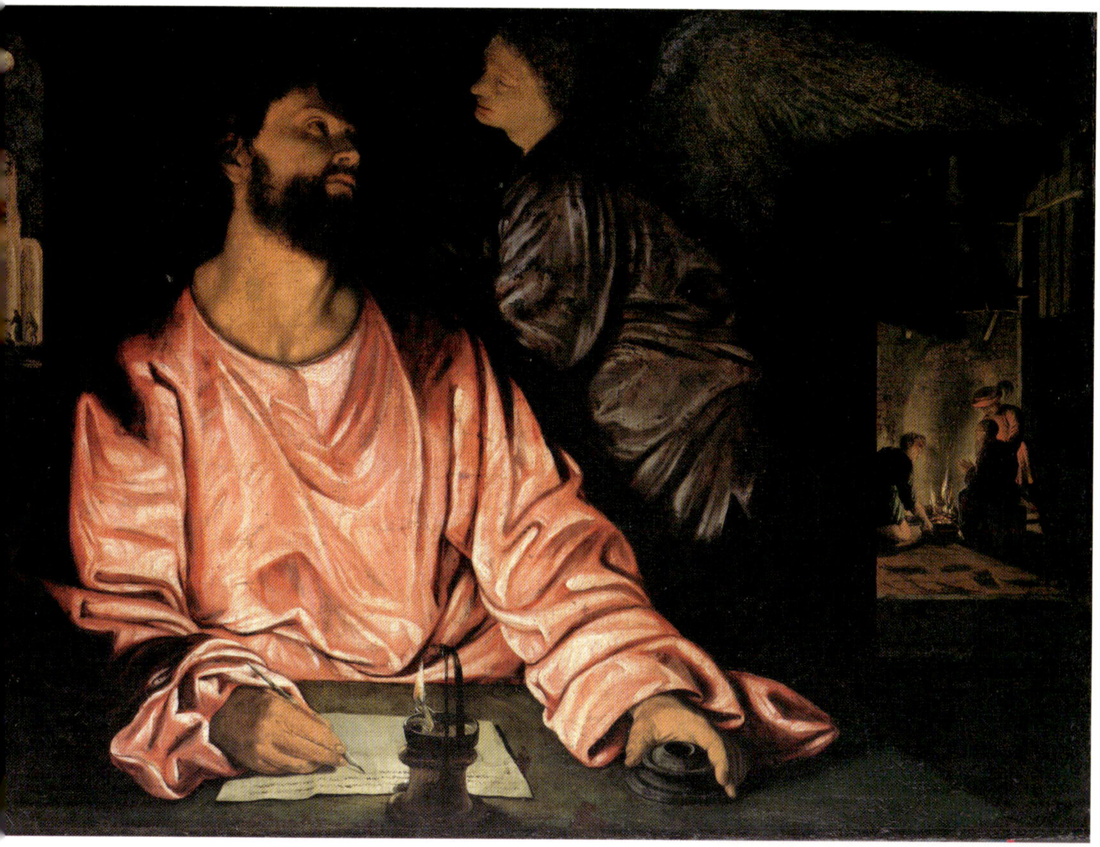

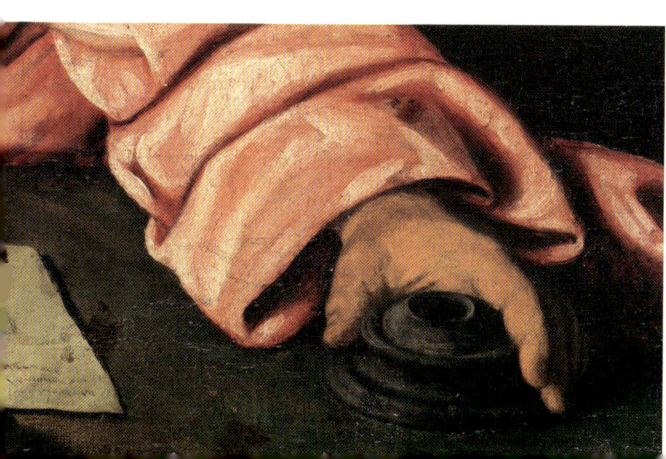

► The figures in the background warm themselves around a small fire that multiplies the effects of light in this intriguing night scene. Moreover, this humble detail brings the tone of the painting back to simple, everyday truth. With the attention to everyday reality typical of 16th-century Lombard painters, Savoldo constitutes an important stylistic precedent to Caravaggio.

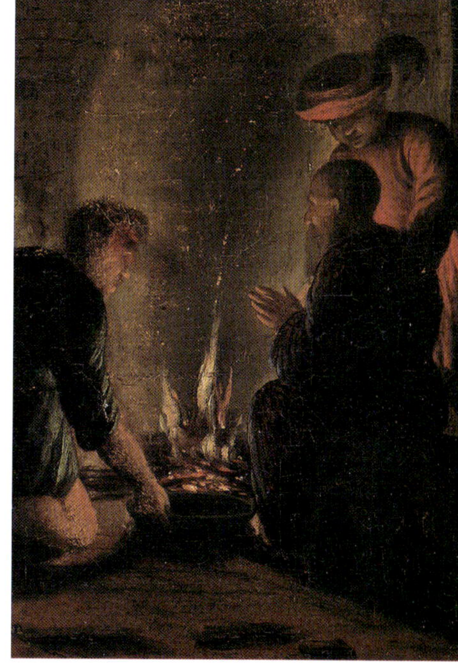

Historicized Portrait

Lorenzo Lotto
*Portrait of a Woman Dressed
as Lucretia*
1533

Oil on canvas, 95 × 110 cm
London, National Gallery

For artist biography, see page 274.

In Renaissance portraiture, the sitter sometimes assumes the appearance and characteristics of a memorable figure from the past. Drawn from the classical sources of Livy and Ovid, the dramatic account of Lucretia – a married woman who was assaulted and raped by Sextus Tarquinius and then took her own life – is one of the memorable stories of the private and civic Antique virtue believed to have formed the basis of Rome's strength and power. The episode's popularity made it an iconographic 'standard' in Renaissance and Baroque painting. The event is presented in a moral and symbolic key: on the one hand, the man's blind violence is condemned, and on the other, Lucretia becomes a model of virtue, a martyr to honour, ready to sacrifice herself for the good of her country. This splendid portrait by Lorenzo Lotto, probably executed on the occasion of the wedding of a young lady named Lucrezia, makes the concept clear through words as well as pictorial references.

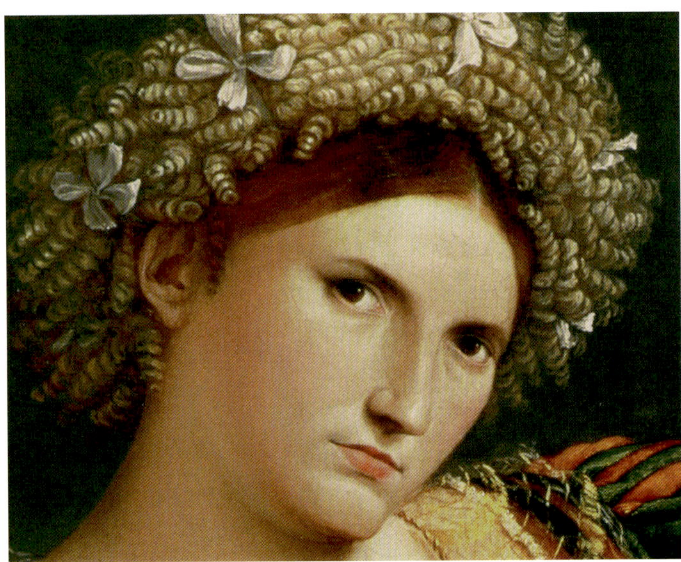

▲ The woman looks the viewer in the eye, and her gesture is explicit: the example of Lucretia invites all women to accept marital fidelity as supreme happiness, and to resist treachery. She also calls viewers to admire the Roman matron's courage.

▼ The way the figure fully occupies the space, the insistent clarity with which the details of clothing and hairstyle are depicted, and the intensity of the sitter's expression make this one of Lotto's most successful portraits.

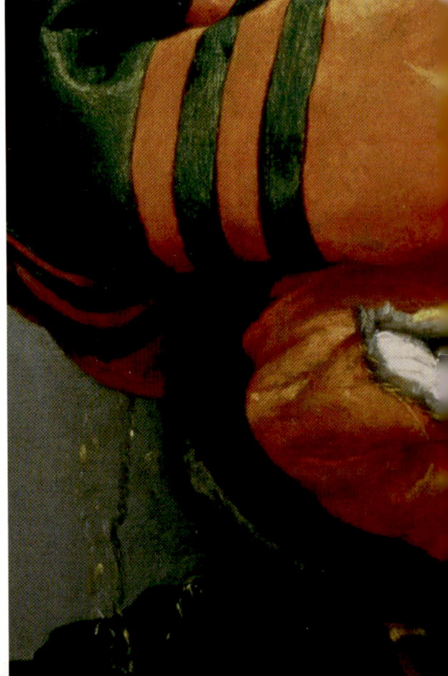

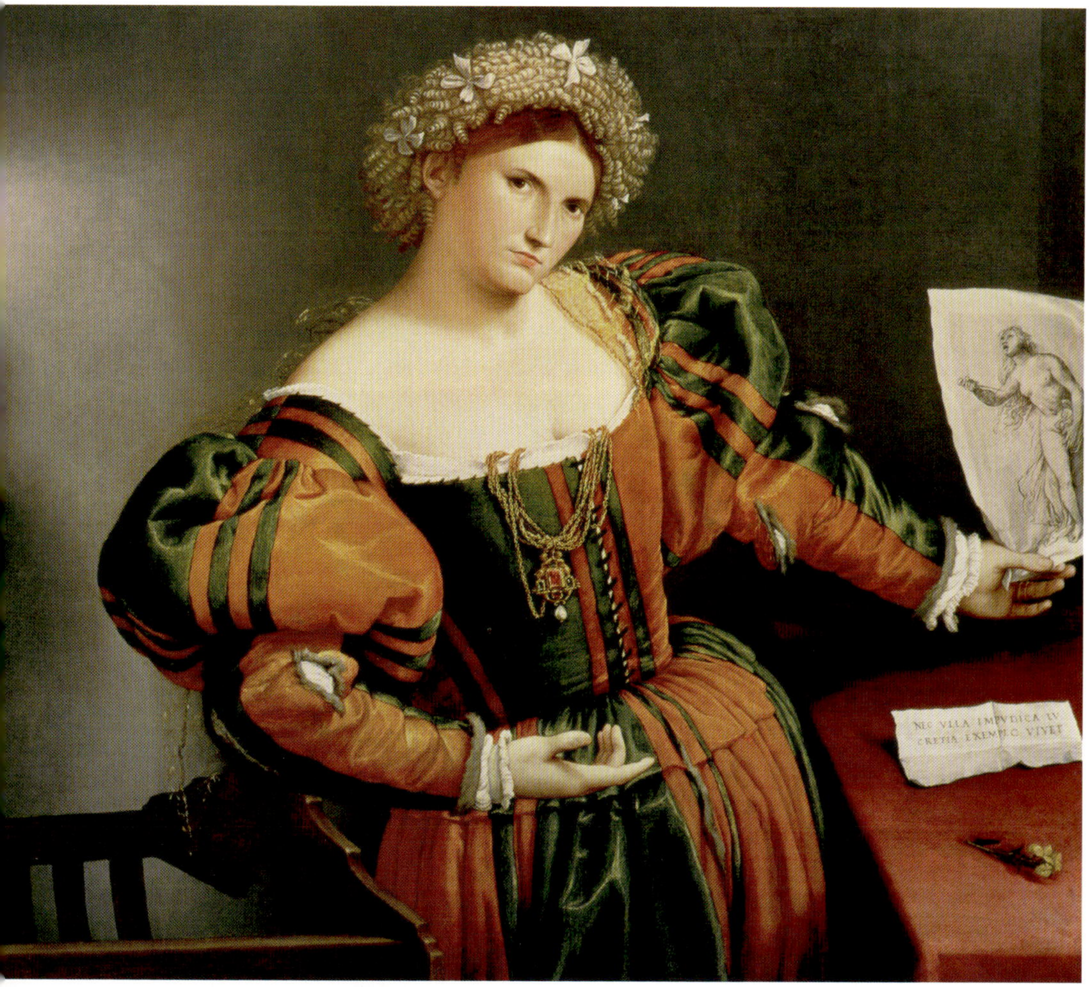

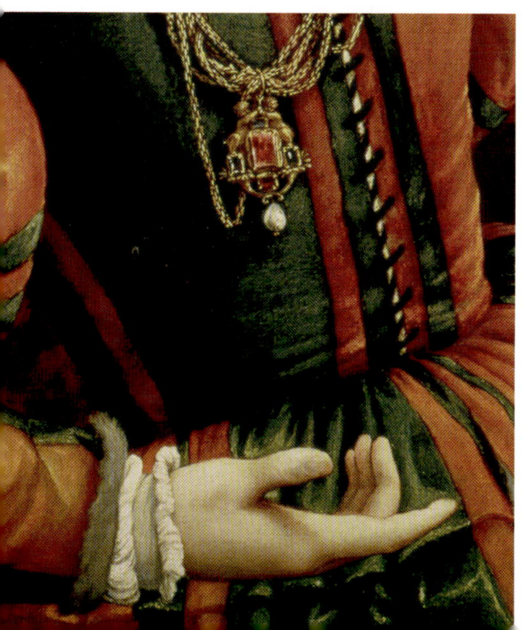

▲ ▶ Resting her elbow on the back of a Savonarola-type folding chair, the sitter compares herself to the exemplary Lucretia, holding a drawing of her suicide in her fingers. The inscription on the scrap of paper on the table also recalls that the exemplary courage of the Roman matron has nothing to do with indecent women, but only those of virtue.

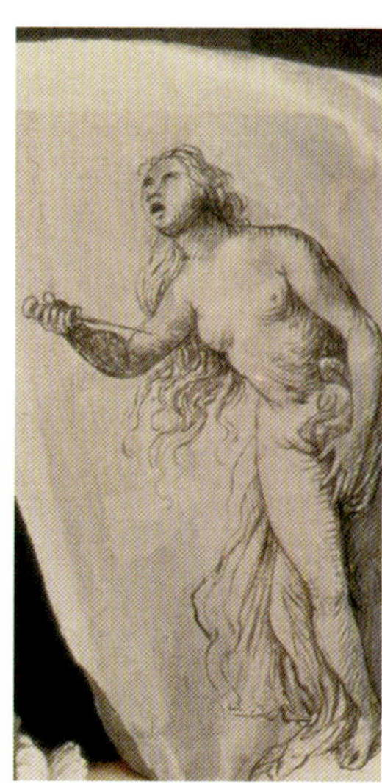

Ambiguity

Parmigianino
Madonna of the Long Neck
1534

Oil on panel, 216 × 132 cm

Florence, Galleria degli Uffizi

For artist biography, see page 280.

From the 1530s, Mannerist painters increasingly produce difficult-to-decipher images veiled in elitist symbolism. N easier to understand today than when they were first painte the figurative references are elusive, leading to various interpretations and ambiguity. The so-called *Madonna of the Long Ne* is Parmigianino's crowning masterpiece. In a sophisticate elegant setting, the painter stretches anatomical verisimilitu to the limits with the figure's unnaturally elongated limb Perplexing presences and mysterious symbols impart an esote value and conceal meanings which the artist has reserved f a select audience.

► The Madonna touches her clothed breast with spindly fingers, and the viewer is left to intuit the nipple. She prepares to nurse the Child, who is in a deep, deathlike sleep. Fascinating but also troubling is the contrast between the little Jesus's livid head and the Madonna's unusual hairstyle gathered and tied with a ribbon.

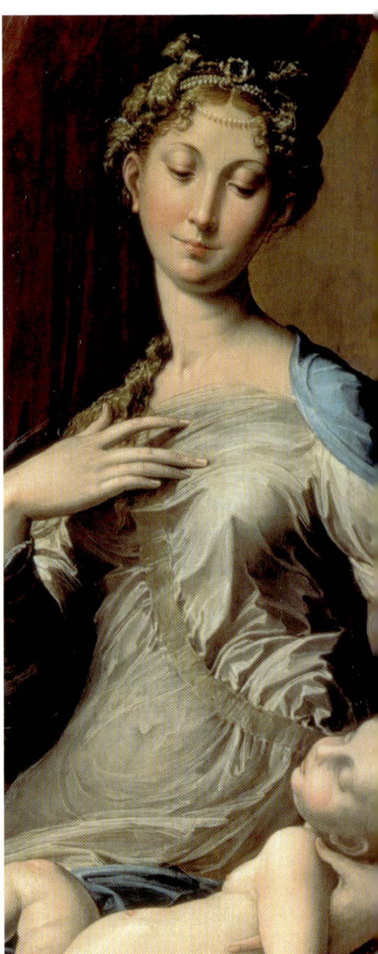

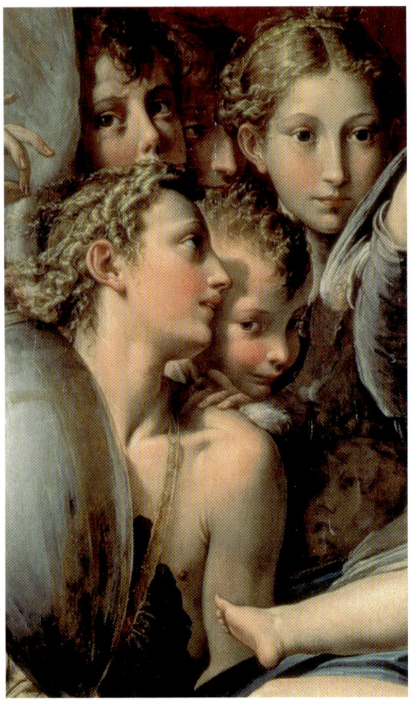

◄ At the left side of the painting is a throng of angels of different ages and statures. Faces and limbs of perfect solidity emerge from the shadows of the drapery. One of the angels in the foreground holds a mysterious, shiny vessel. Old copies and prints after the painting more distinctly show the Cross on the vessel: a reference to the future Passion of Christ. In the original, this detail is barely perceptible today.

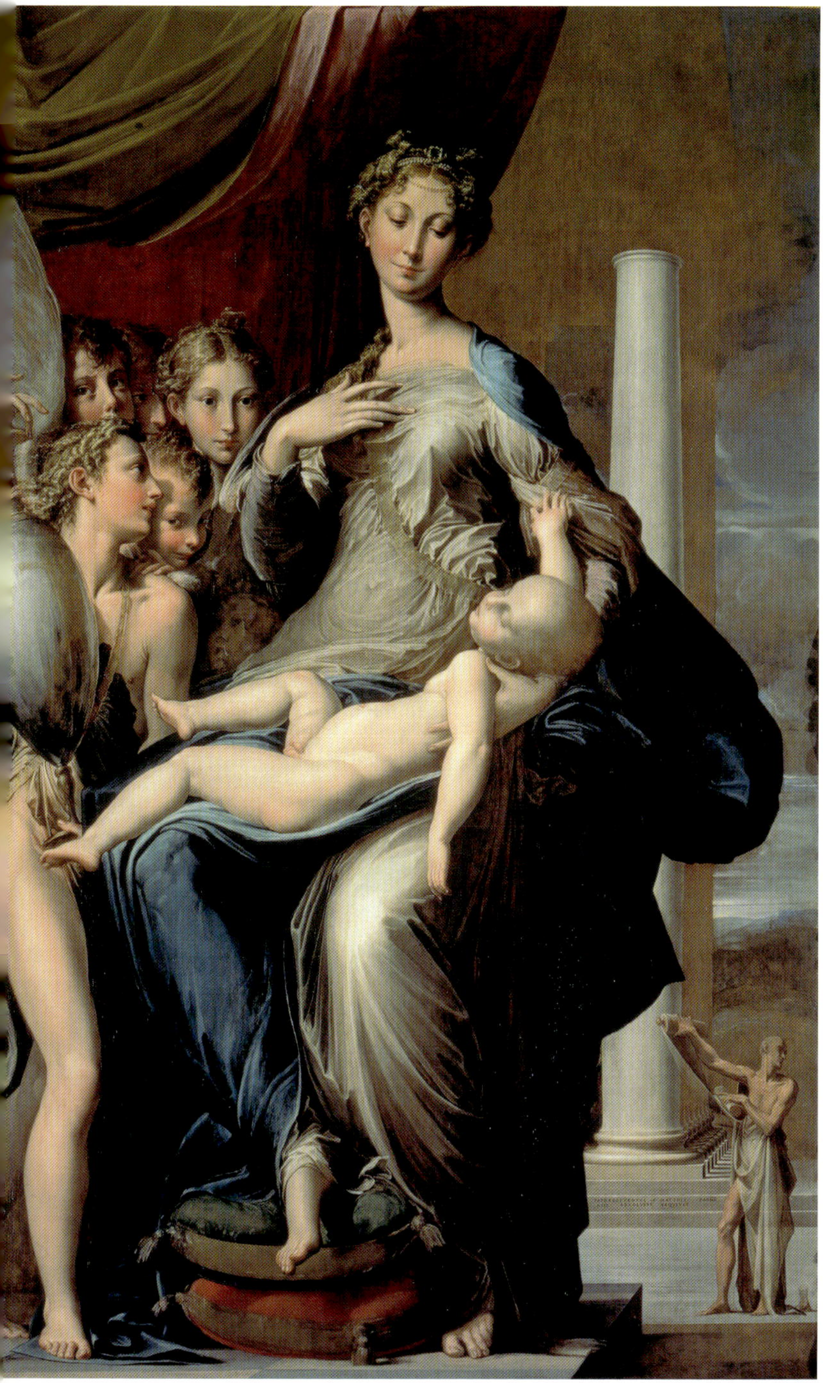

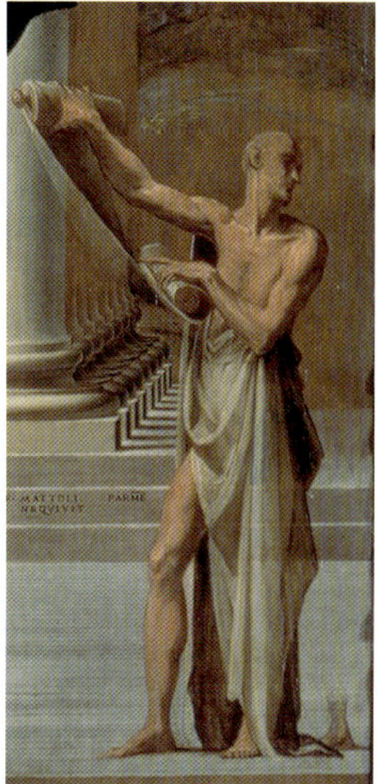

▲ Despite an apparently
long and deeply felt execution,
the painting is unfinished.
Incongruous details such as
the colonnade and the feet
in the background indicate a
figure that was never painted,
and heighten the sense of
ambiguity.

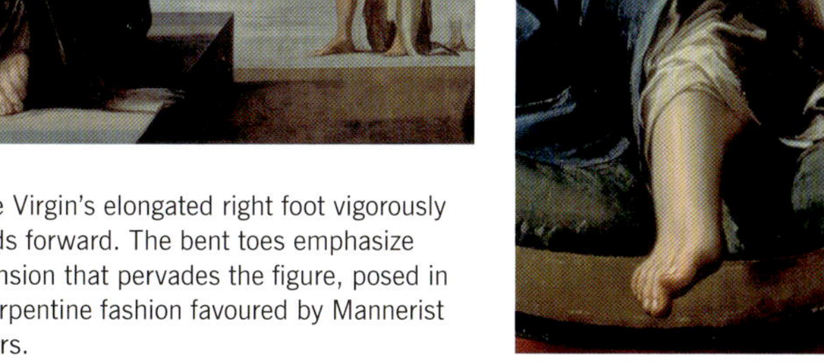

► The Virgin's elongated right foot vigorously
extends forward. The bent toes emphasize
the tension that pervades the figure, posed in
the serpentine fashion favoured by Mannerist
painters.

Sensuality

Titian
Urbino Venus
1536–8

Oil on canvas, 119 × 165 cm

Florence, Galleria degli Uffizi

For artist biography, see page 224.

Titian is one of the artists who most thoroughly investigated the theme of sensual pleasure, painting numerous captivating female nudes in a variety of narrative and symbolic contexts. A comparison of the *Urbino Venus* and the *Dresden Venus* (left, unfinished by Giorgione and finished by Titian in 1510; see pages 222–3) shows how, using an almost identical reclining pose, one nude figure can convey serene contemplation and another, quivering sensuality. While one Venus sleeps in the calm of nature, the other hurls a lightning bolt of seduction at the viewer with her dark, almond-shaped eyes. The title recalls that the painting was made for Francesco Maria della Rovere, Duke of Urbino. The paintings collected by the rulers of Urbino entered the Uffizi collection in 1631 (see also pages 80–1).

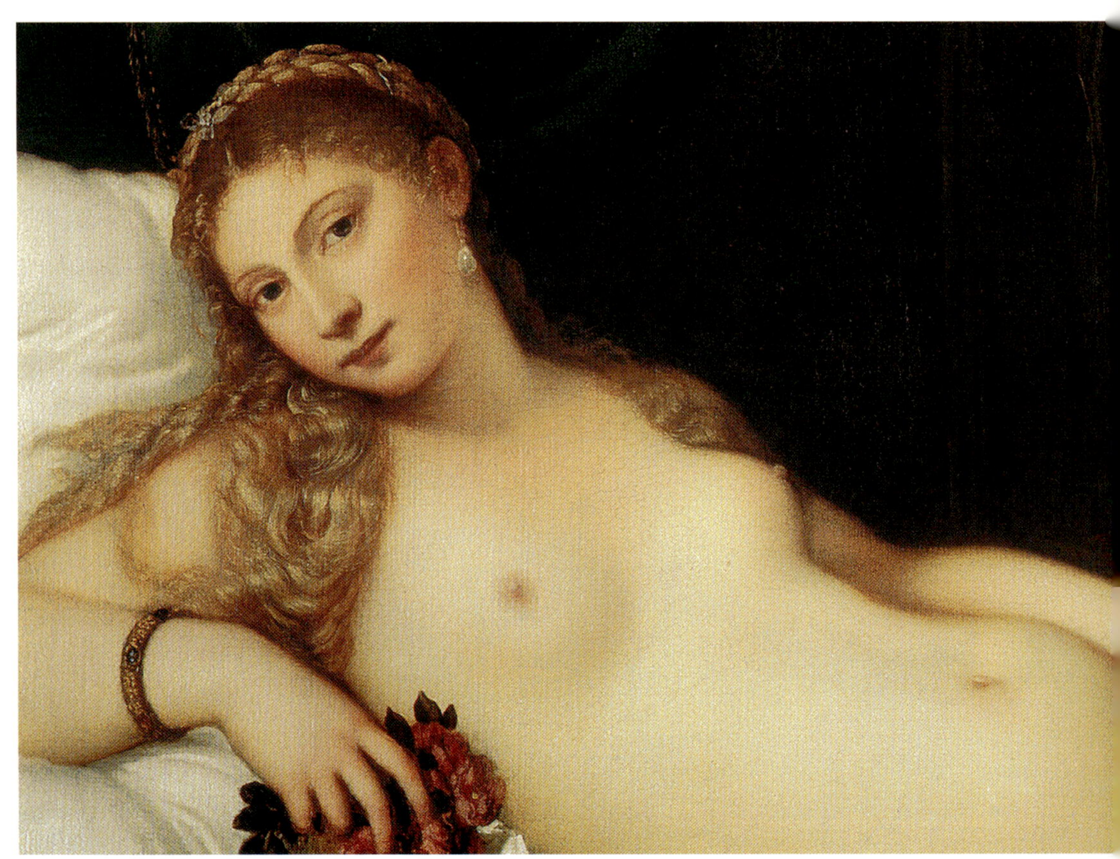

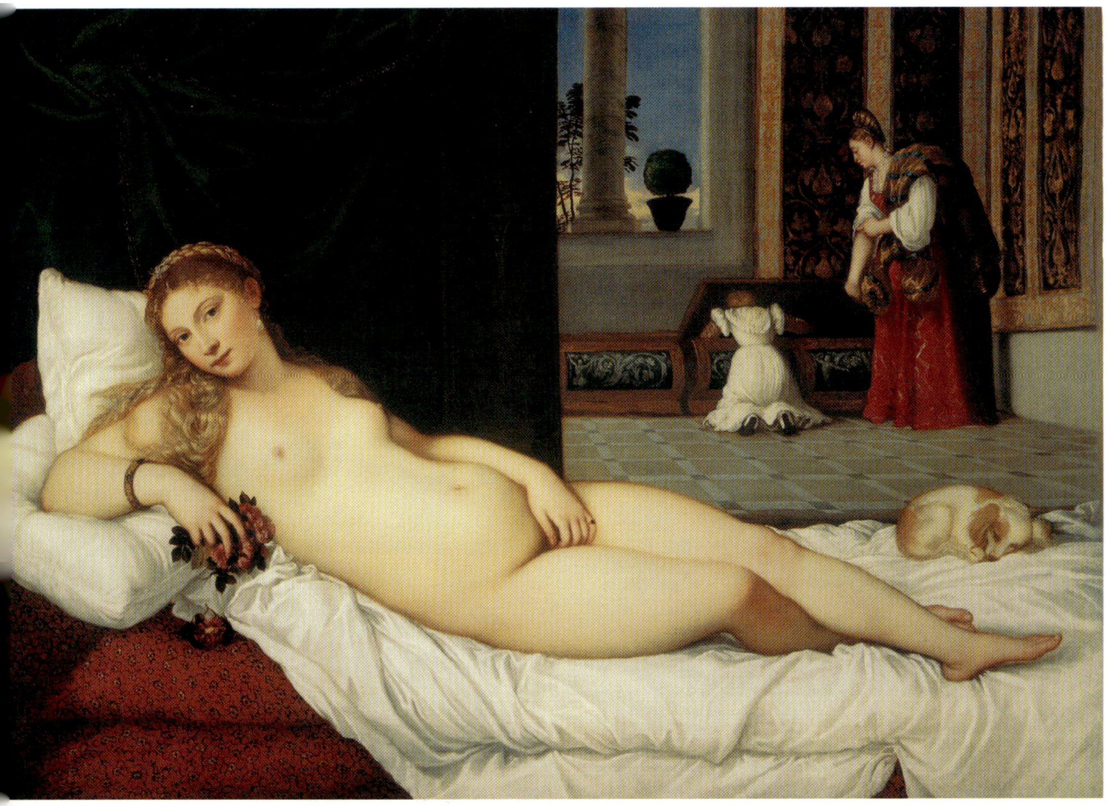

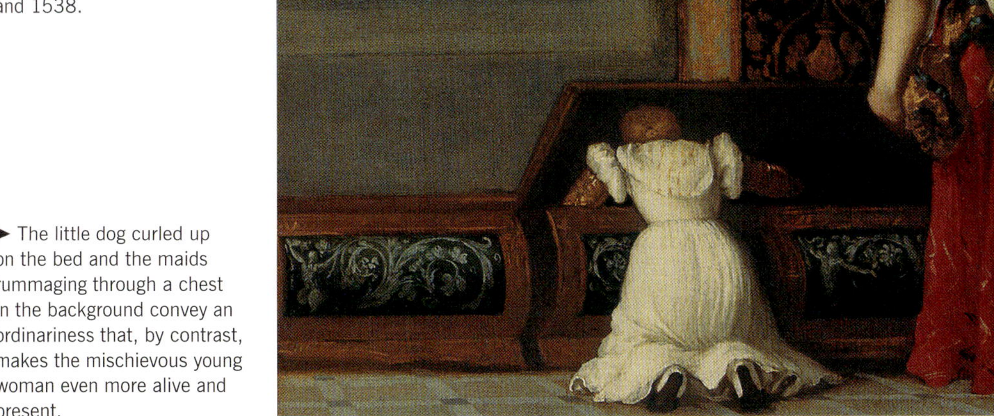

◄ Stretched out on a bed invitingly strewn with plump pillows, the young woman is slenderer than the customary Junoesque figures favoured by painters in the Veneto. The same model, with long, auburn hair and eyes of an unmistakable, almond shape, posed for Titian on various occasions between 1536 and 1538.

► The little dog curled up on the bed and the maids rummaging through a chest in the background convey an ordinariness that, by contrast, makes the mischievous young woman even more alive and present.

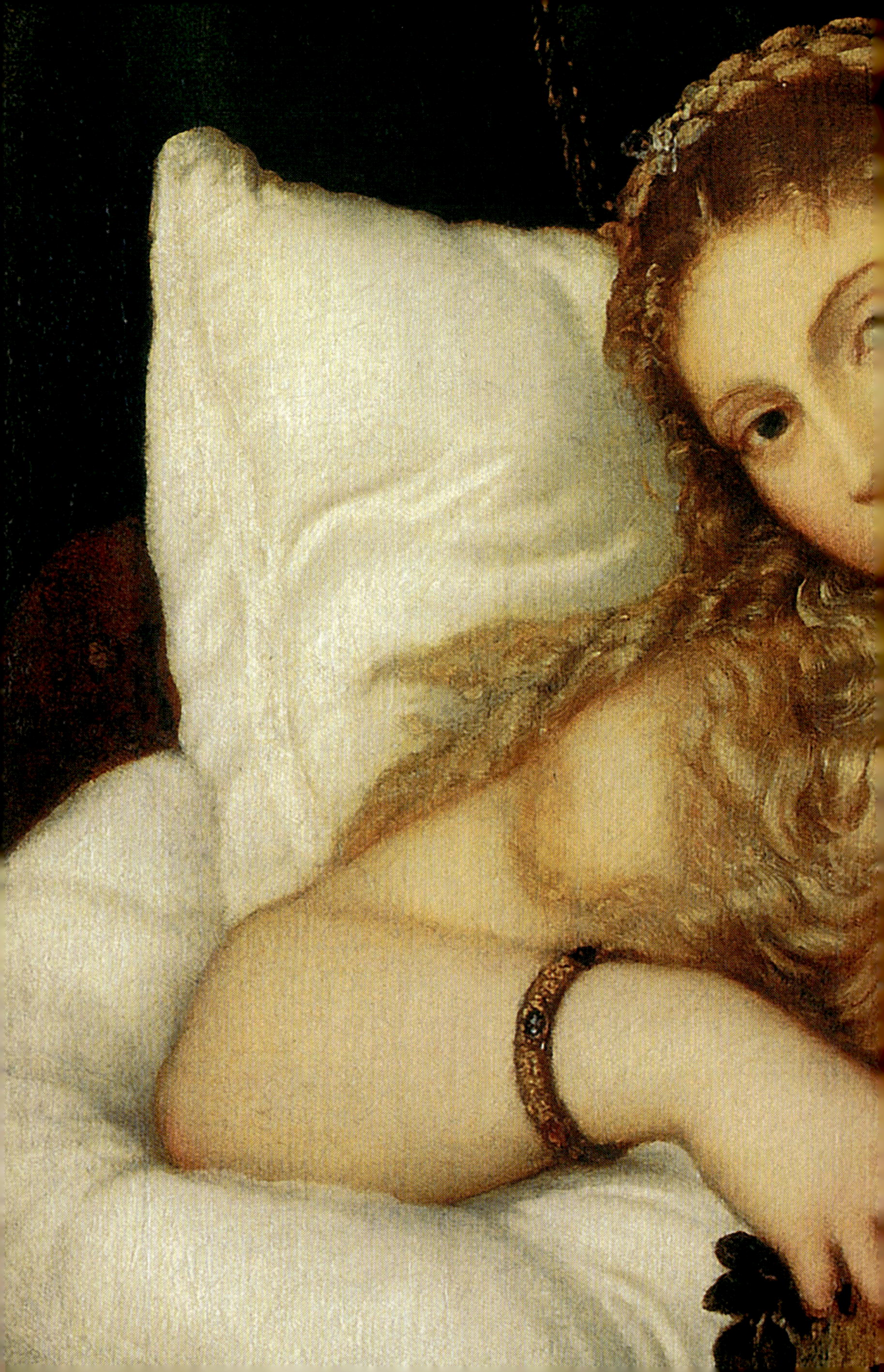

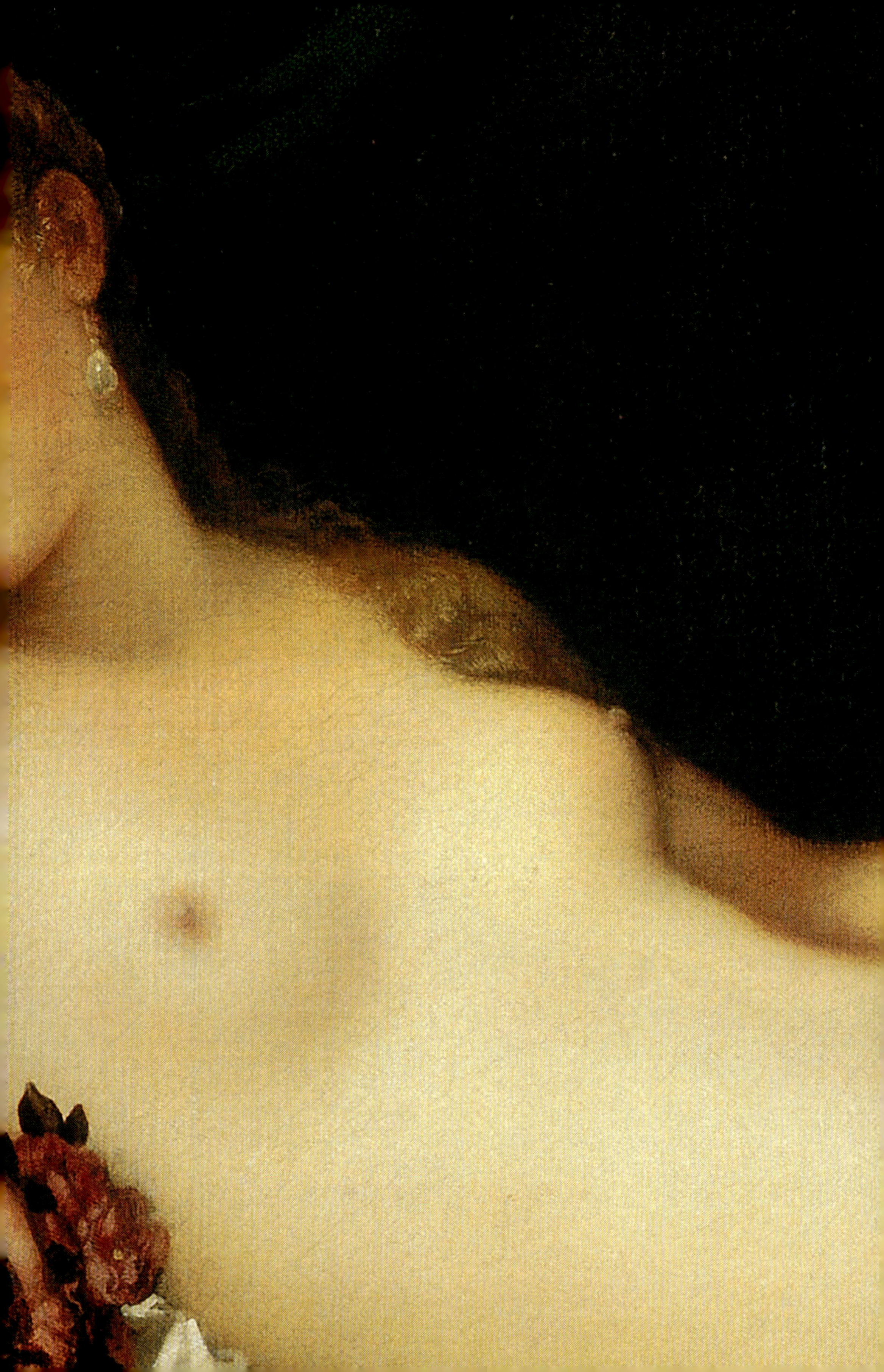

Crisis

Michelangelo
The Last Judgment
1536–41

Fresco, 1370 × 1220 cm

Vatican City, Musei Vaticani,
Sistine Chapel

For artist biography, see page 190.

Preparation for this fresco on the back wall of the Sistine Chapel began in 1535 with the destruction of the existing frescoes and the erection of a new supporting wall. After extended work on the drawings, Michelangelo began to paint *The Last Judgment* in 1537, and the fresco was inaugurated on 31 October 1541, when the artist was 66 years old. The contrast with the ceiling fresco that Michelangelo had executed 30 years earlier (see pages 212–13) is striking: God the Creator has been transformed into the no less dynamic image of Christ the Judge, dividing the damned from the blessed. On the ceiling, Michelangelo exalted the beauty of the human body; here he depicts it undone, anguished and cast into the abyss. The Judgment sweeps away both soul and flesh. Humankind, which had dominated nature through intelligence, rediscovered the values of the classical world, and placed strength and trust in the ideals of justice and beauty – that strong, secure humankind exalted by Michelangelo in the figures on the ceiling – was now finished, broken. For all practical purposes, the dreams and ideals of the Renaissance came to an end with this fresco.

▼ The saints crowd around a youthful, beardless Christ. These awestruck, large and entirely nude figures witness the implacability of divine justice in powerless wonder. Even the Virgin Mary seems to quail beside Christ the Judge.

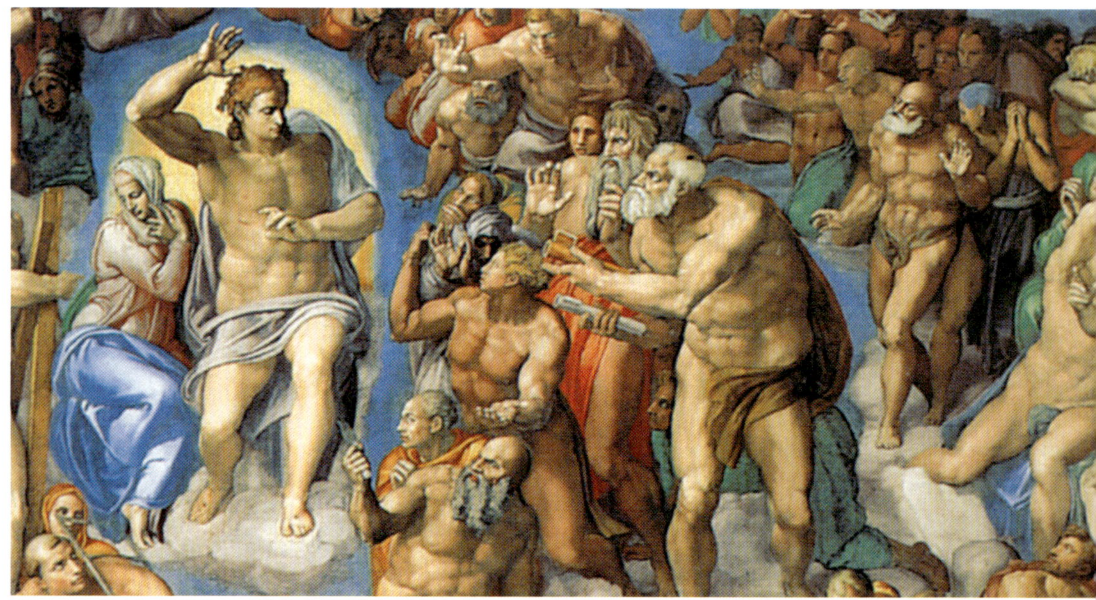

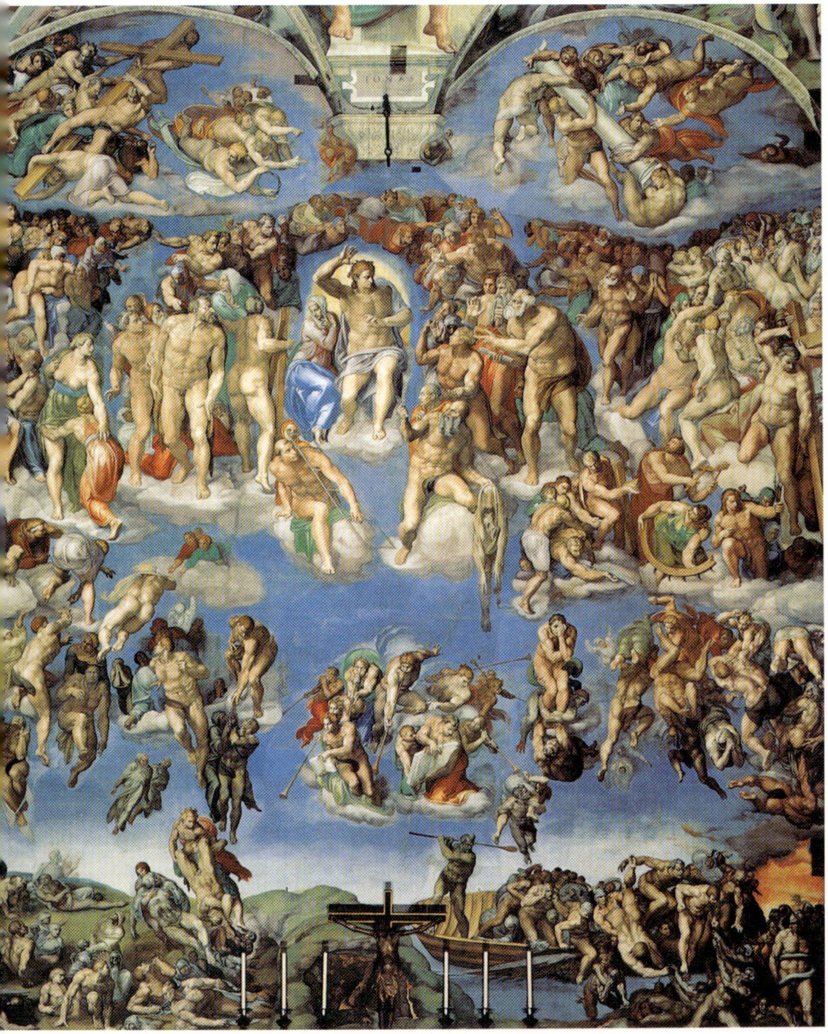

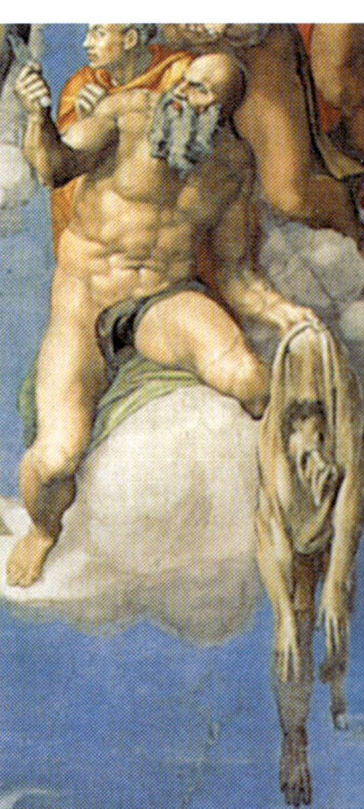

▼ One of the most impressive figures is St Bartholomew, who holds his own skin in his hands. Michelangelo painted a dramatic self-portrait on the flayed figure's fleshless mask, as if the artist himself had been depleted and broken by the fresco's cosmic message.

▲ Under a dense, even sky, where time and space are obliterated, Hell combines with Heaven, the Resurrection of the Flesh with the Last Judgment, angels with devils, and the blessed with the damned in a frightening vision crowded with some 400 figures. By 1564, not long before Michelangelo's death, the painter Daniele da Volterra had covered those examples of 'nudity' considered most scandalous with veils and drapes.

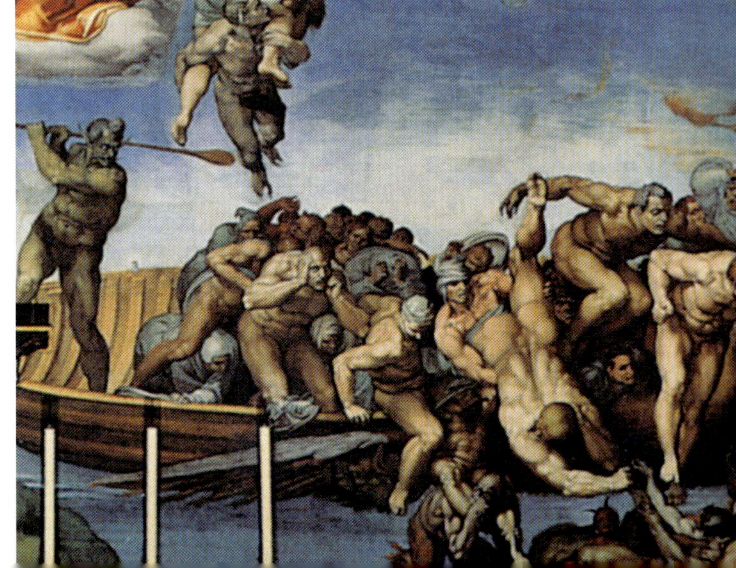

► Along the bottom of the fresco, just above the altar, Michelangelo inserted a visual quote from Dante's *Divine Comedy*: Charon, with flaming eyes, ferries the damned to Hell and strikes those who lag behind with his oar.

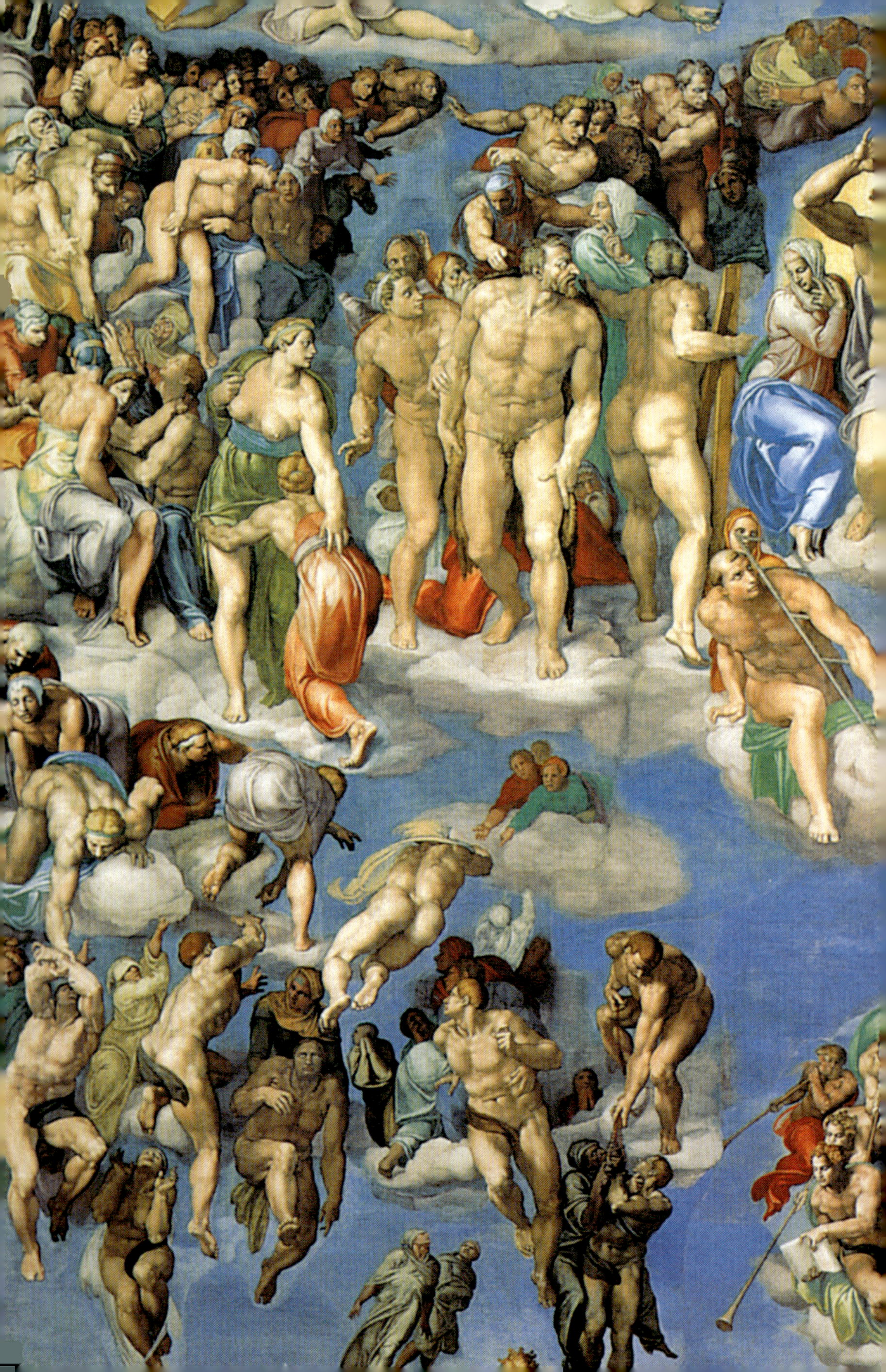

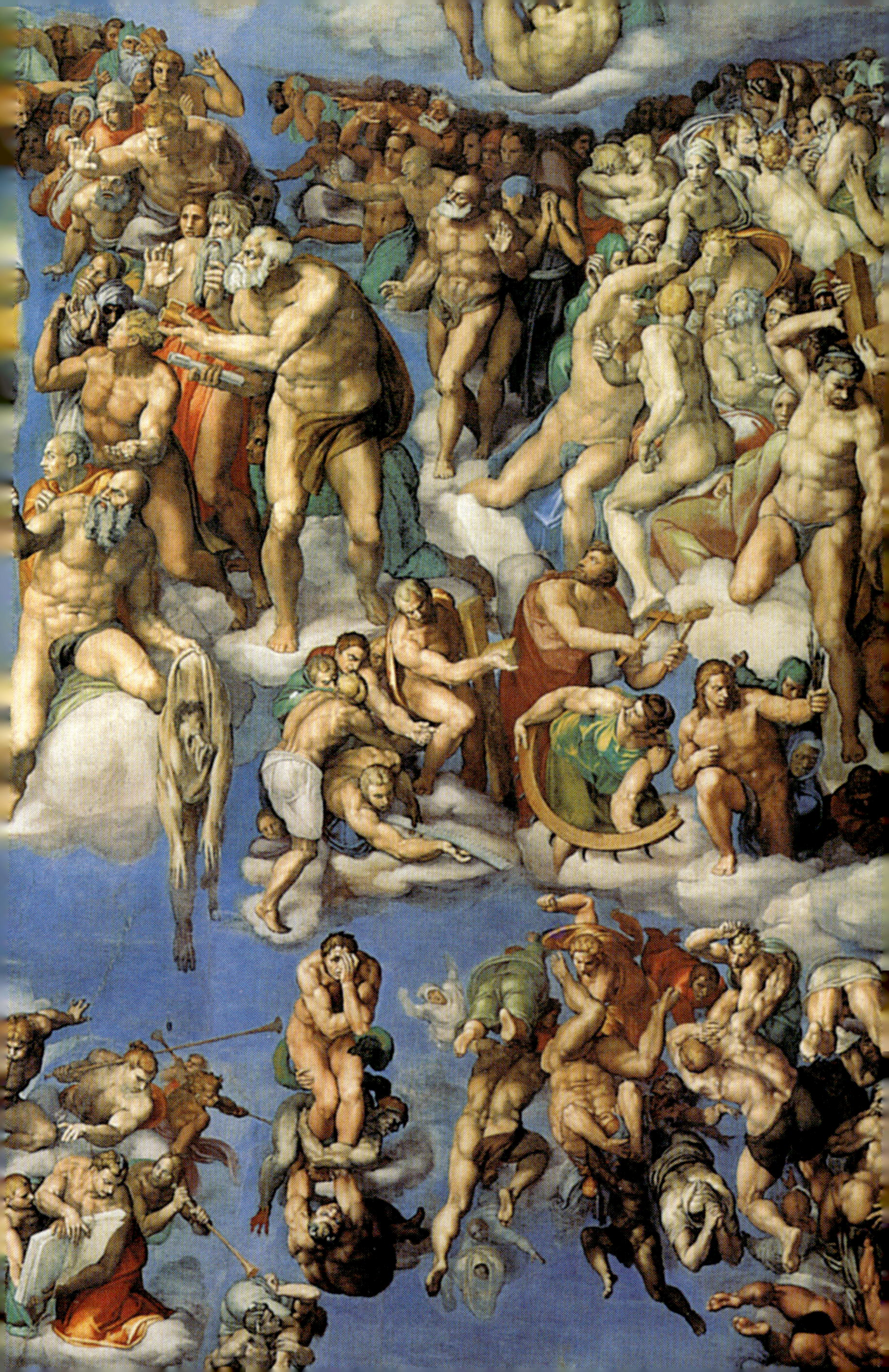

Allegory

Agnolo Bronzino
Allegory
1540

Oil on panel, 147 × 117 cm

London, National Gallery

Agnolo Bronzino

(Agnolo di Cosimo di Mariano Tori)

Florence, 1503–72

The career of Bronzino, whose paintings typify the taste of the grand duchy of Florence in the mid-15th century, sums up the history of Mannerism – from its initial revolt against traditional models to its consolidation as an intellectual expression of the regime and, ultimately, its transformation into a style aimed at a discriminating but restricted cultural aristocracy. A pupil of Pontormo, Bronzino collaborated with his master on important projects in Florence during the 1520s. In 1530, he began painting portraits at the Della Rovere court in Urbino, developing an individual style characterized by clean, compact, enamel-like colours and by the figures' almost total lack of movement. By about 1540, he had become the favourite painter of the Medici court and the Florentine aristocracy, appreciated for his literary as well as artistic gifts. In addition to his increasingly refined portraits of nobles, Bronzino also took on large decorative projects such as the frescoes in the Medici villas, paintings destined for the grand duke's apartments at Palazzo Vecchio and cartoons for the grand duke's tapestries.

Esteemed for his ability to devise stimulating, intellectually complex allegories, Agnolo Bronzino assumed a high-profile role in the Medici court in Florence. The frequent absence from the city of Vasari and Salviati (in addition to the now permanent absence of Michelangelo) made Bronzino easily the city's foremost painter and, more generally, the leading exponent of the style favoured by the international courts. This *Allegory* – a quintessential example of international Mannerism's combination of refined intellectualism with a distinctly sensual component – possesses a strong moral content.

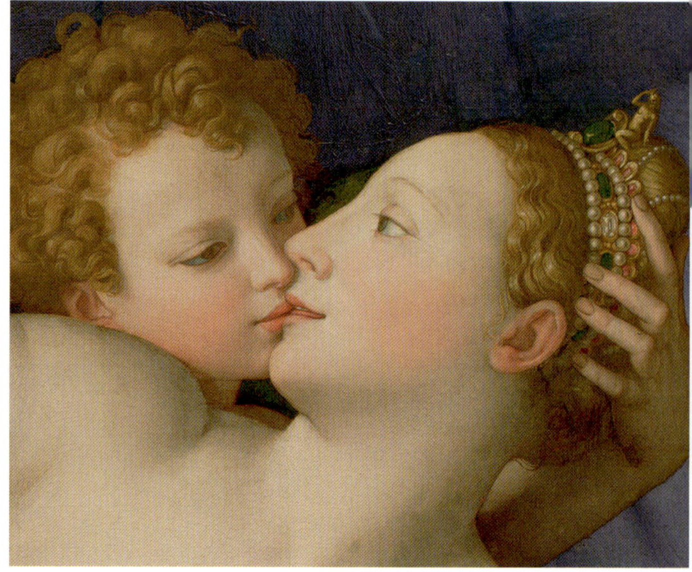

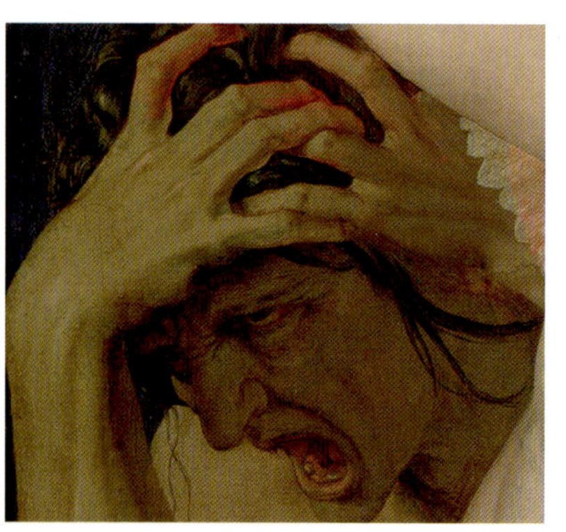

◄ Each and every detail of the painting, even the choice of colours, has allegorical significance. Jealousy, whom Bronzino represents as the inevitable result of Love, has a greenish cast and the distorted facial features of a madman.

▲ The three main figures are Venus and Cupid, who are kissing (an allusion to Lust), and behind them, on the right, Joy, represented as a carefree, smiling cherub.

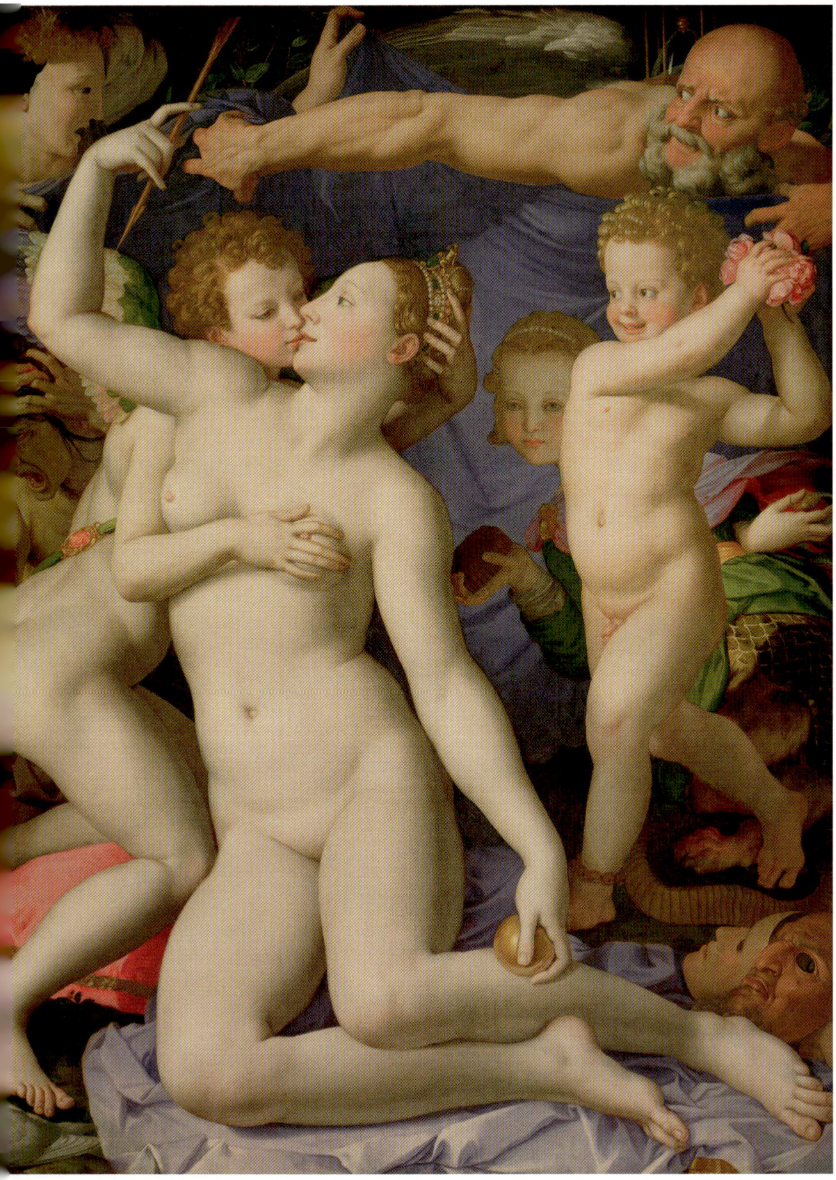

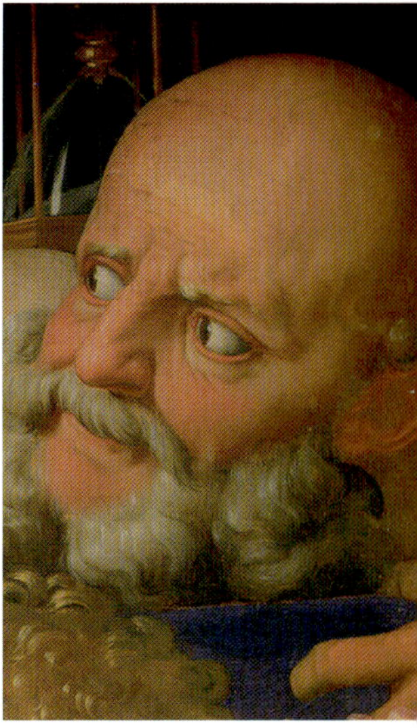

▲ In the upper part, the figures that symbolize Truth (on the left) and Time (the old man) are prepared to cover Venus's beauty with a blue veil.

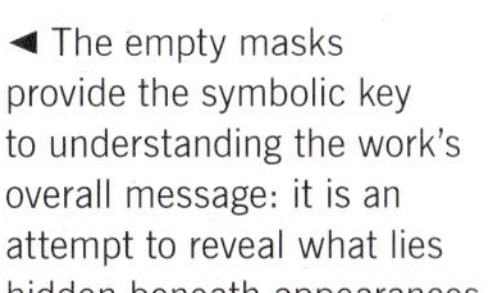

◄ The empty masks provide the symbolic key to understanding the work's overall message: it is an attempt to reveal what lies hidden beneath appearances.

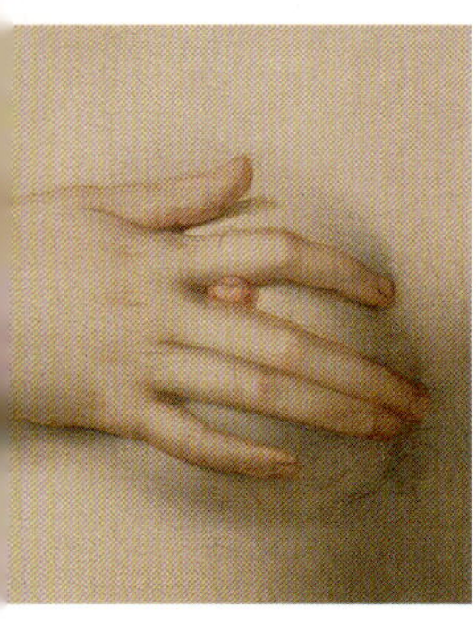

◄ The intricate subject matter is conveyed in a highly formal manner, with flawlessly smooth brushwork that is almost varnish-like. A strong erotic charge permeates the scene. Cupid's hand on Venus's breast recalls Parmigianino's precedent of 1534 (see pages 306–7).

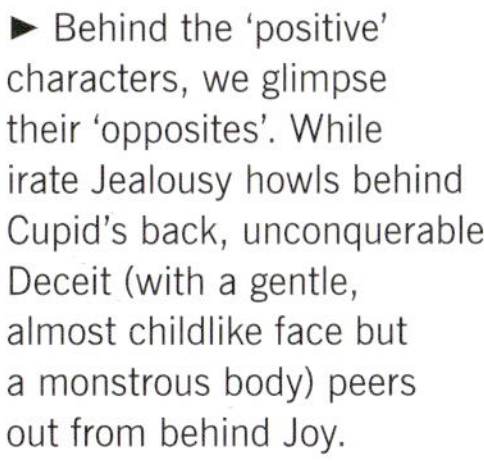

► Behind the 'positive' characters, we glimpse their 'opposites'. While irate Jealousy howls behind Cupid's back, unconquerable Deceit (with a gentle, almost childlike face but a monstrous body) peers out from behind Joy.

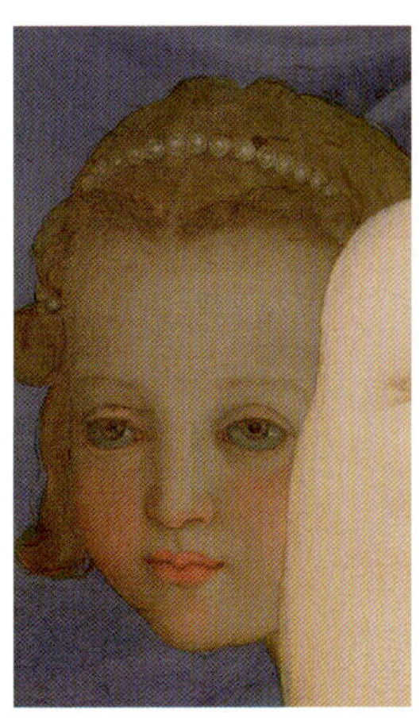

Melancholy

Moretto da Brescia
Portrait of Count Fortunato
Martinengo Cesaresco (?)
1540–2

Oil on canvas, 114 × 94 cm
London, National Gallery

Moretto da Brescia

(Alessandro Bonvicino)

Brescia, c. 1490–1554

An elegant and knowledgeable painter, Moretto perfectly illustrates the vitality that characterized the 'provincial' schools of Italian painting during the 16th century. Along with Romanino and Savoldo, Moretto initiated a period of brilliancy in his native Brescia, working independently yet fully aware of the advances being made by Titian and Lorenzo Lotto, who was active in nearby Bergamo. In the middle of his career, Moretto developed an erudite, classicizing style and adopted a Mannerist approach. However, he soon reoriented himself towards an incisive realism, depicting in his portraits and altarpieces solemn-faced models in serenely domestic settings. Moretto is considered one of the most direct forerunners of Caravaggio, and in his later years he painted sacred works that were already attuned to the visual dictates of the Counter-Reformation.

As we have already seen, a mood of melancholy is not uncommon in 16th-century portraits. According to the Aristotelian doctrine of the four humours that flow through the human body (and whose imbalance can have profound consequences), melancholy is produced by an excess of black bile (in Greek *melan cholè*) and manifests itself in a negative or even pathological state of mind. In a famous engraving from 1514, Dürer suggested a new psychological interpretation of 'melancholy': from a condition of initially unwelcome pensive solitude, an inner strength emerges, gradually leading to the creation of great works. An eloquent example of aristocratic 'melancholy' is Moretto's portrait of a gentleman, tentatively identified as Count Martinengo Cesaresco.

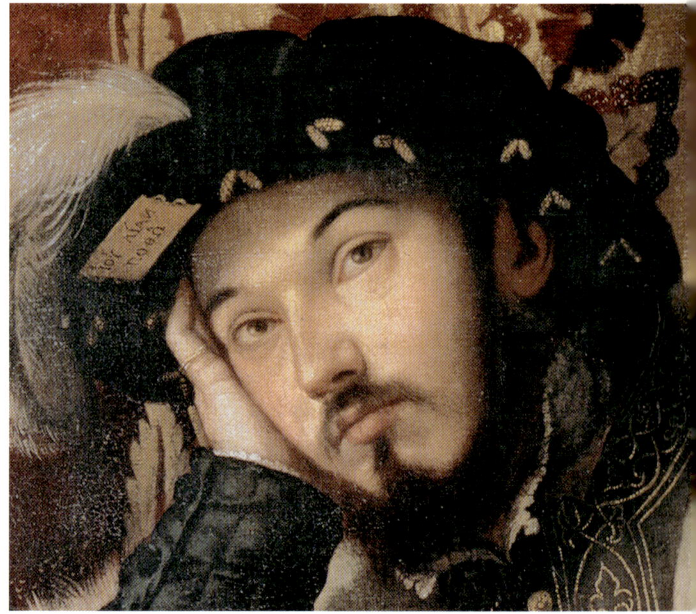

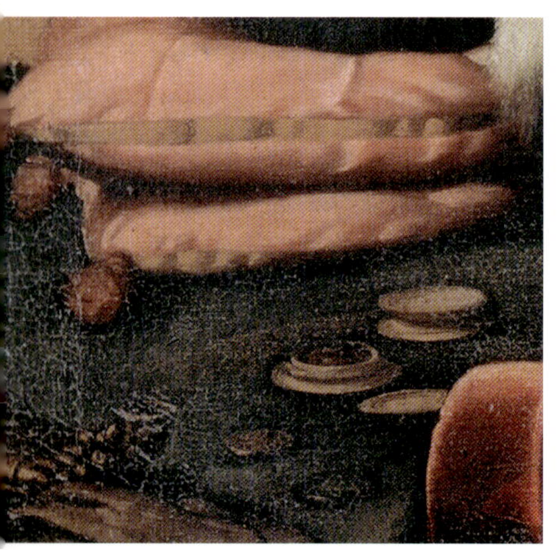

◀ The scene is set in a collector's study. As in the portrait of Andrea Odoni by Lotto (see pages 286–7), ancient coins and antiquarian objects are scattered across the table.

▲ The count's pose echoes that of a figure in an earlier work by Giorgione (see pages 220–1), with the tilted head resting on the palm of one hand, characteristic of the melancholic. A Greek motto on the man's hat explains the reason for his dejection: 'I desire too much.' It is not clear whether these words refer to love or, less commonly, to an awareness of the limits of knowledge and human possibility.

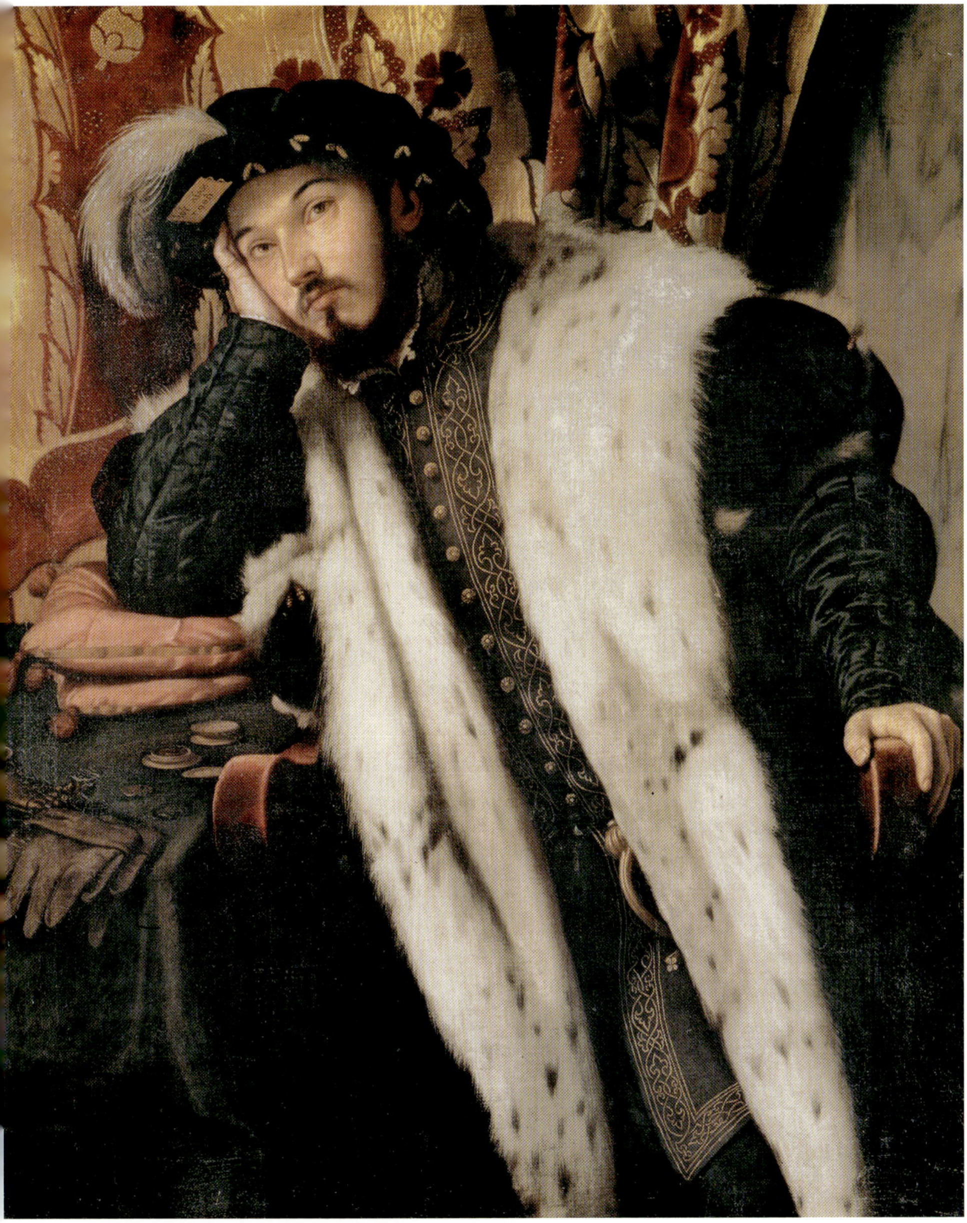

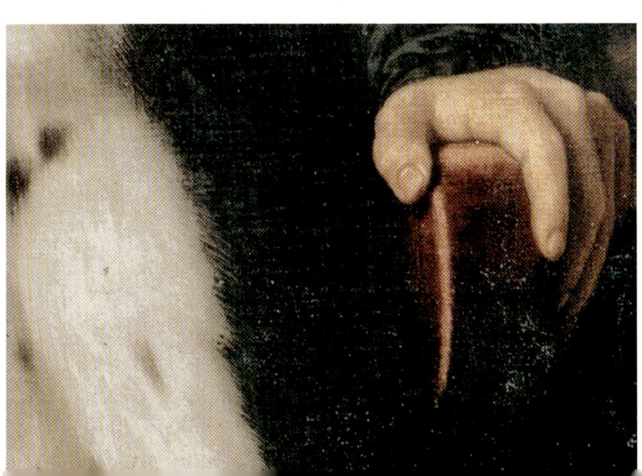

◄ The details of the clothing, furniture and furnishings underscore the elevated rank, wealth and good taste of this Brescian gentleman. Nonetheless, his material good fortune is evidently not enough to uplift his melancholy spirits.

Stage Scenery

Paris Bordone
Bathsheba
1540

Oil on canvas, 234 × 217 cm

Cologne, Wallraf-Richartz-Museum

Paris Bordone

Treviso, 1500–Venice, 1571

A representative of the Veneto school, Paris Bordone pursued a two-track career. In his native region, he resided and worked in the provinces, only occasionally undertaking projects in Venice (such as *The Presentation of the Ring of St Mark to the Doge*, now at the Gallerie dell'Accademia). On the other hand, he executed many important works during extended stays elsewhere: Milan, Mantua, Fontainebleau (in the service of Francis I) and Augsburg, where the Fugger family greatly admired him. The Trevisan painter's early style, which shows a penchant for colour linked to his training under Titian, gradually evolved towards compact forms, reflected light with a metallic quality and perspectival settings that reveal a familiarity with the expressive explorations of international Mannerism.

In the court art tradition, painters were responsible for the production of spectacles, festivals and ephemeral ornamental constructions. With the passing of time, set decoration took on the status of an independent art. Probably as early as the 1520s, the architect and painter Baldassare Peruzzi made painted perspective backdrops for plays performed in palazzo courtyards, urban spaces and private gardens. In the *Second Book of Perspective* (1545), the architect Sebastiano Serlio codified three basic types of scenery: tragic, comic and rustic. In the engravings that illustrate this treatise, set designers and painters found an indispensable source of inspiration.

► The architectural backdrop seen here is drawn directly from Sebastiano Serlio's set design treatises. In fact, Paris Bordone has reproduced exactly the model for the 'tragic set', characterized by austere classical buildings; an obelisk rises in their midst.

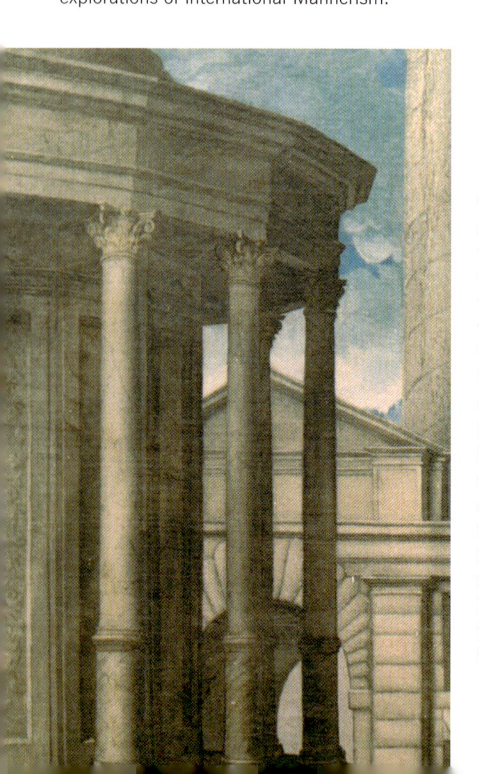

◄ At the time that Paris Bordone made this painting, permanent indoor theatres with stock scenery did not yet exist in Italy. Performances took place in temporary venues. The first 'modern' theatre, the Teatro Olimpico that Andrea Palladio built in Vicenza, was inaugurated in 1585, after its architect's death. It was soon followed by the one that Vincenzo Scamozzi erected in the small town of Sabbioneta, a Gonzaga principality known for the cultivated tastes of many of its citizens. The Sabbioneta theatre's scenery backdrop is very similar to the one represented in this painting.

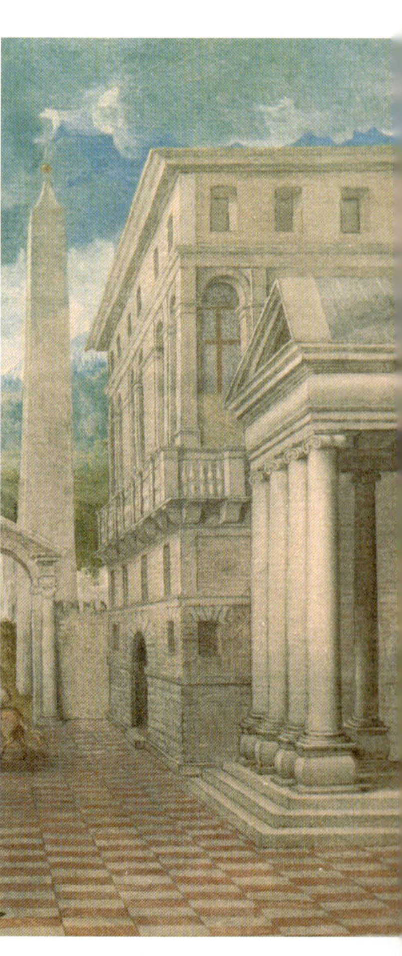

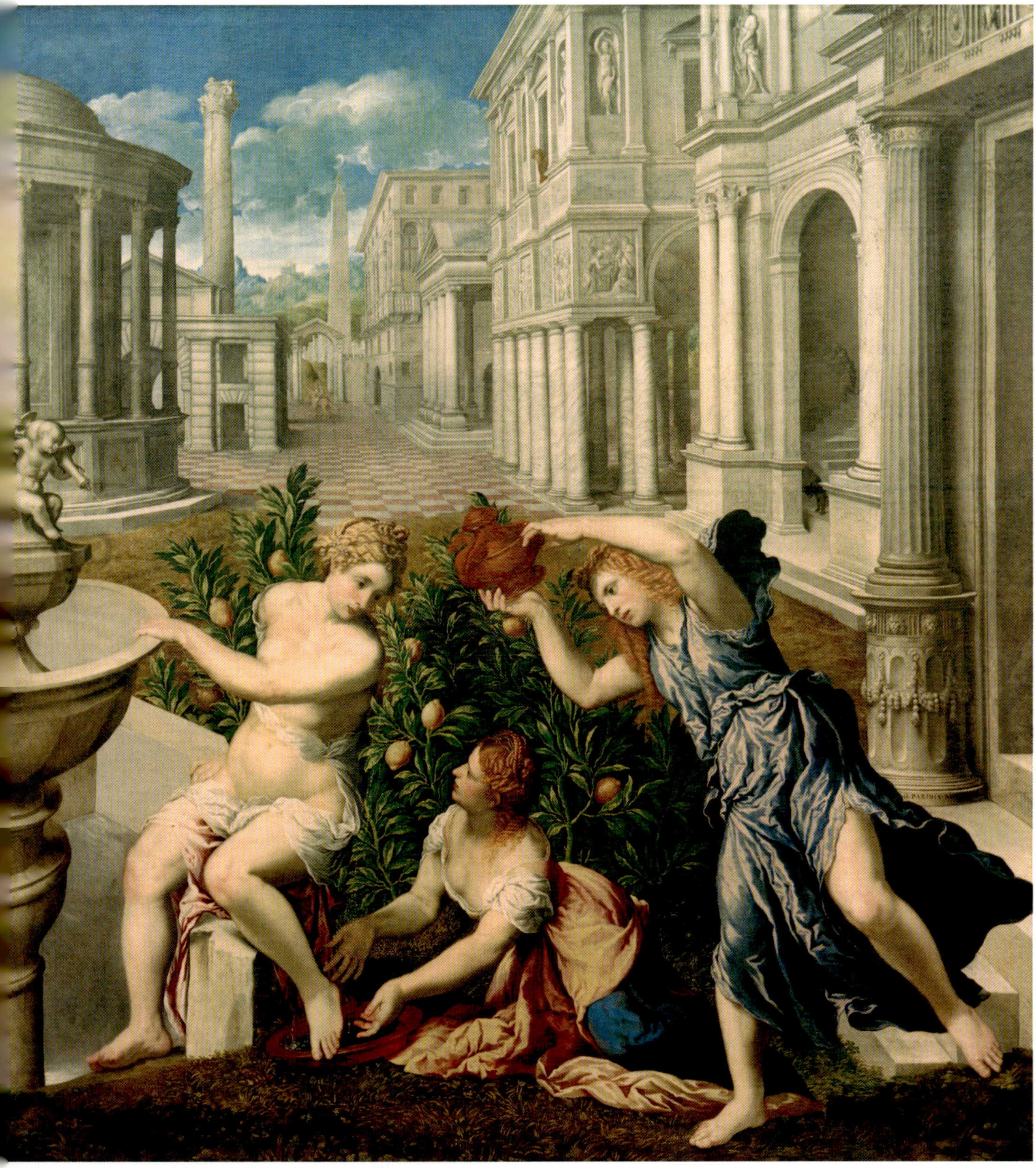

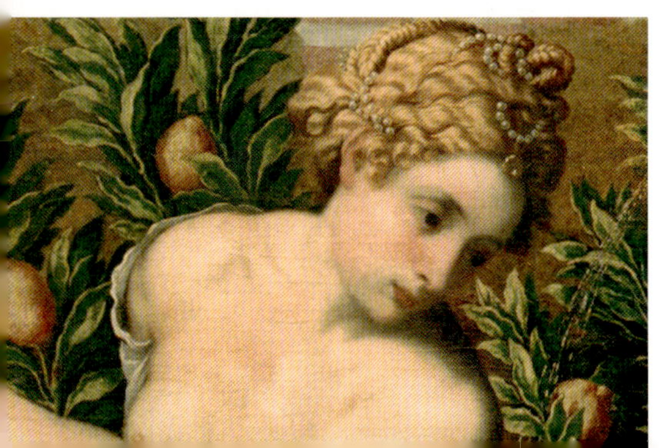

◄ The slightly unnatural poses of the figures in the foreground, 'acting out' the biblical episode, seem to emphasize the essential theatricality of an onstage performance. Even the garden in which the events take place leaves the impression of a temporary structure, rather than a natural setting.

Power

Titian
Portrait of Doge Andrea Gritti
c. 1540

Oil on canvas, 133 × 103 cm
Washington, National Gallery of Art

For artist biography, see page 224.

Titian introduced a new interpretation of the 'official' portrait, establishing models that would be followed for centuries and would even shape the preferred image of certain 20th-century dictators. When portraying leading international political figures, he tried to identify their personality and resolve by choosing dynamic moments, fleeting gestures and telling expressions. This approach paid tribute to the actions that characterize distinguished men – emperor or pope, commander or doge – and their influence in the world and in history. Titian's unequalled mastery as a portraitist comes not only from his skill in creating close likenesses but also from his ability to capture the will and spirit of his subjects.

▼ Andrea Gritti, who was elected doge of Venice in 1523 and died in 1538 after governing the Serenissima for 15 years, is one of the most important figures in 16th-century Venetian history. He was responsible for encouraging the new classical trend in architecture, a distinguishing characteristic of Venice at the height of the Renaissance.

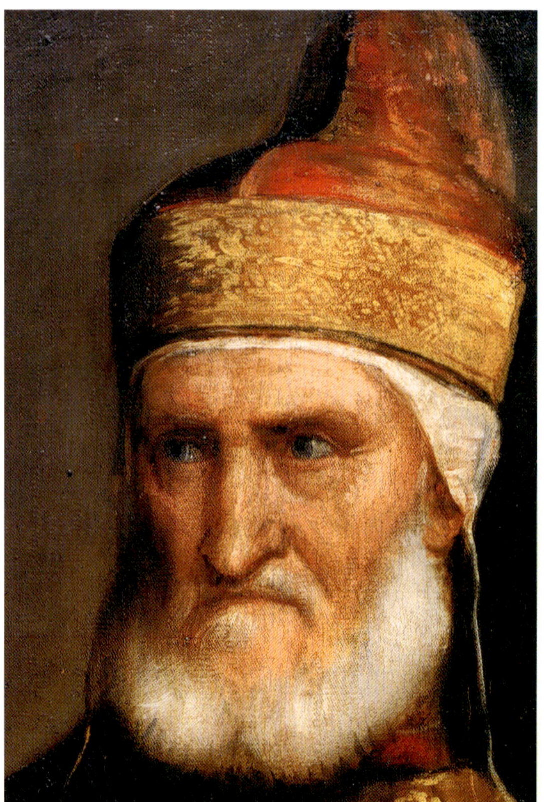

► Titian's painting of the deceased doge is a 'monument' to his memory and not an official portrait. This explains the energetic torsion, absent from more conventional portraits, and especially the experimental quality of the brushwork (see pages 332–3). Titian did not apply the simple, unsatisfying formula of a eulogistic portrait celebrating the idea of power itself. On the contrary, his paintings capture an explosive force composed of thought, psychology, agitation and intellect.

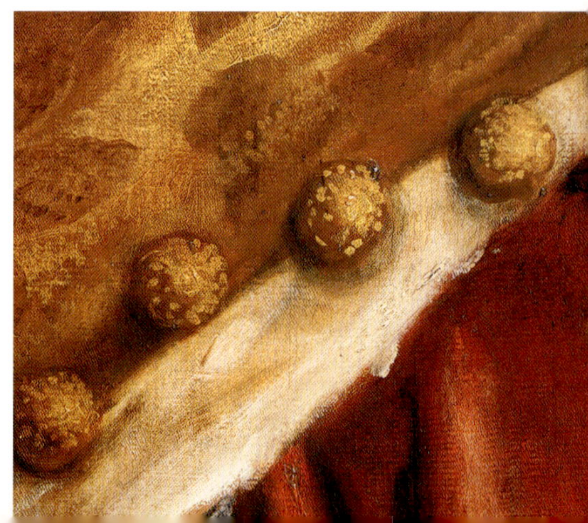

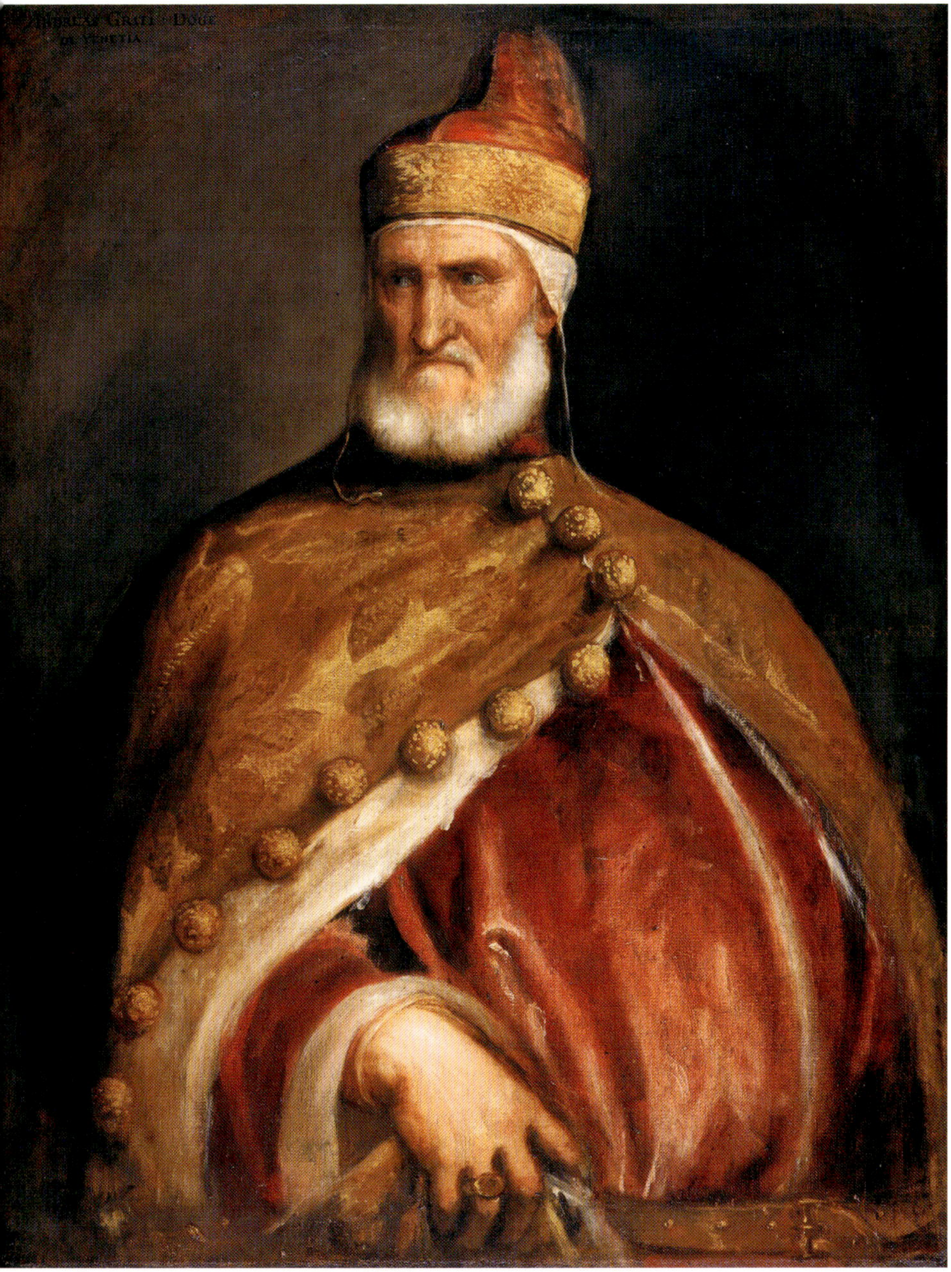

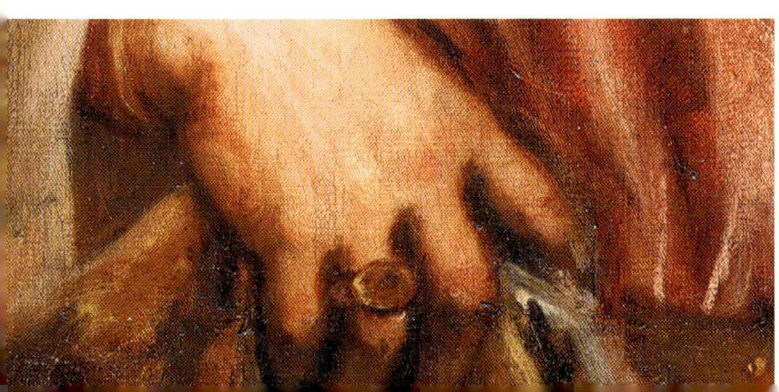

◄◄ This painting's excellent state of preservation allows us to observe the most unusual feature of its brushwork: rather than being polished and smooth, the paint forms dense, three-dimensional clumps, particularly visible on the buttons of the doge's mantle.

Academy

Francesco Salviati
Charity
1543

Oil on panel, 156 × 122 cm

Florence, Galleria degli Uffizi

Francesco Salviati

(Francesco de' Rossi)

Florence, c. 1509–Rome, 1563

An influential exponent of the second
generation of Mannerism, Francesco
Salviati contributed to its rise as the
official style of central Italian painting in
the mid-16th century. Trained in Florence
but working principally in Rome, Salviati
sought refined elegance in quotations
from classical models, rich ornamental
friezes and displays of anatomy inspired
by Michelangelo. As a draughtsman, he
created poses of an almost unimaginable
complexity, resulting in a sophisticated,
virtuosic abstraction. Salviati and his
workshop participated in all the major
Mannerist decoration projects undertaken
in Rome during the mid-16th century.
Moreover, his travels to Venice (1539–41)
and France (1555–7), in addition to his
long stay in Florence (1543–9) to paint
frescoes (including those in the Sala
dell'Udienza of the Palazzo Vecchio),
played a significant part in the spread
of Mannerism.

About the middle of the 16th century, the rigorous, refine
Mannerist aesthetic became the leading international currer
in painting, transforming the restless manner of the Florentin
painters of the previous decade into a solemn expression o
power. Henceforth, the painted figure conveyed a symboli
mental 'idea' that was codified through teaching, the practic
of drawing, and the frequent exchanges between artists and in
tellectuals. This was the birth of the concept of the 'academy'
understood as a school and a stylistic form shared by variou
artists. The first 'Academy of Drawing' opened in Florence a
the instigation of Giorgio Vasari in 1563.

▼ Salviati offers a sophisticated image that
was copied by young artists and admired
by the select audience who could appreciate
its 'timeless' figures. The subject, the figures'
gestures and the features are secondary to
the painter's obligation to present flawlessly
idealized models.

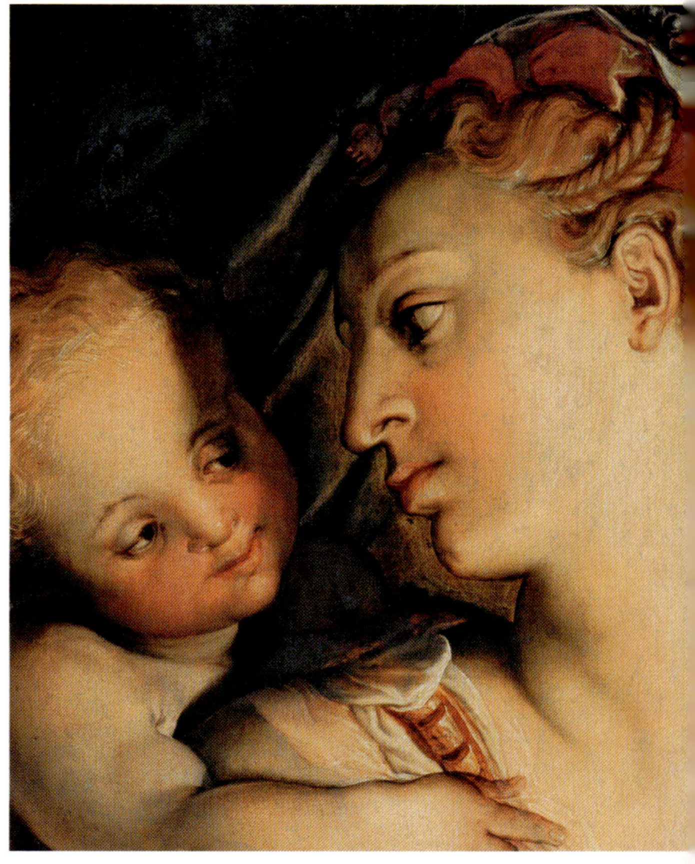

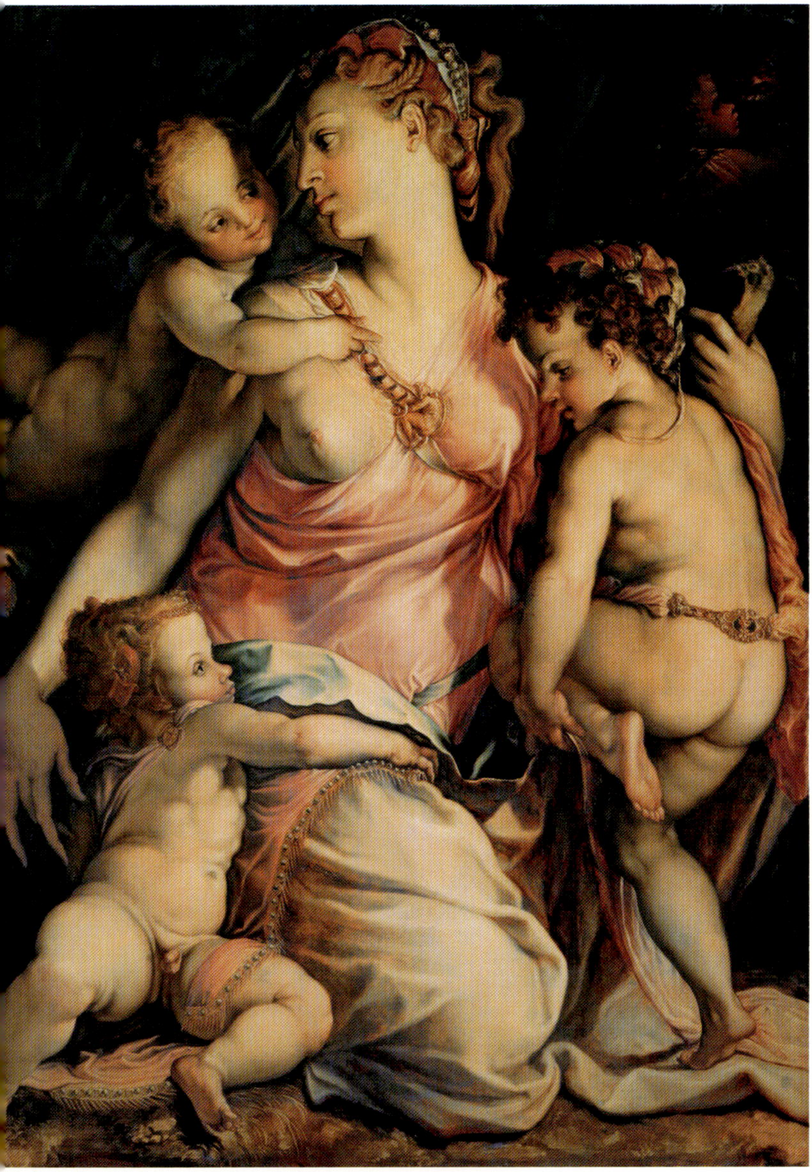

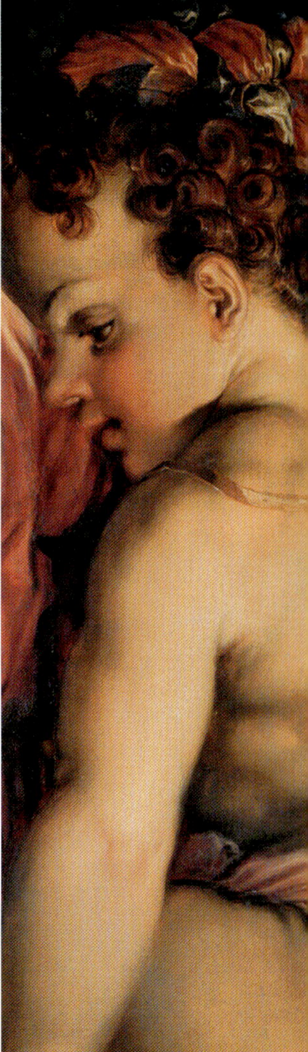

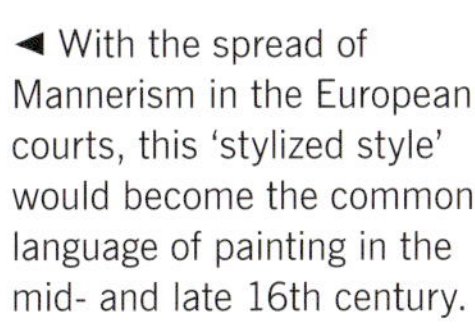

◀ With the spread of Mannerism in the European courts, this 'stylized style' would become the common language of painting in the mid- and late 16th century.

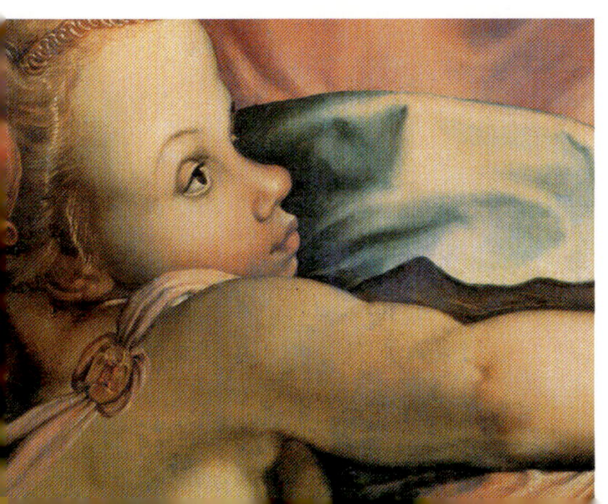

Family

Titian
Votive Painting of the
Vendramin Family
1544–7

Oil on canvas, 206 × 288 cm
London, National Gallery

For artist biography, see page 224.

During the 16th century, the place of women in society broadened to offer unprecedented possibilities and opportunities. Still, the hierarchical family structure continued to favour the males, and discussion of 'family' was understood to refer only to men. In official portraits, a woman's basic role remained that of the quiet 'angel of the household', the submissive, faithful wife and solicitous mother, a chaste and sober lady; at very best she would be exhibited by her proud husband as a splendid household 'ornament' until she assumed her definitive status as the producer of abundant offspring. Images of female sovereigns, the few women who wielded actual power, fell outside this range, however. Official portraits of Elizabeth I of England, for example, bury any appearance of femininity under a mountain of symbols, including those for domination, glory, energy and resilience.

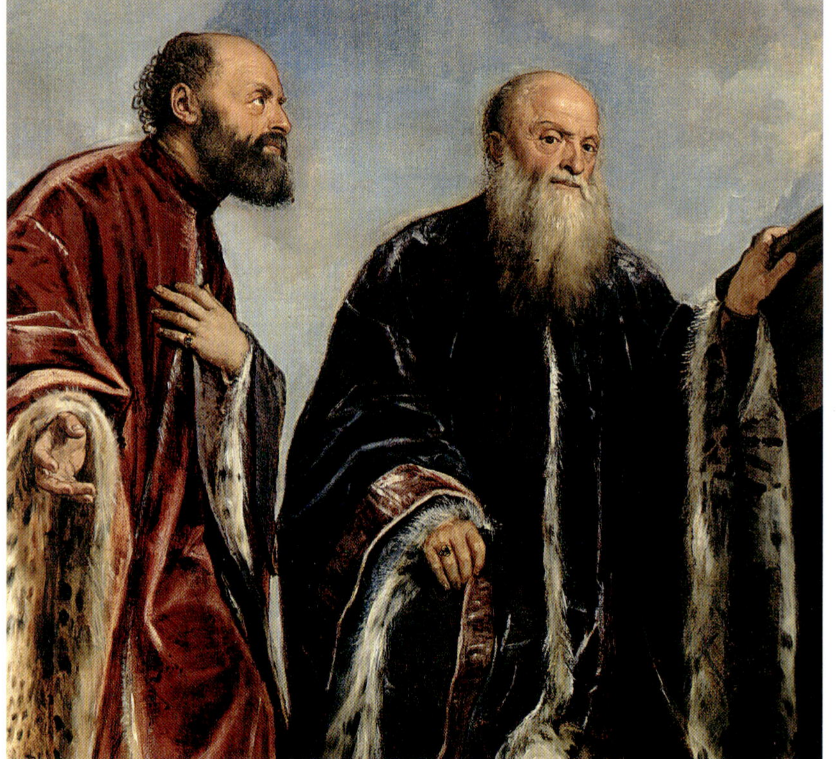

◄ The elderly senator Gabriele Vendramin, who commissioned this portrait, holds the place of honour in the centre and is presented as the head of a family group that includes eight other males of the noble Venetian line. His younger brother Andrea, beside him, wears a sumptuous red, fur-lined cloak. His attitude of intense devotion, his gaze directed towards the reliquary and his separation from the other figures all seem to allude to Andrea's premature death in 1547.

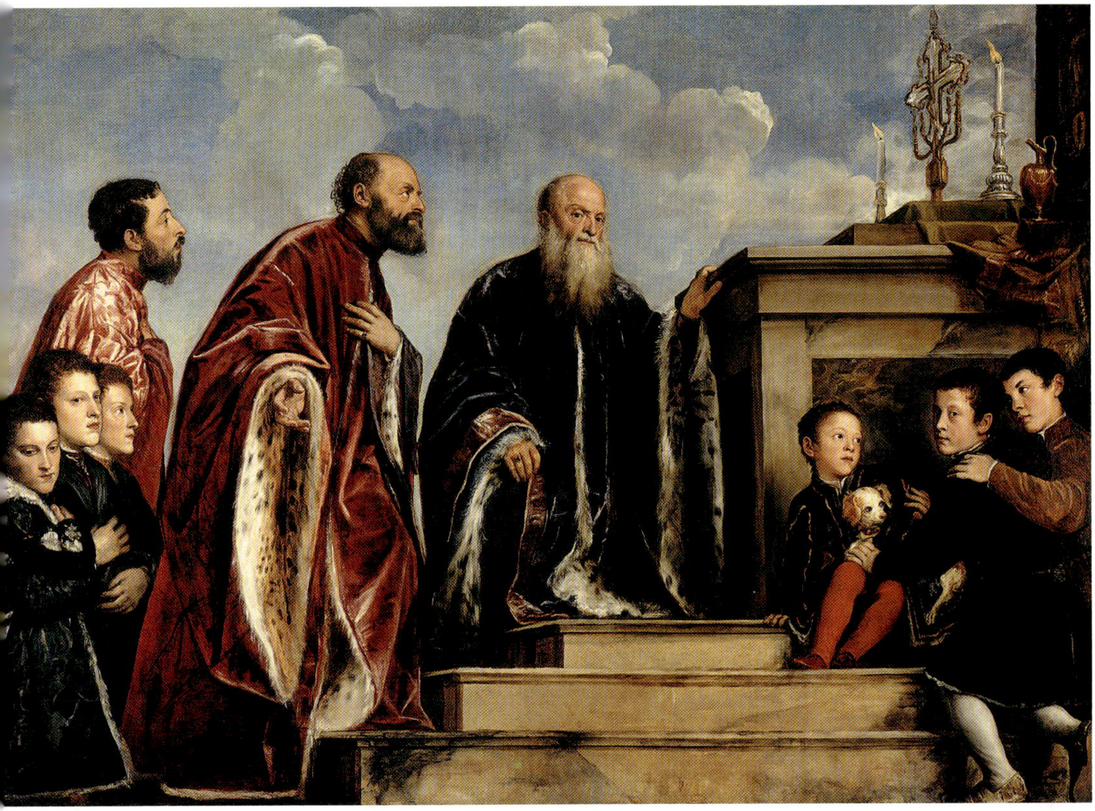

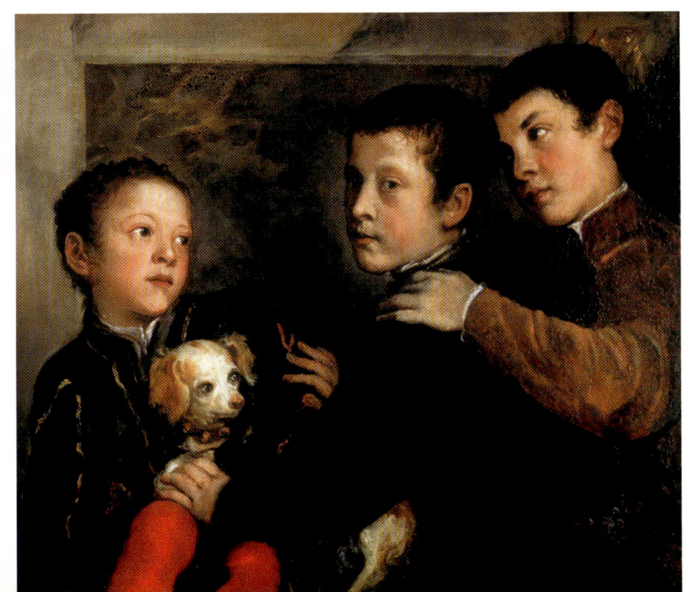

▼ As with the *Pesaro Altarpiece* (see pages 258–9), painted almost 30 years earlier, Titian has represented the men of a noble Venetian family in a devout attitude. Here, however, the young boys are not confined by overly stiff poses but move naturally and spontaneously.

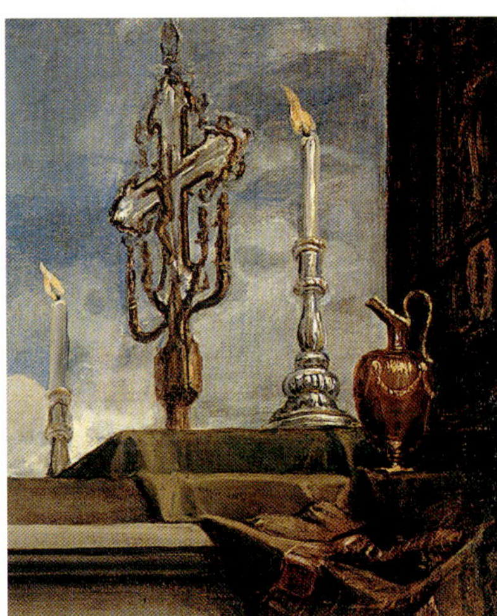

▲ In the 14th century, a relic of the True Cross had been entrusted to the keeping of Andrea Vendramin, *guardiano grande* of the Scuola di San Giovanni Evangelista. The Vendramins upheld their devotion to the 'family' relic, displayed on the altar along with various liturgical objects.

Fashion

Agnolo Bronzino
Portrait of Eleanor of Toledo
c. 1545

Oil on panel, 115 × 96 cm
Florence, Galleria degli Uffizi

For artist biography, see page 316.

In 1539, on the occasion of the marriage between Cosimo I and Eleanor of Toledo, Bronzino became the trusted painter to the Medici. Among the many portraits he made of members of the grand duke's family, the one of Eleanor of Toledo is the most unforgettable. Wearing a stunningly beautiful dress, she is portrayed alongside her son Giovanni, who was destined for a career in the Church. It is an impressive and magnetic image, charged with calculated suggestion. The grand duchess, exuding unattainable perfection, is immobile against a background that seems to glow with the dense, hard smoothness of lapis lazuli. Nobility, self-control, composure, severity, detachment: all feeling is restrained and filtered by the unyielding mask of aristocracy.

▼ ► In contrast to Titian's treatment of children (see pages 326–7), Bronzino immobilizes the two-year-old, who stands rigidly and wears a dazed, unnatural expression, his large eyes open wide, one hand clenched at his side and the other vainly seeking a sign of warmth or affection from his mother.

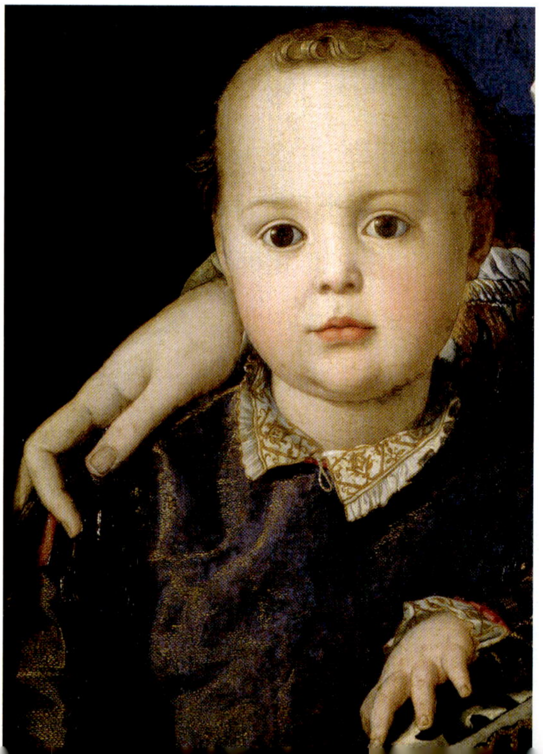

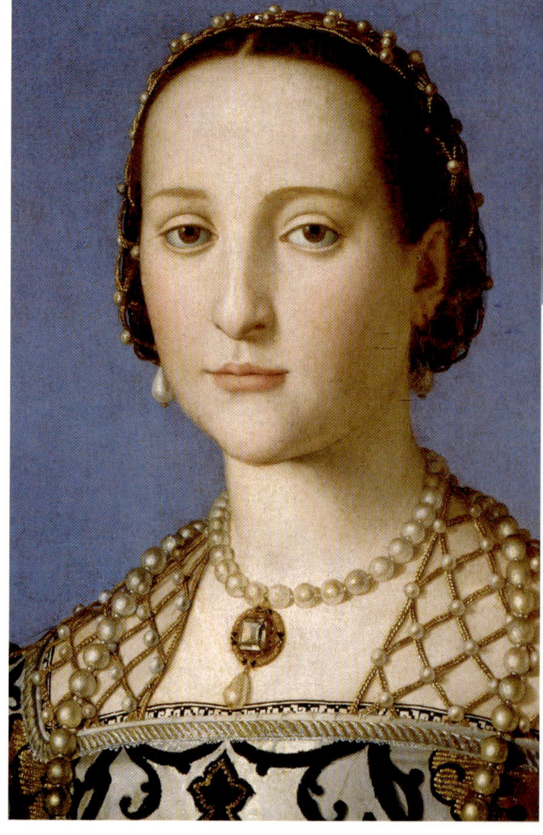

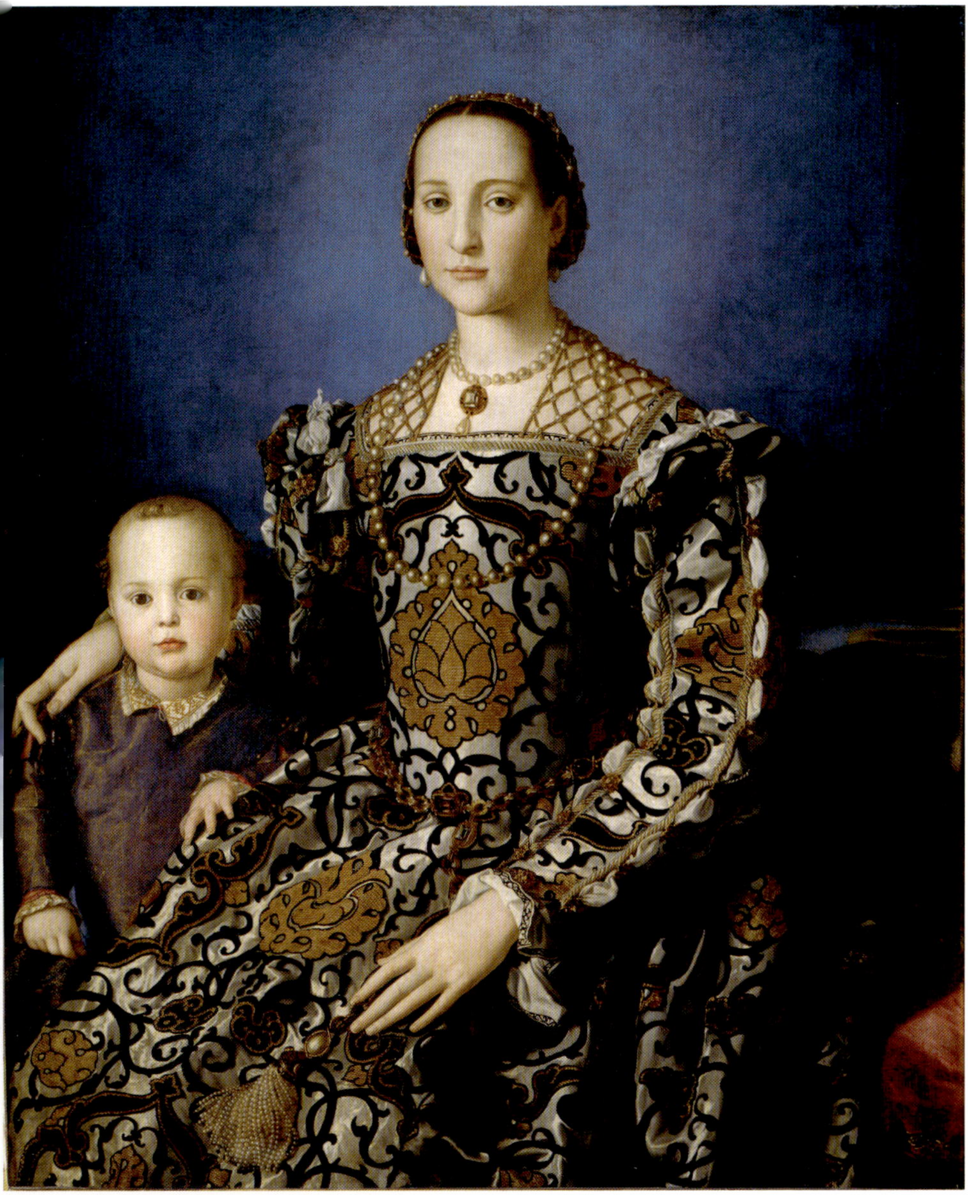

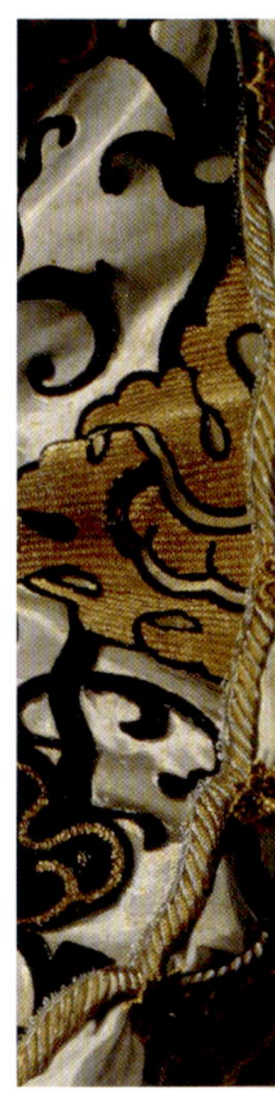

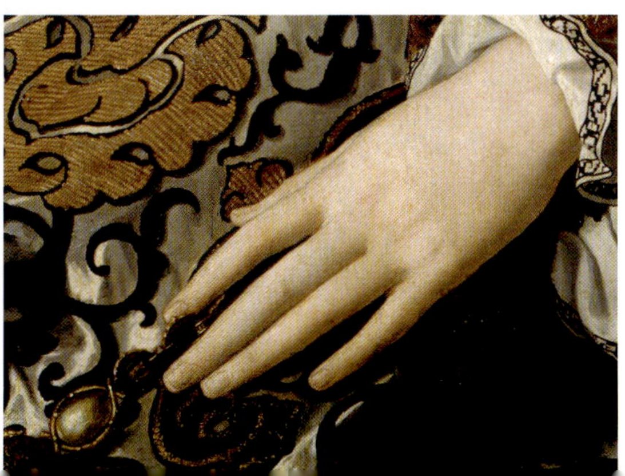

◀ While 15th-century courtiers placed great emphasis on wit and intellect (see pages 136–7), the aristocratic world of Mannerism, closed and exclusive, imposed a rigid etiquette and demanded a model of absolute composure.

◀ The magnificent dress of gold brocade with a pomegranate pattern resembles the one found when Eleanor of Toledo's tomb was opened.

Nepotism

Titian
Portrait of Paul III with His Nephews
1545

Oil on canvas, 210 × 174 cm
Naples, Museo Nazionale di Capodimonte

For artist biography, see page 224.

At the end of the 15th century, Pope Alexander VI (Rodrigo Borgia) had strongly supported the careers and ruthless conquests of his illegitimate children Lucretia and Cesare Borgia. Throughout the Renaissance, popes had supported members of their families, especially 'nephew cardinals' (as these illicit children were often called), by offering them rich prebends or even by setting up actual states. The duchy of Parma and Picenza, for example, was 'carved out' for the Farnese. With this painting Titian has left a dazzling image of the climate of the Roman Curia. The composition of the *Portrait of Paul III with His Nephews* (see pages 256–7) is inspired by Raphael's portrait of Pope Leo X with two nephews, revisited with an extraordinarily bold inventiveness.

Titian and the Farnese Family: Failed Hopes and Unforthcoming Privileges

Titian hoped for certain privileges from his relationship with the Farnese, a household that was taking its place as one of the most notable and influential of the late Renaissance because of the papacy of Paul III (Alessandro Farnese) and the skill of his nephew Cardinal Alessandro. Between 1541 and 1545, Titian made many paintings for the Farnese (today mostly in the Museo Nazionale di Capodimonte in Naples) and organized many meetings with various members of the increasingly powerful household. The material outcome was somewhat disappointing, however. Pietro Aretino, familiar with the power games that went on within the walls of Roman palazzos, had warned his painter friend against harbouring illusions about his relationship with the Farnese, especially in regard to the longed-for ecclesiastical benefice that would have provided employment for Titian's wastrel son Pomponio. In a memorable letter, Aretino advised Titian not to let himself be blinded by the splendour and welcome given him by the pope and other members of the family, adding: 'It is a particular grace of the Farnese household to be generous with flattery. But it is well known that such is the mother of despair; found in nature through the intercourse of men who cling to false promises, always certain though mired in doubt.'

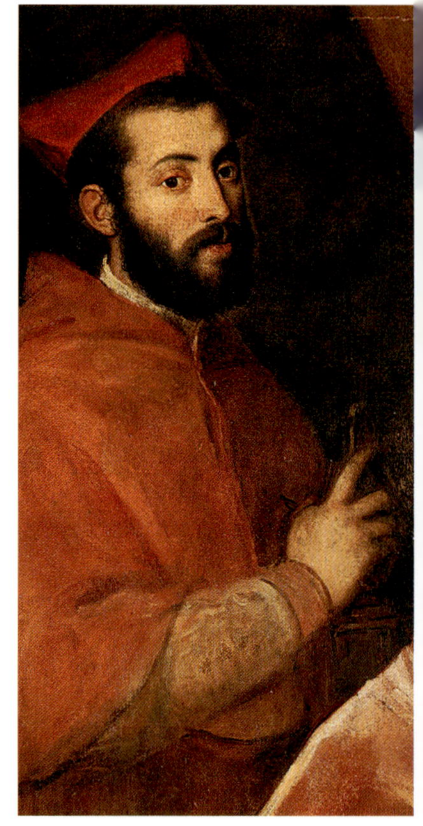

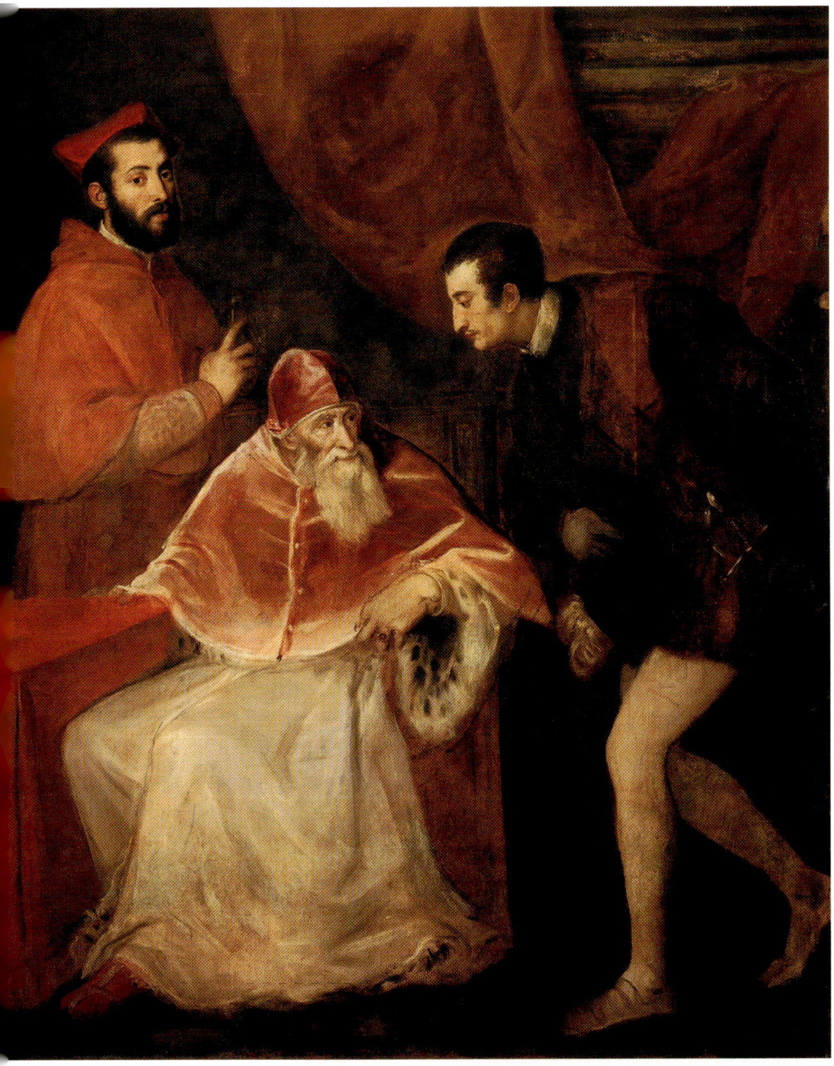

▼ This large portrait is the most important work Titian executed during his stay in Rome in 1545–6. Ottavio Farnese's pose parodies that of Myron's *Discus Thrower*, a well-known Antique sculpture.

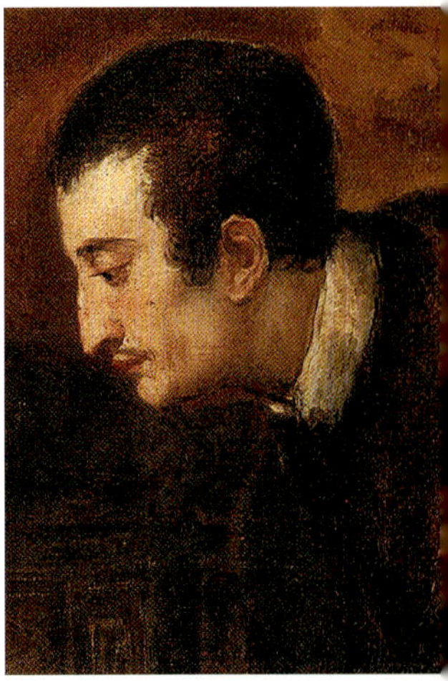

◄ Leaving many details in a sketchy state and employing loose brushwork to create a grainy effect, Titian evokes an atmosphere of intrigue and suspicion that combines unctuous family ceremony, a sense of power, nepotism and a caustic state of mind.

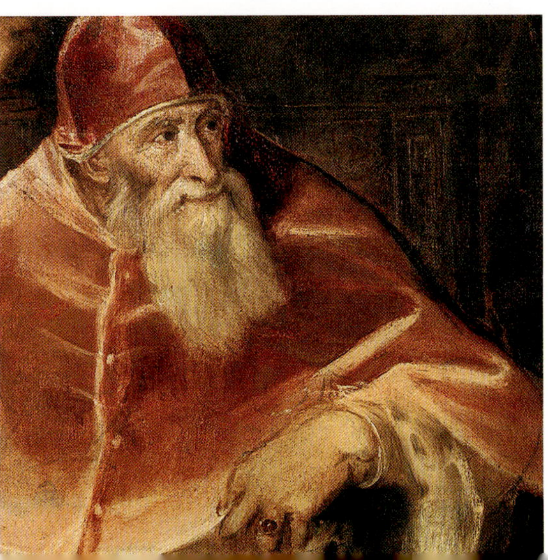

◄▲ The three figures form a psychological triangle worthy of Shakespeare. In the centre is the aged pope, frail-looking but with a piercing gaze; to his left his red-robed nephew Cardinal Alessandro (25 years old), aware of his own power but resting a hand on his uncle's chair with affected nonchalance; and to his right the bowing Ottavio, the other nephew.

Non finito

Titian
Portrait of Pietro Aretino
1545

Oil on canvas, 108 × 76 cm

Florence, Galleria Palatina

For artist biography, see page 224.

Though the two terms appear synonymous, 'unfinished' (*no finito*) does not mean 'incomplete'. Instead, *non finito* is th technique typical of Titian's mature period when, reminiscen of Michelangelo's approach in sculpture, the figures' outlines ar no longer precisely defined and broad brushstrokes are laid o in evident haste, as if to suggest the subject more than describ it. In the portrait of his friend Pietro Aretino, a man of letters Titian displays a technical freedom and experimental handlin he could not have allowed himself with another client. Th result is a vivid, entirely unprecedented sense of animation tha seems at odds with the pedantic style of the second-generatior Mannerists. In a letter written in October 1545, even Aretinc himself admitted to being disconcerted before a canvas that tc his eyes looked more like a quick sketch.

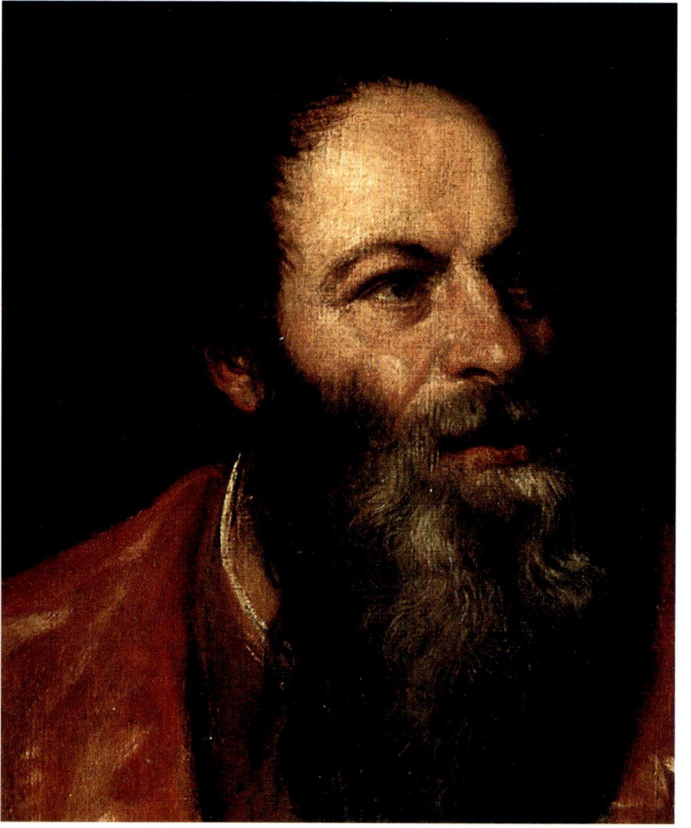

◄ Titian completed this 'private' portrait just before he went to Rome. It is tangible evidence of his close friendship and professional association with the controversial, much-feared Tuscan writer, who through his copious international correspondence ensured Titian's contact with the principal courts of Italy and Europe.

▼ In this painting and that of Doge Gritti (see pages 322–3), Titian adopts a technique called *non finito*. The result is an entirely unprecedented and controversial liveliness that sharply contrasts with a more calculated stylistic approach.

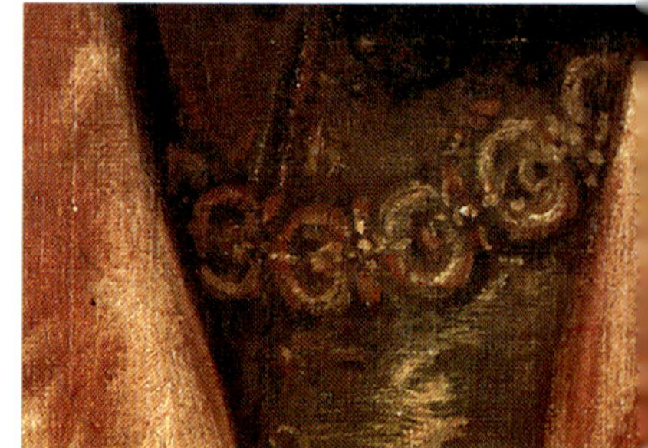

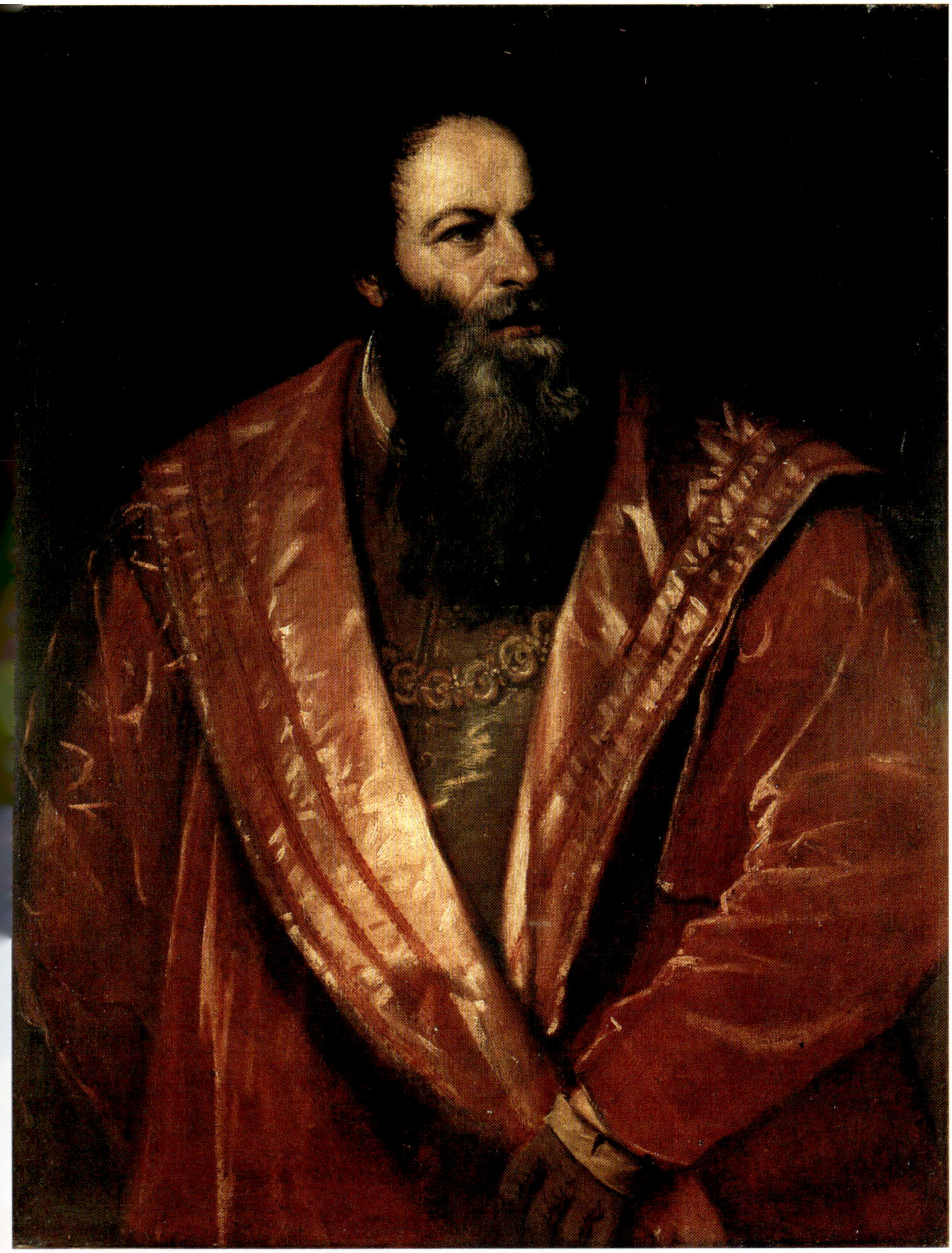

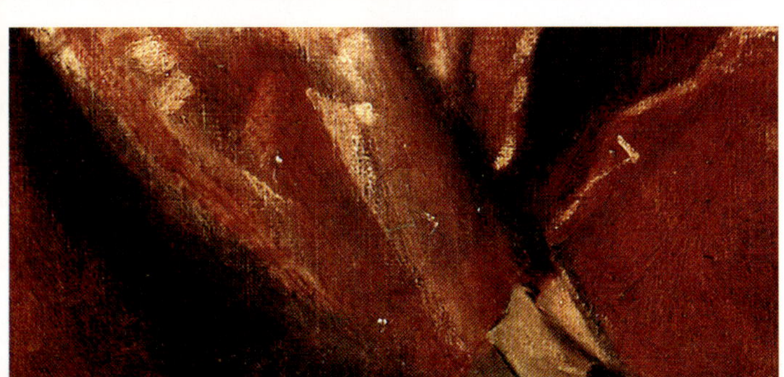

◄ Though Aretino was initially surprised by the sketch-like quality of this portrait, later he called it 'an awesome marvel' and concluded that 'it breathes, its pulse beats and its spirit moves, just as I do myself in life'.

Sinuosity

Andrea Schiavone
The Adoration of the Magi
1548

Oil on canvas, 184 × 222 cm

Milan, Pinacoteca Ambrosiana

Andrea Schiavone

(Andrea Meldolla)

Zara, *c.* 1518–Venice, 1563

Characterized by elongated, twisting figures, Schiavone's unusual manner found a place in Venetian private collections in the mid-16th century, even though the Dalmatian-born painter had difficulty winning major religious commissions owing to competition from Jacopo Tintoretto and hostility from Venetian intellectuals. With his refined approach, Schiavone steered a middle course between the Venetian tradition, Parmigianino's nervous elegance and the lighter style of such Tuscan Mannerists as Salviati and Vasari, active in Venice in the 1540s. A noteworthy draughtsman and engraver, Schiavone created three *tondi* for the ceiling of the Libreria Marciana in Venice (1556).

The most popular proportional model of the human body in the late 15th century was the so-called 'Vitruvian man', an immobilized figure inscribed within a circle and a square. Fifty years later, the refined aesthetic of the 'modern manner' preferred 'serpentine movement', a moving form that unfurled in a twisting spiral. Highly influential models were provided by Raphael and Michelangelo, but the tendency continued and grew more intense as Mannerism developed internationally. The arrival of Tuscan painters like Salviati and Vasari in Venice in about 1540 spurred direct comparison with what was happening in central Italy. Elongated, coiling figures were adopted mainly by younger painters like Tintoretto and the Dalmatian Andrea Schiavone, in contrast to the local tradition embodied by Titian.

► Schiavone's twisting, fluted columns have a troubled internal rhythm, a kind of upward eddying movement. During the 1540s, the models of central Italy indirectly influenced even Jacopo Tintoretto and Jacopo Bassano, though without achieving Schiavone's fantastic effects, in which Mannerism's 'serpentine' poses are exaggerated to the point of absurdity.

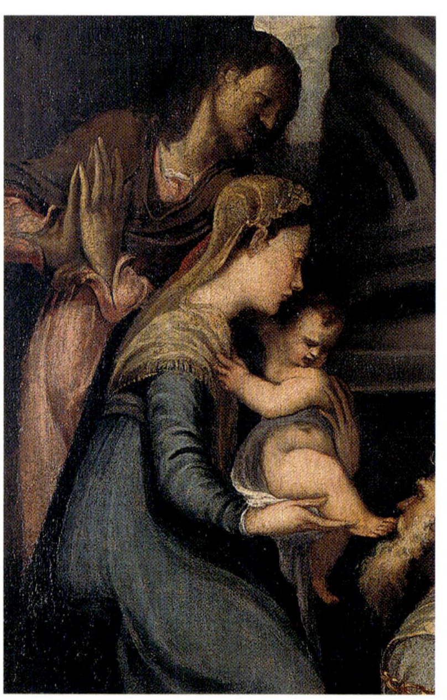

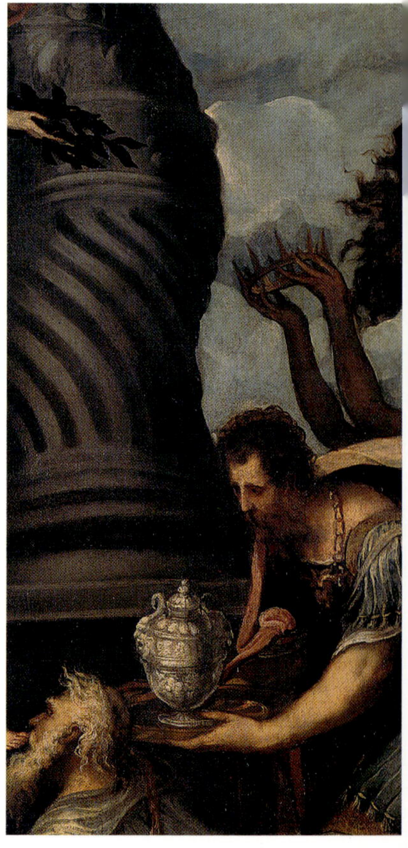

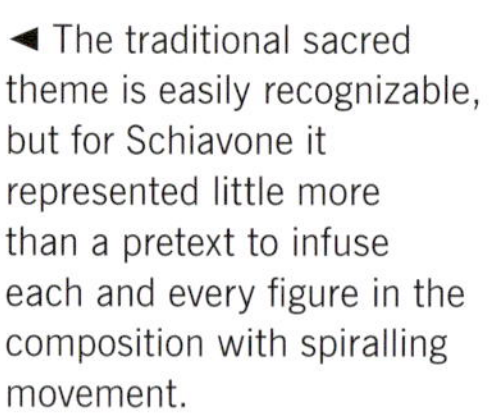

◄ The traditional sacred theme is easily recognizable, but for Schiavone it represented little more than a pretext to infuse each and every figure in the composition with spiralling movement.

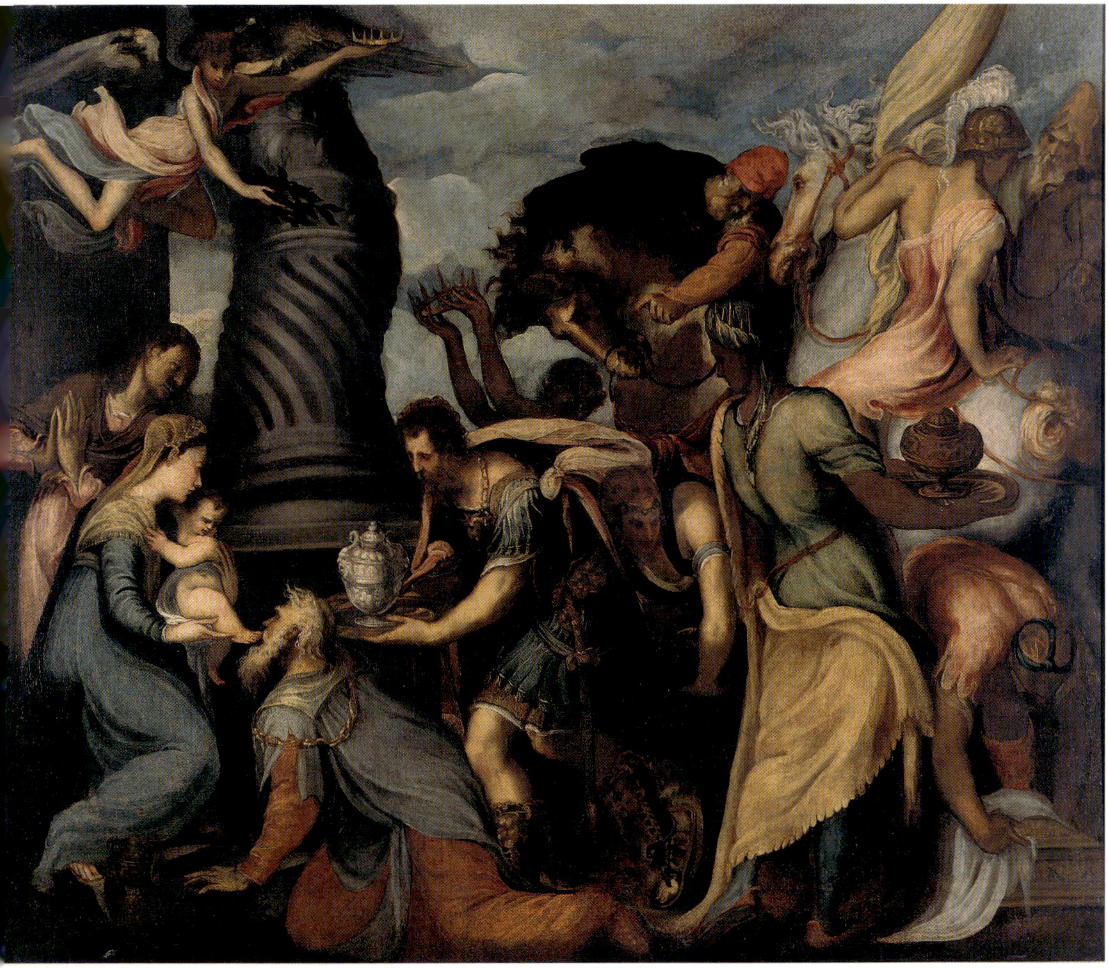

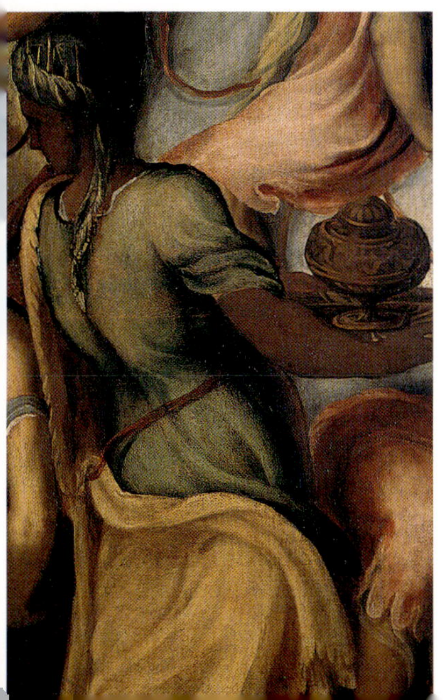

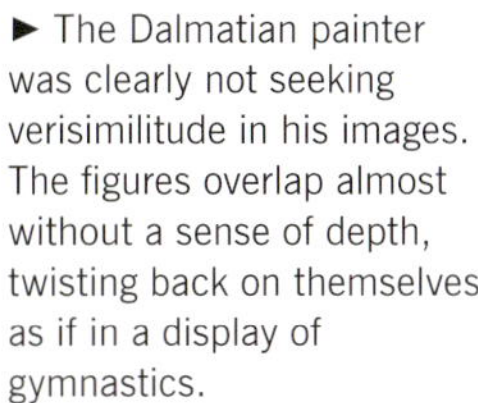

◄ Although Schiavone's 'extremist' works achieved only partial success in Venice, they are nevertheless considered important precedents for the future development of El Greco.

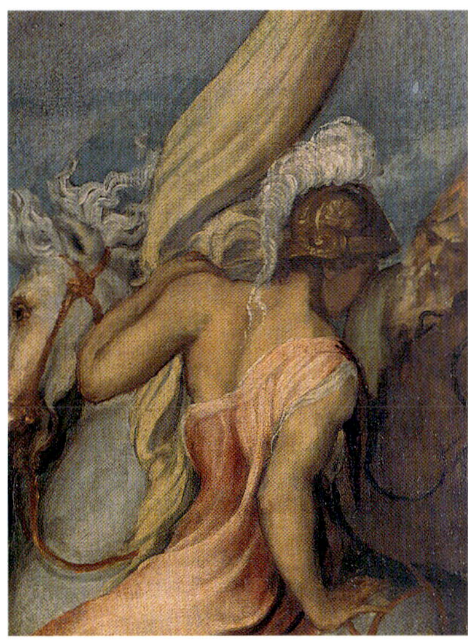

► The Dalmatian painter was clearly not seeking verisimilitude in his images. The figures overlap almost without a sense of depth, twisting back on themselves as if in a display of gymnastics.

Equestrian Portrait

Titian
Charles V at the Battle of Mühlberg
1548

Oil on canvas, 332 × 279 cm
Madrid, Museo Nacional del Prado

For artist biography, see page 224.

Painted during a stay in the German city of Augsburg, to celebrate Charles V's decisive victory over the Protestant princes a[t] Mühlberg, this is the supreme prototype for equestrian portrait[s] to come in subsequent centuries. Titian concentrates entirel[y] on the figure of the emperor – who is the only person to b[e] seen in the entire canvas, which was also intended to represen[t] victory on the battlefield. The impression of human physica[l] frailty conveyed by the portrait is countered by the sense o[f] an absolute will, the only true virtue that Charles was read[y] to acknowledge in himself. Similarly, the image of the passin[g] hours of a dying day is transformed into a vision of eternit[y] within the pages of history.

▼ This portrait of the emperor reveals his tenacity and perseverance, the only virtues Charles was willing to recognize in himself. His expression, anything but triumphant, invites the viewer to look beyond the specific subject of the painting to scrutinize the sovereign's innermost nature.

Advice (Fortunately) Ignored

Titian's friend and adviser, the loquacious man of letters Pietro Aretino, had become aware that the artist had painted the equestrian portrait of Charles V. Writing to Titian in April 1548, Aretino suggested introducing two allegorical figures, Religion and Fame, alongside the mounted emperor. His idea was that they would support the 'monarch who battles and is at pains not only summer and winter, but also day and night, enduring war and the evil indispositions it inflicts upon him'. Titian preferred not to heed this advice, and the strength of the resulting portrait in fact resides in the solemn isolation of a character capable of overcoming delicate health and anxiety by extraordinary force of will.

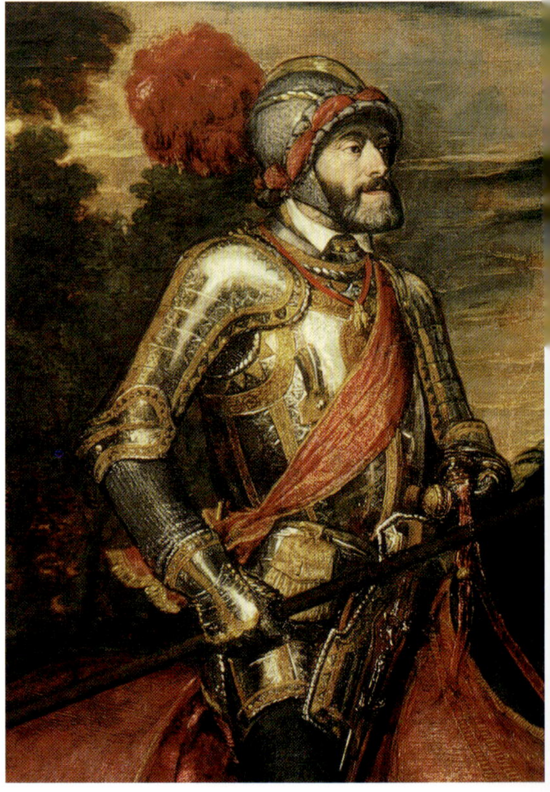

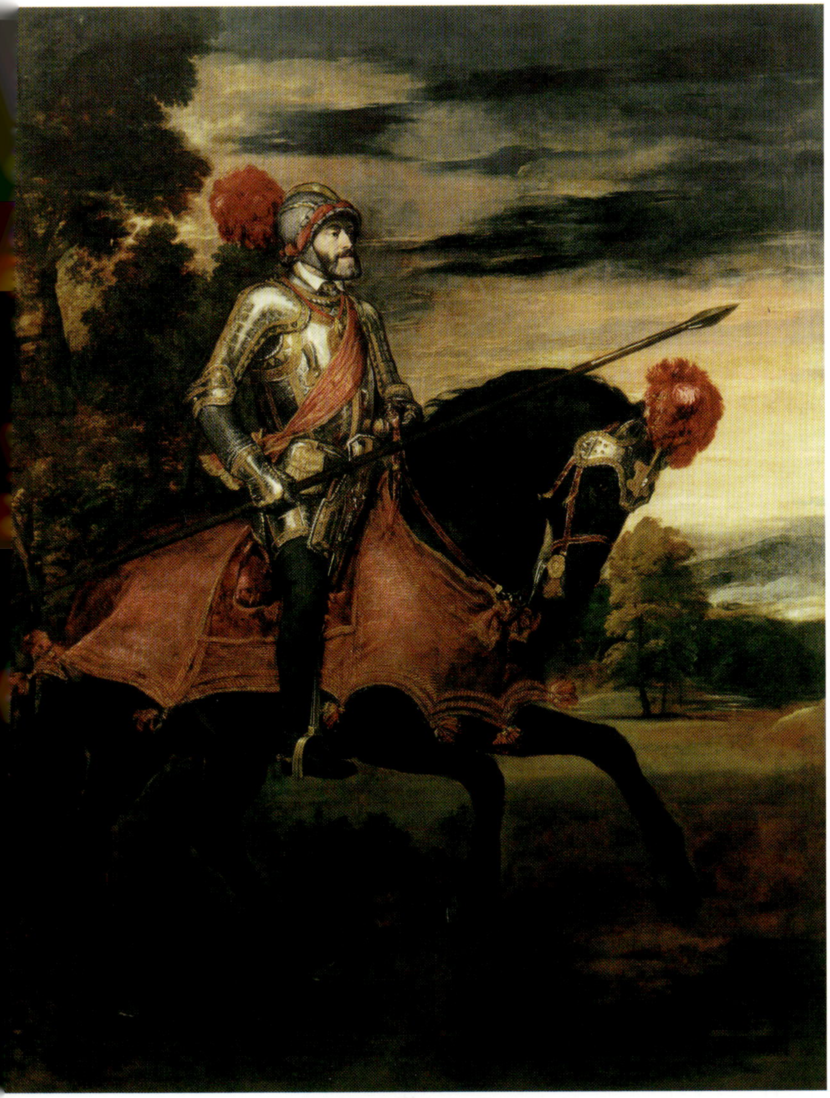

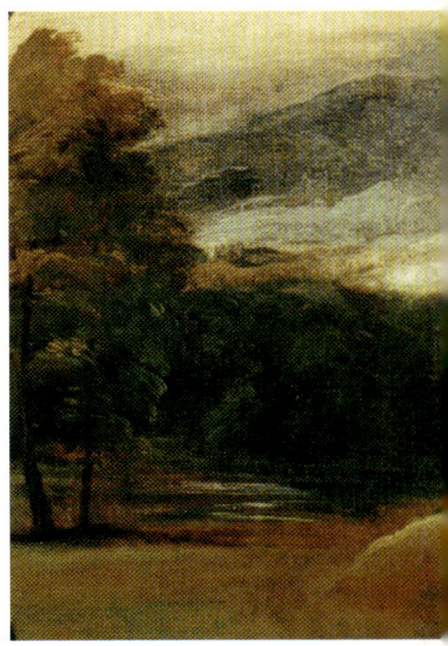

◄ ▲ Dressed in gleaming armour, indifferent to the movements of the restless horse that agitates its wine-coloured trappings, Charles V is presented as a solitary hero on the edge of a sun-reddened landscape that fades into the distant horizon.

► For centuries, Titian's large painting stood as the illustrious and unsurpassed prototype for a series of equestrian portraits by artists from Rubens to Van Dyck, Rembrandt to Velázquez, David to Manet.

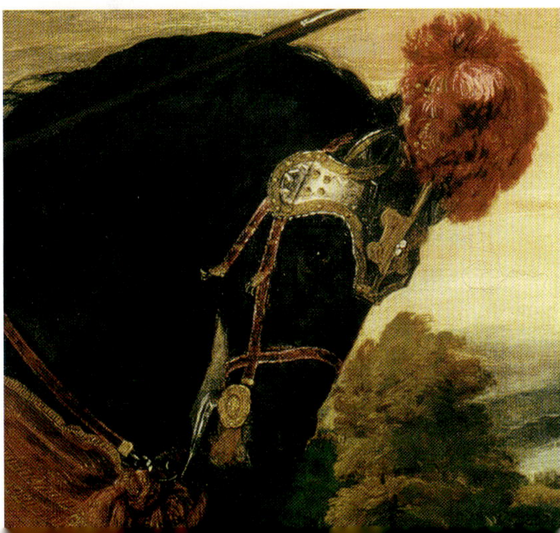

337

Michelangelesque

Pellegrino Tibaldi
The Adoration of the Shepherds
1549

Oil on canvas, 158 × 105 cm
Rome, Galleria Borghese

Pellegrino Tibaldi

Puria in Valsolda, Como, 1527–Milan,
1596

Destined to become one of the reference
points of the Counter-Reformation, Tibaldi
trained in Bologna, both as a painter and
as an architect, studying the innovations
of Giulio Romano and Sebastiano Serlio.
During a stay in Rome (1547–9), he
came into contact with the work of
Michelangelo and collaborated with
Perino del Vaga at the Castel Sant'Angelo.
In Bologna, he painted frescoes of the
story of Ulysses at the Palazzo Poggi
(1549) and then went to Lombardy, where
he worked mainly as an architect. With
the support of Charles Borromeo, the
powerful archbishop of Milan, he obtained
important commissions in Milan, Pavia,
Saronno and Novara, giving form to new
patterns of religious architecture adapted
to the requirements of the Counter-
Reformation. He also designed many
civil buildings. Appointed architect of the
cathedral of Milan, Tibaldi pursued an
active career as a designer and technical
consultant. He eventually returned to
painting. At the request of Philip II of
Spain, he painted frescoes in the cloister
and library of the Escorial (1588–95).

The completion of *The Last Judgment* in the Sistine Chapel con
firmed Michelangelo's absolutely central role in Italian art of th
mid-16th century. The controversy that raged over the 'obscen
ity' of the work's conspicuously placed nudes led to their partia
covering by Daniele da Volterra in 1564. However, discussion
among artists, writers and intellectuals gave further boost to th
paradigmatic status of the masterpiece, whose fame was ensure
by the abundant circulation of reduced copies, reproduction
and prints. Italian painters, with the partial exception of thos
in the area around Venice, largely adopted the eloquent poses
powerful musculature and scowling earnestness of Michelangelo
figures. A sort of 'gigantism' now characterized religious painting
leading at times to exaggeration and what seems like a contes
of mighty athletic physiques.

► Although motifs derived
from Michelangelo clearly
predominate, Tibaldi includes
another reference as well:
the Madonna's face, with
its delicate, almost shy
expression, closely recalls
the painting of Raphael.

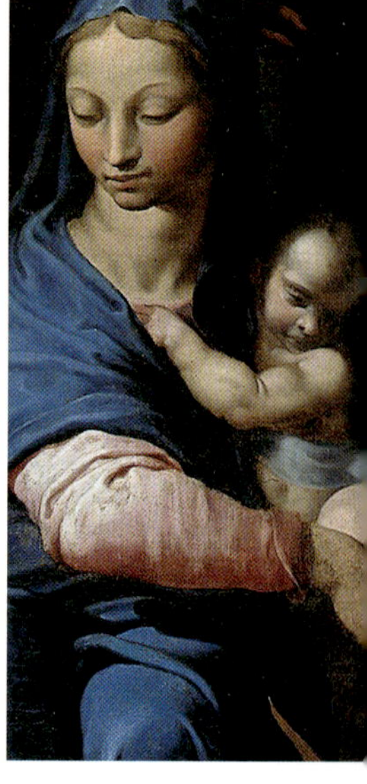

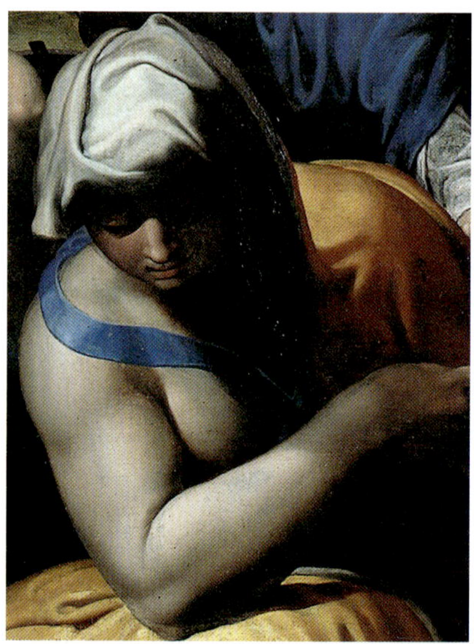

◄ Tibaldi also reused the
physical dimensions and
introverted expressions
of the Sibyls painted by
Michelangelo (see pages
212–13).

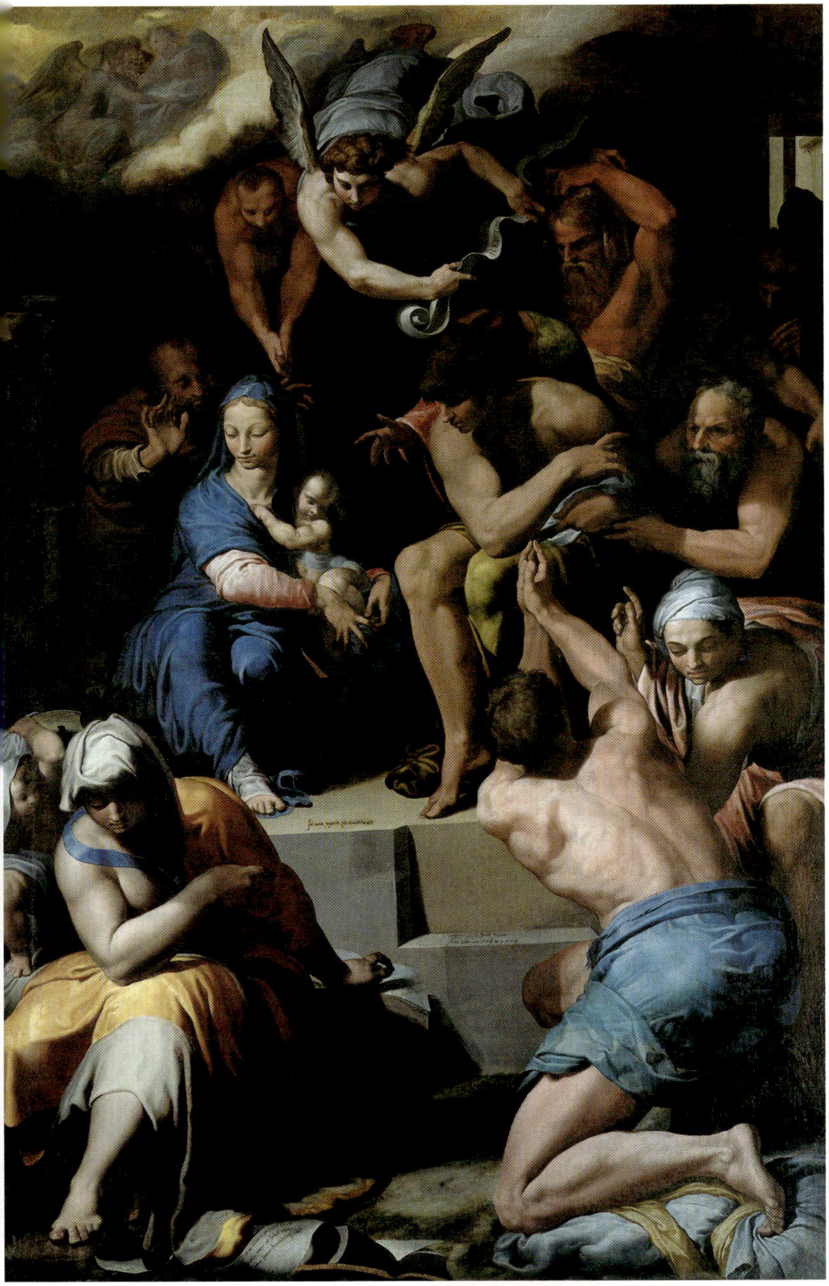

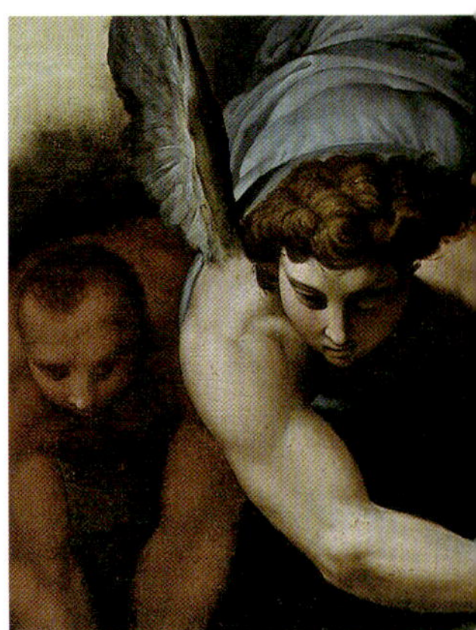

▲ The musculature of the figures, many of whom look like athletes, is exhibited in the broad, carefully worked-out poses, which convey the sculptural power of the human physique in relief.

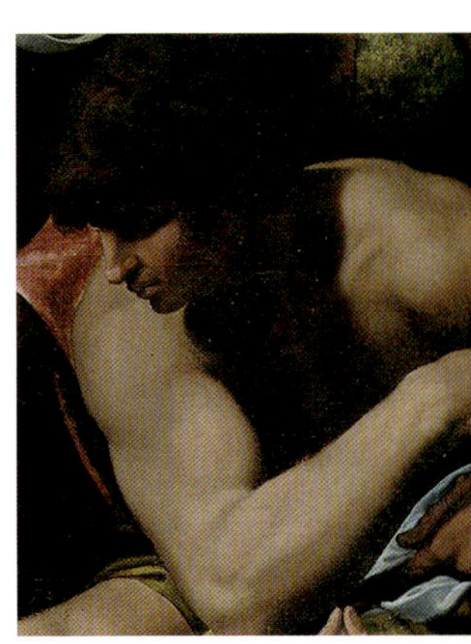

▲ The composition's asymmetry, its ill-defined space and the contorted, entangled figures reflect the loss of certainty on the part of a humanity in crisis after the adventure of the Renaissance.

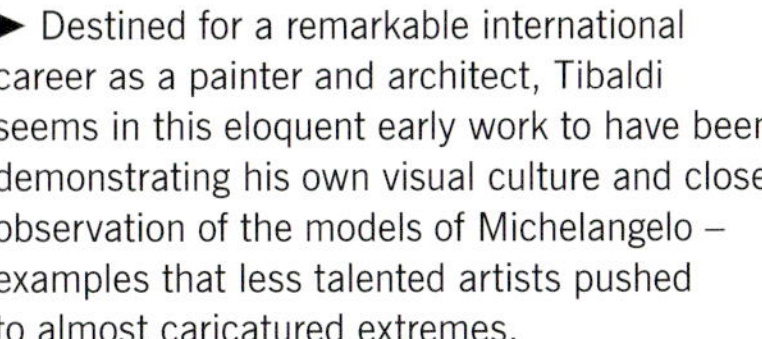

► Destined for a remarkable international career as a painter and architect, Tibaldi seems in this eloquent early work to have been demonstrating his own visual culture and close observation of the models of Michelangelo – examples that less talented artists pushed to almost caricatured extremes.

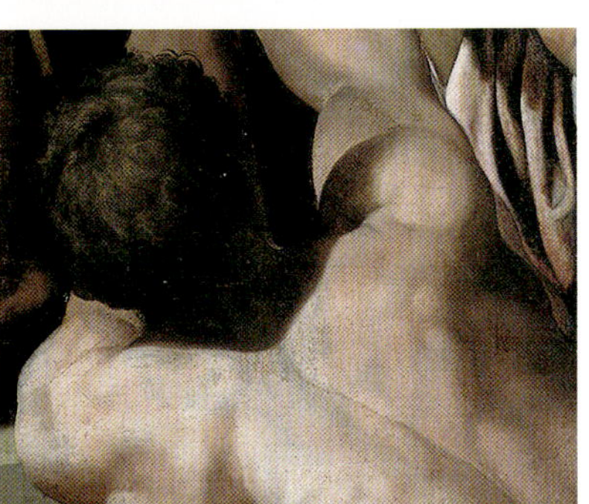

Romanists

Maerten van Heemskerck
Self-portrait with the Colosseum
1553

Oil on panel, 42 × 54 cm

Cambridge, Fitzwilliam Museum

Maerten van Heemskerck

Heemskerk, Utrecht, 1498–Haarlem, 1574

The stylistic and thematic eclecticism of Van Heemskerck offers a fine example of the rapid evolution in Netherlandish art during the mid-16th century. Trained in the Haarlem workshop of Van Scorel, Van Heemskerck began by painting a number of well-received portraits. The student's rapid success aroused the jealousy of Van Scorel, who urged him to go to Rome (1532–6). Van Heemskerck's ability to learn and his remarkable gifts as a draughtsman made him one of the most knowledgeable and original northern European masters, able to play the intermediary between the generic Raphaelism preferred by the Antwerp 'Romanists' and the dramatic plastic force of Michelangelo and classical sculpture. Back in his native country, Van Heemskerck founded a particular sort of Mannerism characterized by a nervous graphic technique that recalls Pontormo and Parmigianino.

Beginning in the first decades of the 16th century, parallel to developments taking place in Italy and Germany, an epoch-making shift occurred in the art of the Low Countries. With the demise of the previous generation of masters of the Flemish tradition, the influence of Italian artistic innovations triggered a current of renewal. Northern painters, experiencing Italian art directly as the result of their travels to the south, reinterpreted it in a style that featured an abundance of decoration and descriptive detail. With the death of Leo X, an exceptional opportunity presented itself to artists of the Low Countries: the election of Adrian VI of Utrecht (Adriaan Florensz, tutor of Charles V), who was, until John Paul II, the only non-Italian pope for more than half a millennium. During Adrian VI's brief papacy, his fellow countryman Jan van Scorel assumed the prestigious position, previously held by Raphael, of curator of Vatican antiquities. However, northern painters did not visit Italy simply to seek suggestions and absorb influences. They also made a decisive contribution to the evolution of painting at the height of the Renaissance and to the birth of the 'modern manner'.

▶ Turning towards the viewer with a hint of a smile, Van Heemskerck explicitly alludes to his long stay in Rome 20 years earlier. The painter conceived images that were far from conventional in the field of portraiture, combining skilful composition with touches of spontaneity and human truth. In this painting, he even gives himself a physical resemblance to Michelangelo.

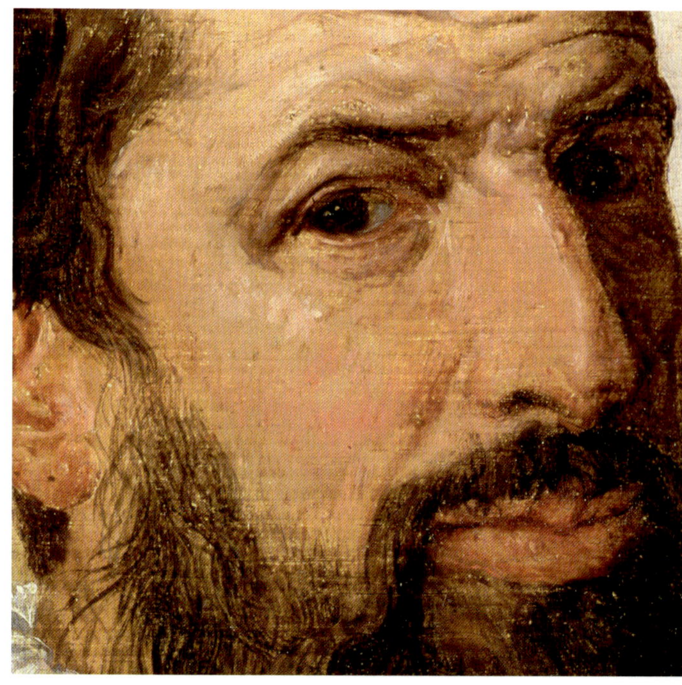

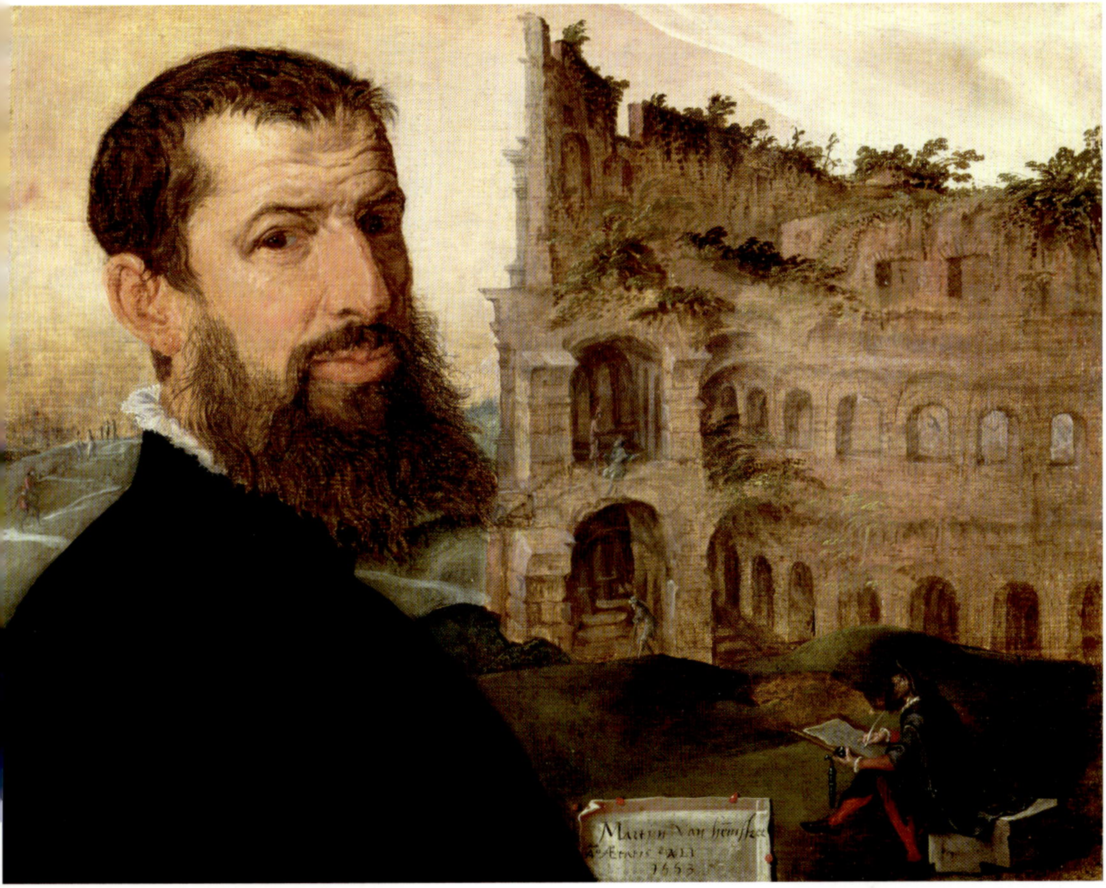

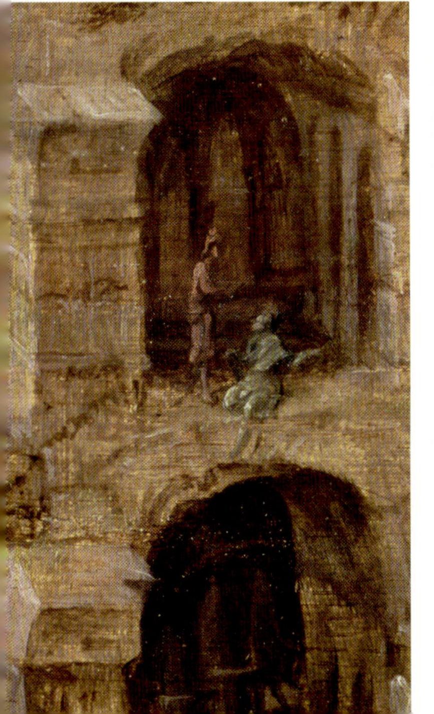

◄ ► In the four years that Van Heemskerck spent in Rome, he carefully recorded the ancient monuments in a series of lucid drawings that provide the most reliable documentation we have on the state of the city's architecture in the mid-16th century. In this self-portrait the painter shows himself as a man of mature years, soberly dressed in dark clothing – but also, in the small figure at right, himself 20 years earlier, when as a young artist he tried to capture in a drawing the immense skeleton of the Colosseum.

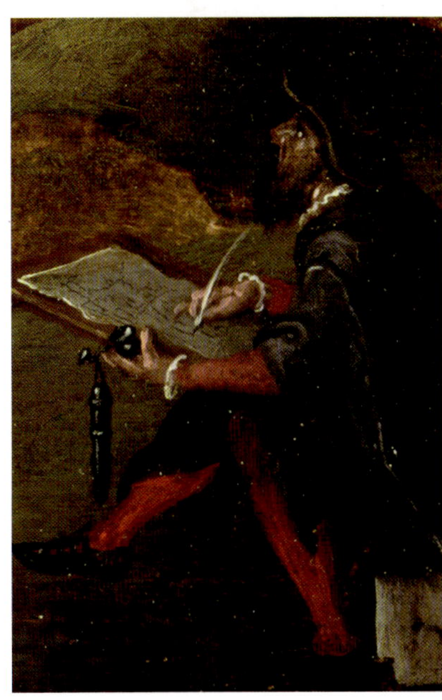

Sofonisba Anguissola
Game of Chess
1555

Oil on canvas, 72 × 97 cm

Pozna, Muzeum Narodowe

Sofonisba Anguissola

Cremona, *c.* 1532–Palermo, 1625

Cited in Vasari's 'Lives', Sofonisba Anguissola was the first woman artist to boast a solid, independent professional career. Trained in her native city of Cremona, the main centre of artistic activity in Lombardy in the second half of the 16th century, she specialized in portraiture, demonstrating a lively sensitivity to psychology and the 'movements of the soul'. Her favourite subjects were the members of her own family – two of her sisters were also good painters. In 1559, at the peak of her career, she was called to the court of Philip II in Madrid to teach art to the Infanta. She married a Sicilian nobleman and in the 1570s moved to Palermo. Widowed in 1579, she went to Genoa with her second husband, Orazio Lomellini. Her contact with Luca Cambiaso and the emerging Genoese school of painting dates to this period. Antony van Dyck visited Anguissola in Genoa when she was in her 90s, and again in Palermo, and admiringly recorded the aged portraitist's advice in his diary.

An important indication of the status of women in the late Renaissance is the appearance of female artists. At this stage they were courageous pioneers, active mainly in northern Italian cities like Cremona, Bologna, Venice and Milan. Sofonisba Anguissola was the very first female Italian painter to achieve international success. Born around 1532 in Cremona, Anguissola earned a local reputation as a refined portrait painter early on, before quickly gaining recognition on a European scale. In 1559 she went to Madrid, where she played an official role in the court of Philip II. Later she returned to Italy, working in Palermo and Genoa. Her flawlessly correct portraits contain a delicate glimmer of personality, sometimes somewhat inhibited. In Lombardy, she provided a link between the 'movements of the soul' sought by Leonardo and the immediacy of emotion expressed by Caravaggio.

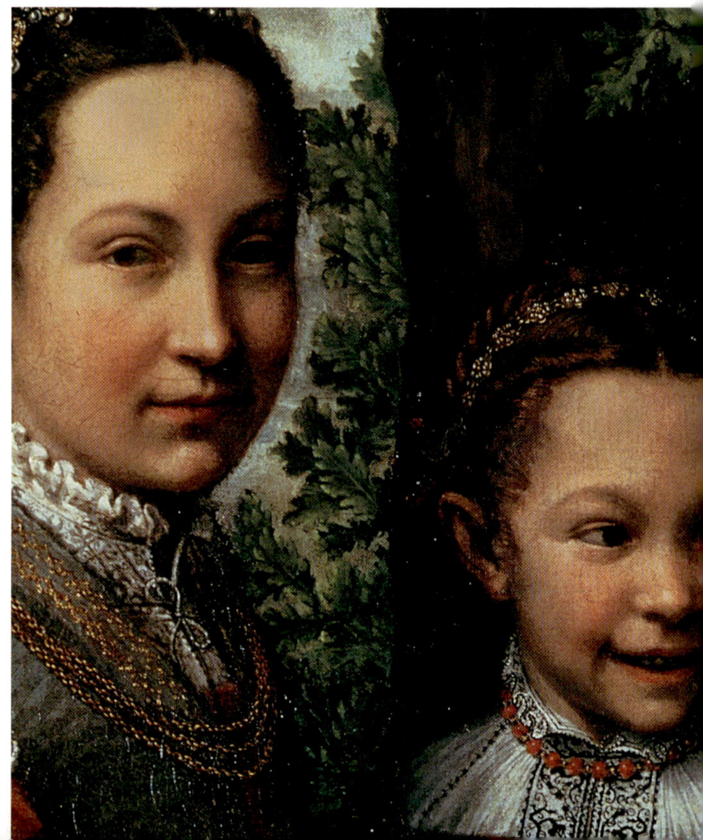

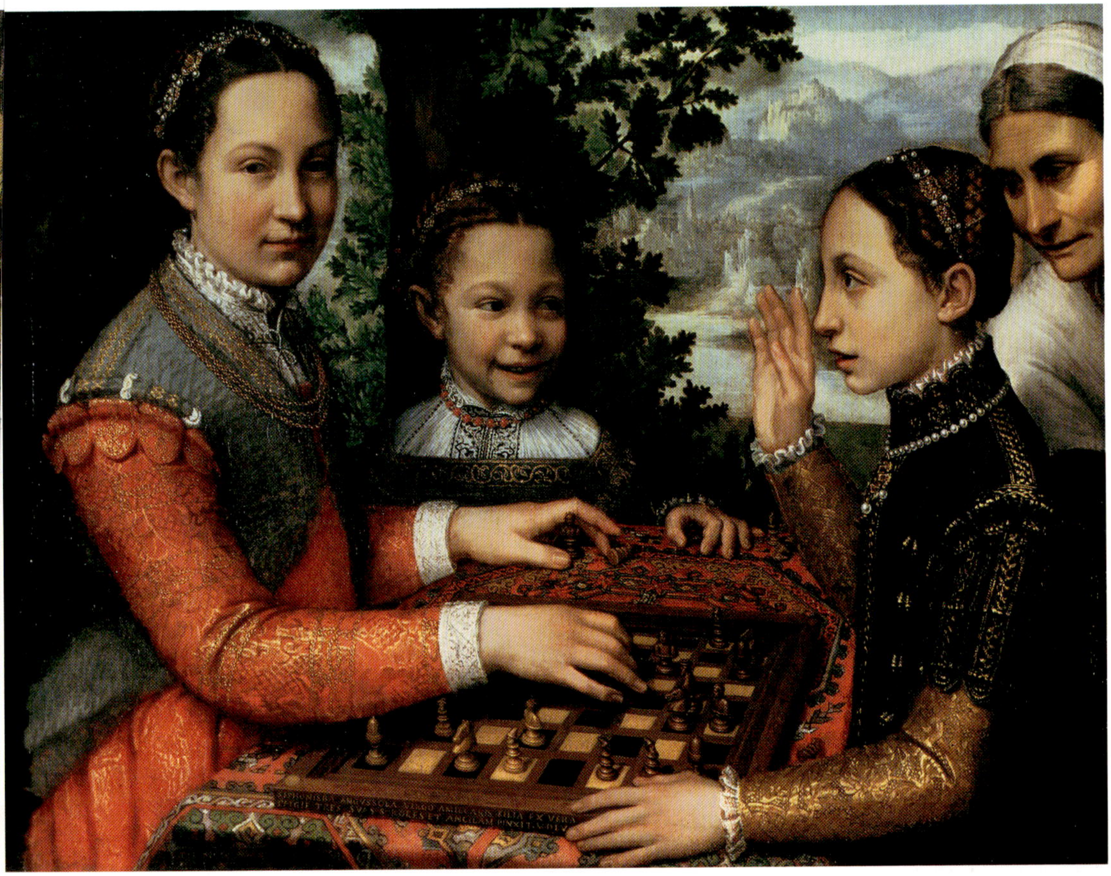

► A third sister, Europa, appears astonished by Lucia's winning move on the chessboard, while the elderly, grey-haired governess looks on from behind. Sofonisba Anguissola was exceptionally skilled in capturing fleeting gestures and expressions, which vary according to age and social status.

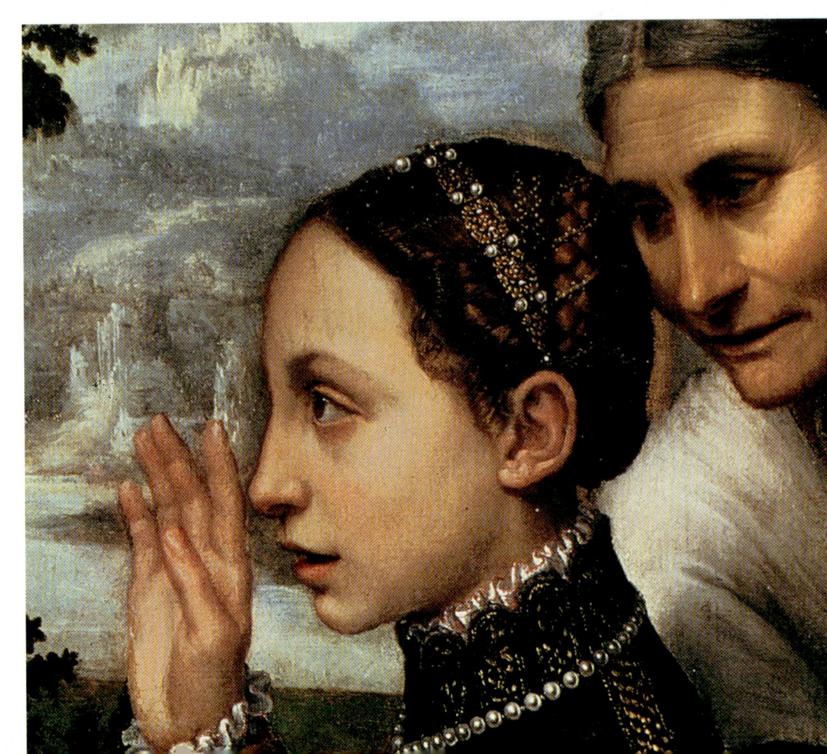

◄ The girls on the left are the painter's sisters Lucia and Minerva. Lucia, who died young, was also a subtle painter. This painting's most interesting and innovative aspect is the way it overcomes the schematic pattern of the family portrait by involving all the participants in a narrative scene.

Ut pictura poesis

Titian
Diana and Actaeon
c. 1555

Oil on canvas, 184 × 202 cm
Edinburgh, National Gallery of Scotland

For artist biography, see page 224.

By the mid-16th century, the 'equal dignity' of poets and painters was thoroughly accepted, as summed up by the phrase *ut pictura poesis* – 'as is painting so is poetry'. Titian was thus justified in defining the canvases he painted for Philip II during the 1550s as 'poetry' – free and exuberant interpretations of mythological episodes, conceived not as erudite illustrations but as images of deep human feeling. Titian did not know Latin, and despite spending time in the company of poets and men of letters, his education remained full of gaps. This limitation resulted in an expressive freedom when it came to the normally unimpeachable authority of the classics. Titian allowed himself to be guided by his own sensibilities: he had no interest in the pedantic literary retelling of myth, but instead focused on a highly sensitive evocation of its human content.

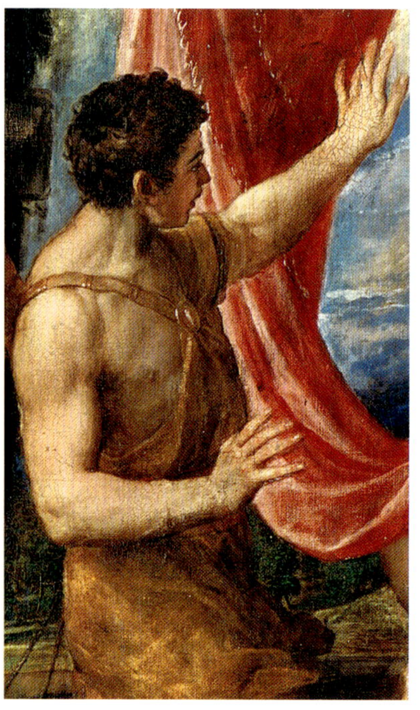

◄ According to the story, the hunter Actaeon, having penetrated a wood, discovers Diana and her companions while they are bathing unclothed in a pond, and this involuntary sighting condemns him to death. Titian does not aim for the visual transcription of a literary source (see pages 154–5) dear to the humanist painters, but allows himself to be guided by his own sensitivities, using the popular translations of Ovid's *Metamorphoses* (see pages 78–9) as a starting point. With Titian, mythological tales become metaphors for human situations, feelings and passions, often focusing on destiny and unjust suffering.

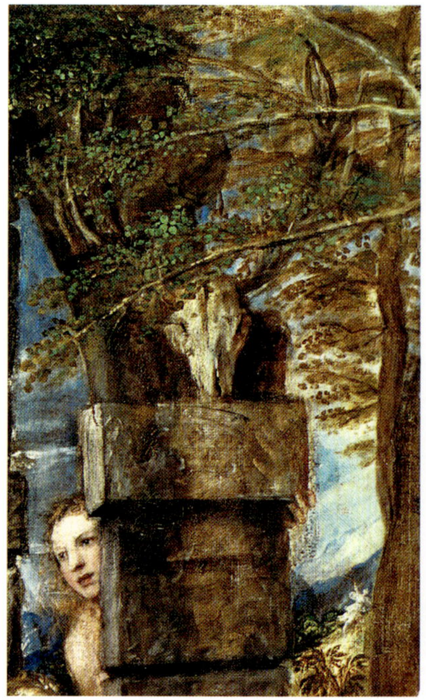

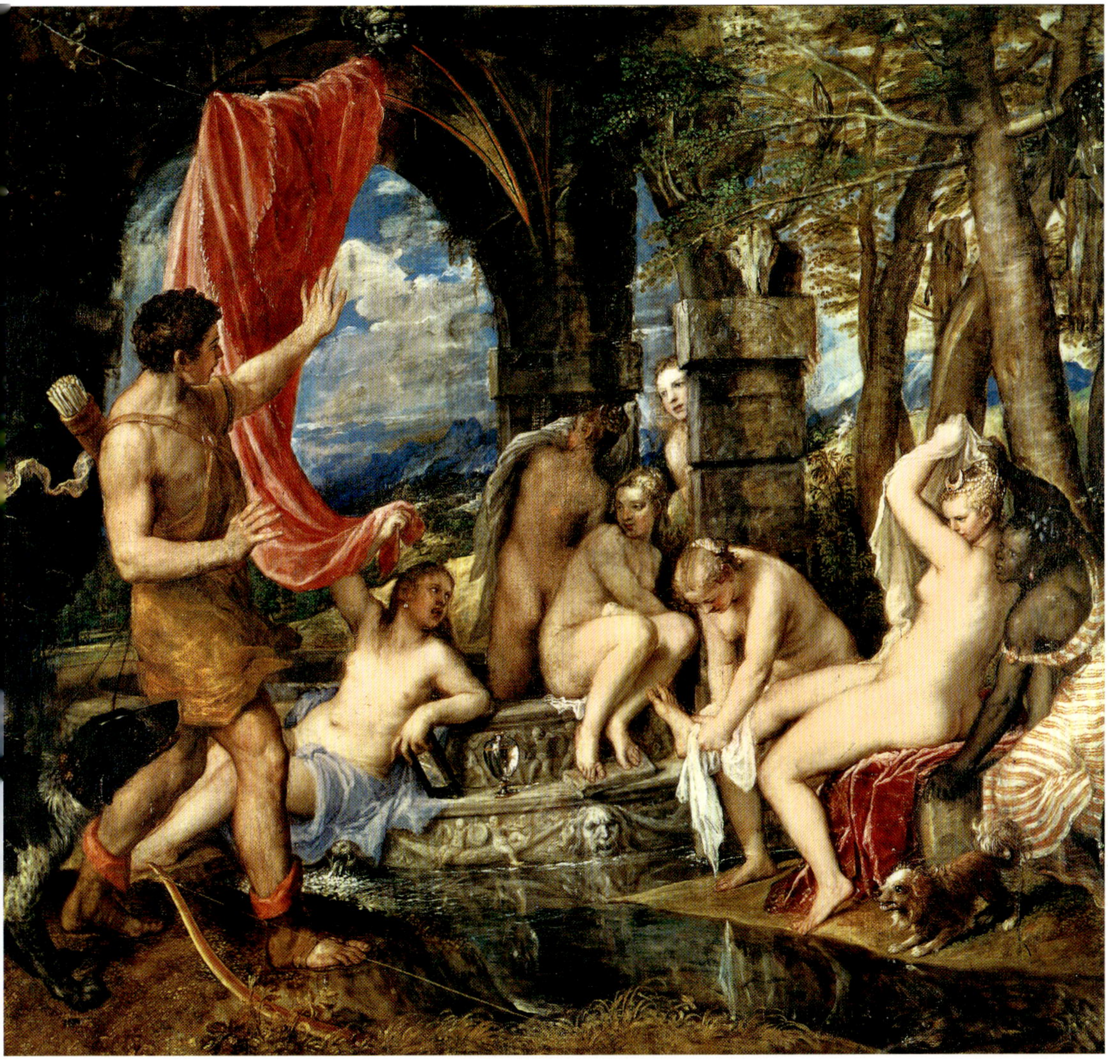

◄▲ The masterpiece of the series of 'poems'
sent to Philip II, the story of Diana illustrates
the merciless punishment inflicted by the
goddess: the deer's skull is a macabre
foreshadowing of the terrible fate of Actaeon,
who will be transformed into a hart and torn
to pieces by his own dogs. The situation is
strikingly different from the happy, Dionysian
Bacchanals Titian painted almost 40 years
earlier for Alfonso d'Este (see pages 272–3).

► The goddess, her nudity discovered by
Actaeon, glares at the intrusive hunter with a
gaze like lightning. The contrast between the
blonde Diana's luminous body and that of the
African handmaid is striking.

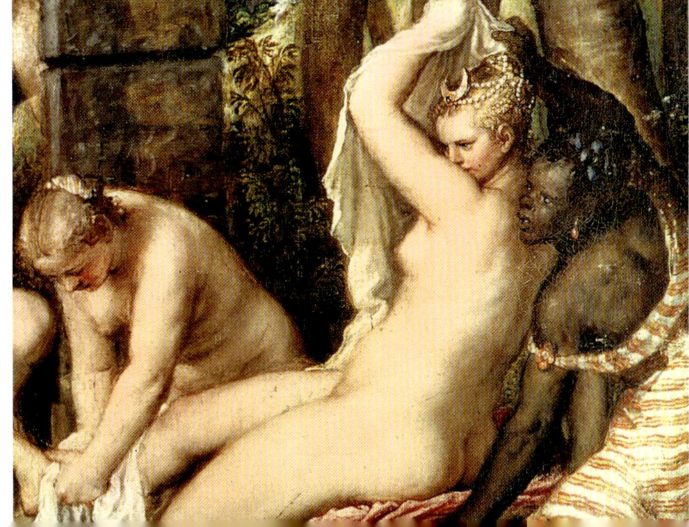

Treatises

Giorgio Vasari
Self-portrait
1560

Oil on canvas, 100.5 × 80 cm
Florence, Galleria degli Uffizi

Giorgio Vasari

Arezzo, 1511–Florence, 1574

In 1524, having first studied art and letters in his native city, Giorgio Vasari went to Florence, where he attended the workshops of Andrea del Sarto and Baccio Bandinelli. In 1527, expelled along with the Medici, he returned to Arezzo. Vasari was active in various cities until 1531, when he followed Cardinal Ippolito de' Medici to Rome. During his stay there, and subsequently from 1532 to 1536 in Florence, he continued to apply himself to painting but also took up the study of architecture. A trip to Venice in 1541 acquainted him with the frescoes of Giulio Romano in Mantua and those of Correggio in Parma, as well as the paintings of Titian and the other Venetian masters. Nevertheless, these experiences did not divert him from his Tuscan–Roman Mannerist style. Returning to Rome, he lived there until 1553 under the protection of Cardinal Alessandro Farnese. During this period, he associated closely with leading men of letters and was friendly with Michelangelo, who urged him to devote greater attention to architecture. From 1554, Cosimo de' Medici entrusted him with many commissions: in Florence, the painted decoration of Palazzo Vecchio and the construction of the Uffizi; and in Pisa, the building of the palazzo and the church of the Knights of St Steven. In the meantime, however, he also worked in Rome, where Pius V commissioned him to paint frescoes of the Battle of Lepanto in the Cappella Regia of the Vatican. While Vasari's painting is deemed a minor product of Mannerism, his work as an architect is more highly regarded. However, he is best known for his historical writings. In 1540, he began to collect information about the life and works of artists, and in 1550 he published the first edition of his *Lives of the Most Eminent Italian Architects, Painters and Sculptors from Cimabue until Our Time* in Rome. A second edition of the work, corrected and updated, was published in 1568.

During the 16th century, the art public broadened and critical debate increased. One of the reasons for this was the growing number of published writings and treatises, some of which were quite controversial. The century opened with the debate between Leonardo and Michelangelo over the supremacy of painting or sculpture. Later, Titian, supported by the writings of Pietro Aretino and Ludovico Dolce, defended his taste for rich, mellow colour against the 'primacy of drawing' that held sway in Florence and Rome. Serlio, Palladio and Vignola meanwhile published major treatises on architecture. Giorgio Vasari proposed placing the three arts 'of drawing' (painting, sculpture and architecture) at the pinnacle and explored the tension between the imitation of nature and the application of rules. As his paradigm, he uses the lives and works of the painters, sculptors and architects who had succeeded one another from the end of the 13th century onward. His obvious predilection for the Tuscan masters is somewhat counterbalanced by the treatises of the Lombard Giovanni Paolo Lomazzo, who a few years later asserted the equal importance of the painters from the Veneto and northern Italy.

Vasari's *Lives*

Notwithstanding his significant activity as a painter and architect, Giorgio Vasari's fame is linked to the book that, perhaps inaccurately, is considered the first art-historical text. Published in 1550, it presents the biographies of painters, sculptors and architects from Cimabue to Michelangelo, organized along an evolutionary path. The premise is that after art reached its nadir in the Middle Ages, it gradually rose again, with stages marked by the progressive conquest of nature, perspective and the human body. The central figure of the first 'epoch', inaugurated by Cimabue, was Giotto. The second period coincides with the 15th century, running from Masaccio to Botticelli and Perugino. The third phase opens with Leonardo and Raphael and reaches its peak with Michelangelo. According to Vasari, no one would ever again be able to surpass the sublime style of this last master, especially in the perfection with which he represented that loftiest of subjects, the male nude. As for media, Vasari explicitly prefers marble sculpture and fresco, which allow no correction or reworking. A marked partiality for the Tuscan masters, hyperbole and some inaccurate anecdotes and details do not eclipse the importance of Vasari's volume, which is both an invaluable source and the expression of the taste of Tuscan Renaissance culture at its height.

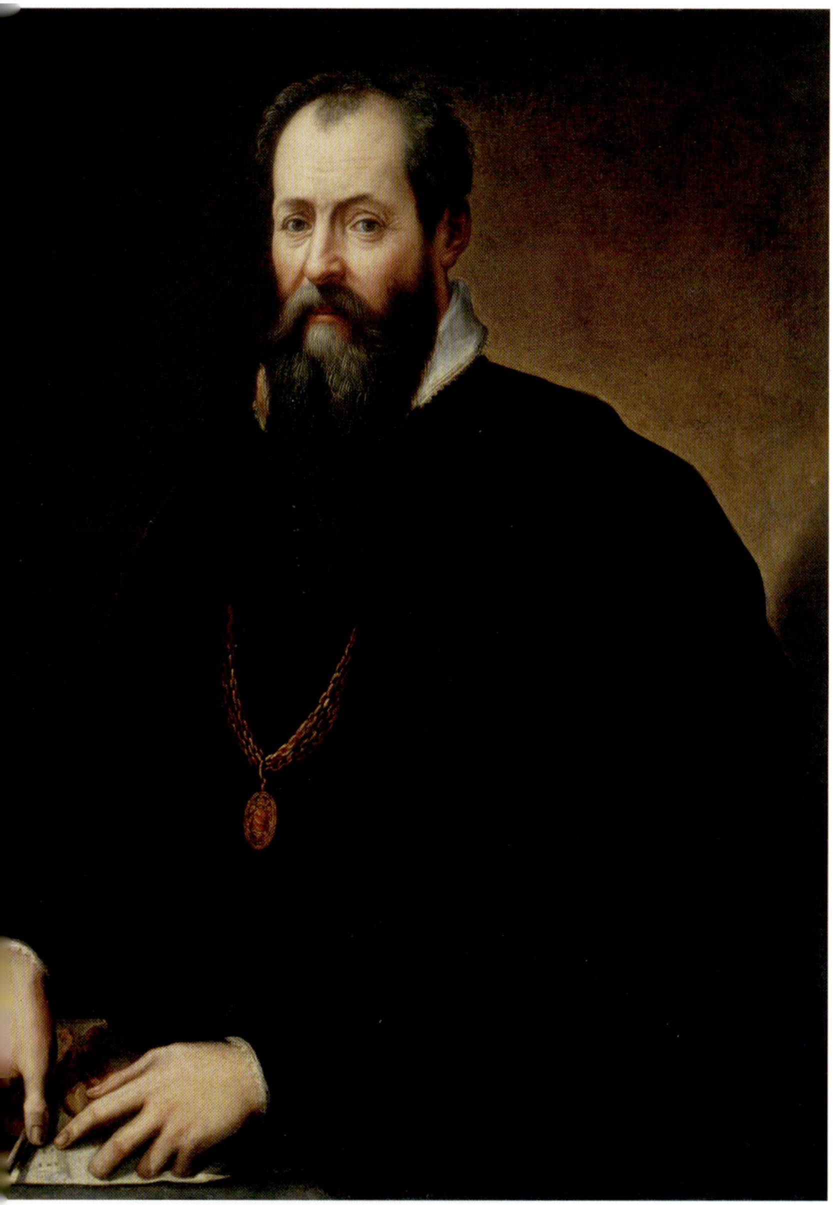

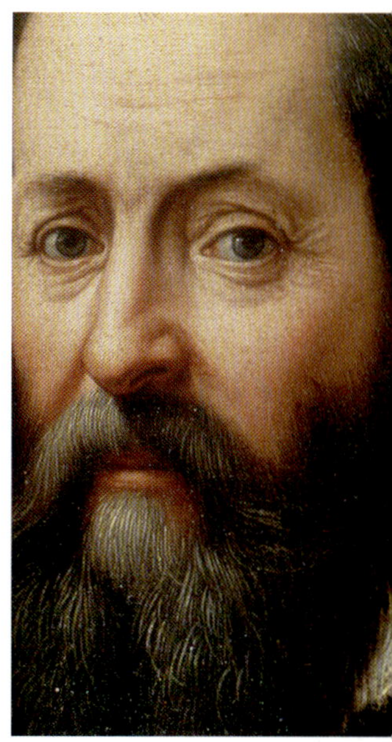

▲ It is very probable that in the execution of this portrait, Vasari was assisted by one of his brilliant collaborators, the Netherlandish painter and engraver Jan van der Straet (1523–1605), who had settled in Florence and was known by his Italianized name Giovanni Stradano.

▼ Dressed in austere but impeccable dark robes adorned with a heavy gold chain, Vasari presents himself as the quintessential 16th-century 'courtier'.

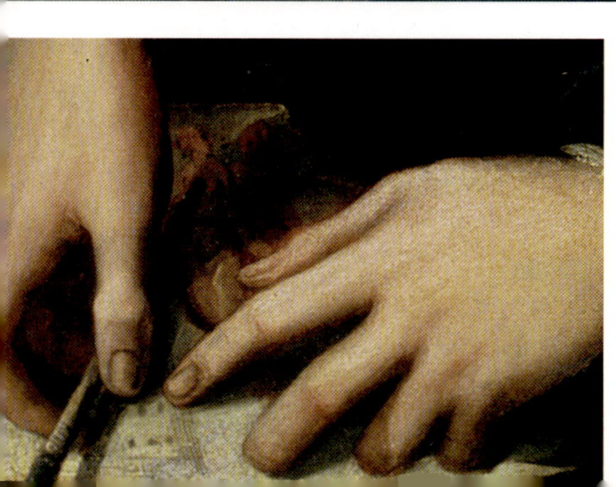

◄ The subject's own preference for graphic art and painting is evident from the sheet of drawings and the brush in the foreground. However, it must be admitted that Vasari's painting does not rise above the constricting rules of Mannerism. His work as an architect is far more original.

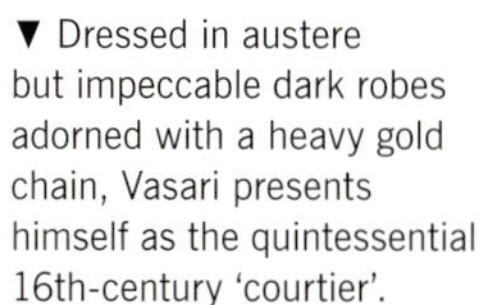

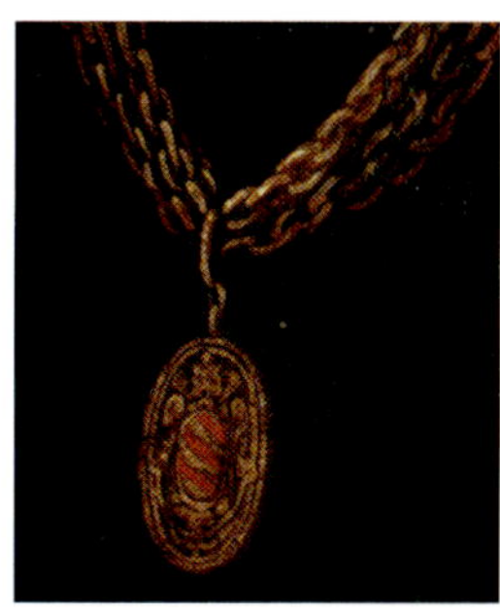

Pastorale

Jacopo Bassano
Sowing Grain
1560

Oil on canvas, 139 × 129 cm
Madrid, Museo Thyssen-Bornemisza

Jacopo Bassano

(Jacopo da Ponte)

Bassano del Grappa, Vicenza,
c. 1510–92

Prolific, long-lived and a leading figure among 16th-century painters in the Veneto, Jacopo Bassano was the son and father of painters. Choosing to remain in his native town rather than work in Venice, he nonetheless remained in touch with the latest international developments in painting and possessed a visual culture comparable to that of his contemporaries Veronese and Tintoretto. Always inspired by a realistic narrative sense, which he enlivened through direct references to daily life in the countryside, Bassano drew from the tradition of the Veneto but combined it with other sources. Spurred by his knowledge of prints and drawings by northern as well as Roman artists, he measured himself against Parmigianino and tried his hand at Mannerism. He alternately painted rural scenes, figures and scintillating studies in colour, characterized by gleams of light that anticipate El Greco. In the 1560s, his Mannerist phase at an end, Jacopo Bassano again chose Titian as a model, preferring to paint 'genre' pictures, often assisted by his sons.

As the 16th century advanced, the re-evaluation of country life as opposed to the predominant urban dimension of humanism became a social, economic and cultural theme. Its expressive subject matter ranged from country idylls of a classical cast to everyday peasant life, from the elegant villas designed by Palladio to dilapidated barns. Born and raised a provincial town-dweller, Jacopo Bassano found inspiration in peasant life in the Veneto countryside, and he offered an important alternative to the grandiloquent 'official' art of the masters active in Venice. The canvases that he painted for private collectors are filled with realistic details, from animals and landscape features to reflections and accurately rendered natural materials.

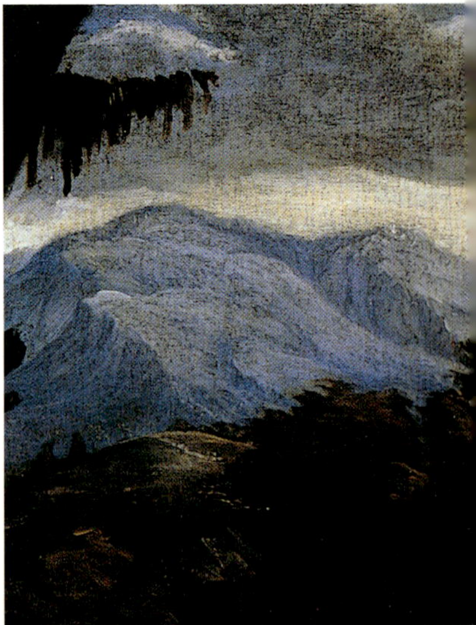

► The painter lived and worked in the shelter of the mountains, which are often the setting for his paintings. The pale blues of the mountains in the background, and the cloud-streaked sky, convey an impression of fresh air that is quite different from the atmosphere of paintings set in Venice or elsewhere on the Lagoon.

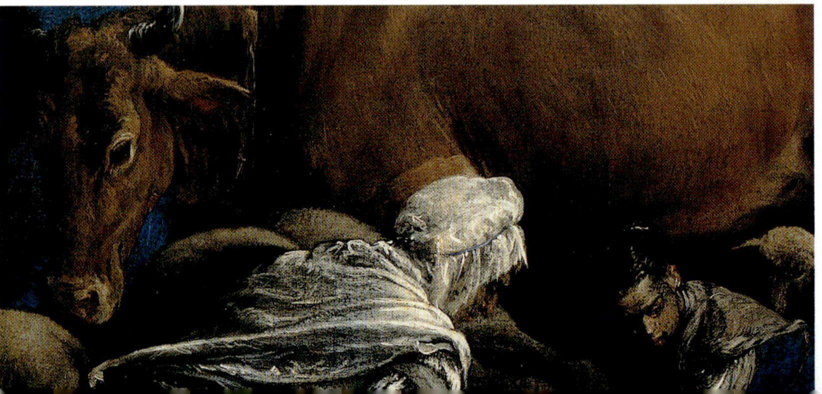

◄ This canvas depicts a recurrent situation in the life of those who worked in the fields: while the father sows, his wife and children tend the sheep and cows. The peasants' hard labour involved the whole family, even the young children.

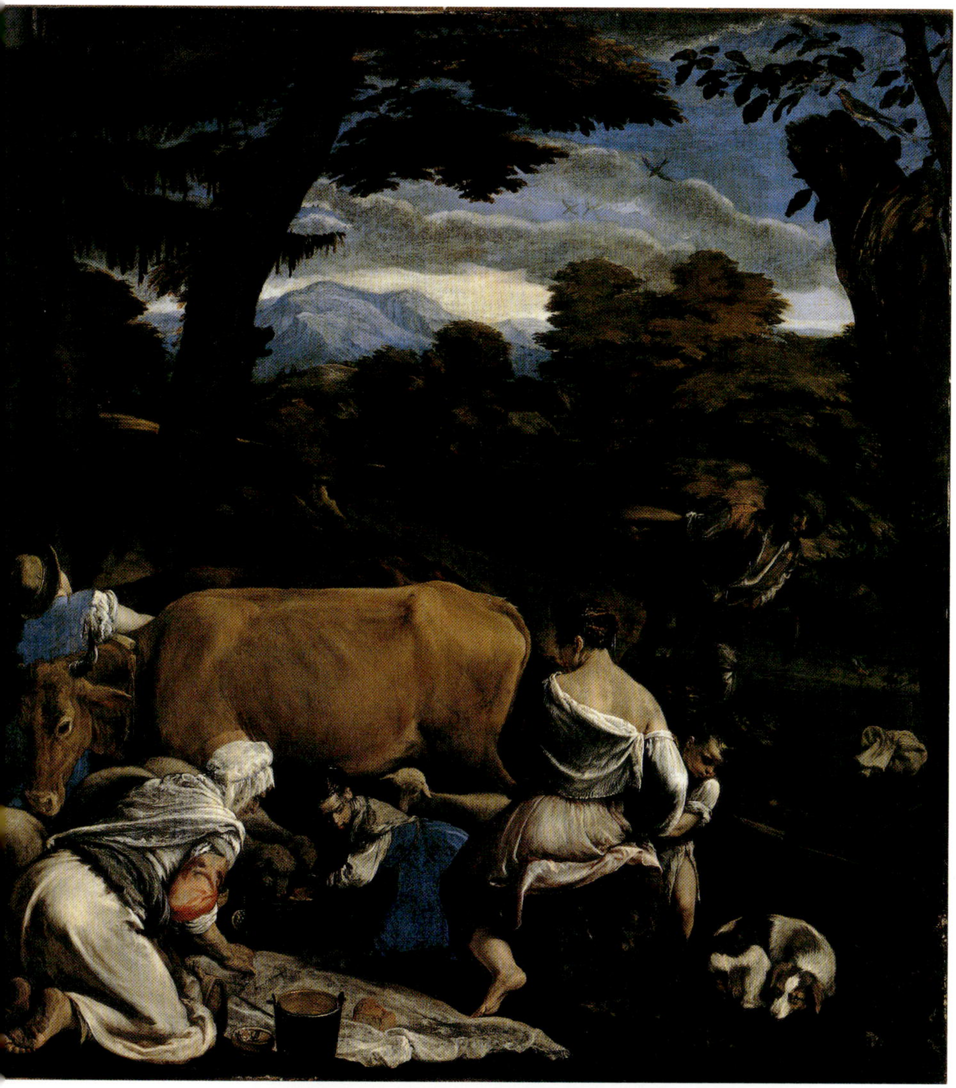

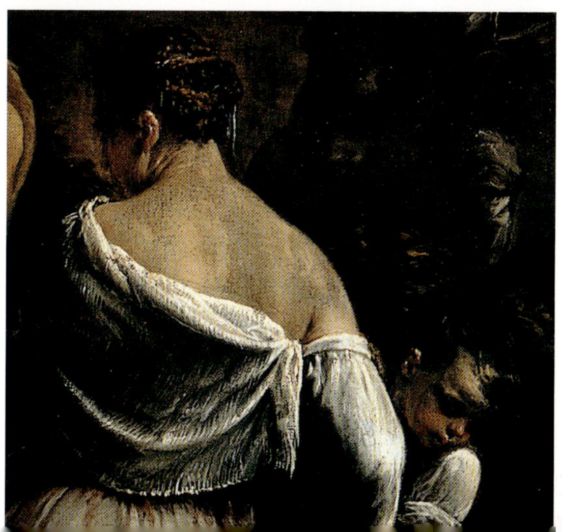

▼ Like Titian (also born
in northern Veneto), Jacopo
Bassano had a great fondness
for dogs, which appear in
almost all his compositions.

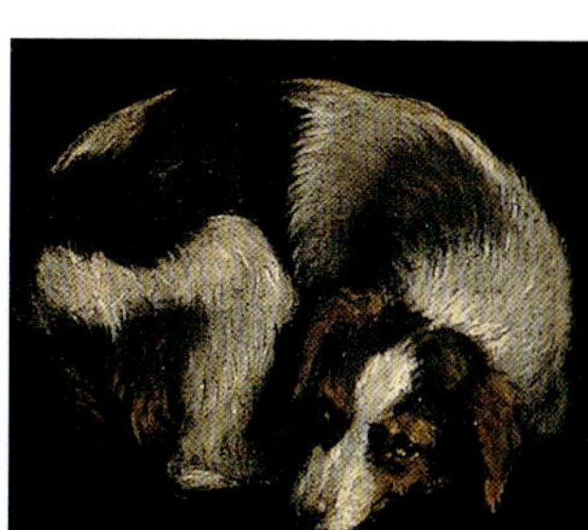

Theatre

Jacopo Tintoretto
Finding the Body of St Mark
1562–6

Oil on canvas, 396 × 400 cm

Milan, Pinacoteca di Brera

For artist biography, see page 344.

Painters created backdrops, scenery and other ephemeral decorations for theatre and opera. From the beginning of the 16th century, treatise writers, painters and architects alike were ever more fascinated by their relationship with the performing arts, and devised new approaches to perspective, monumental backdrops, symbolic references and comparisons with classical theatre. Painting began to reflect the hypothetical viewpoint of a theatre spectator. Some painters, such as Tintoretto, even built scale models and stage sets, in which he placed wax figurines in order to study perspective and lighting.

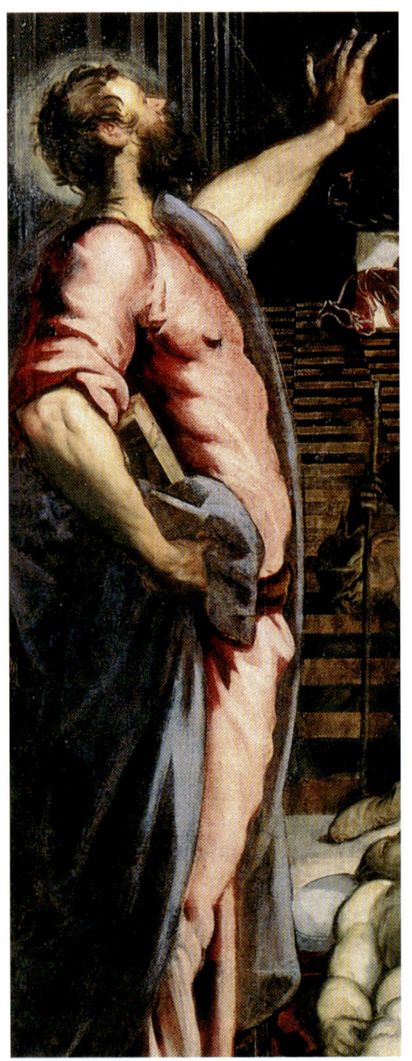

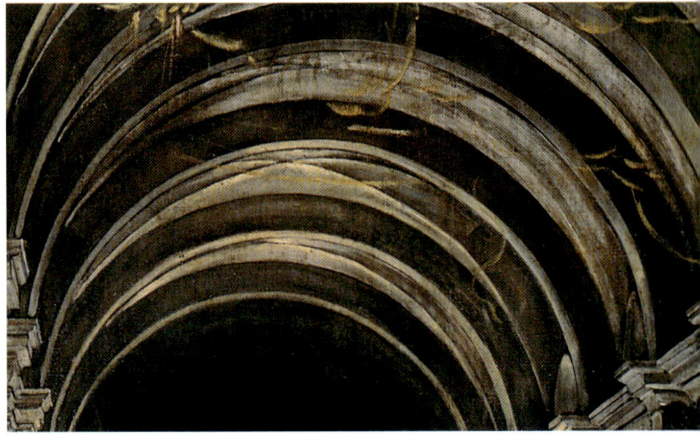

◄ ► The ghost of St Mark suddenly appears to the citizens of Venice at night, as they search for the remains of their patron saint among the cadavers buried in a church graveyard. The ghost interrupts their search with an imperious gesture. At his feet, in an extraordinary foreshortening possibly derived from Mantegna (see pages 116–17), a livid nude corpse lies on a carpet.

▲ The scene is part of a cycle prepared by Jacopo Tintoretto for the Scuola Grande di San Marco in Venice, the same Scuola for which Gentile and Giovanni Bellini had painted *St Mark Preaching in Alexandria* (see pages 196–7). This intensely visionary canvas illustrates the climax of the search for the saint's relics. Tintoretto has set the scene in a theatrical single-point perspective.

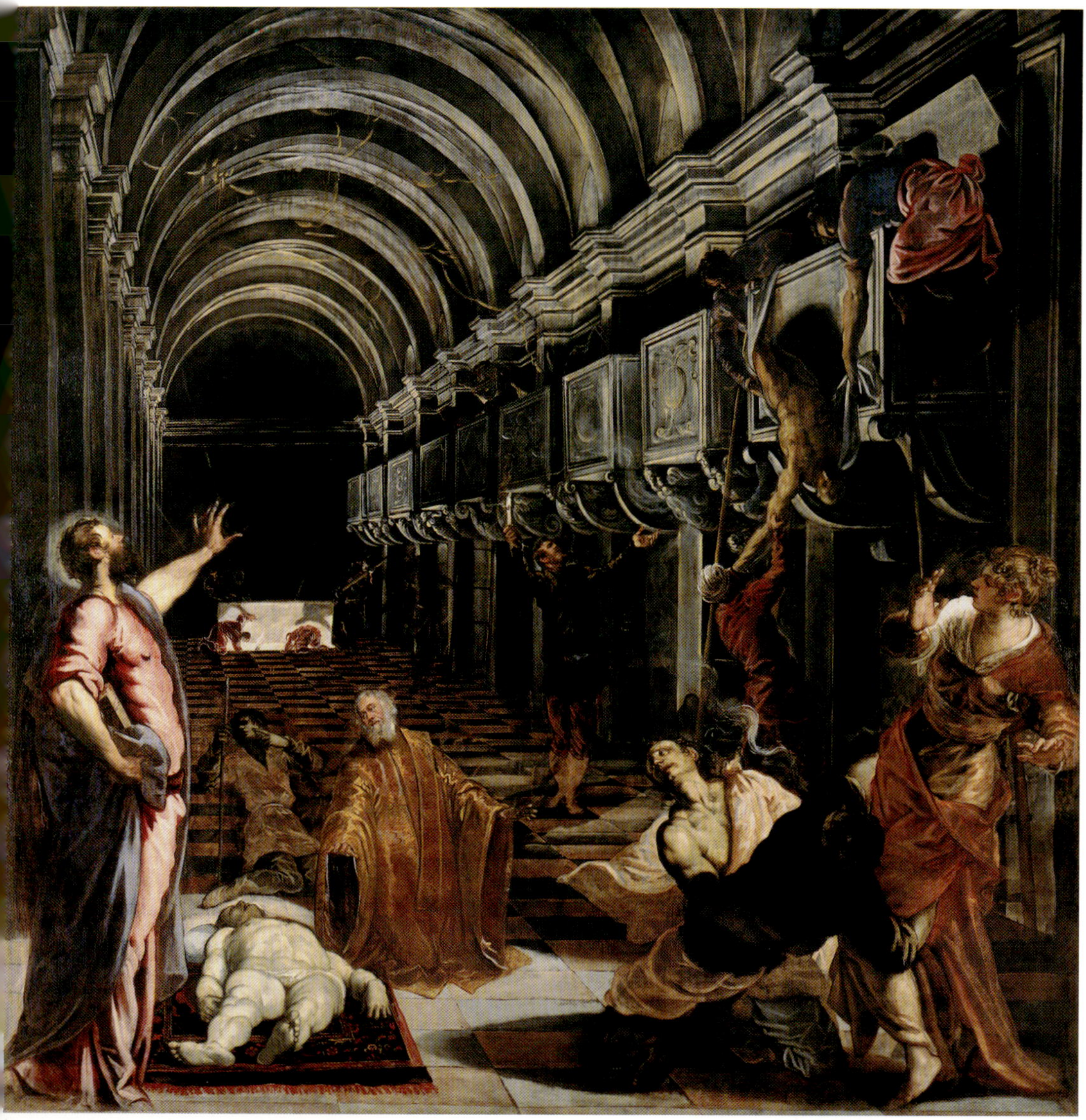

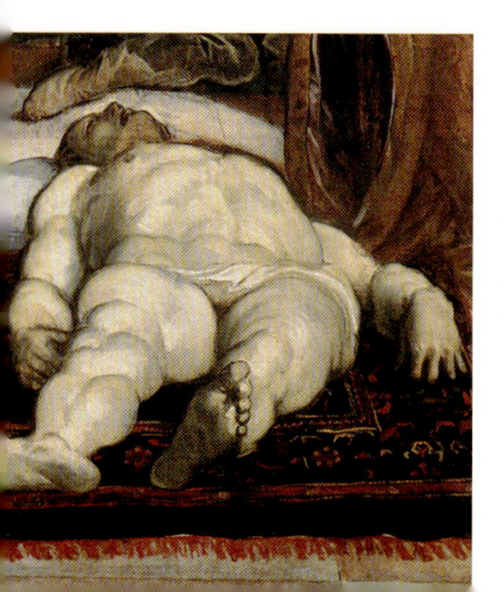

▶ A half-naked man struggles to support a possessed man, whose contortions indicate the presence of the saint's relics. The figures' gestures, the forthright asymmetry of the sharply diagonal space and the flashes of light in the dark night make this work one of the freest inventions of painting in the Veneto at the height of the Renaissance.

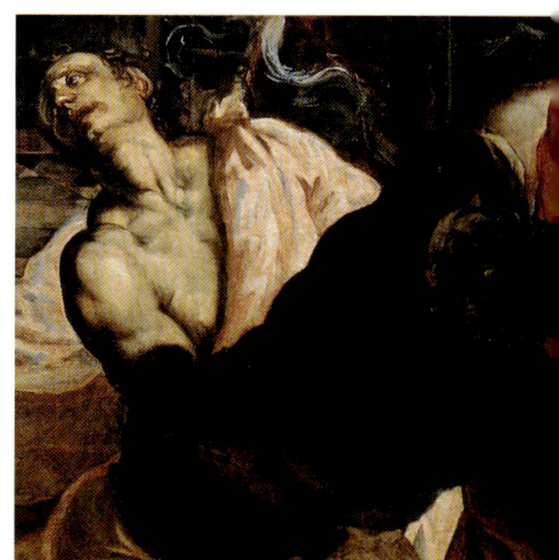

Antiquarian

Titian
Portrait of Jacopo Strada
c. 1567

Oil on canvas, 125 × 95 cm
Vienna, Kunsthistorisches Museum

For artist biography, see page 224.

The specialist art dealer really came into being in the second half of the 16th century, as the Italian art market broadened to include the international scene. The traditional, direct relationship between artist and patron gradually became a commercial transaction that called for the intervention of a professional. The word 'antiquarian' had once referred to a collector, not a vendor, of works of art and antiquities. True connoisseurs cultivated and refined, but also unabashedly commercial, these new art dealers competed for works, artists and clients. Titian was considered the art market's 'star' in the late 16th century.

The International Career of a Brilliant Intermediary

Mantuan by birth and Venetian by adoption, Jacopo Strada was a brilliant, well-to-do art dealer of Dutch parentage (his real name was Jacob van der Straat). He managed a stellar 'client portfolio': Pope Paul III, the Fuggers, the Habsburgs. Thanks to him, Titian made contact with Maximilian II, who had become the ruler of the Austrian part of the Habsburg empire after his brother Charles V abdicated. With great efficiency, Strada organized a meeting in Venice with Veit von Dornberg, who managed Maximilian II's affairs, to offer him seven mythological canvases by Titian, complete with expert appraisals. In short, Jacopo Strada was an able and successful professional. The image that Titian transmitted, in a portrait that is perhaps the last of his career, affirms this with commanding effectiveness. Jacopo Strada's son followed in his father's footsteps. A portrait of Ottavio Strada, painted by Jacopo Tintoretto, is at the Rijksmuseum in Amsterdam.

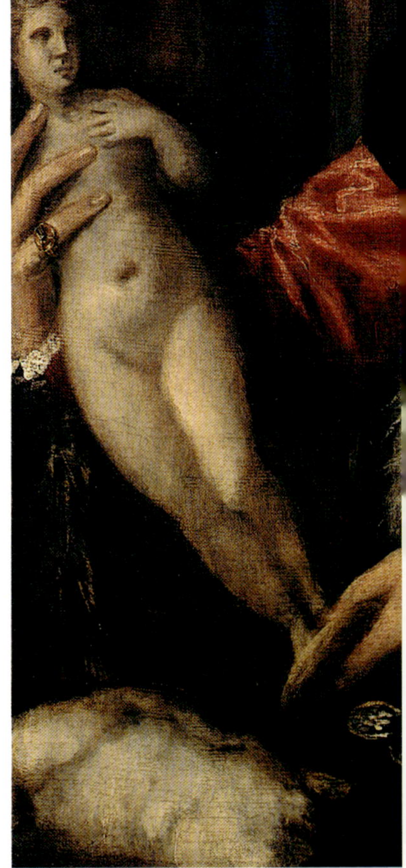

► Titian hastily captures Jacopo Strada's confident expression and innate elegance, but lingers over the loving care with which the art dealer handles an antique statue as he shows it to an imaginary client.

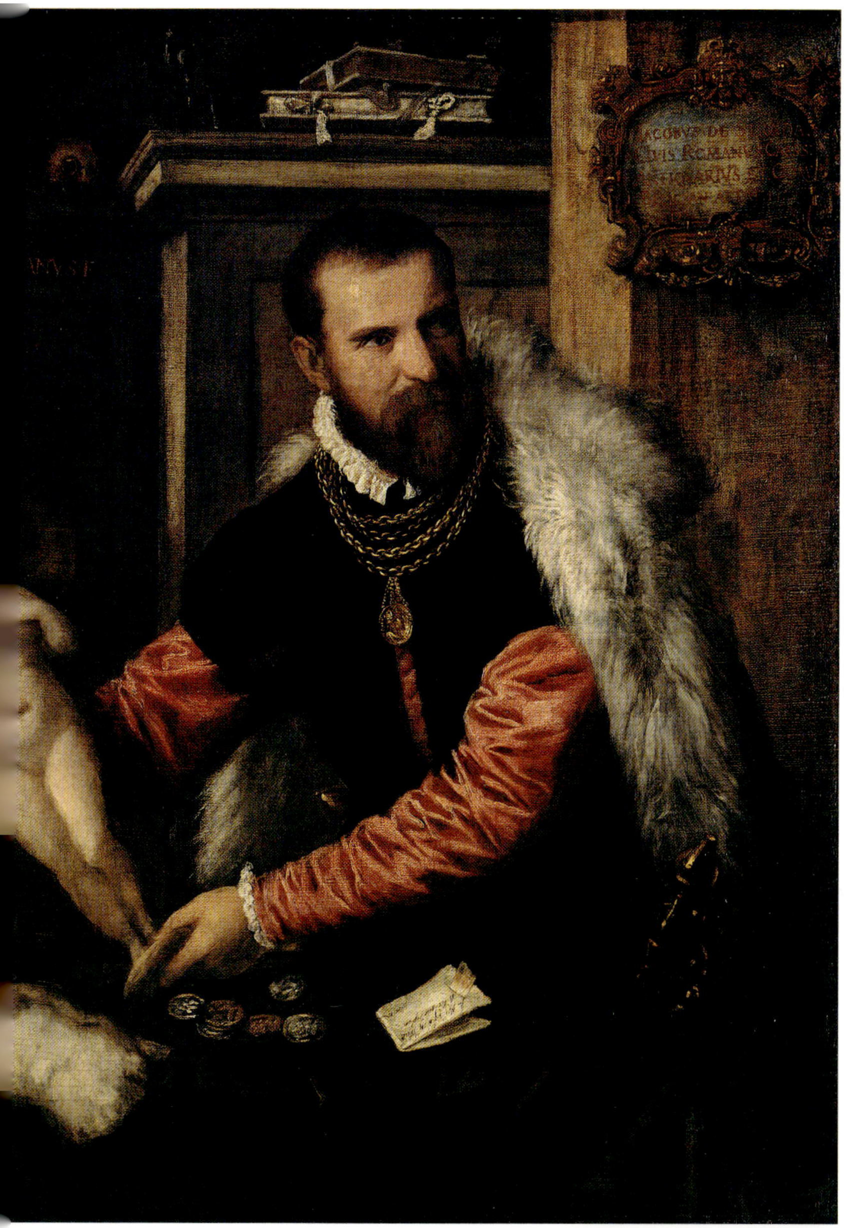

▲ An eye-catching precious stone hangs from an opulent chain that passes around Strada's neck four times.

► Titian portrays the antiquarian surrounded not only by priceless objects but also by symbols of prestige: the sword at his side identifies him as a gentleman, and a letter in the foreground is evidence of relationships with distant purchasers.

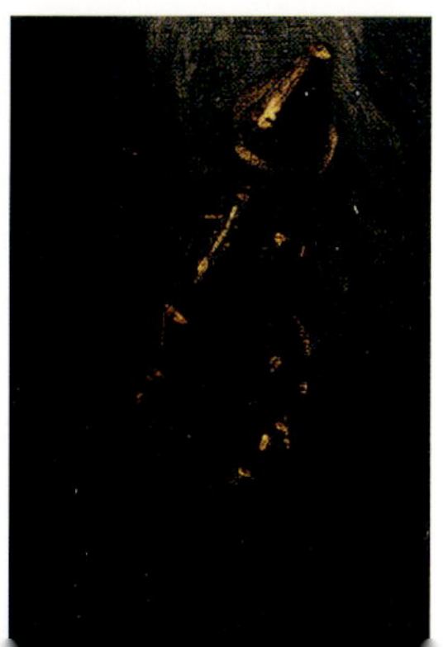

Federico Barocci
The Deposition
1569

Oil on canvas, 412 × 232 cm
Perugia, cathedral

Federico Barocci

(Federico Fiori)

Urbino, 1535–1612

The pleasantly accessible, luminous paintings of Federico Barocci, from the Marche region, made him one of the main exponents of the Counter-Reformation's expressive requirements as well as a bridge between the great Renaissance masters and the new art of the early 17th century, from the Carracci to Rubens. Having grown up in Urbino with the memory of Raphael, Barocci pursued his training on several journeys that exposed him to Correggio, whose warm colours he studied. Meeting with scant success in Rome, in 1565 Barocci returned permanently to Urbino. Despite this somewhat peripheral location, his reputation widened – as a remarkable painter of portraits and especially for his large sacred scenes, which adhere perfectly to the 'instructions' the Council of Trent had issued governing sacred art. His altar paintings convey concepts that are at once noble and – by including realistic, everyday details – simple and direct. The later compositions are increasingly spiritual and contemplative in content, anticipating the Baroque.

The Council of Trent, through which the Catholic Church clarified and defined a wide range of practices and doctrines ran from 1545 to 1563. In addition to significant innovation in the liturgy and the organization of the religious orders, the Council's final documents contain 'instructions' for the revitalization of religious art. The Counter-Reformation proposed to make the places and people of the faith visible and recognizable through an art capable of 'speaking' to everyone. Great churches and sanctuaries – towering symbols of Catholic presence – rose up in small towns below the Alps. To counter the Lutherans rejection of the cult of the saints, the Council encouraged a revival of devotion to popular religious figures through spectacular illustrations of their lives and martyrdom in sculpture and painting. It specifically suggested a change of direction for sacred painting: it was to be easily understandable and include didactic features that provided examples of Christian virtue with which viewers could identify. Figures and details were to be drawn from contemporary daily life, not the distant past. The Counter-Reformation's standards for religious art marked a turning point and formed the basis of the transition from Renaissance to Baroque.

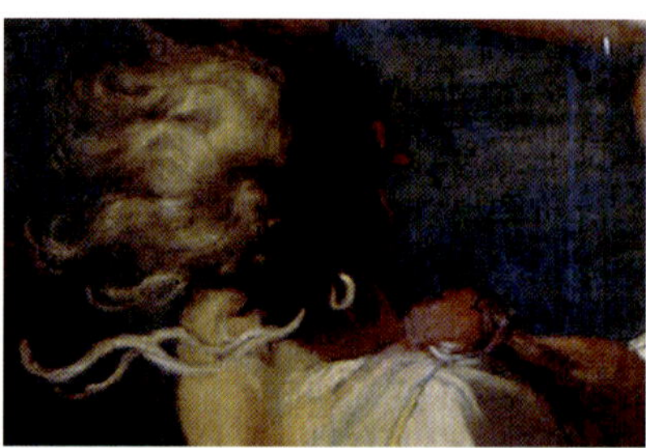

◄ In an effective dramatic contrivance, a gust of wind agitates the outlines, ruffles the hair and stirs the drapery of the figures.

▼ With theatricality and even a note of sensuality, the Holy Women hasten to support the swooning Virgin Mary.

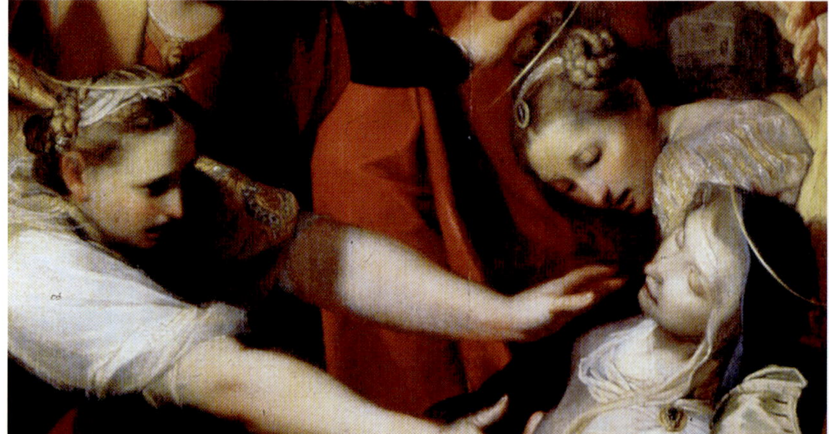

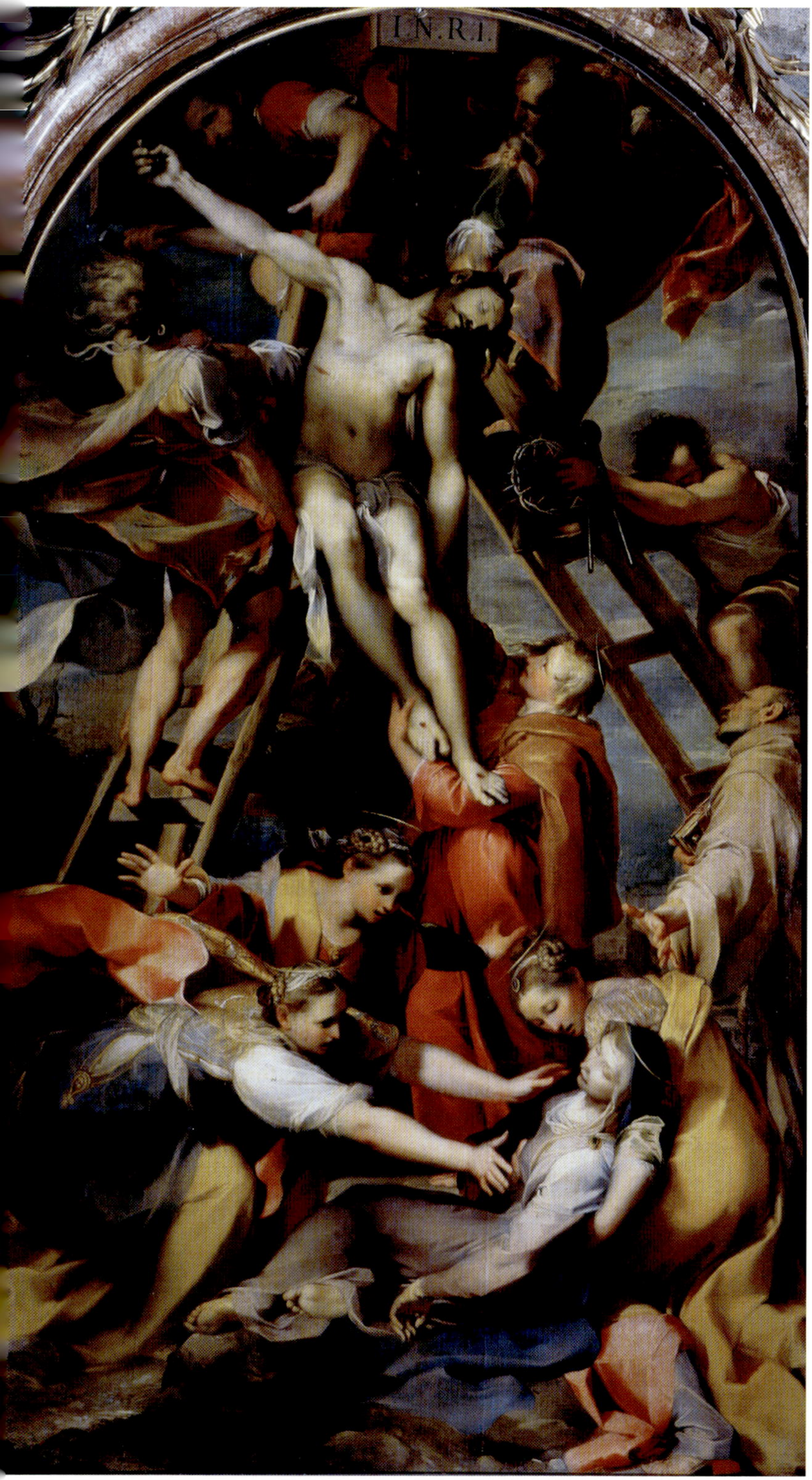

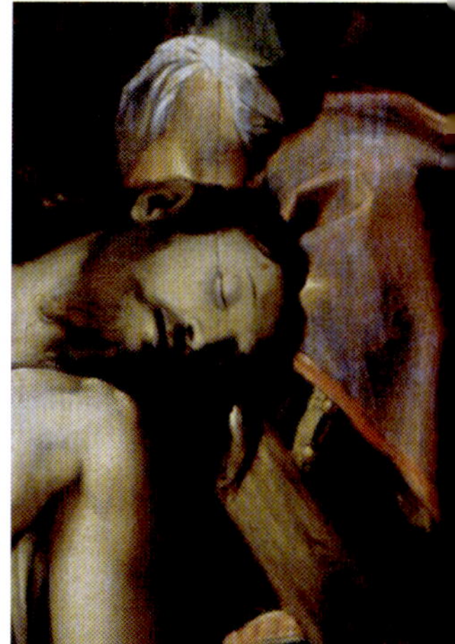

▲ This *Deposition* reuses motifs from the altarpiece painted almost 50 years earlier by Rosso Fiorentino in Volterra (see pages 270–1), but with an effusion of sentiment far different from that cool, angular Mannerist composition. The figure of Christ would in turn be reused in Rubens's painting of this subject, about 40 years later, for the cathedral in Antwerp.

▼ Barocci's narrative clarity, sentimental mood and sense of devoted participation are perfectly in keeping with the precepts set forth by the Council of Trent regarding religious images.

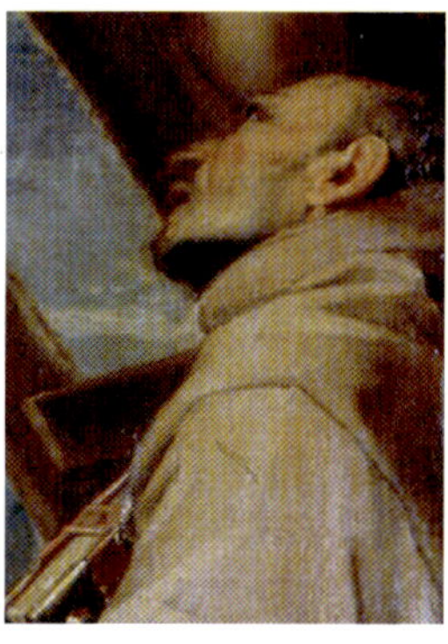

Realism

Giovanni Battista Moroni
The Tailor
c. 1570

Oil on canvas, 97 × 74 cm
London, National Gallery

Giovanni Battista Moroni

Albino, Bergamo, 1520/4–1578

Although his paintings of sacred themes lack originality, Moroni's portraits are considered among the finest painted in 16th-century Italy. His extraordinary capacity to identify with his subjects gives the portraits an astonishing vitality and directness. After an apprenticeship with Moretto in Brescia, Giovanni Battista Moroni spent his entire career around Bergamo, where he was naturally measured against the memory of Lorenzo Lotto. Two sojourns in Trent (in 1548 and 1551) bear mention: while the Council was in session, Moroni painted various works and came in direct contact with the episcopal Madruzzo family and Titian.

'Painting of reality' was an essential component of Lombard visual culture (even though the Milan-born Caravaggio, the greatest interpreter of the 'natural', did not work in Lombardy). A strong element of naturalism runs through the entire 16th century, first entering into dialogue with the Counter-Reformation's doctrinal requirements for sacred art and then continuing on to a convincing and impressive encounter with the Sacro Monte. Though admired for the altarpieces and devotional works inspired by the dictates of the Council of Trent, Moroni excelled above all as a portraitist whose colloquialism, sometimes anxious humanity and concrete sense of reality are linked to Lorenzo Lotto's legacy.

▼ In Moroni's gallery of forceful portraits, that of a tailor at work stands out for its honesty and vivacity. The sitter scarcely raises his eyes as he goes about cutting a piece of black cloth with large fabric scissors. In a brilliant choice of composition, the painter places the figure slightly in perspective, beyond the table.

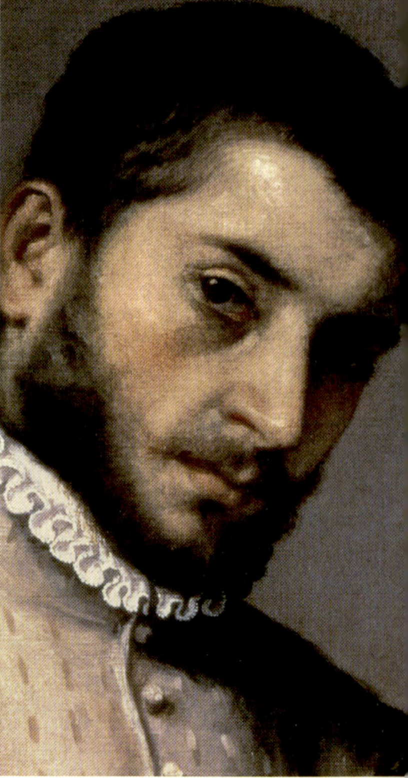

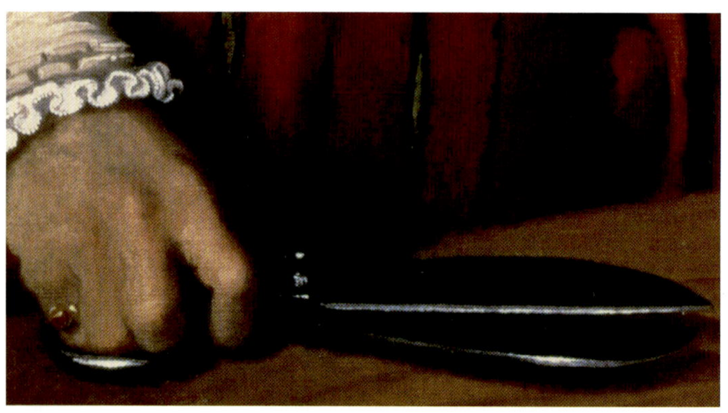

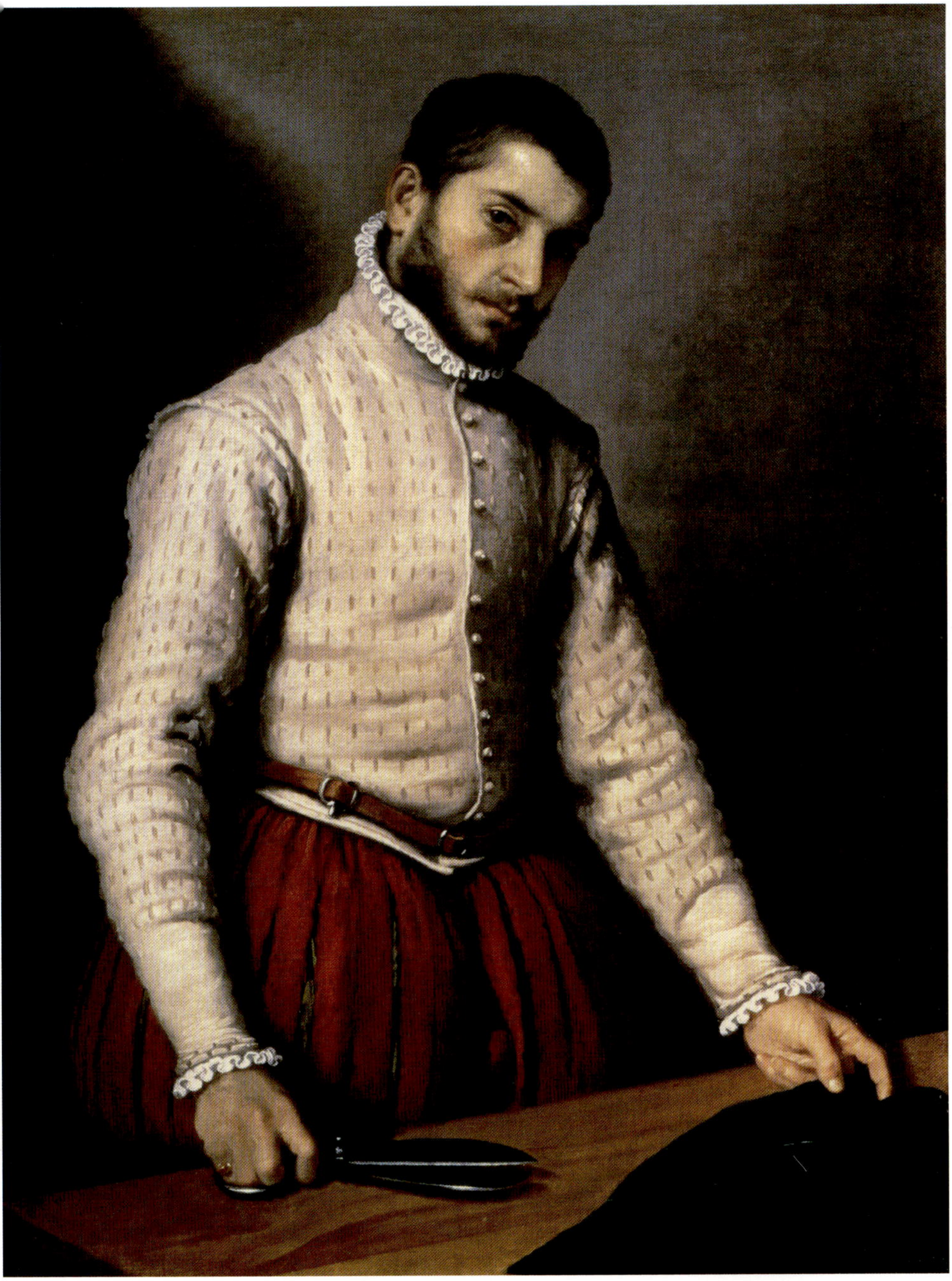

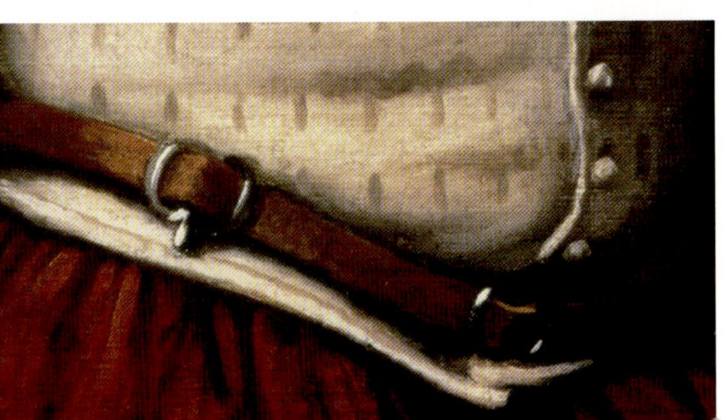

◄ Realistic portraits were an important social innovation. Especially in Italy, patrons belonged to a restricted elite, except for a few merchants and fellow artists.

◄ This anonymous tailor, whose impeccable costume is proof of his professional mastery, is one of the first portraits of the 'middle class'.

Night Scene

Luca Cambiaso
Christ before Caiaphas
1570

Oil on canvas, 188 × 138 cm

Genoa, Museo dell'Accademia Ligustica di Belle Arti

Luca Cambiaso

Moneglia, Genoa, 1527–Madrid, 1585

The most important Genoese painter of the second half of the 16th century, Cambiaso may be considered the founder of the local school, which thanks to him also took on an international dimension. Cambiaso's painting intelligently unites various visual ideas from the height of the Renaissance – the Mannerist experience of Perino del Vaga, the soft *sfumato* of Correggio, the colours of the Venetian masters – and anticipates themes that were to typify the Baroque, such as candlelit night scenes and the intense pathos of some religious scenes. The artist's career took place largely in Genoa and Liguria, where he painted sacred and profane fresco cycles, altarpieces and canvases for collectors, with the support of the local patrons. In 1583, Philip II called him to Spain, to work as a court painter at the Escorial, but he died two years after moving to Madrid. One of his successors in Spain was Pellegrino Tibaldi.

Preceded by a few experiments in northern Italy, a pictorial vein devoted to candlelit scenes began towards the end of the 16th century. The success of the genre spread in the following century. Starting with Caravaggio and his followers, the flame and burning coals, usually against a background evoking the darkness of night, would become 'classics' in European Baroque art. The Genoese artist Luca Cambiaso, known internationally because of the trade between Genoa and Spain, was a precursor in this trend.

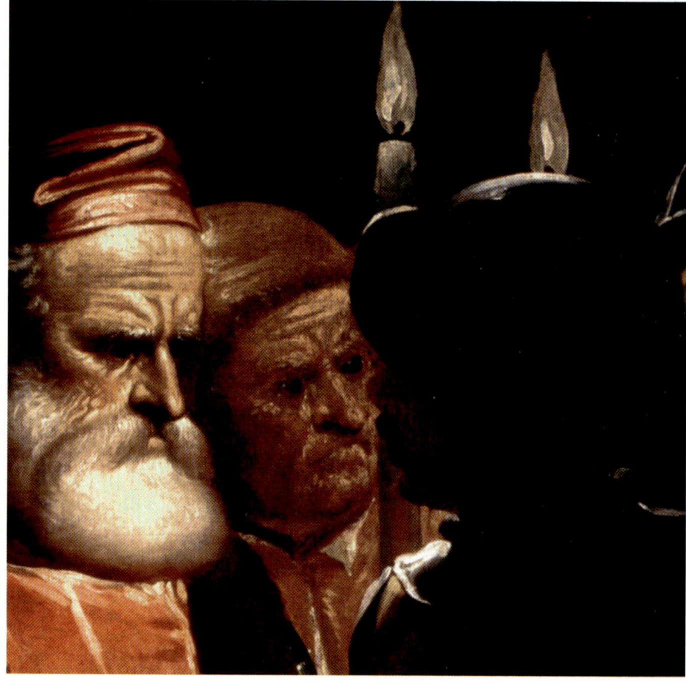

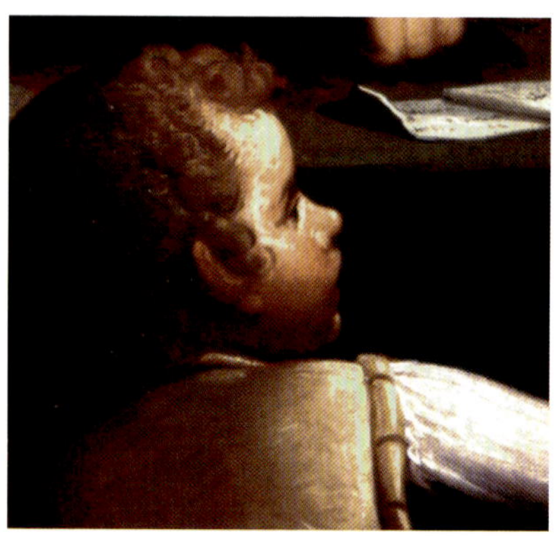

◄ In the early 17th century, this painting belonged to the celebrated collection of Marchese and Marchesa Giustiniani (Genoans living in Rome). Not coincidentally, they were also protectors and collectors of Caravaggio.

▲ Cambiaso's many visual sources – a kind of summary of 16th-century northern Italian painting – are revealed in the faint light of the candles. Cambiaso had an original way of combining the expressive draughtsmanship of Leonardo, the realistic effects of the Lombard masters, and the colour and light of Titian and Jacopo Bassano.

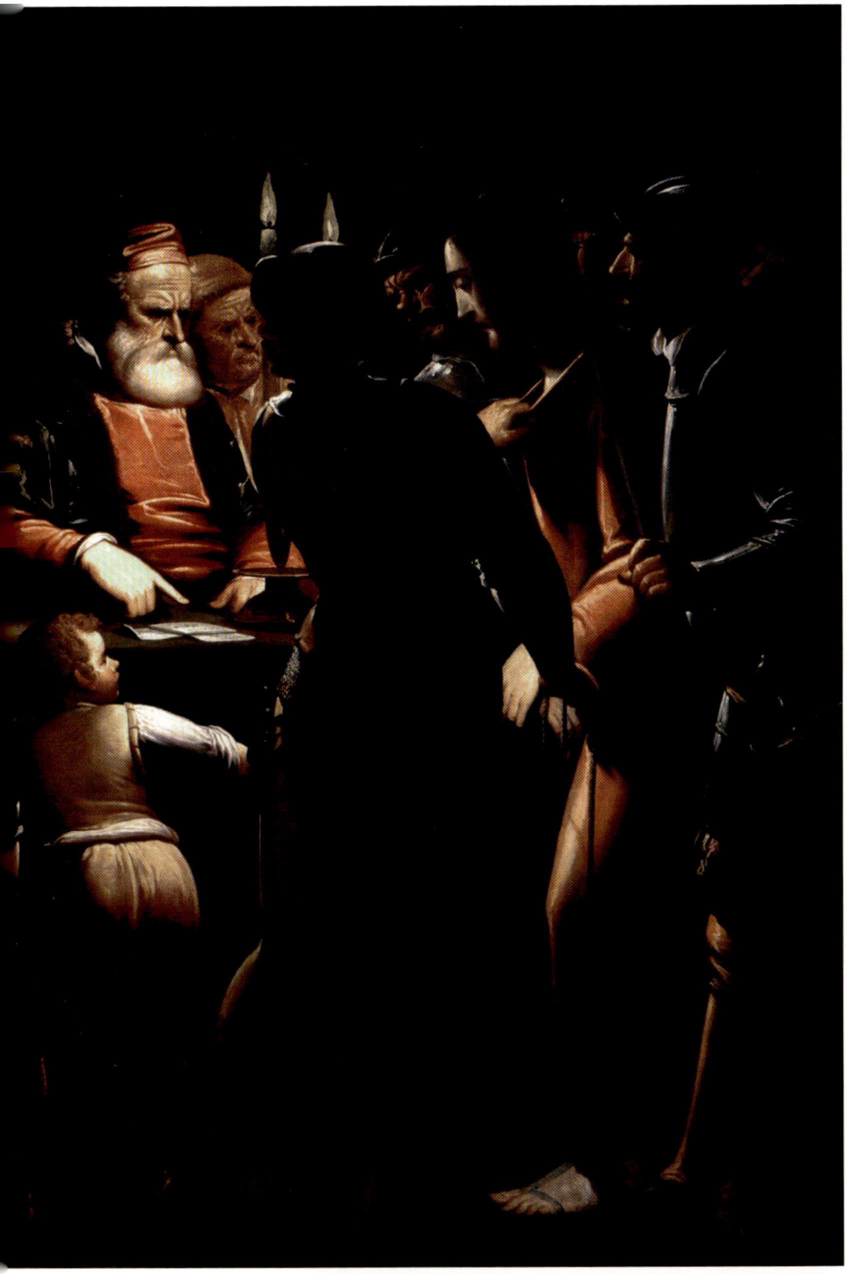

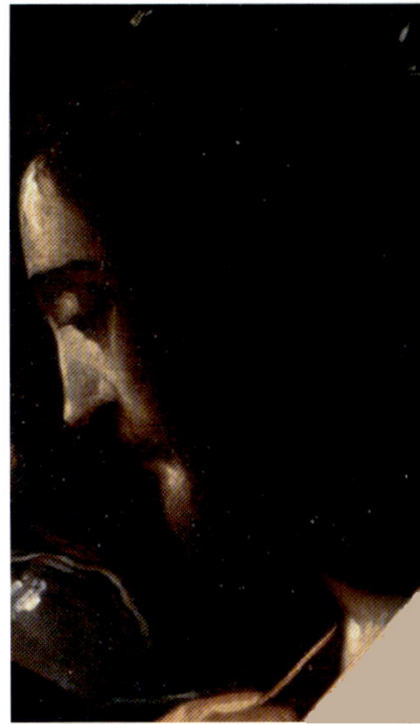

▲ In the palest flesh tones, Christ's melancholy profile is a typical example of Luca Cambiaso's silent, introspective devotion. The night setting heightens the Genoese painter's particular form of sadness. From a stylistic point of view, the effect of backlighting lengthens the figures' thin, tapering proportions. Luca Cambiaso echoes the Mannerist lessons from the works that Raphael's pupil Perino del Vaga painted in Genoa (see pages 300–1).

► The backlighting produced by the candles in the centre of the painting recalls Giovanni Girolamo Savoldo's experiments from the 1530s (see pages 302–3).

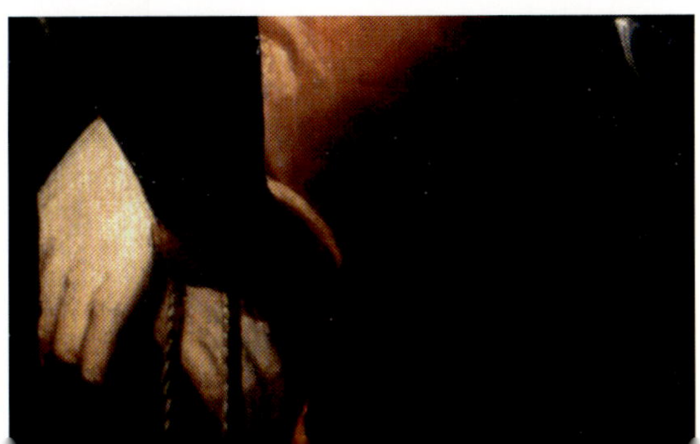

Palladianism

Paolo Veronese
The Feast in the House of Levi
1573

Oil on canvas, 555 × 1280 cm
Venice, Gallerie dell'Accademia

For artist biography, see page 366.

Around 1560, Paolo Veronese painted a splendid cycle of frescoes inside Villa Barbaro, built by Andrea Palladio in Maser, in the foothills of Treviso. Through direct contact with the great architect, Veronese developed a new sense of space and light, and his compositions took on an intense clarity. Veronese demonstrated that the joyful sense of the scenes painted in Maser could be transposed to religious painting, laying out his large, crowded 'suppers' as if on a stage: a set with deep wings, large arcades, stairways with a balustrade and other architectural elements of a Palladian flavour.

Legal Trouble for Veronese

Venice had a well-deserved reputation for tolerance and openness. Nonetheless, after the Council of Trent and with the added tensions caused by war with the Turks, the Inquisition's net tightened around the Lagoon as well. Paolo Veronese paid the price: a painting of his, delivered in 1573 to the monastery of San Zanipolo, perplexed the Dominican inquisitors, who summoned him to defend himself against accusations of heresy. When quizzed about the profane tone of the huge canvas (originally entitled The Last Supper*) and its excessive number of figures, Veronese skilfully defended himself, explaining that he had painted so many figures because the canvas was large and could accommodate them. In a fit of pride, the artist then stated, 'We painters take the same liberties as poets and madmen', thereby claiming creative licence and exalting the 'freedom' that bypasses canons, dictates and rules. Veronese won his case, and was required only to alter the context of the painting and change the title. Today, the canvas hangs in the main gallery of the Gallerie dell'Accademia in Venice, and is called* The Feast in the House of Levi.

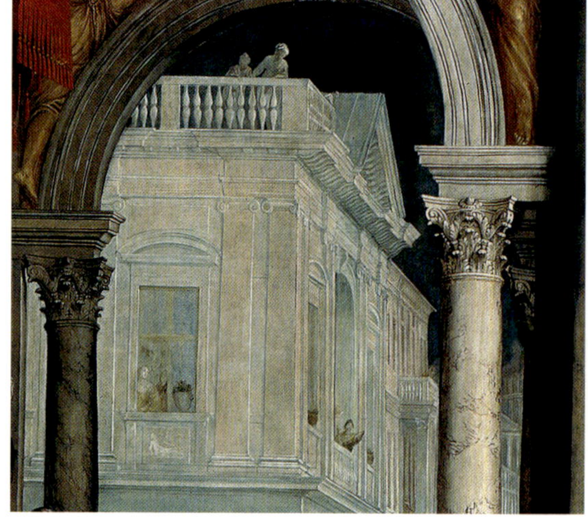

▲ Veronese laid out the scene amid three large, well-lit Corinthian arcades of obviously Palladian style that form a setting similar to the one the architect later built for the Teatro Olimpico in Vicenza. Compared with the arcades' energy, the buildings in the background seem impalpable and distant, like a stage set.

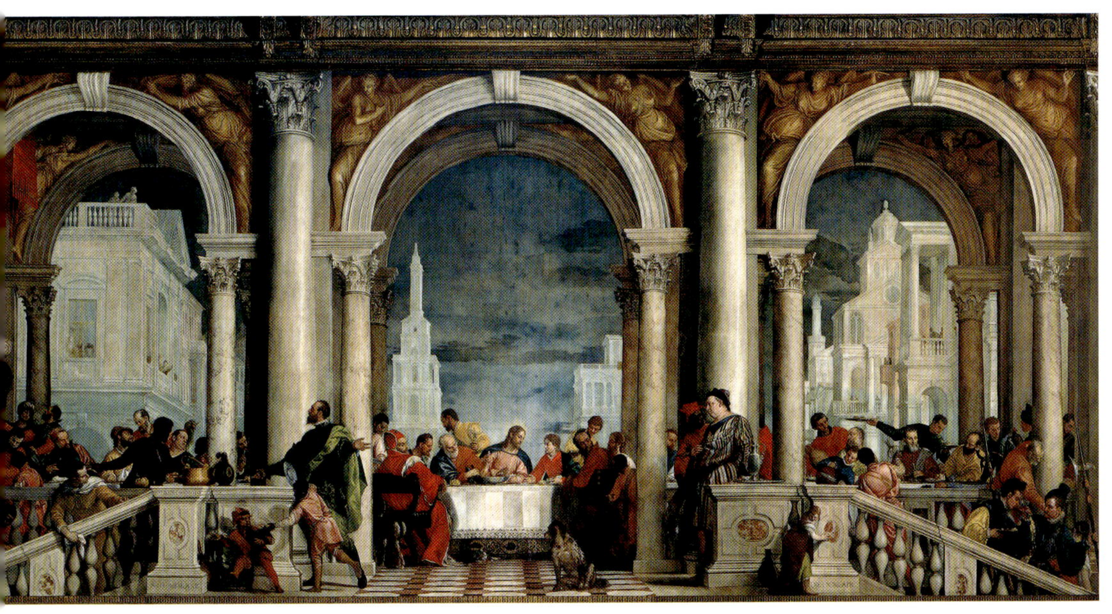

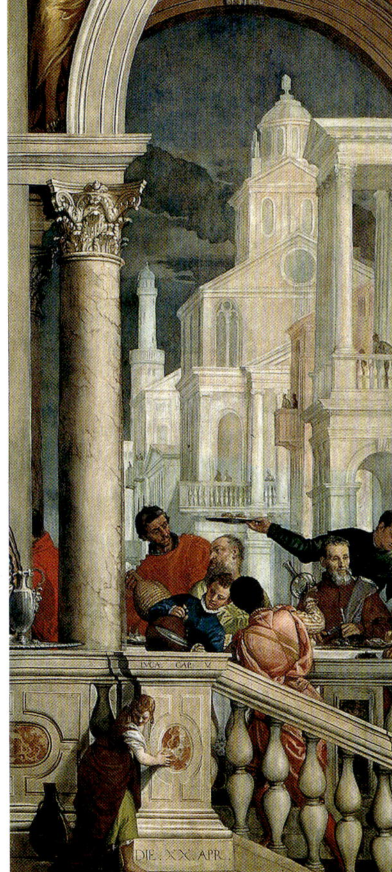

▼ In addition to the main characters, a host of others circulate, wearing contemporary dress and exhibiting uninhibited attitudes, creating an impression of a lavish reception. A good number of these figures do in fact seem quite unimportant to the Gospel episode even if, Veronese emphasized the perfect, unambiguous figure of Christ at the centre of the scene.

► The staircases crowded with servants, jesters and guests are particularly spectacular, suggesting a lavish banquet entirely different from Tintoretto's mystical, dramatic, nocturnal interpretation (see pages 382–3).

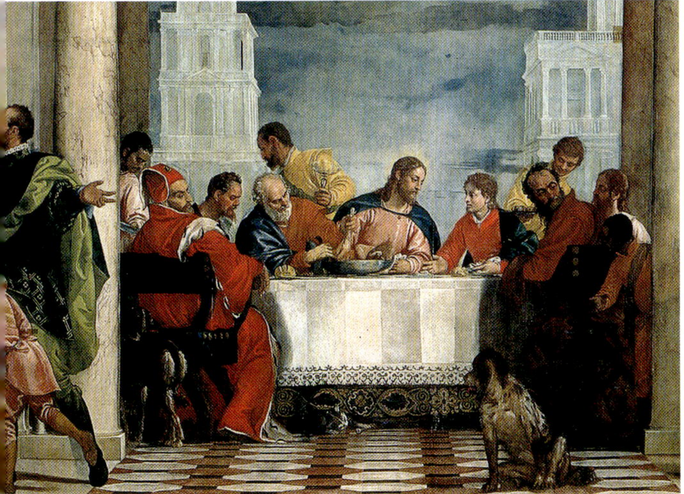

Provincial

Jacopo Bassano
St Valentine Baptizing St Lucille
1575

Oil on canvas, 183 × 130 cm

Bassano del Grappa, Vicenza,
Museo Civico

For artist biography, see page 350.

In the last quarter of the 16th century, the geography of art in Italy changed: Florence lost its relevance, Rome expanded, Venice was in decline, Bologna and Milan were centres of the Counter-Reformation, and significant contributions continued to come from the 'periphery'. Bassano's luminism was less theatrical and violent than that of Tintoretto. The details and figures drawn from peasant life give his canvases a remarkable realism, not only in scenes of everyday life but also in paintings of sacred subjects. The later masterpiece *St Valentine Baptizing St Lucille* blends this realism with almost magical effects.

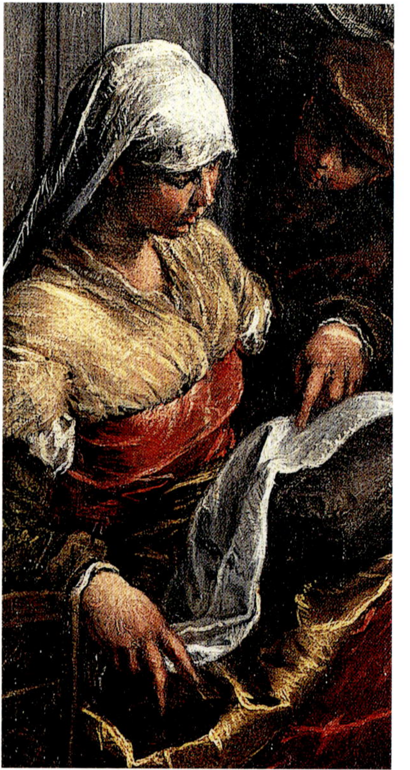

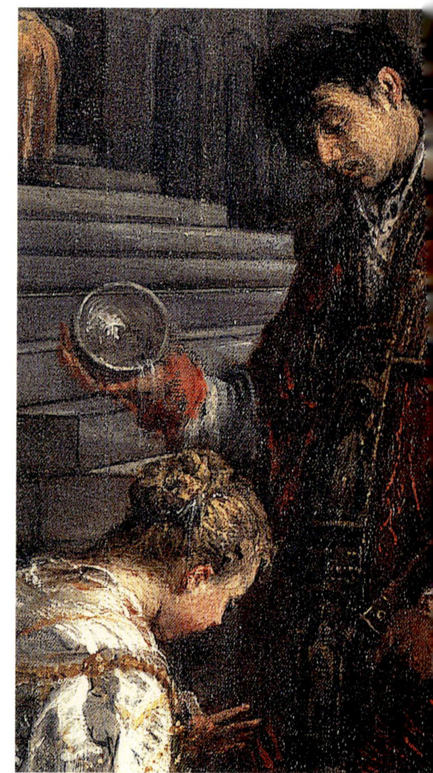

◀ Portrayals of ordinary folk, observed directly from life, are an unmistakable characteristic of Bassano's paintings.

► Radiant with light and colour, the main figures are painted in the sumptuous style of the Veneto in the 16th century, although the long, thin brushstrokes anticipate El Greco. In spite of its obscure location, this altarpiece has been admired for centuries because of its wonderful effects of colour: the great 18th-century painter Giovanni Battista Tiepolo would write to his son Giandomenico, 'I wish you to know, Domenico, that in my journey I have seen a miracle – a black cloth that appears white.'

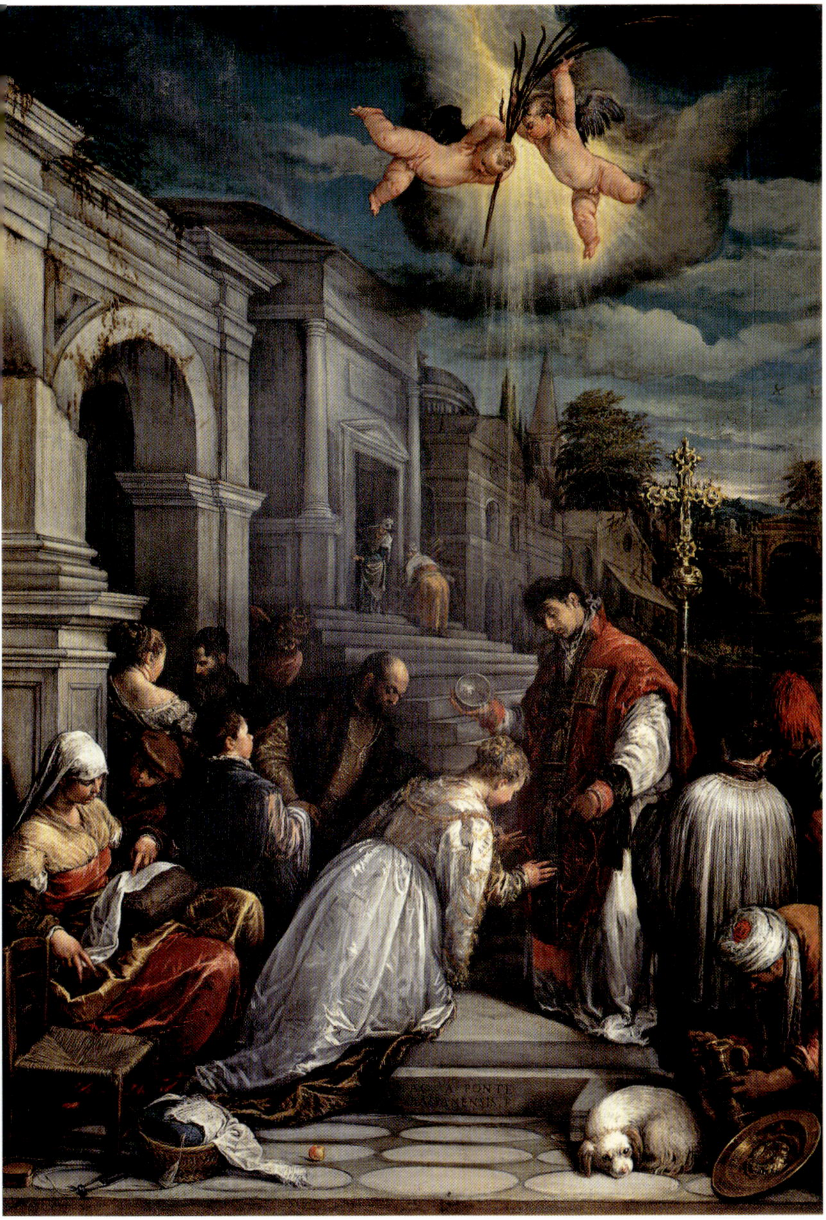

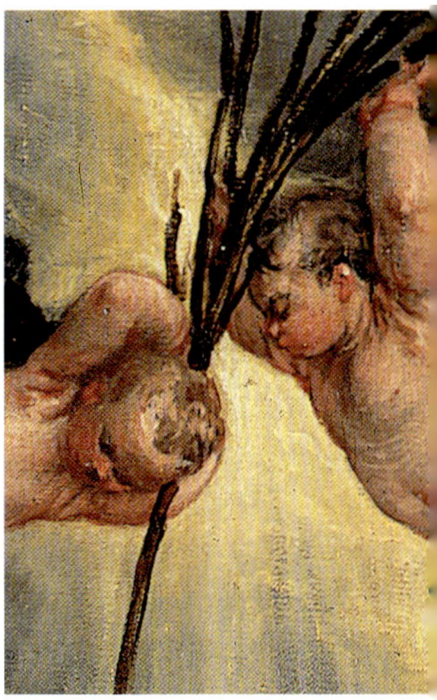

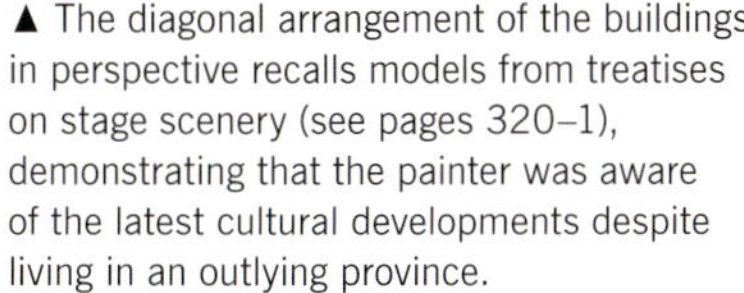

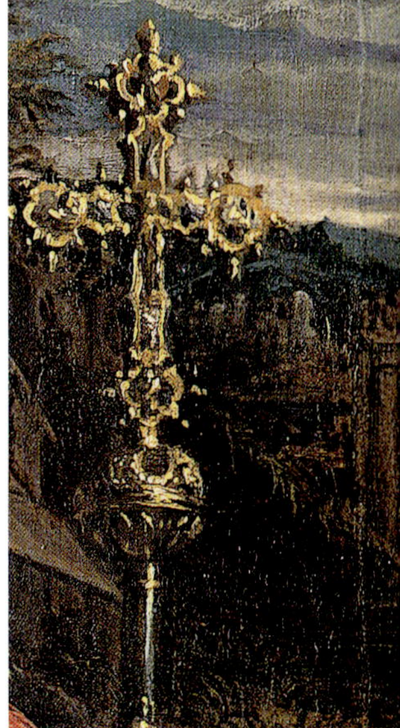

▲ A miraculous source
of light contrasts with the
muted sunset and makes
the silks and metal shimmer.
This effect would be studied,
admired and reused by
El Greco during his training
in Italy, before he moved
permanently to Spain.

▲ The diagonal arrangement of the buildings
in perspective recalls models from treatises
on stage scenery (see pages 320–1),
demonstrating that the painter was aware
of the latest cultural developments despite
living in an outlying province.

► The golden cross recalls the reliquary in
Titian's portrait of the Vendrami family (see
pages 326–7). The sharply described details
increase the work's realism. This constant
characteristic of Jacopo Bassano's painting
appears in both the sacred works and
those that illustrate life in the countryside
(see pages 350–1).

Apotheosis

Paolo Veronese
The Apotheosis of Venice
1577

Oil on canvas, 904 × 579 cm
Venice, Palazzo Ducale

Paolo Veronese

(Paolo Caliari)

Verona, 1528–Venice, 1588

Paolo Veronese, the sunniest personality and the most spectacular master of the 16th century in Venice, trained in his native city of Verona. From an early age, Paolo willingly took part in collective works, initiating an association with his fellow citizen Giovanni Battista Zelotti, a brilliant creator of frescoes in cities throughout the Veneto. Veronese met with success soon after moving to Venice in 1551, and in 1553 was given the important task of decorating the Sala del Consiglio dei Dieci at the ducal palace. His magnificent, bright painting, based on classical symmetry and radiant colours, ensured an increasing number of prestigious commissions, among them cycles of canvases for his favourite church, San Sebastiano. His masterly decoration of the Villa Barbaro in Maser (Treviso) resulted from a meeting with Andrea Palladio. Huge banquet scenes from the Gospels, with crowds of figures in action, were Veronese's typical subject matter. Consternation aroused by the Inquisition over *The Feast in the House of Levi* (Venice, Gallerie dell'Accademia; see pages 362–3) prompted him to restrain the exuberance of his religious paintings, which gradually became more reflective. Meanwhile, state commissions continued, especially in connection with the reconstruction and redecoration of the ducal palace, devastated by fire in 1577.

► The spiral columns give added thrust. This device had also been adopted by Andrea Schiavone in Venice a few years earlier, but with a feverish Mannerist effect, different from Veronese's solemnity (see pages 334–5). Because the painting was to be located on the ceiling, Veronese conceived it to be viewed from below.

The treatment of certain subjects in an exalted or grand manner – known as apotheosis – would become one of the hallmarks of painting of the Baroque era. Towards the end of the Renaissance we already find major allegorical and political scenes celebrating states and cities, just at the time when large segments of Italian territory were being annexed to foreign kingdoms, with the surviving autonomous localities now too small to play a leading role on the international scene. The fire that devastated the ducal palace in 1577 seemed to seal the demise of the glory of Venice, which had just suffered a terrible plague. An entire wing of the building burned to the ground. It decisively scorched the Sala del Maggio Consiglio, a symbol of the government of the Most Serene Republic, and destroyed many works of art, among them masterpieces by Titian and Giovanni Bellini.

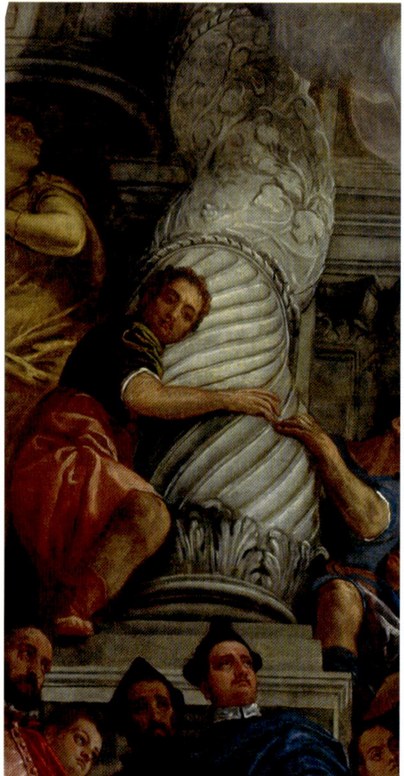

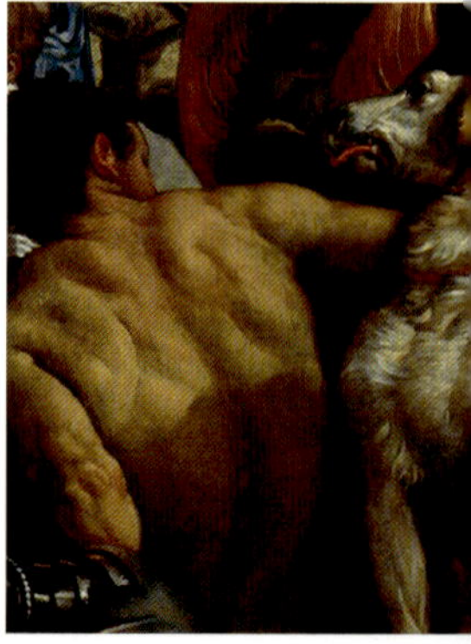

▼ The redecoration of the ducal palace, a collective operation coordinated by Jacopo Tintoretto, absorbed the greater amount of the Venetian painters' energies in the last 20 years of the 16th century. The more important rooms for the administration of the state had ceilings of richly gilt wood, with inserted canvases with celebratory themes.

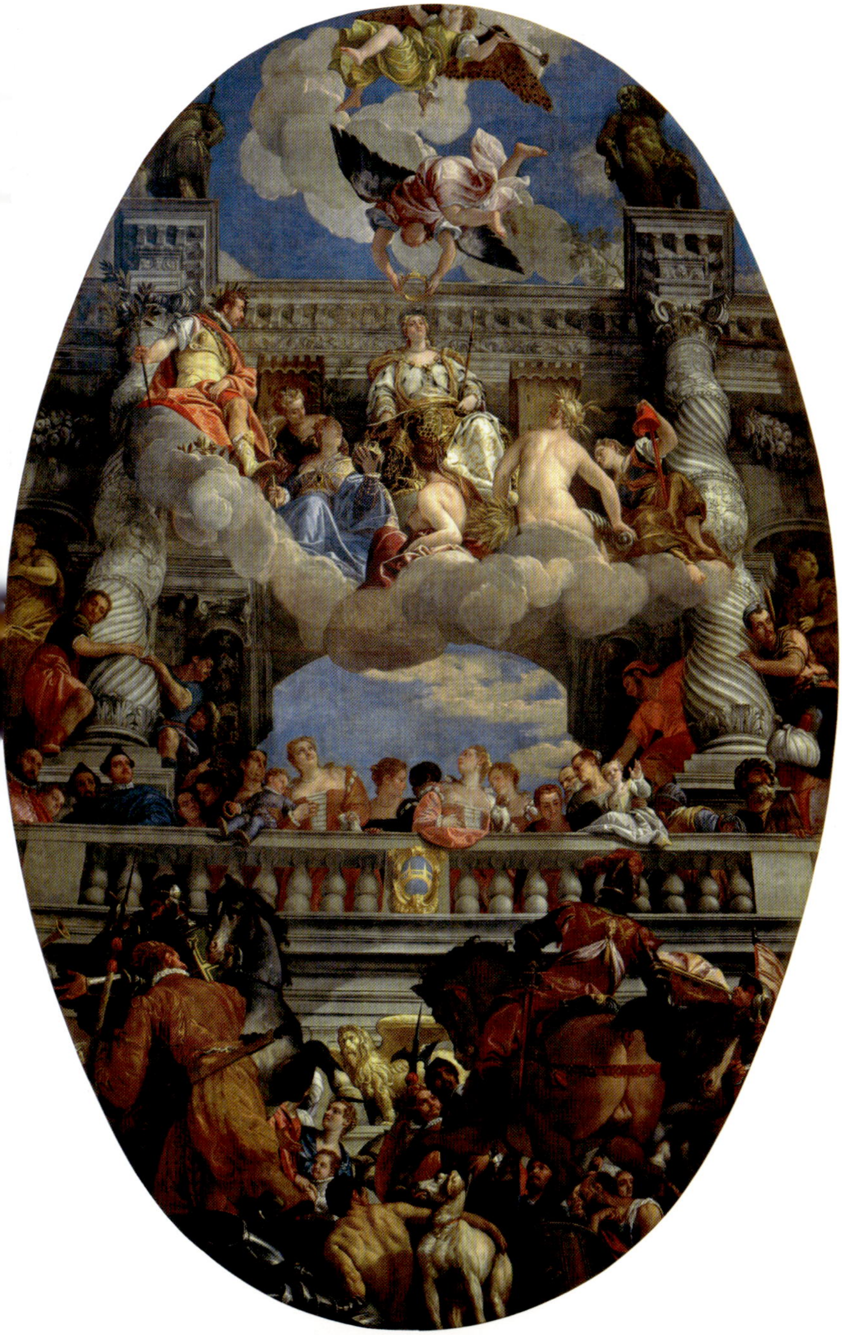

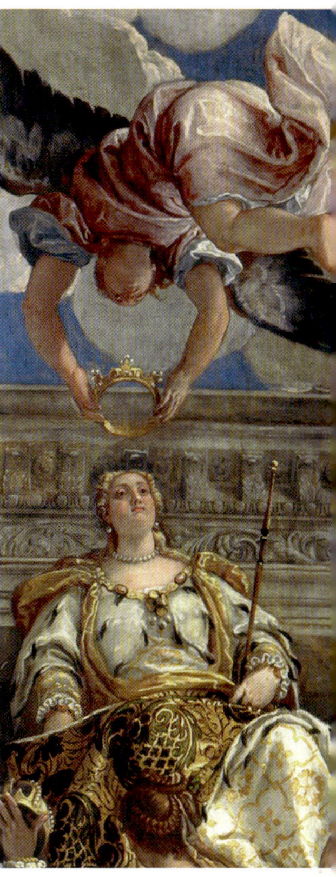

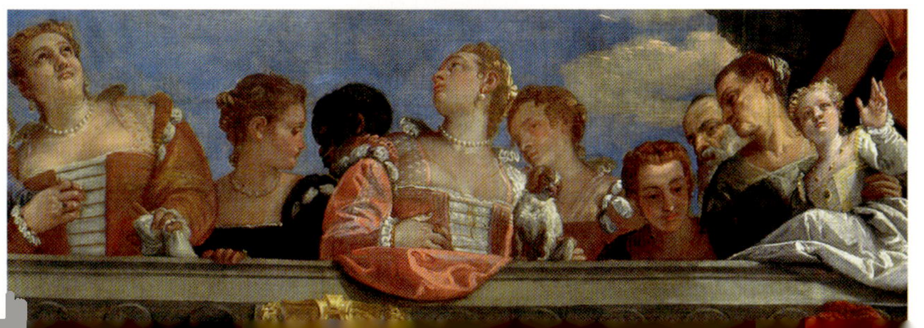

◄ ▲ The oval is dominated
by allegorical figure of Venice
seated on clouds, surrounded
by the gods of Olympus and
crowned with Glory. Set in
the centre of the ceiling
of the main meeting room of
the Venetian aristocracy, the
magnificent canvas celebrates
the splendour of the Republic
of Venice in a sumptuous
but not particularly festive
manner. It seems to warn that
things were changing. After
the conquest of Cyprus by the
Turks (1574) and the plague
of 1576, Venice's economy
was in poor shape, and from
the viewpoint of history there
remained little to celebrate.

◄ Veronese's paintings always
teem with animated, festive
figures such as the women
who appear on the balcony
here.

Still Life

Vincenzo Campi
The Fruit Seller
c. 1580

Oil on canvas, 145 × 215 cm
Milan, Pinacoteca di Brera

Vincenzo Campi

Cremona, *c.* 1536–91

A brother of the prolific painters Antonio and Giulio, Vincenzo Campi grew up in Cremona, which was among the most active cultural centres in Lombardy during the Counter-Reformation. Although he participated in various major sacred art projects, Vincenzo pursued a more naturalistic style than his brothers, which made him one of the first Italian 'genre' painters and a direct forerunner of Caravaggio. After Antonio's sudden death (1587), Vincenzo completed the frescoes in the church of San Paolo Converso (today deconsecrated) in Milan. Reusing motifs from Correggio, Vincenzo painted figures with extreme foreshortening, and also architecture with surprising perspectival effects. His activity as a genre painter is attested above all in the cycle at the Pinacoteca di Brera in Milan and by various other works on popular themes, interpreted in a realistic rather than a caricatural mode.

While the 'artificial' Mannerist taste was developing in Europe, certain painters and patrons in northern Italy turned their interest to the 'natural'. Lombard artists returned to some of Leonardo's ideas, adapting them to the times. Flowers, fruit and inanimate objects were no longer seen as a chance to show off a painter's skills, but also as vehicles of allegorical, symbolic and moral significance. The independent genre of the 'still life' had arrived. The Cremonese painter Vincenzo Campi's successful market scenes, so much in demand by collectors that they were replicated in various forms, indulge neither in the 'picturesque' nor in caricature, but are formulated according to strict compositional principles.

▼ The sober tone of this canvas makes Vincenzo Campi the forerunner of a profound reform in the basic concept of the work of art: subject matter alone no longer determines a work's 'value'. Authors of treatises at the height of the Renaissance considered religious, mythological and literary themes more noble and important, while scenes of everyday life were of a less elevated rank. In the late 16th century, however, new genres such as still life began to assert themselves, in part thanks to Lombard painters such as Campi.

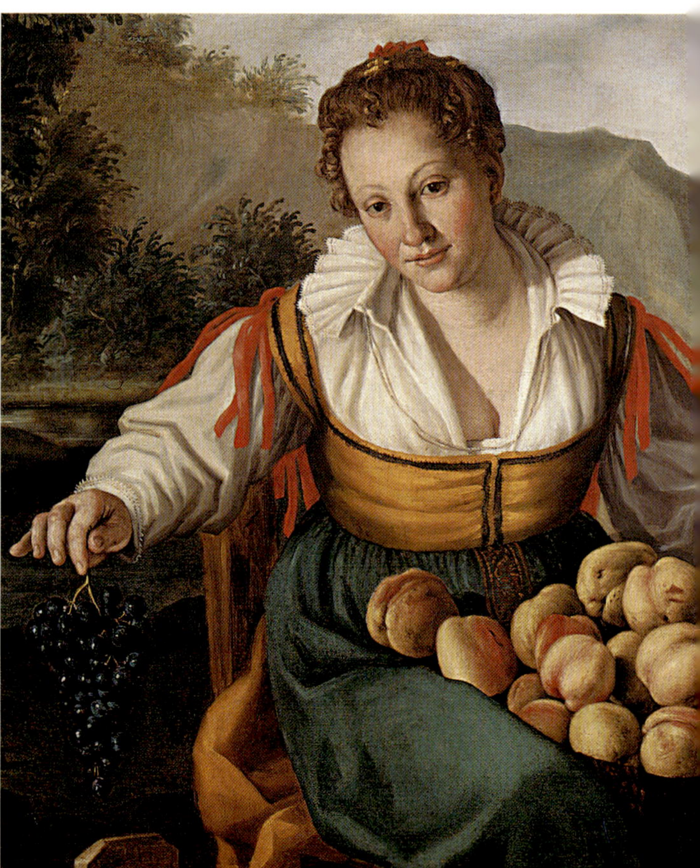

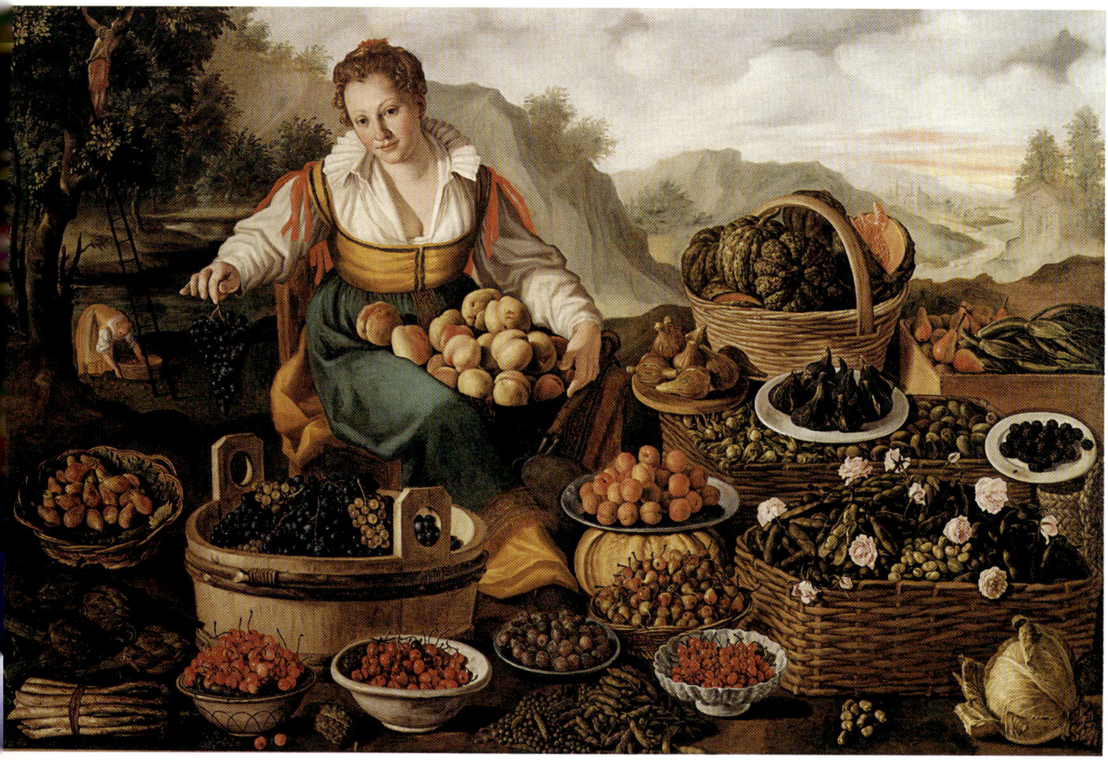

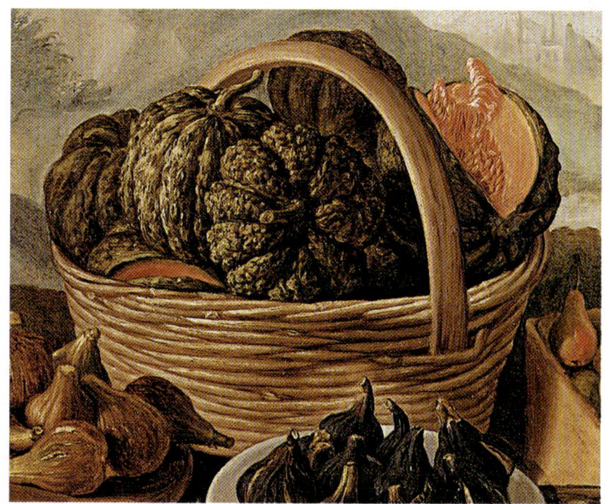

▲ The girl offers a bunch of grapes to an imaginary customer. Vincenzo Campi's quest for direct dialogue with the viewer sprang from the same cultural background as Caravaggio, as did Annibale Carracci's call for painting of 'the natural' in Bologna (see pages 372–3).

▼ ► While the artist still felt the need to include a human figure, the subject is largely a 'still life', with fruit and vegetables exhibited in various containers, creating an elegant balance between the rich and varied taste for naturalistic reproduction and a concern for overall composition.

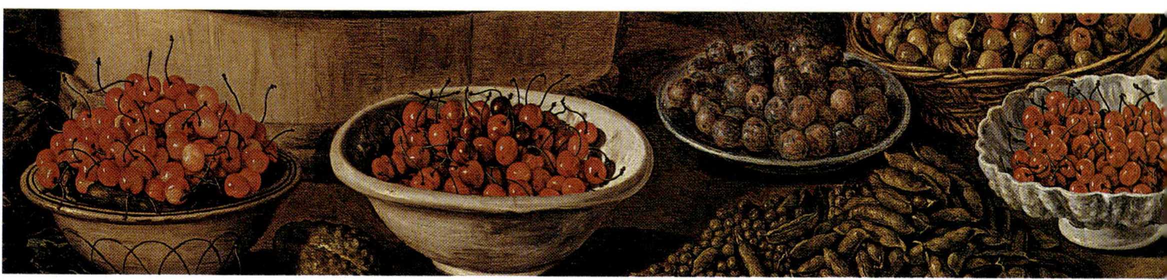

Caricature

Bartolomeo Passarotti
The Butcher's Stall
1578

Oil on canvas, 112 × 152 cm
Rome, Galleria Nazionale d'Arte Antica

Bartolomeo Passarotti

Bologna, 1529–92

A leading figure on the Bolognese art scene in the second half of the 16th century, the intriguing and multifaceted painter Bartolomeo Passarotti took particular interest in the natural sciences. Trained in the fold of Roman Mannerism, he then worked alongside Taddeo Zuccari in Rome. Passarotti (who signed his paintings with a little drawing of a sparrow – *passera* in Italian), created a number of altar paintings in Bologna, suitably inspired by the dictates of the Counter-Reformation. However, his work as a portrait painter and an early exponent of the genre scene is far more engaging. The accurately depicted fish, animals and various other objects in Passarotti's tavern and market scenes reveal a naturalist's attentive eye, and the facial features and expressions even include caricature and sexual references. His approach contrasts with the early work of Annibale Carracci, also in Bologna, who granted great dignity to tradespeople and labourers.

In the late 16th century, 'scholarly' Bologna – the seat of one of the oldest and most illustrious universities – was a cradle of avant-garde movements and important stylistic experiments. Caricature, which had an illustrious precedent in Leonardo's drawings, was among the innovations that took root. By observing physiognomic aspects, caricature accentuated and distorted appearances with surprising, odd or humorous results. For precisely these reasons, the practice of caricature (in drawing, painting and sculpture) would undergo remarkable development in the Baroque era. Bartolomeo Passarotti specialized in painting elegant portraits and scenes of everyday life showing an appetite for anecdote and the grotesque.

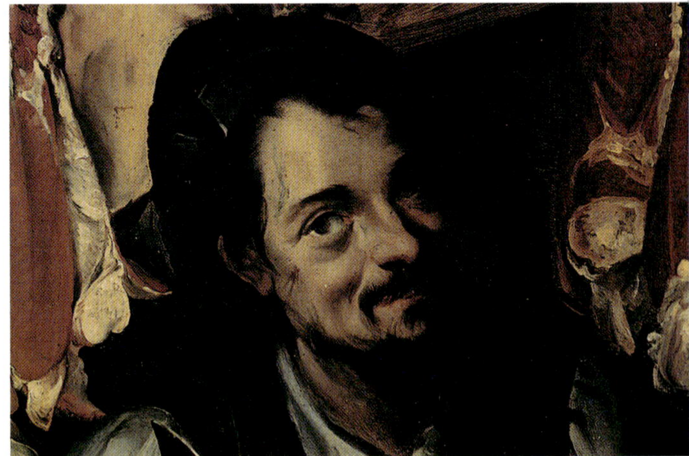

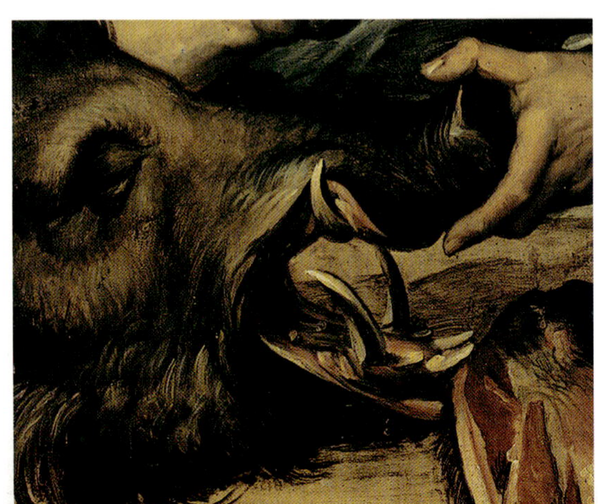

◄▲ In his successful paintings of market stalls, Passarotti frequently exaggerates the expressions and physical characteristics of the shopkeepers, or even the merchandise, as if to mark the social distance separating the painting's purchaser from the setting and people depicted (here, a butcher with a twinkle in his eye points to a wild boar's monstrous tusks). The contrast with Annibale Carracci's more sober, 'natural' formulation is telling (see pages 372–3).

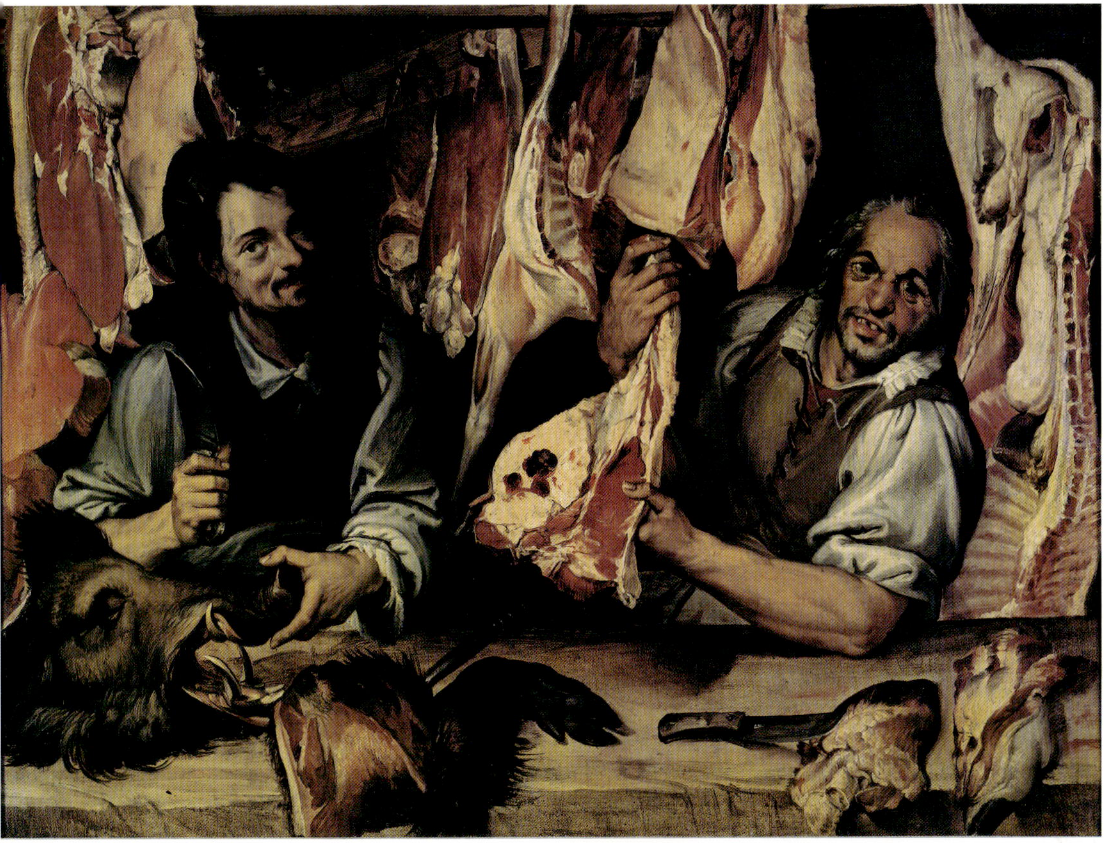

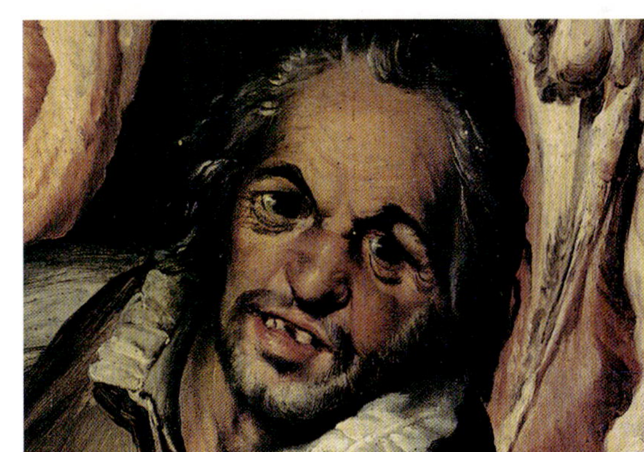

▼ ► Passarotti's exploration of caricature was solidly based on his gifts as a portraitist and an amusing ability to depict qualities of goods, objects and animals. Comparison with Passarotti's fellow citizen Annibale Carracci and Vincenzo Campi of Cremona shows that around 1580, artists in northern Italy who specialized in secular painting were bent on moving past Mannerism and finding an everyday subject matter.

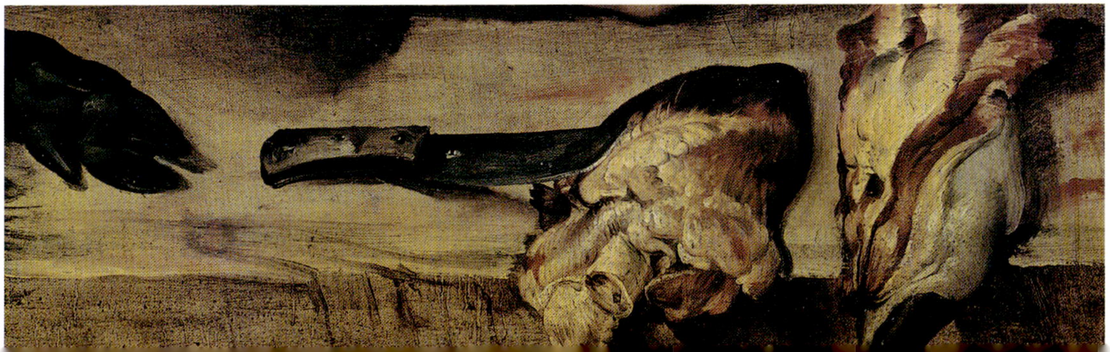

Naturalism

Annibale Carracci
The Butcher's Shop
1583

Oil on canvas, 185 × 266 cm
Oxford, Christ Church Collection

Annibale Carracci

Bologna, 1560–Rome, 1609

Annibale Carracci's career covered a rich and eclectic range of styles, from the simple, sincere realism of his early works to the classical grand finale of the Farnese Gallery. Annibale probably trained with his older cousin Ludovico, collaborating on various works with his brother Agostino. In Bologna, the second-largest city in the Papal States and an important cultural centre during the Counter-Reformation, Annibale and Ludovico shared the desire to return to 'natural' painting, unencumbered by the intellectual trappings of Mannerism. Annibale extended the radius of his references, studied Correggio and Titian, and developed an increasingly elegant style in terms of both drawing and colour. Around 1590, he settled in Rome, where he was fascinated not only by classical art but also by the tradition of Raphael and Michelangelo. The ideal synthesis and, for centuries, the irreplaceable academic model, was the decoration of the gallery of the Palazzo Farnese. Exhausted by this undertaking – physically and intellectually – Annibale Carracci never recovered. He died in 1609, one year before Caravaggio.

This canvas expresses the determination with which Annibale sought to represent everyday life in a simple, candid and natural manner. Comparison with Bartolomeo Passarotti's humorously distorted interpretation of the same subject (see the preceding pages) is instructive. In Annibale Carracci's canvas the butchers are presented not as burlesque caricatures but with dignity. In comparison with Netherlandish and Lombard market scenes, Annibale Carracci's butcher's shop is a clean, sober place with neatly arranged cuts of meat. The painter's uncles were butchers, and so this subject was familiar to him.

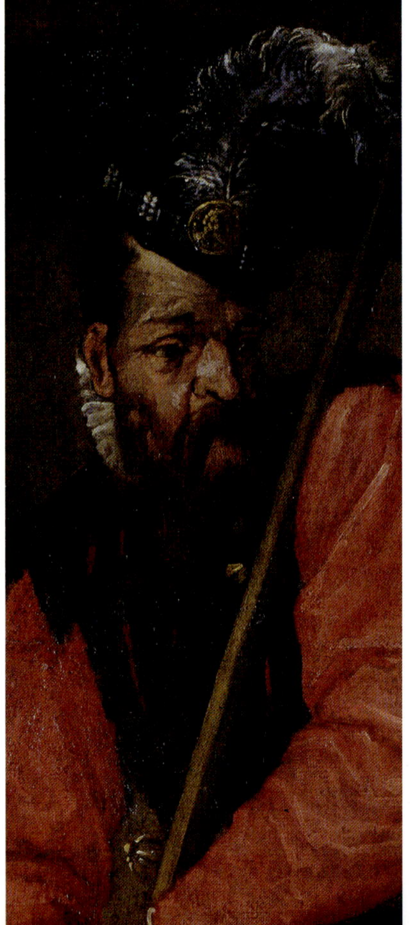

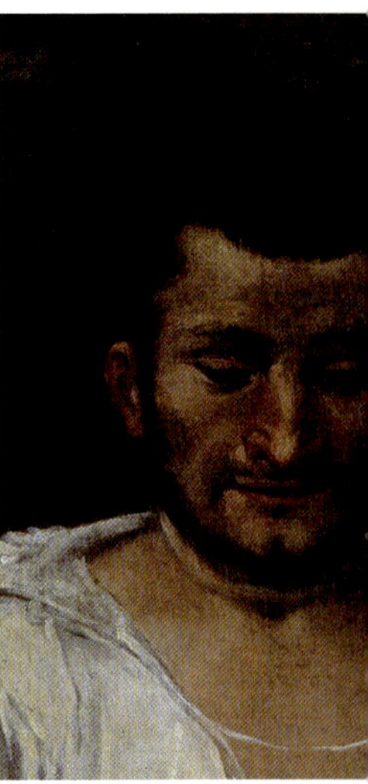

◄▲ Annibale Carracci overturned the traditional roles: the butchers are sober, composed figures, while the customer who clumsily gropes for the coin in his purse is depicted with a certain measure of humour.

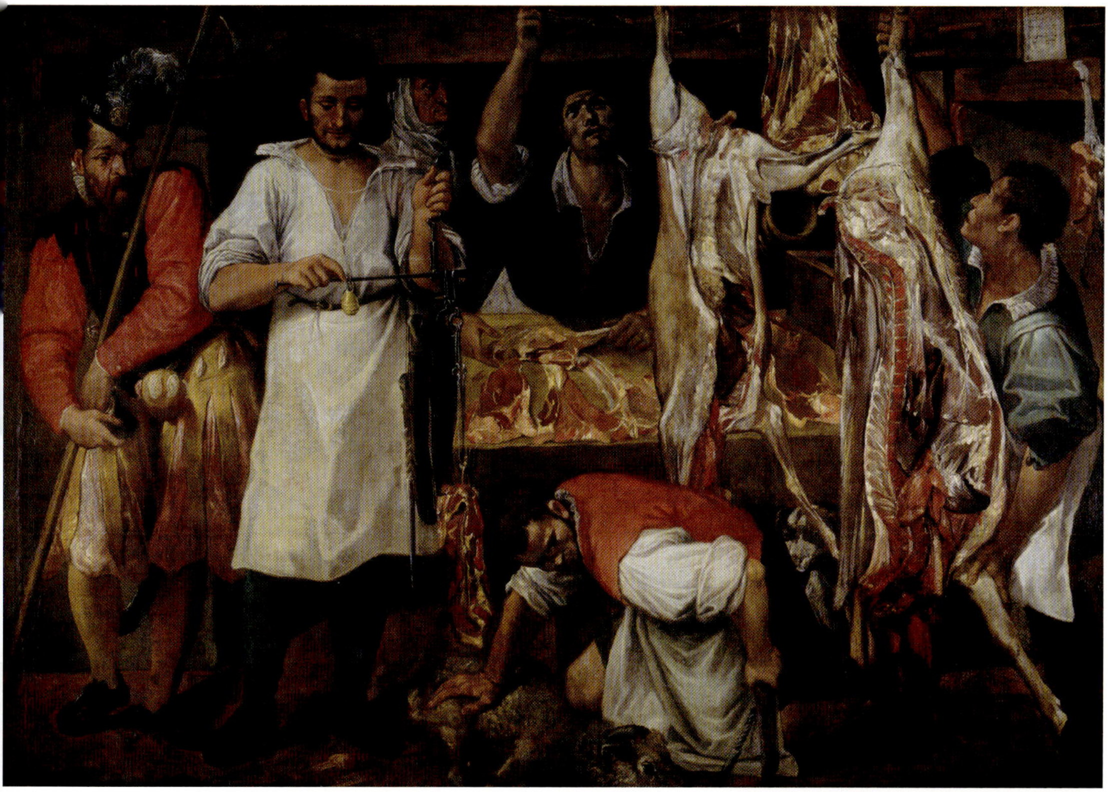

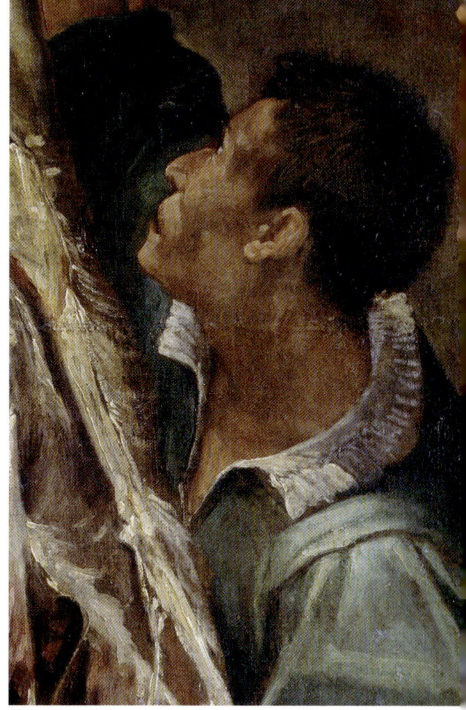

▼ ► This painting is the masterpiece of Annibale Carracci's early career and one of the most unusual works of the late Renaissance. Because of its monumental dimensions and the solemnity of the main characters, it has been likened to an altarpiece. In fact, some details can be related to sacred iconography: the butcher weighs the meat with the same concentration as the archangel Michael weighs souls, and in the foreground, a lamb – the symbol of Christ – is about to be slaughtered.

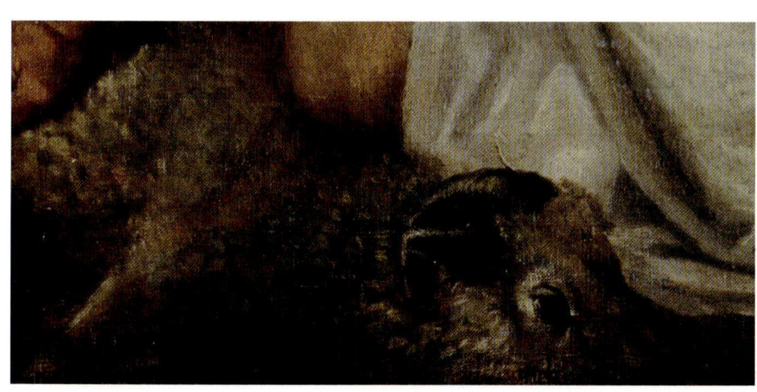

Council of Trent

Ludovico Carracci
The Annunciation
1583

Oil on canvas, 178 × 218 cm
Bologna, Pinacoteca Nazionale

Ludovico Carracci

Bologna, 1555–1619

A cousin of Annibale, Ludovico decided rather than embrace his cousin's eclecticism, to remain faithful to a simple, direct painting in pace with the latest developments of the 16th century in the Veneto, in particular those of Titian and Tintoretto. He based his style on the precepts of clarity and devotion suggested for sacred art by Gabriele Paleotti, cardinal of Bologna. After the secular fresco cycles of his early career in various residences in Bologna (Palazzo Magnani, Palazzo Fava), Ludovico produced works of deeply felt devotional content, such as the delicate *Annunciation*, and other more animated and dramatic paintings like the *Conversion of St Paul* (1588, Bologna, Pinacoteca Nazionale). After Annibale moved to Rome, the destiny of the Academy was in the hands of Ludovico who steered it from the Florentine to the Bolognese school of painting. In 1602, he briefly visited Rome, but the experience did not influence his already mature style.

The Council of Trent ended in 1563. In addition to important liturgical innovations that led to the renovation or complete rebuilding of churches, the Council issued specific 'instructions' for the renewal of religious art. According to the cardinal of Bologna, Gabriele Paleotti, art must 'illuminate the intellect, arouse devotion and touch the heart' through order, clarity, simplicity, formal control and the rejection of the refined but increasingly extravagant Mannerism. Bologna, the largest city in the Papal States after Rome, is where the Carracci initiated this 'reform'. In comparison with the composed, essentially cool style of the early interpreters of Counter-Reformation precepts, the cousins Ludovico and Annibale Carracci proposed uncomplicated, legible images.

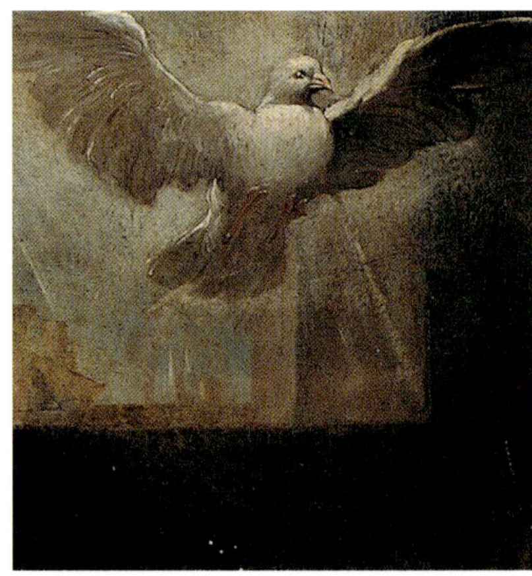

◄ Traditional symbols such as the dove of the Holy Spirit and the white lily held by the angel – an allusion to the purity of the Virgin Mary – are clearly emphasized by the composition's extreme austerity.

▼ The angel of the Annunciation appears smiling and friendly, as in the altar paintings of Correggio.

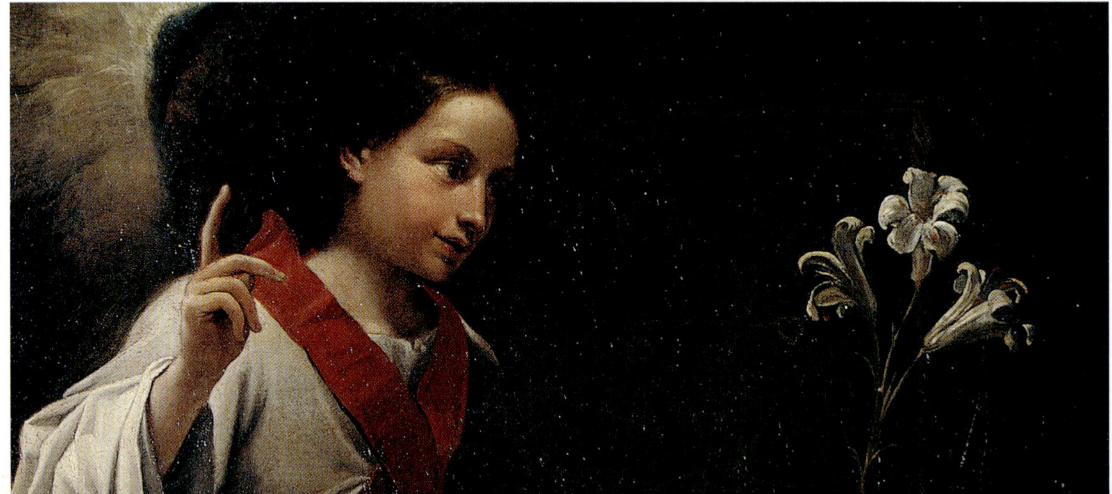

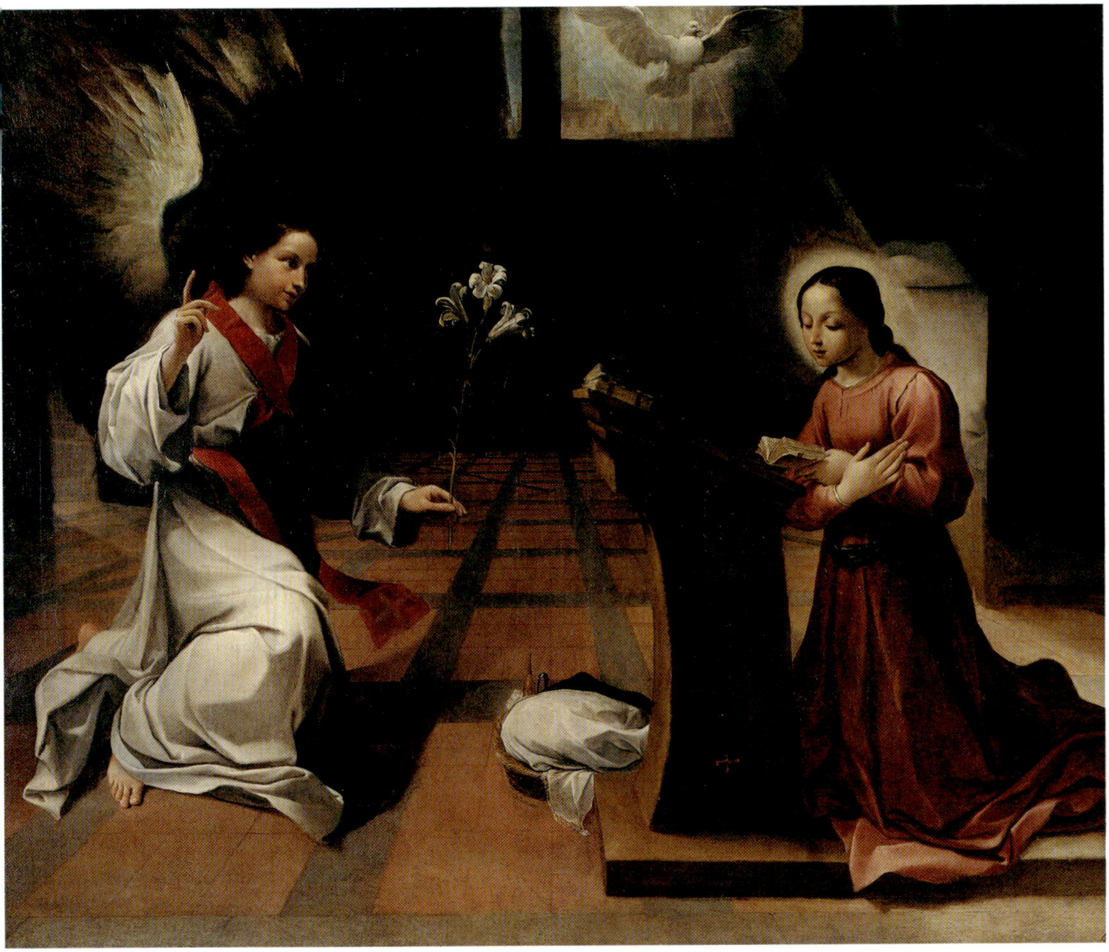

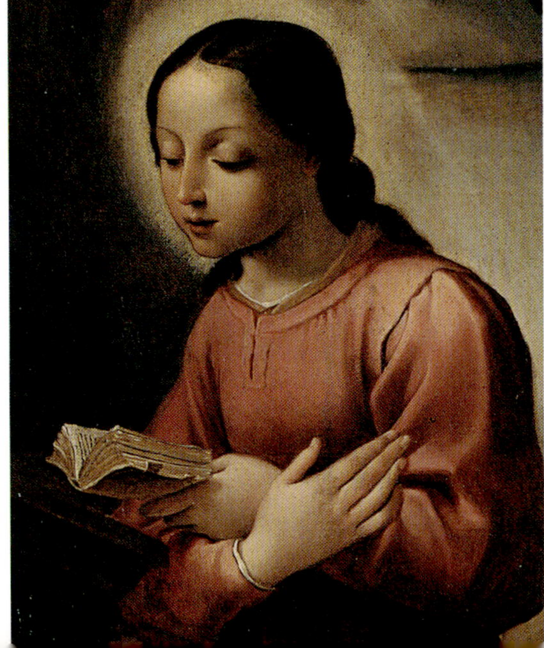

▼ ► The painting's tone is sweet, simple and domestic. The little sewing basket and *prie-dieu* are evidence of Mary's industry and devotion. Lorenzo Lotto took a very different, more dramatic, approach (see pages 284–5).

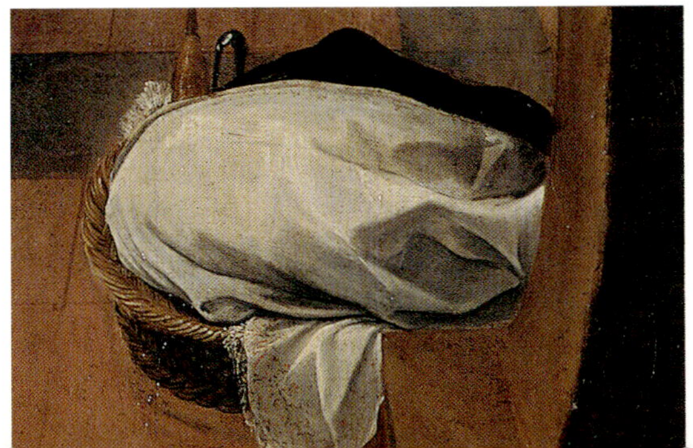

Landscape

Jacopo Tintoretto
St Mary of Egypt
1583–7

Oil on canvas, 425 × 211 cm

Venice, Scuola di San Rocco

For artist biography, see page 344.

In parallel with developments in the Low Countries, late Renaissance Italy saw the birth of the landscape as a subject for painting in its own right. Although Rome was to become the centre for landscape painting in the following decades, it is easy to understand that the genre's initial point of reference was the Venetian school, with its tradition of sensitivity to the effects of nature and atmosphere. The mysterious, visionary works that Jacopo Tintoretto created in his old age set a new horizon of emotion in their freely painted depictions of nature in the wild. With assured, light brushstrokes that are allowed to flow over the canvas, the landscape becomes a voice in an inner dialogue.

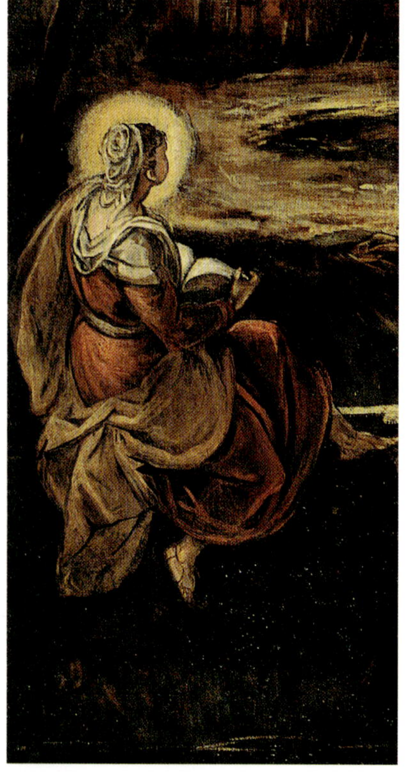

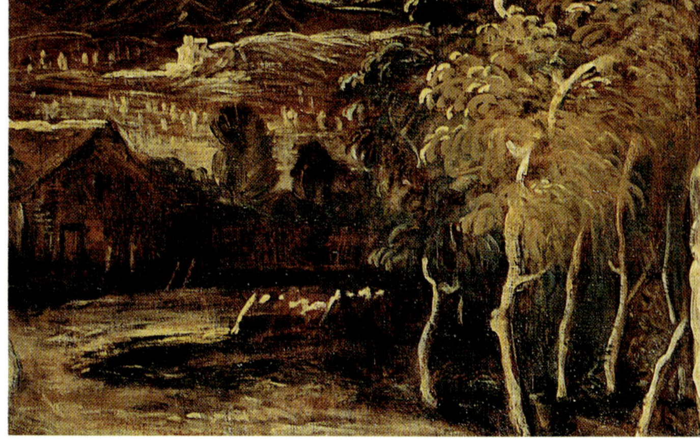

◄ Viewers do not enter into direct communication with the saint, who is seen from behind; instead, they are enveloped by the magic of the momentary but marvellous light, and invited to ponder Man's role in nature.

▲ The saint seems to contemplate the magnificent spectacle of a sunset through the woods. Mysterious presences, discernible in the quiver of the leaves, the white streaks of the trunks and the tremor of the bushes, permeate the golden-red light of the setting sun.

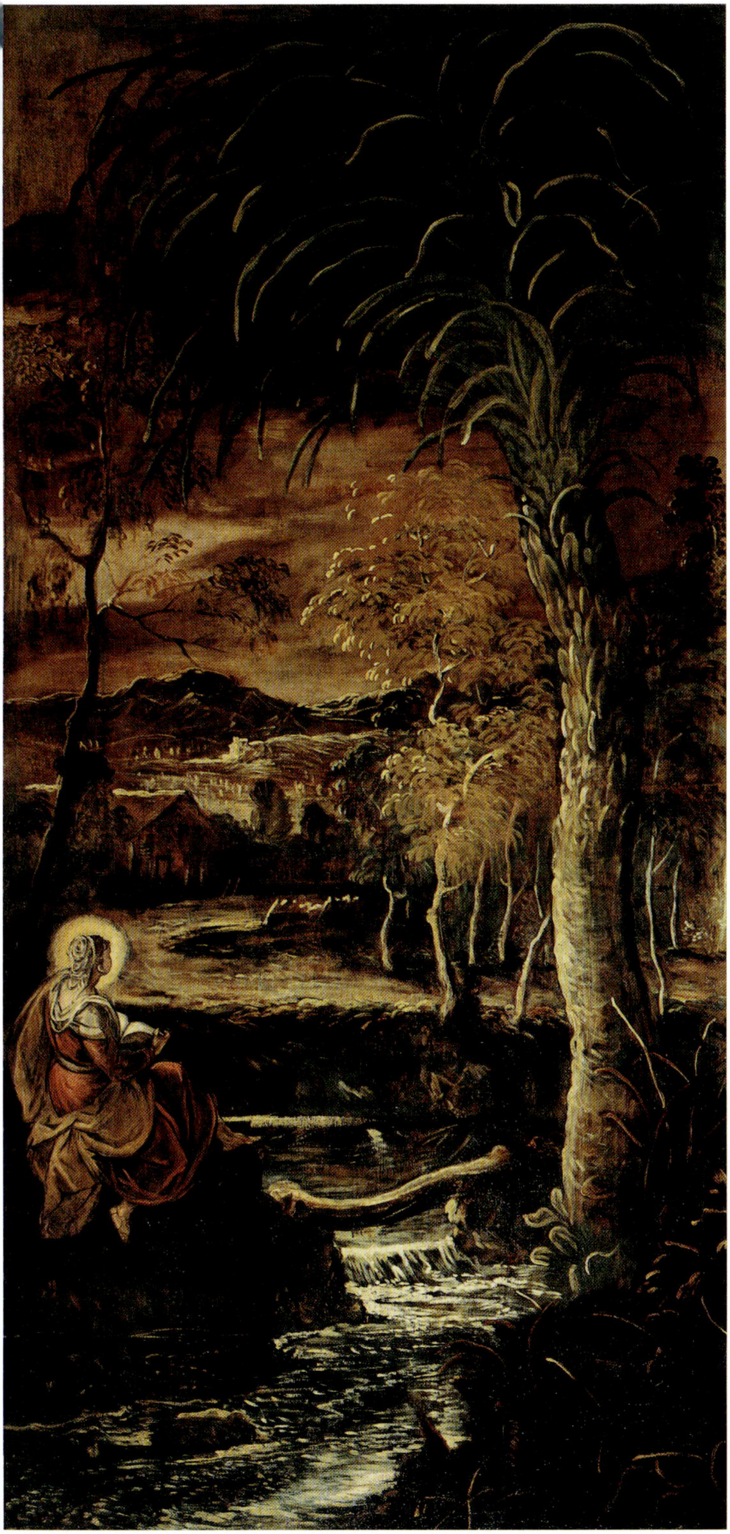

▼ Between 1583 and 1587, Tintoretto
created his third and last cycle for the
Scuola di San Rocco in Venice: eight
panels between the windows of the
large ground-floor room. This series of
episodes in the life of Mary signals the
last important turning point of Venetian
art in the late Renaissance as Tintoretto
achieves a new, more spiritual and
poetic dimension. In keeping with
the Counter-Reformation (see pages
356–7), Tintoretto turned to simple,
immediate devotional painting in a
popular vein.

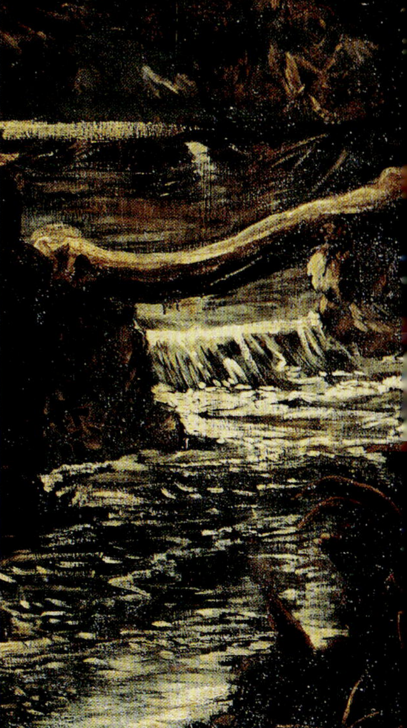

Popularism

Annibale Carracci
The Bean Eater
1584

Oil on canvas, 57 × 68 cm

Rome, Galleria Colonna

For artist biography, see page 372.

The withering of Mannerism's creative vein – which by the 1580s was obsessively focused on intellectual formalism – and the excessive discipline imposed upon Counter-Reformation religious painting led to a desire for 'truth' in explicit, direct painting. 'Popular' subjects, peripheral during the Renaissance and usually depicted only by artists in 'provincial' areas, now took centre stage. Annibale Carracci, raised in a family of middle-class artists and with an ample visual culture rooted in the great masters of the early 16th century, was among the precursors of the renewal of 'popular' painting. A few years later, Caravaggio would share and further develop this courageous endeavour. Controversies blossomed, however: many patrons and collectors did not appreciate the absence of 'decorum' in canvases depicting the awkward manners, simple desires and ragged clothing of peasants and the poor.

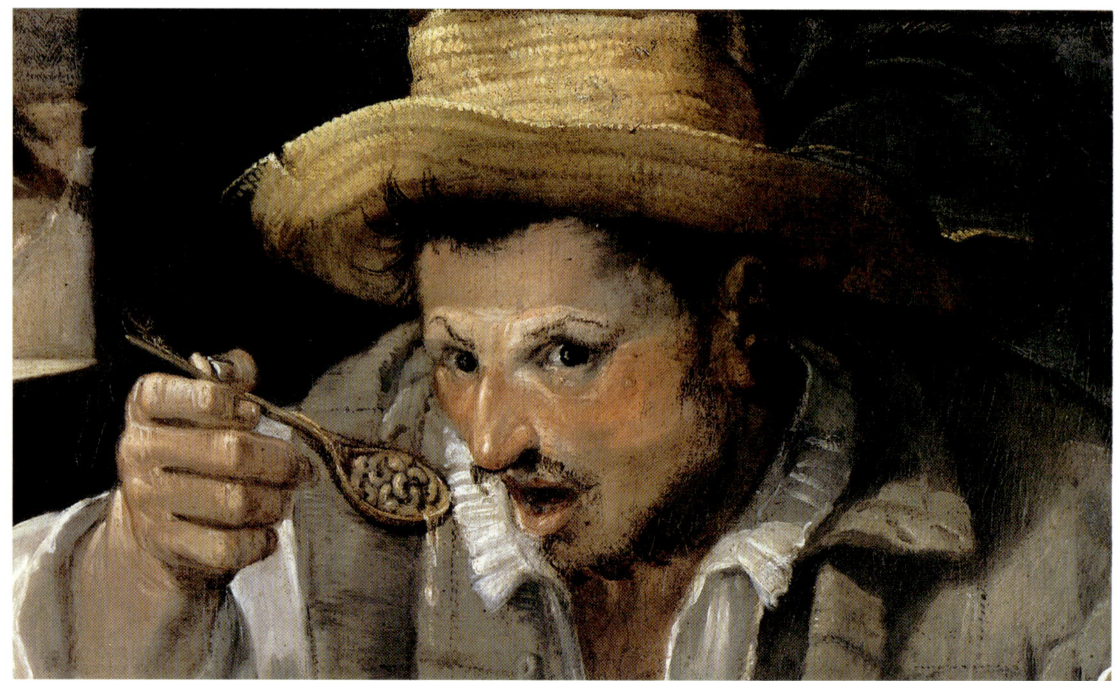

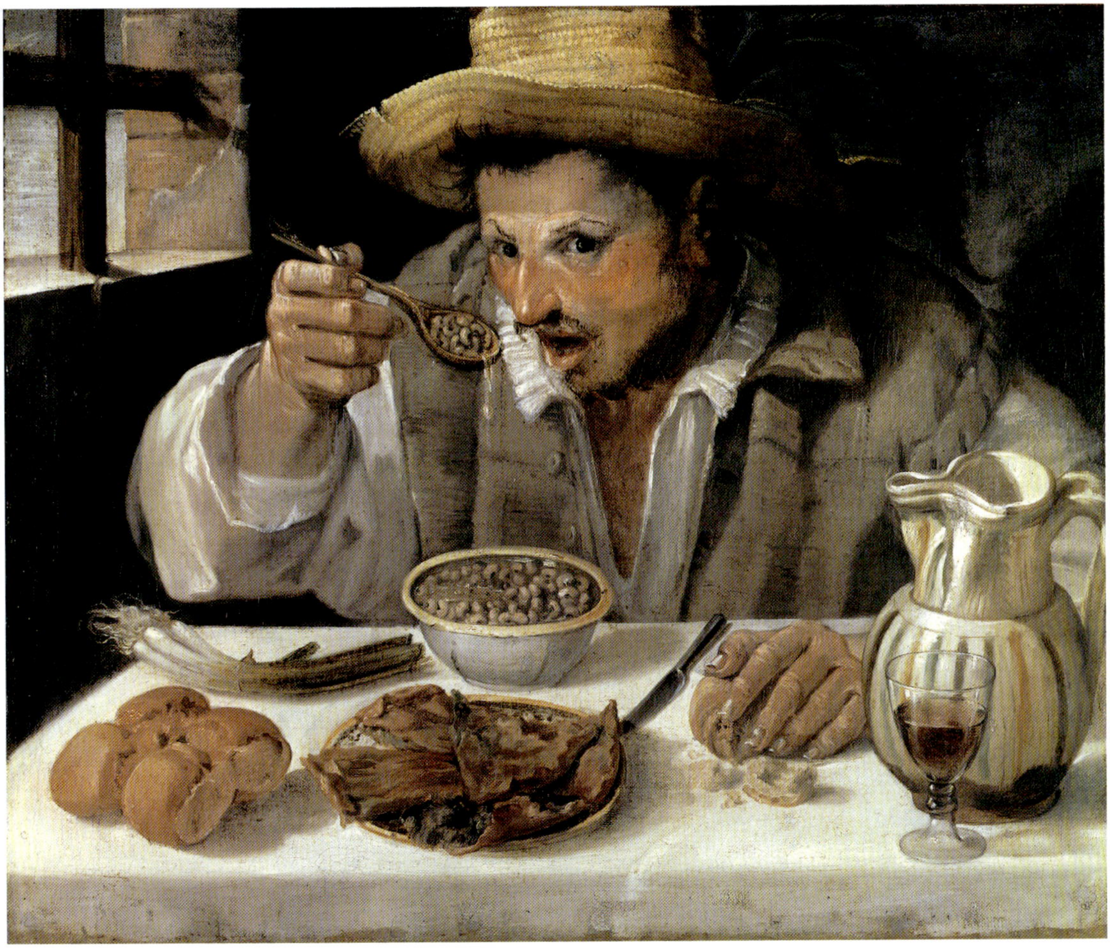

◄ The immediacy of the
'popular' paintings executed
by the young Annibale Carracci
contrasts with the refined
and 'classical' style that he
subsequently developed (see
pages 390–1).

▼ ► The main course of this man's simple
but hearty meal is a bowl of bean soup.
A detail that reveals his social condition as
well as his appetite is the tight hold he keeps
on the bread: he has just bitten into it, and
seems to fear that it might be stolen. The glass
of red wine next to a simple earthenware
pitcher would become a common feature
in still-life paintings.

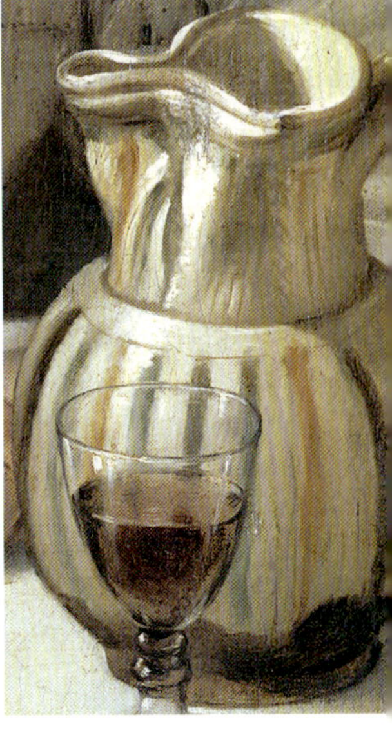

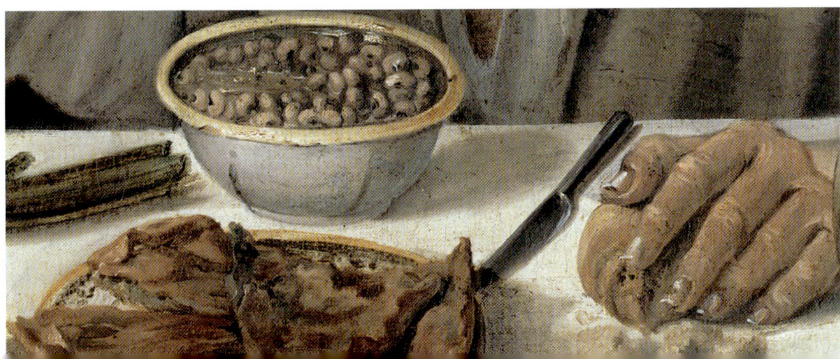

Bizarrerie

Giuseppe Arcimboldi
Rudolf II as Vertumnus
1591

Oil on panel, 70.5 × 57.5 cm

Bålsta, Stockholm, Skoklosters Slott

Giuseppe Arcimboldi

Milan, 1527–93

Known for his unmistakable 'composed heads' – unique allegorical portraits formed from flowers, fruits and objects of every type – Arcimboldi's early production, frescoes and cartoons for stained glass and tapestries in various Lombard cities, gave no hint of his extremely unusual later inclination. Called to the imperial court in Prague in 1562, Arcimboldi unexpectedly revealed an almost surreal imagination, albeit one backed up by a quality of execution that clearly distinguishes his work from later imitations. A characteristic expression of the international artistic culture at the close of the Renaissance, Arcimboldi's paintings show a new attention to the phenomenon of collecting and the scientific study of nature. The Milanese painter also designed costumes, scenery and decorations for the Prague court, which was always open to the whimsical and the magical. Emperor Rudolf II made Arcimboldi responsible for locating and acquiring works of art and natural curiosities, and repeatedly commissioned paintings from him. In 1587, Arcimboldi returned to Milan but did not lose touch with the emperor, who in 1592 conferred the office of Count Palatine upon him for his artistic merit.

By the middle of the 16th century, the Mannerist models had spread to all the courts and cultural centres of Europe. An elegant, intellectual art, rich in literary references and symbolism, it was aimed at a select audience who were in a position to grasp its allusions, and always on the lookout for something new to add to their *Wunderkammer* – cabinet of curiosities, for the display of collections of natural rarities, 'monstrosities' and refined creations in unusual materials. At the Prague court of Rudolf II, Arcimboldi took his place as a leading figure in the most cosmopolitan, exclusive venue of European late Mannerism. His 'composite heads' – portraits and allegories composed of flowers, fruit, animals and disparate objects – are immediately recognizable. His bizarre art struck a chord in the Habsburg court, which valued novelty and experimentation.

▼ The allegorical portrait of Rudolf II was originally set in the centre of a series of canvases that included images of the Seasons and the Elements. It was the crowning moment of the allegories Arcimboldi painted for the emperor, a unified cycle in which Rudolf II was to appear as the alchemical lord of time and of the elements.

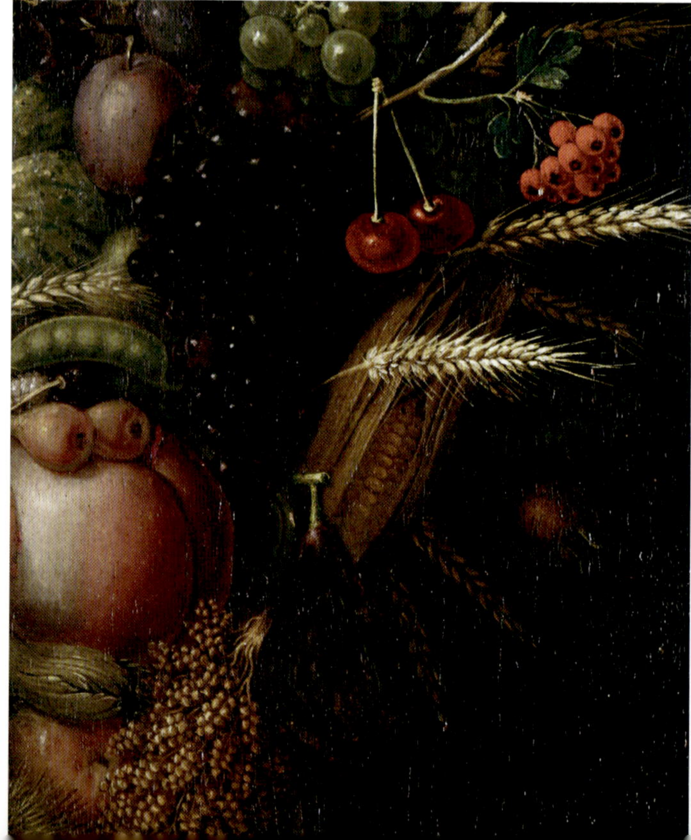

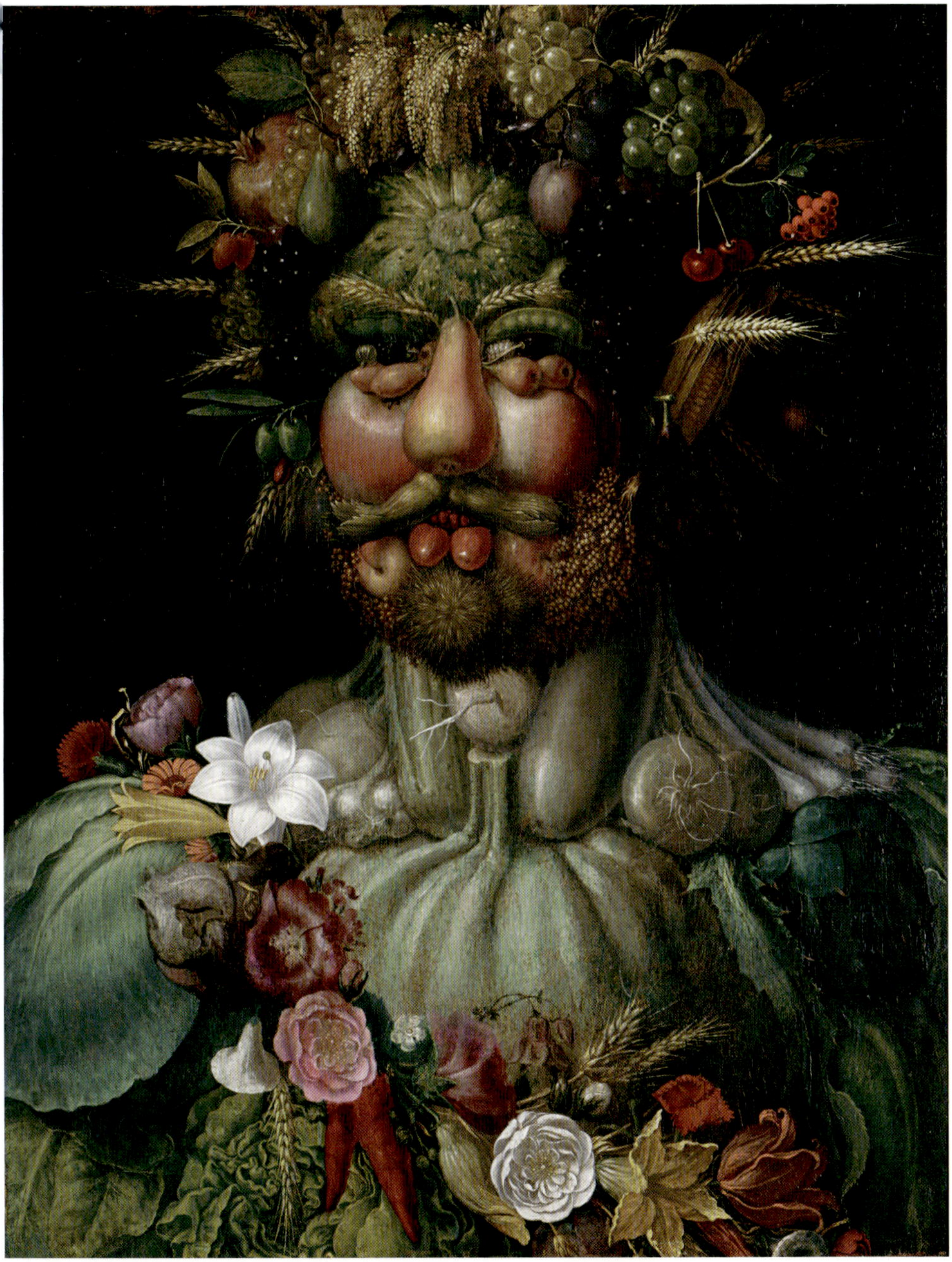

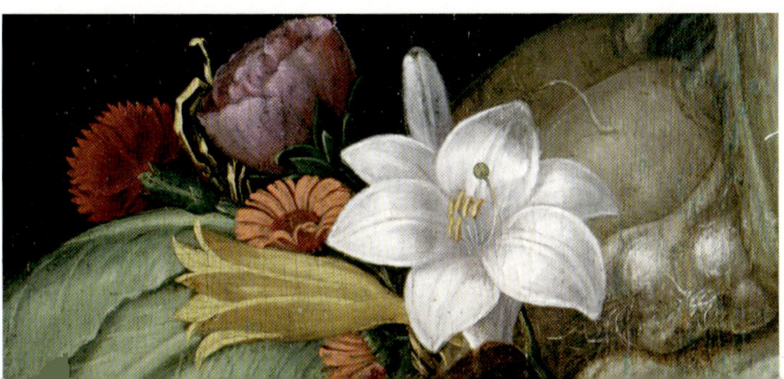

◄ Rudolf II is represented as the mythological god Vertumnus, symbol of the inexhaustible transformations of nature made possible by agriculture. The prodigious man-to-plant metamorphosis is heightened by the presence in the same image of fruits and flowers that grow in different seasons.

Jacopo Tintoretto
The Last Supper
1592

Oil on canvas, 365 × 568 cm

Venice, San Giorgio Maggiore

For artist biography, see page 344.

The long history of single-point perspective, promoted in the mid-15th century by Alberti and Piero della Francesca as the ideal structure for a painting, came to an end in the late 16th century. Tintoretto, who had reached the end of an exhausting career that lasted nearly half a century, completed the experimental process that led to an alternative to traditional perspective. His *Last Supper* for San Giorgio Maggiore is the most unusual version of a subject he had painted repeatedly. The table is placed on the diagonal in an indeterminate setting. The painting's compositional structure, subjected to an unexpected tilting of the axis of perspective, is entirely different from Veronese's centrally oriented sets for theatre (see pages 362–3).

▼ *The Last Supper* is part of a cycle of canvases executed for the Palladian basilica of San Giorgio Maggiore. It is the final effort of Tintoretto, who had reached the end of an almost 50-year career spent entirely in Venice. The artist died in 1594, not long after he completed this painting, and is buried in his favourite church, the Madonna dell'Orto.

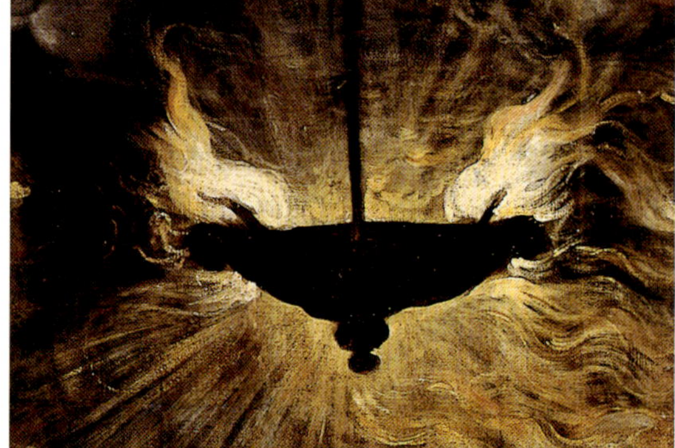

▲ Mysterious presences flutter around the flaming oil lamp – transparent, evanescent angels suspended between solid ground and an ineffable, celestial world.

► Although Christ stands at the middle of the table and in the centre of the group of guests, his radiant face, recognizable by the gleaming halo, appears in a surprising place – in the background.

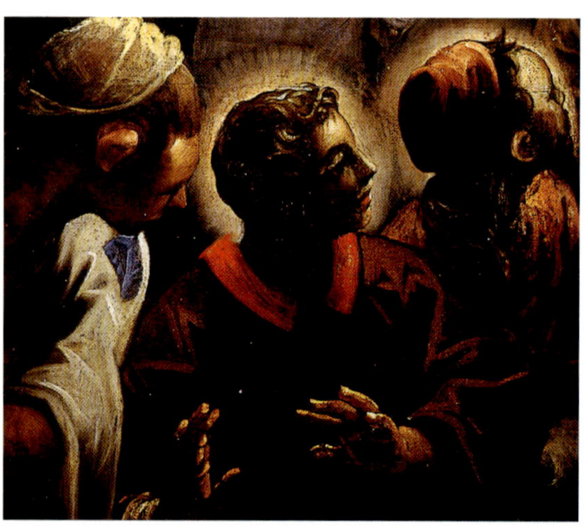

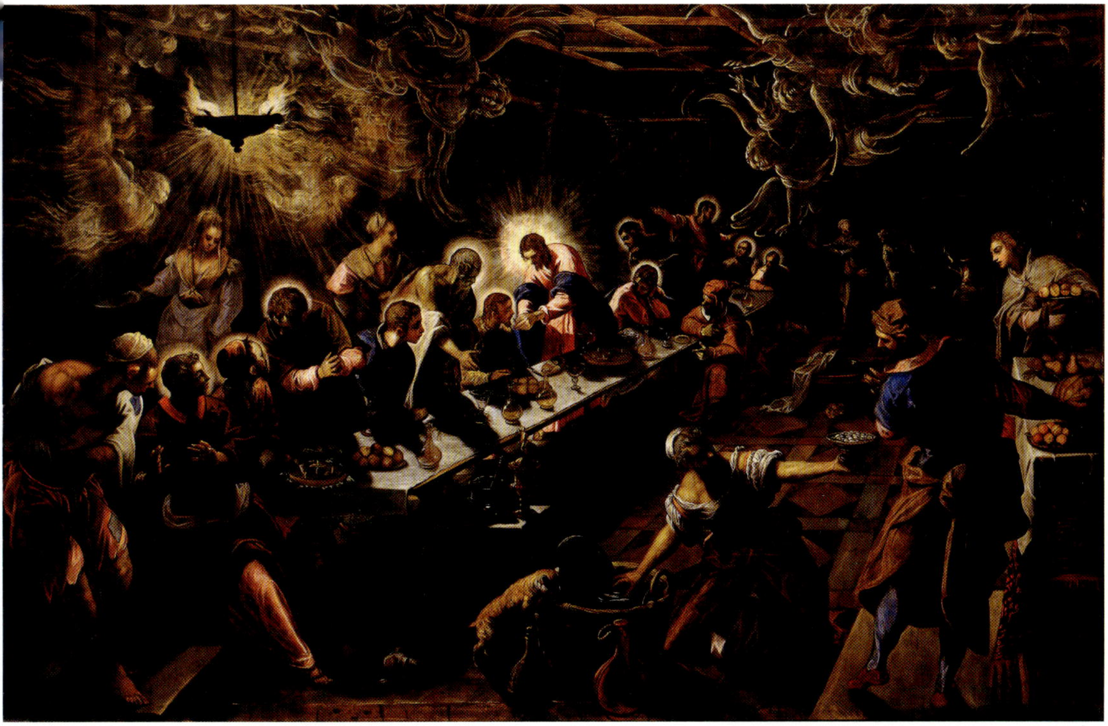

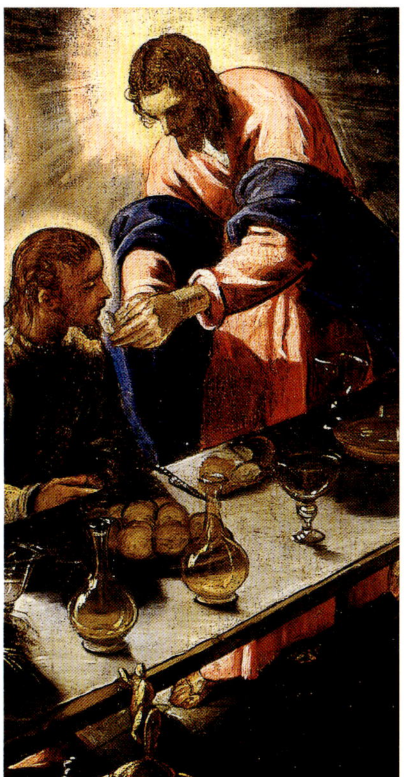

▲ ► Set on a slant, the table of the Eucharist sharply rotates the painting's axis of perspective. Perfectly aware of the unusual nature of this diagonal construction, Tintoretto 'corrected' the scene, balancing it with another plane of support at the far right – a serving table surrounded by various secondary figures. Tintoretto paid great attention to the gestures and poses of the servants who occupy the foreground, and are larger than Christ and his Apostles in the background with the group of diners.

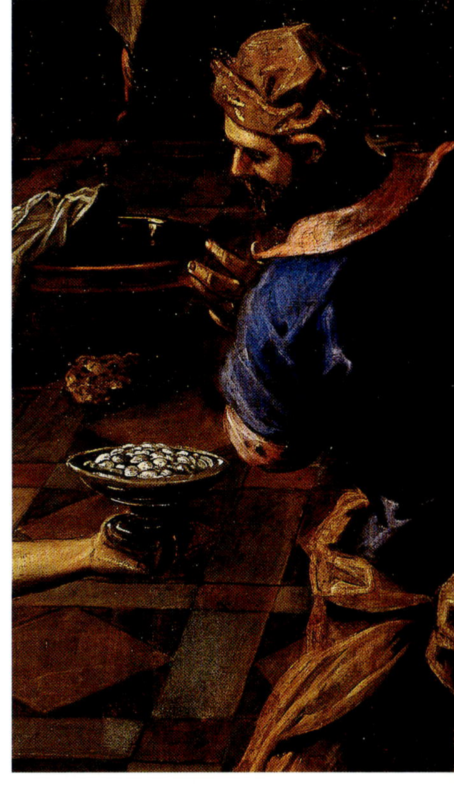

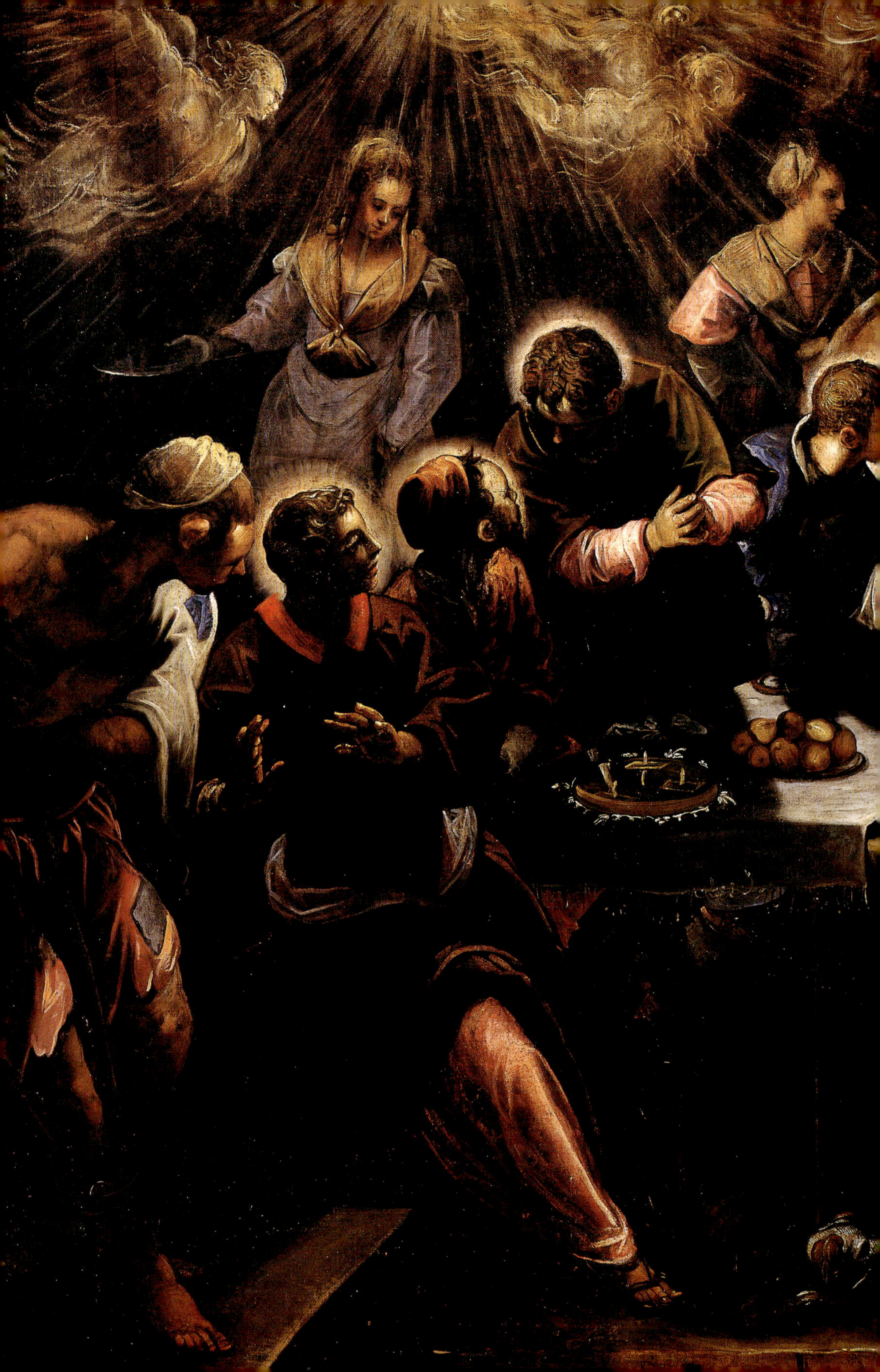

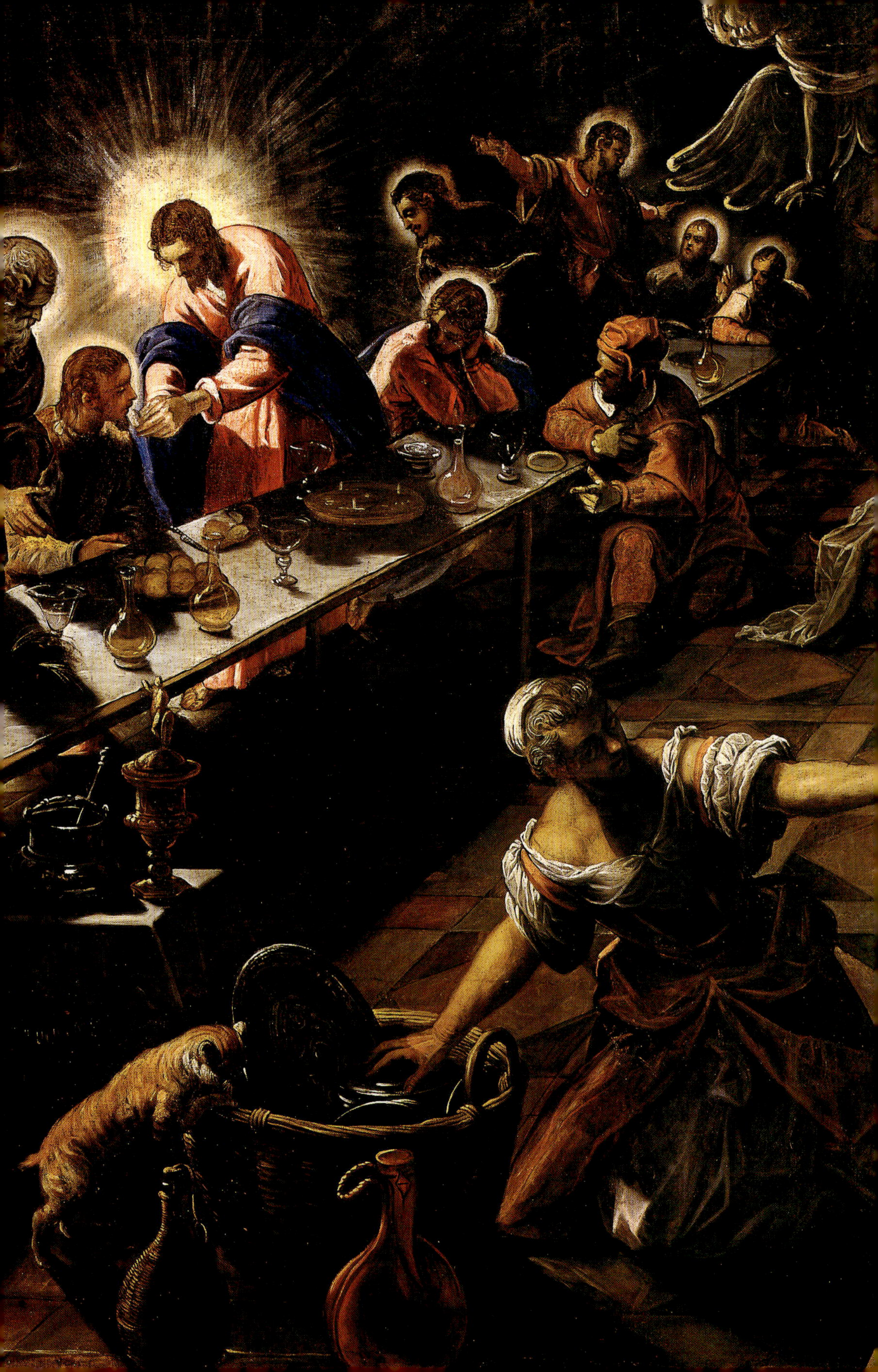

Genre Painting

Caravaggio
The Cardsharps
1594

Oil on canvas, 94.2 × 130.9 cm

Fort Worth, Kimbell Art Museum

Caravaggio

(Michelangelo Merisi da Caravaggio)

Milan, 1571–Porto Ercole, Agricento, 1610

Caravaggio was born in Milan: the recently rediscovered baptismal certificate unequivocally confirms his place and date of birth. He studied under Simone Peterzano but above all admired the Lombard works of Leonardo, Titian and the 16th-century Brescian masters. Their stylistic elements strongly directed him – against the backdrop of the Counter-Reformation and St Charles Borromeo's ideas about art – towards a sense of reality, the expression of feeling and the quest for light. Around 1590, Caravaggio moved to Rome, where he took the name of his family's native city as his nickname and instigated a true revolution in art. The figures featured in Caravaggio's early paintings are card players, gypsy girls, prostitutes, labourers and street musicians. Around 1600, Caravaggio went on to paint unequivocally revolutionary altarpieces and large, sacred paintings with raw, immediate realism. Some patrons, deeming the canvases indecorous, rejected them. Sentenced to death for murder in 1606, Caravaggio fled Rome, making his way from Naples to Malta and Sicily. His dramatic style, the dark shadows and the human intensity of his last works would serve as a lesson to 17th-century Europe. After an incredible sequence of events, Caravaggio died of malaria in the sunny seaside town of Porto Ercole.

The opening up of the art market stimulated the emergence of new subject matter to cater for broader tastes; similarly, the new class of private collectors did not insist upon the pomp and celebration favoured by aristocrats, but simply wanted to decorate their homes in a pleasing manner. The result was paintings that rejected memorable religious, mythological or historical events in favour of everyday contemporary reality, as well as still lifes and landscapes. Caravaggio's first Roman works, with a few figures against a dark background crossed by a ray of diagonal light, are examples of this type. Caravaggio did not draw upon the classical models that Rome offered in abundance but instead observed and painted the life of the streets and inns. Thanks to the warm reception from patrons and the activity of notable painters in northern central Europe, such works would soon have an enormous international success, fostering copies, replicas, imitations and the birth of an entire new genre of European painting in the early 17th century.

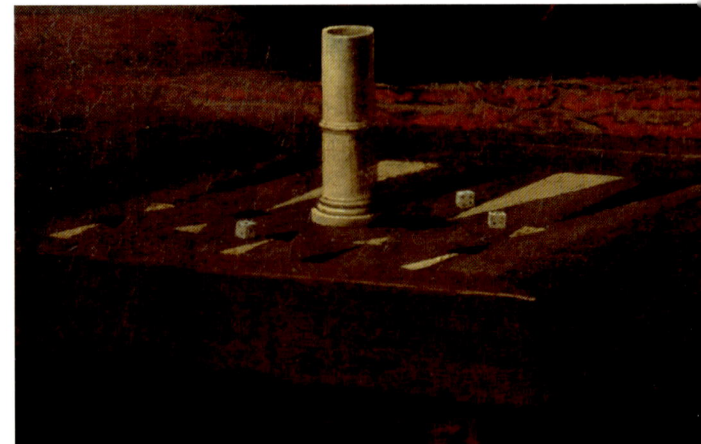

▲ The subject, drawn from everyday reality, met with extraordinary success among collectors, copyists and the international disciples of Caravaggio.

► Caravaggio constructed the scene by combining everyday realism with the memory of paintings of card and chess players he had seen in Lombardy (see pages 342–3). The whole is unified by the light that permeates the pale, neutral background.

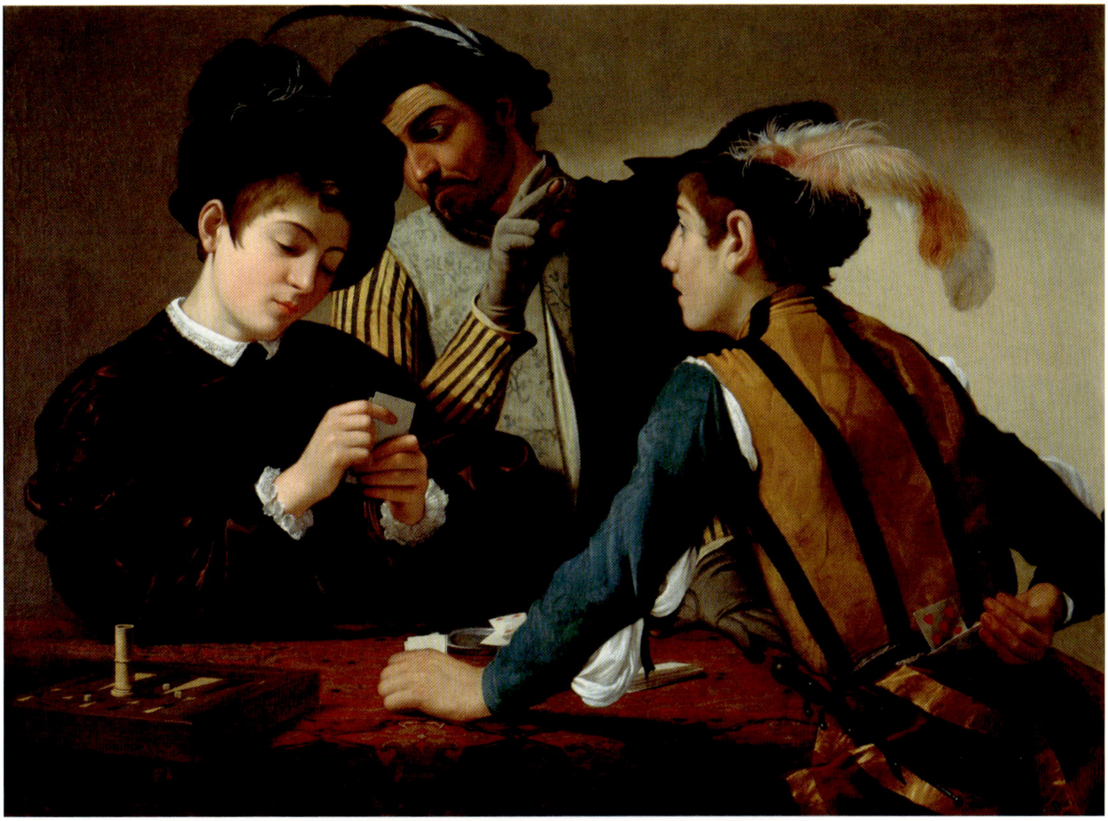

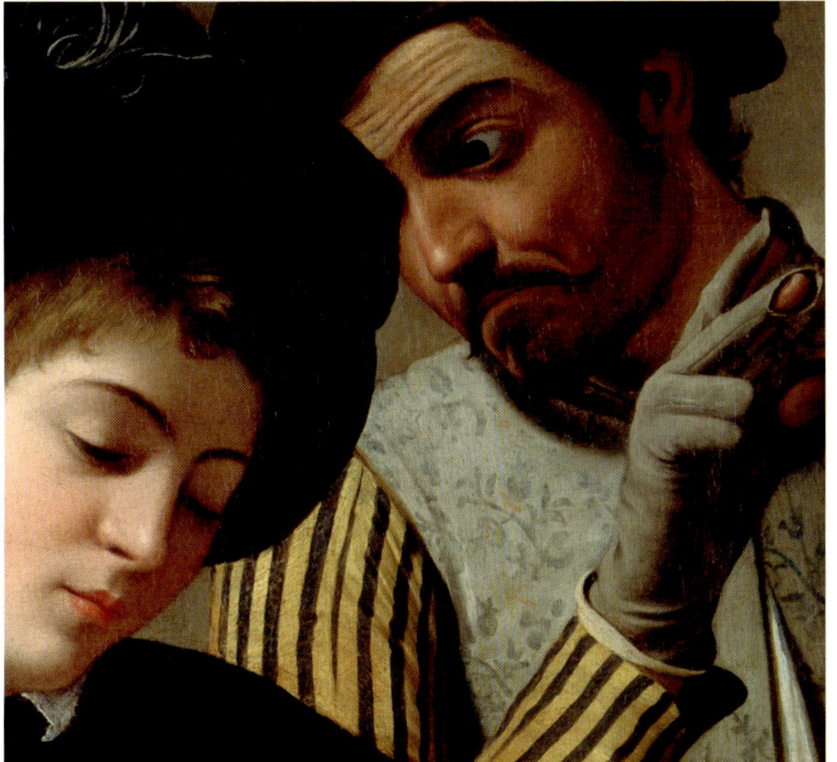

▼ Two cardsharps are cheating an innocent youth. One peeks at the cards and gives hints; the other removes cards from behind his belt. One of Caravaggio's most complex early works, it is enriched by many details – the plumes in the hats, the dagger, the backgammon board on the left, the holes in the older cardsharp's glove, the gestures, grimaces and pallor of the players on the far side of the table.

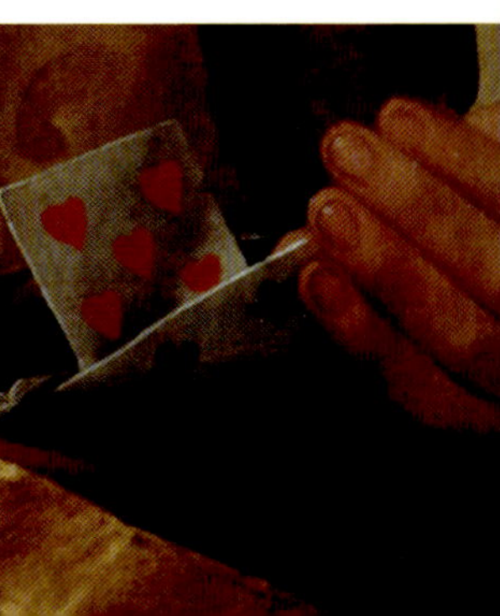

Scream

Caravaggio
Boy Bitten by a Lizard
1594

Oil on canvas, 65.8 × 52.3 cm

Florence, Fondazione di Studi di Storia dell'Arte Roberto Longhi

For artist biography, see page 386.

The education of the ideal Renaissance courtier cultivated the ability to hide emotions behind an imperturbable sobriety; the moral rigour and severity introduced with Spanish fashion in the second half of the 16th century resulted in ever sterner expressions in Counter-Reformation painting. Caravaggio, following the uninterrupted realist tradition of his native Lombardy, forcefully revived the full, direct expression of emotion. On the threshold of Baroque painting, the 'movements of the soul' dear to Leonardo became violent outlets in the work of Caravaggio, sudden outbursts in which the immediate transcription of reality is grafted onto an unmatched theatricality. In various contexts, the painter did not hesitate to depict figures with their mouths open, crying out in pain or fear.

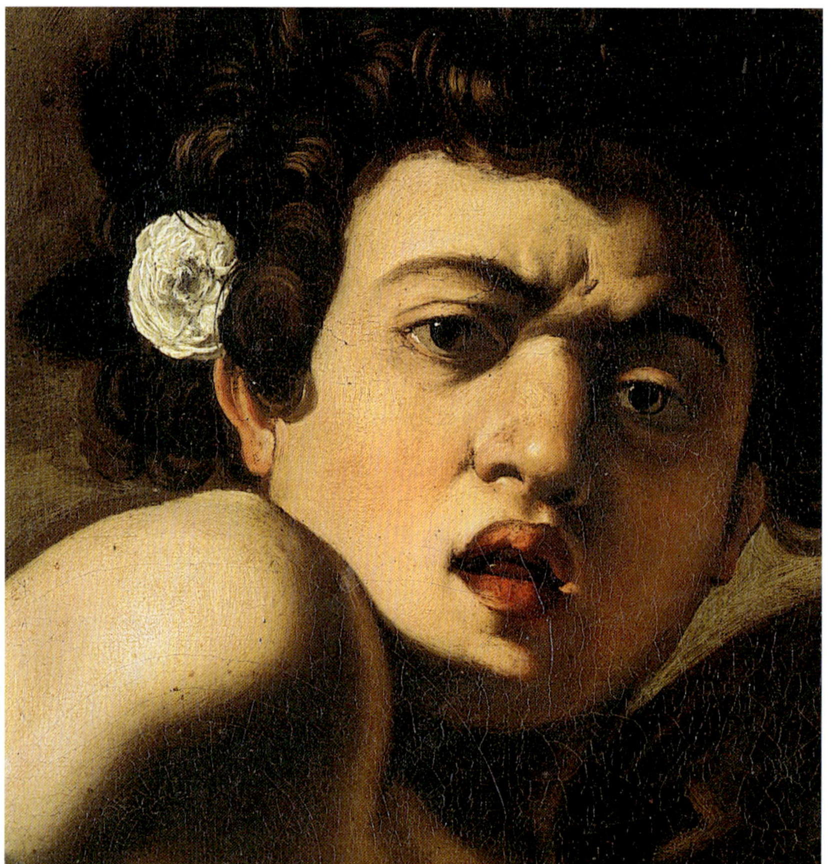

◄ As he stretches his hand towards some ripe fruit, the boy is bitten on a finger by a lizard emerging from the leaves. The counterbalancing of obvious youth and sudden pain makes us reflect upon life's fragility, vanity and the snares and ills that lurk behind alluring earthly goods.

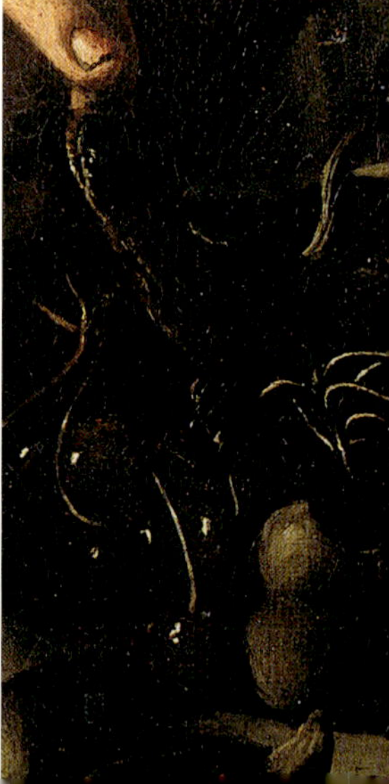

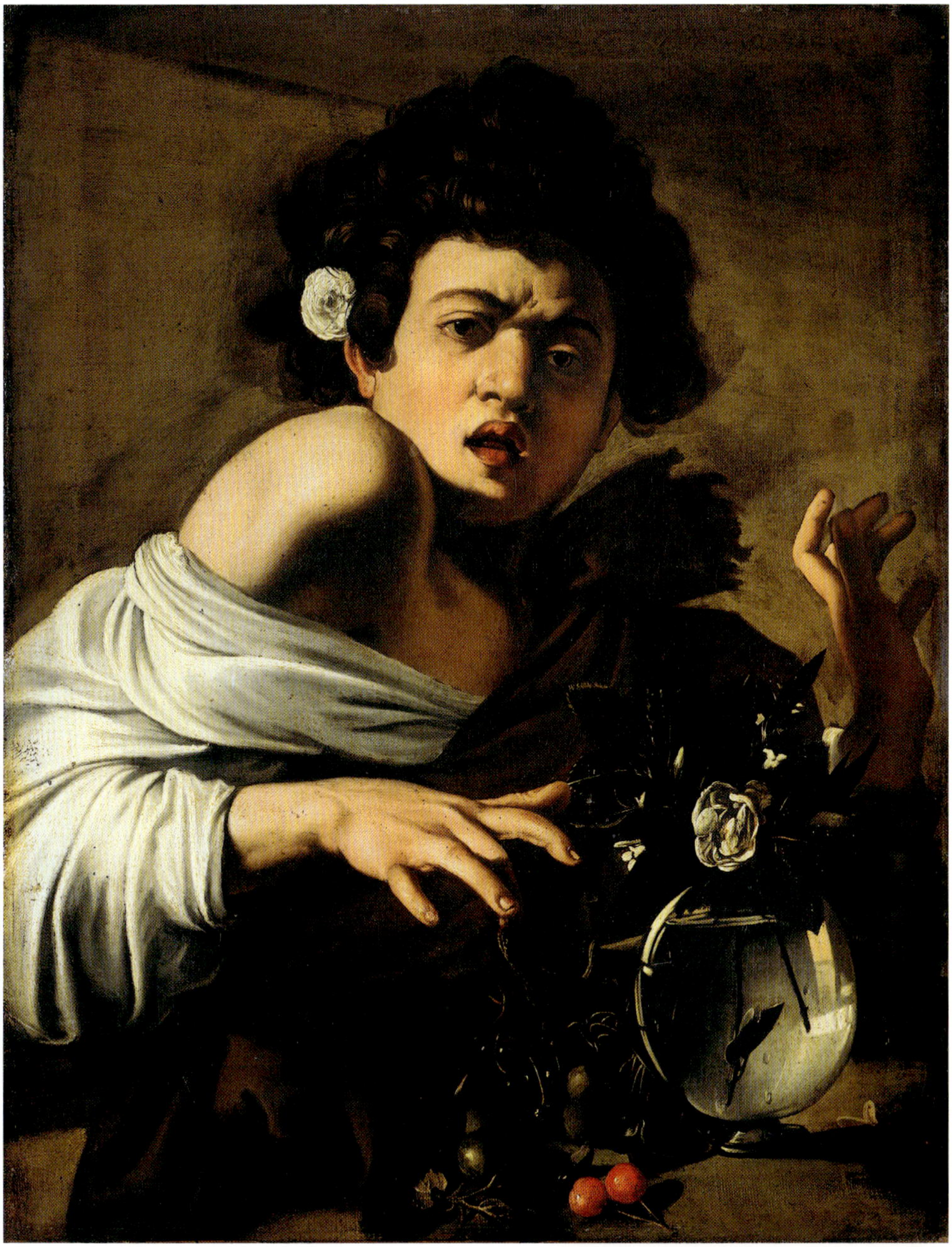

◄ It is not easy to see the little reptile camouflaged against the dark background. But if you look at the boy's middle finger, you will see the lizard attached to the tip.

► The image is effective in its combination of the expression of the youngster seized by unexpected pain and the 'still life' with the glass globe reflecting a window, which reveals the source of the light that strikes the scene from the left.

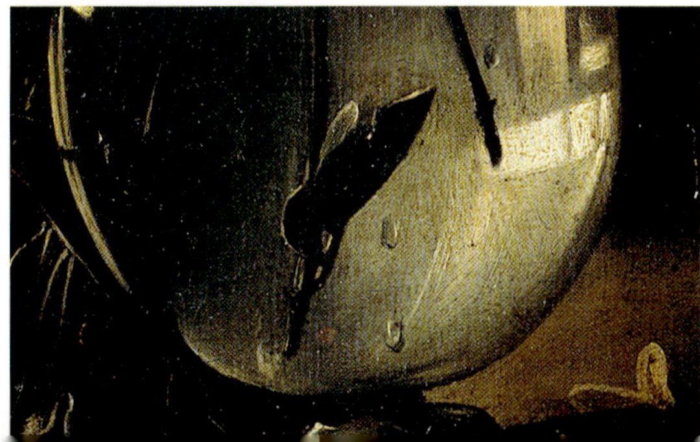

Gallery

**Annibale Carracci
The Farnese Gallery
1595–8**

Fresco
Rome, Palazzo Farnese

For artist biography, see page 372.

The crowning achievement of Annibale Carracci's career, the Farnese Gallery incapacitated and almost completely consumed the artist. The *salone* marked the end of the Italian Renaissance and heralded the advent of classicism, one of the main currents of European Baroque art. Annibale chose to simulate a princely painting gallery, with paintings embedded in the ceiling between stucco and sculpted decoration. He placed the largest picture, *The Triumph of Bacchus and Ariadne*, in the centre of the ceiling, arranging other mythological scenes along the walls. The many explicit visual references (Raphael, Michelangelo, Correggio, Titian, ancient sculpture) are harmonized in a fluid, luminous, idealized style. In the quest for ideal yet natural beauty, Annibale freely drew upon tradition, and succeeded in capturing the grace and delightful liveliness of ancient myths. *Trompe l'oeil* gilt and stucco frames surround some episodes, while others are bounded by large 'atlantes' that imitate ancient stone sculpture, alternating with nude youths in flesh tones who hold up medallions and garlands.

▼ *The Triumph of Bacchus and Ariadne*, frescoed in the main panel, is based on the *Bacchanals* that Titian painted about 70 years earlier for the Ferrara court of the Este family (see pages 272–3). In a radiant, sunny world, an entourage of satyrs, nymphs and bacchanalian Maenads accompanies the carriage where Bacchus and Ariadne sit in celebration of love and sensual beauty.

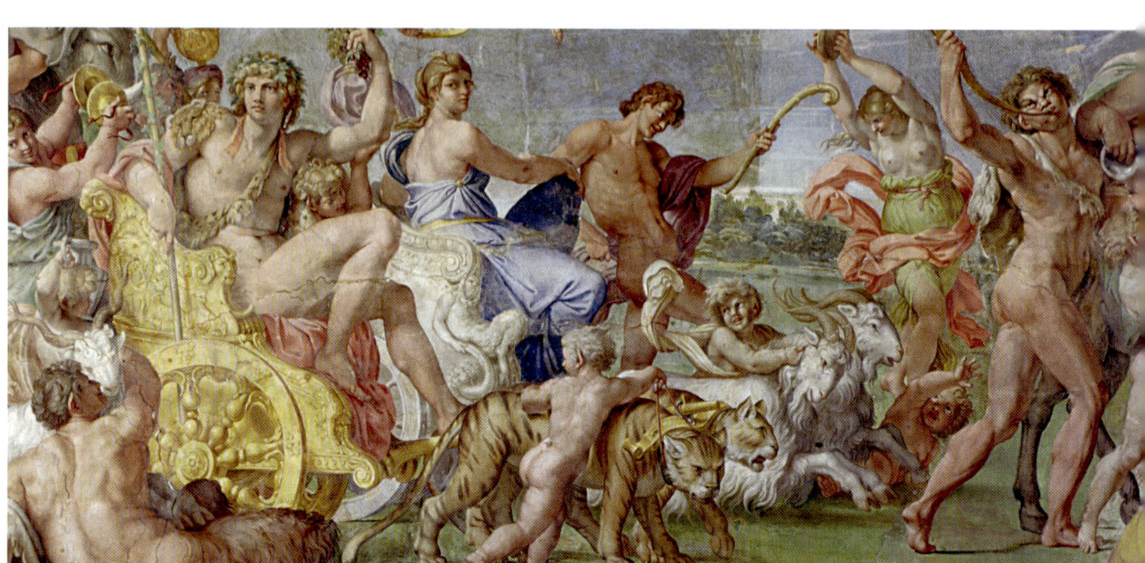

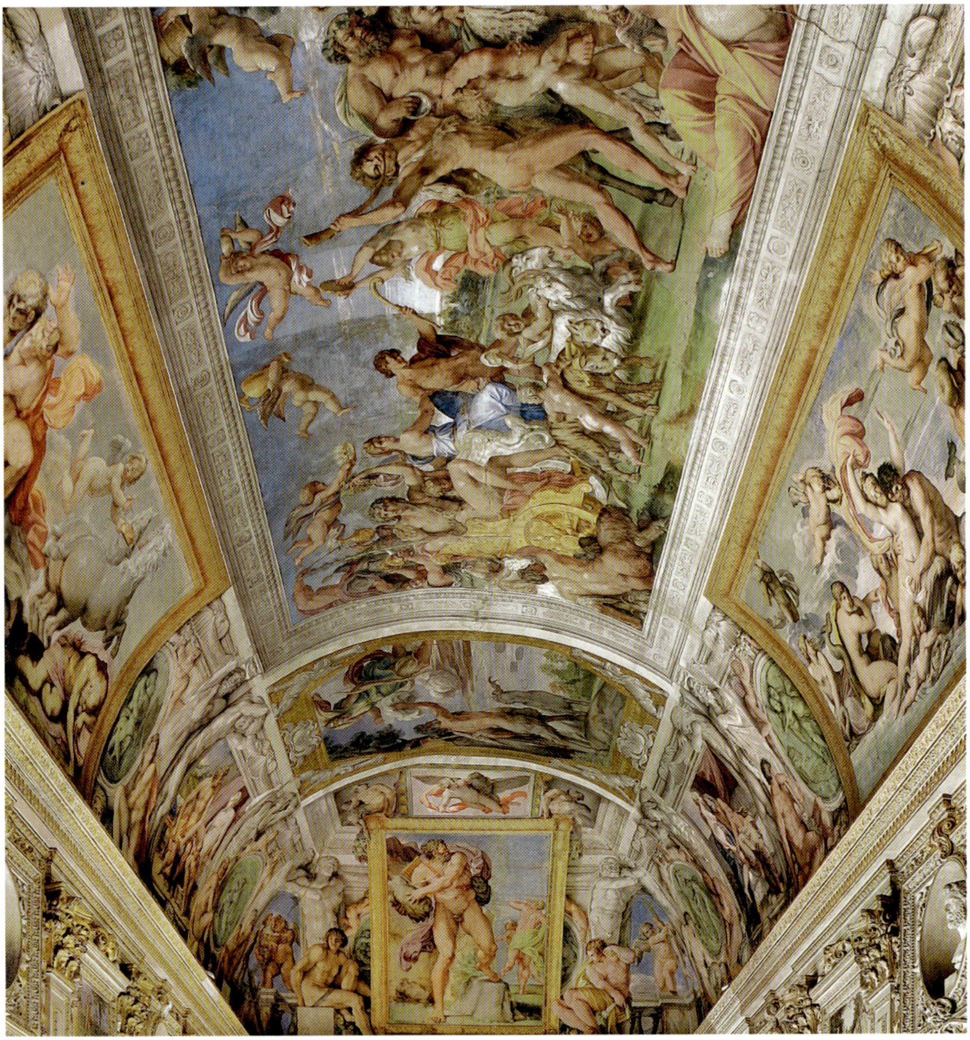

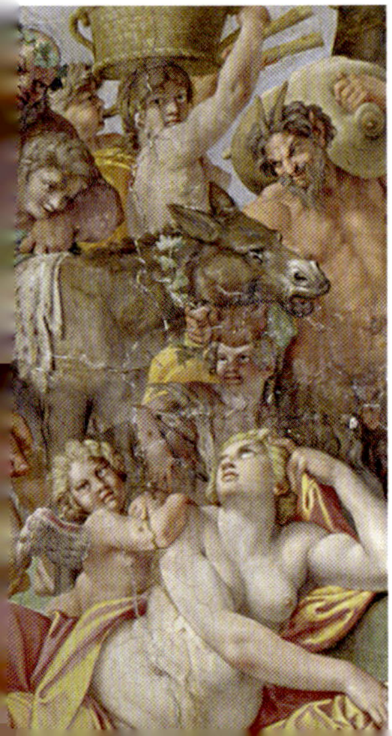

► The overall effect produced by the Farnese Gallery is that of a lavish collection of mythological paintings, symmetrically placed above an elegant, intricate architectural structure. Within this framework, the figures' liveliness and the scenes' sensual charge provided abundant source material for the imminent Baroque.

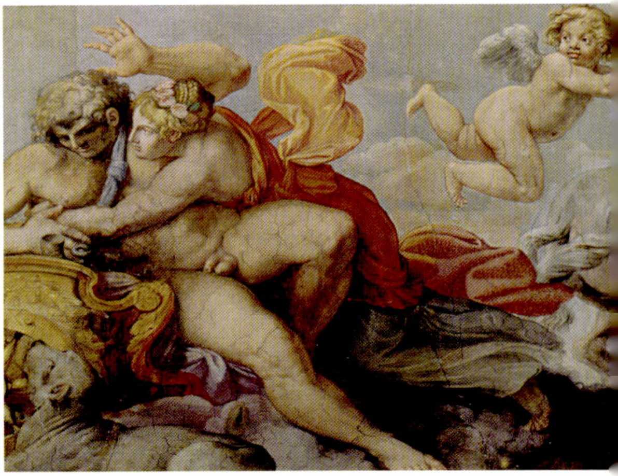

Sunset

Caravaggio
The Rest on the Flight into Egypt
_c._ 1595

Oil on canvas, 135.5 × 166.5 cm
Rome, Galleria Doria Pamphilj

For artist biography, see page 386.

As can be seen in Tintoretto's last works at the Scuola di San Rocco in Venice (see pages 376–7), the 16th century closed with a renewed sensitivity towards nature. The independent landscape – a favourite subject in Baroque painting – was already coming into its own. In one of his rather infrequent paintings in a natural setting, Caravaggio returns – after three generations – to the example of Leonardo and Giorgione, finding an unforgettable accent in the light of the setting sun. It would be difficult to imagine a more effective symbol for the decline of an era. Here, divine enchantment and human truth meet. It seems that time is coming to a close, that in this twilight hour, nature holds its breath to listen to the notes played by the angel violinist – a celestial lullaby for the tender Christ Child who is held in close embrace by his tired and loving mother.

► The magic of evening light, emitting a delicate, pale harmony of colours, permeates this enchanting masterpiece. The day fades into the sound of the violin played by the angel, a slender youth wrapped in a white robe that seems to be sliding from his haunches. The contrast with the rustic St Joseph, who holds up the score, and the donkey peering out from between the branches, is striking and decidedly bold.

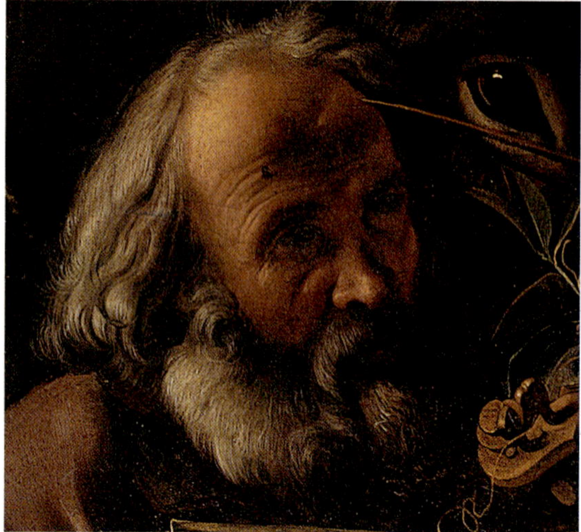

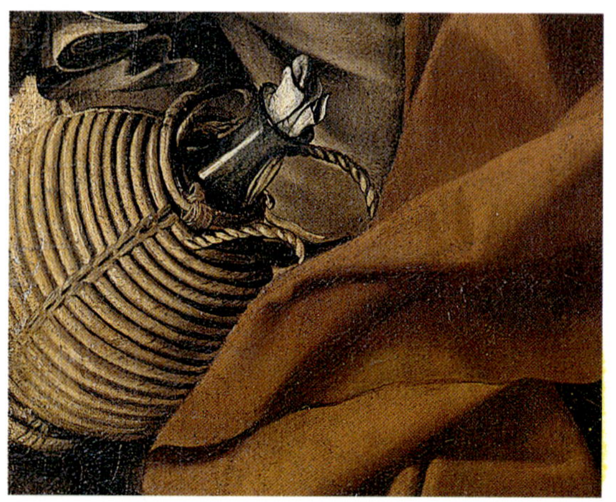

◄ All is painted with extreme care, down to the slightest details of objects and nature. The straw flask, closed with a scrap of paper folded to make a stopper, adds a note of rustic veracity and a further tactile sensation. The feel of the roughness of straw under one's fingers is combined with the almost painful juxtaposition of the angel's delicate feet and the angular rocks in the foreground.

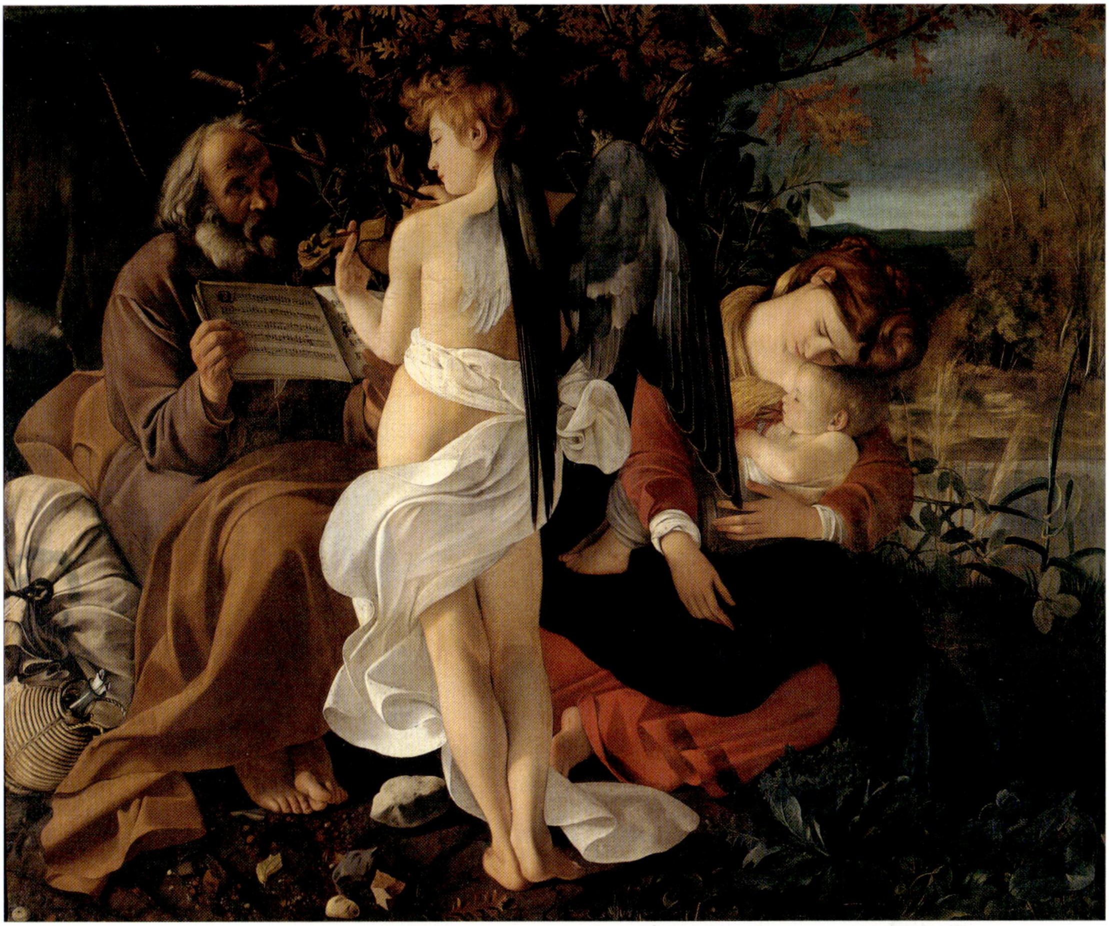

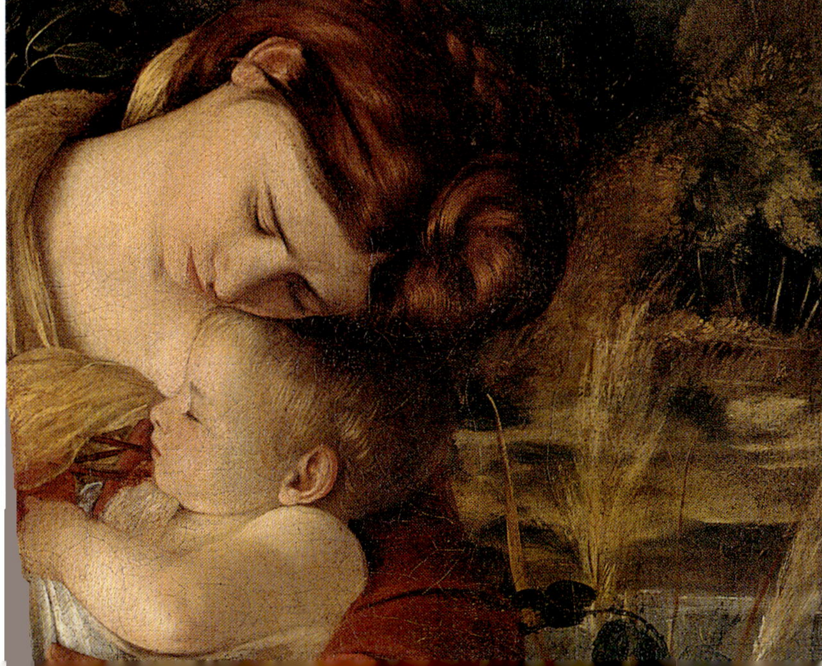

► In portraying this sacred subject, Caravaggio adheres to the same natural truth that predominates in his secular paintings. Mary, with uncharacteristic red hair, appears exhausted yet gentle as she cradles her sleeping son.

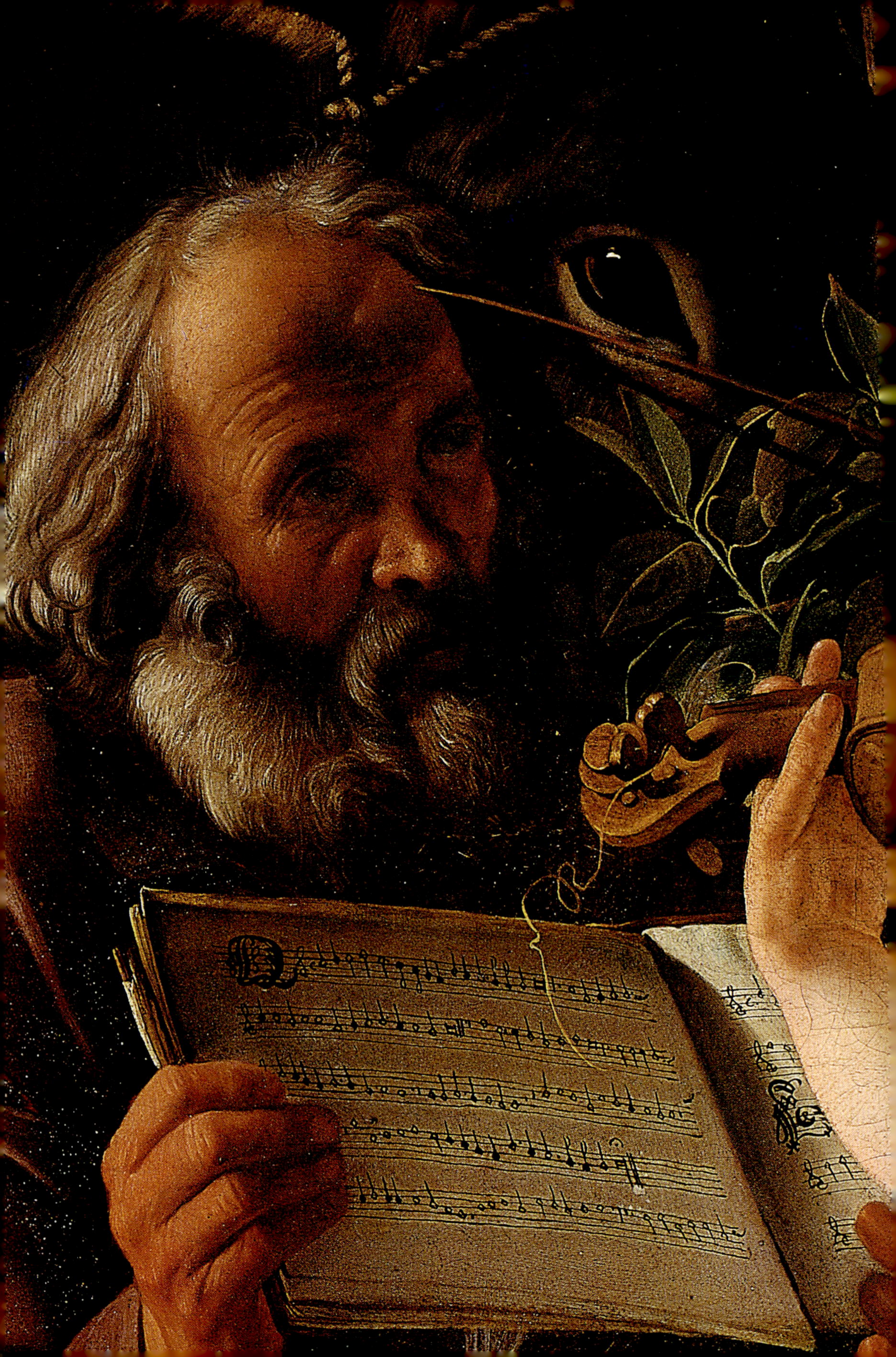

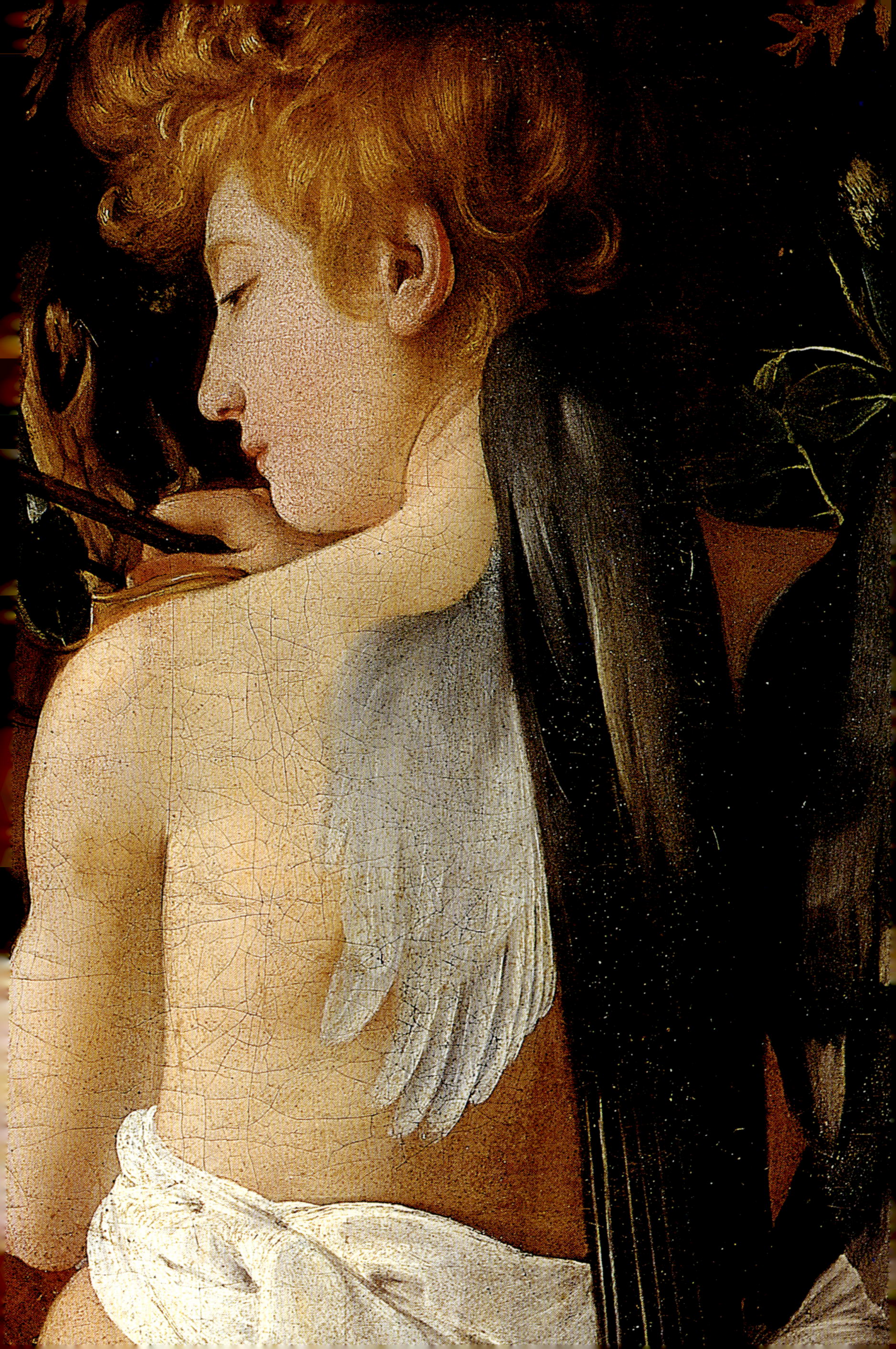

INDEX OF ARTISTS AND THEIR WORKS

Page numbers in italic indicate illustrations.

Fra Angelico 32
The Deposition (Santa Trinita Altarpiece) *32*
Madonna of the Shadows 56
The Mocking of Christ 34
Sofonisba Anguissola 342
Game of Chess 342
Antonello da Messina 100
St Jerome in his Study 100
St Sebastian 110
The Virgin Annunciate 106
Giuseppe Arcimboldo 380
Rudolf II as Vertumnus 380

Jacopo de' Barbari 172
Portrait of Luca Pacioli 172
Federico Barocci 356
The Deposition 356
Fra Bartolomeo 210
*Apparition of God the Father to St Mary
Magdalene and St Catherine* 210
Jacopo Bassano 350
St Valentine Baptizing St Lucille 364
Sowing Grain 350
Gentile Bellini 166
Procession in Piazza San Marco 166
St Mark Preaching in Alexandria 196
Giovanni Bellini 144
Crucifixion with Cemetery 178
Frari Triptych 144
St Mark Preaching in Alexandria 196
Young Woman Combing her Hair 244
Pedro Berruguete 112
Portrait of Federico da Montefeltro 112
Giovanni Antonio Boltraffio 146
Madonna of the Rose 146
Paris Bordone 320
Bathsheba 320
Ambrogio Borgognone 136
Madonna of the Milk 136
Sandro Botticelli 102
The Adoration of the Magi 104
The Birth of Venus 132
The Calumny of Apelles 152
Pallas and the Centaur 128
*Portrait of a Man with a Medal
of Cosimo the Elder* 102
Spring (*Primavera*) 124
Angelo Bronzino 316
Allegory 316
Portrait of Eleanor of Toledo 328

Luca Cambiaso 360
Christ before Caiaphas 360
Vincenzo Campi 368
The Fruit Seller 368
Caravaggio 386
Boy Bitten by a Lizard 388
The Cardsharps 386
The Rest on the Flight into Egypt 392
Vittore Carpaccio 184
*The Meeting and Departure of
the Betrothed Couple* 162
St Augustine in his Study 184
Annibale Carracci 372
The Bean Eater 378
The Butcher's Shop 372
The Farnese Gallery 390
Ludovico Carracci 374
The Annunciation 374
Andrea del Castagno 44
Dante, Boccaccio and Pipo of Ozora 52
The Last Supper 44
Niccolò Antonio Colantonio 40
St Jerome in his Study 40
Correggio 268
Danae 298
Jupiter and Io 294
The Madonna with St Jerome 282
The Vision of St John the Evangelist 268
Francesco del Cossa 88
The Triumph of Venus (Detail from the
Month of April) 88
Carlo Crivelli 150
Madonna of the Candle 150

Domenico Veneziano 46
Santa Lucia de' Magnoli Altarpiece 46
Dosso Dossi 262
Melissa 262
Albrecht Dürer 202
The Feast of the Rosary 202

Gentile da Fabriano 12
The Adoration of the Magi 14
Valleromita Polyptych 12
Gaudenzio Ferrari 234
Crucifixion (Detail from the *Story
of the Life and Passion of Christ*) 234

Domenico Ghirlandaio 140
The Birth of the Virgin (Detail from
the *Story of the Virgin*) 140

Portrait of a Grandfather and His Grandson 148
Portrait of Giovanna Tornabuoni 142
Giorgione 198
Castelfranco Altarpiece 200
Double Portrait 220
Dresden Venus 222
The Old Woman 204
The Tempest 206
The Three Philosophers 198
Giovanni di Ser Giovanni 36
Cassone Adimari 36
Giulio Romano 288
The Fall of the Titans 288
Hugo van der Goes 108
Portinari Triptych 108
Benozzo Gozzoli 70
The Procession of the Magi 70

Maarten van Heemskerck 340
Self-portrait with the Colosseum 340

Leonardo da Vinci 130
The Baptism of Christ 92
Lady with an Ermine 138
The Last Supper 160
Mona Lisa (*La Gioconda*) 192
The Virgin and St Anne 180
The Virgin of the Rocks 130
The Vitruvian Man 174
Filippino Lippi 134
The Vision of St Bernard 134
Fra Filippo Lippi 38
The Annunciation 38
The Annunciation 58
The Dance of Salome 74
Lorenzo Lotto 274
The Annunciation 284
Madonna and Child with Saints
  (*Sacra Conversazione*) 274
Portrait of Andrea Odoni 286
Portrait of a Woman Dressed as Lucretia 304

Andrea Mantegna 76
The Court of the Gonzagas 76
The Dead Christ 116
Minerva Expelling the Vices from
  the Garden of Virtue 186
Oculus in the Ceiling of the
  Camera degli Sposi 82
St Sebastian 120

Masaccio 16
The Adoration of the Magi
  (*Predella of the Pisa Polyptych*) 18
The Expulsion from Eden 16
The Tribute Money (Detail from the
  Stories of Peter) 16
The Trinity 20
Masolino 18
The Banquet of Herod (Detail from
  the *Story of St John the Baptist*) 26
The Temptation of Adam 18
Meester van de Pala Sforzesca 158
Sforzesca Altarpiece 158
Melozzo da Forlì 114
Pope Sixtus IV Appoints Bartolomeo Platina
  Prefect of the Vatican Library 114
Michelangelo 190
Ceiling of the Sistine Chapel 212
The Creation of Adam (Detail from the
  Story of Genesis) 216
Doni Tondo 190
The Last Judgment 312
Moretto da Brescia 318
Portrait of Count Fortunato Martinengo Cesaresco (?) 318
Giovanni Battista Moroni 358
The Tailor 358

Jacopo Palma Vecchio 264
The Three Sisters 264
Parmigianino 280
Cupid Carving His Bow 296
Madonna of the Long Neck 306
The Vision of St Jerome 280
Bartolomeo Passarotti 370
The Butcher's Stall 370
Perino del Vaga 300
The Fall of the Titans 300
Pietro Perugino 152
Apollo and Marsyas (or *Apollo and Daphnis*) 152
The Delivery of the Keys (Detail from the
  Story of Christ) 122
The Lamentation 164
Self-portrait 168
The Virgin Appearing to St Bernard 156
Piero della Francesca 42
The Baptism of Christ 50
The Combat of Heraclius and Khosrau
  (Detail from the *Story of the True Cross*) 60
The Flagellation 66
Madonna of Mercy (Central panel of the
  Polyptych of the Madonna of Mercy) 42

Montefeltro Altarpiece 96
Solomon and the Queen of Sheba (Detail from the
    Story of the True Cross) *62*
    The Urbino Diptych (*Portrait of Federico
    da Montefeltro and Battista Sforza*) *80*
Piero di Cosimo 174
The Death of Procris 174
Bernardino Pinturicchio 168
Self-portrait (Detail from *The Annunciation*) *168*
Details from the *Story of Pius II Piccolomini 188*
Pisanello 28
St George and the Dragon (right side) *28*
The Vision of St Eustace 30
Antonio del Pollaiuolo 78
Apollo and Daphne 78
Portrait of a Woman 90
Jacopo Pontormo 276
The Bearing of Christ's Body to the Tomb 276
The Visitation 292
Pordenone 266
Crucifixion 266

Raphael 194
The Bearing of Christ's Body to the Tomb 208
Cartoon for the School of Athens 226
Disputation of the Holy Sacrament 218
The Fire in the Borgo 240
Madonna of the Chair 236
The Marriage of the Virgin 194
Portrait of Leo X with Two Cardinals 256
The School of Athens 228
Self-portrait with a Friend 254
Sistine Madonna 232
The Transfiguration 252
Rosso Fiorentino 270
The Dead Christ with Angels 278
The Deposition 270

Francesco Salviati 324
Charity 324
Andrea del Sarto 248
Baptism of the People 252
Madonna of the Harpies 248
Giovanni Girolamo Savoldo 260
Portrait of a Man in Armour (Self-portrait?) 260
St Matthew and the Angel 302
Andrea Schiavone 334
The Adoration of the Magi 334
Sebastiano del Piombo 252
The Raising of Lazarus 252

Luca Signorelli 170
The Resurrection of the Flesh (Detail from
    the *Story of the Apocalypse*) *170*

Pellegrino Tibaldi 338
The Adoration of the Shepherds 338
Jacopo Tintoretto 344
Finding the Body of St Mark 352
The Last Supper 382
St Mary of Egypt 376
Susanna and the Elders 344
Tiziano Vecellio, called **Titian** 224
The Arrival of Bacchus on the Island of Andros 272
The Assumption 246
Charles V at the Battle of Mühlberg 336
Diana and Actaeon 346
Pastoral Concert 224
Pesaro Altarpiece 258
Portrait of a Gentleman (*Ariosto*) *230*
Portrait of Doge Andrea Gritti 322
Portrait of Jacopo Strada 354
Portrait of Paul III with His Nephews 330
Portrait of Pietro Aretino 332
Sacred Love and Profane Love 242
The Three Ages of Man 238
Urbino Venus 308
Votive Painting of the Vendramin Family 326
Cosimo Tura 72
The Muse Erato (or *Spring*) *72*
St George and the Dragon 86

Paolo Uccello 68
The Battle of San Romano 68

Giorgio Vasari 348
Self-portrait 348
Paolo Veronese 366
The Feast in the House of Levi 362
The Glory of Venice 366
Andrea del Verrocchio 92
The Baptism of Christ 92

PHOTOGRAPHIC CREDITS

© 2008, Her Majesty Queen Elizabeth II 286–287

© Accademia Carrara – Galleria d'Arte Moderna
e Contemporanea, Bergamo 136–137

© Archivio dell'Arte Luciano Pedicini, Naples
40–41, 172–173

© Alte Pinakothek, Munich 156–157

© Arti Doria Pamphilj, Rome 300–301

© Cameraphoto, Venice 184–185, 366–367

© Christ Church Collection, Oxford 372–373

© Contrasto/Eric Lessing, Milan 5, 138–139,
244–245, 264–265, 380–381

© Fototeca Civica, Ferrara 86–87

Galleria Borghese, Rome © photo Scala,
Firenze – courtesy Ministero per i Beni
e le Attività Culturali 242–243

© Galleria Colonna, Rome 378–379

Galleria degli Uffizi, Florence 108–109

Galleria Palatina, Palazzo Pitti, Florence 332–333

Gallerie Nazionali di Capodimonte, Naples © photo
Scala, Florence – courtesy Ministero per i Beni e le
Attività Culturali 330–331

© Gemäldegalerie Alte Meister, Staatliche
Kunstsammlungen, Dresden 110–111

Gemäldegalerie, Kunsthistorisches Museum,
Vienna 354–355

Musée du Louvre, Paris © RMN /
Hervé Lewandowski 224–225

© Musei e Gallerie Pontificie, Vatican City 114–115,
122–123, 212–213, 214–215, 218–219, 228–229,
240–241

© Museo dell'Accademia Ligustica, Genoa 360–361

Museo Nacional del Prado, Madrid 272–273, 336–337

© Museo Poldi Pezzoli/Mauro Magliano, Milan 146–147

© Museo Thyssen-Bornemisza, Madrid 350–351

© Museum of Fine Arts, Boston 278–279

National Gallery of Art, Washington DC 322–323

National Gallery of Scotland (on loan from the
Duke of Scotland), Edinburgh 238–239, 346–347

© Opera del Duomo, Orvieto 170–171

© PhotoserviceElecta, Milan 28–29, 42–43, 58–59,
60–61, 62–63, 64–65, 88–89, 90–91, 134–135,
142–143, 168, 226–227, 232–233, 234–235,
258–259, 268–269, 276–277, 284–285, 290–291,
292–293, 382–383, 384–385, 388–389

© PhotoserviceElecta courtesy Ministero per i Beni
e le Attività culturali 12–13, 46–47, 92–93, 94–95,
96–97, 98–99, 102–103, 104–105, 112–113,
116–117, 118–119, 150–151, 154–155, 158–159,
161–163, 164–165, 166–167, 174–175, 190–191,
196–197, 204–205, 208–209, 210–211, 236–237,
256–257, 262–263, 282–283, 298–299, 338–339,
352–353, 362–363, 368–369, 370–371, 374–375

© PhotoserviceElecta/AKG Images 32–33, 100–101,
320–321

© PhotoserviceElecta/Colantoni 390–391 above

© PhotoserviceElecta/Leemage 19 right, 22–23,
36–37, 38–39, 52–53, 54–55, 80–81, 120–121,
148–149, 152–153, 180–181, 182–183, 288–289,
328–329, 386–387

© PhotoserviceElecta/Manusardi 26–27, 194–195

© PhotoserviceElecta/Quattrone 19 left, 34–35,
44–45, 56–57, 70–71, 74–75, 76–77, 82–83, 84–85,
106–107, 131 left, 144–145, 178–179, 186–187,
200–201, 248–249, 250–251, 270–271, 274–275

© PhotoserviceElecta/Quattrone courtesy Ministero
per i Beni e le Attività culturali 128–129

© PhotoserviceElecta/Ranzani 266–267

© Pinacoteca Ambrosiana, Milan 334–335

© PubbliPhoto, Palermo 48–49

Santa Maria Gloriosa dei Frari, Venice © photo
Scala, Florence 246–247

© Scala Archives, Florence 14–15, 16–17,
132–133, 140–141, 160–161, 192–193, 216–217

© Staatliche Museen, Berlin 20–21

© with kind permission of the Direzione del Museo
Biblioteca Archivio di Bassano del Grappa 364–365

© The Art Archive / Cathedral Perugia / Alfredo Dagli
Orti 356–357

© The Bridgeman Art Library, London 24–25, 30–31,
50–51, 66–67, 68–69, 72–73, 78–79, 124–125,
126–127, 131 right, 169, 176–177, 188–189, 198–199,
202–203, 206–207, 220–221, 222–223, 252–253,
254–255, 260–261, 294–295, 296–297, 304–305,
306–307, 308–309, 310–311, 312–313, 314–315,
316–317, 318–319, 324–325, 340–341, 342–343,
344–345, 348–349, 358–359, 376–377, 390–391
below, 392–393, 394–395

© The Metropolitan Museum of Art, New York 302–303

The National Gallery, London 230–231, 280–281,
326–327